Troubleshooting Remote Access Networks

Plamen Nedeltchev, Ph.D.

Cisco Press

201 W 103rd Street
Indianapolis, IN 46290 USA

Troubleshooting Remote Access Networks

Plamen Nedeltchev

Copyright© 2003 Cisco Systems, Inc.

Published by:
Cisco Press
201 West 103rd Street
Indianapolis, IN 46290 USA

Printed in the United States of America 1 2 3 4 5 6 7 8 9 0

First Printing November 2002

Library of Congress Cataloging-in-Publication Number: 2001096586

ISBN: 1-58705-076-5

Warning and Disclaimer

This book is designed to provide information about troubleshooting remote access networks. Every effort has been made to make this book as complete and as accurate as possible, but no warranty or fitness is implied.

The information is provided on an "as is" basis. The author, Cisco Press, and Cisco Systems, Inc. shall have neither liability nor responsibility to any person or entity with respect to any loss or damages arising from the information contained in this book or from the use of the discs or programs that may accompany it.

The opinions expressed in this book belong to the author and are not necessarily those of Cisco Systems, Inc.

Trademark Acknowledgments

All terms mentioned in this book that are known to be trademarks or service marks have been appropriately capitalized. Cisco Press or Cisco Systems, Inc. cannot attest to the accuracy of this information. Use of a term in this book should not be regarded as affecting the validity of any trademark or service mark.

Feedback Information

At Cisco Press, our goal is to create in-depth technical books of the highest quality and value. Each book is crafted with care and precision, undergoing rigorous development that involves the unique expertise of members from the professional technical community.

Readers' feedback is a natural continuation of this process. If you have any comments regarding how we could improve the quality of this book, or otherwise alter it to better suit your needs, you can contact us through e-mail at feedback@ciscopress.com. Please make sure to include the book title and ISBN in your message.

We greatly appreciate your assistance.

Publisher	John Wait
Editor-in-Chief	John Kane
Executive Editor	Brett Bartow
Cisco Representative	Anthony Wolfenden
Cisco Press Program Manager	Sonia Torres Chavez
Cisco Marketing Communications Manager	Tom Geitner
Cisco Marketing Program Manager	Edie Quiroz
Production Manager	Patrick Kanouse
Development Editor	Andrew Cupp
Senior Project Editor	Sheri Cain
Copy Editor	Cris Mattison
Technical Editors	Brian Feeny
	Brian Morgan
	William R Wagner
	Jonathan Zung
Team Coordinator	Tammi Ross
Cover Designer	Louisa Adair
Composition	Argosy Publishing
Indexer	Tim Wright

CISCO SYSTEMS

Corporate Headquarters
Cisco Systems, Inc.
170 West Tasman Drive
San Jose, CA 95134-1706
USA
http://www.cisco.com
Tel: 408 526-4000
       800 553-NETS (6387)
Fax: 408 526-4100

European Headquarters
Cisco Systems Europe
11 Rue Camille Desmoulins
92782 Issy-les-Moulineaux
Cedex 9
France
http://www-europe.cisco.com
Tel: 33 1 58 04 60 00
Fax: 33 1 58 04 61 00

Americas Headquarters
Cisco Systems, Inc.
170 West Tasman Drive
San Jose, CA 95134-1706
USA
http://www.cisco.com
Tel: 408 526-7660
Fax: 408 527-0883

Asia Pacific Headquarters
Cisco Systems Australia, Pty.,
Ltd
Level 17, 99 Walker Street
North Sydney
NSW 2059 Australia
http://www.cisco.com
Tel: +61 2 8448 7100
Fax: +61 2 9957 4350

Cisco Systems has more than 200 offices in the following countries. Addresses, phone numbers, and fax numbers are listed on the Cisco Web site at www.cisco.com/go/offices

Argentina • Australia • Austria • Belgium • Brazil • Bulgaria • Canada • Chile • China • Colombia • Costa Rica • Croatia • Czech Republic • Denmark • Dubai, UAE • Finland • France • Germany • Greece • Hong Kong • Hungary • India • Indonesia • Ireland • Israel • Italy • Japan • Korea • Luxembourg • Malaysia • Mexico • The Netherlands • New Zealand • Norway • Peru • Philippines • Poland • Portugal • Puerto Rico • Romania • Russia • Saudi Arabia • Scotland • Singapore • Slovakia • Slovenia • South Africa • Spain Sweden • Switzerland • Taiwan • Thailand • Turkey • Ukraine • United Kingdom • United States • Venezuela • Vietnam • Zimbabwe

About the Author

Plamen Nedeltchev was born in February 1954 in Silistra, Bulgaria. He graduated from high school as valedictorian in 1972. In 1980, he received an M.S. (Summa Cum Laude) from Saint Petersburg State Electro-Technical University. In 1989, he received his Ph.D. from the Bulgarian Academy of Science, Sofia, Bulgaria.

Plamen worked as the chief information officer of VMT (a division of the Ministry of Transport of Bulgaria) in his country of origin. He joined Sprint E-Solutions in 1999 as a senior network architect. The same year, he joined Cisco's Remote Access team as a technical consultant. During his career, he has published more than 40 publications in English, Russian, and Bulgarian, including four recent articles in the Cisco *Packet* Magazine. He speaks five languages and has one technical patent. The scope of his technical expertise and interests includes bridging, switching, routing, capacity planning, compression, multicast, QoS, content networking, SOHO, ROBO, design/modeling/simulation, ISDN, Frame Relay, VPN, xDSL, cable modem, dial, wireless, and troubleshooting. In his spare time, he enjoys political history, philosophy, literature, sports, and music.

About the Technical Reviewers

Brian Feeny (CCIE No. 8036) is the senior network engineer for ShreveNet Inc., an Internet service provider, where he has been working for the last six years. He is also a Partner in Netjam LLC, which specializes in sales and support of Cisco network equipment. Brian has more than ten years experience in the networking industry.

Brian Morgan (CCIE No. 4865) is a Cisco Press author (*CCNP Remote Access Exam Certification Guide*) and a frequent contributor in both editing and content. He has been in the networking industry for over ten years as a consultant in large internetworking environments. He has also spent much of the last five years as an instructor for Cisco Learning Partners teaching ICND, BSCN/I, BCRAN, CATM, CVOICE, CCIE/CCNP bootcamps, and other courses.

William R Wagner works as a Cisco Certified System Instructor for Skyline Computer Corp. He has 23 years of computer programming and data communication experience. He has worked for corporations and companies such as Independent Computer Consultants, Numerax, McGraw-Hill/Numerax, and Standard and Poors. He has teaching experience with the Chubb Institute, Protocol Interface Inc., Geotrain, Mentor Technologies, and he is currently teaching at Skyline Computers Corp. William also holds a degree in Computer Science, is a CNE, and currently holds his CCNA and CCNP from Cisco.

Jonathan Zung (CCNP, CCDP, working towards CCIE) has been at Cisco for nearly five years. He started at Cisco as a UNIX systems administrator, but for the last four years at Cisco, he has been working as a network engineer supporting Cisco's internal remote access environment. He graduated from California Polytechnic State University at San Luis Obispo with a B.S. in MIS and a minor in Computer Science in 1997.

In addition to being one of the book's technical reviewers who helped me with all phases to improve the content, Jonathan is the principal author of the design and troubleshooting content of Multi-Chassis Multilink Point-to-Point Protocol (MMP) in Chapter 10, "ISDN Design Solutions" and Chapter 12, "ISDN BRI Troubleshooting" of this book.

Dedication

I dedicate this book to one of the most amazing people I have ever met, my wife Tatiana, for her sincere moral support and help through all these years.

I dedicate this book to my kids, Nickolay and Irina, who make me a very proud father.

—Plamen

Acknowledgments

To my managers:

This book wouldn't be possible if I didn't have the continuous and unconditional support of my managers: Felicia Brych, who devoted her time for months to make this book happen, and Chuck Trent and Henry White, who encouraged me and created an unmatchable atmosphere of trust and encouragement to ensure the success of this project. Special appreciation goes to my Sprint E-Solutions manager, Debra Wieland, and to Chris Starsiak for believing in me and for the support.

To the Cisco Press team:

Many thanks to Brett Bartow for giving me the chance to write for Cisco Press, and Drew Cupp for his assistance, persistence, and remarkable language skills during the creation of this book. I would also like to thank Sheri Cain for her excellent work in managing this book through the production process. Finally, I want to thank Jill Batistick, Ginny Bess Munroe, Christopher Cleveland, Cris Mattison, Doug Ingersoll, and Marianne Huff for providing me with assistance, formatting, and editing the content, improving the language, and for technical corrections.

To the technical editors of this book:

My special appreciation goes to Brian Feeny (CCIE No. 8036), Brian Morgan (CCIE No. 4865), Bill Wagner (CCSI), and especially to Jonathan Zung (CCDP, CCNP) for their valuable comments, devotion and time, and helping me to make this book better.

To my colleagues who helped write and edit:

Many thanks to my colleagues from the Remote Access team at Cisco, who are some of the most talented engineers I've ever worked with in my carrier. All of them are at different stages of achieving the highest Cisco certifications, but all together, they make what usually is referred to as "The Team" and as such, everyone has their own technical strengths, preferences, and proven techniques. Some of them have written part of this book, some of them have reviewed the content, and some of them did both. Overall, sharing this collective experience, in my understanding, adds value to this book and serves the readers' needs best. As a result, this book includes only the proven best practices type of information and proven troubleshooting scenarios from more than tens of thousands of cases in the recent years. I would like to thank the following team members and note their contributions to this book:

Felicia Brych (BComm, MPM) is from Canada and holds degrees from Memorial University of Newfoundland and the University of Quebec. Felicia managed Cisco's Internal Remote Access Services department from December 1999 to August 2001, with successes that included the global deployment of VPN and significant cost reduction for all remote access solutions. Prior to working for Cisco, she managed Remote Access and Technology Services for Revenue Canada. Felicia currently leads IT initiatives involving collaboration infrastructure and IP telephony for the home. In her spare time, Felicia enjoys gardening and spending time with her husband, three stepchildren, and two Labrador Retrievers.

Felicia is the principal author of the foreword and the "Management Considerations" section for Chapter 1 of this book. Felicia edited the entire content of this book for style and language.

Chuck Cardamon is an IT analyst in Infrastructure, Carrier Services & Provisioning. He has an AOS degree in Culinary Arts and is a veteran, retiring as a U.S. Navy SEAL after 20 years of service. He is a proponent of organ donation and was a live liver donor to save the life of a friend. In his spare time, he rides motorcycles and fly fishes. He has been married for 26 years and has 4 adult children.

Chuck is the principal author of the "Provisioning of Enterprise Remote Access Services" section for Chapter 1.

Jered T. Huegen is a network engineer supporting remote access services for Cisco Systems. He has been working towards his CCIE in Communications and Services and passed the written exam. Jered has helped to facilitate the growth of the remote access infrastructure from a few hundred clients to accommodate 40,000 clients. He has a college background in math and accounting. In his spare time, Jered enjoys being a pit crewmember and making split-second setup decisions for a dirt-track race team. He was married in September 2002.

Jered is the principal author of the following chapters:

- Chapter 5, "Dial Technology Background"
- Chapter 6, "Dial Design and Configuration Solutions"
- Chapter 7, "Dial Troubleshooting"
- Chapter 8, "Dial Troubleshooting Scenarios"

Omid Kaabipour (CCNA) has a B.S. in Business Administration (MIS) from San Jose State University. As a lead engineer for Frame Relay with the Remote Access group, he participated in design, support, and troubleshooting Frame Relay, ISDN, VPN, and Dial. Recently, Omid has been working with the Cisco Northeast Transport Group on transport technologies across a wide range of Cisco platforms, including WAN, LAN, MAN and Frame Relay troubleshooting, design, and maintenance. In his spare time, he thrives on listening to classical music and enjoys going to movies.

Omid is the principal author of the Frame Relay host migration scenario in Chapter 18 of this book and helped with the technical review of this book at its final phase.

David Iacobacci is a network engineer in the Cisco IT Remote Access Services group and has been the technical lead of the team for about two years. He has been working toward his CCIE in Security. A native New Yorker, he lived in Japan for over nine years, working for Nihon Cisco Systems and Procter & Gamble Far East, Inc., after obtaining an MBA from the International University of Japan. He also holds a BS in Mechanical Engineering from Rutgers University and has worked for Citigoup, FMC Corporation, and the U.S. Navy. When not working, David enjoys his free time with his wife and daughter.

David is the principal author of the following chapters:

- Chapter 20, "Remote Access VPN Design and Configuration Solutions"
- Chapter 21, "Remote Access VPN Troubleshooting"

Zack Schaefer (CCNP, CCDP) is currently working on his CCIE. He has spent a majority of his post college career working for Cisco in its Remote Access department. Throughout his entire career at Cisco, he has helped support Cisco's entire VPN infrastructure, solving thousands of VPN problems yearly. He is currently a network engineer supporting WAN, LAN, MAN, and remote access for Latin America and the Central and Southeast United States. Additionally, he routinely performs VPN troubleshooting training for fellow Cisco employees.

Zack is the principal author of Chapter 22, "Remote Access VPN Troubleshooting Scenarios."

James Michael Thompson (CCNP, CCDA) made a move from the music industry to the networking industry in the late 1980s. Before working with the Cisco Remote Access team, Jim worked as a WAN engineer and as a CNE at a network integration company. Jim passed the CCIE qualifying exam and is scheduled to take the lab exam in the near future. He lives in Sonora, California, with hobbies such as photography, hiking, mountain biking, kayaking, and still enjoys making music.

Jim helped with the technical review of this book at its final phase.

Lainie van Doornewaard has been with Cisco Systems, Inc. for approx. five and a half years after leaving a career in law enforcement. She worked as the team lead for support for the engineering community, then joined the Network Operations Team, which is responsible for Cisco's corporate LAN, WAN, and MAN infrastructure. She transferred to the Remote Access team in July of 2000 and has been the backup engineer for VPN and lead engineer for xDSL for almost two years. She is currently a team lead for the Remote Access Engineering team in San Jose.

Lainie helped with the technical review of this book at its final phase.

I'd like to acknowledge the contributions of some of the founders of the Remote Access environment at Cisco: Yinpo Wong, BS, BA, MBA, currently Engineering Manager at Cisco Systems, Inc., John B Cornell III, currently Member of Technical Staff (IT) at Cisco Systems, Inc., and Craig Huegen, CCIE #2100, who is currently Chief Network Architect for Cisco Systems .

Finally, this book enjoyed the encouragement of many people, and I'd like to thank Dave Holloway, Kristine Smith, Lanny Ripple, Julie Martinez, Jeff Galisky, Terrance Blackman, Lilyan Gonzalez, Albert Soeherman, Diana Perez, Sidney Thompson, Damian Morris, Al Roethlisberger, Jawahar Sivasankaran (CCIE 8870), Doug Gober, Kathleen O'Looney, and many others.

Contents at a Glance

Foreword   xxiii

Introduction   xxv

Part I   Remote Access Fundamentals   3

Chapter 1   Remote Access Overview   5

Chapter 2   Telecommunication Basics   37

Chapter 3   The Cloud   69

Chapter 4   Troubleshooting Approaches, Models, and Tools   95

Part II   Dial   123

Chapter 5   Dial Technology Background   125

Chapter 6   Dial Design and Configuration Solutions   141

Chapter 7   Dial Troubleshooting   181

Chapter 8   Dial Troubleshooting Scenarios   219

Part III   ISDN   231

Chapter 9   ISDN Technology Background   233

Chapter 10   ISDN Design Solutions   257

Chapter 11   Cisco ISDN Configuration Solutions   289

Chapter 12   ISDN BRI Troubleshooting   313

Chapter 13   Troubleshooting Scenarios for ISDN BRI   359

Part IV   Frame Relay   411

Chapter 14   Frame Relay Technology Background   413

Chapter 15   Frame Relay Design Solutions   433

Chapter 16   Basic and Advanced Frame Relay Configurations   457

Chapter 17   Frame Relay Troubleshooting   491

Chapter 18   Frame Relay Troubleshooting Scenarios   547

Part V   VPN   589

Chapter 19   VPN Technology Background   591

Chapter 20   Remote Access VPN Design and Configuration Solutions   633

Chapter 21   Remote Access VPN Troubleshooting   675

Chapter 22   Remote Access VPN Troubleshooting Scenarios   765

Appendix A   Answers to Review Questions   807

Index   835

Contents

Foreword   xxiii

Introduction   xxv

Part I   Remote Access Fundamentals   3

Chapter 1   Remote Access Overview   5

Management Considerations   6
   Cost   6
   Availability   7
   Support   7
   In-Sourcing Versus Outsourcing   7
   Billing and Charge Backs   7
   User-Managed Versus Corporate-Managed   8
   Security   8
   Applications   8
   Home Access Versus Mobility   8

Defining the Remote Access User Population   9

Remote Access Service Options   9
   Analog Dialup Services   12
   ISDN Services   14
   Frame Relay Services   17
   VPN Services   18

VPN Service Vehicles   20
   Cable Modem Services   20
   xDSL Services   22
   Wireless Broadband Services   25
   Satellite Services   28

Provisioning of Enterprise Remote Access Services   30

Summary   35

Review Questions   35

Chapter 2   Telecommunication Basics   37

Shannon's Capacity Theorem   38

Modulation and Line-Coding Techniques in Wired Networks   39
   Amplitude, Frequency, and Phase Modulations   40
   Quadrature Amplitude Modulation   41
   xDSL Coding Techniques   42

Modulation and Line-Coding Techniques in Wireless LANs   44
   Infrared   45
   Ultra-High Frequency Narrowband Technologies and WLAN   46
   Synthesized Radio Technology   46
   Multiple Frequency Operation   46
   Ultra Wideband and WLANs   47
   WLAN Modulations and Coding Techniques   48

Modulation and Line-Coding Techniques in Hybrid Networks   53

Clocking, Line Coding, and Framing in Carrier Systems   54
   Clocking   55
   Pseudo-Ternary and Two Binary One Quaternary Signaling   55
   T1 Digital Coding and Framing   59
   T1 and T3 Framing   62
   PRI—1.544-Mbps Interface   64
   PRI—2.048-Mbps Interface   65

End Notes   66

Summary   66

Review Questions   66

Chapter 3   The Cloud   69

Carriers, Service Providers, and How Traffic Is Carried   69

FDM   71

Digitalization of the Signal and Pulse Code Modulation   72

TDM   73

T-Carriers   75
   T1/E1 and Primary Rate Interfaces, T1s, and DS   75
   T1s and DS and TDM Hierarchy   77
   E1   77
   Network Signaling Systems and SS7   78

SONET, Synchronous Transport Signal, and Synchronous Digital Hierarchy   79
   The Optical Fiber Hierarchy of Circuits   80

Carrier's Facilities and Switching Systems   80
   First-Tier Exchange Carriers   80
   Inside the CO   81
   Second Layer Exchange Carriers—IXC   81
   Switches and Tandems   82
   LEC/IXC Operations   82
   Tandem Office and Tool Office   83

ISPs and ASPs   85

Data Centers and Internet Hosting Services   87

The Future of Service Providers   89
   Service Offering   90
   The Last-Mile Problem   90
   The 3G Wireless Alternative   91

End Note   92

Summary   92

Review Questions   92

Chapter 4   Troubleshooting Approaches, Models, and Tools   95

Interconnection Models   96
   Department of Defense Model   97
   Seven-Layer OSI Model   98

Troubleshooting Models and the Baseline   101
   Troubleshooting Models   101
   The Baseline   103

Common and Cisco-Specific Tools   109
   Ping and Privileged (Extended) Ping Commands   110
   The Traceroute and Privileged (Extended) Traceroute Commands   114
   The Netcat Utility   115
   Service Assurance Agent   117
   The IOS Commands show and debug   118

End Notes   119

Summary   119

Review Questions   119

Part II   Dial   123

Chapter 5   Dial Technology Background   125

Overview of Modems   125

Telco Issues   128
   Digital Pad   129
   Line Code Errors   130

Authentication Options   132

PPP   134
    Link Dead (Physical Layer Not Ready)   135
    Link Establishment Phase   135
    Authentication Phase   136
    Network Layer Protocol Phase   136
    Link Termination Phase   137
    PPP Troubleshooting Considerations   137

End Notes   138

Summary   138

Review Questions   138

Chapter 6   Dial Design and Configuration Solutions   141

Dial Design Solutions   142
    Text Dial-In Network   143
    PPP Dial-In Network   143
    Text Dial-Out Network   144
    PPP Dial-Out Network   145
    Large-Scale Dial-Out Network   146
    Dial-On-Demand Backup Network   147

Dial Configuration Solutions   149
    Text Dial-In Configuration   150
    PPP Dial-In Configuration   151
    Large-Scale Dial-In Configuration   159
    Text Dial-Out Configuration   164
    PPP Dial-Out Configuration   168
    Large-Scale Dial-Out Configuration   171
    Dial-On-Demand Backup Configuration   173

Summary   177

Review Questions   177

Chapter 7   Dial Troubleshooting   181

Troubleshooting NAS WAN Links   181
    Troubleshooting T1 Circuits   181
    Troubleshooting PRI Circuits   188

Troubleshooting Dial-In Service   190
    Step One: Verify that the Modem Is Ready to Accept Calls   191
    Step Two: Verify Type of Incoming Connection   192
    Step Three: Verify PPP Negotiation   194

Troubleshooting Dial-Out Service   200

AS5x00 Specific Commands and Debugs   205
    AS5200 Specific Commands and Debugs   207
    AS5300 Specific Commands and Debugs   209
    AS5400 Specific Commands and Debugs   214

Summary   215

Review Questions   215

Chapter 8   Dial Troubleshooting Scenarios   219

Scenario 1: Authentication Time Outs—Part I   219

Scenario 2: Authentication Time Outs—Part II   221

Scenario 3: Frequent Retrains and Disconnects   221

Scenario 4: Dirty Phone Line   223

Scenario 5: Bad Modem   225

Frequently Asked Questions and Answers   226

Summary   228

Part III   ISDN   231

Chapter 9   ISDN Technology Background   233

ISDN Standards   233
    E-Series   233
    I-Series   234
    Q-Series   234

ISDN Channels   234

ISDN Planes: ISDN Layer Architecture   236
    Layer 1: BRI   237
    The Layer 2 D Channel: LAPD   242
    Layer 3 in the D Channel: Q.931 and Message Format   248

ISDN Switch Types   252

Summary   253

Review Questions   253

Chapter 10   ISDN Design Solutions   257

Enterprise and ISP Designs   258
   Setting the ISDN Switch Type   259
   Setting SPIDs and LDNs   260

IP Pool Design   262

NAT and PAT   265
   PAT   266
   NAT   267

Per-User (Per Function) Configuration   272
   Virtual Interface Templates   272
   Virtual Profiles   273

MLP   273

MMP   278
   MMP Configuration   281
   MMP Sample Implementation   282
   Verifying MMP   284

Summary   285

Review Questions   286

Chapter 11   Cisco ISDN Configuration Solutions   289

Cisco ISDN Cost-Effective Solutions   289
   Spoofing   290
   Snapshot Routing and OSPF Demand Circuits   290
   DDR   293
   PPP Callback for ISDN   303

ISDN Security   305

Configuring the POTS (Telephone) Interfaces   306
   Creating Dial Peers   307
   Advanced Telephone Features   308

Summary   310

Review Questions   310

Chapter 12   ISDN BRI Troubleshooting   313

Troubleshooting the Physical Layer   314

Troubleshooting the Data Link Layer   319

Troubleshooting the Network Layer   324

Troubleshooting PPP   335
    Troubleshooting PPP LCP   335
    Troubleshooting PPP Authentication   340
    Troubleshooting PPP Network Control Protocols   341
    PPP: Termination of the Connection   352

Troubleshooting Telephone Interfaces   353

End Notes   356

Summary   356

Review Questions   356

Chapter 13   Troubleshooting Scenarios for ISDN BRI   359

Recommendations for Practical Troubleshooting of ISDN Remote Services   359
    Using #show isdn status to View Service Layers   360
    Preconfiguring the Routers on Both Ends   364
    Accessing the Remote User's Router   365

Scenario 1: New Install Problems   369

Scenario 2: Dial-Out Problems   372

Scenario 3: ISDN Performance Problems   376
    Short-Term Routing Issues   377
    Line Problems   377
    Configuration Setting Problems   382
    LEC Switch Problems   382

Scenario 4: End-to-End Communication Problems   386
    The LEC's ISDN Switch Settings   387
    LCP Problems and the Magic 22 Seconds   387
    Authentication Problems   396
    End-to-End Routing Problems   399

Scenario 5: Windows 2000 DDR Issue   399
    Step 1: Implement the Manufacturer's Recommendations and Determine if They Are
      Effective   400
    Step 2: Monitor and Sniff All Traffic and Try to Find Patterns and Characteristics of the
      Traffic   402
    Step 3: Use a Cisco Knowledge Base to Remedy any Identified Problems   406
    Step 4: Select a Solution and Test It   407

Summary   408

Part IV   Frame Relay   411

Chapter 14   Frame Relay Technology Background 413

Frame Relay Standards   415

Frame Relay Service Architecture   417

Frame Relay Protocols   419
   LAPF   419

End Notes   429

Summary   429

Review Questions   429

Chapter 15   Frame Relay Design Solutions 433

Design Parameters   434
   CIR Options   435
   UNI   438
   NNI   438
   Voice over Frame Relay   440
   Frame Relay Multicast   440

Frame Relay Topologies and Congestion Control   441
   Partial-Mesh and Full-Mesh Frame Relay Designs   441
   User and Frame Relay Switch Operations Under Congestion   441
   Congestion and Windowing   443
   Frame Relay Performance Criteria   444

Frame Relay and Upper-Layer Protocols   445
   Encapsulating IP, Q.933, and SNAP   447
   Encapsulating Other Protocols over Frame Relay   448
   Frame Relay Fragmentation   448

LMI   449
   Consortium (Cisco) LMI Type   451
   Annex D (ANSI) LMI Type   451
   ITU-T Q.933 Annex A LMI Type   453

Address Resolution: ARP, Reverse ARP, and Inverse ARP   453
   ARP   453
   Reverse ARP   454
   Inverse ARP   454

End Notes   454

Summary   455

Review Questions   455

Chapter 16   Basic and Advanced Frame Relay Configurations   457

Basic Frame Relay Configurations   458
Point-to-Multipoint Configurations   458
Point-to-Point Configurations   461
Maximum Number of DLCIs Per Interface   466
Routing Protocols and Frame Relay Configurations   467
Frame Relay Broadcast Queue   468

Advanced Frame Relay Configurations   469
Configuring IP Unnumbered Frame Relay   469
Frame Switching   469
Frame Relay and ISDN Backup Configuration   471
Frame Relay and Bridging   474
Frame Relay Compression   476
Frame Relay and IP Multicast Configuration   482
Frame Relay and Traffic Shaping   483

Summary   488

Review Questions   489

Chapter 17   Frame Relay Troubleshooting   491

Beginning the Frame Relay Troubleshooting Process   492

Physical Layer Troubleshooting   493
Line and Clocking Problems   493
Serial Interface 0 and Line Protocol Is Down   498
Performance Issues Related to the Physical Layer   501

Data Link Layer Troubleshooting   506
PVC Configuration Issues   507
LMI Issues   513

Performance Problems   526
Flapping Links   526
End-to-End Problems   528
Frame Relay Shaping Problems   534
Troubleshooting Compression Over Frame Relay   537

End Notes   544

Summary   544

Review Questions   544

Chapter 18   Frame Relay Troubleshooting Scenarios   547

Scenario 1: New Install Issues   548

Scenario 2: Mismatched DLCI Settings   556

Scenario 3: Performance Issues from Flapping Lines and Traffic Shaping Issues   562
   Flapping Lines   563
   Traffic Shaping Issues   566

Scenario 4: IP Multicast Issues in Frame Relay   573

Scenario 5: Frame Relay Host Migration   580
   Working with Your Vendor   580
   Preparing the Host   581
   Routing Options   583
   Endpoint Migration   584

Summary   585

Part V   VPN   589

Chapter 19   VPN Technology Background   591

Service Provider, Dedicated, and Access VPNs   591

Enterprise VPNs Overview   593

Enterprise VPN Categories   595
   Functional VPN Categories   595
   Technology Category   598

Network Layer (Layer 3) VPNs   604
   Layer 3 Tunneling   605
   Security Associations and Security Policy for IKE and IPSec   605
   Negotiations of ISAKMP and IPSec Phases and Modes   607
   Mutable and Immutable Fields and the ICV   608
   Fragmentation, Path MTU Discovery, and ICMP Processing   610
   IPSec Modes   612
   IPSec Protocols   613
   Authentication in VPN   619

End Notes   628

Summary   629

Review Questions   629

Chapter 20   Remote Access VPN Design and Configuration Solutions   633

Remote Access VPN Design Solutions   633
   Remote Access VPN Design Objectives   634
   Remote Access VPN Management   635
   Remote Access VPN Security Considerations   636
   Remote Access VPN Termination Equipment Design Considerations   641

VPN Configuration Considerations   648
   Configuration of the VPN 3000 Concentrator   648
   Cisco Remote Access VPN Clients   662

End Notes   671

Summary   672

Review Questions   672

Chapter 21   Remote Access VPN Troubleshooting   675

Troubleshooting Cisco Remote Access VPN Clients   676
   Cisco VPN Unity SW Client   676
   Cisco 3002 HW Client Troubleshooting   706
   Cisco Easy VPN Client   713
   Cisco PIX VPN Client   721

Internet Technologies and Remote Access VPNs   732
   VPN and ADSL   732
   VPN and Internet Access Through a Cable TV Infrastructure   740
   VPN and Internet Access over Satellite and Wireless Systems   745

LAN and General Networking Issues Affecting Remote Access VPNs   753
   Multiple VPN Clients Behind a NAT Device   753
   MTU—A Critical Factor for Troubleshooting Internet IPSec Connectivity   754
   Slow or Inaccessible Login to Kerberos Active Directory   760

End Notes   761

Summary   761

Review Questions   762

Chapter 22   Remote Access VPN Troubleshooting Scenarios 765

Warming Up with Preliminary Troubleshooting Steps   766
   Step 1: Determine if There Is an Internet Connection   767
   Step 2: Ensure that the VPN Client Is Properly Installed   771
   Step 3: Check or Create Your Profiles   772

Scenario 1: Cannot Authenticate   773
    Case 1: Bad Group Name or Group Password   774
    Case 2: Prompted Multiple Times for Username and Password   775
    Case 3: Firewall Software   777
    Case 4: MTU Set High   779
    Case 5: MTU Set Low   784

Scenario 2: Can Authenticate but Problems Passing Data   784
    Case 1: Cannot Pass Traffic and Using NAT Connection Entry   785
    Case 2: MTU Causing Packet Loss   786
    Case 3: Connection Keeps Dropping   786
    Case 4: Cannot Browse the Internal Domain   787

Scenario 3: PPPoE Software/Hardware Problems   790
    Case 1: PPPoE Software Issues   791
    Case 2: IOS-Based PPPoE Issues   793

Scenario 4: 3002 Connection Problems   795
    Check the Interfaces Status on the 3002   797
    Confirm the Group Name and Password Are Correct   800
    Problems with User Authentication   800

Scenario 5: Extranet Issues   801
    Protocol 50—ESP   801
    UDP 500—ISAKMP   801
    UDP 10,000 (Allow IPSec Through NAT)   802
    Tunnel Keepalives   802
    Dead Peer Detection   803

Summary   805

Appendix A   Answers to Review Questions   807

Index   835

Foreword

Cisco Systems Inc. is built on the philosophy of changing the way we work, live, play, and learn. The ability to telecommute and work remotely from any location is a large part of this change. Telecommuting is not a new concept; employees have been able to work remotely for decades. Significant benefits are associated with this practice.

Today, the ability to be productive while working remotely can occur only when required office applications and tools are accessed and used as if you were physically present in the office. The early days of dialup networking are replaced with high-speed access to the home at prices that are more cost effective. The requirement to telecommute and to access the corporate network while on business travel has played a significant role in creating an entire industry around remote access. Future trends include more prevalent broadband connectivity available from hotels, airports, and other public locations.

Over the last five years, the Information Technology organization of Cisco Systems created and maintained a dedicated Remote Access Services (RAS) department to provide support to Cisco employees in the U.S. The team, which was based at the San Jose campus in California, grew in responsibility for design, engineering, and support of remote access solutions in the Americas. The IT organizations outside of the Americas provided local remote access support to employees within their regions. The remote and corporate organizations work jointly together to develop global standards strategies and solutions.

Through the years, the team implemented and supported services that consisted of analog dial, ISDN, Frame Relay, xDSL, and VPN. In total, through a combination of in-sourced and outsourced services, the team supported 30,000 dialup users and over 16,000 users with high-speed access to their homes. This RAS team of 15 engineers, provisioners, analysts, and project managers supported more users and services than most medium-sized Internet service providers (ISPs) in the U.S. A separate helpdesk organization provided all first-level support for users globally.

I had the privilege of leading the Remote Access Services team for a 20-month period during 2000 and 2001. They are the most professional, hard-working group of individuals I have ever worked with. Providing remote access support can be thankless and frustrating when dealing with end users who believe their individual remote connectivity should have high level of support with a four-hour mean time to repair. Furthermore, supporting an engineering user base further complicates matters because home networking requirements become more complex to accommodate.

Unlike most enterprises, RAS responsibilities for Cisco also included testing and implementing new Cisco products to showcase their use within our own networks. One could say most of our network was a living lab and, although we were making frequent changes to the infrastructure, the RAS team consistently maintained greater than 99.925 percent availability each quarter. The team contributed to making product improvements and enhanced the testing of new hardware and software by identifying product bugs that were fixed before a customer encountered the problem.

The team achieved significant results during the last fiscal year that included increasing the number of users who have broadband connectivity at home by 62 percent while decreasing average cost per user by 50 percent. The team also improved support ratios for broadband users from 1000 users per engineer to 1700 users per engineer. A member of the team, Plamen Nedeltchev, also developed a solution to address the problems with the huge number of transactions a Windows 2000 network generates, especially for an ISDN usage-based environment. His solution significantly reduced the usage costs for ISDN users and the corporation, and was significantly better than any solution recommended by Microsoft.

Plamen is a key contributor to the enhancements implemented in our remote access network, especially to addressing the requirements of development engineers who work full time from home. It was his vision to write this book for Cisco Press to address the gap of available remote access troubleshooting techniques. It is a compilation of the current knowledge and practices of one of the world's best remote access teams.

In August 2001, a reorganization of IT Infrastructure resulted in the restructuring of remote access within Cisco. Although the centralized RAS team is now disbanded, this book is a testament to their achievements and a legacy to the knowledge they possess for developing and running leading-edge remote access networks. I am proud to be associated with remote access services, and the experience I gained in my former position within Cisco will always be one of the highlights of my career.

Felicia Brych
Manager
Cisco Remote Access Services
December 1999–August 2001

Introduction

In my career, telecommunications came into existence in the beginning of the 1970s. In high school, the army, and later in college, where I had my first contact with big and mini computers, I made my first attempts to grasp the technology. The emerging LANs in the 1980s, bridges, decentralized computing, change of computer generations, Token Ring, and, of course, CSMA with all flavors and modifications, and the emerging IP with its promising end-to-end versus hop-by-hop networking, were among the most intriguing events in my career. The phenomenon of the Internet, the super-media, during the last decade of the 20th century, has without a doubt been one of the principal, not only technical, but also social, events for generations that still stirs my curiosity.

The remote access to corporate resources, located far away from your location, always amazed and fascinated me. I remember when, at the beginning of the 1980s, I was able to not only dial in from Plovdiv, but to read my inbox located on a server in Sofia...I was the happiest man in the world.

NOTE   Sofia is the capital of Bulgaria. Plovdiv is the second biggest city in Bulgaria. The distance between the two cities is about 150 km.

I always wanted to write this book. Years and years of looking at computer screens always wondering if it is possible to put together a concise description of all these numbers, abbreviations, and symbols. Meanwhile, I was always collecting pieces here and there, writing short manuals for myself. Working in the remote access environment at Cisco, I finally had the chance to write this book, which started from an article about ISDN troubleshooting one night in November 2000. (The article was published in the Cisco *Packet* Magazine in Q2 2001.) Brett Bartow's proposal for writing a book about remote access troubleshooting came just in time.

Remote access is about buckets of technologies. Remote access is about how to reach the remote LAN. The uniqueness of working on remote access is the opportunity to enhance your knowledge and to design, implement, configure, and support the variety of technologies used for remote access solutions today. Your troubleshooting ability changes based on your position or location in the classical trio of remote access—whether you are a remote user, a service provider site, or at the corporate site. As a troubleshooting engineer, maybe the best position you can choose is the last one. The uniqueness of the enterprise remote access is that you have limited visibility into the cloud, but you can see both ends of the remote access service and you control the headend side. Of course, troubleshooting is maybe more about hunches, about right-and-wrong, and about experience, but knowledge definitely helps. Combined with passion, it can make troubleshooting a genuine craft.

One of the main challenges of this book was to provide the reader with the minimum technology background sufficient to understand the technology basics. This challenge came from the fact that numerous studies and books published in the last 20 to 30 years have produced an abundance of information, which is almost impossible to synthesize in a limited number of pages for each technology in this book. Combining this information with trouble-shooting techniques and recommendations was another challenge that this book needed to meet.

This book was written with appreciation of generations of scientists and engineers, constantly developing standards, coding and signaling schemes, hardware/software designs, and configurations to provide remote users with full access to their resources, sometimes thousands of miles away. This book was certainly written with an appreciation to Cisco's contribution to the technology over the last decade.

This book is written with appreciation to remote access solutions, where wired networks made possible the most common design solutions today. That's why Part I concentrates on the fundamentals, whereas Parts II, III, and IV deal with commonly available technologies, such as dial, ISDN, and Frame Relay.

However, we are about to witness and participate in a significant change in the existing remote access solutions. *Panta rhei*—as every technology continuously changes its features, the remote access environment is no different. Today's VPN (in all flavors) is only the first wave of moving away from legacy remote access, which is primarily based on permanent circuits. That's why Part V, "VPN," is a bridge to the future—towards using locally available Internet services to access the corporate resources remotely.

The evolving mobility adds a new dimension to remote access technologies. Overcoming the tyranny of cables will transform remote access into ubiquitous access sooner rather than later.

Objectives of This Book

The main objective of this book is to offer a concise version of troubleshooting remote access networks. Whether you are an enterprise network manager or administrator, network or consulting engineer, or a remote access help-desk consultant, you will have access to both sides of the connection. If you are troubleshooting both end-user and core-environment issues, you will find the book useful because it provides you with the maximum reasonable descriptions, explanations, and examples possible.

Secondly, this book's focus is on the remote end of the connection instead of on the corporate side. In my imagination, I always see a user, whose remote access service—his lifeline to the corporation—is down and he is desperately trying to restore it to meet his deadline. I've been there. I know what that's like. That's why, even if you are an end user working with your local service provider or ISP, this book will enhance your knowledge and troubleshooting skills.

Who Should Read This Book?

This book is not about the big picture, but about engineers whose day-to-day operations require remote troubleshooting. This book is for those who, sitting behind non-working routers, are trying to figure out where to start and how to approach a problem. This book is intended for any engineer who is contemplating changing his qualification to become a network engineer. This book is for network engineers who already have a certain level of qualification and experience and are trying to enhance their knowledge in remote access technologies. Finally, this book provides helpful remote access troubleshooting information for engineers working toward CCNP and CCIE certifications. This book is written assuming the reader has a level of networking experience equivalent to that of a CCNA.

The Organization of This Book

This book is based on the premise that if you really want to troubleshoot, you need to go through some preliminary phases first. You need to start with the technology basics, progress through design and configuration solutions, and finally get to the troubleshooting methodologies, techniques, and tools. Every chapter of this book is organized according to this concept, and every chapter includes review questions. Finally, the examples and the scenarios in Parts II, III, IV, and V are live-based and represent the best proven practices from more than tens of thousands of cases handled by the Cisco Remote Access team.

Part I: Remote Access Fundamentals

Part I, which describes the fundamentals of remote access networks, is the technological foundation of this book. This part includes management considerations and remote access service options. It provides relatively extensive information about telecommunications basics, modulations, and coding techniques in wired, wireless, and hybrid environments. An integral part of this discussion is the clocking, line coding, and framing in carrier systems, including the most common T1s and PRIs. An important section of Part I is the discussion about the cloud, and how the carriers and service providers handle the traffic. The information about the future of the service and the last-mile initiative of Cisco is provided as well.

Although the first three chapters are about the remote access environment, the last chapter in Part I is about remote access inter-network layered models, methodology, and tools. In this chapter, the layer-by-layer model of troubleshooting is introduced as one systematic approach to troubleshooting issues.

Part II: Dial

Part II is devoted to one of the most traditional remote access technologies: dial networking. The initial technology information is designated to underline some of the fundamentals and specifics of dial, in addition to the information provided in Part I. The detailed description of modems and the overview of possible provider issues, as well as the detailed description of Point-to-Point Protocol (PPP), is among the main topics covered. The design chapter includes information about text dialin network, PPP dialin network, text dial-out network, PPP dial-out network, large scale dial-out network, and dial-on-demand backup network, all of which are well-known design solutions in the industry today. The same set of design solutions is also presented from a configuration point of view, with the necessary explanations, tips, and notes. The dial troubleshooting section includes information on troubleshooting T1 and PRI circuits, dialin service, dial-out service, and important access server (AS5x00) specific commands and debugs.

The troubleshooting scenario chapter focuses on authentication problems, frequent retrains and disconnects, and dirty phone lines and bad modems.

Part III: ISDN

Part III is about Integrated Services Digital Network (ISDN)—especially ISDN BRI. This part provides concise ISDN technology background information about standards, channels, and ISDN architecture. The necessary troubleshooting information about reference points, interfaces, and initializing of layers one, two, and three is provided here, as is information about ISDN switch types. The common ISDN design solutions are focused on NAT/PAT configurations and virtual profiles and interfaces. Separate sections are designated to provide detailed discussion about Multilink Point-to-Point Protocol (MP) and Multi-Chassis Multilink Point-to-Point Protocol (MMP) designs. The configuration chapter focuses on ISDN cost-effective solutions, such as spoofing, snapshot routing, and dial-on-demand routing (DDR). The ISDN troubleshooting chapter illustrates the layer-by-layer approach and includes detailed discussion about each and every layer, as well as extended information about troubleshooting MP, MMP, and telephone interfaces.

The troubleshooting scenarios include new install problems, dial-out problems, performance issues, end-to-end problems, and Windows 2000 and Cisco DDR controversy.

Part IV: Frame Relay

The main focus of Part IV is Frame Relay. More information is provided about the end user's side of the design than about the corporate side. The Frame Relay standards, protocols, and service architecture are the main foundation topics. The Frame Relay design provides detailed information about User-Network Interface (UNI) and Network-to-Network Interface (NNI). Frame Relay performance criteria, fragmentations, Inverse ARP, upper-layer protocols, and Local Management Interface (LMI) are among the design objectives of Part IV. The Frame Relay configuration provides some common configuration solutions and explanations. The advanced configuration section includes IP unnumbered solution, frame switching, Frame Relay backup, compression, multicast, and traffic shaping. The Frame Relay troubleshooting chapter applies the layer-by-layer approach and discusses Layer 1 and 2 problems, performance, end-to-end issues, compression, and traffic-shaping problems.

The Frame Relay troubleshooting scenarios in Chapter 18 focus on new installs, wrong DLCI, LMI settings, and performance and multicast issues. Rehosting of Frame Relay service is included as well.

Part V: VPN

Virtual Private Network (VPN) is about running private data over public networks. Part V provides the minimum initial background for all versions of VPN, but focuses on remote access solutions. PPTP, L2TP, IPSec, and key agreements are discussed in detail. The common design solutions, the termination points, software and hardware VPN clients, EzVPN, and PIX-based solutions are explained concisely. All available remote access VPN solutions and their configurations are another important part here. They include Cisco VPN 3000 Series Concentrator configuration and Cisco VPN client configuration (including Cisco Unity VPN Client, Cisco VPN 3002 HW Client, Cisco Easy VPN IOS, and Cisco PIX 501 and 506 Client). The VPN troubleshooting chapter includes extensive and detailed explanations, divided into three main groups: Cisco VPN client issues, VPN and Internet technologies issues, and VPN and LAN issues affecting remote access VPN.

The scenarios in Chapter 22 include VPN over PPPOE, authentication problems and cannot pass data issues, hardware VPN client issues, and extranet issues.

Command Syntax Conventions

The command syntax in this book conforms to the following conventions:

- Commands, keywords, and actual values for arguments are **bold**.
- Arguments (which need to be supplied with an actual value) are *italic*.
- Optional keywords and arguments are in brackets [].
- A choice of mandatory keywords and arguments is in braces {}.

These conventions are for syntax only.

References and Additional Reading

You might find the following list of resources helpful in your further study of remote access technologies:

Abe, George. *Residential Broadband*, Second Edition. Cisco Press, 2000.

Adams, Michael. *OpenCable Architecture*. Cisco Press, 2000.

Alwayn, Vivek. *Advanced MPLS Design and Implementation*. Cisco Press, 2001.

American National Standards Institute. ANSI T1.601.1994. "ISDN Basic Access Interface for Use on Metallic Loops for Applications on the Network Side of the NT."

Bingham, John A. C. *ADSL, VDSL, and Multicarrier Modulation*. John Wiley and Sons Inc., 2000.

Birkner, Matthew H. *Cisco Internetwork Design*. Cisco Press, 2000.

Black, Ulysses D. *Frame Relay Networks: Specifications and Implementations*. McGraw Hill, 1998.

— — —. *ISDN and SS7: Architecture for Digital Signaling Networks*. Prentice Hall, 1997.

Boyles, Tim and David Hucaby. *CCNP Switching Exam Certification Guide*. Cisco Press, 2000.

Buckwalter, Jeff T. *Frame Relay: Technology and Practice*. Addison-Wesley Longman Inc., 1999.

Chappel, Laura. *Advanced Cisco Router Configuration*. Cisco Press, 1999.

Chappel, Laura and Dan Farkas. *Cisco Internetwork Troubleshooting*. Cisco Press, 1999.

Cisco Systems, Inc. *Cisco IOS 12.0: Wide-Area Networking Solutions*. Cisco Press, 1999.

— — —. *Dictionary of Internetworking Terms and Acronyms*. Cisco Press, 2001.

— — —. *Internetworking Technologies Handbook*, Third Edition. Cisco Press, 2000.

— — —. *Network Design and Case Studies (CCIE Fundamentals)*, Second Edition. Cisco Press, 2000.

— — —. "Cisco 700 Series Command Reference." 1996-1997.

— — —. "Cisco 700 Series Installation and Configuration Guide." 1997.

Conover, J. "80211a: Making Space for Speed." Network Computing, January 2001.

Cooperman, G., E. Jessen, and G. Michler (eds.). *Workshop on Wide-Area Networks and High Performance Computing*. Springer, 1999.

Coutinho, S. C. *The Mathematics of Ciphers: Number Theory and RSA Cryptography*. A K Peters, Ltd., 1999.

Flanagan, William A. *ISDN: A Practical Guide to Getting Up and Running*. CMP Books, 2000.

Frame Relay Forum, FRF.1.1. "User-to-Network Interface (UNI) Implementation Agreement." January 1996.

Goralski, Walter. *Frame Relay for High-Speed Networks*. John Wiley and Sons Inc., 1999.

Gough, Clare. *CCNP Routing Exam Certification Guide*. Cisco Press, 2001.

Held, Gilbert. *Frame Relay Networking*. John Wiley and Sons Inc., 1999.

Jones, Burton W. *Modular Arithmetic*. Blaisdell Publishing Company, 1964.

Kessler, Gary, and Peter Southwick. *ISDN Concepts, Facilities, and Services*, Third Edition. McGraw Hill, 1996.

Khan, Ahmed S. *The Telecommunications Fact Book and Illustrated Dictionary.* Delma Publishers Inc, 1992.

Knuth, Donald E. *Art of Computer Programming,* Volume III: *Sorting and Searching* (Second Edition). Addison-Wesley Longman, 1998.

McClain, Gary R. *Handbook of Networking and Connectivity.* AP Professional Academic Press, 1994.

Mervana, Sanjeev and Chris Le. *Design and Implementation of DSL-Based Access Solutions.* Cisco Press, 2002.

Miller, Mark. *Analyzing Broadband Networks: ISDN, Frame Relay, SMDS, and ATM.* John Wiley and Sons, Inc., 1996.

Morgan, Brian and Craig Dennis. *CCNP Remote Access Exam Certification Guide.* Cisco Press, 2000.

Oppenheimer, Priscilla. *Top-Down Network Design.* Cisco Press, 1999.

Pecar, Joseph A. and David A. Garbin. *The New McGraw-Hill Telecom Factbook*, Second Edition. McGraw-Hill Professional Publishing, 2000.

Pepelnjak, Ivan and Jim Guichard. *MPLS and VPN Architectures.* Cisco Press, 2000.

Nedeltchev, Plamen. "Troubleshooting ISDN." Cisco Packet Magazine, Q2 2001.

———. "Wireless LAN Ready for Prime Time." Cisco Packet Magazine, Q3 2001.

Nedeltchev, Plamen and Radoslav Ratchkov. "IPSec and Related Algorithms." Cisco Packet Magazine, Q2 2002.

Ranjbar, Amir S. *CCNP Support Exam Certification Guide.* Cisco Press, 2000.

Retana, A. Slice, D., and White, R. *Advanced IP Network Design (CCIE Professional Development).* Cisco Press, 1999.

RFC 1191. "Path MTU Discovery."

RFC 1918. "Address Allocation for Private Internets."

RFC 2401. "Security Architecture for the Internet Protocol."

RFC 2402. "IP Authentication Header."

RFC 2403. "The Use of HMAC-MD5-96 Within ESP and AH."

RFC 2404. "The Use of HMAC-SHA-1-96 Within ESP and AH."

RFC 2405. "The ESP DES-CBC Cipher Algorithm with Explicit IV."

RFC 2406. "IP Encapsulating Security Payload (ESP)."

RFC 2407. "The Internet IP Security Domain of Interpretation for ISAKMP."

RFC 2408. "Internet Security Association and Key Management Protocol (ISAKMP)."

RFC 2409. "The Internet Key Exchange (IKE)."

RFC 2410. "The NULL Encryption Algorithm and Its Use with IPSec."

RFC 2411. "IP Security Document Roadmap."

RFC 2412. "The OAKLEY Key Determination Protocol."

RFC 2637. "Point-to-Point Tunneling Protocol."

RFC 2661. "Layer Two Tunneling Protocol 'L2TP'."

RFC 3078. "Microsoft Point-To-Point Encryption (MPPE) Protocol."

Sapien, Mike, and Greg Piedmo. *Mastering ISDN*. Sybex, 1997.

Schneier, Bruc. *Applied Cryptography: Protocols, Algorithms, and Source Code in C*, Second Edition. John Wiley and Sons Inc., 1996.

Srisuresh, P. and M. Holdrege. "IP Network Address Translator (NAT) Terminology and Considerations." RFC 2663, August 1999.

Stallings, W. *Data and Computer Communications*, Fifth Edition. Prentice Hall, 1997.

Stallings, William. *ISDN and Broadband ISDN with Frame Relay and ATM*. Prentice Hall, 1999.

Tittel, Ed, and Steve James. *ISDN Networking Essentials*. AP Professional Academic Press, 1996.

Williamson, Beau. *Developing IP Multicast Networks*, Volume I. Cisco Press, 2000.

Wright, Robert. *IP Routing Primer*. Cisco Press, 1998.

www.itu.int/ITU-T/

Wynston, Michael. *Cisco Enterprise Management Solutions*, Volume I. Cisco Press, 2001.

PART I

Remote Access Fundamentals

Chapter 1   Remote Access Overview

Chapter 2   Telecommunication Basics

Chapter 3   The Cloud

Chapter 4   Troubleshooting Approaches, Models, and Tools

Remote Access Overview

Remote access is a term that pertains to communication with a data processing facility from a remote location or facility through a data link. This chapter introduces remote access environment specifics and provides brief descriptions of remote access options in the following aspects:

- Management considerations and the pros and cons of remote access solutions
- Defining the remote access population
- Legacy remote access solutions
- Virtual Private Networks (VPNs) over some of the most popular technologies, such as cable modems, xDSL, wireless, and satellite services
- Provisioning of the corporate circuits

As a network administrator or network engineer, you need to identify the specifics of the environment and know the specifics of the solution that you are troubleshooting to set up your expectations accordingly.

Remote access networks are often described as the most difficult type of network to support. In corporate local-area networks (LANs) and wide-area networks (WANs), data centers and network operations centers safeguard the networking infrastructure. However, remote access to an employee's home or from locations while an employee is traveling or working from a customer's premises introduces many components not under a corporation's control.

Within a user's home, there can be wiring problems or limited copper pairs, which can complicate the installation and troubleshooting process. Users can power off their home routers or modems, referred to as customer premises equipment (CPE), at any time. This makes proactive monitoring extremely difficult, if not impossible. Users can install any hardware and software on their home network or computer that might interfere with, or not integrate with, the remote access solution. It is difficult to control the security aspects of a user's home network. Finally, a user might be technically proficient enough to modify the CPE configuration, which can result in additional problems.

While an employee is working on the road from either a hotel or a customer premises, additional complications exist, and sometimes getting answers to specific troubleshooting questions can be impossible. The phone system in a hotel often contributes to dialup connectivity problems. A broadband service offering in a hotel or a customer's firewall can block IPSec traffic for VPN users who are trying to reach their destination point through the Internet.

Some services that the remote user is accustomed to in the corporate environment might be unavailable, not permissible, or have a degradation of quality because of bandwidth, latency, or policy limitations from remote locations. Some of these circumstances might require special setups to meet users' expectations.

For all these reasons, troubleshooting remote access problems can be a difficult and time-consuming process. The purpose of this book is to provide networking professionals with a collection of proven and current troubleshooting techniques for Cisco Systems remote access products and for most remote access service options. Technologies addressed in this book include analog dial, ISDN, Frame Relay, and VPN.

Management Considerations

As a network manager, deciding on the type of remote access services to provide to your organization depends on numerous factors. For each of them, there might be an easy answer based on general knowledge of the organization, or you might be required to obtain specific business requirements that limit service options. For many large enterprises, there is no one-size-fits-all service that meets all user requirements. The categories described in this section are the most common ones that an organization should consider when making remote access service decisions. (They are listed in no particular order.)

Cost

The budget for remote access can limit the options available. The organization must determine what base of users will be granted access, what capacity and growth estimates are required, and how the costs will be allocated internally. To form the basis for a remote access budget and funding approach, answer the following questions:

- Who will cover the initial capital and installation costs?
- What costs are required to deploy the solution?
- Are there any training costs?
- How will any monthly circuit costs for the back-end environment be funded?
- Should a user's organization be charged for the user's monthly access fees and any usage-based services?
- Is an approval process required for users to request remote access?
- Will the organization set a maximum limit on the monthly amount that a user can expense, and the user personally covers any additional costs?
- Should an internal fee be charged to fund the on-going operational support?
- Should the fee differ depending on the service or the level of support required?

Availability

An organization must define the geographic area (local, regional, national, or global) to which service must be supplied and determine the availability of network options within that area. Besides rural areas, many metropolitan areas do not have options for high-speed access to the home that include ISDN, Frame Relay, xDSL, cable, wireless, and satellite. The demise of many of the competitive local exchange carriers (CLECs) in the U.S., and an economic downturn during 2000 and 2001, has further impacted the build out of high-speed network access to residential neighborhoods. You must understand what options and technologies are available and whether or not you must restrict the options to one or more providers/carriers based on availability.

Support

Support options can weigh heavily on the remote access option you choose. You must define the service level for supporting the back end infrastructure and for supporting the end user. Different profiles of users can require different levels of support. Plan to set user expectations up front. The decision to in-source versus outsource must also be considered. The organization must have the available resources with the right skill sets to support the selected service. Training might be required for support staff. Local language and in-country support can be important. Determine if you need consultants to help fill the skill or resource gap. Assess whether the existing helpdesk organization can assume part of the support requirement. As part of your deployment plan, ensure that you include the time required to develop support processes and to train support personnel.

In-Sourcing Versus Outsourcing

The decision to in-source versus outsource depends on the core competency of your IT organization. Besides support considerations, the time and effort to develop and deploy a solution is a factor in the outsourcing decision. Determine if the organization has the available resources with the right skill sets to develop, deploy, provision, and support the selected service. Are resources available in the deployment locations or will team members be required to travel? Will security policies restrict the components that can be supported internally versus externally? What contracting process do you need to follow and how long will this take (that is, do you need to conduct a Request for Information or a Request for Proposal)? You need to solicit several bids from potential vendors and prepare a service and cost comparison of the internal versus external vendor options as part of the decision-making process.

Billing and Charge Backs

The decision or ability to charge back expenses to a user's organization was mentioned in the preceding section, "Cost." If you decide to charge back for user services rather than funding centrally, you must ensure that the necessary processes and systems are in place to handle the financial transactions. Is there a process currently available for remote access purposes? Will the vendor provide the billing information in the required format or medium? Should the corporation centrally manage the bills or should they be sent to the user who submits an expense report to cover the charge? Should there be a maximum limit set on the amount to be expensed? How will exceptions and anomalies be dealt with? What reports are necessary and who must receive them? Be prepared to handle the administrative overhead to manage the billing function.

User-Managed Versus Corporate-Managed

As part of the service offering, the organization must determine if it wants to restrict users to a limited number of vendors or open it up to any vendor and let the end user choose the provider. This concept has been used to implement VPN services where a user can select any Internet service provider (ISP) available in the local area, and choose the provider based on the criteria that are important to the user. When the user rather than the corporation orders high-speed access, the user becomes responsible for dealing with the vendor when the service is down or experiencing problems. The user also receives the monthly bill and is expected to submit an expense report up to an approved amount.

Security

The security policies of an organization are a significant factor in determining the solution. Based on the sensitivity of the information managed by the corporation, policies surrounding authentication, encryption, architecture, and outsourcing vary. Ensure that the security organization is included in the initial planning of the remote access service.

Applications

The applications that must be accessed remotely might restrict the technology alternatives or might affect the network architecture. Some applications can be useless if latency is too great or if the available bandwidth is insufficient. Other applications might not function properly if accessed through a VPN connection. Ensure that you work with the functional areas of the business to identify and test all the core applications that are required to be accessed remotely and to set user expectations on performance.

Home Access Versus Mobility

The final criterion to be considered is the need to access the corporate network from home, and from on the road while in a hotel, convention center, airport, or a customer/business partner premises. Depending on the organization's remote access requirement, a mobile solution might be a necessary part of the overall remote access service offering. The Cisco Mobile Office initiative addresses the solutions and considerations that differ based on the need to work on the road, at home, or at work (see www.cisco.com/warp/public/779/smbiz/mobility/). The next generation of at home solutions will include voice and video over IP, and improved conferencing and collaboration solutions.

Defining the Remote Access User Population

Several profiles of users typically require different solutions for remote connectivity. For each of these profiles, a different solution and possibly a different level of support might be required to meet their remote access needs:

- Full-time telecommuters usually are supported with enough IP addresses to meet their requirements. For them, /32 with NAT, /30, or even /29 address space can be assigned.

- Day extenders use their home environment as an extension to the existing office environment. They are connected an average of two to four hours to the corporate network, usually exchanging e-mails, downloading or uploading files from the server, or browsing the Internet.

- Road warriors typically spend most of their workday out of the office traveling to multiple locations. They require a mobile or wireless solution to access their applications on the network.

- Engineers might extend their office/lab environment at home. If this is the case, they can require up to a /28 IP address space to accommodate their requirements.

Another possible classification here is based on the user's job instead of whether they are full-time or part-time telecommuters. A full-time telecommuter doing HR or marketing work probably will not need five IP addresses, and a part-time engineer might still need a /29, /28, or maybe a NAT private network.

Remote Access Service Options

Building remote access networks is not only related to management, but also to some fundamental technical choices that include last mile decisions, WAN technologies, and subscribed services. These choices can be made based on capacity planning analysis, expected functionality, baselines, and simulative models.

The viable service options offered by practically all service providers include dial-in, ISDN, and Frame Relay. During the last several years in the U.S. market, new technologies, such as xDSL, cable modems, and wireless broadband services, have emerged. Literally all available narrowband and broadband services can be used for future remote access designs. A wireline and wireless classification of the offered services is another possible way of reviewing remote access offerings.

NOTE   Narrowband, or baseband, service offerings refer to subvoice channels that can carry data starting from 64 kbps, fractions of T1, and T1. The term is used for legacy plain old telephone systems (POTS) and non-video-capable systems. Broadband refers to systems that are capable of carrying a wide range of frequencies and services. The cable systems are a classic example.

Figure 1-1 depicts several Cisco remote access services. The scope of enterprise remote access can be broad. The lower portion of Figure 1-1 shows traditional solutions, and the upper portion of Figure 1-1 shows the available VPN options. (In Figure 1-1, the reason that there are two separate dial designs is not technical, but cost-based.)

Figure 1-1   *Cisco Remote Access Services*

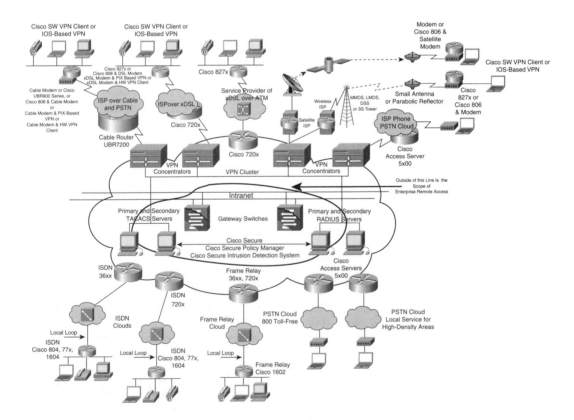

A more recent approach to remote access is the VPN, which is making significant progress in the market by replacing the permanent circuit offering typical of all legacy technologies. In a sense, the VPN offering (VPNs are covered in Part V of this book) became a super vehicle, and the service now includes VPN over ISDN, VPN over dial-in, and so on, where enterprises are not necessarily ordering permanent circuits, but instead are taking advantage of the existing baseband or broadband services of remote users to build VPN tunnels to corporate intranets. VPN is an evolving technology, and some analysts predict it will become a $10 billion market by 2005. Although today, most legacy and some new services compose the bulk of the service provider's offering to the enterprise market.

Table 1-1 provides a summary of each remote access technology option.

Table 1-1   *Remote Access Options*

Remote Access Option		Transmission Medium	Bandwidth	Limitations
Analog		1 pair copper / Standard phone line	56 kbps down / 33.6 kbps up	Available everywhere
ISDN		1 pair copper / Standard phone line	56/64 or 112/128 kbps both directions	Several miles with repeaters
Frame Relay		2 pair copper / Standard phone line	56/64 kbps or fractional T1 up to 1.5 Mbps both directions	Several miles with repeaters for 56 kbps / T1 limitation requires repeater every mile
xDSL family	ISDN DSL (IDSL)	1 pair copper / Standard phone line	144 kbps	Symmetric / <18,000 feet from CO
	Asymmetric DSL (ADSL)	1 pair copper	1.5 to 8 Mbps down / 16 to 800 kbps up	Asymmetric / <18,000 feet from CO
	Single-line DSL (SDSL) (symmetric)	1 pair copper	768 kbps	Symmetric
	Rate adaptive DSL (RADSL)	1 pair copper	1.5 to 8 Mbps down / 16 to 800 kbps up	Adaptive to the line parameters
	Consumer DSL (CDSL)	1 pair copper	Up to 1 Mbps down / 16 to 640 kbps up	Does not need remote equipment
	High-data-rate DSL (HDSL)	2 pairs copper	1.544 Mbps	Symmetric
	High-data-rate DSL2 (HDSL2)	1 pair copper	2.048 Mbps	Symmetric
	Very-high-data-rate DSL (VDSL)	Fiber feeder and ATM	13 to 52 Mbps down / 1.5 to 6 Mbps up	<4500 feet over twisted pair / >4500 feet over fiber

continues

Table 1-1 *Remote Access Options (Continued)*

Remote Access Option	Transmission Medium	Bandwidth	Limitations
Cable modem	Coax	384 kbps to 4 Mbps down	Requires TV cable
		128 kbps to 4 Mbps up	Speed varies significantly with the subscriber load
Multichannel Multi-point Distribution System (MMDS)	Wireless	500 to 600 kbps down 128 kbps up	Requires line of site and antenna
Local Multipoint Distribution Service (LMDS) (on the horizon)	Wireless	0.5 to 4 Mbps both directions	Requires antenna
Satellite	Wireless	400 kbps to 1 Mbps down 64 to 128 kbps up	Requires dish antenna

For more information, see *ADSL and DSL Technologies*, by Walter Goralski.

Analog Dialup Services

The analog modem dialup service gained popularity because of constant increases in speed and support from modem manufacturers. The initial offering started with speeds from 300 to 2400 bps, then to 9600 bps, 14.4 kbps, and so on. The term modem is an abbreviation for modulator–demodulator. Because the modem operates in the 4-kHz bandwidth, it requires analog to digital and digital to analog conversion on both ends. Part of this technology uses extended code correction and compression, which allows the speed to increase up to a factor of 4.

A significant event of the modem offering was in 1968, when the Federal Communications Commission (FCC) regulations permitted CPE to be connected to the Public Switched Telephone Network (PSTN). Another major event in the history of network communications was a paper written in 1948 by Claude Shannon, which established the theoretical limits of the speed that the modem can operate. The equation (see Chapter 2, "Telecommunication Basics") is called Shannon's limit, or Shannon's Law, and defines the upper theoretical limit of the data rate if proper technology is used.

The first attempt for standardization occurred in 1968, where the Comité Consultatif International Téléphonique et Télégraphique (CCITT), which is today called the International Telecommunication Union Telecommunication Standardization Sector (ITU-T), established a recommendation known as V.21, which defines the 200 (300 bps) modem speed. V.21 is still in use today as part of the V.34 and V.8 handshake that establishes basic modem compatibility. In 1984, the V.32 standard defined echo-cancellation and trellis coding. These standards provide some degree of forward error correction (FEC) techniques, and V.32b defines data rates of up to 14.4 kbps. The V.34 standard supports data rates of 24,

28.8, and 33.6 kbps, and coding 10 bits in one sinusoid (10 bits/Hz), which approaches the theoretical limit of Shannon's Law.

The announcement of 56 k modems by US Robotics, based on using T-carriers for dial-in service, was a major breakthrough. Analog modems operate over non-conditional circuits; not all 256 levels of pulse code modulation (PCM) coding are recognizable. The modems use 7 instead of 8 bits, which yields 128 levels of PCM and consequently 7 bits $\times$ 8000 = 56 kbps. Without any special requirements, this service requires a T1 or ISDN digital trunk on one end that supports 56/64 kbps, and a regular analog line on the other end. Both ends of the connection are usually asymmetric. From the modem side, the downstream connection has a fairly good chance to achieve 56 kbps most of the time because quantizing digital to analog is not susceptible to noise and interference on the line (see the section, "PCM" in Chapter 2).

Nevertheless, such things as local loop issues, bridge taps, crosstalk, and so on usually decrease the data rate to a more common 48 to 50+ kbps. The upstream direction is different. Analog to digital transformation is susceptible to different types of interference. Regardless of the connection speed reported by the dial management applications, the upstream speed is usually 28.8 or 33.6 kbps. This fact is not visible to the end user because the Internet is more of a downstream than upstream service.

A remote access implementation is usually based on access servers, or remote access servers, from which the remote user connects to the corporate network access server (NAS) by using a designated phone number(s). (See more about access servers at www.cisco.com/warp/public/44/jump/access_servers.shtml.)

Some telecommunication companies that provide global dialup service from all over the world use global dialer software, where the user chooses the country and the available phone numbers within the country to connect to the corporate network. The dial numbers are predefined and populated in a dial manager application that is standard on a user's laptop or PC.

In the U.S., an option for dial services is to use 800 toll-free numbers, where the enterprise owns the toll-free number, and pays a fixed per-minute usage fee. The 800 numbers eliminate the need for a more expensive and cumbersome calling card option to connect from long distance locations. Be aware that many hotels now charge a usage fee for 800 calls made from the room, which can significantly increase the dialup cost.

Another analog dial option is to use any ISP to connect to the Internet and use VPN-based solutions to connect to the corporate network. This solution is the most cost-effective and all signs in the dial market show that VPN will be the preferable dial solution in the near future. One significant feature of using a dedicated concentrator for VPN over dial is the option to use compression (LZS, STAC), so that the overhead of VPN packets can be overcome and yield better performance. Also, today's VPN client software is built right into many popular operating systems.

You learn more about dialup technologies in Part II, "Dial."

Benefits of Analog Dialup Services

Today, the dialup solution is the most common solution for remote users, road warriors traveling on business, and home teleworkers. Dialup technology does not require any changes to the CPE side, even if the remote user is using a 56-kbps modem. Plenty of tools exist, including web tools, which are offered by manufacturers to measure the maximum connection speed in any particular location.

Another feature of the technology is that when the maximum speed cannot be achieved, the 56-kbps flex modem can use its backward compatibility. If, for any reason, the maximum speed is not achievable, the 56 k technology can decrease the speed and perform V.34 data connections of 33.6 kbps, which is achievable from many locations around the world. One of the most successful aspects of this technology is that many users have some experience with modems, which significantly decreases enterprise support costs. The high availability for minimum cost is the main advantage so far.

Limitations of Analog Dialup Services

When considering the drawbacks of the technology, the data rate needs to be mentioned first. At this point in technology development, connection speeds under 100 kbps seem outdated and can be ineffective with some types of applications. At the same time, competing technologies, such as 3Com's X2 and 56 k flex that is supported by Lucent Technologies, Motorola, and Rockwell, result in a lack of unified standards and interoperability problems. The dialup modem technology has reached its theoretical maximum.

There was an attempt to unify the X2 and K-flex technologies under V.90, and now there is V.92. In today's market, however, V.90 is much more common for high-speed dialup than X2 or K-flex, especially because a lot of those were software flash upgradable to the V.90 standard when it was released.

ISDN Services

ISDN is considered to be the first advancement from analog dialup service. The ISDN standard is well developed and there are a variety of solutions that make ISDN the most commonly available service offering from telecommunication companies.

The T sector of the ITU-T is responsible for issuing protocols for the E-Series, I-Series, and Q-Series, and for components of the X-series that are related to ISDN, broadband ISDN (B-ISDN), and Signaling System 7 (SS7).

E-Series protocols cover the standardization of the recommended telephone network for ISDN. ITU-T recommendation E.164 (I.331), for example, defines the formats of ISDN addresses. I-Series protocols cover the standardization of concepts, terminology, and general methods. I.431, for example, defines the Primary Rate Interface (PRI), and I.432

defines the Basic Rate Interface (BRI). Q-Series protocols deal with the standardization of switching and signaling schemes and techniques. The Q.921 protocol describes the ISDN data-link processes of LAPD, which functions like Layer-2 processes in the International Organization for Standardization/Open System Interconnection (ISO/OSI) reference model. Q.931 specifies ISO/OSI reference model Layer-3 functions.

Because of the level of standardization in ISDN, the technology has a significant presence in the U.S., Canada, Japan, Europe, and all over the world. The fast setup of calls, sometimes referred to as fast-dial, has a call setup phase of less than one second. Some ISDN switches were developed before the standards and there are a variety of ISDN switches in different parts of the world. This diversity requires special attention in the design, configuration, and operational phases of remote access solutions.

From an enterprise perspective, the technology is fully suited for most remote access objectives, offering BRI services (2B+D channels) for end users, with an overall band-width of 112/128 kbps for user data. Service providers usually offer ISDN service with two data/voice channels for the end user.

You learn more about ISDN in Part III, "ISDN."

Benefits of ISDN Services

Some older Cisco routers do not have voice capable ports, such as the 1000 series routers. Also, the 770 and 800 series routers provide analog phone ports and the 1600s provide an S-bus port for ISDN phones but not analog phones. Also, video conferencing is an embedded function because ISDN is designed for voice, data, and video. The technology is defined as a viable alternative when the end user requires more bandwidth than dial-in, a variety of data and voice services, and administrative functions such as exchanging data, sending e-mails, and surfing the Internet. The technology supports corporate connectivity for a small office, home office (SOHO) environment, or a remote office, branch office (ROBO) environment.

Cisco's ISDN solutions are cost effective because of the scalable nature of ISDN that allows you to scale in increments of 64 kbps, or incremental B channels. The most common design solutions include the following:

- Dial-on-demand routing (DDR)
- Snapshot routing
- ISDN backup solution
- Multilink Point-to-Point Protocol (PPP) and multichasis PPP
- Callback solutions

The head end or back end of the enterprise ISDN service is usually developed by using PRIs, or channelized T1/PRIs. Cisco's IOS capability offers more advanced features including the following:

- **Non-Facility Associated Signaling (NFAS) with a D channel backup feature**— ISDN NFAS allows a single D channel to control multiple PRI interfaces. A backup D channel can be configured for use when the primary NFAS D channel fails.

- **Bandwidth Allocation Control Protocol (BACP)**—The BACP provides multilink PPP peers with the ability to govern link use. The Bandwidth Allocation Protocol (BAP), a subset of BACP, provides a set of rules that govern dynamic bandwidth allocation through call control. It also defines a method for adding and removing links from a multilink bundle for multilink PPP.

In the U.S., the local providers that offer ISDN include both local ISDN and Centrex services. A flat rate is offered only in some areas. Typically, the providers charge a per minute rate, at least for data usage. The Centrex solution is possible and preferred when the service is local or an inter-local access and transport area (LATA), as defined in Chapter 3, "The Cloud." Centrex is preferred in a remote access environment because of the significant reduction in cost from a usage-based service. If the inter-exchange carrier (IXC) is involved, the better solution is to subscribe for local ISDN service for Internet access, and VPN to connect to the corporate network. In this scenario, only the voice portion of the bill can cause high usage, not the data part. To date, no drawbacks or problems are identified for ISDN with IPSec VPN solutions.

ISDN is also well suited for multicasting, voice over IP (VoIP), compression, and if the LEC and IXC can commit a rate, a quality of service (QoS) solution can also be implemented.

Limitations of ISDN Services

One of the concerns of ISDN is related to standards. Besides the differences in ISDN switch type, there are interface compatibility limitations. The U-interface, which is available in the U.S. and Canada where the end terminator (NT1) is part of the CPE, is not available in other parts of the world where the S and T reference points, or S/T interface, is the termination solution and the NT1 devices are governed by the local carriers. This difference requires two types of routers to be produced, one suitable for each particular market, or two interfaces in Cisco's 77x ISDN routers (see the Cisco 804/1604 and the Cisco 803/1603 at www.cisco.com).

Another limitation is cost. Initially conceived with huge enthusiasm, the technology has proven to be expensive because of the dialup nature of ISDN. It is usually based on a usage rate; the carriers use metrics on which to base the rate. Usually, the metrics are based on the number of outgoing calls and their duration. When the IXC portion is included in the design, the ratio bandwidth/price can be unfavorable for this solution.

Frame Relay Services

Frame Relay technology is considered to be a derivative of ISDN. It is a connectionless service, however, which means that the frames traveling the network do not require the initial phase of establishing the connection, because the frames carry the address information. This solution is referred to as a permanent virtual circuit (PVC).

Frame switching is the other alternative, where the call setup phase of the connection is necessary, and consequently the technology is based on switched virtual circuits (SVCs). However, the vast majority of existing service offerings are PVC-based.

The requirement for higher connection speeds is one of the reasons for developing Frame Relay technology. The data transmission shift from mainly text exchanges to graphics is one of the driving factors, because graphics and video require peak bandwidth availability and lower response time. The requirement for dynamic bandwidth is another factor in Frame Relay development. The demand for more reliability and less overhead from existing digital facilities, and the requirement for handling bursty traffic are other factors that influenced the creation of the new technology at the end of the 1980s.

You learn more about Frame Relay in Part IV, "Frame Relay."

Frame Relay Standards

A specific feature of Frame Relay technology is the ability to use packet sizes that are greater than 1500 bytes, which are common in LAN environments. Some estimates show that the packet size can be up to 16 kilobytes, remembering that the embedded frame check sequence (FCS) can handle up to 4-kilobyte packets. (See Part IV for more information.)

Frame Relay combines the statistical multiplexing and port sharing of X.25 with the high-speed and low-delay characteristics of time-division multiplexing (TDM) circuit switching. X.25 is considered the predecessor of Frame Relay, but unlike X.25, Frame Relay eliminates the Layer-3 protocols of X.25 and concentrates the addressing and multiplexing in Layer 2. The architecture model is more compliant with the OSI model, where the second layer deals with frames but not with packets. And of course what's really going on to improve efficiency is removing the store and forward/error correction out of the picture (Layer 2), something that modern network technology has allowed. As a result, Frame Relay achieves 45 Mbps and it is available even in 155 Mbps service.

NOTE	Frame Relay and ISDN have common roots. Other derivatives of ISDN are Switched Multimegabit Digital Service (SMDS) with typical speeds of 155 Mbps, and Asynchronous Transfer Mode (ATM) with target rates of 622 Mbps. All fall under the category of B-ISDN services. Today, 10 Gbps (9953 Mbps) and 2.5 Gbps ATM links are available, and soon there will be a 40 Gbps capable interface.

Only a few Layer-2 functions, the so-called core aspects, are used in the most common PVC-based networks. These functions include checking for valid error-free frames, but not requesting retransmission if any error is found. Thus, many high-level protocol functions, such as sequencing, windowing, acknowledgments, and supervisory frames are not duplicated within a Frame Relay network. The omission of these functions dramatically increases the throughput because each frame requires much less processing time.

Benefits of Frame Relay

Enterprise remote access solutions are composed of a variety of components, including technology, hardware, software, standards, and architecture to provide Frame Relay services within the enterprise environment. Examples of these components include data, voice over Frame Relay, Frame Relay multicast, IP multicast, and compression.

Frame Relay technology poses fewer issues when covering longer distances for the remote user who is far from the central office (CO). The technology is fully compatible with T1/T3 carrier systems; however, existing distance limitations apply.

The ability to provision services from 56 kbps, or fractions of a T1 starting from 64 kbps, gives a sense of flexibility to the network designers. Although the ability to order 256-kbps and 384-kbps circuits is possible, the user requirements must be justified to warrant the additional cost because Frame Relay pricing depends on distance. The number of PVCs, the committed information rate (CIR), and port rate all factor into that final cost.

Limitations of Frame Relay

The pricing of Frame Relay services can range from $250 to over $1000 per month, and in many circumstances this does not justify the cost for providing such services to remote access users. When run over T1 circuits, it inherits the limitations of T1s because of repeaters placed in every mile.

VPN Services

VPN is not a new term in the computer and communication world. However, the new phase of VPN is due to new IP-based solutions and a set of protocols, such as L2TP, Point-to-Point Tunneling Protocol (PPTP), and IPSec. The new VPN technology can be thought of as a wire in the cloud, which changes the way enterprises approach remote access challenges. Generally speaking, the most common challenges are as follows:

- A fast growing number of mobile computing devices, demanding ubiquitous access
- A growing demand for home and branch office connectivity
- An emerging requirement to deploy extranets that support unpredictable relationships between enterprises and their business partners

VPN offers solutions for these dilemmas by providing immediate remote access to the corporate Intranet, and by taking advantage of the services provided by ISPs, application service providers (ASPs), and others.

You learn more about VPNs in Part V, "VPN."

Benefits of VPNs

In general, VPN solutions follow two basic models: service-provider dependant and service-provider independent. From a remote access perspective, both models are available, and of course, ISPs and telecommunication companies actively promote the first model. As for which model the enterprise should choose, the following considerations must be analyzed first:

* Expected (committed) performance
* Security requirements
* Network management and access control solutions
* Customer support and service-level agreements (SLAs)
* Billing requirements
* Cost

The expected cost reduction of migrating users from legacy remote access services such as ISDN, Frame Relay, and dialup to VPN can be at least 20 to 50 percent. Another driving factor here is unprecedented mobility—the user with VPN software can establish a tunnel to corporate from many different locations. The demand for VPN solutions is what drives the industry toward more and faster last-mile solutions, such as faster xDSL and more flexible wireless solutions.

Limitations of VPNs

From a desktop perspective, several software products can interfere with the proper functioning of a VPN client solution. Software distribution and management becomes more critical for VPN client solutions than any other remote access medium. Hardware-based and IOS-based VPN clients are less susceptible to incompatibilities with other network applications, but they pose different sets of limitations. (See Part V for more details about this topic.)

VPN Service Vehicles

NOTE	The following sections should be considered only in the context of using these technologies as a vehicle for VPN solutions, but not as an alternative to legacy solutions, unless the solution is based on a provider-dependent VPNs. Based on this premise, the following discussion is fairly limited.

Cable Modem Services

Cable modem technology has been in the market for a long time, but the Internet generation has imposed new features on it. The technology uses cable, which has been used by cable TV operators to deliver TV services. The cable modem converts the digital signals over the cable into analog signals, and it also carries data packets on radio frequencies (RFs), which enables it to carry video streams. When the network includes a fiber segment, the systems are called hybrid systems. When the network consists of fiber and coaxial cable, it is called a hybrid fiber-coaxial (HFC) network. Cable networks use bandwidth much greater than 4-kHz narrowband and most systems operate at 1 GHz (broadband). These systems can perform full-duplex communications and add analog voice to the spectrum of services.

To deliver data services over a cable network, one television channel (of about 6 MHz) in the 50 to 750 MHz band is allocated for downstream traffic to remote users, and another channel (of about 6 MHz) in the 5 to 42 MHz band carries upstream signals to the host routers. A single downstream channel of 6 MHz can support up to 27 Mbps by using 64 quadrature amplitude modulation (QAM) transmission technology. Upstream channels can deliver 500 kbps to 10 Mbps from homes by using 16 QAM or quadrature phase-shift keying (QPSK) modulation technique.

Benefits of Cable Modem Services

The most significant benefit of cable is the enormous bandwidth that can be shared between many users. Active subscribers that are connected to a given cable network segment typically include 500 to 2000 homes on a modern HFC network. An individual cable subscriber can easily use bandwidth up to 10 Mbps downstream. FCC regulations have restricted the bandwidth to between 5 to 50 MHz for interactive services only.

Another advantage of cable modems that are based on coax cable is that most traditional copper-based network problems are eliminated. These problems include analog loops and coils, trunking capacity, and switching resources. The coax cable from a user's home is aggregated in remote fiber units, and from there they can be terminated directly to the Internet routers in the cable TV headend equipment. If voice services are provided concurrently, only the voice traffic is directed to the PSTN networks. The best alternative is when the cable provider is also a LEC, and the voice switch is next to the cable router in the CO.

Another benefit is that the analog nature of the signals provide one type of signaling for all data, voice, and video services, which creates fewer signal transformations from type A-D and D-A, and improves the quality. The cable can connect to the user's LAN environment by using a standard 10Base-T Ethernet card, a Universal Serial Bus (USB) connection, or a transparent combination of them. Internal standard PCI modems are also available in the market. The integration of PC and TV in services such as Internet TV and PC-TV provide the convergence of voice, video, and data. The relatively inexpensive RF devices and the ability of service providers to easily transform the type of services they deliver is another advantage of cable.

Manufacturers can provide a wide range of services, available at the headend, which are based on modularity and service compatibility. The Cisco ubr7200 Series routers (www-search.cisco.com/pcgi-bin/search/public.pl?q=cable&searchselector=0&num=10) support cable telephony, streaming video, data services, VPN, telecommuting, and multiple dwelling units (high-speed integrated data, voice, and video services within apartment buildings and business complexes). Supported standards include all major standards such as Data-over-Cable Service Interface Specifications (DOCSIS) 1.0, EuroDOCSIS, and the upcoming DOCSIS 1.1 standard. Cable operators can choose the appropriate services and devices to optimize their capital investment with a single platform. A variety of radio frequency modem cards provide multiple downstream and upstream port densities over hybrid fiber-coaxial networks, and the fixed wireless card uses next-generation wireless technology to deliver the highest available data rates over obstructed links.

Cable technology for enterprise remote access using a fully outsourced model is possible but rarely used. Cable providers typically focus on the consumer market. The headend routers atypically are at the Internet provider's premises.

Limitations of Cable Modem Services

On the CPE side, most home-owned splitters and drop cables need to be re-installed because of the ingress noise that can cause serious performance degradations. The 5 to 42 or 5 to 50 MHz band is susceptible to interference from appliances such as refrigerators, vacuums, or other home devices that create concentrated radiation in this bandwidth, making it unusable. To address this situation, cable providers prefer to use filters, or normal PSTN modems to provide upstream communication. In turn, the latter solution creates problems when using a VPN over cable service.

Maybe the most serious drawback for cable technology is the lack of a committed rate and contention. Depending on the subscription and usage in a particular area, an overabundance of concurrent users who are using the same upstream direction creates congestion and over-use concerns. For enterprises, this creates a next to impossible situation for capacity planning, where consequently all planning and management of the available bandwidth cannot be handled successfully.

Cable technologies raise another concern about security. In a shared-media environment, the security design requires extra attention because transmissions can be intercepted within the neighborhood. However, VPN solutions are changing this situation by enabling the remote user to securely connect to the corporate network over VPN (refer to Figure 1-1). Instruct users to clearly understand the terms and conditions of their ISP contract because many providers are now restricting the use of IPSec-based solutions over their consumer grade services, which requires the user to upgrade to business-class service.

xDSL Services

Historically, the vast majority of residential copper lines were installed with the presumption of only carrying narrowband (4 kHz) voice signals. The access network consists of the local loops and associated equipment that connects the user's location to the CO. This network typically consists of cable bundles that carry thousands of twisted wire pairs to Feeder Distribution Interfaces (FDIs). FDIs are points where dedicated cable is extended out to the individual user's neighborhood. Some homes are located a long way from the CO and require a long local loop, which creates attenuation problems with the signals that must be corrected. LECs have three primary ways to deal with long loops:

- Use loading coils to modify the electrical characteristics of the local loop, which allows better quality voice frequency transmission over extended distances (typically greater than 18,000 feet). In this extended distance scenario, loading coils are placed every 6000 feet on the line.

- Set up remote termination points where the signals can be terminated at an intermediate point, and aggregated and backhauled to the CO where the switching equipment is located.

- Build a serving wire center (SWC) that does not have switching equipment, but does have the transmission equipment that connects to other central offices. The backhaul to the CO or SWC through T1/E1 circuits can be based on copper or fiber-based technologies.

Ironically, the same techniques later prevented high-speed features over the same copper circuits. Re-inspection of long loops is based on a technique called local loop qualification, which was created to significantly increase the bandwidth of available copper loops. The techniques that conduct loop qualification include the following:

- Accurately testing the length of the loop is important. Even if the loop does not contain shorts, opens, and bridged taps, the wire itself has loss. The longer the loop, the more loss, which affects the transmission rates. The transmission rate is in inverse relationship to the length of the loop, so it is imperative to know the length of the subscriber loop. The techniques are single-ended capacitive or resistance measurement (based on Ohm's law). Because the latter technique requires a short on the CPE, the preferred option is the tone measurement.

- Determining if loading coils are present is essential. Loading coils are in-line inductors, which are used as a low bandwidth filter to balance voice transmission. They are installed in all local loops longer than 18,000 feet. In many cases, they still exist and are DSL-killers because by balancing the line, they also reduce the available bandwidth.

- Detecting the presence of bridged taps is necessary. They are lengths of open wire that are connected in parallel with the loop. They can exist anywhere and can be part of unused pairs, loose pairs, or they can exist between the CO and the CPE.

- Testing for crosstalk is necessary. Long cables, power cables, or cables running side by side with other cabling systems are susceptible to crosstalk. This is because crosstalk-induced signals combine with signals that are intended for transmission over the copper wire loop. The result is a slightly different shaped waveform than was originally transmitted. Crosstalk can be categorized in one of two forms. Near-end crosstalk (NEXT) is the most significant because the high-energy signal from an adjacent system can induce relatively significant crosstalk into the primary signal. Far-end crosstalk (FEXT) is typically less of an issue because the far-end interfering signal is attenuated as it traverses the loop.

A standard device for evaluating the subscriber line is called a *time domain reflectometer (TDR)*, which can detect short and open circuits, loading coils, and bridged taps. The best way to visually analyze the quality of the loop is to use a spectrum analyzer, which provides a clear picture of the feasibility of using a particular loop for xDSL service.

These measures ensure that the typical local loop, which is well designed for low voice bands, can achieve a broader spectrum at 1000 kHz and higher. ADSL uses frequency-division multiplexing (FDM) or echo-cancellation techniques to divide the available bandwidth. In the case of FDM, if the band is 1000-kHz wide, it is divided into three bands: The lower end (0 to 20 kHz) is designated for POTS, the 25 to 200-kHz band is used for upstream transmission, and the last portion is used for downstream transmissions. Two guard bands at 5 kHz and 50 kHz separate them. In the case of echo cancellation, the 25 to 1000 kHz-band is designated for data communications and the upstream direction is part of the downstream band. Both techniques have advantages and disadvantages, but it is important to know that ADSL provides a range up to 5.5 km (18,000 feet), depending on the cable quality.

The following are brief descriptions of the established xDSL technologies, where one of the differentiators is symmetric (the same speed in both directions) and asymmetric (refer to Table 1-1).

IDSL

IDSL technology is the first DSL technology, based on the 2B1Q coding scheme (see Chapter 2), to bundle two 64-k channels and to use the D channel for data transfer, which yields 144 kbps. It runs over one pair of copper wires up to a maximum of 18,000 feet.

ADSL

This is an asymmetric type of broadband service, which usually uses different coding schemes to reach 18,000 feet. The Cisco 827 series ADSL router, for example, uses the following coding schemes:

- **ANSI-DMT**—ANSI full rate mode
- **Auto**—Auto detect mode
- **ITU-DMT**—ITU full rate mode
- **Splitterless**—G.lite mode

SDSL

SDSL is the best opportunity to reuse the existing one pair analog lines. The line is typically provisioned for 768 kbps. It is expected to be replaced by SHDSL.

RADSL

RADSL contains adaptive features. When lines are tested but do not behave in an expected way, the Discrete Multi-Tone (DMT)-based technology of RADSL is preferred.

CDSL

CDSL is a relative of RADSL and ADSL. It is more modest in terms of data rates, especially in the upstream direction. It is a no-splitter type of DSL, where the splitters and the extra wiring are not necessary. This differs from ADSL and RADSL, where splitters split the frequency bands and prevent interference between different frequency bands, which ultimately protects the standard 4-kHz voice frequency band from interference.

HDSL/HDSL2

HDSL is deployed over T1 in the U.S., and E1 in Europe. A combination with DMT is also available. The HDSL technology runs over 2 copper pairs, and HDSL2 runs over 1 copper pair. Both provide service if the user's home is closer than 15,000 feet from the CO.

VDSL

VDSL is the fastest of all DSL technologies, but has distance limitations of 4500 feet using copper pairs, and requires ATM over fiber for distances greater than 4500 feet.

Benefits of xDSL Services

From a remote access perspective, xDSL offers great data rates, a variety of services, and future integration with all available carriers in the market, including Frame Relay and ATM networks, T1/E1, and T3/E3-carriers.

Limitations of xDSL Services

The availability of xDSL, even in the U.S. market, is limited and the ability of ILECs to deliver xDSL service remains to be proven. Loop limitations are preventing existing copper pairs from running higher frequency data transmissions and, according to some sources, more than 700 to 800 thousand U.S. households experience these limitations with their DSL service. Some estimates show that, in any given LATA, more than 20 percent of local loops need to be reinspected. (See www.dsl.com.)

Wireless Broadband Services

Fixed wireless technologies are emerging wireless alternatives that offer high-speed broadband access for data services. The decision to deploy broadband wireless services, whether the choice includes Local Multipoint Distribution Service (LMDS), Multichannel Multipoint Distribution System (MMDS), or unlicensed spectrum systems, also depends on the availability of other broadband access solutions and the suitability of these solutions to customer bandwidth and service requirements. Broadband wireless offers a high-speed alternative for bridging the critical last mile between high-speed IP backbones and customers of high-speed data services.

MMDS

MMDS includes various services and bandwidths. Deployed in a point-to-multipoint topology, MMDS generally provides a maximum of 10 Mbps speeds per customer. MMDS signals generally carry 30 to 35 miles from the transmitter with single cell coverage of 2800 to 3800 square miles. The service comprises 33 channels, which are broken down in a way to provide different types of services. Twenty out of 33 channels are used for a component, called Instructional Television Fixed Service (ITFS), where the service provider maps the channels to the subscriber's CPE by transparent switching. In turn, the subscriber must be eligible for the service, and subscribe for a certain amount of hours of service.

The next 11 channels are assigned to MMDS and the remaining 2 channels to Multipoint Distribution System (MDS). The U.S. market primarily uses this technology, combined with cable, which is referred to as wireless cable. As for the international market, the demand is greater and growing faster for pure MMDS. Coax cable is the most expensive way of delivering TV signals. MMDS offers an alternative by delivering a complete package of services in the 2.5 to 2.7 GHz frequency range. It is important to install the antennas at the highest peaks in the area, to ensure maximum coverage. At the receiver side, the remote user uses a small antenna or parabolic reflector. The transformation of UHF and VHF signals to microwave and vice versa occurs on both the sender and receiver side.

Across the U.S., only a handful of operators have started to provide broadband services over a MMDS infrastructure. Recently, carriers such as Sprint, Verizon, and SBC have invested in these solutions and, as a result, the market and variety of services are expected to grow.

The Cisco uBR7246 Universal Broadband Router combines the functionality of the Cisco 7200 router and a headend wireless modem in one integrated platform. An end-to-end wireless architecture is also constructed to support residential locations. Cisco Aironet 350 Series wireless local-area products can be combined with a MMDS broadband wireless local loop to provide an end-to-end wireless architecture that supports high-speed Internet access for the consumer located in multidwelling units. Using this architecture, Cisco Aironet wireless products connect to broadband wireless enabled routers.

Cisco solutions also include a wireless line card (uBR-MCW-MDA), which fits in a 7223 or 7246 uBR or VXR router, and a MMDS transverter (SX11127A) with duplexor. CPE gear includes either a 2600 or 3600 family router for MxU, or a 950 family router for smaller SMB prospects. Wireless technology gives service providers an alternative last-mile access solution that complements more traditional broadband access technology offerings such as DSL and cable. Cisco MMDS-based solutions are part of the Architecture for Voice, Video and Integrated data (AVVID).

LMDS

On the horizon is LMDS, a multi-cell, point-to-multipoint wireless distribution system, which operates initially in the 27.5 to 29.5 GHz frequency band in the U.S., and the 24 to –40 GHz band overseas. Using a higher than MMDS frequency band, LMDS covers areas only 3 to 6 miles in diameter and can be deployed in asymmetric and symmetric configurations. Compared with two-way communications, LMDS has smaller coverage area, but it can provide faster data rates.

LMDS provides bandwidth in the OC-1 to OC-12 range, which is considerably greater than other wireless services. It is designed to provide the last mile from a carrier of data services to a large building or complex, where it is less costly to set up LMDS transceivers on rooftops than to dig up the ground to install optical fiber. Cells cover the area, and the technology can be considered cellular cable TV. The cell structure overcomes some of the line-of-sight issues of MMDS. Passive and active repeaters and passive reflectors cover the shadow areas. The adjacent cells use the same frequencies but with different polarization.

LDMS uses frequency modulation (FM), not the standard amplitude modulation (AM) that is typical for cable systems. FM provides higher quality, and combined with the cell structure, requires only a small six-inch square antenna for signal exchange.

Benefits of Wireless Broadband Services

From a remote access point of view, it is important to consider these technologies as a viable alternative to the existing environment. It is clear that the future belongs to wireless technologies. The current MMDS and LMDS solutions provide data rates of 40 to 54 Mbps downstream. If MMDS and LMDS are the future technologies for wireless, what future advancements should you expect? The price and innovation of these technologies are expected to play a major role in defining future remote access solutions.

Limitations of Wireless Broadband Services

Both technologies are focused in urban areas where population concentrations are high. They also inherit the limitations of line-of-sight technologies, which results in limited availability.

Scalability of this service is not easy. It depends on the density of the population in the area and their willingness to subscribe to a new technology that traditionally offers one-way (downstream) data delivery, with a voice option still not available.

Using VPN over MMDS and LMDS should not create any issues because the technologies do not have any impact on the third-layer protocols and they create a transparent environment for IPSec-based solutions. (See www.sprintbroadbanddirect.com/.) However, the increased latency (many times more than in a wired network) creates some issues when used for time-sensitive applications, including interactive, terminal-based designs, Voice over IP, and multicast. Also, security and QoS/contention issues associated with cable are also present with wireless.

Unlicensed Frequencies

Based on wireless LAN equipment, unlicensed point-to-point radios capable of 100 Mbps throughputs currently exist. At these speeds, however, distance limitations are great. Twenty-mile links are currently possible with unlicensed spectrum radios on a point-to-point basis. Time and cost savings, in the absence of licensing, favor the use of these frequencies. However, the possibility of signal interference and various technical limitations make these systems less appealing. Unlicensed spectrum radios have been deployed (approximately 200 deployments) by ISPs in the US in rural areas, where broadband service might be otherwise unavailable. The Cisco WT-2750 system operates not only at MMDS, but Unlicensed National Information Infrastructure (U-NII) bands as well. The Cisco WT-2710 system operates in the U-NII band only. U-NII provides both point-to-point (up to 20 miles) and point-to-multipoint solutions (up to 7 miles), and operates in the 5.7 GHz band.

Satellite Services

Direct Broadband Satellite (DBS) is a typical service for satellite communications. The system is capable of delivering downstream data at a rate of 23 Mbps by using one-way communication. All solutions are based on MPEG I Layer II audio encoding and use extensive compression methods. The upstream directions in early deployment for data were based on PSTN-wired modems, which was not a successful solution, especially combined with VPN technology. The most common speed offering is 400 kbps to 1 Mbps for a single user (www.directpc.com), or 400 kbps to 1 Mbps downstream and 64 to 128 kbps upstream (www.starband.com). The satellites are in geosynchronous earth orbit (GEO) and evidently for remote access purposes, there are latency issues. From measurements taken of the latter provider's service, a latency of 0.7 seconds for one-way is typical.

Reliability and latency are factors that concern most satellite providers. Most of today's satellite systems are reliable; however, satellite links also suffer a 1 to 2 percent packet loss. (See www.internettrafficreport.com/.) The satellite round-trip time (RTT) is 540 ms and the terrestrial side is about 150 ms; thus, the total RTT for the TCP connection is about 700 ms.

NOTE   My measurements show that the error level is a bit higher. Here is a Pchar output from a satellite connection, showing about 6 to 8 percent reliability (depending on if it is day or night), and about 0.8s one way RTT:

```
...
XXX.78.249.254 (misc-XXX-78-249-254.pool.starband.net)
    Partial loss:      12 / 138 (8%)
    Partial char:      rtt = 813.546203 ms, (b = 0.189682 ms/B), r2 = 0.149781
                       stddev rtt = 99.374317, stddev b = 0.070578
    Partial queueing:  avg = 0.369341 ms (133278 bytes)
    Hop char:          rtt = 739.066865 ms, bw = 42.346064 kbps
    Hop queueing:      avg = 0.362248 ms (1917 bytes)
```

Measurements show that regardless of the latency and reliability factors, the service can achieve speeds in the range of 500 kbps to 1 Mbps download, and approximately 128 kbps upload. The solution, implemented by StarBand, is based on an upper-layer solution called Internet Page Accelerator (IPA). In terms of the client/server technology, the Remote Page Accelerator (RPA) client is installed on the computer and connects to the satellite modem. The server side is located in the Network Operations Center (NOC), and is called the Host Page Accelerator (HPA). Together, these two individual units make up the IPA (see Figure 1-2). (See www.starband.com.)

A possible solution for acceleration of the performance characteristics is based on Flash Networks' proprietary protocol, called Boosted Session Transport (BST) and its product line NettGain. NettGain products are implemented by organizations such as StarBand, VSAT, NASA, and SAT-TEL.

Figure 1-2   *Remote and Host Page Accelerators (RPAs and HPAs) create the Internet Page Acceleration (IPA) of StarBand*

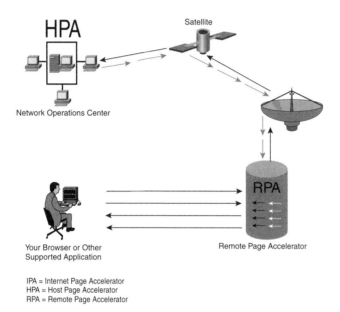

The BST protocol is a TCP-like reliable protocol that replaces TCP over the path where performance optimization is needed. TCP packets from a source location are transformed from TCP to BST and sent to the destination. There they are transformed back into TCP and sent to the originally intended target. NettGain manages both BST and TCP flow control and data queues to allow a full protocol conversion.

Another possible solution is the Cisco Content Engine 500 Series. Different techniques are combined in Cisco Application and Content Networking Software, which offer more complex solutions and allow certain content to be boosted and achieve better throughput times in high-latency networks. (See www.cisco.com/univercd/cc/td/doc/product/ webscale/content/ce500/index.htm.)

The accelerators are not always compatible with IPSec-based VPNs because the Integrity Check Value (ICV) is calculated based on the immutable fields of the TCP/IP stack. A satisfactory resolution is not available so far and research continues.

Satellite-based solutions with IPSsec VPN have proven to be a good solution for applications such as web browsing, e-mails, and data transfer. If used for time-sensitive applications, such as VoIP or interactive client/server applications, they are not the best remote access solution. Cost is another concern when this solution is chosen for remote access services because of higher hardware cost.

The next generation of low earth orbit satellites (LEO), driven by companies such as Hughes Communications, CyberStar and Motorola, are designed to reduce latency issues, but not to replace the GEO satellites.

Another alternative satellite solution is described in Chapter 2 in the section, "Modulation and Line-Coding Techniques in Hybrid Networks."

Provisioning of Enterprise Remote Access Services

A key function of IT planning and design includes provisioning of remote access services for employees. Remote work is defined as work conducted away from corporate facilities. The provisioning activities described in this section support remote workers in a home office (telecommuting), as opposed to another type of virtual office (for example, a satellite or hotel office), instead of commuting to a corporate facility. Cisco's internal remote access offering has changed over the last couple of years; however, the following information describes the processes that Cisco used to provision services for Frame Relay, ISDN, DSL, and VPN.

NOTE	Up to 80 percent of Cisco employees currently work remotely at least one day of their regular workweek.

All successful remote work arrangements meet the needs of the business while enabling employees to maximize productivity in an advantageous work environment. Working remotely can positively impact job satisfaction, maximize the use of on-site workspace, decrease facilities costs, reduce traffic congestion and enhance air quality, attract and retain key employees, expand the pool of potential candidates, and provide opportunities to showcase Cisco's technology.

Cisco's internal remote access services are categorized as Cisco-managed, vendor-managed, and user-managed. The Cisco-managed services account for the Frame Relay, ISDN, and dialup services, where an internal Cisco IT team provided support for the end-to-end solution. The vendor-managed solution was an outsourced private DSL network where all support services were provided by the vendor. The user-managed solution was created for the internal VPN deployment, and it was a hybrid solution where end users managed the home connection with their selected ISP, and Cisco IT support managed the headend VPN concentrators. For Cisco-managed services, the provisioning IT analysts provide dual functions of administration and provisioning, which include installation, deactivation, and move location of services. Within Cisco, the provisioning of all remote access services requires the approval of the employee's manager. An automated approval process was used to manage this process.

Over the course of time, the policies and procedures have changed from a totally manual process to a semi-automated process. The type of technologies offered, and the employees to whom the services are offered changed as the business climate grew in size and authority. In general, the provisioning process includes the following:

- Installation procedures (sometimes called new installs)
- Automated disconnect procedures
- Billing procedures

Frame Relay circuits were usually provisioned for full-time telecommuters, who have no office space and work entirely from home. The full-time usage could usually justify the high monthly service charge, and was more cost effective than a usage based solution. In some cases, the employee's unique business requirements limited the remote access solution to a Frame Relay connection. A single vendor provides service and the charge is based on linear distance from the employee home to a vendor point of presence (POP). These circuits are piped directly into Cisco from that POP, providing speeds starting from 56 kbps and including fractional T1.

Part-time telecommuters, those needing higher bandwidth than dialup, could be authorized for an ISDN service to be installed in their home. ISDN is mostly usage based and depending on the employee's usage requirements, would be more cost effective than Frame Relay. This service usually is provided by the ILEC for the region, offering speeds of 128 kbps and providing two analog phones for analog telephone calls, negating the need for an additional wire pair to make business calls.

The necessary steps for provisioning Frame Relay and ISDN circuits for enterprise remote access needs are shown in Figure 1-3. Figure 1-3 shows the provisioning process for Frame Relay and ISDN. Some of the descriptions are based on an automated system for provisioning, used by Cisco.

Figure 1-3 is a graphic overview of the manual provisioning order process for the installation of Frame Relay and ISDN. A client requests a remote access service through an internal web-based application. After posting the required information to a template, the request is forwarded to management for approval. After it is approved, a case is opened in a case management tool and the request is sent to the provisioning team. The provisioning team member takes action in several areas:

- **Case management tool action**—Updates the case with the appropriate language to document the process and timelines needed to track the installation of the order, and to set realistic expectations for the client.
- **Provisioning page action**—Reviews the order template for accuracy and sends to the appropriate vendor.
- **Administrative page action**—Updates the database with the referenced case number.

Figure 1-3   *The Provisioning Process for Frame Relay and ISDN*

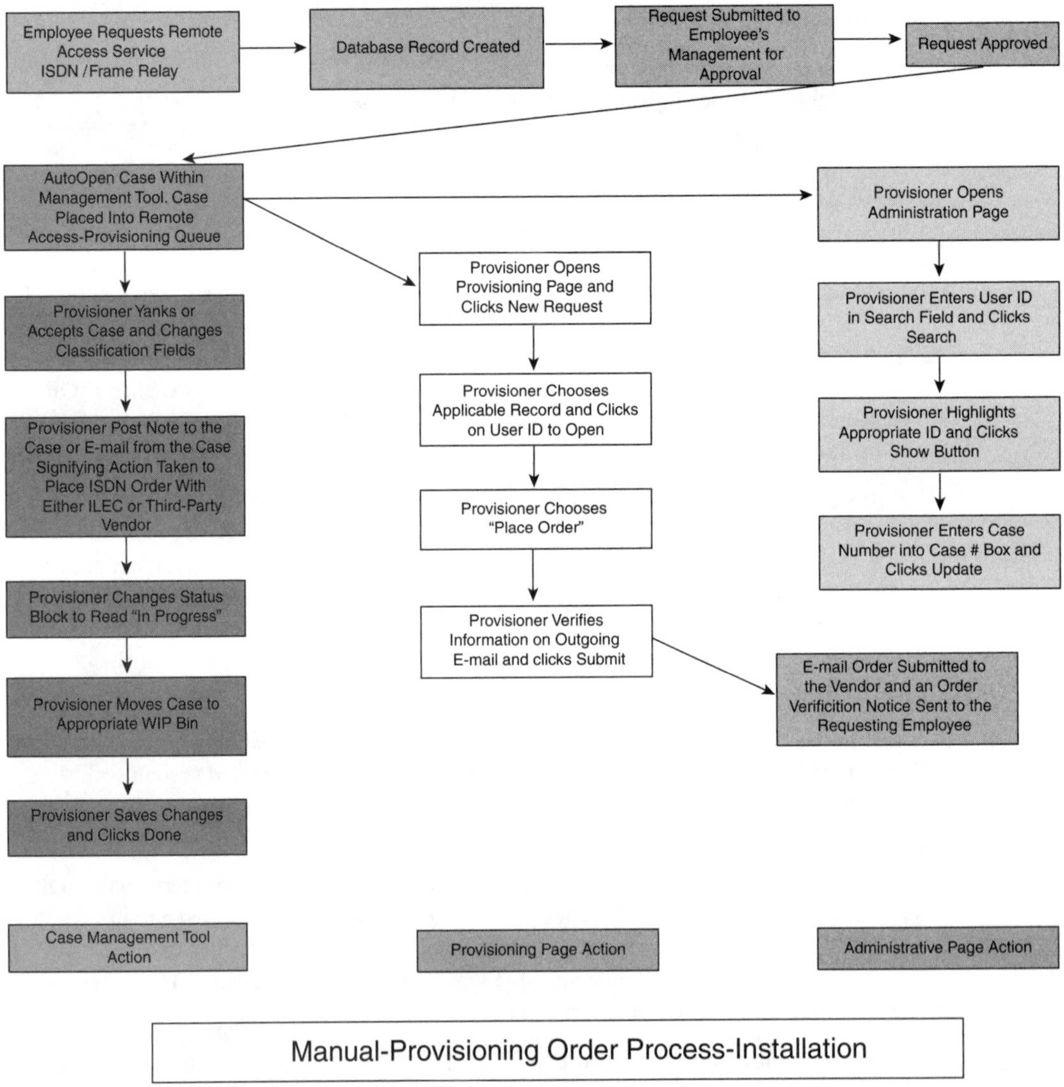

```
┌────────────────────┐     ┌────────────────────┐     ┌────────────────────┐     ┌────────────────────┐
│ Employee Requests  │     │                    │     │ Request Submitted  │     │                    │
│  Remote Access     │────▶│ Database Record    │────▶│ to Employee's      │────▶│ Request Approved   │
│  Service           │     │ Created            │     │ Management for     │     │                    │
│ ISDN /Frame Relay  │     │                    │     │ Approval           │     │                    │
└────────────────────┘     └────────────────────┘     └────────────────────┘     └────────────────────┘
```

Case Management Tool Action	Provisioning Page Action	Administrative Page Action

Flow boxes:

- AutoOpen Case Within Management Tool. Case Placed Into Remote Access-Provisioning Queue
- Provisioner Yanks or Accepts Case and Changes Classification Fields
- Provisioner Post Note to the Case or E-mail from the Case Signifying Action Taken to Place ISDN Order With Either ILEC or Third-Party Vendor
- Provisioner Changes Status Block to Read "In Progress"
- Provisioner Moves Case to Appropriate WIP Bin
- Provisioner Saves Changes and Clicks Done

- Provisioner Opens Provisioning Page and Clicks New Request
- Provisioner Chooses Applicable Record and Clicks on User ID to Open
- Provisioner Chooses "Place Order"
- Provisioner Verifies Information on Outgoing E-mail and clicks Submit

- Provisioner Opens Administration Page
- Provisioner Enters User ID in Search Field and Clicks Search
- Provisioner Highlights Appropriate ID and Clicks Show Button
- Provisioner Enters Case Number into Case # Box and Clicks Update

- E-mail Order Submitted to the Vendor and an Order Verificition Notice Sent to the Requesting Employee

---

Manual-Provisioning Order Process-Installation

As availability for xDSL services expanded, DSL became a vendor-managed remote access option with fixed rates and lower cost than either ISDN or Frame Relay. It was preferred to have a contractual relationship with a single vendor to provide a low cost, fixed rate private DSL network. Bandwidth varied from 128 k to 512 k depending on the distance from the residence to the provider's DSLAM in the ILEC CO. IDSL and ADSL services were available, and with ADSL bandwidths in excess of 384 k, a Cisco IP telephone could be used effectively from home. This option is shown in Figure 1-1, where the xDSL service is hosted to the corporate-managed router (upper half).

Apart from the vendor-managed private solution, xDSL should be considered in the VPN context as a transport medium. This option is shown in Figure 1-1 in the upper half, where an ISP hosts the xDSL service, but the tunnel to the corporate network is terminated on the VPN concentrator. This type of solution is expected to be the pre-dominant remote access solution of the future.

With new technologies driving down the price of Internet access, Cisco's user-managed VPN solution provides the necessary set of options for VPN over technologies. The solution is technology independent and works with any ISP that provides access to the Internet through cable, xDSL, ISDN, satellite, or wireless technologies.

Through the manual process, a provisioning IT analyst received an e-mail or telephone request, and assessed the need for a remote access service (refer to Figure 1-3). After the type of service need was determined, an order was placed with the ILEC or with a third-party vendor who, in turn, placed the order with an ILEC. In heavily Cisco populated areas, agreements were made with the ILEC to accept these orders. In rural or sparsely Cisco populated areas, an agreement went to a third-party vendor to act on Cisco's behalf to place those orders.

NOTE	The following text provides some Cisco specifics, which definitely can be addressed differently as necessary. This section concerns how Cisco is dealing with provisioning.

Cisco IT uses an internally developed semi-automated, fully integrated online management system that assists with the provisioning of ISDN/FR services for employees. This allowed for the following:

- Automates the provisioning process
- Automates vendor/order communication
- Provides a central, uniform repository for ISDN and Frame Relay related data
- Improves asset-tracking measures

The implementation of this system provided the following:

- Labor cost savings
- Improved delivery timeframes
- Improved data accuracy/integrity
- Improved vendor tracking measures
- Improved asset management

Automated order e-mail templates were created to meet the processing demands of each ILEC and the requirements of Cisco:

- The service orders were standard for Frame Relay at 56 k and 128 k. The circuit was directed into Cisco's Intranet, using Cisco as the employee's ISP.

- The service orders were standard for ISDN, the speed was 128 k with 256 k B channels. The second channel was given voice priority over data when an analog phone was used in conjunction with the Cisco router. Long distance for ISDN was standard in accordance with a Cisco-vendor contract. The circuit was directed into Cisco's Intranet, using Cisco as the employee's ISP.

- The service orders were standard for the vendor-managed DSL. After management approval of a DSL service request, the vendor processed the order and the vendor communicated directly with the Cisco employee. Cisco provisioning analysts only provided follow-up and expediting when deemed necessary.

- The service orders for DSL are standard, providing the maximum bandwidth available to the employee, based on the employee distance to the ILEC DSLAM. The circuit is directed into Cisco's Intranet, using Cisco as the employee's ISP.

NOTE   Installation of any of these services would normally take 4–6 weeks from the date the order was placed.

After order verification was received from the ILEC for ISDN/Frame Relay, the remote access engineers could configure a Cisco router designed for the intended service and ship it to the user. DSL routers are configured and shipped by the contracted vendor.

Routing for Frame Relay services would be over a dedicated service provider-based private network into Cisco (see more in Chapter 3, and Chapter 18, "Frame Relay Troubleshooting Scenarios"). Routing for ISDN would be one of several different ways: local Centrex for employees living in the immediate vicinity to the Cisco campus in San Jose or RTP, local long distance for other intra-LATA employees, or local long distance for local inter-LATA employees. All others would be routed on a Cisco contracted 800 number service into a Cisco campus. The routing and distance would determine monthly and usage service rates.

At the time of writing this book, Frame Relay and ISDN are no longer offered as a standard Cisco provided service. The provisioning mechanisms are still available, but not activated for employee access, although special cases are handled as needed. The standard remote access offering is the user-managed service that uses VPN to gain access to the Cisco Intranet.

Summary

In this chapter, you learned the specifics of the remote access environment, and the management considerations when different remote access designs are considered. The definition of the remote access population here is based on a legacy criteria. As previously stated, different approaches also can be applied, based on the job functions of the employee.

This chapter provided a brief description of remote access options in the following aspects: management considerations and the pros and cons of remote access solutions; defining the remote access population; legacy remote access solutions, and VPNs over some of the most popular technologies, such as cable modems, xDSL, wireless, and satellite services. Finally, the chapter explained one possible approach to the provisioning of corporate circuits which, without any doubt, will affect your troubleshooting efforts, especially in new-install cases, as explained in the following chapters.

Review Questions

Answers to the review questions can be found in Appendix A, "Answers to Review Questions."

1 Why are remote access networks considered the most difficult type of network to support?

2 What are the main categories that the management should consider when making remote access service decisions?

3 Give an example for narrowband, baseband, and broadband services.

4 Explain what MMDS and LMDS stand for.

5 Name two benefits of dial-in modem technology for remote access.

6 Name two limitations of dial-in modem technology for remote access.

7 Name two benefits of ISDN for remote access.

8 Name two limitations of ISDN technology for remote access.

9 Name two benefits of Frame Relay for remote access.

10 Name two limitations of Frame Relay technology for remote access.

11 Name two benefits of VPN for remote access.

12 Name two benefits of cable modems for remote access.

13 Name two benefits of xDSL for remote access.

14 Name two limitations of wireless and satellite for remote access.

CHAPTER 2

Telecommunication Basics

The discussion in this chapter covers modulations, line-coding schemes, and techniques for wired, hybrid, wireless, and emerging media. Emerging wireless local-area network (LAN) coding techniques require special attention, and they are covered in detail. The importance of this chapter is to provide you with the fundamental information required for troubleshooting different technical solutions.

Information needs to be transformed into signals to be exchanged over the telecommunication media. When troubleshooting in an enterprise environment, it is important to have a relatively broad understanding of how the information is transformed from one form to another and how the information is carried over the provider's network. This chapter focuses on representing the following:

- Legacy modulations, line-coding schemes, and techniques for the wired media with special attention to the evolving xDSL techniques.

- Extended discussion about some of the emerging wireless modulations and coding schemes because of the expected growth of end-to-end wireless solutions and hybrid solutions.

- Detailed information about clocking, line coding, and framing in the carrier's system, and discussion about T1/Primary Rate Interfaces (PRIs).

In telecommunications, the transfer of information from one point to another is based on signals that can be classified as continuous and discrete, or analog and digital. Analog signals are continuous and carry distinguishable states, called constellations, that can be interpreted as different from each other, such as positive and negative components of the sinusoid, or analog waves with a different amplitude, frequency, or phase. The Public Switched Telephone Network (PSTN), which was developed in the early 1960s, is primarily an analog network. Analog signals are characterized by amplitude, phase, and frequency. The analog transmission can degenerate from changes in the electrical characteristics of the wire that are caused by thunderstorms, snow, rain, and electrical charges.

Discrete, or digital, signals carry the information in defined discrete moments or discrete states. In digital systems, the terminology is based on the base 2 numerical system (1 and 0), where the digital signal has at least two distinguishable states, which are interpreted as

1 or 0. Although the analog transmission's quality can degrade because of interference with other sources, the digital transmission is generally more reliable because error-correcting codes can be applied. Every correction code adds extra bits to the user transmission, and the general rule is that the bigger the correction code, the greater its ability to find and recover from the error. The trade-off is that less user data can be transmitted. The optimum balance must be determined.

Shannon's Capacity Theorem

Error-correcting codes can alleviate some errors, but cannot alleviate all the errors introduced by the channel in a digital communications system. Shannon's Capacity Theorem states that error-free transmission is possible as long as the transmitter does not exceed the channel's capacity. N bits constitute a block of information bits that have K bits of error correction tacked on. In terms of the bit error probability (p), the probability of an error can reach 0 as N becomes larger if the following is true:

- The ratio $N / (N + K) = R$, the rate (R) is kept constant.
- R is less than the channel's capacity (C).
- $C = 1 + p\log_2 p + (1 - p)\log_2(1 - p)$.

Thus, if a repetition code has a rate of 1/3, and if you used more data bits and repeated them twice, you could transmit them through a channel error-free, if the error probability is less than $2^{(1-R)}$. The capacity sets a limit on your ability to transmit digital information through a channel. The converse to the Capacity Theorem states that if $R > C$, the probability of a word error approaches 1 as N becomes greater. The Capacity theorem can also be stated in terms of transmission rates, by dividing the coding rate (and the capacity) by the duration of the bit interval.

Shannon showed that the capacity of an additive white Gaussian noise channel is given by the following:

$C = BW \log_2 (1 + S / N)$
C—Channel capacity in kbps
BW—Bandwidth of transmission medium
S—Power of signal at the transmitting device
N—Power of noise received at the destination

Therefore, the telephone channel with BW = 3 kHz and S / N = 1000, yields a capacity of about 30,000 bits per second (bps). The bandwidth of a twisted pair is 4 kHz, which covers the frequency spectrum for voice. Assuming a signal-to-noise ratio (SNR) of (P0/Pn) equals 1000, (30 dB), the Shannon channel capacity is as follows:

$C = 4000 \times \log_2 (1 + 1000) = 40 \text{ kbps}$

The following sections are based on the assumption that the modulation techniques in wired, wireless, and hybrid media differ from each other. This classification is symbolic and is not precisely correct. The sole purpose of this classification is to represent the most common technical solutions for each media.

Modulation and Line-Coding Techniques in Wired Networks

Modulation and demodulation are processes of converting the analog signals to digital signals and vice versa. The signal transformation from analog form to digital form is based on analog signal-to-discrete signal converters, which are known as analog-to-digital converters (ADCs), digital-to-analog converters (DACs), coder-decoders (codecs), and data service unit/channel service units (DSU/CSUs). The analog systems can still carry voice, data, and video, but are mostly designed for voice communications. The most used technique for voice digitalization is pulse code modulation (PCM). In PCM, at least 8000 analog samples of voice are required to characterize the human voice. The previous suggestion is based on the following two theorems:

First, Nyquist's Theorem defines the following law:

$C = 2 \times BW$
C — Transmission speed (bps) of the channel or channel capacity
BW — Bandwidth (bps) of the noiseless channel

Second, Nyquist's sampling theorem requires the following:

$fs \geq 2fa$
fa — Sampling frequency
fs — Highest frequency of the analog signal

NOTE   A source for Nyquist's sampling theorem is *The Telecommunications Fact Book and Illustrated Dictionary* by Khan S. Ahmed (Delma Publishers Inc., 1992).

Nyquist's sampling theorem states that digital sampling must take place at twice the highest frequency to reconstruct the analog signal accurately. As a result, the sampling theorem requires that, given $fa = 4$-kHz frequency band, $fs \geq 4000 \times 2 = 8000$ Hz.

To convert analog to digital, a binary code needs to be assigned to every analog sample. An 8-bit code provides 256 levels, and enables the quality of the recovered voice to be comparable with the analog voice. The 8000 samples/second times 8 bits per sample, yields the 64 kbps necessary for a single voice channel. Good voice reproduction can be achieved using a 7-bit code per sample, and the resulting overall voice channel is 8000 samples/

second times 7 bits per sample, yielding 56 kbps. Regeneration of the signal is primarily based on the use of repeaters that are necessary because of attenuation of the signal.

Amplitude, Frequency, and Phase Modulations

In general, modulation and demodulation are always related to one of the three characteristics of the signal—amplitude, frequency, and phase—or a combination of all or some of these characteristics. Modulation, or shifting, of any of these characteristics creates a recognizable, adequate (or sometimes called constellation) state of the signal, interprets these states as 1 or 0, and digitalizes them.

In amplitude-shift keying (ASK), the 1 and 0 are represented by two different amplitudes, as shown in Figure 2-1. In some cases, instead of using two amplitudes it is more acceptable to use an amplitude and no signal, in which case the timing is crucial. ASK can be used to code more than one bit. In cases when two recognizable amplitudes are generated, the technique can code-decode 2 bits with 4 stable states: 00, 01, 10, and 11. In copper lines this technique is considered inefficient because amplitude changes (power, attenuation, interference) can generate errors. In fiber media, where the attenuation of the signal is less of a consideration, 1 can be represented as a shot pulse of light, or high-amplitude light, and 0 can be low-amplitude light or the absence of light.

Figure 2-1   *Amplitude-Shift Keying (ASK) Scheme*

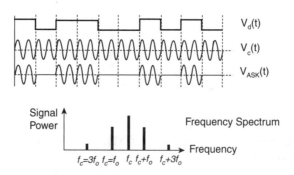

Frequency-shift keying (FSK) uses at least two different frequencies to represent 1 and 0, as shown in Figure 2-2. The scheme is less susceptible to errors than ASK and it is used for low-speed data transmissions.

In phase-shift keying (PSK), 1 and 0 are coded using different phases of the signal, as shown in Figure 2-3. The signal burst of the same phase represents 0, and the signal burst of the opposite phase represents 1. This technique is more resistant to errors than ASK and FSK, but it can still be used for low-rate data transmissions.

Figure 2-2   *Frequency-Shift Keying (FSK) Scheme*

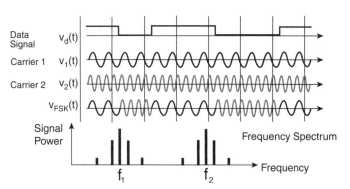

Figure 2-3   *Phase-Shift Keying (PSK) Scheme*

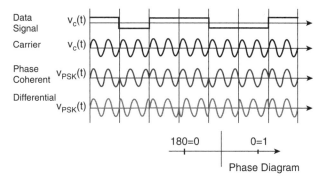

Quadrature Amplitude Modulation

Quadrature amplitude modulation (QAM) is a line-coding technique that has been used in modems for over twenty years. This technology can also be referred to as 16QAM or 4/4QAM. QAM takes advantage of the fact that if two signals are shifted to 90 degrees from each other, they can be sent simultaneously over the same frequency band. The two signals are ASK modulated, but on the receiving side they are de-shifted and the original binary codes are obtained. In general, the signal is divided by 2 and the resulting signal S(t) can be represented as the following:

$$S(t) = d_1(t)\cos w_c t + d_2(t)\sin w_c t$$

In simple terms, QAM modulates the amplitudes of two waves, and instead of using +-1, QAM uses 4 different amplitudes for each of the waves. As a result, there are four instead of two amplitude modulations: A1, A2, A3, and A4. The full combination of amplitude modulations and S(t) provides 16 combinations per Hertz, which is otherwise called 4 bps or 4 baud. The 16 established constellations look like 0000, 0001, ... (to 1111).

xDSL Coding Techniques

The emergence of digital subscriber line (DSL) technology increased the need for more modulation techniques. Unlike other technologies, DSL uses a set of protocols that are suitable for the different types of DSL technologies. Asymmetric DSL (ADSL), in particular, refers to the family of coding schemes where the emerging Internet technologies usually require higher bandwidth in the downstream direction than in the upstream direction (see the section, "xDSL Services" in Chapter 1, "Remote Access Overview"). This fact provides the need to divide the available bandwidth asymmetrically and to provide different data rates for each direction. In terms of Cisco IOS, Cisco ADSL solutions support the following DSL operating modes: ansi-dmt, auto detect mode, itu-dmt, and splitterless (G.lite) mode.

Discrete Multi-Tone

Discrete Multi-Tone (DMT) uses multiple carrier signals at different frequencies, sending some bits on each channel. The term DMT comes from the fact that each discrete bin is at a specific frequency or tone. The available transmission band is divided into several base-band carriers, sometimes called subchannels. Upon the initialization phase, the DMT modulator sends out a test signal on each subchannel to determine the signal–to-noise ratio. The modulator then assigns more bits to channels with better signal transmission quality and less to the channels with poorer quality. DMT modulation is actually a form of frequency-division multiplexing (FDM). The input data stream is split into 256 channels that have the same bandwidth, but a different center frequency, otherwise called the channel number.

Cisco uses the following standard DMT modulations in its products—ITU-DMT(G.992.1 TU G.DMT), ITU-T G.992.2 (G.lite), ANSI-DMT(ANSI Standard T1.413) and auto-recognition ADSL mode. Example 2-1 shows a sample of Cisco's ADSL 827 router showing the content of the bins.

Example 2-1   *A Sample of Cisco's ADSL 827 Router Showing the Content of the Bins*

```
pnedeltc-dsl#sh controllers atm 0

<output omitted>
DMT Bits Per Bin
00: 0 0 0 0 0 0 5 4 5 5 5 6 6 6 6
10: 6 6 6 6 6 5 6 5 6 6 5 6 5 6 6 0
20: 0 0 0 0 0 4 5 5 6 6 6 7 7 7 8
30: 8 7 8 8 8 8 8 8 8 8 8 8 8 8 8
40: 9 9 9 9 9 9 9 9 9 9 9 9 A A A A
50: A A A A A A 2 A A A A A A A A A
```

Example 2-1 *A Sample of Cisco's ADSL 827 Router Showing the Content of the Bins (Continued)*

```
60: 9 A 9 9 9 9 9 9 9 9 9 9 9 9 9 9
70: 9 9 9 9 9 9 9 9 9 9 9 9 9 9 9 9
80: 9 9 9 9 8 8 9 9 8 8 8 8 8 8 8 8
90: 8 8 8 8 8 8 8 8 8 8 8 8 8 8 8 8
A0: 8 8 8 8 8 8 8 8 8 8 8 7 7 7 7
B0: 7 7 7 7 7 7 7 7 7 7 7 5 7 7 7
C0: 7 7 7 7 7 7 7 7 7 7 7 7 7 7 7 7
D0: 7 7 7 7 7 7 7 7 7 7 7 7 7 7 6 6
E0: 6 6 6 6 6 6 6 6 6 6 6 6 6 6 6 6
F0: 6 6 5 5 5 4 4 2 2 0 0 0 0 0 0 0
<output omitted>
```

Every row has 16 (10h) columns (bins), where the first seven 0s are the voice (POTS) and guard channels. The following 24 non-zero bins, which results in about a 103-MHz band, are the upstream channels, followed by 6 bins of guard channels. The last group of 224 bins represent 224 downstream channels. Every bin is QAM modulated, and every value is calculated, based on the following formula:

$$\#\text{bits/sub\_symbol}\#k = \text{Round} \left[\log_2 (3 * SNR(k)/Q^{-1}(BER)^2 + 1) \right]$$

  SNR—Signal-to-noise ratio
  k—DMT tone index
  Q—Error function (erf function)
  BER—Bit error rate

Using multiple narrowband (baseband) channels results in the following advantages:

- All channels become independent regardless of line characteristics. Thus channels can be individually decoded.

- The optimum decoder for each channel uses less memory and it is easy to implement.

- Theoretical channel capacity, as calculated by Shannon's information theory, can be approached by this line code with reasonable complexity.

The ANSI ADSL system uses 256 frequency channels or bins. Data is separately modulated into each bin based on how much data each bin can hold. The amount of data each bin can hold is a function of loop characteristics and frequency. All channels have a bandwidth of 4.3125 kHz and the frequency difference between two successive channels is also 4.3125 kHz. This technology uses frequency bands above the POTS spectrum to pass ADSL data both upstream and downstream. The upstream band is from approximately 25 kHz to about 138 kHz, and the downstream band starts at 142 kHz (25 kHz if echo cancellation is used) and extends to 1.1 MHz. Each of these bands is further subdivided into 4.3125-kHz bins. Data is separately modulated into each bin based on how much data each bin can hold. The amount of data each bin can hold is a function of loop characteristics and frequency. A new batch of data is sent in each bin 4000 times a second. At the next layer up in the protocol stack, a Super Frame (SF) structure is defined. The SF structure defines how the payload data and overhead data is assembled. Additionally, it defines how the data in the SF is allocated to the bins—here, Cisco defines interleave mode and fast mode, where interleave mode performs Reed-Solomon error correction.

DMT is generally accepted to be better at rate adaptation (changing speed because of line conditions), varying loop conditions (bridge taps, mixed gauges), noise and crosstalk handling, and it is better for voice purposes.

Carrierless Amplitude/Phase Modulation

Carrierless amplitude/phase modulation (CAP) (also referred to as ATR-R) enables simple echo cancellation (although many CAP products use FDM), provides less delay (only 25 percent compared to DMT), and provides simplicity and maturity (because it is based on QAM). CAP can be referred to as an improved or suppressed QAM because, unlike QAM, CAP does not send a carrier over the line because the carrier does not carry any information. Generally speaking, if you add a rotation to the receiver side and suppress the carrier from the sender, you can get CAP from QAM. The technology is based on phase shifting (see the beginning of this chapter), but the phase of the wave changes under certain angles and it is measured from the current phase of the carrier, and not from some absolute reference phase. Because it is not absolute phase shifting, it is differential. In the simplest scenario with two phases, 1 is shifting (rotating) the phase to 180 degrees, and 0 is shifting to 0 degrees, or vice versa. This can be improved if you add two more established constellations. Because of quadrature phase-shift keying (QPSK), the signal is already sent as a combination of sine waves and cosine waves at carrier frequency, and they are already shifted by 90 degrees. QPSK as a coding technique takes its name from the term perpendicular, or quadrature. However, there is no phase shifting because the two waves are already shifted (phased, rotated), and CAP simply modulates the two amplitudes. Recently, CAP has been driven primarily by ANSI and is considered an option to DMT.

Modulation and Line-Coding Techniques in Wireless LANs

The emerging wireless LAN (WLAN) technologies offer a wide range of modulations, coding schemes, and technologies.[1] WLANs hold the promise of ubiquitous access to network resources without the physical limitations of the wired network. In WLANs, (otherwise popularly known as wi-fi [wireless-fidelity]) users can move freely about their offices or access network resources from conference rooms, lobbies, cafeterias, and campus buildings. WLANs use radio frequency (RF) waves instead of a cable infrastructure, and ensure mobile, cost-effective solutions that significantly reduce the network installation cost per user.

Infrared

Infrared (IR) radio-channel falls under the visible band of radiation that exists at the lower end of the visible spectrum. It is most effective when a clear line-of-sight can be achieved between the transmitter and the receiver. The technology has two available solutions: diffused-beam and direct-beam (or line-of-sight). Currently, direct-beam WLANs offer a faster data rate than diffused-beam networks, but direct-beam is more directional because diffused-beam technology uses reflected rays to transmit/receive a data signal. IR achieves lower data rates in the 1- to 2-Mbps range. IR optical signals are often used in remote control device applications.

Photonic Wireless Transmission

The only implementation of photonic WLANs use IR light transmission at the 850 to 950 Nm band of IR light with a peak power of 2 watts. The physical layer supports 1- to 2-Mbps data rates. Although photonic wireless systems potentially offer higher transmission rates than RF-based systems, they also have some distinct limitations:

- IR light is restricted to line-of-sight operations; however, the use of diffuse propagation can reduce this restriction by allowing the beam to bounce off passive reflective surfaces.

- The power output (2 watts) is low to reduce damage to the human eye; however, it limits transmissions to about 25 meters.

- Sensors (receivers) need to be laid out accurately otherwise the signal might not be picked up.

Photonic-based WLANs are inherently secure and are immune (as are optical fiber networks) from electromagnetic interference, which can interfere with cable and RF-based systems.

Diffused IR

Diffused IR communications are described as both indirect and non-line-of-sight. The diffused IR signal, which is emitted from the transmitter, fills an enclosed area like light and does not require line-of-sight transmission. You can point the IR adapters at the ceiling or at an angle and the signal bounces off the walls and ceiling. Changing the location of the receiver does not disrupt the signal. Many diffused IR products also offer roaming capabilities, which enables you to connect several access points to the network, and connect your mobile computer to any of these access points or move between them without losing your network connection. Usually diffused IR provides a radius of 25 to 35 feet and a speed of 1 to 2 Mbps.

IR Summary

Overall, the advantages of IR include no government regulations controlling use and its immunity to electromagnetic interference (EMI) and RF interference. Disadvantages of IR include that it is generally a short-range technology (30-50 ft radius under ideal conditions), signals cannot penetrate solid objects, and signals can be affected by light, snow, ice, fog, and dirt. Because of its significant limitations, IR is not a commonly used technology for WLANs.

Ultra-High Frequency Narrowband Technologies and WLAN

The term narrowband describes a technology in which the RF signal is sent in a narrow bandwidth, typically 12.5 kHz or 25 kHz. Power levels range from 1 to 2 watts for narrowband RF data systems. This narrow bandwidth combined with high power results in larger transmission distances than are available from 900-MHz or 2.4-GHz spread spectrum (SS) systems, which have lower power levels and wider bandwidths. UHF wireless data communication systems have been available since the early 1980s. These systems normally transmit in the 430- to 470-MHz frequency range, with rare systems using segments of the 800-MHz range. The lower portion of this band, 430 to 450 MHz, is often referenced as the unprotected (unlicensed) band and 450 to 470 MHz is referred to as the protected (licensed) band.

In the unprotected band, RF licenses are not granted for specific frequencies and anyone is allowed to use any frequency in the band. In the protected band, RF licenses are granted for specific frequencies, which gives customers some assurance that they will have complete use of that frequency. Other terms for UHF include narrowband and 400 MHz RF. Because independent narrowband RF systems cannot coexist on the same frequency, government agencies allocate specific radio frequencies to users through RF site licenses. A limited amount of the unlicensed spectrum is also available in some countries. To have many frequencies that can be allocated to users, the bandwidth given to a specific user is small.

Synthesized Radio Technology

The term synthesized radio technology refers to the crystal-controlled products in legacy UHF products, which require factory installation of unique crystals for each possible channel frequency. Synthesized technology uses a single, standard crystal frequency. The required channel frequency is calculated by either dividing or multiplying the standard crystal frequency. Synthesized UHF-based solutions provide the ability to install standard equipment without replacing the hardware, which provides less complexity and the ability to tune each device.

Multiple Frequency Operation

Modern UHF systems allow access points to be individually configured for operation on one of several pre-programmed frequencies. Wireless stations can be programmed with a list of all the frequencies used in the installed access points, which allows them to change frequencies when roaming. To increase throughput, access points can be installed with overlapping coverage but using different frequencies.

Advantages include a longer range, and it is considered a low cost solution for large sites with low to medium data throughput requirements. The disadvantages include low through-put, no interoperability, and a higher potential for interference. License requirements for protected bands and larger radio and antennas that increase wireless client size are also limiting factors.

Ultra Wideband and WLANs

The origin of ultra wideband (UWB) technology stems from work in time-domain electromagnetics that started in 1962 as a simple concept. Instead of characterizing a linear time-invariant (LTI) system by the more conventional means of a swept frequency response (which is amplitude and phase measurements versus frequency), an LTI system is alternatively characterized by its impulse response. The FCC approved the technology in February 2002, and this could have a significant impact on the WLAN industry. It could transform the industry from mainly limited radar or global positioning systems (GPSs) to more business communications. Wireless technologies, such as the 802.11 family and short-range BlueTooth radios, might be replaced by a UWB technology that has a throughput tens of thousands of times greater than the 802.11b standard.

UWB energy pulses operate in the same frequency spectrum as electronic noise that is typical of printers, chips, and widespread personal electronic equipment. The implications are significant:

- The UWB does not use a carrier and consequently does not require a designated band from any of the overcrowded spectrums.
- It is less expensive and easier to build such devices.
- The electromagnetic noise requires little power (in the order of milliwatts, which is thousands of times less than cellular phones). There is less power, radiation, and distance, but there are available techniques to increase the range.
- A high level of security exists because it is almost impossible to filter pulse signals from the regular noise.

Disadvantages of UWB that should be considered include the following:

- Concerns among academics and the industry about devices operating under the 2.4-GHz band. These pulses can interfere with existing broadcasts such as GPS and public safety nets.
- A high dependence on the way transmitters are tuned, timed, and powered.

UWB is an RF wireless technology, and as such is still subject to the same laws of physics as every other RF technology. Obvious tradeoffs can be made in signal-to-noise ratio versus bandwidth, and in range versus peak, depending on power levels.

WLAN Modulations and Coding Techniques

WLANs are significantly driving the industry. The short-range BlueTooth and HiperLAN/2 are among the key contributors. The standards defined by the IEEE 802.11 Task Force are making the most significant impact.

At the physical layer, IEEE 802.11 defines three physical techniques for WLANs:

- Diffused IR

- Frequency hopping spread spectrum (FH or FHSS)

- Direct sequence spread spectrum (DS or DSSS)

Although the IR technique operates at the baseband, the other two radio-based techniques operate at the 2.4-GHz band. They can operate WLAN devices without the need for end-user licenses. For wireless devices to be interoperable, they must conform to the same physical layer standard. All three techniques specify support for 1-Mbps and 2-Mbps data rates.

Spread Spectrum RF Transmissions

Spread Spectrum (SS) RF systems are true WLANs, which use radio frequency (RF wireless) transmission as the physical layer medium. Two major subsystems exist: FHSS and DSSS. DSSS is primarily an inter-building technology, and FHSS is primarily an intra-building technology. The actual technique of SS transmission was developed by the military in an attempt to reduce jamming and eavesdropping. SS transmission takes a digital signal and expands, or spreads, it so as to make it appear more similar to random background noise rather than a data signal transmission. Coding takes place either by using FSK or PSK. Both methods increase the size of the data signal and the bandwidth. Although the signal appears louder (more bandwidth) and easier to detect, the signal is unintelligible and appears as background noise unless the receiver is tuned to the correct parameters.

FHSS

FHSS is analogous to FM radio transmission as the data signal is superimposed on, or carried by, a narrowband carrier that can change frequency. The IEEE 802.11 standard provides 22 hop patterns, or frequency shifts, to choose from in the 2.4-GHz ISM band. Each channel is 1 MHz and the signal must shift frequency, or hop, at a fixed hop rate (U.S. minimum is 2.5 hops/sec). This technology modulates a radio signal by shifting it from frequency to frequency at near-random intervals. This modulation protects the signal from interference that concentrates around one frequency. To decode the signal, the receiver must know the rate and the sequence of the frequency shifts, thereby providing added security and encryption.

FHSS products can send signals as quickly as 1.2 to 2 Mbps and as far as 620 miles. Increasing the bandwidth (up to 24 Mbps) can be achieved by installing multiple access points on the network. In FS, the 2.4-GHz band is divided into 75 1-MHz subchannels. To minimize the probability that two senders are going to use the same subchannel simultaneously, frequency hopping provides a different hopping pattern for every data exchange. The sender and receiver agree on a hopping pattern, and data is sent over a sequence of subchannels according to the pattern. FCC regulations require bandwidth up to 1 MHz for every subchannel that forces the FHSS technique to spread the patterns across the entire 2.4-GHz band, which results in more hops and a high amount of overhead.

FHSS is considered an economic solution because it provides lower cost ratios, is half the cost of a DSSS system per-node, and can scale above 10 Mbps by adding more access points. Another good point regarding FHSS is its ability to overcome noisy environments, such as metro areas. Because of hopping, it can deal with interference better.

DSSS

SS was first developed by the military as a secure wireless technology. It modulates (changes) a radio signal pseudo-randomly so it is difficult to decode. This modulation provides some security; however, because the signal can be sent great distances, you do risk interception. To provide complete security, most SS products include encryption.

DSSS works by taking a data stream of 0s and 1s and modulating it with a second pattern, the chipping sequence. The sequence is also known as the Barker code, which is an 11-bit sequence (10110111000). The chipping, or spreading, code generates a redundant bit pattern to be transmitted, and the resulting signal appears as wideband noise to the unintended receiver. One of the advantages of using spreading codes is that even if one or more of the bits in the chip are lost during transmission, statistical techniques embedded in the radio can recover the original data without the need for retransmission. The ratio between the data and width of the spreading code is called processing gain. It is 16 times the width of the spreading code and increases the number of possible patterns to 2^{16} (64 k), which reduces the chance of cracking the transmission.

The DSSS signaling technique divides the 2.4-GHz band into 14 22-MHz channels, of which 11 adjacent channels overlap partially and the remaining three do not overlap. Data is sent across one of these 22-MHz channels without hopping to other channels, which causes noise on the given channel. To reduce the number of retransmissions and noise, chipping converts each bit of user data into a series of redundant bit patterns called chips. The inherent redundancy of each chip, combined with spreading the signal across the 22-MHz channel, provides error checking and correction functionality to recover the data.

SS products are often interoperable because many are based on the IEEE 802.11 standard for wireless networks. DSSS is primarily an inter-building technology, and FHSS is primarily an intra-building technology. DSSS products can be fast and far reaching.

DSSS is best suited for large coverage areas, ensures higher data rates, requires fewer access points, and the total system cost is lower.

IEEE 802.11b—The Next Step

All previously mentioned, coding techniques for 802.11 provide a speed of 1 to 2 Mbps, which is lower than the widespread IEEE 802.3 standard speed of 10 Mbps. The only technique (with regards to FCC rules) that is capable of providing a higher speed is DSSS, which was selected as a standard physical layer technique that supports 1 to 2 Mbps and two new speeds of 5.5 and 11 Mbps.

The original 802.11 DSSS standard specifies the 11-bit chipping, or Barker sequence, to encode all data sent over the air. Each 11-chip sequence represents a single data bit (1 or 0), and is converted to a waveform, called a symbol, that can be sent over the air. These symbols are transmitted at 1 MSps (1 million symbols per second) by using a sophisticated technique called binary phase-shift keying (BPSK). In the case of 2 Mbps, you use the more sophisticated implementation, QPSK, which doubles the data rate available in BPSK with improved efficiency in the use of the radio bandwidth.

To increase the data rate in the 802.11b standard, in 1998, Lucent Technologies and Harris Semiconductor proposed to IEEE a standard called Complementary Code Keying (CCK). Rather than the two 11-bit Barker code, CCK uses a set of 64 8-bit unique code words, thus up to 6 bits can be represented by any code word (instead of the 1 bit represented by a Barker symbol). As a set, these code words have unique mathematical properties that allow them to be correctly distinguished from one another by a receiver, even in the presence of substantial noise and multi-path interference (such as interference caused by receiving multiple radio reflections within a building).

The 5.5-Mbps rate uses CCK to encode 4 bits per carrier, and the 11-Mbps rate encodes 8 bits per carrier. Both speeds use QPSK as the modulation technique and signal at 1.375 MSps. QPSK uses four rotations (0, 90, 180 and 270 degrees) to encode 2 bits of information in the same space as BPSK encodes 1. The trade-off is that you must increase power or decrease range to maintain signal quality. Because the FCC regulates the output power of portable radios to 1 watt Effective Isotropic Radiated Power (EIRP), range is the only remaining factor that can change. Thus, for 802.11 devices, as you move away from the radio, the radio adapts and uses a less complex (and slower) encoding mechanism to send data, resulting in the lower data rates. Table 2-1 identifies the differences.

Table 2-1   *802.11b Standard Options*

Data Rate	Code and Code Length	Modulation	Symbol Rate	Bits/Symbol
1 Mbps	11 (Barker sequence)	BPSK	1 MSps	1
2 Mbps	11 (Barker sequence)	QPSK	1 MSps	2
5.5 Mbps	8 (CCK)	QPSK	1.375 MSps	4
11 Mbps	8 (CCK)	QPSK	1.375 MSps	8

802.11a and 802.11g—The New 5-GHz Band

The 802.11b standard for a coding technique is based on DSSS, a technology developed by the military for secure wireless transmission.

Unlike 802.11b, 802.11a was designed to operate in the more recently allocated 5-GHz Unlicensed National Information Infrastructure (UNII) band. Unlike the ISM band, which offers about 83 MHz in the 2.4-GHz spectrum, IEEE 802.11a uses almost four times that of the ISM band because the UNII band offers 300 MHz of relatively interference free spectrum. And unlike 802.11b, the 802.11a standard uses a FDM technique, which is expected to be more efficient in inter-building environments. The FCC allocates 300 MHz of spectrum for UNII in the 5-GHz block, 200 MHz of which is at 5150 MHz to 5350 MHz, with the other 100 MHz at 5725 MHz to 5825 MHz, as shown in Figure 2-4.

Figure 2-4   *5-GHz Frequency Band*

Independent Clear Channels

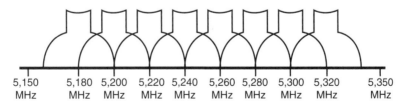

| 5,150 MHz | 5,180 MHz | 5,200 MHz | 5,220 MHz | 5,240 MHz | 5,260 MHz | 5,280 MHz | 5,300 MHz | 5,320 MHz | 5,350 MHz |

There are eight independent clear channels in the lower 200 MHz of the 5-GHz spectrum.

The first advantage of 802.11a over 802.11b is that the standard operates in the 5.4-GHz spectrum, which gives it the performance advantage of the higher frequencies. But frequency, radiated power, and distance together are in an inverse relationship, so moving up the 5-GHz spectrum from 2.4 GHz results in shorter distances and requirements for more power. That is why the 802.11a standard increases the EIRP to the maximum of 50 mW. The 5.4-GHz spectrum is split into three working domains and every domain has restrictions for maximum power.

The second advantage relies on the coding technique used by 802.11a.[2] 802.11a uses an encoding scheme called coded orthogonal FDM (COFDM or OFDM). Each subchannel in the COFDM implementation is about 300-kHz wide. COFDM works by breaking one high-speed data carrier into several lower-speed subcarriers, which are then transmitted in parallel. Each high-speed carrier is 20-MHz wide and is broken up into 52 subchannels, each approximately 300-kHz wide (see Figure 2-5).

Figure 2-5   *Orthogonal Frequency Division Multiplexing (OFDM)*

Subchannels

52 Carriers per Channel

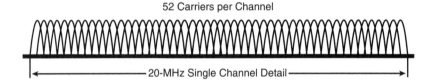

|←——————————— 20-MHz Single Channel Detail ———————————→|

Each channel is subdivided into 52 subchannels, each about 300-KHz wide.

COFDM uses 48 of these subchannels for data, while the remaining four are used for error correction. COFDM delivers higher data rates and a high degree of signal recovery, thanks to its encoding scheme and error correction. Each subchannel in the COFDM implementation is about 300-kHz wide. To encode 125 kbps, the well-known BPSK is used, which yields a 6000-kbps data rate. Using QPSK, it is possible to encode up to 250 kbps per channel, which combined achieves a 12-Mbps data rate. By using 16-level QAM encoding 4 bits per hertz, and achieving data rates of 24 Mbps, the standard defines basic speeds of 6.12 and 24 Mbps that every 802.11a-compliant product must support. Data rates of 54 Mbps are achieved by using 64 QAM, which yields 8 to 10 bits per cycle, and a total of up to 1.125 Mbps per 300-kHz channel. With 48 channels, this results in a 54-Mbps data rate; however, the maximum theoretical data rate of COFDM is considered to be 108 Mbps.

NOTE   802.11a is not backward compatible with 802.11b. As a result, the 802.11a deployment in an already deployed 802.11b environment can be complicated. One possible solution here is the Cisco 1200 product, which supports both standards.

802.11g is an extension of 802.11b, and will broaden 802.11b's data rates to 54 Mbps by using the same OFDM technology as 802.11a within the 2.4-GHz band. Because of backward compatibility, an 802.11b radio card interfaces directly with an 802.11g access point (and vice versa) at 11 Mbps or lower depending on the range. Similar to 802.11b,

802.11g operates in the 2.4-GHz band, and the transmitted signal uses approximately 30 MHz, which is one third of the band. This limits the number of non-overlapping 802.11g access points to three, which is the same as 802.11b. This means that the same difficulties exist with the 802.11g channel assignment as with the 802.11b when covering a large area with a high density of users. Another big issue here is the considerable RF interference from other 2.4-GHz devices. The 802.11g standard is still under development and the release of 802.11g radio cards and access points can be expected by late 2002 or early 2003.

NOTE   The newly accepted IEEE 802.11e adds multimedia, quality of service (QoS), and enhanced security to the current IEEE 802.11 wireless standard. IEEE 802.11e is a Media Access Control (MAC) level enhancement that works with both 802.11b (2.4 GHz) and 802.11a (5 GHz) physical layers, and with the upcoming IEEE 802.11g physical layer specification. Significant elements of ShareWave's patented Whitecamp network protocol have been incorporated into the IEEE 802.11e specification. Recently, ShareWave announced, "The Bodega Wireless LAN Platform Features Whitecap2 Technology, which Adds Wi-Fi (802.11b) Compliance to Multimedia and QoS Capabilities."

Modulation and Line-Coding Techniques in Hybrid Networks

To prevent confusion, hybrid terminology refers to a combination of wired and wireless technologies. These technologies are available in today's market and offer some unique features. The wireless modem works as an integrated part of the Cisco uBR7200 Series Universal Broadband routers, primarily designed for the cable core router product line. The new product is a hardware adapter and it can be plugged to the existing platform. It creates a combined solution of cable and wireless technology, which creates a hybrid networking solution.

Their variety and combinations can vary significantly from solution to solution, but here is another example of a hybrid solution, based on signaling and protocols, as initially designed for other technologies. It is called Cisco's Firestorm Multichannel Multipoint Distribution System (MMDS. This is a Broadband Fixed Wireless (BBFW) point-to-multiPoint (P2MP) headend (HE) and customer premises equipment (CPE) solution that is suited primarily for residential environments, which is designed to provide licensed broadband wireless access to a market not served by fiber or copper, which also will provide geographic coverage not possible with competitive unlicensed BBFW systems. For the HE, Cisco offers a wireless line card (uBR-MCW-MDA) which fits in a 7223 or 7246 uBR or VXR router, and a MMDS transverter (SX11127A) with duplexor. The CPE gear includes either a 951 router for data only or a 952 router for voice enhanced residential use. This BBFW P2MP solution operates at Layer 3, has non line of site (NLOS) capabilities (through the RF component), and can provide voice and differentiated services. Extraordinary co-channel resolution and multi-path signal mitigation is based on signaling protocols QAM 64 downstream with OFDM modulation and 16 QAM upstream modulation schemes, plus optional spatial antenna diversity for NLOS at both the HE or CPE. Also, a co-channel resolution capability is offered with Data-over-Cable Service Interface Specifications (DOCSIS) for subscriber management.

Another solution involves using the licensed and license-free U-UNI spectrums with a fixed wireless solution and terrestrial OC-3 backbone. This alliance was announced by WiFi Metro, Inc. in April 2002. WiFi is a wireless ISP (WISP) that owns a network of over 50 wireless hotspot locations and Gatespeed Broadband, Inc. The wireless HotZone of WiFi Metro, which provides high-speed Internet access to subscribers within a fifteen-mile radius of a centralized Wireless Internet Point of Presence (WIPOP), is combined with the fixed wireless solution of GateSpeed. The 2.4-GHz licensed spectrum runs the IEEE 802.11 protocol. The 5.2-GHz license-free spectrum is used for U-NII, and these two spectrum bands support nationwide deployment. This solution is fully compatible with existing Cisco Aironet 350 series and Cisco 1200 Series products.

Satellite communications can use another approach to provide Internet access, such as the DOCSIS 1.1 standard. It is well known that the primary focus of the DOCSIS standard is cable modem service, but the standard can be used for satellite with a specially designed DOSCIS terminal for emerging Ku-band satellite systems.

Another example here is Sprint, who is using hybrid networks that are based on a proprietary cable modem network in the Bay Area. It is basically a cable modem system, which has been frequency shifted to operate over wireless; it has all the same bandwidth sharing issues as cable modems.

The list of examples is much wider and includes Frame Relay over wireless, L2TP, Multiprotocol Label Switching (MPLS), GRE-based Virtual Private Network (VPN) in fixed wireless networks, Point-to-Point Protocol over Ethernet (PPPoE), and L2TP to MPLS conversions for fixed wireless networks. The bottom line is that market conditions in the U.S. have proved that these types of hybrid solutions can be successful, based on the fact that they combine existing with emerging or evolving technologies and require less of an investment, which provides new solutions and covers more user-based demand areas.

Clocking, Line Coding, and Framing in Carrier Systems

In digital transmissions, three major elements need to be considered:

- Clocking
- Line coding (signaling)
- Framing

They are the differentiators between analog and digital transmission.

Clocking

Analog interfaces do not require that specific timing be configured. However, digital T1 interfaces require that not only the timing be set, but also that the origination of the timing source be considered. Line and internal timing (clocking) are the available options to address this requirement. Clocking refers to both timing and synchronization of the T1 and it is an essential part of the proper functioning. The timing is encoded in the frames and provides synchronization for the circuit and for every synchronous transmission. It is preferred to derive the clocking from the service provider, where the local exchange carrier (LEC) clocking serves as the master and the router clocking serves as a slave. When more than one provider is involved in delivering the T1, clock slips can occur. In this case, it is important to have a master clock to provide reliable time-division multiplexing (TDM) synchronization and alignment.

Pseudo-Ternary and Two Binary One Quaternary Signaling

ISDN and Frame Relay use a coding scheme called pseudo-ternary signaling, which is associated with the S/T interface.

The two binary one quaternary (2B1Q) coding scheme, which in turn is associated with the U-interface, is specific for U.S. ISDN, ISDN DSL (IDSL), high-data-rate DSL (HDSL), and single-line DSL (SDSL) local-loop specifications.

Pseudo-Ternary Line Coding and the S/T Interface

ISDN and the first layer of Frame Relay use a coding scheme called pseudo-ternary signaling, which is used by the S/T interface. This technique provides DC balance and non-voltage drifting procedures for signaling by using positive and negative 0s. In pseudo-signaling, 0 is represented as a line signal of approximately 750 millivolts that alternates between positive and negative polarity, and the 1 represents the absence of voltage. As you can see from Figure 2-6, synchronization is important because there must be a way to recognize the two consecutive 1s from 0s, where two or more consecutive 0s change the polarity. The synchronization is based on the bipolar violation (BPV), which is two consecutive 0s. In pseudo-ternary signaling, the binary values show a 0 as negative or positive, and 1 as the absence of signal.

Figure 2-6   *Pseudo-Ternary Signaling*

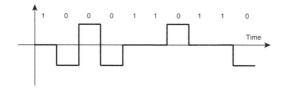

The frame structure is organized into blocks of bits. Figure 2-7 shows the short physical layer frame format. From the CPE terminal equipment (TE), the outgoing frames have 2 bits offset from incoming frames. The network timing drives the process. The TE cannot activate the line (activation bit A), as only the NT confirms the activation. Figure 2-7 shows a significant difference between incoming and outgoing frame formats. Each frame contains 16 bits from every B channel and 4 bits from the D channel.

Figure 2-7   *Short and Detailed Frame Formats*

Short Frame Format

Channel	B1	D	B2	D	B1	D	B2	D
Number of Bits	8	1	8	1	8	1	8	1

Detailed Frame Format

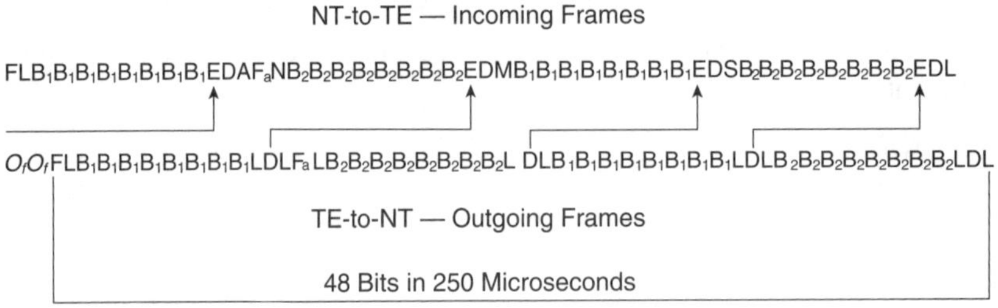

NT-to-TE — Incoming Frames

$FLB_1B_1B_1B_1B_1B_1B_1EDAF_aNB_2B_2B_2B_2B_2B_2B_2EDMB_1B_1B_1B_1B_1B_1B_1EDSB_2B_2B_2B_2B_2B_2B_2EDL$

$O_fO_fFLB_1B_1B_1B_1B_1B_1B_1LDLF_aLB_2B_2B_2B_2B_2B_2B_2L\ DLB_1B_1B_1B_1B_1B_1B_1LDLB_2B_2B_2B_2B_2B_2B_2LDL$

TE-to-NT — Outgoing Frames

48 Bits in 250 Microseconds

The full description of the bits and rules follows:

- **Of**—Offset.
- **F**—Framing bit. Always positive 0 and is based on the BPV, which is used for timing.
- **L**—DC balancing bit. Independent DC balanced; can be +0,-0, or 1.
- **D**—D channel bit. +0, -0, or 1 in the first format; 1,-0 in the second.
- **E**—Echo D channel bit. Can be +0, -0, or 1; exists only in the first format.
- **F$_a$**—Auxiliary framing bit. Only in the first format.
- **A**—Activation bit. Can be +0, -0, or 1; only in the first format.
- **N**—Complement to Fa. Can be +0, -0, or 1; only in the first format.
- **B1, B2**—Data bit within B1 and B2 channels respectively; can be +0, -0, or 1.
- **S**—Reserved.
- **M**—Multiframing bit. Can be +0, -0, or 1; only in the first format. I.430 specifies multiframe, which is a group of 20 I.430 frames. M-bit and F$_a$ are used in the multiframing procedures. The M-bit is set to 1 in the first 20 frames, which are 48 bits each, and set to 0 in every other frame. The I.430 also specifies that the first 0-bit transmitted F and L bits are another BPV.

For every 250 ms, 48 bits are transmitted through the channel, yielding a total of 4000 frames per second. 4000 frames × 48 bits each results in a total rate of 192 kb. For every 16 B-bits, the channel transmits 4 D-bits. Therefore in a Basic Rate Interface (BRI), if every B channel is 64 kbps, the D channel is 16 kbps. A BRI is also known as 2B+D. This signaling is not contention-free, so a simple contention-resolution mechanism was designed to prevent contentions. It is based on the following traffic considerations:

- **B channel traffic**—No additional functionality is necessary to control access to the two B channels because each channel is dedicated to a given TE at any particular time.

- **Incoming D channel traffic**—The D channel is available for use on all member TEs. The Link Access Procedure on the D channel (LAPD) addressing scheme (described later) is sufficient to resolve any unit and its destination, based on the fact that each LAPD frame includes an explicit address of every destination TE. All TEs can read this address and determine whether the frame was sent to them.

- **Outgoing D channel traffic**—Access must be regulated, so that only one device transmits frames at a time.

The following is how the contention resolutions works:

- When the TE is ready to transmit an LAPD frame, it listens to the stream of incoming D channel echo bits. If it detects a string of 1s of equal length to a threshold value Xi, where i = priority class for this LAPD frame, it can transmit. Otherwise, it waits because another TE is transmitting.

- If several TEs transmit 0 at the same time, all are using the same polarity. Sending 1 means no signal. The TEs are attached to the bus in parallel. Based on Ohm's law, the total voltages are not a sum of all voltages. Therefore, 1 is detected if all TEs apply 1 (no voltage) and 0 is detected if one or more TEs apply a voltage. This process uses the logical AND function.

- A NT-to-TE frame carries an E-bit, which is an echoed D-bit in the opposite direction. The E-bit performs an important contention mechanism, especially in the p2mp designs. The mechanism ensures that only one TE is transmitting frames in the TE-to-NT direction. If more than one TE tries to transmit, a collision can result. To avoid a collision, a transmitting TE monitors the echo bit with the transmitted bit. If the E-bit is different from the last transmitted D-bit by this TE, the TE knows that it does not control the D channel and ceases the transmission. This procedure is called *perfect scheduling*.

Two Binary One Quaternary Coding, the Frame Format, and the U-Interface

ANSI standard T1.601 is used in the U.S. to provide the necessary specifications for the U-reference point because the International Telecommunication Union Telecommunication Standardization Sector (ITU-T) does not define the local loop specifications between NT and the LE across U-reference points, or the otherwise called U-interface. The interface and line coding is specific for U.S. ISDN, IDSL, HDSL and SDSL local loop specifications. The physical connection over twisted pair provides distances up to 5.5 km (18,000 ft). The U-interface supports serial, synchronous, full-duplex, and point-to-point designs. The signaling technique associated with the U-interface is called two binary one quaternary (2B1Q), as shown in Figure 2-8.

Figure 2-8   *Two Binary One Quaternary (2B1Q) Signaling*

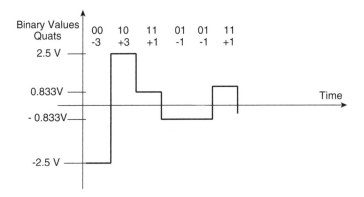

2B1Q is a four-level, single-symbol code. Every combination of two bits (first two columns), where the first bit represents the polarity and the second one the magnitude, has a voltage representation and Q symbol representation called a quat. The frame format in the U-access point (often called the U-interface) is different, as shown in Figure 2-9.

Figure 2-9   *2B1Q Frame Format*

Synchronization Word	12 Groups of (2B+D) Each	Overhead (M Channel)
9 Quats, 18 Bits	108 Quats, 216 Bits	3 Quats, 6 Bits

The Synchronization Word (SW) is a self-explanatory term, which is used for physical layer synchronization and frame alignment. B and D channel information is formed into 12 groups that contain data and control information as follows: B1 (8 bits), B2 (8 bits), and D (2 bits). Therefore, 18 (8 + 8 + 2) multiplied by 12 yields 216 bits, representing 108 quats. The overhead field is used for channel maintenance, limited bit error detection, and power status indication. Using two different interfaces, S/T and U, requires signal transformation that is performed by the device known as the network termination type 1 or NT1. The timing for the NT1 in a U-interface (reference point) is still provided by the LE.

Unlike a S/T reference point, the U-access point operates at 160 kbps and sends 666.666 frames per second, or one frame every 1.5 ms. Every eight groups of frames is a SF. To indicate the beginning of the SF, the technique uses an inverted SW. The 6 overhead bits of all frames represent a 48-bit (8 frames × 6 bits) block, called a M-channel. This block is capable of increased error-detection, signaling maintenance, and power error detection.

T1 Digital Coding and Framing

Analog interfaces do not require a specific line-coding configuration. Digital interfaces do require that the alternate mark inversion (AMI), bipolar 8-zero substitution (B8ZS), B3ZS, B6ZS, or high density binary 3 (HDB3) be configured. These values must match the values of the private branch exchange (PBX) or central office (CO) that connects to the Digital T1/T3 Packet Voice Trunk Module.

A large variety of coding schemes can be used that are based on well-established research and standards. The following are a few of these coding schemes:

- Unipolar non-return to zero (NRZ)
- Unipolar return to zero
- Polar NRZ
- Polar NRZ inverted (NRZI)
- Bipolar return to zero
- B3ZS
- B6ZS
- Manchester code

Some of these are included in Figure 2-10.

Choosing one or another scheme is always based on design considerations, such as the following:

- Does the line code provide good synchronization?
- Does the line code allow a DC buildup in transmission?
- Does the line code provide any error detection capability?

Figure 2-10 *Line-Coding Schemes*

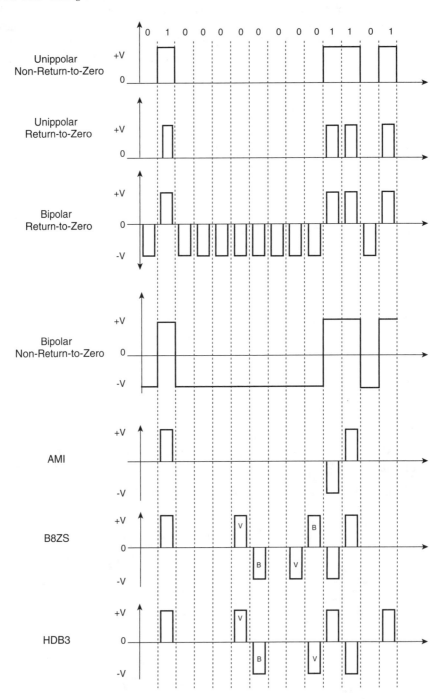

Alternate Mark Inversion

Cisco routers support the following coding schemes:

```
7200-router(config-controller)#linecode ?
ami   AMI encoding
b8zs  B8ZS encoding
```

One of the most widespread coding techniques for T1 carriers is *alternate mark inversion* (*AMI*). By using AMI, pulses correspond to binary 1s and 0s and alternate at 3V (+3/-3V). The presence of a signal is 1, and the absence of a signal is 0. A benefit of this encoding is a built-in method of error detection. When consecutive pulses are detected to have the same polarity, the condition is considered to be a BPV. As a result, the carrier and the CPE indicate that the frame is experiencing some type of error. A problem with this coding scheme is the way that 0 is interpreted as a no-signal condition. Therefore, an absence of pulses (all 0s) can force repeaters and network equipment to lose frame synchronization. To prevent this, all T1s are required to meet the 1's density requirement, which states that no more than 15 consecutive 0s can be transmitted to the line. (In the old days, the FCC actually said you could have 15 0s in a row. Now, the FCC says that you can have up to about 40 0s without harming the network. For all practical purposes, 7 consecutive 0s is the maximum today. See *Newton's Telecom Dictionary: The Authoritative Resource for Telecommunications, Networking, the Internet, and Information Technology* (18th Edition), Harry Newton and Ray Horak.) One solution to this requirement is alternate space inversion (ASI), which reverts the pulses. 1 becomes a no-signal state and the data is inverted for high-level data link control (HDLC) framed packets. However, this isn't commonly used. More often, you find CPE equipment configured to only use 7 of the 8 bits of each T1 timeslot. This effectively brings your data rate down from 64 k to 56 k per channel.

Zero-Suppression Schemes

The most widespread remedies for the density requirements of T1s are zero-suppression codes. They use certain rules, where if a predefined pattern is detected, the network equipment corrects it by inserting another pattern in the data stream to maintain ones density.

B8ZS and T1

B8ZS is one of the most widespread zero-suppression coding techniques. It is implemented to prevent degradation because of long strings of 0s. B8ZS replaces a block of eight consecutive 0s with a code that contains BPVs in the fourth and seventh bits. When eight 0s appear, they are replaced with the B8ZS code before being multiplexed onto the T1 line. At the receiver, detection of the BPV is replaced with eight 0s, which allows the full 64 kbps of the DS0 to be used. This is the most common technique; all major U.S. carriers support it.

B3ZS and B6ZS for T3

Other well-known zero suppressing schemes are B3ZS and B6ZS line codes. These coding schemes are typical for T3 (digital service 3 [DS3]) circuits.

In B3ZS, each pattern of 000 is replaced by 00V or B0V. The choice depends on whether the number of bipolar pulses between violations (V) is an odd number. In this case, V is positive or negative and chosen to cause a BPV, and B is also positive or negative, and is chosen to meet the bipolar conditions.

In B6ZS, each pattern of 000000 is replaced by 0VB0VB. Again, the choice depends on whether the number of bipolar pulses between Vs is an odd number. Here, as in the previous case, V is positive or negative, and is chosen to cause a BPV; and B is positive or negative, and is chosen to meet the bipolar conditions.

T1 and T3 Framing

Analog interfaces do not require that specific framing be configured. Digital T1 interfaces do require that either SF (also called SF or D4 framing) or Extended SF (ESF) be configured. These values must match the values of the PBX or CO that connects to the Digital T1 Packet Voice Trunk Module.

Cisco routers support the following frame formats for T1 connections:

```
7200-router(config-controller)#framing ?
esf  Extended Superframe
sf   Superframe
```

T1 SF Signal Format

The recent D3/Mode 3 D4 format for framing and channelization is, by far, the most popular format. The bit stream is organized into SFs, each consisting of 12 frames. Every frame consists of channel information, where every channel is 8 bits plus framing bits. Framing bits are marked differently. Terminal framing bits (BFt) mark odd frames that produce a sequence of alternating 1s and 0s. Even-numbered signaling frame bits (BFs) produce groups of three 1s, followed by three 0s, repeating. The framing bits, which are every 193rd bit and the last bit in each frame, are inserted between the 24th and 1st channel word. Each channel word consists of 8 bits (B1 through B8) every 0.65 nsec. Channel words represent 8-bit samples, taken at the rate of 8000 samples per second, and correspond to 24 different sources of voice or data information.

Signaling information is information that is exchanged between components of a telecommunication system to establish, monitor, or release connections. For voice transmissions, signaling information must be transmitted with the channel voice samples. This is accomplished by sharing the last significant bit (B8) between voice and signaling. This process is called robbed bit signaling (RBS). The B8 bit carries voice information for five frames, followed by one frame of signaling information. This pattern of B8 assignment to voice and signaling is repeated during each successful group of six frames. Using this technique, 24 channels × (8000 samples/channel/second) × (8 bits per frame) + 8000 BFs/second, yields a total speed of 1.544 Mbps.

T1 ESF Signal Formats

The SF of ESF is extended from 12 to 24 frames with 24 framing bits. Of the 24 framing bits in an ESF, six bits are used for synchronization, six bits for error checking, and the remaining 12 bits are used for a 4-kbps facility data link (FDL), which is a communication link between CSUs and the telephone company's monitoring devices. The framing bits are used for different purposes than in SF. The ESF takes advantage of new more-reliable conduits (just an analogy with X.25 and Frame Relay standards), where not every bit needs to be used for framing and synchronization. To permit error detection, the sending CSU examines all the 4608 data bits within ESF and generates a cyclic redundancy check (CRC). The receiver calculates its own CRC and compares both. If there is a match, there are no errors. CRC is known to report approximately 98 percent of all possible bit errors. This information is stored in counters and considered when there is a trend in speed degradation. This process results in increased availability and uptime for T1s. Some reports show that the expected availability of T1s for most phone companies is greater than 95 percent.

NOTE   The troubleshooting of T1s is covered in Part II, "Dial."

M23 Frame Format

The digital signal level 3 (DS-3) (T3) interface operates at 44.736 Mbps over coax cable, which is compliant with Asynchronous Transfer Mode (ATM) Forum UNI specifications. Three standards for DS-3 framing exist: M23, C-bit parity, and SYNTRAN. The M23 multiplex scheme provides for the transmission of seven DS-2 channels. A T3 is 28 T1s, and the first layer multiplexor (M12) serves four T1s. The seven second-layer multiplexors are connected to the end multiplexor (M23). Because each DS-2 channel can contain four DS-1 signals, a total of 28 DS-1 signals (670 DS-0 signals) are transported in a DS-3 facility. The current DS-3 signal format is a result of a multi-step, partially synchronous, partially asynchronous multiplexing sequence. Cisco routers support the following frame formats:

```
7200-router(config)#contr t3 2/0
7200-router(config-controller)#framing ?
auto-detect  Application Identification Channel Signal
c-bit        C-Bit Parity Framing
m23          M23 Framing Format
```

The DS-3 signal is partitioned into M-frames of 4760 bits each. The M-frames are divided into seven M-subframes, each containing 680 bits. Each subframe is further divided into eight blocks of 85 bits each, with the first bit used for control and the rest for payload. 56 frame overhead bits handle functions such as M-frame alignment, M-subframe alignment, performance monitoring, alarms, and source application channels.

PRI—1.544-Mbps Interface

The ITU-T recommendation I.431 defines the physical layer protocol of PRI for both 1.544 and 2.048 Mbps. The electrical characteristics are defined in G.703 and G.704. The primary use of PRIs are as the trunk and trunk groups, and not as the TEs. Usually, LECs have separate service groups for BRIs and PRIs, which is based on the nature of their usage (see Figure 2-11).

Figure 2-11 *ITU-T I.431 Recommendation*

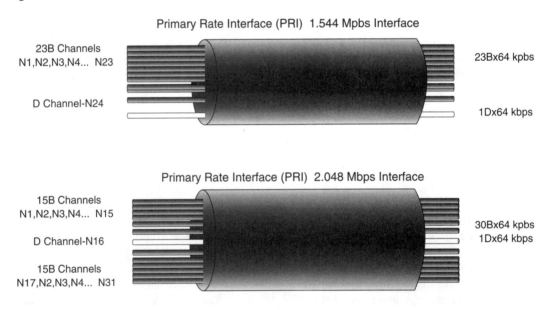

Primary Rate Interface (PRI) 1.544 Mpbs Interface

23B Channels
N1,N2,N3,N4... N23

D Channel-N24

23Bx64 kpbs

1Dx64 kbps

Primary Rate Interface (PRI) 2.048 Mbps Interface

15B Channels
N1,N2,N3,N4... N15

D Channel-N16

15B Channels
N17,N2,N3,N4... N31

30Bx64 kpbs
1Dx64 kbps

The PRI, unlike a BRI does not support p2mp configurations, but only point-to-point. In terms of ISDN, usually it is defined at the T reference point, where a digital PBX or LAN connection device controls multiple ISDN TEs, and provides multiplexing for them. The PRI is based on the DS1 transmission structure and T1 services.

The PRI multiplexes 24 channels, 64 kbps each. When it is configured as 23 B+D channels, the D channel is used for signaling, and when it is configured as 24 B channels, another D channel is available to do the signaling.

NOTE   Out-of-band signaling uses frequencies outside of the normal frequency band for signaling; this is the core of the Signaling System 7 (SS7). In contrast, in-band signaling relies on using certain bits out of the frame format in the frequency band, and can be referred to as bit robbing signaling.

When the PRI is configured for 24 B channels, the PRI frame contains one framing bit plus a single 8-bit pulse code modulation (PCM) sample from each of the 24 channels. These 193 bits, multiplied by 8000 frames per second, yield a total bit rate of 1.544 Mbps. The 24 frames are grouped together to form a multiframe, as described in the ESF frame format. One multiframe is 24 bits and performs the following functions:

- **Frame alignment sequence (FAS)** — FAS ensures the synchronization of frames and is represented by a repeated pattern of 001011.... In case of losing proper synchronization, the receiver needs to listen to five consecutive SFs and find the correct sequence to synchronize.

- **Flow Sequence Control (FSC)** — FSC ensures that no bit errors occurred in the previous multiframe. The sequence detects and reports, but does not correct the errors.

- **Maintenance channel (M)** — The use of M remains to be determined; it is not currently used in PRIs.

In I.431, one bit of every octet is required to meet the density requirement, resulting in a 56-kbps channel rate. To overcome this drawback, B8ZS is used and all 0 octets are replaced by a combination of 000110011, where the BPV occurs in the fourth and seventh bits. If the last 1 was a positive 1, the replacement looks like 000pn0np, where *n* and *p* represent negative and positive polarity. If the previous appearance of 1 was negative, the combination is 000np0pn, and *n* and *p* are negative and positive polarities. The new pattern is injected in a way that all V and B are paired, so that the new code is DC-balanced.

NOTE   The troubleshooting of PRIs can be seen in Part II.

PRI—2.048-Mbps Interface

Similar to the 1.544-Mbps PRI used in the U.S. and based on the T1 carrier, the 2.048-Mbps PRI is typical for Europe and is based on Computer Emergency Response Team (CERT) 1, or the E1 carrier. E1, in the configuration of 30B+D, is the most common remote access solution for ISDN access services. Thirty B-channels and configurations such as 30B+D are more likely to be used for home remote access solutions. The numeration of the channels differs from the previous design (see Figure 2-11). Channels 1 to 15 are B channels, followed by a D channel (number 16), and another set of 15 B channels. Every frame contains 31 slots, and every slot is a single 8-bit sample. The duration of the frame is still 125 seconds, but 256 bits. So, 8000 frames per second with 256 bits each, plus framing bits, yield 2.048 Mbps with 1.9984 Mbps for the user data rate. Unlike AMI in the previous design, the zero-suppression scheme is called HDB3. HDB3 replaces a string of four consecutive 0s with a pattern of x00V, where V is the violation bit, and x is the bit which can be 1 or 0, depending on the requirement to keep the code DC-balanced.

The line-coding and framing techniques described previously include the most common and established ones, but not all of them. The main objective is to provide you with background and details to prepare for the next chapter.

End Notes

1 Plamen Nedeltchev. "Wireless LAN Ready for Prime Time." Cisco Packet Magazine. Q3, 2001.

[2] Network Computing. "80211a: Making Space for Speed." J. Conover. January 2001.

Summary

In this chapter, you learned about clocking, line coding, and framing in the carrier's system, which is an integral part of your knowledge as a troubleshooting engineer. The wired solutions, wireless solutions, and hybrid solutions are well represented in today's enterprise environments. The importance of this chapter is to give you more information about the variety of existing standards in the industry, to help you to recognize the different techniques and solutions, and to assist you in designing, configuring, and troubleshooting your environment.

Review Questions

Answers to the review questions can be found in Appendix A, "Answers to Review Questions."

1 What does Shannon's Law state?

2 What does the Nyquist sampling theorem state?

3 What does DMT stand for? How many subchannels does the standard (ANSI) ADSL define?

4 Why is CAP modulation sometimes called suppressed QAM?

5 What is the typical speed in the 802.11b standard? What coding techniques provide these speeds?

6 How wide is the high carrier in 802.11a; how many subchannels does it have, and how wide is each subchannel?

7 How does the 802.11g standard relate to 802.11a and 802.11b?

8 What is the relation between the terms clocking, timing, and synchronization?

9 What interface uses the pseudo-ternary coding technique? What is the size of the frame?

10 What does 2B1Q stand for and which interface does it use? What is the size of the frame?

11 What is perfect scheduling in the physical layer?

12 How do T1 circuits meet the ones density requirements?

13 Explain how the 24 framing bits in ESF are broken down and how they are used.

CHAPTER 3

The Cloud

In telecommunications, a public or semi-public space on transmission lines (such as T1 or T3) that exists between the endpoints of a transmission is referred to as the cloud or the network cloud. Data that is transmitted across a wide-area network (WAN) enters the network from one endpoint by using a standard protocol suite. The data then enters the network cloud where it shares space with other data transmissions. Within the cloud, the data can be encapsulated, translated, and transported in different ways, but it emerges in the same format as it entered the cloud. A network cloud represents a packet-switched network (PSN), where no two packets necessarily follow the same physical path.

Another understanding of this term as a troubleshooting engineer is that you have no visibility of the internal structure and procedures over the cloud, which traditionally belongs and is managed by a carrier or a local service provider. The term carrier is a legacy term that comes from voice technology, where channels are carried over multiplexed systems and don't appear in their natural band of 0.3-3.4 kHz until the signal reaches the receiver. Today, the term carrier includes not only legacy, but additional services, which are explained in more detail in the following pages.

Having learned about telecommunication basics, this chapter provides you with fundamental knowledge for when you are dealing with service providers. The focus of this chapter covers the following topics:

- Carriers, service providers, and how the traffic is carried

- T-carriers, E-carriers, Signaling System 7 (SS7), and Synchronous Optical Network (SONET)

- Carrier's facilities and switching system

- Internet service providers (ISPs) and application service providers (ASPs)

- Future features to be expected from service providers

Carriers, Service Providers, and How Traffic Is Carried

In telecommunications, transferring information from one point to another is based on transferring signals that by nature can be continuous and discrete, or analog and digital. The typical Public Switched Telephone Network (PSTN) of the early 1960s is primarily an analog network. Discrete or digital signal terminology is based on the base 2 numerical system (1 and 0), where a digital signal has at least two recognizable states that can be interpreted as 1 and 0.

Carriers build networks that differ from each other based on the way that the carrier switches the traffic and reroutes it to the requested destination. The carrier's switching systems can be classified as follows:

- **Circuit switching**—The physical resources of the time, space, and frequency spectrum are dedicated to a single call for the duration of the call. The network handles the resources based on physical availability, thus restricting and blocking the call requests that exceed the physical limitations of the network.

- **Message switching**—Each switch can store and delay incoming messages, and rather than block the requests, the switch uses the available bandwidth by using rate adoption algorithms, multiplexing, or both. Packet switching is a special case of message switching, where messages are formalized and length-restricted by using maximum transmission or receive unit (MTU, MRU) conventions, or by using standards-based message exchanges to minimize the content-based calculations.

- **Packet switching**—Packet switching is slightly different from message switching. Message switching passes messages from the sender to the receiver through intermediate nodes. Packet switching relies on a large number of trunks attached to the switches and thus balances the traffic load around busy trunks and lines.

- **Cell switching**—Cell switching is primarily based on Asynchronous Transfer Mode (ATM), where a standard, fixed-length 53-byte packet that is called a cell can deliver data, voice, and video in a uniform fashion. Traditional switching methods are defined by the two dimensions of the physical conduit and the subchannel (subinterface). Cell switching uses additional dimensions that define the physical conduit, virtual path, and virtual channel, where the intermediate dimension of the virtual path is composed of all the virtual channels that are pointing in the same direction.

Cell switching terminology can be a bit confusing because the term asynchronous is part of the name. In asynchronous data communications, the synchronization is not necessary because the synchronization is part of the frame format. Each character (5 or 8 bits long) requires a start and a stop bit and, in some cases, the stop bit can be 1.5 times longer than the start bit. Considered a reliable form of communication, the asynchronous transfer creates high overhead and thus restricts high bandwidth rates. In the case of synchronous data communications, precise synchronization is mandatory.

NOTE Have you ever heard a technician from the central office (CO) say, "The line cannot sync"? This is the most common reason that the first layer does not come up and/or the clocking is not available.

Synchronous data transmission offers high-speed rates because instead of start and stop procedures, both customer premises equipment (CPE) and local exchange carrier (LEC) equipment must synchronize their exchange, which is based on special frames or bits that indicate the beginning and end of transmitted user data. ATM is called asynchronous because of the sporadic presence of user data. If user data needs to be sent, it is transformed into cells and sent over the line. If there is no user data, only keepalive cell types are sent and received.

The choices that need to be made in analog versus digital communications are related to analog or digital signaling. Historically, the analog versus digital arguments seemed to be a waste of time, because digital technologies are vigorously gaining new market shares. The new technologies of cable, WAN satellite, and wireless LANs (WLANs) are reinventing some of the advantages of analog transmission. The advantages of digital transmission over analog includes better quality of service (QoS), simplified maintenance, synergy with digital switching, powerful digital signal processing, simplified multiplexing, and it is well matched to fiber-optic and device technology. The disadvantages of digital transmission include the need for larger bandwidth, accurate network synchronization, and a costly interface with existing analog networks.

Carrier systems can be split into analog carrier systems and digital carrier systems.

Analog carrier systems use active or passive repeaters to recreate the signal, so any losses or attenuations are corrected while the signal is propagated along the line. Analog systems carry voice, data, and video information, and they exchange supervisory and maintenance information between each other. These carriers are best suited for voice signals; they operate over multi-pair cables, N-carriers, coaxial cables, and L carriers. There are a growing number of radio-channel carriers whose market share is increasing faster than the classic analog carriers.

Digital carrier systems are based primarily on the regeneration of signals. Besides regenerators, these systems use multiplexing and demultiplexing techniques to use broadband signals over a single circuit. The two most significant methods are frequency-division multiplexing (FDM) and time-division multiplexing (TDM).

FDM

FDM is a technique where all signals are transmitted simultaneously, but over different frequency bands. FDM obeys the rule "*some* bandwidth *all* of the time," where the broadband is divided into a number of narrowbands, and every subband is called a channel. Special requirements must be met to prevent interference between the subbands (channels) and to reduce the number of erroneous transmissions. Typical implementations of FDM include voice, AM and FM bands, cable TV, and TV tuners. The bandwidth of a FM channel obeys Carson's rule, which is explained through the following equation:

$$BW(FM) = 2(\Delta f + fm)$$

If the frequencies are separated from each other and don't overlap or interfere, a number of signals can be carried simultaneously. Separation is achieved through a guard band, which uses the unused portion of the spectrum. In voice channels that require a 0.3 to 3.4-kHz channel, the band is 4-kHz wide, where 3.1 kHz are used for the voice channel and 900 Hz are available for the guard channel. To divide the band, one pair of a multiplexor/ demultiplexor is installed on both ends of the transmission facility. For North America, a standard voice multiplexing scheme is twelve 4-kHz voice channels from 60 to 108 kHz (f1, f2, f3, ... f12). Figure 3-1 shows how the input is transformed from serial to parallel and how the encoding is sent to 12 modulators. The lower part of the figure shows how the bandwidth is used.

Figure 3-1   *Frequency-Division Multiplexing (FDM)*

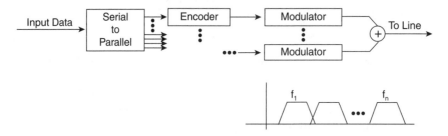

FDM works best with analog signals. In the U.S., common terminology includes the following terms: A group with 12 analog voice channels is called a N-carrier. A supergroup is composed of five groups with 12 channels each, totaling 60 channels. Ten supergroups are combined to produce a mastergroup of 600 voice channels, and a jumbogroup is comprised of six mastergroups with 3600 voice channels. The grouping usually is available over coaxial cables and it forms a family that is referred to as the E-carrier.

Digitalization of the Signal and Pulse Code Modulation

In general, the process of digitizing the signal creates an adequate digital model for a non-digital process. The challenge is trying to represent a real-life scenario as an algorithm. In some cases, the task appears to be much easier because of the existence of repeated samples.

Human voice transfer requires a 4-kHz frequency band. Based on the Nyquist sampling theorem, digital sampling must take place at least twice the highest frequency to reconstruct the analog signal accurately. As a result, the sampling theorem requires that, given that fa equals a 4-kHz frequency band, fs is greater or equal to $4000 \times 2 = 8000$ Hz.

Digitalization of voice as an analog signal includes several steps:

Step 1 Sampling of the analog waves. The process of sampling involves adequately transforming the analog wave in a way that after recreating the signal from the sample, there is an accurate waveform of the signal. Internationally, the sampling requires 8000 times per second, or 8 kHz.

Step 2 Quantization of the analog waves. The waves need to be quantized by adequately assigning 1s or 0s to the samples. Each input sample is assigned to a quantization interval that is closest to the amplitude height of the analog wave. A standard of 8 bits per sample is accepted as an international standard.

NOTE

The choice of 8 bits per sample, given the fact that even the existing microprocessors use a 32- and 64-bit architecture, seems outdated.

Step 3 Coding of the bits. The bits must be coded in forms or frames to be transmitted over the links. All standards must support at least 64 kbps because 8000 samples $\times$ 8 bits / sample = 64 kbps.

A unit called a channel bank can perform sampling, quantization, and coding.

A coder-decoder (codec) device performs the first two functions of pulse code modulation (PCM), and the coding is performed by a data service unit/channel service unit (DSU/CSU). The process is effective and is much less vulnerable to noise, but it is more expensive. The digitalized voice is called PCM voice.

TDM

Unlike FDM, TDM is based on the time-division of the channel, which performs time-sharing rather than frequency-sharing, and obeys the rule "*all* the bandwidth, *some* of the time." This concept is shown in Figure 3-2, where a digital signal level 1 (DS-1) is subdivided into 24 channels.

Figure 3-2   *Time-Division Multiplexing (TDM) Technology Where 24 DS0 (64 kbps) Channels Are Time-Sharing a 1.544-Mbps DS-1*

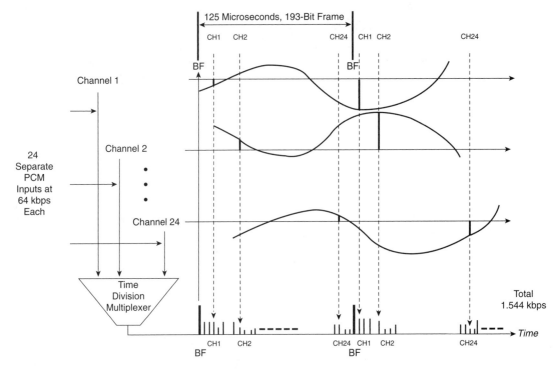

Note:
- The BF bit is the framing bit. It is the last (193rd) bit in every frame.
- The analog signal is transformed from 24 separate signals with 4 kHz bandwidth each to 24 separate PCM signals.
- The sampling interval (125 ms) is calculated on the premise of a sampling rate of 8 kHz.
- The speed 1.544 Mbps = (24 separate PCM channels) x (8000 samples per channel per second) x (8 bits per sample) + (8000 BF bits per second).

Each of the PCM samples is interleaved in time sequence into a single high-speed digital signal that begins with a signal that is referred to as channel 1 and ends with a signal that is referred to as channel 24. The process is repeated for 8-bit samples from each channel for $24 \times 8 = 192$ bits. The following bit (number 193) is the framing bit; it is used for time synchronization. The frame is a sequence of time slots, with each slot containing a sample from one of the channels. Given an 8-kHz frame rate, the sampling interval is 125 micro-seconds, and each frame consists of 24 time slots. Therefore, 24 channels multiplied by 64 kbps for each PCM input yields 1.535 Mbps. If you add the BF bit for every sampling interval, the overall rate is 1.544 Mbps.

The multiplexor loads the time slots with bits and the de-multiplexor removes them on the receiving side. The recipient of the bits is determined by the position of the bits in the data stream. The exchange of bits in a predefined time slot is also known as synchronous TDM, and refers to the fact that the time slots are fixed and preassigned. This scheme requires perfect timing and synchronization between sources. TDM is not limited to digital signals because analog signals can be interleaved too. Unlike synchronous TDM, asynchronous TDM allows time slots to be allocated dynamically. It is possible to combine FDM and TDM in one medium, where the transmission media can be subdivided into a number of channels and every one divided by time for TDM.

T-Carriers

Digitalization of voice is the breaking point of the transition from analog to digital carriers. PCM voice made this possible without a large investment and having to run new cables and trunks to double the available capacity over the same copper pairs.

NOTE   Don't forget: The N-carrier of an analog system runs 12 voice channels over the existing copper pairs, and TDM runs 24 channels.

The initial enormous expense for codecs and DSU/CSUs is now offset by relatively inexpensive facility changes and as a result, an increased trunking capacity of the carriers. As previously mentioned, replacing the N-carriers with T-carriers doubles the capacity over the same two pairs, and 24 simultaneous voice calls can be handled from the CO. The digital trunks led to the production of digital switches, and replaced the analog switchboards with its related personnel and problems. The remaining component of the transition process is the last mile, also referred as a local loop. The twisted copper pairs to local residences and businesses make up the vast majority of the existing wires. Copper pairs prevail over digital, fiber, or any other contemporary solution, which creates an opportunity for the emergence of xDSL technologies.

T1/E1 and Primary Rate Interfaces, T1s, and DS

Usage of T1s is still a growing LEC and inter-exchange carrier (IXC) service. The T1 signal can be transmitted one mile before requiring a repeater, which regenerates the signals, recovers the timing, and sends the regenerated version of the coding sequence.

A T1 signal is referred to as a DSX-1 interface (digital signal crossconnection point for DS-1 signals), which is capable of sending/receiving the T1 signal up to 655 feet. The maximum distance between the CSU and the last network repeater should not exceed 3000 feet. Network repeaters are installed every 6000 feet within the T1 carrier network to compensate for signal loss. The signal loss, called *attenuation of the signal*, requires that a CSU be set to automatically adjust attenuation values depending on the received transmission level. To adjust power levels, Cisco routers support interface configuration commands called **cablelength short** and **cablelength long**, with short-haul being the 655 ft run (max of 1310 ft) and long-haul being the more typical CO to CPE run of 6000 ft (repeated every 3000 ft).

T1 carriers support 24 full-duplex voice channels that only use two pairs of unshielded twisted pair (UTP). The control signals are generated within the CPE. T1 circuits can be terminated at the premises in a number of ways including DS3, SONET, or high-data-rate DSL (HDSL), among others. Typically, the local provider installs some type of network interface unit (NIU) or card to deliver the T1 to the CPE. This device could be a smartjack, M13 multiplexor, or HDSL device, and it usually terminates the circuit through a punchdown. The T1s are terminated by using two twisted-pair circuits. CSUs, and possibly DSUs, are required to connect the CPE to the DS1 service.

CSU functions include conditioning and equalization, error control, and the ability to test local and loopback circuits. For a phone company, line conditioning and equalization is the spacing and operation of amplifiers, so the gain provided by the amplifiers for each transmission frequency compensates for the line signal loss at the same frequency. DSUs provide transmit and receive control logic, synchronization, and timing recovery across the T1 and the other digital circuits (when these signals are not implemented in the CPE). A DSU also converts ordinary binary signals that are generated by the CPE to special bipolar signals. These signals are designed specifically to facilitate transmission at 1.544-Mbps rates over UTP cable, which was a media originally intended for 3-kHz voice band signals (see Figure 3-3). A typical DSU has a legacy serial interface (such as a RS232, or V.35, and so on) and a T1 interface.

Figure 3-3   *How Data Service Unit/Channel Service Unit (DSU/CSU) Works*

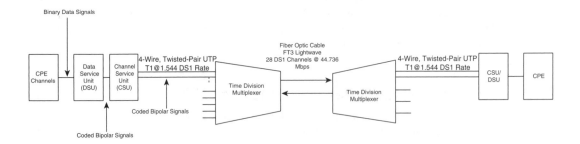

The DSU and CSU may or may not be part of the CPE. On the left and right side of Figure 3-3, you can see the same devices, but on the left side, they are separated. Usually, Cisco routers have DSU/CSU devices built-in and external devices are not necessary. Cisco routers that contain a built-in CSU can attach directly to this termination point through external cabling. If the router does not contain a built-in CSU, an external CSU must be purchased to connect to the carrier network.

T1s and DS and TDM Hierarchy

T1 frames consist of 24 8-bit words plus a framing bit. Each time slot of the frame contains 8 bits of binary information and is called DS0, which is sampled 8000 times per second. Because each DS0 contains 64 kbps (8 k samples/sec × 8 bits/sample) of user information and 24 DS0s are in a T1 frame, this 1544-kbps signal is commonly referred to as DS1. (DS-1 refers to digital signal level 1, which is a framing specification.) T1 refers to the digital transmission system that happens to operate at DS1 rates. Unlike DS1, T1 specifically includes physical transport definitions and line-coding schemes, and as with every other technology, there is a T-carrier hierarchy (see Table 3-1). A T3 carries 28 T1s, yielding 672 channels over one coaxial cable, and can be considered an analog E-carrier.

Table 3-1   *TDM Hierarchy*

Digital Signal Level *n*	North America	Japan	Europe
DS-1	1.544 Mbps—24 channels	1.544 Mbps—24 channels	2.048 Mbps—30 channels
DS-2	6.312 Mbps—96 channels	6.312 Mbps—96 channels	8.448 Mbps—120 channels
DS-3	44.736 Mbps—672 channels	32.064 Mbps—480 channels	34.368 Mbps—480 channels
DS-4	274.176 Mbps—4032 channels	97.728 Mbps—1440 channels	139.264 Mbps—1820 channels
DS-5	Not available	400.352 Mbps—5760 channels	560.000 Mbps—7680 channels

E1

As you can see from Table 3-1, Europe uses another format at the DS-1 level. This format is in compliance with the European Postal and Telecommunications administration, known as the Computer Emergency Response Team (CERT). In the frame format known as E1, CERT defines 32 time slots that are multiplexed in a way to yield a frame of 256 bits in 125 microseconds. One of the time slots is used for signaling, another one is used for alignment and synchronization, and the remaining 30 time slots are used for data, yielding a user data rate of 1.920 Mbps, and an overall data rate of 2.048 Mbps.

NOTE   A key standard for managing digital access lines is RFC 1406 "Definitions of Managed Objects for DS1 and ES1 Interface Types." It defines a set of Management Information Bases (MIBs) and can be used for Transmission Control Protocol/Internet Protocol (TCP/IP) Simple Network Management Protocol (SNMP). The MIBs track the error conditions, performance defects and parameters, and failure states. When a carrier provides proactive monitoring of circuits for enterprises, they basically implement MIBs for reporting.

Network Signaling Systems and SS7

Although totally hidden from the end user, the carrier's signaling systems are similar to a central nervous system in the human body. Signaling systems provide essential information between switches to exchange link status, connection control (signaling), and routing information. Robbed bit signaling (RBS), which was typical in the early 1970s, was replaced with out-of-band signaling, which eventually became a de facto standard for the exchange of signaling information.

NOTE   Out-of-band signaling uses frequencies outside of the normal frequency band for signaling, and it is the core of SS7. In contrast, in-band signaling relies on using certain bits out of each frame in the frequency band, which is why it is called RBS.

Common channel signaling (CCS) was another type of signaling that historically dominated the way carriers exchanged supervisory, addressing, and call information. One of the benefits of the new system (SS7) was that it reduced the time for call setup from between 15 to 20 seconds, to 1 to 3 seconds. In 1976, the system was called Common Channel Interoffice System No. 6, as it was based on signaling system No. 6 (SS6) from the International Telecommunication Union Telecommunication Standardization Sector (ITU-T). It offered a wide range of services for end users, such as callback and 800 (INWATS) capabilities. Because SS6 was not flexible enough for the emerging ISDN standards and services of the mid 1970s, a new standard called SS7 was developed.

The Q.700 recommendations from ITU-T and ANSI's T1.110-Series standards define the SS7 specification. The architectural model is composed of four layers. The lower three levels are part of the message transfer part (MTP), and provide reliable connectionless routing for user data through the network. MTP includes the following:

- Signaling data link, which corresponds to Open System Interconnection (OSI) Layer 1
- Signaling link, which corresponds to OSI Layer 2
- Signaling network

MTP does not provide all the functions of the first three layers of OSI, especially when it comes to connection-oriented services. In 1984, a module called the Signaling Connection Control Part (SCCP) was added and today these four layers are called the Network Service Part (NSP), and perform functions typical of the first three layers of the OSI model. An important element of the model is the ISDN User Part (ISUP), which was developed to provide control signaling for ISDN and related subscriber lines, calls and functions, and which covers layers from SCCP all the way to the top of the OSI model. The higher layers of the SS7 architecture include the transaction capabilities applications part (TCAP), for transaction-oriented as opposed to connection-oriented applications and functions. Also, operations, administration, management, and provisioning (OAM&P) and a set of application service elements (ASEs) defined the remaining layers and defined support for other applications.

In SS7, the control messages are routed through the network to perform call management, such as call setup, call maintenance, and call termination. These messages are standardized blocks of data that are routed throughout the network, and consequently the circuit-switched networks are running packet-switched messages, which transform legacy functions to a new set of features.

SS7 defines control and information planes of operation, where the control plane is responsible for the call setup and for managing the connection, and the information plane is responsible for phases after the call setup, to route additional control information between communicating parties. The latter deals with local exchanges and transit centers, where the core of the control plane signals elements of the network.

From a troubleshooting point of view, the signaling network elements are the most important parts, and include the following:

- **Signaling point (SP)**—The remote user connects to the SP, obeying the rules of User-Network Interface (UNI) and signaling conventions such as Q.931. SP is capable of handling the control messages.

- **Signal transfer point (STP)**—A SP connects to one or more STPs. This is an element that is capable of routing signal messages that are received from one signaling link to another signaling link.

- **Signaling links**—This is a data link that connects SPs.

When a connection is requested by a remote user, it occurs over the D channel, uses Q.931 messaging, and is between the user and the LE. For this purpose, the LE acts as a SP. The Q.931 message is converted to SS7 and the user-requested action establishes and maintains the connection. This process can involve one or more signaling points and STPs. After the connection is set up, the information flows from one end to another, under the control of the information plane.

SONET, Synchronous Transport Signal, and Synchronous Digital Hierarchy

SONET is a fiber-optic-based network specification that is capable of speeds up to 2 Gbps. SONET is based on using optical media, and as such has numerous advantages in comparison to copper conduits. SONET uses STS Level 1 (STS-1) as a basic building block and, like any standard STS-1, assures interoperability of equipment from multiple vendors.

The Optical Fiber Hierarchy of Circuits

The digital hierarchy of SONET is based on Optical Carrier Level 1 (OC-1), which defines transmission rates of 51.84 Mbps. Therefore, the hierarchy starts with data rates of close to T3 speeds of 51.840 Mbps. The transmission rate of 51.840 Mbps is also called STS-1. Every OC-x transmission rate of SONET is the exact multiple of the basic speed, which creates a straightforward way of multiplexing the higher speed formats. The international hierarchy is known as SDH, with starting data rates of OC-3. The optical fiber hierarchy is shown in Table 3-2.

Table 3-2   *Hierarchy of Optical Transmission Rates*

OC-Level (Optical)	STS Level (Electrical)	SDH Equivalent	Line Rate (Mbps)
OC-1	STS-1	—	51.840
OC-3	STS-3	STM-1	155.520
OC-12	STS-12	STM-4	622.080
OC-24	STS-24	STM-8	1244.160
OC-48	STS-48	STM-16	2488.320
OC-192	STS-192	STM-64	9953.280

Carrier's Facilities and Switching Systems

This section provides you with more information about LECs, IXCs, their facilities, areas of operation, and their switching systems.

First-Tier Exchange Carriers

Since the Telecommunications Act of 1996 in the U.S., a service provider can be any provider of telecommunications services that is certified by individual states to become a LEC. The newly certified companies acquired the name of competitive LEC (CLEC), and the existing (former) companies are called incumbent LECs (ILECs). There are several other LECs (OLECs) and some other abbreviations, but for simplicity, only first-layer carriers are referred to as LECs. Recently, more than 1300 LECs were in operation in different parts of the U.S. The country is divided into 240 areas that are called local access and transport areas (LATAs or LATs), which are based on approximately an equal number of calls in each area. A LEC refers to any company that operates in the LATA boundaries, providing Intra-LATA services and functions. LECs can operate in many LATAs, but can't carry traffic between separate LATAs.

Inside the CO

Access lines from CPEs and trunks to other switches enter the local exchange, otherwise called central office (CO), usually with rare exceptions below ground level. This sub-basement is known as a cable vault, and in some metropolitan areas their number can exceed tens of thousands of lines and trunks. The lines and trunks eventually make their way up to the main distribution frame (MDF), which is a facility usually called a wire center. An IXC uses the same term differently, where the MDF is a large, two-dimensional patch panel, and every line or trunk has a unique horizontal and vertical number.

The number and variety of switches in the U.S. and other countries is enormous, and it is practically impossible to provide any kind of precise classification. It is important to remember that the purpose of patching is to adequately identify each connection; this identification is required to assign each connection to the port of the switch. The switching in the CO is always port-to-port, bandwidth-to-bandwidth, and is transparent to any of the bits or packets exchanged over the lines and trunks.

In general, there are two ways to switch data in the CO:

- Leased line
- Switched

The term "nailed-up" refers to a situation when the lines are patched in such a way that they always transfer data from port A to port B. This is leased-line terminology, which is typical for Frame Relay solutions using FT1 and T1/E1. The data can be transferred through the PSTN or redirected to equipment called a Digital Crossconnect System (DCS). This facility, which is also known as private line (non-switched) service, bypasses the PSTN switch, and transfers data from the access lines straight to the trunk system.

A private line solution ensures privacy of the data exchange and is one of the provider-dependant Virtual Private Network (VPN) solutions. DCS is a digital type of equipment that operates over digital access lines, but not over analog local loops. To provide analog local loop conversion to DCS, the signals must first be converted to digital form.

Data that is switched through the CO uses a local switch(s) that is based on the dialup phone number from the call originator. This solution is related to dialup, ISDN, and other services that require an initial call setup phase before proceeding any further.

Each circuit that must be switched must first have a port assigned on the switch. As soon as the originator issues a call, the call is redirected to the requested destination, without adding anything to the content of the user data.

Second Layer Exchange Carriers—IXC

In the U.S., segmentation of the telecommunication network is related to the area in which they operate, and is governed by a single carrier (LATA). To distinguish between different areas and services, there is another set of terms related to the interconnection of different carriers and their zone of responsibility. As previously mentioned, the first layer carriers operate in the LATAs. If calls cross LATA boundaries, they need to be handled by an IXC, sometimes called IECs or long-distance carriers. To provide this long-distance service, IXCs need to maintain a point of presence (POP), or switching office within the LATA. Based on FCC issued licenses, more than 700 companies operate as IXCs today. AT&T and Sprint hold the largest market presence in the U.S. Interestingly enough, Sprint still maintains a few LECs in areas such as North Carolina and Nevada, which creates an unusual mix between LEC and IXC. If, in any particular area, the IXC does not have a POP, based on the rules of equal access, the long-distance can be handled by another IXC, which charges back for the service.

Switches and Tandems

From the carrier's point of view, every carrier system can be broken down into switching systems, transmission facilities and CPE. The CPE (or station equipment) includes all available equipment on the customer side. The dividing line between provider access services and the CPE is called the network point of termination (POT), network interface (NI), Demarcation Point (D-mark), or minimum point of entry (MPOE). The transmission facilities include loop and interoffice. Loop transmission facilities provide clocking, switching, and signaling for the CPE. This part is often called a local loop, subscriber line, subscriber loop, or line. Interoffice transmission facilities connect the carrier's switching system. In this design, the term trunk refers to the communication path between two switches. The available options are to create full-mesh or partial mesh systems, with either no switching (leased lines), endpoint switching, or central switching, based on CO facilities. It is important to consider the carrier's telecommunication network as two segments working together: access services and transport services.

NOTE   When working with carriers, you can often see how they include different groups in the troubleshooting process, depending on the issue. When the local loop is down, you usually deal with technical CO personnel, but when your calls are not going through, the transport personnel must be involved in the troubleshooting process.

LEC/IXC Operations

When the CPE requires service, IXC involvement is not necessary if the problem deals with a LATA local phone call, a local long-distance voice call, data calls through dialup, and ISDN, or if a switched virtual circuit (SVC) is made to the local phone number. This reflects the tariffs of the service and the performance characteristics. When the same scenario includes different area codes in the connection (long distance), there is an interaction between carriers that must be considered in the design process.

The efficiency of interacting with different carriers depends on the way that their networks are structured, and their ability to provide immediate and high quality call transfer. Calls are metered by their number and duration. The fewer switches (hops) in the path of the call, the faster the call. At the same time, it is hard to maintain a full set of trunks from an IXC to every single LEC, creating a fully meshed structure not only within the IXC network, but also outside of it.

Tandem Office and Tool Office

Trunks are not directly run to another LEC's facilities, but to more centrally located LEs that are intermediate points equally convenient for all parties. These LEs are equipped with a secondary switch called a tandem that provides switching trunk-to-trunk, instead of local loop-to-local loop or local loop-to-trunk. It is provisioned for equal access from both parties and for providing services to them. Tandem is a telephony term that means "to connect in series." Thus, a tandem switch connects one trunk to another. A tandem switch is an intermediate switch or connection between an originating telephone call or location and the final destination of the call. The practice of trunk-to-trunk switching received the name of toll office, and a call routed through this office is called a toll call. Unlike long-distance calls, these calls stay within the LATA and do not cross LATA boundaries. This solution architecturally alleviates the challenges of an IXC, which instead of running trunks from anywhere-to-anywhere now runs trunks from their network to the nearest tandem office.

From an IXC's perspective, the toll office is called a service wire center, which provides services for POPs. Most IXCs maintain more than one center within the LATA, to provide redundancy for their services. LECs cannot provide Inter-LATA calls on their own because LEs are designed to provide service for all carriers within the LATA, and the LEC must route all Inter-LATA calls to trunks that are terminated by the IXC's POP (see Figure 3-4). Of the LEC's switches, the last switch pointing to the IXC is called an end office (EO), and it must be configured to point to the specific IXC (101010 for AT&T, 333 for Sprint, and so on). The IXC POP has access to more than one EO within the LATA. When the IXC's switch or LEC's switch is partitioned and certain trunks are designated for specific users, this is referred to as a VPN.

Figure 3-4 shows the LATA boundaries, IXC area of operation, the locations of IXC POPs, network points of termination (POTs), and network points of interface (POIs). In the lower end, LECs provide line-to-trunk connectivity for CPEs; the upper half shows the interaction between LECs and IXCs through tandem (trunk-to-trunk) switches. The book *The New McGraw-Hill Telecom Factbook* by Joseph A. Pecar and David A. Garbin (McGraw-Hill Professional Publishing, 2000) is an excellent reference for different designs and details, and conveys a complex technical subject in an easy-to-understand manner.

Figure 3-4   *Design Example of Inter- and Intra-LATA Carriers Interaction*

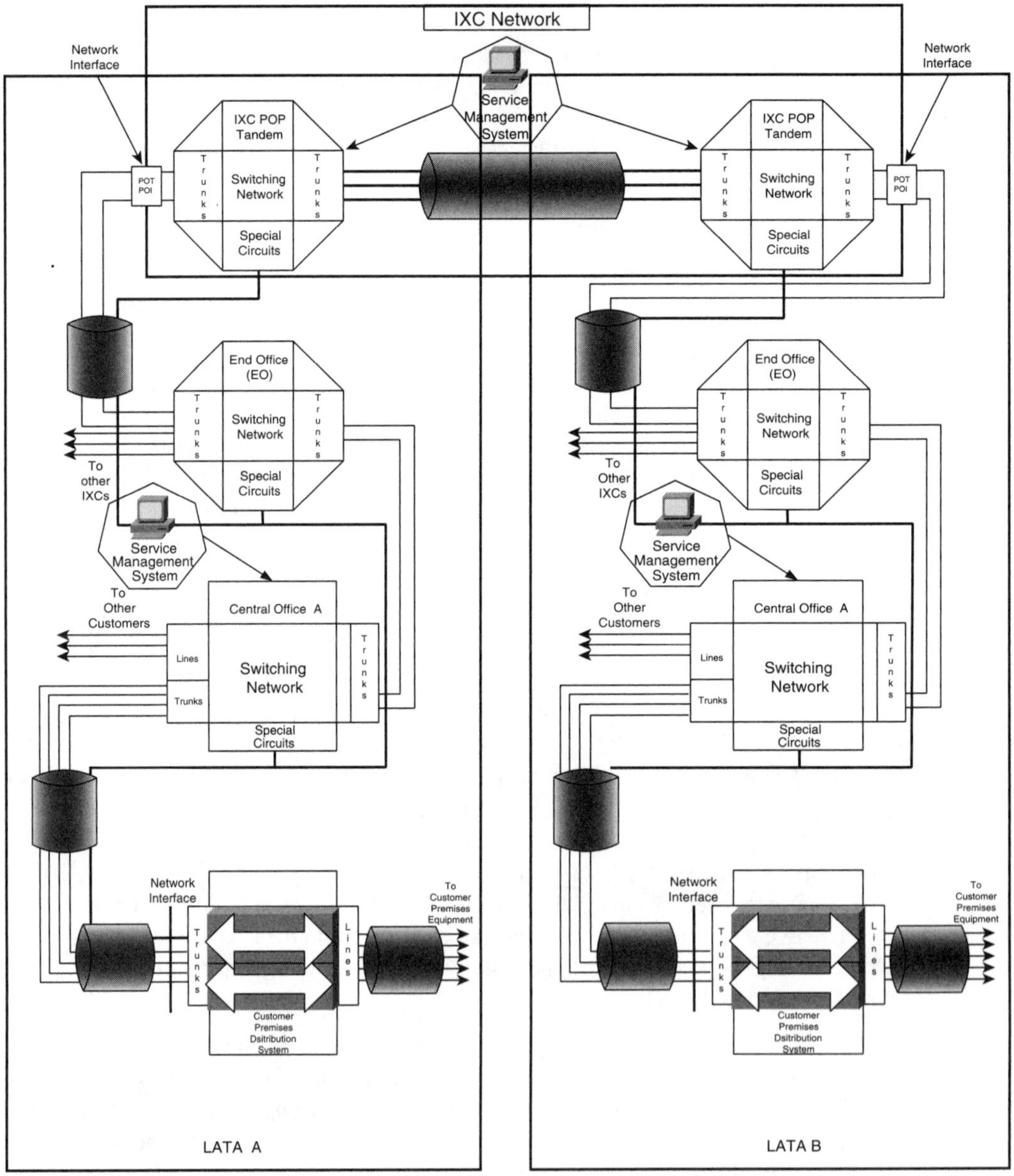

An example of interaction between the LEC and IXC for billing purposes is shown in Figure 3-5.

Figure 3-5   *Example Showing an Interconnection Between SBC as a LEC and Sprint as an IXC in the San Jose, California Area (Courtesy of Cisco Provisioning)*

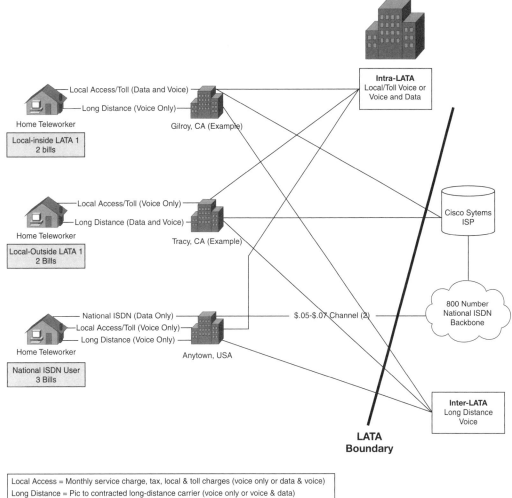

ISPs and ASPs

From the standpoint of LECs, the ISP is another service that provides dedicated services through host routers with access to Internet backbone routers. LECs consider these services as point-to-point, bypassing the PSTN-switched facilities. Usually, the analog dialup ISPs require trunks in a 10:1 user to port ratio, to keep the users/monthly charges ratio in the profitable range. Adding more trunks does not necessarily mean more bandwidth, but definitely means more charges. These lines are patched in a way to redirect the calls to access servers, which are routers with enough modem capacity. They are sometimes called terminal servers. The other connection from the router usually links to another major ISP, or directly to one of the core Internet routers. This core router is usually called a network access point (NAP). NAPs are common for the larger ISPs but rare for the small ISPs. The link is usually T1, or some other T1 hierarchy line, depending on the technical solution. This part of the network is relatively transparent for the end user. The other part of the ISP's network, such as web servers, mail servers, and news servers are located behind the firewall, and remote user access is restricted based on the contract between the two parties.

Over the last several years, there has been a tendency to change the way ISPs operate and to combine the typical LEC and IXC functions with ISP functions. In this case, the ISPs supply the Internet access straight to the local loops and trunks, and then onto leased trunks and lines of the ISP's POP.

NOTE   Can you see the terminology change? Earlier, POP referred to the presence of a long-distance feature, and now POP refers to the presence of Internet access. This is not the first terminology change, nor the last one. It is common to use legacy terms to explain new features in order to alleviate the complexity of the transformation process.

After 1994 and the World Wide Web's (WWW) technology boom, another service trend was Application Service Provider (ASP) and web hosting. Within an IT organization, there is a function to create, design, maintain, and support the IT infrastructure. In early 1997, some analysts showed that it is expensive to support an IT infrastructure because it is not created as a revenue-generating unit. The estimates demonstrated that most investments, including facilities, support groups, power supply, and even some of the design functions, can be outsourced to reduce the cost to the enterprise, according to some authors, by more than 50 percent. Thus, the choice to outsource IT versus supporting IT in-house became a valid alternative to existing solutions. Two of the main elements of this scenario are as follows:

- Availability of specific facilities (data centers) that provide not only ISP, but also ASP features. These services usually require a significant investment to build and support this infrastructure, which is generally only affordable by large companies such as AT&T and Sprint. Therefore, large web-hosting companies (Yahoo.com, for example) can rent private areas in these facilities and host server farms, and achieve high-availability, security, fast access, and other objectives without excessive spending.

NOTE   In 2001 alone, Sprint was planning to invest over $2 billion in expanding and improving its IP businesses for its 18 new Internet centers that are to be completed by the end of 2002.

- Availability of professional services organizations (EDS, IBM, Sprint) able to deliver complex projects for enterprises.

The latter group of services is beyond the scope of this book, but additional information on the services provided by data centers is documented in the next section.

NOTE   History shows that during the early days of computing, there was a tendency for concentrated, centralized computing power. The next generation of computing was driven by decentralized computer power systems. Now, the pendulum has swung back and computing power is once again becoming centralized (data centers, data farms); however, it still has aspects of a decentralized environment (multiple functions and dispersed geographically). The challenge for you is to determine the next trend.

Data Centers and Internet Hosting Services

Data centers usually provide physical facilities, installation and maintenance, environment management equipment (electrical/mechanical/temperature), power management, generators, uninterrupted power supply (UPS), electrical supply, fiber access, security, network services, monitoring, and management. The main factors that affect the enterprise in its decision to use outsourced data centers as part of its remote access plans are the following:

- National presence of the provider with multiple data center facilities
- Solid management structure and practices
- Extensive network management and support expertise
- Financial stability and experience in supporting businesses of all sizes while demonstrating fiscal competence
- Absolute commitment to quality and customer satisfaction

The benefits to the enterprise for this type of solution include the following:

- **Improved response with real-time, load balancing**—Tools dynamically balance the load between the Internet centers and the servers within those centers. Even when a user is in the middle of a session, this technology automatically routes a request to another server when a server experiences either planned or unplanned downtime. The result is improved response and enhanced performance.

- **True site mirroring for enhanced reliability and performance**—For customers desiring geographic redundancy, multiple servers are geographically distributed across server sites. This redundancy translates into a highly reliable, fault tolerant environment that ensures that visitors to the web site experience no disruptions during their session.

- **Robust web interface**—Each customer is provided secure, encrypted, access to the control center through the public Internet or through a provider-based VPN IP network.

- **Complete flexibility for unique solutions**—Customers can run and manage their own applications on a provider's managed hardware. The private application segment also allows customers to connect to their premises for interoperability with legacy systems.

- **Database support**—Additional services for database support is available for varied database management systems.

Unlike legacy LEC/IXC solutions (see Figure 3-4), the main difference of the data center is the existence of an Internet (POP), which is equipped with highly sophisticated hardware. Sprint, for example, offers the following hosting packages for potential customers: enterprise hosting, standard commerce hosting, enterprise commerce hosting, and custom hosting. One possible solution for custom hosting is when Company Y requests hosting services from Sprint (see Figure 3-6).

Figure 3-6   *The Web-Hosting Architecture for a Company Y Requesting Service from the Data Center of Sprint in Two Different Geographical Locations*

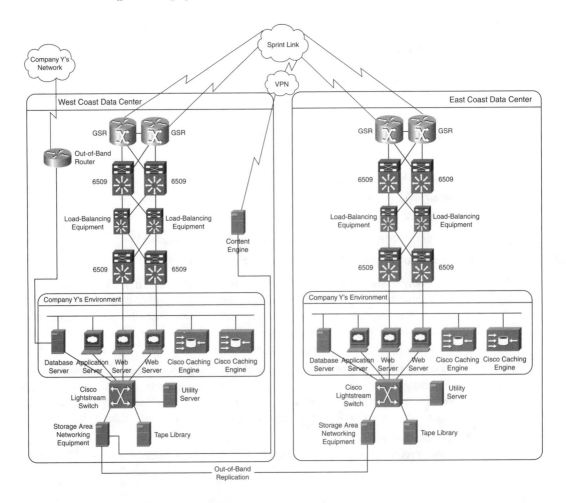

Figure 3-6 shows the extensive use of Cisco equipment, including Gigabit Switch Routers (GSRs) and Cisco 6509s, Content Engines, and Cisco fiber-optic switches in the data center and customer environment. Beyond data-center equipment, the outsourcing company has the freedom to deploy and install any other equipment necessary for its normal operations. The parts of the data center not shown in this figure include private branch exchanges (PBXs), and highly sophisticated UPSs.

Part of every enterprise agreement is the network services agreement and service-level agreement (SLA). In the case of Sprint, they are as follows:

- **Direct connections to Sprint's OC-48 Internet backbone with a range of LAN and WAN connectivity options**—Sprint is also deploying dense wavelength division multiplexing (DWDM) equipment that provides Sprint with virtual fiber by splitting light waves into separate, distinct channels. Sprint deployed 40-channel DWDM equipment that is scalable to 96 channels or 240 Gbps. In 2001, Sprint began deployment of 80-channel DWDM systems with each channel capable of supporting an OC-48 or OC-192 signal.

- **Industry leading SLA guarantees**—A quote from one of the Sprint SLAs is as follows:

  Leading service level agreements—With geographically redundant web servers, you're guaranteed 100% web site availability. Sites without geographic redundancy are guaranteed to be available 99.5% of the time. This guarantee applies to Sprint-provided and managed hardware and software. Sprint will credit up to 50% of the monthly recurring charge should the site become unavailable.

(Taken from www.sprintesolutions.com/solutions/infrastructure/managed_hosting/about.html#Leading.)

Because Company Y is using an outsourced data center model, some caveats must be addressed in the early design stage. The considerations include concerns about commitment of the other party and the level of control. Company Y depends on the outsourcer to obtain, integrate, and support the technology from their premises; to link with the company's operations; and to recruit, train and supervise staff in their support centers. Also, it must consider the management of its most precious asset, its customer data, to an outside firm.

The Future of Service Providers

Remote access design is usually implemented to meet the business need for a longer rather than shorter period. This decision requires an answer to the question "how will service providers change in the future?" Emerging technologies will continue to require that enhanced and complex services be supported by providers.

Service Offering

One of the main directions in the service offering for remote access is Multiprotocol Label Switching VPN (RA to MPLS VPN). This service enables users to connect to the corporate network and handles remote access connectivity for mobile users, telecommuters, and small offices through dial, ISDN, DSL, cable, and wireless technologies (see more in Chapter 19). The increase of IP-based transport changes the focus of the transport from TDM to packet-based services. The connection-oriented restrictions of TDM systems will be overcome with connectionless technologies by providing higher versatility and multiservice support features. These technologies include Media Gateway Control Protocol (MGCP), HTML, Voice XML (VXML), session initiation protocol (SIP), and Automatic Speech Recognition (ASR). These technologies enable service offerings that can be tailored to any combination to meet the customer's needs.

The Last-Mile Problem

In July 2001, a group called IEEE 802.3ah Ethernet in the First Mile Task Force (http:// grouper.ieee.org/groups/802/3/efm/public/) was established to provide solutions for the so-called last-mile issue. Currently, a wide variety of protocols provide services to the last mile. They include ISDN, DSL, cable modems, satellite, and broadband wireless solutions, which offer speeds under 10 Mbps. However, existing Intranets use technologies such as Fast and Giga-Ethernet with speeds several Gbps and higher. Therefore, to interconnect these two environments, a fairly sophisticated protocol conversion is required.

To achieve the conversion goal, the Task Force planned to bring Ethernet to home users. For this purpose, IEEE 803.3ah defines three access layers: home network, access/distribution layer, and a core layer. IEEE also defines three main topologies (the analogy with the Cisco design model is obvious).[1] The topologies are based on two main factors for media and for configuration of the access/distribution layer:

- Ethernet over a point-to-point copper line is expected to adopt the very-high-data-rate DSL (VDSL) and Media Access Control (MAC) protocol on the top of the VDSL physical specification. This should be able to deliver speeds ranging from 10 Mbps and higher over existing copper cabling.

- Gigabit Ethernet over point-to-point fiber is supposed to deliver speeds up to 1 Gbps for distances up to 10 km (6.25 miles).

- Point-to-multipoint fiber topology—The multipoint part is an aggregation point, called an access switch, which provides services for up to 16 passive splitters that are connected to optical network terminators. This topology is designed to deliver speeds starting from 30 to 60 Mbps, up to 100 to 200 Mbps for business and residential customers.

Cisco Systems announced the Optical Ethernet to the First Mile (EFM) Cisco Catalyst 4000 Family in December 2001. The Cisco Catalyst 4000 Series includes a 48-Port 1000BASE-

LX Gigabit Ethernet Line Card, a 48-Port 100Base-FX Line Card and a Cisco ONT 1000 Gigabit Ethernet. All solutions work with the Cisco Ethernet Subscriber Solution Engine 1105 (Cisco ESSE 1105), which is a hardware-based management system for metro access networks and the Cisco Secure Access Control Server (ACS) Version 3.0 centralized access control.

The 3G Wireless Alternative

A bit of a battle is shaping up inside the industry over 2G, 2.5G, and 2.75G solutions. Verizon and Sprint are backing (code division multiple access) CDMA2000 technology. AT&T Wireless, Cingular Wireless, and VoiceStream are backing the Global System of Mobility/General Packet Radio Service (GSM/GPRS) systems, which provide speeds that range from 15 to 40 kbps. Nextel is backing its iDEN (Motorola proprietary version of TDMA with its unique push-to-talk radio capability).

The Wireless 3-th Generation (3G) solution is seen as an evolutionary new path in telecommunications. CDMA2000 1xEV-DO was standardized by the Telecommunications Industry Association (TIA) in October 2000. 1xEV-DO was recognized by the ITU-R WP8F as an IMT-2000 standard.

The first CDMA2000 networks were launched in Korea in October 2000, providing 144-kbps data rates to subscribing customers and delivering nearly twice the voice capacity that operators experienced with their cdmaOne (IS-95) systems. The success of the CDMA2000 1X system in Korea has encouraged many operators in the Americas and Asia to follow through with their plans to launch CDMA2000 this year.

Although the arguments about true 3G solutions in the U.S. are underway, Verizon Wireless with its Express Networks became the first carrier to launch 3G wireless in the U.S. in January 2002—primarily in the Bay Area, East Coast, and Salt Lake City—offering speeds up to 144 kbps, with an average of 40-60 kbps. Meanwhile, Sprint PSC, working with partners such as Samsung and Hitachi, announced its plans and launched nationwide (U.S. market), a 3G solution in August 2002 called PCS Vision.

According to the ITU, a 3G link must be able to send data at rates of up to 144 kbps while mobile, at rates of up to 384 kbps at walking speeds, and at rates of up to 2.4 Mbps when stationary. These speeds are expected to be exceeded soon. The available sources show that plans are underway for variations on CDMA2000, which will change 3G systems dramatically. The wider band, commonly referred to as CDMA2000 3X or 3XRTT will be replaced by a two-phase strategy called CDMA2000 1xEV. 1xEV stands for 1X evolution, or evolution using 1.25 MHz, which is typical for today's CDMA2000 1X systems based on a standard 1.25 MHz carrier for delivering high data rates and increased voice capacity peak data rates of 2.4 Mbps. The 1xEV includes two phases, labeled 1xEV-DO (DO-data only) and 1xEV-DV (DV-data and voice). The CDMA2000 1xEV-DO can provide customers with peak data rates of 2.4 Mbps. However, to implement 1xEV-DO, operators will have to install a separate carrier that's dedicated to data-only use at each cell location where high-speed data services are demanded. Still, customers will be able to hand off seamlessly from a 1X to a 1xEV-DO carrier.

As long as the demand for high-speed wireless high-speed access grows in the years ahead, all the carriers are expected to upgrade their systems to provide 3G services.

E-mail exchange, instant messaging, and Internet browsing are the major forces behind the demand for 3G services.

End Note

[1] Birkner, Matthew H. *Cisco Internetwork Design*. Cisco Press, 2000.

Summary

As a troubleshooting engineer, you need to interact with your service provider(s) almost on a daily basis. It is important to know how the cloud and remote access design solutions interact between each other; how providers operate, engineer their circuits and services, what their areas of responsibility are, and many other factors. This will help you be more successful in your troubleshooting efforts. Besides, it is always beneficial to know the specifics of your local or long-distance provider and what services it offers now or will have available in the near future for your organization.

Review Questions

Answers to the review questions can be found in Appendix A, "Answers to Review Questions."

1 Is Asynchronous Transfer Mode (ATM) a synchronous or asynchronous technique? Explain.

2 Name three of the advantages of digital signaling over analog signaling?

3 What does FDM stand for? What rule does FDM obey?

4 In North America, how many voice channels are in a standard multiplexing scheme for FDM?

5 Describe the main phases of pulse code modulation (PCM).

6 What does TDM stand for? What rule does the TDM obey?

7 What is the purpose of bit number 193 in TDM?

8 What is a frame in TDM?

9 What do DS1 and DS-1 stand for? What is the difference between DS1 and DS-1?

10 What is out-of-band signaling? What is robbed bit signaling?

11 What do CO, LEC, CLEC, and ILEC stand for? What do they have in common?

12 What is the role of tandem switches in carrier networks?

13 What are the main caveats when the enterprise outsources service with the service provider?

14 What are the three main topologies in Cisco's Ethernet to the First Mile (EFM)?

15 What does CDMA stand for? Name the 3G minimum speed requirements, as defined by ITU.

CHAPTER 4

Troubleshooting Approaches, Models, and Tools

This is the final chapter of Part I, "Remote Access Fundamentals." The rest of the book covers material related to troubleshooting dial, ISDN, Frame Relay, and Virtual Private Network (VPN) solutions. Remote access troubleshooting in this book is focused more on the communication subsystem of the Open System Interconnection (OSI) model than on higher levels of the model. Some common models, approaches, and troubleshooting tools are available for the test engineers, which need to be clarified before covering troubleshooting specific remote access networks. This chapter covers these models, approaches, and troubleshooting tools so that this material doesn't need to be repeated for each remote access technology covered hereafter. As such, this chapter outlines fundamental troubleshooting information that the remaining chapters will assume that you are familiar with. The main topics covered in this chapter are as follows:

- **Interconnection models** — The Department of Defense (DoD)model and the seven-layer OSI model
- **Troubleshooting models** — The layer-by-layer approach
- Common troubleshooting tools and techniques
- Cisco-specific troubleshooting tools

Troubleshooting is often considered an intuitive activity, where knowledge is sometimes not enough to successfully and effectively perform the task. However, knowledge and hands-on experience plays a decisive role in the troubleshooting process.

This book's focus is to help the troubleshooting engineer in day-to-day operations. Sometimes, your soft skills are as important as your technical skills, so here are some brief reminders about approaching troubleshooting in general:

- Be passionate, but professional. Be ready to go the extra mile for your user, but don't get personally involved.
- Know the technology. When working with providers, knowledge beyond just your piece of the puzzle might save you a lot of frustration. Be familiar with and use professional terms and acronyms. Understand your provider's internal procedures and specifics and be supportive.
- Try to build mutual trust in your relationship with your customer; the customer is in trouble, but you can get in trouble, too. Show that you care for the customer's problem. Work with the customer as your partner.

- Know your options. Be ready to say no if a request goes against rules, procedures, or policies.

Beyond your technical knowledge, all these components define your professionalism and these soft skills can be decisive in your next troubleshooting case.

A troubleshooting engineer needs to have a systematic approach for analyzing issues. Typically, in the case of an enterprise remote access environment where the engineer sees both ends of the connection, it is convenient to reduce the number of focus points to two or three: the remote user, the cloud, and the core router. Depending on your perspective or location, these also can be referred to as the near end of the connection, the far end of the connection, and the cloud in between. Based on this, some authors recognize the following approaches to troubleshooting:

- Start from the near end
- Start from the far end
- Divide by half and start toward the near end or toward the far end

These approaches seem to be logical and systematic, given the fact that some networks can be complex. When troubleshooting, it is best to focus on one issue rather than jumping randomly from hop to hop, virtually dividing the network to three pseudo-independent segments: remote end, service provider(s), and near end. VPN solutions might seem to be an exception to this rule, but they are not. The remote user (equipment or client), Internet, and enterprise termination point create the same triad of components—a simplified version of a complex solution.

Given the fact that all components of every remote access design conform to one or more industry agreements (standards and protocols), another approach to troubleshooting is feasible. It is based on the industry's accepted layered models. The troubleshooting process can start from any end, but you should follow a layer-by-layer troubleshooting process, starting with layer one. This technology-based approach is used throughout later parts of this book.

NOTE   Of course, you can choose many other troubleshooting approaches. Regardless, it's most important that the method be systematic and consistent, and that you are comfortable using it.

Interconnection Models

The goal of every interconnection model is to provide standards to which all computer hardware and software vendors can adhere so that the present multiplicity of interconnection and interface practices is reduced, thus reducing the costs of designing and producing both hardware and software. The existing models are covered in literally hundreds of sources in great detail, but the following section provides a short description of the DoD model and the seven-layer OSI model from a standpoint of understanding the troubleshooting process.

Department of Defense Model

The efforts to create an interface model for internetworking started with the four-layer Department of Defense (DoD) model, which was developed by the Department of Defense in the 1970s for the Defense Advanced Research Projects Agency (DARPA) Internetwork Project (see Figure 4-1). The core Internet protocols adhere to this model, although the OSI model is preferred for new designs.

Figure 4-1   *The Four Layers of the Department of Defense (DoD) Model*

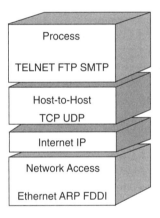

The four layers of the DoD model, from bottom to top, are as follows:

- **Network access layer**—Responsible for delivering data over the hardware media. Different protocols are selected from this layer, depending on the type of physical network.

- **Internet layer**—Responsible for delivering data across a series of different physical networks that interconnect a source and a destination machine. Routing protocols are most closely associated with this layer, as is the Internet Protocol (IP), which is the Internet's fundamental protocol.

- **Host-to-host layer**—Handles connection rendezvous, flow control, retransmission of lost data, and other generic data flow management. The mutually exclusive Transmission Control Protocol (TCP) and User Datagram Protocol (UDP) are this layer's most important members.

- **Process layer**—Contains protocols that implement user-level functions, such as mail delivery, file transfer, and remote login.

Seven-Layer OSI Model

In the 1980s, the European-dominated International Standards Organization (ISO) began to develop its OSI networking suite. OSI has two major components: an abstract model of networking (the basic reference model, or *seven-layer model*), and a set of concrete protocols. This model eventually grew into the Internet, to which the core Internet protocols adhere. This section discusses the layers of the OSI model.

The physical layer is concerned with transmitting raw bits over a communication channel. The design issues are related to timing, line coding, and framing. Categories of the physical layer include simplex, half duplex, and full duplex. The layer deals with the physical (electrical and mechanical) aspects of transmitting data (such as voltage levels, pin-connector design, cable lengths, and grounding arrangements).

The main activity of the data link layer is to deal with the transmission of data frames over a physical link between network entities, including the incorporation of error-correcting coding into the data frames. It accomplishes this task by having the sender fragment the input data into data frames (typically a few hundred bytes), transmit the frames sequentially, and process the acknowledgment frames that are sent back by the receiver. It is up to the data link layer to create and recognize frame boundaries that can be accomplished by attaching special bit patterns to the beginning and end of the frame. If there is a chance that these bit patterns might occur within the data, special care is taken to avoid confusion. This layer is responsible for error control between adjacent nodes, and consequently, flow regulation and error handling are integrated.

The network layer controls the operation of the subnet. The network layer establishes paths for data between a pair of computers, handles any switching among alternative routes between the computers, and also contains definitions of how to break the data segments up into individual packets of data. In this way, packets can be transmitted and reassembled. A key design issue is determining how packets are routed from source to destination. Routes can be static, when the routing does not depend on network conditions, and dynamic, when routes can be dynamically determined based on routing protocol decisions that reflect network conditions. An excessive number of packets in the subnet require sophisticated congestion control, which is another function of the network layer. When a packet has to travel from one network to another to get to its destination, many problems can arise. The addressing used by the second network might be different from the first one. The second one might not accept the packet at all because it is too large, or the protocols might differ, and so on. It is up to the network layer to overcome all routing problems to allow heterogeneous networks to be interconnected. In broadcast designs, the routing problems are simple, and as a result the functions of this layer are reduced.

The basic function of the transport layer is to accept data from the session layer, split it up into smaller units if necessary, pass these to the network layer, and ensure that the pieces (segments) all arrive correctly at the other end, performing the mandatory flow control. If the transport connection requires a high throughput, the transport layer might create multiple network connections by dividing the data among the network connections to improve throughput. The transport layer also determines what type of service to provide to the session layer, and ultimately, the users of the network. The most popular type of transport connection is an error-free point-to-point channel that delivers messages in the order in which they were sent, based on connection-oriented service. In terms of the TCP/IP suite, this function is performed by the TCP protocol. Other kinds of transport protocols transport isolated messages with no guarantee (best-effort type) about the order of delivery or the broadcasting of messages to multiple destinations. This type of connection is connectionless, and in terms of the TCP/IP suite, it is performed by the UDP. The transport header carries information on what message belongs to which process, thus providing multiplexing for the processes. Also, there is a mechanism to regulate information flow, so that a fast host cannot overrun a slow one. Flow control between hosts is distinct from flow control between switches, although similar principles apply to both.

The session layer enables users on different machines to establish sessions between them. A session allows a user to log into a remote time-sharing system or to transfer a file between two machines. One of the services of the session layer is dialogue control. Sessions can allow traffic to flow in both directions at the same time, or in only one direction at a time. If traffic can only go one way at a time, the session layer helps to keep track of whose turn it is. A related session service is token management. For some protocols, it is essential that both sides do not attempt the same operation at the same time. To manage these activities, the session layer provides tokens that can be exchanged. Another session service is synchronization, which inserts checkpoints into the data stream and ensures that after excessive data transfer, if the session has been interrupted, only the data after the last checkpoint is repeated. Another example here can be when one application process requests access to another applications process (e.g., Microsoft Word importing a chart from Excel).

The presentation layer performs functions to ensure consistent syntax and semantics of the transmitted information. It deals with syntactic representation of data, such as agreement on character code (ASCII, extensions to ASCII, Unicode); .doc, .txt, .gif, and .jpg formats; data-compression and data-encryption methods, and representations of graphics (such as files using the .pic or .bmp formats). The presentation layer is also concerned with other aspects of information representation. For example, data compression can reduce the number of bits to be transmitted, and cryptography is frequently required for privacy and authentication.

The application layer deals with data generation and contains a variety of protocols that are commonly needed, such as terminal emulation based on virtual terminal software. Another application layer function is file transfer because different file systems have different naming conventions and ways of representing text lines. Transferring a file between two different systems requires handling these and other incompatibilities.

Each layer of the OSI model receives data from the layer beneath it and provides service for the layer above it. The exchange of information between layers is based on protocol data units (PDUs) and the encapsulation of the user data occurs in every layer. Therefore, every layer adds extra information (headers and trailers) to perform its functions.

In reality, data is passed from one layer down to the next lower layer at the sending computer, until the physical layer finally transmits it onto the network cable. As the data is passed down to a lower layer, it is encapsulated into a larger unit because additional layer information is added. At the receiving end, the message is passed upwards to the desired layer, and as it passes upwards through each layer, the encapsulation information is stripped off.

As an industry standard, OSI is a framework that every new product complies with because it is already accepted and widely adopted. A variety of other specifications, including IEEE (www.ieee.org), RFC (www.ietf.org/rfc.html), Asynchronous Transfer Mode (ATM) Forum (www.atmforum.org), DSL Forum (www.dslforum.org), and the Internet Engineering Task Force (www.ietf.org) create sublayers and define different model structures. It is important to remember the definition of the communication subsystem (see Figure 4-2) that includes up to the first three OSI layers, because it is the main focus of remote access troubleshooting.

Figure 4-2   *The Open System Interconnection (OSI) Model, Including Some of the Related Protocols and the Communications Subsystem*

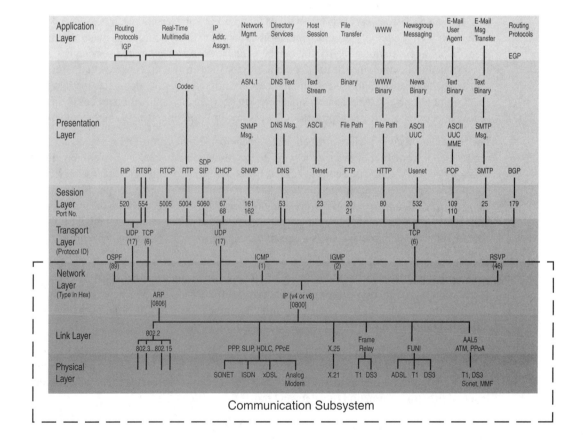

Troubleshooting Models and the Baseline

The purpose of every troubleshooting model is to find a common denominator for all possible issues and to offer a common approach or problem-solving model. The objective is to represent (reduce) a complex problem into a couple or even one point of failure, and then to restore the functionality of the whole system. You are faced with the question: which is better, analysis or synthesis?

Troubleshooting Models

There is more than one Cisco troubleshooting model defined in numerous books and conferences. One such model is defined in the book *Cisco Internetwork Troubleshooting* (by Laura Chappel and Dan Farkas, Cisco Press, 1999), where an eight-step problem solving model is recommended. Some of the commonly accepted troubleshooting steps and tips, recommended by the Cisco troubleshooting society, are available on Cisco.com. Some of the more relevant practices from these resources follow.

The following are basic troubleshooting steps:

1 Identify how it should work.

2 Review your topology.

3 Identify the symptoms.

4 Ask the right questions.

5 Develop a plan of attack.

6 Document your actions.

NOTE   My experience when troubleshooting is, if you understand the design and configuration of the network, gathering the right information is key to finding a resolution. Knowing the baseline performance of the network and asking the right question is 50 percent of the solution.

The following are basic troubleshooting tips:

- Don't panic.
- Understand your network.
- Develop network baselines.
- Gather the right information from your users.
- Work methodically and document all of your actions.

- Learn how to effectively use tools.
- Figure out what tools and what options work best for each problem.
- Use access lists when enabling debug commands.

Based on the sources, many find common ground in the actions of understanding the baseline and topology, gathering information, asking the right questions, learning tools, implementing solutions, and documenting changes. These are the main steps of the troubleshooting process. Later in the discussion, you learn about some common and some Cisco-specific troubleshooting tools (Cisco IOS-based), which are designed to alleviate the process.

IOS Commands

You should assume that all troubleshooting techniques described in this book are Cisco IOS-based. Despite your expertise in IOS, remember that IOS is constantly developing. The syntax of IOS is multioptional and sometimes can be complex. You must continue to study IOS on a regular basis and keep apprised of changes. One of the best sources for information is *Cisco IOS Releases: The Complete Reference* by Mack Coulibaly (Cisco Press, 2000), and the Cisco software center at www.cisco.com/public/sw-center/.

Short Format (Truncation) of IOS Commands

Typing the full version of commands is rare in Cisco-based troubleshooting. For example, most engineers won't type **show running-config**. Instead, they simply type **show run** or even **sh run**. Using such truncated commands can help you save time. Become familiar with the short form of commands so that you can work quicker and understand when others use them. A review of IOS terminology and commands at www.cisco.com is highly recommended.

Device Abbreviations Used in This Book

The abbreviations in this book about the devices and technologies are developed to be self-explanatory. For example, 5300-Dial means Cisco Access Server 5300 for dial, 804-isdn means Cisco 804 ISDN router for remote user, and 1602-frame means Cisco 1602 router for Frame Relay service.

There is no universal troubleshooting tool. The choice of the right tool depends on your hands-on experience. Every tool provides information for one or more aspects of the network, and it is good practice to use several or a combination of tools in the trouble-shooting process. Nevertheless, some tools related to issues such as latency measurement, performance measurement, or reach ability of a certain hop can provide more common results. Some issues, such as how to measure the performance of the network, have more than one answer, and it is recommended to apply a comparative approach whenever possible. If it is possible to use the same tool (i.e., the ping utility), compare the results obtained from different technologies or segments of the network.

The Baseline

The baseline is the expected behavior of the system that you are about to troubleshoot. The baseline is an important factor, but it is hidden in the beginning of the troubleshooting process. In general, the baseline includes performance characteristics, number and type of hops, and expected round-trip times (RTTs). It might include some yes or no questions, such as compression, multicast, Voice over IP (VoIP), quality of service (QoS), and so on. The baseline should be technology and architecture based. You should set expectations before starting the troubleshooting process. One key factor is to have a map of the network topology. The following sections discuss aspects of the network baseline and tools for helping you establishing the baseline.

Network Topology

At a minimum, you need to have a documented network topology. For Internet connections, Internet service providers (ISPs) apply different methods to prevent end users from discovering the topology, assuming that this is one of the first steps in preventing denial of service (DOS) attacks from hackers.

One recommended tool to discover the network topology is to run the Cisco Discovery Protocol (CDP). CDP is a Cisco proprietary protocol that runs on the data link layer (Layer 2) between directly connected and adjacent devices (neighbors), including routers, bridges, switches, access servers, and virtually all Cisco IOS devices. CDP works not only for IOS-based, but non-IOS devices such as IP phones and Aironet access points (APs). CDP is enabled by default on all broadcast interfaces. It is useful for debugging connectivity issues and building topology maps.

The high-level data link control (HDLC) protocol type 0x2000 is assigned to CDP. It uses a second layer multicast Media Access Control (MAC) address 01-00-0C-CC-CC to send and receive periodic messages and to collect data. Using a multicast address prevents the routing because Cisco routers and some switches do not forward this traffic unless specifically configured. If any information has changed since the last packet was received, the new one is cached, ignoring the Time To Live (TTL) value. In this way, CDP provides a quick state discovery. The recommended commands for topology discovery are as follows:

```
Router#show cdp neighbors
Router#show cdp neighbors detail
```

The output from these commands returns specific details including device type, IP address, active interface (Ethernet, serial), port type, and port number. The first command provides short output, and the second command provides detailed information about adjacent topology specifics, as shown in Example 4-1.

Example 4-1 *The* **show cdp neighbors detail** *Command Output*

```
Router#show cdp neighbors detail
<output omitted>
Device ID: access-gateway.cisco.com
Entry address(es):
IP address: 10.10.0.7
Platform: cisco Catalyst 6000,  Capabilities: Router Switch IGMP
Interface: FastEthernet0/0,  Port ID (outgoing port): FastEthernet3/21
Holdtime : 136 sec

Version :
Cisco Internetwork Operating System Software
IOS (tm) c6sup1_rp Software (c6sup1_rp-JK2SV-M), Version 12.1(8b)E9,

Copyright  1986-2002 by cisco Systems, Inc.
Compiled Sun 17-Feb-02 11:22 by erlang

advertisement version: 2
VTP Management Domain: ''
Native VLAN: 10
Duplex: full
<output omitted>
```

Extensive information from the CDP output requires the CDP to be disabled in interfaces that cannot be controlled or that are user-owned or requested, such as dialer interfaces. To disable the CDP on a dialer interface, the following command has to be configured:

```
Router(config-if)#no cdp enable
```

Another source of topology information can be the routing protocol. All routing protocols support information for their neighbors, and link-based routing protocols, such as Open Shortest Path First (OSPF) and Enhanced Interior Gateway Routing Protocol (EIGRP), support topology information. As soon as all members are running routing protocols (instead of static routing), these commands can be informative. Information for neighbors is usually more concise. The following command is an example:

```
Router#show ip eigrp neighbors detail
```

The topology output is usually detailed and relatively complex. It is not discussed in this book. It is up to you to know what type of information is required and what topology command to use.[1]

It is common for a consulting engineer to start troubleshooting in a new environment where the topology of the network is not available. Tools used in combination, such as **telnet**,

ping, **cdp**, and **traceroute** commands, produce information that can create a network topology before starting the troubleshooting process.

Overall, the collected baseline information provides you not only with topology information, but also with IOS versions, types of devices, IP addressing conventions, and both routed and routing protocols.

Performance Characteristics and Path Characteristics

The baseline is related to the expected behavior of the system, including performance characteristics, latency, and expected RTTs. A useful and multioptional tool for establishing baseline performance is the path characteristics (PathChar or Pchar) utility.

Pchar is designed to baseline the network performance. The utility enables you to stress test each hop and provides the ability to collect detailed information. It is based on the path characterization model of Van Jacobson. Pchar measures network performance on a per-hop and a total path basis. It supports IPv4 and IPv6, and it is useful in isolating performance problems. Some of the drawbacks are that the latency figures might not be accurate when measuring application performance, and Internet Control Message Protocol (ICMP) messages can be filtered or respond differently (typical in the case of satellite-based connections).

The utility runs on UNIX, Linux, and Solaris platforms. The options are listed in Table 4-1. The following shows the usage of Pchar:

```
UNIX-host:/users/pnedeltc> ./pchar
Usage: ./pchar [-a analysis] [-b burst] [-c] [-d debuglevel] [-g gap]
[-G gaptype] [-h] [-H hops] [-I increment] [-m mtu] [-n] [-p protocol]
[-P port] [-q] [-R reps] [-s hop] [-t timeout] [-T tos] [-v] [-V] [-w file]
 -r file | host]
```

Table 4-1   *Path Characteristics (Pchar) Options*

Pchar Option	Description
-a	Analysis—Set analysis type (default is **lsq**):
	lsq—Least sum of squares linear fit
	kendall—Linear fit using Kendall's test statistic
	lms—Least median of squares linear fit
	lmsint—Least median of squares linear fit (integer computations)
-b	Burst size (default is **1**)
-c	Ignore route changes (useful for load-balancing situations)
-d	Debug level—Set debugging output level
-g	Gap—Inter-test gap in seconds (default is **0.25**)

continues

Table 4-1   *Path Characteristics (Pchar) Options (Continued)*

Pchar Option	Description
-G	Gap type—Inter-test gap type (default is **fixed**): **fixed**—Fixed gap **exp**—Exponentially distributed random
-H	Hops—Maximum number of hops (default is **30**)
-h	Print this help information
-I	Increment—Packet size increment (default is **32**)
-l	Host—Set origin address of probes (defaults to **hostname**)
-m	Maximum transmission unit (MTU)—Maximum packet size to check (default is **1500**)
-M	Mode—Operational mode (defaults to **pchar**): **pchar**—Path characteristics **trout**—Tiny traceroute
-n	Don't resolve addresses to hostnames
-p	Protocol—Network protocol (default is **ipv4udp**). Specifies the protocol that Pchar uses: **ipv4udp** (default) **ipv4raw** **ipv4icmp** **ipv4tcp** **ipv6icmp** **ipv6udp**
-P	Port—Starting port number (default is **32768**)
-q	Quiet output
-r	File—Read data from a file (- for **stdin**)
-R	Reps—Repetitions per hop (default is **32**)
-s	Hop—Starting hop number (default is **1**)
-S	Do Simple Network Management Protocol (SNMP) queries at each hop to determine the next–hop interface characteristics
-t	Timeout—ICMP timeout in seconds (default is **3**)
-T	Type of service (ToS)—Set IP ToS field (default is **0**)
-v	Verbose output
-V	Print version information
-w file	Write data to file (- for **stdout**)

Table 4-2 shows some performance measurements from Cisco users of different technologies in the U.S. that connect to the corporate network.

Table 4-2   *Pchar and a Baseline Measurement*

Technology	Speed	RTT	Path Bottleneck
Dial	56 kbps	125.6 ms	31 kbps
ISDN	128 kbps	22.8 ms	118 kbps
Frame (FT1)	128 kbps	13.8 ms	118 kbps
Frame (56K)	56 kbps	61.2 ms	52.8 kbps
Asymmetric DSL (ADSL)	~ 600 kbps down ~ 250 kbps up	11.6 ms	568.5 kbps
StarBand Satellite	~ 600 kbps down ~128 kbps up	813.5 ms	42 kbps
Cable Modem	10 Mbps	13.6 ms	7912 kbps
Sprint BroadBand	~ 500 kbps down ~ 128 kbps up	76.6 ms	720 kbps
Ethernet	10 Mbps	1.2 ms	~
Fiber Distributed Data Interface (FDDI)	100 Mbps	120 us	~
T1	1.54 Mbps	4.5 ms	1509 kbps
T3	45 Mbps	267 us	~
OC-3	150 Mbps	80 us	~
OC-12	622 Mbps	19 us	~

Usually, the bottleneck is at the last hop in the test, but not always. In the following examples (see Figure 4-3 and Example 4-2), the Cisco 350 AP is connected to an 804 ISDN router, which in turn is calling a 7206VXR core router. A Microsoft Windows 2000 laptop (IP: 161.70.209.86) is associated with the AP (IP: 161.70.209.82), and the speed between them is 11 Mbps.

Figure 4-3 *Functional Model for Bottleneck Discovery*

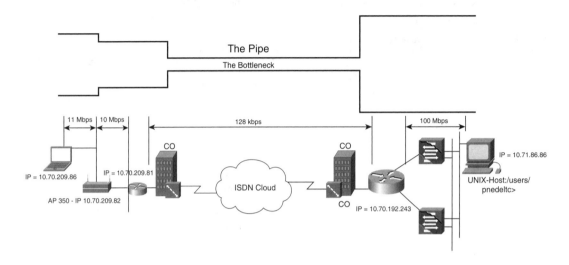

Example 4-2 *Pchar Discovers a Bottleneck*

```
UNIX-host:/users/pnedeltc> ./pchar -p ipv4icmp -v -R 3 -s 8 10.70.209.86
-p - protocol ipv4icmp; -v - verbose; -R-3 repetitions per hop;
   -s -starting from hop 8
pchar to 10.70.209.86 (10.70.209.86) using ICMP/IPv4 (raw sockets)
Using raw socket input
Packet size increments from 32 to 1500 by 32
46 test(s) per repetition
3 repetition(s) per hop
 7: 10.71.86.86 (UNIX-Host)
    Partial loss:      0 / 138 (0%)
    Partial char:      rtt = 1.359319 ms, (b = -0.000003 ms/B), r2 = 0.000210
                       stddev rtt = 0.021433, stddev b = 0.000027
    Partial queueing:  avg = 0.000052 ms (0 bytes)
 8: 10.70.192.243 (Cisco-isdn.cisco.com)
    Partial loss:      0 / 138 (0%)
    Partial char:      rtt = 25.581711 ms, (b = 0.072820 ms/B), r2 = 0.999766
                       stddev rtt = 0.135654, stddev b = 0.000168
    Partial queueing:  avg = 0.029341 ms (402 bytes)
    Hop char:          rtt = 24.222391 ms, bw = 109.855819 Kbps
    Hop queueing:      avg = 0.029288 ms (402 bytes)
 9: 10.70.209.81 (pnedeltc-isdn.cisco.com)
 ! 6% loss:
    Partial loss:      9 / 138 (6%)
    Partial char:      rtt = 25.566884 ms, (b = 0.075063 ms/B), r2 = 0.999448
                       stddev rtt = 0.387928, stddev b = 0.000276
    Partial queueing:  avg = 0.029208 ms (402 bytes)
    Hop char:          rtt = --.--- ms, bw = 3566.545092 Kbps
    Hop queueing:      avg = -0.000133 ms (0 bytes)
```

Example 4-2   *Pchar Discovers a Bottleneck (Continued)*

```
The connection between 10.70.209.81 and 10.70.209.86 is wireless 11 Mbps.
10: 10.70.209.86 (pnedeltc-isdn5.cisco.com)
    Path length:        10 hops
    Path char:          rtt = 25.566884 ms r2 = 0.999448
! This bottleneck matches the bandwidth of
! the core router 7206-isdn (see step 8):
    Path bottleneck:    109.855819 Kbps
    Path pipe:          351 bytes
    Path queueing:      average = 0.029208 ms (402 bytes)
    Start time:         Fri Dec 21 07:48:33 2001
    End time:           Fri Dec 21 07:51:43 2001
executor:/users/pnedeltc>
```

The Pchar is run from 10.71.86.86 towards 10.70.209.86 with the options **-p – protocol ipv4icmp; -v – verbose; -R-3 repetitions per hop; -s –starting from hop 8**. Because of configuration options, the utility performs an initial reachability test and assigns hop 7 to the source (IP: 10.71.86.86), hop 8 to the core ISDN router (IP: 10.70.192.243), 804 ISDN router (IP: 10.70.209.81), and reaches the final hop—Cisco AP 350 (IP: 10.70.209.86). The **interesting** spots are the level of loss—about 6 percent in hop 9 and the comparison between hop 8 and the last report, where the bottleneck is discovered to be at hop 8—see the message bw = 109.855819 kbps.

NOTE   In Example 4-2, you can see **stddev rtt = 0.387928**. This measurement is the standard deviation of the RTT. The standard deviation is the most commonly used measure of the spread. The calculation is based on variance, mean, and standard deviation. If the RTT = 1, 2, 3, the variance is $\sigma = [(1 \times 2)^2 + (2 \times 2)^2 + (3 \times 2)^2] /3 \sim 0.667$, and 2 is the mean. The standard deviation is the square root of the variance, which in this case, is $\sigma^{1/2} \sim 0.816$.

The Pchar utility has two limitations: the utility has difficulties when the hop is a multipath type and when there are transparent hops because of bridges or ATM links on the path.

Common and Cisco-Specific Tools

A variety of tools are available under different platforms. It is worthwhile to explore each of them, and to create a set of pros and cons for each one. This type of research is worth a separate book. One possible approach to classify all tools is the following:

- Network monitoring tools such as local-area network (LAN) and wide-area network (WAN) analyzers and sniffers, such as Sniffer Pro from Network Associates or EtherPeek.

- Remote control software, such as pcAnywhere from www.symantec.com, or Virtual Network Computing (VNC) software, which is used widely throughout the industry.

- Simulative equipment and software. Usually new solutions require lab environment testing before testing in production. The same logic applies to some unique problems when you need to recreate the problem and test the resolution prior to implementing any solution. A convenient tool for this purpose is a hardware simulator. ADTRAN Inc. (www.adtran.com) offers a comprehensive line of WAN test equipment that enables quick and economical deployment of fiber, T3, DSL, T1, E1, Frame Relay, VPN, ISDN, Digital Data Service (DDS), and wireless digital networks.

- Some of the best troubleshooting tools, such as Output Interpreter (www.cisco.com/support/OutputInterpreter/parser.html), are available and updated at Cisco.com.

Network analyzers and sniffers are extremely useful when troubleshooting data link layer and network layer issues such as frame formats, segmentations, and access control lists. (For more information, see Chapter 13, "Troubleshooting Scenarios for ISDN BRI.") Remote control software can be particularly useful for troubleshooting some applications when basic connectivity is available so that you can see what remote users see on their screen. Simulators and software that recreates the problem are recommended tools for the preproduction environment or for the pilot stage of the deployment of new products or services.

Each of the tools listed here requires some investment and it is up to you to define the purpose for each tool and to learn to use it effectively. A common set of tools is widely available for UNIX, Microsoft, and Cisco platforms that can be used for basic trouble-shooting. Some of the more common tools are listed in the following sections.

Ping and Privileged (Extended) Ping Commands

These commands are available for Cisco, Microsoft, and UNIX platforms.

The ping utility can determine basic connectivity. It is based on the specifications for RFC 1256 and RFC 791. Ping is assigned a low priority. It is not an indicator of performance, and it is not used for other more sophisticated tests. During a ping test, the host sends an ICMP echo packet and receives a reply ICMP message if basic connectivity exists.

NOTE   An ICMPv6 is available for the IPv6 protocol (see RFC 1885).

The IOS-based ping can be used in two modes: user mode and ping EXEC mode (or Privileged Ping). The user mode **ping** command is for users who do not have privileged mode access to the device. The command syntax is as follows:

```
Router>ping [protocol] [host | address]
```

The *protocol* option allows you to define several options such as IP, source-route bridging (SRB), and tag. Only the non-verbose form is available, and if the host address can be resolved by the Domain Name System (DNS) server, the **ping** command returns !!!!!. If it cannot be resolved by DNS, the host returns ...... If it fails, it is always a good idea to try to ping by IP address and bypass possible DNS issues. The command returns success rate in percent and RTT in minimum, average, and maximum. For example, if you see a RTT value equal to 50 ms, 500 ms, and 5 seconds, your next questions is: Is this what I should expect, or is this far from the baseline? These questions can be answered by using ping and knowing the topology of the network, the baseline, the expected performance character-istics, and the way that the traffic is carried (local exchange carriers [LECs], inter-exchange carriers [IXCs], local loop, and if it is dial, ISDN, Frame Relay, or any other technology). As an example, for satellite-based VPN connections, 0.7 seconds RTT is what you should expect; however, this RTT is unacceptable for Frame Relay.

The extended ping is much more useful and interesting for troubleshooting. The command provides a variety of options for protocols such as IP, Internetwork Packet Exchange (IPX), AppleTalk, Connectionless Network Service (CLNS), Digital Equipment Corporation net (DECnet), *Virtual Integrated Network Service (VINES)*, and Xerox Network Systems (XNS). The results can be interpreted differently (see Example 4-3).

Example 4-3 *Example of Extended Ping to 10.68.10.70*

```
Router#ping
Protocol [ip]:
Target IP address: 10.68.10.70
Repeat count [5]: 100
Datagram size [100]: 3000
Timeout in seconds [2]: 3
Extended commands [n]: y
Source address or interface:
Type of service [0]:
Set DF bit in IP header? [no]:
Validate reply data? [no]:
Data pattern [0xABCD]: 0x0000
Loose, Strict, Record, Timestamp, Verbose[none]:
Sweep range of sizes [n]:
Type escape sequence to abort.
Sending 100, 3000-byte ICMP Echoes to 10.68.10.70, timeout is 3 seconds:
Packet has data pattern 0x0000
```

The first important consideration is the ability to modify the repeat count (the default is 5), datagram size, and the timeout period (the default is 2). A higher number of ICMP echoes creates traffic for a longer period of time, and combined with the increased size of the packet (3000 bytes), allows you to test Point-to-Point Protocol (PPP), Multilink PPP (MPPP), and Multichassis Multilink PPP (MMP) (see Part II, "Dial," and Part III, "ISDN," for more detail on PPP, MPPP, and MMP) for dialup or ISDN connections, and for thresholds, reliability, txload, and rxload in some interfaces. It is rare to receive a timeout greater than two seconds in wired networks; however, the option is available and can be used accordingly in a wireless environment. One indicator for successfully running compression over a WAN connection is a non-proportional increase in RTT, when you increase the packet size following every test. This is based on the fact that the compression ratio is not a linear function of the packet size.

RFC 791 defines different types of reports that can be used to analyze connectivity issues. The reports are Loose, Strict, Record, Timestamp, and Verbose, and are based on the content of the IP packet. The same is true for TOS parameters and for setting the fragmentation bit. The latter plays a significant role in some connectivity issues and MTU issues in VPN solutions. This, combined with the sweep range of sizes, automatically modifies the packet size and determines the minimum MTU in the path.

NOTE   More about MTU is discussed in Chapter 21, "Remote Access VPN Troubleshooting."

Regarding data patterns, in some instances, it is not appropriate to use the Cisco standard 0xABCD sequence because some connectivity tests are much more productive based on certain specifics of the technology. In T1 and Primary Rate Interface (PRI) connectivity issues, the ones density requirement requires a certain number of 1s to be available. Their absence is referred to as a loss of signal (LOS) (see Chapter 3, "The Cloud"). Running 0x0000 or 0xffff provides more information than a standard Cisco sample. Another example for the same purpose is 0xAAAA, 0xA5A5, and 0x4040. Because of the specifics of T1 lines, it is recommended that you use the 0x0000 pattern for testing. Long series of 0s are indistinguishable from LOS (see Chapter 3 and Chapter 7, "Dial Troubleshooting"), so if the T1 is functional, a zero-insertion procedure is in effect (see Part IV, "Frame Relay"). 0xFFFF helps to localize repeater power problems, and 0x4040 is recommended for timing problems. It is also recommended to use different patterns when testing the compression ratio in a lab environment because of the deficiencies in the standard 0xABCD pattern.

In general, ping returns the following replies:

- **.**—Timed out; waiting for reply
- **!**—Reply received
- **U**—Destination unreachable
- **N**—Network unreachable
- **P**—Protocol unreachable
- **Q**—Source quench
- **M**—Could not fragment
- **?**—Unknown packet type

ICMP type messages are listed in Table 4-3.

When the ICMP type is 3 (destination unreachable), the ICMP codes identify the failure. The failures are defined in Table 4-4.

Table 4-3   *ICMP Type Messages and Descriptions*

ICMP Type Message	Description of ICMP Types
0	Echo Reply
3	Destination Unreachable
4	Source Quench
5	Redirect Message
8	Echo Request
11	Time Exceeded
12	Parameter Problem
13	Timestamp Request
14	Timestamp Reply
15	Information Request (No Longer Used)
16	Information Reply (No Longer Used)
17	Address Mask Request
18	Address Mask Reply

Table 4-4   *ICMP Codes When the ICMP TYPE Is 3—Destination Unreachable*

ICMP Codes for the ICMP Message Type = 3—Destination Unreachable	Description
0	Network unreachable
1	Host unreachable
2	Protocol unreachable
3	Port unreachable
4	Fragment needed and Don't Fragment (DF) bit set
5	Source route failed
6	Network unknown
7	Host unknown
8	Source Host isolated
9	Communication with destination network is administratively prohibited
10	Communication with destination is administratively prohibited
11	Bad type of service for destination network
12	Bad type of service for destination host
13	Administratively blocked by filter

Ping tests the end-to-end connectivity, but if the ping fails, it does not provide you with information on where the possible problem exists. The hop-by-hop information is available in the **traceroute** command, which in a sense extends ping's functionality.

The Traceroute and Privileged (Extended) Traceroute Commands

Available as **traceroute** in Cisco and UNIX based-platforms, and **tracert** in Microsoft-based platforms. The **traceroute** (Cisco/UNIX) and **tracert** (Microsoft) commands differ slightly. Cisco/UNIX uses UDP packets, and Microsoft uses ICMP packets, which are more likely to be filtered.

The **traceroute** command tests the connectivity of the path between two devices (hops). It narrows down connectivity issues, helps to discover routing loops, and determines baseline network layer performance on a hop-by-hop basis.

NOTE   The **traceroute** command is considered a baseline tool. This suggestion is not exactly correct because every router contains links, switching-forwarding engines, and queues. The mathematical model for traceroute does not consider the queues that are typical for every hop when there is competing traffic. This is why it is more precise to refer to traceroute as a hop-discovery tool.

The traceroute mechanism is based on the TTL field of an IP packet. This field is initialized by the sender. If the field is decremented to 0, the packet is discarded and an error indication packet (an ICMP time exceeded) is sent back to the sender. The source address of the ICMP error packet identifies the hop that discarded the data packet. This is the mechanism that identifies every hop. The sending host sets the TTL initially to 1. Every hop in the path decreases the TTL by 1. So for the first hop in the path, the TTL is decreased by 1, and because TTL now equals 0, the error message containing the hop information packet is sent back to the sender. The source then increases the TTL to 2, and after two hops it is sent back. The sender now tries using 3, and so on. The traceroute repeats itself until the command terminates when either the host is reached, the escape sequence (**Ctrl-Shift-^**) is triggered, the TTL reaches 30 (default TTL for Cisco), or the TTL exceeds the set amount. If the timer goes off before the response from the probe packet is back, the symbol * is displayed. The traceroute command can be used with the following protocols:

```
clns       ISO CLNS Trace
ip         IP Trace
ipx        IPX Trace
oldvines   Vines Trace (Cisco)
vines      Vines Trace (Banyan)
```

The privileged **traceroute** command offers some additional features, as shown in Example 4-4.

Example 4-4 *The Privileged* **traceroute** *Command*

```
router#traceroute
Protocol [ip]:
Target IP address: 10.68.10.70
Source address:
Numeric display [n]:
Timeout in seconds [3]:
Probe count [3]:
Minimum Time to Live [1]:
Maximum Time to Live [30]:
Port Number [33434]:
Loose, Strict, Record, Timestamp, Verbose[none]:
Type escape sequence to abort.
```

The options are self-explanatory and a detailed description of expected output from this command is listed in Table 4-5.

Table 4-5 *Traceroute Output Description*

Output	Description of the Output
nn msec	RTT in ms for each number of probes
*	Probe TTL expired
?	Unknown packet type
Q	Source quench
P, N, U, H	Protocol, network, port, host unreachable

The Netcat Utility

The Netcat utility takes advantage of the fact that telnet cannot test UDP connections, but Netcat can. It offers better functionality than telnet and can be used as a replacement because it does not inject too much data into the network. It can also test application connectivity and it is available in UNIX and Microsoft platforms.

The following are some of the options of the Netcat utility for the Microsoft NT platform (see Table 4-6):

```
C:\cisco\pnedeltc\tools\netcat>nc -h
[v1.10 NT]
connect to somewhere:   nc [-options] hostname port[s] [ports] ...
listen for inbound:     nc -l -p port [options] [hostname] [port]
options:
```

Table 4-6   *Netcat Utility Options for Windows NT 4.0 and Windows 2000*

Netcat Option	Description
-d	Detach from console, stealth mode.
-e	Execute inbound program.
-g	Gateway; source-routing hop point(s), up to 8.
-G	Number for source-routing pointer: 4, 8, 12, ...
-i	Delay interval in seconds for lines sent, ports scanned.
-I	Causes Netcat to listen to a given port (as specified with the –p Flag); this option is useful for creating mock services to test throughput or connectivity; use with the –u flag to create a UDP server.
-l	Listen mode, for inbound connects.
-L	Listen harder; relisten on socket close.
-n	Numeric IP address.
-o	Hex dump of the traffic.
-p	Local port number; when Netcat is run with the -I flag, use the specified port and IP address respectively.
-r	Randomize local and remote ports.
-s	Local source address; when Netcat is run with the -I flag, use the specified port and IP address respectively.
-t	Answer TELNET negotiation.
-u	UDP mode; tell Netcat to use UDP instead of TCP; Netcat simulates a UDP connection.
-v	Verbose (use twice to be more verbose).
-w	Timeout for connects and final net reads in seconds; changes the network inactivity timeout; changing this to at least 3 is useful when checking web or gopher services.
-z	Zero—Input/Output (I/O) mode (used for scanning).

Port numbers can be individual or a range: m-n (inclusive).

A simple example of using Netcat is to pull down a web page from a web server. With Netcat, you see the full HTTP header to see what web server a particular site is running. The command line is as follows:

```
C:\cisco\pnedeltc\tools\netcat>nc -v www.website.com 80 < get.txt
```

Netcat makes a connection to port 80, sends the text contained in the file get.txt, and provides the web server's response to stdout. The **-v** stands for verbose.

Another combination is the **-l** or listen option and the **-e** or execute option that instructs Netcat to listen on a particular port for a connection. When a connection is made, Netcat executes the program of your choice and connects the stdin and stdout of the program to the network connection.

```
C:\cisco\pnedeltc\tools\netcat>nc -l -p 23 -t -e cmd.exe
```

The **telnet** equivalent here is as follows:

```
C:\cisco\pnedeltc\tools\netcat>nc 110.71.87.84 23
```

You can listen on any port that gives you an opportunity, even to determine if the firewall you might be behind lets port 53 through. To run Netcat listening behind the firewall on port 53, use the following:

```
C:\cisco\pnedeltc\tools\netcat>nc -L -p 53 -e cmd.exe
```

Then from outside the firewall, connect to the listening machine by using the following command:

```
C:\outside\pnedeltc\tools>nc -v 10.71.87.84 53
```

The extended set of features for different platforms is widely available over the Internet. This particular version was written by Weld Pond (weld@l0pht.com).

Service Assurance Agent

A sophisticated Cisco IOS-based tool is available in IOS versions 12.2 or higher. The Service Assurance Agent (SAA) feature replaces the Response Time Reporter (RTR) in earlier IOS versions and provides extra capabilities such as VoIP metrics, response time, availability of HTTP (port 80) applications, and QoS based on the precedence field of the IP packet. The feature allows you to monitor network performance between a Cisco router and a remote device, which can be another Cisco router, an IP host, or a mainframe host, by measuring key Service Level Agreement (SLA) metrics such as response time, network resources, availability, jitter, connect time, packet loss, and application performance. SAA enables you to perform troubleshooting, problem analysis, and notification based on the statistics collected by the SAA. Example 4-5 shows a sample using IOS 12.2(6) that is configuring the HTTP traffic monitoring to www.cisco.com, and scheduling the data collection.

Example 4-5 *SAA Sample*

```
Router#conf t
Enter configuration commands, one per line.  End with CNTL/Z.
Router(config)#rtr 1
Router(config-rtr)#type http operation get url http://www.cisco.com
Router(config-rtr)#exit
Router(config)#rtr schedule 1 start-time now
Router(config)#^Z
Router#wr
```

continues

Example 4-5 *SAA Sample (Continued)*

```
Router#show rtr collection-statistics
        Collected Statistics

Entry Number: 1
HTTP URL: http://www.cisco.com
Start Time: *00:15:04.000 UTC Mon NOV 1 2001

        Comps: 0           RTTMin: 0
        OvrTh: 0           RTTMax: 0
        DNSTimeOut: 0      RTTSum: 0
        TCPTimeOut: 0      RTTSum2: 0
        TraTimeOut: 0      DNSRTT: 0
        DNSError: 0        TCPConRTT: 0
        HTTPError: 0       TransRTT: 0
        IntError: 8        MesgSize: 0
```

It is recommended to place the SAA in strategic areas of your network (in the core or
distribution layer) to ensure monitoring and to receive performance metrics for the network
functionality. The SAA feature provides an extended set of **#show** and **#debug** features.

The IOS Commands show and debug

The **#show** and **#debug** features of the IOS are the main Cisco-specific tools that have to
be continually learned by troubleshooting engineers to obtain the maximum available
information from the devices. Cisco defined seven severity levels of report of certain events
in Cisco routers. One important point here is to understand that by default the **#debug**
command provides information for a certain severity level and higher. The default severity
level can be changed with the command in Example 4-6.

Example 4-6 *Changing the Default Severity Level*

```
804-isdn(config)#logging console ?
  <0-7>          Logging                          severity level
  emergencies    System is unusable               (severity=0)
  alerts         Immediate action needed          (severity=1)
  critical       Critical conditions              (severity=2)
  errors         Error conditions                 (severity=3)
  warnings       Warning conditions               (severity=4)
  notifications  Normal but significant conditions (severity=5)
  informational  Informational messages           (severity=6)
  debugging      Debugging messages               (severity=7)
  guaranteed     Guarantee console messages
```

The #**show** and #**debug** commands are widely used in the troubleshooting process. Another important preliminary rule for the #**debug** command is that when debugging, some of the debug commands have chatty output and if mishandled, can crash the router. You can even cancel the terminal monitoring with Router#**terminal no monitor,** but this does not cancel the debug process. It is recommended that you open a secondary session (Telnet, Secure Shell [SSH]) to the same router and prepare to cancel the debugging with the shortest command you know. Remember that some debug commands can be used only if the utilization is low (use #**show processes cpu [history]** command), or in a non-production environment.

These commands are widely described in the following chapters to demonstrate some of the most common and recommended Cisco tools for a remote access environment.

End Notes

[1]Retana, Slice, and White. *Advanced IP Network Design (CCIE Professional Development)*. Cisco Press, 1999.

Summary

This chapter focused on troubleshooting models, tools, and approaches. You should be familiar with this preliminary information before you approach the technology-specific troubleshooting covered in the following parts of this book. Part of the discussion was about layered interconnection models because the following discussion in the book is based on the layer-by-layer troubleshooting model, starting from Layer 1. You have learned about baseline, performance characteristics, and some common and Cisco-specific trouble-shooting tools. The PathChar utility, NetCat utility, and SAA of Cisco are discussed in more detail and are recommended for different aspects of the troubleshooting process.

Review Questions

Answers to the review questions can be found in Appendix A, "Answers to Review Questions."

1   What is the name of the layer above the network layer in the DoD model?

2   Name at least one keyword for each of Layer 2, Layer 3, and Layer 4 of the OSI model.

3   What is the communication subsystem in the seven-layer OSI model?

4   What is the baseline of the system?

5   Name at least five of the key concepts in the troubleshooting process.

6 What are the complete and the shortest IOS commands to save the running configuration to the NVRAM?

7 What are the complete and the shortest IOS commands to cancel all debugging in the router?

8 Why does the CDP use a multicast address?

9 When troubleshooting the serial interface, you see HDLC protocol type 0x2000, what is it?

10 Is it recommended that you disable the CDP over the dialer interface? If so, what is the command?

11 What is the measurement of the spread when measuring the path characteristics with Pchar?

12 What does ICMP type 3 mean?

13 What is the command to see the statistics when using Service Assurance Agent (SAA)?

PART II

Dial

Chapter 5   Dial Technology Background

Chapter 6   Dial Design and Configuration Solutions

Chapter 7   Dial Troubleshooting

Chapter 8   Dial Troubleshooting Scenarios

Dial Technology Background

Dial is an essential part of remote access infrastructures because it is one of the easiest means by which a traveling user can obtain network access. For connectivity at home, in most cases, it provides the cheapest form of Internet access. Dial also provides an inexpensive, reliable backup solution when broadband alternatives are not available because of circuit outages or maintenance windows.

Dialup networking seems simplistic in terms of how it works. The steps to establish a connection include modem train-up, authentication, and establishment of a Point-to-Point Protocol (PPP). After you complete these steps, you have a PPP connection from client to server, which allows you to pass traffic.

The difficult part of dialup networking is overcoming its limitations to get the best possible connection speed and the most stable connection. Dial is a technology that everyone has at their fingertips, but it is limited in certain areas because of the telephone company (telco) infrastructure. This chapter covers some of the details regarding dial and its limitations. It also provides some tips on how to overcome these limitations. The main focus of this chapter is not the detailed, but the essential technology background information, which is, in most cases, sufficient when troubleshooting dial issues. This chapter includes the following sections:

- Overview of existing modems
- Typical telco issues, including digital pads and line code errors
- Authentication options for dial
- Extensive information about one of the most commonly used protocols in dial environment—PPP

Overview of Modems

In general, modulator-demodulators (modems) are devices that modulate digital signals into audible sounds and demodulate audible sounds into digital signals. Included in this section are some basic facts about telephone companies, how telephone companies deal with switched services, and the limitations that this places on data connections. Besides the information provided in Chapter 1, "Remote Access Overview," and Chapter 3, "The Cloud," this section also includes information on ways that telcos are improving connection parameters.

A local telco takes the signal from the analog line that terminates at a remote user's residence and digitizes it to 64 kilobits per second (kbps). This is done so that each call can take the same amount of bandwidth and can be easily placed into larger circuits, such as a Primary Rate Interface (PRI) or channelized digital service 3 (DS3). A 64-kb bandwidth per call is limiting in the amount of data that a modem can push. However, this bandwidth assists the telephone company because they can multiplex hundreds of calls together for ease of transport from one central office (CO) to another.

The quality of digital signals sent over long distances is better than that of analog signals sent over long distances. This is an advantage for modems when calling outside your local CO. Digital signals can be amplified by a device called a repeater. When the signal-to-noise ratio (SNR) drops below acceptable margins, repeaters are often inserted into the line. While amplifying analog signals, the noise is part of the analog signal and is also amplified, which results in lost data because of the noise at a point further down the line.

There are two different types of basic modems. The first is an analog modem, which is the type of modem installed on a user's computer. These can be internal (hardware card installed on a system, motherboard) or external (independent, free-standing hardware). Examples of these modems are 3Com/US Robotics Sportster, Lucent WinModems, and Best Data V.90 modems. These modems demodulate the signals coming from an analog line and pass that data off to your computer. They also modulate the data into analog signals and send it down the analog line to your provider.

The second type of modem is a digital modem. Digital modems are found in most dial access servers that interface directly with the 64-kbps trunks from the telco in the form of a PRI or a channelized DS3. They decode the digital signals directly off the 64-kbps trunk and pass them to the dial-in server. They also place the digital signals directly on the 64-kbps trunk and pass them to the end user.

Digital modems were key to breaking the 33.6-kbps speed barrier that analog modem to analog modem calls could not surpass. With digital modem to analog modem calls, the digital modem can send up to 53,333 bps to the analog modem by placing the digital signals directly on the line, but the analog modem can only send at speeds up to 33,600 bps back to the digital modem because it has to perform a digital to analog conversion prior to sending the data.

Table 5-1 describes the different standards that have evolved modems to today's speeds. The different modulations and the speeds achieved by each of them throughout the years are listed in Table 5-1.

Table 5-1   *Modulations and Their Connection Speeds*

Standard	Speeds Achieved
CCITT V.21	300 bps (falls back to 150 and 110 bps)
CCITT V.22	1200 bps (falls back to 600 bps)
CCITT V.22 bis	2400 bps
CCITT V.32	9600 bps (falls back to 7200, 4800, and 2400 bps)
CCITT V.32 bis	14,400 bps (falls back to 12000 bps and V.32)
V.32 ter (terbo)*	20,000 bps
V.Fast*	28,800 bps—Preliminary implementations of V.34
V.FC*	28,800 bps—An attempt to make V.Fast more compatible between different implementations
ITU-T V.34	28,800 bps (falls back to 26,400, 24,000, 21,600, 19,200, 16,800, and 14,400 bps; V.32 bis; and V.32)
X2*	U.S. Robotics 56,000 bps
K56Flex*	56,000 bps
ITU-T V.90	56,000 bps—FCC limited to 53,333 bps (falls back to 52,000, 50,667, 49,333, 48,000, 46,667, 45,333, 44,000, 42,667, 41,333, 40,000, 38,667, 38,400, 37,333, 34,667, 34,000, 33,600, 33,333, 32,000, 31,200, 30,667, and 29,333 bps and V.34)
ITU-T V.92	56,000 bps—Same as V.90 with added features including Modem on Hold and Quick Connect

* Not a standard, but worth mentioning because they helped pave the way for the standards to evolve.

NOTE   CCITT (Consultative Committee for International Telegraph and Telephone) changed its name to ITU-T (International Telecommunications Union Telecommunication Standardization Sector) on March 1, 1993.

The analog signal loss mentioned previously is easy to notice with modems because they are noise-sensitive devices. After you reach a range of about 15,000 cable feet from your CO, the quality drops to a point where 56k/V.90 is no longer available. The further out you are from the CO, the slower the connection speed becomes.

NOTE   The worst case I have recorded is 42,800 cable feet from a CO, where most modems did not train-up at all, and the ones that did only connected at 4800 to 9600 baud at best. Surprisingly, this was in the city of San Jose, California—one of the most populous and up-to-date areas in terms of carrier services.

As speeds increase towards the 56 k limit, the factors that affect a modem's ability to connect and remain at those speeds become more apparent. The number one limiting factor is distance from the CO. The second limiting factor is the SNR (S/N ratio). If there is a lot of crosstalk from other lines, your line will have more noise, which limits your connections. Another factor is the telco's cloud that your call travels across on its way to its final destination.

Telco Issues

This section discusses some modem issues that are not so easy to identify. Before getting to this, having a lot of information can help to determine the fastest speeds you can get by analyzing what your modem sees after a connection is established. Any form of landline should achieve a V.34 connection, but the two key components of a good V.34 connection are the SNR and the amount of usable voice spectrum. For a connection of 33600 baud, the SNR must be 38 dB or higher and the usable spectrum must range from 244 to 3674 Hz. Otherwise, the speaking signal strength to noise strength ratio has to be higher than 79.44. Anything below these standards degrades service.

NOTE | The decibel (dB) is a unit of measuring the strength of the signal, or of a sound. From "Newton's Telecom Dictionary" (Harry Newton, 1999), "The power in telecommunications is low and normally is measured in milliwatts. However, the milliwatt is not a convenient way to express differences in power level between circuits. Voice frequency circuits are designed around the human ear, which has a logarithmic response to changes in power. Therefore, in telephony, the decibel, which is logarithmic rather than linear measurement, is used as a measure between circuits or transmission level points." As you well know, $1 db = 20 \times \log(\text{signal/noise})$.

At least eight factors can reduce the SNR, frequency response, or both:

- Robbed bit signaling reduces the SNR.
- Extra analog to digital conversions reduce the SNR.
- Load coils on the local loop reduce the frequency response.
- Long local loops reduce frequency response and reduce the SNR.
- Bridged taps create a loss in signal strength and reduce the SNR. Most of the industry analysts determine bridged taps to be as prominent as on 75 percent of existing copper lines (www.teradyne.com/prods/btd/articles/adsl_test.html).
- Electrical disturbances including crosstalk, corroded connectors, lines running parallel to fluorescent lights or power cables, and equipment sharing the same power jack as the modem can all reduce the SNR.

- Voice circuits that pass through any sub-64 k coding reduce the frequency response. Most circuits with sub-64 k coding result in speeds of less than 16,800 baud.

- If incorrectly configured, Subscriber Loop Concentrators (SLCs), which multiplex multiple loops into a trunk, can limit the voice spectrum and subsequently create a low SNR ratio.

With these and other limitations mentioned later, a V.90 connection rarely obtains its maximum speed. First, only one analog to digital conversion can exist on a circuit, which means that from the moment the call from the client modem hits the first digital switch, the call must stay in digital form over a DS0 all the way until it hits the network access server (NAS). This also indicates that the NAS must interface with only DS0s in the form of a PRI or a channelized T1 (DS1).

The ideal scenario for a V.90 call is a 3200 Hz response range and the local loop should not be longer than 3 miles. At 3.5 miles in the U.S., a load coil is usually applied to the line, which degrades frequency response and in turn eliminates any chance for a V.90 connection. The SNR from the client modem should be 40 dB (40 dB is a SNR of 100), or higher.

Digital Pad

A telephone line connected to a remote user's minimum point of entry (MPOE) or to a telecommuter's hotel room carries a full-duplex call on a single pair of wires. This means that both send and receive signals are transmitted simultaneously, but on individual wires. When the send and receive signals are broken apart from each other, there is a leakage of audible sound from send to receive and vice versa. This leakage is heard as an echo and becomes more noticeable as the distance increases from source to destination. Because analog lines are primarily used for voice, this echo must be quieted through the use of a pad to remove the echo.

Placement of a pad can cause issues with a 56-bps connection. Both analog and digital pads act as a volume control for both sides of the line. Although a digital pad uses the digital data to adjust the volume, it can affect the speed, but should not prevent a connection. Analog pads have to convert digital data to analog, adjust the volume, and convert back to digital. An analog pad that is located between a residence and the CO can introduce another analog-to-digital conversion into your segment and might prevent a 56-kbps modem connection, although some testing suggests that modems are not adversely affected.

The following are three different call scenarios that demonstrate these issues:

- In cases where your call originates and terminates within the same CO, there is no pad applied to the line. The distance between source and destination is so small that the echo is not heard and a pad is not required.

- If your call travels through a long-distance provider to get from source to destination, there is most likely a 6-dB pad on the line. 6 dB (6 dB is a SNR of 2) is only a general rule and can be different depending on your carrier.

- If your call stays within the same local carrier, but travels from one CO to another, there is a 3-dB pad on the line (signal to noise ratio of approx. 1.4). Again, this is only a general rule and can differ from carrier to carrier. In most cases, this is the type of call that customers make to an Internet service provider (ISP), and an ISP does not generally have equipment at every CO. ISPs do usually have equipment at one CO within a certain calling area or hub, and back haul the traffic from neighboring COs to the location where the equipment resides.

  The reason that the 3-dB pad was mentioned is because it seems to interfere with a lot of 56 k modems in terms of speed and connection quality. There is a way to change your pad to 6 db to see if it makes the connection quality any better. If you dial 1 + area code + number instead of just dialing the number, you are telling the carrier that this is a long-distance call, and that it needs to have a 6-dB pad. If the connection quality is any better, the 3-dB pad is causing the issues.

There is no available data to explain why a 3-dB digital pad adversely affects the connection, nor is there any way to correct this through access server configurations. A carrier can change the padding on a line, but it is uncommon for them to change it for residential customers. In fact, many of the first level support staff that handle trouble calls won't know what this is. A telco technician is the best person to answer these questions and to make this change.

Line Code Errors

On both a PRI and a T1, time slots exist for each of the 64-kbps channels. (See Chapter 2, "Telecommunication Basics," for more information.) As the data is received, a time slot generator places the bits into these time slots. There can never be more than seven 0s in a row, even across time slots, and this is where line coding must be considered. If eight 0s are in a row, the time slot generator converts the eight 0s to a combination of 0s and 1s, depending on the line code. (See Figure 2-10 for a comparison of different coding schemes.)

Alternate mark inversion (AMI) is based on a pseudoternary or three level system signal, which represents binary digits, in which successive marks (logical 1s) are of alternately positive and negative polarity pulses, and the absolute values of their amplitudes are normally equal, and spaces (logical 0s) are of 0 amplitude, or no symbol. Each pulse is approximately 3 volts in amplitude and has a 50 percent duty cycle, which means that it takes up half of the time slot for pulse transmission. Pulses have a tendency to spread out in the time domain as they travel down a line. Restricting the initial transmission to occupy half the time slot helps the repeaters, and the receiving end, find the middle of each time slot and stay synchronized. In AMI, the pattern of bits "1 0 0 0 0 1 1 0" encodes to " + 0 0 0 0 - + 0".

A problem with this coding scheme is the way 0 is interpreted as a no-signal condition. Therefore, an absence of pulses (all 0s) can force repeaters and network equipment (the carriers facility Digital Phase-Locked Loop (DPLL) to lose frame synchronization. To prevent this, all T1s are required to meet the ones density (pulse density) requirement, in which the FCC rule states that no more than 15 consecutive 0s can be transmitted to the line (40 according to some sources). In fact, Cisco and other carriers define the ones density scheme so as to allow a channel service unit/data service unit (CSU/DSU) to recover the data clock reliably, as "no more than eight consecutive 0s." The CSU/DSU derives the data clock from the data that passes through it. To recover the clock, the CSU/DSU hardware must receive at least one 1-bit value for every 8 bits of data that pass through it. The rule is also called pulse density. Often, the carriers use the eighth bit (least significant bit [LSB]) for supervision, which leaves only 7 of the 8 bits for user data, which provide a (7 bits × 8000 frames per second =) 56,000-bps data channel. With AMI, the bits are changed to 0000000P in all time slots when data is being transmitted no matter the bit pattern.

NOTE   In the combination 0000000P, P is a pulse with the opposite polarity as the previous pulse.

The LSB is always 1, which yields a 56-kbps time slot. Only the LSB is altered.

With AMI, throughput suffers when the eighth bit is blindly stuffed with a 1. Maintaining synchronization requires only that enough pulses are sent down the line. Bipolar 8-zero substitution (B8ZS) can transmit an arbitrary bit sequence. When eight consecutive 0 bits are scheduled for transmission, a B8ZS transmitter replaces the eight 0s with a code word that contains intentional bipolar violations (BPVs), as shown in Figure 5-1. This technique guarantees a ones density independent of the data stream.

Figure 5-1   *B8ZS Guaranties that Ones Density Is Independent of the Data Stream*

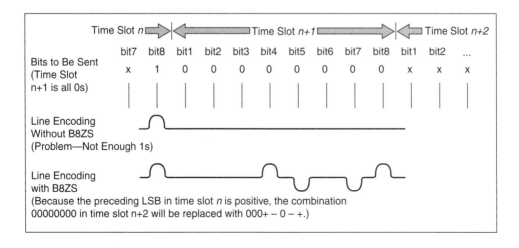

The combination of 00000000 is always replaced with the combination 000VP0VP, but the polarity of V and P can differ, based on a polarity of the preceding LSB. In Figure 5-1, the preceding bit in time slot *n* is positive, and the 0000000 in slot *n + 1* is replaced with 000+-0-+. If the polarity of the preceding lsb is negative, the resulting combination will be 000-+0+-.

The most commonly used coding scheme in Europe and Japan is called high density binary 3 (HDB3). This scheme is based again on AMI encoding, but the string of consecutive four 0 is replaced with a sequence that contains one or two pulses. In each case, the fourth bit is replaced with a code violation (v) signal. An additional rule is introduced to ensure effective violation, based on the polarity of the preceding pulse and the number of bipolar pulses since the last substitution:

If the preceding polarity is negative and

- The number of bipolar pulses since the last substitution is odd, the combination 0000 is represented as 000V (V-negative).

- The number of bipolar pulses since the last substitution is even, the combination 0000 is represented as V00V (V-positive).

If the preceding polarity is positive and

- The number of bipolar pulses since the last substitution is odd, the combination 0000 is represented as 000V (V-positive).

- The number of bipolar pulses since the last substitution is even, the combination 0000 is represented as V00V (V-negative).

Now imagine that an AS5300 router is using B8ZS line coding. The integral CSU/DSU in the router modifies the data prior to sending it across the wire to the telephone company. The other side is expecting AMI coding. It is not difficult to understand that the side using AMI coding will misinterpret the incoming combination in time slot *n + 1*. While the B8ZS is sending 000VP0VP, the AMI side is expecting 0000000P, because only the LSB is altered in AMI, and as a result, this site passes the data without recognizing that the original combination is eight 0s. The same logic applies if AS5300 is using HDB3. The inaccurate transfer of data doesn't significantly affect voice, but it does extensively interfere with a modem. The challenge of finding this type of problem is that it is well masked. The 108 Bert Test, which is supposed to find any and all possible problems with a T1 or a PRI, never transmits more than seven bits set to zero in a row. This will never force the substitution algorithm and therefore never detect this problem. These types of errors are reported in RFC 1232 (see the BPV errors in Table 7-1 in Chapter 7). However, it is vital in the troubleshooting process to make sure that both sides are using the same coding scheme.

Authentication Options

Authentication for dial can be implemented in many different ways. It can be within PPP or outside of PPP, such as in the form of a login script or an after-dial terminal window. Within PPP, authentication can range from Password Authentication Protocol (PAP) to

Challenge Handshake Authentication Protocol (CHAP) to Microsoft Challenge Handshake Authentication Protocol (MSCHAP). The username and password combinations can be stored on the router, a Remote Authentication Dial-In User Service (RADIUS) server, a Terminal Access Controller Access Control System (TACACS) server, or an Extended TACACS (TACACS+) server. You can also use any combination of these.

Because there are a myriad of possibilities, additional considerations are highlighted here to help you decide what form of authentication is best to use for your specific application and requirements.

NOTE   The authentication options are fully applicable for both dialup and ISDN technologies. See Part III, "ISDN" for more information on ISDN service.

The first and easiest decision to make is whether to use an authentication server, such as TACACS or RADIUS, or to configure fixed usernames and passwords directly on the router.

Authentication servers can centrally manage authentications for thousands of users who are dispersed geographically and connecting to the NASs. They include added features for handling static or dynamic Internet Protocol (IP) allocation, dial-out scenarios, and account lockouts for account misuse or terminations.

Having the authentication parameters all locally stored on the router is appealing for dial-on-demand backup scenarios where usernames, passwords, and phone numbers are static unless manually changed.

Next, you choose if you want PPP, a terminal window after connection, or a combination of both to handle authentication. This can be easily answered by reviewing your user-base and their needs. In almost all customer-oriented applications, you will most likely choose authentication through PPP only. However, in enterprise situations where some users have unique requirements, such as text-based dialup, you use a combination of both.

If you decide to use PPP, you can determine which form of authentication to use inside of PPP. The most common form is PAP, but in areas where security is a concern you might opt for MS-CHAP or CHAP. CHAP offers the highest level of security out of the three methods. CHAP is the most common form of authentication for dial-on-demand applications. As before, you can use a combination of all of these. For example, if your typical user dials in with Microsoft Dial-Up Networking, the default settings for authentication are PAP over PPP. You might have some users, especially non-Windows users, connecting through text, and you can configure the lines to auto-select text or PPP. If the core router uses a dial-on-demand link in the event of an outage, you can configure the backup link on the router with a static CHAP username and password.

The most common authentication for Internet Access (connecting to an ISP) is PAP. This is what most people are using when they connect to the Internet. In the corporate world and internal to a business, PAP is also used, but with one-time password tokens. This allows for simplistic end user setup along with the added security of an ever-changing password. In places where static (non-changing) passwords exist in the corporate world, CHAP prevails.

Finally, there is one last form of authentication that is potentially a more secure form. It uses dial-back authentication. In this case, the user places a call to the server. After it is authenticated, the server dials back to the client and authenticates again by using the client's phone number as an added security measure. Unfortunately, this type of authentication requires a fixed phone number, which is not possible for individuals who are traveling.

The configurations for the different types of authentication are covered in Chapter 6, "Dial Design and Configuration Solutions."

PPP

PPP is defined in RFC 1661 and replaces the Serial Line Internet Protocol (SLIP) because of its deficiencies. SLIP only supports the IP protocol, and does not allow authentication and dynamic assignment of routed protocols. Unlike SLIP, PPP provides a standard method for transporting multiprotocol datagrams over point-to-point links. PPP is composed of three main components:

- A method for encapsulating multiprotocol datagrams
- A link control protocol (LCP) for establishing, configuring, and testing the data-link connection
- A family of Network Control Protocols (NCPs) for establishing and configuring different network-layer protocols [1]

The PPP protocol falls under the definitions of the second, or data link layer, of the Open System Interconnection (OSI) model. The format of the PPP frame is shown in Figure 5-2.

Figure 5-2 *The Format of the PPP Frame*

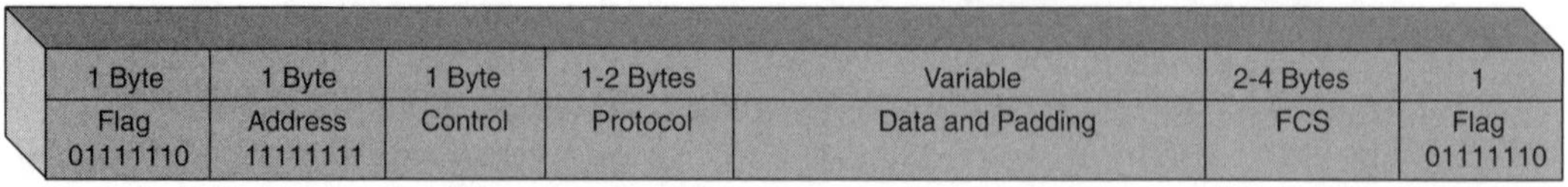

The descriptions of the fields in Figure 5-2 are as follows:

- **Flag**—Similar to the one for high-level data link control (HDLC), the Flag indicates the beginning and the end of the PPP frame. Its value is 01111110.
- **Address**—Because PPP is used for a point-to-point connection, the Address field uses the broadcast address of HDLC, 11111111, to avoid the data-link address in the protocol.

- **Control**—The Control field uses the format of the U-frame in HDLC. The value is 11000000 to show that the frame does not contain any sequence numbers, and that there is no flow and error control.

- **Protocol**—This field defines what is being carried in the Data field. Some valid values of the Protocol field include the following:
    - **c021**—LCP
    - **c023**—PAP
    - **c025**—Link Quality Report
    - **c223**—CHAP

- **Data field**—The user data or NCP packets are carried by the Data field, sometimes called the Payload field.

- **FCS**—The Frame Check Sequence (FCS) field is the same as in HDLC. It contains a 2- or 4-byte cyclic redundancy check (CRC).

During the process of establishing the protocol, the PPP link goes through several distinct phases, which are specified as follows:

- Link Dead (physical layer not ready)
- Link Establishment phase
- Authentication phase
- Network-Layer Protocol phase
- Link Termination phase

The following sections summarize these phases.

Link Dead (Physical Layer Not Ready)

The link necessarily begins and ends with this phase. When an external event, such as a Carrier Detect (CD) Up event, indicates that the physical layer is ready to be used, PPP proceeds to the Link Establishment phase. During this phase, the LCP automation (described later) is in the initial or starting state.

Link Establishment Phase

LCP establishes the connection through an exchange of configure packets. As soon as the Protocol field contains c021h, the phase is changed to link establishment. After a Configure-Ack packet is both sent and received, the exchange is complete and the LCP Opened state begins. The LCP codes are 1-byte long and are listed in Table 5-2.

Table 5-2 *LCP Codes, Packet Types, and Descriptions*

Code (Hex)	Packet Type	Description
01	Configure-Request	List of proposed link configuration options
02	Configure-Ack	Acknowledge the proposed configuration options
03	Configure-Nak	Does not acknowledge the proposed configuration options
04	Configure-Rej	Unknown configuration option—Reject
05	Terminate-Request	Request to terminate the phase
06	Terminate-Ack	Acknowledges the termination request
07	Code-Rej	Unknown code—Reject
08	Protocol-Rej	Unknown protocol—Reject
09	Echo-Request	Checks if the other end is Up
0A	Echo-Replay	Response to Echo-Request
0B	Discard-Request	Discard the request

Any non-LCP packets received during the Link Establishment phase must be silently discarded.

Authentication Phase

By default, authentication is not mandatory unless the protocol number used is c023 (PAP) or c223 (CHAP). The authentication negotiation occurs during the Link Establishment phase, where only LCP, authentication protocol, and link quality monitoring packets (protocol type c025—Link Quality Report) are allowed. All other packets received during this phase are discarded.

In PAP, one side supplies both a username and password in clear-text to the peer that is authenticating it. In CHAP, one peer challenges the other peer, and the latter one must be able to respond with the correct answer to the challenge before passing authentication. The password in CHAP creates the answer to the challenge and is never transmitted across the wire, which makes it inherently more secure. Also, there is MS-CHAP, which is similar to CHAP with the only exception being that MS-CHAP uses Microsoft's version of the protocol.

Network Layer Protocol Phase

After the link is established and optional facilities are negotiated as needed by the LCP, PPP must send NCP packets to choose and configure one or more network-layer protocols (such as IP, Internetwork Packet Exchange [IPX], or AppleTalk). After it is configured, datagrams from each network layer protocol can be sent over the link. The link remains configured for communications until explicit LCP or NCP packets close the link down. Each NCP can be opened and closed at any time. After an NCP reaches the Opened state, PPP carries the corresponding network-layer protocol packets. One example for NCP is the IP Control Protocol (IPCP). Its format is shown in Figure 5-3. The value of the Protocol field for a PPP packet is 8021h. [2]

Figure 5-3   *The Format of an IPCP Frame*

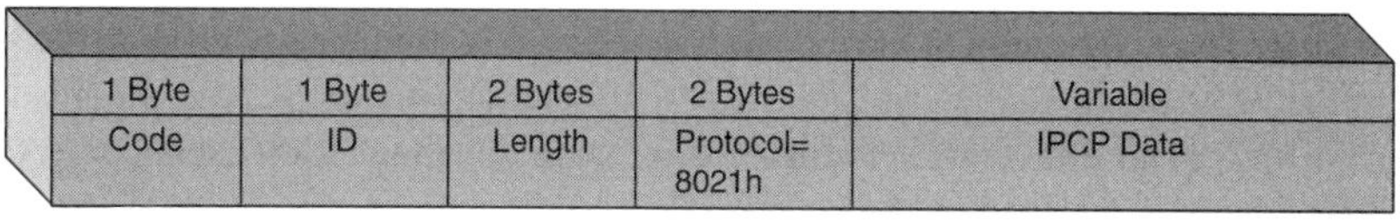

1 Byte	1 Byte	2 Bytes	2 Bytes	Variable
Code	ID	Length	Protocol= 8021h	IPCP Data

Because every NCP negotiates its own phases, reaching levels of Open and Close, Code values are defined in the Code field to facilitate the process. The Code field is 1-byte and the valid values are identified in Table 5-3.

Table 5-3   *Code Values of an IPCP Protocol*

Code (Hex)	Packet Type	Description
01	Configure-Request	List of proposed link configuration options
02	Configure-Ack	Acknowledge the proposed configuration options
03	Configure-Nak	Does not acknowledge the proposed configuration options
04	Configure-Rej	Unknown configuration option—Reject
05	Terminate-Request	Request to terminate the phase
06	Terminate-Ack	Acknowledges the termination request
07	Code-Rej	Unknown code—Reject

Link Termination Phase

PPP can terminate the link at any time. Possible reasons include loss of carrier, authentication failure, link quality failure, expiration of an idle-period timer, and the administrative closing of the link. LCP closes the link through an exchange of terminate packets (see LCP packets 05h and 06h). While the link is closing, PPP informs the network-layer protocols so that they can take appropriate action.

PPP Troubleshooting Considerations

For practical purposes, engineers often consider PPP as a four-phase protocol, ignoring the very first phase (Link Dead). This does not make a difference for troubleshooting purposes. [3]

NOTE	PPP over different technologies, such as dial, ISDN, and Frame Relay, poses different requirements to ensure inter-operability with the PPP protocol. For additional information, see RFC 1618 or Parts III and IV, "Frame Relay," of this book.

One of the most resource-intensive procedures in PPP negotiation occurs during the LCP negotiation. Previously, Cisco IOS created a statically configurable number of processes to authenticate calls. Each of these processes handles a single call, but in some situations, the limited number of processes cannot keep up with the incoming call rate, resulting in some calls timing out (the empiric numbers were showing about 1300 users per NAS). The AAA-PPP-VPDN Non-Blocking feature, introduced in IOS release 12.2(4)T, changed the software architecture such that the number of processes does not limit the rate of call handling. Async HDLC framing (the frame type defined in RFC 1662) engine for the R1.1 release is compatible with the 7200 platform and ensures that each Packet Data Serving Node (PDSN) can handle 8000 active PPP sessions on the 7200 platform.

End Notes

[1] RFC 1661. "The Point-to-Point Protocol (PPP)." W. Simpson, Editor, 1994.

[2] RFC 1332. "PPP Internet Protocol Control Protocol (IPCP)." McGregor, G. 1992.

[3] Cisco Systems, Inc. *CCIE Fundamentals: Network Design and Case Studies*, Second Edition. Cisco Press, 2000.

Summary

This chapter focused on essential background information to give you a better understanding of the main components of dial technology. This chapter provided an overview of existing modems and dial standards and discusses some typical telco issues, such as digital pads and line code errors. This chapter also detailed authentication options for a dial environment and provided a relatively detailed section on the PPP, which is the main protocol, used for dial connections. Some troubleshooting techniques were also included to increase the knowledge of engineers who will need to troubleshoot dial environments.

Review Questions

Answers to the review questions can be found in Appendix A, "Answers to Review Questions."

1 Name two added features in ITU-T V.92 standard, compared to ITU-T V.90.

2 Name two limiting factors for the ability of the modem to connect.

3 If the SNR is 40, how many times higher is the signal strength than noise strength?

4 How would you troubleshoot a case in which a pad of 3dB might be the root of the problem?

5 If AMI needs to transmit the octet 1 0 0 1 0 1 1 0, and the first mark is +, what are the next marks? Write the entire octet.

6 If the preceding LSB in B8ZS is positive, what is the combination for 00000000?

7 What is the main disadvantage of dial-back authentication?

8 Name the main phases of the PPP protocol.

9 What is the value 0xC223 in the protocol field of PPP?

10 Which protocol in the PPP suite establishes and configures the data-link connection?

11 What is the address field value of the PPP protocol?

12 Which packet types of LCP terminate the data-link connection?

CHAPTER 6

Dial Design and Configuration Solutions

Most commonly, modem dial access is used for dial-in network connectivity, dial-out network connectivity, and dial-on-demand routing (DDR). These specific instances are covered in the dial design solutions portion of this chapter, along with dial-out for support purposes and large-scale dial-out services. Fax server capability is another common use for dial, but is not covered here because it is more of a specialized service.

The main topics covered in the design portion of this chapter are as follows:

- Dial-in network design
- Dial-out network design
- Dial-on-demand backup options
- Dial-in configuration essentials
- Dial-out configuration essentials
- Dial-on-demand backup configuration essentials

This part aims at teaching the dial-in and dial-out design essentials. It also teaches the basic configuration options that are required to configure a dial server to either accept or place calls for the particular needs of the network that you are building. Dial-on-demand is also covered here in both design and configuration for use as a backup connection.

Following the design portion of this chapter is an extensive section on dial configuration solutions. The following topics in the configuration portion of this chapter give you detailed information about the common and specific dial configurations, including the following:

- Text dial-in configuration
- Point-to-Point Protocol (PPP) dial-in configuration
- Large-scale dial-in configuration
- Text dial-out configuration
- PPP dial-out configuration
- Large-scale dial-out configuration
- Dial-on-demand backup configuration

Dial Design Solutions

In the design part of this chapter, some design components remain constant. Dial (in, out, or on-demand) is generally served out of an access server that is connected to the network. Usually, there is an authentication server of some kind to offload the authentication processing from the router, making it centrally manageable.

Design considerations need to also include the backbone architecture. If dial is a component of a remote access solution for your company, it is a small part of the overall network and should tie into the backbone accordingly. Large service provider dial networks should be designed accordingly as well. Going into greater detail is not practical because of the wide variety of existing services. However, the best way to manage dial networks is to use a hub and spoke design. The hub is a gateway that ties the spokes (dial routers) into the backbone. This gateway is usually a Layer 3 switching device.

In cases where the dial routers are just components of a remote access solution, not a large service provider network, it might be appropriate to include all remote access services as spokes behind the hub. These services can include home Frame Relay, ISDN, xDSL, and perhaps Virtual Private Network (VPN). This approach works well because backbone networks change frequently because of the rapid advancements of local-area network/wide-area network (LAN/WAN) equipment. Remote access devices generally do not increase speeds as dramatically because the WAN piece of remote access solutions is slowly evolving by comparison. An example of the hub and spoke design for an enterprise is shown in Figure 6-1.

Figure 6-1 *Hub and Spoke Backbone Design for Remote Access Services, Including Dial, Frame Relay, ISDN, and a xDSL Gateway*

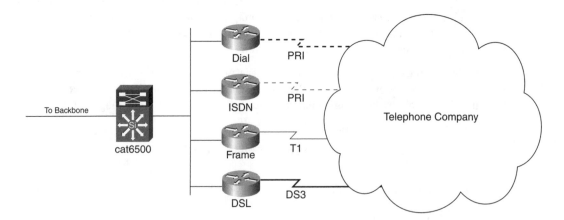

Text Dial-In Network

Text-based dial-in networks are generally for support purposes. Typically, modems are attached to the aux port of a router and set up as a console. If you want to add text-based authentication to PPP dial-in services, go to the section, "PPP Dial-In Network."

The text dial-in design used for remote consoles is relatively simple and the architecture only varies slightly from one implementation to the next. Figure 6-2 shows a modem connected to the aux port of a router. In most cases, this is done using a rolled cable and an RJ45 to DB15 connector. The modem is connected to the telephone company by using a POTS line.

Figure 6-2 *Text Dial-In Network Used as a Remote Console*

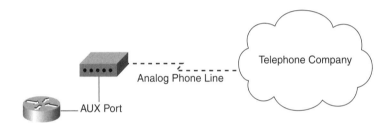

PPP Dial-In Network

PPP dial-in networks can vary significantly from situation to situation; however, the hardware and way it is connected into each network is similar in all cases. Each dial-in router has either a number of async interfaces or group-async interfaces and connects back into the network by an Ethernet or a serial connection. To facilitate centrally managed authentication, an authentication server should also exist on the network. If not, local authentication can be configured on the router, but at the cost of not having the service centrally managed, which can also be difficult to maintain.

Figure 6-3 shows an AS5300, an AS5400, or an AS5800 router configured for PPP dial-in. This router has eight Primary Rate Interfaces (PRIs) to the telephone company (telco), which can take in 23 calls each. These PRIs are connected to the Controller T1 ports of the router. The router processes, authenticates, and routes the traffic back into the corporate network through a Fast Ethernet connection. In Figure 6-3, only one PRI is shown; the other seven are connected in exactly the same way.

Figure 6-3 *PPP Dial-In Network Diagram of an Access Server Connected to the Telephone Company and the Network*

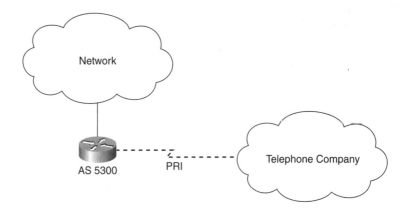

In the case of text-based authentication, the architecture does not change but the configuration changes slightly to allow for text authentication. These configuration changes are noted later in this chapter.

Text Dial-Out Network

Dial-out networks are commonly used for support purposes. They are used in conjunction with routers that are configured for text dial-in as remote consoles, and for access to these routers when their primary links are down. They can also be used as a way to script dial-out for polling pieces of equipment that are attached to modems in any geographic location. This includes using a dial-out system to test the functionality of dial-in servers.

Cisco's Technical Assistance Center (TAC) uses a text-based dial-out service to dial into customer equipment and perform troubleshooting. This is a key resource that the TAC uses and relies upon to do its job daily. This is one way that a TAC can gain access to your equipment.

A text-based dial-out server makes quick connections to modems from a place on the network where an analog line does not exist. The typical user-base of a text-based dial-out server must know modem AT commands, or at least the basic AT commands to dial-out, break, and hang-up.

The network itself is straightforward. You can use the same network as described in the previous section, "PPP Dial-In Network." Figure 6-4 shows an alternate network that you can also use. This figure includes a router with external modems, connected to Async ports through rolled cables, and separate analog lines rather than PRI.

Figure 6-4   *Text Dial-Out Network Using a 2500 Series Router and External Modems*

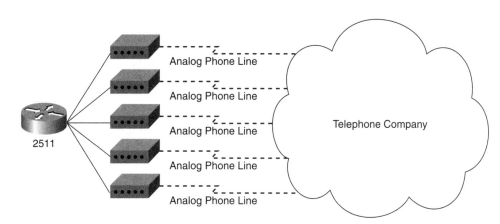

PPP Dial-Out Network

Two types of PPP dial-out solutions exist, depending on the user requirement: on net dial-out using a software client versus off net dial-out using a router.

On Net Dial-Out

The first type of dial-out service involves setting up a text-based dial-out server and using a software client to virtually attach a modem from that server to a PC via a LAN. This type of PPP dial-out uses the same configuration as the text dial-out service mentioned earlier. The only difference is that a user of a PPP dial-out service has a software client installed on their machine that emulates a modem connected to a virtual COM port. This client uses the resources of a dial-out server as a directly connected virtual modem, even for fax use.

No additional configuration lines are required to set up this service, but you must purchase a software client that can do this. The solution is recommended for companies who frequently use PPP dial-out, potentially saving a significant amount of money rather than purchasing separate analog lines for everyone that requires them.

For the current TAC recommended dial-out software, search Cisco.com by using the keyword CiscoDialOut. Consult the software documentation for the recommended IOS version.

Off Net Dial-Out

The second kind of PPP dial-out service connects to an Internet service provider (ISP) using a router as the connecting device. This network design is typical for a home network, when you want more than one PC to access the Internet. It is also similar to a home ISDN design.

The setup consists of a modem hanging off of an async interface or an aux port, which dials into a service provider. On the other side of the router is an Ethernet interface where a home computer is connected. The router most likely takes care of Network Address Translation (NAT) to serve each of the computers behind it. It is also possible to set up routing of a subnet through this connection but only if it is set up by your service provider in advance. Figure 6-5 shows the typical network design for this type of connection.

Figure 6-5   *PPP Dial-Out Design for Off Net*

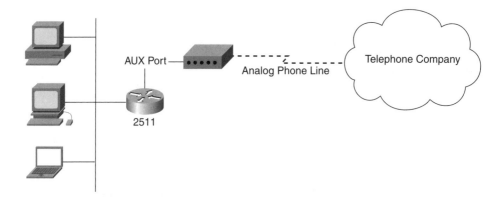

Large-Scale Dial-Out Network

Large-scale dial-out places many calls to multiple locations, mostly for polling purposes. In this scenario, you can do one of two things: include all the phone numbers and locations on the router in the form of dialer maps or place them on a Terminal Access Controller Access Control System (TACACS+) or Remote Authentication Dial-In User Service (RADIUS) server to pass to the dial-out server during the router's boot sequence. Both situations are covered later in this chapter.

Figure 6-6 demonstrates that the network design is identical to the text dial-out network. The only difference is in the configuration. The configuration changes are covered in the section, "Large-Scale Dial-Out Configuration" later in this chapter. In many cases, you can use the same router for both purposes, which saves hardware and circuit costs by sharing the same set of circuits.

Figure 6-6   *Large-Scale Dial-Out Network Using an AS5300 Configured to Place Calls over PRI Circuits*

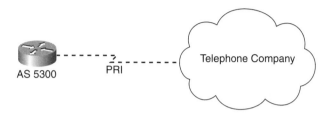

Dial-On-Demand Backup Network

Dial-on demand backup routing is similar to the second form of PPP dial-out covered previously. The section, "PPP Dial-Out Network" did not cover routing, how to bring up the line when a primary circuit fails, and how to tear it down again when the primary circuit comes back up. There are three different ways to configure DDR:

- Using a backup interface
- Using a floating static route
- Using a dialer watch

All three options have advantages and disadvantages. Each option is explained here.

Backup Interface

A backup interface's main advantage is that it is independent of routing protocols, which means that it is not affected by route convergence or stability. The most common use for a backup interface is on a WAN router at a remote site where the only route is a static route back to headquarters. When the primary WAN interface protocol changes its state to down, the backup interface takes over. The router then dials, connects, and passes traffic over the backup.

A backup interface's major downfall is that it is dependent on an interface's physical state or protocol to change the state to down before the backup link is activated. In the case of Frame Relay, the permanent virtual circuit (PVC) can go down while the circuit is still up, and the backup link is not activated. Using a backup interface also requires interesting traffic to bring up a connection. It can also back up only a single interface on a router, which means that, if one site is connected to two locations, you need a backup interface for each main connection, excluding interfaces from other uses.

Floating Static Route

Floating static routes are weighted heavier than the routes that are normally used. It does require a routing protocol, but it does not rely on the physical state or line protocol dropping to trigger a backup connection. For the floating static route to trigger the backup connection, the routing protocol must remove the primary route from the routing table. The speed at which the routing table converges determines how fast the backup connection is triggered. A route showing as possibly down does not trigger the call. Floating static routes still rely on interesting traffic to bring up the line when the primary connection is lost.

A good example of a floating static route is on a WAN router running Enhanced Interior Gateway Routing Protocol (EIGRP). In most cases, the floating static route is a default route. When the primary WAN link goes down, the default route is lost, and the floating static default route sends traffic through the backup connection.

Dialer Watch

Dialer watch provides backup connectivity without relying on interesting traffic. With dialer watch, the router monitors the existence of a specified route, and if that route is not present, it initiates dialing on the backup link. It is more difficult to configure and requires either the EIGRP or Open Shortest Path First (OSPF) routing protocol. The main advantage of this solution is that the router dials immediately when the primary route is lost. Dialer watch does not depend on line protocol, encapsulation type, or interesting traffic. The backup dial link stays active until the primary link comes back up, and can be configured to stay up longer in case of flapping routes. The details required to configure Dialer Watch are covered in a later section of this chapter, "Dial-On-Demand Backup Configuration."

Summary of Each Backup Solution

Table 6-1 summarizes each backup solution.

Table 6-1   *Summary of Each Type of Backup Solution and Relevant Information on Each One*

Factor	Backup Interface	Floating Static Route	Dialer Watch
Determination of when to place the backup call	Dependent on the line protocol status of primary interface and requires that the primary interface go down.	Employs static routes with a higher administrative distance to trigger a dial-on-demand routing (DDR) call.	Watches specific routes in the routing table and initiates a backup link if the route is missing.
Encapsulation	Encapsulation is a factor, for example, a Frame Relay backup might not work correctly with a backup interface.	Encapsulation independent.	Encapsulation independent.

Table 6-1 *Summary of Each Type of Backup Solution and Relevant Information on Each One (Continued)*

Factor	Backup Interface	Floating Static Route	Dialer Watch
Limitations of determining when to place the backup call	Does not consider end-to-end connectivity. Problems with end-to-end connectivity, such as routing errors, do not trigger backup links.	Evaluates the status of primary links based on the existence of routes to the peer. Hence, it considers primary link status based on the ability to pass traffic to the peer.	Evaluates the status of primary links based on the existence of routes to the peer. Hence, it considers primary link status based on the ability to pass traffic to the peer.
Backup triggers	Needs interesting traffic to trigger dialing the backup link.	Needs interesting traffic to trigger dialing the backup link, even after the route to the peer is lost.	Does not rely on interesting packets to trigger dialing. Dialing the backup link is done immediately when the primary route is lost.
Routing protocol dependence	Does not depend on the routing protocol.	Dependent on the routing protocol convergence time.	Dependent on the routing protocol convergence time.
Supported routing protocols	Routing protocol independent.	All routing protocols supported.	EIGRP/OSPF supported.
Interface/router limitations	Limited to one router, one interface.	Typically limited to single router, but with multiple interface/networks.	Supports multiple router backup scenario. For example, one router monitors the link between two other routers and starts the backup if that link fails.
Bandwidth on demand	Can be used to provide bandwidth on demand. The backup interface can be set up to activate when the primary link reaches a specified threshold.	Bandwidth on demand is not possible because the route to the peer exists regardless of the load on the primary link.	Bandwidth on demand is not possible because the route to the peer exists regardless of the load on the primary link.

Dial Configuration Solutions

A dial network can be as small as a single modem on a router or as large as millions of modems across a continent. From modest to grand, the configuration skeleton remains relatively the same. IOS lists the configurations in a standard way because of the hierarchy that is predefined in the system. By no means are you expected to write a configuration the way IOS displays it. In fact, the approach used in this chapter to create dial configurations is a logical approach where the configuration commands are covered in an order that's more direct than the way IOS displays them.

Text Dial-In Configuration

To create a text dial-in configuration, start by creating a fresh configuration in which a modem is connected to the AUX port of a router for remote console purposes. The router needs to be configured to allow text-based authentication. Because you are using a remote console, which means that the authentication servers might not be reachable, you have the choice of using local usernames and passwords, line passwords, or the enable secret as the password. AAA is optional, but because of its flexibility, it's used in the following example. The authentication method name used for the following is console, which allows only the enable secret to log in:

```
3600-wan(config)#aaa authentication login console enable
3600-wan(config)#line aux 0
3600-wan(config-line)#login authentication console
```

Next, add the lines necessary to configure the modem. In this case, a US Robotics Sportster modem is used. You can configure the modem by using the discovery method, using one of the defined modemcaps, or by creating your own modemcap. To see the list of predefined modemcaps, use the command **show modemcap**. The output from the **#show modemcap** command is shown in Example 6-1.

Example 6-1 *Output of the Command* **show modemcap**

```
3600-wan#show modemcap
default
codex_3260
usr_courier
usr_sportster
hayes_optima
global_village
viva
telebit_t3000
microcom_hdms
microcom_server
nec_v34
nec_v110
nec_piafs
cisco_v110
microcom_mimic
mica
```

The **modem autoconfigure** line configuration command performs a series of AT commands that are associated with a modemcap. These are either predefined in IOS or user defined by the **modemcap** global configuration command. The following shows the configuration commands necessary to configure the modem using the predefined modemcap for a US Robotics Sportster modem:

```
3600-wan(config)#line aux 0
3600-wan(config-line)#modem autoconfigure type usr_sportster
```

Finally, the command **modem InOut** sets the line up to allow incoming and outgoing calls. For only outgoing calls, such as setting up a router to dial into an ISP, you use the command

modem host. The following shows this router being set up to answer calls using the line configuration command **modem InOut**:

```
3600-wan(config)#line aux 0
3600-wan(config-line)#modem InOut
```

The display of a full configuration for a remote console through a modem is shown in Example 6-2.

NOTE   Example 6-2 is the full configuration required for the console section only. The rest of the router must still be configured to address your requirements.

Example 6-2 *Text Dial-In Configuration as a Remote Console*

```
3600-wan#show running-config
aaa new-model
aaa authentication login console enable
enable secret 5 $1$VzVJ$B6sbqGo8e2HJDBQ.gxGZp/
!
line aux 0
 login authentication console
 modem InOut
 modem autoconfigure type usr_sportster
 speed 115200
!
end
```

PPP Dial-In Configuration

All PPP dial-in configurations must have a set of the same elements, whether only one or one hundred modems are attached. The first key element is authentication. This can be done locally with a fixed username and password configured on the router or with an authentication, authorization, and accounting (AAA) server. AAA servers can run TACACS+ or RADIUS services for authentication. To apply any aaa configuration, you must first issue the command **aaa new-model**. This instructs the router to user the local username/password if there are no other aaa statements. You can use the following command for general purposes, such as allowing any dial-in authentication:

```
3600-dialin(config)#aaa new-model
3600-dialin(config)#aaa authentication ppp dial group auth
```

The preceding command simply states that the PPP authentication type named dial is to use the authentication servers in the group named auth. To define the group auth as a TACACS+ group, you need to add the following lines:

```
3600-dialin(config)#aaa group server tacacs+ auth
3600-dialin(config-sg-tacacs+)#server 192.168.100.1
3600-dialin(config-sg-tacacs+)#server 192.168.100.2
```

Also, you must specify other characteristics about the TACACS+ servers, such as the port number, key, and timeout, by using the following command structure. For the example, use the default TACACS+ port with a timeout of 18 and a key of 0u812:

```
3600-dialin(config)#tacacs-server host 192.168.100.1 timeout 18 key 0u812
3600-dialin(config)#tacacs-server host 192.168.100.2 timeout 18 key 0u812
```

When using a RADIUS group with a slightly different key, the lines change a bit, as shown in Example 6-3.

Example 6-3 *RADIUS AAA Group Configuration*

```
3600-dialin(config)#aaa group server radius auth
3600-dialin(config-sg-radius)#server 192.168.100.1
3600-dialin(config-sg-radius)#server 192.168.100.2
3600-dialin(config-sg-radius)#exit
3600-dialin(config)#radius-server host 192.168.100.1 timeout 18 key a10u8
3600-dialin(config)#radius-server host 192.168.100.2 timeout 18 key a10u8
```

Review the AAA authentication and determine how it works using RADIUS configuration as the example. The dial authentication type for PPP uses the group called auth. This group contains two RADIUS servers, 192.168.100.1 and 192.168.100.2, both of which have a timeout of 18 seconds and a key of a10u8.

Other authentication requirements can be met by configuring additional features. For example, if you want to put a local username and password on the router for testing purposes, but still use the auth group for all other authentications, you could use the following line. This can be added to the same configuration because its authentication list has a different name. The name for this authentication list is testing, and the previous one is named dial:

```
3600-dialin(config)#aaa authentication ppp testing local group auth
```

Authentication is configured in a particular order. In this case, if the username that tries to pass authentication is not found within the router configuration, the authentication is done by using the group named auth. It is worth mentioning that if a username is set in the router's configuration, the router never passes the authentication for this username to the authentication servers, whether it is correct or incorrect. In other words, after an authentication passes or fails, it never passes through to the next authentication method.

The router determines which named authentication method to use based on what is stated in the interface configuration that is listed later in the full configuration, which is why you can have both the dial and the testing named methods in the same configuration.

All dial-in routers that support PPP must have an Async interface. It is much easier to work with a Group-Async interface in any environment that has multiple modems with the same interface configuration. In either case, the commands are exactly the same. The Group-Async interface applies its subcommands to every Async interface in its group range. The **group-range** command at the end of the list identifies what Async interfaces to apply the subcommands. Example 6-4 shows three separate Async interfaces that are configured the same.

Example 6-4 *Three Async Interfaces Configured for PPP Dial-In*

```
3600-dialin(config)#interface Async1
3600-dialin(config-if)#ip unnumbered Loopback0
3600-dialin(config-if)#encapsulation ppp
3600-dialin(config-if)#async mode dedicated
3600-dialin(config-if)#ppp authentication pap dial
3600-dialin(config-if)#exit
3600-dialin(config)#interface Async2
3600-dialin(config-if)#ip unnumbered Loopback0
3600-dialin(config-if)#encapsulation ppp
3600-dialin(config-if)#async mode dedicated
3600-dialin(config-if)#ppp authentication pap dial
3600-dialin(config-if)#exit
3600-dialin(config)#interface Async3
3600-dialin(config-if)#ip unnumbered Loopback0
3600-dialin(config-if)#encapsulation ppp
3600-dialin(config-if)#async mode dedicated
3600-dialin(config-if)#ppp authentication pap dial
```

The preceding three interfaces were all configured the same way. They could have been easily consolidated into the commands in Example 6-5.

Example 6-5 *Group-Async Interface to Consolidate Individual Async Interfaces*

```
3600-dialin(config)#interface Group-Async1
3600-dialin(config-if)#ip unnumbered Loopback0
3600-dialin(config-if)#encapsulation ppp
3600-dialin(config-if)#async mode dedicated
3600-dialin(config-if)#ppp authentication pap dial
3600-dialin(config-if)#group-range 1 3
```

In both examples, all three Async interfaces use the IP address of Loopback0, use PPP as the encapsulation type, are dedicated to async mode (not interactive), and also authenticate through PPP using the dial named authentication method.

While configuring the Async interfaces, add the lines necessary to configure the modem; this case uses US Robotics Sportster modems as the example. You can configure the lines on which these modems reside by either using the discovery method, the defined modemcaps, or by creating your own modemcap. To see the list of predefined modemcaps in Cisco IOS, use the command **show modemcap**. The following configures this modem with the predefined modemcap built into an IOS named usr sportster:

```
3600-dialin(config)#line 1 3
3600-dialin(config-line)#modem autoconfigure type usr_sportster
```

The following shows the command **modem InOut** being configured to allow incoming modem calls in the same way as it was done in the text dial-in scenario:

```
3600-dialin(config)#line 1 3
3600-dialin(config-line)#modem InOut
```

There are still a few more components to add to this configuration to provide client modems with all the information they require. First, you must provide an IP address from a specified pool:

```
3600-dialin(config)#ip local pool dialpool 192.168.0.250 192.168.0.254
```

The first line specifies the pool named dialpool. It defines an address pool range starting with 192.168.0.250 and ending with 192.168.0.254. For this pool to be used, it must be applied to the Group-Async interface using the following commands:

```
3600-dialin(config)#interface Group-Async1
3600-dialin(config-if)#peer default ip address pool dialpool
```

After it is applied to the interface, the client modems can get an IP address from the range specified. Because the interface Loopback0 still does not have an IP address, however, the client modems do not have a default gateway that works. Therefore, you must assign an IP address for that interface using the following commands:

```
3600-dialin(config)#interface Loopback0
3600-dialin(config-if)#ip address 192.168.0.249 255.255.255.248
```

The interface for Loopback0 is given the first address in the subnet. This address is not contained within the dialpool address pool, but is still within the same subnet. By not including it in the pool, you ensure that the IP is not inadvertently given to a host, thus causing a conflict.

Now, the connecting modems can now get an IP address, but some services still need to be configured. The connecting clients now require Domain Name System (DNS) and Windows Internet Naming Service (WINS) server information, and default gateway and subnet mask information:

```
3600-dialin(config)#async-bootp dns-server 192.168.100.3 192.168.100.4
3600-dialin(config)#async-bootp nbns-server 192.168.100.5 192.168.100.6
3600-dialin(config)#async-bootp gateway 192.168.0.249
3600-dialin(config)#async-bootp subnet-mask 255.255.255.248
```

The connecting modem has all the information that it needs to connect and route, and to use DNS and WINS services. Now, you must configure this dial-in router to route all traffic to the backbone. In most cases, you use a routing protocol that handles this issue for you; however, because this is a single-homed router, static routing is preferred.

On the dial-in core router, the Ethernet0/0 interface shown in these examples connects to the backbone and uses IP address 192.168.0.246/30. Your connection will use different IP addresses. You must add a default route to the device on the other side, which in this example uses the IP address 192.168.0.245:

```
3600-dialin(config)#interface Ethernet0/0
3600-dialin(config-if)#ip address 192.168.0.246 255.255.255.252
3600-dialin(config-if)#exit
3600-dialin(config)#ip route 0.0.0.0 0.0.0.0 192.168.0.245
```

Finally, issue the command **show ip interface brief** to ensure that all the interfaces on the router are not in shutdown state. If they are, you must issue the **no shutdown** command on each interface. Example 6-6 shows the output from this command. You'll notice that all the individual Async interfaces exist in the output, even though their configuration is consolidated under the Group-Async1 interface. These interfaces remain in a down/down state until they are connected.

Example 6-6   *Output from the PPP Dial-In Command* **show ip interface brief**

```
3600-dialin#show ip interface brief
Interface     IP-Address     OK?   Method   Status   Protocol
Ethernet0/0   192.168.0.246  YES   manual   up       up
Async1        192.168.0.249  YES   NVRAM    down     down
Async2        192.168.0.249  YES   NVRAM    down     down
Async3        192.168.0.249  YES   NVRAM    down     down
Group-Async1  192.168.0.249  YES   unset    down     down
Loopback0     192.168.0.249  YES   manual   up       up
```

The basic PPP dial-in configuration is now complete and Example 6-7 is the output of the full configuration.

Example 6-7   *PPP Dial-In Configuration*

```
3600-dialin#show running-config
version 12.2
service timestamps debug uptime
service timestamps log uptime
no service password-encryption
!
hostname 3600-dialin
!
boot system flash
aaa new-model
!
! The authentication type is specified here:
aaa group server radius auth
 server 192.168.100.1 auth-port 1645 acct-port 1646
 server 192.168.100.2 auth-port 1645 acct-port 1646
!
aaa authentication ppp dial group auth
aaa authentication ppp testing local group auth
aaa session-id common
!
ip subnet-zero
!
async-bootp subnet-mask 255.255.255.248
async-bootp gateway 192.168.0.249
async-bootp dns-server 192.168.100.3 192.168.100.4
async-bootp nbns-server 192.168.100.5 192.168.100.6
```

continues

Example 6-7 *PPP Dial-In Configuration (Continued)*

```
!
! Begin interface configurations:
interface Loopback0
 ip address 192.168.0.249 255.255.255.248
!
interface Ethernet0/0
 ip address 192.168.0.246 255.255.255.252
!
! Notice that Async Group requires only one configuration section.
! These configurations apply to all Async interfaces, members of the group.
interface Group-Async1
 ip unnumbered Loopback0
 encapsulation ppp
 async mode dedicated
 peer default ip address pool dialpool
 ppp authentication pap dial
 group-range 1 3
!
ip local pool dialpool 192.168.0.250 192.168.0.254
ip classless
ip route 0.0.0.0 0.0.0.0 192.168.0.245
!
! Authentication server specifications:

radius-server host 192.168.100.1 auth-port 1645 acct-port 1646 timeout 18 key a10u8
radius-server host 192.168.100.2 auth-port 1645 acct-port 1646 timeout 18 key a10u8
radius-server retransmit 3
!
line con 0
 exec-timeout 0 0
line 1 3
 modem InOut
 modem autoconfigure type usr_sportster
 speed 115200
line aux 0
line vty 0 4
!
end
```

You can also use text authentication in conjunction with standard dial-in services to allow for modem scripts, and with any client that uses after-dial terminal windows for authentication. For the following example, the configuration from Example 6-7 on PPP dial-in services is used as the base configuration for text-based authentication; all subsequent commands are added to it.

To enable an interactive text session, you must configure the Async interface to allow interactive use. To do this, use the command **async mode interactive**. Again, you can use the configuration created in the last example as a base configuration:

```
3600-dialin(config)#interface group-async1
3600-dialin(config-if)#async mode interactive
```

The preceding commands enable a connecting modem to connect directly to the VTY line instead of the Async interface. Now, you must configure authentication and the lines associated with the Async interfaces that were just made interactive. First, set the same authentication for the line as previously set for PPP. You must also include the testing line in the event that you want to test or connect using a local username and password in the future:

```
3600-dialin(config)#aaa authentication login dial group auth
3600-dialin(config)#aaa authentication login testing local group auth
```

Here's an important step that's often forgotten: If you authenticated already via text, you do not want to force authentication in PPP as well. The **if-needed** parameter tells the router to only authenticate via PPP, as long as the user has not been authenticated by another method already. If configuring this feature, these commands replace the previous ones:

```
3600-dialin(config)#aaa authentication ppp dial if-needed group auth
3600-dialin(config)#aaa authentication ppp testing if-needed local group auth
```

Then, apply the authentication method to the VTY lines by using the following command:

```
3600-dialin(config)#line 1 3
3600-dialin(config-line)#login authentication dial
```

Next, you must configure the lines to accept a dial-in call. Because the preceding **async mode interactive** command sends the call to the line first, the line must be configured to automatically determine if the client is using PPP or text authentication.

The following lines determine what automatic selection criteria you want the router to use:

```
3600-dialin(config)#line 1 3
3600-dialin(config-line)#autoselect during-login
3600-dialin(config-line)#autoselect ppp
```

First, **autoselect during login** tells the router to do the automatic selection at the username and password prompt. Then, **autoselect ppp** tells the router to check for PPP when it performs the automatic selection. You can also configure it to do automatic selection of Serial Line Internet Protocol (SLIP) and AppleTalk Remote Access Protocol (ARAP) with the commands **autoselect slip** and **autoselect arap** respectively.

To prompt for username and password from the line, the router must allow an exec session by configuring the command **exec** on the line:

```
3600-dialin(config)#line 1 3
3600-dialin(config-line)#exec
```

The added **exec** command starts an exec process, or enables you to have access to a router prompt. The prompt issued after authentication is not an enable prompt, but a user can enable it by entering the enable secret. For security purposes, an ISP uses a command that automatically executes after the user logs in, so that the user does not have access to a router prompt. In most cases, the command you want to automatically execute is **ppp default**, which starts a PPP session. To automatically execute this command, you need to select the preferred lines and configure the **autocommand ppp default** command:

```
3600-dialin(config)#line 1 3
3600-dialin(config-line)#autocommand ppp default
```

The new router configuration is shown in Example 6-8. This configuration allows dial-in using either PPP or text authentication.

Example 6-8 *Text and PPP Dial-In Configuration*

```
version 12.2
service timestamps debug uptime
service timestamps log uptime
no service password-encryption
!
hostname 3600-dialin
!
boot system flash
aaa new-model
!
! RADIUS authentication and server specifications
aaa group server radius auth
 server 192.168.100.1 auth-port 1645 acct-port 1646
 server 192.168.100.2 auth-port 1645 acct-port 1646
!
! Local group access configuration:
aaa authentication login dial group auth
aaa authentication login testing local-case group auth
aaa authentication ppp dial if-needed group auth
aaa authentication ppp testing if-needed local-case group auth
aaa session-id common
!
ip subnet-zero
!
async-bootp subnet-mask 255.255.255.248
async-bootp gateway 192.168.0.249
async-bootp dns-server 192.168.100.3 192.168.100.4
async-bootp nbns-server 192.168.100.5 192.168.100.6
!
interface Loopback0
 ip address 192.168.0.249 255.255.255.248
!
interface Ethernet0/0
 ip address 192.168.0.246 255.255.255.252
!
interface Group-Async1
 ip unnumbered Loopback0
 encapsulation ppp
 async mode interactive
 peer default ip address pool dialpool
 ppp authentication pap dial
 group-range 1 3
!
ip local pool dialpool 192.168.0.250 192.168.0.254
ip classless
ip route 0.0.0.0 0.0.0.0 192.168.0.245
!
radius-server host 192.168.100.1 auth-port 1645 acct-port 1646 timeout 18 key a10u8
```

Example 6-8 *Text and PPP Dial-In Configuration (Continued)*

```
radius-server host 192.168.100.2 auth-port 1645 acct-port 1646 timeout 18 key a10u8
radius-server retransmit 3
!
line con 0
 exec-timeout 0 0
! Line configuration to allow dial group login:
line 1 3
 login authentication dial
 modem InOut
 modem autoconfigure type usr_sportster
 autocommand  ppp default
 autoselect during-login
 autoselect ppp
 speed 115200
line aux 0
line vty 0 4
!
end
```

Large-Scale Dial-In Configuration

A large-scale dial-in configuration does not significantly differ from a regular dial-in configuration. In most cases, it just requires that you use an access server, which provides extended capacity versus any router with a few async ports.

To configure an access server such as an AS5300 or AS5400, use the same PPP or text and PPP dial-in configuration as covered in the previous section. The group range of the group-async interface must increase to include all modems in the router. The IP pool set aside for dial-in users must be increased to handle the number of digital service 0s (DS0s) terminating on the device. Also, the automatic configuration of the modem must be set to the type of modem in the server.

There is also additional configuration information that must be added for large-scale dial-in servers. The phone lines no longer attach directly to the modems; instead, a PRI circuit carries the calls from the central office (CO) to your equipment. Because of this design, the first thing to configure is the PRI. There are two sections to configure: the controller and the serial interface. Example 6-9 shows a sample T1 controller configuration.

Example 6-9 *Controller T1 Configuration*

```
5300-dialin(config)#controller T1 0
5300-dialin(config-controller)#framing esf
5300-dialin(config-controller)#linecode b8zs
5300-dialin(config-controller)#pri-group timeslots 1-24
5300-dialin(config-controller)#no shutdown
```

To begin with, the controller must be configured according to the way that the circuit was provisioned. In most cases where the circuit is a PRI, the framing is Extended Superframe (ESF), and the linecode is bipolar 8-zero substitution (B8ZS). After framing and linecode are configured, you must specify what time slots are to be used. Generally, all time slots are used for PRI DS0s, and they are configured as stated previously. Finally, you can bring the controller up.

Non-Facility-Associated Signaling (NFAS) allows a single D channel to control multiple PRI interfaces. Allowing multiple PRIs to use a single D channel permits the use of an extra DS0 per PRI member of an NFAS group. Also, a backup D channel can be configured for use when the primary NFAS D channel fails. All NFAS members of a group must terminate on the same dial router. To configure NFAS, you must know the circuit with the primary D channel, the circuit with the backup D channel (if there is one), and all NFAS members in order.

The easiest way to configure NFAS is to plug the circuits into the router in order. For example, if you have four circuits in an NFAS group with the primary D channel plugged into controller T1 4, you plug the circuit with the backup D channel into T1 5, and the following two into T1 6 and T1 7, in the order that they are configured from the telco. The controller configuration for this example is shown in Example 6-10.

Example 6-10 *Controller Configuration for NFAS Circuits*

```
5300-dialin(config)#controller T1 4
5300-dialin(config-controller)#framing esf
5300-dialin(config-controller)#linecode b8zs
5300-dialin(config-controller)#pri-group timeslots 1-24 nfas_d primary nfas_int
    0 nfas_group 0
5300-dialin(config-controller)#exit
5300-dialin(config)#controller T1 5
5300-dialin(config-controller)#framing esf
5300-dialin(config-controller)#linecode b8zs
5300-dialin(config-controller)#pri-group timeslots 1-24 nfas_d backup nfas_int
    1 nfas_group 0
5300-dialin(config-controller)#exit
5300-dialin(config)#controller T1 6
5300-dialin(config-controller)#framing esf
5300-dialin(config-controller)#linecode b8zs
5300-dialin(config-controller)#pri-group timeslots 1-24 nfas_d none nfas_int
    2 nfas_group 0
5300-dialin(config-controller)#exit
5300-dialin(config)#controller T1 7
5300-dialin(config-controller)#framing esf
5300-dialin(config-controller)#linecode b8zs
5300-dialin(config-controller)#pri-group timeslots 1-24 nfas_d none nfas_int
    3 nfas_group 0
```

You can have up to 37 different NFAS groups on the same router. Each PRI within each group must have a unique interface number, starting with zero and increasing by one for each PRI in the group. A maximum of 20 PRIs can exist in an NFAS group. D channels are marked as primary, backup, or none.

NOTE   The NFAS considerations shown for a dial environment are fully applicable to the NFAS configuration and utilization rules as in an ISDN environment.

Each PRI and each NFAS group has a serial interface that corresponds to it and that needs to be configured. The serial interface number is the same as the controller number of the circuit with the D channel, with a :23 appended to the end of it. This is done because the D channel on a PRI is the 24th channel, starting with channel number 0—refer to Figure 2-9 in Chapter 2. In the case of an NFAS group, the only serial interface that exists is the one with the D channel. The serial interface for the previously configured NFAS group is shown here:

```
5300-dialin(config)#interface Serial0:23
5300-dialin(config-if)#isdn switch-type primary-4ess
5300-dialin(config-if)#isdn incoming-voice modem
5300-dialin(config-if)#no shutdown
```

The serial interface contains a few components that must be set:

- The first component to be configured is the switch type, which needs to match what the telephone company configured on their side of the circuit.

- Next, the command **isdn incoming-voice modem** is crucial, as it tells the router that any voice call (non-ISDN) must be sent to a modem.

- Finally, you must bring the interface up with the **no shutdown** command. The NFAS group is configured the same way:

```
5300-dialin(config)#interface Serial4:23
5300-dialin(config-if)#isdn switch-type primary-4ess
5300-dialin(config-if)#isdn incoming-voice modem
5300-dialin(config-if)#no shutdown
```

That completes the configuration for a large-scale dial-in service. Example 6-11 shows the full configuration, including four PRI and one NFAS group that contains four circuits.

Example 6-11 *Large-Scale Dial-In Configuration*

```
version 12.2
service timestamps debug uptime
service timestamps log uptime
no service password-encryption
!
hostname 5300-dialin
!
boot system flash
aaa new-model
!
```

continues

Example 6-11 *Large-Scale Dial-In Configuration (Continued)*

```
aaa group server radius auth
 server 192.168.100.1 auth-port 1645 acct-port 1646
 server 192.168.100.2 auth-port 1645 acct-port 1646
!
aaa authentication login dial group auth
aaa authentication login testing local-case group auth
aaa authentication ppp dial if-needed group auth
aaa authentication ppp testing if-needed local-case group auth
aaa session-id common
!
ip subnet-zero
!
async-bootp subnet-mask 255.255.255.0
async-bootp gateway 192.168.1.1
async-bootp dns-server 192.168.100.3 192.168.100.4
async-bootp nbns-server 192.168.100.5 192.168.100.6
!
! Begin controller configurations:
controller T1 0
 framing esf
 clock source line primary
 linecode b8zs
 pri-group timeslots 1-24
!
controller T1 1
 framing esf
 clock source line secondary
 linecode b8zs
 pri-group timeslots 1-24
!
controller T1 2
 framing esf
 linecode b8zs
 pri-group timeslots 1-24
!
controller T1 3
 framing esf
 linecode b8zs
 pri-group timeslots 1-24
!
! NFAS configuration with primary and backup interfaces specified respectively:
controller T1 4
 framing esf
 linecode b8zs
 pri-group timeslots 1-24 nfas_d primary nfas_int 0 nfas_group 0
!
controller T1 5
 framing esf
 clock source line primary
 linecode b8zs
 pri-group timeslots 1-24 nfas_d backup nfas_int 1 nfas_group 0
!
```

Example 6-11 *Large-Scale Dial-In Configuration (Continued)*

```
controller T1 6
 framing esf
 clock source line primary
 linecode b8zs
 pri-group timeslots 1-24 nfas_d none nfas_int 2 nfas_group 0
!
controller T1 7
 framing esf
 clock source line primary
 linecode b8zs
 pri-group timeslots 1-24 nfas_d none nfas_int 3 nfas_group 0
!
interface Loopback0
 ip address 192.168.1.1 255.255.255.0
!
interface Ethernet0/0
 ip address 192.168.0.246 255.255.255.252
!
interface Serial0:23
 no ip address
 isdn switch-type primary-4ess
 isdn incoming-voice modem
!
interface Serial1:23
 no ip address
 isdn switch-type primary-4ess
 isdn incoming-voice modem
!
interface Serial2:23
 no ip address
 isdn switch-type primary-4ess
 isdn incoming-voice modem
!
interface Serial3:23
 no ip address
 isdn switch-type primary-4ess
 isdn incoming-voice modem
!
! The D-channel of this T1 is configured as a primary D-channel.
! When this channel goes down, the T1 #5, which is configured as a
! backup D-channel, inherits this configuration.

interface Serial4:23
 no ip address
 isdn switch-type primary-4ess
 isdn incoming-voice modem
!
! Serial 5:23, 6:23 and 7:23 interfaces don't need to be configured, because
! T1 5, T1 6 and T1 7 belong to the NFAS group.
interface Group-Async1
 ip unnumbered Loopback0
```

continues

Example 6-11 *Large-Scale Dial-In Configuration (Continued)*

```
 encapsulation ppp
 async mode interactive
 peer default ip address pool dialpool
 ppp authentication pap dial
 group-range 1 240
 !
ip local pool dialpool 192.168.1.2 192.168.1.254
ip classless
ip route 0.0.0.0 0.0.0.0 192.168.0.245
 !
radius-server host 192.168.100.1 auth-port 1645 acct-port 1646 timeout 18 key a10u8
radius-server host 192.168.100.2 auth-port 1645 acct-port 1646 timeout 18 key a10u8
radius-server retransmit 3
 !
line con 0
 exec-timeout 0 0
line 1 240
 login authentication dial
 modem InOut
 modem autoconfigure type mica
 autocommand  ppp default
 autoselect during-login
 autoselect ppp
 speed 115200
line aux 0
line vty 0 4
 !
end
```

Text Dial-Out Configuration

For a text dial-out service, you must first make a decision on whether to use local authentication on the router or to use an authentication server. These users do not call into the modems, so security is probably not as much of a concern as a dial-in pool. In the case of dial-out, the user connects through text on a VTY port, which means that the type of authentication is login.

A small fictitious insurance company is used as the example. The company has eight WAN sites, all on dedicated links, and there is no backup implemented because of costs. The routers at each of the WAN sites have modems attached to the AUX ports, and an analog line attached to the modem, so that in the case of any site going down, support personnel can log into the WAN router to troubleshoot the connection from both ends. There are only four headcounts to support the network, so they choose to use local authentication on the router. For a larger company, this could easily be changed to allow for an authentication server.

The configuration lines in Example 6-12 specify the authentication component. The name given to the authentication type is dialout, and it uses local passwords. Usernames and passwords are also configured.

Example 6-12 *Local Authentication Configuration*

```
3600-dialout(config)#aaa new-model
3600-dialout(config)#aaa authentication login dialout local
3600-dialout(config)#username jbrown password james
3600-dialout(config)#username jbob password joe
3600-dialout(config)#username ksmith password keith
3600-dialout(config)#username wclark password will
```

Because of the size of the company, the dial numbers are in the incoming banner to make it easy for anyone to place a call to a site that is down. Therefore, when a support person logs in, that person has all the numbers for the WAN sites listed. They assume that no more than one or two sites would ever be down at once, so they planned the dial-out server to handle three outbound connections at once, thus placing three modems in the dial-out rotary (in this case, lines 1-2).

The configuration lines in Example 6-13 provide the authentication for the three dial-out lines. Also, the banner is put in place listing the office console phone numbers.

Example 6-13 *Authentication and Banner Configuration*

```
3600-dialout(config)#line 1 3
3600-dialout(config-line)#login authentication dialout
3600-dialout(config-line)#exit
3600-dialout(config)#Banner incoming ^
Enter TEXT message.  End with the character '^'.
    Site                    Router Console Number
    ---------------------   ----------------------------
    Dallas Office           231-444-8282
    Oakland Office          415-663-9012
    Las Vegas Office        772-404-9923
    Minneapolis Office      416-223-9245
    St. Louis Office        314-677-4378
    Chicago Office          294-229-3943
    New York Office         723-655-8966
    Atlanta Office          404-339-6774

Use modem AT commands to dial-out.
^
```

Next, configure the modem lines for a typical dial-out setup. In this case, the requirement is for databits set to 8, stopbits set to 1, and parity set to none. Also, set up the lines in rotary group number one, and set the input to be telnet, which sets the router up to allow a reverse telnet directly onto the modem. Finally, turn off exec, which does not allow a router prompt to anyone who tries to dial into this server. Example 6-14 shows dial-out modem configuration commands for a typical text dial-out router.

Example 6-14 *Text Dial-Out Line Configuration*

```
3600-dialout(config)#line 1 3
3600-dialout(config-line)#databits 8
3600-dialout(config-line)#parity none
3600-dialout(config-line)#stopbits 1
3600-dialout(config-line)#modem host
3600-dialout(config-line)#rotary 1
3600-dialout(config-line)#transport input telnet
3600-dialout(config-line)#no exec
```

Then, you must give the router an IP address and put it on the network:

```
3600-dialout(config)#interface Ethernet0/0
3600-dialout(config-if)#ip address 192.168.0.10 255.255.255.248
```

Use another IP address on the Ethernet segment to create an alias to the rotary group, by using the following command:

```
3600-dialout(config)#ip alias 192.168.0.11 3001
```

Telnet to the Ethernet address on port 3001 and connect to the first available modem in rotary group 1. This command allows direct telnet to 192.168.0.11 by using the default port (23), and it connects as if they telnet to port 3001 on the Ethernet address. Port 3002 lands on rotary group number two, which is not configured.

Example 6-15 shows the final configuration used for this small company to access their WAN routers in the event that the WAN links are down.

Example 6-15 *Text Dial-Out Configuration*

```
version 12.2
service timestamps debug datetime msec
service timestamps log uptime
service password-encryption
!
hostname 3600-dialout
!
aaa new-model
!
!
aaa authentication login dialout local
aaa session-id common
enable secret 5 $1$VzVJ$B6sbqGo8e2HJDBQ.gxGZp/
!
! Local username and password files for local login as specified by
! aaa authentication login dialout local configuration command.
username jbrown password 7 000E120B0148
username jbob password 7 020C0B5E
username ksmith password 7 050003063544
username wclark password 7 02110D5707
!
ip subnet-zero
```

Example 6-15 *Text Dial-Out Configuration (Continued)*

```
!
interface Ethernet0/0
 ip address 192.168.0.10 255.255.255.248
!
ip classless
ip route 0.0.0.0 0.0.0.0 Ethernet0/0 192.168.0.9
ip alias 192.168.0.11 3001
no ip http server
!
banner incoming ^
    Site                       Router Console Number
    ----------------------     ----------------------------
    Dallas Office              231-444-8282
    Oakland Office             415-663-9012
    Las Vegas Office           772-404-9923
    Minneapolis Office         416-223-9245
    St. Louis Office           314-677-4378
    Chicago Office             294-229-3943
    New York Office            723-655-8966
    Atlanta Office             404-339-6774

Use modem AT commands to dial-out.
^
!
line con 0
line 1 3
 no exec
 login authentication dialout
 modem autoconfigure type nextport
 rotary 1
 transport input telnet
 stopbits 1
 speed 115200
line aux 0
line vty 0 4
!
end
```

Now that the router is configured, it must be tested. If you do not see characters appearing when you type AT and press Enter, but you do see OK being returned, the modem is not echoing local commands, but all else works correctly. Consult the owner's manual for the modem to turn this feature on. Example 6-16 shows the dial-out test being performed. In the example, a call is placed to the WAN router in Atlanta.

Example 6-16 *Text Dial-Out Test to Verify Functionality*

```
Trying 192.168.0.11 ... Open

User Access Verification
```

continues

Example 6-16 *Text Dial-Out Test to Verify Functionality (Continued)*

```
Username: jbrown
Password:

    Site                        Router Console Number
    ----------------------      ----------------------------
    Dallas Office               231-444-8282
    Oakland Office              415-663-9012
    Las Vegas Office            772-404-9923
    Minneapolis Office          416-223-9245
    St. Louis Office            314-677-4378
    Chicago Office              294-229-3943
    New York Office             723-655-8966
    Atlanta Office              404-339-6774

Use modem AT commands to dial-out.
at
OK
atdt14043396774
CONNECT 26400/REL

atlanta-wan line 65

User Access Verification

Username: jbrown
Password:

atlanta-wan>exit
NO CARRIER
```

The call was placed when user jbrown typed atdt14043396774. It was successfully answered when the modem echoed CONNECT 26400/REL. At that point, the atlanta-wan router asked for authentication. User jbrown logged in and everything worked as planned.

PPP Dial-Out Configuration

The following PPP dial-out configuration section refers to the second type of PPP dial-out mentioned earlier in this chapter, where the router dials into a service provider to gain access to the LAN behind the router.

First, a fixed password is required for this type of configuration, and you must gather a few pieces of information about your service provider. Dialup the provider with a PC and gather the DNS server addresses, the WINS server addresses (if any), and the domain name assigned to you.

Unless you previously arranged to route a network to the service provider, you must use NAT on the router to provide all the computers on your LAN access to the Internet. This example uses NAT and the modem is an external US Robotics Sportster that is attached to the AUX port of a router. Start by assigning an RFC 1918 subnet to your local network. Give an IP address from this network to the Ethernet interface, and set up Dynamic Host Configuration Protocol (DHCP) for the client computers as shown in Example 6-17.

Example 6-17 *Configuration of DHCP on a Local LAN Segment*

```
2500-dialout(config)#interface Ethernet 0/0
2500-dialout(config-if)#ip address 192.168.1.1 255.255.255.0
2500-dialout(config-if)#no shutdown
2500-dialout(config-if)#ip dhcp pool pool1
2500-dialout(dhcp-config)#network 192.168.1.0 255.255.255.0
2500-dialout(dhcp-config)#default-router 192.168.1.1
2500-dialout(dhcp-config)#dns-server 207.217.126.41 207.217.77.42
2500-dialout(dhcp-config)#domain-name earthlink.net
```

In this case, no WINS servers are configured because the ISP does not offer these services. If they had assigned WINS servers, you would use the DHCP configuration command **netbios-name-server** *ip_address_1 ip_address_2* to configure them on your router.

The next action is to put the service provider information into the async interface. The phone number to dial, along with a username and password, is also required. In this example, the router dials up to a typical service provider where the IP address is supplied. The interface is set up to be in dialer-group 1. Also, a dialer hold-queue is added to queue packets in case the modem speedshifts, retrains, or needs to completely reconnect. Example 6-18 shows the configuration lines needed to dial into the provider's network.

Example 6-18 *Async Interface Configuration for PPP Dial-Out Access*

```
2500-dialout(config)#interface async65
2500-dialout(config-if)#ip address negotiated
2500-dialout(config-if)#dialer in-band
2500-dialout(config-if)#dialer string 6222230
2500-dialout(config-if)#encapsulation ppp
2500-dialout(config-if)#ppp pap sent-username jhuegen password test
2500-dialout(config-if)#dialer-group 1
2500-dialout(config-if)#dialer hold-queue 100
```

Configure the line for dial-out and set up the modem through the **autoconfigure** command. Additionally, you might include the **no exec** command for security reasons. This prevents someone from connecting if they try to dial into the router:

```
2500-dialout(config)#line aux 0
2500-dialout(config-line)#modem autoconfigure type usr_sportster
2500-dialout(config-line)#modem InOut
2500-dialout(config-line)#no exec
```

Next, configure NAT so that traffic on the Ethernet interface translates to the IP address negotiated for the async interface:

```
2500-dialout(config)#access-list 1 permit 192.168.1.0 0.0.0.31
2500-dialout(config)#ip nat inside source list 1 interface asy65 overload
```

Then, assign NAT as either inside or outside to all configured interfaces, and configure a default route to the service provider, as shown in Example 6-19.

Example 6-19 *NAT Inside, NAT Outside, and Default Route Configuration Commands*

```
2500-dialout(config)#interface async65
2500-dialout(config-if)#ip nat outside
2500-dialout(config-if)#exit
2500-dialout(config)#interface ethernet0/0
2500-dialout(config-if)#ip nat inside
2500-dialout(config-if)#exit
2500-dialout(config)#ip route 0.0.0.0 0.0.0.0 async65
```

Finally, identify on the router what traffic to mark as interesting, which limits the traffic allowed to bring up the line. In this example, all IP traffic is identified as interesting. You can use an access control list (ACL) to only allow certain types of traffic with the command **dialer-list 1 protocol ip list** *access-list-number*:

```
2500-dialout(config-if)#dialer-list 1 protocol ip permit
```

This completes the configuration for PPP dial-out to a service provider. The full configuration is shown in Example 6-20.

Example 6-20 *PPP Dial-Out Configuration for Connecting to a Service Provider*

```
version 12.2
service timestamps debug datetime msec
service timestamps log uptime
service password-encryption
!
hostname 2500-dialout
!
boot system flash
!
enable secret 5 $1$VzVJ$B6sbqGo8e2HJDBQ.gxGZp/
!
ip subnet-zero
!
! local DHCP service configuration parameters:
ip dhcp pool pool1
   network 192.168.1.0 255.255.255.0
   default-router 192.168.1.1
   dns-server 207.217.126.41 207.217.77.42
   netbios-name-server 207.217.126.42 207.217.77.43
   domain-name earthlink.net
!
```

Example 6-20 *PPP Dial-Out Configuration for Connecting to a Service Provider (Continued)*

```
interface Ethernet0/0
 ip address 192.168.1.1 255.255.255.0
 ip nat inside
!
interface Async65
 ip address negotiated
 ip nat outside
 encapsulation ppp
 dialer in-band
 dialer string 6222230
 dialer hold-queue 100
 dialer-group 1
 ppp pap sent-username jhuegen password 7 044F0E151B
!
! NAT configuration with default route identified:

ip nat inside source list 1 interface Async65 overload
ip classless
ip route 0.0.0.0 0.0.0.0 Async65
!
! Access list configured to allow traffic to/from your Ethernet interface:

access-list 1 permit 192.168.1.0 0.0.0.31
dialer-list 1 protocol ip permit
!
line con 0
line aux 0
 no exec
 modem InOut
 modem autoconfigure type usr_sportster
line vty 0 4
!
end
```

Large-Scale Dial-Out Configuration

Two types of large-scale dial-out configurations exist. The first uses static dialer maps put into a dialer interface, where they exist within the router configuration. The second type uses the AAA system for storing the dialer maps.

In the first example that follows, static dialer maps dial out to each individual client. The number of configurable clients is limited by the size of the configuration. After the configuration is full, no more clients can be added. Although this limitation exists, it is still the easiest way to prepare for large-scale dial-out.

Example 6-21 shows a sample Group-Async interface configuration with dialer maps for large-scale dial-out.

Example 6-21 *Large-Scale Dial-Out Interface Configuration with Dialer Map Statements*

```
5300-dialout(config)#interface Group-Async1
5300-dialout(config-if)#ip address 64.221.12.1
5300-dialout(config-if)#encapsulation ppp
5300-dialout(config-if)#dialer in-band
5300-dialout(config-if)#dialer idle-timeout 30
5300-dialout(config-if)#dialer map ip 64.221.12.2 name ID127361 16632047789
5300-dialout(config-if)#dialer map ip 64.221.12.3 name ID127364 17366224431
5300-dialout(config-if)#dialer map ip 64.221.12.4 name ID127365 12232718341
5300-dialout(config-if)#dialer map ip 64.221.12.5 name ID127367 12812123434
<output omitted>
5300-dialout(config-if)#dialer map ip 64.221.12.253 name ID196458 14732812238
5300-dialout(config-if)#dialer map ip 64.221.12.254 name ID196459 15123848161
5300-dialout(config-if)#dialer hold-queue 100
5300-dialout(config-if)#dialer-group 1
```

As you can see, this can take up much space in the configuration. There is also a manageability issue with removing old customers and adding new ones because it is a manual and time-consuming process. Unfortunately, there's no easy way to keep a configuration like this up to date.

This limitation is where a AAA large-scale dial-out setup is an alternative because AAA is already in a database format. Therefore, you can add information to this database that can be used for other purposes, such as billing and running reports against active and non-active customers.

To set up a large scale dial-out in this manner, the AAA database must be populated with the phone numbers and IP addresses of the remote hosts. The router must be set up for either TACACS+ or RADIUS authentication. TACACS+ is used in the following example:

```
5300-dialout(config)#aaa new-model
5300-dialout(config)#aaa authentication ppp default group tacacs+
5300-dialout(config)#aaa authorization network default group tacacs+
5300-dialout(config)#aaa authorization configuration default group tacacs+
```

The Group-Async interface is configured as in the earlier example; however, instead of the dialer map statements, you use the command **dialer aaa**. Example 6-22 shows the configuration of the Group-Async interface using AAA for large-scale dial-out.

Example 6-22 *Group-Async Interface Using AAA for Large-Scale Dial-Out*

```
5300-dialout(config)#interface Group-Async1
5300-dialout(config-if)#ip address 64.221.12.1
5300-dialout(config-if)#encapsulation ppp
5300-dialout(config-if)#dialer in-band
5300-dialout(config-if)#dialer idle-timeout 30
5300-dialout(config-if)#dialer aaa
5300-dialout(config-if)#dialer hold-queue 100
5300-dialout(config-if)#dialer-group 1
```

Finally, use the following command to download all the routes from the AAA server. In the example, it's set to update the downloaded table every 60 minutes; however, you might opt for a different frequency (remember that the size of the table can make this an intensive process):

```
5300-dialout(config)#aaa route download 60
```

To verify that everything works correctly, turn on terminal monitoring. A temporary debug comes up with the important information about this particular call. Example 6-23 shows the temporary debug. If this does not happen, turn on other AAA debugs to determine the problem.

Example 6-23 *Large-Scale Dial-Out Temporary Debug*

```
5300-dialout#ping 64.221.12.253

Type escape sequence to abort.
Sending 5, 100-byte ICMP Echos to 64.221.12.253, timeout is 2 seconds:
Mar  9 03:59:35.173: %LSdialout: temporary debug to verify the data integrity
Mar  9 03:59:35.177:     dial number = 14732812238
Mar  9 03:59:35.177:     dialnum_count = 1
Mar  9 03:59:35.177:     force_56 = 0
Mar  9 03:59:35.181:     routing = 0
Mar  9 03:59:35.181:     data_svc = -1
Mar  9 03:59:35.181:     port_type = -1
Mar  9 03:59:35.185:     map_class =
Mar  9 03:59:35.185:     ip_address = 64.221.12.253
Mar  9 03:59:35.189:     send_secret = hs7BsL1p
Mar  9 03:59:35.189:     send_auth = 3
```

You have now verified that the dial-out server is collecting the correct information from the AAA server to perform a successful dial-out. From here, basic PPP dial-out must take place for traffic to pass.

Dial-On-Demand Backup Configuration

In the configuration example provided, a WAN router is used with a fractional T1 to the main office and a modem for DDR. When the fractional T1 goes down, you want the modem to place a call to the DDR server at the main office and continue to support the flow of traffic.

Although it is not the easiest to configure, using dialer watch is an effective way to perform dial-on-demand backup. Dialer watch checks on a route that is supposed to be in the routing table, and if the route disappears for any reason, the router believes it is disconnected from the network and dials.

First, you want the router to watch a route that is up as long as the circuit back to head-quarters is up. The easiest way to do this is to put a loopback address on the router on the other end of the circuit. Then, use a routing protocol to propagate that route through the fractional T1 to the router at the WAN site (the one you are configuring). In this case, EIGRP 68 propagates the route for the loopback address 64.213.9.10:

```
<output omitted>
D       64.213.9.10/32 [90/409600] via 64.213.8.41, 00:05:20, Serial0/2.10
<output omitted>
```

Then set up dial-on demand with a dialer-map statement to connect to the hq-ddr router that accepts calls for backup. The router uses Challenge-Handshake Authentication Protocol (CHAP) authentication with a local username and password. Example 6-24 shows the configuration for dialing and authenticating through CHAP to the hq-ddr router.

Example 6-24 *Configuration to Dial and Authenticate to hq-ddr*

```
3600-ddr(config)#aaa authentication ppp default local
! Local username and password for hq-ddr:
3600-ddr(config)#username hq-ddr password helpme
3600-ddr(config)#interface async65
3600-ddr(config-if)#ip address 64.213.10.12 255.255.255.240
3600-ddr(config-if)#encapsulation ppp
3600-ddr(config-if)#dialer in-band
! Maps ip for hq-ddr with calling number for access:
3600-ddr(config-if)#dialer map ip 64.213.10.1 name hq-ddr 16686222230
3600-ddr(config-if)#dialer hold-queue 100
3600-ddr(config-if)#dialer-group 1
3600-ddr(config-if)#ppp authentication chap
```

Next, verify that the route you want to monitor is in the routing table. To do this, issue the command **show ip route** *ip address*. After it is verified, proceed with configuring the rest of the dialer watch commands.

The first of the commands required for dialer watch sets the idle-timeout on the link to 30 seconds. The link does not disconnect every 30 seconds, but instead checks to determine if the route to the watched IP address specified is in place every 30 seconds:

```
3600-ddr(config-if)#dialer idle-timeout 30
```

Next, add a dialer map for the watched IP address by using the same name and phone number as the one configured earlier. This tells the router where to dial when the watched IP address is removed from the routing table:

```
3600-ddr(config-if)#dialer map ip 64.213.9.10 name hq-ddr 16686222230
```

Then, add the interface to a watch group. Because no watch groups were defined before, start with group number 1 (one):

```
3600-ddr(config-if)#dialer watch-group 1
```

Create a dialer watch list that includes the IP address that you want to watch:

```
3600-ddr(config)#dialer watch-list 1 ip 64.213.9.10 255.255.255.255
```

Finally, set all traffic to non-interesting:

```
3600-ddr(config)#dialer-list 1 protocol ip deny
```

The interface dials based on whether or not the watched IP address is in the routing table, not based on whether the traffic is interesting or not. This is an added measure to keep the dial-on-demand link down whenever it is not needed. Example 6-25 shows the final configuration of this WAN router using dial-on-demand backup.

Example 6-25 *Dial-on-Demand Configuration Using Dialer Watch*

```
version 12.2
service timestamps debug datetime msec
service timestamps log uptime
service password-encryption
!
hostname 3600-ddr
!
boot system flash
aaa new-model
!
aaa authentication ppp default local
!
enable secret 5 $1$VzVJ$B6sbqGo8e2HJDBQ.gxGZp/
!
username hq-ddr password 7 08294942191400
!
ip subnet-zero
!
interface Ethernet0/0
 ip address 64.213.11.193 255.255.255.192
 no keepalive
!
interface Serial0/2
 bandwidth 256
 no ip address
 encapsulation frame-relay IETF
 frame-relay lmi-type ansi
!
interface Serial0/2.10 point-to-point
 bandwidth 256
 ip address 64.213.8.42 255.255.255.252
 no arp frame-relay
 frame-relay interface-dlci 20
!
! Specifies watch-group and hq-ddr numbers for backup:
interface Async65
 ip address 64.213.10.12 255.255.255.240
 encapsulation ppp
 dialer in-band
 dialer idle-timeout 30
 dialer map ip 64.213.10.1 name hq-ddr broadcast 16686222230
```

continues

Example 6-25 *Dial-on-Demand Configuration Using Dialer Watch (Continued)*

```
 dialer map ip 64.213.9.10 name hq-ddr broadcast 16686222230
 dialer hold-queue 100
 dialer watch-group 1
 dialer-group 1
 ppp authentication chap
!
router eigrp 68
 network 64.213.8.0 0.0.3.255
 no auto-summary
!
ip classless
!
no ip http server
!
! Watch-list to match watch-group already specified on Async interface:
access-list 1 permit 192.168.0.0 0.0.0.31
dialer watch-list 1 ip 64.213.9.10 255.255.255.255
dialer-list 1 protocol ip deny
!
line con 0
 exec-timeout 0 0
line aux 0
 modem InOut
 modem autoconfigure type usr_sportster
 speed 115200
line vty 0 4
!
end
```

Example 6-26 is a debug to show you what happens during an outage, and what happens
when the primary circuit comes back up. To simulate this force, the serial interface goes
down by unplugging the cable.

Example 6-26 *Dial-on-Demand Routing Debug—Part I*

```
00:12:38: %LINEPROTO-5-UPDOWN: Line protocol on Interface Serial0/2.10, changed
  state to down
Mar  1 00:12:38.023: DDR: Dialer Watch: watch-group = 1
Mar  1 00:12:38.023: DDR:         network 64.213.9.10/255.255.255.255 DOWN,
Mar  1 00:12:38.023: DDR:         primary DOWN
Mar  1 00:12:38.023: DDR: Dialer Watch: Dial Reason: Primary of group 1 DOWN
Mar  1 00:12:38.023: DDR: Dialer Watch: watch-group = 1,
Mar  1 00:12:38.023: DDR:         dialing secondary by dialer map 64.213.9.10 on As65
Mar  1 00:12:38.023: As65 DDR: Attempting to dial 16686222230
```

This starts a typical PPP dial-out connection and after it is authenticated, the network
continues passing traffic through the DDR system. Example 6-27 shows what occurs when
the serial interface is fixed and comes back up; in this case, you plug the cable back in.

Example 6-27 *Dial-on-Demand Routing Debug—Part II*

```
00:13:20: %LINEPROTO-5-UPDOWN: Line protocol on Interface Serial0/2.10, changed
    state to up
Mar  1 00:13:21.819: DDR: Dialer Watch: watch-group = 1
Mar  1 00:13:21.819: DDR:        network 64.213.9.10/255.255.255.255 UP,
Mar  1 00:13:21.819: DDR:        primary UP
```

Shortly following, the call is disconnected and traffic resumes over the serial interface.

Summary

This chapter is divided into two separate sections that cover dial design solutions and dial configuration solutions.

The dial design solutions section covered the essentials of dial-in network connectivity, dial-out network connectivity, and DDR along with dial-out for support purposes and large-scale dial-out services.

The dial configuration solutions section provided detailed information about common and specific dial configurations, including the following:

- Text dial-in configuration
- PPP dial-in configuration
- Large-scale dial-in configuration
- Text dial-out configuration
- PPP dial-out configuration
- Large-scale dial-out configuration
- Dial-on-demand backup configuration

Before the troubleshooting process starts, it is important to understand entirely the design and configuration specifics of the dial solution. This gives you a better understanding of the troubleshooting methodology that's used for dial in the next chapter.

Review Questions

Answers to the review questions can be found in Appendix A, "Answers to Review Questions."

1 List three ways for using dial as a backup solution.

2 What is the main advantage of the dialer watch solution?

3 What is the line configuration command to configure a modem to use the modemcap usr_sportster?

4 What is the global configuration command to define a group named dial as a TACACS+ group?

5 What is the default protocol and port number of RADIUS authentication and accounting?

6 What is the line configuration command to automatically select the PPP protocol during text authentication?

7 What is NFAS and what is its function?

8 What is the interface configuration command to ensure that voice calls are sent to a modem?

9 What is the purpose of the command **no exec**?

10 What is the best way to test a backup solution?

11 How would you connect to a network access server to connect as a text dial-out device?

12 True or False: PC software is required to use a router to perform PPP dial-out.

13 What is the most scaleable way to use large-scale dial-out?

14 What is the main purpose of a group-async interface?

15 What does the interface command **group-range** do?

CHAPTER 7

Dial Troubleshooting

The troubleshooting approach in this chapter demonstrates the layer-by-layer and phase-by-phase approach to dial issues. It is important to be systematic and go step-by-step, starting with the physical layer from both ends. Unlike service provider-based remote access solutions, both ends of the connection are available for troubleshooting in an enterprise remote access scenario. This chapter focuses on the following main topics:

- Detailed troubleshooting network access server (NAS) wide-area network (WAN) links, including T1 circuits and PRIs

- Troubleshooting dial-in services

- Troubleshooting dial-out services

- Specific commands and debugs for NAS 5x00 routers, including Cisco 5200, 5300, and 5400

With this chapter, you can enhance your knowledge about T1s and PRIs. This information is relevant to all parts of this book and should be reviewed as necessary. The dial-in and dial-out troubleshooting techniques are explained in detail, from the viewpoint of the NAS, which gives you the best understanding about the nature of the processes. Troubleshooting the modem operational status is demonstrated in great detail. The specifics of the different platforms provided in this chapter should help you to improve your skill set in dial technology.

Troubleshooting NAS WAN Links

A NAS is the key piece of equipment that accepts incoming calls, authenticates the caller, and routes traffic for each call. The NAS is connected to the telephone company cloud by using a variety of leased lines that range from Basic Rate Interfaces (BRIs) to digital service 3s (DS3s). Typical design solutions include T1s and Primary Rate Interfaces (PRIs), which is why more detailed explanations about troubleshooting them are included in this section.

Troubleshooting T1 Circuits

When you notice a problem with a T1 line, it's recommended that you start troubleshooting with the core end to determine where the problem exists. Start with the physical layer first.

Controller and Line Status

Start with the physical condition and integrity of the T1 line. Always check the status of the T1 controllers and verify that you do not receive any errors. The command that displays the status is **show controllers t1**, as shown in Example 7-1.

Example 7-1 *Output of the Command* **show controllers t1**

```
5300-dial#show controllers t1 0
! The circuit is up according to the next line:
T1 0 is up.
  Applique type is Channelized T1
! Cable length is shown next. If the circuit is not long, it needs to
! be configured differently:
  Cablelength is long gain36 0db
  Description: T1 with Pacific Bell.
! Alarms are shown in the next line.
! If an alarm exists, there is a major problem in the circuit:
  No alarms detected.
  Version info of slot 0:  HW: 1, PLD Rev: 11
  Framer Version: 0x8

Manufacture Cookie Info:
 EEPROM Type 0x0001, EEPROM Version 0x01, Board ID 0x48,
 Board Hardware Version 1.0, Item Number 800-3883-01,
 Board Revision A0, Serial Number 11692119,
 PLD/ISP Version 0.1,  Manufacture Date 6-May-1999.

  Framing is ESF, Line Code is B8ZS, Clock Source is Line Secondary.
! The following 4 lines show that no errors occurred in the last 10 seconds:
  Data in current interval (10 seconds elapsed):
     0 Line Code Violations, 0 Path Code Violations
     0 Slip Secs, 0 Fr Loss Secs, 0 Line Err Secs, 0 Degraded Mins
     0 Errored Secs, 0 Bursty Err Secs, 0 Severely Err Secs, 0 Unavail Secs
! The following 4 lines show a mostly clean line, but there
! were 9 Slip Seconds and 9 Errored Seconds in the last 24 hours:
  Total Data (last 24 hours)
     0 Line Code Violations, 0 Path Code Violations,
     9 Slip Secs, 0 Fr Loss Secs, 0 Line Err Secs, 0 Degraded Mins,
     9 Errored Secs, 0 Bursty Err Secs, 0 Severely Err Secs, 0 Unavail Secs
```

The first line shows line status and tells you if the T1 is either up, down, or administratively down. The first section of the output also alerts you of any alarms that are on the circuit. On the next line, you find your configured cable length. Make sure that this is configured correctly. If the observed output is not correct, the following options are available under the controller configuration mode:

```
5300-dial(config-controller)#cablelength {long [gain26 | gain36]
   [0db | -7.5db | -15db | -22.5db] | short [133 | 266 | 399 | 533 | 655]}
```

Cable length is defined as either long or short with long being anything over 655 feet in length. Length is the distance of the entire circuit from the closest repeater or switch to the NAS. In most cases, the closest repeater is not local, so you use the default **long** with a gain or a boost of 36 decibels (**gain36**). For shorter long cable lengths, the signal is stronger and you might only need **gain26**. The second part of defining a long cable length is transmitting attenuation. The default is **0db**, which is the strongest transmit signal. If the circuit provider tells you that your signal is too strong, you can lower the transmit signal by using **–7.5db**, **-15db**, or **–22db**.

A short cable length is defined in distance by feet from the NAS and closest repeater. You use the value of 133 for distances that range from 1 foot to 133 feet. The value of 266 is for distances that range from 134 to 266 feet. For distances of 267 to 399 feet, use 399. Use 533 for distances from 400 to 533. Finally, use 655 for anything between 534 and 655 feet in length.

NOTE   In modular routers (7200, 1600, and 1700 series), the command **show service-module serial** *slot/port* provides detailed information about the condition of the line. Examples of this command are included in Chapter 17, "Frame Relay Troubleshooting."

Loopback Features

If you have difficulty with any of Cisco's DS1 adapters or network modules with an internal CSU, you can troubleshoot by using the **loopback** command. The three main loopback modes that are configurable are diagnostic, local, and remote. Local loopback can be configured as either line or payload. Remote loopback can be configured as in-band bit-oriented code (IBOC) or Extended Superframe (ESF). Specify the loopback format using one of the following controller configuration commands:

```
5300-dial(config-controller)#loopback [diagnostic | local | remote]
5300-dial(config-controller)#loopback [local {payload | line}]
5300-dial(config-controller)#loopback [remote {esf line | iboc | esf paylaod}]
```

Check Bit Errors with a Bit Error Rate Tester

A bit error rate tester (BERT) alerts you of any issues on the line. Although a circuit can be operational and passing data, some data might be flawed, which can be detected by using a BERT.

A BERT is not an available option on every piece of Cisco hardware. If the option is not available, the proper way to perform this test is to put a tester directly on the circuit. To use a BERT to check for bit errors, if the router supports it, use the following controller configuration command:

```
5300-dial(config-controller)# bert pattern test pattern interval minutes
```

The available options for *test pattern* are the following:

- **0s** — All 0s test pattern
- **1s** — All 1s test pattern
- **2^11** — 2^11-1 test pattern
- **2^15** — 2^15-1 O.151 test pattern
- **2^20-O153** — 2^20-1 O.153 test pattern
- **2^20-QRSS** — 2^20-1 QRSS O.151 test pattern
- **2^23** — 2^23-1 O.151 test pattern
- **alt-0-1** — Alternating 0s and 1s test pattern

A further explanation of the most commonly used BERT test patterns include the following:

- 2^15 is an exponential number that represents a pseudo-random repeating pattern that is 32,767 bits long.
- 2^20 is a pseudo-random repeating pattern that is 1,048,575 bits long.
- 2^23 is a pseudo-random repeating pattern that is 8,388,607 bits long.
- 0s is a pattern of all 0s.
- 1s is a pattern of all 1s.

The *minutes* argument can be 1-14400, which designates the time that the BERT runs.

BERT testing can only be done over a framed T1 signal. The test cannot run if the T1 is in an alarm state where "Receiver has loss of frame (or signal)." Additionally, it can only be run on one port at a time.

Physical Layer Alarms

The alarm section of the output from **show controllers t1** is important as it tells you what type of problem might be present on the line. The presence of any alarm indicates a serious problem on the line (see Figure 7-1 and Table 7-1). In Figure 7-1, each WAN link is represented by a pair of cross-connected receivers and transmitters.

Figure 7-1   *A Functional Model of Physical Layer Alarm Messages*

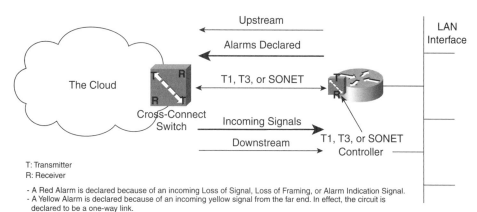

T: Transmitter
R: Receiver

- A Red Alarm is declared because of an incoming Loss of Signal, Loss of Framing, or Alarm Indication Signal.
- A Yellow Alarm is declared because of an incoming yellow signal from the far end. In effect, the circuit is declared to be a one-way link.
- A Blue Alarm is declared because of incoming Alarm Indication Signal (AIS). The Blue Alarm indicates a problem upstream. If you shut down one side of the connection, a Blue Alarm is sent to the other side.

When you have a T1 in an alarm state, verify that the framing and linecoding parameters are configured correctly. A common message in the alarm field is "receiver has loss of frame." Some routers also report a loss of frame (LOF) even when it should be a loss of signal (LOS). Therefore, ensure whenever you receive these errors that the T1 signal is present and the framing is correct. There are three types of alarms:

- **Blue alarm**—Another message you might receive is that the receiver is getting an Alarm Indication Signal (AIS), which means that a blue alarm indication signal is received. This generally indicates that there is a problem upstream. This is a framed or unframed all-ones signal, in both SF and ESF formats, which is transmitted to maintain transmission continuity. It typically occurs when the far-end channel service unit (CSU) has lost its terminal side equipment. For example, if you shut down your side of the connection, a blue alarm is sent to the remote side.

- **Yellow alarm**—The receiver has a remote alarm that indicates the presence of a yellow alarm. This means that the downstream CSU is in a LOF or LOS state. It is also a remote site alarm indication (RAI). When the receiver experiences LOS, the transmitter sends a yellow alarm. For SF-formats, a remote alarm is declared when bit 6 on all channels is set to 0 for at least 35 seconds. The alarm is cleared if the same bit is non-zero for 5 seconds or less (usually 1 second). When the format is ESF, a remote alarm indicates if the yellow alarm pattern exists in at least seven out of ten continuous 16-bit intervals. The alarm is cleared if this condition no longer exists for the same time intervals.

- **Red alarm**—Another typical failure is called a red alarm. A red alarm is usually indicated on the opposite end of the yellow alarm. The red alarm means that the receiver experiences LOS, LOF, or an AIS. A LOS failure is defined in RFC 1406 as "is declared upon observing 175 +/- 75 contiguous pulse positions with no pulses of either positive or negative polarity. The LOS failure is cleared upon observing an average pulse density of at least 12.5% over a period of 175 +/- 75 contiguous pulse positions starting with the receipt of a pulse. For E1 links, the LOS failure is declared when greater than 10 consecutive zeroes are detected." After a red alarm is declared, the device sends a yellow signal to the far end. When the far end receives the yellow signal, it declares a yellow alarm. This message is accompanied by a "receiver has loss of frame" message.

TIP   Always verify the framing and T1 signal when troubleshooting.

NOTE   Regardless of the leased line connection that you are troubleshooting, whether a T1, T3, or Synchronous Optical Network (SONET), the alarm signals and their interpretations remain the same. The alarm states are always based on the presence or lack of signals or certain patterns. This is why the alarm states in this section apply to all circuits in the book.

Linecode Violations

These violations occur when either a bipolar violation (BPV) or excessive zero error event is present. BPVs are inserted as a means of synchronizing circuits with bipolar 8-zero substitution (B8ZS) linecoding. Linecode errors occur when BPVs that are not used for synchronization are received. Excessive zero errors occur when eight or more 0s in a row are received on a circuit where alternate mark inversion (AMI) linecoding is being used. The errors might occur because of an AMI/B8ZS configuration problem or there might be points along the transmission path that do not have all the linecoding parameters set correctly.

Pathcode Violations

Two examples for pathcode violations are frame synchronization errors for SF and cyclic redundancy check (CRC) errors for ESF. Typically, both pathcode violations and linecode violations are present simultaneously, so always that verify the linecoding is correct. Some smartjacks (and mux equipment) might need to be specifically configured for AMI/B8ZS because of problems with automatic linecode detection. Be aware that some amount of errors on your T1 can occur because of impulse noise; therefore, the errors might appear only a few times a day and the effects might be miniscule.

Slip Seconds

The presence of slips on a T1 line indicates a clocking problem. The network provides the clocking with which the customer premises equipment (CPE) must synchronize. If you see slips on the line, verify that you are deriving your clocking from the telephone company (telco) (clock source line). It is possible that only one side of the T1 is experiencing errors, so contact the provider to ensure that they are not seeing errors on their side of the circuit.

T1 Errors

RFC 1232 defines the managed objects for the DS1 interface type and standardizes the DS1 terminology and descriptions of error conditions on a T1 or E1 circuit. Table 7-1 shows the RFC 1232 categories, errors, and their descriptions.

Table 7-1   *RFC 1232 Categories, Errors, and Their Descriptions*

Object	Description
Out of Frame event	Declared when the receiver detects two or more framing-bit errors within a three millisecond period, or two or more errors out of five or less consecutive framing-bits. At this time, the framer enters the Out of Frame state, and starts searching for a correct framing pattern. The Out of Frame state ends when reframe occurs.
Loss of Signal	This event is declared upon observing 175 +/- 75 contiguous pulse positions with no pulses of either positive or negative polarity (also called keepalive).
Code Violation Error Event	The occurrence of a received CRC code that is not identical to the corresponding locally calculated code.
Bipolar Violation	A BPV for B8ZS-coded signals is the occurrence of a received BPV that is not part of a zero-substitution code. It also includes other error patterns such as eight or more consecutive 0s, and incorrect parity.
Errored Seconds	A second with one or more Code Violation Error events or one or more Out of Frame events. The presence of BPVs also triggers an Errored Second.
Severely Errored Seconds	A second with 320 or more Code Violation Error events or one or more Out of Frame events.
Severely Errored Framing Second	A Severely Errored Framing Second is a second with one or more Out of Frame events.
Unavailable Signal State	Declared at the onset of 10 consecutive Severely Errored Seconds. It is cleared at the onset of ten consecutive seconds with no Severely Errored Seconds.
Unavailable Seconds	Calculated by counting the number of seconds that the CSU is in the Unavailable Signal State, including the initial ten seconds to enter the state, but not including the ten seconds to exit the state.
Yellow Alarm	Declared because of an incoming Yellow signal from the far end. In effect, the circuit is declared to be a one-way link.
Red Alarm	Declared because of an incoming LOS, LOF, or an AIS. After a Red Alarm is declared, the device sends a yellow signal to the far end. When the far end receives the yellow signal, it declares a Yellow Alarm.
Circuit Identifier	This is a character string that is specified by the circuit vendor, and is useful when communicating with the vendor during the troubleshooting process.

Troubleshooting PRI Circuits

A PRI is actually an ISDN connection that uses a type of signaling to channelize a T1 without robbing signaling bits from each channel; instead, the signaling is done on the last (24th) channel. The first step in troubleshooting problems with a PRI is to use the **show isdn status** command as shown in Example 7-2.

Example 7-2 *Output of* **show isdn status**

```
5300-dialin#show isdn status
Global ISDN Switchtype = primary-5ess
ISDN Serial0:23 interface
        dsl 0, interface ISDN Switchtype = primary-5ess
    Layer 1 Status:
        ACTIVE
    Layer 2 Status:
        TEI - 0, Ces - 1, SAPI = 0, State = MULTIPLE_FRAME_ESTABLISHED
    Layer 3 Status:
        0 Active Layer 3 Call(s)
<output omitted>
```

The following sections explain this output.

Layer 1 Status

The Layer 1 status portion of the output shows whether the T1 access circuit that the PRI signaling rides on is up or not. If it is not in an active state, go to the beginning of this chapter and troubleshoot the T1 portion of the circuit first.

Layer 2 Status

If the Layer 2 state does not show MULTIPLE_FRAME_ESTABLISHED, check the T1 circuit for incrementing errors and treat this situation as any T1 problem. More information about troubleshooting measures is covered in the section, "Troubleshooting T1 Circuits." If the T1 checks out okay, verify that the ISDN switch type and PRI group time slots were set up the same as the circuit was provisioned. Then check the serial interface associated with the PRI by using the command **show interface serial** *x***:23**, where *X* is the associated T1 port number. A sample output is shown in Example 7-3.

Example 7-3 *Output of* **show interface serial 0:23**

```
S5200-dialin>show interface serial 0:23
 Serial2:23 is up, line protocol is up (spoofing)
  Hardware is DSX1
  MTU 1500 bytes, BW 64 Kbit, DLY 20000 usec,
     reliability 128/255, txload 1/255, rxload 1/255
```

Example 7-3 *Output of* **show interface serial 0:23** *(Continued)*

```
    Encapsulation HDLC, loopback not set
    DTR is pulsed for 1 seconds on reset
    Last input 00:00:20, output never, output hang never
    Last clearing of "show interface" counters never
    Input queue: 0/75/0/0 (size/max/drops/flushes); Total output drops: 0
<output omitted>e
```

Verify that the D channel is up and not in a loopback state. If the state of Layer 2 is still not MULTIPLE_FRAME_ESTABLISHED, you need to call your service provider. However, if you receive this message but you are still experiencing problems, turn on ISDN Q921 debugs. After using **debug isdn q921** and **show debug**, ensure that the output is similar to that in Example 7-4.

Example 7-4 *Output of* **show debug** *Indicates That* **debug isdn q921** *Is On*

```
5300-dialin#show debug
ISDN:
  ISDN Q921 packets debugging is on
  ISDN Q921 packets debug DSLs. (On/Off/No DSL:1/0/-)
  DSL  0 --> 7

  1 1 1 1 1 1 1 1
```

If you are not directly connected to the console port, you have to enable **terminal monitor** to see the output from debug commands.

Also, verify that the only activity you see is similar to that in Example 7-5.

Example 7-5 *Debug Output Showing ISDN q921 Activity*

```
5300-dialin#terminal monitor
Jan  6 03:44:01.653: ISDN Se0:23: RX <- RRf sapi = 0  tei = 0  nr = 4
Jan  6 03:44:05.669: ISDN Se1:23: TX -> RRp sapi = 0  tei = 0 nr = 113
Jan  6 03:44:05.677: ISDN Se1:23: RX <- RRf sapi = 0  tei = 0  nr = 1
Jan  6 03:44:14.981: ISDN Se2:23: TX -> RRp sapi = 0  tei = 0 nr = 0
Jan  6 03:44:14.989: ISDN Se2:23: RX <- RRf sapi = 0  tei = 0  nr = 0
Jan  6 03:44:16.169: ISDN Se3:23: TX -> RRp sapi = 0  tei = 0 nr = 79
Jan  6 03:44:16.185: ISDN Se3:23: RX <- RRf sapi = 0  tei = 0  nr = 79
```

A service access point identifier (SAPI) has a value assigned to it. This value determines the data type coming from the device at the other end. The data types are as follows:

- **0**—Q931 (signaling information)
- **1**—Telemetry
- **16**—X.25 on the D channel
- **63**—Data-link management

A terminal endpoint identifier (TEI) is an address used at Layer 2 that manages individual devices that are connecting to the ISDN network. The TEI is typically dynamically negotiated with the ISDN switch. The range is from 0 to 127. The following shows what each TEI number means:

- **0**—Point-to-point service (as it is for PRI)
- **1-63**—Fixed assigned
- **64-126**—Dynamically assigned by telco switch
- **127**—Broadcast (send frame to all attached devices)

NOTE   The correct TEI for PRI is always 0.

If Set Asynchronous Balanced Mode Extended (SABME) messages appear, the switch-type or PRI time slots are set incorrectly. SABME messages in the debug appear as follows:

```
Jan  6 03:45:16.185: ISDN Se0:23: TX -> SABMEp sapi = 0 tei = 0
Jan  6 03:45:16.662: ISDN Se0:23: RX <- BAD FRAME(0x00017F)Line may be looped!
```

See Chapter 12, "ISDN BRI Troubleshooting," for additional information about the Q921 protocol.

Troubleshooting Dial-In Service

In this section, detail is provided on what you can do to determine the cause of the dial-in connection problems. The troubleshooting techniques include commands for use on a modem, outputs from debug commands, and some common recommendations. This section does not include debugs from Cisco AS5x00 series routers because this is covered in a subsequent section later in this chapter.

When troubleshooting a connection problem, try to piece together everything that is expected to occur throughout the process. Use a step-by-step approach to outline all activities from start to finish, and in the correct sequence.

You might be required to make some assumptions as part of the process. First, assume that the analog lines connected to the modems are working, their phone numbers are correct, and a call placed from one end to the other occurs successfully (the switched services work correctly). Obviously, if a problem exists with an analog line, it's a switched service problem, and your telephone provider must correct the issue. This section covers the following steps that are used to troubleshoot a problem with the NAS:

- Step One: Verify that the modem is ready to accept incoming calls.
- Step Two: Verify the type of connection.
- Step Three: Verify Point-to-Point Protocol (PPP) negotiation.

Step One: Verify that the Modem Is Ready to Accept Calls

The first event to occur is that the modem must pick up the call. If it is an external modem, increase the volume so that you can hear it. Place a call from a telephone to the modem to make sure it answers. If it does not, check the cabling between the modem and the router. The type of cable can differ between modems, so the easiest way to check is through the **show line** *line-number* command. The line you must check is the following:

```
Modem state: Idle
```

If the modem is ready to take an incoming call, but there is no call on the line, the state should be idle. If the state is anything other than idle, the modem will not answer the call. Several different signals (modem states) have to interact properly for the modem to be ready to accept a call. The Modem Hardware State are

- **CTS (Clear To Send)**—Provided by the data communications equipment (DCE). The DCE signals to the data terminal equipment (DTE) that the DCE accepts data.

- **DSR (Data Set Ready)**—Provided by the DCE.

- **DTR (Data Terminal Ready)**—Provided by the DTE. The DTE indicates to the DCE that it accept calls.

- **RTS (Request To Send)**—Provided by the DTE. The DTE signals that the DTE accepts data.

Modem Hardware State: CTS noDSR DTR RTS

In this example, the Modem Hardware State is correct, but the modem is in a ready state instead of an idle state, as indicated by noDSR.

If an active session is on the line, the modem cannot answer a new call. It displays a ready state. The **show users** command shows you if there is an active session. You can then clear the active session with the privileged command **clear line**.

The second reason for noDSR can be because modem control is not configured on the line. Configure the line with either **modem Dialin** or **modem InOut**.

Lastly, DSR might be high, which results from a cabling problem or if the modem is configured where Data Carrier Detect-Provided (DCD) is always high. Fix the cabling problem or reconfigure the modem so that DCD is only high when carrier detection (CD) is successful, which should clear the problem.

Modem Hardware State: noCTS noDSR DTR RTS

In cases where noCTS replaces CTS in the correct state, three different possibilities exist: the modem is turned off, a cabling problem exists, or hardware flow control on the modem is turned off. The line configuration command **no flowcontrol hardware** fixes the last of these three problems.

Modem Hardware State: CTS DSR DTR RTS

In cases where DSR replaces noDSR in the correct state, there can be a cable problem. Also, DCD can always be configured on the modem as high. Reconfigure the modem to correct this and ensure that either the line configuration command **modem Dialin** or **modem InOut** exists.

Now that the cable connection from router to modem is operational, you must also ensure that the modem is set to auto answer. Consult the modems owner's manual to set this up. This concludes the troubleshooting required if a modem does not answer.

Step Two: Verify Type of Incoming Connection

After step one, where the connection is a fact, perform the second step from the core router (NAS). The Cisco IOS features give you much more insight about the type of the connection than any other approach. Start the incoming type verification by using the **debug modem** command. The first debug reflects the configuration from a basic PPP dial-in service in Chapter 6, "Dial Design and Configuration Solutions."

When dialing into an external modem, one that does not have out-of-band signaling, the first line should read as follows:

```
17:11:38: TTY1: DSR came up
```

This signifies that the modem has trained up successfully. If this does not take place, there was a problem with the modem train-up. Line issues or modem incompatibilities can cause a train-up failure. To cure any modem incompatibility problem, ensure that the modems on both ends have the latest firmware and drivers.

The following line indicates a change in modem state:

```
17:11:38: tty1: Modem: IDLE->(unknown)
```

The modem in this example happens to be external, so the router does not know which state the modem changed to. If it had been an internal modem with out-of-band functionality, you would have seen the following:

```
17:11:38: tty1: Modem: IDLE->READY
```

At this point, if you have the interface configured with **async mode dedicated**, the connection immediately jumps into PPP. The PPP debugs are covered later in this section. If the line was configured for text authentication and no PPP, such as a modem in an AUX port, the debug output in Example 7-6 would be displayed.

Example 7-6   *Debug Output for Exec Creation*

```
! The router starts an exec session:
17:11:43: TTY1: EXEC creation
! The following two lines are used when prompting for authentication:
17:11:43: TTY1: set timer type 10, 30 seconds
```

Example 7-6 *Debug Output for Exec Creation (Continued)*

```
17:11:56: TTY1: set timer type 10, 30 seconds
17:11:67: TTY1: create timer type 1, 600 seconds
```

The **type 10 timer** is used for username and password prompts. The fourth line in the output
sets a 30-second timer for the username prompt and the fifth line places another 30-second
timer for the password prompt. The last line in the output is an exec timer. The default **exec-
timeout** set on a line is 10 minutes, or 600 seconds.

In the preceding example, the modem changed state from idle to unknown. If the async
interface was configured with **async mode interactive** and the line was configured with
autoselect ppp and **autoselect during-login**, the debug is different, as shown in Example 7-7.

Example 7-7 *Debug Output of Modem Autoselect for PPP*

```
22:52:59: TTY1: EXEC creation
22:52:59: TTY1: set timer type 10, 30 seconds
22:53:01: TTY1: Autoselect(2) sample 7E
22:53:01: TTY1: Autoselect(2) sample 7EFF
22:53:01: TTY1: Autoselect(2) sample 7EFF7D
22:53:01: TTY1: Autoselect(2) sample 7EFF7D23
22:53:01: TTY1 Autoselect cmd:  ppp negotiate
```

During the username prompt, the router checks incoming characters to see if they are PPP
or if they are part of a username. The autoselect samples shown in Example 7-7 are in
hexadecimal format. If translated to ASCII, they show the text received over a line. There
is an autoselect sample for each character that arrives. The router displays up to four
characters in each new autoselect sample line and includes the three previous characters,
followed by the last character entered as shown.

The four autoselect characters in Example 7-7, if translated into ASCII, are ~ÿ}#, which is
the typical representation of a PPP link control protocol (LCP) packet. For this reason, the
last line in the debug shows that autoselect executed the command **ppp negotiate**, which
instructs the router to negotiate PPP.

The sample output in Example 7-8 uses the same configuration as before, except that the
login was done through text. This can either be from typing it manually or from running a
login script.

Example 7-8 *Debug Output of Modem Autoselect for Text*

```
23:15:22: TTY1: EXEC creation
23:15:22: TTY1: set timer type 10, 30 seconds
! Username entry of six characters, followed by carriage return
23:15:23: TTY1: Autoselect(2) sample 6A
23:15:24: TTY1: Autoselect(2) sample 6A68
23:15:24: TTY1: Autoselect(2) sample 6A6875
```

continues

Example 7-8   *Debug Output of Modem Autoselect for Text (Continued)*

```
23:15:24: TTY1: Autoselect(2) sample 6A687565
23:15:24: TTY1: Autoselect(2) sample 68756567
23:15:24: TTY1: Autoselect(2) sample 75656765
23:15:24: TTY1: Autoselect(2) sample 6567656E
23:15:25: TTY1: Autoselect(2) sample 67656E0D
23:15:25: TTY1: set timer type 10, 30 seconds
! The following lines state [suppressed--line is not echoing], because
! the password prompt never echoed the characters entered.
23:15:26: TTY1: Autoselect(2) sample [suppressed--line is not echoing]
23:15:26: TTY1: Autoselect(2) sample [suppressed--line is not echoing]
23:15:27: TTY1: Autoselect(2) sample [suppressed--line is not echoing]
23:15:27: TTY1: Autoselect(2) sample [suppressed--line is not echoing]
23:15:27: TTY1: Autoselect(2) sample [suppressed--line is not echoing]
```

In this case, the username entered is six characters followed by a carriage return. You can decode the incoming text for usernames by converting the hexadecimal characters in the sample to ASCII. The hexadecimal string can be pieced together to form 6A 68 75 65 67 65 6E 0D. When changed to ASCII, it spells jhuegen followed by 0D, which is a carriage return. The following lines states "[suppressed--line is not echoing]" because the password prompt never echoes the characters entered; however, you can make the assumption that the password entered was four characters followed by a carriage return (to make up the five lines).

Step Three: Verify PPP Negotiation

After the call connects, PPP negotiation starts. The following output is from **debug PPP negotiation**. It is split into the major steps, which are explained:

```
Mar  2 13:32:45.354: %LINK-3-UPDOWN: Interface Async1, changed state to up
Mar  2 13:32:45.354: As1 PPP: Treating connection as a dedicated line
Mar  2 13:32:45.354: As1 PPP: Phase is ESTABLISHING, Active Open
```

NOTE   The Link Dead (physical layer not ready) transition state changes to the Link Establishment phase only if an external event, such as a carrier detect (CD), is up.

LCP Phase of PPP

The following explanations are based on the output you see if you type the **debug ppp negotiation** command to troubleshoot LCP issues. The first part of the output identifies how PPP treats the connection. For every dial case, it is treated as a dedicated line. The first step in LCP takes place when the dial server sends an outgoing configuration request (O CONFREQ), as shown in Example 7-9.

Example 7-9 *Debug Output of PPP Outgoing Configuration Request*

```
Mar  2 13:32:45.354: As1 LCP: O CONFREQ [Closed] id 33 len 24
Mar  2 13:32:45.354: As1 LCP:    ACCM 0x000A0000 (0x0206000A0000)
Mar  2 13:32:45.358: As1 LCP:    AuthProto PAP (0x0304C023)
Mar  2 13:32:45.358: As1 LCP:    MagicNumber 0xE82CFF9C (0x0506E82CFF9C)
Mar  2 13:32:45.358: As1 LCP:    PFC (0x0702)
Mar  2 13:32:45.358: As1 LCP:    ACFC (0x0802)
```

The server expects a reply and the reply should be similar to the Example 7-10, which is an incoming configuration acknowledgment (I CONFACK).

Example 7-10 *Debug Output of PPP Incoming Configuration Acknowledgment*

```
Mar  2 13:32:45.546: As1 LCP: I CONFACK [REQsent] id 33 len 24
Mar  2 13:32:45.546: As1 LCP:    ACCM 0x000A0000 (0x0206000A0000)
Mar  2 13:32:45.546: As1 LCP:    AuthProto PAP (0x0304C023)
Mar  2 13:32:45.546: As1 LCP:    MagicNumber 0xE82CFF9C (0x0506E82CFF9C)
Mar  2 13:32:45.546: As1 LCP:    PFC (0x0702)
Mar  2 13:32:45.546: As1 LCP:    ACFC (0x0802)
```

Next, the incoming configuration request (I CONFREQ) from the connecting client is received. At this point, the client tries to negotiate the callback protocol, as shown in Example 7-11.

Example 7-11 *Debug Output of PPP Request for Callback*

```
Mar  2 13:32:46.402: As1 LCP: I CONFREQ [ACKrcvd] id 2 len 50
Mar  2 13:32:46.402: As1 LCP:    ACCM 0x00000000 (0x020600000000)
Mar  2 13:32:46.406: As1 LCP:    MagicNumber 0x588D5503 (0x0506588D5503)
Mar  2 13:32:46.406: As1 LCP:    PFC (0x0702)
Mar  2 13:32:46.406: As1 LCP:    ACFC (0x0802)
Mar  2 13:32:46.406: As1 LCP:    Callback 6  (0x0D0306)
Mar  2 13:32:46.406: As1 LCP:    MRRU 1614 (0x1104064E)
Mar  2 13:32:46.406: As1 LCP:    EndpointDisc 1 Local
Mar  2 13:32:46.406: As1 LCP:      (0x131701F9358C5F03D643118C9B7AC7F0)
Mar  2 13:32:46.406: As1 LCP:      (0x70629C00000000)
```

The dial server then sends an outgoing rejection (O CONFREJ) because callback authentication is not turned on, as shown in Example 7-12.

Example 7-12 *Debug Output of PPP Rejection for Callback*

```
Mar  2 13:32:46.406: As1 LCP: O CONFREJ [ACKrcvd] id 2 len 11
Mar  2 13:32:46.406: As1 LCP:    Callback 6  (0x0D0306)
Mar  2 13:32:46.406: As1 LCP:    MRRU 1614 (0x1104064E)
```

The client then requests a new set of options. This is an incoming configuration request (I CONFREQ), as shown in Example 7-13.

Example 7-13 *Debug Output of PPP Incoming Configuration Request*

```
Mar  2 13:32:46.594: As1 LCP: I CONFREQ [ACKrcvd] id 3 len 43
Mar  2 13:32:46.594: As1 LCP:    ACCM 0x00000000 (0x020600000000)
Mar  2 13:32:46.594: As1 LCP:    MagicNumber 0x588D5503 (0x0506588D5503)
Mar  2 13:32:46.594: As1 LCP:    PFC (0x0702)
Mar  2 13:32:46.594: As1 LCP:    ACFC (0x0802)
Mar  2 13:32:46.594: As1 LCP:    EndpointDisc 1 Local
Mar  2 13:32:46.594: As1 LCP:      (0x131701F9358C5F03D643118C9B7AC7F0)
Mar  2 13:32:46.594: As1 LCP:      (0x70629C00000000)
```

The server then acknowledges this by sending an outgoing configuration acknowledgement (O CONFACK), as shown in Example 7-14.

Example 7-14 *Debug of PPP Outgoing Configuration Acknowledgment*

```
Mar  2 13:32:46.598: As1 LCP: O CONFACK [ACKrcvd] id 3 len 43
Mar  2 13:32:46.598: As1 LCP:    ACCM 0x00000000 (0x020600000000)
Mar  2 13:32:46.598: As1 LCP:    MagicNumber 0x588D5503 (0x0506588D5503)
Mar  2 13:32:46.598: As1 LCP:    PFC (0x0702)
Mar  2 13:32:46.598: As1 LCP:    ACFC (0x0802)
Mar  2 13:32:46.598: As1 LCP:    EndpointDisc 1 Local
Mar  2 13:32:46.598: As1 LCP:      (0x131701F9358C5F03D643118C9B7AC7F0)
Mar  2 13:32:46.598: As1 LCP:      (0x70629C00000000)
```

Next, LCP changes state to open. At this point, both sides agree that the server will provide a configuration for the client. LCP is then complete.

```
! The LCP is Open:
Mar  2 13:32:46.598: As1 LCP: State is Open
```

IF LCP never completes and does not change state to open, a few problems can possibly exist:

- First, LCP timeouts can be caused by a speed problem between the router and modem. A symptom of this problem is that either one or both of the peers do not see any incoming LCP packets. This occurs only if there is a speed issue between the router and an external modem.

- The second type of LCP problem is caused when both peers are not able to agree on authentication. The client and server must agree on authentication type, which is Password Authentication Protocol (PAP), Challenge Handshake Authentication Protocol (CHAP), or Microsoft CHAP (MS CHAP). For example, if the server side is set to authenticate through CHAP and the client is configured for PAP authentication, LCP times out while trying to negotiate.

- LCP can also fail because of a maximum transmission unit (MTU) mismatch. Make sure that MTU is defined as the same on both peers. If necessary, reduce the MTU on both sides until LCP succeeds.

The Authentication Phase of PPP

After LCP finishes and its state is open, the next step in the process is authentication. During this phase, you can see the authenticating party and whether or not authentication has passed. Example 7-15 shows the output of a successful PPP PAP authentication. This output is a result of the **debug ppp authentication** command.

Example 7-15 *Debug Output of a Successful PPP PAP Authentication*

```
Mar  2 13:32:46.598: As1 PPP: Phase is AUTHENTICATING, by this end
Mar  2 13:32:46.842: As1 PAP: I AUTH-REQ id 7 len 17 from "jhuegen"
Mar  2 13:32:46.846: As1 PAP: Authenticating peer jhuegen
Mar  2 13:32:46.846: As1 PPP: Phase is FORWARDING, Attempting Forward
Mar  2 13:32:46.846: As1 PPP: Phase is AUTHENTICATING, Unauthenticated User
Mar  2 13:32:46.850: As1 PPP: Phase is FORWARDING, Attempting Forward
Mar  2 13:32:46.850: As1 PPP: Phase is AUTHENTICATING, Authenticated User
Mar  2 13:32:46.850: As1 PAP: O AUTH-ACK id 7 len 5
Mar  2 13:32:46.850: As1 PPP: Phase is UP
```

Network Control Protocol Phase of PPP

When the PPP phase is up, authentication has completed successfully. Then, Network Control Protocol (NCP) negotiates Layer 3 protocols, including IP Control Protocol (IPCP). In the case of dial, IPCP negotiates IP addresses for the peer IP address, the Domain Name System (DNS) servers, and the Windows Internet Naming Service (WINS) servers. The following explanations are based on the output from the command **debug ppp negotiation**. Remember that the output can be long and you see these lines only if the previous (authentication) phase is successful. First, an outgoing configuration request is sent to the peer that contains its own IP address:

```
Mar  2 13:32:46.854: As1 IPCP: O CONFREQ [Closed] id 7 len 10
Mar  2 13:32:46.854: As1 IPCP:    Address 192.168.0.249 (0x0306C0A800F9)
```

The peer then sends a request to the NAS to do Compression Control Protocol (CCP):

```
Mar  2 13:32:47.010: As1 CCP: I CONFREQ [Not negotiated] id 6 len 10
Mar  2 13:32:47.014: As1 CCP:    MS-PPC supported bits 0x00000001 (0x120600000001)
```

CCP is then rejected by an outgoing protocol rejection (O PROTREJ) packet. The peer should not attempt to renegotiate CCP:

```
Mar  2 13:32:47.014: As1 LCP: O PROTREJ [Open] id 34 len 16 protocol CCP
 (0x80FD0106000A120600000001)
```

An incoming configuration request is received, and the peer requests VJ 15 header compression and IP addresses for the peer, including the Primary DNS, Primary WINS, Secondary DNS, and Secondary WINS servers, as shown in Example 7-16.

Example 7-16 *Debug Output of IPCP Incoming Configuration Request*

```
Mar  2 13:32:47.058: As1 IPCP: I CONFREQ [REQsent] id 7 len 40
Mar  2 13:32:47.058: As1 IPCP:    CompressType VJ 15 slots CompressSlotID
 (0x0206002D0F01)
Mar  2 13:32:47.058: As1 IPCP:    Address 0.0.0.0 (0x030600000000)
Mar  2 13:32:47.058: As1 IPCP:    PrimaryDNS 0.0.0.0 (0x810600000000)
Mar  2 13:32:47.058: As1 IPCP:    PrimaryWINS 0.0.0.0 (0x820600000000)
Mar  2 13:32:47.058: As1 IPCP:    SecondaryDNS 0.0.0.0 (0x830600000000)
Mar  2 13:32:47.058: As1 IPCP:    SecondaryWINS 0.0.0.0 (0x840600000000)
```

NOTE   VJ compression is Van Jacobsen TCP header compression, which is a widely accepted compression method. See Part IV, "Frame Relay" for more information.

An outgoing configuration reject (O CONFREJ) is sent to reject VJ 15 header compression:

```
Mar  2 13:32:47.058: As1 IPCP: O CONFREJ [REQsent] id 7 len 10
Mar  2 13:32:47.058: As1 IPCP:    CompressType VJ 15 slots CompressSlotID
 (0x0206002D0F01)
```

An incoming configuration acknowledgment (I CONFACK) is received and the peer acknowledges the IP address of the NAS:

```
Mar  2 13:32:47.062: As1 IPCP: I CONFACK [REQsent] id 7 len 10
Mar  2 13:32:47.062: As1 IPCP:    Address 192.168.0.249 (0x0306C0A800F9)
```

Because VJ 15 header compression was rejected, so was the request for IP addresses for the peer and those of the DNS and WINS servers. The peer then sends another configuration request packet because the first was rejected, only this time, it asks for addressing without asking for header compression, as shown in Example 7-17.

Example 7-17 *Debug Output of IPCP Incoming Configuration Request Without Compression*

```
Mar  2 13:32:47.246: As1 IPCP: I CONFREQ [ACKrcvd] id 8 len 34
Mar  2 13:32:47.246: As1 IPCP:    Address 0.0.0.0 (0x030600000000)
Mar  2 13:32:47.246: As1 IPCP:    PrimaryDNS 0.0.0.0 (0x810600000000)
Mar  2 13:32:47.246: As1 IPCP:    PrimaryWINS 0.0.0.0 (0x820600000000)
Mar  2 13:32:47.246: As1 IPCP:    SecondaryDNS 0.0.0.0 (0x830600000000)
Mar  2 13:32:47.246: As1 IPCP:    SecondaryWINS 0.0.0.0 (0x840600000000)
```

Confusion occurs when the router sends a configuration non-acknowledgment, which actually refuses the request for the peer to use 0.0.0.0 as every address. Along with this non-acknowledgment (NAK), the NAS sends the peer the IP address and those of the DNS and WINS servers that it wants the peer to use, as shown in Example 7-18.

Example 7-18 *Debug Output of Outgoing Non-Acknowledgment with Server Assigned Addressing*

```
Mar  2 13:32:47.250: As1 IPCP: O CONFNAK [ACKrcvd] id 8 len 34
Mar  2 13:32:47.250: As1 IPCP:    Address 192.168.0.251 (0x0306C0A800FB)
Mar  2 13:32:47.250: As1 IPCP:    PrimaryDNS 192.168.100.3 (0x8106C0A86403)
Mar  2 13:32:47.250: As1 IPCP:    PrimaryWINS 192.168.100.5 (0x8206C0A86405)
Mar  2 13:32:47.250: As1 IPCP:    SecondaryDNS 192.168.100.4 (0x8306C0A86404)
Mar  2 13:32:47.250: As1 IPCP:    SecondaryWINS 192.168.100.6 (0x8406C0A86406)
```

The peer responds to the NAK with yet another configuration request to use the IP addresses provided with the previous NAK. Example 7-19 shows the expected output for this exchange.

Example 7-19 *Debug Output of Incoming Request with Server Assigned Addressing*

```
Mar  2 13:32:47.446: As1 IPCP: I CONFREQ [ACKrcvd] id 9 len 34
Mar  2 13:32:47.446: As1 IPCP:    Address 192.168.0.251 (0x0306C0A800FB)
Mar  2 13:32:47.446: As1 IPCP:    PrimaryDNS 192.168.100.3 (0x8106C0A86403)
Mar  2 13:32:47.446: As1 IPCP:    PrimaryWINS 192.168.100.5 (0x8206C0A86405)
Mar  2 13:32:47.446: As1 IPCP:    SecondaryDNS 192.168.100.4 (0x8306C0A86404)
Mar  2 13:32:47.450: As1 IPCP:    SecondaryWINS 192.168.100.6 (0x8406C0A86406)
```

The NAS then acknowledges the peer as configured correctly by sending an outgoing configuration acknowledgment packet, as shown in Example 7-20.

Example 7-20 *Debug Output of Outgoing Acknowledgment with Server Assigned Addressing*

```
Mar  2 13:32:47.450: As1 IPCP: O CONFACK [ACKrcvd] id 9 len 34
Mar  2 13:32:47.450: As1 IPCP:    Address 192.168.0.251 (0x0306C0A800FB)
Mar  2 13:32:47.450: As1 IPCP:    PrimaryDNS 192.168.100.3 (0x8106C0A86403)
Mar  2 13:32:47.450: As1 IPCP:    PrimaryWINS 192.168.100.5 (0x8206C0A86405)
Mar  2 13:32:47.450: As1 IPCP:    SecondaryDNS 192.168.100.4 (0x8306C0A86404)
Mar  2 13:32:47.450: As1 IPCP:    SecondaryWINS 192.168.100.6 (0x8406C0A86406)
```

When both sides agree on the addressing, IPCP changes state to open and installs the directly connected route to the dialup peer:

```
Mar  2 13:32:47.450: As1 IPCP: State is Open
Mar  2 13:32:47.454: As1 IPCP: Install route to 192.168.0.251
Mar  2 13:32:47.454: %LINEPROTO-5-UPDOWN: Line protocol on Interface Async1, changed
   state to up
```

NOTE   To troubleshoot a problem during NCP negotiation, ensure that all required IP addresses and protocols are configured.

Two of the most common issues that occur during the NCP stage of PPP negotiation are the following:

- The IP address is not configured on the group-async interface on the NAS. In most cases, you are not able to configure an IP address directly on the interface; therefore, you need to configure a loopback interface with an IP address. Use the command **ip unnumbered** *interface* on your group-async interface, where *interface* refers to your loopback interface. This instructs the group-async interface to use the IP address of the loopback.

- Verify the availability of pool IP addressing for the client. If all addresses in the pool are already allocated, NCP fails by not providing the peer with an IP address.

NOTE   The typical dial oversubscription ratio for Internet service providers (ISPs) is about ten users to one DS0, and scaling beyond this number is not recommended. In the case of an enterprise environment, remote users tend to dial up more often, and this ratio can be as low as 5 to 1. Oversubscription ratios for enterprises that provide a wide variety of remote access services might find it easier to base their oversubscription rate on percentages. For example, an enterprise might try to keep an average of 40 percent of DS0s available throughout a typical day. This 40 percent is there to handle the spikes in daily usage and holidays, when dial usage is normally much higher than on average.

- Verify that DNS and WINS server IP addresses are configured to respond to BOOTP requests. Use the global configuration commands **async-bootp dns-server** *address(es)* and **async-bootp nbns-server** *address(es)* to configure this feature.

After PPP negotiation is complete, the dial connection is complete and traffic is able to pass, unless of course routing problems exist in the network.

Troubleshooting Dial-Out Service

When an outbound call is placed, the output in Example 7-21 is generated from dial-on-demand events and PPP protocol negotiation debugging. The commands that enable this debugging include #**debug dialer** and #**debug ppp negotiation**.

Example 7-21 *Debug Output of Dialer and PPP Negotiation for an Outgoing Call*

```
Mar  1 00:11:15.975: As65 DDR: place call
Mar  1 00:11:15.975: As65 DDR: Dialing cause ip (s=192.168.0.2, d=216.115.102.82)
Mar  1 00:11:15.975: As65 DDR: Attempting to dial 6222230
Mar  1 00:11:15.975: CHAT65: Attempting async line dialer script
Mar  1 00:11:15.983: CHAT65: no matching chat script found for 6222230
Mar  1 00:11:15.983: CHAT65: Dialing using Modem script: d0efault-d0ials0cript
      & System script: none
Mar  1 00:11:15.987: CHAT65: process started
Mar  1 00:11:15.987: CHAT65: Asserting DTR
Mar  1 00:11:15.987: CHAT65: Chat script d0efault-d0ials0cript started
```

To place a call, some interesting traffic must be routed out the async65 interface. In the output shown in Example 7-21, the source address 192.168.0.2 (a host on the Ethernet segment) sent a packet to 216.115.102.82, which caused the router to attempt to dial.

In most cases, you do not need a dial chat script and the default works. The default dial script simply performs the modem AT commands to cause the modem connect and then hands the connection over to the async interface. If the modem does not attempt to dial, check for cabling problems or the correct line configuration. The line must be set for **modem InOut** and the async interface requires a dialer string. Also, ensure that the phone line is active because without a dial tone the modem cannot dial.

At this point, the modem should train up. Once this is successful, the script ends and the interface changes state to up, as shown in the output in Example 7-22.

Example 7-22 *Continuation of Debug from Example 7-21*

```
Mar  1 00:11:39.731: CHAT65: Chat script d0efault-d0ials0cript finished,
    status = success
00:11:41: %LINK-3-UPDOWN: Interface Async65, changed state to up
Mar  1 00:11:41.735: As65 DDR: Dialer state change to up
Mar  1 00:11:41.735: As65 DDR: Dialer call has been placed
Mar  1 00:11:41.735: As65 PPP: Treating connection as a callout
Mar  1 00:11:41.735: As65 PPP: Phase is ESTABLISHING, Active Open
Mar  1 00:11:41.735: As65 PPP: No remote authentication for call-out
```

After the interface is up, PPP negotiation takes place. By default with PAP and CHAP, the router attempts to authenticate the remote side, even on outbound calls. However, this router is configured to only authenticate inbound calls and does not authenticate the server that it is dialing into. To configure this, the word **callin** must be added to the **ppp authentication** interface configuration command.

From this point, the PPP negotiation is exactly the opposite from the previous section because the router acts as a client, and not as the server. The dial-out router sends an outgoing configuration request to the NAS to advise it has connected, as shown in Example 7-23.

Example 7-23 *Debug Output of PPP Outgoing Configuration Request*

```
Mar  1 00:11:41.739: As65 LCP: O CONFREQ [Closed] id 12 len 20
Mar  1 00:11:41.739: As65 LCP:    ACCM 0x000A0000 (0x0206000A0000)
Mar  1 00:11:41.739: As65 LCP:    MagicNumber 0xE0293F01 (0x0506E0293F01)
Mar  1 00:11:41.739: As65 LCP:    PFC (0x0702)
Mar  1 00:11:41.739: As65 LCP:    ACFC (0x0802)
```

Then, the NAS sends the dial-out router a configuration request asking to authenticate through PAP, as shown in Example 7-24.

Example 7-24 *Debug Output of Incoming Request for PAP*

```
Mar  1 00:11:41.915: As65 LCP: I CONFREQ [REQsent] id 253 len 28
Mar  1 00:11:41.915: As65 LCP:    MRU 1500 (0x010405DC)
Mar  1 00:11:41.915: As65 LCP:    ACCM 0x000A0000 (0x0206000A0000)
Mar  1 00:11:41.919: As65 LCP:    MagicNumber 0x01000000 (0x050601000000)
Mar  1 00:11:41.919: As65 LCP:    PFC (0x0702)
Mar  1 00:11:41.919: As65 LCP:    ACFC (0x0802)
Mar  1 00:11:41.919: As65 LCP:    AuthProto PAP (0x0304C023)
```

The router responds to the configuration request for PAP with a configuration acknowledgment, as shown in Example 7-25.

Example 7-25 *Debug Output of Outgoing Acknowledgment for PAP*

```
Mar  1 00:11:41.919: As65 LCP: O CONFACK [REQsent] id 253 len 28
Mar  1 00:11:41.919: As65 LCP:    MRU 1500 (0x010405DC)
Mar  1 00:11:41.919: As65 LCP:    ACCM 0x000A0000 (0x0206000A0000)
Mar  1 00:11:41.919: As65 LCP:    MagicNumber 0x01000000 (0x050601000000)
Mar  1 00:11:41.919: As65 LCP:    PFC (0x0702)
Mar  1 00:11:41.919: As65 LCP:    ACFC (0x0802)
Mar  1 00:11:41.919: As65 LCP:    AuthProto PAP (0x0304C023)
```

The NAS then responds with a configuration acknowledgment and LCP is complete, as shown in Example 7-26.

Example 7-26 *Debug Output of Incoming Acknowledgment for PAP*

```
Mar  1 00:11:41.923: As65 LCP: I CONFACK [ACKsent] id 12 len 20
Mar  1 00:11:41.923: As65 LCP:    ACCM 0x000A0000 (0x0206000A0000)
Mar  1 00:11:41.927: As65 LCP:    MagicNumber 0xE0293F01 (0x0506E0293F01)
Mar  1 00:11:41.927: As65 LCP:    PFC (0x0702)
Mar  1 00:11:41.927: As65 LCP:    ACFC (0x0802)
Mar  1 00:11:41.927: As65 LCP: State is Open
```

After the LCP phase is completed, the router and NAS start authentication. First, the router sends an outgoing authentication request with the username and password. The following shows the username in the debug output:

```
Mar  1 00:11:41.927: As65 PPP: Phase is AUTHENTICATING, by the peer
Mar  1 00:11:41.927: As65 PAP: O AUTH-REQ id 1 len 37 from "jhuegen"
```

Next, the router receives an incoming authentication acknowledgment, which indicates that authentication is successful. If authentication had failed, a NAK would have been received along with a reason, which is usually authentication failure:

```
Mar  1 00:11:43.883: As65 PAP: I AUTH-ACK id 1 len 5
```

The following output shows that authentication is now complete, and the router moves on to the NCP stage of PPP negotiation:

```
Mar  1 00:11:43.883: As65 PPP: Phase is FORWARDING, Attempting Forward
Mar  1 00:11:43.887: As65 PPP: Phase is ESTABLISHING, Finish LCP
Mar  1 00:11:43.887: As65 PPP: Phase is UP
```

The router now sends an outgoing configuration request stating its intent to use IP address 0.0.0.0. The router expects this request will be refused and a real address will be assigned to it:

```
Mar  1 00:11:43.887: As65 IPCP: O CONFREQ [Closed] id 1 len 10
Mar  1 00:11:43.887: As65 IPCP:    Address 0.0.0.0 (0x030600000000)
```

Next, the dial-out router receives an incoming configuration request to use VJ 15 header compression. Also in this configuration request, the NAS sends its IP address:

```
Mar  1 00:11:43.891: As65 IPCP: I CONFREQ [REQsent] id 254 len 16
Mar  1 00:11:43.895: As65 IPCP:    CompressType VJ 15 slots CompressSlotID
  (0x0206002D0F01)
Mar  1 00:11:43.895: As65 IPCP:    Address 216.192.135.254 (0x0306D8C087FE)
```

The router then rejects the header compression, and by doing so it rejects the IP address of the NAS. This is sent back to the dial-out router another time without the compression request:

```
Mar  1 00:11:43.895: As65 IPCP: O CONFREJ [REQsent] id 254 len 10
Mar  1 00:11:43.895: As65 IPCP:    CompressType VJ 15 slots CompressSlotID
  (0x0206002D0F01)
```

The NAS rejects the requested IP address of 0.0.0.0 and offers 216.192.135.145 to the router for use:

```
Mar  1 00:11:44.007: As65 IPCP: I CONFNAK [REQsent] id 1 len 10
Mar  1 00:11:44.007: As65 IPCP:    Address 216.192.135.145 (0x0306D8C08791)
```

In return, the router requests that the NAS allow it to use the address it offered in the previous configuration request:

```
Mar  1 00:11:44.007: As65 IPCP: O CONFREQ [REQsent] id 2 len 10
Mar  1 00:11:44.007: As65 IPCP:    Address 216.192.135.145 (0x0306D8C08791)
```

The NAS then resends its IP address to the router; this time without requesting header compression:

```
Mar  1 00:11:44.011: As65 IPCP: I CONFREQ [REQsent] id 255 len 10
Mar  1 00:11:44.011: As65 IPCP:    Address 216.192.135.254 (0x0306D8C087FE)
```

The dial-out router replies and acknowledges the IP address of the NAS as follows:

```
Mar  1 00:11:44.015: As65 IPCP: O CONFACK [REQsent] id 255 len 10
Mar  1 00:11:44.015: As65 IPCP:    Address 216.192.135.254 (0x0306D8C087FE)
```

Next, the NAS acknowledges the requested IP address of the dial-out router, which it offered to the router in the first place:

```
Mar  1 00:11:44.123: As65 IPCP: I CONFACK [ACKsent] id 2 len 10
Mar  1 00:11:44.123: As65 IPCP:    Address 216.192.135.145 (0x0306D8C08791)
```

Finally, the NCP state of PPP negotiation is completed, as signaled by the State is Open statement:

```
Mar  1 00:11:44.123: As65 IPCP: State is Open
Mar  1 00:11:44.123: As65 IPCP: Install negotiated IP interface address
  216.192.135.145
```

NOTE   The router did not request DNS and WINS server information. It is configured this way
because there is no way to automatically provide negotiated information to PCs upon
connection. Therefore, this information was obtained ahead of time, and statically
configured into the Dynamic Host Configuration Protocol (DHCP) server in the router.

When PPP is up, the router forwards the packets it was holding in the dialer hold-queue
during the train-up, authentication, and PPP negotiation phases to their destination. The
router also installs a route to the peer on the other end of the connection, as shown in the
third line of the output:

```
Mar  1 00:11:44.127: As65 DDR: dialer protocol up
Mar  1 00:11:44.127: As65 DDR: Call connected, 5 packets unqueued, 5 transmitted,
  0 discarded
Mar  1 00:11:44.131: As65 IPCP: Install route to 216.192.135.254
00:11:44: %LINEPROTO-5-UPDOWN: Line protocol on Interface Async65, changed state
  to up
```

The command **show ip interface brief** shows the async interface with its negotiated IP
address, and the method by which this IP address was received. Because in this case the IP
address is a result of successful PPP negotiation, it shows IPCP as the method. This
command and output is demonstrated in Example 7-27.

Example 7-27 *Output of* **show ip interface brief**

```
Router#show ip interface brief
Interface            IP-Address      OK? Method Status      Protocol
Async65              216.192.135.145 YES IPCP   up          up
Ethernet0/0          192.168.0.1     YES NVRAM  up          up
```

If PPP does not fully negotiate, it is most likely not caused by a LCP timeout issue on the
NAS site. This is because a line speed issue prevents the modem from dialing in the first
place. If you receive LCP timeouts as covered in the section, "Troubleshooting Dial-In
Service," the service provider is most likely the source of the issue.

Another issue is an authentication problem caused when the username and password
combination fails. If this occurs, reconfigure the username and password and, if necessary,
verify it with the provider.

The last issue that can cause problems is the router trying to authenticate the NAS. Because
the router is the connecting party, and no provider allows a connecting party to authenticate
them (unless this is arranged in advance), check the configuration for **ppp authentication**
type. This command should not be included in the async interface configuration because it
will try to authenticate the NAS. If this is the case, your debug should display the output,
as shown in Example 7-28.

Example 7-28 *Authentication Type Mismatch*

```
Mar  1 00:09:29.507: As65 LCP: O CONFREQ [ACKsent] id 2 len 24
Mar  1 00:09:29.511: As65 LCP:    ACCM 0x000A0000 (0x0206000A0000)
Mar  1 00:09:29.511: As65 LCP:    AuthProto PAP (0x0304C023)
Mar  1 00:09:29.511: As65 LCP:    MagicNumber 0xE0273903 (0x0506E0273903)
Mar  1 00:09:29.511: As65 LCP:    PFC (0x0702)
Mar  1 00:09:29.511: As65 LCP:    ACFC (0x0802)
Mar  1 00:09:29.827: As65 LCP: I CONFREJ [ACKsent] id 2 len 8
Mar  1 00:09:29.831: As65 LCP:    AuthProto PAP (0x0304C023)
Mar  1 00:09:29.831: As65 LCP: O CONFREQ [ACKsent] id 3 len 24
Mar  1 00:09:29.831: As65 LCP:    ACCM 0x000A0000 (0x0206000A0000)
Mar  1 00:09:29.831: As65 LCP:    AuthProto PAP (0x0304C023)
Mar  1 00:09:29.831: As65 LCP:    MagicNumber 0xE0273903 (0x0506E0273903)
Mar  1 00:09:29.831: As65 LCP:    PFC (0x0702)
Mar  1 00:09:29.831: As65 LCP:    ACFC (0x0802)
Mar  1 00:09:30.083: As65 LCP: I CONFREJ [ACKsent] id 3 len 8
Mar  1 00:09:30.083: As65 LCP:    AuthProto PAP (0x0304C023)
```

In the debug in Example 7-28, the router requests PAP authentication from the NAS. The NAS rejects the request, and because authentication is required, the router requests it again. This process continues in a loop until the router is disconnected for exceeding the connect timer.

AS5x00 Specific Commands and Debugs

High-density Cisco dial routers include the AS5100, AS5200, AS5300, AS5400, and AS5800 series routers. These devices were all developed for an ISP to provide dial-in services for a wide variety of customers. All these devices are modular so that if a modem or a group of modems is faulty, a feature card can be replaced instead of the entire router.

The AS5100 series router is no longer in production, but was solely a router with a lot of external modems on line cards connected to it, all in one chassis; not modular. In fact, phone lines were connected to each of the individual modem line cards on the router. Because the AS5100 is no longer in production and was essentially the same as the router used for the examples on Basic PPP Dial-In Service, it is not covered in detail in this chapter.

The AS5200 series was the first Cisco product in this line to introduce 56 k modems. The router used Microcom modems that were software upgradeable using a digital signal processor (DSP) and firmware files available from the Cisco Systems web site. This server was also the first Cisco dial router to use channelized T1s or PRIs to handle incoming calls. This router has since reached the end of the production cycle.

The AS5300 opened the door to out-of-band signaling. Although the AS5200 had limited out-of-band signaling, the AS5300 (with the MICA modems) allows for polling all kinds of data from the modem that was not previously available. This includes real-time band-width measurements, line shape measurements, serial-to-noise ratio, as well as many other parameters that are key to troubleshooting real-time. Most, if not all competitor dial servers do not provide for this real-time data, and it must be extracted from the modems via the AT command **ati11** after the call is completed. The AS5300 can handle a total of 8 PRIs worth of calls in its 2U chassis.

The AS5400 provides the same out of band signaling, but it has taken port density to a new level. At the time this book was written, the AS5400 can receive a CT3 worth of calls (552 calls if split into 24 PRIs with 23 available channels each) in a router that only consumes 2U worth of rack space. This is possible because of the new NextPort modems included in the AS5400. The AS5350 shares these modems in a 1U chassis that can handle 16 PRIs worth of calls.

The AS5800 was developed with the AS5300 and provided the same functionality as the AS5300, but in a higher density package. It is a large 48VDC unit that was designed for the service provider environment. As well as the use of the MICA modems, all configuration commands are the same as the AS5300.

The AS5850 shares the new NextPort modems with the AS5400 and AS5350, but in a larger chassis developed for sizeable deployments. The AS5850 is a 14U rack mount unit that can handle up to 3360 calls (5xCT3s), 96 T1s or 86 E1s. While not as dense as the AS5400 in terms of ports per unit of rack space, the AS5850 was developed to handle six times its current density.

One of the most commonly used maintenance procedures for all earlier platforms is to upgrade the modem firmware. Although it is relatively straightforward, the procedure requires some steps that are included in the following example.

To upgrade modem software on the routers, you must first know what version of IOS is running on the router. There are two different scenarios for upgrading modem firmware, depending on the IOS version. Each step is covered here.

The first step in upgrading modem firmware is to get the latest version from Cisco.com and put it on your TFTP server. Next, copy it to the flash on the router that requires the update. Be sure not to erase the original contents of the flash memory when copying the upgrade to flash. Example 7-29 shows how to copy an image file to flash.

Example 7-29 *Output from the* **copy tftp flash** *Command*

```
5300-dialin#copy tftp flash
Address or name of remote host []? 192.168.1.17
! Enter the image file name you want to copy:
Source filename []? mica-modem-pw.2.7.3.0.bin
Destination filename [mica-modem-pw.2.7.3.0.bin]?
Accessing tftp://www-emp/ mica-modem-pw.2.7.3.0.bin...
Erase flash: before copying? [confirm]n
Loading mica-modem-pw.2.7.3.0.bin from 192.168.1.17 (via FastEthernet0):
!!!!!!!!!!!!!!!!!!!!!!!!!!!!!!!!!!!!!!!!!!!!!!!!!!!!!!!!!!!!!!!!!!!!!!!!!!!!!!!!!!!!
    !!!!!!!!!!!!!!!
[OK - 474939/949248 bytes]

Verifying checksum...  OK (0xCB52)
```

The image must reside in flash because the modems load this software each time the router is restarted. For IOS versions earlier than 12.0(5), the modem upgrade is done through the **copy flash modem** command, at an enabled prompt, but not in configuration mode. The following is an illustration of that process:

```
5300-dialin#copy flash modem
Modem Numbers (/[-/] | group | all)? all
Name of file to copy? mica-modem-pw.2.7.3.0.bin
Type of service [busyout/reboot] reboot
```

NOTE   Using **reboot** as the type of service does not upgrade the modems until the next time the router is reloaded. This is handy if there are prescheduled maintenance windows. You can then use the **reload at** command to schedule the reload for a specific time, in advance.

As a precaution, only use **busyout** if call volume on the router is low. The router upgrades the modems by busying out all modems and upgrading the groups that have no calls on them. These groups contain either six or 12 modems, depending on type. If calls currently connected prevent modems from upgrading, inbound calls can be rejected with a fast-busy signal because no modems are available.

To confirm the upgrade, use the command **show modem version** to verify that the modems have the new version.

For IOS releases later than 12.0(5), the upgrade is done in Software Port Entry (SPE) configuration mode. Use the command **show spe version** to see what firmware versions are stored in flash on the router and determine which ones require an upgrade. The following lines show the configuration commands required to upgrade spe software:

```
5300-dialin#configure terminal
5300-dialin(config)#spe 1/0 2/9
5300-dialin(config-spe)#firmware upgrade reboot
5300-dialin(config-spe)#firmware location flash:mica-modem-pw.2.7.3.0.bin
```

If you want to use **reboot** as the type of upgrade service, specify this before specifying the location of the firmware. After the location of the firmware is specified, the router begins the upgrade. Because the default is **busyout**, you can easily busy out every modem on a busy access server if you do not specify this beforehand.

To confirm the upgrade, use the command **show spe modem** to verify that the modems have the new version.

AS5200 Specific Commands and Debugs

There are numerous additional commands for modems in the AS5200 series. Although this product has reached the end of life (EOL), it is still in widespread use so these commands are still worth covering. Only the most useful and most commonly used commands are covered.

The first of these commands is **show modem**, which shows a list of all modems along with the number of successful and failed incoming call attempts, outgoing call attempts, and a percentage of successful calls. In addition, it displays the current status of every modem: active, busied out, bad, downloading firmware, or pending download.

If you prefer to only see the summary of this information, use the command **show modem summary**. You can almost immediately tell if there is a problem by looking at the success percentage. Most dial-in pools have a 90 percent or higher success rate.

Using the same **show modem** *slot/port* command (including a specific modem) shows you much more detail about the specified modem, along with all the connection speeds reached with that modem.

The **show modem call-stats** command displays the statistics for all modems and includes reasons for disconnect, compression, number of retrains, and a summary of all the information.

Another useful command is **show modem connect-speeds**, which shows the total number of connections at each speed throughout the range for both receive and transmit. A summary along with percentages is also provided later in the section. This is useful to get a quick glimpse of what your clients are experiencing.

A command that you use often when reporting problems to the Technical Assistance Center (TAC) is **show modem csm** *slot/port*, which provides the TAC a view of exactly what is occurring with a call switching module (CSM) at that precise point in time.

Another command that the TAC often uses to help debug problems is **show modem log** *slot/port*. It provides all information about what the modem has done previously. The data is purged on a first in first out basis, so use this show command immediately after the problem occurs. The command shows all RS232 events, modem state events, modem analog signal events, and connection events. It also contains information on train-up speeds, modulation, and serial-to-noise ratio.

The last of the **show** commands created for the AS5200 is **show modem version**, which shows what version of software is on the modems. Always keep this software up to date to obtain the best possible connection for remote users. A separate procedure exists for each kind of modem (see www.cisco.com for further details).

The AS5200s also have several added debugging modes. The first is **debug modem oob**, which shows information about a modem's out-of-band port that polls modem events. The **debug modem csm** command displays information about the CSM that connects calls. It shows all information about calls coming in from the PRI and what modem it lands on.

Perhaps one of the most useful debug commands in dial routers is **debug modem trace**. With this debug, you can select normal, abnormal, or all reasons for call termination. To gather all abnormal call terminations on the entire router, use the command **debug modem trace abnormal**. If you want to gather all terminations from a specific modem, in the event that you think a particular modem is malfunctioning, use the command **debug modem**

trace all *slot/port*. When disconnecting a call that matched the debug, a trace is sent to the screen including everything that took place with the call, down to the finest detail.

Finally, there is one other command that is neither a show command nor a debug command. This command is **test modem back-to-back** *slot/port slot/port*. It performs a test from one modem to the other to ensure that it can train up and pass data. This test is only done at V.34 speeds.

AS5300 Specific Commands and Debugs

The commands for the AS5200 also work with the AS5300. The AS5300 added MICA modems along with some unique out-of-band functionality. This allowed for a few more commands to provide real-time information that was not possible before. Most of these commands provide little information, but assist the TAC in quickly determining a problem.

The first of these new commands is **show modem configuration**, which shows the setup of the modem. Any changes you make to the modem through a modemcap, appears in the output of this command.

Another command for the AS5300 is **show modem mica** *slot/port*. This is another command that the TAC reviews to help determine a problem.

The **show modem operational-status** *slot/port* command assists you in determining some problems, without the help of TAC engineers. The following is sample output from this command with additional comments provided to assist with troubleshooting:

```
5300-dial#show modem operational-status 1/13
Modem(1/13) Operational-Status:

 Parameter #0  Disconnect Reason Info:  (0x0)
       Type (=0 ):  <unknown>
      Class (=0 ):  Other
     Reason (=0 ):  no disconnect has yet occurred
```

The parameter #0 of the output shows a disconnect reason that identifies the type of disconnect, the class of disconnect, and the reason that the disconnect took place. If there is an issue with a user frequently getting disconnected, determine what modem the user was last connected on, and perform this command to obtain information about the disconnection.

Parameters #1 and #2 cover the connection protocol and compression:

```
 Parameter #1  Connect Protocol:  LAP-M
 Parameter #2  Compression:  V.42bis both
```

Parameter #3 displays the error correction (EC) retransmission count, or the number of times that the modem has gone into error recovery in the transmit direction for a particular connection. Compare this parameter against the count produced by Parameter #36 (EC packets transmitted, received) to determine if a problem really exists.

```
Parameter #3  EC Retransmission Count:  193
```

Parameter #4 shows the error count received during a back-to-back modem test. During any normal active call, this number is 0:

```
Parameter #4  Self Test Error Count:  0
```

Parameter #5 shows how long the call is connected in seconds. This client is connected for just over 3 hours and 44 minutes:

```
Parameter #5  Call Timer:  13491 secs
```

Parameter #6 shows the number of retrains done by the modems. A high number of retrains identifies that the connection made by the client is not stable. This can happen from a dirty phone line, low signal-to-noise ratio (SNR), or even from someone picking up the phone and setting it back down while a modem call is in place over that line:

```
Parameter #6  Total Retrains:  4
```

Parameter #7 displays the measure of the receive signal quality (SQ) bit error rate for the current modulation, as estimated by the DSP. A value of 0 has the highest number of errors and 7 has the lowest. This value is used in conjunction with some S values configured on the modem to determine when to speed shift or retrain. If the SQ value reported in this parameter drops to the value of S32 (SQ Threshold) for longer than the value of S35 in seconds, the DSP attempts a downward speed shift or retrain. Similarly, if the SQ value goes above the threshold for longer than the value of S34 in seconds, an upward speed shift or retrain occurs.

Parameters #8 and #9 show the connection standard and current connection speed of the modem. This real-time data and might not be the same for the connecting client. The client uses a modem that does not have out-of-band signaling and only knows the initial connection speed:

```
Parameter #7  Sq Value:  3
Parameter #8  Connected Standard:  V.90
Parameter #9  TX,RX Bit Rate:  50666, 28800
```

Parameter #11 displays the transmit symbol rate that transmits samples to the line and the receive symbol rate that receives samples from the line:

```
Parameter #11 TX,RX Symbol Rate:  8000, 3200
```

Parameter #13 displays the transmit carrier frequency in Hertz that the local DCE uses and the receive carrier frequency that the remote DCE uses:

```
Parameter #13 TX,RX Carrier Frequency:  0, 1829
```

Parameter #15 shows trellis coding. Trellis coding adds dependency between symbols to make the detection in noise more robust (forward error correction [FEC]). Trellis coding is displayed in values. The value of 0 correlates to a connection standard V.22, V.22*bis*, V.21,

Bell212, Bell103, V.29, or V.27. The value of 8 correlates to a connection standard of V.32, V.32*bis*, or V.17. The value of 16, 32, or 64 correlates to a connection standard of V.34, V.34+, V.90, or K56Flex:

```
Parameter #15 TX,RX Trellis Coding:  0, 16
```

Parameter #16 shows the preemphasis index, which involves shaping the raw transmit spectrum to deal with spectrum roll-offs. A zero denotes no reshaping. This index is used only with V.34 and V.34+ connection standards:

```
Parameter #16 TX,RX Preemphasis Index:  22, 0
```

Parameter #17 shows if constellation shaping is used. Constellation shaping is a technique for improving noise immunity by using a probability distribution for transmitted signal points. The signal states predict the sensitivity to certain transmission impairments. Constellation shaping is used only with the V.34 and V.34+ connection standards. Values displayed by this parameter are either Off or On:

```
Parameter #17 TX,RX Constellation Shaping:  Off, Off
```

Parameter #18 shows if nonlinear encoding is used. Nonlinear encoding occurs during the training phase and moves the outer points of the constellation away to deal with nonlinear distortion. Nonlinear distortion tends to affect the higher-powered signals. Moving the outer constellation points out reduces the chance of error. Nonlinear encoding is used only with the V.34 and V.34+ connection standards. Values displayed by this parameter are either Off or On:

```
Parameter #18 TX,RX Nonlinear Encoding:  Off, Off
```

Parameter #19 shows if precoding is used. Precoding serves the same purpose as the preemphasis index, but instead manages the bits and not the raw transmit signals. This management is done only when asked for and therefore occurs only in the receive mode. Precoding is used only with the V.34 and V.34+ connection standards. Values displayed by this parameter are either Off or On:

```
Parameter #19 TX,RX Precoding:  Off, Off
```

Parameter #20 shows the transmit level reduction. The transmit level affects the transmit signal by reducing it in a range of 0 to 15 dBm. If nonlinear distortion is detected on either end, the modem detecting this distortion requests a lower-powered transmit signal. Transmit level reduction is used with the V.34 and V.34+ connection standards:

```
Parameter #20 TX,RX Xmit Level Reduction:  0, 0 dBm
```

Parameter #21 shows the SNR. This is the ratio on the server side and should not change. The SNR on the client side is determined by issuing the command **ati11** on the modem after disconnect. The higher the number, the better:

```
Parameter #21 Signal Noise Ratio:  36 dB
```

Parameter #22 shows that the power of the received signal ranges from 0 to -128. The optimum range for the receive level displayed by this parameter is from -12 dBm to -24 dBm:

```
Parameter #22 Receive Level:  -23 dBm
```

Parameter #23 shows the frequency offset, which is a shift in the receive spectrum between the expected carrier frequency and the actual carrier frequency. The typical value is 0 Hz:

```
Parameter #23 Frequency Offset:  0 Hz
```

Parameters #24 and #25 deal with phase jitter. This is found only in analog trunk circuits. Typical frequencies are power generation frequencies and their harmonics (that is, 60 and 120 Hz within the U.S; 50 and 100 Hz international). MICA modems cancel all frequencies of phase jitter:

```
Parameter #24 Phase Jitter Frequency:  0 Hz
Parameter #25 Phase Jitter Level:  0 degrees
```

Parameter #26 displays the far-end echo level (the portion of the transmitted analog signal that has bounced off of the analog front end of the remote modem), which can range from 0 to -90 dBm. A MICA modem cannot handle near-end echo if far-end echo is present and the round-trip delay is greater than ten microseconds. This constraint comes from the number of taps in the echo canceller of MICA modems. The reported far-end echo level must be less than -55 dBm to achieve a V.34+ connection. A greater echo level indicates a digital-to-analog conversion in the path between the MICA modem and the switch:

```
Parameter #26 Far End Echo Level:  -47 dBm
```

A form of this signal/constellation pattern echoes off equipment at the central office and is sent back to the MICA modem. However, the constellation shape might be rotated from its original position. This rotation is called the phase roll. It is shown in degrees of rotation in Parameter #27. The echoed signal consists of a frequency component and a phase component. If the frequency component changes at all, a correction is needed for echo cancellation to work correctly. The typical value is 0 or close to 0:

```
Parameter #27 Phase Roll:  0 degrees
```

Parameter #28 shows round-trip delay, which is the total round-trip from modem to modem in microseconds. This delay is important for proper echo cancellation:

```
Parameter #28 Round Trip Delay:  7 msecs
```

Parameter #30 displays the total count of characters sent and received before any modem compression takes place:

```
Parameter #30 Characters transmitted, received:  11116387, 2693386
```

Parameter #32 is included but not used. Other parameters, such as 10, 12, 14, 34, and 37 do not even show up in the output:

```
Parameter #32 General Portware Information:  22
```

Parameters #33 and #35 show the number of packets transmitted and received by the dial server from the client modem. This is useful in determining whether or not the modems are passing traffic to each other:

```
Parameter #33 PPP/SLIP packets transmitted, received:  24080, 23583
Parameter #35 PPP/SLIP packets received (BAD/ABORTED):  0
```

Parameter #36 displays the number of EC packets transmitted and the number of EC packets received:

```
Parameter #36 EC packets transmitted, received OK:  53258, 48144
```

Parameter #38 shows the moving average of EC packets. One way to determine if the connection has gotten better or worse with speedshifts and retrains is to check the moving average several times over the duration of a call. If the value decreases, the connection has become more stable:

```
Parameter #38 Moving Average of EC packets (Received BAD/ABORTED):  88
```

Parameter #39 shows what robbed bit signaling pattern is used. If robbed bit signaling is detected, the dial server must run a pattern so that the missing bit does not affect data transfer. As long as this is a 0, there is no RBS line between the server and the client:

```
Parameter #39 Robbed Bit Signalling (RBS) pattern:  0
```

Chapter 5, "Dial Technology Background," provided an explanation of the digital pad. Cisco dial servers try to avoid the problems incurred by the use of digital pads on a link. Parameter #40 shows if the dial server detected a digital pad and the compensation status:

```
Parameter #40 Digital Pad:  6.0   dB,  Digital Pad Compensation: Enabled
```

Parameters 41 through 44 deal with V.110 calls. These parameters show frames received bad, frames received good, frames transmitted, and number of times synchronization has been lost. Because this is a V.90 call, the values are always 0:

```
Parameter #41 V110/PIAFS frames received bad:  0
Parameter #42 V110/PIAFS frames received good:  0
Parameter #43 V110/PIAFS frames transmitted:  0
Parameter #44 V110/PIAFS sync lost:  0
```

The last piece of information to specifically review from the **show modem operational-status** output is the line shape. The MICA modems use the V.90 Digital Impairment Learning (DIL) sequence to determine the quality of the line and how much of the line is usable for data. Even if the DIL shows that V.90 is not feasible for the client modem connecting, it does store this information and trains up in V.34 mode.

When reviewing the line shape, you want the vertical line created by the asterisks to be as straight as possible. As the line is more curved at the beginning and the end, the maximum attainable connection speed drops. Example 7-30 shows the line shape output.

Example 7-30 *Line Shape*

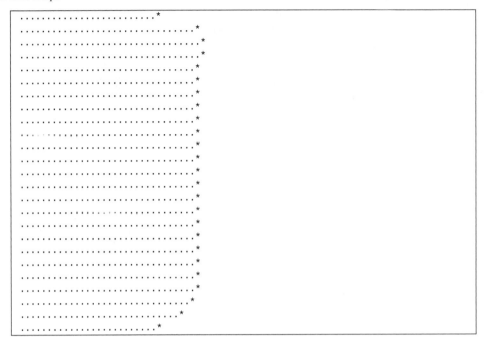

In this case, the line is mostly straight. Also, if you noticed the speed from parameter 9, the connection speed attained in the example is 50,666 baud, which is almost as good as you can get with a 56 k modem.

The only debugs added for the AS5300s are MICA modem debugs. The command **debug modem mica** displays the status of software downloads to the modems.

AS5400 Specific Commands and Debugs

With the introduction of the AS5400, most of the modem commands changed. The following is a list of the commands from the AS5200 and AS5300 that exist in the AS5400 under a different command:

- **show modem** changed to **show spe modem**.

- **show modem version** changed to **show spe version**.

- **show modem log** changed to **show spe log**.

- **show modem summary** changed to **show spe modem csr summary**.

- **show modem connect-speeds** changed to two separate commands:

   — **show spe modem high** shows high-speed modulation connects.

   — **show spe modem low** shows low-speed modulation connects.

The first of the two newly added show commands is **show spe modem active** *slot/spe*. It is not really a new command, but because modem types changed from MICA to NextPort modems, this command replaces the **show modem operational-status** from the AS5300s. Unfortunately, this command only works when the modem is active. To view the disconnect reason for a specific disconnected modem, refer to the command **show spe log** *slot/spe*.

The other helpful command is **show spe modem disconnect-reason** [*slot/port* | **summary**]. This command reveals the allocation of disconnect reasons that the particular slot and/or port on that specific modem has encountered. When reviewing the summary, it displays the total number of disconnects for each disconnect reason. This provides a quick indication of how many modem train-up failures took place.

Show commands are not the only thing that changed between the AS5300 and the AS5400. Most of the debug commands changed or are no longer available. The **debug modem csm** changed to **debug csm modem** and the **debug modem trace** command changed to **debug spe modem trace**.

Many specialized debugs added for the AS5400 deal with the NextPort engine and modules. The details of each are more than this book can cover. If you are experiencing a problem where these debugs are required for troubleshooting, the TAC can instruct you on which debugs to run and provide the required output.

Summary

This chapter follows the troubleshooting methodology suggested in Chapter 4, "Troubleshooting Approaches, Models, and Tools," with a layer-by-layer, phase-by-phase approach to remote access dial issues. Some of the topics of the chapter, such as detailed troubleshooting NAS WAN Links and T1s PRIs, are relevant to other parts of the book. This chapter includes an extensive amount of information about troubleshooting dial-in and dial-out services, where the modem's operational status is covered in greatest detail. The specifics of the different NAS platforms provided in this chapter can serve as a practical troubleshooting manual when dealing with all the different platforms of 5x00 NASs.

Review Questions

Answers to the review questions can be found in Appendix A, "Answers to Review Questions."

 1 What SQ value shows up in the output of **show modem operational-status**, indicating the most stable connection possible?

 2 True or False: Upgraded modem firmware does not have to be stored in flash after it is copied to the modem.

3 What is the controller configuration command required to correctly configure the distance of a circuit that is 639 feet?

```
Router(config-controller)#cablelength short 655
```

4 If you are receiving a blue alarm, what bit pattern is the equipment receiving?

5 What color is an alarm in which the controller status shows "Receiver has loss of Frame"?

6 What happens if one end of a T1 receives a yellow signal?

7 What information is negotiated in the IPCP stage of NCP of a modem dial call?

8 What modem AT command shows the connection information for a call that was previously disconnected?

9 What does BERT stand for?

10 What is the primary advantage that the AS5300 MICA modems have over the Microcom modems in the AS5200 series?

11 What does the call timer show?

12 What command on an AS 5200 and AS5300 shows a summary of all disconnect reasons and the number of disconnects for every reason?

13 What does CSM stand for and what is the command to show the processes of this device?

CHAPTER 8

Dial Troubleshooting Scenarios

Many problems can occur through the train-up, authentication, and Point-to-Point Protocol (PPP) negotiation phases when making a dialup connection. In all cases, it is best to take a step-by-step approach through the connection until you find the area where the problem occurs. This book cannot cover the details of all that can occur in the case of train-up failures or slow speed connections, but it does provide many helpful hints, tips, and tricks to assist with dial troubleshooting.

The authentication and PPP negotiation stages can be resolved to the point of finding the exact cause of the problem almost every time. In certain cases, the provider or telephone company (telco) might be required to fix the issue.

Five troubleshooting scenarios are provided in this chapter. Each scenario covers the most common troubleshooting issues that occur and how to pinpoint the exact causes of the problems. Following the scenarios are frequently asked questions with answers that can help you with common troubleshooting issues that don't always have clear solutions, or that have causes that cannot be pinpointed without more expertise. The topics covered in this chapter are as follows:

- Scenario 1: Authentication Time Outs—Part I
- Scenario 2: Authentication Time Outs—Part II
- Scenario 3: Frequent Retrains and Disconnects
- Scenario 4: Dirty Phone Line
- Scenario 5: Bad Modem
- Frequently Asked Questions and Answers

Scenario 1: Authentication Time Outs—Part I

A user calls in to report that his modem won't authenticate successfully. It seems to be stuck at the verifying username and password stage. First, you use the command **#debug ppp negotiation** to debug the problem.

After debugging the problem, the output in Example 8-1 is produced.

Example 8-1 *Output from* **debug ppp negotiation** *for Authentication Time Outs—Part I*

```
Mar  2 13:38:46.291: As1 LCP: I CONFREQ [ACKrcvd] id 66 len 14
Mar  2 13:38:46.291: As1 LCP: As1 LCP:   AuthProto PAP (0x0304C023)
Mar  2 13:38:46.291: As1 LCP:   MagicNumber 0xBC6B9F91 (0x0506BC6B9F91)
Mar  2 13:38:46.862: As1 LCP: O CONFNAK [ACKrcvd] id 66 len 9
Mar  2 13:38:46.862: As1 LCP:   AuthProto CHAP (0x0305C22305)
Mar  2 13:38:47.394: As1 LCP: I CONFREQ [ACKrcvd] id 67 len 14
Mar  2 13:38:47.394: As1 LCP:   AuthProto PAP (0x0304C023)
Mar  2 13:38:47.394: As1 LCP:   MagicNumber 0xDC6B9F91 (0x0506BC6B9F91)
Mar  2 13:38:47.919: As1 LCP: O CONFNAK [ACKrcvd] id 67 len 9
Mar  2 13:38:47.919: As1 LCP:   AuthProto CHAP (0x0305C22305)
Mar  2 13:38:48.488: As1 LCP: I CONFREQ [ACKrcvd] id 68 len 14
Mar  2 13:38:48.488: As1 LCP:   AuthProto PAP (0x0304C023)
Mar  2 13:38:48.488: As1 LCP:   MagicNumber 0xBC6B9F91 (0x0506BC6B9F91)
Mar  2 13:38:48.812: As1 LCP: O CONFNAK [ACKrcvd] id 68 len 9
Mar  2 13:38:48.812: As1 LCP:   AuthProto CHAP (0x0305C22305)
```

The output in Example 8-1 continues until the modems disconnect. In this example, the link control protocol (LCP) never completes and does not change to an open state. The client and server must agree on the authentication type (Password Authentication Protocol [PAP], Challenge Handshake Authentication Protocol [CHAP], or Microsoft CHAP [MS CHAP]) before LCP can change to an open state and allow authentication. In this case, the client requests PAP authentication and the server requires CHAP authentication, as shaded in Example 8-2.

Example 8-2 *Excerpt of Example 8-1 with CHAP and PAP Commentary*

```
! Non-acknowledgment is sent back saying no to PAP and requesting CHAP:
Mar  2 13:38:46.862: As1 LCP: O CONFNAK [ACKrcvd] id 66 len 9
Mar  2 13:38:46.862: As1 LCP:   AuthProto CHAP (0x0305C22305)
! Request comes in asking to authenticate via PAP:
Mar  2 13:38:47.394: As1 LCP: I CONFREQ [ACKrcvd] id 67 len 14
Mar  2 13:38:47.394: As1 LCP:   AuthProto PAP (0x0304C023)
Mar  2 13:38:47.394: As1 LCP:   MagicNumber 0xBC6B9F91 (0x0506BC6B9F91)
```

The client sends a configuration request to the network access server (NAS) requesting PAP authentication. The NAS sends a non-acknowledgment back to the client that denies PAP authentication and asks for CHAP authentication. The client only knows how to authenticate through PAP and resends its request for PAP authentication. This continues in a loop until a disconnect timer ends the call.

The fix is implemented by making sure that the authentication protocols on both ends are the same. If the service is supposed to authenticate through CHAP, the end user must reconfigure the dial client to use CHAP authentication. If the service is supposed to allow PAP authentication, the router must be reconfigured to accept PAP authentication.

In this case, the service was supposed to accept only CHAP, so the end user reconfigured the dial client and then reconnected.

Scenario 2: Authentication Time Outs—Part II

An end user calls up and states that the connection hangs during the verifying username and password stage of the connection. This time, the problem seems to be widespread. Again, the command #**debug ppp negotiation** is used to log the connection while the client tries to dial in. After debugging, you see the LCP information in Example 8-3 repeat itself.

Example 8-3   *Output from* **debug ppp negotiation** *for Authentication Time Outs—Part II*

```
Mar  2 19:58:19.768: As1 LCP: O CONFREQ [REQsent] id 74 len 25
Mar  2 19:58:19.768: As1 LCP: ACCM 0x000A0000 (0x0206000A0000)
Mar  2 19:58:19.768: As1 LCP: AuthProto PAP (0x0304C023)
Mar  2 19:58:19.768: As1 LCP: MagicNumber 0x5779D9D2 (0x05065779D9D2)
Mar  2 19:58:19.768: As1 LCP: PFC (0x0702)
Mar  2 19:58:19.768: As1 LCP: ACFC (0x0802)
Mar  2 19:58:21.768: As1 LCP: TIMEout: State REQsent
```

The debug output in Example 8-3 happens every two seconds until the modems disconnect. If you review the output carefully, the only event that occurs is outgoing LCP packets—O CONFREQ. This type of problem usually occurs because of a speed mismatch between a router and a modem, which is why the problem seems so widespread. Any user connecting to this modem would have the same problem. This should occur only when there is an external modem attached to the router.

The fix involves verifying whether the speed is set the same on both the modem and the router. In this case, the modem is configured with a line speed of 15200 instead of 115200. It is fixed by issuing the line configuration command **speed 115200** on the client modem.

Scenario 3: Frequent Retrains and Disconnects

To the client, frequent retrains or speedshifts are reported as a bad connection, where data flow is interrupted often. In most cases, a client does not hear the modem retrain because the speaker is turned off after the first train-up is successful.

If you encounter a problem such as this, you can easily determine if the modem is retraining frequently. Just look at the output of the **show modem operational-status** command for the modem that this client last connected to or is currently connected to. Pay particular attention to the following output of these connections:

```
Parameter #5  Call Timer:  1001 secs
Parameter #6  Total Retrains:  11
```

This shows that the user has retrained 11 times in the last 1001 seconds. Looking further down the output, other information about the user's connection also helps (only the parameters necessary to review are shown; the other parameters were omitted from the output):

```
Parameter #8  Connected Standard:  V.90
Parameter #9  TX,RX Bit Rate:  49333, 31200
Parameter #21 Signal Noise Ratio:  39 dB
Parameter #39 Robbed Bit Signalling (RBS) pattern:  0
Parameter #40 Digital Pad:  None,  Digital Pad Compensation: Enabled
```

The client achieves a good speed for both upload and download, modulation is V.90, signal-to-noise ratio is good, and no robbed bit signaling or digital pad events are affecting the call. Even further down in the output of the **show modem operational-status** command is a section for line shape. Check the line shape, as shown in Example 8-4.

Example 8-4 *Line Shape of Frequent Retrain and Disconnect Problems*

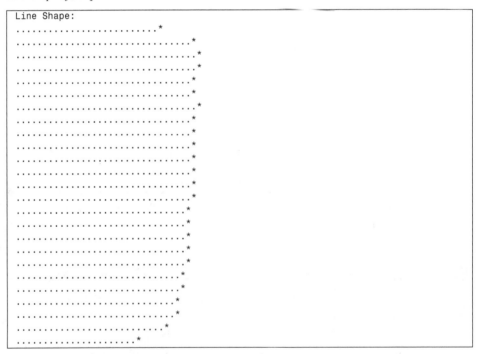

Overall, the line shape is not that bad. Remember, this line must be as vertical as possible. It does tail off slightly at the low and high frequencies, but neither of the extremes is too bad. Because everything checks out except for the retrain number, start with the simplest thing that might eliminate the problem. The first of these is call waiting. Call waiting produces a beep when an incoming call comes in. This beep can upset the connection and force a retrain. Having the user dial *67 before the phone number disables call waiting in most cases. Check with the local telco if this does not work.

A short in the cable that goes from the PC to the wall jack can be another source of trouble. It might be that the cable is fine, but that the PC has been bumped, and the connection has a short, which causes speedshift or retrain problems. This can also occur with other phones around the house. Another quick test is to unplug all the phones that are connected to that line and perform another test call. If two phone lines exist at the same location, a phone line problem can also be ruled out by trying to call over the other phone line.

If none of these solutions helps the problem, software might be a good place to turn next. Because modem software is updated frequently because of bug fixes, technology advancements, and stability improvements, you must make sure that the modems in the NAS are running the latest Technical Assistance Center (TAC) recommended software.

If the modem code on the NAS is up to date, proceed by asking the end user to upgrade his modem code to the latest version. Modems that are driven from software, such as Lucent WinModems, typically have new driver versions available more often than firmware-based modems.

Finally, if all else fails, a modem hardware problem might exist. When all other possible solutions are exhausted, recommend using a different modem to see if the problem disappears.

Scenario 4: Dirty Phone Line

A dirty phone line usually does not have the same symptoms as frequent retrains and disconnects; however, they do occur. In this case, the primary issue that the client reports is that the speed of the connection is unacceptable. The same outputs as "Scenario 3: Frequent Retrains and Disconnects" are provided here, except that these outputs show a modem that is connected to a dirty phone line. Again, the command to use is **show modem operational-status** while having the client attempt a connection. The output is shown in Example 8-5.

Example 8-5 *The* **show modem operational-status** *Output with a Dirty Phone Line*

```
 Parameter #5  Call Timer:  10682 secs
 Parameter #6  Total Retrains:  12
<output  omitted>
 Parameter #8  Connected Standard:  V.34+
 Parameter #9  TX,RX Bit Rate:  26400, 26400
<output  omitted>
 Parameter #21 Signal Noise Ratio:  35 dB
<output  omitted>
 Parameter #39 Robbed Bit Signalling (RBS) pattern:  0
 Parameter #40 Digital Pad:  None,  Digital Pad Compensation: None
```

There are many retrains over the length of the call, the speed is much lower, and the signal-to-noise ratio is lower. The line shape from the end of the **show modem operational-status** output shows just how bad the line is, as shown in Example 8-6.

Example 8-6 *Line Shape from a Dirty Phone Line*

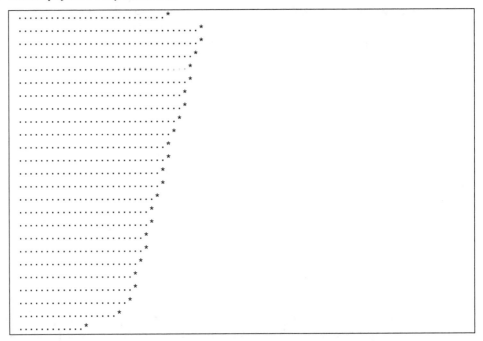

The line tapers off drastically compared to that of a clean line. Because of this reaction, bandwidth is significantly limited, which makes the connection slower. You can use this data to tell the client that their phone line is the problem.

The recommended fix is for the user to notify his telco of this problem and, if possible, have it resolved. In most cases, the telco will first test the line to see where a possible problem might exist. A wide variety of things might need to be fixed, including replacing a bridge tap or repeater. The problem might also exist in a faulty line card at the central office (CO). The telco might even change the pair of wires that your phone is delivered on.

Not all problems can be resolved by the telco. In cases where the distance between the CO and home is too great, there is no fix for slow connections.

Scenario 5: Bad Modem

A bad modem is not something generally reported by your clients. A modem that is experiencing problems usually does not mark itself as defective unless there is an obvious hardware problem. Instead, you must analyze the modem with the **show modem** command.

An output from **show modem** is provided in Example 8-7, where a group of six modems are obviously bad. In the AS5300 access server, modems generally become faulty in groups of six or 12, depending on the types of modems in the device.

Example 8-7 *Output of* **show modem** *Showing a Bad Modem Card*

	Avg Hold	Inc calls		Out calls		Busied	Failed	No	Succ
Mdm	Time	Succ	Fail	Succ	Fail	Out	Dial	Answer	Pct.
* 1/0	00:57:37	408	7	0	0	0	0	0	98%
* 1/1	01:02:03	397	8	0	0	0	0	0	98%
* 1/2	01:08:09	374	8	0	0	0	0	0	98%
* 1/3	00:52:28	419	7	0	0	0	0	0	98%
* 1/4	00:48:24	434	8	0	0	0	0	0	98%
* 1/5	00:57:55	417	5	0	0	0	0	0	99%
<output omitted>									
* 1/30	01:04:09	350	36	0	0	0	0	30	91%
* 1/31	00:46:53	409	41	0	0	0	0	30	91%
* 1/32	00:53:40	366	43	0	0	0	0	30	89%
* 1/33	00:53:00	384	37	0	0	0	0	29	91%
* 1/34	00:48:18	393	38	0	0	0	0	30	91%
* 1/35	00:58:22	362	39	0	0	0	0	30	90%

The first six modems perform as they are supposed to. There are always a few bad calls because of people dialing the number with a telephone, calls cancelled after they have been placed, or other user initiated errors. However, when a group of modems in sequence (in groups of six with Modem ISDN channel aggregation [MICA]) are all showing a much higher number of failed incoming calls, the modems are not working properly.

What is of interest in determining a bad modem can be seen in the next group of six. The call success ratio dropped eight to ten percent below that of the good modems. Also, these modems have not answered some calls, as noted by the column labeled No Answer. These modems likely became faulty recently because the output shows that they also have received many successful calls. Approximately the last 30 calls were answered by each modem, but not connected, which forced the customer to place the call again.

To fix this problem, these modems must be replaced. For companies that have a scheduled maintenance period, you can mark the modems as bad until the defective hex modem modules are replaced. To mark the modem as bad, use the line configuration command **modem bad**. This stops any future calls from being accepted on these modems:

```
5300-dialin(config)#line 31 36
5300-dialin(config-line)#modem bad
```

Frequently Asked Questions and Answers

The questions and answers in this section apply to the majority of users. These solutions will generally fix the problems you or your clients are experiencing. If you still have a problem after taking into account everything listed here, search Cisco's web site for more recent troubleshooting information and, if required, open a TAC case for further investigation.

Question: How can I achieve faster connection speeds?

Answer: To start, some situations simply cannot be helped or improved. First, make sure that the point of presence (POP) that you are dialing is V.90- or V.92-enabled by asking your provider. Line quality and the distance of the user from the CO limit connection speeds and quality. More than any other factor, this is the most important to remember.

With that being said, other reasons exist for slow connection speeds. If applicable, always start by making sure that the connecting modem has the latest drivers and firmware. As with client modems, ensure that the dial servers are running the latest TAC recommended software. Although the modems might not be new, the software running on them is constantly being upgraded to support new features such as modem call waiting and quick connections.

The distance to your CO is measured in cable feet. It is good to know how far away you are from the CO. Anything under three miles should achieve an acceptable connection speed with V.90 modulation, unless there is a line quality issue. You can have the telco check your line for the signal-to-noise ratio, which should be at least 40 decibels.

If you are dialing a local POP and still receive poor connection speeds, it might be a pad issue. Dial the full 10 digits to see if changing the pad to 6 dB fixes the problem. This is the extent of what you can try to improve a slow connection speed. If you feel there is something still wrong, you can open a case with the TAC to investigate specific issues.

Question: My clients complain about getting disconnected frequently. What can be done to stop this?

Answer: The answer to this question is the same as for the previous question. Slow connections and frequent disconnects are both caused by incompatible modems. First, rule out any simple problems such as an idle-timeout, call waiting, a bad phone cable between a jack and PC, or another phone causing the problem. If it is not one of these factors, it is most likely a software problem that can be fixed by upgrading drivers on the client modem or modem firmware on the dial router.

Question: When dialing in, my clients receive a fast busy signal. How can I fix this?

Answer: Two possible causes exist for this problem. The easiest way to troubleshoot this is to turn on ISDN Q931 debugs to determine if calls are reaching the router. If the calls are not reaching the router, the fast busy is generated by a problem in the telco, possibly because of an overloaded switch or switch path.

If the call successfully reaches the router, this indicates that the router does not know what to do with the call. The first thing to check is that every Primary Rate Interface (PRI) has the line **isdn incoming-voice modem** in its serial interface configuration. This command instructs the router to send any voice calls that come in over that PRI to a modem.

The next thing to check is that there are enough modems in each router for the total number of digital service 0s (DS0s). If you only have 60 modems and 92 DS0s (4 PRI worth), the 61st voice (modem) call received will get a fast busy signal.

Question: My clients receive a slow busy signal but plenty of modems are free. How can I fix this?

Answer: It could be possible that the DS0s are at peak capacity, but that modems are still available. If this is the case, it is time to order more circuits from the telco.

If DS0s are available, use the command **show isdn status** to verify that Layer 2 is MULTIPLE_FRAMES_ESTABLISHED. If not, see Chapter 7, "Dial Troubleshooting," for PRI troubleshooting.

If the PRI is up and working, use the command **show isdn service** to determine if any of the channels are out of service. Channels of a PRI are usually idle or busy. If they are out of service, you must open up a ticket with the provider to clear the out of service channels.

Question: I have a large Non-Facility Associated Signaling (NFAS) group configured on a dial router. According to the D channel, calls are successfully connected, but some of the NFAS circuits don't ever seem to take calls. How can I troubleshoot what is happening with the calls?

Answer: Because the D channel is one circuit that controls the incoming calls on all the other circuits, it is possible to have two or more circuits that contain out of order B channels. If they are out of order, the D channel still receives the incoming call notification, but it opens up the wrong B channel for data transfer. This results in the true incoming call being unable to connect because the call is not mapped to a modem. The solution is to verify the correct location for each circuit by any means possible, including tracing cables and getting help from your provider.

Question: When dialing in, some users do not get IP addresses. How can I troubleshoot this?

Answer: If you are using a locally configured pool of addresses, perform the command **show ip local pool** *pool name*, which shows both the in-use addresses and the addresses not in use. The in-use addresses show the username using that address. The addresses that are not in-use show the username of the last person to get that IP address. If all IP addresses in the pool are in use, the pool range is too small and must be increased.

If you are using a Dynamic Host Configuration Protocol (DHCP) server to provide IP addressing, verify that the DHCP server is reachable and verify that it has enough addressing for the number of DS0s in your dial router. Also, verify that leases do not stay active too long. The lease should expire when the client disconnects.

Question: When some of my clients dial up, they get classful subnet masks. Does this affect anything?

Answer: No. PPP is a Point-to-Point Protocol, which means that the client modems send everything down the pipe. Even if they have the wrong subnet mask, their peer (the dial router) knows how to route the traffic correctly and this should not adversely affect them.

Question: How much of a problem do one-time passwords pose for dial-in users?

Answer: First, having one time passwords means that the end users have an extra step in dialing up. This generates trouble tickets by itself. Also, you must remember the type of one-time password that you're using because two different types exist: time-based and single-use.

Time-based passwords are only good for a certain period of time, so be careful not to limit the time too much because of the 20-30 seconds it takes for the modems to train-up. Using 60- or 120-second passwords seems to work well and anything less generates numerous trouble tickets.

Single-use passwords rely on an algorithm that puts passwords in order. These tend to be more user-friendly because the end user can take as much time between getting the password and connecting.

Question: How does Virtual Private Networking (VPN) over dial affect throughput and latency?

Answer: As always, this depends on the Internet, which can provide both positive and negative aspects. If you connect at any speed above 28,800 bps, the VPN overhead is minimal, especially if you use compression over the VPN connection. Latency is affected by the delay between the POP and the VPN concentrator. Most of the time, this is less than 50 ms, which is hardly noticeable over dial. One factor that usually suffers with VPN over dial is real-time applications, such as Telnet, Secure Shell, and any other command-line interface.

Summary

This chapter included some common, real-life scenarios designed to demonstrate the dial troubleshooting techniques discussed in Chapter 7. Another objective of this chapter is to give the troubleshooting engineer some practical recommendations and answers to some of the most commonly asked questions.

PART III

ISDN

Chapter 9   ISDN Technology Background

Chapter 10   ISDN Design Solutions

Chapter 11   Cisco ISDN Configuration Solutions

Chapter 12   ISDN BRI Troubleshooting

Chapter 13   Troubleshooting Scenarios for ISDN BRI

ISDN Technology Background

ISDN was developed by telephone companies (telcos) as an end-to-end out-of-band digital technology well suited for data, voice, and video streams. Connectivity over ISDN offers end users increased bandwidth, reduced call setup time, reduced latency, and gave a lower signal-to-noise ratio (SNR). Being a dialup service (fast dial *is* another name for ISDN), the technology carries digital signaling. In the United States, the ISDN definitions are described in National ISDN standards (NI) to ensure interoperability between a variety of services and providers. The standard defines architecture layers, services, protocols, channels, reference points, and devices. The main topics of this chapter are as follows:

- ISDN standards, ISDN channels, and ISDN layered architecture
- Layer 1, Basic Rate Interface (BRI)
- ISDN devices, reference points, and interfaces
- Layer 2 in D channel Link Access Procedure on the D channel (LAPD)
- Layer 3 in D channel Q.931
- ISDN switch types

ISDN Standards

From the end of the 1960s and up to the mid 1980s, a comprehensive set of standards defined the ISDN technology. The T sector of the International Telecommunication Union (ITU-T) was created in 1993 as a replacement for the former Comité Consultatif International Téléphonique et Télégraphique (CCITT) with an initial 15 study groups. This organization issued protocols in three different series as defined in the sections that follow.

E-Series

E-Series protocols, developed for overall network operation, telephone service, service operation, and human factors, standardize the telephone networks for ISDN. ITU-T recommendation E.167 for example, defines the ISDN network identification codes.

I-Series

I-Series protocols are grouped into three main categories and are designed for the standardization of concepts, terminology, and general methods related to users, User-Network Interfaces (UNIs), and Network-to-Network Interfaces (NNIs). I-Series standards, which are designed for ISDN, start from I.110 and end with I.762. I.431, for example, defines the Primary Rate Interface (PRI), and I.432 defines the BRI.

Q-Series

Q-Series protocols, which are designed for switching and signaling, define the standards of switching and signaling schemes and techniques. The Q.921 standard, for example, describes the ISDN data-link processes of LAPD, which functions as Layer-2 processes in the International Organization for Standardization/Open System Interconnection (ISO/OSI) reference model. Q.931 specifies ISO/OSI reference model Layer 3 functions.

ISDN Channels

In ISDN, the local loop carries only digital signals that represent signaling information and user data. The local loop typically carries voice, data, or video. The term channel, unlike other techniques, means a unidirectional conduit that carries signaling and user information. Three basic channels are defined by the standards:

- **D channel (Delta channel, signaling channel)**—The D channel is a packet-switched channel that carries signaling and control information for B channels between the customer premises equipment (CPE) and the network. It can also be used for user data. Typically, the D channel provides signaling for one or more ISDN access points. When providing signaling for more than one ISDN access point, the D channel saves equipment and resources (see "NFAS Groups" in Chapter 12, "ISDN BRI Troubleshooting," Scenario 4). It operates at 16 or 64 kbps, depending on the implementation.

- **B channel (Bearer channel)**—The B channel carries user data, including data, voice, and video. It operates at digital signal level 0 (DS-0) rates (64 kbps). It can be used for both circuit and packet-switching. The B channel also provides additional services depending on the signaling information from the D channel.

- **H channel (Hybrid channel)**—The standard defines H_0, H_{10}, H_{11} and H_{12}, which operate at rates of 384 kbps, 1.472 Mbps, 1.536 Mbps, and 1.920 Mbps respectively. The H_0 channel is a logical grouping of six B channels, and the H_{11} is equivalent to four H_0 channels. The H channels are used for user information that requires higher speeds such as high quality video, high-speed data, and facsimile.

NOTE   D, B, and H channels were defined in the first ISDN standard and are known as *narrowband ISDN (NISDN)*. A later set of standards called communication services was defined to provide data rates for up to 622 Mbps. These services were designed for multimedia services and are known as *Broadband ISDN (BISDN)*. The focus of this book is on NISDN.

All types of channels share one physical medium. B and D channels define the BRI, as shown in Figure 9-1. For the BRI, the D channel uses time-division multiplexing (TDM) technology to provide the signaling. The same applies for the PRI, but unlike BRI, PRI in the U.S. and Canada uses 23 B channels (from number 1 to number 23 and one D channel (number 24). For its practical use, the D channel can be the following:

0 = Idle
1 = Propose
2 = Busy
3 = Reserved
4 = Restart
5 = Maint_Pend

There is a predefined time slot for every channel, which is typical of synchronous TDM. See Chapter 3, "The Cloud" for more information on synchronous TDM. The PRI is defined differently for European and Asian countries.

Figure 9-1   *ISDN BRI and PRI Channels*

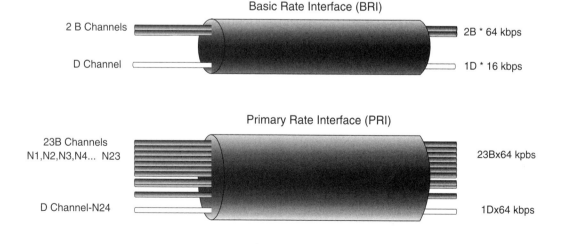

The ISDN network architecture is a roadmap that provides detail sufficient to guide ongoing network planning, design, and implementation. At the same time, the ISDN layered architecture matches the suggested layer-by-layer approach to troubleshooting in this book.

ISDN Planes: ISDN Layer Architecture

As with every technology, the ISDN architecture creates a framework for more informed decision making, including appropriate investments in network technologies, products, and services. The CCITT defines the ISDN architecture to consist of four planes:

- **C-plane**—Control plane
- **U-plane**—User plane
- **T-plane**—Transport plane
- **M-plane**—Management plane

The C-plane primarily deals with UNIs and establishing and tearing down the calls, and, the U-plane deals with User-Network data carried by the B channel. When troubleshooting ISDN, it is important to remember how the ISDN protocol architecture relates to the OSI reference model. Unlike other technologies, ISDN covers the physical, data link, and network layers, which match the first three layers of the OSI model. The three protocol layers for the B and D channel are defined in the following list and in Table 9-1:

- **Layer 1**—Defines the physical connection between the terminal equipment (TE) and the network termination (NT) including connectors, linecoding schemes, framing, and electrical characteristics. The physical connection can be point-to-point or point-to-multipoint with a short or extended passive bus.

- **Layer 2**—Describes the LAPD, also known as Q921, which provides error-free communication over the physical link and defines the communication between the user and the network. It also defines the rules for multiplexing in point-to-multipoint implementations.

- **Layer 3**—Defines the signaling messages for the initial call setup and the termination of the call as defined in Q.931.

Table 9-1   *OSI and ISDN Layers*

OSI Layer	ISDN Layer	ISDN Protocols	Description	Channel
Physical	Layer 1	I.430	Layer-1 specifications	Shared between B and D channels
		I.431	PRI	
		I.432	BRI	

Table 9-1   *OSI and ISDN Layers (Continued)*

OSI Layer	ISDN Layer	ISDN Protocols	Description	Channel
Data Link	Layer 2	Q.920(I.440) Q.921(I.441) Q.921bis	Data link layer general aspects LAPD specifications LAPD conformance testing	D channel
		Point-to-Point Protocol (PPP), (high-level data link control (HDLC)		B channels
Network	Layer 3	Q.930 Q.931 (I.450) Q.931bis Q.932 (I.451)	Layer-3 general aspects Basic call control Conformance testing Supplementary services	D channel
		AppleTalk, Connectionless Network Service (CLNS), DECnet, Internet Protocol (IP), Internetwork Packet Exchange (IPX), Banyan Virtual Integrated Network Service (VINES), Xerox Network Systems (XNS)		B channel

In the point-to-point physical connections, the NT (NT1 or NT2) and the TE (TE1 or TA) can be 1 km (3300 ft) apart. The passive bus (no repeaters or any active devices) point-to-multipoint design allows up to eight devices to be connected to a single NT on a bus length that can be up to 200 m (667 ft). The extended bus supports up to eight devices clustered together at the end of the passive bus and can be up to 1 km (3300 ft) apart from the NT.

The sections that follow discuss all three ISDN layers in greater detail.

Layer 1: BRI

ISDN standards require the availability of three types of services for end-to-end connections by the local exchange carrier (LEC):

- Circuit-switched services on B channels
- Circuit-switched or packet-switched services on D channels
- Packet-switched services on B channels

To use them, the ITU-T defined BRI and PRI access interfaces, and the operation speed and the number and type of channels. The BRI is also referred to as 2B+D, and typically operates over two 64-kbps B channels and one 16-kbps D channel. It can also be provisioned as 1B+D, and even 0B+D for low speed (9.6 kbps) data. As you can see, the D channel in BRI operates at 16 K, but in its S/T implementation, the speed is 192 Kbps. It looks like we are losing 48 Kbps. We're actually not. The remaining 48 Kbps can be used for out-of-band forward error correction (OOB FEC).

The following sections cover the elements of a typical ISDN BRI architecture:

- Devices
- Reference points
- Interfaces
- BRI initialization

ISDN Devices

The hardware that is part of an ISDN service includes the following:

- **TE1**—A device compatible with an ISDN network and that connects to NT type 1 or 2 devices. TE1 devices include ISDN routers, modems, and ISDN phones.

- **TE2**—A device not compatible with an ISDN network and that requires a terminal adapter to connect, such as a regular telephone's old-time terminal and other non-ISDN devices.

- **Terminal adapter (TA)**—Converts non-ISDN signaling to ISDN signaling.

- **NT1**—Connects four-wire ISDN subscriber line wiring to the conventional two-wire local loop facility. In North America, it is common to find an NT1 at a user's location inside of a networking device (router or modem). In Europe and Asia, NT1 is not part of the ISDN device at the user's location because it belongs to the LEC.

- **NT2**—Directs traffic from different subscriber devices and from the NT1. The device performs switching and concentrating, and similar to the NT1, it converts wiring within the telephone carrier (four-wire) network to the (two-wire) local loop. The NT2 adds data link layer and network layer functionality to a NT1, and it is usually used with connecting private branch exchange (PBX) devices. CPE can be considered an NT2 device.

- **Local Exchange (LE)**—Includes Local Termination (LT) and Exchange Termination (ET) on the provider's site.

In the CPE site, the local loop is terminated by using an NT1, which is responsible for performance monitoring, timing, physical signaling, protocol conversion, power transfer, and multiplexing of the D and B channels, as shown in Figure 9-2.

The NT1 devices in Europe and Asia belong to the LEC. It is an external device for the router.

Figure 9-2 *ISDN Devices and Access Points*

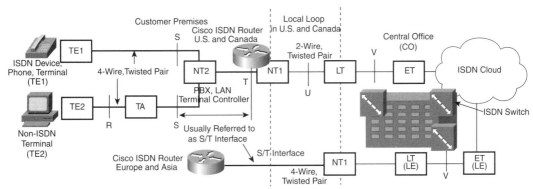

R, S, T, U, V: ISDN Reference Points

ISDN Local Loop Reference Points: ISDN Interfaces

ISDN service providers (those providing the last mile or the local loop of the ISDN connection) refer to reference points when troubleshooting parts of the local loop. To connect devices that perform specific functions, the devices need to support specific interfaces, which can vary from CPE to CPE. As a result, the ISDN standards do not define interfaces in terms of hardware, but refer to them as reference points. However, for trouble-shooting purposes, it is more reasonable to refer to interfaces. Every ISDN compatible router provides information about the type of connection or interface; and Cisco 77x, 80x, 25xx, and 40xx series routers are examples. These interfaces are as follows:

- **R-reference point, or R-interface**—This is between the non-ISDN device (TA2) and the TA. The TA allows the TE2 to appear to the ISDN network as an ISDN device.

- **S/T reference point or S/T interface**—This is usually considered together, where the S-reference point is between the TE1 and NT2, or between the TA and the NT2. The T-reference point is the four-wire (one pair for transmit and one for receive) interface between the customer site switching equipment (NT2) and the local loop termination (NT1). If there's no NT2 equipment, which is common, the UNI is usually called the S/T reference point. S/T is typical for Europe and Asia.

- **U-reference point or U-interface**—This is a two-wire facility that uses frequency-division multiplexing (FDM) and echo cancellation. It is typical for the U.S. and Canada, and the routers produced for these countries, to have a built-in U-interface. The NT1 device converts the four wire S/T interface to a two-wire U-interface. In Europe and Asia, the NT1 device is in the provider's central office (CO).

- **V-reference point**—This defines the interface in the LE between the LT and the ET.

The real structure of every ISDN design includes numerous implementations. For troubleshooting purposes, it is preferable to simplify the diagram of reference points and interfaces to the illustration (refer to Figure 9-2). In most common cases, consider the simpler structure. For residential and Centrex applications, the NT2 is absent.

NOTE	The book *Analyzing Broadband Networks*, now in its third edition, provides some excellent examples of ISDN architecture and design.

Both the S/T and U-interfaces achieve full-duplex connections. The current wiring rules follow the ISO 8877 standard. RJ-45 is an 8-pin connector. Table 9-2 shows the wiring rules for the S/T interface and Table 9-3 shows the U-interface wiring rules. The polarity is important only for the S/T interface.

Table 9-2   *ISDN RJ-45 Pins for the S/T Interface*

Pin	TE Pin	NT Pin	Required
1	Power source 3(+)	Power sink 3 (+)	No
2	Power source 3(-)	Power sink 3 (-)	No
3	Transmit (+)	Receive (+)	Yes
4	Receive (+)	Transmit (+)	Yes
5	Receive (-)	Transmit (-)	Yes
6	Transmit (-)	Receive (-)	Yes
7	Power sink 2 (-)	Power source 2 (-)	No
8	Power sink 2 (+)	Power source 2 (+)	No

Table 9-3   *ISDN RJ-45 Pins for the U-Interface*

Pin	Function
1	Not used
2	Not used
3	Not used
4	U interface network connection (Tip)
5	U interface network connection (Ring)
6	Not used
7	Not used
8	Not used

Chapter 3 covers the S/T interface and U-interface line codes and frame formats in greater detail. Table 9-4 describes the physical characteristics of both interfaces and their differences.

Table 9-4   *Standards Defining the Physical Characteristics of the S/T and U-Interfaces*

Reference Point	S or T or S/T Interface	U-Interface
Defining standard	CCITT I.430	ANSI T1.601
Devices	TE1/TA to NT	NT1 to LE
Distance	1 km	5.5 km
Physical configuration	Point-to-point or point-to-multipoint	Point-to-point
Bit rate	192 kbps	160 Kbps
User data rate	144 kbps	144 Kbps
Line code	Pseudo-ternary	2B1Q
Signaling rate	192 Kbaud	80 Kbaud
Maximum voltage	+- 750 mV	+- 2.5 V
Timing source	NT	LE
Number of wire pairs	2	1
Full-duplex method	One pair for each direction	Echo cancellation
Interleaving scheme	$B1_8 D_1 B2_8 D_1$	$B1_8 B2_8 D_2$
Number of bits per frame[*]	48	240
Number of bits—user data	36	216
Number of bits—overhead	12	24
Number of frames per second	4000	666.666

[*]Referring to frames in the physical layer is not ISO compliant and could be confusing for network engineers; however, to be consistent with the ISDN standard, the adopted terminology is preferred for this and any other technology.

For more information, see *ISDN Concepts, Facilities, and Services*, Third Edition (McGraw-Hill, 1996).

Initializing BRI

Activation of the BRI is based on the exchange of INFO messages and on the performance of a straightforward handshake mechanism. I.430 defines 5 INFO (0-4) messages that perform different roles in the activation process.

As Figure 9-3 shows, the process starts with the TE sending INFO1 to the LE. The A bit that's set to 1 indicates that the line is activated. The INFO0, which is not shown in this figure, indicates "no signal."

Figure 9-3 *Initializing the Physical Link*

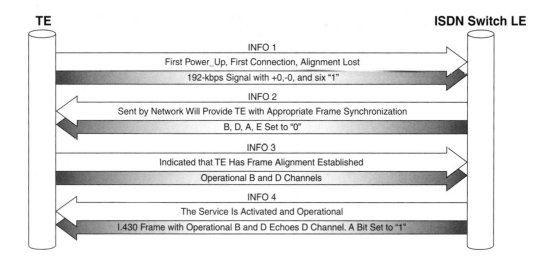

The Layer 2 D Channel: LAPD

As discussed previously, on the second layer of the layered model, ISDN uses a protocol called LAPD. The protocol's general principles are defined in the Q.920 (I.440) and the Q.921 (I.441) standards.

The following is a discussion of Layer 2 frame formats, logical link establishment, and logical link parameter negotiation, which are related to Layer 2 troubleshooting later in this part.

LAPD Frame Formats (A and B)

Two formats, A and B, are defined in LAPD. Format A differs from B, and it is used where the information field is not necessary. Because Format A is a subset of Format B (Format B is identical to Format A with the addition of an Information field), the following explanation will apply to both.

Figure 9-4 shows the format of every transmission unit (frame).

The first row represents the number of octets, and the second row the actual fields. Unlike other frame types, the low-order bit of each octet is transmitted first. In this case, it is the last bit (0) in the Flag field, the last bit of the first octet of the Address field, and so forth.

Figure 9-4 *LAPD Format B Frame*

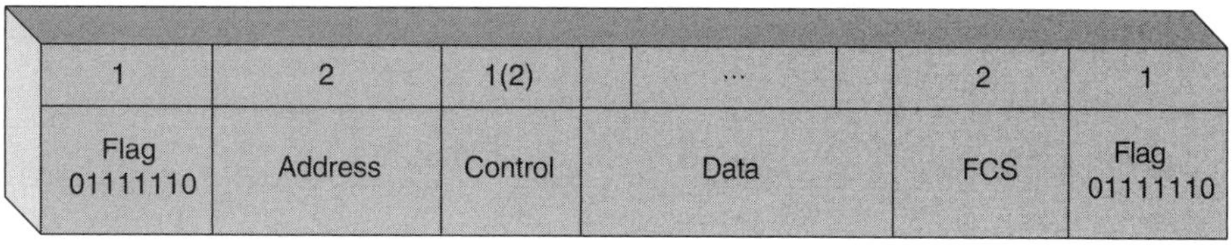

1	2	1(2)	...	2	1
Flag 01111110	Address	Control	Data	FCS	Flag 01111110

Flag Field

The Flag field has a standard value of 0x7E(01111110) and indicates the beginning and the end of the frame. The combination 0x7F(01111111) represents the abort signal, and the combination 0xFF (11111111) represents an idle channel. The Flag begins and ends the frame.

Address Field

The Address field identifies the user device and protocol, and it plays a significant role in the troubleshooting process. It is always two octets. The structure is shown in Figure 9-5. Note that the remaining 13 bits represent the data-link connection identifier (DLCI)—a combination of the TEI and service access point identifier (SAPI) fields. The terminal endpoint identifier (TEI) is designed to maintain a separate logical link over the D channel with the peer process in the LE.

Figure 9-5 *The Structure of the Address Field. The TEI and SAPI Fields Represent a 13-Bit DLCI*

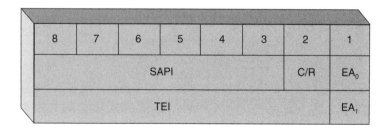

8	7	6	5	4	3	2	1
SAPI						C/R	EA$_0$
TEI							EA$_1$

The Address field has the following subfields:

- TE is a 7-bit subfield of the Address field that can be in the range of 0–127. Three types of TEs exist:
  - 0–63 range is allocated for non-automatic TE assignment.
  - 64–126 range is randomly and automatically assigned value by the LE.
  - A TE equal to 127 is a broadcast.

The maximum number of TEs per BRI is limited to eight by the ITU-T.

- SAPI is a 6-bit subfield. Table 9-5 shows the SAPI values.

Table 9-5 *The SAPI Values*

SAPI Value	Layer-3 Management Entity
0	Call control procedure
1–15	Reserved for future standardization
16	Packet mode, used by X.25
17–31	Reserved for future standardization
32–61	Frame Relay communications
63	Layer 2 management procedure
All others	Not available for Q.921

- C/R is the Command/Response field bit. It is defined in Table 9-6.

Table 9-6 *The C/R Filed Values*

Command/Response	Direction	C/R Value
Command	Network -> User	1
	User -> Network	0
Response	Network -> User	0
	User -> Network	1

- EA0 and EA1 is the Address field extension bit.

Control Field

The Control field of LAPD is used for frame identification. The field can be one or two octets, and provides messages that perform some of the typical functions for the Transmission Control Protocol (TCP), such as ACK and SEQ#. The Control field uses three frame formats, which are indicated by the first two bits of the field: Information, Supervisory and Unnumbered. Information (I) is a two-octet frame field that carries signaling or user data information from higher ISDN layers. Supervisory (S) is also a two-octet field format that controls the exchange of the I-frames. When troubleshooting, it is not easy to recognize the message types. The following descriptions help with the identification.

NOTE   Every message is either a command or a response (R), based on its purpose. P/F is a poll/final bit, S is S-frame type, and M is U-frame type.

Based on the content of messages in the Control field of LAPD, three categories of messages exist:

- Information transfer messages are command messages, where C and R refer to command and response (R) messages. Information transfer messages consist of the following:

  - **N(S) (Send sequence number)** — This message contains 7 bits with 0 at the end.

  - **N(R) (Receive sequence number)** — This message contains 7 bits and a P bit at the end.

- Supervisory messages consist of two bytes where the second byte is N(R), and whose last bit is a P/F bit. These messages can be command or response (R). Supervisory messages consist of the following:

  - **RR (Receive Ready)** — The message can be C or R type. The message means "Ready for more frames."

  - **RNR (Receive not ready)** — This message can be C or R type and means "Busy for more I-frames."

  - **REJ (Reject)** — The message can be C or R, and can be seen when an I-frame is received and not expected and rejected as a result.

- Unnumbered messages. These messages are one byte in length and they can be both C and R types:

  - **SABME (Set Asynchronous Balance Mode Extended)** — This message is only type C and means "Establishes the logical link = Xmod(128)."

  - **DM (Disconnected Mode)** — This message shows error condition and can be only R type.

  - **UI (Unnumbered Information)** — This message can be only C type and means "Transfers Layer 3 management information."

  - **DISC (Disconnect)** — This is only a C type message and means "Terminates the logical link."

  - **UA (Unnumbered Acknowledgment)** — This is a response (R) message and indicates "The Unnumbered (U) frame field is establishing and terminating the logical connection."

- **FRMR (Frame Reject)** — This is a response (R) type of message, which indicates that "Error condition and frame is rejected."

  - **XID (Exchange Identification)** — The message can be C or R type and it links control parameters for negotiation.

Data Field

The Data field contains Q.931 messages, user data, or LAPD management information. The Data field has a variable, octet-aligned length, and it might not exist in all frames.

FCS Field

The frame check sequence (FCS) field is two bytes and it is used for bit error detection.

Logical Link Establishment

The next step of achieving full functionality of ISDN service, immediately after the activation of the physical link, is the logical link establishment. Here, LAPD ensures the TEI and SAPI assignments, which are the core of the logical link establishment, as shown in Figure 9-6. The figure represents another handshake link procedure.

Figure 9-6   *Logical Link Establishment Sequence*

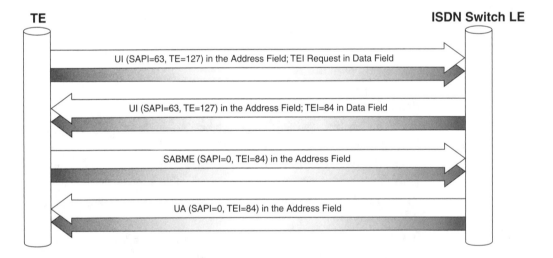

You can distinguish two main phases in the process:

- **First phase**—As soon as the physical link is activated, it sends two broadcast messages in the Address field: SAPI = 63 (broadcast) and TEI=127(broadcast). The ISDN switch responds with randomly and automatically assigned TEI = 84, and repeats the broadcast messages with SAPI = 63 and TEI = 127.

- **Second phase**—The router sends a SABME message, indicating the purpose with SAPI = 0 (third layer data), and confirms the assigned TEI = 84. The ISDN switch then sends a Unnumbered Acknowledgment (UA) frame for SAPI = 0 (call establishment can start) and TEI = 84 to indicate the end of the process.

In the most common 2B+D design of a BRI, this procedure executes twice, once for each B channel. Therefore, by the end of the exchange, every B channel has an assigned TEI = xx and SAPI = 0.

Logical Link Parameter Negotiation

The logical link establishment is more complicated than a physical connectivity establishment. One of the reasons is that the router and the ISDN switch need to negotiate some parameters. There is a mechanism to negotiate some timers values and counters values to adjust the service to the line parameters.

In LAPD, the parameters' negotiation function is accomplished through a system of timers and parameters that are exchanged between parties with a U-type XID frame. One device sends the XID frame with its parameters, and if the other device does not respond with another XID, the first one considers the negotiation complete by using the default parameters. Some of the system parameters and their default values are listed here:

- **N200**—Maximum number of times to retransmit the frame. The default value is 3.
- **N201**—Maximum length of an Information field. The default value is 260 octets.
- **N202**—Maximum number of times to request TEI assignment. The default is 3.
- **K**—Maximum number of unacknowledged I-frames. The default is 1 for SAPI = 0 and 3 for SAPI ≠ 0.

Some of the system timers and their parameters are as follows:

- **T200**—Reply timer. The default is 1s.
- **T201**—Minimum time between TEI identity check messages. The default is 1s.
- **T202**—Minimum time between TEI identity request messages. The default is 2s.
- **T203**—Maximum time without frame exchange. The default is 10s.

In addition to the perfect scheduling mechanism for the LAPD layer mentioned earlier, another mechanism makes sure that no TE has full control over the D channel. This technique is based on analyzing the SAPI content and creating a priority mechanism based on classes. In this case, the signaling SAPI = 0 messages are class 0, and non-zero SAPIs are class 2. Both normal and low priority classes exist, which are based on the number of consecutive 1s in the frame.

Using ISDN in an IP environment is usually related to the PPP and to one of the phases of the PPP protocol, called the Link Control Protocol (LCP), which are discussed in detail in Chapter 5, "Dial Technology Background," and Chapter 13, "Troubleshooting Scenarios for ISDN BRI." It is important to know that LCP does not replace, but works together, with parameter negotiation mechanisms of ISDN. RFC 1618 was created to ensure this feature.

Layer 3 in the D Channel: Q.931 and Message Format

The term Layer 3 protocols comes from the network layer in OSI, and the Q.931 recommendations provide call routing and congestion control for calls between a user's TE and the network (between the terminal endpoint and the local ISDN switch). However, this protocol does not impose an end-to-end recommendation, and various ISDN providers and switch types use various implementations of Q.931. Also, some switch types were developed before the standards groups finalized this standard. For these reasons, the proper specification of the switch in Cisco routers is important.

The recommended Q.931 message formats represent data blocks, called information elements. SS7 provides telephone switches with the out-of-band signaling capabilities for telephone trunks (switch-to-switch 64-kbps connections). Unlike old in-band signaling standards, out-of-band Signaling System 7 (SS7) provides reduced call setup time, 64-kbps data, caller ID, dialed number information (DNIS), bearer capability, and other progress indicators. The Q.931 protocol typically provides the information shown in Figure 9-7. ISDN Layer 3 messages are carried in the Information field of LAPD I-frames. Q.931 messages are used in the debugging process with Cisco routers and deserve detailed attention.

Figure 9-7 *Message Format of the Q.931 Protocol*

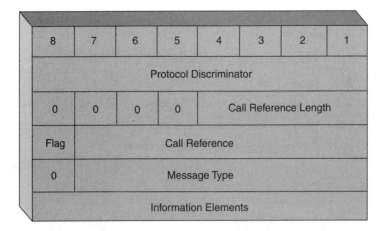

Protocol Discriminator Field

The first field of the Q.931 message format depicted in Figure 9-7 is the Protocol Discriminator field. It identifies the protocol type such as Q.931, X.25, and others. The protocol discriminator has a few values that are used by ISDN:

- **0x00 through 0x03**—Assigned in Q.931 for user-user information
- **0x04**—Q.931 user-network call control message
- **0x10 through 0x3F**—Reserved for other Layer 3 protocols

Call Reference Field

The second field is the Call Reference (CR). It identifies the relationship between the call and the message, where the number identifies the active calls. CR or the Call Reference Value (CRV) is a per-session/per-connection value that is assigned at the beginning of the call, and remains the same until the call is completed. Often the only indicator of whether or not the call goes through is tracing the call and testing with the LEC. Typically, a BRI uses one octet CR length, and a PRI uses two. The high-end bit of the second octet is called a Flag. To prevent the assignment of one CR to two different calls, the Flag is set as follows:

- **0**—From call originator
- **1**—To call originator (destination)

A special CR is defined with 0 value to indicate a broadcast, which is assigned to all active calls in the user-network interface.

Message Type Field

The Message Type value indicates the type of Layer 3 message that the transmission represents. Call establishment message types in Q.931 are as follows:

- **SETUP**—Initial call request
- **SETUP_ACK**—Setup received, more information required
- **CONNECT**—Call establishment phase completed
- **CONNECT_ACK**—Acknowledges CONNECT
- **CALL_PROC**—Shows the call is proceeding
- **ALERTING**—Ring indication

Figure 9-8 shows the process of connecting a call.

The initiator of the call (the router) sends a SETUP message, and usually provides the bearer capability, the calling party number, and the number of the B channel that is starting the call. The bearer capability defines the type of service requested, such as 64-kbps data, 56-kbps data, or 56-kbps voice. The SETUP message also contains the channel identification element, which is designed to be negotiated with the switch, depending on where the call hits the network. After this is completed, both parties know each other's per-session numbers. After receiving the SETUP message and checking for correctness, the LE usually requests any missing information with the SETUP_ACK. Then, the router provides this information (see the arrow "INFORMATION" in the figure). If the information is correct and sufficient, the LE responds with CALL_PROC (call proceeding). So according to Figure 9-8, it should be read as either of the following:

- SETUP—CALL_PROC
- SETUP—SETUP_ACK INFORMATION—CALL_PROC

Figure 9-8   *The Call Setup Procedure: The Switch Handles Both Directions*

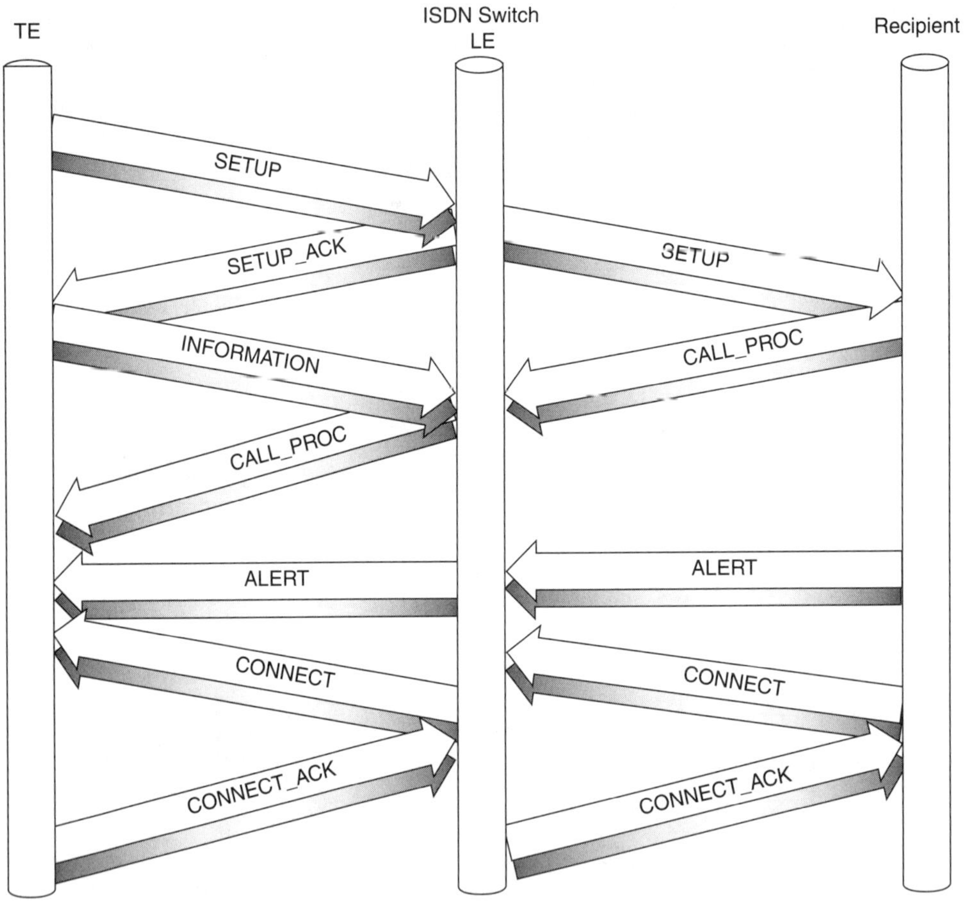

The LE generates a different SETUP message and sends it to the Recipient, which can be thought of as a PRI connecting to the core router. If the Recipient cannot accept the call, it sends an ALERT to the LE, which in turn generates another ALERT message from the LE to the CPE. When the Recipient accepts the call, it sends a CONNECT to the LE and the LE responds with a CONNECT_ACK. In turn, the LE generates a CONNECT message, which informs the router that the call is accepted and the router responds with a CONNECT_ACK.

The call clearing messages are as follows:

- **DISCONNECT**—Hangs up the call
- **RELEASE**—Releases the call

- **RELEASE_COMP**—Acknowledges completion of the RELEASE
- **RESTART**—Restarts Layer 3 protocol
- **RESTART_ACK**—Acknowledges RESTART

The call clearing can be started by any party by sending a DISCONNECT message. Figure 9-9 shows the call clearing procedure, where the DISCONNECT is initiated by the router. After the router sends the DISCONNECT, it disconnects itself from the B channel. The LE returns a RELEASE and in turn, sends a DISCONNECT message to the Recipient. While the Initiator completes the process by sending RELEASE_COMP, the LE releases the B channel. On the other side, after the LE and the Recipient exchange RELEASE and RELEASE_COMP messages, the facility is released for new calls.

Figure 9-9   *The Call Clearing (Tear Down) Process*

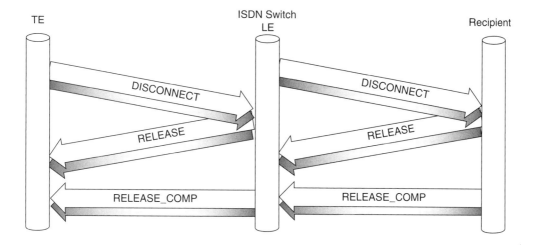

Information Elements Field

As previously mentioned, the data is carried in the Information Elements (IE), which are the Q.931 parameters. Unlike other protocols, Q.931 does not define a fixed length for this field that reflects the actual length of the field. Different content and different length works with different LECs. For this reason, this field might contain a length indicator, defined as Type 1 and Type 2 IE. The Type 1 IE defines a 3-bit identifier and 4 bits for the content of IE, and Type 2 contains a 7-bit IE identifier. The most common IEs are listed here and more are described in Q.922:

- **0x04**—Bearer capability
- **0x2C**—Keypad facility (used to send on 5ESS and NI switches)
- **0x6C**—Calling party number

- **0x70**—Called party number
- **0x3A**—Service profile identifier (SPID)

Layer 3 Summary

The Layer 3 procedures are designed to provide the full functionality of handling the calls, including establishing, connects and disconnects, releasing the facilities for the next calls, and so forth. As discussed earlier, all these functions are performed between two or more parties, but the main role always belongs to the ISDN switch, which naturally leads to the topic of the next section.

ISDN Switch Types

There are many standards for switches because most standards were released during or after the deployment of most ISDN switches. Therefore, a variety of ISDN switch manufacturers pose different requirements for configuring CPE. In Table 9-7, the Cisco supported switches from the latest IOS release are listed.

Table 9-7   *ISDN Switch Types*

Switch Type	Description
basic-1tr6	1TR6 switch type for Germany
basic-5ess	Lucent 5ESS switch type for the U.S.
basic-dms100	Northern Telecom DMS-100 switch type for the U.S.
basic-net3	NET3 switch type for UK, Europe, Asia, and Australia
basic-ni1	National ISDN switch type for the U.S.
basic-qsig	QSIG switch type
basic-ts013	TS013 switch type for Australia (obsolete)
ntt	NTT switch type for Japan
vn3	VN3 and VN4 switch types for France

In the U.S. and Canada, two settings have high importance when you are trying to set up the switch-BRI interoperations: SPID, and Local Directory Numbers (LDNs). The SPID represents a subscriber number and subscriber address. Although the number is defined as a regular phone number with format xxx-xxx-xxxx, the address's purpose is to assign a unique number to the endpoint (such as a terminal). The service provider assigns the SPIDs and they must be configured on the router in exactly the same way as the LEC provides them. Depending on the switch type connected to the CPE, SPIDs might not be necessary.

In the U.S., National ISDN-1 and DMS-100 ISDN switches require SPIDs to be configured, but the AT&T 5ess switch does not.

If they are required, the SPID number is usually a ten-digit telephone number plus two or four extra digits, for example, SPID = 40847647400100 and 40847647410200 represent the following:

- **408**—Area code
- **476**—CO (exchange) code
- **4740 and 4741**—Station IDs for each B channel
- **01 and 02**—Terminal identifiers

Another part of the setting is the LDN. The LDN is configured to receive incoming calls. For example, LDN1 = 4764740 and LDN2 = 4764741, represent the following:

- **476**—Exchange code
- **4740 and 4741**—Station ID

With AT&T switch-type 5ESS, only one LDN is necessary to identify the service. For more information about switch settings, see Chapter 10, "ISDN Design Solutions."

Summary

The importance of this chapter is based on the fact that in ISDN some technical solutions were implemented during or even before some standards were available. That's why for the troubleshooting engineer the information about standards, switches, settings, and provider-specifics is helpful. At the same time, the detailed description of ISDN architecture, reference points, devices, and interfaces in this chapter provides the necessary minimum to ensure that you are familiar with the technology basics of one of the most complicated technologies in today's market.

Review Questions

Answers to the review questions can be found in Appendix A, "Answers to Review Questions."

1   What is the scope of the I.431 and I.432 standards?

2   Where does the name D channel come from? What are the operational speeds of the D channel for BRI and PRI?

3   What is a V-reference point in ISDN?

4   What are the important pins in a S/T interface?

5   What is the modulation of the ISDN U-interface?

6 What is the bit rate of the S/T interface and U-interface?

7 How many INFO messages participate in the BRI's Layer 1 initialization? What does INFO0 mean?

8 Which bit in the ISDN frame indicates line activation?

9 What makes up DLCI in ISDN? What is the length of DLCI, TE, and SAPI?

10 What are the two indicators that Layer 2 is active?

11 What does TE = 127 mean?

12 What is the dynamic range of TEI?

13 What does SAPI = 0 indicate?

14 How do you distinguish an incoming from an outgoing call?

15 Which ISDN protocol provides information about Bearer capability. Name three basic types of Bearer capabilities.

CHAPTER 10

ISDN Design Solutions

Typically, the hub and spoke design is the most commonly used in remote access solutions. The hub and spoke terminology can be used for ISDN design solutions; however, it is more common for designers to use network access server (NAS) and remote node as typical terms that describe the design. Typically, the hub site is referred to as the core or core router, and the spoke side is referred to as the end-user router, or remote user.

The objectives of this chapter are to give you more information about the typical ISDN design solutions. The main topics of the chapter can be summarized as follows:

- Enterprise and Internet service provider (ISP) design
- Setting the ISDN switch type, service profile identifiers (SPIDs) and local directory numbers (LDNs)
- Network address translation (NAT) and Port Address Translation (PAT)
- Per-user (per function) design, virtual templates, and profiles
- Multilink Point-to-Point Protocol (MLP)
- Multichassis Multilink PPP (MMP)

Hub and spoke design, typical for remote access ISDN (see Figure 10-1), is beneficial because of increased manageability and the capability to apply policies to the environment. In this design, the core router is usually connected to two switches that provide the necessary redundancy for remote users who are accessing the company's intranet. At the same time, the core router can be a single point of failure, which raises questions about availability and scalability, and bandwidth aggregation.

Figure 10-1 *Hub and Spoke Design for a Remote Access Environment*

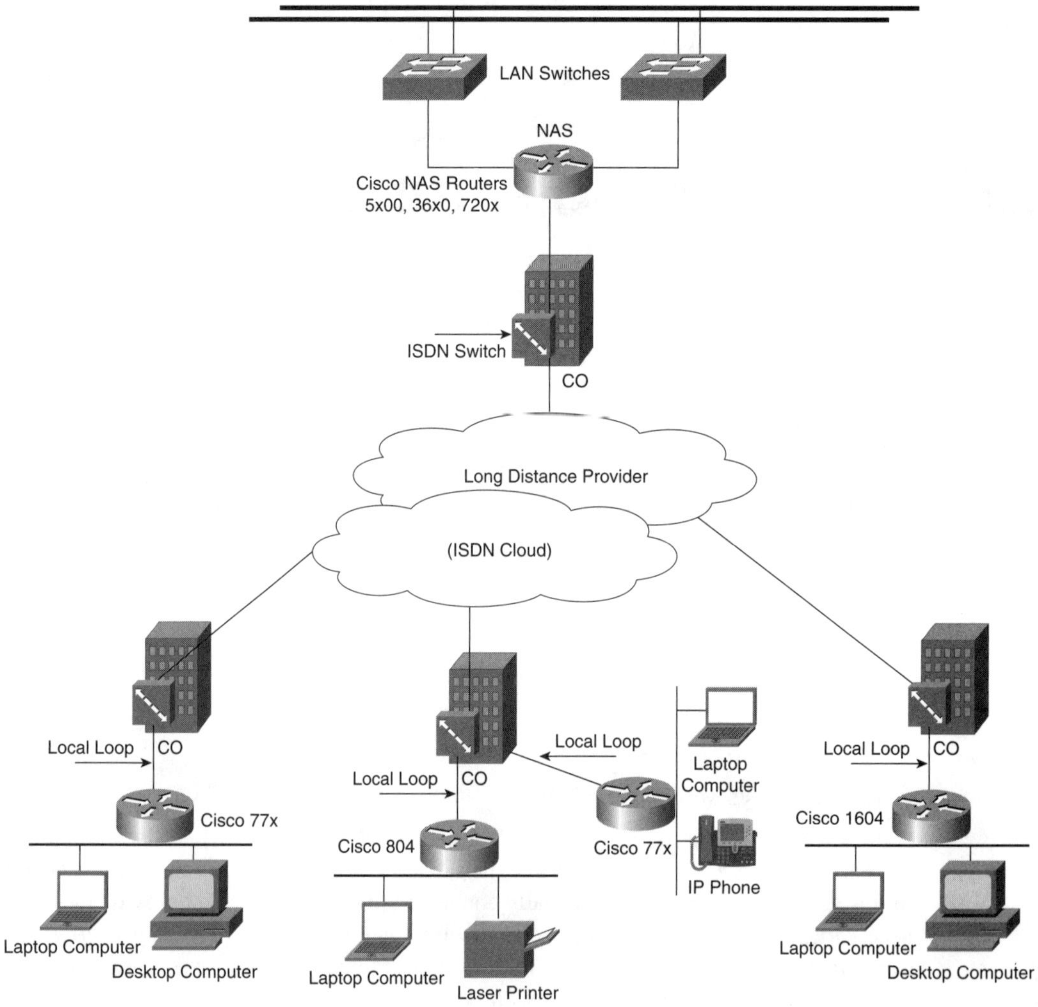

Enterprise and ISP Designs

From an application point of view, you can break down ISDN into the following main categories. Based on the structure of the core side, you can recognize a separate enterprise design and an ISP design in these categories:

- ISPs, more often than enterprises, use the MMP, which is not mandatory for an enterprise solution.

- ISPs often use a pool of IP addresses, whereas enterprises often assign an IP subnet from their routable or private address space for remote users based on their needs.

- ISPs use NAT/PAT techniques or assign a subnet for an extra charge, and an enterprise, using NAT/PAT, assigns a /32, /30, /29, or even a /28 subnet to the remote user. NAT/PAT is more common on the end user side, performing the NAT/PAT on their customer premises equipment (CPE). ISPs rarely perform NAT/PAT for the remote user on their own routers.

- ISPs use one-way authentication so that they can troubleshoot the CPE remotely without configuring the Challenge Handshake Authentication Protocol (CHAP) host name of the core router on the remote user's router. Enterprises use two-way authentication, or more sophisticated authentication schemes.

- ISPs do not make outgoing calls, and enterprises do allow outgoing calls.

- ISPs can apply a flat rate fee for the service; however, enterprises usually pay usage-based charges with volume discounts and usually the charges are charged by the ISP to the enterprise.

Often, combinations of these categories exist in a design. You might want to review some of the basic design techniques, but before that, review the basic ISDN configuration of the ISDN switch type, SPID(s), and LDN(s). They might seem easy to configure, but the reality is that they can cause serious issues, especially when the service is a new-install. Each of these is discussed in the following sections.

Setting the ISDN Switch Type

The switch types supported in the latest versions of IOS (12.1.x. and later) are outlined in Example 10-1. The most commonly used types in the U.S. and Canada are basic-5ess, basic-dms100, and basic-ni1.

Example 10-1 *Determining the ISDN Switch Type*

```
804-isdn(config)#isdn switch-type ?
basic-1tr6        1TR6 switch type for Germany
basic-5ess        Lucent 5ESS switch type for the US
basic-dms100      Northern Telecom DMS-100 switch type for the US
basic-net3        NET3 switch type for the UK, Europe, Asia and Australia
basic-ni          National ISDN switch type for the US
basic-qsig        QSIG switch type
basic-ts013       TS013 switch type for Australia (obsolete)
ntt               NTT switch type for Japan
vn3               VN3 and VN4 switch types for France
```

Besides the listed switches, there is a category of custom design switches for the U.S. and Canada:

```
custom-5ess          Lucent 5ESS switch type for the US
custom-dms100        Northern Telecom DMS-100 switch type for the US
```

The custom design switches are point-to-point designs and usually do not require SPID and LDN information. It is common to define only a phone number.

The command and options for setting the switch types for 776 routers are as follows:

SEt SWitch 5Ess | DMS | NI-1 | PERM64 | PERM128 | PERM2X64

If you don't specify any switch type, the router's default is 5Ess.

In 77x routers the switch type 5Ess applies to all types of 5Ess switches. It is convenient when custom switch types need to be configured because all you need to know is that the switch is 5Ess. This setting is part of the general configuration of the router, which is called the system level in 77x terminology.

For Cisco IOS Software scenarios, the configuration command for switch type National ISDN-1 (NI-1 or N11) is as follows:

```
804-isdn(config)#isdn switch-type basic-ni
```

You can configure more than one switch type in one router configuration by using Cisco IOS Software Release 12.0 and later. An example of a BRI0 interface configuration is as follows:

```
804-isdn(config-if)#isdn switch-type basic-5ess
```

The global configuration mode and the interface configuration mode settings work together and follow the logic that if an interface (BRI0, BRI1, BRI2, and so on) is configured for different switch types, it takes precedence over the settings in the global configuration mode. If not, the BRIx interface takes the switch type from the global configuration mode as a default one.

Additionally, the switch type can be different from the profile that the LEC is using or emulating on the switch. You can have DMS100 running NI1 or any other combination. It is common to see the DMS and 5ess switches running in NI mode in North America. When using Cisco 77x routers, it is preferable to configure the router, based on the provider's profile name, coded as NI or 5E, and if it does not work, configure the switch type. In the case of Cisco IOS Software, either set both global and interface configurations to the type of the local exchange carrier's (LEC's) profile (NI1), or set the switch type (DMS100) in the global configuration, and set the LEC's profile type (NI1) under the Basic Rate Interface (BRI).

Setting SPIDs and LDNs

When an LEC installs the local loop (installing the ISDN service), there is always minimum information available to the user, including SPIDs, LDNs, and the switch type. The NI-1 and the DMS100 both require SPIDs. Basic-5ESS is a point-to-multipoint switch, which is capable of providing up to eight SPIDs per service. As previously mentioned, custom-5ESS is point-to-point and does not require SPIDs, and by default, they do not provide a voice capability. When working with LECs, the network professional might see different settings for voice and data, such as the following:

- A service might not be provided (voice or data).

- Calls might be restricted by rejecting the third call, if two channels are up and running.

- All incoming calls might be forwarded to let the router decide how to handle the priority of the call (voice and data).

The variety of settings and the use of different names by providers (for example, GTE has a setting called Umbrella or U setting) is a real challenge for network engineers, and requires maximum attention to the details of the configuration.

The LDN is not a mandatory part of the configuration, unless the service is provisioned for both voice and data.

Example 10-2, Example 10-3, and Example 10-4 provide examples of valid ISDN settings for 77x router images that use Software Version c760-in.r.US 4.4(2). Example 10-5 uses a Cisco IOS Software router, which is provisioned for voice and data.

Example 10-2   *A Valid SPID Setting Example for 77x Router for Switch Type NI1*

```
776-isdn>set switch ni1
776-isdn>set 1 spid 40857647400101
776-isdn>set 1 directorynumber 5764740
776-isdn>set phone1 = 5764740
776-isdn>set 2 spid 40857647410101
776-isdn>set 2 directorynumber 5764741
776-isdn>set phone2 = 5764741
```

Example 10-3   *A Valid SPID Setting Example for 77x Router for Point-to-Point Switch Type 5ESS*

```
776-isdn>set switch 5ess
776-isdn>set 1 directorynumber 4920672
776-isdn>set phone1 4920672
```

Example 10-4   *A Valid SPID Setting Example for Point-to-Multipoint Switch Type 5Ess*

```
776-isdn>set switch 5ess
776-isdn>set ppp multilink on
776-isdn>set 1 spid 0173125470
776-isdn>set 2 spid 0173125480
776-isdn>set 1 directorynumber 7312547
776-isdn>set 2 directorynumber 7312548
776-isdn>set phone1 7312547
776-isdn>set phone2 7312548
```

In the case of Cisco IOS Software Release 12.0 and later, under the BRIx interface, you usually see the configuration in Example 10-5.

Example 10-5 *Cisco IOS SPID Settings for Interface BRI0*

```
804-isdn(config-if)#isdn switch-type basic-ni
804-isdn(config-if)#isdn spid1 53075358360101 7535836
804-isdn(config-if)#isdn spid2 53075358600101 7535860
```

A relatively new feature of IOS (available in IOS 12.1(6), for example) sets the switch type, and not the SPIDs. A command available under the BRI0 interface is **isdn autodetect**, which enables the router to request the SPID assignment from the switch. The router reports **no LDN, spid1 NOT sent, spid1 NOT valid**, but the indicator state equals 8, which is a valid state (see Table 13-1). The router responds with **MULTIPLE_FRAME_ESTABLISHED** for both terminal endpoint identifiers (TEIs), and the configuration is fully operational.

The user's router needs to be configured to meet the requirements of the core router. The end user requires the following minimum information to configure routers:

- Host name.
- Password. Password Authentication Protocol (PAP) or CHAP host name password (depends on enterprise's choice for authentication method).
- SPIDs, LDNs (optional), and switch type.
- DNS server IP address of the ISP and the domain name (optional). These settings are not relevant to ISDN connectivity, but to DHCP server settings in the configuration.
- NAT/PAT configuration or the subnet of addresses (optional). Another option here can be if the IP address is dynamically obtained (negotiated).

As mentioned, the IP address of the CPE can be statically or dynamically assigned, can be part of the enterprise's IP range, or can be a NAT/PAT address. Some of the common techniques here are designing a pool of IP addresses, or performing PAT or NAT translation to assign an IP address to the remote user.

IP Pool Design

The purpose of the IP pool is to create and assign a group of addresses, so that when the remote user calls, after the user is authenticated, an IP address is provided from a predefined set of IP addresses. The IP pool assignment in the core router is relatively simple to configure, as shown in Example 10-6.

Example 10-6 *Configuration Setting for an IP Pool*

```
<output omitted>
interface Dialer1
description HOME_ISDN_USERS
ip unnumbered Loopback0
encapsulation ppp
no ip mroute-cache
no keepalive
```

Example 10-6 *Configuration Setting for an IP Pool (Continued)*

```
dialer in-band
dialer idle-timeout 3600
dialer-group 8
peer default ip address pool HOME_ISDN_USERS
fair-queue
ppp authentication chap callin
ppp multilink
!
ip local pool HOME_ISDN_USERS 20.18.15.1 20.18.15.62
<output omitted>
```

Under the dialer 1 interface, the definition for the IP address pool is specified. The definition is related to the last statement in the example, which defines the IP pool from 20.18.15.1 to 20.18.15.62 with 62 addresses, or a /26 subnet. The bold statements must match, and it is important not to oversubscribe. Because ISDN is still a dial-in service, expect both peak and non-used hours. It is common practice to use a 10:1 ratio of users to channels. In some cases when it makes business sense, it is better to use a lower ratio to increase the availability of the circuits.

NOTE   In the Cisco ISDN environment for home users, a ratio of 5:1 up to 7:1 works well and does not cause any disconnects or busy signals during peak hours.

To check the status of the pool, use the **show ip local pool** command, as shown in Example 10-7.

Example 10-7 *Checking IP Pool Status*

```
4500-isdn#show ip local pool
Pool              Begin         End            Free    In use
HOME_ISDN_USERS   20.18.15.1    20.18.15.62    59      3
4500-isdn#
```

To check on who the three users are who are currently connected, use the **show users all** command, as shown in Example 10-8.

Example 10-8 *Determining the Users of the IP Pool*

```
4500-isdn#show users all
<output omitted>
Interface   User         Mode                 Idle       Peer Address
Vi13        804-isdn-56  Virtual PPP (Bundle) 00:00:45   10.70.219.20
```
continues

Example 10-8   *Determining the Users of the IP Pool (Continued)*

```
Vi17      804-isdn-1     Virtual PPP (Bundle)     00:00:00     10.99.251.217
Vi19      776-isdn-3     Virtual PPP (Bundle)     00:02:44     10.121.5.185"
<output omitted>
```

The command shows information about all users, including the information about incative ports.

Another option here is to show detailed information about every multilink bundle with the **show ppp multilink** command, as shown in Example 10-9.

Example 10-9   *Collecting Multilink Bundle Information*

```
4500-isdn#show ppp multilink
<output omitted>
Virtual-Access17, bundle name is 804-isdn-1
  Bundle up for 00:01:46
  Dialer interface is Dialer1
  0 lost fragments, 0 reordered, 0 unassigned
  0 discarded, 0 lost received, 1/255 load
  0x0 received sequence, 0x0 sent sequence
  Member links: 1 (max not set, min not set)
    Serial0:21, since 00:01:46

Virtual-Access19, bundle name is 776-isdn-3
  Bundle up for 12:58:58
  Dialer interface is Dialer1
  0 lost fragments, 16 reordered, 0 unassigned
  0 discarded, 0 lost received, 1/255 load
  0x1AA3 received sequence, 0x5392 sent sequence
  Member links: 2 (max not set, min not set)
    Serial0:7, since 12:58:58
    Serial0:22, since 00:00:31

Virtual-Access13, bundle name is 804-isdn-56
  Bundle up for 1d11h
  Dialer interface is Dialer1
  0 lost fragments, 864 reordered, 0 unassigned
  0 discarded, 0 lost received, 1/255 load
  0x300C received sequence, 0x6463 sent sequence
  Member links: 1 (max not set, min not set)
    Serial0:12, since 1d11h
<output omitted>
```

To check which addresses are taken from the pool, use the **show ip route** command, as shown in Example 10-10.

Example 10-10 *Determining Addresses Taken from an IP Pool*

```
4500-isdn#show ip route
<output omitted>
C       20.18.15.3/32 is directly connected, Dialer1
! This IP is taken
D       10.18.15.0/26 is a summary, 00:09:45, Null0
C       20.18.15.51/32 is directly connected, Dialer1 -
! This IP is taken
C       20.18.15.37/32 is directly connected, Dialer1 -
! This IP is taken
C       20.18.254.131/32 is directly connected, Loopback0
D       20.85.130.72/32 [90/409600] via 161.68.99.1, 00:09:45, Ethernet0
S*   0.0.0.0/0 [1/0] via 161.68.99.1
4500-isdn#
```

A better option here is to use the **show ip local pool** *name* command, as shown in Example 10-11.

Example 10-11 *Determining Addresses Within an IP Pool*

```
4500-isdn#show ip local pool HOME_ISDN_USERS
Pool             Begin          End           Free    In use   Cache Size
HOME_ISDN_USERS  20.18.15.1     20.18.15.62    59       3          20
Available addresses:
   20.18.15.3        Vi13                     804-isdn-56
   20.18.15.51       Vi19                     776-isdn-3
   20.18.15.37       Vi17                     804-isdn-1
<output omitted>
```

This command displays the available addresses in the pool. Also, the command shows the IP addresses that are currently in use and the virtual interface that is assigned to the user of that IP address.

NAT and PAT

NAT and PAT are design solutions that create private address space, in the sense that these addresses only exist inside the private network and not in the public address space. These techniques allow designers of future network implementations to achieve some important goals, including the following:

- Conserve IP address space
- Provide scalability
- Provide a firewall technique
- Reduce time and cost by simplifying IP address management

In its simplest configuration, NAT operates on a router that connects two networks together. One of these networks (designated as inside or private) is addressed with either private or obsolete addresses that must be converted into public addresses before packets are forwarded onto the other network (designated as outside or public). The translation operates in conjunction with routing, so that NAT can simply be enabled on a customer-side Internet access router when translation is desired.)

PAT is a configuration with a subset of features from the NAT technique, and it is available in later versions of Cisco IOS Software Release 11.2. Both PAT and NAT are discussed in more detail in the sections that follow.

PAT

Several internal addresses can be NATed to only one or a few external addresses by using a feature called overload, which is also referred to as PAT. PAT is a subset of NAT functionality, where it maps several internal addresses (up to about 4000) to a single external address. PAT statically uses unique port numbers on a single outside IP address to distinguish between the various translations. The total number of these ports is theoretically 2^{16}, or 65,536. PAT-only enabled Cisco IOS Software images do not support full NAT functionality that is required where one-to-one static or dynamic translations are required.

Example 10-12 shows a simple PAT configuration for a 77x router, where a private address space type /28 has to be assigned and ports from 6000–6005 have to be mapped to one IP address (in this case, 10.0.0.2).

Example 10-12 *Simple PAT Configuration*

```
under user "Internal", type
set ip netmask 255.255.255.240
set ip address 10.0.0.1
! If the core router's chap hostname is 'gateway,' then the user will need
! to be name 'gateway' as well.
set user gateway
set ip pat on
```

Assign the ports and private IP addresses as in Example 10-13.

Example 10-13 *Assigning Ports/Private IP Addresses*

```
set dhcp address 10.0.0.2 13
set dhcp netmask 255.255.255.240
set dhcp gateway primary 10.0.0.1
set ip pat porthandler 6000 10.0.0.2
set ip pat porthandler 6001 10.0.0.2
set ip pat porthandler 6002 10.0.0.2
set ip pat porthandler 6003 10.0.0.2
set ip pat porthandler 6004 10.0.0.2
set ip pat porthandler 6005 10.0.0.2
```

NOTE   In Example 10-13, ports 6000–6005 are assigned to PAT transformation statically.

Use the **show ip pat** command to check or troubleshoot the PAT functions on a 77x router, as shown in Example 10-14.

Example 10-14 *Determining PAT Functions for Troubleshooting Purposes*

```
776-isdn> show ip pat

Dropped - icmp 0, udp 15, tcp 0, map 0, frag 0
Timeout - udp 5 minutes, tcp 30 minutes
Port handlers [no default]:

Port    Handler        Service
-------------------------------------
21       10.0.0.2      FTP
6000    10.0.0.2
6001    10.0.0.2
6002    10.0.0.2
6003    10.0.0.2
6004    10.0.0.2
6005    10.0.0.2
23       Router         TELNET
67       Router         DHCP Server
68       Router         DHCP Client
69       Router         TFTP
161     Router         SNMP
162     Router         SNMP-TRAP
520     Router         RIP
Translation Table - 16 Entries.
Inside          Outside        Orig. Port/ID    Trans. Port/ID  Timeout
----------------------------------------------------------------------
10.0.0.2        161.68.235.228  0x89c3           0xfff9          1
10.0.0.2        161.69.2.87     0x89cb           0xfff2          2
10.0.0.2        161.68.235.228  0x89cb           0xfff5          2
10.0.0.2        161.69.2.87     0x89cd           0xffee          3
10.0.0.2        161.68.235.228  0x89cd           0xffef          2
10.0.0.2        161.68.222.255  0x9b1            0x9b1           4
```

NAT

NAT was initially described in RFC 1631. In its simplest configuration, it operates on a router that connects two networks together, where one of these networks is designated as inside or private, and the other is outside or public. As part of a global address plan, each of these networks can use either unique addresses, private addresses (RFC 1918), or addresses that have been officially assigned to some other organization as their private addresses. One of these networks is addressed with addresses that must be translated before packets are forwarded onto the other network. If required, NAT can also perform bidirectionally, translating both the source and destination addresses. Full NAT functionality is required where one-to-one static and dynamic translations are required.

Both static and dynamic address translations are supported by Cisco IOS Software NAT, alone or in conjunction with one another. Static address translations require an administrator to explicitly map an external address to an internal address. Dynamic translations use an allocated IP pool, and each new IP address to be translated is dynamically mapped to another IP address from the pool in a round-robin fashion. Static translations generally allow access to a particular device through the NAT. For example, if a network has an internal Domain Name System (DNS) server that needs to communicate with an external DNS server, one configures a static translation to enable connectivity. The NAT then allows traffic to be passed between these statically known, but translated addresses. Addresses in static translations must explicitly be omitted from the dynamic translation pool.

An IP packet that traverses a NAT can have both its source and destination addresses translated by the NAT. RFC 1918 defines the address space to be allocated for private Internets. The documents state: "The Internet Assigned Numbers Authority (IANA) has reserved the following three blocks of the IP address space for private internets":

```
10.0.0.0 - 10.255.255.255   (10/8 prefix)
172.16.0.0 - 172.31.255.255   (172.16/12 prefix)
192.168.0.0 - 192.168.255.255 (192.168/16 prefix)
```

NOTE   The IANA is now called the American Registry for Internet Numbers (ARIN).

The first block is referred to as the 24-bit block, the second as the 20-bit block, and the third as the 16-bit block. The first block is nothing but a single class A network number, the second block is a set of 16 contiguous class B network numbers, and the third block is a set of 256 contiguous Class C network numbers. The full document can be found in the available literature or at www.faqs.org/rfcs/rfc1918.html.

Under the Ethernet0 interface, a sample config of Cisco IOS Software NAT requires the configuration in Example 10-15.

Example 10-15 *Cisco IOS Software NAT Configuration*

```
!
interface Ethernet0
<output omitted>
ip nat inside
no shutdown
```

```
Under the Dialer 1 interface:
```

Example 10-15 *Cisco IOS Software NAT Configuration (Continued)*

```
<output omitted>
ip nat outside
<output omitted>
```

Example 10-16 shows the configuration in global configuration mode.

Example 10-16 *Cisco IOS Software NAT Configuration: Global Configuration Mode*

```
ip nat inside source list  111 interface Dialer1 overload
access-list 10 permit ip any any
access-list 111 deny    udp any eq netbios-dgm any
access-list 111 deny    udp any eq netbios-ns any
access-list 111 deny    udp any eq netbios-ss any
access-list 111 deny    tcp any eq 137 any
access-list 111 deny    tcp any eq 138 any
access-list 111 deny    tcp any eq 139 any
access-list 111 permit ip any any time-range TIME
dialer-list 1 protocol ip permit
<output omitted>
```

TIP

Before starting the troubleshooting process, use the command **clear ip nat translations**, which is helpful in the NAT debug process.

To troubleshoot the solution, you can use the debug in Example 10-17.

Example 10-17 *Debug for NAT*

```
804-isdn#debug ip nat
*Mar  1 00:03:43.065: NAT: o: icmp (10.0.0.1, 5574) -> (10.0.0.2, 5574) [0]
*Mar  1 00:03:44.565: NAT: o: icmp (10.0.0.1, 5575) -> (10.0.0.2, 5575) [1]
*Mar  1 00:03:49.065: NAT: i: udp (10.0.0.2, 137) -> (161.68.235.228, 137) [18082]
*Mar  1 00:03:50.565: NAT: i: udp (10.0.0.2, 137) -> (161.68.235.228, 137) [18083]
```

The first two lines show that the default gateway 10.0.0.1 is exchanging Internet Control Message Protocol (ICMP) packets with the newly assigned 10.0.0.2. The second two lines show 10.0.0.2 using port 18082, and exchanging udp port 137 packets with an IP address.

To check the arp-cache transactions, use the debug in Example 10-18.

As soon as the **ip nat debug** is turned on, you can see the standard data exchange and NAT in action.

Example 10-18 *Example of Debugging NAT*

```
804-isdn#show ip nat  translations
804-isdn#debug arp804-isdn
#debug ip nat
IP NAT debugging is on
ARP packet debugging is on
804-isdn#
*Oct 105 01:15:19.198: IP ARP: rcvd req src 10.0.0.2 0050.dabb.c887,
  dst 10.0.0.2 Ethernet0
! IP ARP request from  an IP source with MAC address 0050.dabb.c887.
*Oct 105 01:16:20.166: IP ARP: rcvd req src 10.0.0.2 0050.dabb.c887,
  dst 10.0.0.2 Ethernet0
! Again the same request
*Oct 105 01:15:21.166: IP ARP: rcvd req src 10.0.0.2 0050.dabb.c887,
  dst 10.0.0.2 Ethernet0
! and again
*Oct 105 01:15:23.178: IP ARP: creating entry for IP address: 10.0.0.2,
  hw: 0050.dabb.c887
! The entry in the ARP-cache is created to map IP 10.0.0.2 to MAC 0050.dabb.c887.
*Oct 105 01:15:23.182: IP ARP: sent rep src 10.0.0.1 00b0.64ba.2c81,
  dst 10.0.0.2 0050.dabb.c887 Ethernet0
A confirmation (replicate) is sent to confirm the assignment.
804-isdn#show arp
Protocol  Address          Age (min)  Hardware Addr   Type    Interface
Internet  10.0.0.2                 1  0050.dabb.c887  ARPA    Ethernet0
Internet  10.0.0.1                 -  00b0.64ba.2c81  ARPA    Ethernet0
```

See Example 10-19 to see negotiations of the IP and related ports.

Example 10-19 *Negotiations of the IP and Related Ports in Cisco IOS Software*

```
Oct 105 04:30:31.837: NAT: i: tcp (10.0.0.2, 4734) -> (141.68.235.244, 139)
  [17225]
*Oct 105 04:30:31.885: NAT: o: tcp (141.68.235.244, 139) -> (141.70.209.81, 4734)
  [45847]
! Outside source is sending TCP 139 data to the public address of the user
141.70.209.81.
*Oct 105 04:30:32.029: NAT: i: tcp (10.0.0.2, 4734) -> (141.68.235.244, 139)
  [17226]
*Oct 105 04:30:42.873: NAT: o: udp (192.168.165.15, 496) -> (230.0.1.39, 496)
  [38427]
*Oct 105 04:30:42.889: NAT: o: udp (192.168.165.15, 496) -> (230.0.1.39, 496)
  [38426]
*Oct 105 04:30:57.593: NAT: o: udp (141.69.10.13, 496) -> (230.0.1.40, 496)
  [19018]
*Oct 105 04:30:57.609: NAT: o: udp (141.69.10.13, 496) -> (230.0.1.40, 496)
  [19016]
*Oct 105 04:30:58.097: NAT: o: tcp (141.68.235.244, 139) -> (141.70.209.81, 4734)
  [53804]
*Oct 105 04:30:58.265: NAT: i: tcp (10.0.0.2, 4734) -> (141.68.235.244, 139)
  [17227]
*Oct 105 04:31:04.645: NAT: i: tcp (10.0.0.2, 4734) -> (141.68.235.244, 139)
```

Example 10-19 *Negotiations of the IP and Related Ports in Cisco IOS Software (Continued)*

```
    [17228]
*Oct 105 04:31:04.693: NAT: o: tcp (141.68.235.244, 139) -> (141.70.209.81, 4734)
    [24625]
*Oct 105 04:31:04.877: NAT: i: tcp (10.0.0.2, 4734) -> (141.68.235.244, 139)
    [17229]
*Oct 105 04:31:12.017: NAT: i: udp (10.0.0.2, 4796) -> (141.68.10.70, 53) [17230]
*Oct 105 04:31:12.017: NAT: ipnat_allocate_port: wanted 4796 got 4796
*Oct 105 04:31:12.021: NAT: i: udp (10.0.0.2, 137) -> (141.68.235.228, 137)
    [17231]
*Oct 105 04:31:12.073: NAT: o: udp (141.68.10.70, 53) -> (141.70.209.81, 4796)
    [44539]
! The DNS server is sending DNS confirm - UDP 53 to the public IP of the
! user 141.70.209.81
*Oct 105 04:31:12.077: NAT: i: icmp (10.0.0.2, 512) -> (141.68.222.155, 512)
    [17232]
*Oct 105 04:31:12.081: NAT: ipnat_allocate_port: wanted 512 got 512
! Port 512 allocation example.
*Oct 105 04:31:12.117: NAT: o: icmp (141.68.222.155, 512) -> (141.70.209.81, 512)
    [5514]
*Oct 105 04:31:12.121: NAT: i: tcp (10.0.0.2, 4795) -> (141.68.222.155, 445)
    [17233]
*Oct 105 04:31:12.121: NAT: ipnat_allocate_port: wanted 4795 got 4795
! Port 4795 allocation example.
*Oct 105 04:31:12.157: NAT: o: tcp (141.68.222.155, 445) -> (141.70.209.81, 4795)
    [5534]
*Oct 105 04:31:12.585: NAT: i: tcp (10.0.0.2, 4795) -> (141.68.222.155, 445)
    [17234]
*Oct 105 04:31:12.621: NAT: o: tcp (141.68.222.155, 445) -> (141.70.209.81, 4795)
    [5722]
*Oct 105 04:31:13.089: NAT: i: tcp (10.0.0.2, 4795) -> (141.68.222.155, 445)
    [17235]
*Oct 105 04:31:13.121: NAT: o: tcp (141.68.222.155, 445) -> (141.70.209.81, 4795)
    [5816]
*Oct 105 04:31:13.517: NAT: i: udp (10.0.0.2, 137) -> (141.68.235.228, 137)
    [17236]
```

In this example, the information in the first line reads this way:

> Inside IP 10.0.0.2, using TCP port 4734, is requesting TCP port 139 service from
> 141.68.235.244, and the I-O transformation uses port 17225.

The number of simultaneous NAT translations supported on a given platform is bounded by the amount of available dynamic random-access memory (DRAM) in the router. Each NAT translation consumes about 160 bytes of memory. When using the **overload** function, each time a different stream (identified by an IP address, protocol, and Transmission Control Protocol (TCP) or User Datagram Protocol (UDP) port number) passes through the NAT router, a new entry is created in the table. If traditional address translation is used, each IP address matches to only one IP address and creates a single table entry. Not all traffic is supported by NAT/PAT, which can create an issue for some protocols.

Some of the protocols supported by Cisco IOS Software NAT include HTTP, TFTP, Telnet, Archie, Finger, Network Time Protocol (NTP), Network File System (NFS), rlogin, remote shell (rsh), remote copy (rcp), and any TCP/UDP traffic that does not carry source or destination IP addresses in the application data stream.

Unsupported traffic includes routing table updates, DNS zone transfers, Bootp, talk, ntalk, Simple Network Management Protocol (SNMP), and NetShow. See Cisco.com for the full description of protocols.

Per-User (Per Function) Configuration

The per-user configuration is one of the most advanced Cisco IOS Software features that is related to the scaling techniques. This concept is based on virtuality, where physical and virtual interfaces are related to each other, but the virtual ones do not have permanent physical interfaces associated with them. A virtual configuration uses physical interfaces, but it is flexible, dynamic, and per-function oriented. This Cisco design technique improves scalability and management, and increases router operation efficiency. These techniques are transparent to the design differences and can be used in any environment. From a remote access perspective, two virtual configuration techniques exist, where the first one is a subset of the second one:

- Virtual interface template service
- Virtual profiles

NOTE   The per-user configuration information can supplement or override the generic configuration on a virtual interface.

The sections that follow discuss the two virtual configuration techniques in greater detail.

Virtual Interface Templates

Virtual interface templates are used when the generic interface configuration and router-specific configuration information are combined. These templates provide a certain functionality. For example, when the router receives calls from a remote user, the template applies the predefined settings, such as type of authentication, speed, and IP address from a local pool, to the user. This creates a per-user, per-session (call) configuration. With the remote user call-in, the same template applies with a different IP and when the first user disconnects the call, the template is released and applied to another user request. The advantages for the ISP design are obvious:

- Scalability, because interface configurations can be separated from physical interfaces.

- Function-based, which makes the configuration short and easy to read.
- Efficient router operation and easier management, maintenance, and dynamic configuration assignment.

Virtual Profiles

A virtual profile is another instance of virtuality, which is intended to overcome the limitations of network scalabilty. It is based on the same functionality-specific technique, where the user-specific configuration information can be applied to any remote user. The configuration information for virtual profiles can come from either a virtual interface template, or per-user configuration information that is stored on an access control server (ACS), or both, depending on how the router and ACS are configured. When a user dials in, the virtual profile applies the generic interface configuration and then applies the per-user configuration to create a unique virtual access interface for that specific user.

The concept of virtuality has a significant impact on two of the most commonly used Cisco dial concepts: dial-on-demand routing (DDR) and dialer profiles. In the case of legacy DDR, both parties learn the routes after the connection, but they don't delete them after they are disconnected. In the case of virtual interfaces, because of their dynamic nature, the route is removed as soon as the connection is dropped. Besides, the number of virtual interfaces is not limited by the number of physical interfaces. For example, the Cisco 4500 IOS 12.1 (7) allows 300 dialer profiles, the Cisco 5300 IOS12.0 (7) allows 800 profiles, and the Cisco 7206VXR allows 2896. The number depends on interface descriptor blocks (IDBs).

NOTE   You can find out more about IDBs at the following site:

www.cisco.com/warp/public/63/idb_limit.html

or in the following Cisco Press book:

Inside Cisco IOS Software Architecture

MLP

The MLP is relatively complex and is designed to solve several problems that are related to load balancing multilink wide-area network (WAN) links. The problems it solves include the following:

- Multivendor interoperability, as specified by RFC 1717
- Packet fragmentation, improving the latency of each packet

- Packet sequence
- Load calculation

Cisco IOS Software supports MPPP and takes advantage of ISDN's access technology to split a single connection across two separate circuits. Originally defined in RFC 1717 of the Internet Engineering Task Force (IETF), and updated by RFC 1990, MLP was initially developed to assist emerging ISDN deployments. It is designed to fragment packets and transmit them over parallel connections such as ISDN BRI and Primary Rate Interface (PRI) access lines. This feature provides load balancing over dialer interfaces, including ISDN synchronous and asynchronous interfaces, improving throughput, and reducing latency between systems. Starting with a relatively simple configuration command, such as **ppp multilink**, the feature includes endpoint definitions for the multilink bundle (a multilink logical grouping is called a bundle), fragmentations, interleave, and threshold features.

Figure 10-2 provides an example of how incoming (IN) packets are divided up into fragments, and sent over two separate ISDN lines (or two separate B channels). At the destination, another MLP peer receives the fragments and reassembles them back into the correct order.

Figure 10-2 *Multilink Point-to-Point Protocol (MLP)*

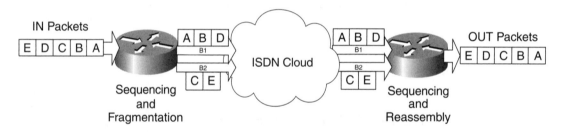

MLP is suitable for a small office/home office (SOHO) environment because of the dynamic nature of bandwidth requirements, and because MLP works over any interface that supports DDR rotary groups and PPP. Multilink systems must do the following:

- Receive protocol data units (PDUs) of a negotiated size
- Combine multiple physical links into one logical link (bundle)
- Receive and reassemble upper-layer PDUs

The MLP feature negotiates the Maximum Received Reconstructed Unit (MRRU) option during the Link Control Protocol (LCP) negotiation, to indicate to its peer that it can combine multiple physical links into a bundle. Also, to indicate that it is willing to multilink by sending the MRRU option as part of the initial LCP option negotiation. In Example 10-20, **I** and **O** are input and output messages of the LCP stage of PPP, and MRRU is the negotiated parameter.

Example 10-20 *Negotiation of MRRU*

```
*Mar  2 06:56:14.744: BR0:1 LCP: O CONFREQ [Closed] id 29 len 30
*Mar  2 06:56:14.744: BR0:1 LCP:    MagicNumber 0xB765FD17 (0x0506B765FD17)
*Mar  2 06:56:14.748: BR0:1 LCP:    MRRU 1524 (0x110405F4)
*Mar  2 06:56:14.748: BR0:1 LCP:    EndpointDisc 1 Local
  (0x131001706E6564656C74632D6973646E)
*Mar  2 06:56:14.776: BR0:1 LCP: I CONFREQ [REQsent] id 249 len 32
*Mar  2 06:56:14.776: BR0:1 LCP:    AuthProto CHAP (0x0305C22305)
*Mar  2 06:56:14.776: BR0:1 LCP:    MagicNumber 0x2101ED36 (0x05062101ED36)
*Mar  2 06:56:14.780: BR0:1 LCP:    MRRU 1524 (0x110405F4)
*Mar  2 06:56:14.780: BR0:1 LCP:    EndpointDisc 1 Local
  (0x130D016163636573732D677731)
*Mar  2 06:56:14.784: BR0:1 LCP: O CONFACK [REQsent] id 249 len 32
*Mar  2 06:56:14.784: BR0:1 LCP:    AuthProto CHAP (0x0305C22305)
*Mar  2 06:56:14.788: BR0:1 LCP:    MagicNumber 0x2101ED36 (0x05062101ED36)
*Mar  2 06:56:14.788: BR0:1 LCP:    MRRU 1524 (0x110405F4)
*Mar  2 06:56:14.788: BR0:1 LCP:    EndpointDisc 1 Local
  (0x130D016163636573732D677731)
*Mar  2 06:56:14.792: BR0:1 LCP: I CONFACK [ACKsent] id 29 len 30
*Mar  2 06:56:14.792: BR0:1 LCP:    MagicNumber 0xB765FD17 (0x0506B765FD17)
*Mar  2 06:56:14.796: BR0:1 LCP:    MRRU 1524 (0x110405F4)
```

After the LCP negotiation has completed successfully, the remote destination must be authenticated, and a dialer map with the remote system name must be configured. The authenticated username (**"804-isdn"**) or callerID determines which bundle to add the link to.

In Example 10-21, one-way authentication with host name authentication is used, where the line ***Mar 2 06:56:15.628: BR0:1 PPP: Phase is VIRTUALIZED** shows that the process is complete, and it starts a new phase—virtualization and MLP is ON.

Example 10-21 *One-Way Authentication of the Remote User Preceding the MLP*

```
*Mar  2 06:56:14.796: BR0:1 LCP:    EndpointDisc 1 Local
  (0x131001706E6564656C74632D6973646E)
*Mar  2 06:56:14.800: BR0:1 LCP: State is Open
*Mar  2 06:56:14.800: BR0:1 PPP: Phase is AUTHENTICATING, by the peer
*Mar  2 06:56:14.816: BR0:1 CHAP: I CHALLENGE id 130 len 31 from gateway
*Mar  2 06:56:14.820: BR0:1 CHAP: O RESPONSE id 130 len 34 from 804-isdn
*Mar  2 06:56:15.628: BR0:1 CHAP: I SUCCESS id 130 len 4
*Mar  2 06:56:15.628: BR0:1 PPP: Phase is VIRTUALIZED
```

To check if MLP is up and running, use the **show ppp multilink** command, as shown in Example 10-22.

Example 10-22 *Determining if MLP Is Up and Running*

```
804-isdn#show ppp multilink
Virtual-Access1, bundle name is access-gw1
  Bundle up for 00:00:18
  Dialer interface is Dialer1
  1 lost fragments, 1 reordered, 0 unassigned
  0 discarded, 0 lost received, 1/255 load
  0x7 received sequence, 0x0 sent sequence
  Member links: 2 (max not set, min not set)
    BRI0:1, since 00:00:18
    BRI0:2, since 00:00:04
804-isdn#
```

The last two lines show two MLP members. Example 10-23 shows the output from the **show negotiation** command.

Example 10-23 *Output from the* **show negotiation** *Command for 776 Router*

```
776-isdn> show negotiation
System Parameters
    PPP Negotiation Parameters
        Integrity Interval       10
        Retry Count               10
        Retry Interval           3000
        Terminate Count        2
        Multilink                ON
! Profile Parameters
        Compression              STAC
        BACP                     ON
        Address Negotiation Local OFF
! Negotiated Parameters
        Connection    1          Virtual
        Connection    2          PPP  IPCP MLCP
        Connection    3          Virtual
```

In the global configuration, MLP supports two functions:

```
multilink bundle-name {authenticated | endpoint | both}
multilink virtual-template 1-25
```

The **virtual-template** function is known to networkers; however, the **multilink bundle-name** endpoint is relatively unknown. This feature was introduced in Cisco IOS Software Release 12.0. During the LCP negotiation of PPP, the endpoint discriminator (ED) option can be negotiated, but it is not required. As previously mentioned, after the LCP negotiation is complete, the remote destination must be authenticated, and a dialer map with the remote system name has to be configured. The dialer maps are not the only solution. See Chapter 11, "Cisco ISDN Configuration Solutions," for more detail. The authenticated username or callerid determines which bundle to add the link. Its primary use is to make a MLP bundle that is unique among different attached users. MLP bundles are either created or supplemented, based on the following four scenarios, and using the ED option in conjunction with an authenticated username. Refer to the output in Example 10-20:

```
*Mar  2 06:56:14.744: BR0:1 LCP: O CONFREQ [Closed] id 29 len 30
*Mar  2 06:56:14.744: BR0:1 LCP:    MagicNumber 0xB765FD17 (0x0506B765FD17)
*Mar  2 06:56:14.748: BR0:1 LCP:    MRRU 1524 (0x110405F4)
*Mar  2 06:56:14.748: BR0:1 LCP:    EndpointDisc 1 Local:
```

- Scenario 1:

  In the first scenario, there is no discriminator, and no authentication; all new links must be joined into one bundle.

  This scenario is not a good idea for any dial service platform where users are not configured to authenticate nor to send an ED. The only time that this is likely to be used is between two fixed systems, where links from an outside device cannot be physically introduced. The **debug ppp negotiation** output shows that **EndpointDisc** is missing. Cisco IOS Software uses the Calling Line ID (CLID) to identify the MLP bundle.

- Scenario 2:

  In the second scenario, there is a discriminator, but no authentication. A discriminator match must join a matching bundle, and a discriminator mismatch must establish a new bundle.

  The **debug ppp negotiation** command shows the endPoint discriminator (**EndpointDisc**) negotiation:

  ```
  Se3/0:2 LCP: EndpointDisc 1 804-isdn (0x1308013137323061) <-- ED
    negotiated
  with Class 1 (Locally Assigned Address), value = Hostname (804-isdn)
  ```

- Scenario 3:

  In the third scenario, there is no discriminator, but there is authentication. The authenticated match must join the matching bundle, and the authenticated mismatch must establish a new bundle. The **debug ppp negotiation** will show that the **EndpointDisc** is missing again.

- Scenario 4:

  In the last scenario, there is a discriminator and user authentication. The discriminator match and authenticated match must join the bundle, and either a discriminator mismatch or authenticated mismatch must establish a new bundle. Again, the command **debug ppp negotiation** command shows that the EndpointDisc is negotiated:

  ```
  Se3/0:2 LCP: EndpointDisc 1 804-isdn (0x1308013137323061) <-- ED
    negotiated
  ```

You can find more detailed information about MLP at Cisco.com.

MMP

With Cisco IOS Software Release 11.2, Cisco provided support for MMP. MLP is enhanced in MMP to enable different MLP links to terminate on different NASs. This enables ISPs and enterprises to design multiple network access servers that process calls for one single phone number, which is usually a telephone company (telco) hunt group, or for the leading phone number of the group of circuits. MMP also allows the network administrator to specify a router with greater CPU capacity to handle the reassembling and resequencing of the MLP packets, while leaving the routers with less CPU capacity to handle the call terminations. Another advantage of this design is scalability because a new NAS can be added to the existing environment to meet user demand, with minimal changes required to the existing design and configuration.

Cisco's Stack Group Bidding Protocol (SGBP) is designed to enable MMP features. As only one router can handle the reassembling and resequencing of MLP packets for any given bundle, a mechanism is required to determine which router in the group (stack) owns the master bundle (also called the call master) to perform the tasks for that bundle. SGBP is used between all members (peers) of the stack group to determine the call master when any PPP link is connected. Each router's seed-bid can be manually configured from 0 to 9999 with the higher number winning the bid to be the call master. If there's a tie, the router that has the physical link is selected as the call master. If neither router has the physical connection, SGBP randomly picks one to be the call master for that user.

After a router wins the bid for a specific user, it changes its bid for that user to 10,000, so it is guaranteed that it will win the bid for all subsequent calls from that user. SGBP uses UDP port 9900 to communicate. When a second call comes in from the same user and is terminated on a different router, a Layer 2 Forwarding (L2F) tunnel is built between the two routers, and the raw PPP data is forwarded over this tunnel from the call terminator to the call master. This is called projecting the PPP link to the call master. Eventually, this will be changed to use L2TP, which is an industry standard. Figure 10-3 shows an example of how SGBP works where RouterA, RouterB, and RouterC are in a stack group with equal seed-bids, and UserA is connecting.

As shown in Figure 10-3, the following 13 steps show the steps which Routers A, B, and C, with no off-load server, bid to be the call-master for UserA's PPP bundle:

1 UserA places the first call. This is Call 1.

2 RouterB answers a call.

3 RouterB negotiates LCP up to the authentication challenge and identifies the caller as UserA.

4 RouterB informs the stack group of a call from UserA.

5 Group members bid for the call, and because all seed-bids are equal, RouterB wins because RouterB terminates the call.

6 RouterB finishes authentication of UserA and finishes PPP negotiation.

7 UserA places a second call. This is Call 2.

8 The new MLP link connects to RouterC.

9 RouterC negotiates LCP up to the authentication challenge and identifies the caller as UserA.

10 RouterC informs the stack group of a call from UserA.

11 The group bids for the call, and because RouterB is already the call master for UserA, RouterB wins.

12 RouterC creates a L2F tunnel to RouterB and projects the PPP link to RouterB.

13 RouterB reassembles and resequences the MPPP packets.

Figure 10-3 *SGBP with No Off-Load Server*

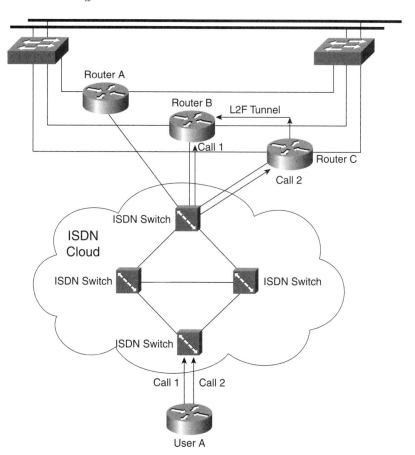

The default seed-bid is 50. A more powerful router can also be configured as an offload server with the seed-bid value, depending on the platform. (For example, a 7200 has a value of 2620, a 3600 has a value of 1050, and a 2500 has a value of 80.) Configuring a seed-bid on a router for forward-only causes the router to never bid for a call. It even hangs up the call rather than win the bid. Figure 10-4 shows an example of SGBP where RouterA, RouterB, and RouterC are in a stack group and RouterA is the off-load server that does not terminate any calls, and UserA is connecting.

Figure 10-4 *SGBP with an Off-Load Server*

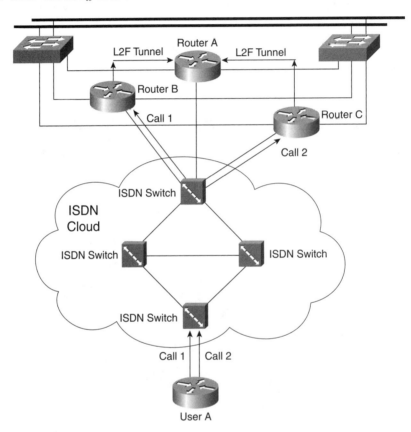

Referring to Figure 10-4, the following 14 steps show the steps that Routers A, B, and C, with A as the off-load server bid, follow to be the call-master for UserA's PPP bundle:

1 UserA starts the first call. This is Call 1.

2 RouterB answers the call.

3 RouterB negotiates LCP up to the authentication challenge and identifies the caller as UserA.

4 RouterB informs the stack group of a call from UserA.

5 Group bids are made for the call, and because RouterA is the off-load, RouterA becomes the call master.

6 RouterB creates a L2F tunnel and forwards the raw PPP data to RouterA.

7 RouterA finishes authentication of UserA and finishes PPP negotiations.

8 UserA starts a second call. This is Call 2.

9 New MLP links connect to RouterC.

10 RouterC negotiates LCP up to the authentication challenge and identifies the caller as UserA.

11 RouterC informs the stack group of a call from UserA.

12 Group bids are made for the call, and because RouterA is already the call master, RouterA wins.

13 RouterC creates a L2F tunnel and forwards the raw PPP data to RouterA.

14 RouterA reassembles and resequences the MLP packets.

All described operations and the protocol interactions are transparent to the end user. From the user's debug information, it is impossible to determine if the other party is using MLP or MMP.

MMP Configuration

Example 10-24 shows the SGBP-related configuration items for each router in Figure 10-4.

Example 10-24 *SGBP-Related Configuration for RouterA, RouterB, and RouterC in Figure 10-4*

```
hostname routerA
!
username dialin-group password cisco
!
sgbp group dialin-group
sgbp seed-bid offload
sgbp member routerB 192.168.0.2
sgbp member routerC 192.168.0.3
sgbp source-ip 192.168.0.1
```

```
hostname routerB
!
username dialin-group password cisco
username userA password knockknock
!
sgbp group dialin-group
```

continues

Example 10-24 *SGBP-Related Configuration for RouterA, RouterB, and RouterC in Figure 10-4 (Continued)*

```
sgbp member routerA 192.168.0.1
sgbp member routerC 192.168.0.3
sgbp source-ip 192.168.0.2
```

```
hostname routerC
!
username dialin-group password cisco
username userA password knockknock
!
sgbp group dialin-group
sgbp member routerA 192.168.0.1
sgbp member routerB 192.168.0.2
sgbp source-ip 192.168.0.3
```

Authentication of the SGBP group, and of the individual users, can be done through Terminal Access Controller Access Control System (TACACS).

NOTE   Each member is authenticating the stack group rather than each other. Also, each router does not specify itself as a member of the stack group, but does need to specify all other members in the stack group to create a fully meshed group.

There is nothing to configure to enable the L2F tunnels. If no dialer interfaces are defined, a virtual template and a virtual template interface must be configured, so that when a virtual access interface needs to be created for each bundle, there is a template to clone.

MMP Sample Implementation

In the sample implementation shown in Example 10-25, you need a solution for a company with thousands of telecommuters across the U.S. who want to connect to the corporate network through an ISDN BRI from each of their homes. You are going to use two 7200 routers (7200-isdn-a and 7200-isdn-b) to terminate the ISDN calls with no offload server.

Example 10-25 *MMP Sample Implementation*

```
hostname 7200-isdn-a
!
username isdnservers password cisco
username user1-isdn password user1
username user2-isdn password user2
!
sgbp group isdnservers
sgbp member 7200-isdn-b 172.30.253.253
```

Example 10-25 *MMP Sample Implementation (Continued)*

```
sgbp source-ip 172.30.253.254
!
! many T1 controllers
!
controller T1 2/0
 framing esf
 linecode b8zs
 pri-group timeslots 1-24
!
! a Serial interface for each T1
!
interface Serial2/0:23
 no ip address
 encapsulation ppp
 dialer rotary-group 1
 isdn switch-type primary-4ess
 no cdp enable
!
interface Dialer1
 bandwidth 128
 ip unnumbered Loopback0
 encapsulation ppp
 dialer in-band
 dialer hold-queue 20
 dialer-group 1
 peer default ip address pool ISDN-POOL
 fair-queue
 no cdp enable
 ppp authentication chap isdn
 ppp chap hostname 7200-isdn
 ppp multilink
!
```

```
hostname 7200-isdn-b
!
username isdnservers password cisco
username user1-isdn password user1
username user2-isdn password user2
!
sgbp group isdnservers
sgbp member 7200-isdn-a 172.30.253.254
sgbp source-ip 172.30.253.253
!
! many T1 controllers
!
controller T1 2/0
 framing esf
 linecode b8zs
 pri-group timeslots 1-24
!
```

continues

Example 10-25 *MMP Sample Implementation (Continued)*

```
! a Serial interface for each T1
!
interface Serial2/0:23
 no ip address
 encapsulation ppp
 dialer rotary-group 1
 isdn switch-type primary-4ess
 no cdp enable
!
interface Dialer1
 bandwidth 128
 ip unnumbered Loopback0
 encapsulation ppp
 dialer in-band
 dialer hold-queue 20
 dialer-group 1
 peer default ip address pool ISDN-POOL
 fair-queue
 no cdp enable
 ppp authentication chap isdn
 ppp chap hostname 7200-isdn
 ppp multilink
!
```

The T1 controller configuration, along with the serial and dialer interface configuration, are standard ISDN and PPP configurations. The MMP-specific commands are the username and passwords for the SGBP group, and the three lines that start with **sgbp** commands.

Verifying MMP

The **show sgbp** command displays the status of the stack group members, as shown in Example 10-26.

Example 10-26 *Displaying Stack Group Member Status*

```
7200-isdn-b#show sgbp
Group Name: isdnservers Ref: 0xC973B000
Seed bid: default, 50, default seed bid setting

  Member Name: 7200-isdn-a State: active Id: 1
  Ref: 0x8ECD9400
  Address: 172.30.253.254
```

The output includes the name of the stack group, the locally configured seed-bid, and each peer and its status. The five possible states for a peer are as follows:

- IDLE
- CONNECTING

- WAIT_INFO
- AUTHOK
- ACTIVE

In Example 10-26, if the state is IDLE, it means that the stack group isdnservers cannot detect 7200-isdn-a as a peer. The other three states are transition states from IDLE to ACTIVE. ACTIVE indicates a fully functional peer. If problems or misconfigurations exist on the local router, all configured peers might be in the IDLE state.

Example 10-27 shows output from 7200-isdn-b, where the master bundle is owned by 7200-isdn-b, and one of the MLP links is connected to 7200-isdn-a. In **show ppp multilink**, the second member link is connected to 7200-isdn-a and is forwarded to the Virtual-Access 17 interface of 7200-isdn-b. In **show users**, that Vi17 is the L2F tunnel.

Example 10-27 *Verifying Master Bundle Ownership, Stack Member Connection Information, and L2F Tunnel Identification*

```
7200-isdn-b#show ppp multilink | begin user2-isdn
Virtual-Access76, bundle name is user2-isdn
  Bundle up for 00:06:35
  Using relaxed lost fragment detection algorithm.
  Dialer interface is Dialer1
  0 lost fragments, 1431 reordered, 0 unassigned
  0 discarded, 0 lost received, 23/255 load
  0x12CC received sequence, 0x8B8 sent sequence
  Member links: 2 (max not set, min not set)
    Serial3/3:20, since 00:06:35, last rcvd seq 0012CB
    7200-isdn-a:Virtual-Access17  (172.30.253.254), since 00:06:25,
    last rcvd seq 0012C4, unsequenced

7200-isdn-b#show users | include user2
  Vi17         user2-isdn   Virtual PPP (L2F   )      -
  Vi76         user2-isdn   Virtual PPP (Bundle) 00:00:00 10.70.200.137
  Se3/3:20     user2-isdn   Sync PPP                  -    Bundle: Vi76
```

On 7200-isdn-a, shown in Example 10-28, you see only the physical link, but nothing else.

Table 10-1 *Output of the **show users** Command Reveals Only the Physical Link*

```
7200-isdn-a#show users | include user2
  Se5/0:8      user2-isdn   Sync PPP                  -
```

Summary

The design solutions provided in this chapter are not the only possible design solutions, but they are the most common and established ones. The main topics here are to enhance knowledge of the troubleshooting engineer in industry-established enterprise and ISP design solutions, ISDN switch types, SPIDs and LDNs, IP pool design, and NAT and PAT solutions. Detailed description for per-user design, virtual templates, and profiles is also provided. Because of the significance of MLP and MMP, a detailed explanation is also provided. This chapter contributes to the identification of the expected behavior of the system, where the routers are expected to perform according to the context of the particular design.

Review Questions

Answers to the review questions can be found in Appendix A, "Answers to Review Questions."

1　Name the most common ISDN switch types in the U.S. and Canada?

2　Type a command that sets up the switch-type NI1 for a Cisco IOS Software ISDN router in global configuration mode.

3　Type a command to define a local pool of 63 IP addresses for your core router, starting with 20.18.15.1, if the pool name is LOCAL_POOL.

4　What is the theoretical maximum number of ports in PAT?

5　How much memory consumes one NAT translation?

6　Name at least five protocols that are supported by Cisco IOS Software NAT.

7　In the case of the virtual interfaces, what happens with the route when the connection is tear-down?

8　Name three main functions of multilink systems.

9　Why would you use multilink PPP between a remote office and corporate headquarters?

10　On which interface types can you use multilink PPP?

11　What does the MRRU stand for and at which stage of the PPP protocol is it used?

12　What is the purpose of using the endpoint discriminator (ED) option in MP?

13　What Cisco IOS Software command displays the status of the stack group members?

14　Name the five possible states of the peer in the stack-group.

CHAPTER 11

Cisco ISDN Configuration Solutions

A wide variety of configuration solutions is available in the existing literature, comprising years of engineering experience. This chapter mainly covers the cost-effective solutions because they are the most common in the existing industry practices, and because Integrated Services Digital Network (ISDN), as a service, is under the pressure of other technologies because of its cost drawbacks in remote access solutions. Most network engineers distinguish the following configuration solutions of ISDN design implementations, and all of them are related to cost efficiency or availability:

- Spoofing
- Snapshot routing
- Dial-on-demand routing (DDR)
- Callback solutions

This chapter provides additional information about some security features of ISDN and advanced phone settings because Voice over ISDN is a widely available service offered by local providers. It also is one of the appealing features of ISDN service.

Cisco ISDN Cost-Effective Solutions

ISDN is offered by most local exchange carriers (LECs). It's used for data, voice, and video exchange. Recently, the use of ISDN for offnet video-conferencing has increased. However, ISDN became less attractive as a cost-effective solution when compared to other emerging technologies, such as digital subscriber line (DSL), cable, wireless, and satellite. The cost of ISDN service is usually composed of an initial installation charge plus usage-based charges. In some cases, a LEC might differentiate pricing of the first minute in comparison to the following minutes. However, all LECs base the per-usage charge on the number and duration of calls. Using special equipment, such as a Centrex, makes it possible to map the calls to other numbers with the same prefix, which reduces the number of digits to dial (for example, five instead of ten), and reduces the cost to a flat-rate service. In some areas, ISDN is still the only alternative providing Basic Rate Interface (BRI) service with two data/voice channels for remote users. The following alternatives are cost-effective solutions that need to be considered.

Spoofing

One of the most popular ISDN techniques is called *spoofing*, which is where the router responds to keepalive packets instead of sending them to the remote party. If the spoofing is "up," the protocol layer is reporting up, as shown in Example 11-1. In order for any interface to report the protocol layer up, the other party must respond to keepalives, but in spoofing, the router itself responds to keepalives. Spoofing is also part of the troubleshooting technique to check the status of the dialer interface. Even when the router does not make a call, the dialer shows a spoofing state.

Example 11-1   show interfaces dialer 1 *Command Output Reveals* **Dialer1 is up (spoofing), line protocol is up (spoofing)**

```
804-isdn# show interfaces dialer 1
Dialer1 is up (spoofing), line protocol is up (spoofing)
  Hardware is Unknown
  Interface is unnumbered. Using address of Ethernet0 (151.70.209.81)
  MTU 1500 bytes, BW 128 Kbit, DLY 20000 usec,
     reliability 255/255, txload 1/255, rxload 1/255
  Encapsulation PPP, loopback not set
  Keepalive set (10 sec)
  DTR is pulsed for 1 seconds on reset
  Last input never, output never, output hang never
  Last clearing of "show interface" counters never
  Input queue: 1/75/0/0 (size/max/drops/flushes); Total output drops: 0
  Queueing strategy: weighted fair
  Output queue: 0/1000/64/0 (size/max total/threshold/drops)
  Conversations  0/0/16 (active/max active/max total)
  Reserved Conversations 0/0 (allocated/max allocated)
  5 minute input rate 0 bits/sec, 0 packets/sec
  5 minute output rate 0 bits/sec, 0 packets/sec
  112555 packets input, 102607119 bytes
  77225 packets output, 9186472 bytes
```

If you monitor the **5 minute input rate** and **5 minute output rate** counters in Example 11-1, you don't see any activity. The spoofing only imitates an active state of the dialer, but this does not mean that the router is connected, or makes a call. This is the cost-saving effect of the spoofing because the router is not connected and there is no charge from the local provider. To clarify, the router makes a call only if the DDR conditions are met.

Snapshot Routing and OSPF Demand Circuits

Another innovative cost-effective ISDN configuration technique is called *snapshot routing*. Before snapshot routing became available in Cisco IOS Software Release 10.2, ISDN interfaces were configured using static routes, which prevent bandwidth from being consumed by routing updates. But, they are difficult to maintain as the network grows. Snapshot routing supports dynamic routes by allowing routing updates to occur during an active period. It also reduces connection cost by suppressing routing updates during a quiet period; thus, snapshot routing is a way to reduce connection time in ISDN networks by suppressing the transfer of routing updates for a configurable period of time. In ISDN, snapshot routing is applicable for distance vector routing protocols, such as Routing Information Protocol (RIP) and Interior Gateway Routing Protocol (IGRP) for IP, RTMP for AppleTalk, RIP and SAP for IPX, and RTP for Vines. Here's why: As you know, the concept of distance vector protocols is based on triggered updates. The goal of snapshot routing is to allow distance vector routing protocols to exchange updates as they normally would.

The nature of snapshot routing is based on the notion that the router learns of routing updates without periodic updates, thus reducing the number and duration of unnecessary calls and reducing cost. Snapshot routing defines active periods and quiet periods. The active period is a time slot that enables the routing updates to be sent over the DDR interface for a short duration of time. After the active period's expiration, the router alternates with a quiet period when the routing tables at both ends of the link are frozen. Snapshot is, therefore, a triggering mechanism that controls routing updates through a DDR exchange. Both periods can be configured based on the traffic, time of day, and cost-effective considerations.

As soon as a call is triggered for any reason, such as interesting traffic in DDR or a DNS lookup, it triggers the active period timer, as shown in Figure 11-1. During that session, both parties update their routing tables. After the active period's expiration, which can be between 5 and 100 minutes, the update is frozen and both parties enter the quiet period. After the expiration of this time slot and if no calls were made, the router triggers another call, sets the timer, and starts another active period exchange. The quiet period can be configured in a large range, which can be between 5 minutes and 65 days. Because of this possible delay, the technique offers another configurable time slot called a retry period, where more updates can be exchanged if no other activity is on the link.

Figure 11-1 *The Active, Quiet, and Retry Period Interaction in Snapshot Routing*

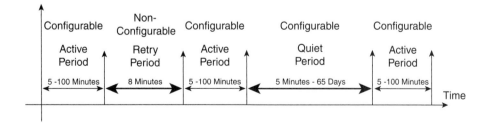

Example 11-2 shows the configuration options for snapshot routing for the dialer 1 interface.

Example 11-2   *Snapshot Routing Options of Cisco IOS Software*

```
804-isdn(config-if)#dialer map snapshot 1 ?
  WORD          Dialer string
  broadcast     Broadcasts should be forwarded to this address
  class         Dialer map class
  modem-script  Specify regular expression to select modem dialing script
  name          Map to a host
  spc           Semi-permanent connections
  speed         Set dialer speed
  system-script Specify regular expression to select system dialing script
```

Another application for the same command line redefines the default speed and then applies the map class to the dialer interface:

```
804-isdn(config-if)#dialer map snapshot 1 class class-name speed [56 | 64]
```

It is almost mandatory to configure the next line under the BRI or dialer interface:

```
804-isdn(config-if)#snapshot [client | server] active-time quiet-time
  [suppress-statechange-updates][dialer]
```

The [**client** | **server**] option must be defined as **client** on the spoke side and **server** on the hub side of the connection.

The *active-time* variable specifies the amount of time, in minutes, that routing updates are regularly exchanged between the client and server routers. This can be an integer in the range 5 to 100. There is no default value. A typical value is 5 minutes.

The *quiet-time* variable specifies the amount of time, in minutes, that routing entries are frozen and remain unchanged between active periods. Routes are not aged during the quiet period, so they remain in the routing table as if they were static entries. This argument can be an integer from 8 to 100,000. There is no default value. The minimum quiet time is generally the active time plus 3.

The **snapshot** command ensures that, if any other event triggers the call out, the snapshot algorithm starts the active period timer and the routing updates will take place.

NOTE   Always start the monitoring of snapshot connections and routing by clearing the appropriate interfaces. **clear dialer** or **clear counters** [**bri** | **dialer**] clears the interface or the previous diagnostic statistics.

Use the following commands to monitor snapshot connections and routing:

- **show dialer** [*interface type number*]—Displays general diagnostics about the interface

- **show interfaces bri 0**—Displays information about the ISDN D-channel

- **clear snapshot quiet-time interface**—Terminates the snapshot routing quiet period on the client router within two minutes

- **show snapshot** [*type number*]—Displays information about snapshot routing parameters

Information about snapshot routing is relatively new. You can find more information about periodic updates at Cisco.com. The key advantages of the snapshot technique are easy evolution, scalability, and manageability.

Snapshot routing is applicable, but not limited, only to ISDN networks. The leased lines can benefit from the reduction of periodic updates that snapshot routing provides.

Snapshot routing is applicable for hub-and-spoke topologies; it's not recommended for meshed topologies. In meshed topologies, configuring static routes is more efficient than configuring snapshot routing.

The link-state protocols, such as Novell Link Services Protocol (NLSP), Open Shortest Path First (OSPF), and Intermediate System-to-Intermediate System (IS-IS) depend on the frequent sending of Hello messages in a short period of time (five or ten seconds) to neighboring routers in order to discover and maintain routes. This fact makes them not suitable for this technique.

For OSPF, which belongs to the family of link-state routing protocols, the "ospf demand circuit" can be thought of as the equivalent to snapshot routing, but with a link-state protocol. The demand circuit options were introduced for OSPF in Cisco IOS Software Release 11.2 in response to the OSPF (RFC 1793). OSPF sends Hellos every 10 seconds and refreshes its link-state advertisements (LSAs) every 30 minutes. These functions, which maintain neighbor relationships and ensure that the link-state databases are accurate, use far less bandwidth than similar functions in RIP and IGRP. However, even this amount of traffic is unwanted on demand circuits. By using the OSPF demand circuit options, which suppresses Hello and LSA refresh functions, OSPF can establish a demand link to form an adjacency and perform initial database synchronization. The adjacency remains active even after Layer 2 of the demand circuit goes down. The two main features of OSPF over demand circuits are

- Suppressed periodic Hellos
- Suppressed periodic LSA refresh

You can find more information about this topic at www.cisco.com/univercd/cc/td/doc/product/software/ios120/12cgcr/np1_c/1cprt1/1cospf.htm.

DDR

DDR is the most common cost-effective technique used in ISDN router configurations. With DDR, all traffic is classified as either interesting or uninteresting. Regardless of the advantages of using dynamic versus static routing, static routing is still a viable solution for a remote access environment and it is commonly used in DDR. One of the reasons is that the dynamic routing updates can trigger the router to call out every time the routing update is necessary.

There are two main options for implementing DDR for routers with ISDN BRIs:

- Dialer maps (sometimes referred to as legacy DDR), which are available for Cisco IOS Software Releases prior to 11.2.

- Dialer profiles, which are available in Cisco IOS Software Release 11.2 and all subsequent versions.

The DDR features discussed in this chapter can be used over ISDN or other dial-up media, as well as over any asynchronous lines.

NOTE
The existence of the dialer interface in the configuration does not necessarily classify it as a dialer profile configuration. The key difference is the mapping and rotary group elements for the legacy DDR versus dialer profiles and pools.

The general concept and function of DDR can be narrowed to the following steps:

1 When the router receives some traffic, it performs a table lookup to determine whether there is a route to the desired destination. Based on the configuration, the outbound interface is identified.

2 If the identified outbound interface is configured for DDR, the router does a lookup to determine whether the traffic is interesting based on the dialer list statement of the configuration.

3 The router then identifies the next hop router and locates the dialing information based on dialer map or dialer profiles configuration.

4 In the case of dialer profiles, the router checks if the dialer is currently connected to the desired remote destination. If so, the traffic is sent and the idle timer is reset to the maximum configured value every time the interesting packet crosses that dialer.

5 In the case of dialer profiles, if the dialer is not currently connected to the desired remote destination, the router determines which physical interfaces are in its dialer pool, "borrows" an interface, makes a call out, applies the map class (if it exists) and dialer interface configuration, establishes a connection, and sets the idle timer to its maximum configured value.

6 After the link is established, the router transmits both interesting and uninteresting traffic. Uninteresting traffic can include data and routing updates.

7 When the time duration between any two consecutive interesting events is greater than the idle timer value, or the idle timer expires, the call is disconnected. In the case of dialer profiles, the physical interface is released and goes back to the dialer pool.

NOTE   DDR is not a traffic filter solution, but a mechanism to force a call setup and call teardown. The moment the interesting traffic triggers a call, the router resets the idle timer to the maximum configured value each time the interesting traffic crosses the interface. As long as the interface is up, however, all traffic is forwarded over that interface. Remember that only the interesting traffic can set or reset the idle timer; otherwise, the idle timer, ticking down by default, expires.

For troubleshooting purposes, refer to one simple procedure, provided in Chapter 7 of *Building Cisco Remote Access Networks* by Catherine Paquet (Cisco Press, 1999).

Obviously, if all traffic is interesting, the router constantly keeps the line up 24 hours a day. This raises questions about how to define interesting traffic and what are the techniques to distinguish it from non-interesting traffic in order to make DDR a cost-effective solution, reducing the up time and, as a result, the duration of the calls.

Both legacy DDR and dialer profiles solutions work simultaneously in existing Cisco production environments. For CPE significance, they are local. As a result, you might have a dialer profiles on the spoke side and legacy DDR on the hub side, or any other combination.

In general, the legacy DDR requires the following steps:

1 Specify interesting traffic. What traffic type should enable the link?

2 Define static routes. What route do you take to get to the destination?

3 Configure the dialer information. What number do you call to get to the next hop router? What service parameters do you use for the call? The key for this configuration is mapping the protocol, address, the remote address name and the phone number with the following command:

```
dialer map ip 161.30.253.254 name gateway broadcast 14085265555
```

These steps can be performed when configuring the dialer profiles, but the content of the dialer information differs.

You can find additional information about legacy DDR at Cisco.com, but for the sake of a complete explanation, here are some of the specifics and limitations of legacy DDR:

- There is one configured interface per ISDN interface. Before dialer profiles, all ISDN B channels inherited the physical interface's configuration.

- Before dialer profiles, one dialer map was required per dialer per protocol, making multiprotocol configurations very complex.

- When a PRI is used to back up an interface, all B channels are down and the entire interface is idle.

- In a packet-switched environment in which many virtual circuits might need to be backed up individually and floating static routes are not desirable, the one-to-one relationship between interfaces and backup interfaces does not scale well.

- Using the concept of rotary groups makes the configuration inflexible and restrictive because the physical interface participates in only one rotary group.

NOTE   The following section focuses on dialer profiles, which conceptually are based on creating virtual interfaces and allow the physical interfaces to belong to many different pools.

When reviewing router hardware, you will not find a physical interface called a dialer. The dialer profile feature enables you to configure dial-on-demand capabilities (in a dialer interface) separate from the physical interface. Because of this separation, the BRI and PRI interfaces can be shared by multiple dialer profile configurations, and the number of dialer profiles can be significant—up to 300 for Cisco 4500 and more than 2800 for Cisco 7206VXR. (See more about this topic in the section, "Virtual Profiles," in Chapter 10, "ISDN Design Solutions.") Dialer profiles enable logical and physical configurations to be bound together dynamically on a per-call requirements basis. Dialer profiles can define encapsulation, access control lists (ACLs), minimum or maximum calls, and turn on and off a variety of features.

With dialer profiles, the physical interfaces become members of a dialer pool, which is configurable and represents a set of interfaces that can be used on an on-demand basis. When a call must be made, the dialer pool borrows a physical interface for the duration of the call, based on the dialer interface configuration. After the call is complete, the physical interface is returned to the dialer pool. Dialer profiles enable BRIs to belong to multiple dialer pools. This eliminates wasting ISDN B channels. Multiple destinations can be bridged to avoid split horizon problems. Remote routers or users' access can be controlled or customized through independent dialer profiles.

The list of features can be extended. The dialer profiles perform the same cost-effective feature of DDR, achieving more flexibility and scalability of the configuration.

The main elements of the dialer profile include the following:

- **Dialer interfaces**—Logical entities used for a per-destination dialer profile. Any number of dialer interfaces can be created in a router. All configuration settings specific to the destination are configurable in the dialer interface configuration.

- **Dialer pool**—Represents a group of physical interfaces associated with a dialer profile. A physical interface can belong to multiple dialer pools. Contention for a specific physical interface is resolved by configuring the optional **priority** command.

- **Physical interfaces**—Configured for encapsulation parameters. The interfaces are configured to identify the dialer pools to which the interfaces belong.

- **Dialer map class (optional)**—The **dialer map-class** command defines specific parameters, such as speed, timers, and so on, and can be applied to different dialer interfaces.

Typically, dialer profiles support PPP and high-level data link control (HDLC) encapsulation.

To configure the dialer profiles for DDR, perform the following steps:

Step 1   Configure the dialer interface.

Step 2   Make every physical interface a member of a dialer pool.

Step 3   Specify the interesting traffic.

Step 4   Define the static route.

Step 5   Optionally, you can define the map class.

The following sections cover each step in detail.

Step 1—Configuring the Dialer Interface

As previously mentioned, the dialer interface is a non-physical interface. It defines the call destination. As is usual for every interface configuration, you have to first configure the interface, its type, and its number. Figure 11-2 shows the network setup and configuration information.

Figure 11-2   *Configuring the Dialer Interface for Cisco IOS-Based ISDN Router on the Remote User's Side and on the Core Router's Side*

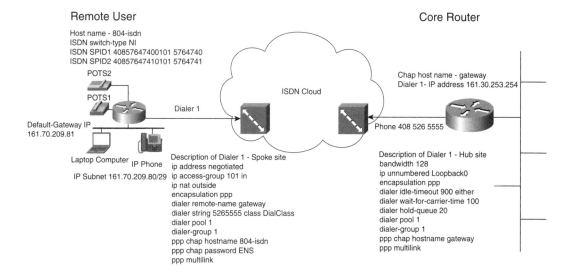

The following text examines some of the more significant aspects of the dialer interface configuration.

For the **encapsulation** *type* command, *type* is typically **ppp**.

For the **ppp authentication** *type* command, *type* can be **pap**, **chap**, or both in specific order. The **chap** type involves configuration of the host name of the other party. Generally speaking, PPP does not need authentication to connect. It requires two conditions to connect:

- A host name
- PPP configuration

As soon as two-way CHAP authentication is defined, however, you must configure the remote host's CHAP name. There are two different options (keep in mind that the remote name is case sensitive):

- Case 1

    ```
    804-isdn(config-if)#dialer remote-name username
    ```

    username, which is the CHAP name of the hub side, is defined as "gateway" in Figure 11-2.

    The remote user's side is configured under the dialer 1 interface with the following:

    ```
    804-isdn(config-if)#ppp chap hostname 804-isdn
    804-isdn(config-if)#ppp chap password ENS
    ```

    where **804-isdn** is the spoke CHAP name and **ENS** is the spoke password.

- Case 2

    The remote name can be defined in the global configuration mode with the following commands:

    ```
    804-isdn(config)#hostname 804-isdn
    804-isdn(config)#username gateway password ENS
    ```

    The parameter **gateway** matches the CHAP name or the host name of the remote party.

Enable the multilink feature of the PPP protocol with **PPP multilink**. The string in the following command represents a phone number:

```
dialer-string string class DialClass
```

In the case of Figure 11-2, the phone number is 526-5555, because the user is calling from the same area. In general, the string includes 1 + area code + 7-digit number of the remote party. In this command, *class* represents the name of the map class, which will apply (map) to this dialer interface.

In the `dialer pool number` command, the *number* parameter represents with which pool the dialer interface is associated.

In the **dialer pool-member** *number* **priority** *number* command, which must be configured for each physical interface, *number* refers to which pool member this physical interface belongs and the second *number* parameter specifies the priority that can fall in the range of 1–255.

The **dialer-group** *number* command assigns the interesting traffic definition to the dialer interface. When applying this line to the dialer interface, ensure that the *number* matches that of the **dialer-list** command.

Step 2—Defining a Physical Interface as a Member of the Dialer Pool

The dialer pool is a set of physical interfaces used when a dialer interface needs to make a call. As previously mentioned, for the physical interface making a call, you can never expect the B channel to make a call. Call establishment, call clearance, and other signaling functions are the prerogative of the D channel in the 2B+D or 23B+D configuration.

NOTE	In general, you must enable in-band dialing to ensure the specified channel makes the call. However, this line is not necessary for the BRI interface because BRI uses out-of-band dialing through the D channel.

The D channel can be assigned to more than one pool, and can be prioritized within each pool to avoid contention. It is more common to assign the D channel of the BRIs (if there are more than one) to different pools, when considering capacity issues or other traffic-dependant issues.

In the case of an 804 ISDN router, there is only one BRI interface. For routers with more than one BRI interface, you must define each of them as a member of any pool with the following command:

```
804-isdn(config-if)# dialer pool-member 4 priority 255
```

The number **4** (from the range of 1–255) is the number of the dialer pool to which the physical interface is assigned. The priority (0–255) is also assigned, where **255** is the highest priority and indicates the dialer interface will choose this physical interface first.

The *priority* parameter is optional. If it is not used and several physical interfaces are members of the same pool, the interface with the lowest port number will be selected first. If that interface is busy, the next lowest port number is selected.

The next important step in Cisco IOS Software-based ISDN BRI0 configuration is to define the encapsulation and authentication under the physical interface, as follows:

- **encapsulation ppp**
- **ppp authentication chap [pap callin]**
- **enable ppp multilink**

As you can see, this step differs from the legacy DDR, where only the command

```
804-isdn(config-if)#encapsulation ppp
```

is required under the physical interface. The reason for configuring the authentication and PPP multilink for dialer profiles DDR is because, based on the authentication information, that is how the router knows which dialer profile to switch the call to. As a result, the authentication must be set on the physical interface as well. If the dialer interface is configured for PPP multilink, it is recommended under the physical interface as well.

If the remote user's CPE is a Cisco 77x router, the role of the interface is performed by a configuration term called user. The user gateway is configured, as shown in Example 11-3.

Example 11-3   *The User Gateway in 77x ISDN Router Performs the Role of Dialer Interface*

```
776-isdn>upload
cd
set user gateway
set ip routing on
set ip framing none
set speed 64
set number 5265555
set ip rip update off
set encapsulation ppp
set ip route destination 0.0.0.0 gateway 0.0.0.0
cd
set ppp authentication incoming chap
set ppp authentication outgoing chap
set ppp secret client
<password>
<password>
set ppp secret host
<password>
<password>
<output omitted>
```

There is a partial analogy to the legacy DDR because all the elements of the DDR are available. The ACL option is discussed in the section, "Step 3—Specifying the Interesting Traffic."

Example 11-4 shows the distribution of dialer pools for a Cisco 3640 router (core side), where interfaces Serial1/0:23 and Serial1/1:23 are members of dialer group 1, while Serial2/0:23 and Serial3/0:23 are members of dialer pools 2 and 3, respectively.

Example 11-4   *The Dialer Pool Member Configuration in the Core Router*

```
3600-isdn#show running-config
interface Serial1/0:23
 description PRI Slot 1:Serial0: D-channel configuration; 408-526-5555
 no ip address
```

Example 11-4   *The Dialer Pool Member Configuration in the Core Router (Continued)*

```
 encapsulation ppp
 ip tcp header-compression passive
 dialer pool-member 1 priority 1
 isdn switch-type primary-5ess
<output omitted>
!
interface Serial1/1:23
description PRI Slot 1:Serial1: D-channel configuration; 408-526-5555
 no ip address
 encapsulation ppp
 ip tcp header-compression passive
 dialer pool-member 1 priority 255
 isdn switch-type primary-5ess
<output omitted>
!
interface Serial2/0:23
description PRI Slot 2:Serial0: D-channel configuration; 408-526-6666
 no ip address
 encapsulation ppp
 ip tcp header-compression passive
 dialer pool-member 2
 isdn switch-type primary-5ess
<Output omitted>
!
interface Serial3/0:23
description PRI Slot 3:Serial0: D-channel configuration; 408-526-7777
 no ip address
 encapsulation ppp
 ip tcp header-compression passive
 dialer pool-member 3
 isdn switch-type primary-5ess
<Output omitted>
```

In this configuration, the Serial1/0:23 and Serial1/1:23 are members of pool 1, but Serial1/1:23 has the highest, whereas Serial1/0:23 has the lowest priority.

Step 3—Specifying the Interesting Traffic

As you already know, the **dialer-list** command and its definition distinguish the interesting from the non-interesting traffic. The dialer list can use ACLs and the associated security mechanisms and techniques for this purposes as well. ACLs can be referred to as standard, extended, named, and temporary. You can find a multitude of resources about ACLs at Cisco.com. Example 11-5 shows a sample ACL for the remote user's side of the connection, based on Cisco IOS ISDN 804 router, where **dialer-list 1** uses ACL 101 to define the interesting traffic.

Example 11-5 **dialer-list 1** *Uses ACL 101 to Define the Interesting Traffic in DDR*

```
access-list 101 deny     icmp any any echo-reply
access-list 101 deny     icmp any any host-unreachable
access-list 101 deny     udp any any eq ntp
access-list 101 deny     igmp any any
access-list 101 deny     ip any host 230.0.0.13
access-list 101 deny     ip any host 230.0.1.39
access-list 101 deny     ip any host 230.0.1.40
access-list 101 deny     ip any host 230.2.127.253
access-list 101 deny     ip any host 230.2.127.254
access-list 101 deny     ip any host 230.2.127.255
access-list 101 deny     ip any host  10.68.235.228
access-list 101 deny     ip any host  11.68.235.229
access-list 101 permit ip any any
dialer-list 1 protocol   ip list 101
```

In Example 11-5, the ACL denies the following:

- Some of the ICMP messages (lines 1 and 2).
- UDP messages exchanging Network Time Protocol (line 3).
- Internet Group Management Protocol (line 4).
- A group of multicast source addresses (lines 5–10).
- Two WINS servers (lines 11 and 12).
- Line 13 permits everything else.
- Line 14 is the dialer-list 1 definition, using ACL 101.

Step 4—Defining the Static Route

The static route can be configured using the following command syntax:

```
804-isdn(config)#ip route prefix mask {address | interface} [distance] [permanent]
```

The following is an example for setting the default route:

```
804-isdn(config)# ip route 0.0.0.0 0.0.0.0 161.68.26.1
```

If the router needs to redistribute IP addresses in the defined range, on the hub side, they need to be redistributed with the appropriate set of commands.

You can find additional discussions related to routing protocols at Cisco.com.

Step 5 (Optional)—Defining the Map Class

Defining the map class is optional, but it is recommended because it creates scalable configurations. Assume the map class is called DialClass and defines the following parameters:

- A class name with a name parameter
- The time to wait before terminating the link when another call must be made
- The amount of time to wait after there is no interesting traffic to send, before terminating the link
- The amount of time to wait for a carrier to pick up the call after dialing the dial string
- The dialer speed that assigns the desired speed to the ISDN line. A short configuration of map class, defining the desired speed, could be the following:

```
804-isdn(config)#map-class dialer DialClass
804-isdn(config-map-cla)#dialer isdn speed 56
```

Then, this map class has to be associated with the **dialer-string** command, discussed in Step 1.

For more detailed configuration rules and explanations, visit Cisco.com.

PPP Callback for ISDN

The PPP LCP Extensions in FRC 1570 defines a callback function, which is negotiated during the LCP phase of PPP.

The callback function of PPP for ISDN interfaces allows a Cisco router using a DDR mechanism and PPP encapsulation to initiate a link to another device and request a callback. A Cisco ISDN router responds to a callback request from a remote device. The process uses the Point-to-Point Protocol (PPP) and the LCP extension specifications in RFC 1570. The callback feature of PPP (introduced in Cisco IOS 11.0) enables the remote user to place a call to the NAS and request the core router to call the remote user back. A typical negotiation would proceed as follows:

1 The remote user's router establishes a connection to the core router.

2 The remote user's router and the core router negotiate PPP Link Control Protocol (LCP) with the remote user's router requesting callback.

3 Both routers authenticate each other using PPP, PAP, or CHAP protocols. It is typical that the initiator of the call to be requested to authenticate itself. In this scenario, this is the remote user's router. The core router's authentication is optional.

4 After authentication, the core router disconnects the call.

5 The core router calls out and establishes a connection with the remote user's router.

The cost-saving effects of an ISDN Cisco IOS Software callback occurs when a difference exists between the usage-based costs associated with the remote user's service and the core router's service. Usually, the corporate site obtains higher discounts from providers because of the expected call volume.

The next example shows how to configure the dialer interfaces of both sites to perform the callback function of PPP for ISDN.

Remote User Router Configuration

Example 11-6 shows a remote user's router configuration.

Example 11-6   *PPP Callback for ISDN: Remote User Router Configuration*

```
804-isdn(config)#interface dialer 1
804-isdn(config-if)#ppp callback request
! If the following line  does not exist, configure:
804-isdn(config-if)#dialer hold-queue 100 timeout 20
```

The **ppp callback request** line specifies that when the interface places a call, it requests a callback. The **dialer hold-queue 100 timeout 20** specifies that up to **100** packets can be held in a queue until the core router returns the call. If the core router does not return the call within 20 seconds, plus the length of the enable timeout (configured on the central site router), the packets are dropped.

Core Router Configuration

Configuring the core router for PPP callback for ISDN involves two separate configurations:

- Defining and naming the map class
- Defining PPP callback for ISDN under the dialer interface

Example 11-7 and Example 11-8 demonstrate these two steps.

Example 11-7   *PPP Callback for ISDN: Core Router Configuration—Defining and Naming the Map Class*

```
7206-isdn(config)#map-class dialer CALLBACK
7206-isdn(config-map-class)#dialer callback-server username
```

Example 11-8   *PPP Callback for ISDN: Core Router Configuration—Defining PPP Callback for ISDN Under the Dialer Interface*

```
7206-isdn(config)#interface dialer 1
7206-isdn(config-if)#ppp callback accept
7206-isdn(config-if)#dialer callback-secure
7206-isdn(config-if)#dialer enable-timeout 5
! If the following line does not exist already, configure:
7206-isdn(config-if)#dialer hold-queue 100
! This is the phone number of the remote user:
7206-isdn(config-if)# dialer map ip 10.19.241.1 name 804-isdn
     speed 56 class CALLBACK 14085764740
```

TIP	The dialer re-enable time must be greater than the serial pulse time.

The **map-class dialer** establishes a quality of service (QoS) parameter that is associated with a static map. The dialer keyword specifies that the map is a dialer map. The **CALLBACK** parameter is a user-defined value (you can name it something other than **CALLBACK**) that creates a map class to which subsequent encapsulation-specific commands apply.

The **dialer callback-server username** enables the interface to return calls when callback is successfully negotiated. The keyword **username** specifies that the interface is to locate the dial string for making the return call. This is done by looking up the authenticated host name in a dialer map command. All phases of PPP must complete successfully.

In **ppp callback accept**, the keyword **accept** enables the interface to accept the callback requests that come into the interface. The request is considered complete if all phases of PPP are successful.

The **dialer callback-secure** command specifies the router will disconnect the initial call and callback only if the dialer map is properly defined for callback with a defined class for the remote router.

If the **dialer callback-secure** command is not present, the core router will not drop the connection.

The **dialer enable-timeout 5** specifies the interface is to wait five seconds after disconnecting the initial call before making the return call.

The **dialer map ip 10.19.241.1 name 804-isdn speed 56 class CALLBACK 14085764740** was modified to include the **class** keyword and the name of the class, as specified in the **map-class** command. The keyword **name** is required so that when the remote user dials in, the interface can locate this dialer map statement in the core router configuration and obtain the dial string for calling back the remote user's router. You can find an example of checking the functionality of the callback feature in Chapter 12, "ISDN BRI Troubleshooting."

ISDN Security

ISDN technology provides some limited security features and, as previously mentioned, SS7 Q.931's frame provides caller ID information and the dialed number identification service (DNIS). Based on this information, two security solutions are available:

- **Caller ID screening**—By using the **isdn caller** interface command, you can define a set of caller telephone numbers that are eligible to make calls to the router. IOS provides additional features, such as exact match and prefix match, where wildcard *x* can also be used. Unmatched calls are rejected.

- **Called-party number verification**—The router can be configured to verify the called-party number and the subaddress provided by the switch as part of the SETUP message by using one of the following configurations:

  ```
  804-isdn(config-if)#isdn answer 1
  ```

  ```
  804-isdn(config-if)#isdn answer 2
  ```

  Configuration commands for the BRI interface enable you to configure the called-party number, subaddress number, or both. If these numbers are not defined, the router accepts all incoming calls. This feature ensures that for one local loop with multiple ISDN devices, the correct ISDN device accepts and handles the call. For more details, visit Cisco.com.

Configuring the POTS (Telephone) Interfaces

Plain old telephone service (POTS) functionality refers to the use of the voice capabilities of the ISDN routers. The ringer equivalent number (REN) consists of a number and a letter that indicates the frequency response of that telephone's ringer. The term *telephone port* refers to the physical port on the router back panel. The *telephone interface* refers to a logical interface that you have to configure to make an analog telephone, fax, or modem connected to the router port (phone 1 and 2) work properly as touch-tone devices.

The set of configuration commands related to the configuration of the physical ports includes the country, resistance of the line, dialing method, disconnect supervision, encoding, and ringing frequency. Most of the default settings are for the U.S. The first thing to check in the global configuration mode of the router is who is providing the tones and how the following command is set up:

```
804-isdn(config)# pots tone-source {local | remote}
```

This command sets who supplies dial, ring back, and busy tones for telephones, fax machines, or modems connected to a Cisco IOS-based ISDN router. The keywords are as follows:

- **local (by default)**—Specifies that the router supplies the tones
- **remote**—Specifies that the ISDN switch supplies the tones

Specifically for supplying the dial tone, another global configuration command is available with same **local** and **remote** options:

```
804-isdn(config)#pots dial-tone {local | remote}
```

In the global configuration command, another command specifies the delay after which a telephone port can be rung after a previous call is disconnected:

```
804-isdn(config)#pots distinctive-ring-guard-time milliseconds
```

The *milliseconds* argument is the number of milliseconds of the delay and ranges from 0 to 1000. The default depends on the chosen country.

You can connect multiple devices (analog telephones, fax machines, and modems) to a router telephone port. The number you can connect depends on the REN of the telephone port (five) or the REN of each device that you plan to connect. If you have five devices and all of them have REN 1, you can connect all of them to the POTS port.

Creating Dial Peers

Dial peers determine the routing of incoming calls to the telephone ports. You can create a total of six dial peers for the two telephone ports. Example 11-9 lists some of the relevant Cisco IOS Software configuration commands.

Example 11-9   *A Common Procedure for Dial Peers Configuration*

```
! This command sets up a tag number (1 to 6):
804-isdn(config)#dial-peer voice tag pots
! This command assigns a local directory number:
804-isdn(config-dial-pe)#destination-pattern ldn
! The number of the port is defined using the following command:
804-isdn(config-dial-pe)#port port-number
! The following command disables  call waiting (optional):
804-isdn(config-dial-pe)#no call-waiting
! This command (optional) sets a custom ring.  Any call coming to that port will
! use that ring. The cadence-number can be 0,1, or 2:
804-isdn(config-dial-pe)#ring cadence-number
```

The configuration is displayed if you type **show dial-peer voice 5**, as shown in Example 11-10.

Example 11-10   *Displaying the Configuration of dialer-peer 5*

```
804-isdn#show dial-peer voice 5
VoiceEncapPeer5
        tag = 5
        destination-pattern = '3335555'
        voice-port = 2
        ring cadence = 0
        call-waiting disabled
        forward_to_unused_port disabled
```

The local directory number (LDN) must be associated with a service profile identifier (SPID). If you do not assign LDN to both SPIDs, you cannot make voice calls simultaneously. If the dial peers are not created, all voice calls are routed to port 1. To ensure you allow incoming and outgoing voice calls under a BRI interface, configure the following command:

```
804-isdn(config-if)#isdn incoming-voice modem
```

The simple configurations enable the basic POTS functionality of the voice portion of ISDN service. There are some advanced features, and their number is continuously changing and growing. Some of them are discussed in the next paragraph.

Advanced Telephone Features

This section provides coverage of some of the more advanced features provided by Cisco IOS Software-based ISND configuration, including the following:

- Setting voice priority
- Enabling supplementary phone services

ISDN Voice Priority

The voice priority feature of IOS handles the data and voice priority. Depending on the user preferences, voice could take precedence over data and vice versa. There are three options:

- **Always**—Always bumps the data call if an outgoing or incoming voice call is initiated.
- **Conditional (by default)**—Voice call bumps data call only if the user has two data connections in the same direction; otherwise, the calling party receives a busy signal.
- **Never/Off**—Voice callers always receive a busy signal.

In Cisco 700 series routers, a set of commands handles the process, as displayed in Example 11-11.

Example 11-11 *Voice Priority Settings for 77x Router*

```
776-isdn>SET VOICEPRIORITY INCOMING INTERFACE PHONE1 CONDITIONAL
776-isdn>SET VOICEPRIORITY OUTGOING INTERFACE PHONE1 CONDITIONAL
776-isdn>SET CALLWAITING INTERFACE PHONE1 ON
776-isdn>SET VOICEPRIORITY INCOMING INTERFACE PHONE2 ALWAYS
776-isdn>SET VOICEPRIORITY OUTGOING INTERFACE PHONE2 ALWAYS
776-isdn>SET CALLWAITING INTERFACE PHONE2 ON
776-isdn>SET CALLTIME VOICE INCOMING OFF
776-isdn>SET CALLTIME VOICE OUTGOING OFF
776-isdn>SET CALLTIME DATA INCOMING OFF
776-isdn>SET CALLTIME DATA OUTGOING OFF
```

The result of this configuration for a Cisco 700 series router is displayed in Example 11-12.

Example 11-12 *Verifying Voice Priority Settings on the 776 Router*

```
776-isdn>show voice
Interface     VoicePriority    VoicePriority     Call      Directory    Ring
              In               Out              Waiting    Number       Cadence
    PHONE1    CONDITIONAL      CONDITIONAL       ON        5764740
    PHONE2    ALWAYS           ALWAYS            ON        5764741
    DOV       N/A              N/A               N/A
    UNSPECIFIED N/A            N/A               N/A
```

For IOS-based routers, the commands are

```
804-isdn#isdn voice-priority ldn {in | out} {always | conditional | off}
```

The **pots dialing-method {overlap | enblock}** command affects the way you receive a busy signal. With the **overlap** option, you hear a fast busy signal. With **enblock,** you initially hear a dial tone followed by a busy signal.

If you cannot make the configuration settings work correctly, it's possible that the LEC is blocking voice calls, the line was provisioned without additional call offering (ACO), or the router is rejecting voice calls due to an incorrect configuration.

Supplementary Phone Services

Cisco supports some supplementary phone services that are available in Cisco IOS Software. Use of these services is possible, but not mandatory; it depends on the way the line is provisioned. Some of the phone services might include the following, depending on the LEC settings:

- **Call holding and retrieving**—By default, this option is set to **number,number #,* but it depends on the LEC settings.

- **Call waiting**—By default, it is enabled with **no call-waiting**. To disable it, enter **number,number#.*

- **Three-way call conferencing**—If the LEC switch type is NI1 or DMS-100 custom, you can activate this feature by using **isdn conference-code** *range,* where *range* is 0 to 999 and the default is 60.

- **Call transfer**—To use this feature, you must request it when you order the line. The feature can then be activated with the command **isdn transfer-code** *range,* where *range* is 0 to 999 and the default code is 61.

- **Call forwarding**—This feature must also be requested from the LEC when you order the line. There are four ways of forwarding available in Cisco routers:

    — Call forwarding unconditional (CFU) forwards all incoming calls unconditionally to another telephone number.

— Call forwarding no reply (CFNR) forwards incoming calls that are not answered within a defined period to another telephone number.

— Call forwarding busy (CFB) forwards incoming calls that get a busy signal to another telephone number. The LEC must provide a number for each forwarding feature such as *#number#*.

— Call forwarding variable (CFV) is available only in the U.S. for NI1 ISDN switch types, and can be turned on or off using numbers provided by the LEC.

Summary

This chapter represented, in reasonable details, the different configurations for Cisco 77x and Cisco IOS-based ISDN routers, including spoofing, snapshot routing, DDR, and callback solutions. Some security features and voice features configurations are part of this chapter as well. There is another typical common solution—ISDN backup, which is explained in the section, "Frame Relay and ISDN Backup Configuration" in Chapter 16, "Basic and Advanced Frame Relay Configurations." The importance of this chapter is related to the so-called expected behavior, or the baseline of the system. It is valuable for the troubleshooting engineer to set up his expectations before starting the troubleshooting process.

Review Questions

Answers to the review questions can be found in Appendix A, "Answers to Review Questions."

1 Type a command to determine if the spoofing is enabled in dialer interface in Cisco IOS ISDN router.

2 Define the active period in snapshot routing. Is it configurable? What is its duration?

3 In a snapshot routing configuration, use an IOS command to ensure termination of a quiet period within two minutes.

4 What are the main elements of the dialer profiles in DDR?

5 Use an IOS command to map the IP address 161.3.2.1 with the destination phone number 773-5555.

6 Define the Dialer1 as a member of pool number 3 with the highest priority.

7 Create an ACL to deny tcp traffic on port 8008. Type the appropriate IOS command.

8 Configure the user's IOS router for callback with 200 packets in the queue and 20 seconds drop time. Explain.

9 In a callback configuration, type the IOS command, specifying that the core router interface will wait five seconds after disconnecting the initial call before making the return call.

10 Type the IOS command to bring the second B channel up after the inbound traffic exceeds 20 percent.

11 What "conditional" priority means in voice features configuration of ISDN?

12 If the user's router has two data calls in progress and it is configured with Router(config)#**pots dialing-method enblock,** what should you expect when making a voice call to any of his LDNs?

CHAPTER 12

ISDN BRI Troubleshooting

From a technology prospective, most of the ISDN fundamentals are covered in the previous chapters of this part. This chapter provides you with a systematic approach to ISDN troubleshooting and demonstrates the suggested layer-by-layer approach to ISDN problems. The approach requires you to start from the physical layer and go up, layer by layer and protocol by protocol, to identify potential issues. This chapter covers the following common issues:

- Troubleshooting the physical layer
- Troubleshooting the data link layer
- Troubleshooting the network layer
- Troubleshooting the Point-to-Point Protocol (PPP), including link control protocol (LCP), authentication, Network Control Protocol (NCP), and the termination of connections
- Troubleshooting MLP, PPP, callback, and MMP
- Troubleshooting telephone interfaces

The layer-by-layer approach in Integrated Services Digital Network (ISDN) trouble-shooting requires that you start at the physical layer. In the enterprise environment, it's best to troubleshoot both ends of the connection—the remote user side and the core side. Before starting the process, however, you need to ensure that you have basic connectivity to the router. See Chapter 4, "Troubleshooting Approaches, Models, and Tools," for tools such as ping and trace. Telnet and SSH are another set of utilities to access the router and some Microsoft Windows-based tools and applications, such as WINIPCFG, IPCONFIG, and HyperTerm.exe can be used also. Most people prefer the console connection. When this is not possbile, just keep in mind that the IOS-based ISDN routers usually are configured for five simultaneous Telnet sessions, whereas 77x routers allow only one by default.

During the troubleshooting process, you might see a significant amount of activity on the screen. This chapter focuses on showing you how to analyze that output.

It is always good to know the exact or relative time of the events. This allows you to recreate the process and understand the chain of events, even if you need to manually set up the clock. One command to remember is **service timestamps**, which applies a timestamp to your log or debug information. It also provides information about when debug events occurred, and it indicates the specific time and duration of an event. The **service timestamps** command has two options: the **debug uptime** and **log datetime msec**. The **log datetime msec** option is the more common of the two options because it logs the date and time in msecs. The following shows the **timeservice command** options:

```
804-isdn# configure terminal
804-isdn(config)#service timestamps debug uptime
804-isdn(config)#service timestamps log datetime msec
```

Another good practice is to turn on and off the following command when you are connected over a Telnet session to the router:

```
804-isdn#terminal monitor
804-isdn#teminal no monitor
```

This command enables you to see or not see the debug output on your screen when you have a Telnet session established with the remote router.

If you are connected through the console port, use the options of the command 804-isdn(config)#**logging console** (described in Chapter 4).

Another useful command, especially when you are monitoring certain events is **logging buffered** *number* **debugging**. To explain the reason, look to a typical case. The user's router intermittently can make calls out in the late evening. Because it is not always possible to monitor the events in the middle of the night, especially when they are intermittent, one good approach is to configure the router with this command and add some issue-related debug commands. In this case, **debug dialer** is the first one to consider. Then, the next morning, even if the end user is not available, you can review the events from the previous night with the **show logging** command.

Before entering the layer-by-layer methodology, keep your main objectives in mind. Two things are important to keep in mind during the troubleshooting process of ISDN:

- If the router can make outgoing calls
- If the router can pass data

Start with the first feature. If the router can make or accept calls, it's an indication that the router is functioning properly. Also, this indicates that the D channel is functional between the customer premises equipment (CPE) and the ISDN switch, and Layers 1, 2, and 3 of the D channel are set up correctly.

If the router cannot pass data, this mainly concerns encapsulating protocols, such as PPP.

Troubleshooting the Physical Layer

The physical layer involves various components, but your main focus is the local loop wiring and clocking. If you have a physical loop, there is clocking, which refers to both timing and synchronization. It is important to understand what's required by the local exchange carrier (LEC) to provide a local loop to the user. Two wires from the line card in the ISDN switch go to a bundle of pairs in the central office (CO) and might split many times into different media, conduits, directions, and multiplexers and/or demultiplexers before finally reaching the field cabinet closest to the user's home. From there, another bundle leads to the user's minimum point of entry (MPOE) or single or split Demarcation Point (D-mark), which is usually a box or cabinet outside the house, in the basement, or in any other easily accessible and protected place. This is the D-mark of the provider's responsibility. Sometimes, especially in rural or hard-to-reach areas, the LEC uses passive or active repeaters. From the MPOE, the CPE zone starts and includes internal wiring (IW) and outlets, such as RJ-11 and RJ-45 connectors. The set of devices and connectors might vary between homes.

To verify the status of the physical layer, it is a good practice to start with the command #**show isdn status** (see Example 12-1).

Example 12-1   **show isdn status** *Output*

```
804-isdn#show isdn status
Global isdn Switchtype = basic-ni
ISDN BRI0 interface
        dsl 0, interface ISDN Switchtype = basic-ni
    Layer 1 Status:
        DEACTIVATED
    Layer 2 Status:
        Layer 2 NOT Activated
```

This command gives you a snapshot of all the layers of the ISDN service. If the first layer is down, the ISDN service is not available. If you are connected to a U interface, the problem is most likely due to the LEC, NT1, or the cable. First, make sure that you are using the proper cable (always check the documentation) from the router to the wall. Look at the front of the router and if the NT1 light is off, the line is down.

The same information is provided on the 700 series routers, as shown in Example 12-2.

Example 12-2   **show status** *Output on the 700 Series Routers*

```
776-isdn>show status
Status    09/01/2000 09:34:30
Line Status
  Line DeActivated
  Terminal Identifier Unassigned  Not Initialized
  Terminal Identifier Unassigned  Not Initialized
Port Status                                      Interface Connection Link
  Ch:  1      Waiting for Call
  Ch:  2      Waiting for Call
```

Both routers are reporting Layer 1 Status DEACTIVATED or Line DeActivated. The local loop appears to not be available, not installed correctly, or nonexistent.

One possible troubleshooting tool is to check the status of the Basic Rate Interface (BRI) controller of the router. The commands to do this, and the resulting output, are displayed in Example 12-3.

Example 12-3   **show controllers bri0** *Output*

```
804-isdn#show controllers bri0
BRI unit 0:BRI unit 0 with U interface and POTS:
Layer 1 internal state is DEACTIVATED
Layer 1 U interface is DEACTIVATED.
ISDN Line Information:
    Current EOC commands:
        RTN - Return to normal
    Received overhead bits:
        AIB=1, UOA=1, SCO=1, DEA=1, ACT=1, M50=1, M51=1, M60=1, FEBE=1
    Errors:  [FEBE]=0, [NEBE]=41
    Errors:  [Superframe Sync Loss]=2, [IDL2 Data Transparency Loss]=0
             [M4 ACT 1 -> 0]=0,
```

Both Layer 1 internal state of the BRI controller and the Layer 1 U interface are deactivated. Another important point is to check the status of the Superframe errors. This value always needs to be 0. In this case, the router is reporting 2 Superframe Sync Losses.

The next logical step is to determine if the LEC is not providing the service or if your equipment is malfunctioning. One sophisticated IOS debug command is recommended to answer the question:

```
804-isdn#debug bri
```

This debug command provides you with information that helps you distinguish between internal and external router problems. This command is the interface between IOS and the ISDN chipset in the router. The output of this command varies between versions of IOS. In some instances, write_sid is sent to the ISDN chipset, which always indicates that the router is trying to bring up the physical layer and set the activation bit (A bit) to 1. At the same time, write_sid instructs the ISDN chipset to generate HDLC flags. Different types of Cisco routers display values such as wrote = E, or wrote = 1B. These values indicate that the ISDN chipset sends HDLC flags. If you cannot see these flags were generated, obviously, you have an internal chipset problem with the router. The sequence of write_sid and wrote=xx, followed by interrupt status reg = C (sent by the chipset to IOS), indicates that the activation bit just turned from 0 to 1. If you type the #**show isdn status** command again, you see LAYER 1 – ACTIVE.[1] As previously mentioned, these indicators might vary from one IOS version or device to another. As shown in Example 12-4, the IOS version 12.0 5(T) for Cisco 804 and Cisco 1604, reports the following sequence.

Example 12-4   *In IOS Version 12.0 5(T), This Is What You See During the Activation of Layer 1*

```
804-isdn#debug bri
*Apr 17 03:13:48.567: BRI0: MC145572 IRQ3: NR1=1
*Apr 17 03:13:48.571: BRI0:MC145572 state handler current state 0 actions
     1000 next state 2
! The MC145572 (chipset) sends NR1=1 to CO
*Apr 17 03:13:51.383: BRI0: MC145572 IRQ3: NR1=B
*Apr 17 03:13:51.383: BRI0:MC145572 state handler current state 2 actions
     2000 next state 2
! The MC145572 (chipset) sends NR1=B to CO - second attempt
*Apr 17 03:13:51.395: BRI0: MC145572 IRQ2: r6=FFF
*Apr 17 03:13:51.399: BRI0:MC145572 state handler current state 2 actions
     A001 next state 3
...
*Apr 17 03:13:55.559: BRI0: MC145572 IRQ1: m4 bits=FF
! Request to set the higher bit to 1 - (A=1)
*Apr 17 03:13:55.563: BRI0:MC145572 state handler current state 3 actions
     A001 next state 3
...
*Apr 17 03:13:55.563: BRI0:M4: received 0xFF - changed bits ACT
! The switch sends confirmation of A=1 and as a result
! the status is set to ACTIVE
*Apr 17 03:13:55.975: BRI0: MC145572 IRQ2: r6=F00
*Apr 17 03:13:55.975: BRI0:EOC HOLD
```

Example 12-5 shows the same procedure for IOS 12.1(4) and a 1604 router.

Example 12-5   *IOS 12.1(4) and a 1604 Router*

```
1604-isdn#debug bri
*Mar  1 01:50:25.629: BRI0:sending C/I AI:Activation Indication
! Sending an activation request
*Mar  1 01:50:25.633: BRI(0):ext ST new state 1
*Mar  1 01:50:25.637: BRI(0):C/I to 2081 AR:Activation Request
*Mar  1 01:50:25.637: BRI0:Unexpected end of mon received data in state 1
*Mar  1 01:50:25.641: BRI(0):C/I from 2081 AR:Activation Request
*Mar  1 01:50:25.645: BRI(0):C/I to 2081 AR:Activation Request
! Activation requests exchanged
...
*Mar  1 01:50:31.637: BRI0:S2091 state handler current state 2 actions 1083
   next state 3
*Mar  1 01:50:31.637: BRI0:receiving C/I AI:Activation Indication
! Here is the indication from the switch for the A=1 setting - line ACTIVE.
*Mar  1 01:50:31.641: BRI0:sending C/I AI:Activation Indication
*Mar  1 01:50:31.645: BRI(0):C/I to 2081 AR:Activation Request
*Mar  1 01:50:31.664: dchan tx start
*Mar  1 01:50:31.668: dchan tx intr
```

Both of the examples distinguish internal from external issues. If the router sends requests to establish the activation bit and a response is not received, the problem is external, such as the cabling, LEC, or NT1. In this case, your recommended action is to open a trouble ticket with your local provider and fix the issue.

If no request is made from the router, continue to analyze it because the problem might be related to a hardware failure or an IOS bug. One possible solution might be to power-cycle the router in order to force the router to resync with the ISDN switch and reset the BRI U MLT timers (TPULSE and T75S). Usually, the IOS-based timer reset is more typical for the PRIs than BRIs because of the simplicity of the latter.

Another possible solution is to clear the D channel with the IOS command #**clear interface bri0**, which resets the BRI controller.

You might want to flush the D channel and see if you can get the D channel to work. The interface BRI0 configuration command is **isdn timeout-signaling**.

If none of these solutions work, consider another CPE.

What you are trying to achieve is the activation of the physical layer (Layer 1). The expected result from the #**show isdn status** command is displayed in Example 12-6.

Example 12-6   show isdn status *Output*

```
804-isdn#show isdn status
Global ISDN Switchtype = basic-5ess
ISDN BRI0 interface
        dsl 0, interface ISDN Switchtype = basic-ni
    Layer 1 Status:
        ACTIVE
! As you can see the line is reported ACTIVE
<output omitted>
```

In the case of a 77x router, the report is as displayed in Example 12-7.

Example 12-7   show status *Output*

```
776-isdn> show status
Status    01/05/1995 02:36:52
Line Status
  Line Activated
! Here the line is reported as a "Activated"
```

Typically, to find out if Layer 1 is active, an engineer checks the status of interfaces. If you apply the same approach here, you see the information displayed in Example 12-8.

Example 12-8   **show interfaces bri 0** *Output*

```
804-isdn#show interfaces bri 0
BRI0 is up (spoofing), line protocol is up (spoofing)
  Hardware is BRI with U interface and POTS
  MTU 1500 bytes, BW 64 Kbit, DLY 20000 usec,
     reliability 255/255, txload 1/255, rxload 1/255
  Encapsulation PPP, loopback not set
  DTR is pulsed for 1 seconds on reset
  Last input 00:01:26, output 00:01:26, output hang never

<output omitted>
```

The BRI0 can be up and the line protocol can be spoofing, but you won't be able to make calls out. As mentioned in Chapter 11, "Cisco ISDN Configuration Solutions," spoofing enables the ISDN router to imitate an active state.

The ISDN configuration that follows includes spoofing. However, DDR becomes active only when interesting traffic triggers a router to place a data call. The status of the D channel is shown in Example 12-9.

Example 12-9   **show interfaces bri 0** *Output*

```
804-isdn#show interfaces bri 0
BRI0 is up/down, line protocol is up (spoofing/down)
  Hardware is BRI with U interface and POTS
  MTU 1500 bytes, BW 64 Kbit, DLY 20000 usec,
     reliability 255/255, txload 1/255, rxload 1/255
  Encapsulation PPP, loopback not set
```

Spoofing does not necessarily mean that the D channel is up and it's not an indication of a properly functioning physical layer. In fact, there might be no line on the interface. Spoofing just implies to the Layer 3 DDR that the routing entry will be maintained in the router, enabling DDR to wake up and make a call out when interesting traffic requires a network connection.

Troubleshooting the Data Link Layer

As previously mentioned, the second layer runs at least two protocols—Link Access Procedure on the D channel (LAPD) and PPP on the B channel. LAPD is also known as Q921; it is the focus of this section.

LAPD is used between the Cisco router and the telco switch to provide a full-duplex error-free link. This protocol is not end-to-end: It can be used only to troubleshoot the connection between the local router (CPE) and the local switch. The troubleshooting of both protocols (LAPD and PPP) must be done separately.

NOTE	Always keep in mind that LAPD (Q921) activation needs to occur before PPP because Q921 signaling is part of the D channel signaling. No data with any encapsulation (including PPP) can be passed if the D channel is not functioning properly.

Using the #**show isdn status** command immediately after Layer 1 activation displays the output shown in Example 12-10.

Example 12-10 show Isdn status *Output*

```
804-isdn#show isdn status
Global ISDN Switchtype = basic-ni
ISDN BRI0 interface
        dsl 0, interface ISDN Switchtype = basic-ni
    Layer 1 Status:
        ACTIVATED
    Layer 2 Status:
        Layer 2 NOT Activated
```

An important part of the second layer activation is the negotiation of the terminal endpoint identifier (TEI). In the BRI environment on a single S/T connection, a single BRI interface can connect up to 8 devices. Each device can have a unique TEI number that's assigned by the local switch. The switch recognizes the devices that are sending and receiving data, and negotiation starts with the router, which sends IDREQ. The switch responds with IDASSN. The IDREQ and IDASSN packets contain two important values—the activation indicator (AI) and the reference indicator (RI). The initial IDREQ sent to the switch is set to 127. This is a broadcast request that asks the switch to assign any TEI. Unlike Primary Rate Interfaces (PRIs), where only one device is connected to the switch and the TEI is always 0, the valid TEI for BRIs is between 64 and 126 (if they are dynamically assigned). The range from 0 to 63 is allocated for fixed or statically assigned TEIs. The RI in the IDREQ packet is a random number that needs to always match an associated IDREQ and IDASSN packet. In Example 12-11, the router sends IDREQ with ri = 86 and broadcast ai = 127. The switch responds with the matching IDASSN ri = 86, and assigns ai = 80, which is a valid TEI. Further down in the output, you can see another IDREQ and IDASSN with ri = 1463 and assigned TEI = 89. Example 12-11 shows the recommended command for troubleshooting and the initialization of Layer 2.

Example 12-11 *Activation of Layer 2 in a Cisco 804 ISDN Router*

```
804-isdn#debug isdn q921
*Mar  1 00:01:14.995: ISDN BR0: TX -> IDREQ  ri = 86  ai = 127 – ID request
*Mar  1 00:01:15.019: ISDN BR0: RX <- IDASSN  ri = 86  ai = 80 – ID assign
*Mar  1 00:01:15.027: ISDN BR0: TX -> SABMEp sapi = 0  tei = 80
! The following line and the preceding line mean LAPD is OK for TEI=80
*Mar  1 00:01:15.043: ISDN BR0: RX <- UAf sapi = 0  tei = 80
```

Example 12-11 *Activation of Layer 2 in a Cisco 804 ISDN Router (Continued)*

```
*Mar  1 00:01:15.047: %ISDN-6-LAYER2UP: Layer 2 for Interface BR0,
    TEI 80 changed to up
*Mar  1 00:01:15.051: ISDN BR0: TX -> INFOc sapi = 0  tei = 80  ns = 0
    nr = 0  i = 0x08007B3A0E3430383537363437343030313031
! Layer 3 exchange
*Mar  1 00:01:15.091: ISDN BR0: RX <- RRr sapi = 0  tei = 80  nr = 1
*Mar  1 00:01:15.095: ISDN BR0: TX -> INFOc sapi = 0  tei = 80  ns = 1
    nr = 0  i = 0x08010105040288901801832C0B31383030373733335303438
*Mar  1 00:01:15.139: ISDN BR0: RX <- INFOc sapi = 0  tei = 80  ns = 0
    nr = 1  i = 0x08007B3B028081
*Mar  1 00:01:15.147: ISDN BR0: RX <- RRr sapi = 0  tei = 80  nr = 2
*Mar  1 00:01:15.151: ISDN BR0: TX -> RRr sapi = 0  tei = 80  nr = 1
*Mar  1 00:01:15.167: ISDN BR0: TX -> IDREQ  ri = 1463  ai = 127
! TEI request
*Mar  1 00:01:15.175: ISDN BR0: RX <- INFOc sapi = 0  tei = 80  ns = 1
    nr = 2  i = 0x08007B952A0480800150
*Mar  1 00:01:15.187: ISDN BR0: TX -> RRr sapi = 0  tei = 80  nr = 2
*Mar  1 00:01:15.191: ISDN BR0: RX <- IDASSN  ri = 1463  ai = 89
! TEI assign
*Mar  1 00:01:15.199: ISDN BR0: TX -> SABMEp sapi = 0  tei = 89
*Mar  1 00:01:15.219: ISDN BR0: RX <- UAf sapi = 0  tei = 89
! The following line and the preceding line mean 89 OK
*Mar  1 00:01:15.219: %ISDN-6-LAYER2UP: Layer 2 for Interface BR0,
    TEI 89 changed to up
*Mar  1 00:01:15.227: ISDN BR0: TX -> INFOc sapi = 0  tei = 89  ns = 0
    nr = 0  i = 0x08007B3A0E3430383537363437343130313031
! Layer 3
*Mar  1 00:01:15.267: ISDN BR0: RX <- RRr sapi = 0  tei = 89  nr = 1
*Mar  1 00:01:15.279: ISDN BR0: RX <- INFOc sapi = 0  tei = 89  ns = 0
    nr = 1  i = 0x08007B3B028181
*Mar  1 00:01:15.287: ISDN BR0: TX -> RRr sapi = 0  tei = 89  nr = 1
*Mar  1 00:01:15.311: ISDN BR0: RX <- INFOc sapi = 0  tei = 89  ns = 1
    nr = 1  i = 0x08007B952A0480800150
*Mar  1 00:01:15.323: ISDN BR0: TX -> RRr sapi = 0  tei = 89  nr = 2
*Mar  1 00:01:15.739: ISDN BR0: RX <- INFOc sapi = 0  tei = 80  ns = 2
    nr = 2  i = 0x08018102180189
*Mar  1 00:01:15.747: ISDN BR0: TX -> RRr sapi = 0  tei = 80  nr = 3
*Mar  1 00:01:17.039: ISDN BR0: RX <- INFOc sapi = 0  tei = 80  ns = 3
    nr = 2  i = 0x08018107
*Mar  1 00:01:17.043: ISDN BR0: TX -> RRr sapi = 0  tei = 80  nr = 4
*Mar  1 00:01:17.051: ISDN BR0: TX -> INFOc sapi = 0  tei = 80  ns = 2
    nr = 4  i = 0x0801010F
```

If negotiation of Layer 2 doesn't occur, IDREQ is transmitted with different random RI and wildcard ri = 127, but you won't see an IDASSN. This indicates that the switch is not responding. Another problem scenario is an invalid TEI from the switch, which can indicate an LEC issue—possibly a malfunctioning switch.

The following message types can be checked during TEI identification:

- ID Request
- ID Assigned
- ID Denied
- ID Check Request
- ID Check Response
- ID Remove
- ID Verify

The only way to change or remove the TEI assigned to the router's BRI interface is to reload the router. Then, the boot code forces the first ISDN TEI first-call flag to be reset. The first call flag affects all switch types, thus forcing incoming and outgoing calls to activate the BRI interface. To enable the router to negotiate the TEI on the first call, use the following configuration command:

```
804-isdn(config)#isdn tei-negotiation first-call
```

NOTE   Some European ISPs remove the TEI assignment during night hours. Then, the user who has a functioning connection during the day cannot make calls out and must power-cycle the router to make it operational during the day. This command is particularly useful for these cases because it allows the TEIs to be re-established during the first call out.

The next step in the activation of Layer 2 is the HDLC connection with the switch. The router sends an asynchronous balance mode extended (SABME) message with TEI xx (in the example, it's 73). In response to SABME, the local switch responds with a series of unnumbered acknowledgments (UAs). At this point, Layer 2 is ACTIVE. If you enter #**show isdn status,** you can see the second layer reported as ACTIVATED.

NOTE   Under normal circumstances, you should not see SABME messages. If you do see them, it is a clear indication that Layer 2 is trying to reinitialize. This is usually seen when transmitting poll requests (RRp) and not receiving a response from the switch (RRf), or vice versa.

After Layer 2 is activated, a sign of normal exchange is the exchange of INFO frames between the router and the local switch. Responses for the INFO messages are RR frames, as shown in Example 12-12.

Example 12-12 **debug isdn q921** *Output*

```
804-isdn#debug isdn q921
*Mar  3 23:59:04.788: ISDN BR0: RX <-  INFOc sapi = 0  tei = 80  ns=0 nr = 1
*Mar  3 23:59:11.736: ISDN BR0: TX ->  RRp sapi = 0  tei = 80  nr = 1
*Mar  3 23:59:11.752: ISDN BR0: RX <-  INFOc sapi = 0  tei =80  ns=0 nr = 1
```

NOTE   Under normal circumstances, you should not see the exchange of any negotiation messages, such as IDREQ or IDASSN, but you should see the exchange shown in the previous output. Also, note that a PRI always uses a Terminal Endpoint Identifier (TEI) of zero because the link is point-to-point only. A TEI uniquely identifies multiple clients on an ISDN bus, which is a BRI.

The INFO frames contain Q931 signaling information and they exchange NS (send sequence number) and NR (next expected sequence number) fields. It is similar to the myseen and yourseen messages on the serial lines. To understand this analogy, look at the idle BRI channel (no user data is exchanged) and you can see a keepalive mechanism, which is when both parties exchange RR frames every 10 to 30 seconds, depending on settings, as shown in Example 12-13.

Example 12-13 *Keepalive Mechanism in* **debug isdn q921** *Output*

```
804-isdn#debug isdn q921
*Mar  4 00:39:11.671: ISDN BR0: TX ->  RRp sapi = 0  tei = 80  nr = 44
*Mar  4 00:39:11.687: ISDN BR0: RX <-  RRf sapi = 0  tei = 80  nr = 1
*Mar  4 00:39:19.675: ISDN BR0: TX ->  RRp sapi = 0  tei = 89 nr = 60
*Mar  4 00:39:19.691: ISDN BR0: RX <-  RRf sapi = 0  tei = 89  nr = 24
```

In active second-layer environments, you can see the messages in Example 12-13. They allow you to conclude that Layer 2 is functioning properly. The final result of the successful establishment of the second layer is shown in Example 12-14's output.

Example 12-14 *The Successful Establishment of the Second Layer*

```
804-isdn#show isdn status
Global ISDN Switchtype = basic-ni
ISDN BRI0 interface
        dsl 0, interface ISDN Switchtype = basic-ni
    Layer 1 Status:
        ACTIVE
    Layer 2 Status:
        TEI = 64, Ces = 1, SAPI = 0, State = MULTIPLE_FRAME_ESTABLISHED
        TEI = 73, Ces = 2, SAPI = 0, State = MULTIPLE_FRAME_ESTABLISHED
```

continues

Example 12-14 *The Successful Establishment of the Second Layer (Continued)*

```
Spid Status:
   TEI 64, ces = 1, state = 5(init)
         spid1 configured, spid1 sent, spid1 valid
         Endpoint ID Info: epsf = 0, usid = 0, tid = 1
   TEI 73, ces = 2, state = 5(init)
         spid2 configured, spid2 sent, spid2 valid
         Endpoint ID Info: epsf = 0, usid = 1, tid = 1,
```

In terms of a Cisco 77x series router, the expected output is displayed in Example 12-15.

Example 12-15 *Cisco 77x Series Router Output*

```
776-isdn> show status
Status     01/03/1995 05:30:24
Line Status
   Line Activated
   Terminal Identifier Assigned    SPID Accepted
   Terminal Identifier Assigned    SPID Accepted
Port Status                                   Interface Connection Link
   Ch:  1        Waiting for Call
   Ch:  2        Waiting for Call
```

NOTE   The output of an IOS command for the second layer must have TEIs in the expected range, SAPI = 0, and State = MULTIPLE_FRAME_ESTABLISHED for each B channel. If only one B channel has the MULTIPLE_FRAME_ESPABLISHED state, ISDN is still operational, but it will only have use of that channel.

After the first and second layers on the D channel are established, you can approach Layer 3. Troubleshooting this layer should be attempted only after you verify that Layer 1 and Layer 2 are active.

Troubleshooting the Network Layer

The third layer protocol on the D channel, or Q.931 messaging, controls connections between various nodes on an ISDN network. These messages contain call setup, call clearing, and various status messaging.

The first Layer 3 activity occurs when the router sends the service profile identifier (SPID) to the switch. Q.931 includes numerous options. You must ensure that you configure the exact type of switch and protocol. Many cases arise when the LEC uses 5ESS or DMS-100, and runs NI-1 protocol. There are other cases when DMS-100 is emulating 4ESS or 5ESS using different profiles. Q.931 has 37 different types of call setups. The SPIDs bind a specific TEI to a specific service profile. If you receive an Invalid IE contents or SPID.x rejected message, that means the handshake procedure between the local switch and the CPE was unsuccessful and the SPID was rejected (see Example 12-16).

Example 12-16 *Handshake Procedure Between the Local Switch and the CPE Was Unsuccessful and the SPID Was Rejected*

```
804-isdn#debug isdn q931
*Mar  1 00:01:10.881: %ISDN-6-LAYER2UP: Layer 2 for Interface BR0,
    TEI 112 changed to up
*Mar  1 00:01:10.885: ISDN BR0: TX -> INFORMATION pd = 8  callref = (null)
       SPID Information i = '40857647400101'
*Mar  1 00:01:10.925: ISDN BR0: RX <- INFORMATION pd = 8  callref = (null)
       ENDPOINT Ident i = 0x8081
*Mar  1 00:01:10.933: ISDN BR0: Received EndPoint ID
*Mar  1 00:01:10.953: ISDN BR0: RX <- INFORMATION pd = 8  callref = (null)
       Locking Shift to Codeset 5
*Mar  1 00:01:10.957:   Codeset 5 IE 0x2A  i = 0x808001, 'P'
*Mar  1 00:01:10.985: %ISDN-6-LAYER2UP: Layer 2 for Interface BR0,
    TEI 65 changed to up
*Mar  1 00:01:10.989: ISDN BR0: TX -> INFORMATION pd = 8  callref = (null)
       SPID Information i = '40857647440101'
*Mar  1 00:01:11.045: ISDN BR0: RX <- INFORMATION pd = 8  callref = (null)
       Cause i = 0x82E43A - Invalid IE contents
*Mar  1 00:01:11.053: %ISDN-4-INVALID_SPID: Interface BR0, Spid2 was rejected
```

The negotiation begins with sending the first SPID information. The SPID information can be in clear text, such as SPID Information i = '40857647400101', for IOS 12.0+, or in ASCII code, such as i = 3631234234545342, for older versions of IOS. The **pd** is the protocol descriptor. Another part of the setting is the local directory number (LDN), which is configured to receive incoming calls. If LDN is not configured on telco's switch, which is because either the switch does not support the voice feature or the ISDN service is not provisioned for voice, the router cannot receive voice calls. In the following examples, you can see the status of the ISDN layers after the second SPID is rejected. Example 12-17 shows the result from the unsuccessful SPID2 negotiation in 776 routers.

Example 12-17 *Examples of SPID Negotiation in 776 Routers*

```
776-isdn> 01/01/1995 00:00:26  L19   1
            Terminal Identifier Unassigned
776-isdn> 01/01/1995 00:00:26  L19   2
            Terminal Identifier Unassigned
776-isdn> 01/01/1995 00:00:26  L12   0
            Disconnected Remotely
776-isdn> 01/01/1995 00:00:26  L18   1
            Terminal Identifier Assigned
776-isdn> 01/01/1995 00:00:26  L22   1
```

continues

Example 12-17 *Examples of SPID Negotiation in 776 Routers (Continued)*

```
       40857647400101  Sending SPID
776-isdn> 01/01/1995 00:00:26  L27  0
             Disconnected
776-isdn> 01/01/1995 00:00:27  L18  2
             Terminal Identifier Assigned
776-isdn> 01/01/1995 00:00:27  L23  1 40857647400101  SPID Accepted
776-isdn> 01/01/1995 00:00:27  L22  2   4085764744  Sending SPID
776-isdn> 01/01/1995 00:00:27  L24  2                SPID Rejected
Cause 100  Invalid Information Element Contents
```

Finally, in terms of 77x router, Example 12-18 shows the status of the ISDN service, including Layer 3's status.

Example 12-18 *The Status of the ISDN Service, Including Layer 3's Status*

```
776-isdn> show status
Status    09/01/2000 11:00:28
Line Status
  Line Activated
    Terminal Identifier Assigned    SPID Accepted
    Terminal Identifier Assigned    SPID Rejected
Port Status                                     Interface Connection Link
  Ch: 1       Waiting for Call
  Ch: 2       Waiting for Call
776-isdn>
```

In terms of IOS, the same information about all layers, including Layer 3, is displayed in Example 12-19.

Example 12-19 **show isdn status** *Output*

```
804-isdn#show isdn status
Global ISDN Switchtype = basic-ni
ISDN BRI0 interface
       dsl 0, interface ISDN Switchtype = basic-ni
    Layer 1 Status:
       ACTIVE
    Layer 2 Status:
       TEI = 112, Ces = 1, SAPI = 0, State = MULTIPLE_FRAME_ESTABLISHED
       TEI = 65, Ces = 2, SAPI = 0, State = MULTIPLE_FRAME_ESTABLISHED
    Spid Status:
       TEI 112, ces = 1, state = 5(init)
          spid1 configured, spid1 sent, spid1 valid
          Endpoint ID Info: epsf = 0, usid = 0, tid = 1
       TEI 65, ces = 2, state = 6(not initialized)
          spid2 configured, spid2 sent, spid2 NOT valid
```

At this point, it is a good idea to carefully review the provisioning information and, if this does not help, work with the service provider to resolve the SPID2 issue.

So far, the information about Layer 3 in this section was about establishing the Layer 3 functionality. The following discussion is about the dynamics of the ISDN Layer 3, which is developed to handle the ISDN calls.

First and foremost of course, you have to make sure that the router can make calls out. This can be done in two ways:

- Generate interesting traffic to force the router to make a call
- Make a manual call out

To generate interesting traffic, you must connect a computer to the router and run an application or open a browser, which is usually configured to be interesting traffic for the router. It's much simpler to generate a manual call, especially when you are troubleshooting remotely, as follows:

- For 77x routers, to make a data call from the first channel, you type the following:

  ```
  776-isdn> call 1 18007735555
  ```

- For IOS ISDN routers, type the following:

  ```
  804-isdn#isdn call interface bri0:1 18007735555
  ```

Another easy way to test the D channel functionality is to use the voice channels on the premise that the ISDN service is provisioned for voice and data. If this is the case, you can work with the remote user to connect a regular phone to the voice ports of the router and try to make a local or long-distance voice call. If there's a dial tone and the user can make calls out at all, the D channel is working properly. If not, you need more detailed troubleshooting.

As previously mentioned, two types of protocols are running on Layer 3:

- D channel protocols Q.931 and Q.932 (optional)
- Routed protocols such as IP, IPX, and AT and all the overhead of routing protocols

No definition of the Layer 2 B channel protocol is in the ISDN standard, but PPP or HDLC (by default) can be used. Q.931 defines a series of messages including the following:

- SETUP
- CONNECT
- RELEASE
- USER INFORMATION
- CANCEL
- STATUS
- CALL_PROC
- DISCONNECT

The router informs the switch that it wants to make a call. The switch transforms the Q.931 messages to SS7 and places a call to the remote switch. The remote switch translates the call to Q.931 signals and calls the remote router.

Q.931 is not an end-to-end protocol, but in terms of troubleshooting, it's more convenient to consider Q.931 as an end-to-end protocol, especially when the ISDN network belongs to a single provider. Layer 2 INFO frames transmit all Q.931 signals and, when the router places a data call, it sends a packet. The setup packet always has a protocol descriptor of pd = 8 and generates a random hex value for the call reference—callref=0x08. The callref is important when troubleshooting with the local or long-distance LEC because the carriers see the same callref and can easily track the call and its history. Also, from the handshaking of transmit (TX->) and receive (RX<-) messages, you can see what call is related to what user. In Example 12-20, you can see the call setup procedure.

Example 12-20 *The Call Setup Procedure*

```
804-isdn#debug isdn q931
*Mar  4 08:12:28.506: ISDN BR0: TX ->  SETUP pd = 8  callref = 0x08
*Mar  4 08:12:28.510:          Bearer Capability i = 0x8890
*Mar  4 08:12:28.510:          Channel ID i = 0x83
*Mar  4 08:12:28.514:          Keypad Facility i = '18007735555'
*Mar  4 08:12:29.646: ISDN BR0: RX <-  CALL_PROC pd = 8  callref = 0x88
*Mar  4 08:12:29.650:          Channel ID i = 0x8A
*Mar  4 08:12:31.930: ISDN BR0: RX <-  CONNECT pd = 8  callref = 0x88
*Mar  4 08:12:31.938: ISDN BR0: TX ->  CONNECT_ACK pd = 8  callref = 0x08
*Mar  4 08:12:31.942: %LINK-3-UPDOWN: Interface BRI0:2, changed state to up
*Mar  4 08:12:31.958: %DIALER-6-BIND: Interface BRI0:2 bound to
    profile Dialer1
*Mar  4 08:12:31.958: %ISDN-6-CONNECT: Interface BRI0:1 is now connected to
    18007735555 gateway
```

To assist with understanding the output from the router, refer to the format of Q.931 in Figure 9-7. From call information of pd = 8 and callref = 0xXX, you can trace the call history and see STATUS pd = 8, DISCONNECT pd = 8, and RELEASE pd = 8. A piece of important information is the Bearer Capability i = 8890, which indicates a 64-kbps data call. The 0x8890218F means it is a 56-kbps data call and the 0x8090A2 means that it's a voice call. Channel ID i = 0x83 is a request from the router to the switch to assign an idle B channel. If the request is not allowed, you can see "isdn_is_bchannel_available: No Free B-channels", which indicates a capacity issue or congestion in the LEC's network. Keypad facility i = '18007735555' is the number called by the router. If it is an incoming call and the line is provisioned so the LEC provides caller_ID (Q.932), you see 'Called Party Number i=0x88 '5764740'. CALL_PROC' , which indicates that the call is proceeding.

To differentiate between TX and RX, callref uses different values for the first digit after the 0x. (0x indicates a hexadecimal value.) Although the second digit is the same for the TX and RX values 0x88 and 0x08, the first digit is different. This fact allows you to differentiate the callref if it is a TX or RX message. Channel ID i = 89 indicates the first channel, and the second channel is indicated as Channel ID i = 8A. The last stage is CONNECT, when the LEC assigns an idle B-channel to the router, and the router receives the following: ISDN BR0: RX <- CONNECT pd = 8 callref = 0x88, with calref = 0x88. The router responds to the same callref = 0x08 with acknowledgment: ISDN BR0: TX -> CONNECT_ACK pd = 8 callref = 0x08. If the call is unsuccessful, the order of the messages is different. If the router places a data call, you might see this message: ISDN BR0: TX -> SETUP pd = 8 callref = 0x08. Later in the Q.931 input, you might see a message RX<- RELEASE_COMP pd = 8 callref = 82. The RELEASE_COMP message is a clear indication that the call is refused.

NOTE   Sometimes, the TX-> release message and RX<- RELEASE_COMP messages can be misleading. The CPE tends to not understand that the call is terminated.

The provided approach for troubleshooting the functionality of the D channel is beneficial when working with the service provider because the Cisco router provides for you the same visibility given to your provider about the details of Q.931 signaling.

The simpler, but still recommended, approach to the D channel functionality is as follows, using another set of IOS debug commands, such as #**debug dialer**:

```
804-isdn#debug dialer ?
  events   Dial on demand events
  packets  Dial on demand traffic
```

In this command, you have two options: to debug the events or the traffic.

It is recommended to turn the debug on and to make a data call out, generating interesting traffic. In Example 12-21, you see output from the command when you are debugging traffic and access list 101 defines the interesting traffic.

Example 12-21 debug dialer packets *Output*

```
804-isdn#debug dialer packets
Mar  3 10:06:46.815: Dialer1 DDR: ip (s=10.19.250.248, d=10.19.92.149),
    41 bytes, outgoing interesting (list 101)
Mar  3 10:06:47.055: Dialer1 DDR: ip (s=10.19.250.248, d=10.19.92.149),
    596 bytes, outgoing interesting (list 101)
```

The output displays the interesting traffic triggering the call, including the source and destination of the information and the TCP port, as well as the number of bytes and the ACL number. Similar information can be seen in Example 12-22 for a 770 series router, with the Software Version c760-in.r.US 4.4(2).

Example 12-22 show packets *Output*

```
776-isdn:gateway> show packets
Packet Statistics for Connection 3
Filtered: 0  Forwarded: 9869  Received: 10773
Dropped: 373 Lost: 27   Corrupted: 0  Misordered: 30
Compression Ratio: 2.38:1
IP Packet that triggered last call
Source Address: 10.0.0.1
Destination Address: 10.19.92.149
Protocol: TCP
Source Port: 23
Destination Port: 3049,
```

For IOS-based ISDN routers, if you want to track the dialer events, use the alternative displayed in Example 12-23.

Example 12-23 debug dialer events *Output*

```
804-isdn#debug dialer events
*Mar  3 10:02:07.699: BRI0 DDR: rotor dialout [priority]
*Mar  3 10:02:07.699: BRI0 DDR: Attempting to dial 18007735555
*Mar  3 10:02:10.643: %LINK-3-UPDOWN: Interface BRI0:2, changed state to up
*Mar  3 10:02:10.659: %DIALER-6-BIND: Interface BRI0:2 bound to profile Dialer1
*Mar  3 10:02:10.663: %ISDN-6-CONNECT: Interface BRI0:1 is now connected to
    18007735555 gateway
*Mar  3 10:02:10.667: isdn_call_connect: Calling lineaction of BRI0:2
*Mar  3 10:02:12.511: %LINEPROTO-5-UPDOWN: Line protocol on Interface BRI0:2,
    changed state to up!!!!!!!
*Mar  3 10:02:16.663: %ISDN-6-CONNECT: Interface BRI0:1 is now connected
    to 18007735555 gateway!!
Success rate is 100 percent (100/100), round-trip min/avg/max = 532/617/992 ms
```

Although the encapsulation discussion appears later in this chapter, it is important to distinguish between calls when they always fail (a Q.931 issue) and calls that might connect for a period of time and then disconnect due to a PPP issue. This is shown in Example 12-24 for a 700 series router, where the first channel has difficulties operating the PPP protocol.

Example 12-24 show status *Output*

```
776-isdn>show status
Status    09/01/2000 09:34:30
Line Status
  Line Activated
  Terminal Identifier Assigned    SPID Accepted
  Terminal Identifier Assigned    SPID Accepted
Port Status Interface             Connection     Link
  Ch:  1    64K Call In Progress  18007735555    DATA    0        0
  Ch:  2    64K Call In Progress  18007735555    DATA    3        1
```

From the previous output, the first channel drops because the PPP negotiation (LCP phase) is unsuccessful. In the Q.931 output, you see the reason for the call rejection and the following output messages: RX<- RELEASE_COMP pd = 8 callref = 82 and Cause i = 0x8295 – Call Rejected. The cause for the rejection is i = 0x8295, and the assigned number (8295) is the hex value of this message.

Usually, the messages from the switch are short decimal values. A brief description of some of the most common decimal values of Q.931, their description and possible cause, received from the NI-1 ISDN switch for 77x routers are provided in Table 12-1.

Table 12-1 *77x ISDN BRI Cause Messages Received from the NI-1 ISDN Switch*

Decimal Value	Description	Cause Messages
Normal Events		
1	Unassigned number	The ISDN number was sent to the switch in the correct format, but the number is not assigned to any destination equipment.
2	No route to the specific transit network	The ISDN exchange routed the call through an unrecognized intermediate network.
3	No route to the destination	The call was routed through an intermediate network that does not serve the destination address.
6	Channel unacceptable	The service quality of the specified channel is insufficient to accept the connection.
7	Call awarded and delivered	The user was assigned an incoming call that was connected to an already established call channel.
16	Normal clearing	Normal call clearing occurred.
17	User busy; BUSY	The called system acknowledges the connection request, but is unable to accept the call because all B channels are in use.
18	No user responding; NO RESPONSE	The connection cannot be completed because the destination does not respond to the call.
19	No answer from user (user alerted); NO ANSWER	The destination responds to the connection request, but fails to complete the connection within the prescribed time. The problem is at the remote end of the connection.
21	Call rejected	The destination is capable of accepting the call, but rejected the call for an unknown reason.
22	Number changed	The ISDN number used to set up the call is not assigned to any BRI. Perhaps an alternate address is assigned to the called equipment.

continues

Table 12-1 *77x ISDN BRI Cause Messages Received from the NI-1 ISDN Switch (Continued)*

Decimal Value	Description	Cause Messages
26	Non-selected user clearing	The destination is capable of accepting the call, but rejected the call because it was not assigned to the user.
27	Destination out of order	The destination cannot be reached because the interface is not functioning correctly, and a signaling message cannot be delivered.
28	Invalid number format (incomplete number)	The connection cannot be established because the destination address was presented in an unrecognizable format.
29	Requested facility rejected	The network cannot provide the facility requested by the user.
30	Response to STATUS Enquiry	The status message is generated in direct response to the prior receipt of a status enquiry message.
31	Normal, unspecified	Reports the occurrence of a normal event when no standard cause applies. No action required.
Network Congestion		
34	No circuit/channel available	No appropriate channel/circuit is available to take the call.
35	Call queued	The call is waiting to be performed.
38	Network out of order	The destination cannot be reached because the network is not functioning correctly.
41	Temporary failure	The network is temporarily not functioning correctly.
42	Network congestion	The network switch is temporarily overloaded.
43	Access information discarded	The network cannot provide the requested access information.
44	Requested circuit/channel not available	The remote equipment cannot provide the requested channel for an unknown reason. It might be temporary.
Service or Option Not Available		
47	Resources unavailable, unspecified	The requested channel or service is unavailable for an unknown reason.
49	Quality of service unavailable	QoS is not available. This could be a subscription problem.
50	Requested facility not subscribed	The remote equipment supports the requested supplementary service, but only by subscription.

Table 12-1   *77x ISDN BRI Cause Messages Received from the NI-1 ISDN Switch (Continued)*

Decimal Value	Description	Cause Messages
52	Outgoing calls barred	The outgoing calls are blocked in the configuration.
54	Incoming calls barred	The incoming calls are blocked in the configuration.
57	Bearer capability not authorized	The user requested bearer capability but is not subscribed to use it.
58	Bearer capability not presently available	The requested bearer capability is not currently available.
63	Service or option not available	The network or remote equipment cannot provide the requested option for an unspecified reason.
Service or Option Not Provisioned or Implemented		
65	Bearer service not implemented	The network cannot support the requested bearer capability.
66	Channel type not implemented	The network or the destination equipment does not support the requested channel type.
69	Requested facility not implemented	The remote site does not support the requested supplementary service.
70	Only restricted digital information bearer is available	The network is unable to provide unrestricted digital bearer capability.
79	Service or option not implemented, unspecified	The service or option cannot be provided for an unspecified reason.
Invalid Messages		
81	Invalid call reference value	The remote equipment received a call with a call reference that is not currently in use on the user-network interface.
82	Identified channel does not exist	The receiving equipment requested to use a channel that is not activated for calls on the interface.
83	A suspended call exists but this call identity does not	The network received a call resume request. It contains call identity information that indicates the call identity is being used for a suspended call.
84	Call identity is use	The network received a call resume request, containing call identity information that indicates it is in use for a suspended call.
85	No call suspended	The network received a call resume request, when there was not a suspended call pending.

continues

Table 12-1 *77x ISDN BRI Cause Messages Received from the NI-1 ISDN Switch (Continued)*

Decimal Value	Description	Cause Messages
86	Call that requested call identity has been cleared	The network received a call resume request. It contains call identity information that identifies the suspended call and then clears the call either by timeout or by the remote user.
88	Incompatible destination	Indicates an attempt to connect to non-ISDN equipment (an analog line).
91	Transit network does not exist/Invalid transit network specified	The ISDN exchange was asked to route the call through an unrecognized intermediate network.
95	Invalid message, unspecified	An invalid message was received, and no standard cause applies. This is usually due to a D channel error.
Protocol and Internetwork Errors		
96	Mandatory information element is missing	This is a D channel error because the Q.931 element is missing.
97	Message type non-existent or not implemented	A D channel error where either the message received is invalid or is valid but not supported. Error 97 is either a remote equipment error or a D channel error.
98	Message not compatible with call state or message type non-existent	A D channel error where the remote side receives an invalid message or no standard cause applies.
99	Information element nonexistent or not implemented.	A D channel error where the remote side receives an information element that cannot be recognized.
100	Invalid information element contents	A D channel error due to invalid information received in the information element.
101	Message not compatible with call state	A D channel error where the remote equipment receives an unexpected message that does not correspond to the current state of the connection.
102	Recovery on timer expiry	An error-handling (recovery) procedure was initiated by a timer expiry.
111	Protocol error, unspecified	The network signals a protocol error and the precise cause is not known.
127	Internetworking, unspecified	The network signals a protocol error and the precise cause is not known.
ALL others/ UNKNOWN	Cause nnn/ Unknown or local error	The error is registered, but the cause and reason are unknown.

As previously mentioned, your second objective is ensuring that the router can pass data. This feature is closely and mainly related to the following discussion about encapsulation options, PPP protocol suite, and its phases.

Troubleshooting PPP

PPP provides a standard method for transporting multiprotocol packets over point-to-point links. Regardless of the PPP definition as a first- and second-layer protocol, for practical purposes, it is more convenient to consider PPP as a third-layer protocol, because the Q.931 negotiation must happen before PPP starts. It is easy to think about ISDN and PPP protocols as a pyramid. For troubleshooting purposes, it's easier to consider the PPP protocol as having four phases: LCP negotiation, authentication, NCP, and termination.

As discussed in Chapter 5, "Dial Technology Background," PPP encapsulates the data over the B channels. Most of the information about PPP settings can be seen in the PPP negotiation process, where the protocol field indicates the upper-layer protocols carried in the information field. Some of the examples of protocol field values are

- **0x0021**—IP
- **0x0029**—AT
- **0x002B**—IPX
- **0x003D**—Multilink
- **0x0201**—802.1d hellos
- **0x8021**—IPCP
- **0x8029**—ATCP
- **0x802B**—IPXCP
- **0xC021**—LCP
- **0xC023**—PAP
- **0xC025**—LQR (link quality report)
- **0xC223**—CHAP

After assessing that the line is active, the next phase of PPP is the Link Establishment Phase, which is controlled by link control protocol (LCP).

Troubleshooting PPP LCP

PPP LCP provides a method of establishing, configuring, maintaining, and terminating the point-to-point connections. LCP goes through four distinct phases:

- Link establishment and configuration negotiation
- Link-quality determination

- Network-layer protocol configuration negotiation
- Link termination

First, link establishment and configuration negotiation occurs before any network layer datagrams (IP, AT, and IPX) are exchanged. LCP first opens the connection and negotiates configuration parameters. At this point, the Layer 2 framing is Layer 2 Generic HDLC. This phase is complete when a configuration-acknowledgment frame is both sent and received. The following parameters and options can be negotiated:

- **Maximum Receive/Transmit Unit (MRU/MTU)**—The default is 1500 bytes.
- **Async Control Character Map**—The control and escape characters on async links.
- **Authentication protocol**—PAP (0xC023) or CHAP (0xC223).
- **Quality protocol**—The process for data-link monitoring.
- **Magic-Number**—The technique to detect loopbacks.
- **MRRU**—The maximum received reconstructed unit.
- **Reserved**—It is reserved for future use.
- **Protocol Field Compression**—Compression of the PPP protocol field.
- **Address and Control Field Compression**—Compression of the PPP address and control field.

The link-establishment and configuration-negotiation phase is followed by link-quality determination, which is an optional phase. In this phase, the link is tested to determine whether the quality is sufficient to bring up the network-layer protocols. LCP can delay transmission of network-layer protocol information until this phase is complete.

Next, network layer protocol configuration negotiation occurs. After LCP finishes the link-quality determination, network-layer protocols can be configured separately by the appropriate NCP and can be brought up and taken down any time. If LCP closes the link, it informs the network-layer protocols so they can take appropriate action. At this point, PPP framing is being used.

Finally, link termination occurs. LCP can terminate the link at any time and it usually is done at the request of a user, but can happen because of a physical event, such as the loss of the carrier or the expiration of the idle-period timer. Three classes of LCP frames exist: link-establishment frames are used to establish and configure the link; link-termination frames are used to terminate a link; and link-maintenance frames are used to manage and debug a link.

For practical purposes, it is better to know the order of the phases. For the Cisco remote access environment, the right procedure is as follows:

1 Q.931 places a data call.

2 The connection is successful.

3 LCP PPP starts and establishes the connection parameters.

4 One- or two-way authentication occurs.

5 The virtual interface is created.

6 The number of the virtual interface (Vix) is assigned.

7 The bundles for IP, CP, and CDP are built.

8 Data transfer occurs.

The sequence is reversed to terminate the call.

During the LCP negotiations, the O CONFREQ proposes certain options. If all options are acceptable, the remote party returns I CONFACK. You should see this procedure twice because all handshaking procedures are two-way negotiations. Turning on some Cisco IOS debug commands displays the real-time negotiation. The O represents outgoing, and I signifies an incoming message.

A detailed description of the first phase is described next. In order to display both Q.931 and PPP negotiation processes together, it is recommended to use the following:

```
804-isdn#debug isdn q931
804-isdn#debug ppp negotiation
```

In Example 12-25, you can see the BR0:1 LCP: State is Open message.

Example 12-25 *LCP Negotiation Process*

```
! Initiation of the call - Q931
Mar 2  04:03:47.900: ISDN BR0: Outgoing call id = 0x8060, dsl 0
Mar 2  04:03:47.904: ISDN BR0: Event: Call to 18007735555 at 64 Kb/s
Mar 2  04:03:47.904: ISDN BR0: process_bri_call(): call id 0x8060,
    called_number  18007735555, speed 64, call type DATA
Mar 2  04:03:47.908: CC_CHAN_GetIdleChanbri: dsl 0
Mar 2 04:03:47.908:     Found idle channel B1
Mar 2 04:03:48.884: ISDN BR0: received HOST_PROCEEDING call_id 0x8060
Mar 2 04:03:50.152: ISDN BR0: received HOST_CONNECT call_id 0x8060
Mar 2 04:03:50.156: %LINK-3-UPDOWN: Interface BRI0:2, changed state to up
Mar 2  04:03:50.172: %ISDN-6-CONNECT: Interface BRI0:2 is now
    connected to 18007735555
! Starting PPP protocol
Mar 2 04:03:50.180: BR0:1 PPP: Treating connection as a callout
Mar 2 04:03:50.180: BR0:1 PPP: Phase is ESTABLISHING, Active Open
Mar 2 04:03:51.139: BR0:2 LCP: O CONFREQ [Closed] id 16 len 33
Mar 2  04:03:51.143: BR0:2 LCP:    AuthProto CHAP (0x0305C22305)
Mar  2 04:03:51.143: BR0:2 LCP:    MagicNumber 0x081C8F7E (0x0506081C8F7E)
Mar  2 04:03:51.143: BR0:2 LCP:    MRRU 1524 (0x110405F4)
Mar  2 04:03:51.147: BR0:2 LCP:    EndpointDisc 1 Local
    (0x130E01706D6172656B2D6973646E)
Mar  2 04:03:51.227: BR0:2 LCP: I CONFREQ [REQsent] id 93 len 32
Mar  2 04:03:51.231: BR0:2 LCP:    AuthProto CHAP (0x0305C22305)
Mar  2 04:03:51.231: BR0:2 LCP:    MagicNumber 0xB699FF25 (0x0506B699FF25)
Mar  2 04:03:51.231: BR0:2 LCP:    MRRU 1524 (0x110405F4)
Mar  2 04:03:51.235: BR0:2 LCP:    EndpointDisc 1 Local
    (0x130D016163636573732D677731)
Mar  2 04:03:51.239: BR0:2 LCP: O CONFACK [REQsent] id 93 len 32
```

continues

Example 12-25 *LCP Negotiation Process (Continued)*

```
Mar  2 04:03:51.239: BR0:2 LCP:    AuthProto CHAP (0x0305C22305)
Mar  2 04:03:51.239: BR0:2 LCP:    MagicNumber 0xB699FF25 (0x0506B699FF25)
Mar  2 04:03:51.243: BR0:2 LCP:    MRRU 1524 (0x110405F4)
Mar  2 04:03:51.243: BR0:2 LCP:    EndpointDisc 1 Local
   (0x130D016163636573732D677731)
Mar  2 04:03:51.243: BR0:2 LCP: I CONFACK [ACKsent] id 16 len 33!
Mar  2 04:03:51.247: BR0:2 LCP:    AuthProto CHAP (0x0305C22305)
Mar  2 04:03:51.247: BR0:2 LCP:    MagicNumber 0x081C8F7E (0x0506081C8F7E)
Mar  2 04:03:51.247: BR0:2 LCP:    MRRU 1524 (0x110405F4)
Mar  2 04:03:51.251: BR0:2 LCP:    EndpointDisc 1 Local
   (0x130E01706U6172656B82DC973646E)
Mar  2 04:03:51.251: BR0:2 LCP: State is Open
```

The information about LCP state is available in the output shown in Example 12-26.

Example 12-26 *Information About LCP State*

```
804-isdn#show interface bri 0 1
BRI0:2 is up, line protocol is up
  Hardware is BRI with U interface and POTS
  MTU 1500 bytes, BW 64 Kbit, DLY 20000 usec,
     reliability 255/255, txload 1/255, rxload 1/255
  Encapsulation PPP, loopback not set
  Keepalive set (10 sec)
  Interface is bound to Dialer1 (Encapsulation PPP)
  LCP Open, multilink Open
  Last input 00:00:00, output 00:00:00, output hang never
  Last clearing of "show interface" counters never
  Queuing strategy: fifo
<output omitted>
```

If LCP is closed, the PPP options are mismatched on both sides. For any negotiation, the LCP can fail, but there are different configuration commands in a 77x series router that reduce the chance of failure:

- 776-isdn>**set ppp nego count 20**—Number of negotiation attempts (default = 10).

- 776-isdn>**set ppp nego integrity 5**—Time between two integrity packets in seconds (default = 10).

- 776-isdn>**set ppp nego retry**—Time between negotiation attempts in milliseconds (default = 5000).

Usually for long-distance connections, the calls are 56 Kbps and the high-order bit of the data is overwritten by the signaling information, causing the called party to possibly report errors. In some solutions, due to the lack of information that the call is 56 Kbps (an old version of SS7), the receiving site treats the call as 64 Kbps, resulting in a common symptom of CRC errors, or probably even "runts" or aborts. The **dialer map** or **map-class dialer** statement enables you to specify the speed of the outgoing call. If the connection is successful and if #**debug isdn q931** is turned on, you can see a message similar to called_number 18007735555, speed 64, call type DATA. In some cases, you need to define the call as not-end-to-end ISDN, as shown in Example 12-27.

Example 12-27 *This Call Is Not End-to-End ISDN*

```
Mar  1 04:50:50.316: ISDN BR0: TX -> SETUP pd = 8  callref = 0x3B
Mar  1 04:50:50.320:          Bearer Capability i = 0x8890
Mar  1 04:50:50.320:          Channel ID i = 0x83
Mar  1 04:50:50.324:          Keypad Facility i = '18007735555'
Mar  1 04:50:51.448: ISDN BR0: RX <- CALL_PROC pd = 8  callref = 0xBB
Mar  1 04:50:51.452:          Channel ID i = 0x89
Mar  1 04:50:55.220: ISDN BR0: RX <- PROGRESS pd = 8  callref = 0xBB
Mar  1 04:50:55.220:          Progress Ind i = 0x8A81 - Call not end-to-end ISDN
Mar  1 04:50:55.224:          Signal i = 0x01 - Ring back tone on
Mar  1 04:51:05.704: ISDN BR0: RX <- DISCONNECT pd = 8  callref = 0xBB
Mar  1 04:51:05.708:          Cause i = 0x839F08 - Normal, unspecified or Speci
Mar  1 04:51:05.720: ISDN BR0: TX -> RELEASE pd = 8  callref = 0x3B
```

If the call hits voice trunks, the output displays "Destination address is not_ISDN", which indicates that you must add the following statement under your BRI interface:

```
804-isdn(config-if)#isdn not-end-to-end
```

NOTE   How do you use the magic numbers for troubleshooting? Part of the LCP negotiation defines the so-called magic numbers. The configuration option of PPP provides a method to detect looped-back links and other Layer 2 anomalies. By default, the magic number is not negotiated. Zero is inserted where a magic number might otherwise be used.

Before the configuration option is requested, the calling party *must* choose its magic number based on an algorithm for random numbers. When a Configure-Request is received with a magic number, the received magic number is compared with the magic number from the last Configure-Request sent to the peer. If the two magic numbers are different, the link is not looped back and the magic number needs to be acknowledged. If the two magic numbers are equal, it's possible that the link is looped back and the Configure-Request is actually the one last sent. To confirm this, a Configure-Nak must be sent with a different magic number value. Reception of a Configure-Nak with a magic number different from the last Configure-Nak proves the link is not looped back. If the magic number is equal to the one sent in the last Configure-Nak, the probability of a looped-back link is increased, and a new magic number must be chosen. If the link is indeed looped back, the same sequence (transmit Configure-Request, receive Configure-Request, transmit Configure-Nak, receive Configure-Nak) will repeat continually. If the link is not looped back, the sequence might occur a few times, but it is extremely unlikely to repeatedly occur.

Troubleshooting PPP Authentication

The next phase of PPP protocol is the authentication phase. By default, PPP authentication is optional and should only be configured after the circuit is known good and IP connectivity has been established. This reduces the number of variables that have to be dealt with in case of a problem. Usually, the protocol number C023- Password Authentication Protocol (PAP) or C223-Challenge Handshake Authentication Protocol (CHAP) is used. If you enter the **debug ppp authentication** command, you can see the next phase of the PPP negotiation, as shown in Example 12-28. (The **authentication** command is a subset of **ppp negotiation** command.)

Example 12-28 debug ppp authentication *Output*

```
804-isdn#debug ppp authentication
Oct 106 06:33:50.248: BR0:1 PPP: Phase is AUTHENTICATING, by both
Oct 106 06:33:50.248: BR0:1 CHAP: O CHALLENGE id 42 len 33 from "804-isdn"
Oct 106 06:33:50.272: BR0:1 CHAP: I CHALLENGE id 218 len 31 from "gateway"
Oct 106 06:33:50.276: BR0:1 CHAP: O RESPONSE id 218 len 33 from "804-isdn"
Oct 106 06:33:50.308: BR0:1 CHAP: I SUCCESS id 218 len 4
Oct 106 06:33:50.312: BR0:1 CHAP: I RESPONSE id 42 len 31 from "gateway"
Oct 106 06:33:50.316: BR0:1 CHAP: O SUCCESS id 42 len 4
```

It's important to make sure the type of the authentication—either PAP or CHAP—is the same on both sides of the connection. It is also important that authentication be configured under the physical interface, even when using dialer profiles, because it is the authentication phase that ultimately determines which dialer profile will be used.

NOTE   If you receive config-nack during the authentication negotiation, it means that one side is configured for PAP and the other is configured for CHAP password authentication.

Most ISPs will use PAP authentication. Also, it is probably going to be one-way PAP using the callin option of Cisco IOS routers, which can be seen in Chapter 11. The preferred PPP authentication choice is CHAP because all parts of the password are encrypted, and it supports the MD5 hash function. CHAP also uses three-way handshaking (as shown in the earlier example with three pairs of I and O messages) and avoids sending the password in clear text on the PPP link. You can see encrypted passwords in the configuration of both routers and in the exchange frame. For these reasons, consider CHAP as the superior authentication protocol. To connect using PPP, both parties do not necessarily require authentication, but if it is required, confirm the following:

- The passwords configured on both the local and remote routers are identical.
- The local and remote router names are configured correctly.

Don't forget that the passwords are case sensitive. If, after authentication, you see the following: BR0:1 CHAP: O SUCCESS, the authentication was successful. If you enter 804-isdn#**sh dialer**, you will see the name of the calling party at the end of the screen.

The PPP authentication operates with names instead of numbers and makes ISDN troubleshooting much easier. As previously mentioned, when you try to trace the call working with your provider, your preferred option is to use calling_party_number, provided by Q.931. Tracing calls with a LEC isn't easy because you don't always know how the line is provisioned. Sometimes, in the router output, you cannot see the calling party number because the LEC might either use prefixes, remove prefixes, or replace the number with dialed number identification service (DNIS) information. Another option is to match the parameter call_ref, which requires your timing to be precisely synchronized with the LEC equipment. The PPP authentication allows you to operate with names, such as gateway or 804-isdn, instead of a numbers. This allows you to trace the call from the core router by using IOS-based search and find features.

Troubleshooting PPP Network Control Protocols

NCPs are a set of protocols that negotiate the upper-layer protocols. Every negotiation is a series of requests and acknowledgments—Vi1 IPCP: I CONFREQ and Vi1 IPCP: I CONFACK [REQsent]. During the negotiation process, you can see IPCP, IPXCP (these are not included in Example 12-29), CDPCP, and CCP negotiating IP, IPX, CDP, and COMPRESSION, respectively. The negotiation depends on the configuration and the process starts by establishing the virtual connection, which is a bundle of channels called Multilink PPP (MLP). Next, LCP negotiates the parameters for the virtual connection. In the next example, you see the building of the bundle for IPCP, the negotiation of CCP, the setting of the LZSDCP history, and the CDPCP rejection.

Example 12-29 *After PPP Is Up, You Can See Part of NCP with IPCP and CCP Negotiation*

```
Oct 106 06:33:50.316: BR0:1 PPP: Phase is VIRTUALIZED
Oct 106 06:33:50.328: %LINK-3-UPDOWN: Interface Virtual-Access1,
    changed state to  up
Oct 106 06:33:50.344: Vi1 PPP: Treating connection as a callout
Oct 106 06:33:50.344: Vi1 PPP: Phase is ESTABLISHING, Active Open
Oct 106 06:33:50.348: Vi1 LCP: O CONFREQ [Closed] id 1 len 34
Oct 106 06:33:50.348: Vi1 LCP:    AuthProto CHAP (0x0305C22305)
Oct 106 06:33:50.352: Vi1 LCP:    MagicNumber 0xCEC4C1DA (0x0506CEC4C1DA)
Oct 106 06:33:50.352: Vi1 LCP:    MRRU 1524 (0x110405F4)
Oct 106 06:33:50.352: Vi1 LCP:    EndpointDisc 1 Local
     (0x130F01727363686966662D6973646E)
Oct 106 06:33:50.356: Vi1 PPP: Phase is UP
Oct 106 06:33:50.360: Vi1 CDPCP: O CONFREQ [Closed] id 1 len 4
Oct 106 06:33:50.360: Vi1 IPCP: O CONFREQ [Closed] id 1 len 10
Oct 106 06:33:50.364: Vi1 IPCP:    Address 10.19.230.89 (0x03060A13E659)
! Building the multilink PPP bundle for IP
```

continues

Example 12-29 *After PPP Is Up, You Can See Part of NCP with IPCP and CCP Negotiation (Continued)*

```
Oct 106 06:33:50.368: BR0:1 IPCP: MLP bundle interface is built,
  process packets now
Oct 106 06:33:50.368: BR0:1 IPCP: Redirect packet to Vi1
Oct 106 06:33:50.368: Vi1 IPCP: I CONFREQ [REQsent BR0:2 PPP:
  Phase is VIRTUALIZED!!!] id 1 len 10
Oct 106 06:33:50.372: Vi1 IPCP:    Address 151.70.196.1 (0x0306AB46C401)
Oct 106 06:33:50.372: Vi1 IPCP: O CONFNAK [REQsent] id 1 len 10
Oct 106 06:33:50.372: Vi1 IPCP:    Address 151.68.26.1 (0x0306AB441A01)
! Building the multilink bundle for stac compress
Oct 106 06:33:50.376: BR0:1 CCP: MLP bundle interface is built,
  process packets now
Oct 106 06:33:50.376: BR0:1 CCP: Redirect packet to Vi1
Oct 106 06:33:50.380: Vi1 CCP: I CONFREQ [Not negotiated] id 1 len 10
Oct 106 06:33:50.380: Vi1 CCP:    LZSDCP history 1 check mode SEQ process
  UNCOMPRESSSED (0x170600010201)
Oct 106 06:33:50.384: Vi1 LCP: O PROTREJ [Open] id 2 len 16 protocol CCP
  (0x80FD0101000A170600010201)
Oct 106 06:33:50.400: BR0:1 LCP: I PROTREJ [Open] id 1 len 10 protocol
  CDPCP (0x820701010004)
! CDPCP rejected
Oct 106 06:33:50.404: Vi1 CDPCP: State is Closed
Oct 106 06:33:50.404: Vi1 IPCP: I CONFACK [REQsent] id 1 len 10
Oct 106 06:33:50.408: Vi1 IPCP:    Address 10.19.230.89 (0x03060A13E659)
Oct 106 06:33:50.408: Vi1 IPCP: I CONFREQ [ACKrcvd] id 2 len 4
Oct 106 06:33:50.412: Vi1 IPCP: O CONFACK [ACKrcvd] id 2 len 4
Oct 106 06:33:50.412: Vi1 IPCP: State is Open
Oct 106 06:33:50.420: Di1 IPCP: Install route to 151.68.26.1
Oct 106 06:33:51.316: %LINEPROTO-5-UPDOWN: Line protocol on Interface BRI0:1,
  changed state to up
```

When troubleshooting the higher-layer protocols, it is important to know which protocol and which port or application is open in the router. One important feature that enables you to find this out is the command #**show tcp brief all**, which shows you what TCP sessions are open to a router.

Sometimes, you need to find out if the utilization of the router's processor is high. Some processes are not running and some use most of the router resources. A fast tool to find this out is

```
804 -isdn#show processes cpu | exclude 0.00
```

This command excludes the processes with utilization 0.00 from the output.

Another important question to answer is which protocol and which port or application is consuming most of the bandwidth. You can find out relatively quickly by using the Cisco IP NetFlow Accounting feature, which makes it possible to quickly identify traffic flows and applications by source and destination port number(s). To do this, you need version 12.2+ of Cisco IOS Software. Follow this procedure:

    1 Type #**ip route-cache flow** under the dialer interface.

    2 Wait a few minutes and execute the #**show ip cache flow** command.

The detailed output provides you with the following information:

- IP packet size distribution and the total number of packets.

- IP flow switching cache, total number in bytes.

- Protocol, type (UDP/TCP) distribution.

- Source and destination IP address of the traffic.

As discussed in Chapter 10, "Cisco ISDN Configuration Solutions," the MLP is a feature providing multivendor interoperability and packet fragmentation, improving the latency of each packet and load calculation. The MLP issues are discussed in the following paragraph.

Troubleshooting MLP

MLP defines a method for sequencing and transmitting packets over multiple physical interfaces. To reduce potential latency issues, MLP defines a method of fragmenting and reassembling large packets. When a packet arrives at an MLP master interface, it is fragmented and transmitted on each physical link in the MLP bundle. Reassembly of the packets occurs on the other side of the connection. MLP is supported, as long as all devices are members of the same rotary group or pool. Usually, designers use load thresholds to define when and for how long MLP will add or remove additional links to the connection. (See Chapters 10 and 11 for more information.)

The easiest way for IOS-based ISDN routers to verify the threshold values of the router is to check the configuration of the IOS ISDN router and look for the value under the command **dialer load-threshold,** or type #**show dialer** and look for "load threshold for dialing additional calls is *x*." A fragment of the output from the second command is shown in Example 12-30.

Example 12-30 **show dialer** *Output*

```
804-isdn#show dialer
BRI0 - dialer type = ISDN
Rotary group 1, priority = 0
0 incoming call(s) have been screened.
0 incoming call(s) rejected for callback.

<output omitted>

Di1 - dialer type = IN-BAND SYNC NO-PARITY
Load threshold for dialing additional calls is 20
Idle timer (60 secs), Fast idle timer (20 secs)
Wait for carrier (30 secs), Re-enable (15 secs)
Number of active calls = 0
```

For a 77x router, the output is displayed in Example 12-31.

Example 12-31 show timeout *Output*

```
776-isdn> show timeout
Demand Calling Parameters        Link 1        Link 2
  Connection Type               Auto ON       Auto ON
  Permanent                         OFF           OFF
  Threshold                       5 kbs        48 kbs
  Duration                        1 sec         1 sec
  Source                            LAN          BOTH
Timeout (call tear down) Parameters
  Threshold                       5 kbs        48 kbs
  Duration                       60 sec        60 sec
  Source                            LAN          BOTH
```

These commands provide the necessary information on how MLP and the thresholds are set. Keep in mind that, for an 800 series router, the threshold value is a fraction of 255, while for a 700 series router, the value is measured in Kbps.

It is important to define not only the conditions of the threshold (level and duration), but also the destination. There are three major options of IN, OUT, or EITHER for IOS-based routers, and LAN, WAN, or BOTH, for 77x series routers.

To set MLP, enter the following:

- 804-isdn(config-if)#**ppp multilink**—For IOS-based routers
- 776-isdn> **set ppp multilink on | off**—For 700 series routers

To check your MLP, you can use one of the following commands:

- 804-isdn#**show ppp multilink**
- 7206-isdn#**show ppp multilink | incl** *name*
- 776-isdn>**show negotiation**—For 77x routers

Troubleshooting PPP Callback for ISDN

As described in Chapter 11, this PPP feature provides a method for an implementation to request a dial-up peer to call back. When callback is successfully negotiated at the LCP phase and the authentication phase of PPP is complete, instead of going to the NCP phase, PPP disconnects the link.

A sample of checking the functionality of the callback feature is shown in Example 12-32.

Example 12-32 *ISDN Callback Output From the* **debug isdn 931** *Command*

```
804-isdn#debug isdn q931
! The remote user requests a connection:
*Oct 10 04:03:00.914: ISDN BR0: TX ->  SETUP pd = 8  callref = 0x0A
*Oct 10 04:03:00.918:         Bearer Capability i = 0x8890
*Oct 10 04:03:00.918:         Channel ID i = 0x83
*Oct 10 04:03:00.922:         Keypad Facility i = '5261783'
*Oct 10 04:03:01.250: ISDN BR0: RX <-  CALL_PROC pd = 8  callref = 0x8A
*Oct 10 04:03:01.250:         Channel ID i = 0x89
*Oct 10 04:03:01.270: ISDN BR0: RX <-  CONNECT pd = 8  callref = 0x8A
*Oct 10 04:03:01.278: ISDN BR0: TX ->  CONNECT_ACK pd = 8  callref = 0x0A
! Incoming and outgoing CONNECT messages - the BRI0:1 is up.
*Oct 10 04:03:01.282: %LINK-3-UPDOWN: Interface BRI0:1, changed state to up
*Oct 10 04:03:01.302: %ISDN-6-CONNECT: Interface BRI0:1 is now connected to
  5261783
*Oct 10 04:03:01.798: %LINK-3-UPDOWN: Interface Virtual-Access1, changed state
    to up
! The fact the virtual-access1 interface is up shows that the authentication
! phase was successful. Now the core disconnects the connection:
*Oct 10 04:03:01.838: ISDN BR0: RX <-  DISCONNECT pd = 8  callref = 0x8A
*Oct 10 04:03:01.842:         Cause i = 0x8090 - Normal call clearing
*Oct 10 04:03:01.854: ISDN BR0: TX ->  RELEASE pd = 8  callref = 0x0A
*Oct 10 04:03:01.858: %LINK-3-UPDOWN: Interface BRI0:1, changed state to down
*Oct 10 04:03:01.886: %LINK-3-UPDOWN: Interface Virtual-Access1,
    changed state to down
*Oct 10 04:03:01.998: ISDN BR0: RX <-  RELEASE_COMP pd = 8  callref = 0x8A
! Now the core router initiates a call to the remote user:
*Oct 10 04:03:16.970: ISDN BR0: RX <-  SETUP pd = 8  callref = 0x10
*Oct 10 04:03:16.974:         Bearer Capability i = 0x8890
*Oct 10 04:03:16.974:         Channel ID i = 0x89
*Oct 10 04:03:16.974:         Signal i = 0x40 - Alerting on - pattern 0
*Oct 10 04:03:16.978:         Called Party Number i = 0xC1, '5764740'
*Oct 10 04:03:16.982:         Locking Shift to Codeset 5
*Oct 10 04:03:16.982:         Codeset 5 IE 0x2A  i = 0x808001039E05,
    'From', 0x208B03, '408', 0x8001098001, '<'
*Oct 10 04:03:16.990: ISDN BR0: Event: Received a DATA call from 408 on B1
    at 64 Kb/s
*Oct 10 04:03:16.998: ISDN BR0: TX ->  CALL_PROC pd = 8  callref = 0x90
*Oct 10 04:03:16.998:         Channel ID i = 0x89
! The remote user's BRI0:1 comes up:
*Oct 10 04:03:17.002: %LINK-3-UPDOWN: Interface BRI0:1, changed state to up
*Oct 10 04:03:17.018: %ISDN-6-CONNECT: Interface BRI0:1 is now connected to 408
*Oct 10 04:03:17.030: ISDN BR0: TX ->  CONNECT pd = 8  callref = 0x90
*Oct 10 04:03:17.034:         Channel ID i = 0x89
*Oct 10 04:03:17.074: ISDN BR0: RX <-  CONNECT_ACK pd = 8  callref = 0x10
*Oct 10 04:03:17.074:         Channel ID i = 0x89
*Oct 10 04:03:17.078:         Signal i = 0x4F - Alerting off
*Oct 10 04:03:17.622: %LINK-3-UPDOWN: Interface Virtual-Access1, changed state
    to up
*Oct 10 04:03:18.610: %LINEPROTO-5-UPDOWN: Line protocol on Interface
    BRI0:1, changed state to up
*Oct 10 04:03:18.642: %LINEPROTO-5-UPDOWN: Line protocol on Interface
```

continues

Example 12-32 *ISDN Callback Output From the* **debug isdn 931** *Command (Continued)*

```
     Virtual-Access1, changed state to up
*Oct 10 04:03:23.022: %ISDN-6-CONNECT: Interface BRI0:1 is now connected
     to 14085265555 access-gw1
804-isdn#
```

As mentioned in Chapter 11, there is a way to set up the configuration so that both channels come up when a call from the core router is received using the #**dialer load-threshold 2 inbound** command. It is interesting to check the functionality of PPP callback feature using the IOS.

One possible solution is to debug the PPP negotiation and ISDN Q931 with the following commands:

```
804-isdn#debug isdn q931
804-isdn#debug ppp negotiation
```

Remember: If you are connected through a telnet session to the remote user's router, make sure that the debug commands are turned on with 804-isdn#**show debug**. Because you will have connects and disconnects during the process, and you will lose the telnet connection, it's recommended that you create a log in the remote user's router configuration to be able to see the entire process afterwards. The output from the log file looks like Example 12-32 (with added PPP negotiation information).

The number 2 in the **dialer load-threshold 2 inbound** command defines that only the incoming traffic will be compared with the threshold, and it is set to 2 (which is ~1% of the bandwidth = 2 / 255 x 100 x bandwidth).

When both channels are up, how do you check that this is due to incoming calls and not outgoing calls? One of the ways is to read the log file for RX<- and TX-> messages to see who is initiating the call. But because this output can be chatty, you might want to try a simpler way, as shown in Example 12-33.

Example 12-33 *Output from the* **sh isdn st** *Used to Check the Reason for the Calls*

```
804-isdn#sh isdn st
Global ISDN Switchtype = basic-5ess
ISDN BRI0 interface
        dsl 0, interface ISDN Switchtype = basic-ni
    Layer 1 Status:
        ACTIVE
    Layer 2 Status:
        TEI = 104, Ces = 2, SAPI = 0, State = MULTIPLE_FRAME_ESTABLISHED
        TEI = 113, Ces = 1, SAPI = 0, State = MULTIPLE_FRAME_ESTABLISHED
    Spid Status:
        TEI 113, ces = 1, state = 5(init)
            spid1 configured, spid1 sent, spid1 valid
            Endpoint ID Info: epsf = 0, usid = 0, tid = 1
        TEI 104, ces = 2, state = 5(init)
```

Example 12-33 *Output from the* **sh isdn st** *Used to Check the Reason for the Calls (Continued)*

```
                  spid2 configured, spid2 sent, spid2 valid
                  Endpoint ID Info: epsf = 0, usid = 1, tid = 1
       Layer 3 Status:
          2 Active Layer 3 Call(s)
       Activated dsl 0 CCBs = 2
! Callid with leading 0:
          CCB:callid=C, sapi=0, ces=1, B-chan=1, calltype=DATA
! Callid with leading 0:
          CCB:callid=D, sapi=0, ces=1, B-chan=2, calltype=DATA
       The Free Channel Mask:  0x80000000
       Total Allocated ISDN CCBs = 2
804-isdn#
```

An explanation for callid can be found in Chapter 9, "ISDN Technology Background." The most significant bit of Q931 is a bit called Flag. When the Flag is 0, the call is initiated from the core router; when Flag is 1, the call is initiated from the remote user's site. The numbers in the output are callid=C and callid=D. Written in binary codes, they have leading 0s, which means that the calls are originated from the core router, thus the callback is working.

Maybe the simplest way to check the callback function is to use the following command:

```
804-isdn#show isdn active
```

With this command, check the call's attribute to see if it is IN or OUT, as shown in Example 12-34.

Example 12-34 *Checking the Call's Attribute*

```
-------------------------------------------------------------------------------
                              ISDN ACTIVE CALLS
-------------------------------------------------------------------------------
Call    Calling     Called      Remote   Seconds Seconds Seconds Charges
Type    Number      Number      Name     Used    Left    Idle    Units/Currency
-------------------------------------------------------------------------------
In     ---N/A---    5764740     gateway  17       .       .            0
In     ---N/A---    5764740     gateway  44       .       .            0
```

The example shows that both calls are incoming, thus the callback works.

As discussed in Chapter 11, another enhancement of MLP is the Multichasis Multilink PPP (MMP), which enables different MLP links to terminate on different NASs.

Troubleshooting MMP

For troubleshooting MMP, it is always recommended that you start with **debug sgbp error**:

```
7200-isdn-a#debug sgbp error
! SGBP errors debugging is on
7200-isdn-b#
Aug  9 22:20:03 PDT: %SGBP-7-NORESP: Failed to respond to 7200-isdn-a
     group isdnservers, may not have password
```

The previous message indicates problems answering the challenges sent by a peer. This should be enough to indicate that the username and password are left out of the stack group, as shown in Example 12-35.

Example 12-35 **debug sgbp hellos** *Output*

```
7200-isdn-a#debug sgbp hellos
! SGBP hellos debugging is on for both routers
7200-isdn-a#
Aug  9 22:29:37 PDT: %SGBP-7-CHALLENGED: Rcv Hello Challenge message from
    member 7200-isdn-b using 152.30.253.253
! Received a hello challenge from 7200-isdn-b from IP address 152.30.253.253
Aug  9 22:29:37 PDT: %SGBP-7-RESPONSE: Send Hello Response to
    7200-isdn-b group isdnservers
! Respond to the challenge
Aug  9 22:29:37 PDT: %SGBP-7-NORESP: Failed to respond to 7200-isdn-b
    group isdnservers, may not have password
! You cannot respond because you do not have a password
Aug  9 22:29:42 PDT: %SGBP-7-CHALLENGE: Send Hello Challenge to 7200-isdn b
    group isdnservers
! You send a challenge to 7200-isdn-b
7200-isdn-b#
Aug  9 22:29:37 PDT: %SGBP-7-CHALLENGE: Send Hello Challenge to 7200-isdn-a
    group isdnservers
Aug  9 22:29:42 PDT: %SGBP-7-CHALLENGED: Rcv Hello Challenge message from member
    7200-isdn-a using 152.30.253.254
Aug  9 22:29:42 PDT: %SGBP-7-RESPONSE: Send Hello Response to 7200-isdn-a
    group isdnservers
Aug  9 22:29:43 PDT: %SGBP-7-NORESP: Failed to respond to 7200-isdn-a
    group isdnservers, may not have password
! The password is mismatched or is missing
```

From the output, each router receives the other's challenge; therefore, you configured the correct host names and IP address for the sgbp peers. Adding the username of isdnservers and the password of cisco to the configuration of both routers fixes the problem indicated in the last line of the previous output stating that the password is mismatched or is missing.

Another possible issue with MMP could be a host name and IP address mismatch. The following message is displayed after entering **debug sgbp hello** on 7200-isdn-b. It usually means that the router has a host name and IP address mismatch, as shown in the following output:

```
Aug 10 01:08:15 PDT: %SGBP-1-MISSCONF: Possible misconfigured member
    7200-isdn-a using 152.30.253.254
```

Correcting the SGBP peer line with the correct IP address fixes this issue.

An incorrect SGBP password prevents peers from authenticating into the SGBP group. The following message means that either the peer's password for the stack group is incorrect or yours is incorrect:

```
Aug 10 01:48:53 PDT: %SGBP-1-AUTHFAILED: Member 7200-isdn-b
    failed authentication
```

The obvious fix is to verify that you have the correct SGBP username and password entered in both routers keeping in mind that they are case sensitive.

As an example, router 7200-isdn-a is receiving hellos from an unknown peer. As a result, both routers are not establishing a peer relationship. Start by using the **debug sgbp error** command again on both routers:

```
SGBP errors debugging is on
7200-isdn-b#
Aug  9 22:59:02 PDT: %SGBP-1-DIFFERENT: Rcv 7200-isdn-a's addr 152.30.253.253
    is different from the hello's addr 152.30.253.254
! Received a hello from 7200-isdn-a, but from 152.30.253.254 instead of what
! was configured in the sgbp member statement
Aug  9 22:59:02 PDT: %SGBP-1-DIFFERENT: Rcv 7200-isdn-a's addr 152.30.253.253
    is different from the hello's addr 152.30.253.254
7200-isdn-a#
```

However, on 7200-isdn-a, there's no output after entering **debug sgbp error**. So you should take a look at the **debug sgbp hello** output.

debug sgbp hello on both routers provides the output in Example 12-36.

Example 12-36 debug sgbp hello *Output*

```
SGBP hellos debugging is on
7200-isdn-b#
Aug  9 23:00:52 PDT: %SGBP-1-DIFFERENT: Rcv 7200-isdn-a's addr 152.30.253.253
    is different from the hello's addr 152.30.253.254
Aug  9 23:00:52 PDT: %SGBP-1-DIFFERENT: Rcv 7200-isdn-a's addr 152.30.253.253
    is different from the hello's addr 152.30.253.254
Aug  9 23:00:52 PDT: %SGBP-7-CHALLENGED: Rcv Hello Challenge message from
    member 7200-isdn-a using 152.30.253.254
Aug  9 23:00:52 PDT: %SGBP-7-RESPONSE: Send Hello Response to
    7200-isdn-a group isdnservers
Aug  9 23:00:54 PDT: %SGBP-7-CHALLENGE: Send Hello Challenge to
    7200-isdn-a group isdnservers
7200-isdn-a#
Aug  9 23:00:08 PDT: %SGBP-7-CHALLENGE: Send Hello Challenge to
    7200-isdn-b group isdnservers
Aug  9 23:00:30 PDT: %SGBP-7-CHALLENGE: Send Hello Challenge to
    7200-isdn-b group isdnservers
```

In Example 12-36's output, 7200-isdn-b's configured peer IP address is different than the one the actual hellos are coming from. In addition to the debug command, the command **show sgbp** tells you that there is another active address for 7200-isdn-a, as shown in Example 12-37.

Example 12-37 show sgbp *Output*

```
7200-isdn-b#show sgbp
Group Name: isdnservers Ref: 0xC973B000
Seed bid: default, 50, default seed bid setting
  Member Name: 7200-isdn-a State: idle Id: 3
  Ref: 0x0
  Address: 152.30.253.253
  Other Active Address: 152.30.253.254
```

In this case, the problem is that a mistake was made on 7200-isdn-b in the IP address of 7200-isdn-a entered in the **sgbp member** statement. From 7200-isdn-a's perspective, only challenges were sent and nothing was received because 7200-isdn-b was sending the replies to the wrong IP address. From 7200-isdn-b's perspective, challenges were sent, but no responses were received. Instead, 7200-isdn-b was getting challenges from 7200-isdn-a with a different IP address than was configured. After the IP address was fixed, **debug sgbp hello** on both routers would just show the keepalives sent every two seconds:

```
Aug 10 00:28:21 PDT: %SGBP-7-KEEPALIVE: Sending Keepalive to
  7200-isdn-b, retry=0
Aug 10 00:28:21 PDT: SGBP: Keepalive ACK rcv from 7200-isdn-b
Aug 10 00:28:23 PDT: %SGBP-7-KEEPALIVE: Sending Keepalive to
  7200-isdn-b, retry=0
Aug 10 00:28:23 PDT: SGBP: Keepalive ACK rcv from 7200-isdn-b
Aug 10 00:28:25 PDT: %SGBP-7-KEEPALIVE: Sending Keepalive to
  7200-isdn-b, retry=0
Aug 10 00:28:25 PDT: SGBP: Keepalive ACK rcv from 7200-isdn-b
```

NOTE   Some versions of IOS displays these debugs differently.

Mismatched IP addresses are especially easy to encounter if the routers have multiple interfaces. If the **sgbp source-ip** command is not used, the hellos would use the outgoing interface's IP address as the source IP address. Therefore, it's good to use the IP addresses of loopback interfaces in the **sgbp source-ip** command to avoid these situations.

The following is not usually something you will see, but it illustrates that missing three keepalives will time out the peer and, in order to re-establish the peer relationship, they must be authenticated again as shown in Example 12-38.

Example 12-38 *Missing Three Keepalives*

```
Aug 10 00:30:37 PDT: %SGBP-7-KEEPALIVE: Sending Keepalive to 7200-isdn-b, retry=0
Aug 10 00:30:37 PDT: SGBP: Keepalive ACK rcv from 7200-isdn-b
Aug 10 00:30:39 PDT: %SGBP-7-KEEPALIVE: Sending Keepalive to 7200-isdn-b, retry=0
Aug 10 00:30:39 PDT: SGBP: Keepalive ACK rcv from 7200-isdn-b
Aug 10 00:30:41 PDT: %SGBP-7-KEEPALIVE: Sending Keepalive to 7200-isdn-b, retry=0
Aug 10 00:30:43 PDT: %SGBP-7-KEEPALIVE: Sending Keepalive to 7200-isdn-b, retry=1
Aug 10 00:30:45 PDT: %SGBP-7-KEEPALIVE: Sending Keepalive to 7200-isdn-b, retry=2
```

Example 12-38 *Missing Three Keepalives (Continued)*

```
! Just missed the third keepalive in a row
Aug 10 00:30:47 PDT: %SGBP-7-KEEPALIVE_TIMEOUT: Keepalive timeout on 7200-isdn-b
! 7200-isdn-b has just timed out and is no longer a functional SGBP peer
Aug 10 00:30:48 PDT: %SGBP-7-CHALLENGE: Send Hello Challenge to
    7200-isdn-b group isdnservers
! Starting hello challenges to try to re-establish 7200-isdn-b as a SGBP peer
Aug 10 00:30:49 PDT: %SGBP-7-CHALLENGE: Send Hello Challenge to
    7200-isdn-b group isdnservers
Aug 10 00:30:50 PDT: %SGBP-7-CHALLENGE: Send Hello Challenge to
    7200-isdn-b group isdnservers
Aug 10 00:30:51 PDT: %SGBP-7-CHALLENGE: Send Hello Challenge to
    7200-isdn-b group isdnservers
```

As mentioned in Chapter 10, the bidding process of SGBP is when the SGBP stack group routers decide who will be the call master for any given MLP bundle. To view the bidding process, you need to debug SGBP queries, as shown in Example 12-39.

Example 12-39 *Debugging SGBP Queries*

```
7200-isdn-a#debug sgbp queries
! Displays the bidding process
Aug 10 14:26:21 PDT: %SGBP-7-NEWP: Peer query #22667 for user1-isdn,
    count 1, peerbid 11, ourbid 10000
! Your peer received a call from user1-isdn and is bidding.
! Your bid is 10000, so you must already be the call master for this user.
Aug 10 14:26:21 PDT: %SGBP-7-DONE: Query #32436 for bundle user1-isdn,
    count 0, master is local
! The call master is local
Aug 10 14:26:21 PDT: %SGBP-7-MQB: Bundle: user1-isdn    State: Done
    OurBid: 10000
Aug 10 14:26:21 PDT: %SGBP-7-PB: 152.30.253.254  State: Closed   Bid: 011
    Retry: 1
```

In this case, the master bundle is on the peer, as shown in Example 12-40.

Example 12-40 *The Master Bundle Is on the Peer*

```
Aug 10 14:27:14 PDT: %SGBP-7-NEWL: Local query #32444 for user2-isdn,
    count 1, ourbid 0
! You received a call from user2-isdn and are starting the bidding process
Aug 10 14:27:14 PDT: %SGBP-7-DONE: Query #32444 for bundle user2-isdn,
    count 1, master is 152.30.253.254
! The call master is 152.30.253.254
Aug 10 14:27:14 PDT: %SGBP-7-MQB:         Bundle: user2-isdn    State: Done
    OurBid: 000
Aug 10 14:27:14 PDT: %SGBP-7-PB:          152.30.253.254  State: Closed
    Bid: 10000  Retry: 0
```

Troubleshooting PPP Compression Control Protocol

Compression Control Protocol (CCP) is a member of the NCP suite and provides a compression session that increases the ISDN throughput. Keep in mind that all compression methods are traffic dependant, so you cannot expect the same compression ratio for different types of traffic. The protocol is referred to as PPP CCP and defines a method for negotiating compression on PPP links over leased lines, and WAN circuit-switched-lines including ISDN. To configure compression, use the following:

- 804-isdn(config-if)#**compress {stac | predictor}**—Under the BRI0 interface

- 776-isdn>**set compression stac | off**

Stac compression defines the LZS Stacker compression algorithm and predictor—the RAND or predictor algorithm. The theory behind these algorithms is extremely complex. More information is available in IETF, Calgary Text Compression Corpus, and the Canterbury Corpus files (http://corpus.canterbury.ac.nz/). It is helpful to know that you can see the compression ratio by entering the following:

- 804-isdn# **show compression**—For IOS 12.1 and higher

- 776-isdn:gateway>**show packets**—For images 4.2 and higher

Example 12-41 displays the output for a 776 router.

Example 12-41   show packets *Output*

```
776-isdn:gateway> show packets
Packet Statistics for Connection 2
Filtered: 0  Forwarded: 2081  Received: 5581
Dropped: 0  Lost: 0   Corrupted: 1  Misordered: 0
Compression Ratio: 1.99:1
776-isdn:gateway>
```

Here, the router is reporting compression ratio 1.99:1 for connection 2, calculated on the base of 2081 forwarded and 5581 received packets.

The last phase of PPP protocol is the teardown, or determination of the connection, which, in turn, should result in releasing the LEC's facilities.

PPP: Termination of the Connection

Consider this example: After a connection is established and there is no further demand for a network connection, the end user's router sends a request for disconnect -BR0:1 LCP: O TERMREQ [Open], which is referred to as a termination request. After the expected acknowledgment - I TERMACK [TERMsent], you can see LCP Closed, PPP down. Example 12-42 shows the PPP termination sequence if the **debug ppp negotiation** command is turned on.

Example 12-42 *PPP Termination Sequence*

```
*Mar  2 04:06:13.755: BR0:1 LCP: O TERMREQ [Open] id 201 len 4
*Mar  2 04:06:13.827: BR0:1 LCP: I TERMACK [TERMsent] id 201 len 4
*Mar  2 04:06:13.827: BR0:1 LCP: State is Closed
*Mar  2 04:06:13.827: BR0:1 PPP: Phase is DOWN
*Mar  2 04:06:13.831: BR0:1 PPP: Treating connection as a callin
*Mar  2 04:06:13.831: BR0:1 PPP: Phase is ESTABLISHING, Passive Open
*Mar  2 04:06:13.831: BR0:1 LCP: State is Listen
*Mar  2 04:06:13.835: %DIALER-6-UNBIND: Interface BRI0:1
    unbound from profile Dialer1
*Mar  2 04:06:13.835: BR0:1 PPP: Phase is ESTABLISHING, Passive Open
*Mar  2 04:06:13.839: %ISDN-6-CONNECT: Interface BRI0:2 is now connected to
    18007735555 gateway
*Mar  2 04:06:13.843: %ISDN-6-DISCONNECT: Interface BRI0:1  disconnected from
    18007735555 gateway, call lasted 243s.
*Mar  2 04:06:14.783: %ISDN-6-CONNECT: Interface BRI0:2 is now connected to
    18007735555  gateway
*Mar  2 04:06:14.787: %LINK-3-UPDOWN: Interface BRI0:1, changed state to down
*Mar  2 04:06:14.803: BR0:1 LCP: State is Closed
*Mar  2 04:06:14.803: BR0:1 PPP: Phase is DOWN
*Mar  2 04:06:14.831: %LINEPROTO-5-UPDOWN: Line protocol on Interface BRI0:1,
    changed state to down
```

The analogous commands for 77x routers to debug (or not) the PPP phases are

```
776-isdn>diag ppp on | off
776-isdn>diag chap on | off
```

These commands turn the debug of PPP on and off.

If the ISDN service is provisioned for data and voice, the voice portion will work as every other regular phone. Now you will see how to approach the possible problems if your regular phone is connected to the voice ports of the router.

Troubleshooting Telephone Interfaces

Cisco IOS includes features that handle data and voice priority. Depending on user preferences, voice can take precedence over data and vice versa. Data and voice alternate on every channel. There are three options for voice priority over data: always, conditional, and never. The choice depends on the configuration, so this is the first thing to check when troubleshooting. The options are shown in the following:

```
804-isdn(config-if)#isdn voice-priority 5764740 out ?
always          always bump data call
conditional     bump data call only if connection is not lost
off             never bump data call
```

The **conditional** option, which is the default, means that the data call will be disconnected only if the network connection can be guaranteed; that is, only if there are two data calls up to the same direction.

NOTE Always advise the user to use POTS2 for voice if he/she is using only one phone because BRI1 is the data channel and comes up first. This way, the user can (for example) exchange data and be on a conference call simultaneously.

The next important consideration is how the line is provisioned. If it is provisioned only for data, there is no voice option. If it is provisioned for voice and data, the ring signal is usually provided by the line (the LEC's switch), but it can also be generated by the router. This should be tested or checked.

To test the ring options of the router and determine if there are any hardware issues, it is always good to have the remote user participating in the troubleshooting process. For this particular part, user participation is mandatory to make voice calls out and to hear the different signals. The following are the possible options:

```
804-isdn#test pots 2 ringer ?
<0-2>  Cadence number
804-isdn#test pots 2 disconnect
! Disconnect tone
```

To test the tone capability of the router, the following are the command options:

```
804-isdn#test pots 1 tone ?
  busy           Busy Tone
  call-waiting   Call Waiting Tone
  dial           Dial Tone
  reorder        Reorder Tone
  ringback       Ringback Tone
  silence        Disable Tones or ringer
```

It is important to check if the line is provisioned for additional call offering (ACO). This usually means that, if you have two B channels up, the switch forwards the next call (data or voice) to the router, and the router makes a decision based on the configuration. To check if the ACO is set up on the following example (where the phone numbers are 4088535983 and 4085764741), first enter the following:

```
804-isdn#debug pots csm
804-isdn#debug pots driver
```

Then enter:

```
804-isdn#show debugging
POTS:
  POTS CSM events debugging is on
  POTS DRIVER debugging is on
```

Then, make a voice call from 4088535983 to 4085764741, and monitor the output from the router (see Example 12-43).

Example 12-43 *The Output of CSM Events and POTS Driver Debugging*

```
804-isdn#
*Mar 22 20:41:54.525: EVENT_FROM_ISDN:dchan_idb=0x27E6F38, call_id=0x68, ces=0x2
   bchan=0x0, event=0x1, cause=0x0
*Mar 22 20:41:54.525: CSM_GET_CALL_INFO_FOR_DN:forward-to-unused-port disabled
   - check the config
! This by default and it is correct
- BY DEFAULTT
*Mar 22 20:41:54.529: CSM_GET_CALL_INFO_FOR_DN:New call forwarded to port 2
! Reporting correct because calling the second number.
! The dial-peer 1 is set up, otherwise the call will go to the first channel
*Mar 22 20:41:54.529: CSM_PROC_IDLE: CSM_EVENT_ISDN_CALL, call id = 0x68,
   port = 2
! Calling the second LDN - check the dial peers
*Mar 22 20:41:54.529: Calling Number:'4088535983'  Called number:'5764741'
! The numbers are correct, so Q931 provides caller ID and called party's ID
*Mar 22 20:41:54.529: POTS DRIVER port=2 activate ringer: cadence=0
   callerId=4088535983
*Mar 22 20:41:54.533: POTS DRIVER port=2 state=Idle drv_event=RING_EVENT
*Mar 22 20:41:54.533: POTS DRIVER port=2 enter_ringing
*Mar 22 20:41:54.573: POTS DRIVER port=2 CallerId Strg=032220414088535983G PCM
   len=129F
*Mar 22 20:41:54.573: POTS DRIVER port=2 cmd=19
*Mar 22 20:41:56.573: POTS DRIVER port=2 cmd=1A
*Mar 22 20:41:57.073: POTS DRIVER port=2 cmd=1B
*Mar 22 20:41:57.073: POTS DRIVER port=2 ts connect: 3 0
*Mar 22 20:42:00.573: POTS DRIVER port=2 cmd=19
*Mar 22 20:42:02.573: POTS DRIVER port=2 cmd=1A
*Mar 22 20:42:06.573: POTS DRIVER port=2 cmd=19
*Mar 22 20:42:07.769: EVENT_FROM_ISDN:dchan_idb=0x27E6F38, call_id=0x68, ces=0x2
   bchan=0xFFFFFFFF, event=0x0, cause=0x10
! The caller is picking the phone
*Mar 22 20:42:07.769: CSM_PROC_RINGING: CSM_EVENT_ISDN_DISCONNECTED,
   call id = 0x68, port = 2
! The caller disconnects
*Mar 22 20:42:07.769: POTS DRIVER port=2 activate disconnect
*Mar 22 20:42:07.773: POTS DRIVER port=2 state=Ringing drv_event=DISCONNECT_EVENT
*Mar 22 20:42:07.773: POTS DRIVER port=2 cmd=1A
*Mar 22 20:42:07.773: POTS DRIVER port=2 enter_idle
*Mar 22 20:42:07.773: POTS DRIVER port=2 ts connect: 0 0
*Mar 22 20:42:07.777: POTS DRIVER port=2 cmd=1B
*Mar 22 20:42:07.777: POTS DRIVER port=2 activate tone=SILENCE_TONE
*Mar 22 20:42:07.777: POTS DRIVER port=2 state=Idle drv_event=TONE_EVENT
*Mar 22 20:42:07.777: POTS DRIVER port=2 activate tone=SILENCE_TONE
*Mar 22 20:42:07.781: POTS DRIVER port=2 state=Idle drv_event=TONE_EVENT
```

The test proves the voice calls hit the router, if BRI2 is idle. To check if the ACO is set up, you need to bring the second channel up and test it again.

The set of voice features of ISDN can be expanded. The important point here is to have a clear understanding about how the voice features, priorities, and services are provisioned and configured. The troubleshooting needs to occur based on the expected feature performance of the ISDN service.

End Notes

[1] Cisco Press. *Network Design and Case Studies (CCIE Fundamentals)*, Second Edition. Cisco Press, 2000.

Summary

This chapter illustrated the layer-by-layer troubleshooting techniques for ISDN. The main focus is to the remote user and the BRI. The systematic approach in this chapter enables you to enhance your knowledge about troubleshooting the most common ISDN solutions and includes information on the following:

- D channel Layer 1, Layer 2, and Layer 3 troubleshooting.

- The PPP protocol troubleshooting in its ISDN implementation. PPP phases and protocols, including PPP callback MLP and MMP protocols and their troubleshooting.

- Troubleshooting techniques for telephone interfaces.

Review Questions

Answers to the review questions can be found in Appendix A, "Answers to Review Questions."

1 What is the command to see the status of the D channel of the IOS-based ISDN router? In which mode of the IOS router can you type the command?

2 If you want to see what IP address has triggered the last call in Cisco 77x router, what command should you type?

3 What do you look for in the output of the IOS command Router#**sh isdn status** to be sure if the physical layer in BRI is functional?

4 What IOS command enables you to distinguish between internal and external ISDN issues?

5 If you want to debug Layer 2 of ISDN, what is the first IOS command you have to type?

6 Under normal circumstances, what messages should you *not* see from the output of Router#**debug isdn q921**?

7 What are you looking for in the output of the IOS command Router#**sh isdn status** to be sure if Layer 2 is functional?

8 In the output from the command Router#**debug isdn q921**, what does TX ->...ai = 127 mean?

9 If you want to debug Layer 3 of ISDN, what is the first IOS command you have to type?

10 What is the bearer capability in Q931 messages for 64 kbps data, 56 kbps data, and voice calls?

11 What is the name of the message indicating that the LCP negotiation is successful?

12 What is the recommended IOS command to troubleshoot the dialer traffic when the router makes outgoing data calls?

13 How many lines of PPP CHAP negotiation indicating success can you see in the output of #**debug ppp authentication**?

14 If you receive config nack during the PPP authentication negotiation, what does it mean?

15 When testing the voice features, what are the two recommended IOS commands you can use?

CHAPTER 13

Troubleshooting Scenarios for ISDN BRI

This chapter provides more specific examples of some of the most common problems when troubleshooting the remote user ISDN BRI connections. This chapter includes the following:

- The common recommendations for the practical troubleshooting of ISDN BRI
- Scenario 1: New Install Problems
- Scenario 2: Dial-Out Problems
- Scenario 3: ISDN Performance Problems
- Scenario 4: End-to-End Communication Problems
- Scenario 5: Windows 2000 DDR Issue

These real-life scenarios illustrate the troubleshooting techniques covered in Chapter 12, "ISDN BRI Troubleshooting."

Recommendations for Practical Troubleshooting of ISDN Remote Services

It is important to understand that most troubleshooting processes occur remotely. The following sections are written with this premise in mind: You are located somewhere else, possibly thousands of miles from the remote user's location. The core router is located somewhere on your campus, or possibly both the core and the end user's router are miles away from you.

NOTE | Make sure that you understand the environment in which you are troubleshooting because troubleshooting is an environment-dependant activity.

After you establish the environment with which you are dealing, you need to set up your own environment. This section focuses on how you should set up your troubleshooting process. Of course, the real world can offer you much less, but any part of these recommendations can help you pinpoint the problem faster. These recommendations include the following:

- Using #**show isdn status** to view service layers
- Preconfiguring the routers on both ends
- Accessing the remote user's router

Using #show isdn status to View Service Layers

If the remote user's ISDN is not functioning correctly, you cannot telnet to the router. Your best chance is to work with the remote user. Take time to help the user (if necessary) by teaching him or her how to use the telnet session or the console connection to the router.

One of the most useful IOS commands for ISDN troubleshooting is **show isdn status,** which provides a snapshot of all layers of the service. Example 13-1 shows an ISDN line in the activation stage. The first layer of this IOS-based router is active, but the second layer negotiation is still in progress.

Example 13-1   *Snapshot of ISDN BRI Layers*

```
804-isdn#show isdn status
Global ISDN Switchtype = basic-5ess
ISDN BRI0 interface
        dsl 0, interface ISDN Switchtype = basic-ni
    Layer 1 Status:
        ACTIVE
    Layer 2 Status:
        TEI = 96, Ces = 1, SAPI = 0, State = TEI_ASSIGNED
        TEI = 105, Ces = 2, SAPI = 0, State = TEI_ASSIGNED
        TEI 96, ces = 1, state = 3(await establishment)
            spid1 configured, spid1 sent, spid1 valid
            Endpoint ID Info: epsf = 0, usid = 0, tid = 1
        TEI 105, ces = 2, state = 1(terminal down)
            spid2 configured, spid2 sent, spid2 valid
            Endpoint ID Info: epsf = 0, usid = 1, tid = 1
    Layer 3 Status:
        0 Active Layer 3 Call(s)
    Active dsl 0 CCBs = 0
    The Free Channel Mask:  0x80000003
    Total Allocated ISDN CCBs = 0
804-isdn#
```

NOTE   The dynamics of ISDN events can be seen using the powerful command 804-isdn#**debug isdn events [interface bri 0]**. This command requires a detailed understanding of the messages on the screen and generates significant output. If you feel confident enough, use it; but when you use it on the core router, limit the duration to less than ten minutes and turn it off.

The #**show isdn status** output in Example 13-2 is of a properly functioning BRI circuit. In Example 13-2, Layer 1 is active and Layer 2 is in a MULTIPLE_FRAME_ESTABLISHED state. The terminal endpoint identifiers (TEIs) are successfully negotiated, and the ISDN Layer 3 is ready to make or receive calls.

Example 13-2   *All Layers of ISDN Are Active*

```
804-isdn#show isdn status
Global ISDN Switchtype = basic-5ess
ISDN BRI0 interface
        dsl 0, interface ISDN Switchtype = basic-ni
    Layer 1 Status:
        ACTIVE
    Layer 2 Status:
        TEI = 96, Ces = 1, SAPI = 0, State = MULTIPLE_FRAME_ESTABLISHED
        TEI = 105, Ces = 2, SAPI = 0, State = MULTIPLE_FRAME_ESTABLISHED
        TEI 96, ces = 1, state = 5(init)
            spid1 configured, spid1 sent, spid1 valid
            Endpoint ID Info: epsf = 0, usid = 0, tid = 1
        TEI 105, ces = 2, state = 5(init)
            spid2 configured, spid2 sent, spid2 valid
            Endpoint ID Info: epsf = 0, usid = 1, tid = 1
    Layer 3 Status:
        0 Active Layer 3 Call(s)
    Active dsl 0 CCBs = 0
    The Free Channel Mask:  0x80000003
    Total Allocated ISDN CCBs = 0
804-isdn#
```

This is an important command. You must understand each line of this output. Table 13-1 provides a detailed description of the output.

Table 13-1   *Output from the #**show isdn status** Command*

Line of the Output	Description
Global ISDN Switchtype	
The current ISDN Switchtype = basic-5ess	Basic-5ess is the switch-type, configured in the general configuration of the router.
ISDN BRI0 interface dsl 0, interface ISDN Switchtype = basic-ni	Basic-NI1 (National) is configured under interface BRI0. This configuration takes precedence over the previous line. If there are more BRI interfaces without a specific switch-type configuration, they will accept the Basic-5ess settings. See Chapter 10, "ISDN Design Solutions."

continues

Table 13-1   *Output from the #***show isdn status** *Command (Continued)*

Line of the Output	Description
Layer 1 status	
ACTIVE	Layer 1 Status: Verifies the physical layer connectivity with the LEC's ISDN switch. This can be ACTIVE or DEACTIVATED. See Chapters 11 and 12 for more information.
Layer 2 Status	
TEI = 96, Ces = 1, SAPI = 0, State = MULTIPLE_FRAME_ESTABLISHED TEI = 105, Ces = 2, SAPI = 0, State = MULTIPLE_FRAME_ESTABLISHED	Status of ISDN Layer 2 with the TEI number and multiframe state. If the switch uses dynamic assignments, the valid TEI numbers are from 64 to 124. If they are static assignments, the numbers are from 1 to 63. TEI=127 stands for broadcast-request. The most common Layer 2 states are MULTIPLE_FRAME_ESTABLISHED and TEI_ASSIGNED. A state=MULTIPLE_FRAME_ESTABLISHED indicates that there is data-link connectivity to the LEC's ISDN switch. You should see this state under normal operation. Any other state indicates a problem on the circuit. A Layer 2 Status of down is indicated by Layer 2 NOT Activated. See Chapter 12 for more information.
Spid Status	
TEI 96, ces = 1, state = 8(established) TEI 106, ces=2, state = 5(init)	TEI number and state. The most common state values are State = 1(terminal down) State = 3(await establishment) State = 5(init) State = 6(not initialized) State = 8(established) Only states 8 and 5 indicate a working BRI circuit. The other states mean the circuit is not properly established.

Table 13-1   *Output from the #**show isdn status** Command (Continued)*

Line of the Output	Description
spid(1 or 2) configured, spid(1 or 2) sent, spid(1 or 2) valid , no LDN	spid(1 or 2) configuration information for a working BRI. The valid combination is shown on the left column and other possible combinations are
	spid(1 or 2) configured, no LDN, spid1 sent, spid1 valid
	spid(1 or 2) NOT configured, spid1 NOT sent, spid1 NOT valid
	spid(1 or 2) configured, spid1 NOT sent, spid1 NOT valid
	spid(1 or 2) configured, spid1 sent, spid1 NOT valid
	The last three states indicate that either the spid was not configured or that it is incorrect.
	No LDN means that the associated LDN(1 or 2) is not configured.
Endpoint ID Info: epsf = 0, usid = 1, tid = 1 Endpoint ID Info: epsf = 0, usid = 3, tid = 1	Endpoint identifier information can be used by the router to decide which channel will answer the call. The message ENDPOINT ID in the isdn q931 format is associated with the usid and tid.
usid	User Service Identifier.
tid	Terminal Identifier.
Layer 3 Status	
2 Active Layer 3 Call(s)	Number of active calls.
CCB:callid=103, sapi=0, ces=1, B-chan=1, calltype=DATA CCB:callid=819B, sapi=0, ces=2, B-chan=2, calltype=DATA	Information about the active calls. The first line is incoming calls to the user's router, and the second line is outgoing calls. For a connected call, it displays the caller ID information, call reference, and the B channel it is occupying.
	The first call's **callid** is a smaller number than the second one. The call type can be DATA or VOICE. Any other type, such as INTERNAL, identifies a problem with the LEC.
Activated dsl 0 CCBs = 2	Number of Digital Signal Link (dsl) activated.
	Number of Call Control Blocks (CCB) in use.
Total Allocated ISDN CCBs = 2	Number of ISDN CCBs that are allocated.

In the enterprise environment—where usually you have deployed limited types of Cisco ISDN routers—you might have more options available, such as ISDN lines and Cisco routers configured for test purposes. The following sections give you details on these.

Preconfiguring the Routers on Both Ends

The first thing you must consider is the router that's immediately available to you. It's a good idea to use any Cisco ISDN router, such as Cisco 776, Cisco 804, Cisco 1604, and so on, to perform initial testing of the remote user's router. If you are a network administrator who is responsible for a relatively big ISDN environment, it's a good idea to have an ISDN line at your desk.

For example, the Cisco 77x router at your desk with a simple configuration can help you perform initial troubleshooting. The following are recommended configuration lines:

```
set system ENS
set ppp secret client
secret
secret
set ppp secret host
secret
secret
set ppp auth out none
```

NOTE   The system name can be anything as long as the system name on both ends (the test side and the remote user side) is the same.

If the remote user has a 77x router, the following configuration needs to be applied to the user's router to allow remote access for troubleshooting:

```
set user ENS
set ppp client ENS
set bridging on
set ppp authentication outgoing chap
set ppp secret client
secret
secret
set ppp secret host
secret
secret
cd
set active ENS
```

NOTE   One possible option is to turn off the authentication on both ends of the link to rule it out as a problem.

The benefit of this configuration is that, if the remote user's router includes this user configuration, you can call the LDN using the 77x router at your desk. The user's router simply prompts you for a password.

NOTE   Remember that the Cisco 77x series router has only one level of password authentication. This is unlike IOS routers, which have more sophisticated password systems, such as vty authentication option, enable password, and secrets.

To verify that the user profile exists and it is active on both sides, enter the **show user** command on both routers, as shown in Example 13-3.

Example 13-3   **show user** *Output*

```
ENS> show user
User                     State       Connection
-----------------------------------------------
LAN                      Active      LAN
Internal                 Active      INTERNAL
Standard                 Active      1
gateway                  Active      2
ENS                      Active      3
ENS>
```

NOTE   The remote user's router must be powered up for testing purposes. Even when trouble-shooting is performed by the LEC, the technician cannot run any tests without the powered-up NT1. If the router has a built-in NT1, the router must be powered on; if not, the power supply for NT1 must be turned on. Most of the line tests by the local providers require looping back the NT1.

Accessing the Remote User's Router

With your router and the user's router setup, you can now make a manual call to the remote user's router from your test router, which will result in a number of typical situations:

- The circuit is not available, and the message from your test router is usually "Cause 34 No Circuit/Channel Available." Typically, after receiving this message, there's nothing to troubleshoot. Either the circuit is disconnected, the service is completely shut down, or you called a non-ISDN number:

```
ENS> call 1 14087785444
02/04/1995 20:54:45  L05  0  14087785444  Outgoing Call Initiated
ENS> ENS> 02/04/1995 20:54:46  L12  1            Disconnected Remotely
Cause 34  No Circuit/Channel Available
ENS> 02/04/1995 20:54:46  L27  1                 Disconnected
ENS>
```

Could this condition be caused by a misconfiguration? It would be prudent to explore this possibility first, and double-check it with the remote user, the switch type, SPIDs, and LDNs.

If everything is okay, it's a good idea to open a trouble ticket with the local provider at this point and double-check how the service is provisioned.

- If you are calling a non-ISDN number, the typical response will be bearer capability error, as shown in the following:

```
ENS> call 1 14083691136
02/04/1995 21:00:21  L05  0  14083691136  Outgoing Call Initiated
ENS> ENS> 02/04/1995 21:00:22  L12  1                Disconnected Remotely
Cause 65  Bearer Capability Error
ENS> 02/04/1995 21:00:22  L27  1                Disconnected
ENS>
```

- The call is rejected. When the channel is already up, you cannot make a call to the remote user's router (unless call waiting is configured on the LEC side). You will receive a Receiver Busy or Call Rejected message. The Call Rejected message is shown here:

```
ENS> call 1 14085764740
02/04/1995 21:04:34  L05  0  14085764740  Outgoing Call Initiated
ENS> ENS> 02/04/1995 21:04:35  L11  1  4085764740  Call Requested
ENS> 02/04/1995 21:04:35  L09  1                Call Rejected
Cause 17  Receiver Busy
ENS> 02/04/1995 21:04:35  L12  1                Disconnected Remotely
Cause 17  Receiver Busy
ENS> 02/04/1995 21:04:35  L27  1                Disconnected
```

For other call rejection messages, see Table 12-1 in Chapter 12.

- The channel that you are calling is idle, so you can make a call. An idle channel and an initiated call is shown here:

```
ENS> call 1 14086175555
01/05/1995 21:34:49  L05  0  14086174271  Outgoing Call Initiated
ENS> ENS> 01/05/1995 21:34:50  L08  1  14086174271  Call Connected
ENS> 01/05/1995 21:34:51  Connection 2 Add     Link 1 Channel 1
! At this point you have a connection
ENS> login remote
ENS> Enter Password:
```

After this point, you are in the remote user's router. If the provided password is correct, you see the remote user's router prompt:

```
776-isdn>
```

Now you have direct access to the user's router without needing the end user to assist you with troubleshooting.

Preliminary Test of Remote IOS-Based ISDN Router with Test 776 Router

If the user's router is an IOS-based ISDN router and you are calling from a 77x router, you can still make a call, but the IOS will not prompt you (by default). To gain access to an IOS router, you usually use a Telnet or Secure Shell (SSH) session. The problem is: How do you use Telnet if the remote user's router cannot pass data? This is the benefit of using a 77x to call an 804 router. If the call is successful, you see the following message:

```
ENS> call 1 14087312598
01/01/1995 00:07:36  L05  0  14087312598  Outgoing Call Initiated
ENS> ENS> 01/01/1995 00:07:37  L08  1  14087312598  Call Connected
ENS> 01/01/1995 00:07:37  L60  1                Password Not Found
ENS> 01/01/1995 00:07:37  L12  1                Disconnected Remotely
Cause 16  Normal Disconnect
```

```
ENS> 01/01/1995 00:07:37  L27  1                    Disconnected
ENS>
```

Your 776 router makes a call to 1 408 731-2598, which is configured in Cisco IOS 804 router. If remote users see the channel1 light, and both the TxD and RxD lights blink, the status of the ISDN service is okay (see the **show isdn status** command later). But the connection drops with the message Password Not Found, which gives you an indication of what the problem is. First of all, this is the expected message and the connection is dropping at the authentication phase of PPP protocol because you are calling from the test router, but not from the core router. This narrows down the probable causes of the problem. Recall from the explanations in Chapter 12 that to reach the PPP authentication phase, the ISDN service goes through all three layers of the D channel, through the LCP stage of PPP, and, just after that, it reaches the authentication phase. At this point, all you have to do is to concentrate on possible PAP/CHAP issues on both the remote user's and core routers.

Preliminary Test of Remote 77x Router with Test IOS-Based ISDN Router

How do you call from an IOS-based router to a 77x router? Example 13-4 shows you how this works. Your test router ENS-isdn is calling 1 831 430-0444 by using your first channel. You are debugging the ppp negotiation with the command #**debug ppp negotiation**.

Example 13-4   *The Output of Calling a 77x Router from an IOS-Based Router*

```
ENS-isdn#isdn call interface bri0:1 18314300444
*Mar  7 02:28:31.895: BR0:1 PPP: Phase is TERMINATING
*Mar  7 02:28:31.899: BR0:1 LCP: O TERMREQ [Open] id 107 len 4
*Mar  7 02:28:31.899: Vi1 CDPCP: State is Closed
*Mar  7 02:28:31.903: Vi1 IPCP: State is Closed
*Mar  7 02:28:31.907: %LINK-3-UPDOWN: Interface Virtual-Access1,
    changed state  to down
*Mar  7 02:28:31.907: Vi1 PPP: Phase is TERMINATING
*Mar  7 02:28:31.911: Vi1 LCP: State is Closed
*Mar  7 02:28:31.911: Vi1 PPP: Phase is DOWN
*Mar  7 02:28:31.911: Di1 IPCP: Remove route to 172.30.253.254
*Mar  7 02:28:32.115: BR0:1 LCP: I TERMACK [TERMsent] id 107 len 4
*Mar  7 02:28:32.115: BR0:1 LCP: State is Closed
*Mar  7 02:28:32.119: BR0:1 PPP: Phase is DOWN
*Mar  7 02:28:32.119: BR0:1 PPP: Phase is ESTABLISHING, Passive Open
*Mar  7 02:28:32.119: BR0:1 LCP: State is Listen
*Mar  7 02:28:32.127: %ISDN-6-DISCONNECT: Interface BRI0:1  disconnected from
   18007735555 access-gw1, call lasted 61 seconds
*Mar  7 02:28:32.319: %LINK-3-UPDOWN: Interface BRI0:1, changed state to down
*Mar  7 02:28:32.331: BR0:1 LCP: State is Closed
*Mar  7 02:28:32.331: BR0:1 PPP: Phase is DOWN8314300444
*Mar  7 02:28:32.895: %LINEPROTO-5-UPDOWN: Line protocol on Interface BRI0:1,
    changed state to down
*Mar  7 02:28:32.907: %LINEPROTO-5-UPDOWN: Line protocol on Interface
   Virtual-Access1, changed state to down
*Mar  7 02:28:35.883: %LINK-3-UPDOWN: Interface BRI0:1, changed state to up
```

continues

Example 13-4 *The Output of Calling a 77x Router from an IOS-Based Router (Continued)*

```
*Mar  7 02:28:35.899: BR0:1 PPP: Treating connection as a callout
*Mar  7 02:28:35.899: BR0:1 PPP: Phase is ESTABLISHING, Active Open
*Mar  7 02:28:35.903: BR0:1 LCP: O CONFREQ [Closed] id 108 len 35
*Mar  7 02:28:35.903: BR0:1 LCP:    AuthProto CHAP (0x0305C22305)
*Mar  7 02:28:35.907: BR0:1 LCP:    MagicNumber 0xD030C260 (0x0506D030C260)
*Mar  7 02:28:35.907: BR0:1 LCP:    MRRU 1524 (0x110405F4)
*Mar  7 02:28:35.907: BR0:1 LCP:    EndpointDisc 1 Local
    (0x131001706E6564656C74632D6973646E)
*Mar  7 02:28:37.539: BR0:1 LCP: I CONFREQ [REQsent] id 89 len 31
*Mar  7 02:28:37.543: BR0:1 LCP:    AuthProto CHAP (0x0305C22305)
*Mar  7 02:28:37.543: BR0:1 LCP:    MagicNumber 0xB13FEF1B (0x0506B13FEF1B)
*Mar  7 02:28:37.543: BR0:1 LCP:    MRRU 1524 (0x110405F4)
*Mar  7 02:28:37.547: BR0:1 LCP:    EndpointDisc 1 Local
    (0x130C01627564692D6973646E)
*Mar  7 02:28:37.551: BR0:1 LCP: O CONFACK [REQsent] id 89 len 31
*Mar  7 02:28:37.551: BR0:1 LCP:    AuthProto CHAP (0x0305C22305)
*Mar  7 02:28:37.551: BR0:1 LCP:    MagicNumber 0xB13FEF1B (0x0506B13FEF1B)
*Mar  7 02:28:37.555: BR0:1 LCP:    MRRU 1524 (0x110405F4)
*Mar  7 02:28:37.555: BR0:1 LCP:    EndpointDisc 1 Local
    (0x130C01627564692D6973646E)
*Mar  7 02:28:37.903: BR0:1 LCP: TIMEout: State ACKsent
*Mar  7 02:28:37.903: BR0:1 LCP: O CONFREQ [ACKsent] id 109 len 35
*Mar  7 02:28:37.903: BR0:1 LCP:    AuthProto CHAP (0x0305C22305)
*Mar  7 02:28:37.907: BR0:1 LCP:    MagicNumber 0xD030C260 (0x0506D030C260)
*Mar  7 02:28:37.907: BR0:1 LCP:    MRRU 1524 (0x110405F4)
*Mar  7 02:28:37.907: BR0:1 LCP:    EndpointDisc 1 Local
    (0x131001706E6564656C74632D6973646E)
*Mar  7 02:28:37.947: BR0:1 LCP: I CONFACK [ACKsent] id 109 len 35
*Mar  7 02:28:37.947: BR0:1 LCP:    AuthProto CHAP (0x0305C22305)
*Mar  7 02:28:37.947: BR0:1 LCP:    MagicNumber 0xD030C260 (0x0506D030C260)
*Mar  7 02:28:37.951: BR0:1 LCP:    MRRU 1524 (0x110405F4)
*Mar  7 02:28:37.951: BR0:1 LCP:    EndpointDisc 1 Local
    (0x131001706E6564656C74632D6973646E)
*Mar  7 02:28:37.955: BR0:1 LCP: State is Open
*Mar  7 02:28:37.955: BR0:1 PPP: Phase is AUTHENTICATING, by both
*Mar  7 02:28:37.955: BR0:1 CHAP: O CHALLENGE id 176 len 34 from "ENS-isdn"
*Mar  7 02:28:37.959: BR0:1 CHAP: I CHALLENGE id 87 len 30 from "804-isdn"
*Mar  7 02:28:37.963: BR0:1 CHAP: Username 804-isdn not found
! Username is not found
*Mar  7 02:28:37.963: BR0:1 CHAP: Unable to authenticate for peer
! Unable to authenticate
*Mar  7 02:28:37.963: BR0:1 PPP: Phase is TERMINATING
*Mar  7 02:28:37.967: BR0:1 LCP: O TERMREQ [Open] id 110 len 4
*Mar  7 02:28:37.995: BR0:1 LCP: I TERMACK [TERMsent] id 110 len 4
*Mar  7 02:28:37.995: BR0:1 LCP: State is Closed
*Mar  7 02:28:37.995: BR0:1 PPP: Phase is DOWN
*Mar  7 02:28:37.995: BR0:1 PPP: Phase is ESTABLISHING, Passive Open
*Mar  7 02:28:37.999: BR0:1 LCP: State is Listen
*Mar  7 02:28:38.003: %ISDN-6-DISCONNECT: Interface BRI0:1  disconnected
    from 18314300475 804-isdn, call lasted 2 seconds
*Mar  7 02:28:38.159: %LINK-3-UPDOWN: Interface BRI0:1, changed state to down
*Mar  7 02:28:38.167: BR0:1 LCP: State is Closed
*Mar  7 02:28:38.167: BR0:1 PPP: Phase is DOWN
ENS-isdn#
```

The procedure is successful until the authentication phase (see Chapter 12 for more information on the authentication phase), at which point the call is dropped in two seconds. This shows that the ISDN layers are okay, PPP is configured, LCP is okay, CHAP is the chosen authentication option, and CHAP is configured two ways. From this point, you can focus on authentication, NCP protocols, and routing.

NOTE It is important to understand that, in this example, username failed because, by default, IOS is trying to use the host name for the CHAP username.

With theses initial recommendations, you are now ready to tackle some of the problems you might face. The following scenarios walk you through typical situations that you might encounter when troubleshooting ISDN remote services.

Scenario 1: New Install Problems

New install problems are related to the way a line is provisioned, and to the way the service is designed and installed. The following are typical new install issues:

- The local loop is installed and the LEC's technician has tested the line, has deemed it as okay, but there's still no ISDN service.

- The service is installed and the user can make local voice calls, but the user cannot connect to the company's core router.

- The user can make calls and can connect one of the channels, but not both channels.

- The user cannot accept voice calls and cannot make voice calls when two channels are making data calls.

There are, of course, many other types of issues. The important thing to recognize is that the provisioning process is critical for new ISDN service. Even if the initial order for the ISDN install is issued correctly and the router is configured accordingly, sometimes a problem can take a long time to correct. An error in the provisioning process can lead to a redesign of the service, and the LEC usually considers a redesign as a new install with new charges and long delays.

NOTE Pay particularly close attention to the provisioning process. Before troubleshooting new install problems, make sure that you know the specifics of the provisioned service. The requested service might be in one of the following stages: requested, ordered, operational, cancelled, deactivated, or pending deactivation. Only spend time troubleshooting if the LEC shows the status as operational, and the requested type of service matches what was provided. For more about provisioning, see Chapter 1, "Remote Access Overview."

NOTE	It is important to note that the type of switch you are connected to is not necessarily the switch type you set in IOS. The technician might know for a fact that the switch is a 5ESS, but it is possible to be provisioned for NI-1. You will need to set up your router likewise. For the U.S., the NI-1 switch setting is by far the most common setting regardless of if the switch is DMS, 5ESS, and so on.

The router is configured based on the provisioning information provided by the LEC. Supposing that the router configuration is correct, Table 13-2 provides some typical new install problems and their respective solutions.

Table 13-2   *Typical New Install Problem Descriptions and Their Solutions*

Problem	Solution
The local loop is installed, the line tested okay, but there is no voice and no data.	The LEC's provisioning/service department needs to turn the service on in the central office (CO) and remove any restrictions from the switch.
The local loop is installed and tested okay, and there is voice, but no data.	Check with the LEC to see if the line is provisioned for VOICE and DATA. Also, because of late payments, the service can be temporarily disabled, which means that the LEC or LD carrier changed the switch settings from "operational" to "maintenance" or "blocked," expecting the end user to contact them.
The local loop is installed and tested okay, and the user can connect to the core router, but the voice service is not available.	Check with the LEC to see if the line is provisioned for VOICE and DATA. Check the switch-type to determine if it supports VOICE. For some providers, the basic service is DATA; VOICE is considered "best effort."
The user can make voice and local data calls, but the user cannot connect to the core router.	Ask the user to make a long-distance voice call. If the long-distance service is not set up, the user will hear either a different LD carrier greeting or a message that states the LD calls are blocked.
How do you check to see if the user's LD service is set up correctly?	Using Sprint LD as an example, an automatic recording system is used. If you make an VOICE call to 1 700 555-4141 and Sprint is the LD carrier, you will hear, "Welcome to Sprint Long-Distance, 54110." The last five digits are called trailing number, which shows the number of the recorder and where the call hits the Sprint network.
The voice service is okay on both channels, but the data is okay only on the first channel.	If the configuration is set up correctly for the type of service (see Scenario 2), the issue is related to the LEC. The switch is not set up to allow two data calls simultaneously.

Table 13-2 *Typical New Install Problem Descriptions and Their Solutions (Continued)*

Problem	Solution
The first channel is okay for data and voice, but when the router brings the second channel up, the user loses the data connection.	There are two possible solutions to this problem: 1. It is most likely that the first channel is picked up by one LD carrier and the second channel is picked up by another carrier by mistake. Sometimes this works, and sometimes it doesn't. The message from the 776 router indicates that there's no route to the destination. The LEC must correct the information on the ISDN switch. For example, 333 indicates that the LD portion is picked up by Sprint. 2. The switch does not allow two data calls simultaneously, which the LEC must correct.
The user has data service, but every incoming voice call hits the first channel.	The dial-peer portion of the configuration probably does not exist, or it is misconfigured in the configuration.
The data service is okay, but the voice portion works only for outgoing calls.	Check to see if the configuration line **isdn incoming-voice modem** exists under the BRI0 interface.
The data and voice portions are okay, but when the router brings both channels up, no incoming calls are available, regardless of the configuration.	The issue is related to the ISDN switch that rejects every other call if two calls are already in progress. The LEC must correct this.
The data and voice portions are okay, but when the first channel is up and someone places a voice call to the first channel of the router, it rings busy.	Check for the command **no forward-to-unused-port** in the dial-peer config blocks. If dial-peers are available in the config, by default, the call should go to the next available channel. Also, this can be related to the voice priority issue rather than an available channel issue. Check the way the voice priority is set up in your configuration.
The data and voice portions are okay, but when both channels are up for data and someone places a voice call to the router, it rings busy.	This can be the correct reaction of the router. If the switch allows every other call to hit the router, the router makes a decision based on the configuration. Check the way the voice priority is set up in your configuration.
The data and voice portions are okay, but there is no ring signal.	The first thing to check is who is generating the signal—the switch or the router. Set the configuration accordingly. If this does not help, the CPE is probably malfunctioning; you might consider getting another one.

These problems and solutions cover the vast majority of the cases that you might encounter for the new-installs category. The next scenario examines dial-out problems.

Scenario 2: Dial-Out Problems

The very first thing the router should be able to do is make outgoing calls and accept incoming ones. A variety of complexities are related to dial functions, but keep in mind that, regardless of first layer functions, a call requires all three layers to be set up correctly.

Begin dial issue troubleshooting with the **show isdn active** command. This command shows the active outgoing calls, called party number, and called remote site name, as displayed in Example 13-5.

Example 13-5   **show isdn active** *Output*

```
804-isdn#show isdn active
                          ISDN ACTIVE CALLS
--------------------------------------------------------------------------
Call   Calling Called     Remote     Seconds Seconds  Seconds  Charges
Type   Number  Number     Name       Used    Left     Idle     Units/Currency
--------------------------------------------------------------------------
Out            +8007735555 gateway   64       -        -        0
Out            +8007735555 gatewaay  31       -        -        0
804-isdn#
```

If you don't see the router calling out, you should see if the remote user router has ever made calls out. For this and other information, use IOS command **show dialer**. Example 13-6 shows the output for this command.

Example 13-6   *Output for the* **show dialer** *Command*

```
804-isdn#show dialer
BRI0 - dialer type = ISDN
Rotary group 1, priority = 0
0 incoming call(s) have been screened.
0 incoming call(s) rejected for callback.
BRI0:1 - dialer type = ISDN
Idle timer (60 secs), Fast idle timer (20 secs)
Wait for carrier (30 secs), Re-enable (15 secs)
Dialer state is multilink member
Connected to 18007735555 (access-gw1)
BRI0:2 - dialer type = ISDN
Idle timer (60 secs), Fast idle timer (20 secs)
Wait for carrier (30 secs), Re-enable (15 secs)
Dialer state is idle
Di1 - dialer type = IN-BAND SYNC NO-PARITY
Load threshold for dialing additional calls is 20
Idle timer (60 secs), Fast idle timer (20 secs)
Wait for carrier (30 secs), Re-enable (15 secs)
Number of active calls = 1
Dial String      Successes    Failures    Last DNIS   Last status
18007735555#             1         164     03:57:41         failed
18007735555             95         165     00:11:05     successful
```

A detailed description of the command line's output is shown in Table 13-3.

Table 13-3 *Description of the Output from the* **show dialer** *Command*

Output	Description
BRI0 - dialer type = ISDN	D channel.
Rotary group 1, priority = 0	Dialer 1 is a member of rotary group 1.
0 incoming call(s) have been screened.	There is no setting in the config for call screening.
0 incoming call(s) rejected for callback.	There is no setting in the configuration for callback.
BRI0:1 - dialer type = ISDN Dialer state is multilink member	BRI1 and BRI2 are defined as a member of MP group.
Di1 - dialer type = IN-BAND SYNC NO-PARITY Load threshold for dialing additional calls is 20	Dialer 1 performs in-band dialing. The threshold for BRI2 is set to 20/255 x bandwidth, which for ISDN is 128 kbps.
Idle timer (60 secs)	The dialer is idle before disconnecting the call. The command line is 804-isdn(config-if)#**dialer idle-timeout [0-2147483]**.
Fast idle timer (20 secs)	The fast-idle timer is activated if there is another packet waiting for a different next hop address. The default is 20 seconds and the command is pnedeltc-isdn(config-if)#**dialer fast-idle [1-2147483]**.
Wait for carrier (30 secs)	Wait for carrier before making a call. pnedeltc-isdn(config-if)#**dialer wait-for-carrier-time [1-2147483]**
Re-enable (15 secs)	Wait interval before redialing. 804-isdn(config-if)#**dialer redial interval [5-2147483]**
Number of active calls = 2	Number of active calls at the moment.
Dial String Successes Failures Last DNIS Last status 18007735048# 1 164 03:57:41 failed 18007735048 95 165 00:11:05 successful	Dialer statistics for every dialer map: String to dial (# indicates secondary) Number of successful calls Number of failures Time from the last call Whether the last call was a failure or success

This is not the only command that can provide information on dial-out issues. The following commands are also recommended:

```
804-isdn#debug dialer
804-isdn#debug dialer [events | packets]
804-isdn#show running-config  interface dialer 1
```

The last command enables you to check the configuration of the dialer 1.

The result of the previous commands usually will allow you to define the problem. The Table 13-4 provides a brief overview of well-known dial issues and their possible resolution.

Table 13-4   *Dial Problems, Reasons, and Solutions*

Problem	Reason/Solution
The router does not call out even if you try a manual call out, you don't see any call activity.	This problem can be due to variety of reasons. If the reasons are not obvious, perform the following step-by-step troubleshooting process.
	First, type the following command:
	804-isdn#**show isdn status**
	This checks to see if each layer of ISDN is okay.
	This step eliminates most issues related to media problems, hardware, cables, ports, SPIDs, and switch-types.
	Check to see if the interface is down. A quick check of interfaces to determine if any are administratively down can be done using the following command:
	804-isdn#**show ip interface brief**
	When it is a new install, it's common for interfaces to be down from the very beginning (by default). Use the previous command to ensure that all interfaces are up.
	To bring an interface up, go to the interface configuration mode and enter the following:
	804-isdn(config-if)#**no shutdown**
	When you change SPIDs and LDNs, instead of power-cycling the router to re-obtain new TEIs, you can enter the following:
	804-isdn#**clear interface BRI0**
	Check if the **dialer map (dialer string)** command exists and is not misconfigured.
	Check if the rotary group (dialer pool) is configured correctly.
	Check for a missing **dialer-list** statement.
	Check for a missing or misconfigured access control list.
	Determine if there is a speed-setting mismatch.
	Always configure the router with a secondary dialer map for **speed 56,** or define a class with options 64 and 56.

Table 13-4 *Dial Problems, Reasons, and Solutions (Continued)*

Problem	Reason/Solution
The second B channel does not come up. The second channel comes up too early or too late.	There is a missing or misconfigured dialer load-threshold command. Enter the following: 804-isdn#**show dialer**
Both channels come up together.	Check the configuration of the dialer interface and specifically check if the **dialer load-threshold** *load* [**outbound** | **inbound** | **either**] command exists under the dialer interface. Make sure you know how it is configured. This command enables you to configure bandwidth on demand and bring up the second channel if necessary. Or refer to the configuration command: 804-isdn#**show run** With IOS routers, the *load* is a fraction of 255, multiplied by the bandwidth (128 kbps). In 77x series routers, it is in kbps. So **25** in IOS indicates about 10 percent of configured interface bandwidth, and in 77x, it indicates 25 kbps. If it is configured for **either** (IOS only) or **both** (77x only), the router calculates load based on inbound + outbound. Use **1** if you want two channels to come up simultaneously. For cost-savings purposes, it is recommended to use **100** or **either**.
The line disconnects too slowly. The line disconnects too quickly.	Check **dialer idle-timeout** [*seconds*]. This timer defines the time (in seconds) between two consecutive interesting events. The timer ticks down between these events. When expires, the router is tearing down the call. It is recommended that you use 180 seconds.
Packets wait too long for a different next-hop address.	This occurs when the fast-idle timer is activated. The command does not appear in the config unless it is configured for different values than the default. The default value is 20. It can be seen under the dialer interface. 804-isdn(config-if)#**dialer fast-idle [1-2147483]**
The router waits too long to connect.	This is probably a configuration issue. If there is no specific configuration, the default value is 30. Check the configuration command under the dialer interface: **dialer wait-for-carrier-time [1-2147483]** Define or change the amount of time to wait for a carrier to pick up the call after dialing the dial string.
The router waits too long before redial.	This is probably a configuration issue. If there is no specific configuration, the default value is 15 seconds, which is the average time for the switch to release the previous call. Check the configuration command under the dialer interface: **dialer redial interval [5-2147483]** Define or change the amount of time is seconds for redial interval.

Table 13-4 is not a complete list of all possible issues, but it covers the most common or well-known problems in this category.

NOTE   The bandwidth on demand in ISDN BRI can be configured with one of the most important commands in every dialer configuration:

```
804-isdn(config-if)#dialer load-threshold load [outbound | inbound | either]
```

Every seconds, the router measures the load in the dialer. The measurement interval is, by default, 300 seconds (5 minutes). To calculate the load at full utilization, the transmission rate of the particular channel is multiplied by the load interval. In general, the rate (input) or (output) is a weighted average calculation that identifies the more-recent load data has more weight in the computation. These computations are made in a time interval called the load interval. To obtain faster results (to bring the interface up faster), or when you test throughput, this interval can be altered.

The 804-isdn(config-if)#**load-interval 30** command alters the load interval of any interface from the default to 30 seconds.

To make a call is one of the main functions of an ISDN router. To pass data is another major function. This function can be accompanied by frustrating performance problems, which are covered in the next scenario.

Scenario 3: ISDN Performance Problems

Usually, a user has bandwidth expectations and uses software or a tester to measure the network speed. If the service is provisioned for $2 \times 56+D$, you can expect a maximum bandwidth of 112 kbps. If the service is provisioned for $2 \times 64+D$, you can expect a maximum of 128 kbps. The user must be educated about the overall bandwidth, which needs to be distinguished from the user's expectations, based on the size of his test files. Don't forget that, in ISDN, a significant part of the frame (1/4) is used for signaling information due to the format of an ISDN frame in the S/T coding technique (Pseudo-Ternary Line Coding) and one tenth in the U-interface coding technique (two binary, one quaternary) (see Chapter 2, "Telecommunication Basics," for more information). Also, given the fact that overhead is associated with all routing and routed protocols, you should set a user's expectations accordingly.

Performance problems don't result immediately from these situations; instead, there is an unexpected degradation of the line speed over a period of time.

The solution to this type of problem requires systematic research of all possible reasons. The problems can be caused by the following:

• Short-term routing issues

- Line problems
- Configuration setting problems
- LEC switch problems

Each issue is discussed in the following sections.

Short-Term Routing Issues

Problems due to routing are related to different aspects of the corporate network, such as routing, server hosting, server availability, and performance. Usually, problems are due to a malfunction of the intranet. A duplicate IP address can severely degrade a user's performance, especially in statically assigned IP subnets, where different subnets can affect each other if there is an overlapping address space. The easiest way to discover the problem is to check the DNS and DHCP pools to determine if access is available, or ping every IP address in the subnet to see if there is a difference in the response time and the number of successful responses.

Line Problems

After you ensure the service is set up correctly and fully operational (the router can make calls), check the status of the BRI service by using the following set of very useful commands:

```
804-isdn#show interface bri0
804-isdn#show interfaces bri0 1 2
```

The detailed output for these commands is explained in Table 13-5. Before you look at this output, note some of the troubleshooting steps you can take for this category of problems:

1 Make sure that the user's router is configured correctly—that it dials out and accepts calls.

NOTE	Always clear the interfaces and counters before testing to limit results to only your actions.

2 Clear the data channels of the user's router before testing by using the following command:

```
804-isdn#clear interface bri0:1
804-isdn#clear interface bri0:2
```

NOTE	Just clearing interface bri0 brings down both channels.

3 From the core router or any server, run the following:

```
server1.cisco.com:/users/pnedeltc>PING 804-isdn 3000
```

If the threshold of the user's router is set to 10 percent of the bandwidth, after 15–20 seconds, you will see the second channel come up. Run 200 packet pings and check the statistics. If the packet loss is greater than 0 percent, a problem exists.

4 Check the information on the D channel, and the BRI0:1 and BRI0:2. Compare the results to the output lines in Table 13-5.

5 Try a 56 K call to determine if the problem still exists. If it does, follow the recommendations in Table 13-5, or work with the LEC to resolve the issue.

Table 13-5 *Explanation of Output from #***show interface bri0** *(D Channel) and #***show interface bri0 1 2** *(For BRI Data Channels 1 and 2)*

Output	Description
BRI0 is up, line protocol is up (spoofing) BRI0:1 is down, line protocol is down	D channel information. It shows that the D channel is spoofing and indicates that the D channel is up and the dial-on-demand is ready. Unlike BRI0:1 and BRI0:2, this interface must be up at all times for DDR to function. BRI0:1 information. The line and protocol are down, which indicates the channel is inactive and does not send or receive data. This does not mean the BRI1 is not functional.
Hardware is BRI with U-interface and POTS	Hardware information that shows the router has a built-in U-interface and supports plain old telephone service (POTS).
MTU 1500 bytes BW 64 Kbit DLY 20000 usec	Maximum transmit unit (MTU) is 1500 bytes. Bandwidth is 64 Kbps. The D channel in 2B+D is 64 Kbps; however, for signaling, it uses only 16 Kbps. A delay of 20,000 microseconds = 20 milliseconds.
reliability 255/255, txload 1/255, rxload 1/255	Reliability, transmit load (txload), and receive load (rxload) are a fraction of 255.
Encapsulation PPP loopback not set	The encapsulation of the interface is Point-to-Point Protocol (PPP). The loopback is not set.
DTR is pulsed for 1 seconds on reset	The Data Terminal Ready (DTR) timer is set to 1 second.
LCP Closed, multilink Closed Closed: CDPCP, IPCP	LCP and multilink can be closed or open. Cisco Discovery Protocol Control Protocol (CDPCP) and IP Control Protocol (IPCP) are part of the NCP suit and can be closed or open as well. These lines exist only for B channels.

Table 13-5   *Explanation of Output from #***show interface bri0** *(D Channel) and #***show interface bri0 1 2**
(For BRI Data Channels 1 and 2) (Continued)

Output	Description
Last input 00:00:24, output 00:00:24,	Number of hours, minutes, and seconds since the last packets were received (input) or sent (output) by this interface.
output hang never	This indicates hours, minutes, seconds, or never since the last reset of this interface. If the time is more than 24 hours, you see 2d3h. But if this format is not sufficient, you will see *****, which indicates that more symbols are required than this format can support.
Last clearing of "show interface" counters 6d23h	Often in troubleshooting, you need to start with "fresh" data. This value indicates the last time in hours:minutes:seconds (or never) that the interface counters were cleared using the command: 804-isdn#**clear interface bri0:1 or bri0:2** The 804-isdn#**clear interface bri0** works as a reset of the D channel and, therefore, works as a reset of the BRI interface.
Input queue: 0/75/0/0 (size/max/ drops/ flushes); Total output drops: 0 Output queue: 0/1000/64/0 (size/max total/ threshold/drops)	Input queue with self-explanatory parameters and the number of dropped packets because of a lack of queue slots. If the number of dropped packets is high, you might want to check the interface buffers with the following: 804-isdn#**show buffers**
Queuing strategy: weighted fair	The queuing strategy.
Conversations 0/1/16 (active/max active/max total) Reserved Conversations 0/0 (allocated/max allocated)	This entry displays the number of conversations in regards to weighted fair queuing (WFQ). If FIFO is configured on the interface, the output would just show output queue and input queue statistics.

The Following Output Is Where the Line Problems Are Reported

5 minute input rate 4200 bits/sec, 1 packets/sec 5 minute output rate 0 bits/sec, 0 packets/sec	The average rate of data exchange, both in and out in five-minute intervals, measured in bits per second and packets per second.
42554 packets input, 187949 bytes, 0 no buffer	Number of packets and bytes passed with no errors. Number of discarded packets because there's no buffer.
Received 0 broadcasts	Total number of received broadcasts on this interface.
0 runts	Number of discarded packets because their size was smaller than the minimum median packet size.
0 giants	Number of packets that were discarded because their size was greater than the maximum median packet size.

continues

Table 13-5 *Explanation of Output from #***show interface bri0** *(D Channel) and #***show interface bri0 1 2** *(For BRI Data Channels 1 and 2) (Continued)*

Output	Description
0 throttles	Number of times the receiver on the port was disabled; possibly due to buffer or processor overload.
81 input errors	Total number of input errors since the last #**clear interface** command.
1 CRC	Cyclic Redundancy Check (CRC) errors usually indicate noise or other transmission problems.
69 frame	Incorrectly received packets, or packets with a non-integer number of octets, which usually indicates noise or other transmission problems.
0 overrun	The number of times the input rate exceeded the receiver's ability to buffer and handle the data.
0 ignored	The number of times the hardware ran low in internal buffers. Broadcast storms and bursts of noise can be the possible cause of the problem.
11 abort	Number of aborts. It shows the illegal number of 1s in the interface. It is an indication of a clocking problem on the interface. (Check the U- or S/T interface cabling.)
42601 packets output, 179159 bytes	Number of output packets and bytes in the interface passed without errors.
0 underruns	Number of times when the transmitter runs faster than the router can handle.
0 output errors	Number of output errors.
0 collisions	Number of collisions on the interface. The collisions can come from the contention failures
9 interface resets	Number of interface resets, which indicate "no signal" in the interface. The router waits ten seconds and then resets the interface trying to trigger the exchange.
0 output buffers failures, 0 output buffers swapped out	Number of buffer failures and swapped output buffers. Use 804-isdn#**show buffers failures** to check the type and the time of failures.
280 carrier transitions	Number of carrier transitions, which is a number that you need to divide by 2 because there are 140 ups and 140 downs in this D channel. This number in the D channel should be much smaller than the same measurement on the B channels because the B channel goes up and down to exchange data, while the D channel stays up (presumably always).

For a Cisco 77x router, the line quality of the ISDN line can be checked with the **show packets** command as displayed in Example 13-7.

Example 13-7 **show packets** *Output*

```
776-isdn:gateway> show 2 packets
Packet Statistics for Connection 2
Filtered: 0   Forwarded: 150   Received: 201
Dropped: 59   Lost: 0   Corrupted: 1   Misordered: 0
Compression Ratio: 0.99:1
IP Packet that triggered last call
Source Address: 151.70.209.82
Destination Address: 151.68.10.140
Protocol: UDP
Source Port: 1242
Destination Port: 53
Date/Time: 01/01/1995 00:00:47
776-isdn:gateway>
```

The line quality information is shown and explained in Table 13-6.

Table 13-6 *Output and Description of* the **show packets** *Output From a 77x Router*

Output	Description
Packet statistics for Connection 2	The packet diagnostic statistics for Link=2.
Filtered	Packets received by the bridge engine and not forwarded.
Forwarded	Packets forwarded to Link=2.
Received	Packets received from Link=2.
The Following Are Where the Problems Are Reported	
Dropped	Packets received from Link=2 and dropped because the queue of packets to be forwarded was too long.
Lost	Packets received from Link=2, but not successfully transmitted (faulty line).
Corrupted	Packets received from Link=2 with bad CRC and discarded as corrupted.
Misordered	Packets received out of sequence when using the ordered or fragmented protocol.
Compression Ratio	If using compression, it shows the compression ratio.

The line-quality issues might be only part of the problem, but they're very significant and can cause frustrating intermittent problems.

NOTE   One of the most unusual cases that I recall involved a user whose MPOE was actually a wooden cabinet in her backyard. On rainy days, her service was intermittent. But every time the LEC technician was onsite testing, everything would be fine. In the end, it turns out that, when the cabinet door was closed, it put pressure on the cable so that moisture caused intermittent connectivity. When the cabinet door was open (such as when the technician was running tests) connectivity was fine.

The interface reports should be interpreted according to the specifics of the service, which can include many and different devices in the local loop. Some configuration settings in the user's router can cause problems as well; they are discussed in the next section.

Configuration Setting Problems

The buffer shortage is included under interface commands and shows the number of successfully passed packets and bytes, as well as the dropped packets due to no buffer. This setting might cause performance problems.

Some simple recommendations that usually work for issues caused by settings include the following:

- If the number of drops increments after clearing the appropriate interfaces and running a ping test from the opposite site, determine what destination is incrementing—input or output, looking to the following lines:

```
Input queue: 0/75/20 (size/max/drops); Total output drops: 30
Output queue: 0/1000/64/0 (size/max total/threshold/drops)
```

  Here, the input queue has dropped 30 packets.

- If any queue drops packets, gradually increase the size of the queue by 25 percent, using either of the commands:

```
804-isdn(config-if)#hold-queue length out
804-isdn(config-if)#hold-queue length in
```

  From the previous example where the input queue dropped 30 packets, you should increase the input queue size.

If you see that the number of dropped packets is decreasing after repeated testing, increase the packets for further testing.

LEC Switch Problems

LEC switch problems are related to the quality of service provided by the LEC. Also, there are different departments within a LEC's organization, and the troubleshooting engineer does not always have visibility to the LEC's internal processes. The following is an example.

A user is taking an e-learning course and experiences slow performance of data and video. The user has a /30 bit (255.255.255.252) subnet assigned on one computer at home—a new notebook.

Here are the troubleshooting steps for this realistic scenario, and the results for this particular case:

1   Gather information from the user. In this case, a conversation with the user determines that the connection is four months old, and has been the same from the beginning.

2   Do a quick check of the configuration, which looks correct for this scenario. The ISDN numbers are

```
isdn spid1 = 56174270270100 LDN1 = 7427027
isdn spid2 = 56174270280100 LDN2 = 7427028
```

3   Do a quick check of the IP subnet in the DNS and DHCP server to see if it looks correct and there is no overlapping. In this case, there is no overlapping.

4   Have the user make two calls out—one from the BRI0:2 VOICE and one from BRI0:1 DATA. Assume that the router reports that the BRI0:1 makes a voice call, but the BRI0:2 is making a data call, as shown in Example 13-8. This is just the opposite of what you expect to see. Remember this!

Example 13-8   show isdn status *Output*

```
804-isdn#show isdn status
Global ISDN Switchtype = basic-ni
ISDN BRI0 interface
        dsl 0, interface ISDN Switchtype = basic-ni
    Layer 1 Status:
        ACTIVE
    Layer 2 Status:
        TEI = 123, Ces = 1, SAPI = 0, State = MULTIPLE_FRAME_ESTABLISHED
        TEI = 124, Ces = 2, SAPI = 0, State = MULTIPLE_FRAME_ESTABLISHED
    Spid Status:
        TEI 123, ces = 1, state = 5(init)
            spid1 configured, spid1 sent, spid1 valid
            Endpoint ID Info: epsf = 0, usid = 1, tid = 0
        TEI 124, ces = 2, state = 5(init)
            spid2 configured, spid2 sent, spid2 valid
            Endpoint ID Info: epsf = 0, usid = 2, tid = 0
    Layer 3 Status:
        1 Active Layer 3 Call(s)
    Activated dsl 0 CCBs = 2
        CCB:callid=8021, sapi=0, ces=1, B-chan=2, calltype=DATA -
! The router reports that BRI0:1 makes a VOICE call, but the BRI0:2 is
! making a data call -- the opposite to what you would expect.
! Remember the word asymmetric.
        CCB:callid=8024, sapi=0, ces=1, B-chan=1, calltype=VOICE
    The Free Channel Mask:  0x80000000
    Total Allocated ISDN CCBs = 2
```

5   Have the user download data and check the interfaces to see if they report any errors. In this case, they don't. The input line errors are not the problem, as you can see from the following fragment from the commands **show interface bri0:1** and **show interface bri0:2**:

```
609 packets input, 3440 bytes, 0 no buffer
        Received 0 broadcasts, 0 runts, 0 giants, 0 throttles
        0 input errors, 0 CRC, 0 frame, 0 overrun, 0 ignored, 0 abort
```

6   Check the dialer interface for errors. Under the Dialer 1 interface, you see the following. Obviously, no input or output errors are reported and they are not the problem:

```
0 input errors, 0 CRC, 0 frame, 0 overrun, 0 ignored
0 input packets with dribble condition detected
6464 packets output, 2178130 bytes, 0 underruns
0 output errors, 0 collisions, 0 interface resets
0 babbles, 0 late collision, 14 deferred
0 lost carrier, 0 no carrier
0 output buffer failures, 0 output buffers swapped out
```

7   Check the error statistics for virtual interface 1 with **show interface dialer 1** command.

The same command provides you with great details, including the five-minute input and output rates on this interface.

Again, recall that the user is downloading data and, for some reason, the router is reporting an asymmetric performance, as shown in the following code fragment:

```
5 minute input rate 2000 bits/sec, 0 packets/sec
5 minute output rate 62000 bits/sec, 0 packets/sec
```

The most concise commands to check the Ethernet 0, Dialer, and Virtual Access 1 interfaces for certain common values is to use the output modifiers of IOS, as follows:

```
804-isdn#show interface ethernet0 | include 5 minute
804-isdn#show interface dialer1 | include 5 minute
804-isdn#show interface virtual-access 1 | include 5 minute
```

8   Ask the user to upload data. The result is again the same asymmetric performance:

```
5 minute input rate 62000 bits/sec, 0 packets/sec
5 minute output rate 2000 bits/sec, 0 packets/sec
```

From the last two tests, you can conclude the tested direction is slow.

9   Do a quick check of the buffers for failures. In this case, it shows that none are present:

```
804-isdn#shows buffers failures
```

Obviously, the buffer failures are not causing any issue.

10   Due to the effect the low size of the MTU can have over the performance, check the E0 interface and computer settings and determine if any MTU is set to less than 1500 for the download direction. In this case, the settings were determined by default. The MTU is not a problem.

11 Check the core router with the following:

```
7206-isdn#show running-config | include 804-isdn
dialer map ip 10.19.236.5 name 804-isdn speed 56 15617427027
```

From this command, you can determine that the core router is calling SPID1, but the call is reaching SPID2. Again, you can see another instance of asymmetric behavior in this particular ISDN service.

12 Given the amount of asymmetric instances, the word asymmetric can characterize this ISDN service. The action plan should now be to make the service symmetric by removing all asymmetric odds from the service and seeing if this corrects the problem.

13 The easiest way to correct the problem is to change the dialer map from the core router from (SPID1), as shown here:

```
7206-isdn(config-if)#dialer map ip 10.19.236.5 name 804-isdn speed 56 15617427027
```

The core router is dialing SPID1 (15617427027).

Make the core router call SPID2 (15617427028) with the following change:

```
7206-isdn(config-if)#dialer map ip 10.19.236.5 name 804-isdn speed 56 15617427028
```

14a Ask the user to download the same information from the same server, as he did in an earlier step. You can check the virtual access interface of the user's router with the following command:

```
804-isdn#show interface virtual-Access 1 | include 5 minute
...
  5 minute input rate 40000 bits/sec, 8 packets/sec
  5 minute output rate 3000 bits/sec, 3 packets/sec
...
```

Recall that the user is downloading. Your testing direction, looking from the remote user's router, is input. If you compare Step 7 and its output with the new report, you can see that the service has improved and the input rate is increasing.

Here is the output from Step 7:

```
5 minute input rate 2000 bits/sec, 0 packets/sec
```

Here is the new, improved output:

```
5 minute input rate 40000 bits/sec, 8 packets/sec
```

If the user is not available to participate in testing, you must consider how to test without him.

14b Run a ping test with a packet size of 3000 and then increase the size to 4200, as shown here:

```
server1.cisco.com:/users/pnedeltc>PING 804-isdn 3000
```

Measure the five-minute rate from the user's router with this:

```
804-isdn#show interface Virtual-Access 1 | incl 5 minu
```

When testing with packet size 3000 bytes, the results are

```
5 minute input rate 24000 bits/sec, 4 packets/sec
5 minute output rate 25000 bits/sec, 4 packets/sec
```

When testing 4500 bytes, the results are

```
5 minute input rate 34000 bits/sec, 4 packets/sec
5 minute output rate 35000 bits/sec, 4 packets/sec
```

For this case, the result of these steps is that now the connection is according with the expected behavior (symmetric), the input rate is increasing, and no packet is lost, as shown in the following fragment from ping 804-isdn 3000 statistics:

```
----804-isdn.cisco.com PING Statistics----
439 packets transmitted, 438 packets received, 0% packet loss
round-trip (ms)  min/avg/max = 654/659/947
```

This example is provided to show how the repeated observation and key impressions of an engineer who doesn't necessarily have knowledge of internal processes of the LEC can still result in resolution of problems.

In this particular case, most probably, you were dealing with the way the circuit was designed by the LEC. Although these types of solutions might not have the perfect technical explanation (after all, the engineer is guessing based on his observations), they often solve the problem regardless.

Scenario 4: End-to-End Communication Problems

A typical ISDN case includes situations where the configuration is okay, the interfaces are configured correctly, and the router makes outgoing calls, but the connection is intermittent, or drops, soon after the connection is established. This scenario is one of the most difficult to troubleshoot for ISDN. As a reminder, end-to-end communications are based on the encapsulation protocol running on the BRI and dialer interfaces. Regardless of the fact that Q.931 is considered to be an end-to-end protocol (as discussed in Chapter 9, "ISDN Technology Background"), after a call is made, the frames are encapsulated by PPP, which takes over and manages the point-to-point and end-to-end communication. Recall that the PPP protocol has five phases (again, for troubleshooting purposes, you might consider there being four phases). Each phase starts after the previous one is open. Every phase and every protocol in that particular phase can create problems. Therefore, if the call out does not drop in the first three seconds, focus on PPP when you're troubleshooting.

The following issues are typical for end-to-end communication problems:

- The LEC's ISDN switch settings
- Link control protocol (LCP) problems and the magic 22 seconds
- Authentication problems
- End-to-end routing problems

Each issue is discussed in the following sections.

The LEC's ISDN Switch Settings

One of the simplest cases is when the router calls out but does not get a response. This situation is typical for new installs. The LEC is responsible for the settings of the switch. An error in the profile can create problems. The easiest way to identify a problem is by using the following:

```
804-isdn#debug isdn events
```

Search for messages with prefix I: (input). If you do not have access to the user's router, work with the end user to determine if the switch passes data from the core router to the user's router (check the RxD lights on the router). If no data is passed, work with the LEC to correct the problem. If the remote user is extremely non-technical, this might make troubleshooting very difficult.

LCP Problems and the Magic 22 Seconds

One of the most complicated issues is when everything works correctly and the router makes calls out, but after the router disconnects, the call results in one of the following:

- If the disconnect is immediately after call out (less than one second), there's either a wrong phone number or it is not provisioned for data. The error messages in Chapter 12 provide more explanations about the possible cause.

- If the call disconnects in two seconds, the other party is not configured to be called from this router (CHAP refused authentication) and the call is rejected.

- The call drops in about 22 seconds.

Because of its importance, the 22 second issue deserves more detailed analyses. This is when the configuration is okay on both sides, the calling router tries to make a call, and the switch responds with call connected, but the call then drops after 22 seconds. Looking at the problem with a 77x router, you see the output that's shown in Example 13-9.

Example 13-9   *The 22 Second Issue*

```
1. Status    01/01/1995 18:34:06
Line Status
  Line Activated
  Terminal Identifier Assigned    SPID Accepted
  Terminal Identifier Assigned    SPID Accepted
Port Status                                    Interface Connection Link
  Ch:  1    64K Call In Progress      20178        DATA        0      0
  Ch:  2    Waiting for call
! The Connection (number) =0 and Link (number) = 0 is a typical sign.
! These values never acquire <>0 (non-zero) value.
 776-isdn: SJB12A75> 01/01/1995 18:34:24  L12  1  Disconnected Remotely
Cause 16  Normal Disconnect
 776-isdn: SJB12A75> 01/01/1995 18:34:25  L27  1  Disconnected
```

continues

Example 13-9 *The 22 Second Issue (Continued)*

```
776-isdn: SJB12A75> 01/01/1995 18:34:33  L05  0  20178  Outgoing Call Initiated
776-isdn: SJB12A75> 01/01/1995 18:34:34  L08  1  20178  Call Connected
776-isdn: SJB12A75> 01/01/1995 18:34:56  L12  1  Disconnected Remotely
Cause 16  Normal Disconnect
```

Another important message from the output of the IOS-based ISDN router is

```
Jul 30 11:01:59 PDT: %ISDN-6-DISCONNECT: Interface BRI0:1
    disconnected from 4086175555 , call lasted 22 seconds.
```

The symptoms are confusing, and checking the call messages does not provide any useful information. The indications from the switch are even more confusing because the switch reports that the call is disconnected and the reason is normal, but the end-to-end communication is not normal. To understand what is occurring, you must review the PPP protocol. As a second-layer protocol, PPP works after Q.931 is complete (the REQUEST and CONNECT messages are sent and confirmed). Once finished (the switch reports a successful connection), and the call is treated as a callout, the next phase of the PPP protocol starts, which is LCP. This protocol establishes various parameters, as described in Chapter 12, and negotiates the line parameters in a typical handshake manner. You can see outgoing requests, incoming requests, and confirmations. In one of the cases, the output of the core router, which of course is reporting the same situation, can be viewed in Example 13-10.

Example 13-10 *The Output of the Core Router*

```
7206-isdn#debug ppp negotiation
Jul 30 11:01:37 PDT: %LINK-3-UPDOWN: Interface Serial2/1:3, changed state to up
Jul 30 11:01:37 PDT: Se2/1:3 PPP: Treating connection as a callin
! The core accepts a call and treats it as an incoming call from a remote user.
Jul 30 11:01:37 PDT: Se2/1:3 PPP: Phase is ESTABLISHING,
    Passive Open [0 sess, 1 load]
Jul 30 11:01:37 PDT: Se2/1:3 CHAP: Using alternate hostname SJB12A75
! The router recognizes the alternate hostname, configured under the user's
! dialer interface, or the hostname, used as a username in the remote
! user's configuration.
Jul 30 11:01:37 PDT: Se2/1:3 LCP: State is Listen
! The LCP is open
Jul 30 11:01:39 PDT: Se2/1:3 LCP: TIMEout: State Listen
! LCP state is listen
Jul 30 11:01:39 PDT: Se2/1:3 CHAP: Using alternate hostname SJB12A75
Jul 30 11:01:39 PDT: Se2/1:3 LCP: O CONFREQ [Listen] id 37 len 30
! First attempt to establish a connection (sending confirmation request OUT)
Jul 30 11:01:39 PDT: Se2/1:3 LCP:    AuthProto CHAP (0x0305C22305)
Jul 30 11:01:39 PDT: Se2/1:3 LCP:    MagicNumber 0x48430C39 (0x050648430C39)
Jul 30 11:01:39 PDT: Se2/1:3 LCP:    MRRU 1524 (0x110405F4)
Jul 30 11:01:39 PDT: Se2/1:3 LCP:    EndpointDisc 1 Local (0x130B01534E564143413031)
Jul 30 11:01:41 PDT: Se2/1:3 LCP: TIMEout: State REQsent
Jul 30 11:01:41 PDT: Se2/1:3 LCP: O CONFREQ [REQsent] id 38 len 30
! Second  attempt to establish a connection (sending confirmation request OUT)
Jul 30 11:01:41 PDT: Se2/1:3 LCP:    AuthProto CHAP (0x0305C22305)
```

Example 13-10 *The Output of the Core Router (Continued)*

```
Jul 30 11:01:41 PDT: Se2/1:3 LCP:    MagicNumber 0x48430C39 (0x050648430C39)
Jul 30 11:01:41 PDT: Se2/1:3 LCP:    MRRU 1524 (0x110405F4)
Jul 30 11:01:41 PDT: Se2/1:3 LCP:    EndpointDisc 1 Local
   (0x130B01534E564143413031)
Jul 30 11:01:43 PDT: %ISDN-6-CONNECT: Interface Serial2/1:3 is now
   connected to 4086174270
Jul 30 11:01:43 PDT: Se2/1:3 LCP: TIMEout: State REQsent
```

Skipping the exact same sequence for attempts 3 through 9, take a look at the last (10)
attempt in Example 13-11.

Example 13-11 *Final Attempt*

```
...
Jul 30 11:01:57 PDT: Se2/1:3 LCP: O CONFREQ [REQsent] id 46 len 30
Jul 30 11:01:57 PDT: Se2/1:3 LCP:    AuthProto CHAP (0x0305C22305)
Jul 30 11:01:57 PDT: Se2/1:3 LCP:    MagicNumber 0x48430C39 (0x050648430C39)
Jul 30 11:01:57 PDT: Se2/1:3 LCP:    MRRU 1524 (0x110405F4)
Jul 30 11:01:57 PDT: Se2/1:3 LCP:    EndpointDisc 1 Local
   (0x130B01534E564143413031)
Jul 30 11:01:59 PDT: Se2/1:3 LCP: TIMEout: State REQsent
Jul 30 11:01:59 PDT: Se2/1:3 LCP: State is Listen
! Last (10th) attempt to establish a connection
! (sending confirmation request OUT)
Jul 30 11:01:59 PDT: %ISDN-6-DISCONNECT: Interface Serial2/1:3
   disconnected from 4086174270 , call lasted 22 seconds
! Again, the same message for "call lasted 22 seconds" and as a result
! "LCP: State is Closed"
Jul 30 11:01:59 PDT: %LINK-3-UPDOWN: Interface Serial2/1:3, changed state to down
Jul 30 11:01:59 PDT: Se2/1:3 LCP: State is Closed
Jul 30 11:01:59 PDT: Se2/1:3 PPP: Phase is DOWN [0 sess, 1 load]
```

The same output can be seen from both ends of the connection; the time interval should
match. The interval between 2 consecutive attempts might vary, but every attempt takes
about 2 seconds (see the timestamps). So, 10 attempts with 2 seconds for each, 1 second at
the beginning, and 1 at the end is equivalent to *22 seconds*. These parameters are adjustable,
but there's no guarantee that if you use non-default parameters, it's going to work. It's
recommended to use the default parameters and investigate further. The same case using a
77x scenario results in 8 attempts, and the interval is a little less than 3 seconds.

In order for LCP to be successful and to report the LCP phase open, both parties expect an
incoming message confirming the parameters from each other, which looks like the
following:

```
Jul 30 11:12:21 PDT: Se2/1:5 LCP: I CONFACK [ACKsent]
   [REQsent] id 118 len 8,
```

The previous line indicates the confirmation acknowledgement and the expected output
from this command is shown in Example 13-12.

Example 13-12 *LCP Is Successfully Opened*

```
Jul 30 11:12:20 PDT: %LINK-3-UPDOWN: Interface Serial2/1:5, changed state to up
Jul 30 11:12:20 PDT: Se2/1:5 PPP: Treating connection as a callin
Jul 30 11:12:20 PDT: Se2/1:5 PPP: Phase is ESTABLISHING, Passive Open
    [0 sess, 0 load]
Jul 30 11:12:20 PDT: Se2/1:5 CHAP: Using alternate hostname SJB12A75
Jul 30 11:12:20 PDT: Se2/1:5 LCP: State is Listen
Jul 30 11:12:21 PDT: Se2/1:5 LCP: T CONFREQ [Listen] id 1 len 36
Jul 30 11:12:21 PDT: Se2/1:5 LCP:    MRU 1522 (0x010405F2)
Jul 30 11:12:21 PDT: Se2/1:5 LCP:    AuthProto CHAP (0x0305C22305)
Jul 30 11:12:21 PDT: Se2/1:5 LCP:    MagicNumber 0x00119790 (0x050600119790)
Jul 30 11:12:21 PDT: Se2/1:5 LCP:    MRRU 1800 (0x11040708)
Jul 30 11:12:21 PDT: Se2/1:5 LCP:    EndpointDisc 3 0040.f913.abc8
    (0x1309030040F913ABC8)
Jul 30 11:12:21 PDT: Se2/1:5 LCP:    LinkDiscriminator 5578 (0x170415CA)
Jul 30 11:12:21 PDT: Se2/1:5 CHAP: Using alternate hostname SJB12A75
Jul 30 11:12:21 PDT: Se2/1:5 LCP: O CONFREQ [Listen] id 118 len 30
Jul 30 11:12:21 PDT: Se2/1:5 LCP:    AuthProto CHAP (0x0305C22305)
Jul 30 11:12:21 PDT: Se2/1:5 LCP:    MagicNumber 0x484CD7F7 (0x0506484CD7F7)
Jul 30 11:12:21 PDT: Se2/1:5 LCP:    MRRU 1524 (0x110405F4)
Jul 30 11:12:21 PDT: Se2/1:5 LCP:    EndpointDisc 1 Local
    (0x130B01534E564143413031)
Jul 30 11:12:21 PDT: Se2/1:5 LCP: O CONFREJ [Listen] id 1 len 8
Jul 30 11:12:21 PDT: Se2/1:5 LCP:    LinkDiscriminator 5578 (0x170415CA)
Jul 30 11:12:21 PDT: Se2/1:5 LCP: I CONFNAK [REQsent] id 118 len 8
Jul 30 11:12:21 PDT: Se2/1:5 LCP:    MRU 1522 (0x010405F2)
Jul 30 11:12:21 PDT: Se2/1:5 LCP: O CONFREQ [REQsent] id 119 len 30
Jul 30 11:12:21 PDT: Se2/1:5 LCP:    AuthProto CHAP (0x0305C22305)
Jul 30 11:12:21 PDT: Se2/1:5 LCP:    MagicNumber 0x484CD7F7 (0x0506484CD7F7)
Jul 30 11:12:21 PDT: Se2/1:5 LCP:    MRRU 1524 (0x110405F4)
Jul 30 11:12:21 PDT: Se2/1:5 LCP:    EndpointDisc 1 Local
    (0x130B01534E564143413031)
Jul 30 11:12:21 PDT: Se2/1:5 LCP: I CONFREQ [REQsent] id 2 len 32
Jul 30 11:12:21 PDT: Se2/1:5 LCP:    MRU 1522 (0x010405F2)
Jul 30 11:12:21 PDT: Se2/1:5 LCP:    AuthProto CHAP (0x0305C22305)
Jul 30 11:12:21 PDT: Se2/1:5 LCP:    MagicNumber 0x00119790 (0x050600119790)
Jul 30 11:12:21 PDT: Se2/1:5 LCP:    MRRU 1800 (0x11040708)
Jul 30 11:12:21 PDT: Se2/1:5 LCP:    EndpointDisc 3 0040.f913.abc8
    (0x1309030040F913ABC8)
Jul 30 11:12:21 PDT: Se2/1:5 LCP: O CONFACK [REQsent] id 2 len 32
Jul 30 11:12:21 PDT: Se2/1:5 LCP:    MRU 1522 (0x010405F2)
Jul 30 11:12:21 PDT: Se2/1:5 LCP:    AuthProto CHAP (0x0305C22305)
Jul 30 11:12:21 PDT: Se2/1:5 LCP:    MagicNumber 0x00119790 (0x050600119790)
Jul 30 11:12:21 PDT: Se2/1:5 LCP:    MRRU 1800 (0x11040708)
Jul 30 11:12:21 PDT: Se2/1:5 LCP:    EndpointDisc 3 0040.f913.abc8
    (0x1309030040F913ABC8)
Jul 30 11:12:21 PDT: Se2/1:5 LCP: I CONFACK [ACKsent] id 119 len 30
Jul 30 11:12:21 PDT: Se2/1:5 LCP:    AuthProto CHAP (0x0305C22305)
Jul 30 11:12:21 PDT: Se2/1:5 LCP:    MagicNumber 0x484CD7F7 (0x0506484CD7F7)
```

Example 13-12 *LCP Is Successfully Opened (Continued)*

```
Jul 30 11:12:21 PDT: Se2/1:5 LCP:    MRRU 1524 (0x110405F4)
Jul 30 11:12:21 PDT: Se2/1:5 LCP:    EndpointDisc 1 Local
   (0x130B01534E564143413031)
Jul 30 11:12:21 PDT: Se2/1:5 LCP: State is Open
! Finally the LCP is successfully opened.
```

Another type of the same problem is when both parties try to establish the LCP parameters and still cannot establish a connection, although both parties exchange messages.

If you trigger the router to make a call out with the following command and you have the #**debug ppp negotiation** command on, you see the ping unsuccessful:

```
804-isdn#ping 151.68.10.70
```

The output from the debug command will appear as displayed in Example 13-13.

Example 13-13 **debug ppp negotiation** *Output*

```
*Aug 22 09::04:21.823: %LINK-3-UPDOWN: Interface BRI0:1, changed state to up
*Aug 22 09::04:21.843: %ISDN-6-CONNECT: Interface BRI0:1 is now connected to
   14087320178 .
*Aug 22 09::04:21.847: BR0:1 PPP: Treating connection as a callout
*Aug 22 09::04:21.847: BR0:1 PPP: Phase is ESTABLISHING, Active Open
*Aug 22 09::04:21.851: BR0:1 LCP: O CONFREQ [Closed] id 12 len 35
*Aug 22 09::04:21.851: BR0:1 LCP:    AuthProto CHAP (0x0305C22305)
*Aug 22 09::04:21.851: BR0:1 LCP:    MagicNumber 0xB0C6897B (0x0506B0C6897B)
*Aug 22 09::04:21.855: BR0:1 LCP:    MRRU 1524 (0x110405F4)
*Aug 22 09::04:21.855: BR0:1 LCP:    EndpointDisc 1 Local
   (0x13100172626561756368652D6973646E)
! The remote user requests confirmation for the first time
! See the O CONFREQ message
*Aug 22 09::04:23.623: BR0:1 LCP: I CONFREQ [REQsent] id 41 len 30
*Aug 22 09::04:23.623: BR0:1 LCP:    AuthProto CHAP (0x0305C22305)
*Aug 22 09::04:23.627: BR0:1 LCP:    MagicNumber 0xBE47D746 (0x0506BE47D746)
*Aug 22 09::04:23.627: BR0:1 LCP:    MRRU 1524 (0x110405F4)
*Aug 22 09::04:23.627: BR0:1 LCP:    EndpointDisc 1 Local
   (0x130B01534E564143413031)
! The core router requests confirmation for the first time
! See the I CONFREQ message
*Aug 22 09::04:23.631: BR0:1 LCP: O CONFACK [REQsent] id 41 len 30
*Aug 22 09::04:23.631: BR0:1 LCP:    AuthProto CHAP (0x0305C22305)
*Aug 22 09::04:23.63.5: BR0:1 LCP:    MagicNumber 0xBE47D746 (0x0506BE47D746)
*Aug 22 09::04:23.635: BR0:1 LCP:    MRRU 1524 (0x110405F4)
*Aug 22 09::04:23.635: BR0:1 LCP:    EndpointDisc 1 Local
   (0x130B01534E564143413031)
*Aug 22 09::04:23.851: BR0:1 LCP: TIMEout: State ACKsent
! The remote user confirms with O CONFAK, but the process times out
! First time, because there is no confirmation from the core router
*Aug 22 09::04:23.851: BR0:1 LCP: O CONFREQ [ACKsent] id 13 len 35
*Aug 22 09::04:23.851: BR0:1 LCP:    AuthProto CHAP (0x0305C22305)
*Aug 22 09::04:23.855: BR0:1 LCP:    MagicNumber 0xB0C6897B (0x0506B0C6897B)
```

continues

Example 13-13 debug ppp negotiation *Output (Continued)*

```
*Aug 22 09::04:23.855: BR0:1 LCP:    MRRU 1524 (0x110405F4)
*Aug 22 09::04:23.855: BR0:1 LCP:    EndpointDisc 1 Local
  (0x131001726265617563686562D6973646E)
! The remote user requests confirmation again
! Second time - see O CONFREQ message
*Aug 22 09::04:25.623: BR0:1 LCP: I CONFREQ [ACKsent] id 42 len 30
*Aug 22 09::04:25.623: BR0:1 LCP:    AuthProto CHAP (0x0305C22305)
*Aug 22 09::04:25.627: BR0:1 LCP:    MagicNumber 0xBE47D746 (0x0506BE47D746)
*Aug 22 09::04:25.627: BR0:1 LCP:    MRRU 1524 (0x110405F4)
*Aug 22 09::04:25.627: BR0:1 LCP:    EndpointDisc 1 Local
  (0x130B01534E564143413031)
! The core router requests confirmation for the second time
! See I CONFREQ for the second time
<output omitted>
*Aug 22 09::04:39.863: BR0:1 LCP: O CONFREQ [ACKsent] id 21 len 35
*Aug 22 09::04:39.863: BR0:1 LCP:    AuthProto CHAP (0x0305C22305)
*Aug 22 09::04:39.867: BR0:1 LCP:    MagicNumber 0xB0C6897B (0x0506B0C6097B)
*Aug 22 09::04:39.867: BR0:1 LCP:    MRRU 1524 (0x110405F4)
*Aug 22 09::04:39.867: BR0:1 LCP:    EndpointDisc 1 Local
  (0x131001726265617563686562D6973646E)
*Aug 22 09::04:41.623: BR0:1 LCP: I CONFREQ [ACKsent] id 50 len 30
*Aug 22 09::04:41.623: BR0:1 LCP:    AuthProto CHAP (0x0305C22305)
*Aug 22 09::04:41.623: BR0:1 LCP:    MagicNumber 0xBE47D746 (0x0506BE47D746)
*Aug 22 09::04:41.627: BR0:1 LCP:    MRRU 1524 (0x110405F4)
*Aug 22 09::04:41.627: BR0:1 LCP:    EndpointDisc 1 Local
  (0x130B01534E564143413031)
*Aug 22 09::04:41.631: BR0:1 LCP: O CONFACK [ACKsent] id 50 len 30
*Aug 22 09::04:41.631: BR0:1 LCP:    AuthProto CHAP (0x0305C22305)
*Aug 22 09::04:41.635: BR0:1 LCP:    MagicNumber 0xBE47D746 (0x0506BE47D746)
*Aug 22 09::04:41.635: BR0:1 LCP:    MRRU 1524 (0x110405F4)
*Aug 22 09::04:41.635: BR0:1 LCP:    EndpointDisc 1 Local
  (0x130B01534E564143413031)
*Aug 22 09::04:41.863: BR0:1 LCP: TIMEout: State ACKsent
! The same message "TIMEout: Stare ACKsent" for the 10th time
*Aug 22 09::04:41.863: BR0:1 LCP: O CONFREQ [ACKsent] id 22 len 35
*Aug 22 09::04:41.863: BR0:1 LCP:    AuthProto CHAP (0x0305C22305)
*Aug 22 09::04:41.867: BR0:1 LCP:    MagicNumber 0xB0C6897B (0x0506B0C6897B)
*Aug 22 09::04:41.867: BR0:1 LCP:    MRRU 1524 (0x110405F4)
*Aug 22 09::04:41.867: BR0:1 LCP:    EndpointDisc 1 Local
  (0x131001726265617563686562D6973646E)
*Aug 22 09::04:43.731: %ISDN-6-DISCONNECT: Interface BRI0:1
  disconnected from 1408735555 gateway, call lasted 22 seconds
*Aug 22 09::04:43.731: %LINK-3-UPDOWN: Interface BRI0:1,
  changed state to down
*Aug 22 09::04:43.751: BR0:1 LCP: State is Closed
*Aug 22 09::04:43.751: BR0:1 PPP: Phase is DOWN
The state LCP: State is Open cannot be reached.
```

The messages "call lasted 22 second" and "The state LCP: State is Open cannot be reached" indicate that the LCP phase cannot be established. The missing message here is the incoming message, I CONFACK [ACKsent], which will confirm that the core router has agreed on parameters that the remote user was proposing.

Here are two important questions to ask when troubleshooting LCP problems:

- Is only one user affected or are multiple users affected?
- What's causing the problem?

The answer to the first question will focus your analysis to either the remote user's set of problems or to the core router and its set of issues. To answer the second question, you need to investigate at least three problem cases:

- 56/64 speed problem
- Cable mapping problem
- Trunk problem

The 56/64 case is related to the 56/64 Kbps settings. In general, it is recommended that 56 kbps be defined and applied as part of the dialer interface or class, to see if it makes a difference. This is especially useful in rural areas or when the circuit runs through old types of switches.

The cable mapping case is related to one of the new features of IOS, called Non-Facility Associated Signaling (NFAS) groups that are a typical set-up for core routers. These groups are comprised of some T1s/PRIs grouped in a way that every single PRI has 24 available data channels and is configured as 24B. Two data channels of the PRIs in the group are designated for D channels and are called primary and backup D channels. They are configured as 23B+D. The other channels are called members, as shown in Example 13-14.

Example 13-14 **show isdn nfas group 0** *Output*

```
7206-isdn#show isdn nfas group 0
        ISDN NFAS GROUP 0 ENTRIES:
        The primary D is Serial2/0:23.
        The backup D is Serial2/1:23.
        The NFAS member is Serial2/2:23.
        The NFAS member is Serial2/3:23.
        The NFAS member is Serial3/0:23.
        The NFAS member is Serial3/1:23.
        The NFAS member is Serial3/2:23.
        The NFAS member is Serial3/3:23.
        There are 8 total nfas members.
        There are 190 total available B channels.
        The primary D-channel is DSL 0 in state IN SERVICE.
        The backup D-channel is DSL 1 in state STANDBY.
        The current active layer 2 DSL is 0.
7206-isdn#
```

Now, recall that the D channel uses TDM technology. One of the features of TDM is that it defines a slot for every data channel (trunk), and an empty slot cannot be used by another.

Also, it's important to note the calls hit a single or NFAS circuit in a particular order (for example Serial1/0, Serial1/1, and Serial2/0). As soon as the first circuit in the switch is in state=2 (busy), the calls roll to available trunks of member circuits. The hunting order set up by the telco should also be known. If it's set up as first available, troubleshooting is easier. But sometimes, the telco uses other hunting methods, such as least busy or round robin, to help spread the calls out and give the modems less of a duty cycle.

It is important to ensure the correct mapping of the circuits between the telco switch configuration and core router configuration. If the cable mapping is mismatched, the calls don't hit the core router in the way the ISDN switch sends them. The TDM cannot handle the D channel signaling correctly and a problem occurs. Monitoring the calls for long periods of time show the call order and it does not usually match the expected order. The easiest way to identify a NFAS group is to disconnect one of the circuits and determine if some of the others are affected. If the cabling is correctly set up, this should not affect any other member of the group, but if there is a mapping problem, you will see at least one of the other members of the group affected. The correct way of setting up the NFAS group and cable mapping is explained in Chapter 6.

The final case is the trunk misconfiguration problem. If it is in the remote user's side, you need to troubleshoot the user's service.

If the core side is affected, here is what happens. Typically, a group of users is trying to connect to the core router, but they have only a 20 percent success rate. As soon as they connect, they can exchange data, but the initial connect rate is low. Sometimes, users are disconnected in the middle of the session.

Here is a typical case for a group of remote users experiencing this problem. After discussing the problem with the end users, you might conclude it is more common during the early morning, and the success rate is higher later at night. It is confusing because no solid pattern or trend exists. When reviewing the core router information, all users call Serial interface 2/1. So, here is the plan of action.

The first thing to do is check the serial 2/1:23, which is the D channel of this interface, as shown in Example 13-15.

Example 13-15 show interface serial2/1:23 *Output*

```
3640-isdn#show interface serial2/1:23
Serial2/1:23 is up, line protocol is up (spoofing)
  Hardware is DSX1
  Description: SJB12A75 72HCQA123132-001 408-732-5555
  MTU 1500 bytes, BW 64 Kbit, DLY 20000 usec,
     reliability 255/255, txload 1/255, rxload 1/255
  Encapsulation PPP, loopback not set
  DTR is pulsed for 1 seconds on reset
  Last input 00:00:25, output 00:27:47, output hang never
  Last clearing of "show interface" counters 1w2d
  Input queue: 0/75/0/0 (size/max/drops/flushes); Total output drops: 0
  Queuing strategy: weighted fair
  Output queue: 0/1000/64/0 (size/max total/threshold/drops)
```

Example 13-15 **show interface serial2/1:23** *Output (Continued)*

```
     Conversations  0/1/16 (active/max active/max total)
     Reserved Conversations 0/0 (allocated/max allocated)
     Available Bandwidth 48 kilobits/sec
  5 minute input rate 0 bits/sec, 0 packets/sec
  5 minute output rate 0 bits/sec, 0 packets/sec
     93069 packets input, 847750 bytes, 0 no buffer
     Received 0 broadcasts, 0 runts, 0 giants, 0 throttles
     9501 input errors, 9010 CRC, 400 frame, 0 overrun, 0 ignored, 31 abort
     93069 packets output, 738440 bytes, 0 underruns
     0 output errors, 0 collisions, 0 interface resets
     0 output buffer failures, 0 output buffers swapped out
     0 carrier transitions
  Timeslot(s) Used:24, Transmitter delay is 0 flags
3640-isdn#
```

If the router reports a high number of errors, you might suggest that it is line quality related. However, there is no significant amount of aborts on the line. The line is not flapping (0 carrier transitions on Serial 2/1:23), and the errors are mainly format errors. You need to find out what is causing the problem and why is it worse in the morning hours versus evening hours.

NOTE   One of the most amazing stories about troubleshooting I've ever encountered was a 3 PM ISDN problem. The connection was fine, except at 3 PM every day, when the connection went down for 15 or 20 minutes. It so happened that the local loop was built under a nearby runway and every day, on schedule, a heavy Hercules aircraft would take off from that runway, which affected the connection for 15 to 20 minutes.

The second thing to do is to find a pattern. Testing with the LEC, trunk by trunk, does not provide any resolution or clues to the nature of the problem. To find a pattern, one of the possible actions here is to take a closer look at the calls, when the remote users are trying to connect to the core router's circuit Serial 2/1. In this case, the following debug commands are recommended:

```
#debug isdn events
```

```
#debug ppp negotiation
```

From the output, you can see that the call failures occur on Serial2/0:0, Serial2/0:1, and Serial2/0:2. You must determine why users calling these channels are experiencing intermittent connections. Reviewing the circuit, you can see up to five users in the morning, but a fully used circuit late in the afternoon. After monitoring the calls of all users, you identify that sometimes some users are connected for a long time, and sometimes the same users are experiencing disconnects. It looks like it's not user related, but trunk (channel) related. You must determine if and which channels cause the disconnects. After a period of monitoring, you determine that the disconnects always result from the same Serial2/0:0 to

Serial2/0:4, and the problem is definitely not user related, but channel related. But, if this is the case, why are the disconnects typical for early hours and the success rate higher for late hours?

The explanation is simple. When the users are experiencing the problem connect in the early morning, they usually connect to the first channels because there are few requests. When they connect at night, more users are connected, and as soon as the monitored users are connected to the higher channels (trunks), they are okay.

The last step is the resolution of this case.

Obviously, the first 5 channels of this particular PRI are failing. The solution is to either redefine the circuit from 23B+D to 18B+D, or busy out the first 5 trunks while working with the LEC to correct. After a few days, you need to check the Serial2/0:23 and you should see no errors, as shown in the following fragment:

```
...
    93069 packets input, 847750 bytes, 0 no buffer
    Received 0 broadcasts, 0 runts, 0 giants, 0 throttles
    0 input errors, 0 CRC, 0 frame, 0 overrun, 0 ignored, 0 abort
...
```

NOTE   Remember that when you are troubleshooting the core router, a significant amount of output is generated by such commands as **debug isdn events** and **debug ppp negotiations**. These debugs can lead to unexpected conditions on the router. The bad news for you will be that you will see more information than is relevant to your particular test plan (in the previous case, the D channel of the serial interface 2/1:23). More helpful will be to apply conditions for the debugging, such as **debug condition interface serial s2/0:23**. After that, you can type **debug isdn events** and the router reports only the ISDN events on the serial 2/0:23.

The final activity is to finish your work with the LEC, fixing the trunks or replacing malfunctioning devices.

Authentication Problems

Before discussing authentication problems, it's important to follow the next rule of the thumb in authentication: Establish the basic IP connectivity prior to implementing any authentication. Verify that the link works, then secure it.

The authentication problems are easier to resolve when used in an enterprise environment. Two basic solutions are available:

- Local authentication is used where the username (host name) and the password are defined in the particular box to which the remote user is trying to connect:

```
username 804-isdn password 7 11456A0119461B02456B
```

The previous statement is necessary in the core router to locally define the user.

- TACACS+ authentication is performed in a designated server.

A detailed description of core router's TACACS+ configuration is provided in Chapter 6 and applies to ISDN as well. In the TACACS+ server, every user has a profile (record). A sample of a user profile in the TACACS+ server is shown in Example 13-16.

Example 13-16 *Sample of a User Profile in the TACACS+ Server*

```
User Profile Information
user = 804-isdn{
profile_id = 5483
profile_cycle = 1
password = chap "********"
service=ppp {
default attribute=permit
allow ".*" ".*" ".*"
protocol=ip {
set addr=10.19.28.137
set routing=true
set route#1="10.19.28.136 255.255.255.252 10.19.28.137"
default attribute=permit
}
protocol=multilink {
default attribute=permit
}
protocol=ccp {
default attribute=permit
}
protocol=lcp {
default attribute=permit
}
}
```

More discussion about authentication can be seen in Chapter 6 and Chapter 20. Visit Cisco.com for more detailed discussion and configuration examples.

For either of these solutions, you need to know what options are available for authentication.

NOTE   PPP authentications follows the LCP stage of the PPP protocol, where you need to receive LCP OPEN, before authentication takes place.

The options for PPP authentication are as follows:

```
ppp authentication chap ms-chap pap [callback] [callin] [callout] [optional]
```

The following steps are recommended when troubleshooting authentication problems.

First, make sure you have the encapsulation type and authentication types defined properly under the BRI and dialer interfaces from both sides:

- **encapsulation ppp**
- **ppp authentication chap**

Second, use the **debug** command to monitor the authentication process:

```
3640-isdn#debug ppp negotiation
```

After the LCP is open, the expected output should look like the output shown in Example 13-17.

Example 13-17 *Output After the LCP Is Open*

```
Jul 30 11:12:21 PDT: Se2/1:5 LCP: I CONFACK [ACKsent] id 119 len 30
Jul 30 11:12:21 PDT: Se2/1:5 LCP:    AuthProto CHAP (0x0305C22305)
Jul 30 11:12:21 PDT: Se2/1:5 LCP:    MagicNumber 0x484CD7F7 (0x0506484CD7F7)
Jul 30 11:12:21 PDT: Se2/1:5 LCP:    MRRU 1524 (0x110405F4)
Jul 30 11:12:21 PDT: Se2/1:5 LCP:    EndpointDisc 1 Local
   (0x130B01534E564143413031)
Jul 30 11:12:21 PDT: Se2/1:5 LCP: State is Open
! The LCP opens successfully, PPP negotiation starts
Jul 30 11:12:21 PDT: Se2/1:5 PPP: Phase is AUTHENTICATING,
   by both [0 sess, 0 load]
Jul 30 11:12:21 PDT: Se2/1:5 CHAP: Using alternate hostname SJB12A75
Jul 30 11:12:21 PDT: Se2/1:5 CHAP: O CHALLENGE id 33 len 29 from " SJB12A75"
Jul 30 11:12:21 PDT: Se2/1:5 CHAP: I CHALLENGE id 1 len 34 from "804-isdn"
!One pair exchanged - Input and Output
Jul 30 11:12:21 PDT: Se2/1:5 CHAP: Waiting for peer to authenticate first
Jul 30 11:12:21 PDT: Se2/1:5 CHAP: I RESPONSE id 33 len 34 from "804-isdn"
Jul 30 11:12:21 PDT: Se2/1:5 CHAP: O SUCCESS id 33 len 4
Jul 30 11:12:21 PDT: Se2/1:5 CHAP: Processing saved Challenge, id 1
Jul 30 11:12:21 PDT: Se2/1:5 CHAP: Using alternate hostname SJB12A75
! Second pair exchanged - Input and Output
Jul 30 11:12:21 PDT: Se2/1:5 CHAP: O RESPONSE id 1 len 29 from " SJB12A75"
Jul 30 11:12:21 PDT: Se2/1:5 CHAP: I SUCCESS id 1 len 36 msg is "chap:
   User SJB12A75 authorized."
! Last pair exchanged - I and O
Jul 30 11:12:21 PDT: Se2/1:5 PPP: Phase is VIRTUALIZED [0 sess, 0 load]
```

There are two SUCCESS messages, and the message Phase is VIRTUALIZED ends the process.

Finally, check the way the passwords are configured. Two things are important here:

- The username in the global configuration of the remote user's router must match the CHAP of the core router. The example includes the host name of the dialer interface of the core router is SJB12A75. This means, for the general configuration mode of the remote user's router, you must have a line starting with 804-isdn#**username**

SJB12A75 password, and the core router must have an authentica-tion part reflecting the host name of the remote user—804-isdn.

- The passwords from both sides must be the same. If the password from the core router is 11456A0119461B02456B (encrypted), or the word "secret" (unencrypted), you can configure the remote user's router with the following:

```
804-isdn(config)#username SJB12A75 password secret
```

Remember that the host names are case sensitive, so when typing or comparing, make sure that the passwords match.

End-to-End Routing Problems

The routing problems are often related to configuration rules and errors.

The first type of problem arises when no default gateway is configured, or it is misconfig-ured. The rule to follow is the default gateway must point to the local router's Ethernet interface. One example is when the local DHCP is defined and part of that definition is the default gateway, as shown in Example 13-18.

Example 13-18 *The Local DHCP Is Defined and Part of that Definition Is the Default Gateway*

```
ip dhcp pool ippool
   network 10.70.209.80 255.255.255.248
   dns-server  20.68.10.70  20.68.10.140
   netbios-name-server  20.68.235.228  20.69.2.87
   domain-name cisco.com
   default-router 10.70.209.81
   lease infinite
!
```

The second case is when there is no route to a remote network. To check if a particular IP address is in the routing table, you can use the command line:

```
804-isdn#show ip route  10.20.30.40
```

If the message returned is % Network not in table, you need to define a static route to the remote party's IP address. See the *Cisco IOS Configuration Guide* for more details.

Scenario 5: Windows 2000 DDR Issue

This scenario covers DDR and the possible issues with interesting traffic that triggers the router to dial out.

In general, the DDR configurations, discussed in detail in Chapter 11, is straightforward. They are usually based on the assumption that the environment is designed and established, and includes certain hardware and software. All potential users, processes, and events are well known and the configuration is a reflection of policies, techniques, and rules. Two major conventional configuration settings are described in this scenario: the **dialer-list** command and the access control list (ACL). The syntax of the **dialer-list** command is

```
dialer-list dialer-group protocol protocol
    {permit | deny | list access-list-number}
```

You must consider what happens when a major change occurs in the environment, such as the addition of new hardware and technology. Typical cases include a new operating system (OS) or a new wireless access points being deployed in the enterprise. This is always a challenge; the DDR must be re-evaluated to meet the new requirement. This is the case (controversy) with a new Microsoft Windows 2000 platform and Cisco DDR.

The problem is that, according to monitoring and billing information, if an idle Windows 2000 (W2K)-based computer is connected to the router, the traffic can increase by as much 60 percent or more, and the number and duration of calls also increases from a reasonable 3 to 4 hours/day to almost 23 to 24 hours/day. For usage-based ISDN charges, this can increase the monthly charges by 10 to 20 times or more.

In this case, the major challenge is to transform the interesting traffic to uninteresting to the router in a way that guarantees the interoperability of the devices connected to the routers, and at the same time, not prevent the W2K-based platforms from operating. The process is iterative. You should follow four easy steps:

Step 1 Read everything available about the new product to be connected to the Cisco router. Try to understand the underlying concept for it and its implications on DDR. Implement the manufacturer's recommendations and determine if they are effective.

Step 2 Monitor and sniff all traffic and try to find patterns and characteristics of the traffic.

Step 3 Use a Cisco knowledge base to remedy any identified problems.

Step 4 Select a solution and test it. Depending on the results, return to Steps 1, 2, or 3 if necessary.

Now, follow the steps to determine if they provide the necessary fix for DDR.

Step 1: Implement the Manufacturer's Recommendations and Determine if They Are Effective

The information provided by Microsoft about the problem and possible remedies can be found at http://support.microsoft.com/directory/overview.asp. Generally speaking, this problem is a legacy issue carried over from Windows NT. It is based on certain periodic exchanges between the workstation and the server. At the URL just given, you can find that Microsoft recognizes the significance of the problem and points to four major factors contributing in the issue:

- Keeping the ISDN line up to ensure interoperability of Windows OS. The directory service client code was changed so that queries are issued once an hour.

- WAN traffic distribution of group policies.

- Browsing and other traffic incurs a high cost over ISDN routers.

- Periodic retransmit times for packets.

A more careful review of the explanations shows that more issues contribute to the problem, including domain browsing, Windows Internet Name Service (WINS) replication, directory replication, user accounts database (SAM) replication, printer browsing, and so on. All periodic retransmissions can be broken down, as Table 13-7 shows.

Table 13-7   *Periodic Retransmissions*

Packet Type	Protocol	Transport	Interval
NetLogon	SMB	TCP/IP & NetBEUI	300 seconds
Browse	SMB	TCP/IP & NetBEUI	300 seconds (Windows NT 3.1)
			720 seconds (Windows NT 3.5x)
KeepAlive	NetBIOS	TCP/IP	60 minutes (Windows NT 3.5x)
SessionAlive	NetBIOS	NetBEUI	30 seconds (LAN Manager)
Poll/Final	LLC	NetBEUI	30 seconds (or ACK to Poll)
KeepAlive	NetBIOS	IPX	30 seconds
Echo SMB	SMB	Direct Host IPX	240 seconds

In general, the recommendation is to check and change the following registry settings:

HKEY_LOCAL_MACHINE\System\CurrentControlSet\Services\NetBT\Parameters

For Windows 2000, the following data type is a string value that specifies the number of times the system will retry NetBIOS name query broadcasts. The default is 3:

BcastNameQueryCount = integer
Data Type: DWORD

For Windows 2000, the following data type is a string value that specifies the period of time that the system will wait before timing out broadcast name queries. The minimum value is 100, and the default is 750:

BcastQueryTimeout = milliseconds
Data Type: DWORD

For Windows 2000, the following data type is a string value that specifies how long NetBIOS names are cached. The minimum is 60,000 milliseconds (1 minute) and the default is 360,000 milliseconds (6 minutes):

CacheTimeout = milliseconds
Data Type: DWORD

For Windows 2000, the following data type is a string value that specifies the UDP port on the name server to send name queries or registrations. The default is 137:

NameServerPort = port
Data Type: DWORD

The following value specifies the number of times the system will try to contact the WINS server for NetBIOS name resolution. The default is 3:

NameSrvQueryCount = integer
Data Type: String

For Windows 98, the following data type is a string value that specifies how long the system waits before timing out a name server query. The minimum is 100 and the default is 750:

NameSrvQueryTimeout = milliseconds
Data Type: DWORD

For Windows 2000, the following data type is a string value that specifies how often to send session keepalive packets on active sessions. The minimum is 60 seconds and the default is 3600 seconds (1 hour):

SessionKeepAlive = milliseconds
Data Type: DWORD

For Windows 2000, the following data type is a string value that specifies how many buffers of various types to preallocate, and the maximum that can be allocated, where 1 = small, 2 = medium, and 3 = large. The default is 1, but if the WINS proxy is enabled, the default is 3:

Size/Small/Medium/Large = 1, 2, or 3
Data Type: DWORD

Step 2: Monitor and Sniff All Traffic and Try to Find Patterns and Characteristics of the Traffic

This part is the most important. It can sometimes take days or months, and hundreds of pages of sniffer information, logs, and analysis. Some examples follow.

When analyzing the service and processes of Windows 2000, you can establish that a service automatically runs as soon as you start the computer. It is called remote procedure call (RPC) and provides the endpoint mapper and other miscellaneous RPC services.

Sniffing the traffic shows the role of RPC in keeping the ISDN line up. The contribution of TCP/IDP port 111 (Cisco keyword sunrpc) is significant and generates more than 19 percent of the additional traffic.

In general, your first contributor for this extra ISDN-traffic situation is RPC (TCP/UDP port 111).

For the sniffing purposes, it's good to know some of the protocol numbers, shown in Table 13-8.

Table 13-8   *Protocol Numbers*

Service	Protocol Number
Internet Control Message Protocol (ICMP)	1
Transmission Control Protocol (TCP)	6
User Datagram Protocol (UDP)	16
General Routing Encapsulation (PPTP data over GRE)	47
Authentication Header (AH) IPSec	51
Encapsulation Security Payload (ESP) IPSec	50
Exterior Gateway Protocol (EGP)	8
Gateway-Gateway Protocol (GGP)	3
Host Monitoring Protocol (HMP)	20
Internet Group Management Protocol (IGMP)	88
MIT Remote Virtual Disk (RVD)	66
Open Shortest Path First (OSPF)	89
PARC Universal Packet Protocol (PUP)	12
Reliable Datagram Protocol (RDP)	27
Reservation Protocol (RSVP) QoS	46
Protocol Independent Multicast (PIM)	103

Also for sniffing (and not only sniffing purposes), it is useful to know the TCP/UDP port numbers. Ports are used in TCP (RFC 793) to name the ends of logical connections that carry long-term conversations. For providing services to unknown callers, a service contact port is defined. This list specifies the port used by the server process as its contact port. These port numbers are divided into three ranges:

- Well-known ports range from 0-1023
- Registered ports range from 1024-49151
- Dynamic and/or private ports range from 49152-65535

Well-known ports are controlled and assigned by the Internet Assigned Numbers Authority (IANA). The IANA is now called American Registry for Internet Numbers (ARIN) and, on most systems, can be used only by the system (or root) processes or by programs executed by privileged users. Table 13-9 shows some of the well-known ports.

Table 13-9   *Some of the Most Important Port Numbers*

Port Number	Port Type	Protocol	Keyword
0	TCP & UDP	Reserved	
1-4	TCP & UDP	Unassigned	
5	TCP & UDP	Remote Job Entry	RJE
7	TCP & UDP	Echo	ECHO
9	TCP & UDP	Discard	DISCARD

continues

11	TCP & UDP	Active Users	USERS
13	TCP & UDP	Daytime	DAYTIME
15	TCP & UDP	Who is up or Netstat	NETSTAT
16	TCP & UDP	Quote of the Day	QUOTE
19	TCP & UDP	Character Generator	CHARGEN
20	TCP & UDP	File Transfer (Default Data)	FTP-DATA
21	TCP & UDP	File Transfer (Control)	FTP
23	TCP & UDP	Telnet	TELNET
25	TCP & UDP	Simple Mail Transfer Protocol	SMTP
37	TCP & UDP	Time	TIME
39	TCP & UDP	Resource Location Protocol	RLP
42	TCP & UDP	Host Name Server	NAMESERVER
43	TCP & UDP	Who Is	NICNAME
49	TCP & UDP	Terminal Access Controller Access Cntrl Sys.	TACACS
53	TCP & UDP	Domain Name Server	DOMAIN
67	TCP & UDP	Bootstrap Protocol Server	BOOTPS
68	TCP & UDP	Bootstrap Protocol Client	BOOTPC
69	TCP & UDP	Trivial File Transfer Protocol	TFTP
70	TCP & UDP	Gopher	GOPHER
75	TCP & UDP	Any private dial-out service	
77	TCP & UDP	Any private RJE service	
79	TCP & UDP	Finger	FINGER
80	TCP & UDP	Hypertext Transfer Protocol (HTTP)	www
87	TCP	Link—commonly used by intruders	
88	TCP & UDP	Kerberos	KERBEROS

Table 13-9   *Some of the Most Important Port Numbers (Continued)*

Port Number	Port Type	Protocol	Keyword
89	TCP & UDP	Open Shortest Path First	OSPF
95	TCP	SUPDUP Protocol	SUPDUP
101	TCP	NIC Host Name Server	HOSTNAME
102	TCP	ISO-TSAP	ISO-TSAP
103	TCP	X400	X400
104	TCP	X400-SND	X400-SND
107	TCP & UDP	Remote Telnet Service	RTELNET
109	TCP	Post Office Protocol v2	POP2
110	TCP	Post Office Protocol v3	POP3
111	TCP & UDP	SUN Remote Procedure Call	SUNRPC
113	TCP & UDP	Authentication Service	AUTH
116	TCP & UDP	UUCP Path Service	UUCP-PATH
119	TCP & UDP	USENET Network News Transfer Protocol	NNTP
123	TCP & UDP	Network Time Protocol (NTP)	Well-Known
133-136	TCP & UDP	Unassigned	
137	UDP	NETBIOS Name Service	NETBIOS-NS
137	TCP	Unassigned	
138	UDP	NETBIOS Datagram Service	NETBIOS-DGM
138	TCP	Unassigned	
139	UDP	NETBIOS Session Service	NETBIOS-SSN
144	TCP	NeWS	Well-Known
161	TCP & UDP	Simple Network Mgmt. Protocol Q/R	SNMP
162	TCP & UDP	SNMP Event Traps	SNMP-TRAP
167	UDP	X Display Manager Control Protocol xdmcp	
169	TCP & UDP	Border Gateway Protocol (BGP)	Well-Known
194	TCP & UDP	Internet Relay Chat	IRC

You already established that RPC is one of the contributors in this process you are trying to analyze. Continuing the same process of sniffing for every protocol and port, you find the following:

- Netbios-ns generates more than 24 percent of the W2K-related traffic.
- Netbios-dgm generates about 1 percent of the W2K-related traffic.

- TCP 445 generates almost 5 percent of the W2K-related traffic.

- PIM generates about 33 percent, and so on.

Your percentage numbers can differ based on characteristics of the traffic.

Step 3: Use a Cisco Knowledge Base to Remedy any Identified Problems

It's time to implement the existing Cisco knowledge base. Based on the available information on Cisco.com for an ACL, you can create the following solution.

For IOS routers, the ACL might include the following:

```
access-list 101 deny    icmp any any echo
access-list 101 deny    icmp any any echo-reply
access-list 101 deny    icmp any any host-unreachable
access-list 101 deny    udp any any eq sunrpc
access-list 101 deny    udp any any eq netbios-ns
access-list 101 deny    udp any any eq netbios-dgm
access-list 101 deny    udp any any eq ntp
access-list 101 deny    tcp any any eq sunrpc
access-list 101 deny    tcp any any eq 445
access-list 101 deny    pim any any
access-list 101 deny    igmp any any
access-list 101 permit ip any any
dialer-list 1 protocol ip list 101
dialer-list 1 protocol netbios deny
```

The 77x version would include the following:

```
set udp111   offset   2 from  udphdr   pattern 00 6f
set udp137   offset   2 from  udphdr   pattern 00 89
set udp138   offset   2 from  udphdr   pattern 00 8a
set udp123   offset   2 from  udphdr   pattern 00 7b
set tcp111   offset   2 from  tcphdr   pattern 00 6f
set tcp139   offset   2 from  tcphdr   pattern 00 8b
set tcp445   offset   2 from  tcphdr   pattern 01 bd
set ip filter icmp out   ignore
set ip filter out udp111     ignore
set ip filter out udp137     ignore
set ip filter out udp138     ignore
set ip filter out udp123     ignore
set ip filter out tcp111     ignore
set ip filter out tcp445     ignore
set ip multicast off
set netbios name spoofing off
set netbios filter on
```

Or the shorter version of the same ACL for 77x router can be the following:

```
set ip filter udp out de=0.0.0.0/0:111 ignore
set ip filter udp out de=0.0.0.0/0:137 ignore
set ip filter udp out de=0.0.0.0/0:138 ignore
set ip filter udp out de=0.0.0.0/0:123 ignore
set ip filter tcp out de=0.0.0.0/0:111 ignore
set ip filter tcp out de=0.0.0.0/0:445 ignore
set ip fiter icmp out ignore
set netbios name spoofing off
set ip multicast of
set bridging of
```

Step 4: Select a Solution and Test It

At this step, you must test your solution. The objective is to prove that you are able to make the extra traffic uninteresting and prevent the router from dialing out. The recommended debug settings are

```
804-isdn#debug arp
ARP packet debugging is on
804-isdn#debug dialer
Dial on demand events debugging is on
804-isdn#debug ip udp
UDP packet debugging is on
804-isdn#debug ip tcp transactions
TCP special event debugging is on
```

The expected result from the debugging the process is displayed in Example 13-19.

Example 13-19 *Debugging Results*

```
804-isdn#
  Aug  1 06:30:25.886: %ISDN-6-LAYER2UP: Layer 2 for Interface BR0,
    TEI 88 changed to up
*Aug  1 06:30:25.910: %ISDN-6-LAYER2UP: Layer 2 for Interface BR0,
    TEI 97 changed to up
! The moment the ISDN line is established, the router is triggering a call
! based on multicast request.
*Aug  1 06:30:28.514: Di1 DDR: ip (s=161.70.209.81, d=230.0.0.1),
    28 bytes, outgoing uninteresting (list 101)
! The traffic is blocked with ACL 101
*Aug  1 06:30:28.518: Di1 DDR: sending broadcast to ip 162.30.253.254 --
    failed, not connected
*Aug  1 06:30:43.278: Di1 DDR: ip (s=161.70.209.82, d=161.68.235.228),
    96 bytes, outgoing uninteresting (list 101)
*Aug  1 06:30:44.778: Di1 DDR: ip (s=161.70.209.82, d=161.68.235.228),
    96 bytes, outgoing uninteresting (list 101)
*Aug  1 06:30:46.278: Di1 DDR: ip (s=161.70.209.82, d=161.68.235.228),
    96 bytes, outgoing uninteresting (list 101)
! The traffic is blocked to 2 WINS servers with ACL 101
*Aug  1 06:30:51.490: Di1 DDR: cdp, 295 bytes, outgoing uninteresting
    (no list matched)
*Aug  1 06:30:51.494: Di1 DDR: sending broadcast to ip 162.30.253.254
    -- failed, not connected
*Aug  1 06:30:55.502: Di1 DDR: ip (s=161.70.209.81, d=230.0.0.13),
    30 bytes, outgoing uninteresting (list 101)
*Aug  1 06:30:55.502: Di1 DDR: sending broadcast to ip 162.30.253.254
    -- failed, not connected
*Aug  1 06:31:25.502: Di1 DDR: ip (s=161.70.209.81, d=230.0.0.13),
    30 bytes, outgoing uninteresting (list 101)
*Aug  1 06:31:25.502: Di1 DDR: sending broadcast to ip 162.30.253.254
    -- failed, not connected
*Aug  1 06:31:51.562: Di1 DDR: cdp, 295 bytes, outgoing uninteresting
    (no list matched)
*Aug  1 06:31:51.566: Di1 DDR: sending broadcast to ip 162.30.253.254
    -- failed, not connected
```

continues

Example 13-19 *Debugging Results (Continued)*

```
*Aug  1 06:31:55.398: Di1 DDR: ip (s=161.70.209.82, d=161.68.222.255),
    116 bytes, outgoing uninteresting (list 101)
*Aug  1 06:31:55.574: Di1 DDR: ip (s=161.70.209.81, d=230.0.0.13),
    30 bytes, outgoing uninteresting (list 101)
*Aug  1 06:31:55.574: Di1 DDR: sending broadcast to ip 162.30.253.254
    -- failed, not connected
*Aug  1 06:32:00.406: Di1 DDR: ip (s=161.70.209.82, d=161.68.222.255),
    116 bytes, outgoing uninteresting (list 101)
*Aug  1 06:32:05.414: Di1 DDR: ip (s=161.70.209.82, d=161.68.222.255),
    116 bytes, outgoing uninteresting (list 101)
*Aug  1 06:32:51.634: Di1 DDR: cdp, 295 bytes, outgoing uninteresting
    (no list matched)
*Aug  1 06:32:51.638: Di1 DDR: sending broadcast to ip 162.30.253.254
    -- failed, not connected
*Aug  1 06:32:55.646: Di1 DDR: ip (s=161.70.209.81, d=230.0.0.13),
    30 bytes, outgoing uninteresting (list 101)
*Aug  1 06:32:55.650: Di1 DDR: sending broadcast to ip 162.30.253.254
    -- failed, not connected .
```

From the previous limited segment, you can see that you are blocking the multicast and preventing the W2K computer with an IP = 161.70.209.82 to trigger a call to the WINS servers of your enterprise. You might consider turning on all the debugging and monitoring the process in more detail and for a longer period of time.

The comparison between the Microsoft provided solution and the Cisco ACL-based solution shows the former one is able to reduce the extra traffic to 50 percent in some instances. However, the Cisco ACL-based solution blocks more than 99 percent of the extra traffic.

The recommended hours for testing the solution are at least 72 hours. It's worth trying the same solution using different hardware, a different set and number of computers, and a different environment to make sure the solution is successful. If this step does not give you the result you are looking for, you need to start from the beginning and iterate the process again.

Summary

This chapter started by covering some recommendations for practical troubleshooting of ISDN remote services. These included using #**show isdn status** to view service layers, preconfiguring the routers on both ends, and accessing the remote user's router. After that general discussion, this chapter presented five scenarios aimed toward helping you learn how to apply ISDN troubleshooting techniques covered earlier in this part:

- Scenario 1: New Install Problems
- Scenario 2: Dial-Out Problems

- Scenario 3: ISDN Performance Problems
- Scenario 4: End-to-End Communication Problems
- Scenario 5: Windows 2000 DDR Issue

PART IV

Frame Relay

Chapter 14 Frame Relay Technology Background

Chapter 15 Frame Relay Design Solutions

Chapter 16 Basic and Advanced Frame Relay Configurations

Chapter 17 Frame Relay Troubleshooting

Chapter 18 Frame Relay Troubleshooting Scenarios

Frame Relay Technology Background

Frame Relay technology includes a combination of hardware, software, standards, and architectures to provide a variety of services. They include data, Voice over Frame Relay (VoFR), Frame Relay multicast, Internet Protocol (IP) multicast over Frame Relay, Frame Relay compression, and others. It is beyond the scope of this book to include all available features of Frame Relay, so the content of Part IV, "Frame Relay," only includes the technology background, common design and configuration solutions for enterprise remote access, and proven troubleshooting techniques and scenarios.

This chapter also provides a more detailed background of Frame Relay technology, including the following:

- Frame Relay standards
- Frame Relay service architecture
- Frame Relay protocols, including Link Access Procedures for Frame Mode Bearer Services (LAPF) core and control protocol

One of the fundamental reasons for creating Frame Relay technology was the need for higher speeds. The other driving factor was the industry change from mainly text exchange, to graphical exchanges, which requires peak bandwidth or dynamic bandwidth and lower response time. Widespread digital facilities demand more reliability and less overhead, and the ability to handle bursty traffic. This combination of factors drove the development of new technology at the end of the 1980s.

Frame Relay combines the statistical multiplexing and port sharing of X.25 with the high-speed and low-delay characteristics of time-division multiplexing (TDM) circuit switching. Conceived as a derivative from X.25, Frame Relay eliminates the Layer 3 protocols of X.25 and concentrates the addressing and multiplexing in Layer 2. The architecture model is more compliant with Open System Interconnection (OSI), where the second layer deals with frames and not with packets. Only a few Layer 2 functions are used in permanent virtual circuit (PVC) solutions, and they are known as the core aspects such as checking for valid error-free frames but not requesting retransmission if an error is found. Therefore, many high-level protocol functions such as sequencing, windowing, acknowledgments, and supervisory frames are not duplicated within Frame Relay.

What Is Statistical Multiplexing?

The term *multiplexing* refers to sharing a single resource among many users. Analog communications typically use frequency-division multiplexing (FDM) to carry multiple conversations. A good example is the 6-MHz TV bandwidth, or simultaneous voice and video. FDM divides the available bandwidth between a narrow voice channel (about 4 kHz) and a wider band for video, and allocates a 900 Hz guard band between them. Digital signaling is mostly based on TDM. TDM allocates a small slot of time for every member sharing the channel. On a round-robin basis, every member gets a dedicated slot.

For more bursty applications (bursty means that the peak data rate is much greater than the average rate), statistical multiplexing is more commonly used because individual applications are supplied with bandwidth on an as needed basis. Thus, the channel is idle if all applications have nothing to send, but if at least one application has data to send, the channel is active. This provides optimal use of available bandwidth, but unlike TDM, cannot guarantee bandwidth for individual applications.

The lack of certain protocol functions in Frame Relay dramatically increases throughput because each frame requires much less processing time. Table 14-1 summarizes the characteristics of these protocols, comparing X.25 switching and Frame Relay.

Table 14-1   *X.25 and Frame Relay Comparison* [1]

Feature	X.25 Packet Switching	Frame Relay
Time-slot multiplexing	No	No
Statistical (virtual circuit) multiplexing	Yes	Yes
Port sharing	Yes	Yes
Packet sequencing	Yes	No
Error checking	Yes	No
Perform flow control	Yes	No, drops frames; on congestion
Network access	300 bps-64 kbps	56-2048 kbps; the technology provides speeds up to 45 Mbps; recent advancements include speeds up to 155 Mbps
Switch delay	10-40 msec	2-6 msec
One-way delay	200-500 msec	40-150 msec

Frame Relay uses a variable length framing structure, which ranges from a few to thousands of bits. This feature affects delay-sensitive user data because the delay is a function of the packet size. Although this is a feature in Frame Relay compression, it is a disadvantage when carrying voice traffic. However, Frame Relay has been adapted to handle the voice traffic, as defined in FRF11.1 (see Table 14-3).

The two factors that make Frame Relay a desirable choice for data transmission are the following:

- Frame Relay virtual circuits consume bandwidth only when they transport data, thus many virtual circuits can exist simultaneously across a given transmission line. Also, each device can use more of the bandwidth as needed, and thus operate at higher speeds.

- The improved reliability of communication lines and increased error-handling sophistication at end stations allows the Frame Relay protocol to discard erroneous frames, and thus eliminates time-consuming error-handling processes.

Frame Relay Standards

All written standards that govern Frame Relay implementations are American National Standards Institute (ANSI), International Telecommunication Union Telecommunication Standardization Sector (ITU-T), or Frame Relay Forum (FRF) standards. Although ANSI and ITU-T standards are based on the ISDN architecture, the FRF documents address implementation issues, ensuring the interoperability of multivendor networks. Table 14-2 summarizes some of the ANSI and ITU-T standards governing Frame Relay.

Table 14-2   *ANSI and ITU-T Standards Governing Frame Relay*

Subject	ANSI	ITU-T
Architecture and service description	T1.606	I.233
Data link layer core aspects	T1.618	Q.922 Annex A
PVC management	T1.617 Annex D	Q.933 Annex A
Congestion management	T1.606a	I.370
Switched virtual connection (SVC) signaling	T1.617	Q.933

The FRF (www.frforum.com) was created to develop Frame Relay technologies, to improve the existing standards, and to facilitate multivendor inter-operability. The FRF's formal documents are called Implementation Agreements (IAs). Table 14-3 shows the current issued agreements.

Table 14-3   *Frame Relay Forum (FRF) Implementation Agreements*

Document	Description
FRF.1.2	User-Network Interface (UNI)
FRF.2.1	Network-to-Network Interface (NNI)
FRF.3.2	Multiprotocol Encapsulation
FRF.4.1	SVC User-Network Interface (UNI)
FRF.5	Frame Relay/ Asynchronous Transfer Mode (ATM) PVC Network Interworking
FRF.6	Frame Relay Service Customer Network Management
FRF.7	Frame Relay PVC Multicast Service and Protocol Description
FRF.8.1	Frame Relay/ATM PVC Service Interworking
FRF.9	Data Compression over Frame Relay
FRF.10.1	Frame Relay Network-to-Network SVC
FRF.11.1	VoFR
FRF.12	Frame Relay Fragmentation
FRF.13	Service Level Definitions
FRF.14	Physical layer Interface
FRF.15	End-to-End Multilink Frame Relay
FRF.16	Multilink Frame Relay UNI/NNI
FRF.17	Frame Relay Privacy
FRF.18	Network-to-Network FR/ATM SVC
FRF.19	Frame Relay Operations, Administration, and Maintenance
FRF.20	Frame Relay IP Header Compression

The RFCs specific to Frame Relay are listed in Table 14-4.

Table 14-4   *IETF Frame Relay Related RFCs*

Document	Description
1604	Definition of Managed Objects from Frame Relay Services
1596	Definition of Managed Objects from Frame Relay Services
1315	Management Information Base for Frame Relay DTEs
1490	Multiprotocol Interconnect over Frame Relay
1294	Multiprotocol Interconnect over Frame Relay
1293	Inverse Address Resolution Protocol (ARP)
1973	Point-to-Point Protocol (PPP) in Frame Relay
2427	Multiprotocol Interconnect over Frame Relay

Frame Relay Service Architecture

The Frame Relay service architecture is defined as two planes: the C-plane (control) and U-plane (user). Both planes are governed by standards, such as ANSI T1.601.[2] Figure 14-1 shows the relationship between the two planes. The Frame Relay and frame switching concepts are shown in Figure 14-2 and Figure 14-3.

Figure 14-1 *C-Plane and U-Plane in Frame Relay Using the ANSI UNI Protocol*

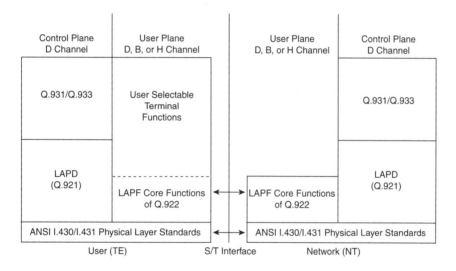

Figure 14-2 *Frame Relay Concept*

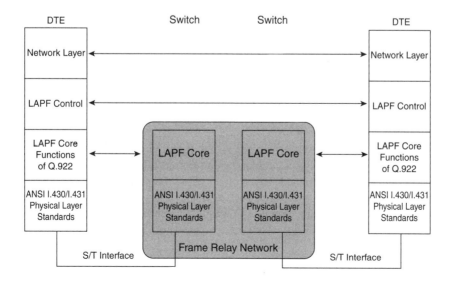

Figure 14-3 *Frame Switching Concept*

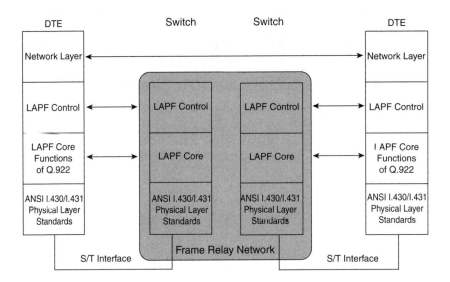

The C-plane uses the Q.921 and Q.931 protocols, and the U-plane deals with the 64-kbps B channel, the 16- or 64-kbps D channel, or the H channel (384, 1472, or 1536 kbps). The main interfaces used today are the following:

- **ITU-T V.35**—A full duplex interface that typically operates at 56 kbps
- **ANSI T1.403**—A metallic interface between carriers and the customer premises equipment (CPE), operating at DS1 or 1.544 Mbps rates

The current version of FRF.1.1[3] adds the following high-speed interfaces:

- **ANSI/EIA/TIA-530-A-1992**—An electrically balanced interface, operating at data rates below 2.1 Mbps, using a 25-pin connector
- **ANSI/EIA/TIA-613-A-1993**—Cisco's High-Speed Serial Interface (HSSI), operating at up to 53 Mbps, using a 50-pin connector
- **ANSI t1.107a**—The DS3 interface, operating at 33,736 Mbps
- **ITU G.703**—The E3 interface, operating at 34.368 Mbps
- **ITUV36/V.37**—An interface operating at 2-10 Mbps, using a 25-pin connector

From the point of view of a troubleshooting engineer, it is good to know that the most commonly available Frame Relay service is the PVC service with typically 56 kbps, or incremented fractions of 64 kbps, such as 64, 128, 384, up to 1544 kbps. Frame Relay supports switched virtual circuit (SVC) and PVC, but SVC is not commonly deployed in Frame Relay.

Frame Relay Protocols

The Frame Relay protocols are designed to reflect the concept of the second layer of the OSI model, based on services from the physical layer and providing services for the higher-layer protocols. At the same time these protocols are not simplistic. They provide a mechanism to maintain PVCs to establish SVCs, and to encapsulate higher-layer protocols.

LAPF

Frame Relay technology provides second layer functions such as framing, error control, and sequence control, and support for third layer functionality such as addressing and multiplexing. This is the core functionality of LAPF, which is defined in Recommendation Q.922. The protocol allows statistical multiplexing of one or more frame connections over a single channel. LAPF can be used over Frame Relay to provide end-to-end error and flow control. LAPF defines core functions and full functionality. The core LAPF is used for Frame Relay, and full LAPF (core LAPF and control LAPF) is used for frame switching.

LAPF Core Protocol and the T1.618 (Q.922 Annex A) Frame Format

LAPF core functions are organized around five elementary procedures:

- Frame Relay must provide services to delimit and align frames and provide transparency of the frame flags with zero-bit stuffing and unstuffing.

- Frame Relay must support virtual circuit multiplexing and demultiplexing through the use of the data-link connection identifier (DLCI) field in the frame.

- The system must inspect the frame to ensure that it aligns itself on an integer number of octets, prior to zero bit insertion and following the unstuffing of the zero bit.

- The system must inspect the frame to ensure that it does not exceed the maximum and minimum frame size (the frame sizes are established by the service provider).

- The systems must be able to detect transmission errors through the use of the Frame Check Sequence (FCS) field.

A Frame Relay network consists of endpoints (PCs, servers, local-area networks [LANs]), Frame Relay access equipment (bridges, routers, hosts and Frame Relay access devices [FRADs]), and network devices (switches, network routers and T1/E1 multiplexers). The protocol interconnecting these devices is a subset of the high-level data link control (HDLC) frame format that is shown in Figure 14-4. The frame consists of five fields:

- Beginning flag field
- Ending flag field
- Two-byte address field
- Variable-length information field
- FCS field, used for error control

NOTE For the purposes of this book, the term router is used later in the discussion as a common name for a Frame Relay access device.

Figure 14-4 *Frame Relay Frame Format*

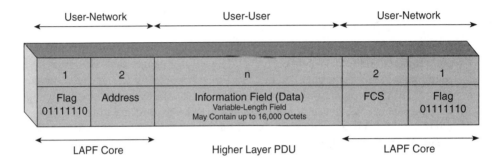

The information field and the FCS fields are no different from most protocol formats.

The information field contains encapsulated upper-layer data. Each frame in this Variable-length field includes a user data or payload field that varies in length as large as 16,000 octets. This field serves to transport the higher-layer protocol packet (protocol data unit [PDU]) through a Frame Relay network.

The FCS precedes the ending flag delimiter and is usually a cyclic redundancy check (CRC) calculation remainder. The CRC calculation is redone in the receiver. If the result differs from the value in the original frame, an error is reported. This field uses a 2-byte CRC sequence with a CRC-16 polynomial. The information field can vary in length up to 16,000 octets, but FCS code provides error detection for frames up to 4096 bytes.

The next sections concentrate on Frame Relay specific format fields such as the Flag field and Address field.

Flag Field

The Flag field is one byte that is a fixed sequence and consists of 01111110 (binary) or 0x7E (7Eh). The Flag indicates the beginning and end of the frame. If the sender needs to send 7Eh as part of the information in the middle of the transmission, but not as a Flag, the sender inspects the data stream for 011111. If found, a 0 is inserted immediately after the fifth 1, which changes the data stream (see Figure 14-5).

This procedure works regardless of the value of bit 7 (0 or 1), because of the content of the next (address) field.

Figure 14-5 *The Zero-Insertion Procedure*

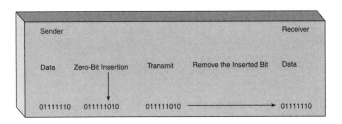

Address Field

The address field has three different formats, shown in Figure 14-6.

Descriptions of the fields follow:

- **DLCI**––Data link connection identifier is a unique number that provides local identification of the connection. The default address field format is 2 bytes or 10 bits. The extended address frame format can be 3 bytes (16 or 17 bits) or 4 bytes (23 bits).

- **C/R**––Command/Response Field provides interconnectivity with higher-layer protocols. Frame Relay does not check it and the router can use this bit for signaling and control.

- **FECN**––Forward explicit congestion notification indicates congestion in the direction of the traffic flow.

- **BECN**––Backward explicit congestion notification indicates congestion in the direction opposite of the traffic flow.

- **DE**––Discard eligible indicates the importance of the packet. If DE = 1, the packet is eligible for discarding, and in the case of congestion it can be dropped without any notification. It is a bit that can be set by the user and by the network. Setting a bit DE = 1 does not necessarily mean that the frame will be dropped; however, the packet is eligible for discard when congestion exists on the network. In fact, in CIR = 0 provisioned networks, you might have up to 99.9 percent of frames delivered.

- **EA**––Extended address extends the addressing structure from a default of 2 bytes, to 3 and 4 bytes. The EA = 0 indicates that more address follows, and EA = 1 indicates that it is the last address byte.

- **D/C**––Data or control field that exists in either the DLCI or the DL-core control indicator.

Two UNI interfaces connect to each other by using a 10-bit DLCI (by default), which provides 2^{10} = 1024 DLCIs, from 0 to 1023 (see Table 14-5).

Figure 14-6 *LAPF Core Formats of the Address Field*

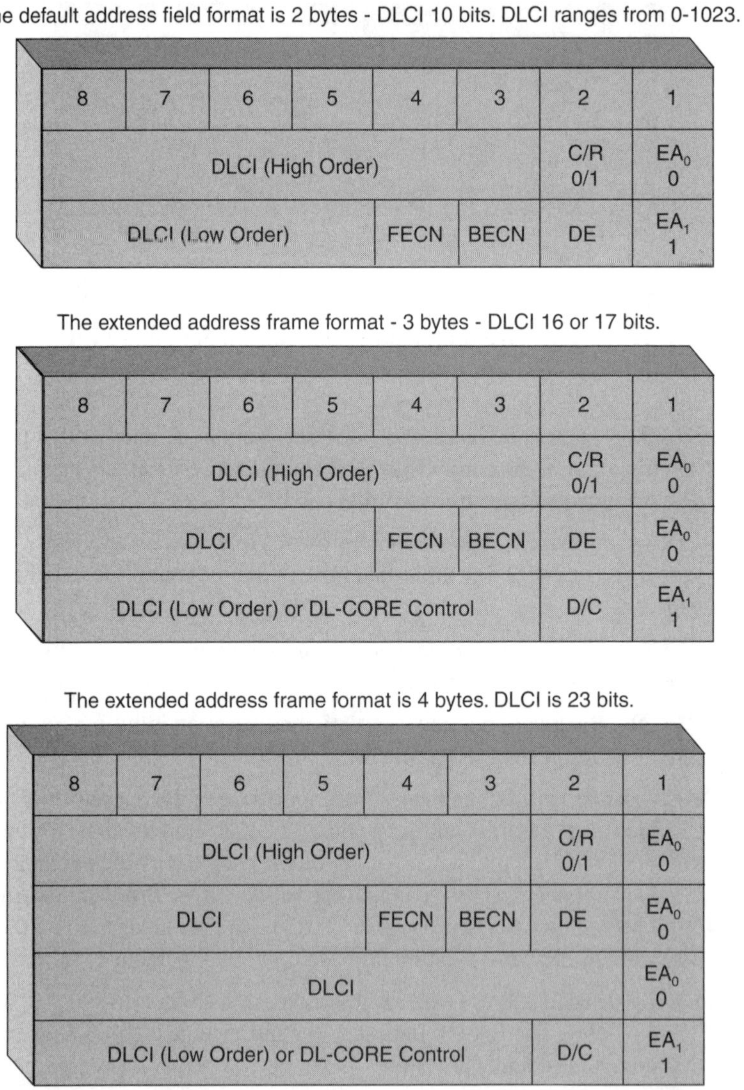

The default address field format is 2 bytes - DLCI 10 bits. DLCI ranges from 0-1023.

8	7	6	5	4	3	2	1
DLCI (High Order)						C/R 0/1	EA$_0$ 0
DLCI (Low Order)				FECN	BECN	DE	EA$_1$ 1

The extended address frame format - 3 bytes - DLCI 16 or 17 bits.

8	7	6	5	4	3	2	1
DLCI (High Order)						C/R 0/1	EA$_0$ 0
DLCI				FECN	BECN	DE	EA$_0$ 0
DLCI (Low Order) or DL-CORE Control						D/C	EA$_1$ 1

The extended address frame format is 4 bytes. DLCI is 23 bits.

8	7	6	5	4	3	2	1
DLCI (High Order)						C/R 0/1	EA$_0$ 0
DLCI				FECN	BECN	DE	EA$_0$ 0
DLCI							EA$_0$ 0
DLCI (Low Order) or DL-CORE Control						D/C	EA$_1$ 1

The core LAPF protocol uses simple logic. The first check of the incoming frame is for a valid/not valid frame. If the frame is valid, the LAPF core checks the known/unknown DLCI. If it is OK, the frame proceeds further. However, a Frame Relay network drops erroneous and non-erroneous frames. The first group of erroneous frames is dropped regardless of the condition of the network and includes packets without opening and closing flag fields, frames with the wrong DLCI, larger and smaller than expected frames, and frames with a FCS error. The second group of drops are frames with DE = 1, if there is network congestion. A third group of non-erroneous frames can be discarded randomly during periods of congestion.

Table 14-5   *Frame Relay Forum (FRF) 10-Bit DLCI Values and Their Functions*

DLCI Values	Function
DLCI Assignments	
0	Reserved for Call Control Signaling; AnnexD Local Management Interface (LMI)
1-15	Reserved
16-1007	Available for PVC
1008-1022	Reserved
1019-1022	Used by some vendors for multicast
1023	Initially defined for LMI by Consortium; used for consolidated link-layer management (CLLM) messages in T1.618
ANSI (T1.618) and ITU-T (Q.922) 10-Bit DLCI Recommendations and Management (LMI)	
0	In-channel signaling
1-15	Reserved
16-991	Assigned, using Frame Relay connection procedure
992- 1007	Layer 2 management of Frame Relay Bearer Services
1008-1022	Reserved
1023	In-channel layer management

Overall, Cisco LMI provides for 992 VCs, and ANSI provides for 976.

NOTE   The original LMI specification defines DLCI 1023 for LMI, but the AnnexD standard assigns DLCI 0 for this function. This change aligns the LMI function with previously defined ISDN, where DLCI 0 is used for signaling (refer to Table 14-5). AnnexD is the most widely accepted for multivendor solutions.

LAPF Control Protocol

For frame switching services, the LAPF control protocol is used along side the LAPF core protocol. This protocol is the full Q.922, and it is implemented both in the user's system and in the network (called the frame handler). Figure 14-4 shows one of the common formats, where the information field carries a higher-layer PDU and represents Frame Relay with other end-to-end protocols above LAPF, thus providing error and flow control. Here again, the Flag and Address fields and FCS are the same as in the LAPF core format. The specific fields for this protocol, the control field and information (data) field are discussed in the following sections.

Control Field

In Figure 14-7 and Figure 14-8, two formats of Q.922 are shown. The only difference between the core format and the control protocol format is the control field. The control field has the same format and identical functionality as the Link Access Procedure on the D channel (LAPD) field. The control protocol provides the functions of error and flow control that are missing from the LAPF core protocol.

Figure 14-7 *LAPF Frame Formats; Frame Relay with End-to-End LAPF Control*

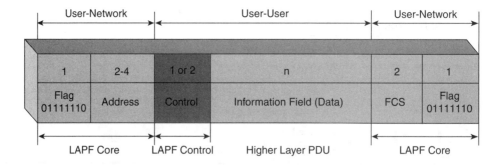

Figure 14-8 *LAPF Frame-Switching Format*

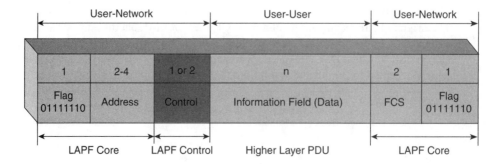

Figure 14-7 represents one possible option for end-to-end flow control and error control, based on the full LAPF protocol frame. The Frame Relay control field is part of the information field of the frame, and because Frame Relay does not monitor the information field, this feature is significant for end-to-end connections. At the same time, the information field can contain network and transport layer PDUs.

Figure 14-8 represents the frame switching bearer service. The control field is visible to the network because it is not part of the information field. Therefore, error control is performed in the user-to-network part of the structure. Regardless of this second layer control feature, the error and flow control functions can still be exercised by the higher-layer protocols.

The different LAPF control formats are shown in Figure 14-9.

Figure 14-9 *LAPF Control Formats*

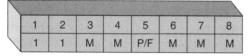

Information Transfer

1	2	3	4	5	6	7	8	9	10	11	12	13	14	15	16
0	N(S)							P/F	N(R)						

Supervisory

1	2	3	4	5	6	7	8	9	10	11	12	13	14	15	16
1	0	S	S	0	0	0	0	P/F	N(R)						

Unnumbered

1	2	3	4	5	6	7	8
1	1	M	M	P/F	M	M	M

N(S)—Transmitter Send Sequence Number
N(R)—Transmitter Receive Sequence Number
P/F—Polling/Final Bit
S—Supervisory Function Bit
M—Modifier Function Bit

NOTE   The control field in LAPF is used between the user and the network; it is not an end-to-end function. End-to-end functions are based on PDUs for the higher-layer protocols, which provide end-to-end flow and error control.

Information (Data) Field of the LAPF Control Protocol Frame

In the LAPF control protocol, the information field carries both non-data (signaling) and user data information.

A Frame Relay network uses four categories of signaling messages:

- LMI messages
- T1.617 AnnexD messages
- CLLM messages
- SVC messages

In general, the information field uses two formats as shown in Figure 14-10. In the figure, IE indicates the information elements.

Figure 14-10   *Information Field Formats*

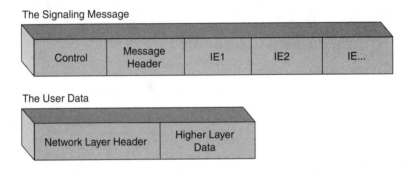

The IE fields carry higher-layer protocol information such as user data and higher-layer overhead and routing updates. It is transparent to the Frame Relay network. There is no inspection or change to this field, which allows the use of new features such as compression, Virtual Private Network (VPN), quality of service (QoS), and VoFR. ANSI T1.618 and FRF.1.1 recommend a maximum negotiated information length up to 1600 bytes to reduce the number of segmentations and re-assembly functions in wide-area network (WAN)-LAN borders. Each of the four categories of signaling messages use a Q.931 header to carry different information.

NOTE   The protocol discriminator field of Q931 (single octet) (refer to Figure 10-7) carries the format of the message that follows. The value **08H** indicates messages defined by ANSI T1.607, and **09H** indicates a Consortium message.

The messages that do not relate to the call establishment disconnect, or status use a Dummy Call Reference in Q.931 header with the field containing all zeros (00H).

Part of the signaling message is the IE, which can follow one of two basic single octet formats: single octet (type 1) and single octet (type 2). The IE can have variable length information. The two single octet types (type 1 and type 2) are shown in Figure 14-11. The single octet basic IE format and the variable-length basic IE format are explained in Table 14-6.

Figure 14-11 *Two Basic Single Octet Formats of IE. The First Format Is the Common Single Octet Format and the Second Two Show Type 1 and Type 2 Formats*

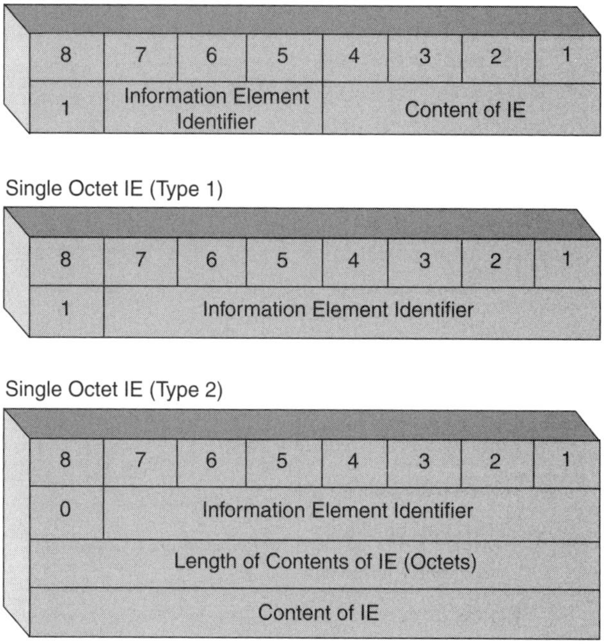

Single Octet IE (Type 1)

Single Octet IE (Type 2)

Table 14-6 *Single Octet and Variable-Length IE Format*[*]

Bits* 8765 4321	Description of the IE Formats	Max Length (Octets)
1xxx xxxx	**Single Octet IE**	
1000 xxxx	Reserved	1
1001 xxxx	Shift	1
1101 xxxx	Repeat indicator	1
0xxx xxxx	**Variable Length IE**	
0000 0001	Report type	3

continues

Table 14-6 *Single Octet and Variable-Length IE Format* [*] *(Continued)*

Bits* 8765 4321	Description of the IE Formats	Max Length (Octets)
0000 0011	Keepalive	4
0000 0100	Bearer capability	5
0000 0111	PVC status	5
0000 1000	Cause	32
0001 0100	Call state	3
0001 1000	Channel ID	n/a
0001 1001	DLCI	6
0001 1010	Link integrity verification	4
0001 1110	Progress indicator	4
0010 0000	Network specific facilities	n/a
0010 1000	Display	82
0100 0010	End-to-end transit delay	11
0100 0100	Packet layer binary parameters	3
0100 1000	Link-layer core parameters	27
0100 1001	Link-layer protocol parameters	9
0100 1100	Connected number	n/a
0100 1101	Connected subaddress	23
0110 1100	Calling party number	n/a
0110 1101	Calling party subaddress	23
0111 0000	Called party number	n/a
0111 0001	Called party subaddress	23
0111 1000	Transit network selection	n/a
0111 1100	Low-layer compatibility	14
0111 1101	High-layer compatibility	4
0111 1110	User-user	131
0111 1111	Escape for extension	n/a

*All other values are reserved; x means the value does not matter. n/a means it is not defined.

There is no commonly implemented minimum or maximum frame size for Frame Relay, although a network must support at least a 262-octet. Generally, each Frame Relay provider specifies an appropriate value for its network. Frame Relay DTE must allow the maximum acceptable frame size to be configurable. The minimum frame size allowed for Frame Relay is five octets between the opening and closing flags, assuming a two-octet Q.922 address field. This minimum increases to six octets for a three-octet Q.922 address and to seven octets for a four-octet Q.922 address format.

The Cisco maximum transmission unit (MTU) is set by default to 1500 bytes. Given the fact that the two flag fields, the default address field and the FCS, are 6 bytes, only a small portion of the size of the packet (up to (1500 – 6) / 1500 = 0.004) is the technology overhead, which is one of the unique features of Frame Relay. (See Chapter 9, "ISDN Technology Background," for a comparison with ISDN overhead.)

End Notes

[1] Held, Gilbert. *Frame Relay Networking*. John Wiley & Son Ltd. 1999.

[2] American National Standards Institute. "ISDN Basic Access Interface for Use on Metallic Loops for Applications on the Network Side of the NT." ANSI T1.601.1994.

[3] Frame Relay Forum. "User-Network Interface (UNI) Implementation Agreement." FRF.1.1, January 1996.

Summary

Frame Relay technology service offerings, which commonly include PVCs provide a variety of services for the enterprise environment, including data, VoFR, Frame Relay multicast, IP multicast over Frame Relay, Frame Relay compression, and others. This chapter gives you a better understanding about Frame Relay standards, architectures, and protocols, such as LAPF core and LAPF control protocol, and also gives you a detailed explanation about common Frame Relay protocol formats.

Review Questions

Answers to the review questions can be found in Appendix A, "Answers to Review Questions."

1   Does Frame Relay perform flow control over the frames?

2   Name the FRF implementation agreement that governs data compression over Frame Relay.

3   Define the main components of the full LAPF protocol.

4   Name the components of the Frame Relay format.

5   What is the maximum frame size that FCS can provide error detection for?

6 What is the zero-insertion procedure and why is it necessary?

7 How many DLCI address field formats are available?

8 What does the DE bit stand for and who can set it?

9 Name the LMI numbers for Consortium and AnnexD specifications.

10 What is the main difference between the core format and control protocol format of LAPF?

11 Name the four categories of signaling messages of the LAPF control protocol.

12 What is the purpose of the Dummy Call Reference in the Q.931 header?

CHAPTER 15

Frame Relay Design Solutions

Frame Relay is a versatile and flexible technology where the provisioned parameters define the way that the service can be manipulated by both the service provider and the enterprise. Provider manipulation is beyond the scope of this chapter, although the enterprise will receive the type of service (ToS) and further ability to manipulate the service, based on the design parameters, topologies, and provisioned parameters. In this chapter, you learn about the following:

- Design parameters of Frame Relay
- User-Network Interface (UNI) and Network-to-Network Interface (NNI)
- Frame Relay topologies
- User and Frame Relay switch under congestion
- Frame Relay performance criteria
- Frame Relay and upper-layer protocols
- Local Management Interface (LMI)
- Inverse Address Resolution Protocol (ARP)

Traffic shaping techniques that do not require any specific design by the enterprise are discussed in Chapter 16, "Basic and Advanced Frame Relay Configurations," and Chapter 17, "Frame Relay Troubleshooting."

To provide an effective Frame Relay service for the enterprise, the Frame Relay network has to solve two main issues: reduce the response time and prevent possible congestion and oversubscription. In the Frame Relay design stage of an enterprise network, it is important to define the design parameters, structural decisions, and both UNI and NNI solutions. It is also important to anticipate the possible multicast and compression solutions, and voice and fragmentation decisions.

Design Parameters

The following parameters must be considered in the Frame Relay design stage:

- **Access rate (AR) or link speed**—This is the data rate, which is measured at the physical interface in bits per second. The link speed determines how rapidly (maximum rate) the end user can inject data into a Frame Relay network.

- **Committed interval (Tc)**—The committed interval represents a time slot over which the rates burst and the committed information rate (CIR) is measured. The measurement is in seconds—usually ranging from 0.5 to 2 seconds. Tc is sometimes called the bandwidth interval. The user and network negotiate and agree on the measurement interval based on the I.370 recommendations:

  - When the CIR equals the AR (E1, T1), the ARs at the ingress and egress points must be equal.

  - When CIR = 0, Bc = 0, Be must be > 0 and Tc = Bc / access rate.

  The ITU-T also recommends that the end user's Frame Relay router should accept and react to the explicit congestion notifications. The router (end-user device) reacts to these notifications because the user's equipment, which is connected to the router, has no way of knowing the conditions of the Frame Relay network.

NOTE   The rule of thumb for Tc is that it should be set to four times the end-to-end transit delay.

- **Committed burst rate (Bc)**—The Bc is the maximum amount of data in bits that the network agrees to transfer, under normal circumstances, over the Tc. The Bc is established (negotiated) during a call setup, or pre-provisioned with a permanent virtual circuit (PVC). Bc defaults to the value of the CIR unless otherwise configured.

- **Excess burst rate (Be)**—The Be is the maximum amount of uncommitted data in bits over and above Bc that the network attempts to deliver in a given Tc. Be is also negotiated during call setup (in frame-switched networks), or pre-provisioned with the PVC. The probability of delivering Be is obviously lower than Bc.

NOTE   When the connection is established (whether it is a PVC or SVC), the user and network establish the CIR, Bc, and Be in the Tc. These three measurements are referred to as network capacity management, which relies on discarding frames (if necessary) at the egress point of the network.

- **Discard eligible (DE)**—The DE is a one-bit field in the Link Access Procedures for Frame-Mode Bearer Services (LAPF) address field, which indicates that the frame can be discarded to relieve congestion (see Figure 14-6 in Chapter 14).

- **CIR**—The CIR is the allowed amount of data that the network is committed to transfer under normal conditions. The rate is averaged over an increment of time Tc. The CIR is also referred to as the minimum acceptable throughput. CIR is one of the most important parameters when designing the network and when subscribing for the service. The measurement is in bps or kbps over the time period of Tc:

  CIR = Bc / Tc

Bc, Be, Tc, and CIR are defined per data-link connection identifier (DLCI). Because of this, the leaky-bucket filter controls the rate per DLCI. The access rate is valid per User-Network Interface (UNI). Bc, Be, and CIR incoming and outgoing values can be distinguished. If the connection is symmetrical, the values in both directions are the same. For PVCs, incoming and outgoing Bc, Be, and CIR are defined at subscription time as follows:

> Peak = DLCI's maximum speed; the bandwidth for that particular DLCI
> Tc = Bc / CIR
> Peak = CIR + Be / Tc = CIR (1 + Be / Bc)

If the Tc is one second:

> Peak = CIR + Be = Bc + Be
> EIR = Be
> Frames sent in excess of Bc have the DE bit set.
> Frames sent in excess of Bc + Be are dropped.

CIR Options

Figure 15-1 provides a general and simplistic view of CIR.[1] The CIR is computed over the minimum increment of Tc. Therefore, if Tc = 1.125s, a CIR of 64 kbps permits a Bc of 72 kbps (72 / 1.125 = 64). If the Bc is 144 kbps and the Tc is 1.125s, the CIR is 128 kbps (128 × 1.125 = 144).

Figure 15-1 *Committed Information Rate (CIR), Excess Information Rate (EIR), and the Service Offering*

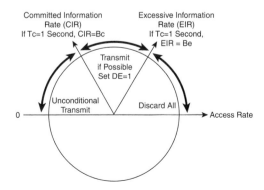

NOTE	Each user's frame is sent at the wire (link) speed (access rate). The end user can be provisioned for a CIR of 128 kbps on a T1 link of 1.544 Mbps, and as a result, the traffic can burst across the link at 1.544 Mbps, which provides low latency in the ingress and egress points.

Several factors must be considered when selecting a CIR from the service provider. Some service providers offer CIRs in increments of 16 kbps, from 0 up to a fractional T1, full T1, and more. Others might not offer CIR = 0 (zero CIR) and might provide CIRs in increments of 4 kbps or 64 kbps. Another choice can be between 56 kbps and fractions of a T1. The cost of the service is proportional to the CIR; therefore, the choice can significantly impact the monthly network charges for the enterprise.

Zero CIR Selection

If the design of the network is to carry only non-delay critical data, you should provision the circuit for CIR = 0. If the CIR = 0, every bit is marked with DE = 1. The fact that every frame is eligible for discard does not mean that the network drops the frame. In fact, service providers generally allow more than 99 percent of frames to flow from end to end. If the frame is dropped, the higher-layer protocols can retransmit the dropped packets. However, the frames can be delayed slightly until the network congestion clears. This is a trade-off for the lower cost of the service.

Also, if all the endpoints are connected to the same Frame Relay switch, only the backplane of the switch is between them, and a CIR of 0 is often all that is needed for wire speed performance. The importance of CIR increases when the topology is more complex, such as in interswitch links. During times of network congestion, DE packets are the first to be discarded, but the data won't be lost because the upper-layer protocols will retransmit them.

Aggregate CIR

Using an aggregate CIR, also referred to as oversubscription, can be a beneficial technique when traffic bursts occur on different PVCs. For example, if a T1 is installed to a core router, and four users are each configured for four slots of 64 kbps ($64 \times 4 = 384$ kbps), two basic line conditions exist in the PVC design: idle and busy. If only two users use the service and the other two are idle, the first two can use the entire rate up to 1.544 Mbps, and because every user is setup for 384 kbps, every extra frame is marked with DE = 1. Regardless of the configured rate, the overall rate is much higher. Now, suppose that every user is configured for 768 kbps. The aggregated rate of all users configured is 2×1.544, which is referred to as an oversubscription. In this example, the ratio is 2:1, where the subscription rate is two times more (2×1.544) than the T1 speed (1.544).

NOTE   Many people are uneasy with the idea of oversubscription, sometimes referred to as *statistical multiplexing*. Telephone companies (telcos) get a bad reputation for doing it, but Internet service providers (ISPs) do it to a much greater extent. Oversubscription of 7:1 or more from an ISP is not uncommon.

Usually, a 3:1 ratio is a sound ratio, depending on usage patterns. The important factor is to have a relatively reliable picture of the traffic distribution during the day, and the estimation that not all users will burst at the same time of day. Then, the 3:1 ratio reflects a traffic prediction that no more than 33 percent of users will use the service during the same period each day.

Asymmetrical CIRs

For interactive query-response types of traffic and for typical client/server operations, the traffic in both directions can differ significantly. For this reason, it makes sense to consider different CIRs in both directions. This is referred to as asymmetrical CIRs. They reduce the organization's service charges if they are appropriate for that organization's traffic.

Adjustable (Flexible) CIR

If the traffic can be planned precisely (for example, trending of the production environment with different shifts and number of users), and if the service provider supports this feature (for an additional fee), it is worth it to request an adjustable CIR. This feature is also known as bandwidth on demand and it can be beneficial when you are trying to satisfy expected changes in bandwidth requirements.

When requesting adjustable CIRs from the service provider, it is important to keep in mind the following parameters:

- **EIR** — A parameter that is measured in bps or kbps that identifies the bits transmitted per second over the time period of Tc, which are beyond the CIR.

- **Offered load** — The amount of data, measured in bits, that the user is ready to request for delivery to the selected destination (DLCI).

- **Explicit congestion notification** — This term refers to the process of explicitly notifying the user of network congestion that is recognized as one of the following states: normal condition (no congestions), mild congestion, and severe congestion.

- **Implicit congestion notification** — This term refers to the high-layer protocol's role in Frame Relay or frame switching, where error and flow control operations depend on the frame congestion condition of the network.

UNI

The Frame Relay standards (refer to FRF 1.2) clearly define bearer services provided by the network to make UNI possible. As shown in Figure 15-2, the UNI operation area is locally defined between the data terminal equipment/data communications equipment (DTE/DCE) peers. In turn, the bearer service definition includes the following:

- Bidirectional frame transfer
- Preservation of the frame order
- Detection of transmission, format, and operational errors
- Transparent transport of user data, with modification of the address and error-control fields only
- No frame acknowledgment

Figure 15-2 *Area of Operation for the User-Network Interface (UNI)*

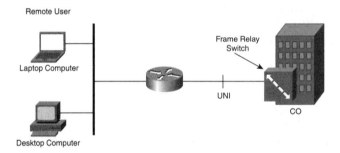

The underlying assumption of Frame Relay is low error rates. Therefore, only a simple, connection-oriented transport service is required. The flow-control and error-recovery functions are beyond the scope of Frame Relay and are provided by higher-layer protocols, such as the Transmission Control Protocol (TCP). Therefore, the reduced overhead of Frame Relay in comparison to other similar technologies is one of its greatest advantages, providing high-rate and large payload connections.

NOTE   The opposite of X.25, which was the transport of choice prior to Frame Relay, TCP's ability to detect errors and the robustness of current carrier quality networks pushed the role of flow control and error recovery from Layer 2 to Layer 3/4.

NNI

FRF2.1 defines the NNI, which extends user communications beyond the scope of UNI. The NNI interface is concerned with the transfer of C-plane and U-plane information between two network nodes that belong to two different Frame Relay networks. Figure 15-3 shows the area of operation of NNI. To keep the architecture functioning in a multivendor environment, network-to-network signaling must exist to keep the PVCs interconnected. To provide this functionality, every pair of adjacent networks (1 and 2; 2 and 3) must support additional provisions to request status information (see details in Chapter 16), and must be able to respond to them. These provisions are called bidirectional procedures. More information about this topic can be found in the Frame Relay Forum's (FRF's) "Frame Relay Network-to-Network Interface Implementation Agreement," or at www.frforum.com.

Figure 15-3 *Area of Operation for the Network-to-Network Interface (NNI)*

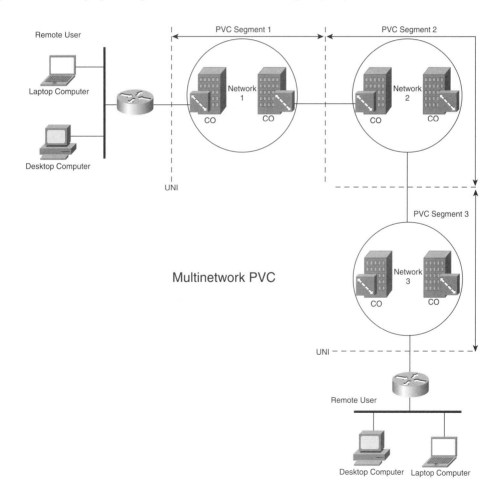

Voice over Frame Relay

Voice over Frame Relay (VoFR) is defined under FRF.11.1. The Frame Relay approach requires the upper-layer protocols, such as the connection-oriented protocol TCP, to ensure end-to-end delivery of frames. However, retransmission results in repeating part of the voice message, which is not acceptable from a user's standpoint. In this case, packetizing and buffering of the frames is required, where the entire message must be stored and played with the appropriate timing.

Imminent transport layer retransmissions are not the only possible issues in VoFR designs. Other issues are related to voice compression, silence suppression, echo cancellation, and the ability to preserve voice quality. Additional information and the latest developments on VoFR are available from the FRF, and at www.cisco.com.

Frame Relay Multicast

The multicast provision exists in most local-area network (LAN) technologies and as part of the Internet Protocol (IP). Multicast is a feature that enables one source to send information to multiple recipients. A typical wide-area network (WAN) uses a point-to-point (unicast) connection, where the user transmits information to only one recipient. Frame Relay multicast is addressed in FRF.7, and this agreement defines one-to-many types of connection, where one sender who provides information to multiple recipients. The architecture is based on the International Telecommunication Union Telecommunication Standardization Sector (ITU-T) recommendation X.6, "Multicast Service Definition." The model defines multicast groups, which includes a multicast server that provides service to all members of the group. In the case of Frame Relay, the server must be internal to the network, so that members can establish multipoint relationships and participate in point-to-multipoint data transfer. Three types of services are defined:

- One-way
- Two-way
- N-way

In one-way service, a central location called a root has a point-to-point relationship with all other members of the group, which are called leaves. The root has a one-to-one connection to the server, as does every single leaf. Two-way multicast doubles the previously described structure, providing a full duplex connection. In N-way service, all members of the group are peers, thus every message is sent to all members of the group. The LMI extension provides the following multicast messages to ensure proper functioning of multicast groups:

- Addition
- Deletion
- Presence

Frame Relay Topologies and Congestion Control

After a discussion about Frame Relay design parameters, an understanding of the various Frame Relay topologies becomes important.

Partial-Mesh and Full-Mesh Frame Relay Designs

Frame Relay networks provide several virtual circuits that form the basis for connections between stations (routers) that are attached to it. The resulting set of interconnected devices form a private Frame Relay group. These groups can be either fully interconnected with a complete mesh of virtual circuits, or only partially interconnected. In either case, each virtual circuit is uniquely identified at each Frame Relay interface by a DLCI.

From an architectural point of view, a Frame Relay topology supports both partial-mesh and full-mesh structures. Because of the permanent nature of the connections, partial-mesh structures contain physical connections to some sites but not to all, thus creating an any-to-some structure. It becomes obvious that a fully meshed structure requires more resources because an any-to-any connection requires n number of sites to be connected to each other. This number can be calculated by using the following formula:

Number of physical connections = $n \times (n - 1) / 2$, where n is the number of connected routers.

NOTE   These topologies might exist not only on the service provider side, but in enterprises that use Frame Relay as a private network solution.

Regardless of the Frame Relay network topology, from an enterprise standpoint, two main configurable connections exist to the Frame Relay network: point-to-point and point-to-multipont configurations, which are addressed in detail in Chapter 16.

User and Frame Relay Switch Operations Under Congestion

The existence of virtual circuits and statistical multiplexing in Frame Relay requires sophisticated methods to deal with congestion. The Frame Relay specifications provide guidelines and rules on how the user should react to forward explicit congestion notifications (FECNs) and backward explicit congestion notifications (BECNs). The Frame Relay switch at the ingress UNI must exercise caution in the amount of traffic that it permits to enter the network. To prevent severe congestion, you need to implement measures not only at the UNI, but at the switch's ingress point, which should know when to implement rate adoption control.

The software at the ingress point should be informed and fast enough to implement a remedy before the traffic load becomes a problem. There are no formal rules for the number of buffers, traffic, and throughput; however, the unofficial rule is the smaller the queue, the lower the delays and better response time.

Two main methods control congestion in Frame Relay networks using explicit notification:

- **Rate adoption algorithm**—The rate adoption algorithm uses both a system of counters and certain ratios of the number of bits to perform rate adjustments. This system is also called the leaky-bucket algorithm. The algorithm maintains a running count of the cumulative number of bits sent during a measurement interval. The counter decrements at a constant rate of 1 per bit, to a minimum value of 0, and increments to the value of the threshold.[2] When the predefined threshold is exceeded, the switch sets the FECN and BECN bits of the passing packet to 1, which notifies both parties that the direction is experiencing congestion.

- **Consolidated link-layer management (CLLM)**—Another congestion method involves using the CLLM message. CLLM transmits management messages over DLCI 1007 (or DLCI 1023 in T1.618), which is reserved for it. Thus, DLCI 1007 (1023) notifies the edge switches that congestion has occurred and that the message contains a list of affected virtual connections. The edge switches then set up the FECNs and BECNs of the appropriate packets or issue another CLLM to end devices that support CLLM.

NOTE   Cisco uses Enhanced LMI (ELMI). Its usage is discussed in Chapter 16.

Figure 15-4 is an illustration of the first method using the rate adoption algorithm. The first Frame Relay network switch (called the Frame Relay Cloud [FRC] switch) experiences congestion. For this illustration, assume that the router connected to edge switch A sends data to both edge switch B and the router connected to edge switch B through the FRC switch. Then assume that there is additional traffic coming from the Frame Relay network to edge switch B. If the FRC switch and edge switch B are connected through a T1 and, at some point, the overall traffic increases and exceeds 1.5 Mbps, the FRC switch notifies all switches of the congestion. For a short period of time, the buffers in the FRC switch overflow and the frames are dropped. This is why the FRC switch sets the FECNs and BECNs to 1, in the manner shown in the figure. When the FRC switch reaches a certain threshold, it sets FECN = 1 in the frames that are coming from edge switch A and that are forwarded by the FRC switch to edge switch B. At the same time, the FRC switch sets BECN = 1 in the frames that are transmitted from edge switch B to edge switch A to identify the network that is experiencing congestion in the opposite direction.

There is no standard criteria for setting BECNs and FECNs. It is obvious that different providers can choose different criteria to set up these bits. In most cases, router A lowers the transmission rate if the incoming messages contain BECN = 1.

Figure 15-4 *The Frame Relay Congestion Mechanism and Use of FECNs and BECNs*

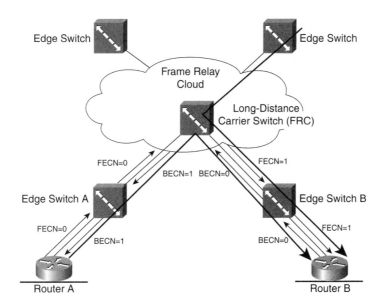

American National Standards Institute (ANSI) Annex A in T1.618 defines guidelines for using BECNs and FECNs by the user and the network. The FRC switch does not set the FECNs and BECNs directly. Instead, the FRC switch generates a CLLM to edge switches A and B, and these switches then decide to either set BECNs or FECNs or to generate another CLLM message to routers A and B. The CLLM messages are incompatible with the initial LMI specification because DLCI 1023 is used, but they are compatible with the Annex D specification.

Congestion and Windowing

Using windowing to manage congestion is suggested in the book *ISDN and SS7: Architectures for Digital Signaling Networks* by Ulysses D. Black. The basic approach resembles the windowing mechanism in the TCP/IP stack, but combines the FECNs and BECNs with the sliding window technique. Unlike TCP, the sliding window technique reduces and increases the size of the window by a factor of 0.125, depending on the network conditions. In Cisco routers, windowing is configurable by parameter K, where K is a maximum number of I-frames that are either outstanding for transmission or transmitted but not acknowledged. The value of K ranges from 1 to 127 frames, with a default of 7. The calculations are based on 2 to the exponent n, where if n = 3, the enumeration of windows is from 0 to 7.

Frame Relay Performance Criteria

The design of Frame Relay requires setting objectives for the future network design, when conducting capacity planning, and developing the ability to measure performance using different criteria. Section 4 of T1.606 contains several definitions of Frame Relay performance parameters. The following sections summarize these performance parameters.

Throughput

The term *throughput* is defined as the number of protocol data units (PDUs) successfully transferred (FCS indicates success) in one direction, per a predefined time period (measurement interval) over a virtual connection. For this definition, the PDU is considered to be all data between the flags of the Frame Relay frame (see Figure 14-4).

Transit Delay

The transit delay is a measurement of the time it takes to send a frame across the link between two points (DCE, Frame Relay access device (FRAD), router). The delay is a function of the access rate of the link, the distance, and the size of the frame. A rough estimate can be obtained by using the following equation:

Delay (seconds) = size (bits) / link access rate (bps)

Transit delay is measured between boundaries, which can be between two adjacent DCEs, two networks, and so forth. Based on the boundary, the measurement starts when the first bit of the PDU leaves the source (t_1), and ends when the last bit of the PDU crosses the other party's boundary (t_2). The transit delay can be measured by the following equation:

Transit delay = $(t_2) - (t_1)$

The virtual circuit transit delay is the sum of all delays across all boundaries of the virtual connection.

Residual Error Rate

Residual error rate (RER) is synonymous with the undetected error ratio of the number of bits incorrectly received and undetected to the total number of bits sent. RER is measured through the exchange of Frame Relay service data units (SDUs), or FSDUs. This measurement can be calculated from the following formula:

RER = 1 − (total correct delivered SDUs / total offered SDUs)

RER is an important component when considering future use of bandwidth demand. The future design must address these parameters when evaluating the service offerings from different providers.

At the same time, RER must be correlated with the user's actual throughput and CIR. If the user constantly exceeds the CIR agreement, a high RER is expected. Conversely, if the design parameters are not exceeded, a lower RER is expected.

Other Performance Parameters

The following parameters are defined by the ITU-T, and are referred to as quality of service (QoS) parameters that affect network performance:

- **Delivered erroneous frames**—The number of frames that are delivered when one or more bits in the frame are discovered erroneous.

- **Delivered duplicate frames**—The number of frames delivered twice or more.

- **Delivered out-of-sequence frames**—The number of frames that are not in the expected sequence.

- **Lost frames**—The number of frames not delivered within the predefined time period.

- **Misdelivered frames**—Frames delivered to the wrong destination.

- **Switched virtual call establishment delay and clearing delay**—These refer respectively to the time required to establish and clear the call across the C-plane.

- **Premature disconnect**—Describes the loss of the PVC.

- **Switching virtual call clearing failure**—Describes a failure to teardown the switched virtual call.

Frame Relay and Upper-Layer Protocols

Flow control and error recovery functions can be performed by the full LAPF protocol. Typically, the full LAPF is not used in PVC circuits. Therefore, these functions must be performed by the higher-layer protocols, which are encapsulated in the PDU as a component of the information field of the frame format. This approach is the most commonly implemented today. To ensure the interoperability of Frame Relay and higher-layer protocols, two major issues must be addressed: multiprotocol support and fragmentation.

Multiprotocol support refers to the encapsulation of higher-layer protocols such as IP, TCP, Internetwork Packet Exchange (IPX), and X.25, in the frame format. FRF.3.2 and RFC 1490, "Multiprotocol Interconnect over Frame Relay" (by Bradley and published by IETF) both address this topic. Fragmentation refers to the process of dividing large network packets into smaller packets and then reassembling them at the receiver site. This subject is governed by ANSI T1.617a Annex A, "Signaling Specification for Frame Relay Bearer Service for Digital Subscriber Signaling System Number 1 (DSS1) Protocol Encapsulation and PICS."

Frame Relay carries two types of data: routed packets and bridged packets. The remote user's router must distinguish between the two types of frames. To assist with this purpose, up to four fields can be added to the T1.618 information field format, as shown in Figure 15-5. They are the Network Layer Protocol ID (NLPID), L2 Protocol ID, L3 Protocol ID, and Subnetwork Access Protocol (SNAP).

Figure 15-5 *Multiprotocol Encapsulation Options*

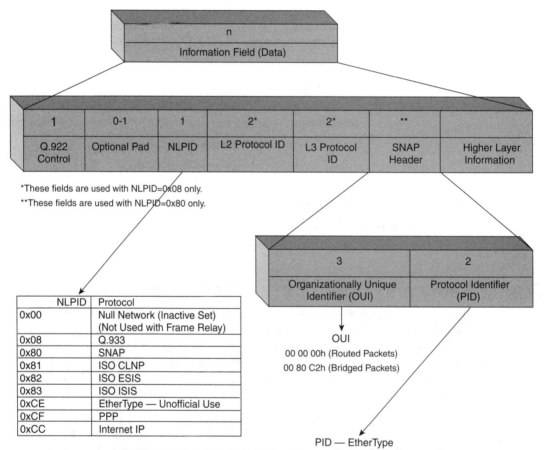

*These fields are used with NLPID=0x08 only.

**These fields are used with NLPID=0x80 only.

NLPID	Protocol
0x00	Null Network (Inactive Set) (Not Used with Frame Relay)
0x08	Q.933
0x80	SNAP
0x81	ISO CLNP
0x82	ISO ESIS
0x83	ISO ISIS
0xCE	EtherType — Unofficial Use
0xCF	PPP
0xCC	Internet IP

OUI

00 00 00h (Routed Packets)

00 80 C2h (Bridged Packets)

PID — EtherType

With Preserved FCS (h)	Without Preserved FCS (h)	Media
00 01	00 07	802.3 /Ethernet
00 02	00 08	802.4
00 03	00 09	802.5
00 04	00 0A	FDDI
00 05	00 0B	802.6
	00 0D	Fragments
	00 0E	BPDUs, Defined by 802.1d or 802.1g
	00 0F	Source Routing BPDUs

The Q.922 Control field specifies an Unnumbered Information (UI), Supervisory (S), or Information (I) frame. The Pad field aligns the rest of the frame on a two-octet boundary and contains up to a single octet with the value 00h. The ISO and ITU-T administer the NLPID, which defines the encapsulation of the protocol that follows. The common values are 08h for Q.933; 80h for SNAP; 81h for ISO Connectionless Network Protocol (CLNP); and CCh (0xCC) for IP. In some cases, Layer 2 and Layer 3 Protocol IDs or a SNAP header follow the NLPID. Some of the encapsulated protocols are covered in the next section.

Encapsulating IP, Q.933, and SNAP

ANSI T1.617a Annex F defines the standards for encapsulating IP, Q.933, and SNAP. When encapsulating IP, an optional pad can be added to align the rest of the frame on a two-octet boundary. No further control information, such as IDs or a SNAP header is required.

The encapsulation format for Q.933 can be used when no specific network protocol is defined.

SNAP is used for encapsulating bridged IEEE 802.3 frames for routed and bridged packets that contain LAN-to-LAN traffic. The NLPID is set to 80h and is followed by a 5-byte SNAP header (3-byte OUI + 2-byte PID). Routed packets use OUI 00 00 00h, and bridged packets use OUI 00 80 C2h to identify the IEEE 802.1. Figure 15-6 shows the encapsulation formats for IP, Q.933, and SNAP.

Figure 15-6 *Encapsulating IP, Q.933, and SNAP*

IP

1	2	1	1	Variable	2	1
Flag 01111110	Address	Q.922 Cntrl (03h)	NLPID (CCh)	IP Datagram	FCS	Flag 01111110

Q933

1	2	1	1	2	2	Variable	2	1
Flag 01111110	Address	Q.922 Cntrl (03h)	NLPID (08h)	L2 Protocol ID	L3 Protocol ID	Protocol Data	FCS	Flag 01111110

SNAP

1	2	1	1	1	3	2	Variable	4	2	1
Flag 01111110	Address	Q.922 Cntrl (03h)	Pad 00h	NLPID (80h)	OUI 00 80 C2h	PID 00 01h or 00 07h	802.3	LAN FSC If PID Is 0001h	FCS	Flag 01111110

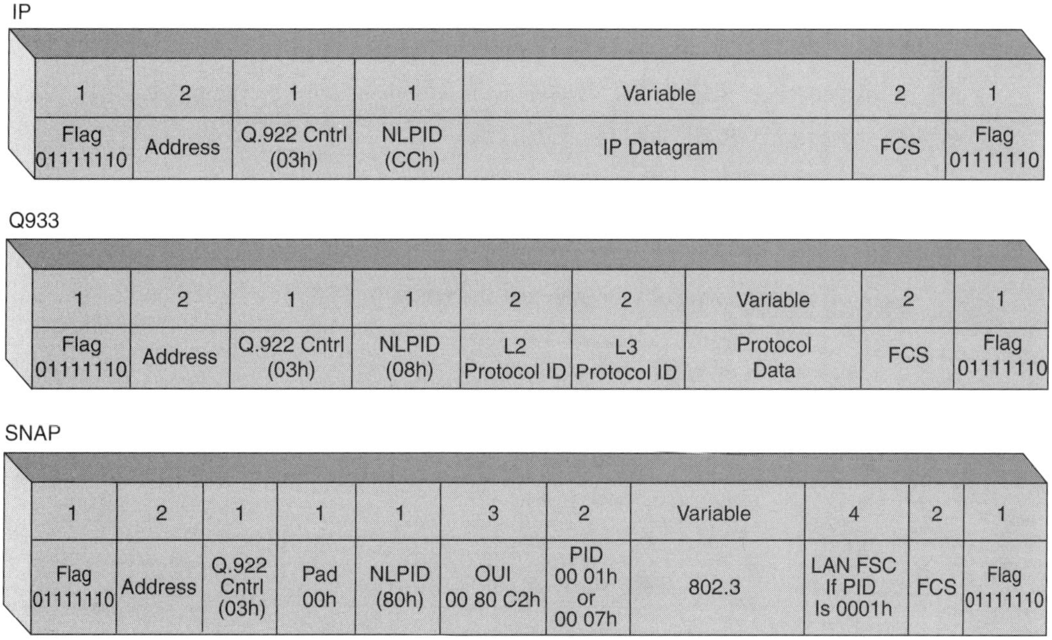

Encapsulating Other Protocols over Frame Relay

To indicate the usage of the ISO CLNP protocol, the NLPID field must be set to 81h. As soon as the NLPID field indicates ISO CLNP, the data packet immediately follows. NLPID is also considered part of the CLNP packet, and as such, it should not be removed before being sent to the upper layers for processing.

IPX does not have a NLPID value defined. For this reason, IPX is encapsulated using the SNAP header. The frame format is in the following order: Initial Q.922 Address and Control field = 03h, then the Pad field is added (00h). NLPID is 80h (SNAP) and OUI – 00 00 00h (routed packets), followed by PID = 8137h, and then the IPX packet itself with possible fragmentation.

FRF.3.2 provides additional encapsulation examples, including Systems Network Architecture (SNA) and NetBios traffic over Frame Relay.

Frame Relay Fragmentation

The upper-layer protocols use different formats and usually the information field contains more than one T1.618 frame. T1.617A Annex F and RFC 1490 address the fragmentation process. When a packet must be fragmented, the fragmentation protocol adds an encapsulation header to it and divides the packet into many smaller fragments, according to network requirements. Each fragment receives a fragmentation header (see Figure 15-7). In the example, the size of the IP packet is greater than the size of the T1.618 frame, and you use the RFC 1490 recommendations.

The fragmentation header consists of four fields:

- A Sequence (Seq.) field (2 bytes) that is incremented for every fragment
- A Reserved (Rsvd) field (4 bits, all 0s)
- A Final bit, which is 0 for the first fragment and 1 for the last one
- An Offset field, which is an 11-bit value that represents the logical offset of this fragment, divided by 32. The first fragment has an offset = 0.

The Cisco recommendations for fragment sizes in Table 15-1 are based on port access rates.

Table 15-1 *Cisco Recommendations for Fragment Sizes*

Port Access Rate	Recommended Data Segmentation Size
64 kbps	80 bytes
128 kbps	160 bytes
256 kbps	320 bytes
512 kbps	640 bytes
1536 (full T1)	1600 bytes
2048 (full E1)	1600 bytes

Figure 15-7 *Fragmented IP Packet in Frame Relay*

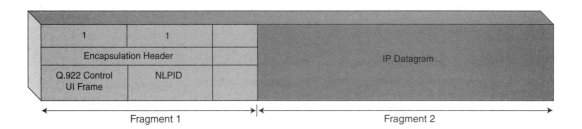

Fragment 1

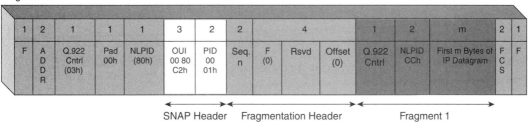

Fragment 2

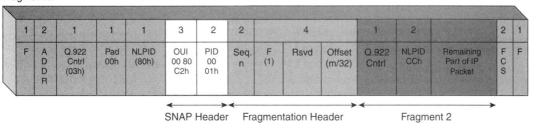

LMI

A consortium of companies known as the *Gang of Four*, which is composed of Cisco Systems, Inc., Digital Equipment Corp, Northern Telecom, and StrataCom, Inc., developed and published the LMI for UNI. The LMI is a set of enhancements to the basic Frame Relay specification that include the following:

- **Virtual circuit status messages** — The only common extension
- **Multicasting messages** — Optional LMI extension
- **Global addressing messages** — Optional LMI extension
- **Simple flow control** — Optional LMI extension

The derivatives of the LMI Consortium were formally adopted as T1.617 Annex D and Q.933 Annex A. The first group of messages, known as the virtual circuit status messages, are the only common LMI (adopted by all vendors) extensions (see Figure 15-8).

Figure 15-8 *The UNI LMI Area of Operation*

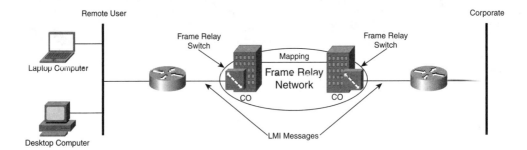

Three different LMI types are supported by Cisco:

- Cisco-Consortium
- ANSI-T1.617 Annex D
- Q.933a-ITU-T Q.933 Annex A

These formats are related to Frame Relay troubleshooting, and their differences are described in the following sections.

The purpose of the Annex D LMI type is to create a multivendor LMI type. The difference between Cisco LMI and Annex D LMI is that, in Annex D, ANSI provides a signaling scheme derived from the initial LMI agreement. To avoid confusion, the Consortium LMI is referred to as the Consortium, and the ANSI T1.617 LMI is referred to as Annex D.[3] The LMI messages periodically poll the network using the Q.931 structure, and are transmitted in HDLC UI frames. To indicate the LMI message, Consortium LMI uses DLCI 1023, whereas Annex D LMI uses DLCI 0. In both cases, the FECN, BECN, and DE bits are set to 0. Within the Q.931 header of Annex D messages, the PD field is set to 08h, and the Consortium LMI sets the PD field to 09h. The Dummy Call Reference and message types are identical, but unlike Consortium, Annex D adds the Locking Shift information element (IE) to the message header.

NOTE   The remaining discussion uses Consortium to refer to the original LMI specifications, and Annex D to refer to ANSI (T1.617 Annex D).

Consortium (Cisco) LMI Type

The Consortium designed the LMI protocol to perform the following functions:

- Allow the network to notify the FRAD about active and present DLCIs
- Allow the network to notify the FRAD if DLCI is removed or fails
- Monitor the status of the router-to-network link in real-time through keepalive messages

The Consortium LMI defines two messages: status enquiry and status. The general format of this LMI type is shown in Figure 15-9.

Figure 15-9 *Format of Consortium LMI Messages*

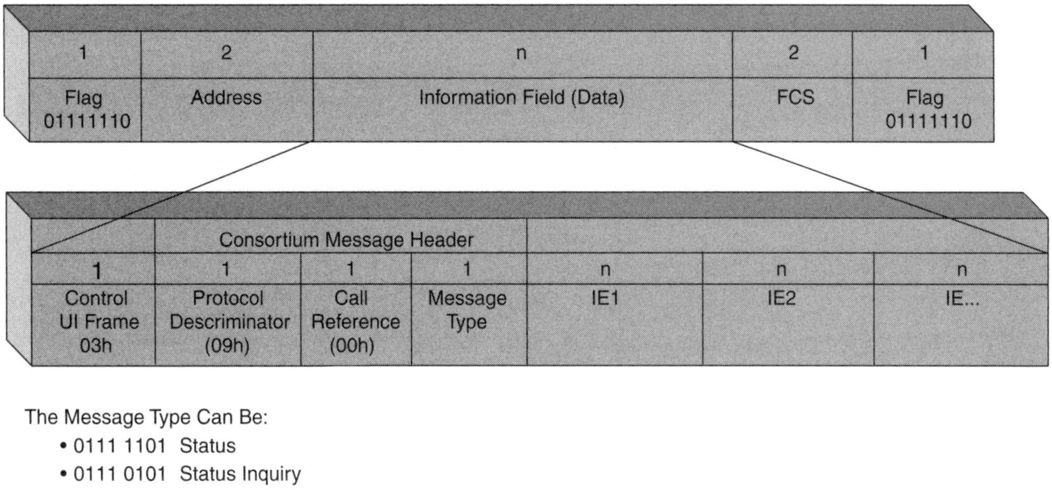

The Message Type Can Be:
- 0111 1101 Status
- 0111 0101 Status Inquiry

Both messages are sent in HDLC UI frames, with a Control field value of 03h. The three-octet message header is based on Q.931 and includes a Protocol Discriminator (09h), a Call Reference Value (00h, also a Dummy Call Reference), and a Message Type indicator. The message types are 75h (0111 0101) to indicate status enquiry, and 7Dh (0111 1101) to indicate status.

Annex D (ANSI) LMI Type

The T1.617 Annex D defines a polling protocol for use between the router and the network to exchange information about the status of the interfaces and the defined PVCs. The functions of the protocol are as follows:

- Notification of the addition of a PVC
- Detection of the deletion of a PVC

- Notification of the availability or unavailability of a configured PVC
- Verification of the integrity of the link (UNI)

The router periodically polls the network, sending a status enquiry message, and the network responds with a status message. The polling period is a negotiable parameter, and ten seconds is the default. The first poll requests a link integrity verification response to determine the status of the in-channel signaling link. Another polling cycle (typically every six polling cycles) occurs when the user requests the status of all PVCs on the interface. The resulting response is a full status message that contains information on each PVC that is configured on that physical channel. The information includes the recent history of the PVC and its availability (inactive or active). The periodic polling for Annex D also detects error conditions, such as reliability errors of DLCI 0, signaling-link protocol errors, or internal network problems. The format of these messages is shown in Figure 15-10.

Figure 15-10 *Format of Annex D LMI Messages*

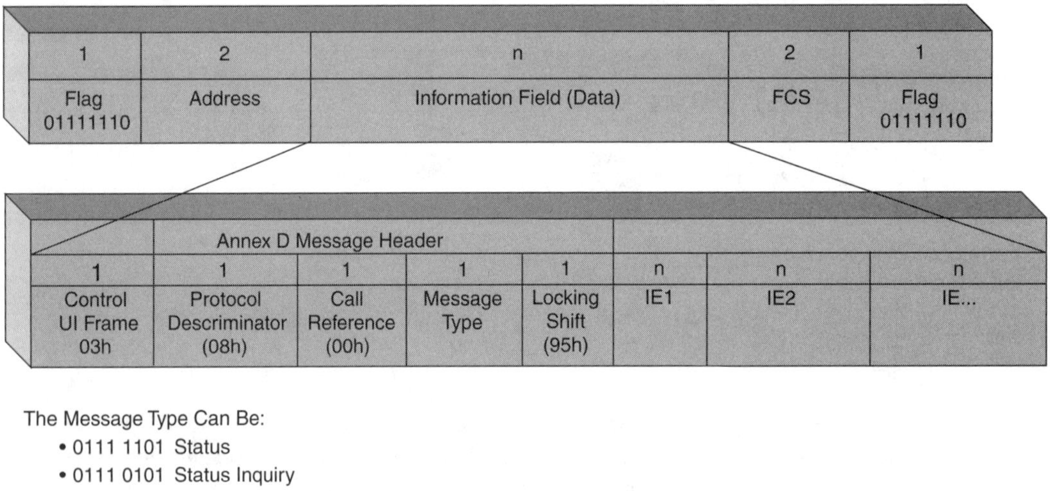

The Message Type Can Be:
- 0111 1101 Status
- 0111 0101 Status Inquiry

Although the Consortium status enquiry messages use the Report Type and Keepalive Sequence IEs, the Annex D status enquiry messages contain Report Type and Link Integrity Verification IEs (see Figure 17-3 and 17-5). The Link Integrity Verification IE (03h) provides an identification ID in the first byte. The second byte indicates the length of the integrity verification content. The third byte is the end sequence number and the fourth byte is the receive sequence number.

ITU-T Q.933 Annex A LMI Type

The vast majority of contemporary Frame Relay solutions are based on PVCs. However, for SVC, the ITU-T Q.933 Annex A LMI type is recommended. For more information, refer to Cisco documentation or the book *Frame Relay for High-Speed Networks*, by Walter Goralski.

In terms of LMI global addressing, Frame Relay resembles a LAN. Address Resolution Protocol (ARP) operates in Frame Relay exactly as it does in a LAN where ARP maps Layer 3 IP to Layer 2 Media Access Control (MAC). The Inverse ARP implementation for Frame Relay is described in the next section.

Address Resolution: ARP, Reverse ARP, and Inverse ARP

The higher-layer protocol encapsulation in Frame Relay formats raises the issue of resolving the upper-layer addresses to Frame Relay addressing schemes. Especially in point-to-multipoint connections, where the hub side has many Layer-3 addresses (typically IPs) assigned, you need to resolve the Layer-2 address (regardless if it is a DLCI or Q.922 address) to the Layer-3 address (IP). The problem can be resolved by polling all subinterfaces for hardware and protocol address resolution, but this method does not seem appropriate. The Frame Relay network provides several virtual circuits that form the basis for connections between stations that are attached to the same Frame Relay network. Every DTE in Frame Relay can have a DLCI, which is the Frame Relay equivalent of a hardware address that is associated with an established PVC, but DTE does not know the protocol address of the other party.

ARP

Address resolution can be accomplished by using the standard ARP encapsulated within a SNAP. DLCIs have a local significance for the Frame Relay networks, but they have no significance whatsoever for the end station (for example, a computer) connected to the Frame Relay router. Therefore, such a station does not have an address to put into the ARP request or reply. The DLCI carried within the Frame Relay header is modified as it traverses the network. When the packet arrives at its destination, the DLCI has been set to the value that, from the standpoint of the receiving station, corresponds to the sending station, but when an ARP message reaches a destination, all hardware addresses are invalid. However, the address found in the frame header is correct. It looks like Frame Relay can use this address in the header as the sender hardware address and still perfom ARP. However, the problem is that the target hardware address in both the ARP request and reply will be also invalid.

Reverse ARP

Could Reverse Address Resolution Protocol (RARP) be a solution? RARP works the same way as ARP. The response to a request returns the protocol address of the requesting station, not the address of the station receiving the request. IP-specific mechanisms are designed to only support the IP protocol.

Obviously, ARP and RARP are not a solution, and a new address resolution variation was developed. This variation is called Inverse ARP (InARP), which is essentially an expanded ARP.

Inverse ARP

InARP enables a Frame Relay station to discover the protocol address of a station that is associated with the virtual circuit. It is more efficient than sending ARP messages over every virtual circuit for every address that the system wants to resolve, and it is more flexible than relying on a static configuration. Basic InARP operates essentially the same as ARP, with the exception that InARP does not broadcast requests. This is because the hardware address of the destination station is already known. A requesting station simply formats a request by inserting its source hardware, protocol addresses, and the known target hardware address. It then zero fills the target protocol address field. Finally, it encapsulates the packet for the specific network and sends it directly to the target station.

In a Frame Relay interface that supports data-link management, an InARP-equipped station that is connected to such an interface sends an InARP request and addresses it to the new virtual circuit. If the other side supports InARP, it can return a response that provides the requested protocol address. In a Frame Relay environment, InARP packets are encapsulated using the NLPID/SNAP format. For more information on the InARP protocol format, see www.faqs.org/rfcs/rfc2390.html. In Cisco routers, the InARP is established by default and does not show up in the configuration. From a configuration point of view, using InARP is referred to as dynamic mapping—see Chapter 16 for more details. InARP does not work without LMIs because it uses LMI messages to determine which PVC to map (remember that LMI carries information for all configured PVCs). If the DLCI is down, the Cisco router still processes and maps an InARP, but does not use it until DLCI is reported as active.

End Notes

[1] Kessler, Gary. *Frame Relay: CIR and Billing Issues*. Network VAR, 1995.

[2] Stallings, W. *ISDN and Broadband ISDN with Frame Relay and ATM*. Prentice Hall, 1998.

[3] American National Standards Institute. "Integrated Services Digital Network (ISDN)–Signaling Specifications for Frame Relay Bearer Services for Digital Subscriber Signaling System Number 1 (DSS1)." ANSI T1.617 Annex D, 1991.

Summary

Frame Relay design is an imminent part of enterprise remote access solutions. In fact, the design and provisioned parameters define the ability of the enterprise to use the versatility and flexibility of Frame Relay for its own benefits.

In this chapter, you learned about design parameters, UNI and NNI interfaces, and VoFR and Frame Relay multicast. Extended information about Frame Relay topologies, congestion control, and performance criteria is another major topic of the chapter. The higher-layer protocol encapsulations and fragmentation are provided in detail. In turn, the higher-layer encapsulation requires resolution of Layer 3 and Layer 2 addresses, where ARP, RARP, and InARP are explained.

Review Questions

Answers to the review questions can be found in Appendix A, "Answers to Review Questions."

1 Define the term access rate (link speed).

2 What is the recommendation for setting the committed interval Tc in Frame Relay?

3 Define the committed information rate (CIR).

4 Define the excess information rate (EIR)

5 Define the explicit congestion notification types.

6 What is the area of operation of UNI in Frame Relay.

7 Define the area of operation of NNI.

8 Name the three Frame Relay multicast messages.

9 If n is the number of connected routers, define the number of physical connections in a full-mesh topology.

10 Name the two main methods to control congestion in Frame Relay networks by using explicit notification:

11 What is transit delay? How do you obtain a rough estimate of transit delay?

12 Name the four main specific and common specifications of LMI.

13 Name the three LMI types that are supported by Cisco.

14 Can InARP run without LMI?

Basic and Advanced Frame Relay Configurations

The configuration options in Frame Relay are derived from the design and provisioning choices made in earlier phases of Frame Relay service. In the configuration phase, it is preferable to apply a Hub/Spoke topology, as described in Chapter 15, "Frame Relay Design Solutions," which is more suitable to the permanent nature of Frame Relay. This chapter provides detailed information about basic and advanced configurations in Cisco Frame Relay routers. The Frame Relay encapsulations (cisco, ietf), DLCI encapsulations (cisco, ietf, ppp, and protocol) and LMI types (cisco, ANSI, and q933a) will not be discussed here. Cisco.com provides detailed information about these topics. This chapter includes two main sections:

- Basic Frame Relay configurations:
    - Point-to-multipoint configurations
    - Point-to-point configurations, their hub side and spoke side
    - Minimum data-link connection identifier (DLCI) recommendations— Frame Relay and the chosen routing protocols
    - The Frame Relay broadcast queue
- The advanced configuration sections include the following:
    - Configuring IP unnumbered Frame Relay
    - Frame switching configuration
    - ISDN as Frame Relay backup configuration, based on dialer profiles and Hot Standby Router Protocol (HSRP) and Enhanced Interior Gateway Routing Protocol (EIGRP)
    - Frame Relay bridging
    - Frame Relay compression, including header compression, per-virtual circuit compression, and hardware compression
    - Frame Relay and IP multicast configuration
    - Frame Relay and traffic shaping with generic traffic shaping, traffic shaping classes, and foresight adaptive shaping with Enhanced Local Management Interface (ELMI)

Basic Frame Relay Configurations

This section covers the basic Frame Relay configuration information including point-to-multipoint configurations, point-to-point configurations, minimum DLCI recommendations, and the Frame Relay broadcast queue.

Point-to-Multipoint Configurations

The basic Frame Relay configurations for point-to-multipoint include the configuration of both the core (hub) and the remote user's (spoke) side. Figure 16-1 shows an example of this configuration.

Figure 16-1 *Hub and Spoke in a Point-to-Multipoint Configuration*

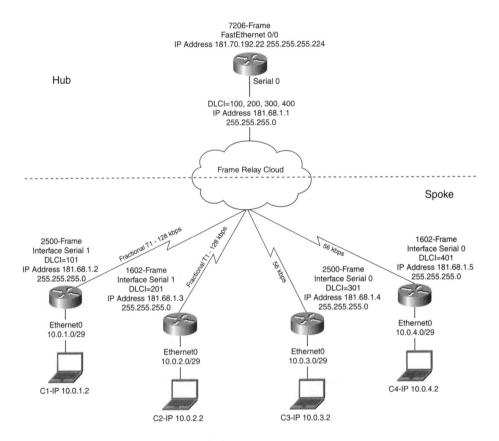

Point-to-Multipoint Configuration of the Hub

Example 16-1 shows a hub side configuration, including the FastEthernet interface and the serial interface of the core router.

Example 16-1   *Basic Hub Configuration in a Point-to-Multipoint Configuration*

```
7206-frame#show running-config
 <output omitted>
interface FastEthernet0/0
 description FastEthernet connection to gateway1
 ip address 181.70.192.22 255.255.255.224
 !
interface Serial0
 ip address 181.68.1.1 255.255.255.0
 encapsulation frame-relay
 frame-relay interface-dlci 100
 frame-relay interface-dlci 200
 frame-relay interface-dlci 300
 frame-relay interface-dlci 400
 !
 !
router eigrp  19
 network 181.68.0.0
 network 181.70.0.0
 !
 <output omitted>
```

In this configuration, the hub side is configured on a Cisco 7206x router (7206-frame) and is connected to four spoke routers with DLCI 100, 200, 300 and 400. The configuration uses dynamic mapping based on Inverse ARP (InARP). InARP is enabled by default and no additional command is required on interface Serial0.

The routers learn the DLCIs from the Frame Relay switch through Local Management Interface (LMI) updates. The routers then use InARP for the remote Internet Protocol (IP) address and create a map of local DLCIs and their associated remote IP addresses (see the section, "Inverse ARP" in Chapter 15). When Frame Relay InARP is enabled, broadcast IP traffic goes out over the connection by default. Using InARP is called *dynamic mapping*. The response from InARP is stored in an address-to-DLCI mapping table on the router that supplies the next hop protocol address for the outgoing interface.

As discussed in Chapter 15, an alternative to using InARP is static mapping. You must use static mapping if the router at the other end either does not support InARP, or does not support InARP for a specific protocol. To establish static mapping according to your network needs, use the commands in Example 16-2. Pay attention to the mapping statements under the Serial0 interface.

In this configuration, the Internet Engineering Task Force (IETF) encapsulation is set up on a per-DLCI Basis. If all DLCIs are using the same encapsulation type, you can use a shorter configuration by configuring the IETF encapsulation on a per-interface basis.

Example 16-2 *Static Mapping Configuration of the Hub Serial Interface*

```
7206-frame#show running-config
<output omitted>
interface Serial0
  ip address 181.68.1.1 255.255.255.0
  encapsulation frame-relay
  frame-relay map ip 181.68.1.2  100 broadcast ietf
  frame-relay map ip 181.68.1.3  200 broadcast ietf
  frame-relay map ip 181.68.1.4  300 broadcast ietf
  frame-relay map ip 181.68.1.5  400 broadcast ietf
<output omitted>
```

NOTE
In the latter case, **encapsulation frame-relay** becomes **encapsulation frame-relay ietf**, and each static mapping statement changes. For example, **frame-relay map ip 181.68.1.2 100 broadcast ietf** becomes **frame-relay map ip 181.68.1.2 100 broadcast**, and so on.

The protocol IP address 181.68.1.2 is bound to DLCI = 100. The command **frame-relay map ip 181.68.1.2 100 broadcast ietf** can be interpreted as saying, "If you want to reach IP 181.68.1.2, use DLCI 100," thus mapping a next hop protocol address to the DLCI that connects to the protocol address. InARP is enabled by default for all protocols that it supports, but it can be disabled for specific protocol-DLCI pairs. When you supply a static map, InARP is automatically disabled for the specified protocol on the specified DLCI.

NOTE
The keyword **broadcast** greatly simplifies the configuration for the Open Shortest Path First (OSPF) protocol. See *Cisco IOS Wide-Area Networking Command Reference* for more information about using the **broadcast** keyword.

You can use dynamic mapping for some protocols and static mapping for other protocols on the same DLCI. You can disable InARP for a protocol-DLCI pair if you know that the protocol is not supported on the other end of the connection.

Point-to-Multipoint Configuration of the Spoke

The configuration on the remote user's router (spoke) is similar to the configuration segment in Example 16-3.

Example 16-3 *Configuring the 2500-Frame Router as a Spoke in a Point-to-Multipoint Configuration*

```
2500-frame#show running-config
<output omitted>
interface Ethernet0
  ip address 10.0.1.1 255.255.255.248
```

Example 16-3   *Configuring the 2500-Frame Router as a Spoke in a Point-to-Multipoint Configuration (Continued)*

```
!
interface Serial1
 ip address  181.68.1.2  255.255.255.0
 encapsulation frame-relay
 frame-relay interface-dlci 101
 !
 !
router eigrp  19
 network 10.0.0.0
 network 181.68.0.0
 !
<output omitted>
```

Similarly, this side can apply InARP or static mapping. If the following command is applied to Interface Serial1, the protocol IP address 181.68.1.2 is bound to DLCI = 101:

```
frame-relay map ip 181.68.1.1  101 broadcast ietf
```

This can be interpreted as saying, "If you want to reach IP 181.68.1.1, use DLCI 101," thus mapping a next-hop protocol address to the DLCI 101 to connect to the protocol address.

Dynamic and static mapping is applicable to this configuration. With a point-to-point configuration, however, only the static mapping solution is applicable.

Point-to-Point Configurations

Configuring a physical interface with multiple subinterfaces or multiple virtual interfaces is another example of the virtuality used in Cisco routers. This approach is commonly used in point-to-point configurations. The benefits of this configuration are realized in partially meshed Frame Relay designs. The concept of subinterfaces was originally created to better handle issues caused by split horizon over nonbroadcast multiaccess (NBMA) networks (such as Frame Relay, Asynchronous Transfer Mode [ATM], Switched Multimegabit Digital Service [SMDS], or X.25), the distance vector-based routing protocols (such as Internetwork Packet Exchange [IPX] Routing Information Protocol/Service Advertisement Protocol [RIP/SAP], AppleTalk, and IP RIP), and transparent bridging. A virtual interface overcomes the rules imposed by split horizon. Because every virtual interface can be considered a separate interface, sending packets back to the same physical interface does not violate the rules of split horizon.

The point-to-point configuration solution allows the transformation from a partially meshed to a de facto, fully meshed configuration. To the routed protocol, each subnetwork now appears to be located on separate interfaces. Routing updates that are received from one side on one logical point-to-point subinterface can be forwarded to another on a separate logical interface without violating split horizon.

NOTE   In the NBMA model, all routers are configured as one logical subnet. As such, NBMA resembles a local-area network (LAN) logical topology.

NOTE   The split horizon rule states the following: Never advertise a route out of the interface through which it was learned.

The basic hub and spoke configuration in a point-to-point configuration is shown in Figure 16-2.

Figure 16-2 *Hub and Spoke in a Point-to-Point Configuration*

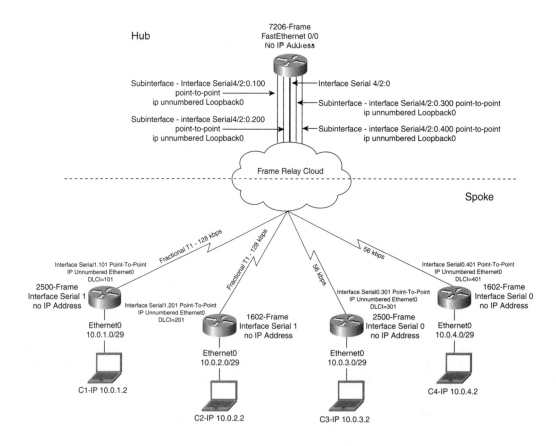

Point-to-Point Configuration of the Hub

The core side is configured according to Example 16-4. Here, the Serial4/2:0 interface, a T1/Channelized Primary Rate Interface (PRI), is configured with four subinterfaces: Serial4/2:0.100, Serial4/2:0.200, Serial4/2:0.300, and Serial4/2:0.400. It is good practice to have the circuit description under the T1/PRI, as in Example 16-4. When working with the service provider, one can reference the interface description for circuit information.

Example 16-4   *Configuration of 7206-Frame as a Hub Router in Point-to-Point Configurations*

```
7206-frame#show running-config
<output omitted>
interface Serial4/2:0
 description Home Frame Relay : NUA :5555555511 : HICAP CID XXXYYZZZ72HCR-001
 no ip address
 encapsulation frame-relay
 no ip route-cache
 no fair-queue
 frame-relay traffic-shaping
 frame-relay lmi-type ansi
 frame-relay broadcast-queue 100 1200 120
!
interface Serial4/2:0.100 point-to-point
 description 2500-frame: 10.0.1.0/29
 bandwidth 128
 ip unnumbered Loopback0
 no ip route-cache
 frame-relay class class-128-new
 frame-relay interface-dlci 100
!
interface Serial4/2:0.200 point-to-point
 description 1602-frame : 10.0.2.0/29 : 14716506 : 3842400259
 bandwidth 128
 ip unnumbered Loopback0
 no ip route-cache
 frame-relay class class-128-new
 frame-relay interface-dlci 200
!
interface Serial4/2:0.300 point-to-point
 description 2500-frame1 : 10.0.3.0/29:  : 3823600256
 bandwidth 56
 ip unnumbered Loopback0
 no ip route-cache
 frame-relay class class-56-new
 frame-relay interface-dlci 300
!
interface Serial4/2:0.400 point-to-point
 description 1602-frame1 : 10.0.4.0/29 : 14787359 : 3872200079
 bandwidth 56
 ip unnumbered Loopback0
 no ip route-cache
 frame-relay class class-56-new
 frame-relay interface-dlci 400
!
interface Loopback0
 description monitoring loopback 0 interface
 ip address 192.3.25.75 255.255.255.255
<output omitted>
```

It is good practice to have a description for every DLCI and user to make remote trouble-shooting easier. You can locate that particular interface quickly by using the different search/find features of IOS.

The line **description 2500-frame: 10.0.1.0/29** explains that this subinterface is configured for a spoke user, called 2500-frame. The rest of the subinterfaces are configured in a similar manner.

Another recommended technique in this configuration is to use the description of the subinterface that is consistent with the DLCI number. It saves time in the troubleshooting process by matching the subinterface number with its associated DLCI.

The configured loopback 0 interface allows any monitoring tool to monitor the status of the 7206-frame router.

The IOS feature IP unnumbered is discussed in the advanced configuration section.

An important part of the hub configuration in point-to-point configurations is to define how routing is performed. For the purposes of this example, dynamic EIGRP routing is used for the hub router, and static routing is used for the spoke routers. The important routing segments of the configuration are shown in Example 16-5 and Example 16-6.

Example 16-5 shows how to prevent other routers on a local network from learning about routes dynamically. One approach here can be to keep routing update messages from being sent through a router interface. This feature applies to all IP-based routing protocols except the Border Gateway Protocol (BGP), and can be configured in the global configuration mode with the following command:

```
Router(config-router)#passive-interface interface-type interface-number
```

Example 16-5 *Configuring the Passive Interfaces in the Hub Router*

```
<output omitted>
 router eigrp 19
 redistribute static
 passive-interface Serial4/2:0.100
 passive-interface Serial4/2:0.200
 passive-interface Serial4/2:0.300
 passive-interface Serial4/2:0.400
 network 10.0.0.0
 no auto-summary
 no eigrp log-neighbor-changes
```

As usual, to configure the static routing statements, you must add the commands shown in Example 16-6.

In this example, there is a next hop address for subinterfaces of 10.0.1.1, 10.0.2.1, 10.0.3.1, and 10.0.4.1. To define the next hop address of the routing statement, you must refer to the advanced configuration section, where it is explained how the subinterface Serial1.201 obtains its IP address from the Ethernet 0 interface of the spoke router.

Example 16-6 *Configuring the Routing Statements in the Hub Router*

```
<output omitted>
ip classless
ip route 10.0.1.0 255.255.255.248 Serial4/2:0.100 10.0.1.1
ip route 10.0.2.0 255.255.255.248 Serial4/2:0.200 10.0.2.1
ip route 10.0.3.0 255.255.255.248 Serial4/2:0.300 10.0.3.1
ip route 10.0.4.0 255.255.255.248 Serial4/2:0.400 10.0.4.1
<output omitted>
```

Point-to-Point Configuration of the Spoke

Next, you configure the spoke router to ensure consistency with the hub router. The Ethernet interface is configured with a static IP address and helper address. The Serial1 interface is configured for 128 kbps (**service-module t1 timeslots 1-2**) with no IP address.

Subinterface Serial1.201 obtains an IP address through the IP unnumbered feature of IOS, which is explained in the advanced configuration section of this chapter. The default route statement points to the Loopback0 address of the hub router (192.3.25.75). The major elements of the configuration can be seen in Example 16-7.

Example 16-7 *The Major Elements of the Spoke Router Configuration*

```
1602-frame#show running-config
interface Ethernet0
 ip address 10.0.2.1 255.255.255.248
 ip helper-address 192.168.221.193
!
 <output omitted>
interface Serial1
 no ip address
 encapsulation frame-relay
 no ip mroute-cache
 no fair-queue
 service-module t1 timeslots 1-2
 frame-relay lmi-type ansi
!
interface Serial1.201 point-to-point
 ip unnumbered Ethernet0
 bandwidth 128
 frame-relay interface-dlci 201
!
ip classless
ip route 0.0.0.0 0.0.0.0 192.3.25.75
ip route 181.70.194.1 255.255.255.255 Serial0.201
ip route 10.0.2.0 255.255.255.248 Ethernet0
<output omitted>
```

The other spoke routers from Figure 16-2 are configured in a similar manner.

In each of the hub and spoke configurations, you must understand how the IP addressing scheme is defined. In the hub configuration, the serial subinterfaces obtain their IP address from the Loopback0 interface. In the spoke configuration, Serial1.201 obtains its IP address from the Ethernet0 interface. This IP preservation technique is only applicable to point-to-point configurations. You are not limited to one Loopback interface.

NOTE	You cannot change the subinterface configurations from point-to-point to point-to-multipoint or vice versa without reloading the router. When a subinterface is configured, IOS defines an interface descriptor block (IDB). The IDBs defined for subinterfaces cannot be changed without a reload. Also, using the **no interface** command shows the subinterfaces as deleted until the router is reloaded, when it disappears from the output. You can also change the encapsulation from Frame Relay to high-level data link control (HDLC) on the interface. This strips out all subinterfaces because HDLC does not support this feature, but you still need to reboot the router.

Maximum Number of DLCIs Per Interface

As you already know from Chapter 14, "Frame Relay Technology Background," the default DLCI address space is 10 bits. Theoretically, $2^{10} = 1024$ DLCIs can be configured on a single physical link. In reality, certain DLCIs are reserved for management and signaling messages. The available DLCIs for permanent virtual circuits (PVCs) range from 16 to 1007 for Consortium and from 16 to 992 for American National Standards Institute/International Telecommunication Union Telecommunication Standardization Sector (ANSI/ITU-T) specifications. However, the LMI protocol requires that the full status report about all PVCs fit into a single packet. This generally limits the number of DLCIs to fewer than 800, and depends on the maximum transmission unit (MTU) size.

If you have the output of a **show frame-relay lmi** command from your Cisco device, you might notice that the report type (RT) information element (IE) is one byte long and the keepalive (KA) IE is 2 bytes long. For the ANSI and Q933a LMIs, the PVC IE is 5 bytes long. For the Cisco LMI, it is 8 bytes long because of the additional bandwidth value. Detailed information from the **debug frame-relay lmi** command is given in Chapter 17. For the purposes of the calculation, consider that the MTU size is equal to the entire LMI packet, which is 1500 bytes. Then, you subtract 13 bytes from the entire LMI packet. 13 bytes = IEs (10 bytes) + RT (1 byte) + KA (2 bytes). Next, divide that number by the length of the PVC IE (5 bytes for ANSI and Q933a, 8 bytes for Cisco) to get the maximum theoretical number of DLCIs for the interface:

For ANSI or Q933a, the formula is

max DLCIs = (MTU – 13) / 5

For Cisco, the formula is

max DLCIs = (MTU – 13) / 8

The calculation for the maximum number of DLCIs per router is available in the Cisco documentation. You can also refer to Appendix C of *Cisco Internetwork Design* by Matthew H. Birkner (Cisco Press, 2000).

Routing Protocols and Frame Relay Configurations

It is well known that every routing protocol adds overhead, which in some cases, can be considerable, and reduces the overall bandwidth. Distance vector protocols, such as RIP and the Interior Gateway Routing Protocol (IGRP), use periodic updates to exchange routing information. RIP updates are exchanged every 30 seconds. RIP IPX updates are exchanged every 60 seconds, which results in the bandwidth consumption reaching 18.7 percent of the access rate of a T1. Some size estimates of the various distance vector routing protocol updates are shown in Table 16-1.

Table 16-1 *Size Estimates for Various Distance Vector Protocols*

Protocol	Bytes
RIP	10
IGRP	14
Novell RIP	12
Novell SAP	85
AppleTalk	6
Virtual Integrated Network Service (VINES) Real-Time Transport Protocol (RTP)	6
Digital Equipment Corporation net (DECnet)	4
IGRP	16
Xerox Network Systems (XNS)	12

Link-state protocols impose other requirements on the configuration. Examples of these protocols include EIGRP for IP, IPX, AppleTalk, OSPF for IP, and Integrated Intermediate System-to-Intermediate System (IS-IS) for IP. Because these protocols do not broadcast large updates regularly, and thereby less frequently affect performance of the normal user data, higher packet and byte rates are acceptable. The queues must be dimensioned properly for the periodic exchange of the full routing/topology tables. Hence, it is recommended that the queue sizes be dimensioned as if a periodic protocol were being used.

If OSPF is chosen as a routing protocol, the **broadcast** command in the static mapping transforms the nonbroadcast Frame Relay to broadcast. This results in forwarding broadcasts when multicasting is not enabled for NBMA networks. This approach allows OSPF to run over Frame Relay as a broadcast network. In point-to-point configurations using EIGRP, the **passive-interface** command prevents all routing updates from being sent to or received from a network through a specific interface, thus reducing the bandwidth consumption for routing overhead. The **passive-interface** command is not applicable for link-state protocols. This command prevents the router from establishing a neighbor adjacency with other routers that are connected to the same link (see Cisco IOS 12.0 documentation for more detail). On most protocols, the **passive-interface** command stops the router from sending updates to a particular neighbor, but it continues to listen to and use its routing updates. In general, the following techniques reduce the update load: update-only routing protocols, routing and SAP filters, longer update timers, longer interval timers, multiple access lines, and higher-speed access lines. (For a detailed description on routing protocols and their requirements and configuration features, refer to Cisco documentation).

Frame Relay Broadcast Queue

Remote access designs are characterized by a large number of spoke routers that terminate into one or a couple of hub routers. The routing updates can create a large amount of traffic and thus seriously affect the overall performance of the entire architecture. One of the possible solutions is the use of a Frame Relay broadcast queue per interface. For Frame Relay, the broadcast queue is separate from the regular interface queue. It has its own buffers, size, rate and is configurable with the command **frame-relay broadcast-queue size byte-rate packet-rate**. The configuration line is as follows:

```
frame-relay broadcast-queue size byte-rate packet-rate
```

The simple configuration procedure for Interface Serial3/0:0 is shown in the following lines:

```
7206-frame#config terminal
7206-frame(config)#interface Serial3/0:0
7206-frame(config-if)#frame-relay broadcast-queue 100 1200 120
```

The default settings of this command are as follows:

- **Queue size**—64
- **Bytes per second**—256,000 bytes per second (2,048,000 bits per second)
- **Packets per second**—36

The actual settings in the configuration can be viewed with the **show interface Serial3/0:0** command.

The broadcast queue has a guaranteed minimum bandwidth allocation. To set the queue size, Cisco recommends starting with 20 packets per DLCI and monitoring the number of drops. Cisco also recommends that the byte rate should be less than both of the following (assuming 250-byte packets):

- N/4 times the minimum remote access rate (measured in bytes per second), where N is the number of DLCIs to which the broadcast must be replicated.
- 1/4 the local access rate (measured in bytes per second).

Advanced Frame Relay Configurations

The represented configuration solutions in the following sections are usually referred to as advanced Frame Relay configurations. They include the following:

- Configuring IP unnumbered
- Frame switching configuration
- Configuring ISDN as Frame Relay backup
- Configuring the bridging in Frame Relay
- Frame Relay compression configuration
- Configuring IP multicast in Frame Relay
- Frame Relay traffic shaping configuration, including foresight adaptive shaping

Configuring IP Unnumbered Frame Relay

One of the IP preservation schemes that is only applicable for point-to-point configurations is to use an unnumbered IP address. In Example 16-4, you can see that for the core router configuration the physical interface is configured with **no ip address** and the IP addresses are assigned to the subinterfaces. These IPs are all obtained from the Loopback0 interface. Given the number of configured subinterfaces, you can see how this approach maximizes the use of available IP address space. The same logic applies to the remote user's router configuration in Example 16-7, where the subinterfaces obtain IPs from the Ethernet0 interface and, thus, the overall solution doubles the number of spared IPs.

Frame Switching

When discussing Frame Relay technology options in Chapter 14, Frame switching and a set of protocols were introduced (refer to Figure 14-2 and Figure 14-3). Typically, a router is configured as data communications equipment (DCE) if it is connecting directly to another router. It can also be configured as DCE when connected to a 90i D4 channel unit, which in turn is connected to a telephone company (telco) channel bank. A variety of configuration solutions exist for frame switching, including the following:

- PVC switching configuration where the DCE router switches frames that are based on DLCI
- Two or more Cisco routers configured as DCE and using Network-to-Network Interface (NNI) signaling between them to provide data terminal equipment (DTE) to DTE switching
- Hybrid configuration where the router is configured as DCE and DTE, and where it switches frames between two or more DCE ports, or DCE and DTE ports
- Switching Frame Relay PVCs over a point-to-point IP tunnel

The full range of configuration examples are beyond the scope of this section, but here are some guidelines about the first and second configuration examples.

The first switch configuration requires three configuration commands. They are **frame-relay switching**, **frame-relay intf-type dce**, and **frame-relay route**. Consequently, the configuration of frame switching (configuring the Cisco router as a DCE device) includes three steps:

Step 1   Enable frame switching

Step 2   Configuration of the DTEs, DCE, or NNI

Step 3   Specification of the static mapping of DLCI to the next hop address

Assume that the top router in Figure 16-2 performs DCE functions for all four of the spoke routers. The DCE configuration rules are as follows:

- The top router must be configured with the following command:

```
7206-frame(config)#frame-relay switching
```

- Every interface connected to the DTE must be configured with the following command:

```
7206-frame(config-if)#frame-relay intf-type dce
```

This configuration line indicates to DTE that it is connected to DCE. Other configuration options for the same command are as follows:

  — **frame-relay intf-type dte**—Configure as a Frame Relay DTE

  — **frame-relay intf-type nni**—Configure as a Frame Relay NNI

- The routing statement must map the *in-dlci* with the *out-dlci* in the interface configuration mode:

```
7206-frame(config-if)# frame-relay route in-dlci interface out-interface out-dlci
```

NOTE   In Cisco IOS Software release 12.1(2)T and later, the **frame-relay route** command is replaced with the **connect** command. This command is defined in global configuration mode, and the format is as follows:

```
7206-frame(config)#connect connection-name interface dlci interface dlci
```

The second configuration allows two or more Cisco routers that are configured as DCE to use NNI signaling between them, and to provide DTE to DTE switching.

Assume that Figure 16-2 has not one, but two top routers. You need to perform a two-step configuration:

Step 1   For each of them, you must ensure that it is configured with NNI
signaling:

```
7206-frame(config-if)# frame-relay intf-type nni
7206-frame(config-if)# frame-relay lmi-type q933a
```

Step 2   Determine who provides the clocking. After you obtain the definitive
answer, configure the particular DCE with the following command:

```
7206-frame(config-if)# clockrate 2048000
```

In case you want to simulate the future architecture before implementing the new
configuration, you might consider using the Adtran simulator as a Frame Relay switch. This
device allows you to simulate a telco channel bank and offers a convenient web-based tool
for mapping DTEs.

Adtran's ATLAS 890 and the $800^{PLUS}/810^{PLUS}$ with Frame Relay Software installed
enable LAN-to-LAN interconnections by using an integral IP router with support for Frame
Relay or PPP traffic (www.adtran.com/all/Public/framemacro?section=products.clec).

Frame Relay and ISDN Backup Configuration

Enterprises that require a wide-area network (WAN) service for long periods of the
workday normally choose Frame Relay as a primary link. To prevent situations where this
link is a single point of failure, and to meet the availability and redundancy requirements of
the design, the ISDN is often used as a backup technology.

In the remote access enterprise environment, remote users don't usually warrant a backup.
It is up to the enterprise to determine if the additional cost of an ISDN backup is worth the
added redundancy. Usually, ISDN backup for Frame Relay is deployed in field sales offices.

The following section provides configuration guidelines for the common ISDN backup,
ISDN backup with dialer profiles, and ISDN backup that is based on HSRP. Other
solutions, such as dialer watch as an alternate backup method, won't be discussed in this
section, but can be seen in Chapter 6 and are applicable in Frame Relay.

Common ISDN Backup Configuration for Frame Relay

The backup ISDN interface can be defined in both point-to-multipoint and point-to-point
interfaces. Depending on the strategy, ISDN BRI0 can back up both the physical and per-
DLCI interface.

In the physical interface backup scenario, losing the PVC does not trigger the backup
mechanism because it only works when there is a complete loss of connectivity (i.e., when
both the interface and line protocol are down). Most probably, this is the reason that this
method is called physical interface backup.

In the per-DLCI scenario, the main interface can stay up, but if the subinterface goes down, the ISDN BRI0 comes up. The physical interface backup (if configured) takes precedence over any other backup configuration. The per-DLCI configuration is the recommended one for practical use.

Assume that you need to back up the DLCI 200 (point-to-point interface) that is included in Figure 16-2, and the top router has an ISDN BRI0 interface. The configuration command sequence must include the commands in Example 16-8.

Example 16-8 *ISDN Per-DLCI Backup Configuration*

```
7206-frame#configure terminal
7206-frame(config)# interface Serial4/2:0.200
7206-frame(config-if)# frame-relay interface-dlci 200
7206-frame(config-if)# backup interface BRI0
7206-frame(config-if)# backup delay 5 10
```

The last command represents the IOS interface configuration command **backup delay** *enable-delay disable-delay.*

This command specifies *enable delay*, which is the number of seconds to wait after the primary link has failed before the backup line is brought up; and *disable-delay*, which is the number of seconds to wait after the primary link is available before the backup line is torn down. In this example, *enable-delay* is five seconds and *disable-delay* is ten seconds.

Cisco recommends two rules of thumb in this situation:

- Wait at least 20 seconds before starting the backup line just in case it was a glitch and the link bounced.

- Wait five seconds after the primary interface comes back up to bring the backup connection down again. This is to ensure that the primary link stays up.

NOTE Load-based backup, based on **load-threshold** calculations, is not available in Frame Relay and is applicable only for ISDN. (See Chapter 11, "Cisco ISDN Configuration Solutions.")

Frame Relay Backup with ISDN Dialer Profiles

This solution is based on creating dialer profiles on both the hub and spoke sides. Assume that you have a configuration with one hub and four spoke routers, as shown in Figure 16-2. If all the spoke routers have ISDN backup links available, they can be configured as shown in Example 16-9.

As soon as Serial1.201 goes down, the backup ISDN interface comes up according to the configuration settings. Here, the backup delay settings are five seconds for *enable-delay* and ten seconds for *disable-delay* parameters (see the line **backup delay 5 10**).

Example 16-9   *Fragment of the Spoke Router Configuration with Per-DLCI Backup Configured Under the Interface Serial1.201*

```
<output omitted>
!
interface Serial1.201 point-to-point
ip unnumbered Ethernet0
bandwidth 128
frame-relay interface-dlci 201
backup delay 5 10
backup interface BRI0
!
<output omitted>
```

Now assume that the core router has one backup Basic Rate Interface (BRI) (BRI0) and you want to configure the dialer profiles for this router. This configuration has two major steps.

The first step is to configure four dialers (D1-D4) to guarantee one BRI channel per spoke router. This step was discussed in Chapter 11.

The second step is to assign BRI interfaces to every pool. Again, refer to Chapter 11 for configurations of dialer pools. The difference here is that to guarantee one BRI channel per every spoke router, you have to restrict the number of channels by using the commands in Example 16-10 under the BRI0 interface.

Example 16-10   *Dialer Pool Member Configuration for the Core Router*

```
dialer pool-member 1 max-link 1
dialer pool-member 2 max-link 1
dialer pool-member 3 max-link 1
dialer pool-member 4 max-link 1
```

If the probability of failure is high, it is better to use a PRI, instead of a group of BRIs, and apply the same configuration rules. In this case, you can consider using **multilink ppp**.

Troubleshooting the solution should follow the methodology described in Chapter 17, "Frame Relay Troubleshooting," and Chapter 12. It is not recommended to use the **shutdown** command on the serial interface to test this solution. Instead, you can emulate a real serial line problem by pulling the cable out from the serial line.

EIGRP- and HSRP-Based Solutions

A more sophisticated backup mechanism is available in Cisco IOS using the EIGRP routing protocol and a combination of floating and static routing. Both one- and two-router based configurations are available. For a full description of the solutions, see the Cisco Press book *Advanced IP Network Design (CCIE Professional Development)* by Alvaro Retana, Don Slice, and Russ White. An important element of the configuration is to prevent an IP route-cache on the ISDN configuration because the router sends traffic over this interface even after the primary connection is restored. A weakness of this solution is that the configuration still relies on the status of the physical connectivity. It is well known that even when the physical layer is up, this does not necessarily mean that IP connectivity is up. In other words, losing IP connectivity might not trigger the backup mechanism.

Another interesting solution is related to HSRP and its functionality. HSRP allows routers to share a virtual IP address between them with only one active HSRP router accepting (and forwarding) traffic destined to that virtual IP. In the latest IOS releases, HSRP provides monitoring and prioritizing capabilities, which result in proper fail-over for devices when a redundant serial link failure occurs on a router. The solution is based on the IOS **track** and **preempt** commands that identify the primary router as a higher priority over the backup one. As soon as the primary link fails (interface Serial3/0:0), the **standby 1 track Serial3/0:0** command reduces the value of priority, so the backup router now has a higher priority value and becomes the primary router. More about this topic can be found at www.cisco.com/warp/public/619/6.html.

Frame Relay and Bridging

When using Frame Relay bridging, there must be a full mesh of Frame Relay virtual circuits between the bridges of a remote bridge group. If the Frame Relay network is not a full mesh, the bridge network must be divided into multiple remote bridge groups. Because LMI transforms the Frame Relay to a LAN-like architecture, this bridging model is identical to the model for remote bridging as described in IEEE P802.1g, which supports the concept of virtual ports. The Frame Relay virtual circuits that interconnect the bridges of a remote bridge group can be combined or used individually to form one or more virtual bridge ports. This solution provides flexibility to treat the Frame Relay interface as either a single virtual bridge port with all virtual circuits in a group, or as a collection of bridge ports (individual or grouped virtual circuits).

The simplest bridge configuration for a Frame Relay network is the LAN view, where all virtual circuits are combined into a single virtual port. Frames, such as Bridge Protocol Data Units (BPDUs), which are broadcast on a LAN, must be flooded to each virtual circuit (or multicast, if configured on the Frame Relay network). Flooding is performed by sending the packet to each relevant DLCI that is associated with the Frame Relay interface. Obviously, this approach is typical for point-to-multipoint configurations.

A second Frame Relay bridging approach for point-to-point configurations treats each Frame Relay virtual circuit as a separate bridge port. Flooding and forwarding packets are significantly less complicated by using the point-to-point approach because each bridge port has only one destination. There is no need to perform artificial flooding or to associate DLCIs with destination Media Access Control (MAC) addresses.

In Example 16-11, a simple bridge configuration (fragment) is provided. The defined subnet of the spoke router is /29 (the subnet mask is 255.255.255.248), and it is a subnet of the core router. Therefore, from the available six addresses for the spoke router, the first address (in this case, 54.161.107.161) is the default route. The spoke is bridging, but the core is routing the packets.

Example 16-11 *Cisco 1602 Router, Configured as a Bridge*

```
1602-frame#show running-config
<output omitted>
!
bridge irb
!
interface Ethernet0
 no ip address
 no cdp enable
 bridge-group 1
 hold-queue 32 in
!
interface Serial1
no ip address
 encapsulation frame-relay
 no ip mroute-cache
 no fair-queue
 service-module t1 timeslots 1-2
 frame-relay lmi-type ansi
!
interface Serial1.201 point-to-point
 ip unnumbered BVI1
 bandwidth 128
 frame-relay interface-dlci 201
 bridge-group 1
!
interface BVI1
 ip address 54.161.107.162 255.255.255.248
 ip nat outside
!
!
ip nat inside source list 1 interface BVI1 overload
```

The first important line in this configuration is the command **bridge irb**. It enables the Integrated Routing and Bridging (IRB) feature. This feature allows a given protocol to be routed between routed interfaces and bridge-groups or between bridge-groups within a single router. Specifically, local or unroutable traffic is bridged among the bridged interfaces in the same bridge-group, and routable traffic is routed to other routed interfaces or bridge-groups. So again, why use IRB? Here are some reasons:

- Interconnect bridged and routed topologies
- Conserve network addresses but maintain connectivity
- Increase performance by keeping bridging traffic local

The second important part of this configuration is the Bridge Group Virtual Interface (BVI). The concept of BVI was created to enable these interfaces to exchange packets for a given protocol. The BVI is a virtual interface within the router that acts just like a normal routed interface. It does not support bridging but represents the corresponding bridge-group within the router. This virtual interface allows routing between a bridge-group and a routed interface. Because bridging is in the data link layer and routing is in the network layer, they have different protocol configuration models. With IP, for example, bridge-group interfaces belong to the same network and have a collective IP network address, and each routed interface represents a distinct network and has its own IP network address.

The interface number of the BVI (#1 in Example 16-11) is the number of the bridge group that this virtual interface represents. The number is the link between this BVI and the bridge group.

When you configure the BVI and enable routing on it, packets that come in on a routed interface are destined for a host on a segment that is in a bridge group that goes through the following processes:

Step 1   The packet is routed to the BVI—Interface BVI1 in Example 16-11.

Step 2   From the BVI, the packet is forwarded to the bridging engine.

Step 3   From the bridging engine, the packet exits through a bridged interface.

Similarly, packets that come in on a bridged interface but that are destined for a host on a routed network first go to the BVI. The BVI then forwards them to the routing engine before sending them out the routed interface.

Interfaces Ethernet 0 and Serial1.201 are members of bridge group 1, as defined by the virtual bridge interface (BVI1). As soon as the BVI1 has an IP address assigned to it, Serial1.201 obtains an IP address. Then the router bridges the frames from E0 to BVI1, and vice versa.

Network Address Translation (NAT) is also an important part of the configuration, but it was already discussed in this book and does not require any further attention.

NOTE   To check if the bridge is working, add and remove an IP routing statement, such as

```
1602-frame(config)#ip route 0.0.0.0 0.0.0.0 BVI1
```

The routing statement should not affect the ability of the router to pass traffic.

Frame Relay Compression

Cisco internetworking devices use the STAC (LZS) and Predictor data compression algorithms.

STAC (LZS) is based on the Lempel-Ziv compression algorithm. Cisco IOS Software uses an optimized version of LZS that provides good compression ratios but requires many CPU cycles. LZS searches the input data stream for redundant strings and replaces them with what is called a token. This token is shorter than the original data string. LZS creates dictionaries. This dictionary is built and begins replacing the redundant strings that are found in the new data streams.

The Predictor compression algorithm tries to predict the next sequence of characters in the data stream by using an index to look up a sequence in the compression dictionary. It then examines the next sequence in the data stream to see if it matches. If it does match, that sequence replaces the looked-up sequence in the dictionary. If not, the algorithm locates the next character sequence in the index and the process begins again. The Predictor data compression algorithm was optimized by Cisco engineers. When compared with LZS, it makes more efficient use of CPU cycles but requires more memory.

The compression alternatives within Frame Relay include two main groups: per-interface compression (also called link compression) and per-virtual circuit compression (also called payload compression). The available Cisco compression solutions for Frame Relay are shown in Figure 16-3.

Depending on which part of the packet you want to compress, several available options exist: header compression (TCP and RTP header compression); payload compression (FRF.9, stacker, predictor; and Microsoft Point to Point Compression [MPPC]). MPPC is based on RFC 2118 and is a per-Point-to-Point Protocol (PPP) connection compression algorithm.

NOTE   Shut down the interface or subinterface prior to adding or changing compression techniques. Although not required, shutting down the interface ensures that it is reset for the new data structures.

Van Jacobson Header Compression

Cisco IOS header compression uses the Van Jacobson Algorithm as defined in RFC 1144. Cisco's header compression product supports X.25, Frame Relay, and dial-on-demand WAN link protocols. Because of the processing overhead, header compression is generally used at 64 kbps. For example, a 50 percent throughput improvement can be achieved with telnet, rlogin, and X Windows traffic on a 64-kbps leased line for TCP/IP, which conforms to RFC 1144.

Example 16-12 shows an interface configured for TCP/IP header compression and an IP map that inherits the compression characteristics. The Frame Relay IP map is not explicitly configured for header compression.

Figure 16-3 *Cisco Frame Relay Compression Solutions*

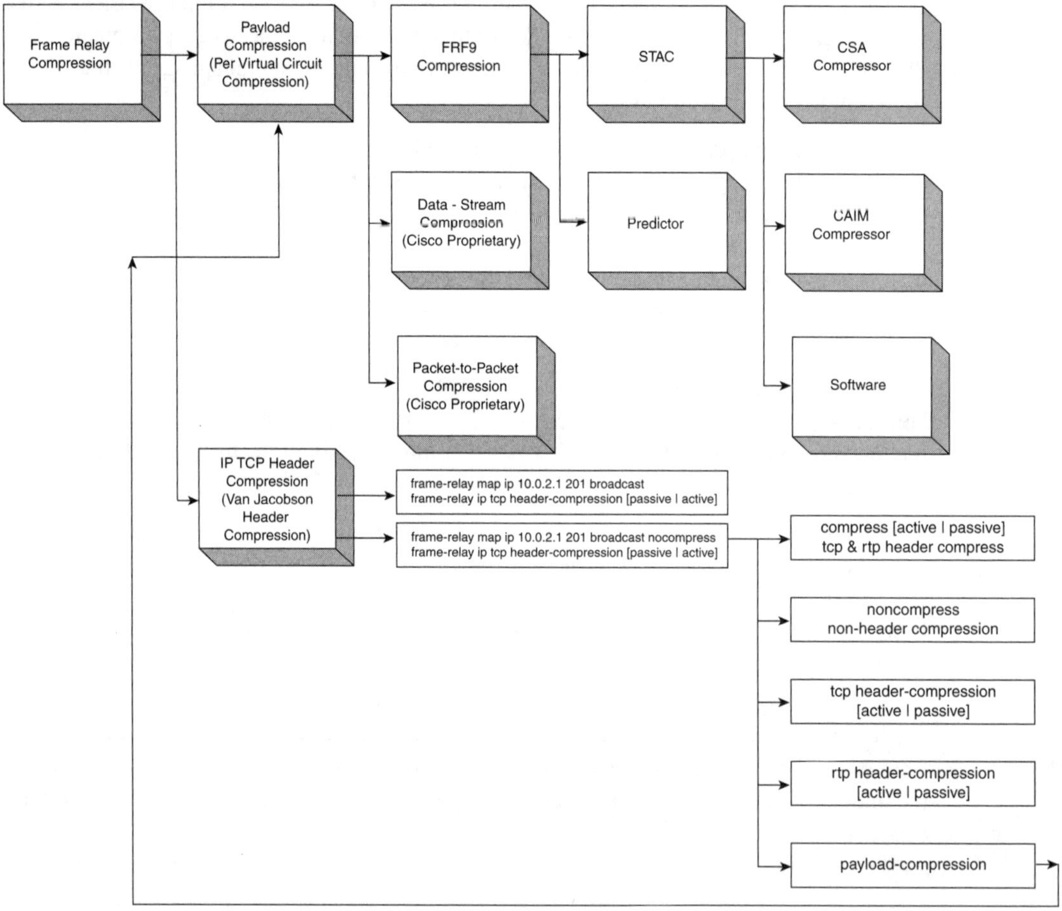

Example 16-12 *The Interface Serial1 and IP MAP with Inherited TCP/IP Header Compression*

```
1602-frame#show running-config
<output omitted>
interface Serial1
 no ip address
 encapsulation frame-relay
 no ip mroute-cache
 no fair-queue
 service-module t1 timeslots 1-2
 frame-relay lmi-type ansi
 frame-relay map ip 10.0.2.1 201 broadcast
 frame-relay ip tcp header-compression passive
<output omitted>
```

NOTE   The **frame-relay ip tcp header-compression** [**passive** | **active**] command has two options. The **passive** option indicates that the TCP header compression is active only for the destinations that are sending compressed headers. The **active** option requires the other side to be configured for the same type of compression.

If you type 1602-frame#**show frame-relay map**, you see a line that looks similar to the following:

```
<output omitted>
dlci 201 (0xC9,0x3090), static,
          broadcast,
          CISCO
          TCP/IP Header Compression (inherited), passive (inherited)
<output omitted>
```

This shows that the IP map has inherited passive TCP/IP header compression. This example also applies to dynamic mappings achieved with the use of InARP on point-to-point subinterfaces, where no Frame Relay maps are explicitly configured.

Another configuration option is to override the compression set on the interfaces, as shown in Example 16-13.

Example 16-13   *Compression, Configured for Interface Serial1 Using an IP Map to Override TCP/IP Header Compression*

```
1602-frame#show running-config
<output omitted>
interface Serial1
 no ip address
 encapsulation frame-relay
 no ip mroute-cache
 no fair-queue
 service-module t1 timeslots 1-2
 frame-relay lmi-type ansi
 frame-relay map ip 10.0.2.1 201 broadcast nocompress
 frame-relay ip tcp header-compression passive
<output omitted>
```

NOTE   If the interface is configured with IETF encapsulation, it cannot be configured for header compression and map compression must be configured. The interface configured for TCP/IP header compression cannot support priority or custom queuing.

Use the **show frame-relay map** command to display the resulting compression and encapsulation characteristics:

```
1602-frame#show frame-relay map

<output omitted>
dlci 201 (0xC9,0x3090), static,
           broadcast,
           CISCO
<output omitted>
```

Because IP map did not inherit the TCP header compression, the keyword **inherited** is not reported in the output.

Per-Virtual Circuit Compression (Payload Compression)

The Frame Relay Forum (FRF) Technical Committee approved an implementation agreement for data compression over Frame Relay called FRF.9. This agreement specifies a standard for compression to ensure multivendor interoperability—see Frame Relay Standards in Chapter 14. FRF.9 is a per-virtual circuit compression mechanism for both switched virtual circuits (SVCs) and permanent virtual circuits (PVCs), which is negotiated at the time that the DLCI is started. Cisco currently supports FRF.9 mode 1 and is evaluating mode 2, which allows more flexibility for parameter negotiation.

Payload compression has several options. From the core side of the router, the available options are shown in Example 16-14.

Example 16-14 *Configuration Interface Serial4/2:0.200 for FRF.9 Payload Compression on the Core Router*

```
7206-frame#show running-config
<output omitted>
!
interface Serial4/2:0.200 point-to-point
 description 1602-frame: 10.0.2.1/29
 bandwidth 128
 ip unnumbered Loopback2
 no ip route-cache
 frame-relay class class-128-new
 frame-relay interface-dlci 200 IETF
 frame-relay payload-compression FRF9 stac csa 2
!
<output omitted>
```

In Example 16-14, subinterface Serial4/2:0.200 uses payload FRF.9 stacker compression, as performed on the compression service adaptor (CSA) hardware module 2(compression service module 2). The syntax of the command is as follows:

```
frame-relay payload-compression encapsulation-option stac compressor-option
```

The values for *encapsulation-option* include the following:

- **FRF9**—For FRF.9 encapsulation
- **data-stream**—For Cisco proprietary encapsulation
- **packet-by-packet**—For Cisco proprietary encapsulation

FRF.9 stacker compression can be performed by a Cisco Advanced Integration Module (CAIM), a CSA, or by the main processor:

```
frame-relay payload-compression  FRF9 stac compressor-option
```

The word **stac** stands for stacker (LZS) compression. The values for *compressor-option* include the following:

- **csa**—CSA compressor, which is available for 7206 and 3640 platforms
- **software**—Force software compression, which is generally available for all platforms
- **caim**—CAIM compressor. CAIM performs the following algorithms:
  - STAC (QIC122) compression algorithms
  - MPPC algorithm
  - FRF.9 Frame Relay Payload Compression
  - Compression Control Protocol (CCP) RFC

NOTE   In the core router, as soon as you use payload compression, switch off the fancy switching. The only available option is to use process switching.

From the spoke perspective, a couple of configuration options are available, as shown in Example 16-15. For 1600 router series, there is no hardware compression module available.

Example 16-15 *Software Compression Configuration of a 1600 Router*

```
1602-frame#show running-config
<output omitted>
!
interface Serial1.200 point-to-point
 bandwidth 128
 ip unnumbered Ethernet0
no ip mroute-cache
 frame-relay interface-dlci 200 IETF
 frame-relay payload-compression FRF9 stac software
<output omitted>
```

In the output in Example 16-15, you can use either the stacker software compression or the Cisco proprietary packet-to-packet compression. Both options are always available. For the

Cisco 2600 series and 3660 series routers, the CAIM is available. For more details about hardware compression modules, see www.cisco.com.

Frame Relay and IP Multicast Configuration

To provide basic multicasting over ISDN and Frame Relay for a remote access environment, you must perform some basic tasks:

- Enable IP multicast routing
- Enable Protocol Independent Multicast (PIM) on an interface
- Configure the router to automatically accept the rendezvous point (Auto-RP) or hardcode the RP's IP address.

In a Frame Relay environment, the following steps provide basic multicast for users.

On the spoke router, the lines in Example 16-16 must be configured.

Example 16-16 *Basic Configuration Steps for IP Multicast on the Spoke Router*

```
1602-frame#configure terminal
1602-frame(config)# ip multicast-routing
1602-frame(config)# ip pim accept-rp auto-rp
1602-frame(config)# interface Serial1.201
1602-frame(config-subif)# ip pim sparse-dense-mode
1602-frame(config-subif)#exit
1602-frame(config)# interface Ethernet 0
1602-frame(config-subif)# ip pim sparse-dense-mode
1602-frame(config-subif)# ^Z
1602-frame# copy running-config startup-config
```

In general, PIM protocol (protocol 103) can be configured for two different modes, which are referred to as dense mode (DM) and sparse mode (SM).

PIM DM uses a process of reverse path flooding that is similar to the Distance Vector Multicast Routing Protocol (DVMRP). Unlike DVMRP, it does not require a particular unicast protocol to determine which interface leads back to the source of a data stream. However, it uses whatever unicast protocol is being used in the network.

PIM SM defines a rendezvous point (RP), which serves as a registration point to facilitate the proper routing of packets. When a sender wants to send data, the next/first hop sends data to the RP. When a receiver wants to receive data, the last hop router registers with the RP. A data stream flows from the sender to the RP, then to the receiver. Afterwards, routers in the path optimize the path automatically to remove any unnecessary hops, including the RP.

The configuration on the hub side router is even simpler because usually the objective is to configure one more user for IP multicast.

If this is the case, **ip multicast-routing** and **ip pim accept-rp auto-rp** already exist in the configuration, as in Example 16-16. Also, at least one of the Ethernet or FastEthernet interfaces is configured with the **ip pim sparse-dense-mode** command. The only interface that needs to be configured now is the serial subinterface.

If the core router requires an entire new configuration for IP multicast, follow the guidelines in Example 16-17. Remember that only the interfaces configured for multicast can participate in the multicast shared tree.

Example 16-17 *Sample IP Multicast Configuration of the Core Router*

```
7206-frame(config)# ip multicast-routing
7206-frame(config)# ip pim accept-rp auto-rp
7206-frame(config)# interface Serial4/2:0.200
7206-frame(config-subif)# ip pim sparse-dense-mode
7206-frame(config-subif)#exit
7206-frame(config)# interface FastEthernet 0
7206-frame(config-subif)# ip pim sparse-dense-mode
7206-frame(config-subif)# ^Z
7206-frame# copy running-config startup-config
```

In both configurations (Example 16-16 and Example 16-17), **ip multicast-routing** is configured in the global configuration mode. This step is mandatory because Cisco routers don't forward broadcast or multicast traffic by default.

The next line allows PIM to accept the **auto-rp**. In general, two options can map RP:

- **Static RP**—RP to be configured on all routers; operates in SM.
- **Auto-RP**—Requires configured candidate RPs and mapping agents.

The next important part is **ip pim sparse-dense-mode**, which defines a dual mode configuration. This mode of Cisco IOS is in fact an interface configuration that allows both DM and SM groups to flow across that interface. It is normally only applied when Auto-RP sends RP information. The configuration in Example 16-17 can include either DM or SM. If you need to choose, Cisco recommends PIM SM, rather than DM.

For Frame Relay, remember that 56 kbps is not the best service for multicast. Even 128 kbps with compression can affect the end user's router performance significantly, and if the wrong configuration settings are used, it can shut the service down completely.

Frame Relay and Traffic Shaping

Traffic shaping enables the router to control the output rate and react to the congestion notification mechanisms according to the traffic shaping settings. In Cisco routers, traffic shaping uses a rate control mechanism called a token bucket filter. The token controls the following expression:

$$(Bc + Be) = \text{Access rate for the virtual circuit}$$

Traffic above the maximum speed is buffered in a traffic shaping queue, which is equal to the size of weighted fair queuing (WFQ). The token bucket filter does not filter traffic. Rather, it controls the rate at which traffic is sent on the outbound interface. The parameters defined in traffic shaping are as follows (see Chapter 14 for more information):

- Committed information rate (CIR)
- Excess information rate (EIR)
- Token bucket (TB), (Bc + Be)
- Committed burst size (Bc, equals sustained burst size)
- Excess burst size (Be)
- Discard eligible (DE)
- Committed interval (Tc)
- Access rate (AR)

Bc, Be, Tc, and CIR are defined per DLCI. Consequently, the token bucket filter controls the rate per DLCI. The access rate is valid per User-Network Interface (UNI). For Bc, Be, and CIR, incoming and outgoing values can be configured. If the connection is symmetrical, the values in both directions are the same. For PVCs, parameters such as incoming and outgoing Bc, Be, and CIR are defined at the time of provisioning.

NOTE   Peak equals the DLCI's maximum speed and represents the bandwidth for that particular DLCI:

Tc = Bc / CIR
Peak = CIR + Be / Tc = CIR (1 + Be / Bc)

If the Tc is one second:

Peak = CIR + Be = Bc + Be and EIR = Be.

Generic Traffic Shaping

The generic traffic shaping feature is a media and encapsulation-independent traffic shaping tool. It helps reduce the flow of outbound traffic when there is congestion within the cloud, on the link, or at the receiving endpoint router. You can set it on interfaces or subinterfaces within a router. See Example 16-18 for the following configuration steps.

First, you need to enable traffic shaping in the main interface (interface Serial4/2:0) with the following command:

```
frame-relay traffic-shaping
```

Then, under the subinterface, you configure the traffic-shape rate. This command configures traffic shaping for outbound traffic on an interface. The full syntax of this command is as follows:

```
traffic-shape rate bit-rate [burst-size [excess-burst-size]] [group access-list]
```

Finally, if the configuration solution requires you to throttle backward explicit congestion notifications (BECNs) on a Frame Relay interface, the following command is required in the interface configuration mode:

```
traffic-shape adaptive [bit-rate]
```

Example 16-18 shows the basic traffic shaping configuration on the hub router, in a point-to-point configuration with DLCI = 100.

Example 16-18 *Configuring General Traffic Shaping on a Core Router*

```
7206-frame# show running-config
<output omitted>
interface Serial4/2:0
description Remote Frame Relay : NUA :3812777777: HICAP CID XXX72HCR-001
 no ip address
 encapsulation frame-relay
 no ip route-cache
 no fair-queue
 frame-relay traffic-shaping
 frame-relay lmi-type ansi
 frame-relay broadcast-queue 100 1200 120
 !
interface Serial4/2:0.100 point-to-point
 description 2500-frame: 10.0.1.0/29
 ip unnumbered Loopback0
 no ip route-cache
 frame-relay interface-dlci 100
 ! Upper limit rate:
 traffic-shape rate 128000
 ! Lower limit rate (CIR value):
 traffic-shape adaptive 64000
<output omitted>
```

NOTE   Traffic shaping must be enabled on the interface with the **traffic-shape rate** command before you can use the **traffic-shape adaptive** command.

In Example 16-18, the expected rate is between 64 kbps and 128 kbps. The **traffic-shape adaptive** command should be configured at both ends of the link because it also configures the device at the slow end to reflect forward explicit congestion notification (FECN) signals as BECNs. This enables the router at the high-speed end to detect and adapt to congestion, even when traffic is flowing primarily in one direction. With generic traffic shaping, you can only specify one peak rate (upper limit) per physical interface and one CIR (lower limit) value per subinterface. With Frame Relay traffic shaping, you start a token bucket filter per virtual circuit.

Traffic Shape Map Classes

The most common technique for traffic shaping is to define the traffic shape map class and apply it to different subinterfaces. This approach is much shorter and easier to manage than defining it under every single interface. In general, Frame Relay traffic shaping has three objectives:

- **Rate enforcement on a per-VC basis**—You can configure a peak rate and EIR.
- **BECN support on a per-VC basis**—The router can monitor BECNs and throttle traffic based on BECN-marked packet feedback from the network.
- **Priority queuing (PQ), custom queuing (CQ), or WFQ support at the VC level**.

The traffic shaping over Frame Relay feature applies to both PVCs and SVCs.

The configuration rules are simple, but first you need to define the map class. An example of a map class, called class-64, is shown in Example 16-19.

Example 16-19 *Configuration Steps for a Map Class Configuration, Called Class-64*

```
7206-frame#config terminal
! Specifies Frame Relay map class named class-64 and
! enters map class configuration mode:
7206-frame(config)#map-class frame-relay class-64

!The next lines can include the following
7206-frame(config-map-class)#frame-relay cir 64000
7206-frame(config-map-class)#frame-relay bc 64000
7206-frame(config-map-class)#frame-relay be 10000
7206-frame(config-map-class)#frame-relay mincir 56000
7206-frame(config-map-class)#end
7206-frame#copy running-config startup-config
```

In this example, the CIR is set to 64,000 bps, the BC is set to 64,000 bits, the BE is set to 10,000 bits and the minimum committed information rate (MINCIR) to 56,000 bps. This example includes some of the commonly used options. After you enter the map class configuration mode, the syntax of the **frame-relay** command is as follows:

```
frame-relay options
```

The possible values for *options* include the following:

- **adaptive-shaping**—Adaptive traffic rate adjustment; default = none
- **bc**—Bc, default = 56,000 bits
- **be**—Be, default = 0 bits

- **cir**—CIR, default = 56,000 bps
- **congestion**—Congestion management parameters
- **custom-queue-list**—Virtual circuit custom queuing
- **end-to-end**—Configure Frame Relay end-to-end virtual circuit parameters
- **fair-queue**—Virtual circuit fair queuing
- **fecn-adapt**—Enable traffic-shaping reflection of FECN as BECN
- **fragment**—Requires Frame Relay traffic shaping to be configured at the interface level
- **holdq**—Hold queue size for virtual circuit
- **interface-queue**—PVC interface queue parameters
- **ip**—Assign a priority queue for RTP streams
- **mincir**—Minimum acceptable CIR; Default = CIR / 2 bps
- **priority-group**—VC priority queuing
- **tc**—Policing Measurement Interval (Tc)
- **traffic-rate**—Virtual circuit traffic rate
- **voice**—Voice options

Next, you apply the map class to the subinterface as shown in Example 16-20. Of course, **frame-relay traffic-shaping** must be enabled on the main interface.

Example 16-20 *Applying the Frame Relay Class to Subinterface Serial4/2:0.100*

```
7206-frame#show running-config interface serial4/2:0.100
interface Serial4/2:0.100 point-to-point
  description AndrewC frame: 10.0.1.0/29 : 2322713474 :
  bandwidth 128
  ip unnumbered Loopback1
  no ip route-cache
! Here the Frame Relay map class from Example 16-19 is applied.
  frame-relay class class-64
  frame-relay interface-dlci 100
```

Frame Relay Foresight Adaptive Shaping with ELMI

ELMI allows the router to adapt the shaping parameters dynamically. ELMI enables the automated exchange of Frame Relay quality of service (QoS) parameter information between the Cisco router and the Cisco switch. Routers can then base congestion management and prioritization decisions on known QoS values such as CIR, Bc, and Be. This enhancement operates between Cisco routers and Cisco switches (BPX/MGX and IGX platforms). You can enable ELMI support on the router by using the **frame-relay qos-autosense** command.

The configuration rules for this feature are simple.

First, you configure the **frame-relay traffic-shaping** and **frame-relay qos-autosense** commands on the main interface, as shown in Example 16-21.

Example 16-21 *Serial4/2:0 Is Configured for Adaptive Shaping*

```
7206-frame# show running-config
<output omitted>
interface Serial4/2:0
 description Home Frame Relay : NUA :3812800174: HICAP CID XXX72HCR-001
 no ip address
 encapsulation frame-relay
 no ip route-cache
 no fair-queue
 frame-relay traffic-shaping
 frame-relay lmi-type ansi
 frame-relay broadcast-queue 100 1200 120
 frame-relay qos-autosense
<output omitted>
```

Then, use the following command to add the existing map class, or create a map class:

```
7206-frame(config-map-class)#frame-relay adaptive-shaping foresight
```

The ELMI feature reduces the manual configuration efforts and ensures consistency of traffic shaping based on the QoS parameters.

Summary

Configuration options in Frame Relay are based on the design and provisioning choices made in the design phase. In this chapter, you learned about basic (common) and advanced configuration options with Cisco Frame Relay routers, including the following:

- Basic Frame Relay configurations, such as point-to-multipoint configurations, point-to-point configurations, and the frame relay broadcast queue. This section also includes minimum DLCIs recommendations, and the effect over Frame Relay service of the chosen routing protocols.

- The advance configuration sections include configuring IP unnumbered Frame Relay, frame switching configurations, ISDN as Frame Relay backup configurations, Frame Relay bridging, and Frame Relay compression and multicast configurations. Frame Relay traffic shaping, because of its importance, is represented in detail, including generic traffic shaping, traffic shaping classes, and foresight adaptive shaping with ELMI.

The Frame Relay encapsulations (cisco, ietf), DLCI encapsulations (cisco, ietf, ppp, and protocol) and LMI types (cisco, ANSI, and q933a) are discussed from a troubleshooting point of view in the following chapter.

Review Questions

Answers to the review questions can be found in Appendix A, "Answers to Review Questions."

1   What is dynamic mapping?

2   For Router-frame, map the IP address 10.0.0.1 to DLCI = 100, using the IETF encapsulation.

3   Can you use IP unnumbered with Frame Relay?

4   Can you ping your own interface address? Can you ping one spoke router from another?

5   What happens to deleted subinterfaces?

6   In point-to-point configurations that are running EIGRP, type the command for Router-frame that prevents all routing updates for interface Serial3/0:0.64?

7   Configure the Frame Relay broadcast queue for Router-frame—subinterface S3/0:0.71 with queue size 100, byte rate 1200, and packet rate 120.

8   Can you configure the Cisco router as a DCE?

9   Under the interface Serial3/0:0.200, what is the backup delay command with enable delay = 5 seconds and disable delay = 10 seconds?

10 For Router-frame and interface Serial1, what is the command for TCP header compression, which is active only for the destinations that are sending compressed headers?

11 For Router-frame and interface Serial4/2:0.200, define that FRF9 payload compression will be performed on CSA 3.

12 Enable the multicast routing in Router-frame.

13 In Router-frame, for interface Serial4/2:0.100, define the upper limit of the rate for traffic shaping to 128000.

14 What Frame Relay timer defines the Cisco autosense feature? How do you configure it?

CHAPTER 17

Frame Relay Troubleshooting

Troubleshooting Frame Relay connections is a design-dependant process, which starts with a clear understanding of the kind of connection you are troubleshooting. You need to know if this is a point-to-point or point-to-multipoint design, if it is a routing or bridging design, if you have a partial-mesh or full-mesh design, if you are using a switched virtual circuit (SVC) or permanent virtual circuit (PVC), how the signaling is maintained, and so on.

The troubleshooting has to be performed as a configuration–context activity as well. You need to start with the configuration solutions, such as access rate (whether it is 56 kbps or fraction T1), expected bandwidth, committed information rate (CIR) and excess information rate (EIR), and many of the other parameters explained in Chapters 14, "Frame Relay Technology Background," 15, "Frame Relay Design Solutions," and 16, "Basic and Advanced Frame Relay Configurations." You must also make sure that the equipment is properly configured for multicast, compression, and Voice over Frame Relay.

This chapter uses the systematic layer-by-layer approach to troubleshooting that is covered in Chapter 4, "Troubleshooting Approaches, Models, and Tools," and contains physical and data link layer troubleshooting techniques, as follows:

- Physical layer troubleshooting:
  - Line and clocking problems
  - Physical layer-related performance issues
- Data link layer troubleshooting:
  - PVC configuration issues, PVC encapsulation, and bandwidth definition issues
  - Local Management Interface (LMI) issues, including LMI types, messages and keepalives, timers, counters, and code types
- Performance problems:
  - Flapping links and end-to-end problems
  - Troubleshooting Frame Relay shaping problems and congestion control
  - Troubleshooting compression over Frame Relay

Beginning the Frame Relay Troubleshooting Process

The minimum information required before starting to troubleshoot includes the characteristics of the service such as: point-to-point or point-to-multipoint design; if routing or bridging is used; what are the remote and local DLCIs; and what is the access rate (link rate), CIR value, and IP addressing scheme. Regardless of the answer to these questions, some common indicators of the status allow you to start with the snapshot commands. The recommended commands are as follows:

```
1602-frame#show ip interface brief
1602-frame#show interface serial 1
```

The latter command depends on the configuration of the 160x router. This command can show the status of Serial 0 (for 56-kbps connections) and Serial 1 (if the router is equipped with a wide-area network interface card [WIC]).

NOTE   The truncated form of **show ip interfaces brief** is **sh ip int brie**.

Using the first command for a 56-kbps access rate service, the output in Example 17-1 is displayed.

Example 17-1   *Output from the* **show ip interface brief** *Command for the 1602 Router, with a Built-In Data Service Unit/Channel Service Unit (DSU/CSU) for a 56-kbps Rate*

```
1604-frame#show ip interface brief
Interface              IP-Address        OK? Method Status              Protocol
Ethernet0              151.68.89.89      YES NVRAM  up                  up
Loopback0              unassigned        YES NVRAM  up                  up
! This is your 56 Kbps connection
Serial0                unassigned        YES NVRAM  up                  up
Serial0.71             171.68.89.89      YES unset  up                  up
```

Example 17-2 shows the output from the **show ip interface brief** command when applied to 128 Kbps service.

Example 17-2   *Output from the* **show ip interface brief** *Command for the 1602 Router, Equipped with a WIC Card*

```
1604-frame#show ip interface brief
Interface              IP-Address        OK? Method Status              Protocol
Ethernet0              121.70.194.209    YES NVRAM  up                  up
Loopback0              unassigned        YES NVRAM  up                  up
Serial0                unassigned        YES NVRAM  administratively down down
! This is your 128 Kbps connection
Serial1                unassigned        YES NVRAM  up                  up
Serial1.37             121.70.194.209    YES unset  up                  up
```

The commands #**show ip interface brief** and #**show interface serial 1(0)** enable you to narrow the scope of the existing problem. The recommended troubleshooting process starts from the first layer (see Figure 14-1 in Chapter 14 and Figure 17-1).

Figure 17-1 *Frame Relay Troubleshooting Tools*

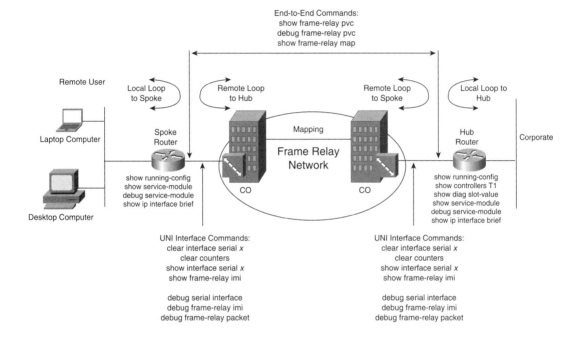

Physical Layer Troubleshooting

Troubleshooting the physical layer starts with checking for cabling issues. The vast majority of these issues can be overcome if you follow the directions in the documentation of your equipment. Usually, cabling problems are evident at the initial implementation of the service and include issues such as the wrong crossover cable or faulty cables. Later in the chapter, some cable pinpoint examples are discussed. Physical problems are probably the number-one suspect on a circuit that has already been installed and turned up and after time has developed an outage. In most cases, if no one has changed the configurations, it is usually a punchdown, bridge clip, line card, or cable break issue.

Line and Clocking Problems

Clocking problems in serial connections can lead to either chronic loss of the connection or to degraded performance. The most common indicators for physical layer problems are shown in Example 17-3.

Example 17-3   *If This Service Is Provisioned for 56-kbps, Check the Status of Serial 0*

```
1604-frame#show ip interface brief
<output omitted>
Serial0    unassigned    YES NVRAM  down down
<output omitted>
```

Under 1602-frame#**show interface serial 0**, the last line reports the status of the physical layer:

```
<output omitted>
DCD=down   DSR=down   DTR=down   RTS=down   CTS=down
<output omitted>
```

These signals are usually referred to as the modem and originally come from RS-232, with the following description:

- **DCD (Data Carrier Detect)**—Provided by DCE
- **DSR (Data Set Ready)**—Provided by DCE
- **DTR (Data Terminal Ready)**—Provided by DTE
- **RTS (Request To Send)**—Provided by DTE
- **CTS (Clear To Send)**—Provided by DCE

Although numerous combinations of up and down signals exist, at this stage it is easy to determine what part of the device is failing. DTE is responsible for **DTR** and **RTS**, and DCE is responsible for the rest of the signals. When the **clockrate** command is missing from the DCE side, DCD, DSR, and CTS are shown as inactive or down.

If the line is functional but is reporting an excessive number of errors, you should be concerned about the quality of the physical layer. Use the command in Example 17-4 to check the physical layer.

Example 17-4   *This Part of the Output Is Your Main Focus*

```
1604-frame#show interfaces serial 0
<output omitted>
237979 packets input, 21491750 bytes, 0 no buffer
Received 0 broadcasts, 0 runts, 5 giants, 0 throttles
! The following line is the part of the output you should review carefully:
198487 input errors, 44907 CRC, 20259 frame, 0 overrun, 0 ignored, 133321 abort
29689 packets output, 3054656 bytes, 0 underruns
0 output errors, 0 collisions, 329 interface res
<output omitted>
```

You should also be concerned about a high number of aborts; as you can see in this case, 133321 aborts represent the vast majority of all input errors (about 70 percent). Start with the configuration on both ends. Check the remote user's end first, for interface availability, as shown in Example 17-5. The output in Example 17-5 can be seen from the **show version** or **show hardware** commands, which shows that this router has one on-board 56-kbps serial interface.

Example 17-5   *Output from the* **show hardware** *Command*

```
1602-frame#show  hardware
<output omitted>
1 Serial network interface(s)
On-board Switched 56K Line Interface.
<output omitted>
```

The clocking issue is addressed in the remote user's router configuration. In the case of a 56-kbps access rate, two configuration commands define the clocking and signaling, as shown in Example 17-6.

Example 17-6   *A Fragment from the 1602 Configuration, Defining the 56-kbps Access Rate*

```
1602-frame#show running-config
<output omitted>
!
interface Serial0
 no ip address
 encapsulation frame-relay IETF
 no fair-queue
 service-module 56k clock source line
 service-module 56k network-type dds
 frame-relay lmi-type ansi
!
<output omitted>
```

The service module built into Cisco routers, including the 16xx, 252x, 26xx, 3600, 4xxx, and 7xxx series, supports two modes of 56-kbps settings for network-type: 56-kbps DSU/CSU and 56-kbps switched modes. The second of the following two commands identifies which side provides the clocking:

```
1602-frame(config-if)#service-module 56k network-type [dds | switched]
1602-frame(config-if)#service-module 56k clock source [line | internal]
```

NOTE   Dataphone Digital Service (DDS) provides digital transmission service between the CPE and the provider's switch at data rates between 2.4 kbps and 56 kbps. The service is available over two twisted pair lines.[1]

The service module report is shown in Example 17-7. The lines are self-explanatory.

Example 17-7   *Verifying the Functionality of the Built-In Service Module*

```
1602-frame#show service-module serial 0
Module type is 4-wire Switched 56K in DDS mode,
Receiver has no alarms.
```

continues

Example 17-7 *Verifying the Functionality of the Built-In Service Module (Continued)*

```
Current line rate is 56 Kbits/sec and role is DSU side,
Last clearing of alarm counters 3d03h
     oos/oof                :   0,
     loss of signal         :   2, last occurred 2d02h
     loss of sealing current:   0,
     CSU/DSU loopback       :   0,
     loopback from remote   :   0,
     DTE loopback           :   0,
     line loopback          :   0,
1602-frame#
```

In the case of a fractional T1 (or full T1) configuration, the expected output from the
configuration should be as displayed in Example 17-8. The output in Example 17-8 can be
seen from the **show hardware** or **show version** commands and shows that this router has
one on-board 56 Kbps interface and one WIC T1-DSU card plugged-in.

Example 17-8 *Output from the* **show version** *Command*

```
1602-frame#show version
<output omitted>
 2 Serial network interface(s)
On-board Switched 56K Line Interface.
WIC T1-DSU
<output omitted>
```

The configuration settings in the remote user's router are shown in Example 17-9.

Example 17-9 *This Fragment of the Configuration Defines a 128-kbps Access Rate (2 Slots × 64 kbps Each)*

```
1602-frame#show running-config
interface Serial1
<output omitted>
encapsulation frame-relay
service-module t1 timeslots 1-2
<output omitted>
```

NOTE   These settings are important and the remote user needs to be aware of which circuit is
ordered and provisioned. A 56-k circuit can be a true 56-k circuit (4 wire or 2 wire), but it
can sometimes be a T1 circuit (4 wire, T1 port speed) with 56-k PVC. The WIC-1DSU-T1
cannot be used for 56-k leased line/DDS service, and of course the 56-k WIC cannot be
used for T1 service.

This configuration defines two slots at 64 kbps each, which results in a 128-kbps access
rate. In case the line is provisioned for 128 kbps, 384 kbps, or any other fraction of a T1,

the built-in service module (serving a 56-kbps port) slows down because the router does not use this clocking (see Example 17-10).

Example 17-10 *The Receiver Has Loss of Signal (LOS) because Serial 0 Is Administratively Down. Meanwhile, the WIC Card Is Functioning Properly*

```
1602-frame#show service-module
Module type is 4-wire Switched 56K in DDS mode,
! You can expect the receiver to lose the signal, because the
! WIC card and DCE will provide the clocking, but not the DDS.
Receiver has loss of signal,
Current line rate is 56 Kbits/sec and role is DSU side,
Last clearing of alarm counters 6w1d
     oos/oof                 :   0,
     loss of signal          :   1, current duration 6w1d
     loss of sealing current:    0,
     CSU/DSU loopback        :   0,
     loopback from remote    :   0,
     DTE loopback            :   0,
     line loopback           :   0,
Module type is T1/fractional
     Hardware revision is 0.88, Software revision is 0.2,
     Image checksum is 0xED22BEC5, Protocol revision is 0.1
! This line usually indicates that the WIC card is functioning properly.
Receiver has no alarms.
Framing is ESF, Line Code is B8ZS, Current clock source is line,
Fraction has 2 timeslots (64 Kbits/sec each), Net bandwidth is 128 Kbits/sec.
Last module self-test (done at startup): Passed
Last clearing of alarm counters 6w1d
     loss of signal          :     0,
     loss of frame           :     0,
     AIS alarm               :     0,
     Remote alarm            :     0,
     Module access errors    :     0,
Total Data (last 96 15 minute intervals):
     0 Line Code Violations, 0 Path Code Violations
     0 Slip Secs, 0 Fr Loss Secs, 0 Line Err Secs, 13 Degraded Mins
     0 Errored Secs, 0 Bursty Err Secs, 0 Severely Err Secs, 0 Unavail Secs
Data in current interval (781 seconds elapsed):
     0 Line Code Violations, 0 Path Code Violations
     0 Slip Secs, 0 Fr Loss Secs, 0 Line Err Secs, 0 Degraded Mins
     0 Errored Secs, 0 Bursty Err Secs, 0 Severely Err Secs, 0 Unavail Secs
1602-frame#
```

NOTE For troubleshooting FT1 and T1s, see Chapter 6, "Dial Design and Configuration Solutions," or RFC 1232.

The clocking and line issues are irrelevant to the situation, when the serial interface reports the output in Example 17-11.

Example 17-11 *A Typical Output When the Interface Is Administratively Shut Down*

```
1602-frame#show interfaces serial 0
<output omitted>
  Serial0 is Administratively Down, Line Protocol is Down
  Hardware is QUICC Serial (with onboard CSU/DSU)
<output omitted>
```

The first command is used for an interface, whereas the second command is used for subinterface. In this case, you need to un-shut the interface with either of the following two commands:

```
1602-frame(config-if)#no shutdown
1602-frame(config-subif)#no shutdown
```

Serial Interface 0 and Line Protocol Is Down

When the interface serial 0 is not administratively down, the clocking problems have to be your primary focus, especially when the router reports the output in Example 17-12.

Example 17-12 *The Line Problems Are Evident from This Output*

```
1602-frame#show interfaces serial 0
Serial0 is Down, Line Protocol is Down
Hardware is QUICC Serial (with onboard CSU/DSU)
<output omitted>
```

In general, this problem occurs because clocking is not available. The following cases describe situations when the serial interface is not administratively down, but the router is still reporting both layers down. This case is typical for new service installations. The root cause of these problems is due to either or both of the following two cases:

- **Case One**—Clocking problems can be because of incorrect cabling, faulty connectors, faulty devices in the D-Mark, and faulty passive or active repeaters. A common problem with the physical wiring is a reversed pair, which shows a line down/protocol down condition. Problems also occur if the CSU/DSU cable is longer than 50 feet [15.24 meters] or is unshielded.

- **Case Two**—Another category of problems result from a faulty DSU/CSU, faulty line cards, an incorrect DSU/CSU configuration, or D-Mark equipment (commonly referred to as smart-jack and is usually on the MPOE, but in case of extended D-marks, can be in another location).

One of the most widespread issues is incorrect cabling. In Table 17-1, the correct cabling is specified for the two most common cases: 56-kbps and fractional T1 WIC cards.

NOTE	Remember that matching pinouts does not mean that the signaling is correct.

Table 17-1   *56-kbps DSU/CSU and WIC T1 Pinpoints*

56-kbps CSU/DSU Pinouts (8-Pin RJ-48S)

Pin Number	Description
1	Transmit
2	Transmit
7	Receive
8	Receive

WIC T1 Pinouts (8-Pin RJ-48S)

Pin Number	Description
1	Transmit
2	Transmit
4	Receive
5	Receive

NOTE   It's always recommended that you refer to the available technical documentation of the customer premises equipment (CPE).

The CSU/DSU derives the data clock from the data that passes through it. Therefore, to recover the clock, the CSU/DSU hardware must receive at least one 1-bit value for every 8 bits of data that pass through it; this is known as ones density. Maintaining ones density allows the hardware to recover the data clock reliably.

Serial communications use a mechanism called serial clock transmit external (SCTE) terminal timing. SCTE is the clock that is echoed back from the data terminal equipment (DTE) device (for example, a router), to the data communications equipment (DCE) device. When the DCE device uses SCTE instead of its internal clock to sample data from the DTE, it is better able to sample the data without error, even if there is a phase shift in the cable between the CSU/DSU and the router. SCTE is an important element in serial transmissions and it uses access rates that are fractions of a T1.

To isolate clocking problems, besides the ones listed earlier, Cisco routers provide a set of tools to troubleshoot the CSU/DSU by using the **show**, **debug**, and **loopback** commands:

```
1602-frame#debug service-module
1602-frame# show service-module
1602-frame(config-if)# loopback dte
1602-frame(config-if)# loopback line
1602-frame(config-if)# loopback remote
```

Refer to Figure 17-1 for the **show service-module** command. Note that, in addition to the listed commands, under the T1 controller of the core router, you can use the following useful command: 7206-frame(config-controller)#**loopback diag**.

The first command reports the functionality of the module, as shown in Example 17-13.

Example 17-13 *Debugging the Service Module*

```
1602-frame#debug service-module
Service module debugging is on
1602-frame#
6w5d: SERVICE_MODULF(0): 1xt441 interrupt 1 status A7 loop 0
6w5d: SERVICE_MODULE(0): 1xt441 interrupt I statuc 87 loop 0
6w5d: SERVICE_MODULE(0): 1xt441 interrupt 1 status A7 loop 0
6w5d: SERVICE_MODULE(0): 1xt441 interrupt 1 status 87 loop 0
```

The output reports that the service module is working properly.

Case One Problem Resolution

It is necessary to perform a series of loopback tests, both local and remote, to determine whether the DSU or CSU is causing the problem. Using the following commands, you can loopback the DTE, line, or the remote site:

```
1602-frame(config-if)# loopback dte
1602-frame(config-if)# loopback line
1602-frame(config-if)# loopback remote
```

It is always good to keep a record of all the different tests performed. In general, when looping and running these tests, always check the number of errors. Different ping tests (samples and sizes) are also recommended during this testing. You must determine whether there is a trend in the accumulation of errors and on what side of the User-Network Interface (UNI) they occur. If errors are accumulating on both ends of the connection (hub site and spoke site), it is most likely because of a DSU problem. If only the DSU end is accumulating errors, there is a problem with that particular end. An excessive number of aborts is a symptom of end-to-end line problems and it is recommended that you work with the local exchange carrier (LEC), who provides the local loop, to isolate the issue. Some Cisco line cards (T1/FT1 WIC) have a loopback button that, when engaged, allows the LEC to loop the spoke side for intrusive testing and clocking.

Case Two Problem Resolution

The problems for this case are related to faulty DSU/CSU, faulty line cards, and incorrect DSU/CSU configurations.

An incorrect CSU configuration is usually related to the clocking source. The following questions should be considered:

- What is the source of clocking (line or internal)?
- Do the impedance parameters match the manufacturer's documentation?

An incorrect DSU configuration is related to several important checkpoints. The following questions should be considered:

- Is SCTE enabled, especially for fractional T1s?
- Is the ones density maintained properly and do the framing and coding schemes match on both sides (Extended Superframe [ESF], bipolar 8-zero substitution [B8ZS], alternate mark inversion [AMI])?
- Although it is not common, is AMI coding configured? If it is, you might need to invert the transmit clock to match the LEC's requirements. For this purpose, Cisco provides an additional command that is set for 4000 series and 7000 series routers, and jumpers in the older versions of the equipment.

NOTE   Always see the Cisco IOS configuration guides and command references for the version of IOS that you are running on your router. You can also refer to available user guides for your CPE.

Performance Issues Related to the Physical Layer

You can experience line problems even if the router reports that the line is not down, as shown in the output in Example 17-14.

Example 17-14 *The Line Shows Up and the Protocol Is Up, But the Performance Issues Exist*

```
1602-frame#show interfaces serial 1
<output omitted>
Serial1 is up, line protocol is up
<output omitted>
```

However, the connection experiences slow performance, intermittent connectivity, and high latency. Some of the most common reasons for poor performance follow:

- Noisy (dirty) serial lines
- Cables longer than 50 feet [15.24 meters] or cables are unshielded
- Noisy or poor patch panel connections
- External EMI sources, such as unshielded cables running too close to EMI sources

A useful tool in this situation is #**show interface serial 0,** which allows you to not only check the status of the line at any moment (snapshot), but to monitor the dynamics of the changes. This command reports the output in Example 17-15 (see Table 17-2 for an explanation).

Example 17-15 *Snapshot of the Serial 0*

```
1602-frame#show interfaces serial 0
Serial0 is up, line protocol is up
  Hardware is QUICC Serial (with onboard CSU/DSU)
  MTU 1500 bytes, BW 1544 Kbit, DLY 20000 usec,
     reliability 255/255, txload 1/255, rxload 1/255
  Encapsulation FRAME-RELAY, loopback not set
  Keepalive set (10 sec)
  LMI enq sent  53714, LMI stat recvd 53710, LMI upd recvd 0, DTE LMI up
  LMI enq recvd 0, LMI stat sent  0, LMI upd sent  0
  LMI DLCI 0  LMI type is ANSI Annex D  frame relay DTE
  FR SVC disabled, LAPF state down
  Broadcast queue 0/64, broadcasts sent/dropped 8958/0, interface broadcasts 3
  Last input 00:00:00, output 00:00:00, output hang never
  Last clearing of "show interface" counters 1w0d
  Queuing strategy: fifo
  Output queue 0/40, 0 drops; input queue 1/75, 0 drops
  5 minute input rate 0 bits/sec, 2 packets/sec
  5 minute output rate 0 bits/sec, 0 packets/sec
     230129 packets input, 44936503 bytes, 0 no buffer
     Received 0 broadcasts, 0 runts, 1 giants, 0 throttles
     7241 input errors, 3594 CRC, 2701 frame, 0 overrun, 0 ignored, 944 abort
     229128 packets output, 49424950 bytes, 0 underruns
     0 output errors, 0 collisions, 2509 interface resets
     0 output buffer failures, 0 output buffers swapped out
     6 carrier transitions
     DCD=up  DSR=up  DTR=up  RTS=up  CTS=up
```

Table 17-2 *The Output From #show **interface serial 0** and Its Description*

Output	Description
Serial0 is [up | down] administratively down	Indicates whether the clocking is presently available or not (matches Data Carrier Detect [DCD] signal in the last line of the output); and whether the line was taken down by the administrator.
Line protocol is [up | down]	Indicates a successful exchange of the configured LMI and keepalives (if they are configured).
Hardware is QUICC Serial (with onboard CSU/DSU)	Hardware information, showing the router has a built-in CSU/DSU-interface.
MTU 1500 bytes	Maximum Transmit Unit (MTU) is 1500 bytes.
BW 1544 Kbit DLY 20000 usec	Bandwidth is 1554 kbps. The routing protocols, such as Interior Gateway Routing Protocol (IGRP) and Enhanced Interior Gateway Routing Protocol (EIGRP), use this parameter to compute the routing metrics. If the bandwith differs from the default value (1544 or 1536), the command 7206-frame(config-if) #**bandwidth** *value* specifies the correct access rate of the line.
	Delay in the interface in milliseconds.

Table 17-2 *The Output From #***show interface serial 0** *and Its Description (Continued)*

Output	Description
reliability 255/255, txload 1/255, rxload 1/255	Reliability, transmit load (txload) and receive load (rxload) are a fraction of 255. Thus, 255/255 is the highest and 1/255 is the lowest.
Encapsulation FRAME-RELAY, loopback not set	The encapsulation of the interface is Frame Relay and the loopback is not set.
Keepalive set (10 sec)	Keepalive messages are set to 10-second intervals.
	In some cases, an interval of 30 seconds is acceptable, in other cases, the engineers set the DSU interval to 8 seconds, which is less than the switch interval, and it is set up this way to prevent the line from flapping. One of the techniques used for troubleshooting is to negate the keepalives with 7206-frame(config-if)#**no keepalive** to prevent the line from flapping reports and to rely only on LMIs.
LMI enq sent 53714	The number of LMI enquiry messages sent by the DTE.
LMI stat recvd 53710	The number of LMI status messages received from the switch.
LMI upd recvd 0	
DTE LMI up	The number of LMI updates received.
	An indication of DTE LMI [up	down].
	(Matches some of the parameters of #**show frame-relay status**)
LMI enq recvd 0	The number of LMI status enquiries received by the switch.
LMI stat sent 0	
LMI upd sent 0	The number of LMI status messages sent to the switch.
	The number of LMI updates sent to the switch.
	(Matches some of the parameters of #**show frame-relay status**)
LMI DLCI 0	The type of LMI signaling (see Chapter 14 or the following chapter).
LMI type is ANSI AnnexD Frame Relay DTE	In this case, DLCI 0 indicates ANSI AnnexD LMI.
	The other options are **cisco** and **q.933**.
FR SVC disabled	This report is for PVC design (frame-relay), but not Frame-Switching. This is why the SVC is down.
Link Access Procedures for Frame-Mode Bearer Services (LAPF) state down	LAPF down means LAPF is not performing the signaling in this circuit. Only the core functions of LAPF are involved.
Broadcast queue 0/64, broadcasts sent/dropped 8958/0, interface broadcasts 3	The line reports the status of the broadcast queue. In Frame Relay, this queue is separate from others.

continues

Table 17-2   *The Output From #***show interface serial 0** *and Its Description (Continued)*

Output	Description
Last input 00:00:00, output 00:00:00	The number of hours, minutes, and seconds since the last packet was received (input) or sent (output) by this interface.
Output hang never	Indicates hours:minutes:seconds or never since the last reset of this interface. If the time is more than 24 hours, you can see 2d3h (2 days and 3 hours), but if this format is not large enough, you can see *****, which indicates more characters than can be expressed in this format.
Last clearing of "show interface" counters 1w0d	Often when troubleshooting, you need to start with fresh data. This value indicates the last time in hours:minutes:seconds (or never) that the interface was cleared by using any of the following commands: 1602-frame#**clear counters serial 0** 7206-frame#**clear counters serial 3/0:0** 7206-frame#**clear interface serial 3/0:0**
Queuing strategy: fifo	The FIFO queuing strategy stands for First-In-First-out. For other queuing strategies, see www.cisco.com.
Output queue 0/40, 0 drops Input queue 1/75, 0 drops	An input queue with self-explanatory parameters and the number of dropped packets because of a lack of queue slots. If the number of dropped packets is high, you might want to check the interface buffers using the following command: 1602-frame#**sh buffers**
Conversations 0/1/16 (active/max active/max total) Reserved conversations 0/0 (allocated/max allocated)	Multiplexing many logical (virtual) interfaces into one physical interface is called data conversations. This information exists only for the D channel. BRI channels do not have signaling functions.
5 minute input rate 0 bits/sec, 2 packets/sec 5 minute output rate 0 bits/sec, 0 packets/sec	The average rate of data exchange in and out in 5-minute intervals, measured in bit/sec and packets/sec. It indicates exponentially weighted values, which are cumulative values and not snapshot values. You only use this parameter as an approximation of the traffic, to check traffic trends, or to compare with other interfaces.
230,129 packets input, 44,936,503 bytes, 0 no buffer Received 0 broadcasts 0 runts 1 giants 0 throttles	The number of successfully received packets and bytes. The number of instances of a lack of input buffer slots. Total number of received broadcasts on this interface. The number of discarded packets because their size was smaller than the minimum packet size.

Table 17-2 *The Output From #***show interface serial 0** *and Its Description (Continued)*

Output	Description
	The number of discarded packets because their size was greater than the maximum packet size.
	The number of times the receiver on the port was disabled, possibly because of buffer or processor overload.
7241 input errors 3594 CRC 2701 frame 0 overrun 0 ignored 944 abort	The total number of input errors since the last **#clear counters** command, which are categorized as follows: Cyclic redundancy check (CRC) errors that usually indicate noise or other transmission problems. Incorrectly received packets, or packets with a non-integer number of octets, which usually indicates noise or other transmission problems. The number of times when the input rate exceeded the receiver's ability to buffer and handle the data. The number of times when the hardware ran low in internal buffers. Broadcast storms and bursts of noise can be the possible cause of this problem. The number of aborts. It shows an illegal number of 1s in the interface, which is an indication of clocking problems on the interface.
229,128 packets output, 49,424,950 bytes 0 underruns 0 output errors 0 collisions 2509 interface resets 0 output buffer failures, 0 output buffers swapped out 6 carrier transitions	The number of output packets and bytes in the interface that were passed without errors. The number of times when the transmitter runs faster than the router can handle. The number of all output errors. The number of collisions on the interface, which might come from the contention failures. A number of collisions more than 4–5 percent should be investigated. The number of interface resets indicates "no signal" in the interface. On the serial line, this is caused by a malfunctioning modem DSU/CSU or a cable problem. If the router sees the DTR up but protocol down, it resets the interface in an effort to trigger the LMI or keepalive exchange. The number of buffer failures and swapped output buffers. The number of carrier transitions, where an excessive number indicates either intrusive testing performed by the LEC, or switch card/line problems that must be investigated with the LEC.

continues

Table 17-2   *The Output From #***show interface serial 0** *and Its Description (Continued)*

Output	Description
DCD = up	DCD clock is up.
DSR = up	Data Set Ready (DSR), an input signal, is up.
DTR = up	Data Terminal Ready, an output signal, is up.
RTS = up	Request To Send (RTS), an output signal, is up.
CTS = up	Clear To Send (CTS), an input signal, is up.
	All five ups indicate that the serial interface is up.

If at any step of the troubleshooting process, the number of errors exceeds an approximate range of 0.5 percent to 2.0 percent of traffic on the interface, clocking problems are likely to exist somewhere in the WAN.

Data Link Layer Troubleshooting

Troubleshooting the second layer in Frame Relay includes the encapsulation types, LMI types and messages, and should be performed just after the physical layer issues are resolved. As previously mentioned #**show ip interface brief** and #**show interfaces serial 1(0)** are the commands that help narrow the scope of troubleshooting. Some typical reports for protocol layer issues are shown in Example 17-16 and Example 17-17.

Example 17-16   *The Serial 1 Interfaces Show Line Up and the Protocol Down*

```
1604-frame#show ip interface brief
Interface       IP-Address       OK? Method Status                 Protocol
Ethernet0       121.70.194.209   YES NVRAM  up                     up
Loopback0       unassigned       YES NVRAM  up                     up
Serial0         unassigned       YES NVRAM  administratively down  down
! The following narrows the scope of possible problems to
! the data link layer issues.
Serial1         unassigned       YES NVRAM  up                     down
Serial1.37      unassigned       YES unset  down                   down
```

Example 17-17   *Data Link Layer Issues Can Be Seen if You Use the* **show interfaces** *Command*

```
7206-frame#show interfaces s3/0:0
Serial0 is up, line protocol is down
  Hardware is QUICC Serial (with onboard CSU/DSU)
<output omitted>
```

PVC Configuration Issues

Configuration issues for a PVC include problems with configuration, encapsulation, and bandwidth definitions. In the case of a 56-kbps configuration shown in Example 17-18, the configuration line is shaded and defines the type of PVC encapsulation.

Example 17-18 *First Step Is to Make Sure the Configuration Is Correct*

```
1602-frame#show running-config
<output omitted>
!
interface Serial0
 no ip address
 ! The frame relay encapsulation and its type (IETF) are your primary focus here
 encapsulation frame-relay IETF
 no fair-queue
 service-module 56k clock source line
 service-module 56k network-type dds
 ! The LMI type is the second point of attention
 frame-relay lmi-type ansi
 !
<output omitted>
```

In the case of fractional T1 (FT1) or T1 configurations, the configuration settings are a little different. The configuration lines are shown in Example 17-19.

Example 17-19 *In Case of Fractional T1, the Encapsulation and the LMI Type Need to Be Your Primary Focus*

```
1602-frame#show running-config
<output omitted>
!
interface Serial1
<output omitted>
 ! The frame relay encapsulation and its type are your primary focus here
 encapsulation frame-relay
 no ip mroute-cache
 no fair-queue
 ! The access rate configuration is your secondary focus.
 service-module t1 timeslots 1-2
 ! The LMI type is the next point of attention
 frame-relay lmi-type ansi
 !
<output omitted>
```

The encapsulation options are shown in Example 17-20.

Example 17-20 *The Encapsulation Options for Cisco 1602 Frame Relay Routers*

```
1602-frame(config-if)#encapsulation ?
  atm-dxi        ATM-DXI encapsulation
  frame-relay    Frame Relay networks
  hdlc           Serial HDLC synchronous
  lapb           LAPB (X.25 Level 2)
  ppp            Point-to-Point protocol
  smds           Switched Megabit Data Service (SMDS)
  x25            X.25
```

Frame Relay encapsulation options are **cisco** and **ietf** (RFC 1490 and RFC 2427). In point-to-point configurations, you need to configure a subinterface, as shown in Example 17-21.

Example 17-21 *Fragment of Configuration of Point-To-Point Interface Serial0.1*

```
interface Serial0.1 point-to-point
 bandwidth 56
 ip unnumbered Ethernet0
 frame-relay interface-dlci 16
```

Encapsulation options are shown in Example 17-22, and if the encapsulation type is omitted, it defaults to **cisco**.

Example 17-22 *Frame Relay DLCI Encapsulation Options*

```
3640-frame(config-fr-dlci)# interface-dlci 16 ?
  cisco       Use CISCO Encapsulation
  ietf        Use RFC1490/RFC2427 Encapsulation
  ppp         Use RFC1973 Encapsulation to support PPP over FR
  protocol    Optional protocol information for remote end,
```

The DLCI types are as follows: **cisco** (Consortium, by default), **ietf** (uses RFC 1490/RFC 2427 encapsulation), **ppp** (uses RFC 1973 encapsulation to support PPP over Frame Relay), and **protocol**.

NOTE   An interesting discussion about different **ppp** options can be found in RFC 1490, "Multiprotocol Interconnect over Frame Relay," by Bradley (July 1995). The **ppp** option is available in Cisco IOS version 12.0(1).T and later versions. The interesting part about **ppp** encapsulation is related to the auto recognition of ppp frames and proposed options for LCP, authentication, and compression techniques.

The first potential problem to check is the access rate definition. The service module definition configures the line as a 2×64-kbps access rate service. If there is any mismatch between both sides of the UNI interface, the report of the line shows the output in Example 17-23.

Example 17-23 *This Output Shows That if the Protocol Layer is Down, the Access Rate Configuration Can Be a Potential Problem*

```
1604-frame#show ip interface brief
Interface        IP-Address      OK? Method Status             Protocol
<output omitted>
Serial1          unassigned      YES NVRAM  up                 down
Serial1.37       unassigned      YES unset  down               down
```

The second important factor is to make sure that the interface is configured with proper encapsulation, and that it matches the encapsulation in the near-end and far-end:

```
1602-frame(config-if)#encapsulation frame-relay [cisco | ietf]
```

The available options in Cisco routers are as follows:

- **cisco**—Uses Cisco's own encapsulation.

- **ietf**—The encapsulation complies with the Internet Engineering Task Force (IETF) standard (RFC 1490). If the chosen encapsulation is IETF, this is an indication that the configuration is designated for a multivendor environment.

NOTE   If the encapsulation is not defined under the serial interface, an attempt to create a subinterface will not work because the default Cisco encapsulation in the serial interface is Cisco Proprietary high-level data link control (HDLC), which does not support subinterfaces.

The correct PVC configuration depends on several factors. The core of the PVC is the DLCI, so you must ensure that the configuration uses the proper DLCI, as it is assigned by the LEC. The DLCI has a local significance, and can be different at each end. At the same time, the DLCI is bound to a certain port on the switch and it cannot be used without the proper settings. When the switch receives a frame, it performs a series of predefined operations. First, it recalculates the FCS and if the value does not match the FCS of the frame, it drops the packet. At the same time, the switch checks the DLCI and the length of the frame. If the DLCI is not correct or the frame is too long, too short, or falls beyond the byte boundary, it discards the frame. After the first check is passed, the switch checks its routing/switching table for proper routing. This routing table consists of port-to-DLCI values, with each pair associated with input or output flows. After the entry is found, the switch changes the incoming DLCI in the frame with the DLCI from the output portion of the table. Using this approach, the incoming DLCI x becomes the outgoing DLCI y and matches the far-end of the connection. Before sending the frame, the switch recalculates the new frame check sequence (FCS), replaces this portion in the outgoing frame, and sends the frame out. If the remote user's equipment is configured with an incorrect DLCI, the indication from the down protocol shows a problem with the DLCI.

NOTE   The line protocol shows down in point-to-point configurations. If the DLCI is misconfigured, the line protocol does not show down if the configuration is point-to-multipoint.

Cisco routers ease the DLCI troubleshooting process. An example of the output from an incorrect DLCI configuration is shown in Example 17-24. In this example, the LEC's switch is configured for DLCI 16, but the router is configured with DLCI 17. There's more than one indication that the configuration is not correct, as shown in the example.

Example 17-24 *The Focus Points, Indicating That There Is an Active DLCI, But There Is Also a Configuration Issue*

```
1602-frame#show frame-relay pvc
PVC Statistics for interface Serial0 (Frame Relay DTE)
! For Serial 0, there is one deleted and one active DLCI
! This should be your first point of attention.
                Active      Inactive    Deleted     Static
  Local         0           0           1           0
  Switched      0           0           0           0
  Unused        1           0           0           0
! Note that DLCI=16 is active, but unused.
! This should be your second point of attention.
DLCI = 16, DLCI USAGE = UNUSED, PVC STATUS = ACTIVE, INTERFACE = Serial0

  input pkts 3            output pkts 0          in bytes 918
  out bytes 0            dropped pkts 0          in FECN pkts 0
  in BECN pkts 0          out FECN pkts 0        out BECN pkts 0
  in DE pkts 0            out DE pkts 0
  out bcast pkts 0        out bcast bytes 0      Num Pkts Switched 0
  pvc create time 00:02:45, last time pvc status changed 00:02:45
! Why is the DLCI reported deleted?
! This should be your third point of attention.
DLCI = 17, DLCI USAGE = LOCAL, PVC STATUS = DELETED, INTERFACE = Serial0.17

  input pkts 0            output pkts 1          in bytes 0
  out bytes 312          dropped pkts 0          in FECN pkts 0
  in BECN pkts 0          out FECN pkts 0        out BECN pkts 0
  in DE pkts 0            out DE pkts 0
  out bcast pkts 1        out bcast bytes 312
  pvc create time 00:03:44, last time pvc status changed 00:02:50
1602-frame#
```

NOTE When checking the DLCI, the other end of the connection is not relevant because DLCI only has a local significance.

NOTE Remember that if the PVC is reported as inactive or deleted, and even if LMI is configured correctly, LMI still does not send packets over the DLCI.

The first group of data (the overall status of the PVCs) provided by the last LMI shows that the serial line has one local and deleted PVC and one active but unused DLCI. (Later in the discussion, you see that LMI must provide the status of all PVCs configured on the interface on every full status message.) The second indication of the DLCI status is its description (see PVC STATUS line). As shown, the configured DLCI = 17 under subinterface Serial0.17 is not correct and the correct one is DLCI = 16.

The overall status of the PVC can be analyzed by using the #**show frame-relay pvc** command as displayed in Example 17-24. Table 17-3 contains a description of the output from this command.

Table 17-3 *Output and Description From the #***show frame-relay pvc** *Command*

Output	Description
This Section Shows the Standard Output	
DLCI	DLCI numbers for the PVC.
DLCI USAGE	Lists SWITCHED when the router or access server is used as a switch, or LOCAL when used as a DTE.
PVC STATUS	Status of the PVC: ACTIVE, INACTIVE, or DELETED.
INTERFACE	Specific subinterface associated with this DLCI.
Input pkts	Number of packets received on this PVC.
Output pkts	Number of packets sent on this PVC.
in bytes	Number of bytes received on this PVC.
out bytes	Number of bytes sent on this PVC.
dropped pkts	Number of incoming and outgoing packets dropped by the router at the Frame Relay level.
in FECN pkts	Number of packets received with the FECN bit set.
in BECN pkts	Number of packets received with the BECN bit set.
out FECN pkts	Number of packets sent with the FECN bit set.
out BECN pkts	Number of packets sent with the BECN bit set.

continues

Table 17-3 *Output and Description From the #***show frame-relay pvc** *Command (Continued)*

Output	Description
in DE pkts	Number of DE packets received.
out DE pkts	Number of DE packets sent.
out bcast pkts	Number of output broadcast packets.
out bcast bytes	Number of output broadcast bytes.
pvc create time	Time the PVC was created.
last time pvc status changed	Time the PVC changed status (active to inactive).
This Section Appears if Voice Is Configured for This PVC	
Service-type	Type of service performed by this PVC. Can be Voice over Frame Relay or Voice over Frame Relay-cisco.
configured voice bandwidth	Amount of bandwidth in bits per second reserved for voice traffic on this PVC.
used voice bandwidth	Amount of bandwidth in bits per second currently being used for voice traffic.
Voice reserved queues	Queue numbers reserved for voice traffic on this PVC. This field was removed in Cisco IOS Release 12.0(5)T.
Fragment type	Type of fragmentation configured for this PVC. The possible types are as follows:
	Voice over Frame Relay-cisco—Fragmented packets contain the Cisco proprietary header.
	Voice over Frame Relay—Fragmented packets contain the FRF.11 Annex C header.
	End-to-end—Fragmented packets contain the standard FRF.12 header.
Fragment size	Size of the fragment payload in bytes.
This Section Appears if the Traffic Shaping Map Class Is Applied to this PVC (Refer to End-to-End Issues Later in This Chapter)	
Cir	Current CIR, in bits per second.
Bc	Current committed burst size, in bits.
Be	Current excess burst size, in bits.
Limit	Maximum number of bytes transmitted per internal interval (excess plus sustained).
Interval	Interval being used internally (can be smaller than the interval derived from Bc/CIR; this occurs when the router determines that traffic flow is more stable with a smaller configured interval).
Mincir	Minimum CIR for the PVC.
Byte increment	Number of bytes that can be sustained per internal interval.
BECN response	Frame Relay has backward explicit congestion notification (BECN) adaptation configured.

Table 17-3   *Output and Description From the #***show frame-relay pvc** *Command (Continued)*

Output	Description
Pkts	Number of packets associated with this PVC that went through the traffic shaping system.
Bytes	Number of bytes associated with this PVC that went through the traffic shaping system.
Pkts delayed	Number of packets associated with this PVC that were delayed by the traffic shaping system.
Bytes delayed	Number of bytes associated with this PVC that were delayed by the traffic shaping system.
Shaping	Shaping is active for all PVCs that are fragmenting data; otherwise, shaping is active if the traffic sent exceeds the CIR for this circuit.
Shaping drops	Number of packets dropped by the traffic shaping process.
Voice queuing stats	Statistics showing the size of packets, the maximum number of packets, and the number of packets dropped in the special voice queue created by using the frame-relay voice bandwidth command queue keyword.
Discard threshold	Maximum number of packets that can be stored in each packet queue. If additional packets are received after a queue is full, they are discarded.
Dynamic queue count	Number of packet queues reserved for best-effort traffic.
Reserved queue count	Number of packet queues reserved for voice traffic.
Output queue size	Size in bytes of each output queue.
max total	Maximum number of packets of all types that can be queued in all queues.
Drops	Number of frames dropped by all output queues.

LMI Issues

The PVC status reports the static or snapshot information, and the LMI provides the dynamics for the troubleshooting process. Some explanations are necessary to understand the outputs on the screen. For troubleshooting purposes, it is important to understand the difference between formats and the underlying concept of LMIs. Local Management Interfaces (LMIs) provide information about the DLCI values and the status of virtual circuits. Three different standards for LMI messages exist: **cisco** LMI (default), which users DLCI 1023 for connection management, **ANSI** LMI, which uses DLCI 0 for connection management, and **Q933a** (ITU).

The Consortium LMI defines two messages: status enqiry and status. The general format of LMI type **cisco** (Consortium) is shown in Figure 17-2.

Both messages are sent in HDLC Unnumbered Information (UI) frames, with a Control field value of 03h. The message header, based on Q.931, is three octets and includes protocol discriminator 09h, call reference value 00h (Dummy Call reference), and message type indicator for the message type: status enquiry 75h (0111 0101) or status 7Dh (0111 1101).

Figure 17-2 *LMI Message Format (Consortium)*

1	2	n	2	1
Flag 01111110	Address	Information Field (Data)	FCS	Flag 0111110

	Consortium Message Header					
1	1	1	1	n	n	n
Control UI Frame 03h	Protocol Descriminator (09h)	Call Reference (00h)	Message Type*	IE1	IE2	IE...

* The Message Type Can Be
  • 0111 1101 Status
  • 0111 0101 Status Inquiry

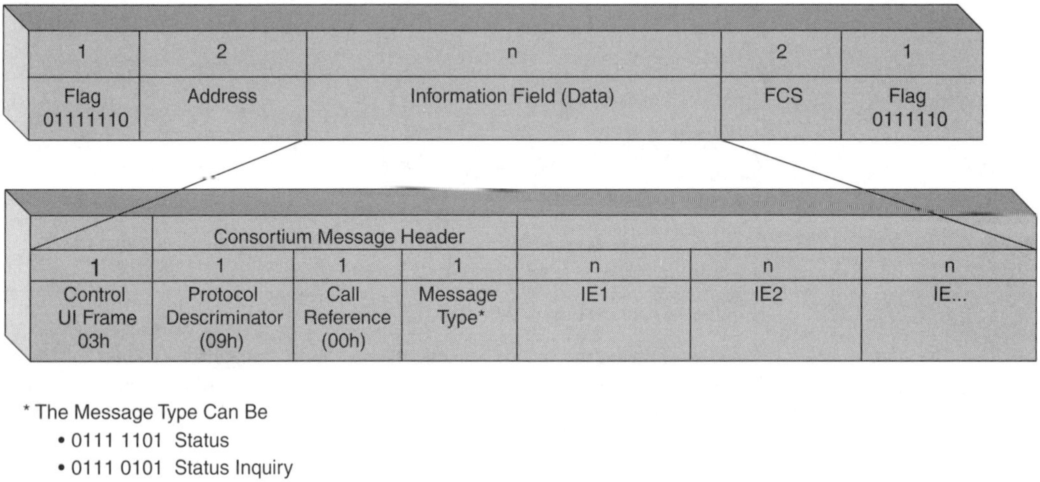

The Consortium LMI Status Enquiry Message Format

The Consortium LMI operates by periodically polling the network, and by using status enquiry messages. The Consortium document defines the polling period as the variable nT1, which ranges from 5 to 30 seconds, where 10 seconds is the default. The message contains two IEs: Report Type and Keepalive Sequence (see Figure 17-3).

Figure 17-3 *LMI Status Enquiry Message Format (Consortium)*

1	2	n	2	1
Flag 01111110	Address	Information Field (Data)	FCS	Flag 01111110

	Consortium Message Header (Mandatory)				
1	1	1	1	3	4
Control UI Frame 03h	Protocol Descriminator (09h)	Call Reference (00h)	Message Type	Report Type (Mandatory)	Keepalive Sequence (Mandatory)

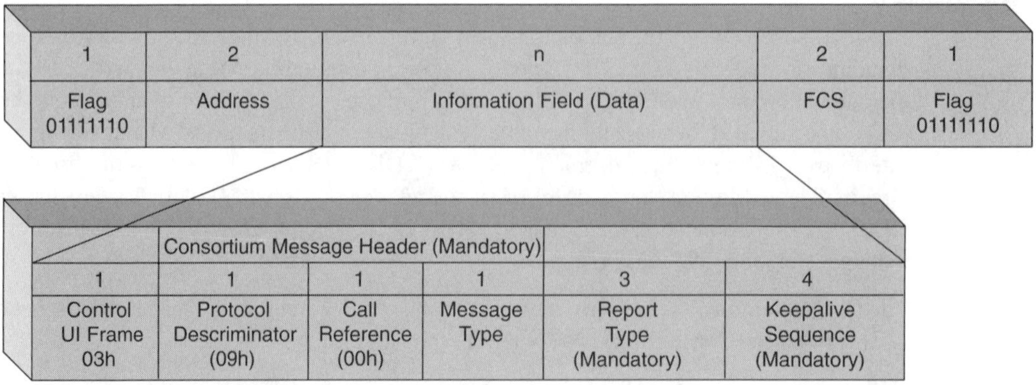

When used with the status enquiry message, the report type defines the content of the network's Status message. The report type IE is identified by 01H in the first byte. The second byte specifies the length of the contents, and the third one identifies the report type. A report type of 00H indicates a full status message, and 01h indicates a sequence number exchange, which verifies the integrity of the link.

NOTE   The Consortium format of the report type is the same as for AnnexD. The difference is AnnexD defines an additional report type, which is the Single PVC Asynchronous Status Report, 02h.

The Keepalive Sequence IE is identified by a 03h in the first octet. The second octet specifies the length of the contents in bytes (02 stands for the second octet), and the last two bytes are Current and Last received sequence numbers. Each time the router or network sends a status enquiry message, it increments its internal sequence number and places the value in the Current received sequence number (byte three). The last sequence number received from the other end of the link is paced in the Last received sequence number (byte four).

NOTE   Less frequently, the Frame Relay access device (router) requests a full status message, which adds one PVC status IE for each PVC configured on the interface. This polling period is defined by the variable nN1, which ranges from 1 to 255 intervals of nT1, with a default of six intervals.

The Consortium LMI Status Message Format

The network sends the status message to the CPE in response to the status enquiry message. Figure 17-4 shows the status message format.

Report type and keepalive sequence IEs are always transmitted with the status message. PVC IEs are added, one per configured PVC, to the status message when the full status message is requested. The PVC status IE is identified by 07h in the first octet and it is either 5 or 8 bytes long. The second octet specifies the length of the contents (3 or 6 bytes). The third and fourth octets carry the DLCI for this PVC, and the fifth octet contains status-bit coding that identifies whether the PVC is new (N = 1) or Active (A = 1). The Consortium defined octets 6 through 8 to optionally carry a 24-bit number, which represents the minimum bandwidth in bits per second that the network has allocated for this PVC.

Figure 17-4 *LMI Status Message (Consortium) Format*

1	2	n	2	1
Flag 01111110	Address	Information Field (Data)	FCS	Flag 01111110

Consortium Message Header (Mandatory)						
1	1	1	1	3	4	5 or 8
Control UI Frame 03h	Protocol Descriminator (09h)	Call Reference (00h)	Message Type	Report Type * (Mandatory)	Keepalive Sequence (Mandatory)	PVC Status (Optional)

* The Report Type IE Includes
- 00h (0000 0000) Full Status Message
- 01h (0000 0001) Sequence Number Exchange Only
- All Others Are Reserved

LMI Type ANSI—T1.617 AnnexD

The Consortium status enquiry messages contain the report type and keepalive sequences, and the AnnexD status enquiry messages contain report type and link integrity verification IEs, as shown in Figure 17-5. The link integrity verification IE has the value of 03h in the Control UI Frame field.

Figure 17-5 *AnnexD Status Enquiry Message*

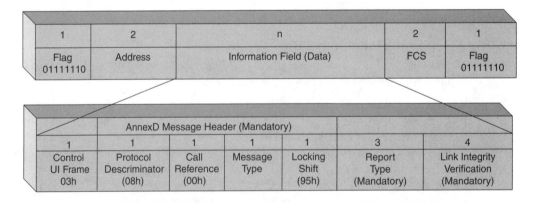

1	2	n	2	1
Flag 01111110	Address	Information Field (Data)	FCS	Flag 01111110

AnnexD Message Header (Mandatory)						
1	1	1	1	1	3	4
Control UI Frame 03h	Protocol Descriminator (08h)	Call Reference (00h)	Message Type	Locking Shift (95h)	Report Type (Mandatory)	Link Integrity Verification (Mandatory)

The link integrity verification IE has an identification ID in the first byte, the length of the integrity verification content in the second byte, send sequence number in the third byte, and receive sequence number in the fourth byte.

The AnnexD status message uses a similar format as Consortium, as shown in Figure 17-6.

Figure 17-6 *AnnexD Status Message Format*

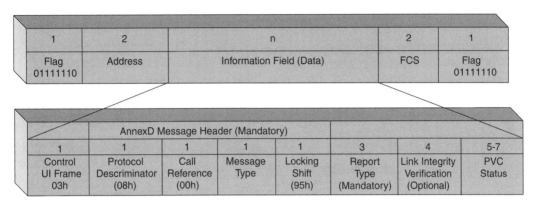

The Report Type IE Coding Is as Follows:
* 0000 0000 Full Status (Status of all PVCs on the Bearer Channel)
* 0000 0001 Link Integrity Verification Only
* 0000 0010 Single PVC Asynchronous Status
* All Other Values Are Reserved

The LMI type configuration is crucial for Frame Relay service. If the DTE configuration does not match the switch configuration, the LMI autosense mode is used, which is supported by Cisco. If the configuration of LMI is not configured explicitly, the router sends out a full status enquiry in all three LMI types to the switch. The order is ANSI, ITU, and Cisco. Cisco can listen on DLCI 0 and DLCI 1023 simultaneously. One of the enquiries receives a status message, but if the autosense is unsuccessful, another status enquiry message is sent every N391 interval (the default is 60 seconds: 6 attempts every 10 seconds) to try to define the LMI type. After a status message is received, Cisco IOS decodes the message and configures the router with the correct LMI type.

When the LMI type is configured, you can use either of the following two options to see the details of the LMI exchange:

```
1602-frame#show frame-relay lmi
1602-frame#debug frame-relay lmi
```

The first command reports the statistics for the time period, after clearing the interface counters, as shown in Example 17-25 and explained in Table 17-4.

Example 17-25 *Output from the* **show frame-relay lmi** *Command*

```
7206-frame#show frame-relay lmi

LMI Statistics for interface Serial3/0:0 (Frame Relay DTE) LMI TYPE = ANSI
  Invalid Unnumbered info 0            Invalid Prot Disc 0
```

continues

Example 17-25 *Output from the* **show frame-relay lmi** *Command (Continued)*

```
Invalid dummy Call Ref 0        Invalid Msg Type 0
Invalid Status Message 0        Invalid Lock Shift 0
Invalid Information ID 0        Invalid Report IE Len 0
Invalid Report Request 0        Invalid Keep IE Len 0
Num Status Enq. Sent 5570       Num Status msgs Rcvd 5570
Num Update Status Rcvd 0        Num Status Timeouts 0
```

Table 17-4 *Output and Description of the #***show frame-relay lmi** *Command*

Output	Description
LMI Statistics	Signaling or LMI specification: CISCO, ANSI, or ITU-T.
Invalid Unnumbered info 0	Number of received LMI messages with invalid unnumbered information field.
Invalid Prot Disc 0	Number of received LMI messages with invalid protocol discriminator.
Invalid Dummy Call Ref 0	Number of received LMI messages with invalid dummy call references.
Invalid Msg Type 0	Number of received LMI messages with invalid message type.
Invalid Status Message 0	Number of received LMI messages with invalid status message.
Invalid Lock Shift 0	Number of received LMI messages with invalid lock shift type. Refer to the LMI ANSI message type.
Invalid Information ID 0	Number of received LMI messages with invalid information identifier.
Invalid Report IE Len 0	Number of received LMI messages with invalid Report IE Length.
Invalid Report Request 0	Number of received LMI messages with invalid Report Request.
Invalid Keep IE Len 0	Number of received LMI messages with invalid Keep IE Length.
Num Status Enq. Sent 5570	Number of LMI status inquiry messages sent. Number of status enquiries successfully sent after the last **clear counters** command.
Num Status Msgs Rcvd 5570	Number of LMI status messages received. Number of status enquiries successfully received after the last **clear counters** command.
Num Update Status Rcvd 0	Number of LMI asynchronous update status messages received.
Num Status Timeouts 0	Number of times the status message was not received within the keepalive time value. Number of resets trying to trigger the exchange.

For troubleshooting purposes, you need to identify non-zero values and, based on the provided figures, analyze the connection. An important consideration is the keepalive (Invalid Keep IE Len) messages and timeouts for status enquiry messages (Num Status Enq. Timeouts), which reflect the number of resets when the interface tries to trigger the exchange within the T392 time interval. All parameters depend on Frame Relay timers and counters, which are listed in Table 17-6.

NOTE   If there are no LMI-related errors, expect Num Status Enq. Sent = 5570 and Num Status msgs Rcvd = 5570 to be the same. In erroneous conditions, Num Status Enq. Sent = Num Status msgs Rcvd + Num Status Timeouts Expect performance issues when this occurs.

The second troubleshooting tool is **debug frame-relay lmi**. The output of this command is not chatty, so it can be used without concern for use of the main CPU in the router. The output from a serial line of 1544 kbps, with Cisco encapsulation for Frame Relays, LMI DLCI 0 with a LMI type of ANSI AnnexD, and the router is DTE, as shown in Example 17-26.

Example 17-26 *Full Status Request Message*

```
7206-frame#debug frame-relay lmi

Aug 26 11:03:25 PDT: Serial4/2:0(out): StEnq, myseq 183, yourseen 182, DTE up
(OUT) Report for serial interface 4/2:0. STATUS ENGUIRY message; myseq=183,
    yourseen=182 out; DTE - up.
Aug 26 11:03:25 PDT: datagramstart = 0x7000214, datagramsize = 14
(OUT) Start of the next datagram; size of the datagram
Aug 26 11:03:25 PDT: FR encap = 0x00010308
(OUT) Frame Relay encapsulation - 0x00010308 - cisco; ( 0xFCF10309 - IETF)
Aug 26 11:03:25 PDT: 00 75 95 01 01 00 03 02 B7 B6
Aug 26 11:03:25 PDT:
Aug 26 11:03:25 PDT: Serial4/2:0(in): Status, myseq 183
(IN) STATUS message from the switch;myseq 183
Aug 26 11:03:25 PDT: RT IE 1, length 1, type 0
(IN) Report Type (RT) Information Element 1, length 1, type 0
Aug 26 11:03:25 PDT: KA IE 3, length 2, yourseq 183, myseq 183
(IN) Keep Alive (integrity verification message); length, yourseq, myseq.
Aug 26 11:03:25 PDT: PVC IE 0x7 , length 0x3 , dlci 35, status 0x2
Aug 26 11:03:25 PDT: PVC IE 0x7 , length 0x3 , dlci 37, status 0x2
Aug 26 11:03:25 PDT: PVC IE 0x7 , length 0x3 , dlci 38, status 0x2
Aug 26 11:03:25 PDT: PVC IE 0x7 , length 0x3 , dlci 40, status 0x2
Aug 26 11:03:25 PDI: PVC IE 0x7 , length 0x3 , dlci 45, status 0x2
Aug 26 11:03:25 PDT: PVC IE 0x7 , length 0x3 , dlci 46, status 0x2
Aug 26 11:03:25 PDT: PVC IE 0x7 , length 0x3 , dlci 55, status 0x2
Aug 26 11:03:25 PDT: PVC IE 0x7 , length 0x3 , dlci 56, status 0x2
Aug 26 11:03:25 PDT: PVC IE 0x7 , length 0x3 , dlci 59, status 0x2
Aug 26 11:03:25 PDT: PVC IE 0x7 , length 0x3 , dlci 64, status 0x2
```

continues

Example 17-26 *Full Status Request Message (Continued)*

```
Aug 26 11:03:25 PDT: PVC IE 0x7 , length 0x3 , dlci 67, status 0x2
Aug 26 11:03:25 PDT: PVC IE 0x7 , length 0x3 , dlci 68, status 0x2
Aug 26 11:03:25 PDT: PVC IE 0x7 , length 0x3 , dlci 72, status 0x2
Aug 26 11:03:25 PDT: PVC IE 0x7 , length 0x3 , dlci 75, status 0x2
Aug 26 11:03:25 PDT: PVC IE 0x7 , length 0x3 , dlci 84, status 0x2
Aug 26 11:03:25 PDT: PVC IE 0x7 , length 0x3 , dlci 90, status 0x2
Aug 26 11:03:25 PDT: PVC IE 0x7 , length 0x3 , dlci 92, status 0x2
! All PVCs are listed because full status message was used.
```

You must know what to expect from various outputs; the expected LMI code values are shown in Table 17-5.

Table 17-5 *LMI Code Values*

Message Type	Binary Value[*]
Status	01111101
Status enquiry	01110101
Update status	01111011
Information Element ID	
Keep Alive Sequence	00000011
Report Type	00000001
PVC status/Modified PVC status	00000111
Multicast status	00000101
Information Definitions	
Report Type	
Full status message	00000000
Sequence number exchange	00000001
Reserved	R—All other values
PVC Status Bit Coding	
New status	00001RXR
PVC already present	00000RXR[**]
PVC active	00000R1R
PVC inactive	00000R0R
Modified PVC Status Bit Codings	
PVC Present	000000XX

Table 17-5 *LMI Code Values (Continued)*

Message Type	Binary Value*
PVC deleted	000001XX
DLCI added	000010XX
PVC active	0000XX1X
PVC inactive	0000XX0X
PVC's buffers above threshold	0000XXX1
PVC's buffers below threshold	0000XXX0
Multicast Status Bit Codings	
Multicast Channel Present	000000XX
Multicast Channel Deleted	000001XX
DLCI added	000010XX
Multicast active	0000XX1X
Multicast inactive	0000XX0X

* R—reserved; X—does not matter.

** Note the PVC status reporting; the PVC present is 0000RXR and is either active or inactive.

For more information, see *Frame Relay Networking* by Gilbert Held (John Wiley and Sons, Inc., 1999).

NOTE   Some common status indications based on the output include status 0xa, which represents a PVC and indicates that the DLCI is passing traffic to the far end; status 0x2, which indicates that the PVC is added and passing traffic; status 0x0, which indicates that the PVC is added but inactive; status 0x4, which identifies that the PVC as deleted; and status 0x8, which indicates that the new PVC is not active.

The appearance of the full status message in the LMI debug is a configurable parameter that is controlled by the value of n391 timers. Because many of the parameters in this exchange are configurable, the optional values and configuration commands are shown in Table 17-6.

The importance of the LMI timer and counter parameters is obvious. One additional aspect to be considered is the situation when you see keepalive mismatches, where both sides of the connection use different keepalive intervals. This solution requires attention to prevent the line from flapping.

Table 17-6 *LMI Timers and Counters*

Timers	Description	Range	Default	Config Command
N391dte	The full status-polling interval, which transmits a status enquiry after expiration. It records an error if STATUS is not received.	1–255	6	**frame-relay lmi-n391dte** *keep-exchange*
N392dce	Set DCE and NNI interface error threshold (declared down), which after expiration, records the error, increments, and restarts.	1–10	2	**frame-relay lmi-n392dce** *threshold*
N392dte	Set DTE and UNI interface error threshold (declared down), which after expiration, records the error, increments, and restarts.	1–10	3	**frame-relay lmi-n392dte** *threshold*
N393dce	Set DCE and NNI monitored event count.	1–10	2	**frame-relay lmi-n393dce** *events*
N393dte	Set DTE and UNI monitored event count (>than N392dte).	1–10	4	**frame-relay lmi-n393dte** *events*
T392dce	Set the polling verification timer in the NNI interface.	5–30	15	**frame-relay lmi-t392dce** *seconds*
K	The maximum number of outstanding or unacknowledged IEs.	1–127	7	**frame-relay lapf t203** *k*
N200	The maximum number for retransmission of a frame.		3	**frame-relay lapf n200** *reties*
N201	The maximum length of the I-frame in LAPF.	1–16,384	260 bytes	**frame-relay lapf n201** *bytes*
T200	The maximum retransmission timer value.	1–100	15	**frame-relay lapf t200** *sec/10*
T203	The idle timer value (has to be T203>T200).	1–65,535	30	**frame-relay lapf t203** *seconds*

NOTE   For troubleshooting purposes, you might sometimes consider verifying the PVC information. One tool to use here is the full status message, which regularly appears every 60 seconds. You can change this interval by using the Cisco IOS command **frame-relay lmi-n391dte 1**. This command requests a Local Management Interface (LMI) full status update every 10 seconds instead every 60 seconds (the default). Remember to turn off the command at the end of the troubleshooting process because this command adds more processing to the router and should be used only if it cannot be avoided.

Some of the timer and counter settings are shown in the output in Example 17-27. Even if SVC is disabled, and as a result the LAPF control protocol is down, some of the timer and counter settings show in the output, as in Example 17-27.

Example 17-27 *Verifying the Status of the LAPF Protocol*

```
1602-frame#show frame-relay lapf

Interface = Serial1 (up),  LAPF state = TEI_ASSIGNED (down)
SVC disabled,  link down cause = SVC disabled,  #link-reset = 0
T200 = 1.5 sec.,  T203 = 30 sec.,  N200 = 3,  k = 7,  N201 = 260
I-frame xmt = 0,  I-frame rcv = 0,  I-frame reXmt = 0
I xmt dropped = 0,  I rcv dropped = 0,  Rcv pak dropped = 0
RR xmt = 0,  RR rcv = 0,  RNR xmt = 0,  RNR rcv = 0
REJ xmt = 0,  REJ rcv = 0,  FRMR xmt = 0,  FRMR rcv = 0
DM xmt = 0,  DM rcv = 0,  DISC xmt = 0,  DISC rcv = 0
SABME xmt = 0,  SABME rcv = 0,  UA xmt = 0,  UA rcv = 0
V(S) = 0,  V(A) = 0,  V(R) = 0,  N(S) = 0,  N(R) = 0
Xmt FRMR at Frame Reject
```

The parameters in Table 17-6 are related to one of the common techniques used by engineers to check the serial line when the LMI exchange is not available and as a result the Frame Relay protocol is reported down. The technique includes setting the encapsulation to HDLC (temporarily) on both ends of the link and then to run the command #**debug interface serial** from the DTE to determine if the keepalive message exchange is successful.

NOTE   The reason for temporarily changing the encapsulation is that LMI carries keepalive messages, and as soon as LMI is not functional, there is no keepalive exchange. To change the encapsulation from Frame Relay to HDLC, just negate the Frame Relay encapsulation. Cisco proprietary HDLC is the default encapsulation in serial lines. The other option is to define HDLC explicitly by entering 1602-frame(config-if)#**encapsulation hdlc**.

Example 17-28 shows the output of the **debug interface serial** command with LMI on.

Example 17-28 *Output of the* **debug interface serial** *Command with LMI On*

```
1602-frame#debug interface serial
6w6d: Serial1(out): StEnq, myseq 137, yourseen 136, DTE up
(OUT) STATUS ENQUIRY, keepalive send by DTE (myseq 137),
keepalive sent by the other side (yourseen 136), DTE is up.
6w6d: Serial1(in): Status, myseq 137
(IN) STATUS, DTE keepalive seen by the other side.
6w6d: Serial1(out): StEnq, myseq 138, yourseen 137, DTE up
```

continues

Example 17-28 *Output of the* **debug interface serial** *Command with LMI On (Continued)*

```
6w6d: Serial1(in): Status, myseq 138
6w6d: Serial1(out): StEnq, myseq 139, yourseen 138, DTE up
6w6d: Serial1(in): Status, myseq 139
6w6d: Serial1(out): StEnq, myseq 140, yourseen 139, DTE up
6w6d: Serial1(in): Status, myseq 140
6w6d: Serial1(out): StEnq, myseq 141, yourseen 140, DTE up
6w6d: Serial1(in): Status, myseq 141
6w6d: Serial1(out): StEnq, myseq 142, yourseen 141, DTE up
6w6d: Serial1(in): Status, myseq 142
6w6d: Serial1(out): StEnq, myseq 143, yourseen 142, DTE up
6w6d: Serial1(in): Status, myseq 143
1602-frame#
```

Example 17-29 shows the output of the **debug interface serial** command with LMI off and HDLC on.

Example 17-29 *Output of the* **debug interface serial** *Command with LMI Off and HDLC On*

```
1602-frame#debug interface serial
*Sep 16 01:26:57 PDT: Serial2/0/1:0: HDLC myseq 20158, mineseen 20158*,
    yourseen 20316, line up
*Sep 16 01:27:07 PDT: Serial2/0/1:0: HDLC myseq 20159, mineseen 20159*,
    yourseen 20317, line up
*Sep 16 01:27:17 PDT: Serial2/0/1:0: HDLC myseq 20160, mineseen 20160*,
    yourseen 20318, line up
*Sep 16 01:27:27 PDT: Serial2/0/1:0: HDLC myseq 20161, mineseen 20161*,
    yourseen 20319, line up
*Sep 16 01:27:37 PDT: Serial2/0/1:0: HDLC myseq 20162, mineseen 20162*,
    yourseen 20320, line up
*Sep 16 01:27:47 PDT: Serial2/0/1:0: HDLC myseq 20163, mineseen 20163*,
    yourseen 20321, line up
*Sep 16 01:27:57 PDT: Serial2/0/1:0: HDLC myseq 20164, mineseen 20164*,
    yourseen 20322, line up
*Sep 16 01:28:17 PDT: Serial2/0/1:0: HDLC myseq 20166, mineseen 20166*,
    yourseen 20324, line up

*Sep 16 01:28:20 PDT: Illegal HDLC serial type code 34915, PC=0x601B7E8C
```

NOTE   It is common at the end of this output to see the message illegal serial line type xxx. The message indicates that the encapsulation is Frame Relay or HDLC, and the router attempts to send a packet with an unknown packet type.

If the (OUT) myseq message matches the other side's (IN) myseq message, the line is up. For N392dte keepalive exchanges, which count N393dte events, if the values do not match, the interface is reported down, the N392dte increments, and the interface restarts. In other words, if in four consecutive exchanges the values do not match, the interface is reported down.

The keepalive sequence IE (Consortium) is identified by a 03h in the first octet. The second octet specifies the length of the contents in bytes (01 stands for 1 octet), and the last two bytes are current and last received sequence numbers. Each time the router or network sends a status enquiry message, it increments its internal sequence number and places the value in the current sequence number (byte three) (see Figure 17-7 and Figure 17-8). The last sequence number received from the other end of the link is placed in the last received sequence number (byte four). Both types of messages are four bytes in length and differ slightly in format, but work the same way.

Figure 17-7 *Keepalive Sequence IE (Consortium)*

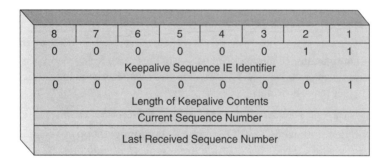

Figure 17-8 *Link Integrity Verification IE (ANSI)*

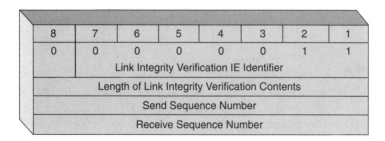

Several commands trim the keepalive messages, as shown in Table 17-7. These commands require a good understanding of the implication that they can have on the Frame Relay functionality and should be used with caution.

Table 17-7   *IOS Keepalive Configuration Commands*

IOS Command	Description	Max/Default
frame-relay end-to-end keepalive error-threshold [**send** | **receive**] *count*	Modifies the error threshold value.	32/2
frame-relay end-to-end keepalive event window [**send** | **receive**] *size*	Modifies the keepalive event window.	32/3
frame-relay end-to-end keepalive mode [**bi-directional** | **request** | **reply** | **passive-replay**]	When the keepalive mode is enabled, default values depend on which mode is selected.	
frame-relay end-to-end keepalive success-events [**send** | **receive**] *count*	Modifies the keepalive success events.	32/2
frame-relay end-to-end keepalive timer [**send** | **receive**] *interval*	Modifies the keepalive timer value.	–/10,15

These configuration commands can be part of the Frame Relay map-class definitions to trim the parameters of the service. Every single command has an output, which can be displayed if you enter the following:

```
3640#show frame-relay end-to-end keepalive interface serial 1
```

The full description of Cisco IOS Frame Relay configuration commands and their output can be found in *Cisco IOS 12.0 Wide Area Networking Solutions* (Cisco Press, 1999).

Performance Problems

Frame Relay performance problems include flapping links, end-to-end problems, shaping problems, and compression over Frame Relay problems. They are described in detail in this section.

Flapping Links

One of the typical problems of poor performance is that the computers connected to the router lose their connection or experience high delay or slow performance. The issue is related to instability in the second layer and the protocol constantly going up and down. The first step in troubleshooting this problem is to check both sides of the connection. The user's end reports the output in Example 17-30.

Example 17-30   *The Status of the Interfaces of the Remote User's Router*

```
1602-frame#show ip interface brief
Interface        IP-Address       OK? Method Status        Protocol
Ethernet0        10.70.194.209    YES NVRAM  up            up
Loopback0        unassigned       YES NVRAM  up            up
```

Example 17-30 *The Status of the Interfaces of the Remote User's Router (Continued)*

```
Serial1            unassigned     YES NVRAM  up                  up
Serial1.37         10.70.194.209  YES unset  up                  up
1602-frame#
```

Meanwhile, the core router is reporting the output in Example 17-31.

Example 17-31 *The Status of the Interfaces of the Core Router*

```
7026-frame#show ip interface brief
Serial4/1:0        unassigned     YES NVRAM  up                  up
<output omitted>
!This interface - Serial 4/1:0.37 - is the peer of the remote user's
! Serial 1.37 interface in this point-to-point configuration.
Serial4/1:0.37     10.68.88.1     YES unset  up                  up
Serial4/1:0.41     10.68.88.1     YES unset  up                  up
Serial4/1:0.44     10.68.88.1     YES unset  up                  up
```

Check the output carefully. If you compare both parts of the history of the PVC (see Chapter 14 to double-check who provides the history information), you can see a significant difference between the time that the PVC is created and the last time the PVC was changed. Enter either of the following commands:

```
1602-frame#show frame-relay pvc
```

```
72060- frame#show frame-relay pvc 37
```

The following PVC information is displayed:

- **PVC create time**—Time the PVC was created

- **Last time PVC status changed**—Time the PVC changed status (active to inactive)

The full display of the output is shown in Example 17-32.

Example 17-32 *Checking the History of Serial 1.37 on a Remote User's Router*

```
1602-frame#show frame-relay pvc 37

PVC Statistics for interface Serial1 (Frame Relay DTE)
DLCI = 37, DLCI USAGE = LOCAL, PVC STATUS = ACTIVE, INTERFACE = Serial1.37

  input pkts 708285       output pkts 97790       in bytes 354082477
  out bytes 20908266      dropped pkts 0          in FECN pkts 0
  in BECN pkts 0          out FECN pkts 0         out BECN pkts 0
  in DE pkts 708285       out DE pkts 0
  out bcast pkts 22619     out bcast bytes 2437086
! The next line shows the PVC was created 7w2d ago, but
! flapped 05:05 minutes ago
  pvc create time 7w2d, last time pvc status changed 00:05:05
! There is no process in Frame Relay that requires the
! PVC to go down systematically.
1602-frame#
```

In Example 17-32, the first time the end user's router was turned on is 7w2d ago, and for some reason, 00:05:05 hours ago the PVC went down again. If you continue to monitor, you will see this measurement going up and down, which is known as flapping.

NOTE   You can monitor Frame Relay permanent virtual circuit's (PVC's) status better if you use the following commands under the serial 0(1) interface:

```
1602-frame(config-if)#logging event ?
  dlci-status-change  DLCICHANGE messages
  link-status         UPDOWN and CHANGE messages
  subif-link-status   Sub-interface UPDOWN and CHANGE messages

1602-frame#
```

These command parameters enable you to report any change in the status of the DLCI, link, or subinterface. This way, you can review the log the following day and be precise in your information as to how many times and when the PVC has changed its status. Remember to set the router clock before testing.

You do not need to check if both sides are reacting the same way. You should not forget that the UNI is a local interface. Common sense dictates that whichever connection is flapping is the one experiencing local loop or other problems. This can be resolved by working with the LEC.

End-to-End Problems

End-to-end issues in Frame Relay are related to factors including congestion, overuse or oversubscription of lines, or incorrect or flapping routes. These factors can be recognized by some indicators such as degradation of performance during a particular time of day or after a period of normal operations. Although the routing problems are the subject of a wide variety of Cisco Press books (such as *CCIE Professional Development: Advanced IP Network Design*, by Retana, Slice, and White [Cisco Press, 1999]), the Frame Relay IOS troubleshooting techniques are the main objective of this section.

NOTE   The enhanced output of #**show interfaces serial 1** provides a wealth of information for analysis. One indicator of excessive use is the reliability 255/255. The comparison between "5 minute input rate 0 bits/sec, 2 packets/sec" and "5 minute output rate 0 bits/sec, 0 packets/sec" and their reliability is a sign of excessive use. Every instance of reliability that trends away from 100 percent raises a red flag.

The first end-to-end tool to use is to check the status of the PVC. When traffic shaping is not on and the interface is inactive, the information in Example 17-33 appears on the screen.

Example 17-33 *The End-To-End Status of PVC*

```
7206-frame#show frame-relay pvc
<output omitted>
DLCI = 65, DLCI USAGE = UNUSED, PVC STATUS = INACTIVE, INTERFACE = Serial3/2:0

  input pkts 0              output pkts 0            in bytes 0
  out bytes 0              dropped pkts 0          in FECN pkts 0
  in BECN pkts 0          out FECN pkts 0        out BECN pkts 0
  in DE pkts 0            out DE pkts 0
  out bcast pkts 0      out bcast bytes 0
  switched pkts 0
  Detailed packet drop counters:
  no out intf 0            out intf down 0          no out PVC 0
  in PVC down 0            out PVC down 0          pkt too big 0
  shaping Q full 0        pkt above DE 0          policing drop 0
  pvc create time 3w0d, last time pvc status changed 3w0d
<output omitted>
```

NOTE   Some of the results of this output can also be displayed using #**show frame-relay route**.

When you want to see the status of any particular PVC, the command requires a DLCI number. Example 17-34 shows a sample of this output and includes all PVCs, with DLCI = 37.

Example 17-34 *Verifying the Status of PVCs = 37*

```
7206-frame#show frame-relay pvc 37
<output omitted>
DLCI = 37, DLCI USAGE = LOCAL, PVC STATUS = ACTIVE, INTERFACE = Serial3/2:0.37

  input pkts 243555        output pkts 253526      in bytes 32877370
  out bytes 158986875      dropped pkts 264        in FECN pkts 0
  in BECN pkts 0          out FECN pkts 0        out BECN pkts 0
  in DE pkts 243555        out DE pkts 0
  out bcast pkts 22834    out bcast bytes 6850200
  pvc create time 3w2d, last time pvc status changed 3d21h
  cir 56000      bc 56000      be 0          byte limit 875      interval 125
  mincir 28000      byte increment 875    Adaptive Shaping none
  pkts 253265      bytes 158969188 pkts delayed 130549      bytes delayed 130688876
  shaping inactive
  traffic shaping drops 0
  Queuing strategy: fifo
  Output queue 0/40, 264 drop, 130549 dequeued
<output omitted>
```

Besides #**show frame-relay pvc**, an important troubleshooting tool is #**debug frame-relay** [**packet** | **events**], as shown in Example 17-35.

NOTE	The #**debug frame-relay** [**packet** I **events**] command is chatty, so when conducting remote troubleshooting it is good practice to have two telnet/SSH sessions open. One session should have both the #**terminal monitor** command and the #**debug frame-relay packet** command. The second session should have the #**undebug all** command ready to enter if necessary. Use these commands only if the router's utilization is low (below 25 percent).

Example 17-35 *Output from the #**debug frame-relay packet** Command*

```
1602-frame#debug frame-relay packet
Frame Relay packet debugging is on
1602-frame#
7w3d: Serial1(i): dlci 37(0x853), NLPID 0x3CC(IP), datagramsize 146
incoming (i), dlci 37(0x851), network layer protocol ID = 3CCh, datagramsize 146
7w3d: Serial1(i): dlci 37(0x853), NLPID 0x3CC(IP), datagramsize 146
7w3d: Serial1(i): dlci 37(0x853), pkt type 0x2000, datagramsize 300
7w3d: Serial1.37(o): dlci 37(0x853), NLPID 0x3CC(IP), datagramsize 580
7w3d: Serial1.37(o): dlci 37(0x851), NLPID 0x3CC(IP), datagramsize 580
7w3d: Serial1.37(o): dlci 37(0x851), NLPID 0x3CC(IP), datagramsize 81
7w3d: Serial1(i): dlci 37(0x851), NLPID 0x3CC(IP), datagramsize 44
7w3d: Serial1(i): dlci 37(0x851), NLPID 0x3CC(IP), datagramsize 44
7w3d: Serial1.37(o): dlci 37(0x851), NLPID 0x3CC(IP), datagramsize 580
7w3d: Serial1.37(o): dlci 37(0x851), NLPID 0x3CC(IP), datagramsize 66
7w3d: Serial1(i): dlci 37(0x851), NLPID 0x3CC(IP), datagramsize 44
7w3d: Serial1.37(o): dlci 37(0x851), NLPID 0x3CC(IP), datagramsize 255
7w3d: Serial1(i): dlci 37(0x851), NLPID 0x3CC(IP), datagramsize 44
7w3d: Serial1.37(o): dlci 37(0x851), NLPID 0x3CC(IP), datagramsize 184
7w3d: Serial1(i): dlci 37(0x851), NLPID 0x3CC(IP), datagramsize 44
7w3d: Serial1.37(o): dlci 37(0x851), NLPID 0x3CC(IP), datagramsize 184
7w3d: Serial1(i): dlci 37(0x851), NLPID 0x3CC(IP), datagramsize 44
7w3d: Serial1.37: Broadcast on DLCI 37 link 65(CDP)
! The router broadcasts on dlci 37, using link 65
7w3d: Serial1.37(o): dlci 37(0x851), pkt type 0x2000(CDP), datagramsize 312
outgoing (o), dlci 37(0x851), packet type 2000h (CDP), datagramsize 312
7w3d: broadcast dequeue
7w3d: Serial1.37(o):Pkt sent on dlci 37(0x851), pkt type 0x2000(CDP),
    datagramsize 312
7w3d: Serial1.37(o): dlci 37(0x851), NLPID 0x3CC(IP), datagramsize 427
7w3d: Serial1(i): dlci 37(0x851), NLPID 0x3CC(IP), datagramsize 44
```

Refer to the beginning of the output, and you can see two different hexadecimal values for the same DLCI. This is not an error. To understand the output, see Figure 17-9, where the DLCI format is shown. If the format of the DLCI is 2 bytes, the values are shown in Figure 17-9.

In this example, the DLCI = 37 (decimal) and the next value is also DLCI = 37 (decimal). The two messages differ because of the value of the DE bit (DE = 1 for the 0x853 message and DE = 0 for the x0851 message). In exactly the same way as Q.922 hexadecimal addresses, examples of the conversion include the following: 50 represents 0x0c21, 60 represents 0x0cc1, and 70 represents 0x1401.

Figure 17-9 *Determining the DLCI from the #debug frame-relay packet Command*

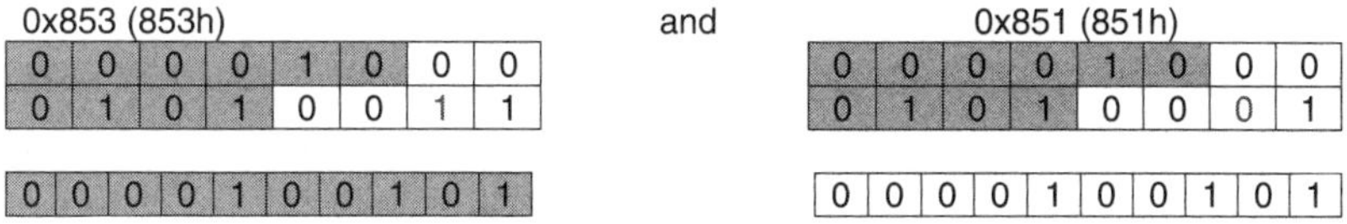

```
0x853 (853h)                   and            0x851 (851h)

 0  0  0  0  1  0  0  0                   0  0  0  0  1  0  0  0
 0  1  0  1  0  0  1  1                   0  1  0  1  0  0  0  1

 0  0  0  0  1  0  0  1  0  1            0  0  0  0  1  0  0  1  0  1
```

Another troubleshooting tool is the chatty #**debug frame-relay events** command, which helps to analyze the incoming packets. It is a useful command when trying to differentiate between the incoming types of traffic. Another useful command is #**debug frame-relay packets** to monitor the outgoing and incoming traffic, as shown in Example 17-36.

NOTE   Both commands generate a high volume of output and should only be used in cases where the overall use on the router is lower than usual. Use 7206-frame#**show processes cpu** to ensure that the CPU utilization for five seconds, one minute, and five minutes is low.

Example 17-36 *Debugging the Frame Relay Packets*

```
7206-frame#debug frame-relay packet

Sep  1 08:32:41 PDT: Serial4/2:0.72(o): dlci 72(0x1081), pkt type 0x800(IP),
    datagramsize 146
Outgoing (o) packet over serail4/2:0.72 subinterface, using DLCI=72,
    packet type IP, datagramsize 146
Sep  1 08:32:41 PDT: Serial4/0:0.76(o): dlci 76(0x10C1), NLPID 0x3CC(IP),
    datagramsize 48
Sep  1 08:32:41 PDT: Serial4/0:0.97(o): dlci 97(0x1811), pkt type 0x800(IP),
    datagramsize 68
Sep  1 08:32:41 PDT: Serial4/0:0.86(o): dlci 86(0x1461), pkt type 0x800(IP),
    datagramsize 272
Sep  1 08:32:41 PDT: Serial4/0:0(i): dlci 53(0xC53), pkt type 0x2000,
    datagramsize 309
Incoming (i) traffic over DLCI=53, subinterface serial4/0:0,
    packet type CDP (0x2000), datagramsize 309
Sep  1 08:32:41 PDT: Serial4/0:0.97(o): dlci 97(0x1811), pkt type 0x800(IP),
    datagramsize 68
Sep  1 08:32:41 PDT: Serial3/0:0(i): dlci 30(0x4E3), pkt type 0x800,
    datagramsize 52
Sep  1 08:32:41 PDT: Serial3/0:0.30(o): dlci 30(0x4E1), pkt type 0x800(IP),
    datagramsize 52
Sep  1 08:32:41 PDT: Serial4/2:0.72(o): dlci 72(0x1081), pkt type 0x800(IP),
    datagramsize 154
Sep  1 08:32:42 PDT: Serial4/0:0.97(o): dlci 97(0x1811), pkt type 0x800(IP),
    datagramsize 60
```

continues

Example 17-36 *Debugging the Frame Relay Packets (Continued)*

```
Sep  1 08:32:42 PDT: Serial4/0:0.202(o): dlci 202(0x30A1), pkt type 0x800(IP),
   datagramsize 48
Sep  1 08:32:42 PDT: Serial4/0:0.47(o): dlci 47(0x8F1), pkt type 0x800(IP),
   datagramsize 1504
Sep  1 08:32:42 PDT: Serial4/0:0.97(o): dlci 97(0x1811), pkt type 0x800(IP),
   datagramsize 68
Sep  1 08:32:42 PDT: Serial4/2:0.72(o): dlci 72(0x1081), pkt type 0x800(IP),
   datagramsize 140
Sep  1 08:32:42 PDT: Serial3/1:0(i): dlci 118(0x1C61),
   pkt encaps 0x0300 0x8000 0x0000 0x2000(CDP), datagramsize 316
```

Other messages you can see from this output include the following:

- **0x308** — Signaling message, valid with DLCI = 0 (AnnexD)
- **0x309** — LMI message of Consortium's DLCI = 1023

The Ethernet-type codes are the following:

- **0x3CC IP, 0x0800** — Internet Protocol (IP) in a 10-Mbps network
- **0x201** — IP in a 3-Mbps network
- **0x0806** — IP Address Resolution Protocol (ARP)
- **0x0808** — Frame Relay ARP
- **0x8035** — Reverse Address Resolution Protocol (RARP)
- **0x809b–** — Apple EtherTalk
- **0x80f3** — AppleTalk ARP
- **0x8038** — Spanning tree
- **0x8137** — Internetwork Packet Exchange (IPX)
- **0x200** — CDP
- **0x9000** — Loopback packet

If the encapsulation is HDLC, the possible packet codes are the following:

- **0x1A58** — IPX
- **0xFEFE** — Connectionless Network Service (CLNS)
- **0xEFEF** — Intermediate System-to-Intermediate System (IS-IS)
- **0x1998** — Uncompressed Transmission Control Protocol (TCP) (header compression)
- **0x1999** — Compressed TCP (header compression)
- **0x6558** — Bridge packets

Another end-to-end troubleshooting command is #**show frame-relay map**. In point-to-multipoint designs, it is a useful tool to see the end-to-end settings and to check the functionality. The Frame Relay mapping information is shown in Example 17-37 and is explained in Table 17-8.

Example 17-37 *End-to-End Settings of DLCI 37*

```
1602-frame# show frame-relay map
<output omitted>
Serial1.37 (up): point-to-point dlci, dlci 37(0x25,0x850), broadcast, IETF
        status defined, active
1602-frame#
<output omitted>
! Or

1602-frame# show frame-relay map
<output omitted>
Serial 1 is up: ip 121.118.117.111
dlci 37 (0xB1,0x2C10), static,
broadcast,
CISCO
TCP/IP Header Compression (inherited), passive (inherited)
<output omitted>
! Or

7206-frame#show frame-relay map

Serial3/1:0.120 (down): point-to-point dlci, dlci 120(0x78,0x1C80),
    broadcast  status deleted
Serial3/1:0.112 (up): point-to-point dlci, dlci 112(0x70,0x1C00),
    broadcast, BW = 56000  status defined, active
Serial3/1:0.17 (up): point-to-point dlci, dlci 17(0x11,0x410),
    broadcast, BW = 128000  status defined, active
Serial3/1:0.121 (up): point-to-point dlci, dlci 121(0x79,0x1C90),
    broadcast, BW = 56000  status defined, active
Serial3/1:0.114 (up): point-to-point dlci, dlci 114(0x72,0x1C20),
    broadcast, BW = 56000  status defined, active
```

Table 17-8 *Output from the* **show frame-relay map** *Command (The Lines Can Vary)*

Output	Description
Serial 1 up; Serial3/1:0.112 (up)	Identifies a Frame Relay interface (subinterface) and its status (up or down).
ip 121.118.117.111	Destination IP address.
point-to-point dlci	Shows if this design is point-to-point.
dlci 112(0x70,0x1C00)	DLCI that identifies the logical connection, which reaches this interface. This line displays three values: its decimal value (122), the hexadecimal value (0x70), and its value as it appears on the wire (0x1C00).

continues

Table 17-8 *Output from the* **show frame-relay map** *Command (The Lines Can Vary) (Continued)*

Output	Description
Static/dynamic	Indicates whether this is a static or dynamic entry.
Cisco/IETF	Indicates the encapsulation type for this entry.
Broadcast	Indicates if it is broadcast/non-broadcast.
status deleted/status defined—active	If the interface is down, it reports a status of deleted. If not, it is defined and active.
BW = 128000	Defines the bandwidth defined for this map.
TCP/IP Header Compression (inherited), passive (inherited)	Indicates whether the TCP/IP header compression characteristics were inherited from the interface or were explicitly configured for the IP map.

Frame Relay Shaping Problems

The traffic shaping feature of Frame Relay is a derivative from the nature of the technology. It is related to the classes of service defined for different types of traffic (see Chapter 16 for more details). If traffic shaping is not configured as part of the initial configuration settings (see the next chapter), they are reported accordingly by the IOS. As previously mentioned, the #**show frame-relay pvc** *DLCI-number,* reports if traffic shaping is on and what the status is of this particular PVC. For convenience, the traffic shaping part of the output is described in Table 17-9.

Table 17-9 *Lines of Output and Descriptions of Traffic Shaping Parameters (This Section Appears if the Traffic Shaping Map Class Is Applied to This PVC)*

Output	Description
Cir	Current CIR, in bits per second.
Bc	Current committed burst size, in bits.
Be	Current excess burst size, in bits.
Limit	Maximum number of bytes transmitted per internal interval (excess plus sustained).
Interval	Interval used internally (can be smaller than the interval derived from Bc/CIR; this occurs when the router determines that traffic flow is more stable with a smaller configured interval).
Mincir	Minimum CIR for the PVC.
Byte increment	Number of bytes that are sustained per internal interval.
Adaptive shaping none	Indicates if the adaptive shaping is ON.
BECN response	Frame Relay has BECN adaptation configured.

Table 17-9   *Lines of Output and Descriptions of Traffic Shaping Parameters (This Section Appears if the Traffic Shaping Map Class Is Applied to This PVC) (Continued)*

Output	Description
Pkts	Number of packets associated with this PVC that went through the traffic shaping system.
Bytes	Number of bytes associated with this PVC that went through the traffic shaping system.
Pkts delayed	Number of packets associated with this PVC that were delayed by the traffic shaping system.
Bytes delayed	Number of bytes associated with this PVC that were delayed by the traffic shaping system.
Shaping	Shaping is active for all PVCs that are fragmenting data; otherwise, shaping is active if the traffic being sent exceeds the CIR for this circuit.
Traffic shaping drops	Number of packets dropped by the traffic shaping process.
Queuing strategy	The queuing strategies can be FIFO, weighted fair, priority queuing, none, or custom.
Output queue 0/40, 264 drop,	The size of the output queue number/maximum slots and number of drops.
130549 dequeued	Number of dequeued packets.

You must know the use of BECNs and forward explicit congestion notifications (FECNs) and their interaction with the Frame Relay switch because a growing number of delays or drops can severely affect performance.

User and Network Reactions to FECNs

The router compares the number of frames in which the FECN bit is set to 1, to the number of frames in which the FECN bit is set to 0 during Tc. If during this period, the number of BECN = 1 > = BECN = 0, the router reduces the throughput to 0.875 of its previous value. Conversely, if the number of frames with BECN = 1 < the number of frames with BECN = 0, the router increases the transmission by 1/16 of its throughput, performing slow start operations. Tc is set to four times the end-to-end transit delay.

The network switch and affiliated software constantly monitors the size of each queue, based on the regeneration cycle. This cycle begins when a queue on an outgoing port goes from idle to busy, and the average queue is computed during the measurement period. When the size exceeds a predefined threshold, the circuit is considered in a state of incipient congestion. At this time, the FECN is set to 1 and remains in this state until the average value is below the threshold. ANSI T1.618 defines an algorithm to compute the average queue length (refer to the ANSI T1.618 standard for more details).

User and Network Reactions to BECNs

If the user receives n consecutive frames with BECN = 1, the traffic from the user is reduced by a step below the current offered rate. This step count (S) is reduced by 0.675 times the throughput, then 0.5 times the throughput, and finally, 0.25 times the throughput. Likewise, traffic can build up after receiving $n/2$ consecutive frames with BECN = 0, and the rate is then increased by a factor of 0.125 times throughput.

The network applies flow control before the traffic becomes a factor and, therefore, it sets BECN = 1 preemptively.

NOTE   The router knows that the data flowing in its direction is experiencing congestion. It cannot control this process, but it can influence it by delaying the acknowledgments. This can delay the flow of incoming data.

You must pay attention to three significant factors when analyzing the possible traffic shaping issues:

- The ratio between the total number of output packets and out bytes to packets delayed and bytes delayed. The higher the ratio, the better. Ratios under 2:1 should be investigated.

- The number of dropped packets should also be analyzed. Remember that DE = 1 indicates eligibility and does not mean a mandatory drop, even in CIR =0 services. Two lines in the beginning of the output that are indicators of line issues are as follows:

```
dropped pkts
Queuing strategy: FIFO Output queue 8/40, ...drop, ...dequeued
```

- Buffer misses and other software problems, especially when implementing voice, compression, and multicast can cause problems. The wrong multicast configuration, for example, can shut the interfaces down and have nothing to do with any kind of line or end-to-end Frame Relay problems.

The recommended action list to overcome the performance issues because of traffic shaping includes the following:

- Work with the LEC to resolve the problem.
- Reduce broadcast traffic.
- Implement priority queuing.
- Adjust the hold queues and buffered sizes.
- Use a protocol analyzer to check if any of your devices are generating specific traffic.
- Check for buffer types and sizes to trim their number.

Troubleshooting Compression Over Frame Relay

Before starting to troubleshoot compression, it is useful to follow some preliminary tips (more detailed information about compression is provided in Chapter 16).

Using #**show hardware** or #**show version** allows you to check what type of compression is available in the router. A Cisco router enables compression in several ways, depending on the product:

- If the router contains a compression service adapter (CSA), compression is performed in the CSA hardware (hardware compression).

- If a CSA is not available, compression is performed in the software installed on the VIP2 card (distributed compression).

- If a VIP2 card is not available, compression is performed in the router's main processor (software compression).

If hardware compression is available, it is identified in the output in Example 17-38.

Example 17-38 *How to Check What Kind of Compression Is Available*

```
3640-frame#show version
Cisco Internetwork Operating System Software
IOS (tm) 7200 Software (C7200-IS-M), Version 12.2(1), RELEASE SOFTWARE (fc2)
Copyright  1986-2001 by cisco Systems, Inc.
Compiled Fri 27-Apr-01 19:23 by cmong
Image text-base: 0x60008960, data-base: 0x6131C000
<output omitted>
Last reset from power-on
Bridging software.
X.25 software, Version 3.0.0.
Primary Rate ISDN software, Version 1.1.
2 FastEthernet/IEEE 802.3 interface(s)
6 Serial network interface(s)
8 Channelized T1/PRI port(s)
! This line shows that the router 7206 has two
! compression service adapters installed.
2 Compression service adapter(s)
125K bytes of non-volatile configuration memory.
4096K bytes of packet SRAM memory.
```

Hardware compression starts in the core router, after the router is rebooted or is turned on. Among the first messages to be displayed (if you are using a console connection) is "Compressor is up" and "Decompressor is up." Subsequently, a message is displayed that indicates that the CSA module or data compression advanced integration module (AIM) has started successfully (see www.cisco.com/univercd/cc/td/doc/pcat/3660__p1.htm). This option is not always available because the router cannot be rebooted every time to see if the compression module is starting. However, you can check the router configuration by using the command in Example 17-39.

Example 17-39 *Diagnostic Information for Compression Engine, Installed on Port 2*

```
7206-frame#show diag 2
Slot 2:
        Compression engine 3M Port adapter
! This next line usually shows that the module functions properly.
        Port adapter is analyzed
        Port adapter insertion time 3w1d ago
        EEPROM contents at hardware discovery:
        Hardware revision 1.0        Board revision A0
        Serial number    6942323     Part number   73-1868-02
        Test history     0x0         RMA number    00-00-00
        EEPROM format version 1
        EEPROM contents (hex):
          0x20: 01 18 01 00 00 69 EE 73 49 07 4C 02 00 00 00 00
          0x30: 50 00 00 00 99 03 12 00 FF FF FF FF FF FF FF FF
```

Before choosing any kind of compression for implementation, it is good to know which one is most appropriate for your particular core router. Because of various reasons (including IOS incompatibility) even if the router configuration is correct, compression might not work properly. As a result, instead of increasing performance, it might degrade it. It is recommended to take a look at the core router's output by using the command 7206-frame#**show compress**. The number of resyncs or resets usually shows a condition, where the router tries to synchronize the content of the vocabularies on both sides. Initially, this process is very intensive and generates a lot of traffic. However, if the trend of incrementing the counter is almost linear, it is not recommended to use this type of compression.

When you are about to configure compression, it is best to shut down the interfaces or subinterfaces first. Otherwise, you see a significant increase in response time, or possibly no end-to-end connection. Shutting down the interface or subinterface prior to adding or changing compression techniques is not required, but it ensures it is reset for the new data structures, and the two vocabularies start their synchronization from the beginning.

Always remember the scalability factor when applying compression. Cisco proprietary packet-to-packet compression takes about 0.5 percent utilization per DCLI, and FRF9 stac software compression shows 6 percent peak utilization per DLCI in short-term reports. The hardware compression module CSA version 2, provides compression for 256 users, and the router and IOS can support more than one module. The test results over some commonly used file types are provided in Figure 17-10.

Don't forget that compression is a traffic-dependant function. If the prevailing type of user traffic is pre-compressed or redundant (IOS images, for example), you cannot expect a high compression ratio from the implementation.

Figure 17-10 *Test Results of Frame Relay Compression*

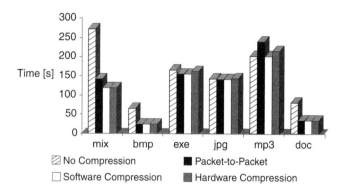

The router reports compression in different ways. As shown earlier in Table 17-8, one of the options for header compression is to use the 7206-frame#**show frame-relay map** command, which displays the resulting compression and encapsulation characteristics; the IP map has inherited passive TCP/IP header compression. Another option is to use the command 7206-frame#**sh frame-relay ip tcp header-compression**. The output is displayed in Example 17-40 and an explanation is provided in Table 17-10.

Example 17-40 *The Status of Header Compression for DLCI = 37*

```
7206-frame# show frame-relay ip tcp header-compression

DLCI 37          Link/Destination info: ip 10.70.194.209
Interface Serial1:
Rcvd:    40 total, 36 compressed, 0 errors
         0 dropped, 0 buffer copies, 0 buffer failures
Sent:    0 total, 0 compressed
         0 bytes saved, 0 bytes sent
Connect: 16 rx slots, 16 tx slots, 0 long searches, 0 misses, 0% hit ratio
         Five minute miss rate 0 misses/sec, 0 max misses/sec
```

Table 17-10 *Header Compression Field Descriptions from the #***show frame-relay ip tcp header-compression*** Command*

Output	Description
Rcvd	Table of details concerning received packets.
Total	Sum of compressed and uncompressed packets received.
compressed	Number of compressed packets received.
Errors	Number of errors caused by errors in the header fields (version, total length, or IP checksum).

continues

Table 17-10 *Header Compression Field Descriptions from the* #**show frame-relay ip tcp header-compression** *Command (Continued)*

Output	Description
dropped	Number of packets discarded; seen only after line errors.
buffer copies	Number of times a new buffer was needed for the uncompressed packet.
buffer failures	Number of times a new buffer was needed but was not obtained.
Sent	Table of details concerning sent packets.
Total	Sum of compressed and uncompressed packets sent.
compressed	Number of compressed packets sent.
bytes saved	Number of bytes reduced because of the compression.
bytes sent	Actual number of bytes transmitted.
Connect	Table of details about the connections.
rx slots, tx slots	Number of states allowed over one TCP connection. A state is recognized by a source address, a destination address, and an IP header length.
long searches	Number of times the connection ID in the incoming packet was not the same as the previous one processed.
Misses	Number of times a matching entry was not found within the connection table and a new entry had to be entered.
hit ratio	Percentage of times a matching entry was found in the compression tables and the header was compressed.
Five minute miss rate	Miss rate computed over the most recent five minutes and the maximum per-second miss rate during that period.

For payload compression, the **show compress** command provides the sample output in Example 17-41.

Example 17-41 *Compression Statistics per DLCI 37*

```
3640-frame#show compress
<output omitted>
     Serial4/1:0 - DLCI: 37
        Software compression enabled
! The total amount of data to be transmitted before compression
        uncompressed bytes xmt/rcv 1962361561/132244042
        compressed   bytes xmt/rcv 498585954/87588960
        1  min avg ratio xmt/rcv 0.705/0.705
 5  min avg ratio xmt/rcv 0.715/0.718
10 min avg ratio xmt/rcv 0.715/0.722
no bufs xmt 0 no bufs rcv 87
```

Example 17-41 *Compression Statistics per DLCI 37 (Continued)*

```
resyncs 448
      Additional Stacker Stats:
! The total amount of data to be transmitted after applying compression
      Transmit bytes:  Uncompressed = 45109432 Compressed =   348114663
      Received bytes:  Compressed =   76914754 Uncompressed =       0
<output omitted>
```

In Table 17-11, some of the descriptions of the line-by-line output are shown from the previous command.

Table 17-11 *Payload Compression Output from #***show compress** *and Field Descriptions*

Output	Description
Serial4/1:0 - DLCI: 37	Identifies a Frame Relay subinterface for software compression.
Software compression enabled	Type of compression.
Uncompressed bytes xmt/rcv 1962361561/132244042	Byte count for sent and received uncompressed data.
Compressed bytes xmt/rcv 498585954/87588960	Byte count for sent and received compressed data.
1 min avg ratio xmt/rcv 0.000/0.000 5 min avg ratio xmt/rcv 0.001/0.001 10 min avg ratio xmt/rcv 0.002/0.001	Ratio of the data throughput gained or lost in the compression routine. Any number less than one indicates that the compression is actually slowing down data throughput. It does not reflect how compressed the data is.
no bufs xmt 0 no bufs rcv 0	Indicates the number of times the compression routine was not able to allocate a transmit or receive buffer to compress or decompress a packet.
resyncs 118	Number of times the compression routine detected that the dictionaries were out of sync and restarted building a dictionary. Line errors are a common cause of restarts.
Additional Stacker Stats: Transmit bytes: Uncompressed = 45109432 Compressed = 348114663 Received bytes: Compressed = 76914754 Uncompressed = 0	The uncompressed value is the amount of data not able to be compressed, which was sent in uncompressed format. The compressed value is the byte-count of the data after it was compressed. The sum of these two values represents the actual number of bytes transmitted on the interface, minus the second layer encapsulation overhead. The compressed value is the byte-count of the compressed data received. The uncompressed value is the amount of data that is received in uncompressed format. The sum of these two values represents the actual byte count received on the interface, minus the Layer 2 encapsulation overhead.

To interpret the transmit output and compression ratio for software compression, there are some simple rules for the calculation.

Based on the information from Example 17-41 and Table 17-11, you can perform the following calculations:

- The total amount of data to be transmitted before you apply the compression routine, based on the following lines, is as follows: 1962361561 + 45109432 = **2007470993**:

```
uncompressed bytes xmt/rcv 1962361561/132244042
Transmit bytes:  Uncompressed = 45109432 Compressed =   348114663
```

- The total amount of data to be transmitted after you apply the compression based on the following line is 45109432 + 348114663 = **393224095**:

```
Transmit bytes:  Uncompressed = 45109432 Compressed =   348114663
```

Therefore, the overall data compression ratio is as follows:

2007470993 / 393224095 = 5.1:1

NOTE   The listed numbers do not represent the real compression ratios, but rather they represent a snapshot figure with redundant traffic types. You should not expect compression ratios higher than 2:1 over a long period of usage, with a variety of traffic types.

The precise calculations of the total amount of output in bytes, can be performed by using the results from the #**show compress** command and by using the number of outgoing/incoming packets from the command #**show interfaces serial 1**:

1 Calculate the total number of transmit bytes from the output of the #**show compress** command.

2 Multiply the number of outgoing packets from the output of the #**show interfaces serial 1** command by 6. (For a 2-byte DLCI frame, the overhead is a 2-byte Flag, a 2-byte Address, and a 2-byte FCS).

3 Add the two results from the previous steps and the resulting number should match the number of total bytes of output in the serial interface from the output of #**show interfaces serial 1**.

In the case of hardware compression, the output is similar with one important exception. The compression ratio is calculated by the compression engine, and some of the calculations are not necessary. Example 17-42 shows the hardware compression statistics for DLCI 64.

Example 17-42 *Hardware Compression Statistics for DLCI 62*

```
7206-frame#show compress detail-ccp
 Serial4/2:0 - DLCI: 64
     Hardware compression enabled
     CSA in slot 2 in use
       uncompressed bytes xmt/rcv 316009631/178259458
       compressed bytes   xmt/rcv 185779090/236163882
     Compressed bytes sent:  185779090 bytes   1 Kbits/sec  ratio: 1.700
     Compressed bytes recv:  236163882 bytes   1 Kbits/sec  ratio: 0.754
 ! Resync represents the number of times the compression routine detected
 ! that the dictionaries were out of sync and restarted building a dictionary.
 ! Line errors are a common cause of restarts.
       resyncs 7509
     last clearing of counters: 1211408 seconds
       Additional Stacker Stats:
       Transmit bytes:  Uncompressed = 88971017 Compressed =   92164757
       Received bytes:  Compressed =    52030283 Uncompressed = 177870511
```

NOTE   The compression ratio is lower than in software compression. If you are using the same type of compression (stacker) in both cases, you will notice that the compression ratios differ significantly. Compare the resyncs in both cases. It is obvious that the hardware compression experiences issues and that the constant resync of vocabularies causes poor performance.

Unlike the previously explained precise calculations of the compression parameters, for troubleshooting purposes it is sometimes useful to see if the compression works at all. Some preliminary indicators follow:

- Non-zero values from the #**show compress** command

- A difference between the five minute rate in the WAN (serial) and local-area network (LAN) (Ethernet) interfaces, as shown in the following example:

```
1602-frame#show interfaces serial 1 | include 5 min
  5 minute input rate 8000 bits/sec, 9 packets/sec
  5 minute output rate 2000 bits/sec, 4 packets/sec
1602-frame#show interfaces ethernet 0 | include 5 min
  5 minute input rate 12000 bits/sec, 2 packets/sec
  5 minute output rate 0 bits/sec, 0 packets/sec
```

- Non-linear increments of the round-trip time (RTT) of the output (using the **ping 1602-frame** *packet_size* command) when linearly incrementing the size of the ping packets

For practical purposes, it is convenient to imagine that the compressor-decompressor engine is located between the WAN and LAN interfaces. As soon as the incoming packet hits the WAN interface (serial interface), it gets decompressed and switched to the LAN interface (Ethernet interface) and vice versa. Every outgoing Ethernet packet gets compressed, sent to the serial interface, sent compressed over the serial link, and decompressed by the other party's decompressor.

End Notes

[1] Cough, L. *Digital and Analog Communications Systems*. Prentice Hall, 1997.

Summary

For every troubleshooting process in this chapter, it is recommended that you start with the maximum information about the existing service. The minimum amount of information that you need to have before even starting to troubleshoot includes the characteristics of the service: point-to-point or point-to-multipoint design, routing or bridging, remote and local DLCIs, access rate (link rate), CIR value, IP addressing scheme, and so on. The chapter follows the recommended layer-by-layer troubleshooting process, including physical layer and data link layer problems, performance problems, PVC and LMI-related troubleshooting, and troubleshooting of traffic shaping and compression over Frame Relay.

Review Questions

Answers to the review questions can be found in Appendix A, "Answers to Review Questions."

1 What are the signals on the physical layer provided by DTE?

2 What are the two available options for 56-kbps configurations for Cisco routers?

3 In the command **service-module 56k network-type dds**, what is DDS and what are the data rates provided by DDS?

4 Serial 1 is configured with the command **service-module t1 timeslots 1-2**. What is the configured bandwidth on Serial 1?

5 Name the WIC T1 Pinouts (8 pin RJ48S).

6 What is the command to loopback your equipment?

7 Name two checkpoints for a failing CSU.

8 In the **show frame-relay map** IOS command, if the DLCI is defined and active, what does this mean?

9 What happens with the incoming DLCI in the switch?

10 How do you know if the DLCI is active but not configured in the router?

11   Under what conditions does the properly configured LMI in a Cisco router not send packets over the DLCI?

12   Which LMI message reports the PVC status for each PVC configured on the interface?

13   What is the order of the Cisco LMI autosense full status enquiry message?

14   How are "Num Status Enq. Sent," "Num Status msgs Rcvd," and "Num Status Timeouts" related in erroneous conditions?

15   When debugging the serial interface, what does the message "illegal serial line type xxx" mean?

CHAPTER 18

Frame Relay Troubleshooting Scenarios

This chapter includes some common, real-life scenarios that are designed to demonstrate the Frame Relay troubleshooting techniques covered in Chapter 17, "Frame Relay Troubleshooting." Another objective of this chapter is to give troubleshooting engineers some practical recommendations that deal with Frame Relay troubleshooting issues and to increase their practical knowledge about typical Frame Relay problems.

The greatest advantage of enterprise troubleshooting is that you always see both sides of the connection, and the necessary information about the development of the service is available to you. It is important that you have access to the proper data to fully understand the environment that you are troubleshooting. This includes the provisioning information, the requirements for the design, the configuration solution, and finally, the expected baseline. It is also important to understand the use of different IOS commands and tools, because the screen outputs from some of the recommended commands may or may not provide the information you require. The scenarios provided in this chapter represent some of the most common Frame Relay issues that you might experience when working with different service providers, routers, and solutions.

Five troubleshooting scenarios are provided in this chapter. Each scenario covers the most common troubleshooting issues that occur and how to pinpoint the exact causes of the problems. The topics covered in this chapter are as follows:

- Scenario 1: New Install Issues
- Scenario 2: Mismatched DLCI Settings
- Scenario 3: Performance Issues from Flapping Lines and Traffic Shaping Issues
- Scenario 4: IP Multicast Issues in Frame Relay
- Scenario 5: Frame Relay Host Migration

NOTE   Most troubleshooting engineers recommend that you have two telnet sessions open for some of the more chatty IOS commands. The reason behind this is that you can force the router to crash if you don't know how much output to expect. One of the sessions is used with the #**terminal monitor** or (config)#**logging console** command and the appropriate debug command. For the second telnet session, have the **undebug all** command ready in case use exceeds reasonable levels. The **logging console** command only logs to the console, so you must have a telnet session open or be directly connected to the console port. Logging to the console is more processor intensive than logging to the terminal because of the default slow speed of the console port. Another alternative is to send the log messages to a syslog server and then view them there without logging on the router at all.

Scenario 1: New Install Issues

To troubleshoot new install issues, you must clearly understand what stage of the installation process you are troubleshooting. The most common scenario is when the provisioning process is complete, and the confirmation of circuit installation is received from the service provider, which indicates that the termination device is installed in the minimum point of entry (MPOE), or the sometimes-called Demarcation Point (D-mark). Also as part of the scenario, the local loop is checked and the technician reports that the line is installed.

The first situation here is when you have an administratively down situation for interfaces. A user might have forgotten to not shut the interface (shutdown is the default condition for a new interface that has not been configured). However, this is a basic step that most engineers won't miss to unshut the interface. If the end user's router configuration is correct, three typical indicators exist for new install issues:

- The line is down, the protocol is down.
- The line is up, the protocol is down.
- The line is up, the protocol is up, the router cannot pass data.

NOTE   In explanations throughout this chapter, you see references to up and down states. When there are two references to these states (such as up, up), the first is referring to the line status and the second is referring to the protocol layer status.

Example 18-1 shows the first case. Example 18-2 shows the second case. Finally, Example 18-3 shows the third case.

In the first case, if the line to the MPOE is reported as operational, you might be dealing with internal wiring problems (IW in the local exchange carrier's [LEC's] terminology) or router cable problems. Review the information pertaining to these problems in Chapter 17.

Example 18-1   *The Line Is Reported Down, the Protocol Layer Is Down*

```
1602-frame#show ip interface brief
Interface            IP-Address      OK? Method Status        Protocol
Ethernet0            10.84.14.169    YES NVRAM  up            up
Serial0              unassigned      YES NVRAM  down          down
Serial0.37           10.84.14.169    YES unset  down          down
1602-frame#
```

Example 18-2   *The Line Is Reported Up, the Protocol Layer Is Down*

```
1602-frame#show ip interface brief
Interface            IP-Address      OK? Method  Status       Protocol
Ethernet0            10.84.14.169    YES NVRAM   up           up
Serial0              unassigned      YES NVRAM   up           down
Serial0.62           10.84.14.169    YES unset   down         down
1602-frame#
```

Example 18-3   *The Line Is Reported Up, the Protocol Layer Is Up, but the Router Cannot Pass Data*

```
1602-frame#show ip interface brief
Interface            IP-Address      OK? Method  Status       Protocol
Ethernet0            10.84.14.169    YES NVRAM   up           up
Serial0              unassigned      YES NVRAM   up           up
Serial0.62           10.84.14.169    YES unset   up           up
1602-frame#
```

A more interesting case for troubleshooting purposes is the second case, where the line is reported up but the protocol layer is reported down. An initial checklist of possible issues include (following the described methodology in Chapter 16, "Basic and Advanced Frame Relay Configurations"):

- Configuration issues:
  - Local router configuration errors
  - Core router configuration errors
  - Existing loopback from the core side
- Service provider issues:
  - The permanent virtual circuit (PVC) is not mapped
  - The switch is in maintenance mode
  - The access rate requirements do not match
  - The Local Management Interface (LMI) type does not match

NOTE	For the purposes of the explanation, both sides are configured to use data-link connection identifier (DLCI) = 62; however, the number does not have to be the same on both ends because DLCI only has a local significance.

Starting with the configuration issues, when analyzing both sides, you see the following.

The remote user's router is configured correctly for 56 kbps, it is defined as Frame Relay Internet Engineering Task Force (IETF) encapsulation, and it is set up for LMI type AnnexD. It also reports the output listed in Example 18-2 with line up and protocol down. The remote user's router is configured as shown in Example 18-4.

Example 18-4 *Fragment of the Remote User Configuration*

```
1602-frame#show running-config
<output omitted>
interface Serial0
 no ip address
! The Frame Relay encapsulation is IETF:
 encapsulation frame-relay IETF
 service-module 56k clock source line
 service-module 56k network-type dds
! The LMI type is ANSI:
 frame-relay lmi-type ansi
 !
interface Serial0.62 point-to-point
 bandwidth 56
 ip unnumbered Ethernet0
! The encapsulation of DLCI 62 is IETF because the Serial0 is IETF
 frame-relay interface-dlci 62
<output omitted>
```

The core router reports the output shown in Example 18-5.

Example 18-5 *Core Router Output*

```
3640-frame#show ip interface brief
Interface         IP-Address      OK? Method Status    Protocol
FastEthernet0/0   10.84.5.111     YES manual up        up
FastEthernet1/0   unassigned      YES NVRAM  up        up
Serial3/2:0.65    unassigned      YES unset  deleted   down
Serial3/2:0.66    10.84.5.111     YES unset  up        up
<output omitted>
Serial3/3:0.59    10.84.5.111     YES unset  up        up
Serial3/3:0.60    10.84.5.111     YES unset  down      down
Serial3/3:0.61    10.84.5.111     YES unset  up        up
Serial3/3:0.62    10.84.5.111     YES unset  up        up
! The connection serial3/3:0.62 is the one that requires troubleshooting:
Serial3/3:0.70    unassigned      YES unset  deleted   down
Serial3/3:0.138   10.84.5.111     YES unset  up        up
Serial4/0:0       unassigned      YES NVRAM  up        up
Serial4/0:0.17    unassigned      YES unset  deleted   down
```

The output in Example 18-6 shows the status of DLCI = 62 on the core router.

Example 18-6   *From the Core Router Perspective, DLCI 62 Is Reported Up, Up*

```
3640-frame#show interfaces serial 3/3:0.62
Serial3/3:0.62 is up, line protocol is up
  Hardware is Multichannel T1
  Description: frame to 1602-frame: 10.84.14.169
  Interface is unnumbered. Using address of FastEthernet0/0 (10.84.5.222)
  MTU 1500 bytes, BW 1536 Kbit, DLY 20000 usec,
     reliability 255/255, txload 6/255, rxload 1/255
  Encapsulation FRAME-RELAY IETF
3640-frame#
```

The service from the core side is configured as point-to-point with unnumbered IP, as shown in Example 18-7.

Example 18-7   *How to Check if the Configuration Is Correct*

```
3640-frame#show running-config interface serial s3/3:0.62
! The configuration of the serial interface matches the
! Encapsulation Frame Relay IETF.
Building configuration...
Current configuration: 236 bytes
!
! Matches the remote user's router settings:
interface Serial3/3:0.62 point-to-point
 description frame-relay service for 1602-frame: 10.84.14.169
! The bandwidth matches:
 bandwidth 56
 ip unnumbered FastEthernet0/0
 no ip route-cache
! DLCI IETF matches the local switch:
 frame-relay interface-dlci 62 IETF
end
3640-frame#
```

Obviously, the core side is connected to the local switch and the User-Network Interface (UNI) is functioning correctly.

NOTE   The way the loopback is set up can affect the way the router reports it. The core router can report the line and protocol up for remote loopback, or if you set a local loopback, it can report looped instead of up. However, if the service provider's test technician sets loopback on the interface, the core router does not indicate loopback and the switch must be checked.

Start with the remote user's router to identify what it is reporting (see Example 18-8).

Example 18-8   *Debugging the LMI*

```
1602-frame#debug frame-relay lmi
Frame Relay LMI debugging is on
Displaying all Frame Relay LMI data
1602-frame#
! The DTE sends myseq 55. It does not receive anything from the switch.
! The DTE is down:
3d07h: Serial0(out): StEnq, myseq 55, yourseen 0, DTE down
3d07h: datagramstart = 0x2B9CD48, datagramsize = 14
! The Frame Relay encapsulation is 0x00010308 (Cisco), (0xFCF10309 IETF):
3d07h: FR encap = 0x00010308
3d07h: 00 75 95 01 01 00 03 02 37 00
3d07h:
! The DTE sends myseq 56. It does not receive anything from the switch.
! The DTE is down:
3d07h: Serial0(out): StEnq, myseq 56, yourseen 0, DTE down
3d07h: datagramstart = 0x2B9CD48, datagramsize = 14
3d07h: FR encap = 0x00010308
3d07h: 00 75 95 01 01 00 03 02 38 00
3d07h:
! The DTE sends myseq 57. It does not receive anything from the switch.
! The DTE is down:
3d07h: Serial0(out): StEnq, myseq 57, yourseen 0, DTE down
<output omitted>
```

Change the encapsulation to high-level data link control (HDLC) and try again (see Example 18-9).

Example 18-9   *Debug of the Serial Interface, After Changing the Encapsulation to HDLC*

```
1602-frame-frame# debug serial interface
Serial network interface debugging is on
1602-frame#
3d07h: Serial0: attempting to restart
3d07h: QUICC_SERIAL(0): Reset from 0x200C8FE
3d07h: Serial0(out): StEnq, myseq 62, yourseen 0, DTE down
3d07h: Serial0(out): StEnq, myseq 63, yourseen 0, DTE down
3d07h: Serial0(out): StEnq, myseq 64, yourseen 0, DTE down
! Increase the number of errors; restart the interface:
3d07h: Serial0: attempting to restart
3d07h: QUICC_SERIAL(0): Reset from 0x200C8FE
3d07h: Serial0(out): StEnq, myseq 65, yourseen 0, DTE down
3d07h: Serial0(out): StEnq, myseq 66, yourseen 0, DTE down
3d07h: Serial0(out): StEnq, myseq 67, yourseen 0, DTE down
! Increase the number of errors; restart the interface:
3d07h: Serial0: attempting to restart
3d07h: QUICC_SERIAL(0): Reset from 0x200C8FE
3d07h: Serial0(out): StEnq, myseq 68, yourseen 0, DTE down
1602-frame#
```

Change the encapsulation back to Frame Relay because the report is the same. When working
with the service provider, the technician explicitly defines the LMI type from none to ANSI
to match the remote user's router settings. As a result, the message in Example 18-10 on the
screen shows the protocol coming back up.

Example 18-10   *Changing the LMI Type to ANSI Brings the Protocol Layer to Up*

```
1602-frame#show ip interface brief
Interface            IP-Address      OK? Method Status       Protocol
Ethernet0            10.84.14.169    YES NVRAM  up           up
Serial0              unassigned      YES NVRAM  up           down
Serial0.62           10.84.14.169    YES unset  down         down
1602-frame#
! The line protocol changed state to up:
3d07h: %LINEPROTO-5-UPDOWN: Line protocol on Interface Serial0, changed state to up
1602-frame#
```

Consequently, the output in Example 18-11 is shown.

Example 18-11   *Checking the Status of the Interfaces of a Remote User's Router*

```
1602-frame#show ip interface brief
Interface            IP-Address      OK? Method  Status      Protocol
Ethernet0            10.84.14.169    YES NVRAM   up          up
Serial0              unassigned      YES NVRAM   up          up
Serial0.62           10.84.14.169    YES unset   up          up
```

The last thing to do is to test the new service, as shown in Example 18-12.

Example 18-12   *Check if the Service Is Functioning Properly and Check the LMI Reports*

```
1602-frame#show interfaces
<output omitted>
Serial0 is up, line protocol is up
  Hardware is QUICC Serial (with onboard CSU/DSU)
  MTU 1500 bytes, BW 1544 Kbit, DLY 20000 usec,
      reliability 255/255, txload 1/255, rxload 1/255
  Encapsulation FRAME-RELAY IETF, loopback not set
  Keepalive set (10 sec)
  LMI enq sent  28694, LMI stat recvd 20, LMI upd recvd 0, DTE LMI up
  LMI enq recvd 0, LMI stat sent  0, LMI upd sent  0
  LMI DLCI 0  LMI type is ANSI Annex D  frame relay DTE
  FR SVC disabled, LAPF state down
  Broadcast queue 0/64, broadcasts sent/dropped 5/0, interface broadcasts 1
  Last input 00:00:00, output 00:00:00, output hang never
  Last clearing of "show interfaces" counters 3d07h
  Input queue: 0/75/0/0 (size/max/drops/flushes); Total output drops: 0
  Queuing strategy: weighted fair
  Output queue: 0/1000/64/0 (size/max total/threshold/drops)
```

continues

Example 18-12 *Check if the Service Is Functioning Properly and Check the LMI Reports (Continued)*

```
               Conversations  0/23/256 (active/max active/max total)
               Reserved Conversations 0/0 (allocated/max allocated)
         5 minute input rate 3000 bits/sec, 6 packets/sec
         5 minute output rate 4000 bits/sec, 6 packets/sec
            68159 packets input, 5690460 bytes, 0 no buffer
            Received 0 broadcasts, 0 runts, 0 giants, 0 throttles
            2629 input errors, 0 CRC, 2615 frame, 0 overrun, 0 ignored, 14 abort
! These errors were displayed when the line was down.
! Now you can ignore them because they are not increasing;
! or you may want to clear the counters and monitor again.
            29578 packets output, 497773 bytes, 0 underruns
            0 output errors, 0 collisions, 9558 interface resets
            0 output buffer failures, 0 output buffers swapped out
            2 carrier transitions
            DCD=up  DSR=up  DTR=up  RTS=up  CTS=up

Serial0.62 is up, line protocol is up
  Hardware is QUICC Serial (with onboard CSU/DSU)
  Interface is unnumbered. Using address of Ethernet0 (10.84.14.169)
  MTU 1500 bytes, BW 56 Kbit, DLY 20000 usec,
     reliability 255/255, txload 1/255, rxload 1/255
  Encapsulation FRAME-RELAY IETF
1602-frame#

1602-frame#show frame-relay lmi

LMI Statistics for interface Serial0 (Frame Relay DTE) LMI TYPE = ANSI
      Invalid Unnumbered info 0          Invalid Prot Disc 0
      Invalid dummy Call Ref 0           Invalid Msg Type 0
      Invalid Status Message 0           Invalid Lock Shift 0
      Invalid Information ID 0           Invalid Report IE Len 0
      Invalid Report Request 0           Invalid Keep IE Len 0
! All invalid message counters are reporting 0s
      Num Status Enq. Sent 28699         Num Status msgs Rcvd 28699
      Num Update Status Rcvd 0           Num Status Timeouts 0
1602-frame#
```

Next, run a ping test to check if the router can pass IP traffic (see Example 18-13).

Example 18-13 *The Ping Test Shows that the Router Passes IP Traffic*

```
3640-frame#ping 10.84.14.169

Type escape sequence to abort.
Sending 5, 100-byte ICMP Echos to 10.84.14.169, timeout is 2 seconds:
!!!!!
Success rate is 100 percent (5/5), round-trip min/avg/max = 36/40/48 ms

3640-frame#ping
Protocol [ip]:
```

Example 18-13 *The Ping Test Shows that the Router Passes IP Traffic (Continued)*

```
Target IP address: 10.84.14.169
Repeat count [5]: 50
Datagram size [100]: 1000
Timeout in seconds [2]:
Extended commands [n]:
Sweep range of sizes [n]:
Type escape sequence to abort.
Sending 50, 1000-byte ICMP Echos to 10.84.14.169, timeout is 2 seconds:
!!!!!!!!!!!!!!!!!!!!!!!!!!!!!!!!!!!!!!!!!!!!!!!!!!!
```

The third case occurs when the interfaces of the remote user report line up, protocol up, but the remote user cannot pass any traffic (ping, telnet, and so on) between the home network and the corporate network. This might be related to a variety of problems, including the following:

- The router on the other end is not configured or not configured properly.
- The router network addressing scheme is incorrect.
- The routing protocol is not configured properly.
- The Frame Relay network is not mapped correctly.

The first action to take in this case is to view both ends of the connection, focusing on the core router. Typically, the core router serial interface is up but the subinterfaces report down, as shown in Example 18-14.

Example 18-14 *This Is How the Troubled Connection Serial 3/0:0.47 Looks from the Core Router Perspective*

```
7206-frame#show interfaces serial 3/0:0.47
Serial3/0:0.47 is down, line protocol is down
  Hardware is Multichannel T1
  Description: 1602-frame: 10.10.253.136/29 : 9833502 : 3814500206
  Interface is unnumbered. Using address of Loopback2 (171.68.88.1)
  MTU 1500 bytes, BW 56 Kbit, DLY 20000 usec,
     reliability 255/255, txload 1/255, rxload 1/255
  Encapsulation FRAME-RELAY
7206-frame#
```

If you check the interfaces from the viewpoint of the remote user, most probably it shows that the interface is up, up, and the subinterface shows up, up.

Checking two ends—the remote side and the core side—points to a conclusion that the PVC is probably not mapped by the service provider or that the remote user is looped back instead of mapping the PVC to the other end.

If everything on the physical and data link layers seems to function correctly, it makes sense to move on and look for another set of possible issues. The most typical ones are routed protocol-related mismatches. In the case of IP, there are generally three groups:

- **Duplicate IP addresses**—IP duplication can take place between subnets and within subnets. Large, fast-growing IP spaces can create this situation, and poor IP management, oversight, and merging networks. In the case of duplicates within a subnet, IOS usually provides a warning before assigning the IP address, when the interface is Ethernet or FastEthernet. In wide-area network (WAN) links, there is no warning (possibly because of bridge configurations). The result of the duplicate IP is either sporadic connectivity or total loss of IP connectivity. One possible action is to check the Domain Name System (DNS) server entries to ensure that there are no duplicate IP addresses (Cisco uses a web-based utility to provide access to the DNS tree). Another solution is to use #**show cdp neighbor detail** (see Chapter 4, "Troubleshooting Approaches, Models, and Tools").

- **Duplicate subnets**—In some cases, when you try to merge two or more subnets or to assign a larger subnet to a remote user, it might result in overlapping or duplicate subnets. This can cause loss of connectivity or intermittent connectivity. Again, the #**show cdp neighbor detail**, #**show ip interface brief**, and #**show ip route** commands, and available DNS utilities, are the recommended tools.

- **Misconfigured masks**—The mask defines what part of the IP address is a network address, and what part is designated for host addresses. The mask plays a significant role in all routing protocols and can be a source of different issues. It is recommended that the troubleshooting of this situation be performed in the context of the chosen routing protocol, such as Open Shortest Path First (OSPF) or Border Gateway Protocol (BGP).

For possible routing issues and overhead, see Chapter 16. DLCI and PVC issues are discussed in the following scenario.

Scenario 2: Mismatched DLCI Settings

The importance of this scenario is based on the fact that the DLCI is a super-identifier in Frame Relay. Recall the extended coverage of DLCI formats in Chapter 14, "Frame Relay Technology Background" and the numerous standards and committees that define the rules and scope of DLCI usage. Additionally, rules exist for the number of DLCIs that are configurable on any particular interface or router, and that are restricted by the amount of available memory.

In this section, one of the simplest situations is covered—when the DLCI does not match the value provisioned by the local service provider.

Use the #**show frame-relay pvc** command to clarify if you have the correct DLCI, as shown in Example 18-15.

Example 18-15 *Output from the Core Router from the* **show frame-relay pvc** *Command*

```
7206-frame#show frame-relay pvc
<output omitted>
DLCI = 54, DLCI USAGE = LOCAL, PVC STATUS = DELETED, INTERFACE = Serial3/0:0.54

  input pkts 0              output pkts 0            in bytes 0
  out bytes 0              dropped pkts 0           in FECN pkts 0
  in BECN pkts 0          out FECN pkts 0          out BECN pkts 0
  in DE pkts 0            out DE pkts 0
  out bcast pkts 0        out bcast bytes 0
  pvc create time 3w3d, last time pvc status changed 3w3d

DLCI = 64, DLCI USAGE = LOCAL, PVC STATUS = ACTIVE, INTERFACE = Serial3/0:0.64

  input pkts 41898         output pkts 39200        in bytes 9673029
  out bytes 17274236      dropped pkts 0           in FECN pkts 0
  in BECN pkts 0          out FECN pkts 0          out BECN pkts 0
  in DE pkts 41898        out DE pkts 0
  out bcast pkts 10818    out bcast bytes 3245400
  pvc create time 3w3d, last time pvc status changed 1d17h

DLCI = 67, DLCI USAGE = UNUSED, PVC STATUS = INACTIVE, INTERFACE = Serial3/0:0.67

  input pkts 0              output pkts 0            in bytes 0
  out bytes 0              dropped pkts 0           in FECN pkts 0
  in BECN pkts 0          out FECN pkts 0          out BECN pkts 0
  in DE pkts 0            out DE pkts 0
  out bcast pkts 0        out bcast bytes 0
  switched pkts 0
  Detailed packet drop counters:
  no out intf 0            out intf down 0          no out PVC 0
  in PVC down 0            out PVC down 0           pkt too big 0
  shaping Q full 0         pkt above DE 0           policing drop 0
  pvc create time 3w3d, last time pvc status changed 3w3d
<output omitted>
```

From this command, you learn details of the DLCI and the PVC status:

- **DLCI**—The DLCI number for this PVC. The usage of the DLCI includes the following:

  — **DLCI USAGE = LOCAL**—Locally configured in the data terminal equipment (DTE).

  — **DLCI USAGE = UNUSED**—If the PVC status is inactive, the DLCI is not linked to an interface.

  — **DLCI USAGE = SWITCHED**—The router is configured as a Frame Relay switch.

- **PVC STATUS**—Reports the status of the PVC, which can be the following:

  — **PVC STATUS = ACTIVE**—DLCI is active and up.

  — **PVC STATUS = INACTIVE**—DLCI is not active, but LMI is reporting it up.

- **PVC STATUS = DELETED**—DLCI is not listed in the periodic LMI exchange.

- **INTERFACE = Serial3/0:0.67, or INTERFACE = Serial3/0:0.54, or INTERFACE = Serial3/0:0.64**—Shows which interface, or in this case subinterface, uses this DLCI.

As shown in Example 18-15, DLCI = 64 is active and appears to be fully functional. If the router (on either end of the PVC) reports differently (inactive or deleted) and the cause is because of wrong DLCI settings that are provided by the service provider, an option for resolution is contacting the provider for the correct DLCI. However, Cisco IOS provides features that help recognize the issue. The remote user's router is used for this example.

First and foremost, check the configuration shown in Example 18-16 to make sure that the DLCI matches the one provisioned by your provider, and that it is configured correctly.

Example 18-16 *Verifying the DLCI Settings in the Router Configuration*

```
1602-frame# show running-config

<output omitted>

interface Serial0
 no ip address
 encapsulation frame-relay IETF
 no ip mroute-cache
 service-module 56k clock source line
 service-module 56k network-type dds
 frame-relay lmi-type ansi
!
interface Serial0.16 point-to-point
 bandwidth 56
 ip unnumbered Ethernet0
 no ip mroute-cache
 frame-relay interface-dlci 17 IETF
!
<output omitted>
```

Next, check the status of the remote user's interfaces with the **show ip interfaces brief** command, as shown in Example 18-17.

Example 18-17 *Verifying the Status of the Interfaces*

```
1602-frame#show ip interfaces brief
Interface        IP-Address       OK? Method Status        Protocol
Ethernet0        10.84.14.169     YES NVRAM  up            up
Serial0          unassigned       YES NVRAM  up            up
! Focus on the next line. What is wrong with serial0.16?
Serial0.16       10.84.14.169     YES unset  down          down
1602-frame#
```

The serial line reports line up, protocol up, but the subinterface is line down, protocol down. To determine what is wrong with the subinterface, identify what the LMI exchanges report, as shown in Example 18-18.

Example 18-18 *The LMI Statistics, as a Result of the* **debug frame-relay lmi** *Command*

```
1602-frame#debug frame-relay lmi
Frame Relay LMI debugging is on
Displaying all Frame Relay LMI data
1602-frame#
1d21h: Serial0(out): StEnq, myseq 175, yourseen 83, DTE up
1d21h: datagramstart = 0x2B9C888, datagramsize = 14
1d21h: FR encap = 0x00010308
1d21h: 00 75 95 01 01 01 03 02 AF 53
1d21h:
1d21h: Serial0(in): Status, myseq 175
1d21h: RT IE 1, length 1, type 1
1d21h: KA IE 3, length 2, yourseq 84, myseq 175
1d21h: Serial0(out): StEnq, myseq 176, yourseen 84, DTE up
1d21h: datagramstart = 0x2B9C888, datagramsize = 14
1d21h: FR encap = 0x00010308
1d21h: 00 75 95 01 01 01 03 02 B0 54
! The keepalive exchanges are correct and the link is operational, but
! the DLCI requires additional attention.
1d21h:
1d21h: Serial0(in): Status, myseq 176
1d21h: RT IE 1, length 1, type 1
1d21h: KA IE 3, length 2, yourseq 85, myseq 176
1d21h: Serial0(out): StEnq, myseq 177, yourseen 85, DTE up
1d21h: datagramstart = 0x2B9C888, datagramsize = 14
1d21h: FR encap = 0x00010308
1d21h: 00 75 95 01 01 00 03 02 B1 55
1d21h:
1d21h: Serial0(in): Status, myseq 177
1d21h: RT IE 1, length 1, type 0
1d21h: KA IE 3, length 2, yourseq 86, myseq 177
! Review the next line, it shows dlci 16
1d21h: PVC IE 0x7 , length 0x3 , dlci 16, status 0x2
1d21h: Serial0(out): StEnq, myseq 178, yourseen 86, DTE up
1d21h: datagramstart = 0x2B9C888, datagramsize = 14
1d21h: FR encap = 0x00010308
1d21h: 00 75 95 01 01 01 03 02 B2 56
! This is an output from full status enquiry, where the listed
! DLCI is 16 and the status is reported 0x2 - active.
! The other value would be Inactive - 0x0.
1d21h:
1d21h: Serial0(in): Status, myseq 178
1d21h: RT IE 1, length 1, type 1
1d21h: KA IE 3, length 2, yourseq 87, myseq 178
1d21h: Serial0(out): StEnq, myseq 179, yourseen 87, DTE up
1d21h: datagramstart = 0x2B9C888, datagramsize = 14
1d21h: FR encap = 0x00010308
1d21h: 00 75 95 01 01 01 03 02 B3 57
```

At the same time, the core router report shows the output in Example 18-19 (the core router's configured DLCI is 62).

Example 18-19 *Verifying the Status of DLCI 62 on the Core Router*

```
7206-frame#show ip interface brief
Serial3/3:0              unassigned      YES NVRAM  up                up
<output omitted>
Serial3/3:0.50          10.84.5.222     YES unset  up                up
Serial3/3:0.53          10.84.5.222     YES unset  up                up
Serial3/3:0.55          10.84.5.222     YES unset  up                up
Serial3/3:0.57          10.84.5.222     YES unset  down              down
Serial3/3.0.61          10.84.5.222     YES unset  down              down
! The serial 3/3:0.62 is reporting UP, UP
Serial3/3:0.62          10.84.5.222     YES unset  up                up
```

Notice that DLCI = 62 is reported as up and up.

The information reported from the remote user's router includes all configured PVCs, except for any PVCs with PVC STATUS = DELETED. So based on the initial service provider's confirmation of the service, the provider seems to have configured DLCI = 16, but DLCI=17 is configured on the remote user's router.

To verify this suggestion, look at the **show frame-relay pvc** output, as shown in Example 18-20.

Example 18-20 *Output from the Remote User's Router After the **show frame-relay pvc** Command*

```
1602-frame#show frame-relay pvc

PVC Statistics for interface Serial0 (Frame Relay DTE)

                    Active      Inactive    Deleted     Static
  Local             0           0           1           0
  Switched          0           0           0           0
  Unused            1           0           0           0

DLCI = 16, DLCI USAGE = UNUSED, PVC STATUS = ACTIVE, INTERFACE = Serial0

  input pkts 3           output pkts 0          in bytes 918
  out bytes 0            dropped pkts 0         in FECN pkts 0
  in BECN pkts 0         out FECN pkts 0        out BECN pkts 0
  in DE pkts 0           out DE pkts 0
  out bcast pkts 0       out bcast bytes 0      Num Pkts Switched 0
  pvc create time 00:02:45, last time pvc status changed 00:02:45

DLCI = 17, DLCI USAGE = LOCAL, PVC STATUS = DELETED, INTERFACE = Serial0.16

  input pkts 0           output pkts 1          in bytes 0
  out bytes 312          dropped pkts 0         in FECN pkts 0
  in BECN pkts 0         out FECN pkts 0        out BECN pkts 0
  in DE pkts 0           out DE pkts 0
  out bcast pkts 1       out bcast bytes 312
  pvc create time 00:03:44, last time pvc status changed 00:02:50
1602-frame#
```

You can clearly see that the non-configured Serial0.16 is ACTIVE, and that Serial0.17 is DELETED. The fix is standard and quick to implement, as shown in Example 18-21.

Example 18-21 *Implementing the Configuration Change—Change DLCI = 17 to DLCI = 16*

```
1602-frame#configure terminal
Enter configuration commands, one per line.  End with CNTL/Z.
1602-frame(config)#interface serial 0.16
1602-frame(config-subif)#frame-relay interface-dlci 16 ietf
1602-frame(config-fr-dlc)#end
1602-frame#write memory
! It is always good practice to check the status of interfaces after
! the change and make sure that the change is successful.
! This is shown in the following output.
1602-frame#show ip interface brief
Interface        IP-Address      OK? Method  Status            Protocol
Ethernet0        10.84.14.169    YES NVRAM   up                up
Serial0          unassigned      YES NVRAM   up                up
Serial0.16       10.84.14.169    YES unset   up                up
1602-frame#
```

After shutting down Serial0.17, verify the PVC status of the remote user's router with the **show frame-relay pvc** command, as shown in Example 18-22.

Example 18-22 *Output from the Remote User's Router, Showing the PVC Status*

```
1602-frame#show frame-relay pvc

PVC Statistics for interface Serial0 (Frame Relay DTE)

               Active      Inactive     Deleted      Static
  Local        1           0            0            0
  Switched     0           0            0            0
  Unused       0           0            0            0

DLCI = 16, DLCI USAGE = LOCAL, PVC STATUS = ACTIVE, INTERFACE = Serial0.16

  input pkts 2829       output pkts 1894      in bytes 505954
  out bytes 524513      dropped pkts 0        in FECN pkts 19
  in BECN pkts 0        out FECN pkts 0       out BECN pkts 0
  in DE pkts 0          out DE pkts 0
  out bcast pkts 95     out bcast bytes 30824
  pvc create time 01:31:33, last time pvc status changed 01:31:33
1602-frame#
```

NOTE   The DLCI = 17 disappears from the configuration and from the show status command's outputs, but not immediately. It disappears only after the box is reloaded.

One of the most common problems related to the same issue is that the remote user's router is unable to ping the core router's serial interface. The recommended steps to follow are verifying the correct network address and its mapping to the correct DLCI by using **show frame-relay map**:

```
7206-frame#show frame-relay map
Serial3/3:0.62 (up): point-to-point dlci, dlci 62(0x3E,0xCE0), broadcast, IETF
        status defined, active
```

This shows the network address, DLCI number, and interface in use. The status message of "defined and active" can be displayed, even if the DLCI is not working. The message actually indicates that the DLCI can carry data and that the router at the far end is active, which is important end-to-end information.

Another important point is to distinguish between different designs, and to realize that you cannot always ping your own Ethernet interface, especially in a multipoint Frame Relay interface. Pings to your own interface address are successful on point-to-point subinterfaces, or HDLC links because the router on the other side of the link knows where to return the Internet Control Message Protocol (ICMP) echo and echo reply packets. Thus, an ICMP is sent and received in the right direction. In point-to-multipoint designs, the multipoint interface has multiple IPs and multiple destinations assigned. Therefore, to successfully send an ICMP reply, the router must have a mapping for every destination. If mapping is not configured, do not expect to receive an ICMP reply because the router does not have any Layer-2 to Layer-3 mapping for its own address and it does not know how to encapsulate the packet.

An encapsulation failure is the typical result. You cannot ping from one spoke to another in a hub and spoke configuration by using multipoint interfaces because there is no mapping for the other spokes' IP addresses. Interestingly enough, the same logic applies when you use Frame Relay or ADSL over Asynchronous Transfer Mode (ATM), and use a spoke and hub configuration. Only the hub's address is learned through Inverse Address Resolution Protocol (InARP). If you configure a static map using the **frame-relay map** command for your IP address or the IP address of a remote spoke, you can ping your interface address and the addresses of other spokes.

Scenario 3: Performance Issues from Flapping Lines and Traffic Shaping Issues

This scenario represents one of the most common and, at the same time, most difficult to pinpoint issues—when performance expectations are not met or the service is good for a period of time but there is no data exchange whatsoever for short periods of time. Some of the most common reasons for these problems are flapping lines and traffic shaping issues.

Flapping Lines

Problems that result from flapping lines are linked to the history of the PVC, as reported by the Frame Relay commands. As previously discussed, the Frame Relay router requests the status of all PVCs on the interface during the periodic polling cycles of LMI, which is typically every six polling cycles. The resulting full-status message response contains information on every PVC that is configured on that physical interface. The information includes the recent history of the PVC and its availability (inactive or active). The term flapping lines refers to the situation when the service continually changes its state from active to inactive, or is flapping. The user tries to exchange data, but the exchange is not available for a period of time, where the user cannot ping, telnet, or reach the other party's router or any party's IP address. After a while, the service comes back up and repeats the cycle.

The typical reports that indicate a flapping line are shown in Example 18-23.

Example 18-23 *The History of the DLCI, Including the Relative Time When the Service Was Created and the Last Time the PVC Status Was Changed*

```
1602-frame#show frame-relay pvc

PVC Statistics for interface Serial0 (Frame Relay DTE)

                Active     Inactive    Deleted      Static
    Local       1          0           0            0
    Switched    0          0           0            0
    Unused      0          0           0            0

DLCI = 74, DLCI USAGE = LOCAL, PVC STATUS = ACTIVE, INTERFACE = Serial0.74

    input pkts 42832        output pkts 49616       in bytes 17904175
    out bytes 9379033       dropped pkts 62         in FECN pkts 0
    in BECN pkts 0          out FECN pkts 0         out BECN pkts 0
    in DE pkts 42832        out DE pkts 0
    out bcast pkts 2580      out bcast bytes 777846
    pvc create time 3w2d, last time pvc status changed 00:15:53
! If the PVC was created 3w2d ago, you must identify what causes
! the pvc status to be changed so often.
1602-frame#

! Use the show service-module command to verify how the line parameters
! are reported:
1602-frame#show service-module
Module type is 4-wire Switched 56K in DDS mode,
Receiver has no alarms.
Current line rate is 56 Kbits/sec and role is DSU side,
Last clearing of alarm counters 1d19h
! This report matches the previous one
    oos/oof                 :   120, last occurred 00:15:53
    loss of signal          :   0,
    loss of sealing current:    0,
```

continues

Example 18-23 *The History of the DLCI, Including the Relative Time When the Service Was Created and the Last Time the PVC Status Was Changed (Continued)*

```
! The last time CSU/DSU was looped back (from you, or from
! the service provider) in order to test the connection
      CSU/DSU loopback        :    107, last occurred 14:11:29
      loopback from remote    :    0,
      DTE loopback            :    0,
      line loopback           :    0,
1602-frame#
```

If you check the serial interfaces, you see a high volume of errors on the input portion of the statistics, as shown in Example 18-24.

Example 18-24 *To See the Number of Input and Output Errors and Their Type, Use the* **show interfaces** *Command in Enabled Mode*

```
1602-frame#show interfaces
Serial0 is up, line protocol is up
  Hardware is QUICC Serial (with onboard CSU/DSU)
  MTU 1500 bytes, BW 1544 Kbit, DLY 20000 usec,
      reliability 255/255, txload 1/255, rxload 1/255
  Encapsulation FRAME-RELAY, loopback not set
  Keepalive set (10 sec)
  LMI enq sent  15696, LMI stat recvd 15107, LMI upd recvd 0, DTE LMI up
  LMI enq recvd 0, LMI stat sent  0, LMI upd sent  0
  LMI DLCI 0  LMI type is ANSI Annex D  frame relay DTE
<output omitted>
  5 minute input rate 2000 bits/sec, 4 packets/sec
  5 minute output rate 2000 bits/sec, 3 packets/sec
     59692 packets input, 19967056 bytes, 0 no buffer
     Received 0 broadcasts, 0 runts, 6 giants, 0 throttles
! Look to the extensive number of errors and especially number of aborts.
     201794 input errors, 11665 CRC, 159475 frame, 0 overrun, 0 ignored, 30654 abort
     65338 packets output, 9595695 bytes, 0 underruns
! The number of interface resets is extremely high as well
     0 output errors, 0 collisions, 11137 interface resets
     0 output buffer failures, 0 output buffers swapped out
     0 carrier transitions
     DCD=up  DSR=up  DTR=up  RTS=up  CTS=up
```

This output shows that you are dealing with second-layer problems, which is the reason that the service went down. Identify which layer of the service is affected and not the first layer. Examine the output from the #**show service-module** command, which shows that the DTE never loses the signal (loss of signal : 0). Also, no carrier transitions exist (0 carrier transitions), which is typical when the line is out of sync. Obviously, the first layer is not affected; thus, focus on the protocol layer and its components and determine which one is causing the service to go down. Recall the way that LMI works and reports the DTE down, then increments the counter and resets the interface. Check the number of interface resets to confirm that the counters were incremented. The number of interface resets does not match the carrier transitions, but CRC and frame errors, which leads you to determine that you are dealing with second-layer issues. Remembering that, verify how the other party — the core router — reports the status of the PVC. The core router is configured for DLCI = 74 in Serial4/1:0. Its status is shown in Example 18-25.

Example 18-25 *Verifying the Status of PVC 74 on the Core Router*

```
7206-frame#show frame-relay pvc 74

PVC Statistics for interface Serial4/1:0 (Frame Relay DTE)

DLCI = 74, DLCI USAGE = LOCAL, PVC STATUS = ACTIVE, INTERFACE = Serial4/1:0.74

  input pkts 167039        output pkts 157077      in bytes 26896506
  out bytes 79023826       dropped pkts 116        in FECN pkts 0
  in BECN pkts 0           out FECN pkts 0         out BECN pkts 0
  in DE pkts 167039        out DE pkts 0
  out bcast pkts 9748      out bcast bytes 2924400
  pvc create time 3w0d, last time pvc status changed 00:17:09
  cir 56000      bc 56000      be 0          byte limit 875     interval 125
  mincir 28000      byte increment 875    Adaptive Shaping none
  pkts 156956      bytes 78972226  pkts delayed 51275      bytes delayed 56957021
  shaping inactive
  traffic shaping drops 0
  Queuing strategy: fifo
  Output queue 0/40, 116 drop, 51275 dequeued
7206-frame#
```

There is nothing unusual from the core side to affect or reflect the issues that the remote side is experiencing.

Further actions to fix the service include the following steps on the remote user's router:

- Check the performance parameters of the router with #**show processes cpu**.
- Check for possible hardware problems using #**show diag** *module_number*.
- Check for failing buffers with #**show buffers fail**.
- Work with the service provider to eliminate the failing device or equipment.

After the successful resolution of this issue, it is good practice to check the status of the service from both sides the next day with the following commands:

```
1602-frame#show frame-relay pvc 74
7206-frame#show frame-relay pvc 74
```

The remote user's router reports the output shown in Example 18-26.

Example 18-26   *The Core Router Report for the Troubled PVC 74*

```
PVC Statistics for interface Serial0 (Frame Relay DTE)

                Active      Inactive    Deleted     Static
    Local       1           0           0           0
    Switched    0           0           0           0
    Unused      0           0           0           0

DLCI = 74, DLCI USAGE = LOCAL, PVC STATUS = ACTIVE, INTERFACE = Serial4/1:0.74

    input pkts 186908        output pkts 175377      in bytes 29752740
    out bytes 89258825       dropped pkts 116        in FECN pkts 0
    in BECN pkts 0           out FECN pkts 0         out BECN pkts 0
    in DE pkts 186908        out DE pkts 0
    out bcast pkts 11055     out bcast bytes 3316500
    ! The last time the pvc status has changed is 17:44.54.
    pvc create time 3w1d, last time pvc status changed 17:44:54
    cir 56000      bc 56000      be 0          byte limit 875     interval 125
    mincir 28000      byte increment 875    Adaptive Shaping none
    pkts 175256      bytes 89207225   pkts delayed 57828      bytes delayed 64737774
    shaping inactive
    traffic shaping drops 0
    Queuing strategy: fifo
    Output queue 0/40, 116 drop, 57828 dequeued
7206-frame#
```

The last time the PVC changed is reported after the fix is implemented (the last time the PVC status changed was 17:44:54). If the number and type of errors is not incrementing from where they were before the changes were implemented, you can consider the case closed—the troubleshooting actions have corrected the problem.

Traffic Shaping Issues

Another important cause of performance issues is related to traffic shaping settings. The two basic cases are no traffic shaping and wrong traffic shaping; both equally affect performance of the service.

The configuration for traffic shaping is covered in Chapter 16. It is a necessary feature if you need to prioritize different types of traffic by trimming the timers and counters, or configuring Bc, Be, and timing intervals.

NOTE	The Enhanced Local Management Interface (ELMI) is an interesting Cisco feature that is well-known for enabling Frame Relay quality of service (QoS) by using the 7206-frame(config-if)# **frame-relay qos-autosense** command. By turning this command on and off, it can perform dynamic traffic shaping. The feature enables the automated exchange of Frame Relay QoS parameter information, between the Cisco router and the Cisco switch (BPX/MGX and IGX platforms). The router uses the QoS values from the switch that are configurable to establish traffic shaping. More about this Cisco IOS feature can be found at www.cisco.com.

Because of the use of traffic shaping, performance issues are recognized in three typical scenarios:

- Unacceptable high round-trip time (RTT)
- The line that was provisioned for certain access rates provides less than expected performance
- Flapping routes

High RTT Numbers

An example of the first case is when the user and the core router are located in the same area, but the test is performed from a remote geographic location. The local carriers are X and Y, and the IXC (long-distance carrier) carries the traffic with one-way latency of about 80 ms. The local loop latency is definitely lower than the two-way latency of the long-distance carrier, given the locations and distance. If you assume that two local loops (core side and the remote user's side) each have latency equal to one-way latency of the local carrier (3×80), you can expect a RTT of about 240 ms. Now, to check the actual results, perform a **ping** with 64 bytes, which means that there is no need for fragmentation/defragmentation (see Example 18-27).

Example 18-27 *A Ping Test Performed to Find Out the RTT*

```
 UNIX.cisco.com:/users/pnedeltc> ping 1602-frame
PING 1602-frame.cisco.com: 56 data bytes
64 bytes from 1602-frame.cisco.com (10.84.11.73): icmp_seq=0. time=6191. ms
64 bytes from 1602-frame.cisco.com (10.84.11.73): icmp_seq=1. time=7424. ms
64 bytes from 1602-frame.cisco.com (10.84.11.73): icmp_seq=2. time=9101. ms
64 bytes from 1602-frame.cisco.com (10.84.11.73): icmp_seq=3. time=11448. ms
64 bytes from 1602-frame.cisco.com (10.84.11.73): icmp_seq=4. time=13887. ms
64 bytes from 1602-frame.cisco.com (10.84.11.73): icmp_seq=5. time=16244. ms
64 bytes from 1602-frame.cisco.com (10.84.11.73): icmp_seq=6. time=18760. ms
64 bytes from 1602-frame.cisco.com (10.84.11.73): icmp_seq=7. time=22428. ms
64 bytes from 1602-frame.cisco.com (10.84.11.73): icmp_seq=8. time=27199. ms
```

continues

Example 18-27 *A Ping Test Performed to Find Out the RTT (Continued)*

```
64 bytes from 1602-frame.cisco.com (10.84.11.73): icmp_seq=9. time=34426. ms
..................
64 bytes from 1602-frame.cisco.com (10.84.11.73): icmp_seq=376. time=114440. ms
^C
----1602-frame.cisco.com PING Statistics----
493 packets transmitted, 135 packets received, 72% packet loss
round-trip (ms)  min/avg/max = 6191/112398/133134
```

As you can see from the output, the RTT values are inconsistent and significantly exceed your expectations.

If you trace the path (see Example 18-28), you see that the long-distance provider carries the trace to the remote site in 80 ms; however, the local service provider carries the trace within a local area in 200 ms. There is a problem with performance on the local loop.

Example 18-28 *A Trace Route Test, Performed to Find the Highest RTT*

```
Starting trace - Aug 27, 2001  10:19:40
Tracing to 1602-frame [10.84.11.73]....
Hops    IP Address           RTT(ms)        DNS Name
1       161.71.86.2          0              hop-dtb-gw1.cisco.com
2       161.71.241.153       0              hop-sbb4-gw1.cisco.com
3       161.71.241.37        0              hop-rbb-gw3.cisco.com
4       161.69.7.217         0              hop-rbb-gw1.cisco.com
5       161.69.7.158         0              hop-gb4-g0-0.cisco.com
6       161.68.86.58         81             hop-sj-pos.cisco.com
7       10.184.5.89          80             hop-rbb-gw1.cisco.com
! The trace reaches the other end, which is the core router.
8       10.84.5.222          80             7206-frame.cisco.com
! The trace reaches the remote user's router
9       10.84.11.73          200            1602-frame.cisco.com
Host reached
! The last hop is 200 ms RTT
```

The tests of the user's router show no buffer or hardware failures. However, if you check whether traffic shaping is applied to DLCI = 60, you can see that DLCI = 60 is not listed, as shown in Example 18-29.

Example 18-29 *Verifying if DLCI = 60 Is Listed Among DLCIs, with Applied Traffic Shaping*

```
7206-frame#show traffic-shape

Interface   Se3/0:0
            Access Target   Byte   Sustain   Excess   Interval  Increment Adapt
VC   List   Rate     Limit  bits/int bits/int (ms)      (bytes)   Active
38          56000    875    7000     0        125       875       -
34          56000    875    7000     0        125       875       -
33          56000    875    7000     0        125       875       -
```

Example 18-29 *Verifying if DLCI = 60 Is Listed Among DLCIs, with Applied Traffic Shaping (Continued)*

```
 32              56000    875    7000    0         125       875      -
 22              56000    875    7000    0         125       875      -
 16              56000    875    7000    0         125       875      -


 Interface   Se3/0:0.17
           Access Target    Byte    Sustain   Excess   Interval  Increment Adapt
 VC        List   Rate      Limit   bits/int  bits/int (ms)      (bytes)   Active
 17               56000     875     7000      0        125       875       -


 Interface   Se3/0:0.18
           Access Target    Byte    Sustain   Excess   Interval  Increment Adapt
 VC        List   Rate      Limit   bits/int  bits/int (ms)      (bytes)   Active
 18               56000     875     7000      0        125       875       -


 Interface   Se3/0:0.20
           Access Target    Byte    Sustain   Excess   Interval  Increment Adapt
 VC        List   Rate      Limit   bits/int  bits/int (ms)      (bytes)   Active
 20               56000     875     7000      0        125       875       -


 Interface   Se3/0:0.23
           Access Target    Byte    Sustain   Excess   Interval  Increment Adapt
 VC        List   Rate      Limit   bits/int  bits/int (ms)      (bytes)   Active
 23               56000     875     7000      0        125       875       -


 Interface   Se3/0:0.24
           Access Target    Byte    Sustain   Excess   Interval  Increment Adapt
 VC        List   Rate      Limit   bits/int  bits/int (ms)      (bytes)   Active
 24               56000     875     7000      0        125       875       -


 <output omitted>


 Interface   Se3/0:0.62
           Access Target    Byte     Sustain   Excess   Interval   Increment Adapt
 VC        List   Rate      Limit    bits/int  bits/int (ms)       (bytes)   Active
 62               384000    6000     384000    0        125        6000      -
```

The first conclusion about this case can lead you to Scenario 1, local loop problems, or
flapping links. After working with LEC, you might conclude that this is a traffic-shaping
issue. The required fix is to implement the appropriate traffic-shaping map class.

Slow Performance

The second traffic shaping issue is when performance is lower than what the user is
expecting. In this scenario, the service is provisioned for an access rate of 384-kbps, but
performance characteristics are closer to a 56-kbps circuit. The service is operational, the
serial lines do not report any errors, and both the remote user's and the core router's
configurations are set up correctly, and report normal. The output in Example 18-30 shows
the DLCI = 98 parameters.

Example 18-30   *Verifying the Serial 4/0:0.98 Configuration on the Core Router*

```
7206-frame#show interfaces serial 4/0:0.98
Serial4/0:0.98 is up, line protocol is up
  Hardware is Multichannel T1
  Description: 1604-frame: 10.21.56.8/29 : 23161309 : 3844600235
  Interface is unnumbered. Using address of Loopback2 (171.68.88.1)
  MTU 1500 bytes, BW 256 Kbit, DLY 20000 usec,
     reliability 255/255, txload 24/255, rxload 5/255
  Encapsulation FRAME-RELAY
```

The output from 7206-frame#**show frame-relay pvc 98** is shown in Example 18-31.

Example 18-31   *Verifying if PVC 98 Has Traffic Shaping Applied to It*

```
7206-frame#show frame-relay pvc 98
DLCI = 98, DLCI USAGE = UNUSED, PVC STATUS = ACTIVE, INTERFACE = Serial4/0:0

    input pkts 167755         output pkts 167552        in bytes 13750582
    out bytes 189232810       dropped pkts 71           in FECN pkts 0
    in BECN pkts 0            out FECN pkts 0           out BECN pkts 0
    in DE pkts 167755         out DE pkts 0
    out bcast pkts 16392      out bcast bytes 4967386
    pvc create time 5d16h, last time pvc status changed 5d16h
  ! These are the parameters, defining the performance.
    cir 28000      bc 7000      be 0         limit 875     interval 125
    mincir 28000      byte increment 875    Adaptive Shaping none
    pkts 167481      bytes 189226266 pkts delayed 128118     bytes delayed 171119678
    shaping inactive
    traffic shaping drops 0
    Serial4/0:0.98 dlci 98 is first come first serve default queuing
    Output queue 0/40, 71 drop, 128118 dequeued
```

Next, you need to take some measurements from the interfaces Ethernet0 and Serial1 of the remote user's router, then ping from the core router or from any server in the same area with a packet size of 3000 bytes. Measure the end user's five-minute rate by entering the following two commands, as shown in Example 18-32:

```
1602-frame#show interfaces ethernet 0 | include 5 min
1602-frame#show interfaces serial 1 | include 5 min
```

Example 18-32   *Measuring the Input and Output Rate on Ethernet0 and Serial1 Interfaces of a Remote User's Router*

```
1602-frame#show interfaces ethernet 0 | include 5 min
  5 minute input rate 7000 bits/sec, 13 packets/sec
  5 minute output rate 8000 bits/sec, 18 packets/sec
1602-frame#show interfaces serial 1 | include 5 min
```

Example 18-32 *Measuring the Input and Output Rate on Ethernet0 and Serial1 Interfaces of a Remote User's Router (Continued)*

```
   5 minute input rate 4000 bits/sec, 22 packets/sec
   5 minute output rate 6000 bits/sec, 14 packets/sec
1602-frame#
```

It is a good idea to monitor the RXD and TXD, and the reliability reports (reliability 255/255) of the 1602-frame router:

```
Serial1 is up, line protocol is up
  Hardware is QUICC Serial (with FT1 CSU/DSU WIC)
  MTU 1500 bytes, BW 128 Kbit, DLY 20000 usec,
     reliability 255/255, txload 7/255, rxload 85/255
```

If you go back to review the previous outputs, you will notice that for a 384-kbps circuit, the core router reports the following:

```
pvc create time 5d16h, last time pvc status changed 5d16h
cir 28000      bc 7000      be 0          limit 875      interval 125
mincir 28000      byte increment 875      Adaptive Shaping none
```

The new config inherits the default settings of Serial4/0:0, where traffic shaping is defined with no classes. The fix is easy to apply.

First, create a map class, as shown in Example 18-33.

Example 18-33 *Example for Class Definition Called* **class-384-new**

```
map-class frame-relay class-384-new
 no frame-relay adaptive-shaping
 frame-relay cir 384000
 frame-relay bc 384000
 frame-relay be 128000
 frame-relay mincir 256000
```

Next, apply the map class, as shown in Example 18-34.

Example 18-34 *The Class* **class-384-new** *Is Applied to the Interface*

```
interface Serial4/0:0.98 point-to-point
 description 1604-frame frame: 10.21.56.8/29 : 23161309 : 3844600235
 bandwidth 384
 ip unnumbered Loopback2
 no ip route-cache
 frame-relay class class-384-new
 frame-relay interface-dlci 98 IETF
```

Repeat the status commands and compare the results, as shown in Example 18-35.

Example 18-35   *Check the Status of PVC 98*

```
7206-frame#show frame-relay pvc 98

PVC Statistics for interface Serial4/0:0 (Frame Relay DTE)

DLCI = 98, DLCI USAGE = LOCAL, PVC STATUS = ACTIVE, INTERFACE = Serial4/0:0.98

  input pkts 536361          output pkts 659230       in bytes 100680624
  out bytes 165617202        dropped pkts 68          in FECN pkts 0
  in BECN pkts 0             out FECN pkts 0          out BECN pkts 0
  in DE pkts 536361          out DE pkts 0
  out bcast pkts 23237        out bcast bytes 1886266
  pvc create time 2d04h, last time pvc status changed 1d05h
! The CIR now is 384000, bc=384000, be=128000.
  cir 384000    bc 384000 be 128000        limit 4000    interval 125
  mincir 256000    byte increment 4000  Adaptive Shaping none
  pkts 659213    bytes 122881018 pkts delayed 20415    bytes delayed 19232012
  shaping inactive
  traffic shaping drops 0
  Serial4/0:0.98 dlci 98 is first come first serve default queuing

  Output queue 0/40, 29 drop, 20415 dequeued
```

Finally, repeat the ping test and compare the results, as shown in Example 18-36.

Example 18-36   *Measuring the Input and Output Rate on Ethernet0 and Serial1 Interfaces of the Remote User's*
Router, After Implementing the Map Class

```
1602-frame#show interfaces ethernet 0 | include 5 min
  5 minute input rate 8000 bits/sec, 15 packets/sec
  5 minute output rate 192000 bits/sec, 30 packets/sec
1602-frame#show interfaces serial 1 | include 5 min
  5 minute input rate 70000 bits/sec, 29 packets/sec
  5 minute output rate 6000 bits/sec, 16 packets/sec
```

The performance has improved significantly.

Flapping Routes

Flapping routes occur during the convergence process when there is instability in the
network. Different routing protocols pose different requirements for Frame Relay, but
sometimes even a lack of memory on the core router when the number of subscribed users
increases can cause this issue. One symptom of network instability is when trace commands
use different paths to reach the destination, indicating either a slow convergence process,
or a change in the topology and a related change in the routing table.

All the routers in the network must converge on the new topology when changes exist in
the network. Toward this end, they begin sharing routing information, and each update

nullifies the previous decision and triggers another update to the other routers. These routers, in turn, adjust their own routing tables and generate new updates, which cause flapping routes. The recommended way of dealing with this situation is far more complex than it appears, and requires additional troubleshooting. One possible solution is powering down the affected routers and slowly allowing convergence in your network, one router at a time. For more information, check www.cisco.com. Powering down production routers is not always feasible. Also, depending on the size and configuration of the routers, it might not work to do it router by router. In extremely large networks, with large routing tables, it might be necessary to shut down all interfaces, power cycle the box, and bring it back online one interface at a time.

Scenario 4: IP Multicast Issues in Frame Relay

Because multicast is a specific area of expertise, it is necessary that you first have a clear understanding of the terminology and underlying concepts of IP multicast. Internet Group Management Protocol (IGMP), Protocol Independent Multicast (PIM), dense mode, sparse mode, sparse-dense mode, rendezvous point (RP), Distance Vector Multicast Routing Protocol (DVMRP), Reverse Path Forwarding (RPF), shortest path tree (SPT) and their interactions are the key elements for troubleshooting multicast in Frame Relay. It is important to have a clear understanding of the group flags, and their role in the management of the process. The group flags include the following:

- **D**—Dense
- **S**—Sparse
- **B**—Bidir Group
- **C**—Connected
- **L**—Local
- **P**—Pruned
- **R**—RP-bit set
- **F**—Register flag
- **T**—SPT-bit set
- **J**—Join SPT
- **M**—MSDP created entry
- **X**—Proxy Join Timer Running
- **A**—Advertised through Multicast Source Discovery Protocol (MSDP)

Recall that IP multicast, unlike unicast and broadcast, provides a scheme where a host sends packets to a subset of all hosts (group transmission), which are known as group members. Instead of listing all the IP addresses of the group members, all members are identified by a single multicast group address. Multicast packets are delivered to a group using best-effort reliability. In this environment, some members send multicast streams and others only listen, but while any host (whether a member of the group or not) can send to the group, only the members of a group receive the multicast streams. Membership in a multicast group is dynamic; hosts can join and leave at any time. A host can be a member of more than one multicast group at a time. For further information about multicast see *Developing IP Multicast Networks*, Volume I, by Beau Williamson (Cisco Press, 2000).

Some of the most common symptoms of existing problems with multicast are documented here. The remote user that's configured under Serial3/2:0.83 interface of the core router does not receive multicast traffic. The multicast software (such as Cisco IP/TV for example), regardless of the configuration efforts, does not report any incoming multicasts, or there is voice but no video.

The first action is to check if the SPT exists. Always start the troubleshooting process with the upstream neighbor of the remote user's router, and check if there is multicast traffic by checking the PIM neighbors using the command in Example 18-37. In this case, the upstream neighbor is the core router.

Example 18-37   *Checking if There Is an Upstream PIM Neighbor Available*

```
7206-frame#show ip pim neighbor
PIM Neighbor Table
Neighbor          Interface             Uptime/Expires        Ver     DR
Address                                                               Prio/Mode
161.70.192.10     FastEthernet0/0       00:04:20/00:01:24 v2    1 / B S
161.70.192.24     FastEthernet0/0       00:04:24/00:01:21 v2    N /
161.70.192.15     FastEthernet0/0       00:04:25/00:01:18 v2    1 / B S
! One of the PIM neighbor's IP is 161.70.192.15.
! The IP is learned through the F0/0 interface.
! The uptime of the neighbor is  04:25 minutes and the timer
! expires after 01:18 minutes. The PIM is version 2.
161.70.192.11     FastEthernet0/0       00:04:33/00:01:41 v2    1 / B S
161.70.192.1      FastEthernet0/0       00:04:33/00:01:41 v2    N /
161.70.192.16     FastEthernet0/0       00:04:35/00:01:40 v2    1 / B S
161.70.192.12     FastEthernet0/0       00:04:37/00:01:37 v2    1 / B S
```

Checking the PIM neighbors is an important step to ensure that the upstream router or switch provides multicast for the core router. The availability of the downstream multicast can be checked by using the **show ip mroute** command, as shown in Example 18-38.

Example 18-38   *Checking the Availability of the Downstream Multicast*

```
7206-frame#show ip mroute
IP Multicast Routing Table
Flags: D - Dense, S - Sparse, B - Bidir Group, s - SSM Group, C - Connected,
       L - Local, P - Pruned, R - RP-bit set, F - Register flag,
       T - SPT-bit set, J - Join SPT, M - MSDP created entry,
       X - Proxy Join Timer Running, A - Advertised via MSDP, U - URD,
       I - Received Source Specific Host Report
```

Example 18-38 *Checking the Availability of the Downstream Multicast (Continued)*

```
Outgoing interface flags: H - Hardware switched
Timers: Uptime/Expires
Interface state: Interface, Next-Hop or VCD, State/Mode
<output omitted>
! The RP cannot be recognized - "RP 0.0.0.0"
(*, 239.255.255.253), 09:39:29/00:02:27, RP 0.0.0.0, flags: S
! Sparse mode indicated RPF neighbor 0.0.0.0
  Incoming interface: Null, RPF nbr 0.0.0.0
  Outgoing interface list:
    Serial3/2:0.83, Forward/Sparse-Dense, 09:39:29/00:02:27
<output omitted>
(*, 224.0.1.39), 3d13h/00:02:00, RP 0.0.0.0, flags: D
  Incoming interface: Null, RPF nbr 0.0.0.0
  Outgoing interface list:
    Serial4/1:0.37, Forward/Sparse-Dense, 3d13h/00:00:00
    Serial3/2:0.83, Forward/Sparse-Dense, 09:40:01/00:00:00
    Serial4/0:0.89, Forward/Sparse-Dense, 02:08:12/00:00:00
    FastEthernet0/0, Forward/Sparse-Dense, 00:03:55/00:00:00
    FastEthernet1/0, Forward/Sparse-Dense, 00:03:43/00:00:00
<output omitted>
```

In the second part of the output, the flag S-Sparse indicates sparse mode and shows RPF
neighbor 0.0.0.0. You can also see that the remote user connected through Serial3/2:0.83
issued a join request and, as a result, an outgoing entry is created in the multicast routing
table. A similar situation is listed in the third group, where more interfaces (members) have
joined, but the incoming interface still reports 0.0.0.0. It seems that the **ip pim sparse-
dense-mode** command is missing in the upstream interfaces, which in this case, is a
FastEthernet interface. After configuring the interfaces, take a look at the multicast routing
table, as shown in Example 18-39.

Example 18-39 *Now the FastEthernet 1/0 Interface Sees Its Upstream Neighbor*

```
7206-frame#show ip mroute
IP Multicast Routing Table
Flags: D - Dense, S - Sparse, B - Bidir Group, s - SSM Group, C - Connected,
       L - Local, P - Pruned, R - RP-bit set, F - Register flag,
       T - SPT-bit set, J - Join SPT, M - MSDP created entry,
       X - Proxy Join Timer Running, A - Advertised via MSDP, U - URD,
       I - Received Source Specific Host Report
Outgoing interface flags: H - Hardware switched
Timers: Uptime/Expires
Interface state: Interface, Next-Hop or VCD, State/Mode

<output omitted>
! The FastEthernet 1/0 interface sees its upstream neighbor
(*, 239.255.255.255), 4w3d/00:00:00, RP 10.68.10.13, flags: SJCL
  Incoming interface: FastEthernet1/0, RPF nbr 161.70.192.33
  Outgoing interface list:
```

continues

Example 18-39 *Now the FastEthernet 1/0 Interface Sees Its Upstream Neighbor (Continued)*

```
        FastEthernet0/0, Forward/Sparse-Dense, 00:25:50/00:00:00
        Serial3/2:0.83, Forward/Sparse-Dense, 00:25:50/00:00:00
        Serial4/0:0.89, Forward/Sparse-Dense, 00:25:51/00:00:00
        Serial4/1:0.37, Forward/Sparse-Dense, 00:25:51/00:00:00
<output omitted>
(192.168.165.15, 224.0.1.39), 00:00:51/00:02:08, flags: PTA
  Incoming interface: FastEthernet1/0, RPF nbr 161.70.192.33
  Outgoing interface list:
    FastEthernet0/0, Prune/Sparse-Dense, 00:00:51/00:02:08
    Serial3/2:0.83, Prune/Sparse-Dense, 00:00:55/00:02:07
    Serial4/0:0.89, Prune/Sparse-Dense, 00:00:55/00:02:07
    Serial4/1:0.37, Prune/Sparse-Dense, 00:00:55/00:02:06
<output omitted>
```

The incoming interface reports a valid IP source, and the join messages from downstream members (including Serial3/2:0.83) are registered as an outgoing interface.

Next, check the remote user's router on the other end. The remote user's service is operational, but is experiencing trouble with multicast. The primary focus is on the remote user's configuration. If it is correct, the next action to take is to launch Cisco IP/TV (or any other multicast software), and check if the user issues a join request to the group (see Example 18-40).

Example 18-40 *Check the IGMP Group Members*

```
1602-frame#show ip igmp group
IGMP Connected Group Membership
Group Address    Interface      Uptime     Expires    Last Reporter
239.193.0.10     Ethernet0      00:00:44   00:02:39   10.10.253.125
239.193.0.5      Ethernet0      00:00:45   00:02:35   10.10.253.125
224.0.1.40       Ethernet0      5w4d       never      10.10.253.121
1602-frame#
```

The result is positive, so it is time to check if the core router has registered the join request, and identifies the downstream router as a neighbor (see Example 18-41).

Example 18-41 *Check the IP PIM Neighbors of the Core Router*

```
7206-frame#show ip pim neighbor
PIM Neighbor Table
Neighbor         Interface         Uptime/Expires      Ver  DR
Address                                                     Prio/Mode
<output omitted>
161.70.192.47    FastEthernet1/0   16:33:17/00:01:20 v2   1 / B S
161.70.192.44    FastEthernet1/0   16:33:17/00:01:17 v2   1 / B S
161.70.192.43    FastEthernet1/0   16:33:17/00:01:16 v2   1 / B S
161.70.192.48    FastEthernet1/0   16:33:17/00:01:39 v2   1 / B S
! The core router sees the downstream neighbor Serial 3/2:0.83
```

Example 18-41   *Check the IP PIM Neighbors of the Core Router (Continued)*

```
10.10.253.121      Serial3/2:0.83          00:27:41/00:01:23 v2    N /
10.21.56.193       Serial4/0:0.89          16:33:15/00:01:43 v2    N /
161.70.194.209     Serial4/1:0.37          16:33:13/00:01:34 v2    N /
7206-frame#
```

The result is positive, so now check how the remote user's router sees the upstream
neighbors (see Example 18-42).

Example 18-42   *Check if the Remote User's Router Sees the Upstream Neighbor, RP and RPF*

```
1602-frame#show ip mroute
IP Multicast Routing Table
Flags: D - Dense, S - Sparse, B - Bidir Group, C - Connected, L - Local,
       P - Pruned, R - RP-bit set, F - Register flag, T - SPT-bit set,
       J - Join SPT, M - MSDP created entry, X - Proxy Join Timer Running
       A - Advertised via MSDP
Outgoing interface flags: H - Hardware switched
Timers: Uptime/Expires
Interface state: Interface, Next-Hop or VCD, State/Mode

(*, 239.193.0.10), 00:18:26/00:02:49, RP 10.68.10.13, flags: SJC
! There is a incoming interface, outgoing interface and a neighbor
  Incoming interface: Serial1.83, RPF nbr 161.68.122.1
  Outgoing interface list:
    Ethernet0, Forward/Sparse-Dense, 00:03:36/00:02:49

(*, 239.193.0.5), 00:18:27/00:02:41, RP 10.68.10.13, flags: SJC
  Incoming interface: Serial1.83, RPF nbr 161.68.122.1
  Outgoing interface list:
    Ethernet0, Forward/Sparse-Dense, 00:03:38/00:02:41
<output omitted>
1602-frame#
```

Next, recall the RPF procedure. For traffic flowing down the source tree, the RPF check
follows several steps. First, the router examines the source address of the arriving multicast
packet to determine whether the packet arrived through an interface that is on the reverse
path back to the source. If the check is successful, it forwards the packet; otherwise, it drops
it. In the case of the PIM protocol, it typically uses the existing unicast routing table to
determine the RPF check. The obvious next step is to compare the trace information
between the two trace tools, which are available in the remote user's router.

A unicast trace uses the existing routing table, and the report is similar to that in
Example 18-43.

The multicast trace report is different and it clearly reports the problem. The multicast
stream is expected from 161.68.88.1, but the next hop is 161.68.86.70 (see Example 18-44).

Example 18-43 *Using Unicast Trace for Multicast Troubleshooting*

```
1602-frame# trace 10.68.10.13
! This address (10.68.10.13) points to the Rendezvous Point

Type escape sequence to abort.
Tracing the route to sj-mbone-loopback0.cisco.com (10.68.10.13)

  1 7206-frame.cisco.com (161.68.88.1) 88 msec 84 msec 84 msec
  2 access-gw1.cisco.com (161.70.192.1) 84 msec 88 msec 84 msec
  3 bbi1-gw2.cisco.com (161.70.192.217) 84 msec 136 msec 128 msec
<output omitted>
-9 sj-mbone-loopback0.cisco.com (10.68.10.13)

1602-frame#
```

Example 18-44 *Using the Multicast Trace (**mtrace** Command) for Multicast Troubleshooting*

```
1602-frame#mtrace 10.68.10.13
Type escape sequence to abort.
Mtrace from 10.68.10.13 to 10.10.253.121 via RPF
From source (sj-mbone-loopback0.cisco.com) to destination (1602-frame.cisco.com)
Querying full reverse path...
  0  1602-frame.cisco.com (10.10.253.121)
 -1  1602-frame.cisco.com (10.10.253.121) PIM  [default]
! This !RPF! indication should not be missed.
 -2  161.68.86.70 PIM  !RPF!161.68.122.1 [default]
 -3  161.68.86.69 PIM  [default]
<output omitted>
 -9  sj-mbone-loopback0.cisco.com (10.68.10.13)
1602-frame#
```

The **mtrace** command output is reporting **-2 161.68.86.70 PIM !RPF!161.68.122.1 [default]**, which indicates some issues with the RPF. RPF is based on the routing table information. Check the routing configuration again. The routing section is configured as shown in Example 18-45.

Example 18-45 *The Configuration of the Static Route in the Remote User's Router*

```
1602-frame#show running-config
<output omitted>
ip classless
ip route 0.0.0.0 0.0.0.0 161.68.122.1
ip route 10.10.253.120 255.255.255.248 Ethernet0
<output omitted>
```

The **mtrace** command is based on the routing statement of the router that points to IP address 161.68.122.1, which is not on the reverse path, and consequently, the packets are discarded.

Finally, replace the routing statement and bound the next hop address in the static route with the outgoing interface, rather than with the IP address of the next hop. Another approach is to replace 161.68.122.1 with 161.68.88.1. After the configuration change, check the result with #**show ip mroute**, as shown in Example 18-46.

Example 18-46   *Output from the* **show ip mroute** *Command Shows a New Neighbor*

```
1602-frame#show ip mroute
IP Multicast Routing Table
Flags: D - Dense, S - Sparse, B - Bidir Group, C - Connected, L - Local,
       P - Pruned, R - RP-bit set, F - Register flag, T - SPT-bit set,
       J - Join SPT, M - MSDP created entry, X - Proxy Join Timer Running
       A - Advertised via MSDP
Outgoing interface flags: H - Hardware switched
Timers: Uptime/Expires
Interface state: Interface, Next-Hop or VCD, State/Mode

(*, 239.193.0.10), 00:30:56/00:02:14, RP 10.68.10.13, flags: SJC
  Incoming interface: Serial1.83, RPF nbr 171.68.88.1
  Outgoing interface list:
    Ethernet0, Forward/Sparse-Dense, 00:16:06/00:02:14

(*, 239.193.0.5), 00:30:57/00:02:59, RP 10.68.10.13, flags: SJC
  Incoming interface: Serial1.83, RPF nbr 171.68.88.1
  Outgoing interface list:
    Ethernet0, Forward/Sparse-Dense, 00:16:07/00:02:18
<output omitted>
```

Consequently, the output of the **mtrace** command is as shown in Example 18-47.

Example 18-47   *Output from the* **mtrace** *Command*

```
1602-frame#mtrace 10.68.10.13

Type escape sequence to abort.
Mtrace from 10.68.10.13 to 10.10.253.121 via RPF
From source (sj-mbone-loopback0.cisco.com) to destination (1602-frame.cisco.com)
Querying full reverse path...
 0  1602-frame.cisco.com (10.10.253.121)
-1  1602-frame.cisco.com (10.10.253.121) PIM  [default]
! The next line shows that the upstream neighbor has changed.
-2  7206-frame-1.cisco.com (171.68.88.1) PIM  [default]
-3  161.70.192.33 PIM  [default]
-4  161.70.192.221 PIM  [10.68.10.13/32]
<output omitted>
-10 sj-mbone-loopback0.cisco.com (10.68.10.13)
```

NOTE   Another recommended command is 1602-frame#**mstat 10.10.253.121 10.68.10.13**.

The result after the configuration changes confirms that the multicast feature is on and the multicast applications are passing IP traffic.

The example provided is one of the possible scenarios, and it is designed to demonstrate the methodology for troubleshooting IP multicast in Frame Relay rather than including all possible issues and their solutions.

Scenario 5: Frame Relay Host Migration

During the ebb and flow of business cycles and reorganizations, many consolidations in plant and office locations can take place. These include office moves and closures, which require existing remote access infrastructures to be relocated. In a small to medium-sized remote access Frame Relay environment, it occasionally might become necessary to rehome your remote users to a new location. The following scenario describes how to manage such a move and the required steps to implement a seamless transition between two Frame Relay hosts in different locations.

The example here works on the premise that an office located in Austin, TX, will be closed in a matter of months and relocated to Phoenix, AZ. Fourty remote access circuits are currently configured on a host in the Austin office. These circuits must be remapped to a host in Phoenix.

Working with Your Vendor

One of the first steps is to speak to your vendor to provision a host circuit in the new location. In this case, a Frame Relay T1 is ordered for Phoenix and it is also necessary to map the endpoints onto this host. The end-user locations are most likely geographically dispersed. Service management is simplified if there is one vendor that provisions and installs the endpoint and host circuits because they most likely cross LEC boundaries.

If you anticipate the time frame necessary for the vendor to deliver the service, you can request that the DLCIs be provisioned on top of existing circuits. This means that although you might currently have an existing DLCI mapped onto the end-user circuit, the vendor has the means of configuring another DLCI and mapping it back to Phoenix. This allows you to carry several point-to-point circuits on one Frame Relay line.

You must provide the vendor with new DLCI numbers for the remote users that differ from the previous ones. Make sure that they are sequential and coincide with the way you want to see the mappings. For example, you might want to choose the DLCI range of 100–139. This provides a simplified migration when building the new host.

At this point, the vendor must perform a series of tasks to migrate the host from Austin to Phoenix. Initially, they must install the host circuit in Phoenix. Secondly, they must build and provision the new mappings for the remote users, which creates another virtual circuit (VC) at the remote end that points back to the Phoenix host while keeping the existing maps back to Austin. After this is completed, you are ready to perform the tasks required to migrate.

Preparing the Host

Supposing that the vendor performed the required tasks, you are now ready to begin the process of migration. In this example, a 3640 host is used with 1602s at the remote user's premise. Initially, you must configure and set up the new host circuit in Phoenix. Essentially, it should look like the existing installation in Austin, unless features and functionality have been added or removed. For the purposes of this example, start by configuring the T1 controller (see Example 18-48).

Example 18-48 *Configuration Commands that Provide Basic Signaling Services for the Frame Relay Host*

```
3640-frame-phoenix#configure terminal
3640-frame-phoenix(config)# controller T1 1/0
3640-fram(config-controller)# description Frame Relay T1-Phoenix, AZ,
    Vendor M Circuit # 83XXXXXXXX
3640-fram(config-controller)# framing esf
3640-fram(config-controller)# fdl ansi
3640-fram(config-controller)# linecode b8zs
3640-fram(config-controller)# channel-group 0 timeslots 1-24 speed 64
```

The vendor provides a circuit that runs coding schemes such as Extended Superframe (ESF) framing and bipolar 8-zero substitution (B8ZS) linecoding.

NOTE   It is a recommended practice to use a description of the circuit in the configuration, in case any issues exist with the line.

Next, the corresponding serial interface must be configured to split the host circuit into its corresponding subinterfaces and DLCIs. Traditional Frame Relay lines look like what is shown in Example 18-49.

Example 18-49 *These Configuration Commands Allow the Serial Interface to Interact with the Controller Previously Configured*

```
3640-frame-phoenix#config terminal
3640-frame-phoenix(config)#interface Serial1/0:0
3640-frame-phoenix(config-if)# description T1 Frame Relay Phoenix,
    AZ: Vendor M / Circuit #: 83XXXXXXXX
3640-frame-phoenix(config-if)# no ip address
3640-frame-phoenix(config-if)# encapsulation frame-relay IETF
3640-frame-phoenix(config-if)# ip mroute-cache
3640-frame-phoenix(config-if)# frame-relay lmi-type ansi
```

An IP address is not used for the host circuit. Frame Relay encapsulation is ANSI LMI. After it is configured, you can check to see if you have the appropriate signaling by performing a **show interfaces** command (see Example 18-50).

Example 18-50 *Output from the* **show interfaces** *Command Should Show the Status of the Serial Interface, the Type of Frame Relay Encapsulation and the Type of LMI*

```
3640-frame-phoenix#show interfaces Serial1/0:0
Serial1/0:0 is up, line protocol is up
  Hardware is DSX1
  Description: T1 Frame Relay Phoenix, AZ: Vendor M / Circuit #: 83XXXXXXXX
  MTU 1500 bytes, BW 1536 Kbit, DLY 20000 usec,
     reliability 255/255, txload 2/255, rxload 1/255
  Encapsulation FRAME-RELAY IETF, loopback not set
  Keepalive set (10 sec)
  LMI enq sent  103431, LMI stat recvd 103431, LMI upd recvd 0, DTE LMI up
  LMI enq recvd 0, LMI stat sent  0, LMI upd sent  0
  LMI DLCI 0  LMI type is ANSI Annex D  frame relay DTE
  Broadcast queue 0/64, broadcasts sent/dropped 2304560/0, interface broadcasts
2011528
  <output omitted>
3640-frame-phoenix#
```

You must also begin the task of configuring the subinterfaces that are mapped to this new host. Enter the commands in Example 18-51, which specify the appropriate subinterfaces and their corresponding DLCIs. The numbering scheme in this example allows the subinterface to correspond to the DLCI of the PVC.

Example 18-51 *These Commands Allow Configuration of the Subinterface. It Is a Good Idea to Create These Subinterfaces from a Text File Template*

```
interface Serial1/0:0.100 point-to-point
 description fr 56k frame to johnsmith
 ip unnumbered loopback1
 frame-relay interface-dlci 100
!
interface Serial1/0:0.101 point-to-point
 description 56k frame to nshumpar
 ip unnumbered loopback1
 frame-relay interface-dlci 101
!
interface Serial1/0:0.102 point-to-point
 description 128k frame to okaabipo
 ip unnumbered loopback1
 frame-relay interface-dlci 102
!
interface Serial1/0:0.103 point-to-point
 description 56k frame to djohnson
 ip unnumbered loopback1
 frame-relay interface-dlci 103
```

Further in this example, Loopback1 provides addressing for the subinterfaces (see Example 18-52).

Example 18-52 *Interface Loopback1 Provides a Routing Pointer for the Endpoints and Conserves Address Space*

```
3640-frame-phoenix#config terminal
3640-frame-phoenix(config)# interface Loopback1
3640-frame-phoenix(config-if)# description Vendor M Frame Relay address placeholder
3640-frame-phoenix(config-if) ip address 10.10.0.1 255.255.255.252
```

This loopback interface allows communication with the rest of the network as it forwards traffic to the connected serial and Ethernet interfaces.

Routing Options

Based on the assumption that no readdressing is going to be performed and that the new environment will mirror the old, two approaches can be taken with respect to routing.

Method 1: Moving Routes with Ethernet Interface in Shutdown State

This method requires the Ethernet interface to be administratively shutdown. A console must be set up on the Phoenix router to bypass the Ethernet interface, which should be shut down to avoid any adverse routing consequences that might result from having both routes in different locations.

After all the subinterfaces are created and the Ethernet interface is administratively shut down, it is a good idea to copy and paste the IP routes from one router to another. When the transition is complete, the Ethernet interface can be turned up to allow routes to be forwarded if necessary.

Method 2: Host by Host Migration

If a previous method creates too much downtime, it is also possible to enter the routes individually as they are migrated. They must also be removed from the router in Austin. This method brings the users up as soon as the route statement is placed in the Phoenix router.

The decision on which method to use is subjective because it depends on the window of time necessary to migrate the remote users. If the first method is used, the larger the number of endpoints, the longer the downtime for users as the migration proceeds.

After the subinterfaces are ready, the task of migrating the remote users can begin.

Endpoint Migration

The host is now ready and work can begin on migrating the endpoints to this new circuit. The endpoint serial configuration for a 56-k frame line is similar to Example 18-53.

Example 18-53 *These Are the Common Command Entries to Configure Endpoint Routers*

```
1602-frame#config terminal
1602-frame(config)# interface Serial0
1602-frame(config-if)# no ip address
1602-frame(config-if)# encapsulation frame-relay IETF
1602-frame(config-if)# service-module 56k clock source line
1602-frame(config-if)# service-module 56k network-type dds
1602-frame(config-if)# frame-relay lmi-type ansi
!
```

The subinterface on 1602 can be configured with an unnumbered interface to conserve IP addresses (see Example 18-54).

Example 18-54 *Subinterface Configuration Commands for Endpoint Routers*

```
1602-frame#config terminal
1602-frame(config)# interface Serial0.1 point-to-point
1602-frame(config-if)# ip unnumbered Ethernet0
1602-frame(config-if)# frame-relay interface-dlci 16
```

To configure a new subinterface, you must use the same commands with a different DLCI. Following the numbering guidelines given to the vendor, the task of configuring new subinterfaces can begin. To configure a new subinterface for the DLCI that is mapped to the host in Phoenix, you can enter the commands in Example 18-55. End with CNTL/Z.

Example 18-55 *New Configuration Commands for the Endpoint Router*

```
1602-frame# configure terminal
1602-frame(config)#interface  serial0.100
1602-frame(config-if)# ip unnumbered  Loopback 1
1602-frame(config-if)# frame-relay interface-dlci 100
1602-frame(config-if)#  end
1602-frame#
```

Perform a **show interfaces** command to make sure that the line is operational and has been turned up by the vendor (see Example 18-56).

After it is verified that the PVC is up, the routing should be changed to the new line. For example, assuming static routes, the routing accounts for a default route to the host network, and one back to the remote network. Example 18-57 shows the configuration for the existing network.

Example 18-56 *Verifying Proper Configuration and PVC Establishment*

```
1602-frame# show interfaces serial0.100
Serial0.100 is up, line protocol is up
  Hardware is QUICC Serial (with onboard CSU/DSU)
  Interface is unnumbered.  Using address of Ethernet0 (10.84.5.105)
  MTU 1500 bytes, BW 56 Kbit, DLY 20000 usec,
  reliability 255/255, txload 1/255, rxload 1/255
  Encapsulation FRAME-RELAY
1602-frame#
```

Example 18-57 *Endpoint and Host Routing Configuration*

```
1602-frame#configure terminal
1602-frame(config)# ip route 0.0.0.0 0.0.0.0 Serial 0.1
1602-frame(config)# ip route 10.10.10.0 255.255.255.248 Ethernet0
```

To migrate this service over the new PVC, a simple routing command must be entered to the core router configuration to complete the migration of this PVC:

```
3640-frame-phoenix(config)#ip route 10.10.10.0 255.255.255.248 Serial 0.100
```

By entering this command, you can now route data over the new PVC rather than the old. If the route statements already exist in the Phoenix host, this service is now operational. The default routes for the old host are replaced in favor of routes to the new host. Additionally, routes from the Austin router must be removed prior to reenabling the interfaces. Now, the Austin router is ready to be decommissioned.

If Method 1 is used to migrate, after all the remote users are moved over, the routes can be removed from the Austin router, and the Ethernet interface for Phoenix can be turned up to advertise the new routes in a different location.

As long as the routes are placed in the new host, the endpoint is reachable from the new location.

Summary

The focus of the scenarios in this chapter is troubleshooting Frame Relay connections. The scenarios focused on end-user issues, particularly the following:

- New install issues
- Mismatch DLCI settings
- Performance issues
- Flapping lines
- Traffic shaping issues

For traffic shaping issues and IP Multicast issues in Frame Relay, you can see that there are also advantages to troubleshooting in enterprise portions of the connection. You need to understand both sides of the connection. The last scenario covers Frame Relay host migration. It gives a clear example for engineers who want to rehost the service from one location to another, where because of the permanent nature of PVCs, some troubleshooting situations might arise.

PART V

VPN

Chapter 19   VPN Technology Background

Chapter 20   Remote Access VPN Design and Configuration Solutions

Chapter 21   Remote Access VPN Troubleshooting

Chapter 22   Remote Access VPN Troubleshooting Scenarios

Appendix A   Answers to Review Questions

VPN Technology Background

A Virtual Private Network (VPN) involves transmitting private data over public networks. It is not a new term for data communications. The term VPN initially came from the specific carrier's design, where a part of the carrier's network (referred to as a cloud) is separated from other parts and is leased by an enterprise for purposes of voice, data, and video communications (see Chapter 3, "The Cloud," for more information). Today, VPN is more like a wire in the cloud type of connection, which is explained in this chapter.

Understanding VPN and its complexities is more challenging than for most other technologies on the market because of the many complex mathematical algorithms, and the wide range and types of both deployed and emerging solutions.

In this chapter, you learn about service provider-based VPNs and enterprise VPNs, and their classifications and categories. The focus of this book is on remote access solutions, so information on service provider VPNs is provided solely for the purpose of discussion.

The main topics of the chapter are related to the overview and classification of the existing industry VPN solutions; however, the main focus is on IP Security (IPSec). The chapter presents a concise description of the following topics:

- Service provider VPNs
- Enterprise VPNs
- VPNs on the data link layer and on the network layer of Open System Interconnection (OSI)
- IPSec and security associations
- IPSec modes and protocols
- Key exchange, hashing, and encryption in IPSec

Service Provider, Dedicated, and Access VPNs

In the old world, service providers emphasized lower-layer transport services, such as leased lines and Frame Relay. In the new world, service providers work with business customers to meet their networking requirements through the use of VPNs. The service provider VPNs, otherwise called provider dependant VPNs, are one of the key technologies that service providers will use to stay competitive in the years ahead. VPNs deliver enterprise-scale connectivity that is deployed on a shared infrastructure with the same policies that are deployed in a private network. A VPN can be built on the Internet or on a service provider's IP, Frame Relay, or Asynchronous Transfer Mode (ATM) infrastructure.

Today, this solution is known as a dedicated VPN. It is related to legacy VPNs, and is built on virtual leased lines.

Another service offering is called Remote Access to Multiprotocol Label Switching Virtual Private Network (RA to MPLS VPN), [1] which enables remote users to connect to the corporate network. This service handles remote access connectivity for mobile users, telecommuters, and small offices through dial, ISDN, DSL, cable, and wireless technologies. This solution is also known as an access VPN. It is shown in Figure 19-1.

Figure 19-1   *The Service Provider Virtual Private Network (VPN)*

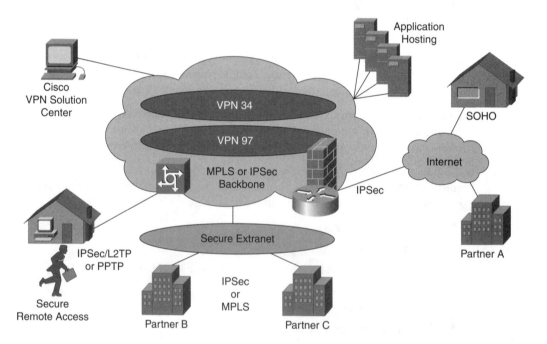

From the standpoint of the service provider, the MPLS is typically a full or partial mesh or hub and spoke topology, depending on how the customer wants to connect their sites. From the standpoint of the potential user, MPLS is typically offered by a service provider as a site-to-site VPN service. The provider builds a private IP-based network, and offers multiple customers IP connectivity between their sites across this network. The technology allows individual customers to view the MPLS service as if they had a private IP network connecting their sites. This scenario offers customers the same advantages of a Layer 2 private network, such as Frame Relay or ATM, but with the scalability and the manage-ability of a Layer 3 network. Also, because MPLS runs across a private IP-based network rather than the Internet, the service provider can provide differentiated levels of service (quality of service [QoS]) and service-level agreements (SLAs) to its customers. However, because MPLS is based on a service provider's private network, the reach of the service is limited to locations where the provider operates.

The RA to MPLS VPN solution provides flexible options to the existing MPLS VPN. Currently, a service provider can create a scalable and efficient VPN across the core of its network for each customer with MPLS VPN through dialup, DSL, and Data-over-Cable Service Interface Specifications (DOCSIS).

NOTE   In January 2002, Cisco received notification that its uBR7246VXR Universal Broadband Router passed CableLabs qualification for DOCSIS 1.1. Based on this qualification, the Cisco uBR7246VXR is the first Layer-3 routed cable modem termination system (CMTS) to receive DOCSIS 1.1 qualification.

With the introduction of RA to their MPLS VPN service, the service provider can now integrate various additional access methods into their VPN services. This permits the service provider to offer an extended bundle of end-to-end VPN service to its Internet service provider (ISP) or enterprise customers. Major new directions are new media, such as wireless and satellite, and multiprotocol VPNs. The newly announced Cisco Any Transport Over MPLS (AToM)[2] integrates Layer 2 tunneling and MPLS networks. By using IP-based MPLS with IPSec/Layer 2 Tunnel Protocol (L2TP) solutions, providers can create virtual leased lines that improve scalability, and implement QoS features that are typical for MPLS.

Enterprise VPNs Overview

Provider-independent or enterprise VPNs provide connectivity that is deployed on a shared (public) infrastructure with the same policies as a private network, where users expect the same or similar performance, applications, and connectivity.

Cisco classifies existing solutions into three major VPN types (see Figure 19-2):

- Cisco remote access VPN solutions
- Cisco site-to-site VPN solutions
- Cisco extranet VPN solutions

Figure 19-2 *Major Cisco VPN Types*

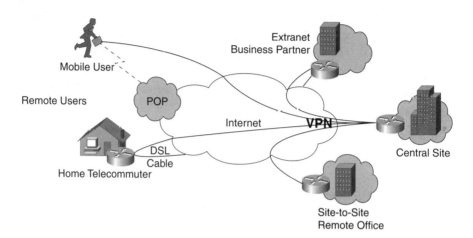

Remote access and site-to-site VPN solutions provide an alterna-tive to building a carrier-based private network for enterprise communication. Companies can cost-effectively extend the corporate network to locations that might not have been justified before because they operate across a shared infrastructure rather than a private network. For example, in many domestic applications and most international applications, VPNs provide significant cost savings over private wide-area network (WAN) connections. Also, rather than having multiple independent circuits terminating at the corporate headend, VPNs allow all traffic to be aggregated into a single connection. This scenario usually results in increased bandwidth and cost savings at the headend, and further savings is achieved from not having to maintain a private network.

VPNs provide the opportunity for additional cost reduction both within and external to the company. The Internet, as a super-medium, allows the enterprise to change the way its networks operate in the following key directions:

- For intranets, most companies, especially large enterprises, maintain costly WANs. It remains to be seen if the constant cost reductions of dedicated leased lines can compete with the VPN's potential cost savings.

- For extranets, the recent solution for large businesses and their business partners require dedicated lines, or slow legacy connections. VPN over the Internet should be seriously considered as an alternative.

- For remote access, rather than using slow dialup links, or more costly services, such as ISDN and Frame Relay, full-time and part-time telecommuters can take advantage of VPN technology through the following:

  — Higher-speed access from DSL and cable services offered by local providers

> — ISDN, dial, Frame Relay, or FT1 as a local service that is offered by the local exchange carrier (LEC) with flat rate pricing

Mobile users can also take advantage of higher-speed Ethernet connections found in many hotels, airports, and convention centers for access to the enterprise network through the Internet and VPN. The cost savings alone, from not having to pay long-distance telephone charges, might justify the use of VPNs in such cases. Another benefit of VPN is that companies can take advantage of the technology to enable new applications and business processes, such as e-commerce, supply chain management, and virtual office concepts.

The Internet, as a supermedia, is not an all-purpose remedy or alternative. Some key components, such as security, QoS, reliability, and manageability are some of the factors currently limiting it from becoming a super-alternative.

Enterprise VPN Categories

Every new technology requires some type of classification to distinguish it from a wide variety of solutions, proposals, and views. Cisco classifies the existing variety of VPN solutions into two main categories:

- Functional, which emphasizes the particular design consideration of the VPN

- Technological, which defines VPN solutions based on the OSI-layered structure and protocol suites for every layer

Functional VPN Categories

The three Cisco enterprise functional groups are remote access VPN, site-to-site VPN, and firewall-based VPN solutions. Each is discussed in the following sections.

NOTE   Each VPN classification has distinguishing features. Other valid classifications of VPNs are remote access VPNs, intranet VPNs, and extranet VPNs. As noted in the article, "SAFEguard for Smaller Networks" (Cisco *Packet*, Q1, 2002), Cisco SAFE categories include 800 series access routers, 1700 series modular routers, PIX firewalls, 3002 VPN Hardware Clients, the VPN Software Client, and the Intrusion Detection System (IDS).

Remote Access VPNs

Remote access VPNs refer to implementations for individual remote users that are running the VPN client software to access the corporate intranet through a gateway, or VPN concentrator, which is also referred to as a server. For this reason, this solution is often called a client/server solution, where telecommuters or mobile users can use traditional methods to start tunnels back to the corporation. These methods include dialup connections to a local service provider or the use of any high-speed or broadband service.

The Cisco last-mile solution, called Ethernet to the First Mile (EFM) (see Cisco's 575 LRE customer premises equipment (CPE) and Cisco last-mile solutions in Chapter 3), when it becomes available, might change the way remote access VPNs are designed.

Another relatively recent development in remote access VPNs is the wireless remote access VPN (see Cisco's Aironet product series), where a mobile worker accesses the corporate network through a wireless connection on a personal digital assistant (PDA). In this design, the wireless connection needs to connect to a wireless termination point and then to the corporate wired network at the remote location. In all cases, the client software on the PC or PDA provides a secure connection, referred to as a tunnel, back to the corporate network. An important part of this solution is the design of the initial authentication, which is designed to ensure a request to establish a tunnel from a trusted source. Usually, this initial phase relies on the same authentication security policies and remote access controls to access corporate resources, including procedures, techniques, and servers (such as Remote Authentication Dial-In User Service [RADIUS], Terminal Access Controller Access Control System Plus [TACACS+], and so on).

Site-to-Site or LAN-to-LAN VPN

Site-to-site or LAN-to-LAN VPN refers to implementations where the network of one location is connected to the network of another location through VPN. In this situation, the initial authentication process for trusted users is between devices on the network, where an initial VPN connection is established between them. These devices then act as gateways, securely passing traffic destined for the other site. Routers or firewalls with VPN capability, and dedicated VPN concentrators all provide this functionality.

LAN-to-LAN VPNs can be considered as intranet or extranet VPNs, from the policy management point of view. If they are under one authority, it can be considered an intranet VPN; otherwise, they are considered as an extranet. Access between sites should be tightly controlled by both entities at their respective sites. The site-to-site solution is not a remote access solution, but was added here for completeness.

The distinction between remote access VPNs and LAN-to-LAN VPNs is rather symbolic, and it is provided solely for the purposes of further discussion. One example is the new hardware-based VPN devices (see the Cisco 3002, described later), where this classification can be interpreted both ways because the hardware-based client can appear as if a single device is accessing the network, although there might be a network with several devices behind the VPN device. Another example includes the extension-mode of the EzVPN solution, by using 806 and 17xx routers.

Firewall-Based VPNs

Firewall-based VPNs are solutions where either the enterprise's security organization owns both the firewall and VPN implementation, or service providers offer enhanced firewall systems to support VPN services. In general, they are based on the Cisco PIX series firewalls, including the PIX 506 for small office, home office (SOHO) environments, the PIX 515 for small- to medium-sized businesses, and the PIX 525 and 535 for enterprise and service provider implementations.

Cisco provides several remote access solutions for VPN clients. These solutions meet different enterprise requirements and are designed for each of the covered functional groups. These solutions include the following:

- **Concentrator-based VPN clients**—Cisco VPN Client 3.x.x and the VPN 3002 software and hardware client

- **Cisco IOS(router)-based VPN solutions**—Cisco 806 and 17xx end-user routers, and EzVPN

- **Cisco PIX firewall-based solutions**—Cisco PIX 501

Another view of Cisco VPN solutions from a software-hardware point of view is as follows (for more details on what operating systems are supported, see www.cisco.com):

- Software clients:
  - VPN client for Microsoft
  - VPN client for Solaris
  - VPN client for Linux
  - VPN client for wireless devices

- Hardware clients:
  - Easy VPN
  - VPN 3002
  - 806 Router
  - PIX 501

The introduction of the PIX 501 VPN solution expands the available choices for the remote user. The hardware options are further defined in Table 19-1. The full list of available VPN 3000 concentrator series products can be found under www.cisco.com/univercd/cc/td/doc/pcat/3000.htm#xtoc1d7.

Table 19-1   *Cisco Enterprise VPN Options*

VPN Group	Large Enterprise	Medium Enterprise	Small Enterprise Branch	SOHO
Cisco remote access VPN 3000	VPN 3060 VPN 3080 Concentrators	VPN 3030 Concentrators	VPN 3015 VPN 3005 Concentrators	3002 Hardware Client VPN Software Client
Site-to-site	7200	7100	3600	800
IOS router	7100	3600	2600	900
			1700	
Firewall-based VPN	PIX 535	PIX 525	PIX 515	PIX 501
PIX firewall	PIX 525	PIX 515	PIX 506	

NOTE   Recently, Cisco announced a comparative approach for classifying remote access VPNs that is based on key element ratings. The key elements are resiliency, scalability, client OS support, management, identity, and a consolidated solution. This classification is more suitable for practical purposes and better reflects the functional category.

Technology Category

From a technology perspective, VPN is not running special types of electrons over the shared switch or network, but it is running packets over networks, which are encrypted and authenticated in a way that distinguishes them from other packets. Often, this is associated with a tunnel in the network.

Earlier solutions included the physical layer division of the circuits in the carrier's switches and main distribution frames (MDFs), which prevents unauthorized access between dedicated lines for separate enterprises, and creates a VPN.

Later solutions included implementing the Secure Socket Layer (SSL) protocol for web browsers and other applications, which enables every application to be protected and provides application confidentiality. This is an encryption VPN solution that resides on the application layer of the Transmission Control Protocol/Internet Protocol (TCP/IP) suite. But in the OSI seven-layer model, the presentation layer is responsible for translation, encryption/decryption, authentication, and compression. To prevent confusion, it is most appropriate to refer to this solution as an upper-layer encryption (see Figure 19-3).

Figure 19-3   *The Layered Models and Encryption*

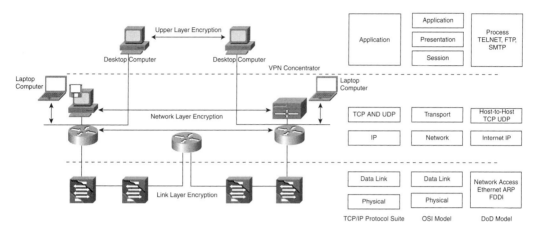

For years, military implementations have used hardware-based link-layer encryption that addresses authentication concerns differently. Every termination of a communication link is protected with end devices. Although it ensures security protection, this solution is difficult to manage and almost impossible to implement in a large-scale public network.

Data Link Layer VPNs

In the public network environment, data-link encryption can be implemented in devices within the private network; however, users must encrypt the traffic before it enters the router or switch. Obviously in this scenario, the traffic must be either bridged or encrypted/decrypted at every hop because the second layer does not provide a unique IP-type addressing scheme. As a result, the data (frames) needs to be encrypted/decrypted several times, which results in increased latency and concerns about trusted providers. ATM and Frame Relay networks are sometimes referred to as VPN networks because they use a shared infrastructure to provide private network services to a large number of users; however, they are viewed more as private network implementations.

Data-link VPN technologies are designed to run on the second layer of the OSI model and include the following:

- Point-to-Point Tunneling Protocol (PPTP) and generic routing encapsulation (GRE)
- L2TP

PPTP and GRE

PPTP is defined by the Internet Engineering Task Force (IETF) in RFC 2637.[3] It is designed by Microsoft to enable a low-cost, private connection to a corporate network through the public Internet. The PPTP session can provide a secure connection through the Internet to the corporate network when dialing a local ISP's phone number, or when using an ISDN device. The local call connects into a hardware device (front-end processor [FEP]), which in turn connects to a Windows NT Server through a WAN connection. The FEP connects by transmitting Point-to-Point Protocol (PPP) packets from the end user, and tunneling them through the WAN.

Because PPTP supports multiple protocols (IP, Internetwork Packet Exchange [IPX], and Network Basic Input/Output System Extended User Interface [NetBEUI]), it can access a wide variety of existing LAN infrastructures. This architectural description includes a typical client/server architecture, where the client is the remote user's PC, running PPTP. On the server side, there is a dial-in router, VPN concentrator, or actual application server. Both sides can start a tunnel. When the remote user starts the tunnel, it is called voluntary mode. When the tunnel is started by the network access server (NAS), it is often referred to as compulsory mode. A NAS can start a tunnel even if the remote user is not running PPTP, which raises security concerns and it is not recommended.

The PPTP encapsulates PPP frames into IP datagrams for transmission over an IP-based network, such as the Internet or a private intranet. PPTP, which is derived from the PPP protocol, inherits the encryption, compression, or both from the PPP protocol. PPTP requires the availability of an IP internetwork between a PPTP client (a VPN client using the PPTP tunneling protocol) and a PPTP server (a VPN server using the PPTP tunneling protocol). The PPTP client might already be attached to an IP internetwork that can reach the PPTP server, or the client might dial into a NAS to establish IP connectivity, as in the case of dialup Internet users.

PPTP uses a TCP connection (known as the PPTP control connection) to create, maintain, and terminate the tunnel. PPTP also uses a modified version of GRE to encapsulate the PPP frames as tunneled data. The payloads of the encapsulated PPP frames can be encrypted, or compressed, or both.

GRE is defined in RFCs 1701 and 1702, and is simply a mechanism for performing encapsulation of an arbitrary network layer protocol over another arbitrary network layer protocol. It was designed to provide a simple, lightweight, general-purpose mechanism for encapsulating data sent over IP networks. Therefore, PPTP can transport various Layer 3 protocols, such as IP, IPX, and NetBEUI.

PPTP assumes the availability of an IP internetwork between a PPTP client and a PPTP server. The client might already be attached to an IP internetwork that can reach the server, or the PPTP client might dial into a NAS to establish IP connectivity, as in the case of dialup Internet users.

Authentication that occurs during the creation of a PPTP-based VPN connection uses the same authentication mechanisms as PPP connections, such as Password Authentication Protocol (PAP) and Challenge Handshake Authentication Protocol (CHAP), which are not considered particularly strong. PAP sends passwords across the link in clear text and is not secure. CHAP is considered more secure than PAP because CHAP issues an encrypted challenge to which the other side must respond to authenticate.

An enhanced version of CHAP, called MS-CHAP, was created by Microsoft to use information within NT domains for security. Another option for authentication is IETF's PPP—Extensible Authentication Protocol (EAP) (refer to RFC 2284). Microsoft has also incorporated a protocol called Microsoft Point-to-Point Encryption (MPPE)[4] to encrypt the traffic across a PPTP link. MPPE is based on the Rovest, Shamir, and Adelman (RSA) RC4 encryption algorithm and provides only link encryption, not end-to-end encryption. End-to-end encryption is data encryption between the client application and the server that is hosting the resource or service accessed by the client application. If end-to-end encryption is required, IPSec can encrypt IP traffic from end-to-end after the PPTP tunnel is established.

For Windows 2000, either EAP-Transport Level Security (EAP-TLS) or MS-CHAP must be used for PPP payloads to be encrypted using MPPE.

PPTP Control Connection and Tunnel Maintenance   The PPTP control connection is between the IP address of the PPTP client that is using a dynamically allocated TCP port, and the IP address of the PPTP server that is using the reserved TCP port 1723. The PPTP control packet (called a connection packet) carries the PPTP call control and management messages that maintain the PPTP tunnel (see Figure 19-4).

Figure 19-4   *PPTP Control Connection Packet Format*

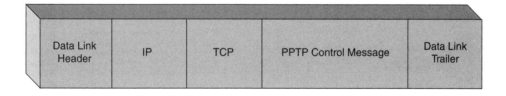

After the initial negotiation, two parties exchange a series of messages that include 12 standard call and connection management messages. For more information about the structure of PPTP control connection messages, see RFC 2637.

PPTP Data Tunneling   PPTP data tunneling is performed through multiple levels of encapsulation. The structure is shown in Figure 19-5. The initial PPP payload is encrypted and encapsulated with a PPP header to create a PPP frame. The PPP frame is then encapsulated with a modified GRE header. GRE uses client protocol ID number 47.

Figure 19-5 *PPTP Data Tunneling*

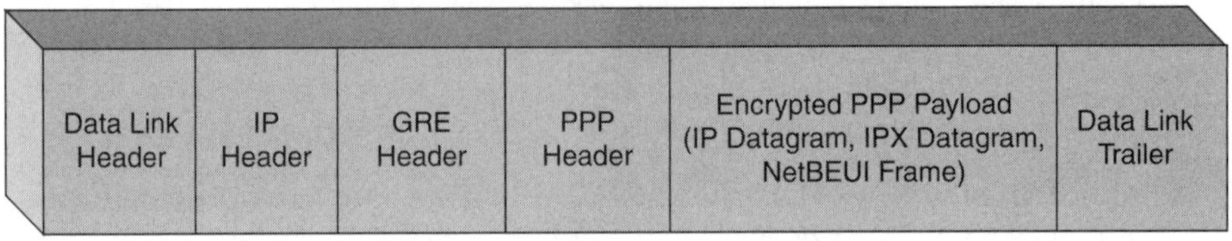

Data Link Header
IP Header
GRE Header
PPP Header
Encrypted PPP Payload (IP Datagram, IPX Datagram, NetBEUI Frame)
Data Link Trailer

NOTE For troubleshooting purposes, it is important to remember that PPTP uses the reserved TCP port 1723. The PPTP control connection carries PPTP call control and management messages that maintain the PPTP tunnel. The GRE protocol ID is 47.

L2TP

L2TP is addressed in IETF's RFC 2661 standard. It combines the best features of two existing tunneling protocols: Cisco's Layer 2 Forwarding (L2F) and Microsoft's PPTP.[5] L2TP is an extension of PPP and is an important component for VPNs. L2TP is considered more scalable than PPTP and it also operates in client-server mode. Similar to PPTP, the L2TP tunnel can be started from the remote PC back to the L2TP network server (LNS), or from the L2TP-enabled access concentrator (LAC) to the LNS (see Figure 19-6). Although L2TP still uses PPP, it defines its own tunneling protocol, depending upon the transport media rather than using GRE.

Figure 19-6 *L2TP Architecture Model*

PPP Remote User
LAC
PSTN or ISDN
ISP or Public Network
L2TP Tunnel
LNS
Corporate Network
AAA Server (RADIUS/TACACS+)
AAA Server (RADIUS/TACACS+)

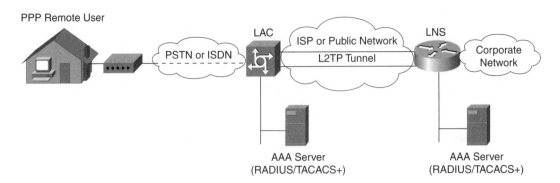

L2TP can also transport various Layer 3 protocols other than IP, although not all implementations support this feature. L2TP can use PAP, CHAP, and EAP for authentication; however, a major difference is support for the use of IPSec, which can secure traffic all the way from the end user's PC to the corporate network.

L2TP uses two types of messages: control and data (see Figure 19-7). Control messages are used in the establishment, maintenance, and clearing of tunnels and calls. Data messages encapsulate PPP frames that are carried over the tunnel. Control messages use a reliable control channel within L2TP to guarantee delivery, while data messages are not retransmitted when packet loss occurs.

Figure 19-7   *L2TP Protocol Structure*

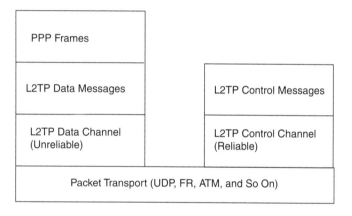

PPP frames are passed over an unreliable data channel and are first encapsulated by an L2TP header, and then by a packet transport such as User Datagram Protocol (UDP), Frame Relay, or Asynchronous Transfer Mode (ATM). Control messages are sent over a reliable L2TP control channel that transmits packets in-band over the same packet transport. Sequence numbers are required in all control messages. The numbers provide reliable delivery on the control channel because the packets can be reordered to detect lost packets.

An example for L2TP encapsulation over high-level data link control (HDLC) and IP is shown in Figure 19-8, and a general tunnel structure is shown in Figure 19-9.

The L2TP protocol is defined in RFC 2661 and is referred to as L2TPv2. The IETF Extension Group recently released version 3. The new standard includes PPP-related changes and the transition from both a 16-bit session ID and control connection ID, to 32-bit IDs. The new RFC 3193 covers "Securing L2TP using IPSec," to build private and authenticated PPP connections over the Internet. This feature is already implemented in IOS 12.2(4).T and results in the interoperability between Windows 2000 and XP, and Cisco routers. (The Microsoft version is called L2TP+IPSec.)

Figure 19-8   *L2TP Encapsulation over HDLC and IP, Where the Maximum Size Is 1500 Bytes*
(L2TP Encapsulation Is in Dark Gray)

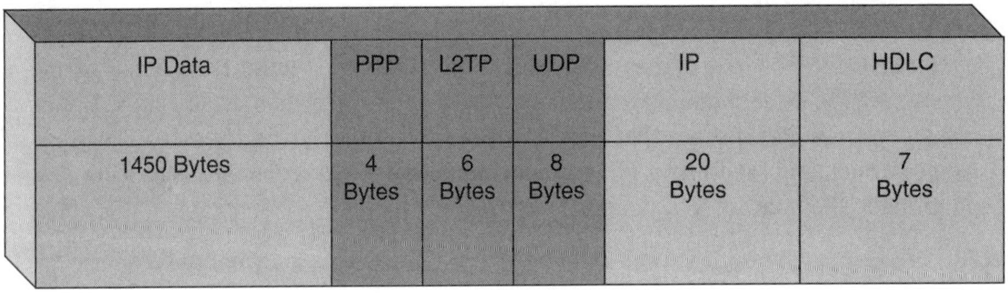

IP Data	PPP	L2TP	UDP	IP	HDLC
1450 Bytes	4 Bytes	6 Bytes	8 Bytes	20 Bytes	7 Bytes

Figure 19-9   *The General Tunnel Structure of L2TP*

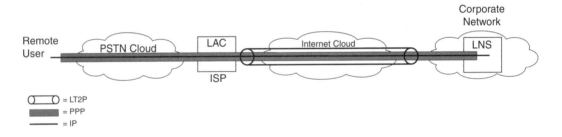

The recent developments in the VPN industry are closely related to Layer 3 and especially IPSec tunneling. The following section focuses on this topic.

Network Layer (Layer 3) VPNs

This section covers the following topics:

- Layer 3 tunneling
- Security associations and security policy for Internet Key Exchange (IKE) and IPSec
- Internet Security Association and Key Management Protocol (ISAKMP) and IPSec phases and modes
- Mutable and immutable fields and the Integrity Check Value (ICV)
- Fragmentation, path maximum transmission unit (MTU) discovery, and Internet Control Message Protocol (ICMP) processing
- IPSec modes
- IPSec protocols
- Authentication in VPN

Layer 3 Tunneling

Because of the abundance of available literature about Layer 3 tunneling, only a short description is provided in the following sections to cover the basics of the technology. A more in-depth analysis would require a separate book.

Layer 3 VPN technologies are designed to run at the network layer of the OSI model. Typically, these VPNs use the IP protocol as the network layer protocol, and they can include Layer 3 VPNs such as *Multiprotocol Label Switching* (MPLS) or IPSec, which is the IETF standard for encryption and encrypted tunnels. MPLS was covered earlier in this chapter. IPSec on Layer 3 is covered in the following sections.

RFC 2764 defines the framework for VPNs running across IP backbones. An IP tunnel operates as an overlay across the IP backbone, and the traffic sent through the tunnel is incomprehensible to the underlying IP backbone. In effect, the IP backbone is used as a link-layer technology, and the tunnel forms a point-to-point connection. Numerous IP tunneling mechanisms exist because Layer 3 tunneling is not a new technology. In fact, GRE with RFC 1701 has existed for a long time. Some protocols were initially not considered as tunneling protocols, such as IP/IP, GRE, and L2TP. Cisco first supported tunneling technology in Cisco IOS version 9.21, and provided IPSec support in Cisco IOS version 11.3(3)T and later versions.

Originally, IPSec was conceived as an extension for IPv4 with added security features. Now, IPSec is a framework of open standards for ensuring secure private communications over IP networks. It is based on an architecture model defined in RFC 2401, which covers the security features and architecture model for IPv4 and IPv6.[6] Now, IPSec VPNs use the services defined within IPSec to ensure confidentiality, integrity, and authenticity of data communications across public networks.

Security Associations and Security Policy for IKE and IPSec

IPSec operates in a peer-to-peer relationship, rather than a client/server relationship. The security association (SA) is a convention (contract) between two parties that facilitates an IPSec-based conversation between two communicating parties. Each party (device, software client) must agree to the policies or rules of their conversation by negotiating these policies with their potential peer.

There are two types of SAs: ISAKMP SAs (also known as IKE SAs) and IPSec SAs (see RFC 2408 and 2409 for more details).

The IKE SA is bidirectional and provides a secure communication channel between the two parties that can negotiate further communications. The term bidirectional means that once established, either party can start Quick Mode, Informational, and New Group Mode exchanges. IKE SA is identified by the initiator's cookie, followed by the responder's cookie, and the role of each party in the Phase 1 exchange dictates what cookie is the initiator's. The cookie order established by the phase 1 exchange continues to identify the

IKE SA, regardless of its direction. The main function of IKE is to establish and maintain the SAs. The following attributes are a minimal set that must be negotiated as part of the ISAKMP SA:

- Encryption algorithm
- Hash algorithm
- Authentication method
- Information about the group required to perform the Diffie-Hellman (DH) key agreement protocol

IKE provides negotiation, peer authentication, key management, and key exchange. IKE negotiates a contract between the two IPSec endpoints and the SA keeps track of all elements of the negotiation for a single IPSec session. After the successful negotiation, the active (valid) SA parameters are stored in the SA Database (SAD).

NOTE   To enable ISAKMP functionality, UDP port 500 must be open on the corporate firewalls.

The ISAKMP is strongly tied to policy management, which offers a different level of granularity. The ability to push or change policies on the user's CPE from the corporate concentrator is a major feature of the enterprise VPN design. The VPN 3000 Series Concentrator provides a configuration mode, which enables sending the remote user centrally controlled policies including Domain Name System (DNS), Windows Internet Naming Service (WINS), IP Address, and default domain name. This mode also provides functionality for save connection password, split tunneling, local LAN access control, remote access load balancing, centralized protection policy (firewall), personal firewall capability (are you there?), and software update notification.

The IPSec SA is unidirectional and is used for the actual communication between devices. Therefore, two-way communication between devices requires at least two IPSec SAs, one in each direction, because IPSec SA is a simplex data connection. For example, when a bidirectional TCP session exists between two systems, A and B, there is one SA from A to B and a separate SA from B to A. If both security protocols, Authentication Header (AH) and Encapsulating Security Payload (ESP), are applied to a unidirectional traffic stream, two SAs are created for the traffic stream.

NOTE   A SA is uniquely identified by an IP destination address, a security protocol (AH or ESP) identifier, and a unique security parameter index (SPI) value. A SPI is a 32-bit number assigned to the initiator of the SA request by the receiving IPSec endpoint. The SPIs for AH and ESP are not the same for a given traffic flow. The SPI value is a field in both the AH and ESP headers, and it identifies the appropriate SA for all the communications between the two end nodes. The three elements of a SA allow the receiving party to associate the received packet appropriately.

Negotiations of ISAKMP and IPSec Phases and Modes

SAs for both IKE and IPSec are negotiated by IKE over various phases and modes. The terms phases and modes denote the steps involved in establishing an IPSec connection. Key exchange and management is an important part of IPSec because of the number of keys that must be exchanged for parties to communicate securely.

Two methods of handling key exchange and management that are specified within IPSec include manual keying and IKE, which is based on ISAKMP/Oakley. IKE provides three modes for exchanging key information and setting up SAs: main, aggressive, and quick modes. The first two modes are phase 1 exchanges (main and aggressive), which set up the initial secure channel—IKE SA. The other mode is the phase 2 exchange (quick), which negotiates IPSec SAs. When identity protection is not required, only the aggressive mode can be used to reduce the time required for negotiation.

In ISAKMP, phase 1 occurs when the two ISAKMP peers establish a secure, authenticated channel for communication. Main and aggressive modes each accomplish a phase 1 exchange, and are only related to phase 1. Phase 2 occurs when SAs are negotiated on behalf of services such as IPSec or other services that require key material or parameter negotiation. Quick mode accomplishes a phase 2 exchange and is used only in phase 2.

In IPSec, phase 1 IKE negotiates IPSec SAs. Two modes can be used for this phase: main mode is used in the vast majority of situations, and aggressive mode is used under some circumstances, given the particular configuration parameters between the two systems. The aggressive mode is typical for situations when authentication is not necessary, or was already performed earlier. (Cisco VPN Client 3.0.4 mainly uses aggressive mode). The user has no control over what mode is chosen; it is automatic and depends on the configuration parameters set up by both peers. In phase 2, IKE negotiates IPSec SAs and the exchange only uses quick mode.

The elements and functions of the IKE and IPSec negotiation, and the differences between modes are shown in Figure 19-10. (Some of the terms are discussed later.)

Figure 19-10 *Elements and Functions of IKE and IPSec*

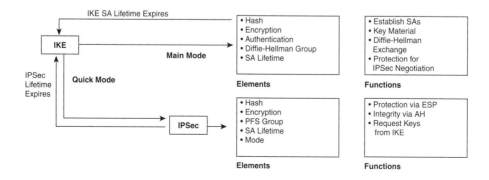

IPSec SAs terminate through deletion or by timing out. When the SAs terminate, the keys are discarded. When subsequent IPSec SAs are needed for flow, IKE performs a new phase 2 and, if necessary, a new phase 1 negotiation. A successful negotiation results in new SAs and new keys. New SAs can be established before the existing SAs expire, so a given flow can continue uninterrupted.

Mutable and Immutable Fields and the ICV

One of the services of IPSec is to provide access control and data integrity, so that no one can change any bits in the packet exchange between the two parties. The service, called *connectionless data integrity*, ensures that the original IP packet is not modified in transit from the source to the destination. However, any packet to be routed can undergo several transformations (changes to the content) to be delivered to the destination.

The ability to read the header of packets for routing purposes, while maintaining security of the data, is a controversy that is addressed by the calculation of the ICV. The ICV is a keyed hash that uses a shared secret value. The computation uses IP header fields that are either immutable in transit or that are predictable in value upon arrival at the endpoint for the SA. The upper-layer protocol data is assumed to be immutable in transit. For the purposes of this computation, the IP datagram fields are divided into three groups: immutable, mutable but predictable, and mutable.

Figure 19-11 shows the original IPv4 packet and the breakdown. The IP datagram is a variable-length packet that can be split into two major parts: the header (20-60 bytes), and the total size of 20-65,536 bytes. The header is designed in a way to provide the necessary information for delivery and routing.

Figure 19-11 *Mutable and Immutable Fields of IPv4 (The Mutable Fields Are in White, the Destination IP Address Is in Light Gray, and the Immutable Fields Are in Dark Gray)*

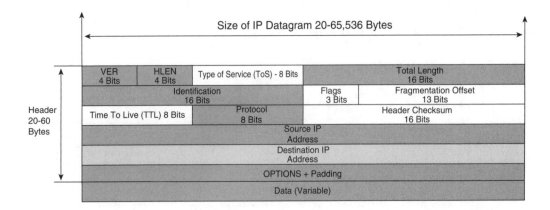

Note the following about Figure 19-11:

- **Version**—The first 4 bits are the version. The IPv4 uses 0100 in this field.

- **Header length (HLEN)**—The value is provided to help calculate the length of the header because IP is a variable length. To determine the length, you must multiply by 4 because with 4 bits, a maximum of four 1s (15) can be coded. Therefore, $15 \times 4 = 60$ is the maximum HLEN.

- **Type of service (TOS)**—Identifies how the datagram should be handled (normal delay, throughput, reliability). This field is mutable because some routers are known to change the value of this field, even though the IP specification does not consider TOS to be a mutable header field.

- **Total length**—Specifies the length, in bytes, of the entire IP packet, including the data and header. It is a 2-byte field, which can code a maximum size of $2^{16} = 65{,}536$ bytes.

- **Identification**—This field is used for fragmentation. To pass large packets through networks with different MTUs, the packet must be fragmented. It identifies the sequence number.

- **Flags**—This is a 3-bit field of which the low-order (least significant) 2 bits control fragmentation. The 3 bits are defined as follows:

  — Low-order bit specifies whether the packet can be fragmented.

  — Middle bit specifies whether the packet is the last fragment in a series of fragmented packets.

  — High-order bit is not used.

  The field is mutable because an intermediate router might set the Don't Fragment (DF) bit, even if the source did not select it.

- **Fragmentation offset**—Provides the offset of the data in the original packet. The field is mutable because AH is applied only to non-fragmented IP packets; therefore, the Offset Field must always be 0 and is excluded (even though it is predictable).

- **Time To Live (TTL)**—If the destination is not reached, it defines the number of hops/seconds that the packet can travel before being discarded. Every hop decrements the initial value by 1, so when the field contains 0 and the destination is not yet reached, the packet is discarded. The field is mutable because it changes due to the normal processing by routers, and therefore its value at the receiver end is not predictable by the sender.

- **Protocol**—Contains information for the upper-layer protocols that are encapsulated in IP. For example, the protocol ID for UDP is 17, and for TCP, it is 6.

- **Header checksum**—This 16-bit field checks the integrity of the header. It is a mutable field because it changes if any of the other fields change, and therefore, its value cannot be predicted by the sender.

- **Source IP address**—This is a 32-bit IP address.

- **Destination IP address**—This is a 32-bit IP address for the destination. It is mutable but predictable with loose or strict source routing.

- **Options**—For IPv4 (unlike IPv6), there is no mechanism for tagging options as mutable in transit. As a result, the IPv4 options are explicitly listed and classified and the entire option is viewed as a unit. So, even though the type and length fields within most options are immutable in transit, if an option is classified as mutable, the entire option is zeroed for ICV computation purposes.

Fragmentation, Path MTU Discovery, and ICMP Processing

The fragmentation in VPN, path MTU discovery, and IPSec-related ICMP messages are discussed in detail in RFC 2401, "Security Architecture for the Internet Protocol." Some other studies, such as IETF MTU Discovery Working Group, and in particular RFC 1191, propose a technique for dynamically discovering the MTU of an arbitrary Internet path.

The fragmentation of the IP datagrams, if required, occurs after IPSec processing within an IPSec implementation. Thus, transport mode AH or ESP is applied only to entire IP datagrams (not to IP fragments). An IP packet to which AH or ESP has been applied can itself be fragmented by intermediate routers, but such fragments must be reassembled prior to IPSec processing at a receiver. In tunnel mode, AH or ESP is applied to an IP packet, the payload of which can be a fragmented IP packet.

Of course, the official minimum MTU (see RFC 791) can process the IP packets, but that would be wasting Internet resources in most cases. In fact, this results in the use of smaller datagrams than necessary because many paths have a Path MTU (PMTU) greater than 576. Furthermore, current practice does not prevent fragmentation in all cases because some path's PMTU is less than 576. These realities essentially emphasize the importance of the fragmentations and related MTU issues. The key suggestion here is that "when one IP host has a large amount of data to send to another host, the data is transmitted as a series of IP datagrams. It is usually preferable that these datagrams be of the largest size that does not require fragmentation anywhere along the path from the source to the destination. This datagram size is referred to as the Path MTU (PMTU), and it is equal to the minimum of the MTUs of each hop in the path. A shortcoming of the current Internet protocol suite is the lack of a standard mechanism for a host to discover the PMTU of an arbitrary path." [7]

The PMTU depends on the different modes and protocols applied to the remote access VPN solution because different protocols and modes add different overhead to the IP datagrams. See the section, "IPSec Protocols" for more details about IPSec protocols. For the purposes of this explanation, the general format of the datagrams in the tunnel mode, in terms of the TCP/IP stack, look similar to the following.

The AH datagram includes the following:

- **IP2**—New (second) IP header

- **AH header**

- **IP1**—Original IP header
- **TCP header**
- **TCP data**

The ESP datagram includes the following:

- **IP2–**—New (second) IP header
- **ESP header**
- **IP1**—Original IP header
- **TCP header**
- **TCP data**
- **ESP trailer**

Information is provided in Chapter 4, "Troubleshooting Approaches, Models, and Tools," about using the ping utility and ICMP protocol to perform the reachibility test between two hops in the network. The same ICMP protocol can perform additional functionality about PMTU discovery. The term PMTU Discovery or ICMP PMTU refers to an ICMP message used for PMTU Discovery.

The suggested approach in RFC 1191 is based on the interaction between certain unused fields in the ICMP header and the maximum segment size (MSS) field of the TCP protocol. After the original IP datagram is encapsulated by any of the IPSec protocols, it changes its format. Also, when used with the ICMP protocol, the format changes in the following fashion:

- IP3 header (third header, which includes source and destination information)
- ICMP header (includes PMTU)
- IP2 header (second header, which includes source and destination information), where:
    - If the protocol is ESP, the minimum of 64 bits includes the security parameter index (SPI) (32 bits), and sequence number (32 bits).
    - If the protocol is AH, the minimum of 64 bits includes the next header (8 bits), payload len (8 bits), reserved (16 bits), and SPI (32 bits).

To make this possible, the ICMP protocol must include the MTU of that next-hop network in the low-order 16 bits of the ICMP header field that is labeled unused" in the ICMP specification. The high-order 16 bits remain unused, and must be set to 0. The format of the ICMP header is shown in Figure 19-12.

Figure 19-12 *ICMP Header Format*

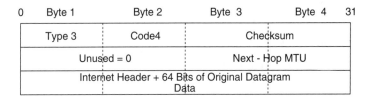

Another approach to the MTU discovery process is based on a simple suggestion that, regardless of the content of the IP datagram after the IPSec encapsulation (MD5-ESP-3DES), the ICMP overhead is always 28 bytes when it is used with ICMP: Type = 0 (Echo reply) and ICMP: Code = 0. For more explanations about approach and how to use it for troubleshooting, see the section, "Determining a Functional MTU Between the VPN Host and Concentrator," in Chapter 21, "Remote Access VPN Troubleshooting," and Case 4 of Chapter 22, "Remote Access VPN Troubleshooting Scenarios."

Both solutions provide successful solutions in most cases. However, they can become complicated if you consider some realities in the existing networks.

One reality is the blocking of ICMP messages from most providers, or enterprise firewalls. Another obstacle for implementation can be the existence of black hole routers. A black hole router does not return ICMP destination unreachable messages when it needs to fragment a TCP packet with the DF bit set. TCP depends on receiving these messages to perform PMTU Discovery. One possible approach here is to modify the TCP in a way that TCP tries to send segments without the DF bit set, if several retransmissions of a segment go unacknowledged. If the segment is acknowledged as a result, the MSS is decreased and the DF bit is set in future packets on the connection. Enabling black hole detection increases the maximum number of retransmissions performed for a given segment. It is disabled by default in Windows.

IPSec Modes

IPSec provides secure communication between two hosts, from a host to a security gateway, or between two security gateways. A security gateway is a device, such as a router, firewall, or a dedicated VPN concentrator, which provides IPSec services (that is, terminates the IPSec connection) and passes traffic through the tunnel to the other side. IPSec can operate in one of two modes to accommodate different types of connections: transport mode and tunnel mode.

With transport mode, the AH or ESP is placed after the original IP header, so only the IP payload is encrypted and the original IP headers are left intact. Transport mode can be used when both end hosts support IPSec. This mode has the advantage of adding only a few bytes to each packet and it also allows devices on the public network to see the final source and destination of the packet. This capability enables special processing (for example, quality of service) in the intermediate network, based on the information on the IP header. However, the Layer 4 header is encrypted, which limits the examination of the packet (see Figure 19-14 and Figure 19-17 later in this chapter).

With tunnel mode, the entire original IP packet is encapsulated within AH or ESP, and a new IP header is placed around it. So, the original IP datagram is encrypted and becomes the payload in a new IP packet. This mode allows a network device, such as a router, to act as an IPSec proxy that performs encryption on behalf of the host. The source's router encrypts packets and forwards them along the IPSec tunnel. The destination's router decrypts the original IP datagram and forwards it on to the destination system. Therefore, the new IP header has the source address of the gateway itself. With tunnel mode operating between two security gateways, the original source and destination addresses can be hidden through the use of encryption. Tunnel mode is used when one or both sides of the IPSec connection are a security gateway and the actual destination hosts behind it do not support IPSec (see Figure 19-15 and Figure 19-18 later in this chapter).

IPSec Protocols

In a TCP/IP environment, IPSec protocols offer security services at the network layer. These services include the following:

- Access control prevents unauthorized use of a resource, such as the network behind a security gateway (router, firewall).
- Authentication service includes the following:
    - Connectionless integrity, which detects any modification to data within individual IP packets, regardless of their position in a data stream.
    - Data origin authentication, which verifies the source of the data.
- Anti-replay protection (optional) occurs when the sender must increment the sequence number, and the receiver (if this option is chosen) must detect the arrival of the duplicate IP sequence packet number.
- Confidentiality protects data from unauthorized disclosure by using encryption. Limited traffic-flow confidentiality occurs by hiding the original source and destination addresses as part of the data when using ESP in tunnel mode.

Because both AH and ESP provide access control, the main decision to make when choosing security services is whether you need authentication or both authentication and encryption.

To give you a better feel for the issues surrounding IPSec protocols, the discussion is divided into the following topics:

- IP authentication header
- IP encapsulating security payload

IP Authentication Header and RFC 2402

The AH provides connectionless data integrity and data origin authentication as part of the authentication of IP packets.

Connectionless data integrity means that the original IP packet was not modified in transit from the source to the destination. AH provides authentication for as much of the IP header as possible, and for upper-level protocol data. However, some IP header fields can change in transit and the value of these fields might not be predictable by the sender, when the packet arrives at the receiver. The values of such fields cannot be protected by AH; therefore, the protection provided to the IP header by AH is not considered strong enough.

AH can be applied alone, in combination with the IP ESP, or in a nested fashion. Security services can be provided between a pair of communicating hosts, security gateways, or between a security gateway and a host. ESP can provide the same security services as AH, but it also provides a confidentiality (encryption) service. The AH header is shown in Figure 19-13.

Figure 19-13 *Authentication Header (AH) Format*

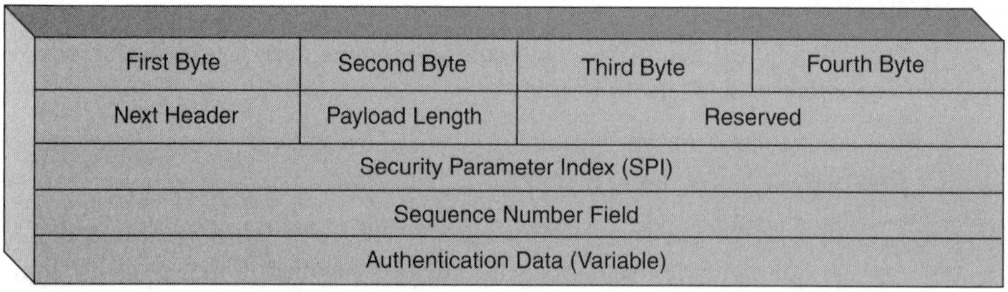

First Byte	Second Byte	Third Byte	Fourth Byte
Next Header	Payload Length	Reserved	
Security Parameter Index (SPI)			
Sequence Number Field			
Authentication Data (Variable)			

NOTE   To ensure AH functionality, protocol 51 must be open in the corporate firewalls.

The AH is inserted into the IP packet between the IP header and the rest of the packet's contents. It contains a cryptographic checksum of the packet's contents, including the parts of the IP header itself that are immutable in transit.

Figure 19-14 shows the IP packet before and after applying the AH in transport mode.

Figure 19-14 *The IP Packet Before and After Applying the AH in Transport Mode*

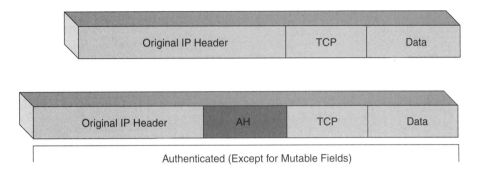

Figure 19-15 shows the IP packet before and after applying the AH in tunnel mode.

Figure 19-15 *The IP Packet Before and After Applying the AH in Tunnel Mode*

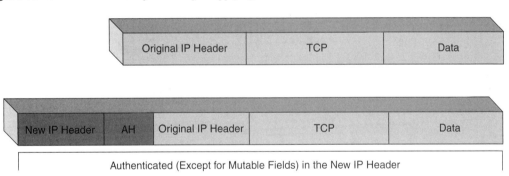

The default cryptographic algorithms for calculating the checksum are hash-based message authentication code (HMAC) coupled with the Message Digest 5 (MD5) hash function, or HMAC coupled with the Secure Hash Algorithm (SHA-1) function. When taking a received message and calculating the same cryptographic checksum, then comparing it with the value received, the receiver can verify that the message has not been altered in transit.

Calculation of ICV in AH

The ICV calculation includes the following components of AH: next header, payload length, reserved, SPI, sequence number, authentication data (which is set to 0 for this computation), and explicit padding bytes (if any) (see Figure 19-13).

AH also provides a limited anti-replay service that counters a denial of service (DoS) attack, based on an attacker intercepting a series of packets and then replaying them. It should be noted that the anti-replay service can affect performance, if the network reorders packets to provide higher QoS for certain types of traffic. If the packets arrive outside the anti-replay window, IPSec rejects them. AH is not widely used for IPSec implementations across the Internet because it does nothing to keep the packet contents confidential. For confidentiality, ESP must be used.

IP ESP and RFC 2406

The ESP header is designed to provide a mix of security services in IPv4 and IPv6. ESP can be applied alone, in combination with AH, or in a nested fashion. Security services can be provided between a pair of communicating hosts, a pair of communicating security gateways, or a security gateway and a host. The ESP objectives reflect the ESP header format that is shown in Figure 19-16.

Figure 19-16 *ESP Header Format*

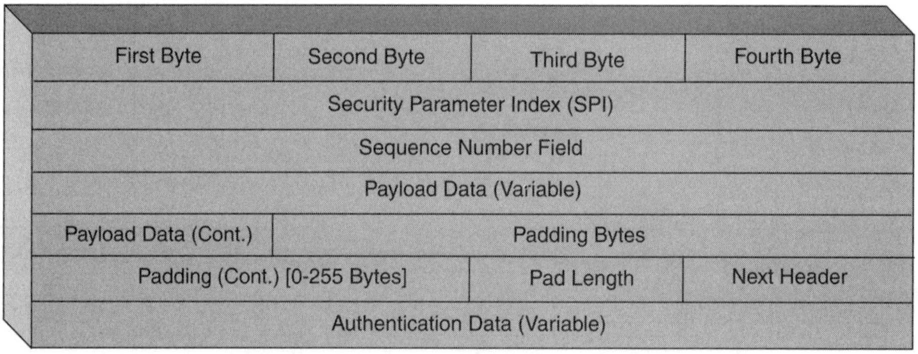

First Byte	Second Byte	Third Byte	Fourth Byte
Security Parameter Index (SPI)			
Sequence Number Field			
Payload Data (Variable)			
Payload Data (Cont.)	Padding Bytes		
Padding (Cont.) [0-255 Bytes]		Pad Length	Next Header
Authentication Data (Variable)			

NOTE To enable ESP functionality, protocol 50 must be open in the corporate firewalls.

ESP provides confidentiality, data origin authentication, connectionless integrity, an anti-replay service (a form of partial sequence integrity), and limited traffic flow confidentiality. The set of services enabled depends on the options selected at the time of SA establishment.

The ESP header is inserted after the IP header and before the upper-layer protocol header (in transport mode), or before an encapsulated IP header (in tunnel mode). Figure 19-17 shows how the IPv4 packet is modified in transport mode, and Figure 19-18 shows the IPv4 packet transformation in tunnel mode.

Confidentiality in ESP is achieved through encryption. Encryption is the process of taking a clear text message, and passing it through a mathematical algorithm to produce what is known as ciphertext. Decryption is the reverse process. Encryption algorithms typically rely on a value, called a key, to encrypt and decrypt the data.

Figure 19-17   *The IP Packet Before and After Applying the ESP in Transport Mode*

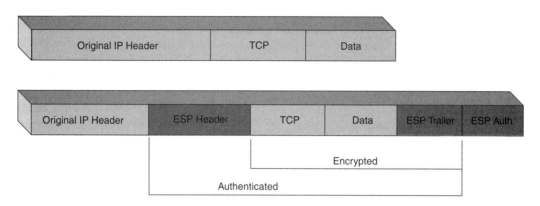

Figure 19-18   *The IP Packet Before and After Applying the ESP in Tunnel Mode*

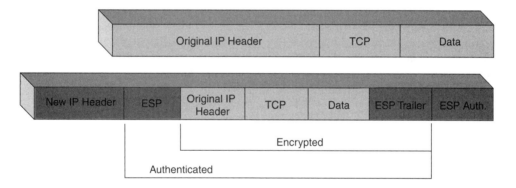

Two major forms of encryption are used today: symmetric encryption (also known as shared-key encryption) and asymmetric encryption (know as public/private key encryption). Symmetric encryption is approximately 1000 times faster than asymmetric encryption, and is therefore used for the bulk encryption of data. Generally, with well-designed encryption algorithms, longer keys result in a higher degree of security because more brute force is required to try every possible key (known as the key space) to decrypt a message.

ESP supports a variety of symmetric encryption algorithms for data encryption. The Data Encryption Standard (DES) is the default algorithm that uses a 56-bit key and has been in use for about 20 years. However, DES has been susceptible to brute-force attacks, so Triple DES (3DES) is now the standard algorithm recommended for most business use because it encrypts the data three times with up to three different keys. ESP encrypts the higher-level protocol information (such as the TCP header) and the actual data itself. The authentication services of ESP do not protect the new IP header of the packet.

On May 26, 2002, the Advanced Encryption Standard (AES) became a finalized Federal Information Processing Standard (FIPS)-approved cryptographic algorithm for purposes of protecting transmissions of electronic data (see FIPS PUB 197). AES is a new, faster, and more secure standard encryption algorithm, and it is being considered by Cisco for future two-phase implementations. The first phase includes the software (IOS) version and the second phase includes the hardware version. AES is expected to be considered as a baseline functionality in mid 2002 and early 2003, and VPN solutions and devices without high-speed AES support will not be considered for many VPN deployments.

The underlying algorithm for AES is called Rijndael. AES specifies three key sizes: 128, 192, and 256 bits. In decimal terms, this indicates that there are approximately the following:

- 3.4×10^{38} possible 128-bit keys
- 6.2×10^{57} possible 192-bit keys
- 1.1×10^{77} possible 256-bit keys

In comparison, DES keys are 56-bits long, which indicates that there are approximately 7.2×10^{16} possible DES keys. Hence, there are on the order of 10^{21} times more AES 128-bit keys than DES 56-bit keys. For more information, see the article, "AES an Approved Cryptographic Algorithm" (Cisco *Packet* Magazine, Q3 2002; also available at www.cisco.com/warp/public/784/packet/standards.html).

NOTE   In the late 1990s, specialized DES Cracker machines were built that could recover a DES key after a few hours. Assuming that someone could build a machine that could recover a DES key in a second (that is, try 2^{55} keys per second), it would take that machine approximately 149 trillion years to crack a 128-bit AES key. To put this in perspective, the universe is believed to be less than 20 billion years old.

The anti-replay service can be used only if data origin authentication is selected, and its election is solely at the discretion of the receiver. However the default requires the sender to increment the sequence number used for anti-replay, and the service is effective only if the receiver checks the sequence number. Traffic flow confidentiality requires the selection of tunnel mode, and it is most effective if implemented at a security gateway, where traffic aggregation can mask true source-destination patterns. Although both confidentiality and authentication are optional, at least one must be selected. Most IPSec VPN implementations today use ESP.

Calculation of ICV in ESP

If authentication is selected for the SA, the ICV calculation includes the following components: SPI, sequence number, payload data, padding (if present), pad length, and next header. In general, the sender computes the ICV over the ESP packet, except for the authentication data. The last four fields are in ciphertext form because encryption is performed prior to authentication.

Authentication in VPN

Authentication in VPN has several aspects that include the following:

- Client authentication, VPN group name, and group password
- User/identity authentication
- Key management, DH algorithm, and methodology
- Cisco and IPSec message authentication (integrity) and confidentiality

The text discusses each in turn.

Client Authentication, VPN Group Name, and Group Password

The group name and group password approach simplifies policy enforcement because a user can be a member of a group of users who have common policy requirements. For example, a single change can be made to a group that affects hundreds of users versus making changes for every single user. Groups and users are core components in managing the security of VPNs, and in configuring the Cisco VPN 3000 Concentrator. They have attributes that determine their access to and use of the VPN. Users are members of groups and groups are members of the base group. Users inherit attributes from groups and groups inherit attributes from the base group. The VPN client can be configured with an active group name and group password to provide a user prompt, and be authenticated by a RADIUS server if the Group Lock feature on the concentrator is turned on.

Groups simplify system management. By configuring the base group first, then specific groups, and finally users as members of groups, you can quickly manage access and usage rights for large numbers of users. Associating users with specific groups simplifies the configuration of the VPN, while providing granular control over who has access to certain resources. When configuring groups and users, only the attributes that differ from those defined in the base group need to be defined and all other attributes are inherited from the base group.

The group name and group password for VPN users are stored locally on the concentrator or server. When the client tries to connect to the concentrator, it has to provide the same group name and password to be recognized as an eligible user. After a successful negotiation, a typical message from the log of both peers is Peer Is a Cisco Unity Compliant Peer, which indicates a successful group name and password authentication.

Another important feature allows the VPN administrator to group different user requirements into different client groups. For example, some users have Network Address Translation (NAT) configured within their home LAN, so that when they connect to the concentrator, it must recognize that the user is NATing and adjust. The concentrator can determine if the user is NATing or not based on the group name and password they used to connect.

User/Identity Authentication

One of the basic functions for key exchange is to ensure that the exchange occurs between trusted sources. This requires user identity verification and it is related to the non-repudiation feature, which prevents a communicating party from later denying having participated. User identity requires proof of identity of the sender and it is based on digital signatures and authentication mechanisms. The Cisco VPN Client (Unity) supports the following digital certificates:

- Simple Certificate Enrollment Protocol (SCEP) and certificates enrolled with Microsoft Internet Explorer.

- Supported certification authorities (CAs) that include Entrust, GTE Cybertrust, Netscape, Baltimore, RSA, Keon, Verisign, and Microsoft.

- Entrust Intelligence Client support.

- Smartcards are supported through MS CAPI (CRYPT_NOHASHOID), and include Activcard (Schlumberger cards), eAladdin, and Gemplus.

Supported authentication mechanisms are as follows:

- RADIUS with support for the following:
    - State/Reply Message attributes (token cards)
    - Security dynamics (RSA SecurID Ready)
    - Microsoft NT domain authentication
    - MSCHAPv2—NT password expiration
    - X.509v3 digital certificates
- Extended Authentication (XAUTH) within IKE provides user authentication of IPSec tunnels within the IKE protocol. XAUTH prompts the user for authentication material (user name + password), and verifies this information through the use of a TACACS+/RADIUS authentication, authorization, and accounting (AAA) server. User authentication occurs between IKE phase 1 and phase 2. If the user successfully authenticates, establishment of the phase 2 SA (IPSec SA) allows the remote user's data to be sent securely to the private network. If the user fails to authenticate, no phase 2 SA is established and the user is not able to send data.

External User Authentication—RADIUS

Individual user authentication information, such as user name and password, can be stored locally, which is more appropriate for small installations. Larger installations must use RADIUS or Terminal Access Controller Access Control System Plus (TACACS+), with an external database capable of supporting a large number of remote users. Larger sites with thousands of users are only limited or restricted by the authentication, authorization, and accounting (AAA) server's capacity.

NOTE   The RADIUS server is based on a protocol for AAA that was developed by Livingston Enterprises, Inc. (see RFC 2866). Cisco has incorporated the RADIUS client into Cisco IOS 11.1.

TACACS was introduced with Cisco products and has been in use for many years. The extension of the original TACACS was commonly called Extended TACACS or XTACACS, and was introduced in 1990. Both are documented in RFC 1492. The third is TACACS+, which despite the name, is a completely new protocol and is not compatible with TACACS or XTACACS.

RADIUS is the main choice for external user authentication in existing VPNs. It is composed of a protocol with a frame format that uses UDP/IP, a server, and a client.

The RADIUS server runs on a central computer, usually at the customer's site, and the clients reside in the access servers that can be distributed throughout the network. The RADIUS client is typically a NAS and the RADIUS server is usually a daemon process, which runs on a UNIX or Windows NT machine. The client passes user information to designated RADIUS servers, and acts on the response that is returned. RADIUS servers receive user connection requests, authenticate the user, and return the configuration information necessary for the client to deliver service to the user. A RADIUS server can act as a proxy client to other RADIUS servers or other kinds of authentication servers.

Packet Encryption

RADIUS only encrypts the password in the access-request packet from the client to the server. The remainder of the packet is in clear text. Information other than the encrypted password, such as username, authorized services, and accounting, can be intercepted by a third party. RADIUS can use encrypted passwords by using UNIX /etc/passwd file; however, this process is slow because of the time consuming linear file searches.

Authentication and Authorization

RADIUS combines authentication and authorization. The access-accept packets sent by the RADIUS server to the client contains authorization information, which makes it difficult to separate authentication from authorization.

NOTE   Starting with release 3.0 of the VPN 3000 Concentrator, you can use TACACS+ for administrative authentication. After configuring TACACS+, ensure that you test authentication before logging out. An incorrect configuration of TACACS+ can lock you out, and require a console port login to disable TACACS+ and rectify the problem.

VPN and RADIUS

VPN uses server authentication that is similar to a dialup environment. The client passes user information to designated RADIUS servers, and acts on the response that is returned. The RADIUS server receives user connection requests, authenticates the user, and returns the configuration information necessary for the client to deliver service to the user (see Figure 19-19).

Figure 19-19   *The VPN Authentication Process Using RADIUS*

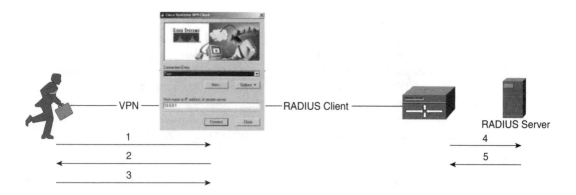

The following summarizes the process:

1 The user starts an IPSec tunnel to the VPN concentrator by using the VPN client.

2 The VPN concentrator prompts for username and password.

3 The user replies.

4 The RADIUS client sends a username and encrypted password to the RADIUS server.

5 The RADIUS server responds with Accept, Reject, or Challenge.

6 The RADIUS client acts upon services and service parameters that are bundled with Accept or Reject.

Every authentication method deserves special attention, which exceeds the objectives of this book. However, the XAUTH within IKE is extensively used by Cisco VPN solutions, and deserves more attention here.

XAUTH

IKE enables a device to set up a secure session by using a bidirectional authentication method, which uses either preshared keys or digital certificates. However, IKE does not provide a method to leverage legacy authentication methods that are widely deployed today. XAUTH is not designed to replace or enhance existing authentication mechanisms, but rather to enable them to be extended by using legacy unidirectional authentication mechanisms such as RADIUS, SecurID, and one-time password (OTP) within IPSec's ISAKMP protocol.[8]

This XAUTH protocol is designed so that the authentication can be accomplished by using any mode of operation for phase 1 (such as main mode or aggressive mode), and as any authentication method supported by IKE. This protocol can also be easily extended to support new modes of authentication methods, but it does require that the phase 1 authentication method be fully secure. XAUTH adds a vendor ID that must be authenticated whenever possible. The vendor ID for this revision of XAUTH is the following 8 bytes:

Vendor ID = 0x09002689DFD6B712

XAUTH provides a mechanism for five basic types of authentication:

- Simple authentication
- Challenge-response authentication
- Two-factor authentication
- OTPs
- User previously authenticated

An example of an authentication mechanism, where the user password is hidden by an encryption mechanism, follows (see Figure 19-20).

Designed for future use, XAUTH supports the following authentication types: 0–Generic, 1-RADIUS-CHAP, 2-OTP, and 3-S/Key. Types 4-32767 are reserved for future use, and types 32768-65545 are reserved for private use.

Figure 19-20 *XAUTH Authentication When the Password Is Encrypted*

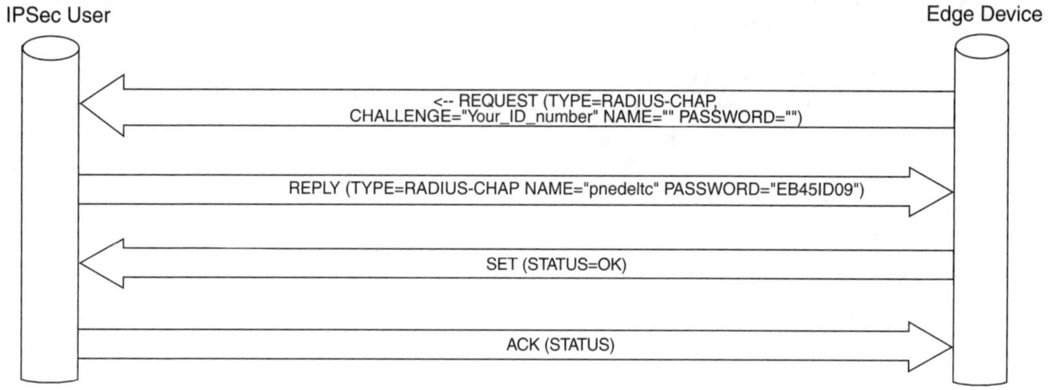

IPSec User   Edge Device

<-- REQUEST (TYPE=RADIUS-CHAP,
CHALLENGE="Your_ID_number" NAME="" PASSWORD="")

REPLY (TYPE=RADIUS-CHAP NAME="pnedeltc" PASSWORD="EB45ID09")

SET (STATUS=OK)

ACK (STATUS)

Key Management, DH Algorithm, and Methodology

Confidentiality services can be selected independent of other services. However, use of confidentiality without integrity/authentication (either in ESP or separately in AH), might subject traffic to certain forms of active attacks that can undermine the confidentiality service. Therefore, authentication is offered as an option in conjunction with confidentiality. RFC 2401 defines two methods of authentication and key management: manual keying, and automated keying through IKE. Valid authentication methods include the following:

- Preshared keys
- Digital signature standard (DSS) signatures
- RSA signatures
- Encryption with RSA
- Revised encryption with RSA

A DH exponential algorithm generates a strong initial key.

NOTE   The Diffie-Hellman key agreement protocol (also called an exponential key agreement) was developed by Whitfield Diffie and Martin Hellman in 1976, and was published in *New Directions in Cryptography*. The protocol enables two users to exchange a secret key over an insecure medium without any prior secrets.

Before IKE proceeds, the parties must agree on how to authenticate themselves to each other. This authentication method is negotiated during the IKE phase main mode exchange. The following mechanisms are in use today:

- Preshared keys that involve the manual installation of the same key on each peer.

- Encrypted nonces that generate an asymmetric encryption public/private key pair for each peer, then manually copy the public key of each peer to every other peer.

- Digital certificates are issued by a trusted third party, called a CA, to validate the authenticity of each peer and to offer the added benefit of non-repudiation, so a peer can verify that a communication actually took place.

When remote access clients are involved, a second level of user authentication occurs after device authentication, which occurs through the IKE SA. The headend starts an XAUTH request to the remote user, which prompts for the username-password/passcode pair.[9] After authentication is completed in the first phase, the second phase connects the remote and local networks.

The DH algorithm is still considered the strongest by the cryptographic society. In the DH key agreement, the two parties, without any prior arrangements, can agree upon a secret key that is known only to them (often called a shared secret or a key encryption key). This secret key can then encrypt further communications between the parties. The shared secret encrypts the symmetric key (or data encryption key—such as DES, Triple DES, CAST, International Data Encryption Algorithm [IDEA], or Blowfish) for secure transmission.

Asymmetric key systems use two keys: the private key, which the user keeps secret, and the public key, which can be shared with the world. Unfortunately, the asymmetric key calculation is extremely slow. Today, it is a typical practice to use a symmetric system to encrypt the data, and an asymmetric system to encrypt the symmetric keys. This is how you use DH.

The basis for the DH algorithm is the difficulty of calculating logs in modular arithmetic (see the following Note). The process begins when each side of the communication generates a private key. Each side then generates a public key, which is a derivative of the private key. The two systems then exchange their public keys, so that each side of the communication now has its own private key and the other system's public key. Because of the complexity of the algorithm, its explanation goes beyond the scope of this book. The methodology of the DH algorithm can be found in the article "IPSec-Based VPNs and Related Algorithms," by P. Nedeltchev and R. Ratchkov (Cisco *Packet* Magazine, Q2 2002; and at www.cisco.com/warp/public/784/packet/apr02/pdfs/plamen.pdf).

NOTE   The expression $x = y \pmod{m}$ reads as "x is equivalent to y, modulo m." The statement $a + kp = a \pmod{p}$ should be fairly obvious. The Chinese Remainder Theorem states that $x = y \pmod{p}$ and $x = y \pmod{q}$ is the same as $x = y \pmod{pq}$, if p and q are coprimes. The Fermat/Euler Theorem rules that if p is prime, $x^p - 1 = 1 \pmod{p}$. RSA correctness rules that if d and e are generated in a way that $de = k(p-1)(q-1) + 1$, and k is an integer, the encryption/decryption process can be written as $x^{ed} \% pq$.[10]

The cost of some methods for computing discrete logarithms depends on the length of the prime, and the cost of others depends on the length of the private value. The intention of selecting a private-value length is to reduce the computation time for key agreement, while maintaining a given level of security. The time to execute the algorithm by software is proportional to D^3, where D is the number of bits of p. Therefore, increasing from 200 to 800 bits raises the complexity by a factor of 64.

The length of the primes that defined DH-Groups, or Oakley Default Groups, are as follows:

Group 1—Default 768-bit (300h)
Group 2—Alternate 1024-bit (400h)—recommended
Group 3—EC2N group on GP[2^{155}]
Group 4—EC2N group on GP[2^{185}]
Group 5—Prime length 1536 bits (600h)

NOTE   The Cisco VPN 3000 Concentrator uses DH group 7 as well. The DH group 7 generates IPSec SA keys that are based on an elliptical curve field (ECC) size of 163 bits. You can use this option with any encryption algorithm and any peer that supports ECC group 7, but it is intended for use with the movianVPN (wireless) client.

The DH key exchange is vulnerable to a man-in-the-middle (MIM) attack because it does not authenticate the participants. The attack consists of someone intercepting both public keys and forwarding bogus public keys of their own. The MIM can potentially intercept encrypted traffic, decrypt it, copy or modify it, re-encrypt it with the bogus key, and forward it on to its destination. If successful, the parties on each end have no idea that there was an unauthorized intermediary. The authenticated DH key agreement protocol, or Station-to-Station (STS) protocol, was developed by Diffie, van Oorschot, and Wiener in 1992, to defeat the MIM attack on the DH key agreement protocol.[11] Immunity is achieved by allowing the two parties to authenticate themselves to each other through the use of digital signatures and public-key certificates.

NOTE   The MIM is addressed in ISAKMP (see RFC 2408), where not only MIM, but two other types of ISAKMP protection, including anti-clogging (DOS) and connection hijacking are addressed.

The longer that a symmetric key is in use, the easier it is to perform a successful crypto-analytic attack against it. Therefore, changing keys frequently is important. Both sides of the communication still have the shared secret and it can be used to encrypt future keys at any time and for any frequency desired.

RFC 2401 defines perfect forward secrecy (PFS), where a shared secret encryption key refresh involves combining the current key with a random number to create a new key. PFS enforces the recalculation of the shared secret key from scratch by using the public and private key generation and DH techniques. It recalculates to avoid the situation where a hacker might have derived a particular secret key. PFS allows a new key to be calculated that has no relationship to the preceding key.

The PFS is closely related to SA Lifetime, where an SA Lifetime determines the period of time that a security association is valid. It also determines how often a key is refreshed or recalculated. A lifetime can be measured in seconds or kilobytes and is applied to both the IKE SA and IPSec SAs.

Cisco and IPSec Message Authentication (Integrity) and Confidentiality

IPSec provides numerous security features that are based on a family of algorithms, which perform transformations over different fields of packets. The content transformation of the packet is governed by HMAC, as defined by RFC 2104. As previously mentioned, it is based on a secret key that is available to both parties and the key material generation precedes the packet content transformation. Codes based on cryptographic hash functions are called HMAC. RFC 2104 defines HMAC as the following:

> **H** (**K** xor opad, **H** (**K** xor ipad, **text**))
> **H**—Denotes a cryptographic hash function
> **K**—Denotes a secret key
> **text**—The input text stream

HMAC can use any cryptographic hash function, such as MD5 and SHA-1, and it is at least as strong as the hash function it uses. This also allows for easy cryptographic analysis of the HMAC, where only the underlying hash function is analyzed. Assuming that **H** is a cryptographic hash function that iterates over a block of data, with byte length B for each block, **ipad** and **opad** are fixed length strings that are defined as follows:

> **ipad** = 0x36 repeated B times
> **opad** = 0x5C repeated B times

The enterprise can define the policy and implement a high level of granularity by using different algorithms. The algorithm's parameters are configurable and include type of data encryption, device authentication and credentials, data integrity, address hiding, and SA key aging. The IPSec standard requires the use of either data integrity or data encryption, and using both is optional. Cisco highly recommends using both encryption and integrity— see the site www.cisco.com/go/safe. Do not use hash functions for encryption. Cisco recommends the use of 3DES for data encryption, and either MD5 or SHA-1 for data integrity (message authentication).

Because of the greater bit strength of SHA-1, it is considered more secure. Cisco recommends the use of SHA-1 mainly for S2S VPNs because the increased security outweighs the slight increase in processor overhead (in fact, SHA-1 is sometimes faster than MD5 in certain hardware implementations).[12]

Both IPSec phases offer the ability to change the lifetime of the SA. You might consider changing the lifetime from the default setting, when the sensitivity of the tunneled data demands replacing the encryption keys and re-authenticating each device on a more aggressive basis. For more information about transformation, hashing, and encryption techniques, see the IPSec family of standards that recommends certain mandatory choices, which are called conformance requirements. The valid choices, supported and recommended by Cisco, are documented in Table 19-2.

Table 19-2 *Cisco Recommended Algorithms (At the Time This Book Was Written)*

Recommended Algorithms	Description of the Recommended Algorithms
ah-md5-hmac	AH-HMAC-MD5 transform
ah-rfc1828	AH-MD5 transform (RFC 1828)
ah-sha-hmac	AH-HMAC-SHA transform
esp-40bitdes	ESP transform using DES cipher (40 bits)
esp-des	ESP transform using DES cipher (56 bits)
esp-md5-hmac	ESP transform using HMAC-MD5 auth
esp-rfc1829	ESP-DES-CBC transform (RFC 1829)—Can't use with an auth Method
esp-sha-hmac	ESP transform using HMAC-SHA auth
esp-3des	ESP transform using 3DES cipher (168 bits)
esp-null	ESP transform using null cipher

In conclusion, Cisco announced major new capabilities in March 2002, for a Unified VPN (UVPN) suite of protocols that will increase service provider reach, and allow enterprises greater choices and flexibility. A first in the industry, UVPN was introduced with complete support for Layer 2 and Layer 3 VPN technologies. The second phase of Unified VPN Suite will support Multiprotocol Label Switching/Border Gateway Protocol based (MPLS/BGP) VPNs, IPSec, and generic routing encapsulation (GRE). It will integrate Layer 2 access VPNs and simplify deployment. As the latest addition to Cisco IOS Software, L2TP version 3 appears to offer a promising path to efficiently deliver Layer 2 services. One of the features in the UVPN is Cisco's EasyVPN, which is discussed in detail in the following chapters.

End Notes

[1] Alwayn, Vivek. *Advanced MPLS Design and Implementation.* Cisco Press, 2001.

[2] Cisco *Packet* Magazine. "Transport to the Future." R. Brown. Q1, 2002.

[3] RFC 2637. "Point-to-Point Tunneling Protocol." K. Hamzeh, G. Pall, W. Verthein, J. Taarud, W. Little, and G. Zorn. 1999.

[4] RFC 3078. "Microsoft Point-To-Point Encryption (MPPE) Protocol." G. Pall, G. Zorn. 2001.

[5] RFC 2661. "Layer Two Tunneling Protocol (L2TP)." W. Townsley, A. Valencia, A. Rubens, G. Pall, G. Zorn, B. Palter. 1999.

[6] RFC 2401. "Security Architecture for the Internet Protocol."

[7] RFC 1191. "Path MTU Discovery." J.C. Mogul and S.E. Deering. 1990.

[8] Cisco Systems Internet Draft. "Extended Authentication Within IKE (XAUTH)." S. Beaulieu and R. Pereira. 2002.

[9] "Extended Authentication within IKE (XAUTH)." www.ietf.org/internet-drafts/draft-beaulieu-ike-xauth-01.txt.

[10] Jones, Burton W. *Modular Arithmetic*. Blaisdell Publishing Company, 1964.

[11] www.sans.org/infosecFAQ/encription/diffie.htm.

[12] Cisco *Packet* Magazine. "IPSec-Based VPNs and Related Algorithms." P. Nedeltchev and R. Ratchkov. Q2 2002. (Also at www.cisco.com/warp/public/784/packet/apr02/pdfs/plamen.pdf.)

Summary

In this chapter, you learned about service provider-based VPNs and enterprise VPNs, the functional and technological categories, and the data link layer and network layer VPNs. The PPTP and L2TP second layer VPNs are explained in reasonable detail. The main focus of the chapter is on remote access VPNs, and especially IPSec-based remote access VPN solutions, because they represent the vast majority of the existing VPN solutions in today's industry. The IPSec sections include security associations, security policies, IKE and IPSec modes and protocols, such as the AH and ESP. The authentication includes group name and password, client, user and message authentication methods, and certificates. The DH exponential algorithm, and the complex hashing and encryption complex mathematical algorithms are represented.

Review Questions

Answers to the review questions can be found in Appendix A, "Answers to Review Questions."

1   Name the major VPN types of Cisco Enterprise VPN solutions.

2   What ports need to be open in the corporate firewall to ensure PPTP functionality?

3 What is the purpose of control messages in the L2TP protocol?

4 Define voluntary mode and compulsory mode in PPTP-based VPN.

5 What is the minimum set of negotiable attributes in IKE SA?

6 What does SPI stand for in IPSec?

7 What are the valid authenticating methods in IPSec?

8 What is the main difference between main mode and aggressive mode?

9 What is the main difference between transport mode and tunnel mode in IPSec?

10 Define the unidirectional and bidirectional security associations (SA). What kind of SA is an IKE SA? An IPSec SA?

11 What is ICV and how is it calculated?

12 Which ports have to open in the company's firewall to ensure ISAKMP, ESP, and AH operation?

13 What is the advantage of XAUTH among other authentication methods? What is type 1 authentication in XAUTH?

14 What is the size of the prime in DH Group 5?

15 What does PFS stand for? Explain PFS.

CHAPTER 20

Remote Access VPN Design and Configuration Solutions

The design of a remote access Virtual Private Network (VPN) solution is concerned with determining the optimum balance between functionality, frugality, and manageability for an organization. All Cisco solutions are competitive in pricing, offer overlapping feature sets, and perform remote access with cryptographic features. As a result, an organization's requirements can be met using a single or combination of Cisco alternatives. This chapter focuses on remote access VPN solutions. The initial part provides more detailed information about the main remote access VPN design objectives, remote access VPN management considerations, and security policies when designing remote access VPN access solutions. This chapter is divided into design and configuration sections.

The remote access VPN design part focuses on a concise description of the following topics:

- Remote access VPN design objectives
- Remote access VPN management considerations
- Security policies, authentication options, IP Security (IPSec) modes, Network Address Translation/Port Address Translation (NAT/PAT) challenges, split tunneling, and firewall functionality
- Remote access VPN core design considerations and architectural guidelines

The remote access VPN configuration part includes the following:

- Configuration of the VPN 3000 Concentrator
- Cisco VPN client configurations, including the VPN Unity Client, the Hardware client, the Easy VPN client, and the PIX-based client

Remote Access VPN Design Solutions

To clarify your need for a remote access VPN solution, you must first differentiate between remote access and site-to-site S2S VPNs, as shown in Table 20-1.

Table 20-1 *Remote Access Versus Site-to-Site VPN Comparison*

Location	Significant Number of Endpoints with Lower-Bandwidth Internet Connections	Limited Number of Endpoints with High-Bandwidth Internet Connections
Mobile	Remote access	Remote access
Fixed	Remote access	Site-to-site

A remote access solution is required to meet the demands for mobility from sales or remote staff who are frequently out of the office. Individual remote users require access to resources on their organization's network, regardless of the fact that they might be at a fixed location or roaming by connecting through high-bandwidth services to the Internet.

However, the distinction between remote access and smaller S2S VPN requirements is starting to blur because Cisco's product offerings in this area provide more flexibility. Today, remote access solutions provide not only Client mode, but also Network-Extension mode (VPN3002, Easy VPN, PIX 501 and 506), which enables a separate private network to be deployed on the client side with addressing that is routable with the organization's network. This expands the initial understanding of a S2S solution.

For large-scale enterprise remote access VPNs, particularly those that must support broadband connections, the key objectives of the design phase of VPNs are as follows:

- Resiliency and availability
- Easy management and flexibility
- Security policies
- Robust architecture and scalability

The most important decisions in the design phase of remote access VPN solutions include outlining the key objectives of the design, understanding how the VPN management processes are implemented, planning the required security policies, and knowing how to create a robust and scalable environment.

Remote Access VPN Design Objectives

Typically, a remote access VPN solution should meet the resiliency and availability standards of other areas of your network. Assuming that your organization has designed its Internet connectivity to provide local and global redundancy, you must consider product features that allow you to maximize service levels for your user base:

- **Flexible deployment**—You should be able to deploy your VPN terminating devices anywhere in your network. Currently, three general network configurations exist for VPN devices: bridge, end-node, and routed. A routed device provides the most redundancy because it participates in your network's dynamic routing processes. End-node devices depend on static routes that have a varying affect on redundancy, depending on how the Internet Protocol (IP) addresses are assigned to VPN clients, and how the pools are routed. If any client can access all network devices without regard to the concentrator or user group, redundancy for end-node devices approaches that for routed devices. Finally, bridged devices have the least flexibility because they must be located directly behind your Internet service provider's (ISP's) gateways.

- **Client transparency**—Upon failure or the inaccessibility of a VPN terminating device, the connection of a remote access VPN user should be seamlessly transferred to another VPN terminating device. Further, the client should be configurable to connect to multiple devices, with automatic connection attempts to backup devices in the event that the first choice is not available. Finally, if failover attempts are unsuccessful, the client should be notified in a timely manner that the connection has failed.

- **Service transparency**—Ideally, clients should be able to point their client to a single Domain Name System (DNS) to access the VPN service, regardless of the location and the corporate Internet access points. A single host name that covers all VPN terminating devices can provide maximum redundancy and perceived uptime from the client perspective. This design can be facilitated with the use of products such as Cisco Content Engines for Internet Content Delivery, which can be seen at the following site: www.cisco.com/warp/public/cc/so/neso/cxne/cceng_ds.htm or Cisco Distributed Director at www.cisco.com/warp/public/cc/pd/cxsr/dd/index.shtml.

The management of VPN solutions is crucial not only to protect the company's resources from unauthorized access, but also to enable a transparent and manageable solution for all categories of potential users, including full-time telecommuters, day-extenders, road-warriors, and engineers who are working from home or from a customer's site. The solution deployed for each category must be evaluated according to the ability to deploy, change, and enforce policy from the central site.

Remote Access VPN Management

Robust VPN management is a crucial factor for any large remote access VPN deployment. The relevant management features can fit into three broad categories: configuration, change, and operations.

Configuration Management

VPN is a sophisticated technology with an extensive number of configuration options. To fully realize the benefits, it must be easier to deploy than earlier solutions. Characteristics of strong configuration management include the following:

- Core devices demonstrate extremely high availability/low failure rates.

- Clients are easy to deploy and use, and end users do not require significant training.

- Existing infrastructures can be leveraged to minimize new investment in supporting technologies such as authentication, which includes the following:
    - Remote Access Dial-In User Server (RADIUS)
    - Terminal Access Controller Access Control System Plus (TACACS+)

Change Management

Inevitably, you will make changes to your VPN implementation. This might be as simple as changing the Simple Network Management Protocol (SNMP) strings on your central equipment, to a complete upgrade of your central devices and clients. The following are examples of requirements to consider when determining your change management needs:

- Changes to core devices do not require stopping/starting the device.
- New SW is verified by the core device before becoming available for operation, and erasing previous versions.
- Client SW upgrades require little to no user intervention.

Operations Management

Day-to-day monitoring and management of the VPN solution should be automated to the fullest extent, and require minimal human interaction to maintain service levels at the highest levels of operational availability. Examples of effective operations management include the following:

- Monitoring the entire service and individual devices
- Failure warnings and alerts that support industry standards
- Self-monitoring, alerts, and failover for proactive management

(See the section, "Redundancy" later in this chapter, which covers redundancy using Virtual Router Redundancy Protocol (VRRP) and load balancing.)

Remote Access VPN Security Considerations

This section covers some of the decision-making aspects when deciding on a remote access VPN solution. Most of these considerations are valid for any VPN design, but the main focus of this section is on remote access solutions.

In particular, the text covers the following:

- User authentication infrastructure
- IPSec transport and tunnel mode
- IPSec data authentication and encryption

- Challenges of NAT/PAT
- Split tunneling
- Performance criteria for VPN termination equipment
- Firewall functionality
- Resiliency and availability
- VPN core design considerations

Some of the following information was presented in detail in Chapter 19, "VPN Technology Background." Its presence here is to show how the different choices and options can or cannot make a difference in the design phase of remote access VPNs.

User Authentication Infrastructure

Ideally, organizations want to use what they already have deployed and are comfortable supporting. This is especially obvious for organizations that have some type of infrastructure to support dialup services. Although relatively few organizations have implemented Public Key Infrastructure (PKI) or digital certificate authentication systems across the entire enterprise, often systems to support RADIUS, TACACS+, NT Domain, and token-based security servers are already in-place. The argument could be made to migrate to VPN and PKI at the same time, but a general recommendation is to migrate to each technology individually to minimize the amount of change for the support organization.

IPSec Transport and Tunnel Mode

If you decide to implement IPSec, theoretically, you must also decide whether to implement Authentication Header (AH), or Encapsulation Security Protocol (ESP), or both. AH provides data integrity and data origin authentication. However, it does not hide the contents of its packets, so it cannot provide data confidentiality. ESP does encrypt the data, but it does not protect the new IP header. Ideally, you use both ESP and AH to gain the benefits of both. In reality, almost all remote access VPN deployments use only ESP.

Whether the IPSec AH or ESP protocol is chosen, the second important decision is whether to use transport or tunnel mode. Transport mode is used when both endpoints support IPSec, as opposed to tunnel mode, where there can be a proxy-like device terminating the tunnel, and then sending traffic on to and from the central network. In transport mode, the AH or ESP header is placed after the original header, and only the payload of the IP packet is encrypted. The original packet headers are left intact, which allows network services, such as quality of service (QoS) to be implemented. Tunnel mode encapsulates the entire IP packet in either AH or ESP, adding a new header, and then the entire datagram is encrypted. Because of its proxy-like capability, tunnel mode is almost exclusively used for all remote access VPN environments.

IPSec Data Authentication and Encryption

Security protocols must ensure that data transmissions are secure after the user is authenticated. This requires special tunneling protocols and encryption services because the remote user's information might be intercepted in transit, and modified by a third party without the knowledge of the user or the application. Packet contents can be inspected and modified, and source and destination addresses can be changed. TCP/IP originally did not offer any method to secure the data stream. Examples of the security protocols include generic routing encapsulation (GRE), Layer 2 Tunnel Protocol (L2TP), Point-to-Point Tunneling Protocol (PPTP), and IPSec.

In some instances, combining security protocols can be a preferable solution, as offered in the Cisco Unified VPN offering that is available in IOS versions 12.0S and 12.2T. For example, second layer tunneling could be more beneficial in high-latency networks, which require special measures to enforce your security policies. Based upon the details covered in Chapter 19, it is generally agreed that IPSec offers the strongest combination of features for tunneling, message authentication, and confidentiality.

A crucial component of authentication and encryption is the generation of keys used for each process. The key exchange between the devices in a remote access VPN session also identifies the participants. The Internet Key Exchange (IKE) (formerly [Internet Security Association and Key Management Protocol] ISAKMP/Oakley) is the recommended solution, and configurable options include the Diffie-Helman (DH) group to be used with a popular public key crypto algorithm. There are some indications that development of a new key exchange algorithm, Fast Key Exchange, is underway.

Data authentication confirms that the data one receives is actually the data that the originator intended to send. As part of IPSec-based VPNs, Cisco recommends data authentication protocols that use keyed hash algorithms. For most remote access environments, the Message Digest 5 (MD5) algorithm is the preferred alternative; however, the Secure Hash Algorithm 1 (SHA-1) is recommended for router-based or S2S solutions. These protocols offer configuration features that simplify their implementation.

Encryption converts the data into a coded form with a key that can only be understood if you have the key and understand the encoding algorithm. Otherwise, you cannot read the original data in the encrypted format. The more common encryption algorithms include the Data Encryption Standard (DES) and Triple-DES (3DES). A recently developed algorithm is the Advanced Encryption Standard (AES), which was approved as a Federal Information Processing Standard (FIPS) by the National Institute of Standards and Technology (NIST) at the end of 2001. Similar to the hashes discussed earlier in this section of this chapter, these data encryption algorithms usually offer configurable parameters.

Challenges of NAT/PAT

Environments that use NAT or PAT present challenges for establishing, transmitting, and receiving data across IPSec tunnels. A one-to-one NAT translation occurs when there is an internal address that is mapped to a unique external address. Although not widely used, this form of NAT is used by organizations that want to hide the identity of the end client. A one-to-many NAT, or a PAT environment, consists of one external address that is mapped to many internal addresses.

The router or firewall that performs the NAT or PAT maintains a translation table that identifies the external destination address with a unique identifier, such as the TCP or User Datagram Protocol (UDP) port numbers, and maps these port numbers to traffic transmitted to specific devices on the internal network. PAT is used extensively on residential and corporate networks, and enables the user to conserve address space and hide the identity of their clients.

Unfortunately, the ESP protocol does not use the concept of ports. Also, information in the packet is encrypted and unavailable, so the translation device cannot obtain the internal addresses from the IPSec packet. As a result, ESP is typically incompatible with this form of NAT.

IPSec over UDP: A Viable Alternative

As a workaround to the NAT issue described earlier in this chapter, Cisco implemented a technique where the IPSec traffic is encapsulated in UDP traffic, on the VPN 3000 series concentrator. By encapsulating the packet in UDP, the NAT translation device can perform the standard port mapping technique to uniquely identify the source and destination traffic flows. Implementing UDP encapsulation requires additional overhead for each packet, but it is relatively small compared to average packet sizes. At this time, a standards-based approach to resolving IPSec over NAT implementations has not been agreed upon. In the meantime, the Cisco alternative of UDP encapsulation is an effective solution.

IPSec over UDP on the Cisco VPN 3000 Concentrator and Clients

To use IPSec over UDP encapsulation, the VPN 3000 Concentrator administrator must configure either the user or a group. If enabled for a specific user, tunnel negotiation between the client and the concentrator occurs automatically by using IKE. The setup includes the UDP port number and the actual requirement for IPSec over UDP. It is configurable on the Cisco VPN Unity Client, but the Cisco VPN 3002 HW client does not offer any configurable options, so the IPSec over UDP feature for these client types must be configured on the Cisco VPN 3000 Concentrator.

As part of enabling the IPSec over UDP option, the core site concentrator must be accessible through the negotiated UDP port; then, data transmissions will be successful from a client behind a device that is performing NAT. If the remote user is behind a firewall, the user must ensure that the firewall rules permit the required traffic, which is necessary for establishing the tunnel over the specified UDP port.

IPSec over TCP

The Cisco VPN 3000 Concentrator, VPN Unity Client, and VPN 3002 HW Client provide the option to encapsulate IPSec traffic in TCP datagrams, which was released in v3.5 of these products. To activate this feature, both the core concentrator and the client must be configured to enable IPSec over TCP on the same TCP port. The benefit of enabling this feature is primarily for clients who try to access the central concentrator, while behind a firewall that only permits outside exchanges of datagrams that are started by internal hosts on well known or specific ports. By encapsulating the traffic over, for example, port 443 (https), the initiator can be reasonably confident that the firewall will permit responses from the core concentrator. This precludes the need to request security changes to accommodate IPSec, ISAKMP or specific UDP port traffic.

Split Tunneling

The split tunneling feature allows clients to simultaneously send and receive data across a VPN tunnel, while also communicating directly with resources on the Internet. Only traffic that is destined for or originating from hosts on the network that are terminating the VPN connection is encrypted and sent across the tunnel. All other IP traffic is sent outside of the VPN connection to hosts connected on the Internet unencrypted.

An organization might find split tunneling beneficial because it reduces the central resources required to support a VPN environment, including ISP bandwidth, and through-put on the local-area network (LAN) and VPN tunnel terminating device. However, many organizations with strict security policies might find the risk of implementing split tunneling too great, and restrict its use.

Concerns might arise as split tunneling could increase the likelihood that an intruder might break into the corporate network by hacking a member's host that is concurrently connected to both the Internet and the corporate network through the VPN. The argument is that the organization does not want to extend their firewall capabilities to the customer premises equipment (CPE) at the remote user's location, and deal with the administration. To possibly address some of these concerns, an integrated stateful firewall was incorporated into v3.5A of the Cisco VPN Unity Client, which can be activated when a VPN connection is attempted or active. With v3.5 the VPN 3000 Concentrator included a configurable option to require or warn connecting SW VPN clients that they must imple-ment a specific SW firewall. Further, with v3.5.1, the concentrator can point to a central server that administers the firewall policy.

Firewall Functionality

Firewalls are designed to protect a network from outside traffic that is determined to be hostile to the organization. Some products provide an integrated solution for both the firewall and the VPN terminating device; however, before covering this in more detail, the following descriptions of firewall types are provided:

- **Packet filter firewalls**—Packet filter firewalls are the simplest type of firewall available today. They require the least amount of resources, but can only perform simple logic such as permit/deny—based on source/destination IP address, protocol, or port. Intruders can thwart the firewall by spoofing the address.

- **Proxy firewalls**—A proxy is a gateway between the source and destination. All traffic that is intended for external hosts is sourced from the proxy address, instead of the originator's address, which provides some anonymity and security to the data transfer. Detailed access controls and traffic reporting are available on proxy firewalls.

- **Stateful inspection firewalls**—Stateful inspection firewalls are the most sophisticated, extending the features of packet-filtering to examine packet flows, and allowing policies to be implemented and checked. An example of this capability is when a TCP acknowledgment (ACK) packet is not preceded by a TCP synchronize (SYN) packet in the correct sequence.

The concentrator rejects any traffic not sourced from one of the allowed protocols or ports. A common deployment for most organizations is to place a stateful inspection firewall in parallel with the VPN concentrator, which offers scaling advantages versus an integrated device. Another advantage of separate devices is the opportunity to implement management interfaces that are optimized independently for each environment. An obvious drawback of this solution is the fact that two different devices with different interfaces require support staff who are trained on both units.

Remote Access VPN Termination Equipment Design Considerations

Cisco recently developed the SAFE Blueprint,[1] which provides the latest information for VPN architecture and designs. An entire series of documents are available online from www.cisco.com. This information should be regularly reviewed to ensure that your networks incorporate the latest suggested designs and features. SAFE discusses various alternatives from the organization's perspective, taking into account the scale of the implementation, and the available resources of the organization. It is recommended that you extensively refer to this site when planning your remote access VPN offering.

Termination Equipment Architecture Guidelines

A quick overview of some suggested items that should be considered for your VPN core device architecture are documented in this section.

For remote access VPNs, determining the number of devices and where they are deployed is a major concern. To address location decisions, you must analyze your organization's firewall locations and determine where the largest numbers of your user community can access your network. Based on this analysis, enterprises usually provide VPN termination capability at these high-traffic Internet points of presence (POPs).

For redundancy, clients can be automatically redirected to VPN core devices at other locations if they cannot access the devices in their chosen location. The number of VPN sites that you implement depends on your remote access strategy, Internet POPs, available bandwidth, and the availability of required support staff and procedures. In most cases, it is usually worthwhile to consolidate into selected sites, where bandwidth is plentiful and cost effective, to reduce the complexity of maintaining a large number of firewalls and demilitarized zone (DMZ) networks. However, this model might not be the best fit in areas of the world where there is little difference in the cost of Internet access versus dedicated bandwidth. Generally speaking, Cisco recommends that you install the VPN device in parallel with your corporate firewall in the DMZ, as shown in Figure 20-1.

Figure 20-1   *Cisco Recommended Architecture for VPN Core Devices*

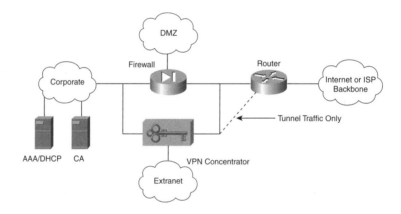

In the dotted-line configuration, only tunneled traffic is routed to the VPN concentrator from the Internet, and the concentrator is protected from denial of service (DOS) attacks. Alternatives are possible, such as placing a firewall behind and parallel to the concentrator to provide additional protection to the internal network from such things as virus-infected VPN clients. Numerous possibilities must be considered. It is recommended that you consult Cisco and network security specialists to determine the architecture that best meets your requirements.

A number of questions can be considered in determining which core device to use as the core VPN tunnel terminating device:

- What are the desired features (NAT transparency, 3DES encryption, and so on)?

- How many clients must be supported by the core device?

- Is an integrated firewall on the concentrator required or desired?

- Would you plan to run a routing protocol on the VPN tunnel-terminating device (Enhanced Interior Gateway Routing Protocol [EIGRP], Routing Information Protocol [RIP], or Open Shortest Path First [OSPF])?

- What are the installation and ongoing support costs between alternative VPN solutions, and when compared to the existing remote access solution?

Core Device Choice Considerations

Cisco IOS-based routers, PIX firewalls, and 3000 VPN Concentrators can all terminate remote access IPSec VPN tunnels (see Figure 20-2). The device(s) you select to implement depends on the scale of your roll out, the number of sites where remote access VPN tunnel terminating devices are located, and the available development and support resources within your organization.

Figure 20-2   *The Possible Combinations of Remote Access VPN Client and Termination Points*

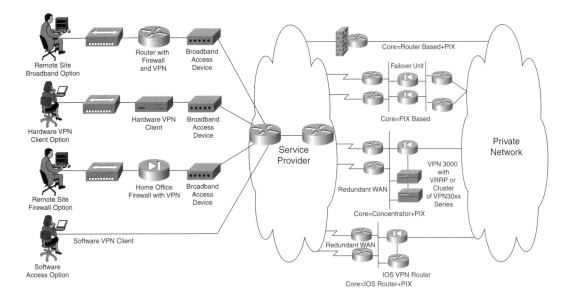

Where scalability is an issue, such as for medium and large-scale deployments with greater than 100 concurrent connections, dedicated devices for terminating the remote access VPN tunnels should be deployed. Generally speaking, for maximum security, the termination device should be in parallel with your corporate firewall. However, this extra security comes with slightly greater support costs because you must manage additional devices, versus a scenario where the terminating device was behind the firewall.

Cisco Remote Access VPN Core Devices

The device that you implement to terminate remote access IPSec VPN tunnels depends on the requirements and resources of the site and your organization. This section provides a brief overview of the Cisco VPN 3000 Series Concentrators. Additional information for the Cisco Easy VPN Server and PIX, as VPN tunnel terminating devices, is also provided. However, you should consult your Cisco resources to determine the latest information available about remote access VPN features in the IOS and PIX devices, and the use of these devices for terminating remote access VPN tunnels.

Cisco VPN 3000 Series Concentrator Features

Functions of the VPN 3000 Concentrator include the following:

- Establishes tunnels

- Negotiates tunnel parameters

- Authenticates users

- Assigns user addresses

- Encrypts and decrypts data

- Manages security keys

- Manages data transfer across the tunnel

- Manages data transfer inbound and outbound as a tunnel endpoint or router [2]

The Cisco VPN 3000 Concentrators, in various models, address the remote access requirements of all organizations of any type and size. The available models and their specific features are listed in Table 20-2.[3] Configuration and selected features of the Cisco VPN 3000 Concentrators are covered in the following discussion.

Table 20-2 *Cisco VPN 3000 Series Concentrator Models and Features*

Feature	Cisco 3005	Cisco 3015	Cisco 3030	Cisco 3060	Cisco 3080
Simultaneous users	100	100	1500	5000	10000
Encryption throughput	4 Mbps	4 Mbps	50 Mbps	100 Mbps	100 Mbps
Encryption method	Software	Software	Hardware	Hardware	Hardware
Encryption (Scalable Encryption Processing [SEP]) module	0	0	1	2	4
Redundant SEP	N/A	N/A	Option	Option	Yes
Available expansion slots	0	4	3	2	N/A
Upgrade capability	No	Yes	Yes	N/A	N/A
System memory	32 MB (fixed)	64 MB	128 MB	256 MB	256 MB
T1 wide-area network (WAN) module	Fixed option	Option	Option	Option	Option
Hardware	1U, Fixed	2U, Scalable	2U, Scalable	2U, Scalable	2U
Dual power supply	Single	Option	Option	Option	Yes
Client license	Unlimited	Unlimited	Unlimited	Unlimited	Unlimited

Easy VPN Server

The Easy VPN Server feature for Cisco routers was first offered in IOS Release 12.2(8)T. It allows a router to act as a VPN head-end device for remote access VPNs, where the remote device can be a Cisco Unity VPN Client, a VPN 3002 HW Client, a PIX501 or PIX506 running PIX OS v6.2 configured as a VPN client, or a Cisco 800 or 1700 series router configured with SW that supports the Easy VPN Client.

Using the Easy VPN Server feature, security policies defined at the head-end can be pushed to the remote access client. The functions of the Easy VPN Server are similar to those of the Cisco VPN 3000 Series Concentrators. A list of the routers that function as an Easy VPN Server are as follows: Cisco 800, 1400, 1600, 1700, 2600, 3600, 7100, 7200, and 7500 series routers, and the uBR905 and uBR925 cable modems (see www.cisco.com/univercd/cc/td/doc/product/software/ios122/122newft/122t/122t8/ftunity.htm).

A selected list of supported IPSec protocol options and attributes, supported by the Easy VPN Server, is listed in Table 20-3. A list of non-supported IPSec protocols and attributes is provided in Table 20-4. Detailed explanations of the attributes can be found in Chapter 19, or in the "Configuration of the VPN 3000 Concentrator" section.

Table 20-3 *Selected IPSec Options and Attributes Supported by the Easy VPN Server*[4]

Options	Attributes
Authentication algorithms	HMAC-MD5
	HMAC-SHA1
Authentication types	Preshared keys
	RSA digital signatures
DH groups	2
	5
Encryption algorithms (IKE)	DES
	3DES
Encryption algorithms (IPSec)	DES
	3DES
	NULL
IPSec protocol	ESP
	IPCOMP-LZS
IPSec protocol mode	Tunnel mode

Table 20-4 *Selected IPSec Protocol Options and Attributes NOT Supported on the Easy VPN Server*[5]

IPSec Protocol Options	Attributes Not Supported
Authentication types	Authentication with public key encryption
	Digital signature standard (DSS)
DH group	1
IPSec protocol	IPSEC_AH
IPSec protocol mode	Transport mode
Miscellaneous	Manual keys
	Perfect forward secrecy (PFS)

PIX 500 Series Firewalls as Remote Access VPN Servers

PIX 500 series firewalls can also be configured as the core device that terminates remote access IPSec VPN tunnels. Concurrent users and throughput for the various PIX firewalls that are configured as core devices are shown in Table 20-5. The PIX firewalls support most of the same attributes as the Cisco Easy VPN Server with a few differences such as support for DH Group 1, but not for Group 5, which Easy VPN supports. Other selected features that PIX supports, but not the Easy VPN Server, are as follows:

- Transport mode (for L2P)
- PFS
- IPComp-L2Z (Compression)

One useful feature that is not supported on both the PIX and the Easy VPN Server is UDP encapsulation for NAT/PAT operating environments.

Table 20-5 *Differences Between the Various PIX Firewalls Configured as Core Devices to Terminate Remote Access IPSec VPN Tunnels*

	501	506	515	525	535
IPSec VPN clients	5	25	2000	2000	2000
SW throughput (3DES-SHA)	3 Mbps	10 Mbps	10 Mbps	30 Mbps	45 Mbps
HW throughput (3DES-SHA)	NA	NA	NA	70 Mbps	95 Mbps

Performance Criteria for VPN Termination Equipment

The device that terminates the VPN tunnel on the corporate network should be the solution that best meets the organization's requirements, while maximizing performance. As is often the case, the factors of cost, productivity, and security must be prioritized to assist with the selection of the most appropriate solution. Of course, financial concerns must be acknowledged, but these should be balanced against improved productivity and security. To evaluate the VPN termination device, compare your requirement's against the VPN device's capabilities.

The device must authenticate users, based on centralized databases that are located on the concentrator, or through a proxy mechanism to central servers. It usually has two interfaces—a public and private. As the names suggest, the public interface is accessible from the Internet or service provider network, and the private is protected by the corporate firewalls or by the concentrator itself. Encrypted traffic is passed through the public interface, and unencrypted traffic flows through the private interface. In most cases, performance is maximized by devices that are dedicated to terminating the VPN tunnel, instead of a shared-purpose device, such as a firewall.

Specifications of the VPN termination equipment that should be carefully reviewed before making any commitments along with some recommendations include the following:

- **Encrypted throughput**—When the preferred method of encryption is implemented, throughput measurements should be taken. If 3DES is the choice, using the largest key available, which is 168-bit, is recommended. If AES is the choice, a 256-bit key is recommended.

- **Data authentication**—Implementing either the SHA-1 or MD5 hash algorithms for data authentication also requires significant processing power. Measurements have to be made, based on the chosen hashing algorithm, and 168-bit 3DES encryption (256-bit AES).

- **Packet size**—In general, the packet size of wired networks is proportional to throughput. It is unrealistic to perform measurements based on 1500, or 64 bytes. An effective measurement should be performed with an average packet size that is commonly found on the Internet.[6]

- **Data throughput**—Most VPN termination devices have two interfaces, but to quote throughput as the sum of the data traffic passing through both the public and private interface at a given moment is misleading. True throughput should be measured as the data transported through the device.

- **Simultaneous connections and throughput**—Theoretically, maximum throughput can be measured with one user connected through a single tunnel to the termination device. However, this is not a realistic representation of a real-world scenario. It is better to increase the number of clients for testing purposes, to better determine the expected throughput after it is deployed.

- **Latency**—As throughput increases, internal packet queues also increase. Unfortunately, this can also impact clients with delay-sensitive applications, such as Voice over IP (VoIP) or terminal emulators. High-performance devices that are specifically designed for terminating the VPN tunnel offer better performance versus a general-purpose device.

- **Actual data**—When comparing throughput of devices, try to use the same data streams. If you measure throughput in terms of user-payload data, this approach avoids any inconsistency that might arise.

- **Packets per second**—Measuring packets per second is an important statistic for comparison purposes. Although it is not as critical as throughput, it does measure the ability to route packets from the private to public interface.

- **Routing capability**—You can select a device that can run a routing protocol used on your network. However, the use of large contiguous address pools might require you to use static routes, but unfortunately, static routes can result in reduced redundancy.

VPN Configuration Considerations

This section covers selected configuration features of the Cisco VPN 3000 Series Concentrator running v3.5.2, which is used as the core device that terminates remote access VPN tunnels for the following clients: Cisco Unity VPN Client, VPN 3002 HW Client, Easy VPN, and the PIX 501 and 506 Clients.

Configuration of the VPN 3000 Concentrator

As indicated, this section does not attempt to cover all aspects of configuring the Cisco VPN 3000 Series Concentrators. Instead, selected features are explored and actual configurations of these features are discussed by using v3.5.2 as the reference.

The concentrator offers a quick configuration menu that allows you to configure it in a matter of minutes, after you determine the values and settings for the unit. The steps required to configure the concentrator are outlined in Table 20-6.[7] The minimum required settings offered by the Quick Configuration option are listed in Table 20-7.[8]

Table 20-6 *Steps Required for Quick Configuration on a VPN 3000 Concentrator*

Step	Task
1	Set the system time, date, and time zone, from the console.
2	Configure the VPN Concentrator Ethernet 1 interface to your private network, from the console.
At this point, you can use a browser that is pointing to the private interface to complete Quick Configuration with the VPN Concentrator Manager.	
3	Configure the other Ethernet interfaces that are connected to a public network or an additional external network.
4	Enter system identification information: system name, date, time, DNS, domain name, and default gateway.
5	Specify tunneling protocols and encryption options.

Table 20-6   *Steps Required for Quick Configuration on a VPN 3000 Concentrator (Continued)*

Step	Task
6	Specify methods for assigning IP addresses to clients as a tunnel is established.
7	Choose and identify the user authentication server: the internal server, RADIUS, NT Domain, or Security Dynamics Incorporated (SDI).
8	If using the internal authentication server, populate the internal user database.
9	If using the IPSec tunneling protocol, assign a name and password to the IPSec tunnel group.
10	Change the **admin** password for security.
11	Save the configuration file. Quick Configuration is now completed.

Table 20-7   *Quick Configuration Settings for a VPN 3000 Concentrator*

Quick Configuration Parameters Screen	Parameter Name	Parameter Description and Use
IP Interfaces	Ethernet 1 (Private)	Specify the IP address and subnet mask, speed, and duplex mode for the VPN Concentrator interface to your private network.
IP Interfaces	Ethernet 2 (Public)	Specify the IP address and subnet mask, speed, and duplex mode for the VPN Concentrator interface to the public network.
IP Interfaces	Ethernet 3 (External)	(For models 3015-3080 only) If so connected, specify the IP address and subnet mask, speed, and duplex mode for the VPN Concentrator interface to an additional external network.
System Info	System Name	Specify a device or system name for the VPN Concentrator (for example, VPN01).
System Info	DNS Server	Specify the IP address of your local DNS server.
System Info	Domain	Specify the registered Internet domain name to use with DNS (for example, cisco.com).
System Info	Default Gateway	Specify the IP address or hostname of the default gateway for packets not otherwise routed.
Address Assignment	DHCP	Server	If you use Dynamic Host Configuration Protocol (DHCP) for remote address assignment, specify the IP address or host name of the DHCP server.
Address Assignment	Configured Pool	Range Start and Range End	If you use the VPN Concentrator to assign addresses, specify the starting and ending IP addresses in its initial configured pool.
Authentication	Choose from the following parameters you see in the following screen. Possible values are as follows: **Internal Server**—Choosing Internal Server means using the internal VPN Concentrator user authentication server. On the User Database screen, specify the username and password for each user.

continues

Table 20-7 *Quick Configuration Settings for a VPN 3000 Concentrator (Continued)*

Quick Configuration Parameters Screen I Parameter Name	Parameter Description and Use
	Additionally, if you specify a per-user address assignment, specify the IP address and subnet mask for each user.
	RADIUS—If you use an external RADIUS user authentication server, specify its IP address or host name, port number, and server secret or password.
	NT Domain—If you use an external Windows NT Domain user authentication server, specify its IP address, port number, and primary domain controller (PDC) hostname.
	SDI—If you use an external SDI user authentication server, specify its IP address and port number.
User Database I Group Name, Password, Verify	If you enable the IPSec tunneling protocol, specify a name and password for the IPSec tunnel group.

System Configuration Highlights

Details of each facet of the concentrator configuration for v3.5 can be found at www.cisco.com/univercd/cc/td/doc/product/vpn/vpn3000/rel3_5_1/config/cfg.pdf.

The following section highlights some of the parameters that can be configured on the VPN 3000 Series Concentrator, under the Configuration, System menu.

Filters and Rules

Filters are assigned to the private (interface 1), public (interface 2), and external (interface 3) interfaces of the concentrator, and to groups or users. The filters provide a means to control traffic that passes through the concentrator.

Three filters can be set (Private, Public and External), besides the option to not set a filter. The filter is configured by assigning rules to it under the Configuration, Policy Management, Traffic Management, Filters menu, as shown in Figure 20-3. This menu also offers the option to modify the existing filter settings, or to create your own filter.

Rules consist of either one of two actions, forward or drop, which you assign to the filter for various types of TCP/IP traffic. The concept is similar to that of access-lists on an IOS router, in which you use permit/deny instead of forward/drop.

Figure 20-3   *Assigning Rules to the Filter Configuration Menu*

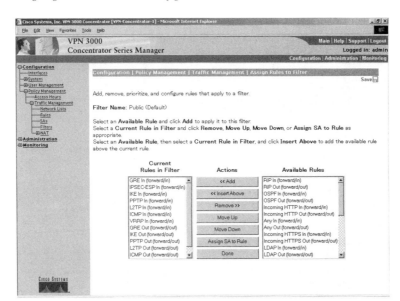

A substantial number of rules are preconfigured on the concentrator for various types of TCP/IP traffic that is specific to whether the traffic is incoming or outgoing. Rules are configured under Configuration, System Management, Policy Management, Traffic Management, Rules, as shown in Figure 20-4. The figure comprises two images. To modify existing rules or to configure your own, you must decide on the following parameters:

- Protocol or port (source and destination)

- Direction (inbound or outbound)

- Action for traffic received over established connections

- Source and destination address information (network and subnet mask)

Figure 20-4 *Configuring Rules*

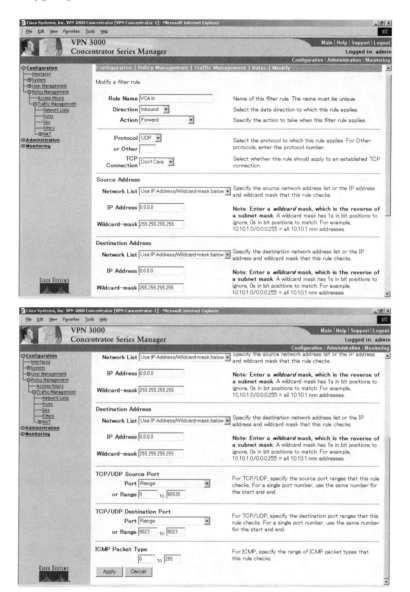

Redundancy

Using VRRP,[9] you can configure redundant concentrators in case the primary concentrator fails. Using this configuration, there are one or more Backup units, and there is one active concentrator, referred to as the Master.

The Backup units behave as hot standby concentrators, by not terminating any tunnels unless the primary concentrator fails. The Master constantly communicates its status to the Backup concentrators, and if the Master concentrator fails, VRRP tries the Backup concentrator(s) in order of precedence.[10]

The Backup concentrators must be configured identically to the Master unit. The IP addresses of the Master concentrators are the virtual IP addresses that must be configured on the Backup units. Further, the Backup and Master concentrators' public interfaces should be on the same subnet. Similarly, the private interfaces should be on the same subnet.

The Backup units do not respond to pings to the virtual IP address; however, if the Master fails, the highest priority Backup unit assumes the role of Master and terminates the IPSec tunnels. From the client perspective, the transfer from the Master to the Backup unit is transparent, and the client session continues without the need to re-establish the IPSec tunnel. Redundancy is configured under the menu Configuration, System, IP Routing, Redundancy, as shown in Figure 20-5.

Figure 20-5   *Redundancy Menu Used to Configure VRRP*

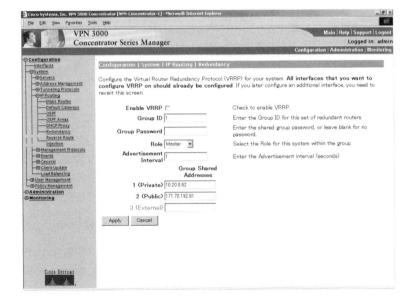

Load Balancing

Load balancing occurs when multiple concentrators are configured to appear as one virtual cluster instead of multiple concentrators. Client connections are established on a round-robin basis, based on the session load on each concentrator. This session load per concentrator is the total number of active connections, divided by the maximum number of sessions configured on the concentrator. As a result, when you first implement load balancing, you might have to reduce the maximum number of sessions per concentrator in the cluster, until the number of active clients approaches a predetermined threshold, when the maximum session count on each concentrator should be re-evaluated. The maximum session count is configured under the Configuration, System, General, Sessions menu.

Each concentrator in the cluster is configured with the IP address of the virtual cluster, which clients use to establish their IPSec tunnels. To configure load balancing, go to Configuration, System, Load Balancing, as shown in Figure 20-6. If you use the default public or private filters, you might be required to change the filter rules to permit the protocol used for the Virtual Cluster Agent (VCA). The default for this protocol is UDP, port 9023.

Figure 20-6 *Menu Used to Configure Load Balancing*

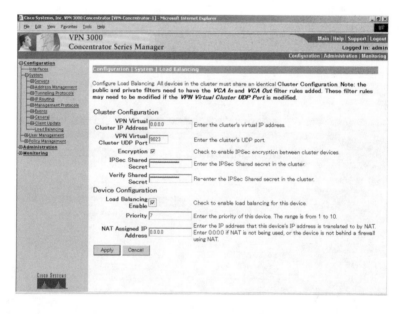

You must set the priority of each concentrator in the virtual cluster, which determines the concentrator that will act as the Master of the cluster. Default priority values are assigned to concentrators that are based on the HW platform, as shown in Table 20-8. Generally, the first concentrator configured and deployed in a cluster is the Master, and if it fails, or if two concentrators are deployed at the same time, the concentrator with the highest priority takes precedence. If the concentrators boot at the same time and have the same priority, the concentrator with the lowest IP is elected Master. After the Master is determined, a new Master is not elected until the current Master fails.

Table 20-8   *Default Priority for VPN 3000 Series Concentrators* [11]

VPN Concentrator Model	Priority
3005	1
3015	3
3030	5
3060	7
3080	10

Unlike the redundancy configuration, if the concentrators are configured for load balancing, a client connection is terminated if their VPN terminating concentrator fails. Clients must re-establish their IPSec tunnel; however, they can still point to the cluster address instead of a specific concentrator.

Reverse Route Injection

The VPN 3000 Concentrators offer reverse route injection, when the concentrator is configured to announce routes on the private interface using OSPF or RIP. Under reverse route injection, the concentrator announces the route of the client. If the Client Reverse Route Injection feature is activated, and if the connection is from a Unity VPN SW Client or a VPN 3002 HW Client configured for PAT mode, the concentrator announces the host route for that specific client. To activate this feature, go to Configuration, System, IP Routing, Reverse Route Injection, as shown in Figure 20-7.

Similarly, if the tunnel between the VPN 3000 Concentrator and the VPN 3002 HW Client is configured for network extension mode, the Network Extension Reverse Route Injection must be configured on the same concentrator menu. The VPN 3000 concentrators can be configured with hold down routes for client addresses. You can use the Generate Hold Down Routes feature to automatically create the routes for all the address pools that are configured on the concentrator.

Figure 20-7 *Reverse Route Configuration Menu*

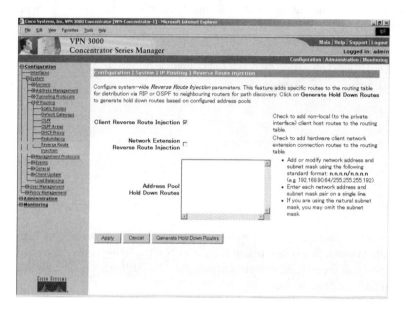

IKE Proposals and Security Associations for IKE and IPSec

IKE proposals are the settings that negotiate the IKE and IPSec Security Associations (SA). As discussed in Chapter 19, IKE SAs negotiate the parameters to establish a secure tunnel, so that the IPSec SAs can negotiate how traffic is managed in the tunnel. The VPN 3000 Concentrator responds to IPSec requests from remote access clients, and checks all active IKE proposals in priority order, to determine if one matches the parameters in the initiator's proposed SA. Some IKE proposals and IKE and IPSec SAs that are compatible with the Cisco VPN Unity Client and VPN 3002 HW Client, are preconfigured on the concentrator, but you can add your own or modify the existing proposals. After you configure the IKE proposals, configure the IPSec SAs and apply them to the specific user or group.

The IKE proposal contains the information required for the Phase 1 IPSec negotiation. IKE proposals are configured under the Configuration, System, Tunneling Protocols, IKE Proposals menu, and the modification menu for a specific IKE proposal is shown in Figure 20-8. Specific attributes for active and inactive preconfigured IKE proposals are listed in Table 20-9.

Figure 20-8   *Modification Menu for a Specific IKE Proposal*

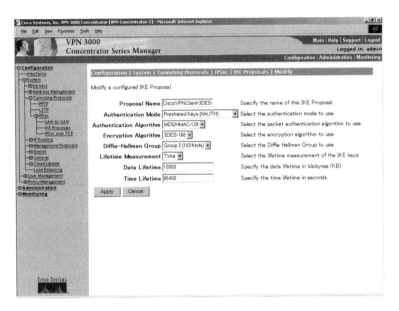

Table 20-9 *Attributes for Preconfigured IKE Proposals* [12]

Proposal Name	Authentication Mode	Authentication Algorithm	Encryption Algorithm	DH Group	Lifetime Measurements	Data Lifetime	Time Lifetime
Proposals Active by Default							
CiscoVPNClient-3DES-MD5	Preshared Keys (XAUTH)	MD5/HMAC-128	3DES-168	Group 2 (1024bits)	Time	10,000 KB	86,400 sec
IKE-3DES-MD5	Preshared Keys	MD5/HMAC-128	3DES-168	Group 2 (1024bits)	Time	10,000 KB	86,400 sec
IKE-3DES-MD5-DH1	Preshared Keys	MD5/HMAC-128	3DES-168	Group 1 (768bits)	Time	10,000 KB	86,400 sec
IKE-DES-MD5	Preshared Keys	MD5/HMAC-128	DES-56	Group 1 (768-bits)	Time	10,000 KB	86,400 sec
IKE-3DES-MD5-DH7	Preshared Keys	MD5/HMAC-128	3DES-168	Group 7 (ECC) (163bits)	Time	10,000 KB	86,400 sec
IKE-3DES-MD5-RSA	RSA Digital Certificate	MD5/HMAC-128	3DES-168	Group 2 (1024bits)	Time	10,000 KB	86,400 sec
Proposals Inactive by Default							
IKE-3DES-MD5-RSA	RSA Digital Certificate	MD5/HMAC-128	3DES-168	Group 2 (1024-bits)	Time	10,000 KB	86,400 sec
IKE-3DES-SHA-DSA	RSA Digital Certificate	SHA/HMAC-160	3DES-168	Group 2 (1024bits)	Time	10,000 KB	86,400 sec
IKE-3DES-MD5-RSA-DH1	RSA Digital Certificate	MD5/HMAC-128	3DES-168	Group 1 (768bits)	Time	10,000 KB	86,400 sec
IKE-DES-MD5-DH7	Preshared Keys	MD5/HMAC-128	DES-56	Group 7 (ECC) (163bits)	Time	10,000 KB	86,400 sec
CiscoVPNClient-3DES-MD5-RSA	RSA Digital Certificate (XAUTH)	MD5/HMAC-128	3DES-168	Group 2 (1024-bits)	Time	10,000 KB	86,400 sec
CiscoVPNClient-3DES-SHA-DSA	DSA Digital Certificate (XAUTH)	SHA/HMAC-160	3DES-168	Group 2 (1024bits)	Time	10,0000 KB	86,400 sec

The various alternatives for the IKE proposal parameters are described in detail in Chapter 19. The minimum and maximum lifetimes for the IKE proposals are 60 and 2,147,483,647 seconds (about 68 years). The minimum and maximum lifetimes for the IKE proposals, if measured by data, are 10 and 2,147,483,647 KB.

DH Group 2 is the default for the 3DES-168 bit encryption algorithm. The Cisco VPN Unity SW Client v3.x is only compatible with DH Group 2. To use DH Group 1 or Group 7 with the VPN 3002 HW client, digital certificates must be used in the Authentication Mode.

SAs

SAs are configured under the Configuration, Policy Management, Traffic Management, SAs menu. The SA modification menu is shown in Figure 20-9. Similar to the IKE proposals, the concentrators are preconfigured with default SAs that are listed in Table 20-10. These SAs were discussed in detail in Chapter 19.

The IPSec parameters negotiate the Phase 2 SAs, and the IKE parameters apply to the Phase 1 SA negotiations. All parameters must be configured on the remote access client and the core, except where noted. However, clients often do not have the same flexibility to support various possibilities for a given parameter. For the remaining parameters, the default settings are usually the best suited for the Cisco VPN Unity SW Client and the VPN 3002 HW Client.

Figure 20-9   *Specific SA Configuration Menu*

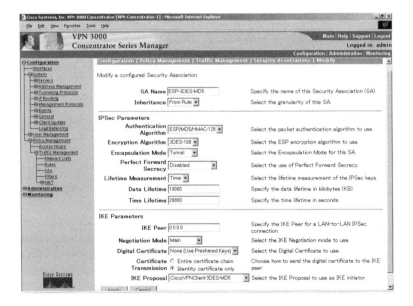

Table 20-10 *Preconfigured SAs for the VPN 3000 Concentrators* [13]

SA Name Parameter	ESP-DES-MD5	ESP-3DES-MD5	ESP/IKE-3DES-MD5	ESP-3DES-NONE	ESP-L2TP-TRANSPORT	ESP-3DES-MD5-DH7
Inheritance	**From Rule**	**From Rule**	**From Rule**	**From Rule**	**From Rule**	**From Rule**
IPSec Parameters						
Authentication algorithm	ESP/MD5/ HMAC-128	ESP/MD5/ HMAC-128	ESP/MD5/ HMAC-128	None	ESP/MD5/ HMAC-128	ESP/MD5/ HMAC-128
Encryption algorithm	DES-56	3DES-168	3DES-168	3DES-168	DES-56	3DES-168
Encapsulation mode	Tunnel	Tunnel	Tunnel	Tunnel	Transport	Tunnel
PFS	Disabled	Disabled	Disabled	Disabled	Disabled	Disabled
Lifetime Measurement	Time	Time	Time	Time	Time	Time
Data lifetime	10,000 KB	10,000 KB	10,000 KB	10,000 KB	10,000 KB	10,000 KB
Time lifetime	28,800 sec	28,800 sec	28,800 sec	28,800 sec	3,600 sec	28,800 sec
IKE Parameters						
IKE peer	0.0.0.0	0.0.0.0	0.0.0.0	0.0.0.0	0.0.0.0	0.0.0.0
Negotiation mode	Main	Main	Main	Main	Main	Aggressive
Digital certificate	None (Use preshared keys)	None (Use preshared keys)	None (Use preshared keys)	None (Use preshared keys)	None (Use preshared keys)	None (Use preshared keys)
IKE proposal	IKE-DES-MD5	IKE-DES-MD5	IKE-3DES-MD5	IKE-3DES-MD5	IKE-3DES-MD5	IKE-3DES-MD5-DH7

Inheritance specifies the number of tunnels that should be built for each connection. It is more applicable for LAN-to-LAN VPN connections than for remote access VPN connections, as the alternatives are From Rule, one tunnel for each rule in the connection, or From Data, one tunnel for every address pair within the address range specified in the rule.

IPSec and IKE SA Parameters

Most parameter options are discussed in detail in Chapter 19; however, the following additional information might be required. The IKE peer is applicable only for LAN-to-LAN VPNs. Configure the digital certificate option only if you are using PKI certificates, and then you must determine if you will send just the identity certificate, or the entire certificate chain. The IKE proposal parameter is applicable for LAN-to-LAN VPN environments, where the concentrator can be the initiator of the IPSec negotiations. In this scenario, the IKE proposal that is entered is the only proposal negotiated by the concentrator. This is opposite to when the concentrator responds to the IPSec negotiations.

User Configuration Highlights

This section highlights selected parameters that can be configured on the VPN 3000 Concentrator under the Configuration, User Management menus. The following specific menus refer to the Configuration, User Management, Groups menu, but the IPSec SA can also be configured for individual users under the Configuration, User Management, Users menu.

IPSec SA

In the previous section of this chapter, the parameters of the IPSec SA were covered. This section provides information when you select the IPSec SA under the IPSec tab of the specific user or group, as shown in Figure 20-10.

Figure 20-10 *IPSec Configuration Menu for User Management*

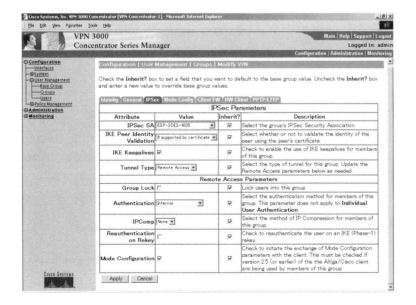

IKE Peer Identity Validation

IKE peer identity validation applies only to tunnel negotiations based on certificates. When configured, it provides an extra measure of security because the concentrator verifies the identity of the client with information in the digital certificate, such as the hostname or IP address. If you want to implement this additional validation for clients, select this feature, as shown in Figure 20-10.

Group Lock

By setting the Group Lock parameter, you can configure the concentrator to authenticate users only if they are members of the group configured on an external RADIUS server. So the VPN client can be configured with an active group name and group password to provide a user prompt, and then be authenticated by a RADIUS server. However, if the server returns information that the user is a member of another group, the user fails authentication.[14] Furthermore, by using this feature, VPN clients who authenticate as members of one group are restricted to use the features of the group that are authenticated, even if the client is a member of another group with different feature sets.

Configuration Mode

Configuration mode refers to the process and communications when the concentrator exchanges certain configuration parameters with the client, such as the DNS and Windows Internet Naming Service (WINS) server addresses, during the SA negotiation. Configuration mode must be configured if you want to implement split tunneling, local LAN access, or UDP encapsulation of IPSec traffic. Third-party VPN clients might not support Configuration mode and its parameters.

Client Firewall

The VPN 3000 Series Concentrators now support interaction with PC-based firewalls. Depending on your preference, you can require clients to use a firewall to allow them to establish a VPN tunnel, to push the firewall policy from the concentrator upon tunnel establishment, or to push the policy from a Zone Labs Integrity Server. Supported personal firewalls include these or later versions: Cisco Integrated Firewall (CIC), ZoneAlarm Pro 2.6, ZoneAlarm 2.6, BlackICE 2.5, and BlackICE Agent 2.5.

Cisco Remote Access VPN Clients

Client features and availability are constantly being updated. As a result, the focus in this section is limited to configuration information for only the following Cisco VPN clients:

- Cisco VPN Unity SW Client (v3.5.1b)
- Cisco VPN 3002 HW Client (v3.5)

- Cisco Easy VPN Client (v12.2(4)YA+)
- Cisco PIX501 and PIX506 configured as a VPN client (v6.2)

NOTE   Information on Cisco VPN products is constantly evolving. It is recommended to track Cisco.com for the most recent announcements.

Cisco VPN Unity Client

The Cisco VPN Unity Client is available for Windows, Linux, Solaris, and Macintosh OS platforms. Table 20-11 indicates the specific requirements for each platform.

Table 20-11 *Cisco VPN Unity Client Compatibility Matrix* [15, 16]

Operating System	Requirement
Windows	Windows 2000, NT 98 (V3.x or later)
	Windows XP V3.1 or later
Linux	Red Hat v6.2 Linux (Intel) or compatible libraries w/glibc v2.1.1-6 or later, using kernel versions 2.2.12 or later
Solaris	Any ultraSPARC running 32-bit Solaris kernel OS version 2.6 or later
Macintosh	Any Mac running OS X version 10.1.0 or later

The focus of this section is on the Windows compatible client. Clients for other operating systems have similar parameters that you must configure to negotiate, establish, and send data over an IPSec VPN tunnel.

Items you must configure on the VPN Client include the following:

- Connection name
- Host name or IP address of remote server
- Authentication parameters of Group Access Information (group name and group password) or Certificate

Options include the following:

- Enabling transparent tunneling of IPSec over the following:
    - **UDP**—To allow IPSec data transmission in NAT/PAT environments
    - **TCP**—Including the specific port enabled on the VPN concentrator (besides UDP encapsulation advantages, it also allows data transmission when you do not have access to the local firewall to permit the UDP encapsulation port, ISAKMP port, and protocol 50 ESP)

- **Allow local LAN access**—If enabled in the VPN concentrators
- **Peer response timeout**—30-480 seconds, and the default is 90 seconds
- Configuration of backup servers (concentrators)

Before configuring your clients, you must decide on all these parameters. The configuration information is stored in a profile, which is represented by a ConnectionName.pcf file, with the ConnectionName representing the connection name that you enter in the client.

The ConnectionName.pcf file is stored in the Profiles folder, under the Cisco VPN Unity Client program folder. The actual number of profiles that you need to configure depends on how you identify the concentrators or clusters to your clients. You can use a product, such as Cisco's DistributedDirector, to enable one DNS entry to represent all of your concentrators or cluster environments. You also might elect to use a different profile for each cluster or concentrator.

The configuration of the backup clusters or concentrators depends on how you configure clients to connect to the primary cluster or concentrator. For example, if you cannot use one entry that relies upon DistributedDirector to redirect clients to the closest cluster, you might want to list each of your specific clusters. However, if you point clients to a specific cluster, you might want to add clusters in order of anticipated latency from the primary cluster.

When users launch the VPN Unity Client (ipsecdialer.exe), they can scroll to their preferred profile. The profiles are listed in alphabetical order and the last profile that is selected by a client is normally the profile that the ipsecdialer.exe uses by default the next time that the client is started.

Upon installation, the Windows VPN Unity Client automatically installs the following utilities to be used with the client:

- **Set MTU**—Changes the maximum transmission unit (MTU) of a network interface
- **Certificate Manager**—Allows clients to install certificates
- **Log Viewer**—Helpful for troubleshooting connectivity issues (refer to Chapter 21, "Remote Access VPN Troubleshooting," and Chapter 22, "Remote Access VPN Troubleshooting Scenarios.")
- **Help**—Browser-based utility that points to a local file on a PC

NOTE   One caveat worth mentioning is that after you have established an IPSec tunnel, the user cannot see the intermediate hops when running the **traceroute** (TRACERT.exe) command. However, if you have enabled and configured split tunneling, traceroutes function correctly over the unencrypted data path.

Cisco VPN 3002 HW Client

The VPN 3002 HW client provides the same functionality as the VPN Unity SW Client; however, it is platform independent because it provides an Ethernet interface for hosts. Actually, two versions of the 3002 exist—one with one port for the private interface and the other with an 8-port switch. Both models have one public interface. The IPSec VPN tunnel is established between the core concentrator and the 3002, so that any device connected to the private interface of the 3002 can access the central network.

The VPN 3002 HW Client does offer two modes of client configuration—Network Extension and PAT. As the name suggests, Network Extension mode is when the private interface is configured with an IP address that is routable in the network and connected to the concentrator that is terminating the VPN tunnel. In PAT mode, the 3002 performs address translation of addresses that are assigned to clients on the private interface. Currently, the advantage of Network Extension mode is that it provides support for a Cisco IP HW Telephone, and hosts on the public interface side can access resources that are connected to the private interface.

The browser and CLI interfaces of the VPN 3002 HW Client are similar to the interface on the VPN 3000 Series Concentrators. The 3002 HW Client has a Quick Configuration feature that allows users to configure the client right out of the box, without requiring a console connection. However, configurable options are different between the HW client and the concentrators.

The Quick Configuration menu has the following options:

- **Time**—Sets date and time on the client.
- **Upload Config**—Allows you to upload the configuration file to the client.
- **Private Interface**—Sets the IP address and subnet mask on the interface, with the option to set the 3002 as a DHCP server with an address pool.
- **Public Interface**—Allows you to configure the 3002 HW client as a DHCP client (default), Point-to-Point Protocol over Ethernet (PPPoE) client, or with a static IP address.
- **IPSec**—Similar to the Unity SW Client; configures preshared secret information or certificates besides tunneling in TCP.
- **PAT**—Configures a client to perform PAT or Network Extension (see next section).
- **DNS**—The IP address of the service provider's DNS server, which can be learned through DHCP or PPPoE.
- **Static Routes**—Normally learned through DHCP or PPPoE; only required if the IP address is statically configured on the 3002.
- **Admin**—Changes password facility.

Additional settings for these parameters can be configured under the Configuration, System menu with the exception of the PAT/Network Extension, which is enabled under the Configuration, Policy Management, Traffic Management menu.

You cannot configure the following DHCP options on the 3002 HW client when it's configured as a DHCP client:

- Subnet mask
- Router
- DNS
- Domain name
- NetBios Name Server(s)/WINS

These DHCP options are configured on the central-site concentrator for the group that is specified for the VPN 3002 Hardware Client. As is the case for all group configuration parameters, the central-site concentrator pushes these values to the VPN 3002 over the tunnel.[17]

Similar to a VPN 3000 Concentrator, the 3002 HW Client offers features to limit access, and to collect operational data under the Configuration, System, Management Protocols and Configuration, System, Events menus.

Cisco Easy VPN IOS Client

The Cisco Easy VPN Client offers most of the functionality of the Cisco VPN 3002 HW client in specific IOS platforms. The Cisco Easy VPN Client feature was first released in Cisco IOS 12.2(4)YA for the following Cisco routers:

- The Cisco 806, 826, 827, and 828 from the 800 series routers
- The Cisco 1700 series routers
- The Cisco uBR905 and uBR925 cable access routers[18]

Similar to the 3002, the Easy VPN Client supports two modes of operation—Client mode and Network Extension mode.

In Client mode, the Easy VPN Client uses NAT/PAT to provide network connectivity to devices that are connected to the Ethernet interface(s). The NAT/PAT feature is automatically created by the router when the VPN tunnel is established. A configuration for a Cisco 806 router, configured as an Easy VPN Client in Client mode, is shown in Example 20-1.

Example 20-1 *Configuration of a Cisco 806 Router That Is Configured as an Easy VPN Client in Client Mode*

```
version 12.2
no service pad
service timestamps debug uptime
```

Example 20-1 *Configuration of a Cisco 806 Router That Is Configured as an Easy VPN Client in Client Mode (Continued)*

```
service timestamps log uptime
no service password-encryption
!
hostname Router
!
ip subnet-zero
ip name-server 192.168.168.183
ip name-server 192.168.226.120
ip dhcp excluded-address 10.10.10.1
!
ip dhcp pool CLIENT
    import all
    network 10.10.10.0 255.255.255.0
    default-router 10.10.10.1
    dns-server 192.168.226.120 192.168.168.183
    lease infinite
!
ip ssh time-out 120
ip ssh authentication-retries 3
!
crypto ipsec client ezvpn test
! The command is crypto ipsec client <name>
 groupname testgroup key grouppw
! The command is group <groupname> key <group-password>
 mode client
! Set for Client mode (change to mode network-extension for
! Network Extension mode)
 peer 192.168.192.81
! Address on the tunnel terminating device (DNS name can also be entered)
!
interface Ethernet0
 ip address 10.10.10.1 255.255.255.0
 hold-queue 100 out
!
interface Ethernet1
 ip address 192.168.87.252 255.255.255.254
 crypto ipsec client ezvpn test
 Assigns the Easy VPN configuration to the interface.
!
ip classless
ip route 0.0.0.0 0.0.0.0 Ethernet1
ip http server
ip pim bidir-enable
!
line con 0
 stopbits 1
line vty 0 4
 login
!
scheduler max-task-time 5000
end
```

NOTE	If NAT/PAT is already configured on the CPE and you start to configure it as an Easy VPN Client, the original NAT/PAT configuration information is automatically overwritten upon establishing the VPN tunnel by using the Easy VPN Client. The **ip nat inside** or the **ip nat outside** commands, under the private and public interfaces for the IOS device, are eliminated from the configuration.

You cannot view the NAT/PAT configurations as you normally do with the **show run** command. Instead, after the connection is established, you can view this information by using the **show access-list** and **show ip nat statistics** commands.

In Network Extension mode, after the tunnel is established, devices behind the Easy VPN Client appear as entities on your organization's network. The Easy VPN Client also supports split tunneling in either Client or Network Extension mode, if the tunnel terminating device is configured to permit this feature.

After configuration of the router as an Easy VPN Client is complete, you can start the Extended Authentication (XAUTH) login sequence by using the **crypto ipsec client ezvpn xauth** command. This command prompts the user to enter their username and password. The user can use the **show crypto ipsec client ezvpn** command to determine if the tunnel has been successfully established. If the VPN tunnel is successfully established, the results of this command are shown in Example 20-2. If the tunnel is not established, the user is prompted with the following response on the Easy VPN router:

```
EZVPN: Pending XAuth Request, Please enter the following command:
EZVPN: crypto ipsec client ezvpn xauth
```

Example 20-2   *Results of Running the* **show crypto ipsec client ezvpn** *Command on an Easy VPN Client Configured for Client Mode, After Establishing a Successful VPN Tunnel*

```
Router#show crypto ipsec client ezvpn
Current State: IPSEC_ACTIVE
Last Event: SOCKET_UP
Address: 10.25.254.1
! Note this address and the following mask are assigned by the VPN
! tunnel terminating device upon authentication for Client Mode only;
! it is not assigned in Network Extension mode.
Mask: 255.255.255.255
DNS Primary: 192.168.226.120
DNS Secondary: 192.168.168.183
NBMS/WINS Primary: 192.168.2.87
NBMS/WINS Secondary: 192.168.235.228
Default Domain: abc.com
```

NOTE   At the time of writing, the Easy VPN Client does not support digital certificates and the PFS feature on the VPN 3000 Concentrators. Similar to the Cisco VPN Unity SW Client, the Easy VPN Client only supports ISAKMP Group 2 policies (DH 1024-bit key). For the latest product information, see Cisco.com.

Cisco PIX 501 and 506 VPN Client

With the release of v6.2 for the PIX operating system (OS), the PIX 501 and PIX 506 provide the functional equivalent to the Cisco VPN 3002 HW Client. Similar to the VPN 3002 HW Client and the Easy VPN IOS Client, the PIX 501 and PIX 506 support both Client and Network Extension modes. Digital certificate support in Client mode is not available at this time.

The commands to configure the PIX as a remote access VPN HW client starts with the keyword **vpnclient**. This feature makes it easier for you to differentiate between commands that are required to configure the PIX as a HW client, as opposed to configuring the PIX as a core device that terminates the remote access VPN tunnels. The commands required to configure the VPN client features on the PIX v6.2OS are shown in Table 20-12.

Table 20-12 *Commands and Their Format for Setting the VPN Client Features on the PIX 501 with v6.2OS*

VPN Client Commands on PIX 501 with v6.2OS	Explanation
vpnclient vpngroup *group_name* **password** *preshared_key*	Sets preshared key
vpnclient username *xauth_username* **password** *xauth_password*	Sets username
vpnclient peer *ip_primary* [*ip_secondary_1...ip_secondary_n*]	Sets IP address of core tunnel terminating device
vpnclient mode {**client-mode** | **network-extension-mode**}	Sets VPN client mode
vpnclient enable	Activates VPN client feature
no vpnclient {**vpngroup** | **username** | **peer** | **mode** | **enable**}	Removes or disables the specified feature
show vpnclient	Displays VPN client configured features
clear vpnclient	Removes all VPN client features

On the PIX 501 console, after establishment of the VPN tunnel, you should see results for Client and Network Extension mode as shown in Example 20-3 and Example 20-4. The PIX client that is configured for Client mode operation includes many parameters that are not pushed down to the client that is configured for Network Extension mode upon establishment of the VPN tunnel.

Example 20-3   *Results of* **show vpnclient** *Command After Establishing a VPN Tunnel in Client Mode*

```
pixfirewall# show vpnclient
Local Configuration
vpnclient vpngroup pix password ********
vpnclient username test password ********
vpnclient peer 192.168.192.81
vpnclient mode client-mode
vpnclient enable

Downloaded Dynamic Policy
! IP address assigned by the VPN tunnel terminating device:
NAT addr        : 10.25.254.1
! Pushed down from tunnel terminating device:
Primary DNS     : 192.168.226.120
! Pushed down from tunnel terminating device:
Secondary DNS   : 192.168.168.183
! Pushed down from tunnel terminating device:
Primary WINS    : 192.168.2.87
! Pushed down from tunnel terminating device:
Secondary WINS  : 192.168.235.228
! Pushed down from tunnel terminating device:
Default Domain  : abc.com
! Note that terminating device did not require PFS:
PFS Enabled     :
Current Peer    : 192.168.192.81
! DNS configured on the PIX, and active if split-tunneling is
! enabled on the VPN tunnel terminating device
Split DNS       : def.com_
```

Example 20-4   *Results of* **show vpnclient** *Command After Establishing a VPN Tunnel in Network Extension Mode*

```
pixfirewall# show vpnclient
Local Configuration
vpnclient vpngroup pix password ********
vpnclient username test password ********
vpnclient peer 192.168.192.81
vpnclient mode network-extension-mode
vpnclient enable

Downloaded Dynamic Policy
PFS Enabled     : No
Current Peer    : 192.168.192.81
Split DNS       : def.com_
```

By default, the PIX 501 with v6.2 is configured as a DHCP server with PAT to enable hosts that are connected to the inside interface to access external hosts. You can configure the VPN client parameters when you attempt to enable the VPN client by using the command

vpnclient enable. You must remove any access-lists and PAT address pools that support PAT/NAT. If you attempt to enable the VPN client feature while PAT/NAT rules or global pools are in effect, you receive a notice indicating that you must attempt to enable the VPN client only after removing those items.

Similar to the VPN 3002 and most of the routers that support the Easy VPN IOS Clients, the PIX 501 can be configured as either a DHCP client on the public interface (default), a PPPoE client, or with a static IP address.

End Notes

[1] SAFE Blueprint. http://wwwin.cisco.com/ent/vsec/safe/.

[2] www.cisco.com/univercd/cc/td/doc/product/vpn/vpn3000/3_5/getting/gs1und.htm#xtocid3.

[3] www.cisco.com/univercd/cc/td/doc/pcat/3000.htm#xtocid2.

[4] www.cisco.com/univercd/cc/td/doc/product/software/ios122/122newft/122t/122t8/ftunity.htm.

[5] www.cisco.com/univercd/cc/td/doc/product/software/ios122/122newft/122t/122t8/ftunity.htm.

[6] Most sources identify 576 as an average size of packets over the Internet (see RFC 1191). Others suggest that 402.7 bytes is the average size (see http://advanced.comms.agilent.com/routertester/member/journal/1MxdPktSzThroughput.html). However, a packet size of 576 is approximately 50 percent of the packet size distribution.

[7] www.cisco.com/univercd/cc/td/doc/product/vpn/vpn3000/3_5/getting/gs2inst.htm#xtocid19.

[8] www.cisco.com/univercd/cc/td/doc/product/vpn/vpn3000/3_5/getting/gs2inst.htm#xtocid20.

[9] RFC 2338.

[10] www.cisco.com/warp/public/471/vrrp.html.

[11] www.cisco.com/warp/public/471/ld_bl_vpn3000_7602.html.

[12] Cisco VPN 3000 Concentrator IKE Proposals Help.

[13] VPN Concentrator 3.5 Help menu, Configuration, Policy Management, Traffic Management, SA.

[14] www.cisco.com/warp/public/471/vpn_3000_auth.html.

[15] Release Notes for Cisco VPN Client for Windows, Release 3.5.1; www.cisco.com/univercd/cc/td/doc/product/vpn/client/rel3_5_1/351_3kcl.htm.

[16] "Installing the VPN Client User Guide for Linux, Solaris, and Mac OS X."
www.cisco.com/univercd/cc/td/doc/product/vpn/client/nonwin35/user_gd/index.htm.

[17] Cisco VPN 3002 Help menu, v3.5.2.

[18] www.cisco.com/univercd/cc/td/doc/product/software/ios122/122newft/122limit/122y/
122ya/122ya4/ftezvpcm.htm.

Summary

This chapter covered remote access VPN design and configuration solutions. The design
part defines the remote access VPN design objectives, considerations, and architectural
guidelines. The configuration part is focused primarily on using the Cisco VPN 3000
Concentrator as a core termination device and VPN clients based upon the Cisco Unity
VPN client, the Hardware Client, the Easy VPN Client, and PIX-based clients.

Review Questions

Answers to the review questions can be found in Appendix A, "Answers to Review
Questions."

1 Why is the AH protocol considered less secure than ESP?

2 Which part of the ESP packet is not protected?

3 What is a one-to-many NAT or PAT?

4 What is split tunneling?

5 Name the three main types of firewalls.

6 Describe how to calculate the session load on the VPN concentrator.

7 What does VRRP stand for?

8 What is Reverse Route Injection?

9 What is the Group Lock configuration in a VPN concentrator?

10 Name the two mandatory settings on your VPN client.

11 Define the network extension mode for the VPN 3002 Client.

12 For the Router-EzVPN, type the IOS command to start the XAUTH login sentence.

13 When typing IOS command **show crypto ipsec client ezvpn,** how do you find out if
IPSec is up and running?

14 In PIX 501, how do you check if you are running Client mode, or Network Extension
mode?

CHAPTER 21

Remote Access VPN Troubleshooting

Virtual Private Network (VPN) is private networking over public networks. In the troubleshooting context, this implies different narrowband and broadband technologies as Internet access alternatives. The technologies discussed in Part II, "Dial," Part III, "ISDN," and Part IV, "Frame Relay," are not known to pose any restrictions over VPN. If they do, it is not technology-related, but a VPN-related issue, and all the principles of VPN troubleshooting apply. For this reason, more detailed information is provided in this chapter for technologies that require specific knowledge and adjustments when used with VPN. The emphasis is on the client side because the client issues and problems supercede all others combined. To facilitate troubleshooting, the entire VPN implementation chain is divided into three areas:

- Troubleshooting of Cisco remote access VPN clients, which includes the following:
  - Cisco VPN Unity software client troubleshooting
  - Cisco 3002 HW client troubleshooting
  - Cisco Easy VPN client troubleshooting
  - Cisco PIX hardware client troubleshooting
- Internet technologies and remote access VPNs sections include VPN-related troubleshooting information for the following technologies:
  - VPN and asymmetric DSL (ADSL)
  - VPN over cable
  - VPN over wireless and satellite
- Local-area networks (LANs) and remote access VPNs sections are focused on common networking issues that affect VPN connections.

The information in this chapter allows you to show and debug some VPN events. Additionally, the VPN clients and the VPN concentrator allow you to review post-factum large log files for troubleshooting purposes. Some of the outputs are provided in this chapter because of their importance, despite their large size. It is important to review your performance criteria before approaching VPN troubleshooting.

Troubleshooting Cisco Remote Access VPN Clients

Cisco's remote access IPSec-based VPN solution includes the Unity software (SW) client, the 3002 VPN Hardware (HW) client, the 806/17xx IOS-based easy VPN and PIX-based VPN clients. See Chapter 19, "VPN Technology Background," and Chapter 20, "Remote Access VPN Design and Configuration Solutions" for details.

In this chapter, common VPN troubleshooting techniques and recommended approaches (methodologies) are provided. The examples are demonstrated using the Cisco 3000 family of concentrators as termination devices for the following remote access solutions:

- Cisco VPN Unity SW client
- Cisco 3002 HW client
- Cisco Easy VPN client
- Cisco PIX VPN client

First, general restrictions and limitations exist for each solution. After these are understood, actual operational issues can be resolved by isolating the components that might affect the establishment of an IPSec VPN tunnel, and the flow of data through the tunnel. By using the initial troubleshooting tools, you isolate the source of the issue to one or more areas, then further investigate until the actual cause is identified and corrective actions are implemented.

Cisco VPN Unity SW Client

In this section, you focus on the Cisco VPN Unity SW client. The following sections address the client in the following order:

- Restrictions and limitations
- Initial problem identification and troubleshooting
- Cisco VPN Unity client event log
- Cisco 3000 concentrator event log

Restrictions and Limitations of the Cisco VPN Unity Software Client

The Cisco VPN Unity client on the Windows 2000 (W2K) host has several restrictions and limitations, which serve as a foundation for the other remote access solutions that are covered in this chapter; specifically, the text includes the 3002 VPN HW client, and the Easy VPN client that operates on a Cisco 806 router. In sections dedicated to these alternative solutions, differences between them and the Cisco VPN Unity client, and any unique circumstances that might be applicable, are highlighted.

The following briefly summarizes the major restrictions and limitations of the Unity client. They are listed in Table 21-1:

- The Cisco VPN Unity client cannot function correctly if installed on a host on which another VPN client has been installed. You can install other VPN clients on the same host and use them, but then you cannot use your Cisco VPN Unity client.

- The native VPN client included in Microsoft W2K and other Windows platforms is not compatible with the IPSec implementation on Cisco 3000 concentrators, which forces you to ensure that on a W2K platform, the MS IPSec Policy Agent is completely disabled.

- If a software firewall, such as Zone Alarm Pro from Zone Labs, is installed on the host, the maximum security setting must not be configured, to allow the VPN client to function. This setting and the terminology varies for each firewall that is compatible with the Unity client.

- You cannot view multicast streams through the VPN client at this time. VPN clients can participate as a client when using Microsoft NetMeeting for data sharing and collaboration applications, but cannot host the meeting. This varies among data collaboration solutions.

NOTE   Although you can configure the Unity client to enable viewing of multicast sessions through applications such as Cisco IP/TV, the configuration requires access to a multicast-enabled UNIX host that is beyond what can be implemented for most clients.

NOTE   Remote users must be made aware of security policies and restrictions such as split tunneling, especially if it is not permitted because the user cannot reach LAN devices when the tunnel is established.

Some of these restrictions might no longer be applicable, and readers are encouraged to review the latest status at www.cisco.com.

- Finally, the security administrator of the network must open the required IP protocol, User Datagram Protocol (UDP) ports, and Transmission Control Protocol (TCP) ports necessary to establish and transmit data across the IPSec tunnel and permit it through the corporate firewalls.

Table 21-1   *Cisco VPN Unity Client Restrictions and Limitations When Choosing MD5-ESP-3DES Tunnel Mode*

Restriction/Limitations	Requirement	Corrective Action
Host		
Only the Cisco VPN client can be installed on the PC.	Verify that no other VPN client is installed on the PC.	Check the Start, Settings, Control Panel, Add/Remove Programs to determine that no other VPN clients have been installed. If they have, you must uninstall that client. To ensure smooth operation, you might want to also uninstall the Cisco VPN Unity client, shut down the PC, and then reinstall it.
MS IPSEC Policy Agent should not be active.	IPSec Policy Service Agent State mode should be stopped and the Start mode should be disabled.	To disable and stop the service: Start, Settings, Network and Dial-Up Connections, "your active network connection," Properties, Internet Protocol (TCP/IP), Advanced, Options, IP Security, Properties, Do not use IPSEC—then restart PC, as shown in Figure 21-1.
		Verify the State and Start Mode of the IPSEC Policy: Start, Programs, Accessories, System Tools, System Information, Software Environment, Services, as shown in Figure 21-2.
TCP/IP filtering does not permit traffic on the required ports to establish a VPN tunnel.	Disable TCP/IP filtering, or if required, permit necessary TCP or UDP Network Address Translation (NAT) encapsulation ports (default is 10,000).	To verify and permit required traffic: Start, Settings, Network and Dial-Up Connections, "your active network connection," Properties, Internet Protocol (TCP/IP), Advanced, Options, TCP/IP filtering, Enable TCP/IP Filtering (all adapters) should not be checked. An alternative is to permit IP protocol 50 (Encapsulating Security Payload [ESP]) and UDP Port 500 (Internet Security Association and Key Management Protocol [ISAKMP]), and if necessary, permit the TCP or UDP port for encapsulation in the respective protocol (default on the concentrator is 10,000 but is configurable on the concentrator) (see Figure 21-3).
Personal firewall blocks access for the client.	Adjust settings on the firewall to maximum security that permits Cisco VPN Unity client to establish tunnel and send/receive data.	As an example, on Zone Alarm Pro from Zone Labs, the Security Settings must be set at medium or low for LAN and Internet access, as shown in Figure 21-4.
Cannot view multicast streams.	The Cisco 3000 concentrators and the Cisco VPN Unity client do not support multicast at the time this book was written.	The multicast traffic flows must be converted to a unicast session. A workaround can be implemented if you have access to a multicast enabled UNIX host.

Table 21-1   *Cisco VPN Unity Client Restrictions and Limitations When Choosing MD5-ESP-3DES Tunnel Mode (Continued)*

Restriction/Limitations	Requirement	Corrective Action
Host		
Cannot host real-time collaboration sessions.	The Cisco VPN Unity client does not permit hosting of real-time collaboration sessions for some applications.	The workaround is to host the session from a user on the corporate intranet and require VPN clients to connect to it, or use a collaboration solution that works with the Unity client, such as Lotus Sametime.
Split-tunneling policy is controlled from the central concentrator.	Clients must be informed that policy is "pushed" from core.	On the core concentrator split tunneling is controlled through Configuration, User Management, Base Group or Groups, Mode Config menu.
LAN		
Local and remote firewalls permit VPN connectivity.	To establish an IPSec VPN tunnel and send traffic over it, local and remote firewalls must permit IP protocol 50 ESP, UDP port 500 ISAKMP, and the TCP or UDP port encapsulation (if applicable).	Verify that the local and remote firewalls allow the required protocols through the firewall. Confirm that the tunnel can be successfully established from behind the firewall. If the core concentrator is configured for UDP or TCP encapsulation, confirm the port set on the client, as shown in Figure 21-5. TCP encapsulation is available in VPN 3.5x and higher.

Figure 21-1   *IPSec Policy Setting*

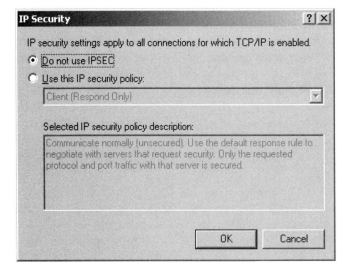

Figure 21-2 *IPSec Policy Agent Setting*

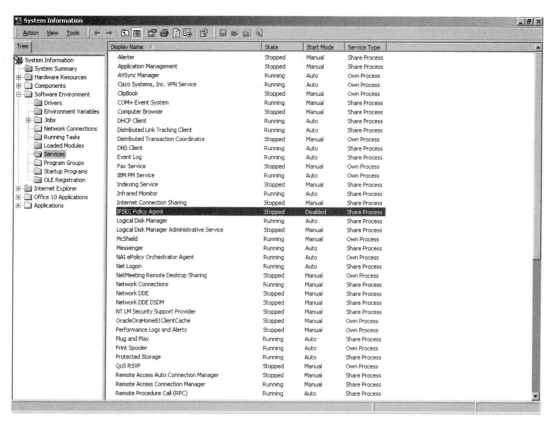

NOTE   To prevent a conflict with other VPN clients and the Cisco VPN Unity client, the VPN 3.5x
            installer (and later versions) automatically issues a warning and permits the user to disable
            the IPSec Policy Agent Service. If this service is not disabled, the error message, "The
            necessary sub-system is not available," is displayed when the user starts the VPN client. See
            Table 21-2 for more information.

Figure 21-3 *TCP/IP Filter Set Menu*

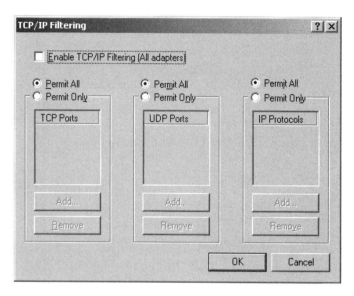

Figure 21-4 *Security Settings on Zone Alarm Client*

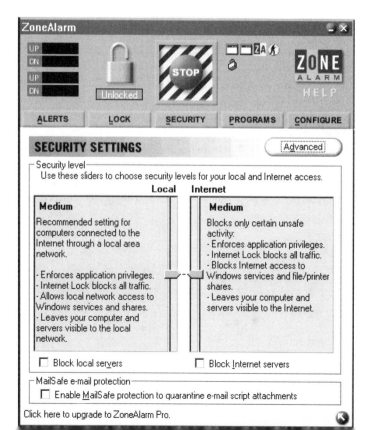

Figure 21-5 *Setting the Tunnel Port on Cisco VPN Unity Client*

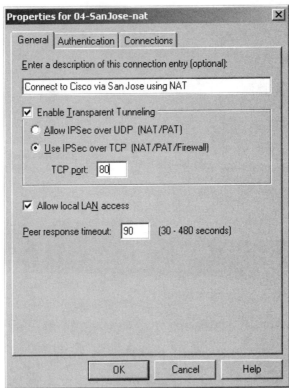

Initial Problem Identification and Troubleshooting with the Cisco VPN Unity SW Client

Assume that you successfully set up the core concentrator and security environment, and confirmed that remote users can successfully establish an IPSec tunnel to send and receive data across the tunnel using the Cisco VPN Unity client. Based on the problem reported by a user experiencing issues, potential sources and suggested corrective action are listed in Table 21-2.

Table 21-2   *Initial Troubleshooting Checklist for Cisco VPN Unity Client*

Issue	Possible Source	Corrective Action
Host		
1. User never receives the "Authenticating user . . ." prompt during the initial dialer connection attempt (see Figure 21-6).	a. Internet Connectivity and Domain Name System (DNS) services. Confirm that the user can access public Internet sites such as www.cisco.com from the host by using ping or a browser.	If the client cannot access public Internet sites, run Start, Run, CMD, IPCONFIG and verify IP address information. If the user cannot ping the local gateway from the host, you must work with a LAN administrator to resolve basic network connectivity, or confirm Point-to-Point Protocol over Ethernet (PPPoE) username and password if using a PPPoE SW client, such as RASPPPoE.
	b. IP address or host name of concentrator might be incorrect.	Verify the host name and IP address entered in the host name or IP address of the remote server block of the Cisco VPN Unity client dialer.
	c. DNS services are not working correctly. User cannot resolve host name of core concentrator from the Cisco VPN Unity client host.	Request user run NSLOOKUP, Go to Start, Run, CMD, NSLOOKUP <Hostname> to verify host lookup function. If the user cannot resolve the hostname of the concentrator from the host, reconfigure the Cisco VPN Unity Client profile with the specific IP address of the core concentrator, and contact LAN support to resolve.
	d. Group name and group password might not match the concentrator.	Verify the groupname and groupname password in the Cisco VPN Unity client profile Options, Properties, Authentication.
	e. Cisco VPN Unity client is not configured with the correct TCP encapsulation port.	Verify that the installed Cisco VPN Unity client is version 3.5 or later, and the profile is configured with one of the TCP encapsulation ports configured on the core concentrator. Options, Properties, General.
	f. Required protocols and ports are not permitted through the local firewall to the Internet. To establish an IPSec VPN tunnel and send traffic over it, local and remote firewalls must permit IP protocol 50 (ESP) and UDP port 500 (ISAKMP), or UDP port 500 and the UDP port used for encapsulation of the	Verify if the remote LAN permits one of the required combinations of traffic: —ESP and ISAKMP —ISAKMP and UDP (default 10,000) encapsulation port configured on the concentrator

continues

Table 21-2   *Initial Troubleshooting Checklist for Cisco VPN Unity Client   (Continued)*

Issue	Possible Source	Corrective Action
	ESP traffic, or the TCP port used for encapsulation of both ESP and ISAKMP traffic. The core concentrator must be configured for encapsulation of UDP or TCP for clients to establish a tunnel through encapsulation.	—TCP encapsulation port configured on the concentrator (usually but not limited to a port already opened for other traffic, such as port 80, 443 or 22)
	g. Gateway router on user's LAN might not correctly handle redirects if trying to connect to a cluster instead of a specific concentrator.	Reconfigure Cisco VPN Unity client profile to connect to a specific concentrator. Verify if IPSec tunnel can be established.
	h. Maximum transmission unit (MTU) must be reduced to =< MTU of the segment with the lowest MTU between the client and the concentrator.	Run SetMTU utility to reduce MTU on network interface card (NIC), or if applicable, change MTU in PPPoE SW client to a size that permits a connection (See the sections, "MTU—A Critical Factor for Troubleshooting Internet IPSec Connectivity," and "VPN and Asymmetric DSL").
2. User is connected and authenticated but cannot pass any traffic.	a. Determine if the host is connected to a device that performs NAT. If yes, verify that the user has a selected profile that supports UDP encapsulation of IPSec traffic on the Cisco VPN 3000.	If host is behind a NAT device, confirm that UDP encapsulation is configured on the concentrator. Also verify that the Cisco VPN Unity client profile on the host supports UDP encapsulation, and is configured with the UDP encapsulation port supported by the concentrator.
	b. MTU must be reduced to =< MTU of the segment with the lowest MTU between the host and the concentrator.	Run SetMTU utility to reduce MTU of the NIC, or if applicable change the MTU in the PPPoE SW client (such as RASPPPoE) to a size that permits a connection (see the sections, "MTU—A Critical Factor for Troubleshooting Internet IPSec Connectivity" and "VPN and Asymmetric DSL").
3. User cannot access devices on the local network behind the NAT device.	Split tunneling might not be enabled by the administrator.	Verify with your system administrator if split tunneling is enabled.
4. User receives the message "VPN Client Subsystem cannot be started."	a. The Cisco VPN Daemon (CVPND) service cannot be started.	Verify that the MS IPSEC Policy Agent is stopped and is disabled (see Figure 21-2).

Table 21-2   *Initial Troubleshooting Checklist for Cisco VPN Unity Client (Continued)*

Issue	Possible Source	Corrective Action
	b. Corrupt installation of Cisco VPN Unity client.	Uninstall the Cisco VPN client. Shut down the host, then reinstall the Cisco VPN Unity client from a different source file.
5. User cannot log in to Windows after installation of the VPN client.	Incompatible Graphical Identification and Authentication (GINA) program.	See the section, "Incompatible GINAs and Workarounds."
6. User cannot establish two concurrent IPSec VPN tunnels from two hosts connected behind the same router to the same concentrator. When the second Cisco VPN Unity client authenticates, the first client is disconnected.	If the router performs NAT/Port Address Translation (PAT), it might be designed to force the ISAKMP UDP source port to 500, for all IPSec tunnels from devices behind the router, regardless if a VPN tunnel is already established.	For the NAT device, switch to a device or SW version that does not require the UDP source port of an ISAKMP exchange to be 500. See the section, "Multiple VPN Clients Behind a NAT Device" in the LAN section of this chapter.

Figure 21-6   *Cisco VPN Unity Client Dialog Box Indicating Authentication Process Has Been Initiated Between the Client and the Concentrator with an IP Address of 192.68.1.2*

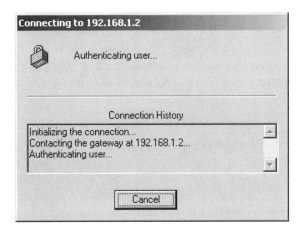

Cisco VPN Unity Client Event Log

The VPN Client Event Log Viewer provides a real-time event log of the VPN client from starting the connection, negotiating authentication, maintaining the connection, and terminating the VPN tunnel. The Log Viewer collects event messages from all processes that contribute to the client-peer connection, and it can be especially helpful if you cannot identify the source of a problem for a client in an environment that you do not have access to or cannot replicate. Also, if you believe you have identified a bug with the client or have other reasons to open a Technical Assistance Center (TAC) case, you will most likely be required to provide a copy of the Log Viewer event log. Sometimes, you might find it helpful to collect and examine the log information on the core concentrator that terminates the remote access VPN session.

For your reference, this section of the text is divided into the following sections:

- Starting the Client Log Viewer
- ISAKMP and Its Phases
- Reviewing a VPN Client Log

Starting the Client Log Viewer

To start the Log Viewer on a W2K host, select Start, Programs, Cisco Systems VPN Client, Log Viewer. The Log Viewer displays its main window upon startup. The VPN client version is indicated under the Help option. To collect the log information, the client must turn on the capture feature, under Options, Capture.

By default, the filter is set to low for the ten log classes identified in the Log Viewer, as shown in Table 21-3. As a result, you might not see the required events displayed in the Log Viewer. To change the filter for a specific event class, select Options, Filter, or click the Filter icon. You should see the screen shown in Figure 21-7. Next, select the event class filters you want to change, right-click your selection and change the filter verbose level to the desired setting. For the purposes of working with remote clients, it is easier to instruct the client to change all filters to high. When using the Log Viewer with the high filter setting, it might impact performance of all applications on the client's PC, but there is no impact to performance when it is not in use.

Table 21-3 *Event Generating Classes in the VPN Client* [1]

Class Name	Definition
CERT	Certificate management process, which handles getting, validating, and renewing certificates from certificate authorities. CERT also displays errors that occur as you use the application.
CLI	Command line interface, which is used instead of Windows ipsecdialer application.
CM	Connection manager, which drives VPN connections. It dials a PPP device, configures IKE for establishing secure connections, and manages connection states.
CVPND	Cisco VPN Daemon (main daemon), which starts client services and controls messaging process and flow.

Table 21-3   *Event Generating Classes in the VPN Client [1] (Continued)*

Class Name	Definition
DIALER	Windows-only component, which handles configuring a profile, initiating a connection, and monitoring.
FIREWALL	Available in versions that support firewall SW client integrated operations with the VPN client.
IKE	Internet Key Exchange module, which manages secure associations.
IPSEC	IPSec module, which obtains network traffic and applies IPSec rules to it.
PPP	Point-to-Point Protocol.
XAUTH	Extended authorization application, which validates a remote user's credentials.

Figure 21-7   *Software VPN Log Filter*

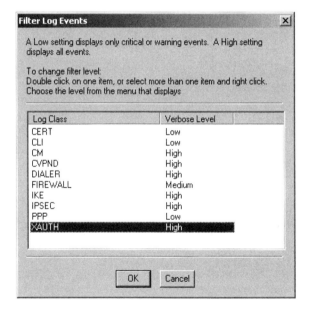

ISAKMP and Its Phases

Before you review the log, a brief review is required of the ISAKMP and IPSec negotiation phases and modes (see Chapter 19 for more information). Recall that ISAKMP has two phases: Phase 1 establishes a secure channel between ISAKMP peers that negotiate the parameters of the Phase 2 services.

Phase 1 has two modes: Main mode and Aggressive mode. After Phase 1 negotiation is successfully completed, Phase 2 negotiation occurs. Phase 2 ISAKMP also negotiates security parameters for the actual data transfer over the secure channel. Phase 2 only has one mode—Quick mode. After Phase 2 negotiation is complete, the VPN peers exchange data over their secure IPSec tunnel.

Reviewing a VPN Client Log

The log of a successful VPN client connection is reviewed in Example 21-1. Example 21-1 is the captured Log Viewer results of a version 3.0 Unity client. Each entry is numbered, has a time and date stamp, is marked with a severity level (1-6) with 1 being the most severe, and is noted with a specific event class and message ID.

Example 21-1 provides detailed output from two separate processes: establishing the VPN connection and termination of the VPN connection. It is relatively large, which is why inline comments help you to comprehend the content. This type of connect-disconnect scenario is rare in the real world. However, when a troubleshooting problem arises and is beyond the scope of well-known issues, this is a possibility with which you need to be familiar.

Example 21-1   *Log Viewer Results for Establishing and Terminating a VPN v3.5.2 Unity Client*

```
*****
1     05:52:44.564  07/15/02  Sev=Info/6
DIALER/0x63300002
Initiating connection.

2     05:52:44.564  07/15/02  Sev=Info/4
CM/0x63100002
Begin connection process

3     05:52:44.584  07/15/02  Sev=Info/4
CM/0x63100004
Establish secure connection using Ethernet

4     05:52:44.584  07/15/02  Sev=Info/4
CM/0x63100026
Attempt connection with server "vpn-concentrator.xyz.com"
! Core VPN concentrator is "vpn-concentrator.xyz.com".

5     05:52:44.604  07/15/02  Sev=Info/6
IKE/0x6300003B
Attempting to establish a connection with 192.68.192.81.
! Core VPN concentrator IP address is 192.168.192.81.

6     05:52:44.644  07/15/02  Sev=Info/4
IKE/0x63000013
SENDING >>> ISAKMP OAK AG (SA, KE, NON, ID, VID, VID, VID) to 192.68.192.81
! OAK=Oakley
```

Example 21-1 *Log Viewer Results for Establishing and Terminating a VPN v3.5.2 Unity Client (Continued)*

```
! AG=Aggressive Mode
! SA=Security Association
! KE=Key Exchange
! NON=Nonce
! ID=Identifier
! HASH
! VID=Vendor Identifier

7     05:52:44.804  07/15/02  Sev=Info/5
IKE/0x6300002F
Received ISAKMP packet: peer = 192.68.192.81

8     05:52:44.804  07/15/02  Sev=Info/4
IKE/0x63000014
RECEIVING <<< ISAKMP OAK AG (SA, KE, NON, ID, HASH, VID, VID, VID, VID)
    from 192.68.192.81

9     05:52:44.804  07/15/02  Sev=Info/5
IKE/0x63000059
Vendor ID payload = 12F5F28C457168A9702D9FE274CC0100

10    05:52:44.804  07/15/02  Sev=Info/5
IKE/0x63000001
Peer is a Cisco-Unity compliant peer
! Client authentication. Successful verification for trusted source.
! Group name and password is verified.

11    05:52:44.804  07/15/02  Sev=Info/5
IKE/0x63000059
Vendor ID payload = 09002689DFD6B712

12    05:52:44.804  07/15/02  Sev=Info/5
IKE/0x63000059
Vendor ID payload = AFCAD71368A1F1C96B8696FC77570100

13    05:52:44.804  07/15/02  Sev=Info/5
IKE/0x63000001
Peer supports DPD
! DPD: Dead Peer Detection. The client will send a series of query
! packets to the core concentrator if it does not receive a
! response to data it has sent.
! If there is no response after a predefined time period,
! (90 seconds is the default) then the client will assume
! the IPSec connection is inactive and tear it down.

14    05:52:44.804  07/15/02  Sev=Info/5
IKE/0x63000059
Vendor ID payload = 1F07F70EAA6514D3B0FA96542A500305

15    05:52:44.834  07/15/02  Sev=Info/4
IKE/0x63000013
SENDING >>> ISAKMP OAK AG *(HASH, NOTIFY:STATUS_INITIAL_CONTACT) to 192.68.192.81
```

continues

Example 21-1 *Log Viewer Results for Establishing and Terminating a VPN v3.5.2 Unity Client (Continued)*

```
16    05:52:44.854  07/15/02  Sev=Info/5
IKE/0x6300002F
Received ISAKMP packet: peer = 192.68.192.81


17    05:52:44.854  07/15/02  Sev=Info/4
IKE/0x63000014
RECEIVING <<< ISAKMP OAK TRANS *(HASH, ATTR) from 192.68.192.81


18    05:52:44.854  07/15/02  Sev=Info/4
CM/0x63100015
Launch xAuth application
! User authentication launched.


19    05:52:45.585  07/15/02  Sev=Info/4
IPSEC/0x63700014
Deleted all keys


20    05:52:51.024  07/15/02  Sev=Info/4
CM/0x63100017
xAuth application returned


21    05:52:51.024  07/15/02  Sev=Info/4
IKE/0x63000013
SENDING >>> ISAKMP OAK TRANS *(HASH, ATTR) to 192.68.192.81


22    05:52:51.334  07/15/02  Sev=Info/5
IKE/0x6300002F
Received ISAKMP packet: peer = 192.68.192.81


23    05:52:51.334  07/15/02  Sev=Info/4
IKE/0x63000014
RECEIVING <<< ISAKMP OAK TRANS *(HASH, ATTR) from 192.68.192.81


24    05:52:51.334  07/15/02  Sev=Info/4
CM/0x6310000E
Established Phase 1 SA.  1 Phase 1 SA in the system
! Phase 1 Security Association has been successfully established.


25    05:52:51.354  07/15/02  Sev=Info/4
IKE/0x63000013
SENDING >>> ISAKMP OAK TRANS *(HASH, ATTR) to 192.68.192.81


26    05:52:51.535  07/15/02  Sev=Info/5
IKE/0x6300005D
Client sending a firewall request to concentrator


27    05:52:51.535  07/15/02  Sev=Info/5
IKE/0x6300005C
Firewall Policy: Product=Cisco Integrated Client, Capability= (Centralized Policy
Push).
! Cisco VPN Unity Client has integrated firewall
```

Example 21-1   *Log Viewer Results for Establishing and Terminating a VPN v3.5.2 Unity Client (Continued)*

```
28    05:52:51.535  07/15/02  Sev=Info/4
IKE/0x63000013
SENDING >>> ISAKMP OAK TRANS *(HASH, ATTR) to 192.68.192.81


29    05:52:51.575  07/15/02  Sev=Info/5
IKE/0x6300002F
Received ISAKMP packet: peer = 192.68.192.81


30    05:52:51.575  07/15/02  Sev=Info/4
IKE/0x63000014
RECEIVING <<< ISAKMP OAK TRANS *(HASH, ATTR) from 192.68.192.81


31    05:52:51.575  07/15/02  Sev=Info/5
IKE/0x63000010
MODE_CFG_REPLY: Attribute = INTERNAL_IPV4_ADDRESS: , value = 10.25.250.2
! IP address assigned to the client by the VPN
! concentrator for the IPSec tunnel.


32    05:52:51.575  07/15/02  Sev=Info/5
IKE/0x63000010
MODE_CFG_REPLY: Attribute = INTERNAL_IPV4_DNS(1): , value = 192.168.226.120
! IP address of the primary DNS server assigned to the
! client by the concentrator.


33    05:52:51.575  07/15/02  Sev=Info/5
IKE/0x63000010
MODE_CFG_REPLY: Attribute = INTERNAL_IPV4_DNS(2): , value = 192.168.168.183
! IP address of the secondary DNS server assigned to the
! client by the concentrator.


34    05:52:51.575  07/15/02  Sev=Info/5
IKE/0x63000010
MODE_CFG_REPLY: Attribute = INTERNAL_IPV4_NBNS(1) (a.k.a. WINS) : , value =
192.168.2.87
! IP address of the primary WINS server assigned to
! the client by the concentrator.


35    05:52:51.575  07/15/02  Sev=Info/5
IKE/0x63000010
MODE_CFG_REPLY: Attribute = INTERNAL_IPV4_NBNS(2) (a.k.a. WINS): , value =
192.168.235.228
! IP address of the secondary WINS server assigned to
! the client by the concentrator.


36    05:52:51.575  07/15/02  Sev=Info/5
IKE/0x6300000E
MODE_CFG_REPLY: Attribute = MODECFG_UNITY_BANNER, value = Unauthorized access is
prohibited.  Connected to vpn-concentrator.
! Banner that Cisco VPN Unity client receives from the concentrator.
! The banner indicated the Configuration mode was done successfully.
```

continues

Example 21-1   *Log Viewer Results for Establishing and Terminating a VPN v3.5.2 Unity Client (Continued)*

```
37    05:52:51.575  07/15/02  Sev=Info/5
IKE/0x6300000D
MODE_CFG_REPLY: Attribute = MODECFG_UNITY_SAVEPWD: , value = 0x00000000


38    05:52:51.575  07/15/02  Sev=Info/5
IKE/0x6300000E
MODE_CFG_REPLY: Attribute = MODECFG_UNITY_DEFDOMAIN: , value = xyz.com
! Domain assigned to the concentrator by the VPN concentrator, xyz.com.


39    05:52:51.575  07/15/02  Sev=Info/5
IKE/0x6300000D
MODE_CFG_REPLY: Attribute = MODECFG_UNITY_PFS: , value = 0x00000000
! PFS=Perfect Forward Secrecy; not being used
! This parameter specifies whether to use Perfect Forward Secrecy
! and the size of the numbers to use in generating Phase 2 IPSec keys.
! Perfect Forward Secrecy is a cryptographic concept;
! each new key is unrelated to any previous key.
! In IPSec negotiations, Phase 2 keys are based on Phase 1 keys unless
! Perfect Forward Secrecy is specified.
! Perfect Forward Secrecy uses Diffie-Hellman techniques to generate the keys.²


40    05:52:51.575  07/15/02  Sev=Info/5
IKE/0x6300000E
MODE_CFG_REPLY: Attribute = APPLICATION_VERSION, value = Cisco Systems, Inc./VPN
3000 Concentrator Version 3.5.2.Rel built by vmurphy on Feb 14 2002 12:10:21


41    05:52:51.575  07/15/02  Sev=Info/4
CM/0x63100019
Mode Config data received


42    05:52:51.595  07/15/02  Sev=Info/5
IKE/0x63000055
Received a key request from Driver for IP address 192.68.192.81, GW IP =
192.68.192.81


43    05:52:51.595  07/15/02  Sev=Info/4
IKE/0x63000013
SENDING >>> ISAKMP OAK QM *(HASH, SA, NON, ID, ID) to 192.68.192.81
! QM=Quick Mode


44    05:52:51.595  07/15/02  Sev=Info/5
IKE/0x63000055
Received a key request from Driver for IP address 10.10.10.255, GW IP = 192.68.192.81


45    05:52:51.595  07/15/02  Sev=Info/4
IKE/0x63000013
SENDING >>> ISAKMP OAK QM *(HASH, SA, NON, ID, ID) to 192.68.192.81


46    05:52:51.595  07/15/02  Sev=Info/4
IPSEC/0x63700014
Deleted all keys
```

Example 21-1   *Log Viewer Results for Establishing and Terminating a VPN v3.5.2 Unity Client (Continued)*

```
47    05:52:51.645  07/15/02  Sev=Info/5
IKE/0x6300002F
Received ISAKMP packet: peer = 192.68.192.81


48    05:52:51.645  07/15/02  Sev=Info/4
IKE/0x63000014
RECEIVING <<< ISAKMP OAK INFO *(HASH, NOTIFY:STATUS_RESP_LIFETIME) from
192.68.192.81


49    05:52:51.645  07/15/02  Sev=Info/5
IKE/0x63000044
RESPONDER-LIFETIME notify has value of 86400 seconds
! Lifetime of IPSec SA keys.  Set by core concentrator


50    05:52:51.645  07/15/02  Sev=Info/5
IKE/0x63000046
This SA has already been alive for 7 seconds, setting expiry to 86393
    seconds from now


51    05:52:51.645  07/15/02  Sev=Info/5
IKE/0x6300002F
Received ISAKMP packet: peer = 192.68.192.81


52    05:52:51.645  07/15/02  Sev=Info/4
IKE/0x63000014RECEIVING <<< ISAKMP OAK QM *(HASH, SA, NON, ID, ID,
    NOTIFY:STATUS_RESP_LIFETIME) from 192.68.192.81


53    05:52:51.645  07/15/02  Sev=Info/5
IKE/0x63000044
RESPONDER-LIFETIME notify has value of 28800 seconds


54    05:52:51.645  07/15/02  Sev=Info/4
IKE/0x63000013
SENDING >>> ISAKMP OAK QM *(HASH) to 192.68.192.81


55    05:52:51.645  07/15/02  Sev=Info/5
IKE/0x63000058
Loading IPsec SA (Message ID = 0xD6D39C1E OUTBOUND SPI = 0x2FC49467
    INBOUND SPI = 0x50A8DB73)


56    05:52:51.645  07/15/02  Sev=Info/5
IKE/0x63000025
Loaded OUTBOUND ESP SPI: 0x2FC49467


57    05:52:51.645  07/15/02  Sev=Info/5
IKE/0x63000026
Loaded INBOUND ESP SPI: 0x50A8DB73
```

continues

Example 21-1   *Log Viewer Results for Establishing and Terminating a VPN v3.5.2 Unity Client (Continued)*

```
58    05:52:51.645  07/15/02  Sev=Info/4
CM/0x6310001A
One secure connection established


59    05:52:51.695  07/15/02  Sev=Info/6
DIALER/0x63300003
Connection established.


60    05:52:51.755  07/15/02  Sev=Info/5
IKE/0x6300002F
Received ISAKMP packet: peer = 192.68.192.81


61    05:52:51.755  07/15/02  Sev=Info/4
IKE/0x63000014
RECEIVING <<< ISAKMP OAK QM *(HASH, SA, NON, ID, ID,
    NOTIFY:STATUS_RESP_LIFETIME) from 192.68.192.81


62    05:52:51.765  07/15/02  Sev=Info/5
IKE/0x63000044
RESPONDER-LIFETIME notify has value of 28800 seconds


63    05:52:51.765  07/15/02  Sev=Info/4
IKE/0x63000013
SENDING >>> ISAKMP OAK QM *(HASH) to 192.68.192.81


64    05:52:51.765  07/15/02  Sev=Info/5
IKE/0x63000058
Loading IPsec SA (Message ID = 0xD765C6C4 OUTBOUND SPI = 0x07742CDC
    INBOUND SPI = 0xCB7C70B2)
! Concentrator connecting to this client will have the same SPI numbers but
! its inbound and outbound SPI's will be reversed as seen in Table 21-3.


65    05:52:51.765  07/15/02  Sev=Info/5
IKE/0x63000025
Loaded OUTBOUND ESP SPI: 0x07742CDC


66    05:52:51.765  07/15/02  Sev=Info/5
IKE/0x63000026
Loaded INBOUND ESP SPI: 0xCB7C70B2


67    05:52:51.765  07/15/02  Sev=Info/4
CM/0x63100022
Additional Phase 2 SA established.
! The Phase 2 SA (IPSec SA) was successfully established.


68    05:52:51.765  07/15/02  Sev=Info/5
IKE/0x63000055
Received a key request from Driver for IP address 192.168.2.87,
    GW IP = 192.68.192.81


69    05:52:51.765  07/15/02  Sev=Info/4
IKE/0x63000013
SENDING >>> ISAKMP OAK QM *(HASH, SA, NON, ID, ID) to 192.68.192.81
```

Example 21-1   *Log Viewer Results for Establishing and Terminating a VPN v3.5.2 Unity Client (Continued)*

```
70    05:52:51.805  07/15/02  Sev=Info/5
IKE/0x6300002F
Received ISAKMP packet: peer = 192.68.192.81


71    05:52:51.805  07/15/02  Sev=Info/4
IKE/0x63000014
RECEIVING <<< ISAKMP OAK QM *(HASH, SA, NON, ID, ID,
    NOTIFY:STATUS_RESP_LIFETIME) from 192.68.192.81


72    05:52:51.805  07/15/02  Sev=Info/5
IKE/0x63000044
RESPONDER-LIFETIME notify has value of 28800 seconds


73    05:52:51.805  07/15/02  Sev=Info/4
IKE/0x63000013
SENDING >>> ISAKMP OAK QM *(HASH) to 192.68.192.81


74    05:52:51.805  07/15/02  Sev=Info/5
IKE/0x63000058
Loading IPsec SA (Message ID = 0x8367341C OUTBOUND SPI = 0x044318D0
    INBOUND SPI = 0x682F214E)


75    05:52:51.805  07/15/02  Sev=Info/5
IKE/0x63000025
Loaded OUTBOUND ESP SPI: 0x044318D0


76    05:52:51.805  07/15/02  Sev=Info/5
IKE/0x63000026
Loaded INBOUND ESP SPI: 0x682F214E


77    05:52:51.805  07/15/02  Sev=Info/4
CM/0x63100022
Additional Phase 2 SA established.


78    05:52:52.807  07/15/02  Sev=Info/4
IPSEC/0x63700010
Created a new key structure
! A new key structure was created.
79    05:52:52.807  07/15/02  Sev=Info/4
IPSEC/0x6370000F
Added key with SPI=0x6794c42f into key list


<Output Omitted>


90    05:52:53.187  07/15/02  Sev=Info/6
DIALER/0x63300008
MAPI32 Information - Outlook not default mail client
! This message does not affect operation of the VPN Client.
! The issue occurs when Microsoft Outlook is installed but not
! configured for email, although it is the default mail client.
```

continues

Example 21-1 *Log Viewer Results for Establishing and Terminating a VPN v3.5.2 Unity Client (Continued)*

```
! It is caused by a Registry Key that is set when the user installs Outlook.
! To eliminate this message, do one of the following:
! -Right-click the Outlook icon, go to Properties, and configure it to use
!  Microsoft Exchange or Internet Mail as the default mail client
! -Use Internet Explorer to configure the system to have no default mail client
! -Configure Outlook as the default mail client (CSCdv67594)[3]

91    05:52:54.189  07/15/02  Sev=Info/4
IPSEC/0x63700019
Activate outbound key with SPI=0xdc2c7407 for inbound key with SPI=0xb2707ccb

92    05:53:21.803  07/15/02  Sev=Info/5
IKE/0x6300002F
Received ISAKMP packet: peer = 192.68.192.81

93    05:53:21.803  07/15/02  Sev=Info/4
IKE/0x63000014
RECEIVING <<< ISAKMP OAK INFO *(HASH, DEL) from 192.68.192.81

94    05:53:21.803  07/15/02  Sev=Info/5
IKE/0x63000018
Deleting IPsec SA: (OUTBOUND SPI = 7742CDC INBOUND SPI = CB7C70B2)

95    05:53:22.734  07/15/02  Sev=Info/4
IPSEC/0x63700013
Delete internal key with SPI=0xb2707ccb

96    05:53:22.734  07/15/02  Sev=Info/4
IPSEC/0x6370000C
Key deleted by SPI 0xb2707ccb

97    05:53:22.734  07/15/02  Sev=Info/4
IPSEC/0x63700013
Delete internal key with SPI=0xdc2c7407

98    05:53:22.734  07/15/02  Sev=Info/4
IPSEC/0x6370000C
Key deleted by SPI 0xdc2c7407

99    05:53:26.741  07/15/02  Sev=Info/4
IPSEC/0x63700019
Activate outbound key with SPI=0xd0184304 for inbound
key with SPI=0x4e212f68

100   05:54:49.903  07/15/02  Sev=Info/6
DIALER/0x63300006
Disconnecting connection.
! Termination process has been initiated.

101   05:54:49.913  07/15/02  Sev=Info/4
CM/0x6310000A
Secure connections terminated
```

Example 21-1   *Log Viewer Results for Establishing and Terminating a VPN v3.5.2 Unity Client (Continued)*

```
102    05:54:49.913  07/15/02  Sev=Info/5
IKE/0x63000018
Deleting IPsec SA: (OUTBOUND SPI = 44318D0 INBOUND SPI = 682F214E)
! Deleting SA - Recall the SA is IP address + IPSec protocol +S PI

103    05:54:49.913  07/15/02  Sev=Info/4
IKE/0x63000013
SENDING >>> ISAKMP OAK INFO *(HASH, DEL) to 192.68.192.81

104    05:54:49.913  07/15/02  Sev=Info/5
IKE/0x63000018
Deleting IPsec SA: (OUTBOUND SPI = 2FC49467 INBOUND SPI = 50A8DB73)

105    05:54:49.913  07/15/02  Sev=Info/4
IKE/0x63000013
SENDING >>> ISAKMP OAK INFO *(HASH, DEL) to 192.68.192.81

106    05:54:49.913  07/15/02  Sev=Info/5
IKE/0x63000017
Marking IKE SA for deletion (COOKIES = FA981A927C24915F AED77DA44D19D140) reason =
DEL_REASON_RESET_SADB
! Reason for disconnect was a reset of the security association data base - SADB.

107    05:54:49.913  07/15/02  Sev=Info/4
IKE/0x63000013
SENDING >>> ISAKMP OAK INFO *(HASH, DEL) to
192.68.192.81

108    05:54:49.913  07/15/02  Sev=Info/4
CM/0x63100013
Phase 1 SA deleted cause by DEL_REASON_RESET_SADB.  0
Phase 1 SA currently in the system

109    05:54:49.973  07/15/02  Sev=Info/5
CM/0x63100029
Initializing CVPNDrv

110    05:54:49.973  07/15/02  Sev=Info/6
CM/0x63100035
Tunnel to headend device vpn-concentrator.xyz.com
disconnected: duration: 0 days 0:1:58

111    05:54:49.973  07/15/02  Sev=Info/5
CM/0x63100029
Initializing CVPNDrv

112    05:54:49.983  07/15/02  Sev=Info/4
IPSEC/0x63700013
Delete internal key with SPI=0x4e212f68
```

continues

Example 21-1 *Log Viewer Results for Establishing and Terminating a VPN v3.5.2 Unity Client (Continued)*

```
113    05:54:49.983  07/15/02  Sev=Info/4
IPSEC/0x63700013
Delete internal key with SPI=0xd0184304

114    05:54:49.983  07/15/02  Sev=Info/4
IPSEC/0x63700013
Delete internal key with SPI=0x73dba850

115    05:54:49.983  07/15/02  Sev=Info/4
IPSEC/0x63700013
Delete internal key with SPI=0x6794c42f

116    05:54:49.983  07/15/02  Sev=Info/4
IPSEC/0x63700014
Deleted all keys

117    05:54:49.983  07/15/02  Sev=Info/4
IPSEC/0x63700010
Created a new key structure

118    05:54:49.983  07/15/02  Sev=Info/4
IPSEC/0x63700013
Delete internal key with SPI=0x00000000

119    05:54:49.983  07/15/02  Sev=Info/4
IPSEC/0x63700014
Deleted all keys

120    05:54:49.983  07/15/02  Sev=Info/4
IPSEC/0x63700014
Deleted all keys

121    05:54:49.983  07/15/02  Sev=Info/4
IPSEC/0x63700014
Deleted all keys

122    05:54:49.983  07/15/02  Sev=Info/5
IKE/0x6300002F
Received ISAKMP packet: peer = 192.68.192.81

123    05:54:49.983  07/15/02  Sev=Warning/2
IKE/0xA3000062
Attempted incoming connection from 192.68.192.81. Inbound connections are
    not allowed.

124    05:54:49.983  07/15/02  Sev=Info/5
IKE/0x63000055
Received a key request from Driver for IP address 192.168.2.87,
    GW IP = 192.68.192.81

125    05:54:49.983  07/15/02  Sev=Warning/3
IKE/0xE3000065
```

Example 21-1   *Log Viewer Results for Establishing and Terminating a VPN v3.5.2 Unity Client (Continued)*

```
Could not find an IKE SA for 192.68.192.81.  KEY_REQ aborted.
! In addition to the termination, this message may appear when the WAN
! IP address has changed due to problems such as flapping WAN connections or
! ISP issues (see Chapter 22 for more information).

126    05:54:50.413  07/15/02  Sev=Info/6
DIALER/0x63300007
Disconnected.
```

Log files showing that a Phase 1 SA cannot be established is an indication that the client cannot successfully communicate with the core concentrator. Clients that cannot establish the Phase 2 SA might be encountering an issue related to MTU size, and the clients need to consider reducing the size. Clients with connections that randomly fail after successfully passing data, and receive an error message similar to the one in Example 21-2, is an indication that connectivity between the client and the VPN concentrator is suspect.

Example 21-2   *Log Entry for Terminating VPN Session*

```
IKE lost contact with remote peer, deleting connection (keepalive type: DPD)
! Cause of termination was loss of Network Connectivity to
! VPN terminating device
```

Cisco 3000 Concentrator Event Log

The concentrator also has a log feature that is helpful in troubleshooting remote access VPN connections. Example 21-3 shows the concentrator log entries for the same client shown in Example 21-1. Example 21-3 shows the benefit of being a troubleshooting engineer in the enterprise environment, where usually you have access to the concentrator and can check the log, which shows the same connection that is shown in Example 21-1 from the other end. For the purposes of the example, the beginning of the negotiation process is skipped and line 29299 starts from the user authentication phase, which allows you to identify the user by login name (smith) in the log. As mentioned in Example 21-1, the log shows the output from the connect-disconnect scenario, and it is provided here solely for the purposes of explanation.

Example 21-3   *Concentrator Log for Unity*

```
VPN SW Client Connection (client v3.5.2, concentrator v3.5)
29299 07/15/2002 05:52:11.970 SEV=4 IKE/52 RPT=4502 12.235.95.31
Group [vpn] User [smith]
User (smith) authenticated.
! 12.235.95.31 is the actual IP address of the client.

29301 07/15/2002 05:52:12.500 SEV=4 AUTH/22 RPT=4691
User smith connected
```

continues

Example 21-3   *Concentrator Log for Unity (Continued)*

```
29302 07/15/2002 05:52:12.500 SEV=4 IKE/119 RPT=15983 12.235.95.31
Group [vpn] User [smith]
PHASE 1 COMPLETED


29304 07/15/2002 05:52:12.500 SEV=5 IKE/25 RPT=39263 12.235.95.31
Group [vpn] User [smith]
Received remote Proxy Host data in ID Payload:
Address 10.25.250.2, Protocol 0, Port 0
! 10.25.250.2 is the IP address assigned to the client by
! the concentrator for the VPN tunnel.


29307 07/15/2002 05:52:12.500 SEV=5 IKE/24 RPT=38566 12.235.95.31
Group [vpn] User [smith]
Received local Proxy Host data in ID Payload:
Address 192.168.192.81, Protocol 0, Port 0
29310 07/15/2002 05:52:12.500 SEV=5 IKE/66 RPT=20250 12.235.95.31
Group [vpn] User [smith]
IKE Remote Peer configured for SA: ESP/IKE-3DES-MD5


29311 07/15/2002 05:52:12.510 SEV=5 IKE/75 RPT=19355 12.235.95.31
Group [vpn] User [smith]
Overriding Initiator's IPSec rekeying duration from 2147483 to 28800 seconds
! The lower value offered for re-keying between both concentrator and
! client is the agreed upon value for key lifetime.


29313 07/15/2002 05:52:12.530 SEV=5 IKE/25 RPT=39264 12.235.95.31
Group [vpn] User [smith]
Received remote Proxy Host data in ID Payload:
Address 10.25.250.2, Protocol 0, Port 0


29316 07/15/2002 05:52:12.530 SEV=5 IKE/34 RPT=47224 12.235.95.31
Group [vpn] User [smith]
Received local IP Proxy Subnet data in ID Payload:
 Address 0.0.0.0, Mask 0.0.0.0, Protocol 0, Port 0


29319 07/15/2002 05:52:12.530 SEV=5 IKE/66 RPT=20251 12.235.95.31
Group [vpn] User [smith]
IKE Remote Peer configured for SA: ESP/IKE-3DES-MD5
! SA protocol ESP, encryption algorithm 3DES, and hash MD5.


29320 07/15/2002 05:52:12.530 SEV=5 IKE/75 RPT=19356 12.235.95.31
Group [vpn] User [smith]
Overriding Initiator's IPSec rekeying duration from 2147483 to 28800 seconds
! The group on the VPN concentrator is set to rekey the keys for
! the IPSec negotiations.


29322 07/15/2002 05:52:12.540 SEV=4 IKE/49 RPT=20311 12.235.95.31
Group [vpn] User [smith]
Security negotiation complete for User (smith)
Responder, Inbound SPI = 0x0db4b5a1, Outbound SPI = 0x7e6fc994
! You can see the SPI's reversed from the client as shown in Example 21-1.
```

Example 21-3   *Concentrator Log for Unity (Continued)*

```
29325 07/15/2002 05:52:12.540 SEV=4 IKE/120 RPT=20311 12.235.95.31
Group [vpn] User [smith]
PHASE 2 COMPLETED (msgid=32e87ed3)


29326 07/15/2002 05:52:12.790 SEV=4 IKE/49 RPT=20312 12.235.95.31
Group [vpn] User [smith]
Security negotiation complete for User (smith)
Responder, Inbound SPI = 0x73558664, Outbound SPI = 0xa9a80dcf


29329 07/15/2002 05:52:12.790 SEV=4 IKE/120 RPT=20312 12.235.95.31
Group [vpn] User [smith]
PHASE 2 COMPLETED (msgid=6fdb7e4d)


29330 07/15/2002 05:52:12.810 SEV=5 IKE/25 RPT=39265 12.235.95.31
Group [vpn] User [smith]
Received remote Proxy Host data in ID Payload:
Address 10.25.250.2, Protocol 0, Port 0


29333 07/15/2002 05:52:12.810 SEV=5 IKE/34 RPT=47225 12.235.95.31
Group [vpn] User [smith]
Received local IP Proxy Subnet data in ID Payload:
 Address 0.0.0.0, Mask 0.0.0.0, Protocol 0, Port 0


29336 07/15/2002 05:52:12.810 SEV=5 IKE/66 RPT=20252 12.235.95.31
Group [vpn] User [smith]
IKE Remote Peer configured for SA: ESP/IKE-3DES-MD5


29337 07/15/2002 05:52:12.810 SEV=5 IKE/75 RPT=19357 12.235.95.31
Group [vpn] User [smith]
Overriding Initiator's IPSec rekeying duration from 2147483 to 28800 seconds


29339 07/15/2002 05:52:12.830 SEV=4 IKE/49 RPT=20313 12.235.95.31
Group [vpn] User [smith]
Security negotiation complete for User (smith)
Responder, Inbound SPI = 0x398539b4, Outbound SPI = 0x7cc8d0c0


29342 07/15/2002 05:52:12.840 SEV=4 IKE/120 RPT=20313 12.235.95.31
Group [vpn] User [smith]
PHASE 2 COMPLETED (msgid=ba313b15)


! Disconnect process follows.
29349 07/15/2002 05:52:22.280 SEV=5 IKE/50 RPT=3452 12.235.95.31
Group [vpn] User [smith]
Connection terminated for peer smith (Peer Terminate)
Remote Proxy 10.25.250.2, Local Proxy 0.0.0.0


29352 07/15/2002 05:52:22.280 SEV=5 IKE/170 RPT=34237 12.235.95.31
Group [vpn] User [smith]
IKE Received delete for rekeyed centry
IKE peer: 10.25.250.2, centry addr: 0727a5f0, msgid: 0x6fdb7e4d
```

continues

Example 21-3   *Concentrator Log for Unity (Continued)*

```
29355 07/15/2002 05:52:22.280 SEV=5 IKE/50 RPT=3453 12.235.95.31
Group [vpn] User [smith]
Connection terminated for peer smith (Peer Terminate)
Remote Proxy 10.25.250.2, Local Proxy 192.168.192.81

29358 07/15/2002 05:52:22.290 SEV=4 AUTH/28 RPT=4322 12.235.95.31
User [smith] disconnected:
 Duration: 0:00:09
 Bytes xmt: 456
 Bytes rcv: 680
 Reason: User Requested
```

The concentrator event classes and corresponding descriptions are found in Table 21-4.

Table 21-4   *VPN Concentrator Event Classes [2]*

Class Name	Class Description (Event Source)
AUTH	Authentication
AUTHDBG	Authentication debugging
AUTHDECODE	Authentication protocol decoding
AUTOUPDATE	Autoupdate subsystem
CAPI	Cryptography subsystem
CERT	Digital certificates subsystem
CONFIG	Configuration subsystem
DHCP	Dynamic Host Configuration Protocol (DHCP) subsystem
DHCPDBG	DHCP debugging
DHCPDECODE	DHCP decoding
DM	Data movement subsystem
DNS	DNS subsystem
DNSDBG	DNS debugging
DNSDECODE	DNS decoding
EVENT	Event subsystem
EVENTDBG	Event subsystem debugging
EVENTMIB	Event Management Information Base (MIB) changes
EXPANSIONCARD	Expansion card (module) subsystem
FILTER	Filter subsystem
FILTERDBG	Filter debugging
FSM	Finite state machine subsystem (for debugging)

Table 21-4   *VPN Concentrator Event Classes [2] (Continued)*

Class Name	Class Description (Event Source)
FTPD	FTP daemon subsystem
GENERAL	Network Time Protocol (NTP) subsystem and other general events
GRE	Generic routing encapsulation (GRE) subsystem
GREDBG	GRE debugging
GREDECODE	GRE decoding
HARDWAREMON	Hardware monitoring (fans, temperature, voltages, and so on)
HTTP	HTTP subsystem
IKE	ISAKMP/Oakley (IKE) subsystem
IKEDBG	ISAKMP/Oakley (IKE) debugging
IKEDECODE	ISAKMP/Oakley (IKE) decoding
IP	IP router subsystem
IPDBG	IP router debugging
IPDECODE	IP packet decoding
IPSEC	IPSec subsystem
IPSECDBG	IPSec debugging
IPSECDECODE	IPSec decoding
L2TP	Layer 2 Tunnel Protocol (L2TP) subsystem
L2TPDBG	L2TP debugging
L2TPDECODE	L2TP decoding
LBSSF	Load balancing subsystem
MIB2TRAP	MIB-II trap subsystem: Simple Network Management Protocol (SNMP) MIB-II traps
OSPF	Open Shortest Path First (OSPF) subsystem
PPP	PPP subsystem
PPPDBG	PPP debugging
PPPDECODE	PPP decoding
PPTP	PPTP subsystem
PPTPDBG	PPTP debugging
PPTPDECODE	PPTP decoding
PSH	Operating system command shell
PSOS	Embedded real-time operating system

continues

Table 21-4 *VPN Concentrator Event Classes [2] (Continued)*

Class Name	Class Description (Event Source)
QUEUE	System queue
REBOOT	System rebooting
RM	Resource manager subsystem
SMTP	Simple Mail Transfer Protocol (SMTP) event handling
SNMP	SNMP trap subsystem
SSH	Secure Shell (SSH) subsystem
SSL	Secure Socket Layer (SSL) subsystem
SYSTEM	Buffer, heap, and other system utilities
TCP	TCP subsystem
TELNET	Telnet subsystem
TELNETDBG	Telnet debugging
TELNETDECODE	Telnet decoding
TIME	System time (clock)
VRRP	Virtual Router Redundancy Protocol (VRRP) subsystem
XML	XML

The impact of these events, or their severity levels, is measured and shown in the event logs per Table 21-5.

Table 21-5 *VPN Concentrator Event Severity Levels [2]*

Level	Category	Description
1	Fault	A crash or non-recoverable error
2	Warning	A pending crash or severe problem that requires user intervention
3	Warning	A potentially serious problem that might require user action
4	Information	An information-only event with few details
5	Information	An information-only event with moderate detail
6	Information	An information-only event with greatest detail
7	Debug	Least amount of debugging detail
8	Debug	Moderate amount of debugging detail
9	Debug	Greatest amount of debugging detail
10	Packet Decode	High-level packet header decoding
11	Packet Decode	Low-level packet header decoding

Table 21-5   *VPN Concentrator Event Severity Levels [2] (Continued)*

Level	Category	Description
12	Packet Decode	Hex dump of header
13	Packet Decode	Hex dump of packet

Cisco indicates that within a severity level category, higher-numbered events provide more details than lower-numbered events. You can change the severity level of the events displayed in the concentrator event log and console, as well as those displayed in the syslog, e-mail and traps, with the concentrator menu Configuration, System, Events, General. An example of a specific event and severity level is shown in Example 21-4, in which the concentrator deletes its connection with User "smith" because of no response using the Dead Peer Detection (DPD) feature. Actually, the concentrator reports two separate events, first no response, then disconnection. For the "no response" event, the severity level is 4 the event class is IKE, and the event number is 123. The disconnection is also classified as severity level 4, and the event class is authentication. RPT stands for repeat and indicates the number of times that the event has occurred since the concentrator was reloaded.[2]

Example 21-4   *Event Log for Deleted Connection Because of No Response from the Client*

```
8157 07/11/2002 12:54:19.140 SEV=4 IKE/123 RPT=6792 128.216.126.77
Group [xyz-vpn] User [smith]
IKE lost contact with remote peer, deleting connection (keepalive type: DPD)

8162 07/11/2002 12:54:19.150 SEV=4 AUTH/28 RPT=16579 128.216.126.77
User [smith] disconnected:
 Duration: 0:51:22
 Bytes xmt: 276824
 Bytes rcv: 311120
 Reason: User Requested
```

Incompatible GINAs and Workarounds

GINA is the system that Microsoft devised to control access to the W2K and NT host environments. GINAs are the modules that force clients to log in to their host. Two types of GINAs are in use: authenticator and filter.[4] There can be multiple filters, but only one authenticator. In this case, the filters chain to each other but the last GINA called in this chain must be the authenticator. The authenticator manages the user login process, and the filters offer additional benefits.

The default GINA for W2K is MSGINA.DLL. Unfortunately, some GINAs cannot coexist and participate in a chain of GINAs. If you install the Cisco VPN Unity client v3.5 or earlier on a host that already has a third party GINA, which is incompatible with the GINA for the Cisco VPN Unity client (CSGINA.DLL), the W2K host might experience a startup failure.[5]

A typical failure message that is as a result of installing incompatible GINAs during the boot process is as follows:

```
SAS window: winlogon.exe - Application Error
The instruction at "0x00000000" referenced memory at "0x00000000".
  The memory could not be "read".
```

You might need to restart your host in Safe mode, and implement the following sequence to restore your host to the state it was in before the Cisco VPN Unity client installed its GINA:

1 Copy CSGINA.DLL in the SYSTEM32 directory to TEMPORARY_CSGINA.DLL.

2 In the same SYSTEM32 directory, copy MSGINA.DLL to CSGINA.DLL.

3 Reboot the host and log into the host as Administrator.

4 Type "run32dll temporary_csgina.dll,GinaUnregister," omitting the quotes at the command line, or use Start, Run.

5 Reboot the host.

This procedure can also result in extended delays for clients who log into Windows NT networks after authenticating their Cisco VPN Unity client. This delay, of up to 30 seconds or more, can occur because the client is preempted by other tasks running on the host. If you want to force the host to disregard any third-party GINAs and to restore the backup method for logging into Windows NT networks, after authenticating the Cisco VPN Unity client, Cisco suggests the following:

1 Copy MSGINA.DLL to CSGINA.DLL in the SYSTEM32 directory.

2 Reboot the host and log in as Administrator.

3 Delete the "HKEY_LOCAL_MACHINE\Software\Microsoft\Windows NT\CurrentVersion\WinLogon" subkey in the Registry editor.

4 Set the "HKEY_LOCAL_MACHINE\Software\Cisco Systems\VPN Client" subkey to 0.

5 Reboot the host.

Cisco 3002 HW Client Troubleshooting

The Cisco VPN 3002 HW client can be configured in either Client mode or Network Extension mode. In Client mode, the 3002 performs as the Cisco VPN Unity SW client, obtaining an IP address from the device terminating the VPN tunnel. PAT/NAT is implemented on the VPN 3002 to direct network traffic to/from hosts connected to its private interface. In Network Extension mode, the VPN 3002 HW client is configured with an IP address subnet that is routable throughout the organization, which provides the capability to remotely access hosts connected to the private interface from the enterprise network.

In this section, you review methods and tools for troubleshooting the VPN 3002 HW client, including the following:

- Initial troubleshooting checklist
- Using the VPN 3002 HW client event log

Initial Troubleshooting Checklist

As with the Cisco VPN Unity client, this section is written under the assumption that the configuration of the 3002 HW client is correct; however, the first steps are to verify the configuration, as suggested in Table 21-6. Issues that clients might encounter are related to end-to-end connectivity, MTU, and address assignment. The end-to-end connectivity and MTU issues are similar to those encountered with the SW client. The address assignment issue is unique to the 3002. At the time of writing this book, Cisco was working to address the MTU and subnet mask assignment issues for the 3002. Other features that most probably will be available in the near future are support for viewing multicast streams and two-way IP telephony when the 3002 HW client is in Client mode.

Table 21-6   *Initial Troubleshooting Checklist for the VPN 3002 HW Client*

Issue	Possible Source	Corrective Action
1. User does not receive login prompt if using XAUTH for unit authentication.	a. VPN 3002 HW client might need to be reset.	Administration, Ping, and attempt to ping an Internet site, such as www.cisco.com. If successful, save the VPN 3002 concentrator configuration and reload the VPN 3002.
	b. VPN 3002 HW client does not have Internet connectivity because it is incorrectly configured.	If VPN 3002 HW client cannot resolve host name, verify DNS server addresses. Next, verify the public interface connectivity. If using PPPoE, verify PPPoE username and password. Check log to verify PPPoE authentication, Monitoring, Filterable Event Log, Get Log. Verify that the VPN 3002 HW client is properly configured or learning correct route(s). If not using PPPoE, verify that the public interface is either learning IP address information through DHCP, or is configured with the correct static IP address information. If applicable, verify Internet connectivity from a router in front of the VPN 3002 HW client.
2. User is authenticated but cannot pass any data.	a. The correct client mode was not selected—either Network Extension or Client mode.	Configuration, Interfaces, Verify the private interface is configured with the correct IP address and subnet mask.

continues

Table 21-6   *Initial Troubleshooting Checklist for the VPN 3002 HW Client (Continued)*

Issue	Possible Source	Corrective Action
	b. If Network Extension mode is used, another client might have an overlapping subnet.	On the core VPN3000 concentrator, the administrator needs to verify the subnet mask for each client with subnets adjacent to the client experiencing the problem: Administration, Administer Sessions. Next, check masks for subnets that might have been mistakenly set. After the device causing the problem is identified, correct the setting and confirm that the 3002 HW client with the original issue can now send/receive data.
3. User is authenticated but cannot send/ receive data for applications with large packet sizes such as HTTP, e-mail or Network File System (NFS).	a. MTU of host is too large (at the time of writing, the VPN 3002 HW client does not have a mechanism to set/ change the MTU on its interfaces).	Reduce the MTU on the network interface for each host exhibiting the issue (see the section, "MTU—A Critical Factor for Troubleshooting Internet IPSec Connectivity").

Using the VPN 30002 HW Client Event Log

Similar to the Cisco VPN Unity client, the Event Console Messages and Event Log for the VPN 3002 HW client can prove useful when troubleshooting remote access connectivity issues. The settings that control the events reported in the VPN 3002 HW Client Event Log are found under Configuration, System, Events. The VPN 3002 HW Client Help menu provides an excellent overview and detailed information of the features of the Event Logging system.

A significant number of event classes exist for the VPN 3002 HW client (see Table 21-7), some of which are designed exclusively for Cisco to provide support. However, some can provide useful information when troubleshooting a VPN 3002 HW client.

Table 21-7   *VPN 3002 HW Client Event Classes for General Users [6]*

Class Name	Class Description (Event Source)
CERT	Digital certificates subsystem
DHCP	DHCP subsystem
DNS	DNS subsystem
FTPD	FTP daemon subsystem

Table 21-7   *VPN 3002 HW Client Event Classes for General Users [6] (Continued)*

Class Name	Class Description (Event Source)
GENERAL	NTP subsystem and other general events
HARDWAREMON	Hardware monitoring (fans, temperature, voltages, and so on)
HTTP	HTTP subsystem
IKE	ISAKMP/Oakley (IKE) subsystem
IP	IP router subsystem
IPSEC	IPSec subsystem
PPP	PPP subsystem
PPPoE	PPPoE subsystem
REBOOT	System rebooting
SNMP	SNMP trap subsystem
SSH	SSH subsystem
SSL	SSL subsystem
TCP	TCP subsystem
TELNET	Telnet subsystem
TIME	System time (clock)

By default, the VPN 3002 displays all events of severity level 1 through 3 on the console. It writes all events of severity level 1 through 5 to the event log. Severity 1 is the most severe and indicates a system crash. Levels 1 to 13 are available, although setting logging for some event classes up to level 13 can cause the concentrator to become inaccessible as a result of processor overuse.

Example 21-5 shows the entries for the Event Log from a 3060 concentrator that successfully authenticates a 3002 VPN HW client and negotiates and establishes a VPN tunnel.

Example 21-5   *Event Log from the VPN 3000 Core Concentrator Authenticating a VPN 3002 HW Client v3.5 in Network Extension Mode (Using Default Event Reporting Settings)*

```
52714 03/04/2002 02:38:10.010 SEV=4 IKE/52 RPT=113 12.234.185.130
Group [TEST] User [smith]
User (smithsmith) authenticated.
!Client IP address= 12.234.185.130
Group name= TEST
Username = smith

52715 03/04/2002 02:38:10.070 SEV=4 AUTH/22 RPT=116
User smith connected
```

continues

Example 21-5 *Event Log from the VPN 3000 Core Concentrator Authenticating a VPN 3002 HW Client v3.5 in Network Extension Mode (Using Default Event Reporting Settings) (Continued)*

```
52716 03/04/2002 02:38:10.070 SEV=4 IKE/119 RPT=185 12.234.185.130
Group [TEST] User [smith]
PHASE 1 COMPLETED


52718 03/04/2002 02:38:10.070 SEV=5 IKE/25 RPT=390 12.234.185.130
Group [TEST] User [smith]
Received remote Proxy Host data in ID Payload:
Address 12.234.185.130, Protocol 0, Port 0


52721 03/04/2002 02:38:10.070 SEV=5 IKE/24 RPT=386 12.234.185.130
Group [TEST] User [smith]
Received local Proxy Host data in ID Payload:
Address 1928.168.192.81, Protocol 0, Port 0
! 192.168.192.81 is IP address of the concentrator


52724 03/04/2002 02:38:10.070 SEV=5 IKE/66 RPT=835 12.234.185.130
Group [TEST] User [smith]
IKE Remote Peer configured for SA: ESP-3DES-MD5
! SA protocol ESP, encryption algorithm 3DES, and hash MD5.
52726 03/04/2002 02:38:10.070 SEV=5 IKE/75 RPT=835 12.234.185.130
Group [TEST] User [smith]
Overriding Initiator's IPSec rekeying duration from 2147483647 to 28800 seconds
! Lifetime of IPSec SA keys.  Set by this concentrator.
52728 03/04/2002 02:38:10.100 SEV=4 IKE/49 RPT=835 12.234.185.130
Group [TEST] User [smith]
Security negotiation complete for User (smith)
Responder, Inbound SPI = 0x72b26536, Outbound SPI = 0x76018499


52731 03/04/2002 02:38:10.100 SEV=4 IKE/120 RPT=835 12.234.185.130
Group [TEST] User [smith]
PHASE 2 COMPLETED (msgid=6573ee0a)


52732 03/04/2002 02:38:10.100 SEV=4 AUTOUPDATE/19 RPT=114
Sending IKE Notify: AutoUpdating clients in group [TEST]
Client delay: 0, instID: 0000046F


52734 03/04/2002 02:38:14.110 SEV=5 IKE/35 RPT=446 12.234.185.130
Group [TEST] User [smith]
Received remote IP Proxy Subnet data in ID Payload:
 Address 10.25.0.128, Mask 255.255.255.240, Protocol 0, Port 0
! IP address subnet configured on the client is 10.25.0.128/28.
! The subnet could also be assigned via a Radius authentication server.


52737 03/04/2002 02:38:14.110 SEV=5 IKE/34 RPT=450 12.234.185.130
Group [TEST] User [smith]
Received local IP Proxy Subnet data in ID Payload:
 Address 0.0.0.0, Mask 0.0.0.0, Protocol 0, Port 0


52740 03/04/2002 02:38:14.110 SEV=5 IKE/66 RPT=836 12.234.185.130
Group [TEST] User [smith]
IKE Remote Peer configured for SA: ESP-3DES-MD5
```

Example 21-5   *Event Log from the VPN 3000 Core Concentrator Authenticating a VPN 3002 HW Client v3.5 in Network Extension Mode (Using Default Event Reporting Settings) (Continued)*

```
52742 03/04/2002 02:38:14.110 SEV=5 IKE/75 RPT=836 12.234.185.130
Group [TEST] User [smith]
Overriding Initiator's IPSec rekeying duration from 2147483647 to 28800 seconds

52744 03/04/2002 02:38:14.150 SEV=4 IKE/49 RPT=836 12.234.185.130
Group [TEST] User [smith]
Security negotiation complete for User (smith)
Responder, Inbound SPI = 0x6f1c24f7, Outbound SPI = 0x25f707f3

52747 03/04/2002 02:38:14.150 SEV=4 IKE/120 RPT=836 12.234.185.130
Group [TEST] User [smith]
PHASE 2 COMPLETED (msgid=6b8ddbe7)
! At this point the IPSec SA was successfully negotiated and
! data can be sent to/from hosts connected behind the VPN 3002 HW Client.

! The disconnect process begins.
54625 03/04/2002 04:10:59.250 SEV=4 IKE/123 RPT=28 12.234.185.130
Group [TEST] User [smith]
IKE lost contact with remote peer, deleting connection (keepalive type: DPD)

54629 03/04/2002 04:10:59.250 SEV=4 AUTH/28 RPT=47 12.234.185.130
User [smith] disconnected:
 Duration: 1:32:49
 Bytes xmt: 156848
 Bytes rcv: 242112
 Reason: User Requested
```

Example 21-6 shows the event log from a 3002 client during its authentication, negotiation, and establishment of a VPN tunnel.

Example 21-6   *Event Log from a VPN 3002 HW Client for Establishing a VPN Tunnel (Using Default Event Reporting Settings)*

```
1235 03/04/2002 02:35:52.520 SEV=4 IKE/41 RPT=156 192.168.192.81
IKE Initiator: New Phase 1, Intf 2, IKE Peer 192.168.192.81
local Proxy Address 12.234.185.130, remote Proxy Address 192.168.192.81,
SA (ESP-3DES-MD5)

1238 03/04/2002 02:36:00.640 SEV=5 DHCP/66 RPT=32
DHCPREQUEST received by server.  MAC Addr: 00.00.86.46.2E.8E.  Requested IP: 10.
25.0.130.
! 3002 VPN HW Client configured as DHCP server.  Receives DHCP request.

1240 03/04/2002 02:36:00.640 SEV=5 DHCP/72 RPT=31
DHCPACK sent by server.  MAC Addr: 00.00.86.46.2E.8E
! 3002 VPN HW Client Responds to DHCP request.

1241 03/04/2002 02:36:23.590 SEV=3 AUTH/24 RPT=3
Tunnel to headend device 192.168.192.81 connected
```

continues

Example 21-6   *Event Log from a VPN 3002 HW Client for Establishing a VPN Tunnel (Using Default Event Reporting Settings) (Continued)*

```
1242 03/04/2002 02:36:23.590 SEV=4 IKE/119 RPT=4 192.168.192.81
Group [192.168.192.81192.168.192.81]
PHASE 1 COMPLETED


1243 03/04/2002 02:36:23.620 SEV=5 IKE/73 RPT=14 192.168.192.81
Group [192.168.192.81]
Responder forcing change of IKE rekeying duration from 2147483647 to 86400 seconds
! Core terminating concentrator forces IKE rekey duration change.


1246 03/04/2002 02:36:23.620 SEV=5 IKE/73 RPT=15 192.168.192.81
Group [192.168.192.81]
Responder forcing change of IPSec rekeying duration from 2147483647 to 28800 seconds


1249 03/04/2002 02:36:23.630 SEV=4 IKE/49 RPT=11 192.168.192.81
Group [192.168.192.81]
Security negotiation complete for peer (192.168.192.81)
Initiator, Inbound SPI = 0x76018499, Outbound SPI = 0x72b26536


1252 03/04/2002 02:36:23.640 SEV=4 IKE/120 RPT=11 192.168.192.81
Group [192.168.192.81]
PHASE 2 COMPLETED (msgid=6573ee0a)


1253 03/04/2002 02:36:23.660 SEV=4 AUTOUPDATE/5 RPT=3
Current version 3.5.Rel is up to date.
! Core terminating concentrator checked SW version running on this
! 3002 HW client and verified it matches its requirement.
! Otherwise it could have been configured to push new SW image to the client.


1254 03/04/2002 02:36:27.640 SEV=4 IKE/41 RPT=157
IKE Initiator: New Phase 2, Intf 2, IKE Peer 1-192.168.192.81
local Proxy Address 10.25.0.128, remote Proxy Address 0.0.0.0,
SA (ESP-3DES-MD5)


1256 03/04/2002 02:36:27.660 SEV=5 IKE/73 RPT=16 192.168.192.81
Group [192.168.192.81]
Responder forcing change of IPSec rekeying duration from 2147483647 to 28800 seconds
1259 03/04/2002 02:36:27.670 SEV=4 IKE/49 RPT=12 192.168.192.81
Group [192.168.192.81]
Security negotiation complete for peer (192.168.192.81)
Initiator, Inbound SPI = 0x25f707f3, Outbound SPI = 0x6f1c24f7


1262 03/04/2002 02:36:27.680 SEV=4 IKE/120 RPT=12 192.168.192.81
Group [192.168.192.81]
PHASE 2 COMPLETED (msgid=6b8ddbe7)
! At this point the IPSec SA was successfully negotiated, and data
!can be sent to/from hosts connected behind the VPN 3002 HW Client.


! The disconnect process begins.
1282 03/04/2002 04:03:55.070 SEV=3 IP/31 RPT=1
Deleting Default Gateway 12.234.184.1 learned via DHCP on interface 2.


1283 03/04/2002 04:03:55.090 SEV=3 AUTH/25 RPT=3 192.168.192.81
Tunnel to headend device 192.168.192.81 disconnected: duration: 1:27:31
```

Cisco Easy VPN Client

In this section, you review information specific to the Cisco Easy VPN client. Similar to the VPN 3002 HW client, an Easy VPN client can be configured to operate in Client or Network Extension mode. However, configuring and troubleshooting an Easy VPN client presents its own unique challenges that you review in this section. In particular, you learn about the following:

- Restrictions and limitations
- Troubleshooting the Cisco Easy VPN client

Restrictions and Limitations of the Cisco Easy VPN Client

Features are constantly being implemented in the Cisco Easy VPN client. At the time this book was written, the Easy VPN client did not yet support NAT transparency (UDP/TCP encapsulation). Additional restrictions and limitations are outlined in Table 21-8. Some are similar to the Cisco VPN Unity client and some are specific to the Cisco Easy VPN client. For the most recent list of restrictions and limitations, consult www.cisco.com.

Table 21-8 *Cisco Easy VPN Client Selected Restrictions and Limitations for an 806 Router Running IOS v12.2(4)YA*

Restriction	Requirement	Corrective Action
Host		
Cisco Easy VPN Client does not support perfect forward secrecy (PFS).	Disable PFS option.	On core concentrator, disable PFS option through Configuration, Policy Management, Traffic Management, Security Associations.
Cisco Easy VPN client uses SA that does not exist in the default configuration of the VPN 3000 concentrator series running v3.5.	Cisco Easy VPN uses a modified form of ESP/IKE-3DES-MD5 on the VPN 3000 concentrator that is modified to use the IKE proposal CiscoVPNClient-3DES-MD5.	Copy the ESP/IKE-3DES-MD5 SA and change the IKE proposal to CiscoVPNClient-3DES-MD5 in the Configuration, Policy Management, Traffic Management, Security Associations menu.
Manual NAT/PAT configuration is not permitted.	Do not configure NAT / PAT on any interface when using the Cisco Easy VPN client.	Remove any manual NAT/PAT configuration on the router.
Digital Certificates are not supported in the release 12.2(4)YA.	Cannot use digital certificates.	Do not use digital certificates for authentication.

continues

Table 21-8   *Cisco Easy VPN Client Selected Restrictions and Limitations for an 806 Router Running IOS v12.2(4)YA (Continued)*

Restriction	Requirement	Corrective Action
Host		
Supports only Group 2 ISAKMP policy (1024 bit Diffie-Hellman (DH) IKE negotiation).	Is not compatible with ISAKMP Group 1 or Group 1 policies.	Configure the core concentrator IKE proposal to use only Group 2 policies (the default for most preconfigured IKE proposals). Select Configuration, System, Tunneling Protocols, IPSEC, IKE Proposals.
Cisco Easy VPN client does not support the transform sets that provide encryption without authentication.	Intended transform set for Cisco Easy VPN clients must include both encryption and authentication.	Confirm that selected transform set supports both encryption and authentication. Do not use preconfigured transform sets that do not provide authentication (ESP-DES and ESP-3DES), or transform sets that do not provide encryption (ESP-NULL, ESP-SHA-HMAC, ESP-NULL, and ESP-MD5-HMAC).
Cannot host real-time collaboration application sessions.	The Cisco Easy VPN client does not permit hosting of real-time collaboration sessions for some applications such as MS NetMeeting.	The workaround is to host the session from a user on the corporate intranet and require VPN clients to connect to it, or select a data collaboration application that supports the Easy VPN client.

Troubleshooting the Cisco Easy VPN Client

Because Easy VPN is a Cisco IOS feature, one of the most effective methods to troubleshoot the Cisco Easy VPN client is through the use of the **show** and **debug** commands. The commands in the following list are specific to the Cisco Easy VPN client to troubleshoot the establishment of the VPN IPSec tunnels, and as data transmission and reception. You can perform the following commands from the console if using a telnet (SSH, if it is configured) session into the router:

- The **show crypto ipsec client ezvpn** command displays the status of the Easy VPN client, as shown in Example 21-8 and Example 21-9.

- The **debug crypto ezvpn** command enables debugging of the Cisco Easy VPN client.

- The **clear crypto ipsec client ezvpn** command resets the VPN connection, as shown in Example 21-10. However, if you have enabled debugging, you might prefer to use the **clear crypto sa** and **clear crypto isakmp** commands.

- The **debug crypto ipsec** and **debug crypto isakmp** commands enable debugging of the IPSec and IKE key events. The results of the **debug crypto isakmp** are shown in Example 21-11.

- The **show crypto engine connections active** command displays the active IPSec VPN connections.

A suggested troubleshooting checklist for the Easy VPN client is presented in Table 21-9.

Table 21-9   *Initial Troubleshooting Checklist for the Cisco Easy VPN Client*

Issue	Possible Source	Corrective Action
1. Cannot establish a VPN IPSec tunnel between the Cisco Easy VPN client and the core VPN 3000 concentrator.	a. Cisco Easy VPN client router does not have Internet connectivity.	Run **show ip interface brief** to verify that the router has IP addresses on both the inside and outside (public) interfaces, as shown in Example 21-7. If applicable, verify the PPPoE configuration (see the section, "ADSL"). Check the DHCP client configuration for outside interface (if appropriate). Confirm that you can ping Internet hosts such as www.cisco.com.
	b. Cisco Easy VPN client is not active.	Run **show crypto ipsec client ezvpn** to verify if the Cisco Easy VPN client is active, as in Example 21-8. If inactive, run **crypto ipsec client ezvpn <name>** to verify output, as shown in Example 21-9.
		Run **debug crypto ipsec client ezvpn** and then clear the active IPSec tunnel using the command **clear crypto ipsec client ezvpn**, as shown in Example 21-10. Run a second debug, **debug crypto isakmp**, and then start a tunnel, as shown in Example 21-11.
		Identify the source of the error from the output and correct accordingly.
	c. Core VPN 3000 concentrator authentication parameter is not set to NONE.	Verify that authentication is set to none under the Configuration, User Management, Base Group, IPSec menu, and in Configuration, User Management, Groups, specific group, IPSec.
2. Data is not transmitted/ received by the hosts connected to the inside (private) interface of the router running the Cisco Easy VPN client.	a. IPSec VPN tunnel has been terminated.	Verify that VPN IPSec tunnel is established using **show crypto ipsec client ezvpn**.

continues

Table 21-9   *Initial Troubleshooting Checklist for the Cisco Easy VPN Client (Continued)*

Issue	Possible Source	Corrective Action
	b. NAT and the access-list configuration on the Cisco Easy VPN client router are invalid. NAT might have been manually configured on the router prior to establishment of the VPN IPSec tunnel.	Verify that NAT is not configured under the interfaces by using **show running-config**, and by identifying if **ip nat inside** or **ip nat outside** is configured.
	c. The DHCP pool is not configured correctly.	Verify the DHCP pool configuration on the router or server for hosts on the inside interface.

Example 21-7   *Output of* **show ip interface brief** *Command*

```
Router-EzVPN#show ip interface brief
Interface       IP-Address      OK? Method      Status      Protocol
Ethernet0       10.1.1.1        YES NVRAM       up          up
Ethernet1       66.127.241.85   YES NVRAM       up          up
! Ethernet1 is the Public interface.
! The address 66.127.241.85 has been assigned by the ISP.
```

Example 21-8   *Output of* **show crypto ipsec client ezvpn** *Command for an Inactive Client*

```
Inactive EzVPN client
Router-EzVPN #show crypto ipsec client ezvpn
Current State: XAUTH_REQ
! Client requests XAUTH response in current state
Last Event: XAUTH_REQUEST
Router-EzVPN#
```

Example 21-9   *Output of* **show crypto ipsec client ezvpn** *Command for an Active Easy VPN Client Configured for Client Mode*

```
Router-EzVPN#show crypto ipsec client ezvpn
Current State: IPSEC_ACTIVE
Last Event: SOCKET_UP
Address: 10.25.250.1
! The IP address obtained from the address pool on the terminating concentrator
Mask: 255.255.255.255
! The subnet mask obtained from the pool, defined in the server configuration.
DNS Primary: 192.168.226.120
DNS Secondary: 192.168.168.183
! The primary and secondary DNS servers defined for the group on the
! concentrator terminating the VPN tunnel
NBMS/WINS Primary: 192.168.2.87
NBMS/WINS Secondary: 192.168.235.228
! The primary and secondary WINS servers defined for the group on the
! concentrator terminating the VPN tunnel
Default Domain: cisco.com
```

Example 21-10 *Output of* **clear crypto ipsec client ezvpn** *Command*

```
Router-EzVPN#clear crypto ipsec client ezvpn
Router-EzVPN#
00:09:25: EZVPN: Current State: IPSEC_ACTIVE
00:09:25: EZVPN: Event: RESET
00:09:25: ezvpn_reconnect_request
00:09:25: ezvpn_close
00:09:25: ezvpn_connect_request
00:09:25: EZVPN: New State: READY
00:09:26: EZVPN: Current State: READY
00:09:26: EZVPN: Event: XAUTH_REQUEST
00:09:26: ezvpn_xauth_request
00:09:26: ezvpn_parse_xauth_msg
00:09:26: EZVPN: Attributes sent in xauth request message:
00:09:26:         XAUTH_TYPE_V2: 0
00:09:26:         XAUTH_USER_NAME_V2:
00:09:26:         XAUTH_USER_PASSWORD_V2:
00:09:26:         XAUTH_MESSAGE_V2 <Enter Username and Password.>
00:09:26: EZVPN: New State: XAUTH_REQ
00:09:27: EZVPN: Pending XAuth Request, Please enter the following command:
00:09:27: EZVPN: crypto ipsec client ezvpn xauth
```

Example 21-11 *Output from a 8xx Router Running 12.2(4)YA, Configured as an Easy VPN Client with* **debug crypto isakmp** *When Attempting to Establish an IPSec VPN Tunnel*

```
Router-EzVPN #debug crypto isakmp
Router-EzVPN#crypto ipsec client ezvpn xauth
Enter Username and Password.: login_name
Password: password.
! The user provides the login name and password
Router-EzVPN#
00:12:48:         xauth-type: 0
00:12:48:         username: login_name
00:12:48:         password: <omitted>
00:12:48:         message <Enter Username and Password.>
00:12:48: ISAKMP (0:7): responding to peer config from 192.168.192.81. ID =
    -252864948
00:12:48: ISAKMP (0:7): sending packet to 192.168.192.81 (I) CONF_XAUTH
00:12:48: ISAKMP (0:7): deleting node -252864948 error FALSE reason
    "done with xauth request/reply exchange"
00:12:48: ISAKMP (0:7): Input = IKE_MESG_INTERNAL, IKE_XAUTH_REPLY_ATTR
Old State = IKE_XAUTH_REPLY_AWAIT  New State = IKE_XAUTH_REPLY_SENT

00:12:48: ISAKMP (0:7): received packet from 192.168.192.81 (I) CONF_XAUTH
00:12:48: ISAKMP: set new node 1465183127 to CONF_XAUTH
! The server confirms the login name and password
! Authentication  is successful
00:12:48: ISAKMP (0:7): processing transaction payload from
    192.168.192.81. message ID = 1465183127
00:12:48: ISAKMP: Config payload SET
00:12:48: ISAKMP (0:7): Xauth process set, status = 1
00:12:48: ISAKMP (0:7): checking SET:
```

continues

Example 21-11 *Output from a 8xx Router Running 12.2(4)YA, Configured as an Easy VPN Client with* **debug crypto isakmp** *When Attempting to Establish an IPSec VPN Tunnel (Continued)*

```
00:12:48: ISAKMP:   XAUTH_STATUS_V2 XAUTH-OK
00:12:48: ISAKMP (0:7): attributes sent in message:
00:12:48:       Status: 1
00:12:48: ISAKMP (0:7): sending packet to 192.168.192.81 (I) CONF_XAUTH
00:12:48: ISAKMP (0:7): deleting node 1465183127 error FALSE reason ""
00:12:48: ISAKMP (0:7): Input = IKE_MESG_FROM_PEER, IKE_CFG_SET
Old State = IKE_XAUTH_REPLY_SENT  New State = IKE_P1_COMPLETE
! IKE phase one completed successfully.
00:12:48: ISAKMP (0:7): Need config/address
00:12:48: ISAKMP (0:7): Need config/address
00:12:48: ISAKMP: set new node 1868961837 to CONF_ADDR
00:12:48: ISAKMP (0:7): initiating peer config to 192.168.192.81. ID = 1868961837
00:12:48: ISAKMP (0:7): sending packet to 192.168.192.81 (I) CONF_ADDR
00:12:48: ISAKMP (0:7): Input = IKE_MESG_INTERNAL, IKE_PHASE1_COMPLETE
Old State = IKE_P1_COMPLETE  New State = IKE_CONFIG_MODE_REQ_SENT
! The end user receives a configuration from the server.
00:12:48: ISAKMP (0:7): received packet from 192.168.192.81 (I) CONF_ADDR
00:12:48: ISAKMP (0:7): processing transaction payload from 192.168.192.81.
    message ID = 1868961837
00:12:48: ISAKMP: Config payload REPLY
00:12:48: ISAKMP(0:7) process config reply
00:12:48: ISAKMP (0:7): deleting node 1868961837 error FALSE reason
    "done with transaction"
00:12:48: ISAKMP (0:7): Input = IKE_MESG_FROM_PEER, IKE_CFG_REPLY
Old State = IKE_CONFIG_MODE_REQ_SENT  New State = IKE_P1_COMPLETE
! Request for configuration mode sent.

00:12:48: ISAKMP (0:7): Input = IKE_MESG_INTERNAL, IKE_PHASE1_COMPLETE
Old State = IKE_P1_COMPLETE  New State = IKE_P1_COMPLETE

00:12:48: ISAKMP: received ke message (1/4)
00:12:48: ISAKMP: set new node 0 to QM_IDLE
00:12:48: ISAKMP (0:7): sitting IDLE. Starting QM immediately (QM_IDLE      )
00:12:48: ISAKMP (0:7): beginning Quick Mode exchange, M-ID of 85557524
! Quick mode begins.

00:12:48: ISAKMP (0:7): sending packet to 192.168.192.81 (I) QM_IDLE
00:12:48: ISAKMP (0:7): Node 85557524, Input = IKE_MESG_INTERNAL, IKE_INIT_QM
Old State = IKE_QM_READY  New State = IKE_QM_I_QM1
00:12:48: ISAKMP (0:7): received packet from 192.168.192.81 (I) QM_IDLE
! Quick mode exchange
00:12:48: ISAKMP (0:7): processing HASH payload. message ID = 85557524
00:12:48: ISAKMP (0:7): processing SA payload. message ID = 85557524
00:12:48: ISAKMP (0:7): Checking IPSec proposal 1
! IPSec proposal 1 sent.
00:12:48: ISAKMP: transform 1, ESP_3DES
00:12:48: ISAKMP:    attributes in transform:
00:12:48: ISAKMP:      SA life type in seconds
00:12:48: ISAKMP:      SA life duration (basic) of 3600
00:12:48: ISAKMP:      SA life type in kilobytes
00:12:48: ISAKMP:      SA life duration (VPI) of  0x0 0x46 0x50 0x0
00:12:48: ISAKMP:      encaps is 1
```

Example 21-11 *Output from a 8xx Router Running 12.2(4)YA, Configured as an Easy VPN Client with* **debug crypto isakmp** *When Attempting to Establish an IPSec VPN Tunnel (Continued)*

```
00:12:48: ISAKMP:      authenticator is HMAC-MD5
00:12:48: ISAKMP (0:7): atts are acceptable.
00:12:48: ISAKMP (0:7): processing NONCE payload. message ID = 85557524
00:12:48: ISAKMP (0:7): processing ID payload. message ID = 85557524
00:12:48: ISAKMP (0:7): processing ID payload. message ID = 85557524
00:12:48: ISAKMP (0:7): Creating IPSec Sas
! Creating the security association, which includes the IP addresses,
! the protocol (ESP or AH), and SPI.
00:12:48:         inbound SA from 192.168.192.81 to 66.127.241.85
! The public IP address
        (proxy 0.0.0.0 to 10.31.17.129)
00:12:48:         has spi 0x9608BACF and conn_id 2000 and flags 4
00:12:48:         lifetime of 3600 seconds
00:12:48:         lifetime of 4608000 kilobytes
00:12:48:         outbound SA from 66.127.241.85      to 192.168.192.81
    (proxy 10.31.17.129    to 0.0.0.0      )
00:12:48:         has spi 703036318 and conn_id 2001 and flags C
00:12:48:         lifetime of 3600 seconds
00:12:48:         lifetime of 4608000 kilobytes
00:12:48: ISAKMP (0:7): sending packet to 192.168.192.81 (I) QM_IDLE
00:12:48: ISAKMP (0:7): deleting node 85557524 error FALSE reason ""
00:12:48: ISAKMP (0:7): Node 85557524, Input = IKE_MESG_FROM_PEER, IKE_QM_EXCH
Old State = IKE_QM_I_QM1  New State = IKE_QM_PHASE2_COMPLETE
! ISAKMP phase 2 complete and the parameters are negotiated.
00:12:48: ISAKMP: received ke message (4/1)
00:12:48: ISAKMP: Locking CONFIG struct 0x80F93638 for
    crypto_ikmp_config_handle_kei_mess, count 3
00:12:48: ISAKMP (0:7): received packet from 192.168.192.81 (I) QM_IDLE
00:12:48: ISAKMP: set new node 1502656406 to QM_IDLE
00:12:48: ISAKMP (0:7): processing HASH payload. message ID = 1502656406
00:12:48: ISAKMP (0:7): processing NOTIFY unknown protocol 1
        spi 0, message ID = 1502656406, sa = 80EB31E8
00:12:48: ISAKMP (0:7): deleting node 1502656406 error FALSE reason
    "informational (in) state 1"
00:12:48: ISAKMP (0:7): Input = IKE_MESG_FROM_PEER, IKE_INFO_NOTIFY
Old State = IKE_P1_COMPLETE  New State = IKE_P1_COMPLETE
```

In addition to the steps outlined in Table 21-9 for troubleshooting connectivity issues, you might find the following commands useful for monitoring the Cisco Easy VPN environment:

- To verify the applied policy, use **show crypto isakmp policy** (see Example 21-12).

- To check the ISAKMP security association, use **show crypto isakmp sa** (see Example 21-13).

- To check the status of the Cisco Easy VPN client profile, use **show crypto ipsec profile** (see Example 21-14).

- To check the status of the IPSec SA, use **show crypto ipsec sa** (see Example 21-15).

- To check the status of the crypto engine connections, use **show crypto engine connections active** (see Example 21-16).

Example 21-12 *Output of* **show crypto isakmp policy** *Command*

```
Router-EzVPN#show crypto isakmp policy
Protection suite of priority 65527
        encryption algorithm:   DES - Data Encryption Standard (56 bit keys).
        hash algorithm:         Secure Hash Standard
        authentication method:
        Diffie-Hellman group:   #2 (1024 bit)
        lifetime:               65535 seconds, no volume limit

<output omitted>

Default protection suite
        encryption algorithm:   DES - Data Encryption Standard (56 bit keys).
        hash algorithm:         Secure Hash Standard
        authentication method:  Rivest-Shamir-Adleman Signature
        Diffie-Hellman group:   #1 (768 bit)
        lifetime:               86400 seconds, no volume limit
```

Example 21-13 *Output of* **show crypto isakmp sa** *Command*

```
Router-EzVPN#show crypto isakmp sa
dst              src             state       conn-id   slot
192.168.192.81   66.127.241.85   QM_IDLE     7         0
```

Example 21-14 *Output of* **show crypto ipsec profile** *Command*

```
Router-EzVPN#show crypto ipsec profile
IPSEC profile ezvpn-profile
        Security association lifetime: 4608000 kilobytes/3600 seconds
        PFS (Y/N): N
        Transform sets={
                ezvpn-profile-autoconfig-transform-0,
                ezvpn-profile-autoconfig-transform-1,
                ezvpn-profile-autoconfig-transform-2,
                ezvpn-profile-autoconfig-transform-3,
        }
```

Example 21-15 *Output of* **show crypto ipsec sa** *Command*

```
Route-EzVPN#show crypto ipsec sa
interface: Ethernet1
    Crypto map tag: Ethernet1-head-0, local addr. 66.127.241.85

    local  ident (addr/mask/prot/port): (192.168.192.81/255.255.255.255/0/0)
    remote ident (addr/mask/prot/port): (0.0.0.0/0.0.0.0/0/0)
    current_peer: 192.168.192.81
      PERMIT, flags={origin_is_acl,}
     #pkts encaps: 0, #pkts encrypt: 0, #pkts digest 0
     #pkts decaps: 0, #pkts decrypt: 0, #pkts verify 0
     #pkts compressed: 0, #pkts decompressed: 0
     #pkts not compressed: 0, #pkts compr. failed: 0, #pkts decompress failed: 0
     #send errors 0, #recv errors 0
```

Example 21-15 *Output of* **show crypto ipsec sa** *Command (Continued)*

```
        local crypto endpt.: 66.127.241.85, remote crypto endpt.: 192.168.192.81
        path mtu 1500, media mtu 1500
        current outbound spi: 36B6AD4B

        inbound esp sas:
! Inbound direction of ESP Security Association
           spi: 0x74FBAEB0(1962651312)
             transform: esp-3des esp-md5-hmac ,
             in use settings ={Tunnel, }
             slot: 0, conn id: 2000, flow_id: 1, crypto map: Ethernet1-head-0
             sa timing: remaining key lifetime (k/sec): (4608000/3374)
             IV size: 8 bytes
             replay detection support: Y

        inbound ah sas:
! The client is not running the AH protocol, so it is empty

        inbound pcp sas:
! The client is not running PCP, so it is empty

        outbound esp sas:
! Outbound direction of ESP SA
           spi: 0x36B6AD4B(917941579)
             transform: esp-3des esp-md5-hmac ,
             in use settings ={Tunnel, }
             slot: 0, conn id: 2001, flow_id: 2, crypto map: Ethernet1-head-0
             sa timing: remaining key lifetime (k/sec): (4608000/3374)
             IV size: 8 bytes
             replay detection support: Y

        outbound ah sas:

        outbound pcp sas:
```

Example 21-16 *Output of* **show crypto engine connections active** *Command*

```
Router-EzVPN #show crypto engine connections active
ID Interface       IP-Address     State  Algorithm       Encrypt  Decrypt
   22 Ethernet1    66.127.241.85  set    HMAC_MD5+3DES_56_C  0         0
2000 Ethernet1     66.127.241.85  set    HMAC_MD5+3DES_56_C  0         0
2001 Ethernet1     66.127.241.85  set    HMAC_MD5+3DES_56_C  0         0
```

Cisco PIX VPN Client

Starting with v6.2, the Pix 501 and 506 can be configured as VPN clients. These platforms can be configured in Client or Network Extension mode, and perform similarly to the Cisco VPN 3002 HW client.

Restrictions and Limitations

The PIX 501 and 506, when configured as VPN clients, share the same restrictions as the VPN 3002 HW client, such as a lack of support for multicast traffic and IP telephony when configured in Client mode. At the time this was written, a notable limitation was the lack of support for NAT transparency. However, most of these features might be addressed by the time this book is available. For the latest feature status, consult www.cisco.com.

Verifying and Troubleshooting the VPN Connection

Assuming that you have correctly configured your PIX 501 or 506 to provide Internet connectivity, you can verify the VPN Client configuration with the command, **show vpnclient**. Results are shown in Example 21-17. All examples in this section were created on a PIX 501 running v6.2 of the PIX operating system.

Example 21-17   *Output of* **show vpnclient** *Command on PIX*

```
pix#show vpnclient

Local Configuration
vpnclient vpngroup pix password ********
vpnclient username smith password ********
vpnclient server 192.168.192.81
! Core device terminating the VPN tunnel.
vpnclient mode client-mode
! PIX can be configured in Client or Network Extension mode.
vpnclient enable
```

At this point, the VPN tunnel is not established. You should be able to establish the VPN tunnel by trying to ping a device on the internal network on the other end of the tunnel. The first few pings might fail but a tunnel should be established. The tunnel information can be viewed with the output from the following commands:

- **show vpnclient** (see Example 21-18)
- **show crypto ipsec sa** (see Example 21-19)
- **show crypto isakmp sa** (see Example 21-20)

If the tunnel is not established, you cannot see any Downloaded Dynamic Policy parameters, and the ESP SA or (SPI) security parameter index is not established. At that point, if you have confirmed the PIX configuration and Internet connectivity, you might want to clear the VPN client information by using the command **clear vpnclient** in the global configuration mode. Then, re-enter the VPN client configuration information.

Example 21-18 *Output from* **show vpnclient** *Command on PIX Configured as a VPN Client after Establishing a VPN Tunnel*

```
pix#show vpnclient

Local Configuration
vpnclient vpngroup pix password ********
! pix was the entered groupname
vpnclient username smith password ********
! smith was the entered username
vpnclient server 192.168.192.81
vpnclient mode network-extension-mode
vpnclient enable

Downloaded Dynamic Policy
Current Server : 192.168.192.81
Primary DNS    : 192.168.226.120
Secondary DNS  : 192.168.168.183
Primary WINS   : 192.168.2.87
Secondary WINS : 192.168.235.228
Default Domain : cisco.com
PFS Enabled    : No
Split DNS      : cisco.com_
```

Example 21-19 *Output from* **show crypto ipsec sa** *Command After Establishment of VPN Tunnel*

```
pix#show crypto ipsec sa

interface: outside
    Crypto map tag: _vpnc_cm, local addr. 12.235.95.31
! 12.235.95.31 is the IP address of outside interface of the PIX

    local  ident (addr/mask/prot/port): (10.25.250.1/255.255.255.255/0/0)
    remote ident (addr/mask/prot/port): (0.0.0.0/0.0.0.0/0/0)
    current_peer: 192.168.192.81
! 192.168.192.81 is IP address of the core VPN terminating device
      PERMIT, flags={origin_is_acl,}
     #pkts encaps: 101, #pkts encrypt: 101, #pkts digest 101
! Number of packets encrypted
     #pkts decaps: 140, #pkts decrypt: 140, #pkts verify 140
     #pkts compressed: 0, #pkts decompressed: 0
     #pkts not compressed: 0, #pkts compr. failed: 0, #pkts decompress failed: 0
     #send errors 1, #recv errors 0

     local crypto endpt.: 12.235.95.31, remote crypto endpt.: 192.168.192.81
     path mtu 1500, ipsec overhead 56, media mtu 1500
     current outbound spi: 321e317b
! SPI has been created

     inbound esp sas:
      spi: 0xb84c8c89(3092024457)
        transform: esp-3des esp-md5-hmac ,
```

continues

Example 21-19 *Output from* **show crypto ipsec sa** *Command After Establishment of VPN Tunnel (Continued)*

```
                in use settings ={Tunnel, }
                slot: 0, conn id: 1, crypto map: _vpnc_cm
                sa timing: remaining key lifetime (k/sec): (4607889/28424)
                IV size: 8 bytes
                replay detection support: Y
! Inbound SA has been created with the esp protocol using
! 3DES encryption, md5 hash


            inbound ah sas:
! Authentication Header (AH) was not an option on the core device
! terminating the VPN connection



            inbound pcp sas:
! Payload Compression Protocol (pcp) was not an option on the core device
! terminating the VPN tunnel⁷


            outbound esp sas:
             spi: 0x321e317b(840839547)
                transform: esp-3des esp-md5-hmac ,
                in use settings ={Tunnel, }
                slot: 0, conn id: 2, crypto map: _vpnc_cm
                sa timing: remaining key lifetime (k/sec): (4607995/28419)
                IV size: 8 bytes
                replay detection support: Y
! Outbound esp SAS

            outbound ah sas:


            outbound pcp sas:




            outbound ah sas:


            outbound pcp sas:

local  ident (addr/mask/prot/port): (12.235.95.31/255.255.255.255/0/0)
      remote ident (addr/mask/prot/port): (0.0.0.0/0.0.0.0/0/0)
      current_peer: 192.168.192.81
        PERMIT, flags={origin_is_acl,}
        #pkts encaps: 0, #pkts encrypt: 0, #pkts digest 0
        #pkts decaps: 0, #pkts decrypt: 0, #pkts verify 0
        #pkts compressed: 0, #pkts decompressed: 0
        #pkts not compressed: 0, #pkts compr. failed: 0, #pkts decompress failed: 0
        #send errors 1, #recv errors 0
```

Example 21-19 *Output from* **show crypto ipsec sa** *Command After Establishment of VPN Tunnel (Continued)*

```
         local crypto endpt.: 12.235.95.31, remote crypto endpt.: 192.168.192.81
         path mtu 1500, ipsec overhead 56, media mtu 1500
         current outbound spi: 76accd0d

         inbound esp sas:
          spi: 0x948b4d0c(2492157196)
            transform: esp-3des esp-md5-hmac ,
            in use settings ={Tunnel, }
            slot: 0, conn id: 3, crypto map: _vpnc_cm
            sa timing: remaining key lifetime (k/sec): (4608000/28706)
            IV size: 8 bytes
            replay detection support: Y


         inbound ah sas:


         inbound pcp sas:


         outbound esp sas:
          spi: 0x76accd0d(1991036173)
            transform: esp-3des esp-md5-hmac ,
            in use settings ={Tunnel, }
            slot: 0, conn id: 4, crypto map: _vpnc_cm
            sa timing: remaining key lifetime (k/sec): (4608000/28706)
            IV size: 8 bytes
            replay detection support: Y


         outbound ah sas:


         outbound pcp sas:
```

Example 21-20 *Output from* **show crypto isakmp sa** *Command After Establishing VPN Tunnel*

```
pix#show crypto isakmp sa
Total    : 1
Embryonic : 0
        dst          src          state       pending     created
    192.168.192.81  12.235.95.31 QM_IDLE         0           2
! If the VPN tunnel had not been established then the created
! entry would have been zero.
```

The log from a VPN 3000 series concentrator that shows the establishment of the VPN tunnel illustrated in the previous two examples is shown in Example 21-21. This again shows how the troubleshooting engineer can analyze the process from the other end, and what the process looks like.

Example 21-21 *Log from a VPN 3000 Series Concentrator for a PIX Client*

```
13160 07/17/2002 08:13:50.200 SEV=4 IKE/52 RPT=4625 12.235.95.31
Group [pix] User [smith]
User (smith) authenticated.

13161 07/17/2002 08:13:51.690 SEV=4 AUTH/22 RPT=4826
User smith connected

13162 07/17/2002 08:13:51.690 SEV=4 IKE/119 RPT=16260 12.235.95.31
Group [pix] User [smith]
PHASE 1 COMPLETED

13164 07/17/2002 08:13:51.690 SEV=5 IKE/25 RPT=39847 12.235.95.31
Group [pix] User [smith]
Received remote Proxy Host data in ID Payload:
Address 10.25.250.1, Protocol 0, Port 0

13167 07/17/2002 08:13:51.690 SEV=5 IKE/34 RPT=47957 12.235.95.31
Group [pix] User [smith]
Received local IP Proxy Subnet data in ID Payload:
 Address 0.0.0.0, Mask 0.0.0.0, Protocol 0, Port 0

13170 07/17/2002 08:13:51.690 SEV=5 IKE/66 RPT=21557 12.235.95.31
Group [pix] User [smith]
IKE Remote Peer configured for SA: ESP/IKE-3DES-MD5

13171 07/17/2002 08:13:51.710 SEV=4 IKE/49 RPT=21627 12.235.95.31
Group [pix] User [smith]
Security negotiation complete for User (smith)
Responder, Inbound SPI = 0x321e317b, Outbound SPI = 0xb84c8c89
! The Inbound and Outbound SPI are reversed compared
! to the log from PIX client.

13174 07/17/2002 08:13:51.710 SEV=4 IKE/120 RPT=21627 12.235.95.31
Group [pix] User [smith]
PHASE 2 COMPLETED (msgid=e367589c)

13181 07/17/2002 08:13:55.270 SEV=5 IKE/25 RPT=39848 12.235.95.31
Group [pix] User [smith]
Received remote Proxy Host data in ID Payload:
Address 12.235.95.31, Protocol 0, Port 0

13184 07/17/2002 08:13:55.270 SEV=5 IKE/34 RPT=47958 12.235.95.31
Group [pix] User [smith]
Received local IP Proxy Subnet data in ID Payload:
 Address 0.0.0.0, Mask 0.0.0.0, Protocol 0, Port 0

13187 07/17/2002 08:13:55.270 SEV=5 IKE/66 RPT=21558 12.235.95.31
Group [pix] User [smith]
IKE Remote Peer configured for SA: ESP/IKE-3DES-MD5

13188 07/17/2002 08:13:55.290 SEV=4 IKE/49 RPT=21628 12.235.95.31
Group [pix] User [smith]
```

Example 21-21   *Log from a VPN 3000 Series Concentrator for a PIX Client (Continued)*

```
Security negotiation complete for User (smith)
Responder, Inbound SPI = 0x76accd0d, Outbound SPI = 0x948b4d0c
! Again, the SPI identifying the IPSec SAs reversed on the PIX client.

13191 07/17/2002 08:13:55.290 SEV=4 IKE/120 RPT=21628 12.235.95.31
Group [pix] User [smith]
PHASE 2 COMPLETED (msgid=3be10994)
```

Two debug commands that can provide detailed information during the negotiation of the VPN tunnels are the following:

- **debug crypto ipsec sa**
- **debug crypto isakmp sa**

Output on the PIX 501 after enabling these debugs before the VPN tunnel negotiation is shown in Example 21-22. By checking this output, you can observe if something is failing during the tunnel negotiation process.

Example 21-22   *Output on PIX After Implementing* **debug crypto ipsec sa** *and* **debug crypto isakmp sa** *and Enabling a VPN Client*

```
pix# debug crypto ipsec
pix# debug crypto isakmp
pix# show debug
debug crypto ipsec 1
debug crypto isakmp 1
pix#config terminal
pix(config)# vpnclient vpngroup pix password abcd
pix(config)# vpnclient server 192.168.192.81
pix(config)# vpnclient mode network
pix(config)# vpnclient username smith password efghij
pix(config)# vpnclient enable
! After this group of configuration commands, you can see the following events:
pViPx(coNnCfig )#C FG: transform set unconfig attempt done
VPNC CLI: no isakmp keepalive 10
VPNC CFG: IKE unconfig successful
VPNC CLI: no crypto map _vpnc_cm
VPNC CFG: crypto map deletion attempt done
VPNC CFG: crypto unconfig successful
VPNC CLI: no global 65001
VPNC CLI: no nat (inside) 0 access-list _vpnc_acl
VPNC CFG: nat unconfig attempt failed
VPNC CLI: no access-list _vpnc_acl
VPNC CFG: ACL deletion attempt failed
VPNC CLI: no crypto      ALT_DEF_DOMAIN
         INTERNAL_IPV_NBNS
         INTERNAL_IPV_DNS
         ALT_SPLIT_INCLUDE
         ALT_SPLITDNS_NAME
```

continues

Example 21-22 *Output on PIX After Implementing* **debug crypto ipsec sa** *and* **debug crypto isakmp sa** *and Enabling a VPN Client (Continued)*

```
         ALT_PFS
map _vpnc_cm interface outside
VPNC CFG: crypto map de/attach failed
VPNC CLI: no sysopt connection permit-ipsec
VPNC CLI: sysopt connection permit-ipsec
VPNC CFG: transform sets configured
VPNC CFG: crypto config successful
VPNC CLI: isakmp keepalive 10
VPNC CFG: IKE config successful
VPNC CLI: no access-list _vpnc_acl
VPNC CFG: ACL deletion attempt failed
VPNC CLI: access-list _vpnc_acl permit ip host 12.235.95.31 host 192.168.192.81
VPNC CLI: crypto map _vpnc_cm 10 match address _vpnc_acl
VPNC CFG: crypto map acl update successful
VPNC CLI: no crypto map _vpnc_cm interface outside
VPNC CLI: crypto map _vpnc_cm interface outside

VPN Peer: ISAKMP: Added new peer: ip:192.168.192.81 Total VPN Peers:1
VPN Peer: ISAKMP: Peer ip:192.168.192.81 Ref cnt incremented to:1 Total
    VPN Peers:1
ISAKMP (0): ID payload
        next-payload : 13
        type         : 11
        protocol     : 17
        port         : 500
        length       : 7
ISAKMP (0): Total payload length: 11
ISAKMP (0): beginning Aggressive Mode exchangeVPNC INF: Request for
    IKE trigger done

crypto_isakmp_process_block: src 192.168.192.81, dest 12.235.95.31
OAK_AG exchange
ISAKMP (0): processing SA payload. message ID = 0

ISAKMP (0): Checking ISAKMP transform 2 against priority 65010 policy
ISAKMP:      encryption 3DES-CBC
ISAKMP:      hash MD5
ISAKMP:      default group 2
ISAKMP:      extended auth pre-share
ISAKMP:      life type in seconds
! Lifetime duration of the ISAKMP SA in seconds
ISAKMP:      life duration (VPI) of  0x0 0x1 0x51 0x80
ISAKMP (0): atts are not acceptable. Next payload is 0
ISAKMP (0): Checking ISAKMP transform 2 against priority 65020 policy
ISAKMP:      encryption 3DES-CBC
ISAKMP:      hash MD5
ISAKMP:      default group 2
ISAKMP:      extended auth pre-share
ISAKMP:      life type in seconds
ISAKMP:      life duration (VPI) of  0x0 0x1 0x51
crypto_isakmp_process_block: src 192.168.192.81, dest 12.235.95.31
```

Example 21-22 *Output on PIX After Implementing* **debug crypto ipsec sa** *and* **debug crypto isakmp sa** *and Enabling a VPN Client (Continued)*

```
ISAKMP_TRANSACTION exchange
ISAKMP (0:0): processing transaction payload from 192.168.192.81.
    message ID = 2158353436
crypto_isakmp_process_block: src 192.168.192.81, dest 12.235.95.31
ISAKMP_TRANSACTION exchange
ISAKMP (0:0): processing transaction payload from 192.168.192.81.
    message ID = 2158353436
ISAKMP: Config payload CFG_SET
ISAKMP (0:0): checking SET:
ISAKMP:    XAUTH_STATUS
ISAKMP (0:0): attributes sent in message:
        Status: 1
return status is IKMP_NO_ERROR
VPNC INF: Constructing policy download req

VPNC INF: Packing attributes for policy request

VPNC INF: Attributes being requested

ISAKMP : attributes being requested

ISAKMP (0:0): initiating peer config to 192.168.192.81. ID =
    3931692763 (0xea58dedb)
crypto_isakmp_process_block: src 192.168.192.81, dest 12.235.95.31
ISAKMP_TRANSACTION exchange
ISAKMP (0:0): processing transaction payload from 192.168.192.81.
    message ID = 2158353436
ISAKMP: Config payload CFG_REPLYVPNC ATTR: INTERNAL_IP4_DNS: 192.168.226.120
VPNC ATTR: INTERNAL_IP4_DNS: 192.168.168.183
VPNC ATTR: INTERNAL_IP4_NBNS: 192.168.2.87
VPNC ATTR: INTERNAL_IP4_NBNS: 192.168.235.228
VPNC ATTR: ALT_DEF_DOMAIN: cisco.com
VPNC ATTR: ALT_SPLITDNS_NAME
        cisco.com_
VPNC ATTR: ALT_PFS: 0

VPNC INF: Received application version 'Cisco Systems, Inc./VPN 3000
    Concentrator Version 3.5.2.Rel built by vmurphy on
    Feb 14 2002 12:10:21
! Version information of VPN 3000 Concentrator terminating the IPSec tunnel
VPNC CLI: no VPNC INF: IPSec rmt mgmt trigger done

ISAKMP (0): beginning Quick Mode exchange, M-ID of 1015758940:3c8b405cIPSEC
    (key_engine): got a queue event...
IPSEC(spi_response): getting spi 0x689d0b46(1755122502) for SA
        from    192.168.192.81 to    12.235.95.31 for prot 3

crypto_isakmp_process_block: src 192.168.192.81, dest 12.235.95.31
OAK_QM exchange
oakley_process_quick_mode:
```

continues

Example 21-22 *Output on PIX After Implementing* **debug crypto ipsec sa** *and* **debug crypto isakmp sa** *and Enabling a VPN Client (Continued)*

```
OAK_QM_IDLE
ISAKMP (0): processing SA payload. message ID = 1015758940

ISAKMP : Checking IPSec proposal 1

ISAKMP: transform 1, ESP_3DES
ISAKMP:    attributes in transform:
ISAKMP:       SA life type in seconds
ISAKMP:       SA life duration (basic) of 28800
ISAKMP:       SA life type in kilobytes
ISAKMP:       SA life duration (VPI) of  0x0 0x46 0x50 0x0
ISAKMP:       encaps is 1
ISAKMP:       authenticator is HMAC-MD5
ISAKMP (0): atts are acceptable.IPSEC(validate_proposal_request):
    proposal part #1,
  (key eng. msg.) dest= 192.168.192.81, src= 12.235.95.31,
    dest_proxy= 0.0.0.0/0.0.0.0/0/0 (type=4),
    src_proxy= 12.235.95.31/255.255.255.255/0/0 (type=1),
    protocol= ESP, transform= esp-3des esp-md5-hmac ,
    lifedur= 0s and 0kb,
    spi= 0x0(0), conn_id= 0, keysize= 0, flags= 0x4

ISAKMP (0): processing NONCE payload. message ID = 1015758940

ISAKMP (0): processing ID payload. message ID = 1015758940
ISAKMP (0): processing ID payload. message ID = 1015758940
ISAKMP (0): Creating IPSec SAs
        inbound SA from   192.168.192.81 to    12.235.95.31 (proxy
        0.0.0.0 to    12.235.95.31)
        has spi 1755122502 and conn_id 4 and flags 4
        lifetime of 28800 seconds
        lifetime of 4608000 kilobytes
        outbound SA from    12.235.95.31 to    192.168.192.81 (proxy
    12.235.95.31 to       0.0.0.0)
        has spi 865892405 and conn_id 3 and flags 4
        lifetime of 28800 seconds
        lifetime of 4608000 kilobytesIPSEC(key_engine): got a queue event...
IPSEC(initialize_sas): ,
  (key eng. msg.) dest= 12.235.95.31, src= 192.168.192.81,
    dest_proxy= 12.235.95.31/255.255.255.255/0/0 (type=1),
    src_proxy= 0.0.0.0/0.0.0.0/0/0 (type=4),
    protocol= ESP, transform= esp-3des esp-md5-hmac ,
    lifedur= 28800s and 4608000kb,
    spi= 0x689d0b46(1755122502), conn_id= 4, keysize= 0, flags= 0x4
IPSEC(initialize_sas): ,
  (key eng. msg.) src= 12.235.95.31, dest= 192.168.192.81,
    src_proxy= 12.235.95.31/255.255.255.255/0/0 (type=1),
    dest_proxy= 0.0.0.0/0.0.0.0/0/0 (type=4),
    protocol= ESP, transform= esp-3des esp-md5-hmac ,
    lifedur= 28800s and 4608000kb,
    spi= 0x339c7835(865892405), conn_id= 3, keysize= 0, flags= 0x4
```

Example 21-22 *Output on PIX After Implementing* **debug crypto ipsec sa** *and* **debug crypto isakmp sa** *and Enabling a VPN Client (Continued)*

```
VPN Peer: IPSEC: Peer ip:192.168.192.81 Ref cnt incremented to:2
    Total VPN Peers:1
VPN Peer: IPSEC: Peer ip:192.168.192.81 Ref cnt incremented to:3
    Total VPN Peers:1
return status is IKMP_NO_ERROR
ISAKMP (0): beginning Quick Mode exchange, M-ID of 1352049028:5096a184IPSEC
    (key_engine): got a queue event...
IPSEC(spi_response): getting spi 0x4dbb61e3(1304125923) for SA
        from   192.168.192.81 to    12.235.95.31 for prot 3

crypto_isakmp_process_block: src 192.168.192.81, dest 12.235.95.31
OAK_QM exchange
oakley_process_quick_mode:
OAK_QM_IDLE
ISAKMP (0): processing SA payload. message ID = 1352049028

ISAKMP : Checking IPSec proposal 1

ISAKMP: transform 1, ESP_3DES
ISAKMP:    attributes in transform:
ISAKMP:       SA life type in seconds
ISAKMP:       SA life duration (basic) of 28800
ISAKMP:       SA life type in kilobytes
ISAKMP:       SA life duration (VPI) of  0x0 0x46 0x50 0x0
ISAKMP:       encaps is 1
ISAKMP:       authenticator is HMAC-MD5
ISAKMP (0): atts are acceptable.IPSEC(validate_proposal_request):
    proposal part #1,
  (key eng. msg.) dest= 192.168.192.81, src= 12.235.95.31,
    dest_proxy= 0.0.0.0/0.0.0.0/0/0 (type=4),
    src_proxy= 10.25.0.128/255.255.255.240/0/0 (type=4),
    protocol= ESP, transform= esp-3des esp-md5-hmac ,
    lifedur= 0s and 0kb,
    spi= 0x0(0), conn_id= 0, keysize= 0, flags= 0x4

ISAKMP (0): processing NONCE payload. message ID = 1352049028

ISAKMP (0): processing ID payload. message ID = 1352049028
ISAKMP (0): processing ID payload. message ID = 1352049028
ISAKMP (0): Creating IPSec SAs
        inbound SA from   192.168.192.81 to    12.235.95.31 (proxy
        0.0.0.0 to    10.25.0.128)
        has spi 1304125923 and conn_id 2 and flags 4
        lifetime of 28800 seconds
        lifetime of 4608000 kilobytes
        outbound SA from    12.235.95.31 to    192.168.192.81 (proxy
    10.25.0.128 to        0.0.0.0)
        has spi 17882921 and conn_id 1 and flags 4
        lifetime of 28800 seconds
        lifetime of 4608000 kilobytesIPSEC(key_engine): got a queue event...
```

continues

Example 21-22 *Output on PIX After Implementing* **debug crypto ipsec sa** *and* **debug crypto isakmp sa** *and Enabling a VPN Client (Continued)*

```
IPSEC(initialize_sas): ,
  (key eng. msg.) dest= 12.235.95.31, src= 192.168.192.81,
    dest_proxy= 10.25.0.128/255.255.255.240/0/0 (type=4),
    src_proxy= 0.0.0.0/0.0.0.0/0/0 (type=4),
    protocol= ESP, transform= esp-3des esp-md5-hmac ,
    lifedur= 28800s and 4608000kb,
    spi= 0x4dbb61e3(1304125923), conn_id= 2, keysize= 0, flags= 0x4
IPSEC(initialize_sas): ,
  (key eng. msg.) src= 12.235.95.31, dest= 192.168.192.81,
    src_proxy= 10.25.0.128/255.255.255.240/0/0 (type=4),
    dest_proxy= 0.0.0.0/0.0.0.0/0/0 (type=4),
    protocol= ESP, transform= esp-3des esp-md5-hmac ,
    lifedur= 28800s and 4608000kb,
    spi= 0x110df29(17882921), conn_id= 1, keysize= 0, flags= 0x4

VPN Peer: IPSEC: Peer ip:192.168.192.81 Ref cnt incremented to:4
    Total VPN Peers:1
VPN Peer: IPSEC: Peer ip:192.168.192.81 Ref cnt incremented to:5
    Total VPN Peers:1
return status is IKMP_NO_ERROR
```

An overall discussion of PIX-based solutions is beyond the scope of this book. The objectives of this section are only to help you troubleshoot PIX-based VPN solutions. For further details on PIX-based VPN solutions as part of the overall security strategy of Cisco, see *Cisco Secure PIX Firewalls* by David W. Chapman and Andy Fox (Cisco Press, 2002).

Internet Technologies and Remote Access VPNs

In this section, issues are briefly covered that are specific to three popular technologies that offer broadband services for most remote access VPNs:

- VPN and ADSL
- VPN and Internet access through cable TV infrastructure
- VPN and Internet access over satellite and wireless systems

VPN and ADSL

A typical ADSL architecture is composed of equipment at the ADSL point of presence (POP) and customer premises equipment (CPE). Network access providers (NAPs) manage Layer 2 network cores, and network service providers (NSPs) manage Layer 3 network cores. These roles are divided or shared among incumbent local exchange carriers (ILECs), competitive local exchange carriers (CLECs), and Tier 1 and Tier 2 Internet service providers (ISPs).

CPEs can consist of PCs or workstations, remote ADSL terminating units (ATU-Rs), and routers. For example, a residential user might have a single PC connected through Ethernet to an ADSL modem. The end-user might also connect their PC or workstations through Ethernet to a router with an integrated ADSL modem, or a two-port Ethernet router that is then connected to a stand-alone ADSL modem.

DSL access multiplexers (DSLAMs) are installed at the ADSL POP, and because the DSLAMs service the local loops between residences and businesses and the POP, they are often located in the ILEC's central office (CO). DSLAMs connect to a local access concentrator (LAC) or the node route processor (NRP). The LAC provides Layer 3 connectivity from the CPE to the NSP or IP network.

More detailed discussion of this topic is divided into the following sections:

- PPPoE
- PPPoE design details
- PPPoE discovery stage
- PPPoE session stage
- Review of the PPPoE discovery and session negotiation
- Common issues for RA VPNs with PPPoE on ADSL

PPPoE

PPPoE is becoming the technology of choice for new DSL installations. It enables providers to conserve IP addresses and use them per connection, and to track the IP address to a specific client. RFC 2516 provides the standard for communicating through PPPoE.

With PPPoE, an ADSL modem acts as an Ethernet-to-wide-area network (WAN) bridge. The PPP network parameters are negotiated and the PPP session is established between the CPE and the LAC or NRP. CPEs that can negotiate PPP parameters and terminate the session include both a host and router. Any host with PPP client software such as RASPPPoE, NTS EnterNet or Windows PPP over Ethernet Client Software Application (WINPoET), can perform this function. A router such as the Cisco 806 dual Ethernet router that sits behind an ADSL modem, or the Cisco 827 that incorporates the ADSL modem and establishes the PPP session, are examples of typical small office/home office (SOHO) CPEs that can handle all facets of the PPP session.

The CPE starts a PPP session by encapsulating PPP frames into a Media Access Control (MAC) frame, then bridging the frame (over Asynchronous Transfer Mode [ATM]/DSL) to the LAC or NRP. As a result, PPP sessions can be established, authenticated, and addressed. The client receives its IP address using IP Control Protocol (IPCP) from the PPP termination point, or the LAC or NRP.

An example of a DSL implementation that uses a PPPoE network architecture is shown in Figure 21-8.

Figure 21-8 *PPPoE over ADSL Architecture Example*[8]

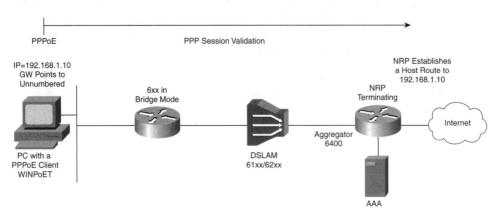

PPPoE Stages

As specified in RFC 2516, PPPoE has two distinct stages, the discovery stage and the PPP session stage.

When a host wants to start a PPPoE session, it must first perform discovery to identify which server can meet this client's request, then identify the Ethernet MAC address of the peer and establish a PPPoE SESSION_ID. Although PPP defines a peer-to-peer relationship, discovery is inherently a client-server relationship. In the discovery process, a host (the client) discovers an access concentrator (AC) (the server). Based on the network topology, more than one AC can communicate with the host. The discovery stage allows the host to discover all ACs and then select one. When discovery is successfully completed, both the host and the selected AC have the information they need to build a point-to-point connection over Ethernet. After a PPP session is established, both the host and the AC must allocate the resources for a PPP virtual interface; however, this might not be the case for all implementations. Finally, to be in compliance with RFC 2516, the IP MTU must be specified as 1492 for PPPoE.

PPPoE Discovery Stage

The discovery stage consists of four steps:

Step 1 The host broadcasting an initiation packet

Step 2 One or more ACs sending offer packets

Step 3 The host sending a unicast session request packet

Step 4 The selected AC sending a confirmation packet

When the host receives the confirmation packet, it proceeds to the PPP session stage, and when the AC sends the confirmation packet, it proceeds to the PPP session stage. At the completion of the discovery stage, both peers know the PPPoE SESSION_ID and the peer's Ethernet address, which together define the PPPoE session uniquely.

The host sends the PPPoE Active Discovery Initiation (PADI) packet with the DESTINATION_ADDR set to the broadcast address. The PADI consists of one tag, indicating what service type it is requesting. When the AC receives a PADI that it can serve, it replies by sending a PPPoE Active Discovery Offer (PADO) packet. The DESTINATION_ADDR is the unicast address of the host that sent the PADI.

If the AC cannot serve the PADI, it must not respond with a PADO. Because the PADI was broadcast, the host can receive more than one PADO. The host reviews the PADO packets it receives and chooses one. The choice can be based on the services offered by each AC. The host then sends one PPPoE Active Discovery Request (PADR) packet to the AC that it has chosen. The DESTINATION_ADDR field is set to the unicast Ethernet address of the AC, or the router that sent the PADO. When the AC receives a PADR packet, it prepares to begin a PPP session. It generates a unique SESSION_ID for the PPPoE session, and replies to the host with a PPPoE Active Discovery Session-confirmation (PADS) packet. The DESTINATION_ADDR field is the unicast Ethernet address of the host that sent the PADR. The PPPoE negotiation process is shown in Figure 21-9.

Figure 21-9 *Negotiation Process for a PPPoE Client*

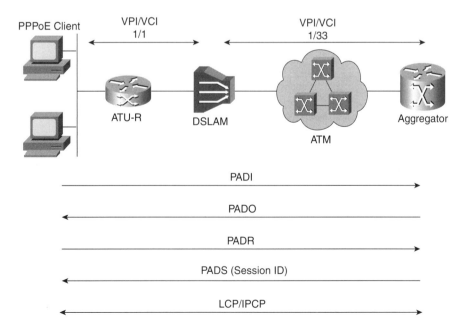

PPPoE Session Stage

After the PPPoE session begins, PPP data is sent as in any other PPP encapsulation. The typical number of steps per exchange in the PPPoe session stage is four steps for link control protocol (LCP), two or four steps for AUTH, and a various number of steps for Network Control Protocol (NCP), it is dependent on the Layer 3 protocols that are in use. At this point, all Ethernet packets are unicast. A PPPoE Active Discovery Terminate (PADT) packet can be sent anytime after a session is established, to indicate that a PPPoE session has been terminated. The packet can be sent by the host or the AC. The DESTINATION_ADDR field is a unicast Ethernet address.

PPPoE Discovery and Session Negotiation

The Cisco 827 router provides an excellent illustration of PPPoE negotiations. The output from the router is shown in Example 21-23. For this example, IOS v12.2(2)XH is used and the following debug commands are activated:

- Dial-on-demand events
- ATM events
- Virtual private dialup network (VPDN) events
- PPPoE protocol
- PPP packet

Example 21-23 shows the output as a result of debugging the dialer events, ATM events, VPDN events, PPPoE events, and PPP packets for a Cisco 827 router.

Example 21-23   *Output from a Cisco 827 Router Showing Successful PPPoE Discovery Stage Negotiation*

```
VPN-dsl#show debug
Dial on demand:
  Dial on demand events debugging is on
Generic ATM:
  ATM events debugging is on
VPN:
  VPDN events debugging is on
  PPPoE protocol events debugging is on
PPP:
  PPP packet display debugging is on

*Oct 18 16:02:18 PST: Sending PADI: vc=0/35
! The router sends its PAD initiation (PADI).
*Oct 18 16:02:18 PST:  padi timer expired
*Oct 18 16:02:18 PST: PPPoE 0: I PADO L:0004.27fd.970e R:0010.6700.b5a0 0/35 AT0
! The router receives the LAC response with the PAD offer (PADO),
! with L: and R: over vc/vp 0/35 ATM0.
! I indicates input, L for local, and R is remote.
! The number strings following these letters are MAC addresses of
! the respective host.
```

Example 21-23 *Output from a Cisco 827 Router Showing Successful PPPoE Discovery Stage Negotiation (Continued)*

```
*Oct 18 16:02:20 PST:  PPPOE: we've got our pado and the pado timer went off
*Oct 18 16:02:20 PST: OUT PADR from PPPoE tunnel
! The router sends PAD request (PADR) out.
*Oct 18 16:02:20 PST: PPPoE 4922: I PADS L:0004.27fd.970e R:0010.6700.b5a0 0/35 AT0
*Oct 18 16:02:20 PST: IN PADS from PPPoE tunnel
! The router receives the PAD session confirmation (PADS).
! The discovery stage is done.
*Oct 18 16:02:20 PST: %DIALER-6-BIND: Interface Vi1 bound to profile Di1
! The virtual interface is created and referred to as Vix
! (in this example, replace x with 1).
! It bonds to the dialer interface to start the PPP Session stage.
*Oct 18 16:02:20 PST: PPPoE: Virtual Access interface obtained.
```

At this point, the router and AC complete the PPPoE discovery stage. If you enter the command **show ip interface brief**, you see that a virtual-interface has been established, as shown in Example 21-24.

Example 21-24 *IP Interface Status After PPPoE Discovery Stage*

```
VPN-dsl#show ip interface brief
Interface        IP-Address      OK? Method    Status     Protocol
ATM0             unassigned      YES NVRAM     up         up
Dialer1          unassigned      YES NVRAM     up         up
Ethernet0        10.10.10.1      YES NVRAM     up         down
Virtual-Access1  unassigned      YES unset     up         up
```

If, for some reason, the router cannot successfully negotiate the first steps in the discovery stage, you might see output similar to that shown in Example 21-25.

Example 21-25 *Output from a Cisco 827 Router for a PPPoE Session Negotiation with a Failed Result*

```
*Oct 18 16:04:38 PST: Sending PADI: vc=0/35
*Oct 18 16:04:38 PST: pppoe_send_padi failed
*Oct 18 16:04:38 PST:  padi timer expired
*Oct 18 16:04:40 PST: Sending PADI: vc=0/35
*Oct 18 16:04:40 PST: pppoe_send_padi failed
*Oct 18 16:04:40 PST:  padi timer expired
*Oct 18 16:04:42 PST: Sending PADI: vc=0/35
*Oct 18 16:04:42 PST: pppoe_send_padi failed
*Oct 18 16:04:42 PST:  padi timer expired
```

Next, you can see the output for the successful negotiation of the PPPoE session stage parameters, as shown in Example 21-26.

At this point, the virtual interface is now assigned an IP address, as shown in Example 21-27, and data transfer can be started.

Example 21-26 *Output from a Cisco 827 Router for Successful PPPoE Negotiation*

```
*Oct 18 16:02:20 PST: Vi1 VPDN: Bind interface direction=2
*Oct 18 16:02:20 PST: Vi1 LCP: O CONFREQ [Closed] id 1 len 10
*Oct 18 16:02:20 PST: Vi1 LCP:    MagicNumber 0x042A23C5 (0x0506042A23C5)
*Oct 18 16:02:20 PST: %LINK-3-UPDOWN: Interface Virtual-Access1,
    changed state to up
*Oct 18 16:02:20 PST: Vi1 DDR: Dialer statechange to up
*Oct 18 16:02:20 PST: Vi1 PPP: I pkt type 0xC021, datagramsize 20
*Oct 18 16:02:20 PST: Vi1 PPP: I pkt type 0xC021, datagramsize 12
*Oct 18 16:02:20 PST: Vi1 LCP: I CONFREQ [REQsent] id 241 len 18
*Oct 18 16:02:20 PST: Vi1 LCP:    MRU 1492 (0x010405D4)
*Oct 18 16:02:20 PST: Vi1 LCP:    AuthProto PAP (0x0304C023)
*Oct 18 16:02:20 PST: Vi1 LCP:    MagicNumber 0x02511B20 (0x050602511B20)
*Oct 18 16:02:20 PST: Vi1 LCP: O CONFNAK [REQsent] id 241 len 8
! The CPE refuses
*Oct 18 16:02:20 PST: Vi1 LCP:    MRU 1500 (0x010405DC)
*Oct 18 16:02:20 PST: Vi1 LCP: I CONFACK [REQsent] id 1 len 10
*Oct 18 16:02:20 PST: Vi1 LCP:    MagicNumber 0x042A23C5 (0x0506042A23C5)
*Oct 18 16:02:20 PST: Vi1 PPP: I pkt type 0xC021, datagramsize 20
*Oct 18 16:02:20 PST: Vi1 LCP: I CONFREQ [ACKrcvd] id 242 len 18
*Oct 18 16:02:20 PST: Vi1 LCP:    MRU 1492 (0x010405D4)
*Oct 18 16:02:20 PST: Vi1 LCP:    AuthProto PAP (0x0304C023)
*Oct 18 16:02:20 PST: Vi1 LCP:    MagicNumber 0x02511B20 (0x050602511B20)
*Oct 18 16:02:20 PST: Vi1 LCP: O CONFNAK [ACKrcvd] id 242 len 8
! CPE refuses again
*Oct 18 16:02:20 PST: Vi1 LCP:    MRU 1500 (0x010405DC)
*Oct 18 16:02:20 PST: Vi1 PPP: I pkt type 0xC021, datagramsize 20
! Finally, the CPE agrees.
*Oct 18 16:02:20 PST: Vi1 PPP: I pkt type 0xC021, datagramsize 16
*Oct 18 16:02:20 PST: Vi1 LCP: I CONFREQ [ACKrcvd] id 247 len 14
*Oct 18 16:02:20 PST: Vi1 LCP:    AuthProto PAP (0x0304C023)
*Oct 18 16:02:20 PST: Vi1 LCP:    MagicNumber 0x02511B20 (0x050602511B20)
*Oct 18 16:02:20 PST: Vi1 LCP: O CONFACK [ACKrcvd] id 247 len 14
*Oct 18 16:02:20 PST: Vi1 LCP:    AuthProto PAP (0x0304C023)
*Oct 18 16:02:20 PST: Vi1 LCP:    MagicNumber 0x02511B20 (0x050602511B20)
*Oct 18 16:02:20 PST: Vi1 PAP: O AUTH-REQ id 1 len 40 from VPN-dsl@xyz.net
! CPE starts the AUTH process with a request.
*Oct 18 16:02:22 PST: Vi1 PPP: I pkt type 0xC023, datagramsize 7
*Oct 18 16:02:22 PST: Vi1 PPP: I pkt type 0xC021, datagramsize 10
*Oct 18 16:02:22 PST: Vi1 LCP: I ECHOREQ [Open] id 0 len 8 magic 0x02511B20
*Oct 18 16:02:22 PST: Vi1 LCP: O ECHOREP [Open] id 0 len 8 magic 0x042A23C5
*Oct 18 16:02:22 PST: Vi1 PPP: I pkt type 0x8021, datagramsize 12
*Oct 18 16:02:22 PST: Vi1 PAP: I AUTH-ACK id 1 len 5
! Access Concentrator agrees on PAP AUTH.
*Oct 18 16:02:22 PST: Vi1 IPCP: I CONFREQ [Closed] id 241 len 10
*Oct 18 16:02:22 PST: Vi1 IPCP:    Address 64.175.247.254 (0x030640AFF7FE)
*Oct 18 16:02:22 PST: Vi1 IPCP: O CONFREQ [Closed] id 1 len 22
*Oct 18 16:02:22 PST: Vi1 IPCP:    Address 0.0.0.0 (0x030600000000)
*Oct 18 16:02:22 PST: Vi1 IPCP:    PrimaryDNS 0.0.0.0 (0x810600000000)
*Oct 18 16:02:22 PST: Vi1 IPCP:    SecondaryDNS 0.0.0.0 (0x830600000000)
*Oct 18 16:02:22 PST: Vi1 PPP: I pkt type 0x8021, datagramsize 24
*Oct 18 16:02:22 PST: Vi1 IPCP: I CONFNAK [REQsent] id 1 len 22
*Oct 18 16:02:22 PST: Vi1 IPCP:    Address 64.175.245.47 (0x030640AFF52F)
```

Example 21-26 *Output from a Cisco 827 Router for Successful PPPoE Negotiation (Continued)*

```
*Oct 18 16:02:22 PST: Vi1 IPCP:    PrimaryDNS 63.203.35.55 (0x81063FCB2337)
*Oct 18 16:02:22 PST: Vi1 IPCP:    SecondaryDNS 206.13.28.12 (0x8306CE0D1C0C)
*Oct 18 16:02:22 PST: Vi1 IPCP: O CONFREQ [REQsent] id 2 len 22
*Oct 18 16:02:22 PST: Vi1 IPCP:    Address 64.175.245.47 (0x030640AFF52F)
*Oct 18 16:02:22 PST: Vi1 IPCP:    PrimaryDNS 63.203.35.55 (0x81063FCB2337)
*Oct 18 16:02:22 PST: Vi1 IPCP:    SecondaryDNS 206.13.28.12 (0x8306CE0D1C0C)
*Oct 18 16:02:22 PST: Vi1 PPP: I pkt type 0x8021, datagramsize 24
*Oct 18 16:02:22 PST: Vi1 IPCP: I CONFACK [REQsent] id 2 len 22
*Oct 18 16:02:22 PST: Vi1 IPCP:    Address 64.175.245.47 (0x030640AFF52F)
*Oct 18 16:02:22 PST: Vi1 IPCP:    PrimaryDNS 63.203.35.55 (0x81063FCB2337)
*Oct 18 16:02:22 PST: Vi1 IPCP:    SecondaryDNS 206.13.28.12 (0x8306CE0D1C0C)
*Oct 18 16:02:23 PST: %LINEPROTO-5-UPDOWN: Line protocol on Interface
    Virtual-Access1, changed state to up
! Virtual interface protocol is up and it is in the IPCP phase.
*Oct 18 16:02:24 PST: Vi1 IPCP: TIMEout: State ACKrcvd
*Oct 18 16:02:24 PST: Vi1 IPCP: O CONFREQ [ACKrcvd] id 3 len 22
*Oct 18 16:02:24 PST: Vi1 IPCP:    Address 64.175.245.47 (0x030640AFF52F)
*Oct 18 16:02:24 PST: Vi1 IPCP:    PrimaryDNS 63.203.35.55 (0x81063FCB2337)
*Oct 18 16:02:24 PST: Vi1 IPCP:    SecondaryDNS 206.13.28.12 (0x8306CE0D1C0C)
*Oct 18 16:02:24 PST: Vi1 PPP: I pkt type 0x8021, datagramsize 24
*Oct 18 16:02:24 PST: Vi1 IPCP: I CONFACK [REQsent] id 3 len 22
! The IP address 64.175.245.47 is assigned to Dialer 1
*Oct 18 16:02:24 PST: Vi1 IPCP:    Address 64.175.245.47 (0x030640AFF52F)
*Oct 18 16:02:24 PST: Vi1 IPCP:    PrimaryDNS 63.203.35.55 (0x81063FCB2337)
*Oct 18 16:02:24 PST: Vi1 IPCP:    SecondaryDNS 206.13.28.12 (0x8306CE0D1C0C)
*Oct 18 16:02:25 PST: Vi1 PPP: I pkt type 0x8021, datagramsize 12
*Oct 18 16:02:25 PST: Vi1 IPCP: I CONFREQ [ACKrcvd] id 241 len 10
*Oct 18 16:02:25 PST: Vi1 IPCP:    Address 64.175.247.254 (0x030640AFF7FE)
*Oct 18 16:02:25 PST: Vi1 IPCP: O CONFACK [ACKrcvd] id 241 len 10
*Oct 18 16:02:25 PST: Vi1 IPCP:    Address 64.175.247.254 (0x030640AFF7FE)
*Oct 18 16:02:25 PST: Vi1 DDR: dialer protocol up
*Oct 18 16:02:25 PST: Vi1 PPP: I pkt type 0xC021, datagramsize 10
```

Example 21-27 *IP Interface Status after Completing PPPoE Session Stage Negotiation*

```
VPN-dsl#sh ip int brie
Interface        IP-Address      OK?   Method   Status   Protocol
ATM0             unassigned      YES   NVRAM    up       up
Dialer1          64.175.245.47   YES   IPCP     up       up
Ethernet0        10.10.10.1      YES   NVRAM    up       down
Virtual-Access1  unassigned      YES   unset    up       up
```

Common Issues for Remote Access VPNs with PPPoE on ADSL

Two of the more common issues that ADSL PPPoE clients encounter are authentication into the provider's network, and the MTU of the PPPoE adapter. Clients can choose to use a router or a SW application on their host to negotiate both the authentication and MTU parameters. In almost all cases, the remote access device must be configured to provide a PPPoE username and password to authenticate with the provider's authentication server. If the client or router cannot negotiate an IP address with the provider, confirm that the PPPoE username and password are correct. If they are correct and you still cannot obtain an IP address, verify the network infrastructure at home. If using a router to negotiate authentication, switch to a host and use one of the SW PPPoE adapters. If you still cannot negotiate an address, you might have to work with the provider to verify that the service is operational and that you have the correct authentication parameters.

In Chapter 22, "Remote Access VPN Troubleshooting Scenarios," a scenario is presented that shows the steps required to change the MTU on some SW PPPoE adapters. Some routers, such as the Cisco827, also provide this feature.

VPN and Internet Access Through a Cable TV Infrastructure

In the last few years, Multiple Service Operators (MSOs) have been upgrading their networks and installing high-speed data communication systems that operate over the cable television (CATV) system to provide Internet broadband connectivity to subscribers. These systems effectively provide a data communications path that is transparent to IP over the last portion of their network. However, exchanging TCP/IP information over the Internet through a CATV network presents it own unique issues and challenges to remote access VPNs, which are addressed in the next section.

Subsequent sections related to this topic cover the following:

- Overview of data transmission over a CATV network
- Cable modems and infrastructure
- Standards for data transmission over cable, and common issues for remote access VPNs over CATV data networks

Overview of Data Transmission over a CATV Network

CATV networks were originally designed and used for one-way distribution of analog television signals, from the operator to the subscriber. Under this configuration, a substantial amount of bandwidth on the CATV infrastructure was unused. By upgrading a portion of the CATV system to fiber optics, it is usually possible to enable signal flow in both directions. Most CATV networks that support two-way data distribution are hybrid fiber-coaxial (HFC) networks. The signals run in fiber-optic cables from the headend center, to node locations near the subscriber. From these nodes, the signal is converted from fiber to coaxial cables that run to the subscribers' premises. Higher frequencies flow toward the subscriber, and the lower frequencies travel in the opposite direction.

Cable Modems and Cable Infrastructure

The term *cable modem* refers to a modem that operates over ordinary CATV networks. Basically, the subscriber connects the cable modem to the outlet for the TV, and the MSO or CATV operator connects a cable modem termination system (CMTS) at their end, commonly known as the head-end, as shown in Figure 21-10. The CMTS supports the data exchange. Normally, a single channel on a CMTS supports approximately 2000 simultaneous cable modem users. If more cable modems are required, additional channels must be added to the CMTS.

Figure 21-10   *High-Level Graphical Representation of a CMTS and Cable Modem Architecture*

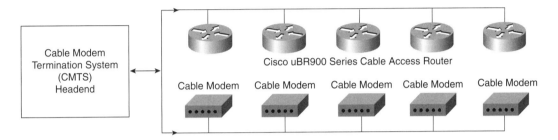

Almost all cable modems are standalone units with Ethernet interfaces; however, some are available that can be installed internally in a host, or that provide a USB port. The term cable modem is somewhat misleading, as you recall experiences with analog or ISDN modems. A cable modem provides a LAN interface and behaves similarly to other network devices. However, cable modems do display some operating characteristics that are similar to traditional modems. Normal operating ranges can be over 100 km, and the typical data throughput of most modems is 3 to 50 Mbps. The modems can act either as MAC layer bridges or as routers.

Major differences between analog and ISDN modems are the online status and speed. Cable modems are online whenever they are powered-up and connected to the cable plant. Cable modems are much faster than conventional telephony modems, which are capable of speeds 25 to 1000 times faster. Remember that this is the speed the subscriber experiences between the modem and the operator's CMTS. Actual performance for a host browsing the web varies based on a number of factors with varying levels of influence. Some of the more common dependencies include the number of cable modems on the segment, the speed of the connection between the operator's network and the Internet, and the deployment and effectiveness of proxy cache servers.

Standards for Data Transmission over Cable

Unfortunately, there is no one industry-wide standard that covers the transmission of data over cable networks. In North America, the Data-Over-Cable Service Interface Specifications (DOCSIS) addresses cable modems and CMTS. DOCSIS was initiated by a consortium of MSOs and has the support of major cable modem manufacturers and network operators. There is an ongoing battle in Europe between the initial DVB/DAVIC and EuroDOCSIS standards. For the purposes of brevity, the DOCSIS standard is discussed in more detail, and any differences between it and the EuroDOCSIS or DVB/DAVIC standards are noted.

The new DOCSIS 1.1 specification is built upon DOCSIS 1.0 (www.cablemodem.com), but differs from it with the following features:

- Quality of service (QoS)
- Dynamic services
- Concatenation
- Fragmentation
- Payload header suppression
- IP multicast
- Cable modem authentication
- SNMPv3
- View-based access control and management (VACM)
- Cable modem account management
- Fault management
- Secure software availability

The emerging DOCSIS 2.0 (in development since late 1998) delivers all the capabilities of DOCSIS 1.1, and by providing greater resilience to noise, DOCSIS 2.0 provides more reliable and efficient service delivery. DOCSIS 2.0 is not only compatible with previous versions of DOCSIS, but allows improved performance of 1.0 and 1.1 modems when DOCSIS 2.0 modems and CMTSs are deployed on the network. DOCSIS 2.0 adds throughput in the upstream portion of the cable plant—from the consumer out to the Internet—which creates a network that has 30-Mbps capacity in two directions. That tripling of data capacity enables services such as videoconferencing and peer-to-peer applications. DOCSIS 2.0 enables operators to create new services for both home and business use, including symmetrical and critical applications. The modulation techniques for DOCSIS 2.0 include synchronous code division multiple access (S-CDMA) and advanced frequency agile time division multiple access (A-TDMA).

Further discussion about VPN over cable is based on the most commonly deployed solutions today—DOCSIS 1.0.

Cable System Architectural Elements

The cable modem typically is connected to a two-way cable RF path over a low-split HFC cable system. In the downstream direction, the cable modem receives signals in a predefined portion of the downstream passband, usually between 50 MHz and a system-dependent upper limit that can be 750 MHz or more. In the upstream direction, or away from the subscriber, the cable modem transmits signals in a predefined portion of the upstream passband, which is between 5 and 42 MHz.

Similar to an Ethernet segment, data sent downstream from the CMTS is received by all cable modems on the CMTS channel segment. However, the various data over cable implementations are significantly more efficient with their bandwidth than Ethernet. Intended recipients can be one, some, or all cable modems on the segment.

DOCSIS Characteristics

The Open System Interconnection (OSI) model for the operator interface of a DOCSIS cable modem is shown in Figure 21-11.

Figure 21-11   *The OSI Model as Applied to the DOCSIS Industry Standard*

OSI Layer	DOCSIS		
Higher Layers	Applications	DOCSIS Control Messages	
Transport Layer	TCP/UDP		
Network Layer	IP		
Data Layer	802.2		
Physical	Upstream	Downstream	
	Minislots Basic Time Slot Unit Used for Bursts of Data Transmission	MPEG-TS Continuous Stream of Data Transmitted	

Physical characteristics of the downstream data are listed in Table 21-10.

Table 21-10   *Downstream DOCSIS Data Transmission Characteristics*

Physical Parameters	Downstream Data Characteristics
Frequency	54–850 MHz (USA) and 65–850 MHz (EU)
Bandwidth	6 MHz (USA) and 8 MHz (EU)
Modulation	64-quadrature amplitude modulation (QAM) with 6 bits per symbol (normal) 256-QAM with 8 bits per symbol (faster, but more sensitive to noise)
Speed	27–56 Mbps
Nature of Data	Continuous stream

Physical characteristics of the upstream data are listed in Table 21-11.

Table 21-11   *Upstream DOCSIS Data Transmission Characteristics*

Physical Parameters	Upstream Data Characteristics
Frequency	5–42 MHz
Bandwidth	2 MHz
Modulation	Quadrature phase-shift keying (QPSK) or 16-QAM
Speed	3 Mbps
Nature of data	Bursts (Variable-length burst: US) (Fixed-length burst: EU)

In Figures 21-9 and 21-10, there is 12 Mhz between the upstream and the downstream bands. This band is known as the guard band.

One downstream channel is normally paired with a number of upstream channels to achieve the balance in required bandwidth. Each modem transmits bursts in time slots that are marked as reserved, contention, or ranging by the CMTS per a vendor-specific algorithm. Characteristics of the CMTS timeslots are highlighted in Table 21-12.

Table 21-12 *Characteristics of CMTS Timeslots*

Time Slot	Description
Reserved	Set aside for a specific modem. Usually for longer transmissions.
Contention	Open to all modems. If collision detected, modems resend after random interval. Usually for short transmissions.
Ranging	Adjusts transmission power level and clock of cable modem.

Common Issues for Remote Access VPNs over CATV Data Networks

There are a limited number of issues to troubleshoot when running VPN over CATV data networks. Two common situations you might encounter when working on remote access VPNs, using the Cisco VPN Unity client over CATV networks, are two-way Internet connections and heartbeats that monitor the CPE.

Two-Way Internet Connections

Two-way Internet connections can be implemented by using either an analog modem integrated in the cable modem (a telephone return cable modem), or a modem on the PC host. In the latter configuration, you normally cannot pass data over a VPN IPSec tunnel. This is because the Ethernet and dial interfaces on the PC have different IP addresses, and to successfully pass data with the Cisco VPN 3000 concentrator, the client must present one address. The former configuration, with the analog modem integrated into the cable modem, allows a Cisco VPN Unity client to pass data over the IPSec connection because the client is aware of only one routable address from the cable modem.

Heartbeats

Most clients that are attached to CATV Internet connections obtain their routable IP address from the operator through DHCP. Some operators then monitor the status of the CPE device that obtained the IP address through the use of a regular ping. If the CPE device fails to respond to the pings after a predetermined time interval, the operator assumes that the CPE device is no longer connected to the operator's network, and returns the IP address to the DHCP pool.

If the CPE device that obtains the IP address is the host that terminates the VPN tunnel, and if split tunneling is not enabled, the CPE does not respond to the pings sent from the operator to the public IP address. The reason for non-response is because the CPE device is assigned an IP address from the concentrator for the duration that the IPSec VPN tunnel is active, and it only responds to IP traffic that is received over the IPSec tunnel. A workaround for this scenario is to use a router to obtain the IP address from the operator, and to configure the router to NAT the host with the VPN client. Select a concentrator and profile that supports IPSec over UDP encapsulation. The router then responds to the operator's pings and you can establish and exchange data over the IPSec tunnel.

VPN and Internet Access over Satellite and Wireless Systems

Satellite and wireless-based communication systems deliver Internet connectivity to users who otherwise do not qualify for typical SOHO and residential broadband solutions, such as DSL and CATV. However, because of their inherent designs and features, IPSec VPNs face unique issues when operated over satellite and wireless solutions. In particular, you learn about the following:

- Satellite and wireless systems specifics
- Performance solutions in satellite networks
- IPSec VPN performance issues over satellite systems

Satellite and Wireless Systems Specifics

Current Satellite (DBS) systems, such as Starband or Directway, are being deployed in greater numbers to provide Internet access. DBS systems are capable of delivering one-way downstream data rates of 23 Mbps or more; however, they do introduce error rates of 1–2 percent (www.internettrafficreport.com). Also, they inherently increase the latency that users experience by a minimum of several hundred milliseconds.

An inherent delay occurs in the delivery of messages over a satellite link because of the finite speed of light and the altitude of communications satellites. Therefore, the propagation time for a radio signal to travel twice that distance (corresponding to a ground station directly below the satellite) is 239.6 milliseconds (ms) (see RFC 2488). The propagation delay for a message and the corresponding reply (one round-trip time [RTT]) is at least 558 ms.

The RTT is not based solely on satellite propagation time; it is increased by other network factors, such as transmission time and propagation time of other links in the network path, and queuing delay in gateways that have terrestrial components. Typically, satellite RTT is 560 ms and the terrestrial side is about 150 ms; hence, the total RTT for the TCP connection is 710 ms (see the following Note). As a result, today's offering can achieve download speeds in the range of 500 kbps to 1 Mbps and upload speeds approaching 128 kbps. Satellite channels are dominated by two fundamental characteristics for noise and bandwidth that are described in subsequent sections of this chapter.

NOTE   Measurements show that the error level is slightly higher. Pchar output follows from a satellite connection, demonstrating 6–8 percent error loss that varies between day and night, and approximately 0.8s one-way RTT:

```
....XXX.78.249.254 (misc-XXX-78-249-254.pool.starband.net)
    Partial loss:       12 / 138 (8%)
    Partial char:       rtt = 813.546203 ms, (b = 0.189682 ms/B), r2 = 0.149781
                        stddev rtt = 99.374317, stddev b = 0.070578
    Partial queueing:   avg = 0.369341 ms (133278 bytes)
    Hop char:           rtt = 739.066865 ms, bw = 42.346064 Kbps
    Hop queueing:       avg = 0.362248 ms (1917 bytes)
```

The text discusses each of the following issues in detail in the subsequent sections:

- Noise
- Bandwidth
- VPN, TCP, and TCP inefficiency over satellite and wireless systems
- TCP characteristics that impact performance

Noise and Satellite and Wireless Systems

The strength of a radio signal falls in proportion to the square of the distance traveled. For a satellite link, the distance is great and the signal weakens before reaching its destination. This results in a low signal-to-noise ratio (SNR) and increased error rate. Typical error control coding, such as Reed Solomon, can be added to existing satellite services and is currently being used by many other services.

Bandwidth and Satellite and Wireless Systems

The radio spectrum is controlled by licenses and the typical carrier frequencies for current, point-to-point, commercial, satellite services are 6 GHz (uplink) and 4 GHz (downlink), also known as C band, and 14/12 GHz (Ku band).

From the point of view of VPN over wireless, existing wireless systems (see Chapter 3, "The Cloud," for more details) offer a different spectrum of challenges. Wireless systems typically have higher bit error rates (BERs) than wire-based carriage systems. Mobile wireless systems also include factors such as signal fade, base-station handover, and variable levels of load. The noise and bandwidth characteristics also apply, but the most important point is the affect both systems have over VPN. More information on this topic is included in the Performance Implications of Link Characteristics (PILC) Group of the Internet Engineering Task Force (IETF) through www.ietf.org/internet-drafts/draft-ietf-pilc-2.5g3g-07.txt.

VPN, TCP, and TCP Inefficiency over Satellite and Wireless Systems

IPSec is an IP-based set of protocols, which interacts with the TCP/IP stack. As stated in Chapter 19, the tunnel mode of VPN essentially uses protocols, such as AH and ESP, to encapsulate the IP packets. TCP is also involved because some of the calculations and headers involve TCP headers (see Figure 21-5). A problem exists when you run VPN over high-latency networks, such as satellite and wireless, where the throughput degrades significantly compared to VPN over wire-based technologies.

What seems to be the problem? TCP was designed using wire-based assumptions that include the following:

- Packet loss is the result of network congestion, rather than bit-level corruption
- Some level of stability in the RTT because TCP uses a method of damping down the changes in the RTT estimate
- A best-path route-selection protocol
- A network with fixed bandwidth circuits, not varying bandwidth
- A switched network with first-in, first-out (FIFO) buffers
- Limited duration of TCP sessions
- Large payloads and adequate bandwidth
- Interaction with other TCP sessions

The full description of TCP assumptions and inefficiencies are available in RFC 2488 and RFC 2760. You can also see RFC 1323.

If these assumptions are challenged, the associated cost is TCP efficiency. If TCP is extended to environments where these assumptions are no longer valid, preserving the integrity of the TCP transfer and maintaining a high level of efficiency can require the TCP operation to be altered. Overall, because satellite and wireless channels have several characteristics that differ from most terrestrial channels, they can degrade TCP performance.

TCP Characteristics That Impact Performance

Many characteristics can impact performance:

- **Congestion avoidance**—A fundamental assumption of TCP is that it treats all packet loss as an indication of network congestion, and it reduces transmission rates drastically until an optimal rate is found for data transmission. In satellite and wireless networks, packet loss is because of link noise or other transient conditions, rather than congestion, which results in slower data transfer.

- **Receive window**—Every TCP-source that sends data is allowed to send as many bytes as are explicitly allowed in the last packet received from the TCP-destination. Therefore, the destination confirms that it has enough space to store the bytes about to be sent, and this value is known as the Advertised Receive Window. If this value is set too low, which is common, it severely limits the top speeds of a TCP connection regardless of the access rate (link speed). The actual bandwidth can be calculated according to the RTT and the window size by using the following calculation:

  Max bandwidth = size of the window / RTT [bps]

- **Three-way handshake**—The TCP three-way handshake requires three RTTs before there is any data sent, and this can take two seconds for each connection on a satellite system.

- **Variable response time**—TCP is heavily dependent on measuring the RTT between the sender and the receiver. Multiple-access satellite networks such as time-division multiplex access (TDMA) or Demand Assigned Multiple Access (DAMA)-based access systems can have variable response times, which in turn can be considered as lost packets and lead to unnecessary retransmissions.

- **TCP acknowledgment**—A significant factor for resource inefficiency is dealing with the sheer volume of ACK packets generated by TCP. This amount can be reduced by using selective ACK, but it cannot be eliminated.

- **Excessive number of concurrent connections**—As part of the TCP protocol suite, HTTP and HTTP/1.0 use a separate TCP connection for each object to be retrieved. Requests are not sent until after the previous object has been completely received. HTTP1.1 enables up to four parallel TCP connections, yet most browsers use only two TCP connections. The time required to download one web page can be calculated from the following:

  Time = RTT × (#Objects / #TCP) + PageSize / Bandwidth

  The result of a large number of connections leads to a reduction in throughput of up to 50 percent, which is primarily because of performing slow-starts at frequent intervals and then usually terminating.

- **Data transmission of small segments**—Related to the previous discussion on HTTP, this protocol and some applications can force TCP to transmit data in segment sizes smaller than the minimum allowed size, which directly results in inefficiencies.

Performance Solutions in Satellite Networks

As explained, TCP was specifically designed as a flexible protocol that operates on various wired networks. However, it is not optimal for wireless or satellite links, and it proves to be a medium where TCP provides marginal service. Because latency is a constant concern of enterprise VPNs, but enterprise VPNs are not the main concern of satellite providers, the only viable option is to increase the throughput, implementing proprietary solutions to improve or resolve issues introduced by using TCP over satellite networks.

To help you understand the nuances of some of the implemented proprietary solutions, the discussion is further divided into the following sections:

- Manipulating (tweaking) the TCP stack
- Boosted session transport protocol
- The FITFEEL transmission protocol

Manipulating (Tweaking) the TCP Stack

One possible solution to improve performance is explained in Chapter 3, and is based on the Internet Page Accelerator (IPA), which allows increased numbers of concurrent HTTP 1.0 and 1.1 sessions.

Another possible solution is tweaking the TCP protocol. Some aspects of this approach are described in RFC 2488. The suggested summary of the recommendations is shown in Table 21-13. FEC stands for forward error correction, PAWS stands for Protection Against Wrapped Sequence Space, and RTTM is Round-Trip Time Measurements.

NOTE   Cisco IOS version 12.2+ allows some functions to be performed on the router's TCP traffic, such as **ip tcp timestamp** or **debug ip tcp sack**. RFC 1323 timestamps help TCP to measure RTT accurately to adjust retransmission timeouts. By default, they are disabled in Windows and are considered ineffective. The **ip tcp timestamp** works with another technique called window scaling, which permits TCP to negotiate a scaling factor for the TCP receive window size. It permits a large TCP receive window of up to 1 GB. This option must be enabled if you want to use receive windows larger than 64 KB. Window scaling is enabled by default in Windows.

Table 21-13 *Recommended Tweaking Mechanisms*

Mechanism	Use	Where
Path-MTU Discovery	Recommended	Sender
FEC	Recommended	Satellite Link
TCP Congestion Control		
Slow Start	Required	Sender
Congestion Avoidance	Required	Sender
Fast Retransmit	Recommended	Sender
Fast Recovery	Recommended	Sender

continues

Table 21-13 *Recommended Tweaking Mechanisms (Continued)*

Mechanism	Use	Where
TCP Large Windows		
Window Scaling	Recommended	Sender, Receiver
PAWS	Recommended	Sender, Receiver
RTTM	Recommended	Sender, Receiver
TCP Selective Acknowledgments (SACKs)	Recommended	Sender, Receiver

Numerous software solutions exist on the market, such as TweakMaster of Hagel Technologies, DrTCP, and others. The effect of these measures is moderate, and there is some reasonable improvement to the responsiveness of applications, even when running VPN, but tweaking techniques don't offer radical solutions for the degradation of speed when it comes to using VPN over wireless or satellite. Why? Because when it comes to an overall solution, according to Table 21-13, in some cases both ends, not only the sender, must perform some procedures. In the default TCP stack installations, this is definitely not the case.

Boosted Session Transport Protocol

One example of a different approach to TCP, related to performance issues, is the implementation of the Boosted Session Transport (BST) protocol (see www.flashnetworks.com/). BST is a connection-oriented protocol used instead of TCP on satellite or wireless segments. TCP traffic is converted to BST flows before being sent across the wireless WAN links, and then is converted back to TCP before being sent to the intended destination, as shown in Figure 21-12. BST is available in the NettGain product line from Flash Networks, and has been implemented in satellite networks by StarBand, NASA, SAT-TEL, and VSAT.

The BST protocol offers numerous enhancements over TCP:

- Pretuned parameters
- Immediate transmission at full speed
- Smart congestion avoidance
- Intelligent bandwidth allocation
- Smart rate control
- Intelligent acknowledgments
- Unlimited window size
- No three-way handshake
- Packet loss recovery

Figure 21-12   *The BST Mechanism*

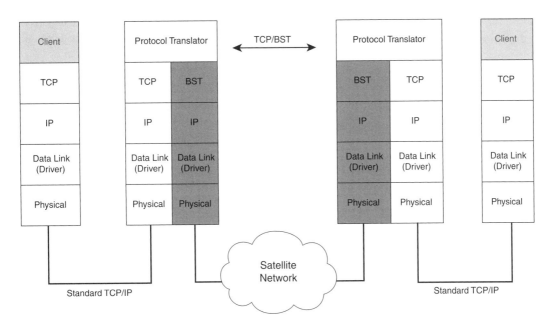

The FITFEEL Transmission Protocol

Another solution to the TCP performance problem was introduced by the authors of the
Fast Information Transfer For Extremely Errored Links (FITFEEL) protocol, which
introduces a simple transmission protocol that performs better than TCP over bad links. The
basic assumption of using the TCP proxy concept is that TCP applications can be used
effectively on poor links without alteration. This is accomplished by translating TCP to a
better protocol over the problematic links, then translating back to TCP at the other end.
The FITFEEL addresses aspects of TCP action when there is either a propagation delay, bit
error, queuing delay, or buffer overflow. The TCP proxy concept is referred to as TCP
boomerangs, and the boomerang effect is achieved with proxy software that talks TCP
language to the initiating host in the role of the destination host, and so forth. Using this
approach, the TCP boomerang trick reflects outgoing TCP packet streams to an IP host,
which simply and reliably handles the TCP protocol by acting in the role of a proxy.

IPSec VPN Performance Issues over Satellite Systems

Both BST and FITFEEL protocols implement a proprietary form of compression. Given the
fact that there is always a transformation of the TCP stack either to the BST stack, or to a

proxy TCP, IPSec-based solutions experience significant degradation of the overall through-put. VPN performance over satellite systems can be disappointing, often limited to dialup speeds. However, a user can make some adjustments to their W2K host to improve perform-ance, but it is significantly lower than the download speeds that users expect when not using VPN. It all depends on the perspective: either the IPSec VPN shows a significant degradation in throughput, or the IPSec VPN cannot take advantage of the boosting protocol mechanisms.

Using traffic boosting protocols does not affect any of the transport layer security protocols, such as Secure Sockets Layer (SSL) or Transport Layer Security (TLS). This is because they do not modify the contents of the TCP payload. It is not known if boosting protocols pose any potential security risk to Layer 2 protocols, such as PPP, because it does not modify the IP information.

On the other hand, they do replace the TCP headers with a new header over the wireless/satellite hop. As a result, potential security issues exist with IPSec because AH and ESP use the Integrity Check Value (ICV) for calculating much of the TCP header information.

NOTE   The Satellite Service Providers use two main strategies when it comes to erroneous packets: They either request repeat, apply error correction, or use both. The author experiments and measurements with Cisco VPNs over satellite show that Concatenated Viterbi and Reed Solomon error-correction codes, used by Spacenet, allow the users to achieve better performance. See www.spacenet.com/ for details.

Possible resolutions include the following:

* Managing two secure and interrelated links, one for the wireless/satellite hop and another over TCP.

* Using a provider's software, allowing non-boosted traffic to pass and using proprietary methods for boosting and compression

* Transforming the existing traffic to UDP or TCP using extra encapsulation.

* The most promising solution is creating an IOS-based boosting engine, which can provide an end-to-end VPN over satellite solution for satellite Internet providers.

Information about the interaction of the FITFEEL protocol with IPSec-based VPN solutions was not available at the time this book was written; however, possible solutions are under study. Some of the issues are addressed in the VPN client versions 3.5.x and higher (NAT/UDP and NAT/TCP encapsulations and transparent tunneling), and some of them might become available with the newest Cisco content engines (CTE 1400 and COE 590). Check www.cisco.com regularly for updates.

Another approach to this problem is checking if the satellite providers move to another coding technique where they don't need to boost the traffic. One possible solution in this direction is the emerging Ku-band technology, which essentially uses DOCSIS 1.1 for wireless broadband services. DOCSIS 1.1-based systems are expected to use Ku-band wireless broadband services with expected rates up to 10 Mbps and transmission rates up to 500 kbps. No known issues exist with IPSec-based VPNs and the DOCSIS 1.1 specification.

LAN and General Networking Issues Affecting Remote Access VPNs

Three LAN related issues are known to affect remote access VPNs: the improper configuration of a NAT device, availability of necessary firewall holes, and the method a NAT device uses to manipulate multiple VPN clients. Configuration of the NAT device is beyond the scope of this discussion. However, if the device is a Cisco product, you can consult www.cisco.com for the configuration commands, examples, and SW versions. The need for necessary firewall holes to be available was previously discussed. Another alternative is to implement TCP encapsulation on well-known ports. Finally, the third case described for the handling of multiple VPN clients connected behind a NAT device warrants further coverage.

Multiple VPN Clients Behind a NAT Device

Depending on the NAT device used, you can establish multiple remote access IPSec VPN connections to the same concentrator or different concentrators. Other times, you might observe that a single client can establish an IPSec VPN connection to a concentrator, but this client is disconnected if a second client establishes a connection to the same concentrator. In an environment that uses a different NAT device, you observe that you can have multiple IPSec client connections to the same concentrator.

The explanations for the different observations are provided now. First, a NAT device in a PAT environment overloads private IP addresses on a single public IP address. To differentiate the traffic destined for each host on the private network, a unique TCP or UDP port is assigned to the private IP address. The NAT device handles all communication with public networks by using its single public IP address, and correctly distributes traffic destined for devices on the private network based on the unique TCP or UDP port assignment.

However, when implementing IKE-based VPNs, several manufacturers misinterpreted the ISAKMP specification. These vendors incorrectly designed their products so that the UDP source port of an ISAKMP exchange must be 500. As a result, instead of the traditional NAT, vendors had to identify the different devices on the private network with IKE-based VPN connections by using the SPI as the identifier. The VPN 3000 concentrators allow multiple ISAKMP connections from the same IP address, if the source port of each of the ISAKMP streams is different. If you use a Cisco 806 IOS-based NAT device, you already know that the source port behavior is configurable. For other NAT devices, it is recommended that you contact the manufacturers of the equipment to learn their specific capabilities and support plans.

MTU—A Critical Factor for Troubleshooting Internet IPSec Connectivity

The MTU, the largest possible size of a network Layer 2 payload or Layer 3 packet, is not constant throughout the Internet. It is the source of many issues for IPSec tunnels. Also, the Path MTU (PMTU) feature of the VPN client might not function if your concentrator is behind a firewall that does not permit Internet Control Message Protocol (ICMP) pings from the Internet. As a result, you need to identify and resolve issues related to the MTU with regards to IPSec communications.

Basically, any intermediary IP routers that are encountered on the Internet (hops), which are set to an MTU less than 1500, often fragment packets, which divides them into smaller units before sending them out the respective interface. In an IPSec tunnel, the VPN client and concentrator are the only parties that can change the size of the packets that they exchange. Any attempt to change the packet content and size being sent in an IPSec tunnel by another router or device causes the IPSec connection to fail because the MTU requirements set by the originator of the packets, either client or concentrator, were not met (see the immutable fields concept in Chapter 19).

The MTU is normally set in conjunction with the maximum segment size (MSS) and the TCP Receive Window (RWIN). MSS is the largest segment of TCP data that the Microsoft Winsock is prepared to receive on a connection. MSS must be smaller than the MTU by at least 40 bytes, which accommodates the IP and TCP headers that are each 20 bytes. RWIN determines how much data the receiving computer is prepared to receive. If RWIN is set too large, it results in greater loss of data if a packet is lost or damaged. If it is set too small, transmission is slow. Normally, RWIN is set to be four, six, or eight times the MSS (see TCP Windows scale option in RFC 1323).

Practical examples in which the MTU is greater or equal to MSS+40 bytes is demonstrated by the following default IOS setting examples, for 8xx series routers running Cisco IOS ver.12.2+:

* Under the E0 interface—**ip tcp adjust-mss 1452**
* Under the D1 and E1 (806 router) interfaces—**ip mtu 1492**

However, it is far more common to set the MTU for all traffic passing through an interface. Some common MTU settings include the following:

* MTU of Ethernet interfaces is usually set to 1500 bytes, which is the maximum payload size of an Ethernet frame (see Figure 21-13).
* MTU of a PPPoE frame is usually set to 1492, because the PPP header is 8 octets: Flag—1 octet, Address—1 octet, Control—1 octet, Protocol ID—2 octets, FSC—2-4 bytes, and Flag—1 octet (see Chapter 5, "Dial Technology Background").

- MTU of frames over dialup connections is usually set to 576 octets, which is the default setting by Microsoft and is based on the average size of Internet packets.
- When using a cable modem, MTU size is not known to cause fragmentation issues.

Figure 21-13 *The Basic IEEE 802.3 MAC Data Frame Format*

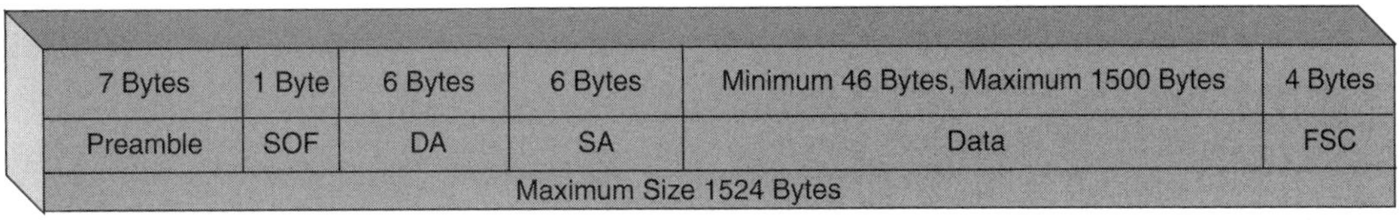

7 Bytes	1 Byte	6 Bytes	6 Bytes	Minimum 46 Bytes, Maximum 1500 Bytes	4 Bytes
Preamble	SOF	DA	SA	Data	FSC
Maximum Size 1524 Bytes					

To illustrate further, the discussion is divided into the following sections:

- Determining a Functional MTU Between the VPN Host and Concentrator
- MTU—What Difference Does It Make?

Determining a Functional MTU Between the VPN Host and Concentrator

The MTU value that you use with the Cisco VPN client is limited by the minimum MTU value of all segments between your host, and the concentrator to which you are trying to establish an IPSec tunnel. To determine the MTU of this path, you must first determine the path, then through a sequential process of pings with specific packet sizes, determine the minimum MTU of all the segments.

In the following example, the ping utility determines a functional MTU from a client in Northern California by using AT&T Broadband Internet over cable, IP address 12.234.185.224, to www.cisco.com, IP address 198.133.219.25.

At the command prompt, enter the following:

```
C:/>ping -f -l [packetsize] [www.cisco.com]
```

The elements are as follows:

- –**f** indicates don't fragment.
- -**l** indicates packetsize.
- *packetsize* is the size of the IP packet that you transmit (between 0 and 1500 octets).
- **www.cisco.com** is the URL (substitute **www.cisco.com** for the public address of the VPN concentrator to which you connect, or any public URL, gateway, or server).

If you exceed the minimum MTU of all the segments, the message you will most likely receive is "Packet needs to be fragmented, but DF set." If you receive this message, you need to decrease the size of the packet and repeat the ping as many times as required until you receive a successful echo reply from the remote host. To extract the MTU size from this information, assuming that the first successful echo reply message is when the *packetsize* is set to 1300, you can examine the results of a ping to 198.133.219.33 from a host with the IP address 12.234.185.224, as shown in Example 21-28.

Example 21-28 *Sniffer Capture Results from the Command*

```
C:/>ping -f -l 1300 198.133.219.33
! Performed from a Win2K host with IP=12.234.185.224.
- - - - - - - - - - - - - - - - - - - - - Frame 1 - - - - - - - - - - - - - - - - - - -
 Frame  Status  Source Address    Dest. Address      Size Rel. Time
      Delta Time    Abs. Time              Summary
      1   M      [12.234.185.224] [198.133.219.25]   1342 0:00:00.000
      0.000.000    02/03/2002 04:17:54   PM DLC: Ethertype=0800, size=1342 bytes
IP:   D=[198.133.219.25] S=[12.234.185.224] LEN=1308 ID=440
ICMP: Echo
DLC:  ----- DLC Header -----
      DLC:
      DLC:  Frame 1 arrived at  16:17:54.2930; frame size is 1342
      (053E hex) bytes.
      DLC:  Destination = Station 00301931778C
      DLC:  Source      = Station GtwCom462E8E
      DLC:  Ethertype   = 0800 (IP)
      DLC:
IP: ----- IP Header -----
      IP:
      IP: Version = 4, header length = 20 bytes
! Indicates the IP header size is 20 bytes.
      IP: Type of service = 00
      IP:      000. ....   = routine
      IP:      ...0 ....   = normal delay
      IP:      .... 0...   = normal throughput
      IP:      .... .0..   = normal reliability
      IP:      .... ..0.   = ECT bit - transport protocol will ignore the CE bit
      IP:      .... ...0   = CE bit - no congestion
      IP: Total length    = 1328 bytes
! The complete IP packet includes the IP header (20 bytes) +
! ICMP header (8 bytes) + ICMP payload (1300 bytes).
      IP: Identification  = 440
      IP: Flags           = 4X
      IP:      .1.. ....   = don't fragment
      IP:      ..0. ....   = last fragment
      IP: Fragment offset = 0 bytes
      IP: Time to live    = 128 seconds/hops
      IP: Protocol        = 1 (ICMP)
      IP: Header checksum = 8BAB (correct)
      IP: Source address     = [12.234.185.224]
      IP: Destination address = [198.133.219.25]
      IP: No options
      IP:
ICMP: ----- ICMP header -----
      ICMP:
      ICMP: Type = 8 (Echo)
```

Example 21-28 *Sniffer Capture Results from the Command (Continued)*

```
      ICMP: Code = 0
      ICMP: Checksum = B5D2 (correct)
      ICMP: Identifier = 512
      ICMP: Sequence number = 6400
! The overall size of all previous fields in the ICMP header is 8 bytes,
! followed by the 1300 byte payload.
      ICMP: [1300 bytes of data]
! Indicates echo ICMP packet requests an echo reply from
! 198.133.219.25 with packet size 1300.
      ICMP:
      ICMP: [Normal end of "ICMP header".]
      ICMP:


! The following is the echo reply from 198.133.219.25.


 - - - - - - - - - - - - - - - - - - - - Frame 3 - - - - - - - - - - - - - - - - - - - -
 Frame Status Source Address   Dest. Address     Size Rel. Time    Delta Time
Abs. Time              Summary
    3       [198.133.219.25]  [12.234.185.224]   1342 0:00:00.018   0.018.214
02/03/2002 04:17:54 PM DLC: Ethertype=0800, size=1342 bytes
IP:  D=[12.234.185.224] S=[198.133.219.25] LEN=1308 ID=440
ICMP: Echo reply
! A successful reply for 1300 bytes from 198.133.219.25
! (the largest size without fragmentation).
DLC:  ----- DLC Header -----
      DLC:
      DLC:  Frame 3 arrived at  16:17:54.3114; frame size is 1342 (053E hex) bytes.
      DLC:  Destination = Station GtwCom462E8E
      DLC:  Source      = Station 00301931778C
      DLC:  Ethertype   = 0800 (IP)
      DLC:
IP:  ----- IP Header -----
      IP:
      IP: Version = 4, header length = 20 bytes
      IP: Type of service = 00
      IP:      000. ....  = routine
      IP:      ...0 ....  = normal delay
      IP:      .... 0...  = normal throughput
      IP:      .... .0..  = normal reliability
      IP:      .... ..0.  = ECT bit - transport protocol will ignore the CE bit
      IP:      .... ...0  = CE bit - no congestion
      IP: Total length    = 1328 bytes
      IP: Identification  = 440
      IP: Flags           = 4X
      IP:      .1.. ....  = don't fragment
      IP:      ..0. ....  = last fragment
      IP: Fragment offset = 0 bytes
      IP: Time to live    = 247 seconds/hops
      IP: Protocol        = 1 (ICMP)
      IP: Header checksum = 14AB (correct)
      IP: Source address      = [198.133.219.25]
      IP: Destination address = [12.234.185.224]
```

continues

Example 21-28 *Sniffer Capture Results from the Command (Continued)*

```
         IP: No options
         IP:
ICMP: ----- ICMP header -----
         ICMP:
         ICMP: Type = 0 (Echo reply)
         ICMP: Code = 0
         ICMP: Checksum = BDD2 (correct)
         ICMP: Identifier = 512
         ICMP: Sequence number = 6400
         ICMP: [1300 bytes of data]
         ICMP:
         ICMP: [Normal end of "ICMP header".]
         ICMP:
```

The MTU exceeds the parameter 1300 with only 20 + 8 = 28 bytes.

NOTE   The rule for setting MTU is that the largest value that does not result in the error "Packet needs to be fragmented, but DF set," is your ISP's MTU less 28 bytes. This excludes the IP (20 bytes) and ICMP (8 bytes) headers.

Based on this rule and the findings from the example, you can set the MTU size of this VPN client to 1300 + 28 = 1328 bytes. 1300 might not be the maximum MTU that allows the VPN client to establish an IPSec tunnel and pass traffic. After you determine a packet size that does not respond with a successful ping, try to ping the router one hop closer to you, which you can identify with the traceroute utility (tracert on W2K hosts). If that's not successful, try to ping the next router one hop closer, and so on until you either receive a successful response or reduce the packet size and start the ping process over again.

Effects of Packet Size on Performance

Data transfer performance is significantly impacted by the packet size, which affects the MTU. In this section, you review how latency and throughput, two parameters that are affected by changes in MTU, affect data transfer performance. In particular, you learn about the following:

- Packet size versus latency
- Throughput versus packet size

Packet Size Versus Latency

In this example, a data transfer over a standard ADSL line with a download speed of 600 kbps is examined using MTU packet sizes of 1500 and 576 on the same line.

The following formula for latency applies:

Latency (per hop) = (MSS + header) × 8 / speed

NOTE   MTU = MSS + (IP header + TCP header).

Using these different MTU sizes (1500 and 576), you can calculate the latency as a function of the packet size, as follows:

Latency for MTU 1500 = (1460 + 40) × 8 / 600,000 = 20 ms delay per hop
Latency for MTU 576 = (536 + 40) × 8 / 600,000 = 7.69 ms delay per hop

Assuming a transfer over 10 hops, the 1500 MTU would yield 200 ms delay, while a 576 MTU would only take 76.9 ms to be downloaded.

It is obvious the smaller packets will be transmitted faster. However, the amount of data transferred will be less by a factor of 1500 / 576 = 2.6 times.

Throughput Versus Packet Size

Using the same formula from the previous example, assume you need to transfer a 1 megabyte file over a T1 line:

1 megabyte = 1024 kilobytes = 1,048,576 bytes

If MTU = 1500, the delay would be 20 ms per hop and the MSS = 1460. 1 megabyte / MSS = 1,048,576 bytes / 1460 = 718.2. 719 packets are required to transfer 1 megabyte. The time required to transfer 1 megabyte = 719 packets × 20 ms per hop = 14.38 seconds per hop. Multiplied by 10 hops, this is 143.8 seconds.

If MTU = 576, the delay would be 7.69 ms per hop and the MSS = 536. 1 megabyte / MSS = 1,048,576 bytes / 536 = 1956.3. 1957 packets are required to transfer 1 megabyte. The time required to transfer 1 megabyte = 1957 packets × 7.69 ms delay per hop = 15.049 seconds per hop. If you are transferring the 1 megabyte file over the same 10 hops, it will take 150.49 seconds.

The difference is because of the fact that, when using larger packets, the overhead is smaller. Every packet carries header information. Smaller packets will require a greater number of packets (more headers) to pass the same amount of data. For example, to transfer 1 megabyte with an MTU of 1500, the overhead would be 719 (packets) × 40 (IP header + TCP header) = 28,760 bytes. If using an MTU of 576, the overhead would be 1957 × 40 = 78,280 bytes; an additional 49,520 bytes of headers are transferred for each megabyte. For the 10-hop transfer, the additional overhead will result in an extra 6.69 seconds difference in transfer time for every megabyte. This difference might be slightly larger in practice when considering TCP options such as sliding windows or TCP Receive window. Also, modern TCP/IP implementations might use larger headers, such as an additional 12-byte header space for timestamps.

The provided calculations are not precisely correct because they are based on the assumption that the available access rate (physical line speed) can be used entirely for data traffic. The fact is that the effective throughput depends upon the way that TCP treats the line and line characteristics, which increases and reduces the TCP window.

Generally, it's logical to assume that larger packets offer improved performance because of the following factors:

- **Network**—Reduced number of headers, as shown in the preceding discussion
- **Routers**—Fewer routing decisions
- **Clients**—Fewer protocol processing and device interrupts

If throughput is not the ultimate goal, however, smaller packets might be more responsive because they require less time to travel throughout the network, and consequently, the probability of effects because of interference or any other factors is lower (geometric probability). This result might be preferred in some solutions, such as satellite and wireless, at the expense of throughput.

The important factor here is how the error-free communication is managed. If every error requires retransmission, especially in wireless or satellite networks given the nature of these communications, the size of the window and MTU can significantly affect the overall throughput. If the error-free strategy assumes and applies correction codes, this can affect the performance model in a different way, and it is another factor to consider when comparing two solutions.

NOTE Experiments with the Cisco Aironet 350 series AP show that the difference between MTU 1400 and MTU 576 can be 1:0.75 in favor of 1400 MTU with an error rate under 5 percent.

Slow or Inaccessible Login to Kerberos Active Directory

Windows 2000 and Windows XP users might be unable to log in or experience unusually long times for logging into a Kerberos Active Directory. This might be the case with either Cisco VPN Unity client or on a host connected through an IPSec VPN tunnel that is started by the Cisco VPN 3002 Hardware client, Cisco Easy VPN client, or Cisco PIX Hardware client. The time to login can exceed 20 minutes.

Source of the Slow Login Is the Use of Kerberos over UDP Fragments

The source of the issue is the use of Kerberos over fragmented UDP packets, and the problem can be especially acute when connected behind a NAT/PAT device that does not handle packet refragmentation correctly.

Resolution—Force Kerberos to Use TCP Instead of UDP

Forcing Kerberos to use TCP instead of UDP packets eliminates this issue. On a Windows 2000 or Windows XP host, you can force Kerberos to use TCP by setting the Registry as follows:

```
HKEY_LOCAL_MACHINE\SYSTEM\CurrentControlSet\Control\Lsa\Kerberos\Parameters
Value Name : MaxPacketSize
                Data Type : REG_DWORD
                Value : 1
```

Starting with v3.5.1c, the Cisco VPN Unity client installation package automatically changes the Registry to force Kerberos to use TCP. If you do not want to force Kerberos to use TCP when installing v3.5.1c or later versions of the client, change the VPN client installation file, oem.ini, as follows: [9]

```
[Main]
DisableKerberosOverTCP = 1
```

End Notes

[1] "Managing the VPN Client" at www.cisco.com.

[2] Help file, VPN 3000 Concentrator, v3.5.

[3] www.cisco.com/univercd/cc/td/doc/product/vpn/client/rel3_5_1/351_3kcl.htm#xtocid40.

[4] "What is a GINA?," Symantec Corporation, http://service4.symantec.com/SUPPORT/pca.nsf/pfdocs/199852785735.

[5] Cisco Systems, Inc., Software Bug ID CSCdt55739.

[6] Help file, VPN 3002 HW Client, v3.5.

[7] www.cisco.com/warp/public/471/pix501506_vpn3k.html.

[8] www.cisco.com/univercd/cc/td/doc/product/dsl_prod/gsol_dsl/dsl_arch/gdslarch.htm#xtocid11.

[9] www.cisco.com/cgi-bin/Support/Bugtool/onebug.pl?bugid=CSCdx06180&Submit=Search.

Summary

This chapter focused on remote access VPN troubleshooting techniques. This chapter provided common troubleshooting recommendations and techniques when using the different VPN clients such as the following:

- Cisco VPN Unity Software client
- Cisco 3002 HW client

- Cisco Easy VPN client
- Cisco PIX Hardware client

By using the existing variety of broadband technologies and running remote access VPN over cable modem technology, xDSL technology and wireless and satellite technologies were another focus of this chapter. Every one of them poses different requirements and challenges when run with VPN. The provided technology details are designated to help troubleshooting engineers in their efforts.

One emphasis of this chapter was to show the different phases and modes of VPN, which provide extensive outputs, using mainly Cisco IOS tools, to outline some of the otherwise hidden steps in the user VPN processes. This information some times can be invaluable when the non-known troubleshooting issue arises.

Review Questions

Answers to the review questions can be found in Appendix A, "Answers to Review Questions."

1 What are the first three steps to check if the user never receives an Authenticating User prompt during the initial dialer connection attempt in the VPN software client?

2 What is the CVPND event class and what is its purpose?

3 Name the main severity categories in the Cisco VPN concentrator?

4 In a 3002 HW VPN client, the user is authenticated but cannot pass any data. What are two possible reasons?

5 Which severity level events are displayed by default on the VPN HW 3002 client?

6 How do you proceed if a NAT/PAT configuration already exists in the router and you are about to configure an Easy VPN client?

7 What is the command for the Easy VPN client to reset the VPN connection?

8 What is the command for Easy VPN to check the status of the Cisco Easy VPN client profile?

9 To verify the applied policy in Cisco Easy VPN, what command do you use?

10 In the PIX-based VPN client, how do you verify if the VPN client is active?

11 In the PIX-based VPN client, how do you check that the VPN tunnel has been established?

12 What are two debug commands to debug the PIX-based VPN establishment of IPSec and ISAKMP?

13 What parameters define the PPPoE session uniquely?

14 Name the modulation techniques for the DOCSIS 2.0 standard.

15 If the TCP protocol is notified for packet loss, how does it react?

CHAPTER 22

Remote Access VPN Troubleshooting Scenarios

This chapter provides real-world scenarios faced by Cisco's internal remote access (RA) group in supporting their Virtual Private Network (VPN) infrastructure. Each scenario is followed by several possible problems or cases, and each case includes one or more solutions. The chosen cases were derived from over 4000 cases solved by the group. Cisco proudly declares that they implement all their own products in their own network. The solutions provided might not be the only ones for that particular problem; however, they are thoroughly tested and are proven to be the most successful.

The scenarios are based on the Cisco VPN 3000 client version 3.0 (also called the Unity client) for Microsoft Windows. Versions of the VPN client 3.5- suport only Windows operating systems. Versions 3.5+ support operating systems other than Windows, including MAC OSX and Solaris 2.6. Also, the VPN client for Linux supports Red Hat version 6.2 Linux (Intel), or compatible libraries with glibc Version 2.1.1-6 or later, using kernel versions 2.2.12 or later. This chapter primarily focuses on the following common troubleshooting scenarios:

- Initial preparation for RA VPN troubleshooting
- Authentication problems and their resolution
- Trouble passing data after successful authentication
- RA VPN and xDSL issues and their troubleshooting
- RA hardware VPN client 3002 issues and their troubleshooting
- Extranet VPN issues and their troubleshooting

These scenarios assist VPN users and VPN network administrators to solve current issues. In some of the following scenarios, the perspective from the user and the core environment are documented to show the troubleshooting steps that a network administrator and a user should take to solve a particular problem. Table 22-1 is a quick reference to help you get started.

Table 22-1   *Scenario Quick Reference Table*

Scenario	Case Details	Location in Chapter
Authentication issues (involving an Internet Service Provider [ISP])	Bad group name or password	See Scenario 1, Case 1
	Prompted multiple times for username and password	See Scenario 1, Case 2
	Firewall software	See Scenario 1, Case 3
	MTU set high	See Scenario 1, Case 4
	MTU set low	See Scenario 1, Case 5
Problems passing data	Cannot pass data—use Network Address Translation (NAT) connection entry	See Scenario 2, Case 1
	Maximum transmission unit (MTU) causing packet loss	See Scenario 2, Case 2
	Connection keeps getting dropped	See Scenario 2, Case 3
	Cannot browse the internal domain	See Scenario 2, Case 4
PPPoE Software/Hardware	Point-to-Point Protocol over Ethernet (PPPoE) software issues	See Scenario 3, Case 1
	IOS-based PPPoE issues	See Scenario 3, Case 2
3002 Connection issues	Cannot connect to the concentrator	See Scenario 4
Extranet problems	Problems connecting through company X's firewall	See Scenario 5

Warming Up with Preliminary Troubleshooting Steps

Before getting started, some naming conventions must be defined when referring to specific devices. These devices are given the same host name and IP address throughout the entire chapter. The following devices are referenced as follows:

- VPN concentrator
  - Host name: vpn-concentrator
  - IP Address: 10.0.0.1
- VPN 3002
  - Host name: vpn-3002
  - Private IP Address: 10.2.2.2
  - Public IP Address: 66.1.1.2
  - Domain Name: company.com

- VPN client

  — IP Address: 10.3.3.3

  — Username: zack

- Firewall

  — Host name: firewall.company.com

  — IP Address: 65.1.1.2

There are three steps you should always take before moving on to the VPN troubleshooting scenarios. If you cannot verify that all these steps are functioning properly, you will not be able to connect with the VPN client. These steps include determining if you have an Internet connection, making sure that the VPN client is working properly, and checking or creating your profiles.

Step 1: Determine if There Is an Internet Connection

When trying to initiate an IPSec tunnel with no Internet connectivity or a bad route to the concentrator, you receive one of two errors. After clicking the Connect button, you are immediately prompted with either "Failed to establish a secure connection to the security gateway" or "Remote peer is no longer responding." The errors are shown in Figure 22-1 and Figure 22-2.

Figure 22-1   *Failure to Connect to Gateway Error*

Figure 22-2   *Remote Peer No Longer Responding*

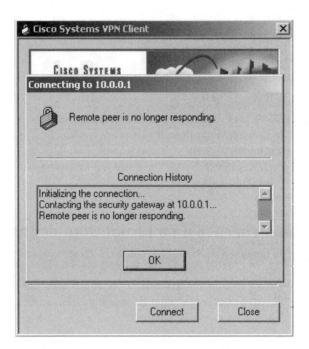

If the error "Failed to establish a secure connection to the gateway" is received, a problem exists with the connection to the Internet. Four things could be wrong:

- No physical connection to gateway device
- Invalid IP addresses of the VPN concentrator or your computer
- Domain Name System (DNS) resolution problems
- Firewall blocking connection

To check the physical connection of the PC to the gateway device, the first thing you do is to make sure that the PC's network interface card (NIC) has a link light. If the left light is glowing (it is usually the left light for most NICs), it means that there is a physical connection. If it is not, make sure that the cables are properly plugged in. In some cases, the connection might require a crossover cable, instead of a straight-through cable. For a detailed explanation of RJ-45 cable types, see www.cisco.com/univercd/cc/td/doc/pcat/rj45__c1.htm.

If there is a physical connection, check the status of the IP address, as listed in Table 22-2.

Table 22-2   *Accessing DOS and IP information in Windows*

OS	How to Access DOS	How to View IP Information
Windows 95	Go to Start, Programs, MSDOS.exe.	Go to Start, Run, and type **winipcfg**.
Windows 98	Go to Start, Programs, MSDOS.exe.	Go to Start, Run, and type **winipcfg**.
Windows NT	Go to Start, Run, type **cmd**, and click OK.	From DOS, type **ipconfig /all**.
Windows 2000	Go to Start, Run, type **cmd**, and click OK.	From DOS, type **ipconfig /all**.

Windows 95/98

Figure 22-3 is an example of **winipcfg**. If you click the More Info button that is circled, you receive information including DNS servers, Windows Internet Naming Service (WINS) servers, Dynamic Host Configuration Protocol (DHCP) servers, and a Media Access Control (MAC) address. The IP address 10.25.0.146 falls under RFC 1918 NAT. For more information on RFC 1918, see Chapter 10, "ISDN Design Solutions."

Figure 22-3   *Windows 95/98* **winipcfg** *Output Information*

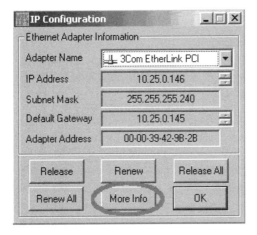

The subnet mask is 255.255.255.240 or /28. The /28 indicates the number of bits allocated for the network.

The default gateway is simply the first hop that all the devices on your subnet go to when they need to access anything outside of your subnet. Lastly, the adapter address is the MAC address of the adapter that you are using.

Windows NT/2000 IP Information

The **ipconfig** output from a Windows NT/2000 DOS prompt is shown in Example 22-1.

Example 22-1   *Windows NT/2000* **ipconfig** *Output Information*

```
C:\>ipconfig
Windows 2000 IP Configuration
Ethernet adapter Local Area Connection:

        Connection-specific DNS Suffix  . : cisco.com
        IP Address. . . . . . . . . . . : 10.25.0.146
! IP address falls in the RFC 1918 address range.
        Subnet Mask . . . . . . . . . : 255.255.255.240
! Subnet mask indicates you have 14 addresses in this subnet.
        Default Gateway . . . . . . . : 10.25.0.145
! The first hop that all devices on your subnet go to first.
```

After you verify the physical connection and check the IP address, make sure that the PC resolves the host name of the concentrator. Open a DOS window and use the **nslookup** command, along with the host name of the concentrator to which you are trying to connect. If it resolves properly, it appears as follows:

```
C:\>nslookup www.cisco.com
Server:  dns-sjk.cisco.com
Address:  171.68.226.120

Name:    www.cisco.com
Address:  198.133.219.25
```

If you receive the error "*** dns.company.com can't find www.cisco.com: Non-existent host/domain," it indicates that the VPN client has problems finding the concentrator. Possible causes to investigate are a bad route or a misspelling in the host name or IP address of remote server window, or a local firewall blockage. To test the route, open a DOS prompt window and try tracing to the concentrator's IP address or to the company's firewall using the **tracert** command.

You trace to your company's firewall because most firewalls are configured to block Internet Control Message Protocol (ICMP) traffic from entering the network. If ICMP traffic is blocked, you will never get a **ping** or **tracert** through to the concentrator.

See the **tracert** in Example 22-2. When you can reach the concentrator or your company's firewall, you should be able to establish an IPSec tunnel by using the VPN client. If you do not know the IP or host name of the firewall, you can simply try to trace to the concentrator, and most likely you will reach the firewall and receive timeouts because firewalls block ICMP packets by default.

The trace shows that because you can route to the company firewall, you should be able to route to the concentrator as long as the firewall is configured to allow IPSec through.

Because you can trace to the firewall successfully, you have proven that your PC can route to your company correctly.

Example 22-2   *Tracing to Your Company's Firewall*

```
C:\>tracert firewall.company.com

Tracing route to firewall.company.com [65.1.1.2]
over a maximum of 30 hops:

  1    30 ms    20 ms    10 ms  adsl.dsl.01.ISP.net [63.12.101.254]
! Three datagrams round-trip time
  2    30 ms    40 ms    40 ms  sl-bb22-sj-5-ISP.net [144.232.18.74]
! Hostname and IP of router
  3    41 ms    40 ms    30 ms  sl-bb20-sj-15-0.ISP.net [144.232.3.2]
  4    30 ms    40 ms    40 ms  sl-gw-ISP.net [144.232.3.1]
  5    30 ms    40 ms    40 ms  sl-company.ISP.net [144.218.1.1]
  6    31 ms    40 ms    40 ms  firewall.company.com [65.1.1.2]
! The firewall is reached
 Trace complete.
```

The **tracert** command is a simple and valuable tool. Three datagrams are sent, each with a Time To Live (TTL) field value set to 1. The TTL value of 1 causes the datagram to timeout as soon as it hits the first router in the path; this router then responds with an ICMP time exceeded message (TEM), which indicates that the TTL has expired. For more information on **tracert** and **ping**, see Chapter 4, "Troubleshooting Approaches, Models, and Tools."

Step 2: Ensure that the VPN Client Is Properly Installed

The next step is to determine if the VPN client is working properly. To do this, check to ensure that the cvpnd.exe process has started and is currently running. You can immediately determine this if you receive the error "The necessary VPN subsystem is not available," when you open the VPN dialer.

To check to see if the cvpnd.exe is running in most Windows versions, simply press Ctrl-Alt-Delete and go to Task Manager. In Task Manager, click the Processes tab, and then click the column called Image Name to sort the process names. If the cvpnd.exe process is not running, two possible problems might have occurred:

• The Cisco Systems VPN Service might be disabled in your Windows services.

• The cvpnd.exe driver might not have been installed properly.

The first problem is slightly easier to remedy than the second. To enable the Cisco Systems, Inc. VPN Service in Windows NT/2000, go to Start, Control Panel, Administrative Tools, Services. Then look for the Cisco Systems. VPN Service, right-click it and select Properties. From the Properties window, change the Startup Type to automatic, and click

Start to start the service. If the cvpnd.exe is now listed in Task Manager's processes, the VPN client should work correctly.

NOTE   The Microsoft IPSec policy agent must be disabled in services for VPN to work. The VPN installer is set up to disable it, but there have been cases where it was still enabled.

If you tried to start the cvpnd.exe in services and it failed, there is a chance that the cvpnd.exe driver was not installed properly or you might have installed the new version over the old version.

NOTE   Before installing a new version of the VPN client, always ensure that older versions are uninstalled prior to installation. Some un-installers might not work in a way you expect. To resolve this issue, uninstall the current version; make sure to use the VPN uninstaller that is located in Start, Programs, Cisco Systems VPN Client, Uninstall VPN Client, and then reboot. After the reboot, reinstall the new VPN client, reboot, and test it.

Step 3: Check or Create Your Profiles

Before you can connect to a concentrator, you must have at least one profile pointing to that concentrator. Typically, the network administrator creates the profiles and distributes them to users. The VPN client software is shipped with a sample user profile. The file is named sample.pcf, and its content is shown in Example 22-3.

The *.pcf files are usually stored under C:\Program Files\Cisco Systems\VPN Client\ Profiles. For specific information on the meaning of each field, see www.cisco.com/ univercd/cc/td/doc/product/ vpn/client/nonwin35/user_gd/profile.htm.

Example 22-3   *A Sample User Profile That Might Be Shipped with the Installer*

```
[main]
Description=sample user profile
Host=10.7.44.1
AuthType=1
GroupName=monkeys
EnableISPConnect=0
ISPConnectType=0
ISPConnect=
ISPCommand=
Username=gawf
SaveUserPassword=0
NTDomain=
EnableBackup=0
```

Example 22-3   *A Sample User Profile That Might Be Shipped with the Installer (Continued)*

```
BackupServer=
EnableNat=0
CertStore=0
CertName=
CertPath=
CertSubjectName=
CertSerialHash=00000000000000000000000000000000
DHGroup=2
ForceKeepAlives=0
```

The easiest way to create a profile is to open sample.pcf with any text editor. Then modify the necessary entries and save it with a different name in the same directory that is called, for example, NEW_CONNECTION.pcf. Make sure you use the .pcf file extension or the VPN client will not read it. When creating a profile, the following fields must be defined at a bare minimum:

- [main] (This does not have to be defined but must be in the file)
- Host
- AuthType
- GroupName
- Username

After a profile is created, you have the option of cloning entries from the VPN client. Choose the connection entry that you want to clone and select options, then select clone entry. After you enter the name of the cloned entry, it creates a duplicate .pcf file in the Profiles folder. After it's created, you can modify the properties on the VPN client by choosing options and then properties.

Scenario 1: Cannot Authenticate

In this scenario, several possible problems are reviewed to demonstrate why authentication might fail when using the VPN software client. Each case identifies a possible problem, one or more solutions. This scenario is based on the assumption that you have completed the preliminary troubleshooting steps and have a working Internet connection. Different reasons exist for why VPN authentication might fail, and they are reviewed in this scenario.

- **Case 1: Bad group name or group password**—A bad group name or group password can cause a connection to fail every time.
- **Case 2: Prompted multiple times for username and password**—Most likely, this is caused by a bad password. This might also be because the deterministic network enhancer (DNE) is not enabled in the Local Area Connection window.
- **Case 3: Firewall software**—Personal firewall software might be blocking the necessary ports or applications that VPN requires to function.

- **Case 4: MTU set high**—A fragmentation issue, because the MTU might be set too high.
- **Case 5: MTU set low**—This can cause authentication issues.

Case 1: Bad Group Name or Group Password

In this case, the possibility of a bad group name or group password is examined. Typically, the user receives the error "Remote peer is no longer responding" or "Failed to establish a secure connection to the security gateway." It is difficult to determine what the problem is based on solely on the connection error messages, because a single error can parent multiple problems.

The group name and group password is not the same as the username and password used for authentication on a Remote Authentication Dial-In User Service (RADIUS) server. The group name and password are stored on the VPN concentrator, and on the VPN client. In essence, it is a way for the VPN administrator to group different user requirements into different client groups and eventually to apply group features or policies to all members of the group. For example, some users' NAT within their home local-area network (LAN). When they connect to the concentrator, it must recognize that the user is NATing and adjust. The concentrator can tell if the user is NATing or not, based on the group name and password used to connect.

The group name and encrypted password are stored on the .pcf file that is located within the C:\Program Files\Cisco Systems\VPN Client\Profiles folder. The best way to re-enter a group name and password for a specific profile is to clone the connection entry because the password is encrypted in the .pcf file, which contains the necessary information for the client to establish an IPSec tunnel to the concentrator. Further analysis on what you can do with .pcf files is included in some of the later cases, but for now, refer to Step 3 in the previous section of this chapter.

The best way to troubleshoot this type of case is to examine the log for multiple Internet Security Association and Key Management Protocol (ISAKMP)/Oakley retransmissions while trying to initiate a connection. Refer to Example 22-4. If multiple retransmissions exist, it is likely that the group password is corrupted.

To re-enter the group name and group password, get the group password from the VPN administrator and clone the connection entry by highlighting the entry you want to clone, then go to Options, Clone Entry. Simply fill in the name of the entry, group name, and password.

Example 22-4   *Example of a Connection Attempt with a Corrupted Group Password*

```
49      00:30:30.482  12/26/01  Sev=Info/6  DIALER/0x63300002
Initiating connection.
<Output Omitted>
```

Example 22-4   *Example of a Connection Attempt with a Corrupted Group Password (Continued)*

```
56     00:30:36.430  12/26/01  Sev=Info/4   IKE/0x63000013
SENDING >>> ISAKMP OAK AG (Retransmission) to 10.0.0.1


57     00:30:41.448  12/26/01  Sev=Info/4   IKE/0x63000013
SENDING >>> ISAKMP OAK AG (Retransmission) to 10.0.0.1


58     00:30:46.465  12/26/01  Sev=Info/4   IKE/0x63000013
SENDING >>> ISAKMP OAK AG (Retransmission) to 10.0.0.1
! After four attempts to initiate an ISAKMP/Oakley key exchange with
! no response, the client stops sending.
59     00:30:51.492  12/26/01  Sev=Warning/2  IKE/0xE3000079
Exceeded 3 IKE SA negotiation retransmits... peer is not responding


60     00:30:51.492  12/26/01  Sev=Info/4   CM/0x63100014
Unable to establish Phase 1 SA with server "10.0.0.1 " because of
    "DEL_REASON_PEER_NOT_RESPONDING"
! The concentrator will never allow a client to begin phase 1 if
! the group password is invalid.
<Output Omitted>
```

When multiple backup concentrators are listed in the .pcf file, and if the VPN client cycles rapidly through all the connection entries and returns with "Failed to establish a secure connection to the security gateway," both the group name and password might be corrupted. If that is the case, clone the connection entry and re-enter the group name and password.

Case 2: Prompted Multiple Times for Username and Password

In this case, you have already tested your Internet connectivity and lowered your MTUs. You are about to connect, but after entering username and password at the VPN username and password prompt, you do not connect. Instead, you continually get prompted for your username and password. This problem can be one of two things: Either there is a problem with the RADIUS username and password, or there might be an issue with one of the DNE miniports.

Bad Username or Password

Ninety-five percent of the time, a bad username or password is related to a bad RADIUS account. Unfortunately, versions below VPN client v3.5 do not identify why you have to re-enter your password, it just keeps prompting you. The solution to this problem is to contact your network administrator (RADIUS administrator) and request a reset of your username and password.

When using the VPN client release 3.5.1, if the RADIUS Expiry option is selected on the VPN 3000 concentrator as the IPSec authentication method for the group, the VPN concentrator can provide enhanced login failure messages to the VPN client describing specific error conditions. These conditions include the following:

- Password expired
- Restricted login hours
- Account disabled
- No dial-in permission
- Error changing password
- Authentication failure

The "password expired" message appears when a user, whose password has expired, first attempts to log in. The other messages appear only after three unsuccessful login attempts. For more information on VPN client release 3.5.1, see www.cisco.com/univercd/cc/td/doc/product/vpn/client/rel3_5_1/351_3kcl.htm.

Problem with the DNE Miniport

To troubleshoot the issue, DNE first must be explained. DNE is a network driver interface specification (NDIS) compliant module, which resides under the NDIS module of the Windows OS and is essentially an extension of NDIS functionality—see more about DNE architecture under www.deterministicnetworks.com/dne.asp. DNE has solved numerous well-known problems when using competitive NDIS intermediate drivers, and it is available for Windows, Linux, HP-UX, and Solaris versions.

DNE appears as a network device driver to all protocol stacks, and as a protocol driver to all network device drivers. It supports all known network protocols and network adapter types. Every physical device listed under the Device Manager of Windows OS, has a supporting DNE driver—one for every LAN adapter (NIC card), USB driver, or wide-area network (WAN) protocol (Internet Protocol [IP], Point-to-Point Tunneling Protocol [PPTP], Layer 2 Tunnel Protocol [L2TP]).

If any physical adapter or protocol has ever been installed and then later removed from any particular system, the DNE supporting driver still exists until it is removed manually. If the DNE extension is installed, the newly installed physical driver or protocol obtains a newly populated DNE driver.

The DNE extension includes DNE plugins, which can be invoked when inbound or outbound packets match prespecified filters. A DNE plugin written for one operating system usually requires only to be recompiled to run on other operating systems. The number of filters is not defined; there can be thousands of them. The DNE plugins provide frame or packet inspection (including MAC-level), to modify, delete, insert, or redirect them. The redirect function is especially important when redirecting packets from a virtual VPN IP to the ISP's IP address.

In DNE-related issues, the user has a valid RADIUS account but still is unable to authenticate. The user gets prompted for username and password multiple times, and cannot authenticate. For this case, you should always check the Windows Device Manager for bad DNE miniports.

To check DNE functionality, first open the Windows Device Manager by right-clicking My Computer, and select properties. From the Properties window, select the tab labeled Hardware, then click Device Manager. Scroll down to the Network Adapters and expand the window by clicking the + next to it. From there, you should see a list of your network adapters.

Remove any extra Ethernet adapters that are bound to a DNE miniport with a red cross through it. There must be at least one functioning DNE miniport bound to each adapter, so make sure not to remove them all. After removing all the extra disabled DNE miniports, try the connection again.

Case 3: Firewall Software

Several different firewall software solutions are available for home users, but the three leaders are ZoneAlarm, Black Ice, and Norton Personal Firewall. Cisco recommends using Zone Lab's ZoneAlarm with the Cisco VPN 3000 client because of its compatibility with the VPN client. Although Cisco recommends ZoneAlarm, we also show you how to configure NetworkIce's BlackICE, another popular software firewall.

Despite what firewall client you choose, you must allow all VPN applications and port numbers.

There are a couple of reasons why Cisco endorses ZoneAlarm, besides the fact that it is compatible with the Cisco VPN client. One major reason is its ease of use, by using applications instead of port numbers to block data. So you see what applications are trying to access your computer, and you can then make better decisions on whether to block them or not. ZoneAlarm Pro is compatible with Microsoft Windows 95/98/Me/NT/2000 and XP. A majority of Cisco employees that use firewall software use ZoneAlarm.

NOTE   As of December 2001, Cisco embedded ZoneAlarm stateful firewall into the new release of the Cisco VPN 3.5 client. For more information, visit www.zonelabs.com/store/content/home.jsp.

ZoneAlarm Configuration

Getting the VPN client to work with ZoneAlarm is actually pretty simple. When ZoneAlarm is first installed, it blocks everything and is in stealth mode; no one on the Internet can see you. As you start bringing up applications that need to access the Internet, it asks you if you would like each application to access the Internet. The first time you try to connect with the VPN client, you are prompted three times to permit access. First, for the cvpnd.exe, second for the ipsecdialer.exe, and lastly for the Extended Authentication (Xauth) application (VPN user authentication). After you approve the application, they are placed into ZoneAlarm's programs, see Figure 22-4. From there, you will need to grant Trusted and Internet Access in ZoneAlarm Plus and Allow Connect in ZoneAlarm Pro. This will allow the VPN client to traverse through ZoneAlarm freely.

Figure 22-4 *Allowing the VPN Client to Pass Through the ZoneAlarm Software Firewall*

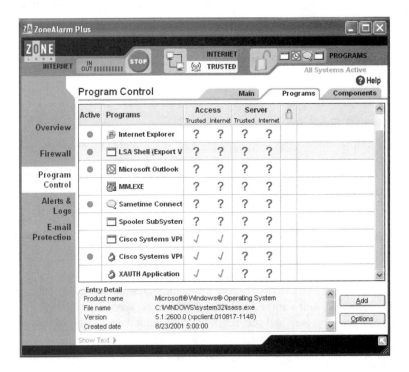

Network ICE BlackICE Defender Configuration

Network ICE BlackICE Defender is a traffic monitoring security product. If you properly configure it, BlackICE Defender can work with the VPN client. It must be configured in Trusting, Nervous, or Cautious mode, and if you use Nervous or Cautious mode, you must add the public IP address of the VPN concentrator to the list of trusted addresses. You can configure the VPN client to work with Paranoid mode when using Tunnel-everything mode. Split Tunneling requires BlackICE to be in Trusting, Nervous, or Cautious mode.

The Cisco VPN client firewall has the following requirements for BlackICE (BlackICE Defender 2.5 or greater, or BlackICE Agent 2.5 or greater). For BlackICE Defender 2.5, copy the BICTRL.DLL file from the Cisco installation release medium to the BlackICE installation directory on the VPN client PC. This is a mandatory step for making a connection with BlackICE.

BlackICE Defender version 2.9 and greater includes the BICTRL.DLL file in the Network ICE distribution medium, so you do not need to copy it from the Cisco installation release medium.

Some types of firewall software require you to enter specific port numbers to access the Internet. The port numbers that the VPN client requires to be open are covered in Scenario 5, Case 1.

Case 4: MTU Set High

If the user has gone through Case 1 and verified that the Internet connectivity and routing is functioning, the next step is to check the MTU. In this case, you analyze why the user cannot authenticate when trying to initiate an IPSec tunnel with the MTU set at 1500. One of two things can happen: Either the user cannot authenticate at all, or the user can pass data successfully. If the user can authenticate but cannot pass any data, see Scenario 2, Case 1.

The size of the MTU is an integral part for a successful VPN connection. The MTU for the most common encapsulation of IP over an Ethernet transmission link (www.faqs.org/rfcs/ rfc894.html) is 1500 bytes. By convention, the MTU includes the entire IP datagram, including all IP headers, but excludes link encapsulation headers. See Chapter 21, "Remote Access VPN Troubleshooting," for details.

IPSec causes major issues with the MTU setting because it lengthens each IP packet by one, or possibly by two IP headers. The length of these headers depends on the type of IPSec protocol that you are using; however, the headers cannot exceed 80 bytes per packet. If an application emitted a 1500-byte packet that must travel though an IPSec tunnel, the added IPSec headers require fragmentation of each packet. See Figure 22-5. Most believe that the only downside to fragmentation in a worst-case scenario is some minor performance issues; however, fragmentation can cause the inability to pass data or the failure to authenticate with VPN.

Figure 22-5   *Fragmented Packets Traversing Through the Network*

The best way to handle this problem is to avoid fragmentation completely. By lowering the interface MTU, your interface does not emit packets that need to be fragmented after IPSec encapsulation for transport through Ethernet-size-capable routers and links, as shown in Figure 22-6.

Figure 22-6 *MTU Emitting 1400-Byte Frames and Not Requiring Fragmentation*

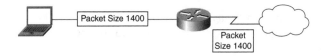

To illustrate the nuances surrounding lowering an MTU, the text discusses the following issues:

- Determining what MTU will work
- Applying the MTU size to the PC
- Adjusting the MTU size in the registry

Determining What MTU Will Work

Remember that 1400 is not always the correct number; you might have to decrease the MTU even further, but 1400 is an excellent starting point. The MTU size depends on your ISP's equipment because your packets must traverse across their routers. To determine what the MTU size is on your connection, at the DOS prompt, type the following:

C:/>ping -f -l [*packetsize*] [**www.***your_isp***.com**]

where

- **-f** is don't fragment; this is the variable that tells DOS not to break the packet into smaller pieces.
- **-l** is an option that allows you to enter [*packetsize*].
- [*packetsize*] is the amount of data that you want to send (valid range is from 0 to 65,500).
- {**www.***your_isp***.com**] is your ISP's URL (you can also use any public URL, gateway, or server).

If you exceed the MTU of the ISP, you receive the message "Packet needs to be fragmented, but DF set." If you receive this message, you must decrease the size of the packet and repeat the ping again. Continue this process until you receive a successful echo reply from the remote host.

Assume that the first successful echo reply message is when the packet size is set to 1372. In calculating the MTU, remember that when you specify -l <n>, the IP packets that you generate are actually <n> + 28 bytes long. So when you apply the MTU size on your interface card, the size is 1372 + 28 = 1400.

Applying the MTU Size to the PC

A few ways exist to apply the MTU to your PC. The most common and simplest way is to use the SetMTU application that comes with the Cisco VPN client. See Figure 22-7. You can also adjust the MTU in the registry, or use applications such as TweakMaster (Rose City Software), but both are substantially more difficult and risky. TweakMaster is similar to the Cisco VPN SetMTU application, and if you are interested you can download it at www.pattersondesigns.com.

Figure 22-7   *The SetMTU Application*

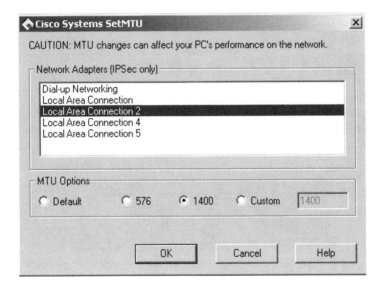

Adjusting the MTU Size in the Registry

In some circumstances, you might find that MTU adjustment applications such as the Cisco VPN client Set MTU or TweakDUN application do not have the capabilities of lowering the MTU on some interfaces. In that case, you have the option of adjusting the MTU in the registry, which is all the MTU applications really do. This next section describes in detail how to lower the MTU in the following versions of the Windows operating system:

- Windows 9x
- Setting the MTU manually in the registry
- Windows XP only

Windows 9x

There is an optional parameter in the registry called MaxMTU that can be associated with adapter bindings. Adding this optional key influences the outbound MTU, as seen by the IP

protocol stack, and the announced maximum segment size (MSS) during Transmission
Control Protocol (TCP) setup. If MaxMTU is missing from a binding, the default MTU for
the adapter (1500 for Ethernet) is assumed. If you see fragmentation problems, set
MaxMTU on your active TCP network interface to 1400. Remember to reboot after you
make any registry changes because they do not take affect until the PC has rebooted.

NOTE   When adjusting settings in the registry, fairly minor changes in your networking
configuration can cause the parameter to disappear. Please read the documentation
suggested in the following links.

The location of the MaxMTU in the Windows 9x registry is as follows:

```
HKEY_LOCAL_MACHINE\System\CurrentControlSet\Services\Class\netTrans\000 n
```

You can learn more about it at http://support.microsoft.com/support/kb/articles/q158/4/
74.asp.

The location of the MaxMTU in the Windows NT registry is as follows:

```
HKEY_LOCAL_MACHINE\SYSTEM\CurrentControlSet\Services
Key: Adapter Name \Parameters\Tcpip
```

For Windows 2000 and later, the MaxMTU value is located under the following key:

```
HKEY_LOCAL_MACHINE\SYSTEM\CurrentControlSet\Services
Key: Tcpip\Parameters\Interfaces\ ID for Adapter
```

NOTE   There is a bug in the SP1 version of W2K, and MaxMTU does not work. Either upgrade to
SP2, or delete MaxMTU from the registry. See http://support.microsoft.com/support/kb/
articles/q120/6/42.asp for more information.

Windows NT/2000

You might prefer to follow the directions from Microsoft's web site. However, some easy
steps to manually set the MTU value in Windows 2000 are described in the following list.
This method is designed for Windows 2000, but it is similar for other Windows operating
systems. You should only perform this process if you suspect that the Cisco VPN client
SetMTU application is not functioning correctly. For example, if you still observe MTU-
related issues, despite the fact that you have lowered the MTU, this is a good way to confirm
that the MTU is set to your intended value. The steps are as follows:

1 Open the registry using **regedt32** (regedit can be used, but this example is designed
for regedt32).

2 From the HKEY_LOCAL_MACHINE window, go to \SYSTEM\CurrentControlSet\
Services\Tcpip\Parameters\Interfaces (these are all the adapters that your PC has,
unfortunately they do not have a name associated with them).

3 Highlight the adapter you want to drop the MTU on, and look in the right window for something called MTU:REG_DWORD:0x514 (it can be a different number from 0x514, this number is the MTU size in hex).

4 In the right window, double-click MTU:REG_DWORD:0x514; a box called DWORD Editor opens.

5 Change the Radix radio button to Decimal; this is your MTU value.

6 Change the MTU to the desired value and close regedt32.

7 Reboot.

If you are unsure of what adapter you are lowering the MTU on, try dropping the MTUs down on all adapters listed. It does not hurt your uplink to have the MTU set to 1400 instead of 1500. If there is no MTU field for that adapter, you can add one by highlighting the adapter, then go to Edit, and Add Value. Choose REG_DWORD from the drop-down menu, name it MTU, and press OK.

Windows XP Only

This example demonstrates how to lower the MTU on a PPPoE adapter.

First, locate the following key:

```
HKLM\SYSTEM\CurrentControlSet\Services\Ndiswan\Parameters\Protocols\0
```

- After you locate the key, add all these values:
- **Value Name**: ProtocolType
  - **Data Type**: REG_DWORD
  - **Value Data**: 0x00000800
- **Value Name**: PPPProtocolType
  - **Data Type**: REG_DWORD
  - **Value Data**: 0x00000021
- **Value Name**: ProtocolMTU
  - **Data Type** REG_DWORD
  - **Value Data**: The appropriate MTU size (in decimal) (we recommend 80 Hex or 128 Decimal)

To do so,

1 Click Start, click Run, type **regedit**, and click OK.

2 Locate and click the following key in the registry:

HKEY_LOCAL_MACHINE\System\CurrentControlSet\Services\Ndiswan\Parameters

3 On the Edit menu, point to New, and click Key.

4 Type **Protocols**, and press ENTER.

5 On the Edit menu, point to New, and click Key.

6 Type **0**, and press ENTER.

7 On the Edit menu, point to New, and click DWORD Value.

8 Type **ProtocolType**, and press ENTER.

9 On the Edit menu, click Modify.

10 Type **800**, and click OK.

11 On the Edit menu, point to New, and click DWORD Value.

12 Type **PPPProtocolType**, and press ENTER.

13 On the Edit menu, click Modify.

14 Type **21**, and click OK.

15 On the Edit menu, point to New, and click DWORD Value.

16 Type **ProtocolMTU**, and press ENTER.

17 On the Edit menu, click Modify.

18 Type the appropriate MTU size (decimal value), and click OK.

19 Quit Registry Editor.

Case 5: MTU Set Low

The last case discussed how lowering the MTU reduces problems with the IPSec connection; however, too low an MTU can inhibit the ability to authenticate. Cisco's remote access team has encountered many cases where the user was familiar with the MTU issue, and lowered their MTU to 576 without trying a higher number such as 1400. These users were trying to save time on reboots (you have to reboot each time you make an MTU change) by lowering it to 576, assuming that the lower the MTU the better the VPN works. This assumption is incorrect for two reasons: First, too low an MTU can inhibit the overall performance of your Internet connection, and second, it can cause the Xauth to fail during VPN authentication.

Scenario 2: Can Authenticate but Problems Passing Data

In this scenario, the user can authenticate on the concentrator, but cannot pass data. The ability to pass data consists of downloading e-mail, browsing the company's internal web sites, and accessing the internal domain. Different things might be wrong based on the characteristics, and each possible issue is covered in the following cases. These cases introduce the following issues:

- Cannot pass traffic and using NAT connection entry
- MTU causing packet loss
- Connection keeps dropping
- Cannot browse the internal domain

Case 1: Cannot Pass Traffic and Using NAT Connection Entry

If you are using NAT on your LAN, you must use a specific connection entry on the VPN client. The concentrator must be aware that you are using NAT, because that might be the main reason for the not passing data issue.

The Internet Assigned Numbers Authority (IANA) RFC 1918 reserved the following three blocks of IP address space for private networks (see www.ietf.org/rfc/rfc1918.txt?number=1918 for more information):

- 10.0.0.0–10.255.255.255
- 172.16.0.0–172.31.255.255
- 192.168.0.0–192.168.255.255

To identify if you are using NAT, check your IP address. Refer to Table 22-2 to determine the IP address that your computer is using. If your address is in any of the three ranges listed above, you are NATing and you must use the NAT connection entry.

The NAT connection entry, or profile, does not point you to a different concentrator from the standard connection entry. The main difference between the two profiles is the group that you are assigned by the concentrator. If you review the two profiles, NAT and standard, you will notice that each has a different group name and password (the password is encrypted). The concentrator has a group set up to allow IPSec clients to operate through a firewall, using NAT through UDP.

The easiest way to create groups is to create a base group. After you have the base group that works with your current network, you can add groups and have them inherit the settings from the base group. Both the standard and NAT groups have the same properties except for the group name, password, and the IPSec over User Datagram Protocol (UDP) box must be checked on the NAT group. It is located under Mode Config. After you have created both groups on the concentrator, users can use the new groups after they have their .pcf files modified. See Chapter 20, "Remote Access VPN Design and Configuration Solutions," for more information about creating groups on the concentrator.

Case 2: MTU Causing Packet Loss

In Scenario 1, Case 1, it was explained how the default MTU size (1500) can cause authentication failures. The method to test MTU size was also explained and although this information was covered in detail already, this case advises you that different types of problems are associated to the MTU setting.

The MTU is the largest number of bytes that a frame can carry, not counting the frame's header and trailer. A frame is a single unit of transportation on the data link layer. It consists of header data, plus data passed down from the network layer, and possibly trailer data. An Ethernet frame has an MTU of 1500 bytes, but the actual size of the basic Ethernet frame can be up to 1524 bytes (20-byte header, 4-byte CRC trailer).

If you can connect with the Cisco VPN client but cannot send or receive data, it is likely an MTU problem. Common failure indicators include the following:

- You can receive data, such as mail, but not send it.
- You can send small messages (about ten lines), but larger ones time out.
- You cannot send attachments in e-mail.
- While browsing the web, you can bring up small pages with mostly text, but the larger graphical sites, or parts of them, do not come up.

If you are experiencing any of these issues, you must lower your MTU. To determine what size to set your MTU and where to set it, see Scenario 1, Case 1.

Case 3: Connection Keeps Dropping

There are a couple of reasons why a VPN connection might be dropping. It can be a problem with the ISP, or ports can be closing on a firewall that you are going through. It is unlikely that the concentrator is dropping your connection, but it is not impossible. In this case, you are shown how to use some tools to help maintain your VPN tunnel, and ways to pinpoint where the problem exists.

The following sections cover these issues:

- Bad ISP connections
- Sending keepalives

Bad ISP Connection

The first thing to determine is the quality of your ISP connection by using the **ping** or **tracert** commands. Set up a continuous ping to your corporate firewall or concentrator (if it is in front of the firewall). This identifies if there is any heavy latency or packet loss along the way, and both of these issues can cause a tunnel to drop.

For certain technologies, such as satellite, you have to expect some degree of latency. Satellite services can result in up to 1500-3000 ms round-trip time (RTT), depending on the packet size. That much latency does not disrupt browsing capabilities to the external web, but it does severely impair the speed of a VPN connection. Some VPN over satellite users have compared it to speeds of analog dialup connections. To set up a continuous ping to your corporate firewall, use the **ping** command from Example 22-5.

Example 22-5   *Continuous* **ping** *to the Corporate Firewall to Determine if There Is Packet Loss*

```
C:\>ping -t -w 4000 firewall.company.com
! The -w sets the ping to 4000 ms before timing out
Pinging firewall.company.com [65.1.1.2] with 32 bytes of data:

Reply from 65.1.1.2: bytes=32 time=240ms TTL=249
! 4000 ms or more may cause a problem
Reply from 65.1.1.2: bytes=32 time=240ms TTL=249
Reply from 65.1.1.2: bytes=32 time=245ms TTL=249
Request timed out.
! Packet loss
Reply from 65.1.1.2: bytes=32 time=242ms TTL=249
Request timed out.
<Output Omitted>
```

If you see any dropped packets, try tracing to the firewall a couple of times. By trace routing to the firewall, you can see exactly where the packets are getting dropped, or where the latency occurs. If you are losing packets and cannot route to your corporate firewall, you must contact your ISP. Provide them information, including how many packets are dropped and the host name of the router that you are experiencing latency connecting to or dropping packets on.

Sending Keepalives

If you run the **ping** and **traceroute** tests and find that your ISP connection is stable, try turning on ForceKeepAlive for that profile. There is a feature in each connection entry profile called ForceKeepAlive, which basically sends out Internet Key Exchange (IKE) and Encapsulating Security Payload (ESP) keepalives for a connection at approximately 20-second intervals. It helps prevent the NAT device or firewall from dropping your connection. Try turning ForceKeepAlive on and see if it helps.

To turn ForceKeepAlive on, open the .pcf file with any text editor for the profile that you typically use. The profiles are located under C:\Program Files\Cisco Systems\VPN Client\Profiles. After it is open, set ForceKeepAlive = 1, which turns it on. It should dramatically reduce the number of dropped connections if it is associated with your firewall or NAT device. The ForceKeepAlive is covered in more detail in Scenario 5, Case 1.

Case 4: Cannot Browse the Internal Domain

In this case, the user can connect to the concentrator and even pass data such as e-mail, and browse internal web sites. However, the one thing that does not work is accessing the internal NT domain (Network Neighborhood or My Network Places), where the user has zero to limited access to the domain. This issue can be frustrating initially because it appears everything except domain access is working. You can take two steps to solve this problem: adding the WINS addresses or further lowering the MTU.

Adding WINS IP

WINS is a NetBIOS name service defined in RFC 1001 and RFC 1002. WINS servers basically maintain a database of computer names to IP addresses. When WINS is configured, a computer first tries to use a WINS server for name registration and resolution. If that fails, the computer then resorts to subnet broadcasts. Unlike LMHOSTS, WINS is useful in a DHCP network where IP addresses are constantly changing because each client, during boot up, registers its name and IP address with the WINS server.

In general, this step is not necessary because when the concentrator performs the configuration mode, it pushes a packet of IP addresses to the client, including WINS IPs. However, because of computer-related issues or version-related bugs, you might consider the following steps. Assign statically the corporate WINS addresses to your TCP/IP settings. The WINS addresses help guide your computer to and through the domain by giving it access to a database of computer locations. This eliminates a lot of the problems with finding the domain controller and other Microsoft issues that you might encounter. To add WINS addresses to your TCP/IP, use the following instructions.

For Windows 95/98,

1 Under Control Panel, double-click Network.

2 Under the Configuration tab, highlight the adapter that you are using with ->TCP/IP next to it (for example 3COM->TCP/IP), then click Properties.

3 Under the WINS tab, enter the WINS IP addresses.

NOTE   On Windows 95/98 workstations, the workgroup name of the workstation must be the same as the domain name that you are trying to log into, or you will not see a browse list.

For Windows NT/2000,

1 Right-click My Network Places, which is located on your desktop and select Properties.

2 Right-click and select Properties on the Local Area Connection that is not crossed out.

3 Highlight TCP/IP, then click Properties.

4 Click Advanced.

5 Under the WINS tab, enter the WINS IP addresses.

Still Cannot Browse Correctly

If you are still having problems browsing the intranet and the domain, you might need to modify some networking settings. In this section, you learn how to fine-tune your network settings to work best with VPN:

- Windows 95/98
- Windows NT/2000
- Lower the MTU

Windows 95/98

A majority of the time, this problem occurs with users who are dialing to an ISP, and connecting with VPN. Most dialup-only users cannot change the browser characteristics because they do not have the file and printer sharing for Microsoft Networks service configured in the Network Control Panel. To install file and printer sharing for Microsoft Networks service, go to Network in the Control Panel, click Install, and select Service. Then, choose Microsoft as the vendor along with file and printer sharing, and click Add.

These settings must be configured and they are different from the File and Print Sharing buttons in the Control Panel. After the settings are installed, you can select the properties for this service under the Advanced tab. Two options can be changed, and setting the Browse Master to disable ensures that the user gets the Browse list more quickly through the tunnel.

NOTE   For information about the rogue master browser problem and for many other good tips for people experiencing the preceding problem, go to www.cisco.com/warp/public/473/winnt_dg.htm#xtocid882960.

Windows NT/2000

NT has a Registry key that indicates to the OS whether or not to maintain a list of servers for the browser function. It also indicates how the node acts in the browser context. If the key value is set to Auto (the default), the PC tries to force an election. When the workstation boots on an isolated LAN segment or for dialup, the result is that it cannot find a master browser (or backup master browser). After the tunnel is up, it sends out subnet broadcasts for a backup server, which gets forwarded across. If these go unanswered, it asks for an election. The Registry key to change is as follows (try setting it to No):

HKEY_LOCAL_MACHINE/SYSTEM/CurrentControlSet/Services/Browser/
Parameters/MaintainServerList

Lower the MTU

After you complete the WINS modifications, and if you are still having problems browsing the domain, try lowering the MTU. This rarely occurs but there have been cases where the MTUs were set just a little too high. Try lowering them by 50 and see if that fixes the issue. For information on how to lower your MTU, refer to Scenario 1, Case 1.

Scenario 3: PPPoE Software/Hardware Problems

PPPoE was covered in great detail in Chapter 21. In this case, the types of problems you might encounter with PPPoE are identified. As you might know, the use of PPPoE software continues to increase, especially in the DSL industry. PPPoE can be used with cable, but it is rarely used by cable ISPs. Companies such as AT&T @Home currently use a static computer name to authenticate their users.

Numerous PPPoE clients are in use today, but only three comprise 90 percent of the market. These three main PPPoE clients are NTS Enternet 300 (SBC), WinPoet (Verizon, Earthlink), and RASPPPoE (Freeware). The subsequent sections cover each client (after first presenting an overview of PPPoE and the MTU issue). This section demonstrates to you how to configure and troubleshoot the following two topics:

- PPPoE Software Issues
- IOS-based PPPoE Issues

PPPoE is similar to a dialup connection: you bring up a dialer on your PC, type a username and password, and hit connect. Your user information is then passed to an authentication server through the access concentrator, and if you are successfully authenticated, you get connected. All PPPoE negotiations are done on the ISP side, so after you get connected, you can connect with your VPN client (see Figure 22-8).

Figure 22-8 *The Basic PPPoE Infrastructure; All the PPPoE Negotiations Are Done on the ISP Side*

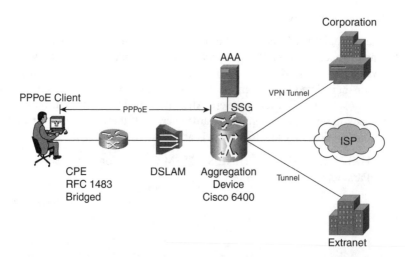

Case 1: PPPoE Software Issues

Based on previous discussions, the MTU issue is one of the greatest problems faced by VPN users, and unfortunately, it also carries over to PPPoE. The MTU settings when using the PPPoE protocol are the main contributor to most of the problems.

NOTE   The Set MTU application in the VPN client does not have the capability to adjust the MTU on a PPPoE virtual adapter. As of October 2002, there are no plans to add PPPoE adjustment capabilities to the VPN 3000 Client Set MTU application.

If you try to connect without lowering the MTU on your PPPoE adapter, you might experience severe problems such as failure to download e-mail, failure to browse the intranet, and failure to browse the internal domain.

In the following three sections, you learn about the steps required to lower the MTU on all three of the major PPPoE clients.

MTU Settings in NTS Enternet 300

NTS Enternet 300 has proven to be one of the dominant PPPoE clients in the market, particularly on the West coast. It is a solid client, easy to configure, and it works well with Cisco's VPN client. This section focuses on configuring NTS Enternet 300 on multiple Windows operating systems.

For Windows 95/98,

1   On the main desktop, right-click My Network Places and go to Properties. The Network window opens.

2   Double-click the Network TeleSystems PPPoE Adapter.

3   On the Network TeleSystems window, click the Advanced tab, and then click MaxFrameSize. Change the value, which varies from case to case but ranges from 1200 to 1400.

4   Reboot the computer.

For Windows NT/2000,

1   On the main desktop, right-click My Network Places and go to Properties. The Network and Dial-Up Connections window opens.

2   Right-click and go to Properties on each connection until you find the connection that has the NTS Enternet PPPoE Adapter.

3   After you find the correct connection, click Configure on the right side of the window.

4   On the next window, click the Advanced tab, then click MaxFrameSize. Change the value, which varies from case to case but ranges from 1200 to 1400.

MTU Settings in WinPoet

Winpoet is another widely used PPPoE client. Although it is widely used it is not considered by most to be a great PPPoE client. It is difficult to modify MTU settings for it to work with the Cisco VPN client. Essentially, the Cisco VPN client and WinPoet do not work well together. Fortunately for the PPPoE users, they can use any PPPoE client. So there are no limitations prohibiting a user from switching PPPoE clients. We have formulated a method to adjust the MTU using WinPoet, which follows; however, Cisco recommends switching to another PPPoE client such as NTS Enternet or RASPPPoE.

WinPoet does not provide user control over the PPPoE MTU under Windows 95/98. But for Windows NT/2000, you can control it by explicitly setting the following registry key:

HKLM/system/currentcontrolset/control/class/*<guid>*/*<adapternumber>*
adapter(000x) :
Value: MaxFrameSize
Value type: DWORD
Data: 1400 (or less)

The *<guid>* and *<adapternumber>* can vary on different systems. Browse through the registry, looking for the MaxFrameSize value.

WARNING Edit the registry only if you are comfortable doing so. Incorrect registry entries can make your PC unstable or unusable. If you are not familiar with editing the registry, contact desktop support for assistance.

MTU Settings in RASPPPoE

RASPPPoE is another good PPPoE client, and it is freeware. It gives users the ability to adjust the MTU without having to touch the registry and has been successfully tested with Cisco's VPN client. If you are interested in downloading or for more information on configuring RASPPPoE, visit http://user.cs.tu-berlin.de/~normanb/.

For Windows 95/98,

  1 On the main desktop, right-click My Network Places and go to Properties. The Network window opens.

  2 Find the PPP over Ethernet Protocol that is bound to the network card in your PC, then double-click it.

  3 Under the General tab, check Override Maximum Transfer Unit. Change the value, which varies from case to case but ranges from 1200 to 1400.

For Windows NT/2000,

1 On the main desktop, right-click My Network Places and go to properties. The Network and Dial-Up Connections window opens.

2 Right-click the connection that the PPPoE Protocol was installed for, and go to Properties.

3 When the window opens, double-click PPP over Ethernet Protocol.

4 Under the General tab, check Override Maximum Transfer Unit. Change the value, which varies from case to case but ranges from 1200 to 1400.

Additional information about this topic can be found at http://user.cs.tu-berlin.de/ ~normanb/README2K.HTM.

Case 2: IOS-Based PPPoE Issues

In today's environment, more and more devices support PPPoE. It is no longer just software and routers that can support PPPoE; devices such as the PIX 501 and 506, and the VPN 3002 hardware client also support PPPoE. There is a long list of Cisco routers that support PPPoE, including the 806, 826, 827, 827-4V, 828, SOHO 77, and SOHO 78. Although each one supports PPPoE, each one meets different needs. For more information on these product specifications, see www.cisco.com/univercd/cc/td/doc/product/access/acs_fix/827/ 827rlnts /820feat.htm.

Hundreds of routers on the market support PPPoE. Although some were built to work with both PPPoE and VPN, others were built to meet the need for only one of the two. The following information provides output from a series of debug commands, which is not possible from a majority of routers on the market.

Cisco 800 Series PPPoE Connection Problem

This case demonstrates how a Cisco 806 router connects to an ISP using PPPoE. The 806 router connects to a generic ADSL modem and there is no other equipment besides the PC. In Example 22-6, the output shows the router trying to complete the PPPoE negotiation, but the Ethernet1 (WAN) interface is bouncing. You can also see what the log viewer displays with all filters set to high. The PPPoE's link control protocol (LCP) sends keepalives to the core. See the shaded comments in Example 22-6.

Example 22-6 *PPPoE Router Trying to Connect While the WAN Link Bounces*

```
806-ADSL#debug vpdn pppoe events and 806-ADSL#debug ppp negotiation
THE LOG VIEWER IS OPEN

04:42:15: Vi1 LCP: echo_cnt 2, sent id 34, line up
```

continues

Example 22-6 *PPPoE Router Trying to Connect While the WAN Link Bounces (Continued)*

```
04:42:25: Vi1 LCP: echo_cnt 3, id 35, line up
04:42:35: Vi1 LCP: echo_cnt 4, sent id 36, line up
04:42:45: Vi1 LCP: echo_cnt 5, sent id 37, line up
04:42:56: Vi1 PPP: Missed 5 keepalives, taking LCP down
! LCP misses 5 keepalive responses and then takes the line down.
! The keepalives act as integrity packets.
04:42:56: Vi1 IPCP: Remove link info for cef entry 165.1.1.1
04:42:56: Vi1 IPCP: State is Closed
04:42:56: Vi1 PPP: Phase is DOWN
04:42:56: PPPoE 12997: Shutting down
04:42:56:  PPPoE : Shutting down client session
04:42:56: PPPoE 12997: O PADT L:0002.1762.ad36 R:0002.3b00.9d43 Et1
04:42:56: %DIALER-6-UNBIND: Interface Vi1 unbound from profile Di1
04:42:56: Vi1 PPP: Phase is ESTABLISHING, Passive Open
04:42:56: Vi1 PPP: No remote authentication for call-out
04:42:56: Vi1 LCP: State is Listen
04:42:56: %LINK-3-UPDOWN: Interface Virtual-Access1, changed state to down
04:42:56: Vi1 LCP: State is Closed
04:42:56: Vi1 PPP: Phase is DOWN
04:42:56: Di1 IPCP: Remove route to 165.1.1.1
04:42:57: %LINEPROTO-5-UPDOWN: Line protocol on Interface Virtual-Access1, changed
state to down
! End of the process for taking down all phases, and
! removes the IP route from the table.

Here the LOG VIEWER reports these events...

2    04:42:24.164  01/31/02  Sev=Warning/3    IKE/0xE3000062
Could not find an IKE SA for 10.0.0.1.  KEY REQ aborted.

! This message usually indicates that at least one of the parameters of
! the SA has changed and as a result, the VPN tunnel is terminated.
! In this particular case, the reason is a flapping WAN connection, which
! results in changing the DHCP-based IP address.

3    04:53:57.140  01/31/02  Sev=Warning/2    IKE/0xE3000080
Received an IKE packet from someone other than the Concentrator that
   we are currently connected to... discarding packet.

4    04:55:06.023  01/31/02  Sev=Warning/3    IKE/0xE3000002
Function initialize_qm failed with an error code of 0x00000000(INITIATE:822)

When you initiate a disconnect, a message similar to
   "The VPN is terminated..." is displayed.

04:43:16:  Sending PADI: Interface = Ethernet1
! Beginning the new negotiation of PADI-PADO
04:43:20:  Sending PADI: Interface = Ethernet1
04:43:20:  padi timer expired
04:43:28:  Sending PADI: Interface = Ethernet1
04:43:28:  padi timer expired
04:43:28: PPPoE 0: I PADO L:0002.1762.ad36 R:0002.3b00.9d43 Et1
04:43:30:  PPPOE: we've got our pado and the pado timer went off
```

Example 22-6   *PPPoE Router Trying to Connect While the WAN Link Bounces (Continued)*

```
04:43:30: OUT PADR from PPPoE tunnel
04:43:30: PPPoE 13380: I PADS L:0002.1762.ad36 R:0002.3b00.9d43 Et1
04:43:30: IN PADS from PPPoE tunnel
04:43:30: %DIALER-6-BIND: Interface Vi1 bound to profile Di1
04:43:30: PPPoE: Virtual Access interface obtained.
04:43:30: Vi1 PPP: Phase is DOWN, Setup
04:43:30: Vi1 PPP: Treating connection as a callout
04:43:30: Vi1 PPP: Phase is ESTABLISHING, Active Open
.........................................
04:43:37: Vi1 IPCP: I CONFREQ [ACKrcvd] id 4 len 10
04:43:37: Vi1 IPCP:    Address 66.1.1.2 (0x030642201A01)
04:43:37: Vi1 IPCP: O CONFACK [ACKrcvd] id 4 len 10
04:43:37: Vi1 IPCP:    Address 66.1.1.2 (0x030642201A01)
04:43:37: Vi1 IPCP: State is Open
04:43:37: Di1 IPCP: Install negotiated IP interface address 66.44.44.1
04:43:37: Di1 IPCP: Install route to 66.1.1.2
04:43:37: Vi1 IPCP: Add link info for cef entry 66.1.1.2
! End of the new negotiation - The new IP is installed under dialer interface.

There is connectivity and  the VPN session can start again.
```

See Chapter 21 for a detailed explanation of PPPoE.

Upgrading the Router's Firmware

Because PPPoE is a relatively new technology, it is still going through growing pains, especially with VPN. Many companies, other than Cisco, who manufacture SOHO routers, are frantically trying to develop products that meet the PPPoE/VPN needs of the consumer. Some of these routers might not function as expected and they might not work with the Cisco VPN client right out of the box.

The best approach when you have problems connecting to a VPN concentrator through a new router is to upgrade the firmware. Almost all companies post a copy of their latest firmware release on their web sites, along with instructions on how to implement it. Immediately upgrade the router's firmware to eliminate this possible cause.

If you use a router with firewall capabilities and the firmware upgrade does not solve the problem, try to open up the firewall completely. If it works, you know you have to work on getting the correct ports open. See Scenario 5, Case 1 for more information on what ports and protocols must be allowed on a firewall.

Scenario 4: 3002 Connection Problems

This scenario is designed to solve some fundamental problems you might run into when deploying a Cisco VPN 3002 solution within your company. The cases focus on establishing the connection to the concentrator, and on some general debugging techniques that you can perform on the 3002. To simplify matters, the Cisco recommendation for authentication is used in the scenarios. However, there are five different authentication mechanisms/ systems that can be used with the Cisco VPN 3000 concentrator, which are as follows:

- NT domain
- RADIUS or RADIUS proxy
- RSA security SecurID (SDI)
- Digital certificates
- Internal authentication

Cisco recommends using RADIUS authentication. As you know, many companies already use RADIUS with their current dialup environment, so they can use the already built infrastructure. Also, the configuration required on the VPN concentrator to authenticate using a RADIUS server is relatively easy.

Using RADIUS to authenticate 3002 clients is more secure than internal authentication because you can deny access to specific users immediately and easily. Internal authentication requires that you add users individually to the concentrator; therefore, users are authenticated by the concentrator itself. It is not the preferred method of authentication because many companies already have a dialup environment that uses RADIUS, so instead of managing two types of user authentication, RADIUS and internal VPN, just use the existing one. With one method, if you need to terminate a user's access to all devices, you can simply terminate one account on the RADIUS server.

The following "Can't connect to the Concentrator" scenario, as shown in Figure 22-9, is entirely based on 3002 authentication by a RADIUS server.

Figure 22-9   *The VPN 3002 Network Model Used in Scenario 4*

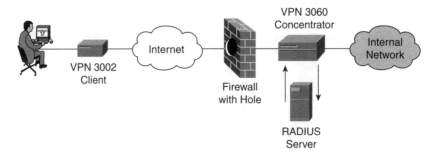

In this case, the user connects the 3002 to a generic DSL modem, and uses PPPoE for the standard DSL connection, and RADIUS for the concentrator. If you are not using PPPoE, the trouble shooting process is less difficult because you either use a static IP address or pull one through DHCP. If not using PPPoE, ignore the PPPoE section. You try to establish a VPN connection with the 3002 client to the concentrator, but are unable to establish a tunnel. You should take three troubleshooting steps to resolve this issue:

- Check the interfaces status on the 3002
- Confirm the group name and password are correct
- Confirm the username and password are valid

Check the Interfaces Status on the 3002

The first thing to check is the status of the interfaces. Are they Up or Down? To view interfaces on the 3002, go to Configuration, Interfaces. From there, if you have been given an IP address, subnet information, and your allocated DNS servers, you can check status (Up/Down). See Figure 22-10.

In Figure 22-10, both the public and private interfaces are Up. The private interface is to your private network (internal LAN), and the public interface is to the public network, which uses the IP address provided by your ISP.

Figure 22-10 *Checking the Interface Status on the VPN 3002*

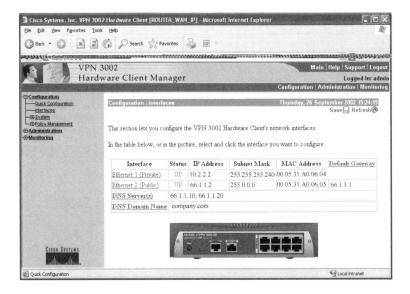

There are a total of nine different operational status messages that can be associated to either Public or Private interfaces. The status messages are as follows:

- **UP (green)**—Configured, enabled, and operational; ready to pass data traffic.
- **DOWN (red)**—Configured but disabled or disconnected.
- **Testing**—In test mode; no regular data traffic can pass.
- **Dormant (red)**—Configured and enabled but waiting for an external action, such as an incoming connection.

- **Not Present (red)**—Missing hardware components.
- **Lower Layer Down**—Not operational because a lower-layer interface is down.
- **Unknown (red)**—Not configured or not able to determine status.
- **Not Configured**—Present but not configured.
- **Waiting for DHCP/PPPoE**—Waiting for DHCP or PPPoE to assign an IP address.

If the interface is Down, the problem can be one of two things. Either there is a problem with the ISP's physical connection or the PPPoE connection is failing. Before calling the ISP, always check to see if you have entered a bad username or password. One way to do this is to run two event classes, PPPOEDBG and PPPOE. To add event classes on the 3002, go to Configuration, System, Events, Classes and click Add. Scroll down the list until you find PPPOEDBG or PPPOE, and change the severity to log to 1-9, then click Add. The severity to log determines what is sent to the log based on the severity level.

After you have the event classes (debugs) set up, go to the Filterable Event Log that is located under Monitoring, Filterable Event Log, and click Get Log. If you see a display similar to Example 22-7, you know it is either the PPPoE username or password. Try re-entering the username and password on the Public interface, then retest. If the PPPoE authentication is still failing, work with your ISP to reset your PPPoE username and password.

Example 22-7 *Log from a VPN 3002 Using PPPOEDBG and PPPOE Event Classes and a Bad PPPoE Username*

```
23 03/02/2002 03:55:36.240 SEV=6 PPPOEDBG/4 RPT=11
Building PADI Packet.
! Usually the first step in the PPPoE connection.

24 03/02/2002 03:55:36.240 SEV=8 PPPOEDBG/11 RPT=19
Sending Packet down to IP.

25 03/02/2002 03:55:36.260 SEV=8 PPPOEDBG/12 RPT=214
Received Packet from IP.

26 03/02/2002 03:55:36.260 SEV=6 PPPOEDBG/7 RPT=9
Processing Received PADO Packet.

27 03/02/2002 03:55:36.260 SEV=6 PPPOEDBG/5 RPT=8
Building PADR Packet.

28 03/02/2002 03:55:36.260 SEV=8 PPPOEDBG/11 RPT=20
Sending Packet down to IP.

29 03/02/2002 03:55:36.280 SEV=8 PPPOEDBG/12 RPT=215
Received Packet from IP.

30 03/02/2002 03:55:36.280 SEV=6 PPPOEDBG/8 RPT=8
Processing Received PADS Packet.
```

Example 22-7   *Log from a VPN 3002 Using PPPOEDBG and PPPOE Event Classes and a Bad PPPoE Username (Continued)*

```
31 03/02/2002 03:55:36.280 SEV=7 PPPOEDBG/10 RPT=8
Building PPP Stream.

32 03/02/2002 03:55:36.310 SEV=8 PPPOEDBG/12 RPT=216
Received Packet from IP.

33 03/02/2002 03:55:36.310 SEV=8 PPPOEDBG/13 RPT=192
Sending Packet to PPP.

34 03/02/2002 03:55:36.310 SEV=8 PPPOEDBG/12 RPT=217
Received Packet from IP.

35 03/02/2002 03:55:36.310 SEV=8 PPPOEDBG/13 RPT=193
Sending Packet to PPP.

36 03/02/2002 03:55:37.710 SEV=8 PPPOEDBG/12 RPT=218
Received Packet from IP.

37 03/02/2002 03:55:37.710 SEV=8 PPPOEDBG/13 RPT=194
Sending Packet to PPP.

38 03/02/2002 03:55:37.710 SEV=2 PPP/39 RPT=8
PAP authentication failed received.. check/verify username/password .
! This indicates either the username or password is incorrectly configured.

39 03/02/2002 03:55:37.710 SEV=8 PPPOEDBG/12 RPT=219
Received Packet from IP.

40 03/02/2002 03:55:37.710 SEV=8 PPPOEDBG/13 RPT=195
Sending Packet to PPP.

41 03/02/2002 03:55:39.720 SEV=8 PPPOEDBG/12 RPT=220
Received Packet from IP.

42 03/02/2002 03:55:39.720 SEV=6 PPPOEDBG/9 RPT=8
Processing Received PADT Packet.

43 03/02/2002 03:55:39.720 SEV=6 PPPOE/6 RPT=18
PPPoE Session Terminated.
! The PPPoE session terminated so there is no connectivity.
```

After you get the public/PPPoE interface up, you should be able to ping external devices such as www.cisco.com. To ping on the 3002, go to Administration, Ping, then enter the host name or IP address of any host (for example, www.cisco.com). If the ping says Alive, you have Internet connectivity.

Confirm the Group Name and Password Are Correct

Now that a physical connection to the Internet is confirmed, try to connect to the concentrator. The best way to ensure that you have the correct username and password stored on the 3002 is to re-enter it. The location of the group name and password is found under Configuration, System, Tunneling Protocols, IPSec. If you do not know the group name and password, contact the network administrator.

Cisco recommends turning on six event classes when troubleshooting this type of case, to cover a wide spectrum of possible issues. Do not set the severity to log level to 1-13, because this would capture too much information to digest at once; 1-9 severity level should suffice. The list of event classes that should run when troubleshooting is below. It is easier to read the output in the log if you run them in coordinating pairs, such as AUTH and AUTHDBG:

- AUTH
- AUTHDBG
- IPSEC
- IPSECDB
- IKE
- IKEDBG

While running the capture log, if there is a bad group name or password, unfortunately there is no error indication; however, many phase 1 initializations are displayed. See Example 22-8.

Example 22-8 *Common Log of Output if There Is a Group Name or Password Failure*

```
5 03/02/2002 05:47:32.410 SEV=4 IKE/41 RPT=368 10.0.0.1
IKE Initiator: New Phase 1, Intf 12, IKE Peer 10.0.0.1
local Proxy Address 66.1.1.2, remote Proxy Address 10.0.0.1,
SA (ESP-3DES-MD5)

6 03/02/2002 05:48:21.211 SEV=4 IKE/41 RPT=368 10.0.0.1
IKE Initiator: New Phase 1, Intf 12, IKE Peer 10.0.0.1
local Proxy Address 66.1.1.2, remote Proxy Address 10.0.0.1,
SA (ESP-3DES-MD5)

7 03/02/2002 05:48:49.182 SEV=4 IKE/41 RPT=368 10.0.0.1
IKE Initiator: New Phase 1, Intf 12, IKE Peer 10.0.0.1
local Proxy Address 66.1.1.2, remote Proxy Address 10.0.0.1,
SA (ESP-3DES-MD5)
```

Problems with User Authentication

Depending on your VPN authentication method, verify that you have a valid corporate username and password with the organization that manages authentication and controls the RADIUS servers, digital certificate servers, NT domain, and VPN 3000 concentrators.

Scenario 5: Extranet Issues

This scenario addresses the requirement for users that have a need to access their corporate network from a location outside of their corporate firewall, such as a customer site. These are the typical Extranet VPN situations. To ensure that your VPN works properly, it requires specific ports on your customer's firewall to be open, and if they are not, your company's VPN concentrator will be unable to communicate with the VPN client. Simply put, these cases can be described as "problems connecting through customer's site firewall."

The typical situation here is that an employee (user) from your company works on a customer site and tries to connect to the concentrator at your company, using your VPN software client (typically). The user can browse the web and ping the corporate firewall, but it cannot connect to the concentrator. When the user hits connect on the VPN client, it cycles through all the back-up concentrators and times out. The client initiates the ISAKMP key exchange but the concentrator cannot reach the client to accept it, and the client receives the error "Remote peer no longer responding."

Typically, most companies block the ports and protocols that VPN requires. In some cases, the firewall might need to allow the IP address of the concentrator that you are connecting to, but that depends on the type of firewall. The ports required to be open on a firewall to support VPN are as follows and are discussed in this section:

- ESP 50
- UDP 500 ISAKMP
- UDP 10,000 (Allow IPSec Through NAT)

In addition, the following issues are discussed:

- Tunnel keepalives
- Dead Peer Detection

Protocol 50—ESP

All IKE 3.x clients require that ESP protocol 50 be enabled on the corporate firewall if encryption is specified in the group's transform, and all 2.x clients require it if encryption is specified in the VPN Group. Macintosh 3.x and 2.x clients also require ESP 50. For a more detailed explanation of ESP and ISAKMP and how they work, see Chapter 19, "VPN Technology Background."

UDP 500—ISAKMP

All IKE clients and LAN-to-LAN IKE tunnels require UDP Port 500 and their respective protocol to establish a tunnel. IKE negotiation uses UDP on port 500. Ensure that your access lists are configured so that UDP port 500 traffic is not blocked at interfaces that are used by IKE and IPSec. In some cases, you might need to add a statement to your access lists to explicitly permit UDP port 500 traffic. If UDP port 500 is being blocked by your firewall, you are unable to establish a VPN tunnel.

UDP 10,000 (Allow IPSec Through NAT)

Unlike the other two ports, this port number is configurable on the VPN concentrator. You have the choice of using a number between 4001 and 49,151; the default is 10,000. See Figure 22-11 to determine where to modify the port number.

Figure 22-11   *The NAT Port Number Configured on the Concentrator*

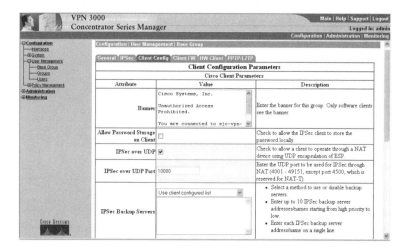

NOTE   In version 3.5x of the VPN client, IPSec can be encapsulated in UDP or TCP packets, which enables secure tunneling through both NAT and Port Address Translation (PAT) devices and firewalls. This feature enables the VPN client to operate in an environment where the standard ESP, Protocol 50 or IKE, UDP 500 cannot normally function, or can only function with modification to the existing firewall configuration. This provides a significant benefit to users who want to VPN from within an external network. This feature does not work with proxy-based firewalls.

Tunnel Keepalives

In some cases, the VPN tunnel can drop when going through a firewall because the port on an ESP-aware NAT/Firewall closes after short periods of inactivity. To reduce the chance of the tunnel dropping, you can modify the .pcf file for that connection. Use a text editor to open the .pcf file for the connection entry that you are using; the .pcf files are located under C:\Program Files\Cisco Systems\VPN Client\Profiles. Then set the **ForceKeepAlives=1**. By turning on the ForceKeepAlive, you direct the VPN client to send IKE and ESP keepalives for a connection at approximately 20-second intervals. This significantly reduces the risk of a firewall closing a port because of inactivity.

Dead Peer Detection

The Cisco VPN client supports the ability to dynamically connect to multiple gateways and uses IKE keepalives or Dead Peer Detection (DPD) to determine tunnel status. The introduction of PIX OS 6.x supports the version of keepalives used by the Cisco VPN client. The same method is used for immediate multiple peer failover with the PIX, as is used for the VPN 3000 series concentrators.

The DPD protocol is the successor to the Keepalive protocol. These protocols systematically test the remote end of a VPN tunnel and notify their host when messages can no longer be passed. DPDs are passed every 30 seconds, and the concentrator drops the connection if it does not receive a reply within five minutes.

From the concentrator log, VPN administrators can see the DPD exchange with the VPN client (see Example 22-9). Both the client and the concentrator agree to use DPD.

Example 22-9   *Concentrator Capture of the DPD Exchange and a DPD Disconnect*

```
30     17:08:51.400  01/25/2002  Sev=Info/5     IKE/0x43000001
Peer supports DPD

<Output Omitted>
83     17:09:13.752  01/25/2002  Sev=Info/6     IKE/0x4300003D
Sending DPD request to 10.3.3.3, seq# = 2948297981


84     17:09:13.752  01/25/2002  Sev=Info/4     IKE/0x43000013
SENDING >>> ISAKMP OAK INFO *(HASH, NOTIFY:DPD_REQUEST) to 10.3.3.3


85     17:09:13.758  01/25/2002  Sev=Info/5     IKE/0x4300002F
Received ISAKMP packet: peer = 10.3.3.3


86     17:09:13.758  01/25/2002  Sev=Info/4     IKE/0x43000014
RECEIVING <<< ISAKMP OAK INFO *(HASH, NOTIFY:DPD_ACK) from 10.3.3.3
<Output Omitted>
584 02/26/2002 17:03:02.300 SEV=4 IKE/123 RPT=35497 10.3.3.3
IKE lost contact with remote peer, deleting connection (keepalive type: DPD)
! Based on DPD keepalives, after 5 minutes of no response from the client,
! the concentrator drops the connection.
<Output Omitted>
```

Extranet issues can vary, depending on software functionality. In the VPN client version 3.5x, there are additional encapsulation options for UDP or TCP, specifically for NAT-based connections (see Figure 21-5). This functionality can reduce firewall-related issues that users experience when trying to connect from an external network, such as a customer's premises. Using the following ports are preferred because these ports are usually open in a company's firewalls: TCP port 80 (http), TCP port 22 (ssh), or TCP port 443 (https).

Extranet issues can vary depending on the software functionality. In the VPN Client version 3.5x, additional encapsulation options exist for UDP or TCP, specifically for NAT-based connections (see Figure 22-12). This functionality can reduce firewall-related issues that users experience when trying to connect from an external network, such as a customer's premises. Using the following ports are preferred because they are usually open in a company's firewalls: TCP port 80 (http), TCP port 22 (ssh), or TCP port 443 (https).

Figure 22-12 *TCP Encapsulation in a NAT Mode for Cisco VPN Software Client*

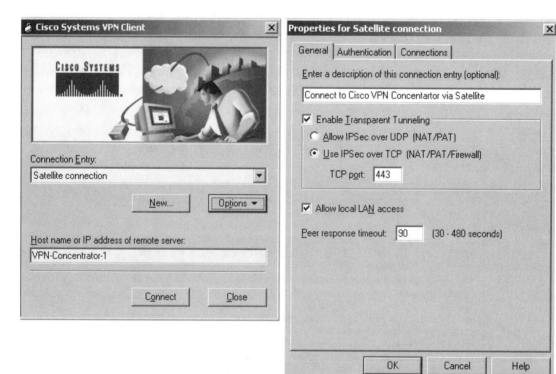

Summary

The provided scenarios reflect about 90 percent of the problems you face with Cisco's RA VPN solutions. This chapter is based on real world examples; everything you just read has been used in real situations. The chapter covers the following:

- **VPN 3000 software client**—Several scenarios and cases on troubleshooting VPN client problems.

- **MTU**—How crucial the MTU is in regards to VPN and several methods to lower it.

- **Software firewalls**—Troubleshooting problems with the VPN client and some of the better-known software firewalls in the market, such as ZoneAlarm.

- **DNE**—What DNE is and its function with VPN.

- **PPPoE**—What PPPoE is and how to get VPN to work several of the commonly used PPPoE clients.

- **VPN 3002 Hardware client**—How to troubleshoot some of the larger problems.

As previously stated, this part does not include solutions that are not specifically for enterprise remote access use. This part does not include any recently announced solutions or expected standards because they are not implemented, and consequently, there is no available information for possible troubleshooting issues. The information provided in Part V, "VPN" reflects troubleshooting practices for remote access VPN solutions that are currently in production at the time of writing this book.

Answers to Review Questions

This appendix contains the answers to the review questions at the end of each chapter (except for the scenarios chapters). Some questions might have multiple correct answers. In those cases, the best answer is supplied here with an explanation. The questions are repeated here for your convenience.

Chapter 1

1 Why are remote access networks considered the most difficult type of network to support?

   Many of the components of the remote user's location are not under an enterprise's control.

2 What are the main categories that the management should consider when making remote access service decisions?

   Cost, availability, support, in-source versus out-source, and billing.

3 Give an example for narrowband, baseband, and broadband services.

   Narrowband and baseband are synonyms and refer to legacy POTS and non-video-capable systems. Cable modems are typical broadband systems.

4 Explain what MMDS and LMDS stand for.

   Multichannel Multipoint Distribution System (MMDS) and Local Multipoint Distribution Service (LMDS) are wireless broadband technologies for Internet access.

5 Name two benefits of dial-in modem technology for remote access.

   Backward compatibility and high availability for minimum cost.

6 Name two limitations of dial-in modem technology for remote access.

   Dial-in modem technology has reached its theoretical maximum and has a low speed.

7 Name two benefits of ISDN for remote access.

The technology is defined as a viable alternative when the end user requires more bandwidth than dial-in. Also, it has a variety of data and voice services.

8 Name two limitations of ISDN technology for remote access.

Interface compatibility limitations and cost.

9 Name two benefits of Frame Relay for remote access.

Provides peak bandwidth availability and lower response time.

10 Name two limitations of Frame Relay technology for remote access.

The cost and when run over T1 circuits it inherits the limitations of T1s for repeaters in every mile.

11 Name two benefits of VPN for remote access.

The expected cost reduction and unprecedented mobility.

12 Name two benefits of cable modems for remote access.

Enormous bandwidth that can be shared between many users. Cable modems that are based on coax cable eliminate most traditional copper-based network problems.

13 Name two benefits of xDSL for remote access.

It offers great data rates and a variety of services.

14 Name two limitations of wireless and satellite for remote access.

High latency and security issues.

Chapter 2

1 What does Shannon's Law state?

Shannon's Law states that error-free transmission is possible as long as the transmitter does not exceed the channel's capacity.

2 What does the Nyquist sampling theorem state?

The Nyquist theorem states that digital sampling must take place at twice the highest frequency, to reconstruct the analog signal accurately.

3 What does DMT stand for? How many subchannels does the standard (ANSI) ADSL define?

DMT stands for Discrete Multitone. The standard (ANSI) ADSL system divides the frequency spectrum into 256 subchannels (subcarriers).

4   Why is CAP modulation sometimes called suppressed QAM?

Because, unlike QAM, CAP is not sending the carrier over the line.

5   What is the typical speed in the 802.11b standard? What coding techniques provide these speeds?

1 and 2 Mbps with 11-bit Barker code. 11 and 22 Mbps with Complementary Code Keying (CCK).

6   How wide is the high carrier in 802.11a; how many subchannels does it have, and how wide is each subchannel?

Each high-speed carrier is 20-MHz wide and is broken up into 52 subchannels, each approximately 300-kHz wide.

7   How does the 802.11g standard relate to 802.11a and 802.11b?

802.11g uses the same OFDM technology as 802.11a and operates in the same 2.4-GHz band as 802.11b.

8   What is the relation between the terms clocking, timing, and synchronization?

Clocking refers to both timing and synchronization.

9   What interface uses the pseudo-ternary coding technique? What is the size of the frame?

The S/T interface. The size is 48 bits.

10   What does 2B1Q stand for and which interface does it use? What is the size of the frame?

Two binary one quaternary (2B1Q) over the U-interface. The frame is 240 bits in length.

11   What is perfect scheduling in the physical layer?

Perfect scheduling is the interaction between the E-bit and D-bit of the frame of the S/T interface that provides a contention mechanism called perfect scheduling.

12   How do T1 circuits meet the ones density requirements?

By using zero-suppression schemes.

13   Explain how the 24 framing bits in ESF are broken down and how they are used.

Of the 24 framing bits in an ESF, 6 bits are used for synchronization, 6 bits for error checking, and the remaining 12 bits are used for a 4-kbps facility data link (FDL).

Chapter 3

1 Is Asynchronous Transfer Mode (ATM) a synchronous or asynchronous technique? Explain.

It is a synchronous technique. The word asynchronous in ATM is not associated with embedded start-stop techniques, but with sporadic presence of user data.

2 Name three of the advantages of digital signaling over analog signaling?

Better quality of service; simplified maintenance; synergy with digital switching.

3 What does FDM stand for? What rule does FDM obey?

FDM stands for frequency-division multiplexing and obeys the rule "some bandwidth all of the time."

4 In North America, how many voice channels are in a standard multiplexing scheme for FDM?

For North America, a standard voice multiplexing scheme is 12 voice channels, 4 kHz each, totaling a bandwidth from 60 to 108 kHz.

5 Describe the main phases of pulse code modulation (PCM).

Sampling, quantization, and coding. The first two functions are performed by a codec device, and the coding is performed by a DSU/CSU.

6 What does TDM stand for? What rule does the TDM obey?

TDM stands for time-division multiplexing and obeys the rule "all the bandwidth, some of the time."

7 What is the purpose of bit number 193 in TDM?

Bit number 193 is a framing bit; it is used for time synchronization.

8 What is a frame in TDM?

A frame is a sequence of time slots, each containing a sample from one of the channels.

9 What do DS1 and DS-1 stand for? What is the difference between DS1 and DS-1?

DS1 stands for digital service 1, which is a digital interface with a 1.544-Mbps data rate. DS-1 stands for digital signal level 1, which is a framing specification for transmitting digital signals at 1.544 Mbps on a T1 facility in the U.S.

10 What is out-of-band signaling? What is robbed bit signaling?

Out-of-band signaling uses frequencies outside of the normal frequency band for signaling; it is the core of SS7. In contrast, in-band signaling relies on using certain bits out of the frame format in the frequency band, which is why it is sometimes called robbed bit signaling (RBS).

11 What do CO, LEC, CLEC, and ILEC stand for? What do they have in common?

CO stands for central office, LEC is local exchange carrier, CLEC is competitive LEC and ILEC stands for incumbent LECs. All of them belong to the first tier of exchange carriers.

12 What is the role of tandem switches in carrier networks?

The secondary switch, called the tandem, provides a trunk-to-trunk switching for both LECs and IXCs.

13 What are the main caveats when the enterprise outsources service with the service provider?

They include the commitment of the other party and control of the information.

14 What are the three main topologies in Cisco's Ethernet to the First Mile (EFM)?

Ethernet over point-to-point copper; Gigabit Ethernet over point-to-point optical fiber; point-to-multipoint optical fiber topology.

15 What does CDMA stand for? Name the 3G minimum speed requirements, as defined by ITU.

CDMA stands for Code Division Multiple Access. 3G, 144 kbps mobile, 384 kbps walking, 2.4 Mbps stationary.

Chapter 4

1 What is the name of the layer above the network layer in the DoD model?

Host-to-host layer.

2 Name at least one keyword for each of Layer 2, Layer 3, and Layer 4 of the OSI model.

Layer 2: Frame; Layer 3: Packet; Layer 4: Segment.

3 What is the communication subsystem in the seven-layer OSI model?

The communication subsystem includes the first three layers of the model.

4 What is the baseline of the system?

The baseline is the expected behavior of the system.

5 Name at least five of the key concepts in the troubleshooting process.

Baseline, topology, gathering, tools, and solutions.

6 What are the complete and the shortest IOS commands to save the running configuration to the NVRAM?

The complete command is #copy running-config startup-config. The shortest command is #wr.

7 What are the complete and the shortest IOS commands to cancel all debugging in the router?

The complete command is #undebug all. The shortest command is #u all.

8 Why does the CDP use a multicast address?

Using a multicast address prevents routing because Cisco routers do not forward this traffic, unless specifically configured.

9 When troubleshooting the serial interface, you see HDLC protocol type 0x2000, what is it?

HDLC protocol type 0x2000 stands for CDP protocol.

10 Is it recommended that you disable the CDP over the dialer interface? If so, what is the command?

The extensive information from CDP output requires the CDP to be disabled in interfaces, which cannot be controlled or user-owned. The command is #no cdp enable.

11 What is the measurement of the spread when measuring the path characteristics with Pchar?

The standard deviation.

12 What does ICMP type 3 mean?

ICMP type 3 means Destination Unreachable.

13 What is the command to see the statistics when using Service Assurance Agent (SAA)?

#show rtr collection-statistics

Chapter 5

1 Name two added features in ITU-T V.92 standard, compared to ITU-T V.90.

Modem on Hold and Quick Connect.

2 Name two limiting factors for the ability of the modem to connect.

The distance from the central office and the signal-to-noise ratio.

3 If the SNR is 40, how many times higher is the signal strength than noise strength?

100.

4 How would you troubleshoot a case in which a pad of 3dB might be the root of the problem?

Make a long-distance call to the same number and see if the quality is better.

5 If AMI needs to transmit the octet 1 0 0 1 0 1 1 0, and the first mark is +, what are the next marks? Write the entire octet.

+00-0+-0.

6 If the preceding LSB in B8ZS is positive, what is the combination for 00000000?

000+-0-+.

7 What is the main disadvantage of dial-back authentication?

This type of authentication requires a fixed phone number, which cannot be used by travelers.

8 Name the main phases of the PPP protocol.

Link Dead, Link Establishment phase, Authentication phase, Network-Layer Protocol phase, Link Termination phase.

9 What is the value 0xC223 in the protocol field of PPP?

0xC223—Challenge Handshake Authentication Protocol (CHAP).

10 Which protocol in the PPP suite establishes and configures the data-link connection?

Link Control Protocol (LCP).

11 What is the address field value of the PPP protocol?

11111111.

12 Which packet types of LCP terminate the data-link connection?

05, Terminate request; and 06, terminate acknowledgement.

Chapter 6

1 List three ways for using dial as a backup solution.

Using a backup interface, using a floating static route, and using a dialer watch.

2 What is the main advantage of the dialer watch solution?

The router dials immediately when the primary route is lost. It does not depend on line protocol, encapsulation, or interesting traffic.

3 What is the line configuration command to configure a modem to use the modemcap usr_sportster?

```
Router(config-line)#modem autoconfigure type usr_sportster
```

4 What is the global configuration command to define a group named dial as a TACACS+ group?

```
Router(config)#aaa group server tacacs+ dial
```

5 What is the default protocol and port number of RADIUS authentication and accounting?

UDP 1645 and UDP 1646.

6 What is the line configuration command to automatically select the PPP protocol during text authentication?

```
Router(config-line)#autoselect ppp
```

7 What is NFAS and what is its function?

Non-Facility Associated Signaling (NFAS) allows a single D channel to control multiple PRI circuits.

8 What is the interface configuration command to ensure that voice calls are sent to a modem?

```
Router(config-if)#isdn incoming-voice modem
```

9 What is the purpose of the command **no exec**?

It prevents a person from obtaining a login prompt when they connect to a line on which it is configured.

10 What is the best way to test a backup solution?

Physically unplug the cable from the main interface.

11 How would you connect to a network access server to connect as a text dial-out device?

Telnet or Secure Shell (if enabled).

12 True or False: PC software is required to use a router to perform PPP dial-out.

False. PC software is only required to attach a network modem to a virtual communications port for dial-out.

13 What is the most scaleable way to use large-scale dial-out?

Store the client information and phone numbers on an AAA server.

14 What is the main purpose of a group-async interface?

It allows you to consolidate many async interfaces into a group for ease of configuration.

15 What does the interface command **group-range** do?

It specifies which lines are part of the group-async interface.

Chapter 7

1 What SQ value shows up in the output of **show modem operational-status**, indicating the most stable connection possible?

0.

2 True or False: Upgraded modem firmware does not have to be stored in flash after it is copied to the modem.

False. The router needs to access the version in flash at the next maintenance period or when the router is reloaded.

3 What is the controller configuration command required to correctly configure the distance of a circuit that is 639 feet?

```
Router(config-controller)#cablelength short 655
```

4 If you are receiving a blue alarm, what bit pattern is the equipment receiving?

All 1s.

5 What color is an alarm in which the controller status shows "Receiver has loss of Frame"?

Red Alarm.

6 What happens if one end of a T1 receives a yellow signal?

A Yellow Alarm is declared because of an incoming yellow signal from the far end. In effect, the circuit is declared to be a one-way link.

7 What information is negotiated in the IPCP stage of NCP of a modem dial call?

IP address, WINS address, and DNS address.

8   What modem AT command shows the connection information for a call that was previously disconnected?

ATI11.

9   What does BERT stand for?

Bit error rate tester.

10   What is the primary advantage that the AS5300 MICA modems have over the Microcom modems in the AS5200 series?

With out-of-band signaling, the router has access to real-time data while the modem is connected.

11   What does the call timer show?

The duration of the current active call in seconds.

12   What command on an AS 5200 and AS5300 shows a summary of all disconnect reasons and the number of disconnects for every reason?

#show modem call-stats.

13   What does CSM stand for and what is the command to show the processes of this device?

CSM stands for call switching module. The #debug modem csm command starts call switch module debugging.

Chapter 9

1   What is the scope of the I.431 and I.432 standards?

I.431 defines the Primary Rate Interface, and I.432 defines the Basic Rate Interface.

2   Where does the name D channel come from? What are the operational speeds of the D channel for BRI and PRI?

The name D channel comes from Delta. It operates at 16 kbps for BRI and 64 kbps for PRI.

3   What is a V-reference point in ISDN?

A V-reference point defines the interface in a Local Exchange (LE) between the Local Termination (LT) and Exchange Termination (ET).

4   What are the important pins in a S/T interface?

3, 4, 5, and 6.

5 What is the modulation of the ISDN U-interface?

The U-Interface uses frequency-division multiplexing and echo cancellation.

6 What is the bit rate of the S/T interface and U-interface?

S/T interface—192 kbps; U-interface—160 kbps.

7 How many INFO messages participate in the BRI's Layer 1 initialization? What does INFO0 mean?

INFO0 to INFO4; INFO0 means "no signal."

8 Which bit in the ISDN frame indicates line activation?

The A bit set to 1 indicates the activation of the line.

9 What makes up DLCI in ISDN? What is the length of DLCI, TE, and SAPI?

TEI and SAPI in the LAPD protocol represent the 13-bit data-link connection identifier (DLCI). TEI is 7 bits; SAPI is 6 bits.

10 What are the two indicators that Layer 2 is active?

Receiving a UA message with SAPI = 0 or TEI = *xxx*, where *xxx* is not 0 or 127.

11 What does TE = 127 mean?

TEI = 127 is a broadcast.

12 What is the dynamic range of TEI?

TEI ranges from 64–126.

13 What does SAPI = 0 indicate?

Call control procedure.

14 How do you distinguish an incoming from an outgoing call?

Check the reference flag in the Q.931 message. A message of 0 is sent by the call originator, and 1 means that the message was sent by the other party.

15 Which ISDN protocol provides information about Bearer capability. Name three basic types of Bearer capabilities.

Bearer capability is part of the format of the ISDN Q.931 protocol, which provides information for the type of the call—56-kbps data, 64-kbps data, or 56-kbps voice.

Chapter 10

1 Name the most common ISDN switch types in the U.S. and Canada.

basic-5ess, basic-dms100, basic-ni1.

2 Type a command that sets up the switch-type NI1 for a Cisco IOS Software ISDN router in global configuration mode.

Router(config)#isdn switch-type basic-ni

3 Type a command to define a local pool of 63 IP addresses for your core router, starting with 20.18.15.1, if the pool name is LOCAL_POOL.

router(config)#ip local pool LOCAL_POOL 20.18.15.1 20.18.15.62

4 What is the theoretical maximum number of ports in PAT?

The total number of these ports is theoretically 2^{16} = 65,536.

5 How much memory consumes one NAT translation?

Each NAT translation consumes about 160 bytes of memory.

6 Name at least five protocols that are supported by Cisco IOS Software NAT.

HTTP, TFTP, Telnet, Archie, Finger, NTP, and NFS.

7 In the case of the virtual interfaces, what happens with the route when the connection is tear-down?

In the case of the virtual interfaces, because of his dynamic nature, the route is gone as soon as the connection is gone.

8 Name three main functions of multilink systems.

Multilink systems must do the following: receive PDUs of a negotiated size; combine multiple physical links into one logical link (bundle); receive and reassemble upper-layer protocol data units (PDUs).

9 Why would you use multilink PPP between a remote office and corporate headquarters?

To increase bandwidth and reduce network latency.

10 On which interface types can you use multilink PPP?

On any interface that supports DDR rotary groups and PPP, including ISDN, synchronous, and asynchronous lines.

11 What does the MRRU stand for and at which stage of the PPP protocol is it used?

MRRU stands for Maximum Received Reconstructed Unit (MRRU). It is used during LCP negotiation to indicate to its peer that it is willing to be included in the multilink bundle.

12 What is the purpose of using the endpoint discriminator (ED) option in MP?

The ED option determines which bundle to add the link to, and its primary use is to generate uniqueness in identifying MP bundles.

13 What Cisco IOS Software command displays the status of the stack group members?

The show sgbp command displays the status of the stack group members.

14 Name the five possible states of the peer in the stack-group.

The five possible states for a peer in the stack-group are the following: IDLE, CONNECTING, WAIT_INFO, AUTHOK, and ACTIVE.

Chapter 11

1 Type a command to determine if the spoofing is enabled in dialer interface in Cisco IOS ISDN router.

Router#show interfaces dialer 1

I should see on the very first line of the output: Dialer1 is up (spoofing), line protocol is up (spoofing).

2 Define the active period in snapshot routing. Is it configurable? What is its duration?

The active period is a time slot when the routing protocols updates can be sent over the interface. It is configurable and can be between 5 and 100 minutes.

3 In a snapshot routing configuration, use an IOS command to ensure termination of a quiet period within two minutes.

Router#clear snapshot quiet-time interface

4 What are the main elements of the dialer profiles in DDR?

The main elements of dialer profiles include dialer interfaces, dialer pools, physical interfaces and dialer map class (optional).

5 Use an IOS command to map the IP address 161.3.2.1 with the destination phone number 773-5555.

Router(config-if)#dialer map ip 161.3.2.1 name gateway broadcast 7735555

6 Define the Dialer1 as a member of pool number 3 with the highest priority.

Router(config-if)#dialer pool-member 3 priority 255

7 Create an ACL to deny tcp traffic on port 8008. Type the appropriate IOS command.

Router(config)#access-list 101 deny tcp any any eq 8008

8 Configure the user's IOS router for callback with 200 packets in the queue and 20 seconds drop time. Explain.

The correct configuration is

Router(config-if)#dialer hold-queue 200 timeout 20

under the dialer interface. The dialer hold-queue 200 timeout 20 specifies that up to 100 packets can be held in a queue until the core router returns the call. If the core router does not return the call within 20 seconds plus the length of the enable timeout on the central site router, the packets are dropped.

9 In a callback configuration, type the IOS command, specifying that the core router interface will wait five seconds after disconnecting the initial call before making the return call.

Router(config-if)#dialer enable-timeout 5

10 Type the IOS command to bring the second B channel up after the inbound traffic exceeds 20 percent.

804-isdn (config-if)#dialer load-threshold 51 inbound

11 What "conditional" priority means in voice features configuration of ISDN?

Conditional means that voice call bumps data call only if the user has two data connections in the same direction; otherwise, the calling party receives a busy signal.

12 If the user's router has two data calls in progress and it is configured with Router(config)#**pots dialing-method enblock,** what should you expect when making a voice call to any of his LDNs?

Initially expect to hear a dial tone, then a busy signal, if the voice priority is not set up to "Always."

Chapter 12

1 What is the command to see the status of the D channel of the IOS-based ISDN router? In which mode of the IOS router can you type the command?

The command is show interfaces bri 0. The command is available for both privileged and user modes.

2 If you want to see what IP address has triggered the last call in Cisco 77x router, what command should you type?

The command is

```
Router>show packet
```

3 What do you look for in the output of the IOS command Router#**sh isdn status** to be sure if the physical layer in BRI is functional?

Look for Layer 1 Status: ACTIVE. Any other message shows physical layer issues.

4 What IOS command enables you to distinguish between internal and external ISDN issues?

The IOS command is Router#debug bri. If the router is sending requests for establishment of the activation bit and the response is not coming back, the possible issues are external. If there is no request from the router, concentrate your attention to it.

5 If you want to debug Layer 2 of ISDN, what is the first IOS command you have to type?

The command is

```
Router#debug isdn Q921
```

6 Under normal circumstances, what messages should you *not* see from the output of Router#**debug isdn q921**?

Under normal circumstances, you should not see SABME, IDREQ, and IDASSN messages. Otherwise, you have a clear indication that Layer 2 is trying to reinitialize.

7 What are you looking for in the output of the IOS command Router#**sh isdn status** to be sure if Layer 2 is functional?

First, TEIs = number, where the number has to be between 64 and 126. Second, SAPI has to be 0. Third, every line should have State = MULTIPLE_FRAME_ESTABLISHED.

8 In the output from the command Router#**debug isdn q921**, what does TX ->...ai = 127 mean?

ai = 127 means that the BRI is broadcasting and requesting TEI assignment from the ISDN switch.

9 If you want to debug Layer 3 of ISDN, what is the first IOS command you have to type?

The command is

```
Router#debug isdn q931
```

10 What is the bearer capability in Q931 messages for 64 kbps data, 56 kbps data, and voice calls?

8890 for 64 kbps data call. 0x8890218F means it is a 56-kbps data call. 0x8090A2 means it is a voice call.

11 What is the name of the message indicating that the LCP negotiation is successful?

Incoming message CONFACK.

12 What is the recommended IOS command to troubleshoot the dialer traffic when the router makes outgoing data calls?

The command is

```
Router#debug dialer packets
```

13 How many lines of PPP CHAP negotiation indicating success can you see in the output of #**debug ppp authentication**?

Two lines if the CHAP negotiation is two ways: one for incoming and one for outgoing. If it is one-way CHAP negotiation, there's only one incoming line.

14 If you receive config nack during the PPP authentication negotiation, what does it mean?

It means that one side is configured for PAP, but the other is configured for CHAP authentication.

15 When testing the voice features, what are the two recommended IOS commands you can use?

The commands are

```
Router#debug pots csm
Router#debug pots driver
```

Chapter 14

1 Does Frame Relay perform flow control over the frames?

No, Frame Relay drops frames on congestion.

2 Name the FRF implementation agreement that governs data compression over Frame Relay.

FRF.9.

3 Define the main components of the full LAPF protocol.

The full LAPF protocol includes core LAPF and control LAPF.

4 Name the components of the Frame Relay format.

Beginning and ending Flag field, Address field, Information (Data) field, and FCS field.

5 What is the maximum frame size that FCS can provide error detection for?

The FCS code provides error detection for frames up to 4096 bytes in length.

6   What is the zero-insertion procedure and why is it necessary?

Zero-insertion is looking for non-flag data pattern 011111. It inserts a zero to distinguish between flags and data.

7   How many DLCI Address field formats are available?

The default Address field format is 2 bytes or 10 bits. The extended address frame format can be 3 bytes (16 or 17 bits) or 4 bytes (23 bits).

8   What does the DE bit stand for and who can set it?

Discard eligible (DE) indicates the importance of the packet. It can be set by the user and by the network.

9   Name the LMI numbers for Consortium and AnnexD specifications.

Consortium uses DLCI = 1023 for LMI. AnnexD uses DLCI = 0 for LMI.

10 What is the main difference between the core format and control protocol format of LAPF?

The main difference between the core format and the control protocol format is the control field.

11 Name the four categories of signaling messages of the LAPF control protocol.

LMIs, T1.617 AnnexD messages, CLLM messages, and SVC messages.

12 What is the purpose of the Dummy Call Reference in the Q.931 header?

To indicate that the message is not a call establishment, disconnect, or status message.

Chapter 15

1   Define the term access rate (link speed).

The link speed determines how rapidly (maximum rate) the end user can inject data into a Frame Relay network.

2   What is the recommendation for setting the committed interval Tc in Frame Relay?

Tc should be set to four times the end-to-end transit delay.

3   Define the committed information rate (CIR).

CIR is the allowed amount of data that the network is committed to transfer under normal conditions.

4   Define the excess information rate (EIR).

EIR identifies the bits transmitted per second, over the time period of Tc, which are beyond the committed information rate.

5 Define the explicit congestion notification types.

Normal, mild, and severe congestion.

6 What is the area of operation of UNI in Frame Relay.

The UNI operation area is locally defined between the DTE/DCE peers.

7 Define the area of operation of NNI.

The NNI interface is concerned with the transfer of information between two network nodes that belong to two different Frame Relay networks.

8 Name the three Frame Relay multicast messages.

Addition, Deletion, Presence.

9 If *n* is the number of connected routers, define the number of physical connections in a full-mesh topology.

n × (n – 1) / 2.

10 Name the two main methods to control congestion in Frame Relay networks by using explicit notification.

Rate adoption algorithm and consolidated link-layer management (CLLM).

11 What is transit delay? How do you obtain a rough estimate of transit delay?

This term refers to the time to send a frame across the link between two points. The delay is a function of the access rate of the link, distance, and the size of the frame. A rough estimate can be obtained by the equation Delay = frame size / link access rate.

12 Name the four main specific and common specifications of LMI.

Virtual circuit status messages, multicasting messages, global addressing messages, and simple flow control.

13 Name the three LMI types that are supported by Cisco.

Cisco, ANSI, Q.933a.

14 Can InARP run without LMI?

No, because InARP LMI messages determine which PVC to map.

Chapter 16

1 What is dynamic mapping?

Using Inverse ARP to request the next hop protocol address for a specific DLCI.

2 For Router-frame, map the IP address 10.0.0.1 to DLCI = 100, using the IETF encapsulation.

```
Router-frame(config-if)#frame-relay map ip 10.0.1.1 100 broadcast ietf
```

3 Can you use IP unnumbered with Frame Relay?

You can, but you must use point-to-point subinterfaces and static routes or dynamic routing for your traffic to get routed.

4 Can you ping your own interface address? Can you ping one spoke router from another?

In point-to-point interfaces, you can. In point-to-multipoint interfaces, you cannot, unless you configure Frame Relay map.

5 What happens to deleted subinterfaces?

Deleted subinterfaces show up as deleted until the router is reloaded.

6 In point-to-point configurations that are running EIGRP, type the command for Router-frame that prevents all routing updates for interface Serial3/0:0.64?

```
Router-frame(config)#passive-interface Serial3/0:0.64
```

7 Configure the Frame Relay broadcast queue for Router-frame—subinterface S3/0:0.71 with queue size 100, byte rate 1200, and packet rate 120.

```
Router-frame(config-if)#frame-relay broadcast-queue 100 1200 120
```

8 Can you configure the Cisco router as a DCE?

You can, if you use the frame-relay intf-type [dce | nni] command in the general configuration mode.

9 Under the interface Serial3/0:0.200, what is the backup delay command with enable delay = 5 seconds and disable delay = 10 seconds?

```
Router-frame(config-if)#backup delay 5 10
```

10 For Router-frame and interface Serial1, what is the command for TCP header compression, which is active only for the destinations that are sending compressed headers?

```
Router-frame(config-if)#frame-relay ip tcp header-compression passive
```

11 For Router-frame and interface Serial4/2:0.200, define that FRF9 payload compression will be performed on CSA 3.

```
Router-frame(config-if)#frame-relay payload-compression FRF9 stac csa 3
```

12 Enable the multicast routing in Router-frame.

```
Router-frame(config)#ip multicast-routing
```

13 In Router-frame, for interface Serial4/2:0.100, define the upper limit of the rate for traffic shaping to 128000.

```
Router-frame(config-if)#traffic-shape rate 128000
```

14 What Frame Relay timer defines the Cisco autosense feature? How do you configure it?

N391. At every N391 interval, LMI autosenses the LMI type. The default is 6 attempts in 60 seconds. It is configurable with the command frame-relay lmi-n391dte *value.*

Chapter 17

1 What are the signals on the physical layer provided by DTE?

Data Terminal Ready (DTR) and Request To Send (RTS).

2 What are the two available options for 56-kbps configurations for Cisco routers?

56-kbps DSU/CSU and 56-kbps switched modes.

3 In the command **service-module 56k network-type dds**, what is DDS and what are the data rates provided by DDS?

DDS stands for Dataphone Digital Service and provides rates between 2.4 Kbps and 56 Kbps.

4 Serial 1 is configured with the command **service-module t1 timeslots 1-2**. What is the configured bandwidth on Serial 1?

$64 \times 2 = 128$ kbps.

5 Name the WIC T1 Pinouts (8 pin RJ48S).

1, 2, 4, and 5.

6 What is the command to loopback your equipment?

loopback dte

7 Name two checkpoints for a failing CSU.

Line or internal clocking and impedance mismatch.

8 In the **show frame-relay map** IOS command, if the DLCI is defined and active, what does this mean?

The message defined and active indicates that the DLCI can carry data and that the router at the far end is active.

9   What happens with the incoming DLCI in the switch?

The incoming DLCI number changes to match the far-end of the connection. Before sending the frame, the switch recalculates the new FCS and replaces this portion in the outgoing frame. It then sends the frame out.

10   How do you know if the DLCI is active but not configured in the router?

Type #show frame-relay pvc and check for an unused, active non-zero value.

11   Under what conditions does the properly configured LMI in a Cisco router not send packets over the DLCI?

When the PVC is listed as inactive or deleted.

12   Which LMI message reports the PVC status for each PVC configured on the interface?

The full status message.

13   What is the order of the Cisco LMI autosense full status enquiry message?

The order is ANSI, ITU, and Cisco.

14   How are "Num Status Enq. Sent," "Num Status msgs Rcvd," and "Num Status Timeouts" related in erroneous conditions?

In erroneous conditions "Num Status Enq. Sent" = "Num Status msgs Rcvd" + "Num Status Timeouts."

15   When debugging the serial interface, what does the message "illegal serial line type xxx" mean?

The message indicates that the encapsulation is Frame Relay or HDLC, and the router attempts to send a packet with an unknown packet type.

Chapter 19

1   Name the major VPN types of Cisco Enterprise VPN solutions?

The major Cisco Enterprise VPN solutions are Cisco remote access VPN, Cisco site-to-site VPN, and extranet VPN solutions.

2   What ports need to be open in the corporate firewall to ensure PPTP functionality?

TCP port 1723 and the GRE protocol ID 47.

3   What is the purpose of control messages in the L2TP protocol?

Control messages are used in the establishment, maintenance, and clearing of tunnels and calls.

 4 Define voluntary mode and compulsory mode in PPTP-based VPN.

When a remote user starts the tunnel, it is called voluntary mode. When the initiation of the tunnel is done by the NAS, it is often referred to as compulsory mode.

 5 What is the minimum set of negotiable attributes in IKE SA?

The minimum set of negotiable attributes are the encryption algorithm, hash algorithm, authentication method, and information about a group over which to perform the Diffie-Hellman key exchange.

 6 What does SPI stand for in IPSec?

SPI stands for security parameter index and is a 32-bit number assigned to the initiator of the SA request by the receiving IPSec endpoint.

 7 What are the valid authenticating methods in IPSec?

The valid authenticating methods in IPSec are preshared key, digital signature standard (DSS) signatures, RSA signatures, encryption with RSA, and revised encryption with RSA.

 8 What is the main difference between main mode and aggressive mode?

Aggressive mode is used when identity protection is not needed.

 9 What is the main difference between transport mode and tunnel mode in IPSec?

In transport mode, only the IP payload is encrypted and the original IP headers are left intact. In tunnel mode, the entire original IP datagram is encrypted and it becomes the payload in a new IP packet.

10 Define the unidirectional and bidirectional security associations (SA). What kind of SA is an IKE SA? An IPSec SA?

Unidirectional means that, for two-way communication between devices, there must be at least two SAs—one in each direction. The term bidirectional means that, once established, either party can initiate Quick Mode, Informational, and New Group Mode exchanges. IPSec SA is unidirectional; IKE SA is bidirectional.

11 What is ICV and how is it calculated?

ICV stands for Integrity Check Value (ICV). The computation of ICV is over IP header fields that are either immutable in transit or that are predictable in value upon arrival at the endpoint for the SA.

12 Which ports have to open in the company's firewall to ensure ISAKMP, ESP, and AH operation?

ISAKMP: UDP port 500; ESP: protocol 50; AH: protocol 51.

13 What is the advantage of XAUTH among other authentication methods? What is type 1 authentication in XAUTH?

XAUTH is designed in a way to provide a method to leverage legacy authentication methods that are widely deployed today with existing and future authentication mechanisms. Type 1 authentication in XAUTH is RADIUS-CHAP.

14 What is the size of the prime in DH Group 5?

1536 bits (600h).

15 What does PFS stand for? Explain PFS.

PFS stands for perfect forward secrecy (PFS). In PFS, a shared secret encryption key can be calculated that has no relationship to the preceding key.

Chapter 20

1 Why is the AH protocol considered less secure than ESP?

AH does not provide data confidentiality.

2 Which part of the ESP packet is not protected?

ESP does not protect the new IP header.

3 What is a one-to-many NAT or PAT?

A one-to-many NAT or PAT consists of one external address being mapped to many internal addresses.

4 What is split tunneling?

Split tunneling is a feature that allows clients to simultaneously send and receive data across a VPN tunnel, while also communicating directly with resources on the Internet.

5 Name the three main types of firewalls.

Packet filter, proxy, and stateful inspection firewalls.

6 Describe how to calculate the session load on the VPN concentrator.

The session load per concentrator is the total number of active connections divided by the maximum number of sessions configured on the concentrator.

7 What does VRRP stand for?

VRRP is Virtual Router Redundancy Protocol (VRRP), which is a standard proposed by IETF that provides IP routing redundancy. It is designed to provide transparent fail-over at the first hop IP router.

8 What is Reverse Route Injection?

Reverse Route Injection is when the concentrator is configured to advertise routes on the private interface by using OSPF or RIP.

9 What is the Group Lock configuration in a VPN concentrator?

Group Lock allows users to be authenticated only if they are members of a particular group.

10 Name the two mandatory settings on your VPN client.

Host name or IP address of remote server and authentication parameters.

11 Define the network extension mode for the VPN 3002 Client.

Network Extension mode is when the private interface is configured with an IP address that is routable in the network connected to the concentrator that is terminating the VPN tunnel.

12 For the Router-EzVPN, type the IOS command to start the XAUTH login sentence.

```
Router-EzVPN#crypto ipsec client ezvpn xauth
```

13 When typing the IOS command **show crypto ipsec client ezvpn**, how do you find out if IPSec is up and running?

Check for the line IPSEC_ACTIVE in the output.

14 In PIX 501, how do you check if you are running client mode, or network extension mode?

Type PIX#show vpnclient and look for a line that starts with vpnclient mode.

Chapter 21

1 What are the first three steps to check if the user never receives an Authenticating User prompt during the initial dialer connection attempt in the VPN software client?

Check if the Internet connection is okay, if the group name and group password are correct, and if the DNS service is resolving the name of the concentrator.

2 What is the CVPND event class and what is its purpose?

CVPND is Cisco VPN Daemon (main daemon), which starts client service and controls messaging process and flow.

3 Name the main severity categories in the Cisco VPN concentrator?

Fault, Warning, Information, Debug, and Packet decode.

4 In a 3002 HW VPN client, the user is authenticated but cannot pass any data. What are two possible reasons?

The correct client mode was not selected, either Network Extension or Client mode. If Network Extension mode is used, another client might have an overlapping subnet.

5 Which severity level events are displayed by default on the VPN HW 3002 client?

By default, the VPN 3002 displays all events of severity level 1 through 3 on the console.

6 How do you proceed if a NAT/PAT configuration already exists in the router and you are about to configure an easy VPN client?

Remove any manual NAT/PAT configuration on the router before configuring the easy VPN client.

7 What is the command for the Easy VPN client to reset the VPN connection?

The command is

```
Router-EzVPN#clear crypto ipsec client ezvpn
```

8 What is the command for Easy VPN to check the status of the Cisco Easy VPN client profile?

The command is

```
Router-EzVPN#show crypto ipsec profile
```

9 To verify the applied policy in Cisco Easy VPN, what command do you use?

The command is

```
Router-EzVPN#show crypto isakmp policy
```

10 In the PIX-based VPN client, how do you verify if the VPN client is active?

Type PIX#show vpnclient and look for the line vpnclient enable.

11 In the PIX-based VPN client, how do you check that the VPN tunnel has been established?

Type the command Router#show crypto isakmp sa, and look to see if the created entry has a non-zero value.

12 What are two debug commands to debug the PIX-based VPN establishment of IPSec and ISAKMP?

The commands are

```
Router#debug crypto ipsec sa
Router#debug crypto isakmp sa
```

13 What parameters define the PPPoE session uniquely?

The PPPoE session ID and the peer's Ethernet address.

14 Name the modulation techniques for the DOCSIS 2.0 standard.

The modulation techniques for DOCSIS 2.0 include S-CDMA (synchronous code division multiple access) and A-TDMA (advanced frequency agile time division multiple access).

15 If the TCP protocol is notified for packet loss, how does it react?

The packet loss for TCP is an indication of congestion. It reduces transmission rates drastically until an optimal rate is found.

INDEX

Numerics

108 Bert Test, 132

11-bit chipping, 50

22 second issue (ISDN), resolving, 387–396

2B+D, 238

2B1Q (two binary one quaternary) signaling, 55, 58–59

3G wireless, 91–92

56-kbps flex modems, 14

5ess switch types (ISDN), 259–260

5-GHz UNII band, 51–52

77x routers, accessing IOS routers, 366–367, 369

800 toll-free numbers, dialup, 13

802.11a specification, 51–52

802.11e specification, 53

802.11g specification, 52

804 routers, calling from 77x routers, 366–369

A

access servers, 13

activating Layer 2 in ISDN routers, 320–321

active periods (snapshot routing), 291

adaptive shaping, 487–488

ADCs (analog-to-digital converters), 39

Address field

    Frame Relay frames, 421–423

    LAPD frames, 244

    PPP frames, 134

addressing, Frame Relay

    ARP, 453

    Inverse ARP, 454

    RARP, 454

adjustable CIRs, 437

administratively down interfaces on Frame Relay new installs, troubleshooting, 548–549

ADSL (asymmetric DSL) , 24, 732

    PPoE, 733

        discovery stage, 735

        negotiations, 736–739

        session stage, 736

advanced Frame Relay configurations

    bridging, 474–476

    compression, 476–477

        payload compression, 480–481

        Van Jacobson header compression, 477–480

    frame switching, 469–470

    generic traffic shaping, 484–486

    IP multicast, 482–483

    IP unnumbered, 469

    ISDN backup, 471–473

    traffic shaping, 483–484

        ELMI, 487–488

        map classes, 486–487

AES (Advanced Encryption Standard), 618

aggregate CIR, 436–437

agile time division multiple access (A-TDMA), 742

AH (Authentication Header) format, 614

    ICV calculation, 615

alarms states of T1 circuits, 184, 186

alternate mark inversion. *See* AMI

AMI (alternate mark inversion), 61, 130

    ones density, 131

amplitude, 40

amplitude-shift keying (ASK), 40

analog dialup services, 12

    limitations of, 14

    VPNs, 13

analog modems, 126

    signal loss, 127

analog pads, echo removal, 129–130

analog-to-digital converters (ADCs), 39

Annex A LMI type, 453

Annex D LMI, 516–520

Annex D LMI type, 451

ANSI (American National Standards Institute) standards, Frame Relay, 415

ANSI T1.617 Annex D LMI, 516–520
application layer (OSI model), 99
Application Service Providers (ASPs), 85–86
applications, accessing remotely, 8
applying timestamps, 313–314
approaches to troubleshooting, models, 101–102
AR (access rate), Frame Relay, 434
architecture
    ISDN
        C-plane, 236
        Layer 1, 237–241
        Layer 2, 242–247
        Layer 3, 248–252
ARP (Address Resolution Protocol), 453
AS5x00 routers, 205–207
    AS5200 router commands, 207, 209
    AS5300 router commands, 209–214
    AS5400 router commands, 215
ASK (amplitude-shift keying), 40
ASPs (Application Service Providers), 85–86
asymmetrical CIR, 437
A-TDMA (agile time division multiple access), 742
authentication
    OTPs, 228
    PAP, 133
    PPP, 340, 396–398
    remote access VPN users, 637
    servers, 133
    timeouts (dialup), 219–221
    VPNs
        client authentication, 619
        DH algorithm, 624–627
        HMAC, 627–628
        key management, 624–627
        RADIUS, 621–623
        user/identity authentication, 620
Authentication phase (PPP), 136, 197
authenticator GINAs, 705
Auto-RP, 483
availability
    of remote access services, 7
    of phone services for ISDN, 309–310

B

B (Bearer) channels (ISDN), 234
    Layer 1, 237–241
        devices, 238
        interfaces, 239–241
    Layer 2, 242
        LAPD frame format, 242–247
        logical link establishment (LAPD),
          246–247
    Layer 3, 248
        Q.931, 248–252
    NFAS, out-of-order detection, 227
B8ZS (bipolar 8-zero substitution), 131–132
    backup interfaces, DDR configuration, 147
BACP (Bandwidth Allocation Control Protocol), 16
bandwidth
    of modems, 126
    on demand, ISDN BRI configuration, 376
Bandwidth Allocation Control Protocol (BACP), 16
bandwidth interval, Frame Relay, 434
Barker sequence, 50
baseline behavior
    network topology, discovering, 103–105
    performance, establishing, 105–109
basic-5ess switch types (ISDN), 259–260
    SPIDs, configuring, 260–262
BBFW (Broadband Fixed Wireless) P2MP
    solutions, 53
Bc (committed burst rate), 434
Be (excess burst rate), 434
bearer services, Frame Relay, 438
BECNs (backward explicit congestion
    notifications), 441–443, 536
    Frame Relay Address field bit, 421
BERTs (bit error rate testers), testing T1 circuits,
    183–184
bidirectional procedures, 439
billing expenses, 7
binary phase-shift keying (BPSK), 50
BISDN (Broadband ISDN), 235
bit errors, checking on T1 circuits, 183–184
bit-robbing signaling, 65

blue alarms, 185
Boosted Session Transport, 29, 750
BPSK (binary phase-shift keying), 50
BRI (Basic Rate Interface), 57, 237–241
    D channel, testing, 327
    developing troubleshooting process in remote
        services environments, 359
            accessing remote user's router, 365–369
            preconfiguring routers on both ends,
                364–365
        end-to-end communications, 386
            routing issues, resolving, 399
            troubleshooting LEC switch settings, 387
    initializing, 241
    keepalive mechanism, 323
    performance issues
        LEC switch problems, 382–386
        line problems, 377–382
        routing, 377
        settings, 382
    service layers, viewing, 360–363
    SPIDs, 253
bridging Frame Relay, 474, 476
broadband wireless services, 25
    limitations of, 27
    LMDS, 26–27
    MMDS, 25–26
    unlicensed frequencies, 27
broadcast queues, Frame Relay configuration, 468
BST (Boosted Session Transport), 29, 750
budgeting remote access costs, 6
bursty traffic, 414

C

C/R (Command/Response) bit, Frame Relay
    Address field, 421
cable modems, 740
    services, 20
        limitations of, 22
        standards, 21

cabling
    long versus short lengths, 183
    shorts, detecting, 223
calculating
    CIR, 435
    ISDN BRI load at full utilization, 376
    maximum DLCIs per interface, 467
    RER, 444
call clearing messages, 251
Call Reference field (Q.931 messages), 249
callback function, PPP, 344–347
    ISDN configuration, 303–305
called-party number verification, 306
caller ID screening, 306
calling IOS routers from IOS 77x routers, 366–369
CAP (carrierless amplitude/phase modulation), 44
Capacity Theorem, 38
captured Log Viewer results, viewing, 688–699
carrierless amplitude/phase modulation (CAP), 44
carriers, 69
    CO, 81
    first-tier exchange carriers, 80
    IXCs, 81
    switching systems, 70–71
    tandem office, 83
    T-carriers, 75
        E1, 77
        T1, 76–77
categories of ISDN network designs, 258–259
CATV (cable TV)
    cable modems, 20–22, 740
    data transmission, 740
        standards, 741–744
    heartbeats, 745
    two-way Internet connections, 744
Cause messages (ISDN BRI), 331–334
CCITT (Comité Consultatif International
    Téléphonique et Télégraphique), 12
CCP (Compression Control Protocol), 352
CCS (common channel signaling), 78
CDMA2000 1xEV, 91
CDP (Cisco Discovery Protocol), discovering
    network topology, 103

CDSL (consumer DSL), 24

cell switching, 70

CERT (Computer Emergency Response Team), 77

Challenge Handshake Authentication Protocol
(CHAP), 340

change management of remote access VPNs, 636

channel banks, 73

channels, ISDN, 234

CHAP (Challenge Handshake Authentication
Protocol), 340

charge backs, 7

Chinese Remainder Theorem, 625

CIR (committed information rate), 435

adjustable CIRs, 437

aggregate CIR, 436–437

asymmetrical CIR, 437

flexible CIR, 437

zero CIR, 436

circuit switching, 70

Cisco Discovery Protocol, 103

Cisco Easy VPN client, 713

client status, displaying, 716

debugging IPSec key events, 717–719

initial troubleshooting checklist, 714, 716

monitoring, 720–721

resetting connection, 717

restrictions, 713–714

Cisco IOS

77x routers, accessing ISDN routers, 366–369

commands, 102

ISDN

available phone services, 309–310

voice privacy, configuring, 308–309

NFAS groups, 393

Cisco Mobile Office initiative, 8–9

Cisco PIX VPN clients

501 VPN Client, configuring, 669–670

506 VPN Client, configuring, 669–671

connectivity, verifying, 722–732

restrictions, 722

Cisco UBR7200 Series routers, 21

Cisco UBR7246 Universal Broadband Router, 26

Cisco VPN 3000 Concentrator, IPSec over UDP, 639

Cisco VPN 3002 router

connection establishment, 795–796

verifying group name/password, 800

verifying interface status, 797–799

HW Client, 706

configuring, 665–666

Event Log, 708–712

initial troubleshooting checklist, 707

Cisco VPN IOS Client, configuring, 666–668

Cisco VPN Unity client, 663–664

Concentrator Event Log, 699–701

event classes, 702–704

event security levels, 704–705

Event Log Viewer, 685

Client Log Viewer, starting, 686

ISAKMP, 688

reviewing captured data, 688–699

incompatible GINAs, 705–706

restrictions, 676–679

troubleshooting checklist, 682–685

classifying

enterprise VPNs, 593–595

data link layer VPNs, 599–603

firewall-based VPNs, 597–598

network VPNs, 604–607

remote access VPNs, 595

site-to-site VPNs, 596

troubleshooting tools, 110

clear interface bri0 command, 318

CLECs (competitive LECs), 80, 732

client authentication, 619

Client mode configuration, Cisco VPN 3002
routers, 706

CLLM (consolidated link-layer management),
442–443

clocking issues, 55

Frame Relay

isolating, 499–500

troubleshooting, 493–498

SCTE, 499

CO (central office), 81

code values for LMIs, 520–521

codecs, 73

coded orthogonal FDM (COFDM), 52

coding schemes

    2B1Q, 55–59

    AMI, 61, 130

    B8ZS, 131–132

    COFDM, 52

    DSL, 41–42

    HDB3, 132

    pseudo-ternary signaling, 55–57

    WLANs, 48

    zero-suppression, 61–62

COFDM (coded orthogonal FDM), 52

Comité Consultatif International Téléphonique et Télégraphique (CCITT), 12

commands

    AS5200 series routers, 207–209

    AS5300 series routers, 209–214

    AS5400 series routers, 215

    clear interface bri0, 318

    debug bri, 316–317

    debug interface serial, 523–524

    debug isdn q931, 325, 328

    debug ppp negotiation, 220–221

    deub ppp authentication, 340

    extended ping, 111

    isdn autodetect, 262

    isdn timeout signaling, 318

    logging console, 548

    loopback, troubleshooting T1 circuits, 183

    mtrace, 578

    ping, 110–114

        replies, 112

        syntax, 110

    service timestamps, 313

    short format, 102

    show cdp neighbors, 103

    show controllers bri0, 316

    show dialer, 373–374

    show interface serial 0, 502–505

    show isdn active, 372

    show isdn status, 315, 320, 360–363

    show modem operational status, 224

    tracert, 114–115

committed burst rate (Bc), 434

committed interval (Tc), 434

comparing

    remote access and site-to-site VPNs, 633–634

    X.25 and Frame Relay features, 414–415

components of Frame Relay networks, 419

compression, Frame Relay, 476–477, 538, 540–543

    hardware compression, 537

    payload compression, 480–481

    software compression, 542–543

    Van Jacobson header compression, 477–480

Concentrator Event Log, 699–701

    event classes, 702–704

    event security levels, 704–705

configuration management of remote access VPNs, 635

configuration negotiation phase (LCP), 335–336

configuring

    DDR

        backup, 173–176

        with backup interfaces, 147

        with dialer watch, 148

        with floating static routes, 148

    dialer profiles, 297, 299–303

    dial-in

        large-scale, 160–164

        PPP dial-in, 151–159

        text dial-in, 150–151

    dial-out

        large-scale, 171–173

        PPP dial-out, 168–171

        text dial-out, 164–168

    Frame Relay

        bridging, 474–476

        broadcast queues, 468

        compression, 476–477

        frame switching, 469–470

        generic traffic shaping, 484–486

        IP multicast, 482–483

        IP unnumbered, 469

        ISDN backup, 471–473

        payload compression, 480–481

        point-to-multipoint connections, 458–461

point-to-point connections, 461–466
routing protocol overhead estimates,
    467–468
traffic shaping, 483–488
Van Jacobson header compression,
    477–480
ISDN
    BRI, bandwidth on demand, 376
    DDR, 294–303
    IP pools, 262–265
    MMP, 278–284
    NAT, 267–271
    PAT, 266–267
    per-user configuration, 272–273
    POTS interfaces, 306–308
    PPP callback, 303–305
    snapshot routing, 290–292
    SPIDs, 260–262
    spoofing, 290
    switch type, 259–260
    voice privacy, 308–309
PPP callback, 304–305
remote access VPNs
    Cisco PIX 501 VPN Client, 669–670
    Cisco PIX 506 VPN Client, 669, 671
    Cisco VPN 3002 HW Client, 665–666
    Cisco VPN IOSClient, 666–668
    Cisco VPN Unity Client, 663–664
VPN 3000 Concentrator, 648–649
    filters and rules, 650–651
    Group Lock, 662
    IKE peer identity validation, 662
    IKE proposals, 656, 658–659
    IPSec SAs, 661
    load balancing, 654–655
    redundancy, 653
    reverse route injection, 655
    SAs, 659–660
congestion control mechanisms, Frame Relay, 441
    BECNs, 536
    CLLM, 443
    FECNs, 535
    rate adoption algorithm, 442

windowing, 443
connection speeds
    increasing, 226
    limitations of, 128
    of modems, 126–127
connection termination phase (PPP), 352–353
connectionless data integrity, 608, 614
connectivity
    of Cisco PIX VPN client, verifying, 722–732
    testing, 110–117
console logging, 548
Consortium LMI, 513–515
    Status Enquiry message format, 514–515
    Status message format, 515
constellations, 40
contention resolution, 57
Control field
    LAPD frames, 244–245
    LAPF control protocol, 424–425
    PPP frames, 135
control LAPF, 419
Control plane. *See* C-plane
core aspects of Frame Relay, 413
core LAPF, 419
core routers, 257
    DLCI settings, verifying, 560–562
    Frame Relay point-to-multipoint configuration,
        458–460
    IP pool assignment, 262, 264–265
    NFAS groups, 393
    point-to-point Frame Relay configuration,
        462–465
corporate managed services, 8
cost-effective ISDN solutions
    DDR, 294–295
        dialer profiles, 296–303
    PPP callback, 303–305
    snapshot routing, 290–292
    spoofing, 290
costs of remote access, budgeting, 6
counter parameters for LMIs, 521, 523
CPE (customer premises equipment), 5
C-plane, 236, 417–418

creating
    dial peers, 307–308
    VPN client profiles, 772
CSU/DSU (channel service unit/data service unit)
    pinouts, 499
custom design ISDN switches, 260
customer premises equipment (CPE), 5

D

D (Delta) channel, 234
    Layer 1, 237–241
        devices, 238
        interfaces, 239–241
    Layer 2, 242
        LAPD frame format, 242–247
        logical link establishment, 246–247
    Layer 3, 248
        Q.931 message format, 248–252
    TDM, 393
    testing, 327
D/C (data/control) bit (Frame Relay Address
    field), 421
DACs (digital-to-analog converters), 39
DARPA (Defense Advanced Research Projects
    Agency), 97
data centers, 87–89
Data Encryption Standard, 617
Data field (LAPD frames), 246
Data field (PPP frames), 135
data link connection identifiers. *See* DLCIs
data link layer (OSI model), 98
    Frame Relay, 506
        LMI issues, 513–526
        misconfigured PVCs, 507–513
    ISDN BRI, 319–324
data link layer protocols, 599–601
    L2TP, 602–603
    PPTP, 600–601
    PPP, 134
        Authentication phase, 136, 396–398
        frame fields, 134–135
        LCP, troubleshooting, 387–396

Link Dead phase, 135
Link Establishment phase, 135–136
Link Termination phase, 137
Network Layer Protocol phase, 137
troubleshooting, 138
data transmission over CATV, standards, 740–744
dB (decibel), 128
DBS (Direct Broadband Satellite) systems, 28
    BST, 29, 750
    FITFEEL protocol, 751
    IPA, 28
    IPSec, 752–753
    LEO satellites, 30
    manipulating TCP stack, 749–750
    performance, 749
    VPNs, 745–746
        bandwidth, 747–748
        error control coding, 746
DDR (dial-on-demand routing), 294–295
    configuring, 173–176
        with backup interfaces, 147
        with dialer watch, 148
        with floating static routes, 148
    dialer profiles, 296
        configuring, 297–303
    Windows 2000, 399–408
DDS (Dataphone Digital Service), 495
DE (discard eligible) bit, Frame Relay Address field,
    421, 434
debug bri command, 316–317
debug information, timestamping, 313–314
debug interface serial command, 523–524
debug isdn q931 command, 325, 328
debug ppp authentication command, 340
debug ppp negotiation command, 220–221
debugging
    Cisco Easy VPN client connection, IPSec key
        events, 717–719
    Frame Relay LMI, 552
Defense Advanced Research Projects Agency
    (DARPA), 97
defining service levels, 9
delivered erroneous frames, 445
demand circuits (OSPF), 293

demodulation, 39

dense mode (PIM), Frame Relay multicast configuration, 482–483

design objectives of remote access VPNs, 634–635

designing

  enterprise services, 30–34

  Frame Relay network parameters, 434

    CIR, 435–437

  ISDN networks

    hub and spoke, 257

    IP pools, 262–265

    MLP, 273–277

    MMP, 278–285

    NAT, 267–271

    PAT, 266–267

    per-user configuration, 272–273

Destination Unreachable messages (ICMP), 113–114

detecting

  dirty phone lines, 223–224

  shorts in modem cables, 223

  source of frequent disconnections, 226

devices

  AS5200 routers, commands, 207, 209

  AS5300 routers, commands, 209–214

  AS5400 routers, commands, 215

  AS5x00 routers, 205–207

  cable modems, 740

  codecs, 73

  Frame Relay, 419

  ISDN, 238

    switch types, 252–253

  modems, 125

    56-k flex modems, 14

    analog, 126

    analog dialup services, 12–13

    bandwidth, 126

    cable modem services, 20

    connection speeds, 126–127

    digital, 126

    malfunctioning, 225

    PCM, 13

    Shannon's Capacity Theorem, 12

repeaters, 126

DH (Diffie-Hellman) algorithm, 624–627

DHCP (Dynamic Host Configuration Protocol) servers, verifying reachability, 227

dial peers, creating, 307–308

dial-back authentication, 134

dialer maps, 294

dialer profiles, 294–296

  configuring, 297–303

dialer watch, DDR configuration, 148

dial-in

  large-scale dial-in, configuring, 160–164

  PPP dial-in

    configuring, 151–159

    network design, 143–144

  text dial-in

    configuring, 150–151

    network design, 143

  troubleshooting procedure

    verifying incoming connection type, 192–194

    verifying modem operability, 191–192

    verifying PPP negotiation, 194–200

dial-on demand backup routing, configuring

  with backup interfaces, 147

  with dialer watch, 148

  with floating static routes, 148

dial-out

  ISDN, 372–374, 376

  large-scalet, 146

    configuring, 171–173

  PPP dial-out

    configuring, 168–171

    network design, 145

  text dial-out

    configuring, 164–168

    network design, 144

  troubleshooting procedure, 200–205

dial up

  800 toll-free numbers, 13

  analog, 12–14

  authentication

    PAP, 133

servers, 133
time outs, 219–221
disconnections, isolating source of, 221–223
Frame Relay, 17
benefits of, 18
limitations of, 18
standards, 17–18
ISDN, 14
benefits of, 15–16
limitations of, 16
PPP, 134
Authentication phase, 136
frame fields, 134–135
Link Dead phase, 135
Link Establishment phase, 135–136
Link Termination phase, 137
Network Layer Protocol phase, 137
troubleshooting, 138
retrains, 221–223
diffused-beam WLANs, 45
digital modems, 126
digital pads, echo cancellation, 129–130
digital sampling, Nyquist's sampling theorem, 39
digital transmissions, clocking, 55
digitalization of voice, 73
digital-to-analog converters (DACs), 39
Direct Broadband Satellite. *See* DBS systems
direct-beam WLANs, 45
direct sequence spread spectrum (DSSS), 49
dirty phone lines, as source of slow line speeds, 223–224
discard eligible (DE), 434
disconnections, troubleshooting, 221–223
Discrete Multi-Tone. *See* DMT
displaying
Cisco Easy VPN client status, 716
ISDN BRI service layers, 360–363
distance vector routing protocols, size estimation, 467

DLCIs (data link connection identifiers), 421
channel assignments, 422–423
CIR, 435
aggregate CIR, 436–437
asymmetrical CIR, 437
flexible CIR, 437
zero CIR, 436
mismatched settings, troubleshooting, 556–562
per interface limitations, 466–467
DMT (Discrete Multi-Tone), 42–44
CAP, 44
SF structure, 43
DOCSIS (Data-Over-Cable Service Interface Specifications), 741–744
satellite communications, 54
DoD (Department of Defense) interconnection model, 97
down interfaces, troubleshooting Frame Relay new installs, 548–552
DPD (Dead Peer Detection), 803–804
dropped calls (ISDN), resolving 22 second issue, 387–396
DS0, 77
DSL (digital subscriber line)
coding schemes, 41–42
PPoE, 733
discovery stage, 735
negotiations, 736–737, 739
session stage, 736
xDSL services, 22
ADSL, 24
CDSL, 24
FDIs, 22–23
HDSL, 24
IDSL, 24
RADSL, 24
SDSL, 24
TDRs, 23
VDSL, 25
DSLAMs (digital subscriber line access multiplexers), 733
DSSS (direct sequence spread spectrum), 49

E

E1, 77

EA (extended address) bit (Frame Relay Address field), 421

echo, removing, 129–130

Effective Isotropic Radiated Power (EIRP), 50

EFM (Ethernet to the First Mile), 596

ELMI (Enhanced Local Management Interface), 567
    Foresight adaptive shaping, 487–488

enabling ForceKeepAlive, 787

encapsulation
    DDR backup solutions, 148
    over Frame Relay, 447

encoding schemes
    2B1Q, 55, 58–59
    AMI, 61
    COFDM, 52
    zero-suppression, 61–62

encryption
    AES, 618
    DES, 617
    remote access VPNs, 638

endpoint migration, Frame Relay, 584–585

end-to-end communications
    Frame Relay, 528–533
    ISDN BRI, 386
        22 second issue, 387–396
        LEC switch settings, 387
        PPP authentication, 396–398
        routing issues, 399

end-user routers (ISDN), 257
    configuring, 262

enterprise ISDN networks, 258–259

enterprise remote access services, provisioning, 30–34
    Frame Relay, 31–33
    ISDN, 31, 33
    xDSL, 33–34

enterprise VPNs, 593–594
    categories of, 595
    data link layer, 599–601

L2TP, 602–603
PPTP, 600–601
firewall-based, 597–598
network layer layer, 604
    Layer 3 tunneling, 605
    SAs, 605–607
remote access, 595
site-to-site, 596

errors on T1 circuits, 187

E-Series protocols, 14, 233

ESF (Extended Super Frame) signal format, 63

ESP header format, 616–618

establishing baseline behavior
    network topology, 103–105
    performance characteristics, 105–109

estimating transit delay, 444

ET (Exchange Termination), 238

Ethernet to the First Mile (EFM), 596

Event Log, Cisco VPN 3002 HW client, 708–712

excess burst rate (Be), 434

expenses, billing, 7

extended bus architecture (ISDN), 237

extended ping command, 111

F

far end, 96

far-end crosstalk (FEXT), 23

fast busy signals, debugging, 226

fast-dial, 15

Fast Information Transfer For Extremely Errored Links (FITFEEL) protocol, 751

FCS (frame check sequence) field
    Frame Relay frames, 420
    LAPD frames, 246
    PPP frames, 135

FDIs (Feeder Distribution Interfaces), 22

FDM (frequency-division multiplexing), 71–72, 414
    DMT, 42

FECNs (forward explicit congestion notifications), 421, 441–443, 535

Feeder Distribution Interfaces (FDIs), 22
Fermat/Euler Theorem, 625
FEXT (far-end crosstalk), 23
FHSS (frequency hopping spread spectrum), 48
fiber-optic networks, SONET, 80
fields
    of ICV, 608–610
    of LAPD frames
        Address field, 244
        Control field, 244–245
        Data field, 246
        FCS field, 246
        Flag field, 243
    of PPP frames, 134–135
filter GINAs, 705
firewall-based VPNs, 597–598
firewalls, implementing in remote access VPNs,
    640–641
first-tier exchange carriers, 80
FITFEEL (Fast Information Transfer For Extremely
    Errored Links) protocol, 751
Flag field
    Frame Relay frames, 420
    LAPD frames, 243
    PPP frames, 134
flapping lines, 562–566
flapping links, 526–528
flapping routes, 572
floating static routes, DDR configuration, 148
ForceKeepAlive, enabling, 787
Foresight adaptive shaping ELMI, 487–488
fragmentation process, 610
    Frame Relay, 448
Frame Relay, 17
    addressing
        ARP, 453
        Inverse ARP, 454
        RARP, 454
    ANSI standards, 415
    benefits of, 18
    bidrectional procedures, 439
    bridging, 474, 476
    broadcast queues, 468

CIR, 435
    aggregate CIR, 436–437
    asymmetrical CIR, 437
    flexible CIR, 437
    zero CIR, 436
compression, 538, 540–543
    configuring, 476–477
    hardware compression, 537
    software compression, 542–543
congestion control mechanisms, 441
    CLLM, 443
    rate adoption algorithm, 442
    windowing, 443
core aspects, 413
C-plane, 417–418
CSU/DSU pinouts, 499
data link layer troubleshooting, 506
    LMI issues, 513–526
    misconfigured PVCs, 507–513
design parameters, 434
DLCIs
    mismatched settings, troubleshooting,
        556–562
    per interface limitations, 466–467
ELMI, 487–488
end-to-end connectivity, 528–533
flapping lines, 563–566
flapping links, 526–528
frame switching configuration, 469–470
full-mesh topology, 441
generic traffic shaping, 484–486
host migration, 580–585
IAs, 415–416
initial troubleshooting steps, 492–493
IP multicast, 440
    checking IGMP group members, 576–577
    checking upstream neighbor availability,
        574–576
    configuring, 471–473
    group flags, 573
    multicast trace reporting, 577–580
    testing remote user's router, 577

IP unnumbered configuration, 469
ISDN backup configuration, 471–473
LAPF
    control protocol, 424
        Control field, 424–425
        Information field, 426–429
    logical frame processing, 422
    T1.618 frame format, 419–423
limitations of, 18
LMIs, 449
    Annex D, 451
    Cisco-Consortium, 451
    code values, 520–521
    counter parameters, 521, 523
    ITU-T Q.933 Annex A, 453
    timers, 522
multiplexing, 414
network components, 419
new install issues, 548–556
NNI, 439
partial-mesh topology, 441
payload compression, configuring, 480–481
performance parameters, 562
    RER, 444
    throughput, 444
    transit delay, 444
physical layer
    clocking problems, 493–498
    DSU/CSU, testing, 501
    loopback testing, 500
    performance issues, 501–505
point-to-point connections
    configuring, 461
    hub configuration, 462, 464
    spoke configuration, 465–466
provisioning enterprise remote access services, 31–33
pseudo-ternary signaling, 55–57
QoS parameters, 445
remote user router, verifying status, 553
serial interface configuration, verifying, 551
service architecture, VCs, 418
service functioning, checking, 553–555

standards, 17–18
traffic shaping, 483–484, 534
    BECNs, 536
    FECNs, 535
    flapping routes, investigating, 572
    high RTT numbers, investigating, 567–569
    map classes, 486–487
    slow performance, investigating, 569–572
    verifying settings, 566
UNI, 438
upper-layer protocol interoperability, 445
    encapsulation, 447
    fragmentation, 448
    multiprotocol support, 445–447
Van Jacobson header compression. configuring, 477–480
variable length framing, 415
VCs, 415
versus X.25, 414–415
VoFR, 440
framing techniques
    ESF, 63
    T1, 62
        ESF signal format, 63
        SF signal format, 62–63
    T3, M23 signal format, 63–64
frequency, 40
frequency-division multiplexing. *See* FDM
frequency-shift keying (FSK), 40
frequent disconnections, detecting source of, 226
FRF (Frame Relay Forum) IAs, 415–416
FSK (frequency shift-keying), 40
full-mesh topology, Frame Relay, 441
funding remote access, 6

G

Gang of Four, 449
generic traffic shaping, 484–486

geographic requirements for remote access
  deployment, 7
GINA, 705
global dialer software, 13
group flags, 573
Group Lock parameter, configuring on VPN 3000
  Concentrators, 662
group members, 573
GSM/GPRS (Global System of Mobility/General
  Packet Radio Service), 91

H

H (Hybrid) channel, ISDN, 234
hardware compression, 537
hardware simulators, 110
Hash-based Message Authentication Code (HMAC),
  627–628
HDB3 (high density binary 3), 132
HDSL (high-data rate DSL), 24
heartbeats, 745
helpdesks, supporting remote access users, 7
HFC (hybrid fiber-coaxial) networks, 20
HMAC (Hash-based Message Authentication Code),
  627–628
host migration, Frame Relay, 580–585
Host Page Accelerator (HPA), 28
hosting services, 87–89
HPA (Host Page Accelerator), 28
hub and spoke network design, 142
    ISDN, 257
hub configuration
    Frame Relay point-to-multipoint configuration,
      458–460
    point-to-point Frame Relay connections, 462,
      464–465
hybrid systems, 20
    line-coding techniques, 53–54
    modulation, 53–54

I

IAs (Implementation Agreements), 415–416
ICMP (Internet Control Message Protocol), message
  types, 112–113
    Destination Unreachable, 113–114
IDBs (interface descriptor blocks), 273
IDSL, 24
IE (information element) fields, LAPF control
  protocol, 426–429
IEEE 802.11a specification, 51–52
IEEE 802.11e specification, 53
IEEE 802.11g specification, 52
IGMP (Internet Group Message Protocol)
    group members, verifying on Frame Relay
      networks, 576–577
IKE (Internet Key Exchange)
    key management, 624–627
    peer identity validation, configuring on VPN
      3000 Concentrators, 662
    proposals, configuring on VPN 3000
      Concentrators, 656–659
    remote access VPN authentication, 638
ILECs (incumbent LECs), 80, 732
illegal serial line type xx messages, 524
immutable ICV fields, 608–610
incompatible GINAs, 705–706
increasing slow connection speeds, 226
Information Elements field (Q.931 messages),
  251–252
Information field
    Frame Relay frames, 420
    LAPF control frames, 426–429
information transfer messages, 245
initial troubleshooting steps, Frame Relay, 492–493
in-sourcing remote access support, 7
installation issues, Frame Relay, 548–556
interconnection models
    DoD, 97
    OSI, 98–100
interfaces, 469
    Frame Relay, broadcast queues, 468
    ISDN, 239–241

internal standard PCI modems, 21
International Telecommunication Union
    Telecommunication Standardization Sector.
        See ITU-T
Internet hosting services, 87–89
Internet Page Accelerator (IPA), 28
interoperability of Frame Relay and upper-layer
    protocols, 445
        encapsulation, 447
        fragmentation, 448
        multiprotocol support, 445–447
Inverse ARP (Address Resolution Protocol), 454
IOS-based troubleshooting methods, 102
IP addressing, ISDN configuration
        NAT, 267–271
        PAT, 266–267
IP datagrams, fragmentation, 610
IP multicast
        Frame Relay networks, 482–483
                multicast trace reporting, 577–580
                remote user's router, testing, 577
                verifying IGMP group members, 576–577
                verifying upstream PIM neighbor
                    availability, 574–576
        group flags, 573
IP pools, defining, 262, 264–265
IP unnumbered Frame Relay configuration, 469
IPA (Internet Page Accelerator), 28
ipconfig command (Windows NT/2000), verifying
    IP addressing configuration, 769–770
IPSec
        AH, 614–615
        authenticating remote access VPNs, 638
        connectionless data integrity, 608
        ESP header, 616–618
        ICMP processing, 611–612
        ICV calculation, 615
        ICV fields, 608–610
        IP fragmentation, 610
        modes, 612
        over satellite systems, 752–753
        over TCP, 640
        PMTU discovery, 610–611

        SAs, configuring on VPN 3000 Concentrators,
            661
        selecting mode for remote access VPNs, 637
IR (infrared) radio-channel, 45
ISAKMP (Internet Security Association and Key
    Management Protocol), 688
ISDN (Integrated Services Digital Network), 14
        accessing routers from IOS 77x routers,
            366–369
        B channel, 234
        benefits of, 15–16
        channels, 234
        C-plane, 236
        custom design switches, 260
        D channel, 234
                TDM, 393
        data link layer, activation procedure, 320–321
        DDR, 294–295
                dialer profiles, 296–303
        design solutions
                NAT, 267–271
                PAT, 266–267
        dial-out, 372–374, 376
        H channel, 234
        hub and spoke design, 257
        IP pools, configuring, 262, 264–265
        Layer 1, 237–238, 241
                devices, 238
                interfaces, 239–241
        Layer 2, 242
                LAPD frame format, 242–247
                logical link establishment, 246–247
        Layer 3, 248
                Q.931 messages, 248–252
        limitations of, 16
        load interval, 376
        local loop, 234
        MLP, 273–277
        MMP, 278, 280
                configuring, 281–282
                sample implementation, 282–284
                verifying, 284–285

network design, categories of, 258–259

new install issues, 369, 371

NISDN, 235

per-user configuration, 272

    virtual interface templates, 272

    virtual profiles, 273

POTS interfaces, configuring, 306–308

PPP

    callback, 303–305

    LCP, 387–396

PRI

    1.544-Mbps interface, 64–65

    2.048-Mbps interface, 65

PRI circuits, 188

    Layer 1 status, verifying, 188

    Layer 2 status, verifying, 188–190

provisioning enterprise remote access services, 31–33

pseudo-ternary signaling, 55–57

security, 305

snapshot routing, 290–292

SPIDs, 253

spoofing, 290

supplementary phone services, 309–310

switch types, 252–253, 259–260

voice privacy, configuring, 308–309

isdn autodetect command, 262

ISDN BRI

    bandwidth on demand, configuring, 376

    developing troubleshooting process in remote services environment, 359

        accessing remote user's router, 365–369

        preconfiguring routers on both ends, 364–365

        viewing service layers, 360–363

    end-to-end communications, 386

        resolving routing issues, 399

        troubleshooting LEC switch settings, 387

    keepalive mechanism, 323

    performance issues

        LEC switch problems, 382–386

        lines, 377–382

        routing, 377

        settings, 382

isdn timeout-signaling command, 318

I-series protocols, 234

isolating Frame Relay clocking problems, 499–500

ISPs, 85–86

    ISDN networks, 258–259

ITFS (Instructional Television Fixed Service), 25

ITU-T (International Telecommunication Union Telecommunication Standardization Sector), 12

    E-series protocols, 233

    I-series protocols, 234

    Frame Relay standards, 415

    Q.933 Annex A, 453

    Q-series protocols, 234

IXCs, 81

J-L

keepalive mechanism

    ISDN BRI, 323

    spoofing, 290

key management, 624–627

L2TP (Layer 2 Tunneling Protocol0, 602–603

LAN-specific VPN issues

    inability to log in, 760

    MTU settings, 754–756, 758

    NAT, multiple client handling, 753

    packet size, 758, 760

LAN-to-LAN VPNs, 596

LAPD (Link Access Procedure on the D channel), 242, 248

    Address field, 244

    Control field, 244–245

    Data field, 246

    FCS field, 246

    Flag field, 243

    frame format, 242–247

    logical link establishment, 246–247

LAPF

    control protocol, 424

        Control field, 424–425

        Information field, 426–429

T1.618 frame format, 419
  Address field, 421–423
  fields, 420
  Flag field, 420
  logical frame processing, 422
large-scale dial-in, configuring, 160–164
large-scale dial-out
  configuring, 171–173
  network design, 146
last mile, 90–91
LATAs (local access and transport areas), 80
layer 1/2 status of PRI circuits, verifying, 188–190
Layer 3 tunneling, 605
layered architecture
  DoD model, 97
  ISDN
    BRI, 237–241
    C-plane, 236
    LAPD, 242–244, 246–248
    Q.931, 248–249, 251–252
  OSI Reference Model, 98–100
layered approach to troubleshooting, 96
LCP (link control protocol) phase of PPP, 194–196
  configuration negotiation phase, 335–336
  magic numbers, 339
  troubleshooting, 335–339
LDN (local directory number), 308
LDNs (Local Directory Numbers), 252
LE (Local Exchange), 238
LEC (local exchange carrier) switch problems,
  ISDN
    end-to-end communications, 387
    performance issues, 382–386
legacy DDR, 294–295
limitations
  of analog dialup services, 14
  of analog modem connection speeds, 128
  of cable modems services, 22
  of Cisco Easy VPN client, 713–714
  of Cisco PIX VPN client, 722
  of Cisco Unity client, 676–679
  of ISDN services, 16
  of wireless broadband services, 27

line coding techniques
  B8ZS, 131–132
  errors, 130
  HDB3, 132
  in hybrid networks, 53–54
  in wireless LANs, 44–45
line problems
  Frame Relay, investigating, 493–498
  ISDN performance issues, 377–382
line provision, verifying, 354
linecode violations of T1 circuits, 186
link compression, 477
Link Dead phase (PPP), 135
Link Establishment phase (PPP), 135–136, 335–339
link speeds, 434
Link Termination phase (PPP), 137
link-state protocols
  OSPF, demand circuits, 293
  size estimation, 467–468
listen option (Netcat utility), 117
LMDS (Local Multipoint Distribution Service),
  25–27
LMIs (Local Manaagement Interfaces), 449
  ANSI T1.617 Annex D, 516, 518–520
  Annex D, 451
  Cisco-Consortium, 451
  code values, 520–521
  Consortium LMI, 513–515
    Status Enquiry message format, 514–515
    Status message format, 515
  counter parameters, 521, 523
  debugging, 552
  ITU-T Q.933 Annex A, 453
  timers, 522
load balancing, configuring on VPN 3000
  Concentrators, 654–655
load interval, 376
local loop, 234
Local Multipoint Distribution Service, 25–27
log files, timestamping, 313–314
logging console command, 548
logical frame processing, LAPF, 422
logical link establishment (LAPD), 246–247

long cable lengths, 183

loopback command, troubleshooting T1
   circuits, 183

loopback testing, Frame Relay, 500
     magic numbers, 339

lost frames, 445

LT (Local Termination), 238

LTI (linear time-invariant) systems, 47

M

magic numbers, 339

malfunctioning modems, detecting, 225

managing Frame Relay host migration, 580–585
     endpoint migration, 583–585
     host preparation, 581–583
     routing options, 583

mandatory user participation, troubleshooting ring
   options, 354–355

map classes, defining, 486–487

marking malfunctioning modems, 225

MDF (main distribution frame), 81

message switching, 70

Message Type field (Q.931 messages), 249–250

messages
     CLLM, 442
     ICMP, 112–113
        Destination Unreachable, 113–114
     illegal serial line type xxx, 524
     ISDN BRI Cause Messages, 331–332, 334
     SABME, 322

M-frames, 63

Microsoft Windows 2000, DDR troubleshooting
   procedures, 399–408

migration strategies, Frame Relay, 580–585
     endpoint migration, 583–585
     host preparation, 581–583
     routing options, 583

minimum acceptable throughput, 435

misconfigured PVCs, troubleshooting, 507–513

misdelivered frames, 445

mismatched DLCI settings, investigating, 556–562

MLP (multilink PPP), 273–277, 343–344

MMDS (Multichannel Multipoint Distribution
   System), 25–26, 53

MMP (Multichassis Multilink PPP), 278–280,
   347–351
     configuring, 281–282
     sample implementation, 282–284
     verifying configuration, 284–285

mobile solutions, 8–9

modems, 125
     56-kbps flex, 14
     analog, 126
        signal loss, 127
     analog dialup services, 12–13
        limitations of, 14
        VPNs, 13
     authentication timeouts, 219–221
     bandwidth, 126
     cable modem services, 20
        limitations of, 22
        standards, 21
     cables
        dirty phone lines as source of slow
           connection speeds, 223–224
        shorts, detecting, 223
     connection speeds, 126–127
        increasing, 226
        limitations of, 128
     digital, 126
     disconnections, 221–223
     fast busy signals, debugging, 226
     internal standard PCI modems, 21
     malfunctioning, 225
     PCM, 13
     Shannon's Capacity Theorem, 12, 38
     slow busy signals, debugging, 227

modes of IPSec operation, 612

modulation, 39
     in hybrid networks, 53–54
     in wireless LANs, 44–45
     WLANs
        DSSS, 49
        FHSS, 48

modulator-demodulators. *See* modems
monitoring
    Cisco Easy VPN client environment, 720–721
    network performance, SAA, 117–119
M-plane (ISDN), 236
MPLS VPN, 90
MPOE (minimum point of entry), 129
mtrace command, 578
multicast
    Frame Relay, 440, 482–483
    group flags, 573
Multichannel Multipoint Distribution System.
    See MMDS
multiple frequency operation (UHF), 47
multiplexing, 414
    FDM, 71–72, 414
    statistical multiplexing, 414
    TDM, 74, 414
mutable ICV fields, 608–610

N

nailed-up, 81
NAPs (network access points), 86
narrowband, 46
narrowband ISDN (NISDN), 235
NASs (Network Access Servers)
    dial-in, 191–200
    dial-out, 200–205
    T1 circuits, 181–187
NAT (Network Address Translation)
    implementing in remote access VPNs, 639–640
    ISDN configuration, 267–271
    multiple client handling, 753
NBMA (nonbroadcast multi-access) model
    point-to-point Frame Relay, 461
NCPs (network control protocols), 197–200,
    341–352
    CCP, 352
    MLP, 343–344
    MMP, 347–351

near end, 96
near-end crosstalk (NEXT), 23
negotiating upper-layer protocols, NCPs, 341–352
    CCP, 352
    MLP, 344
    MMP, 347–351
Netcat utility, 115–117
network design
    DDR, configuring
        with backup interfaces, 147
        with dialer watch, 148
        with floating static routes, 148
    dial-in
        PPP dial-in, 143–144
        text dial-in, 143
    dial-out
        large-scale, 146
        PPP dial-out, 145
        text dial-out, 144
    hub and spoke, 142
    ISDN
        categories of, 258–259
        configuring switch type, 259–260
        hub and spoke, 257
        MLP, 273–277
        MMP, 278, 280–285
        per-user configuration, 272–273
        SPIDs, configuring, 260–262
Network Extension mode, Cisco 3002 HW
    client, 706
network layer (OSI model), 98
    troubleshooting ISDN BRI, 324–334
    VPNs, 604
        Layer 3 tunneling, 605
        SAs, 605–607
Network Layer Protocol phase (PPP), 137
network monitoring tools, 109
new install issues
    ISDN, 369–371
    Frame Relay, 548–556
NEXT (near-end crosstalk), 23
NFAS (Non-Facility-Associated Signaling), 16

D channel, verifying correct circuit locations, 227

groups, 393

NI (National ISDN) standards, 233

NNI (network node interface), 439

Non-Facility-Associated Signaling. *See* NFAS

NT1 (network termination type 1), 58, 238

NT2 (network termination type 2) devices, 238

N-way multicast service, Frame Relay, 440

Nyquist sampling theorem, 72

Nyquist's Theorem, 39

O

off net dial-out, 146

ones density, 131, 499

one-way service, Frame Relay multicast, 440

on-net dial-out, 145

operating systems, Windows 2000

DDR issues, resolving, 399–408

well-known ports, 403–405

operations management of remote access VPNs, 636

optical networks, SONET, 80

OSI model, 98–100

data link layer

correlated Frame Relay protocol functions, 419–420

troubleshooting ISDN BRI, 319–324

network layer, 324–334

physical layer, 314–319

OSPF (Open Shortest Path First) demand circuits, 293

OTPs (one-time passwords), 228

outgoing calls, ISDN, 372–376

out-of-band signaling, 78

outsourcing remote acces support, 7

overload. *See* PAT

oversubscription, 436

P

packet switching, 70

PAP (Password Authentication Protocol), 133

partial-mesh topologies, Frame Relay, 441

passive bus point-to-multipoint architecture (ISDN), 237

passwords

authentication, PPP, 340

OTPs, 228

PAT (Port Address Translation)

in remote access environments, 639–640

ISDN configuration, 266–267

PathChar utility. *See* Pchar

pathcode violations of T1 circuits, 186

payload compression, 477

configuring, 480–481

Pchar

establishing baseline performance, 105–109

options, 105–106

PCM (pulse code modulation), 13, 39, 73

PDUs (protocol data units), 99

per interface limitations of DLCIs, 466–467

perfect scheduling, 57

performance

discovering baseline behavior, 105–109

Frame Relay, physical layer, 501–505, 562

compression, 537–543

end-to-end connectivity, 528–533

flapping lines, 563–566

flapping links, 526–528

RER, 444

throughput, 444

traffic shaping, 534–536, 566–572

transit delay, 444

monitoring with SAA, 117–119

selection criteria for VPN termination equipment, 646–648

per-interface compression, 477

periodic retransmissions, packets sent from W2K systems, 401

permanent virtual circuits. *See* PVCs

per-virtual circuit compression, 477
PFS (perfect forward secrecy), 627
phase modulations, 40
phase-shift keying, 40
photonic WLANs, 45
physical layer
    Frame Relay
        clocking problems, 493–498
        CSU/DSU, testing, 501
        loopback testing, 500
        performance issues, 501–505
    ISDN BRI, 314–319
    T1 circuits
        alarm states, 184, 186
        checking bit errors, 183–184
        errors, 187
        identifying loopback features, 183
        linecode violations, 186
        pathcode violations, 186
        slip seconds, 186
        verifying controller status, 181–183
PIM SM (Protocol Independent Multicast Sparse
    Mode), Frame Relay multicast configuration,
    482–483
ping command, 110–114
PMTU (Path MTU) discovery, 610–612
point-to-multipoint Frame Relay
    hub side configuration, 458, 460
    spoke side configuration, 460–461
point-to-point Frame Relay configuration
    hub configuration, 462, 464
    NBMA model, 461
    spoke configuration, 465–466
ports, 403
POTS (plain old telephone service) interfaces, ISDN
    configuration, 306–308
PPPoE, 733
    discovery stage, 735
    negotiations, 736–739
    session stage, 736
PPP (Point-to-Point Protocol), 134. *See also* MLP
    authentication
        servers, 133

        timeouts, troubleshooting, 220–221
        troubleshooting, 340
    Authentication phase, 136, 396–398
    callback, 303–305, 344–347
    connection termination, 352–353
    dial-in network design, 143–144, 151–159
    dial-out
        configuring, 168–171
        network design, 145
    frame fields, 134–135
    LCP, 335–339
        22 second issue, 387–396
    Link Dead phase, 135
    Link Establishment phase, 135–136
    Link Termination phase, 137
    NCPs, 341–352
    negotiation
        authentication phase, 197
        LCP phase, 194–196
        NCP phase, 197–200
    Network Layer Protocol phase, 137
    protocol field, 335
    troubleshooting, 138
PPTP (Point-to-Point Tunneling Protocol), 600–601
Predictor data compression, 477
premature disconnect, 445
presentation layer (OSI model), 99
PRI (Primary Rate Interface) circuits, 188
    1.544-Mbps interface, 64–65
    2.048-Mbps interface, 65
    Layer 1 status, verifying, 188
    Layer 2 status, verifying, 188–190
profiles (VPN client), creating, 772
projecting PPP link to call master, 278
protected band (RF), 46
Protocol Discriminator field (Q.931 messages), 248
Protocol field (PPP frames), 135, 335
protocol layer (Frame Relay), 506
    LMI issues, 513–526
    misconfigured PVCs, 507–513
    new installs, 549–552
provisioning process, enterprise remote access
    services, 30–31, 33–34

Frame Relay, 31–33
ISDN, 31, 33, 369
xDSL, 33–34
pseudo-ternary signaling, 55, 57
PSK (phase-shift keying), 40
PSTN (Public Switched Telephone Network), 37
pulse code modulation. *See* PCM
pulse density, 131
PVCs (permanent virtual circuits), 17, 418
    DLCIs, per interface limitations, 466–467
    end-to-end connectivity, 528–533
    flapping lines, 563–566
    misconfiguration issues, 507–513
    premature disconnect, 445

Q

Q.921, 242. *See also* LAPD
    LAPD frame format, 242–247
        Address field, 244
        Control field, 244–245
        Data field, 246
        FCS field, 246
        Flag field, 243
    logical link establishment, 246–247
Q.922 protocol, 424
    Control field, 424–425
    Information field, 426–429
Q.931 message format, 248, 331–332, 334
    Call Reference field, 249
    Information Elements field, 251–252
    Message Type field, 249–250
    Protocol Discriminator field, 248
QoS (quality of service) parameters, Frame Relay, 445
QPSK (quaternary phase-shift keying), 44
Q-series protocols, 234
quiet periods (snapshot routing), 291

R

RA to MPLS VPN (Remote Access to Multiprotocol Label Switching Virtual Private Network), 90, 592–593
RADIUS, 621–623
RARP (Reverse Address Resolution Protocol), 454
rate adoption algorithm, 442
RBS (robbed bit signaling), 78
red alarms, 185
redundancy
    configuring on VPN 3000 Concentrators, 653
    ISDN backup for Frame Relay, configuring, 471–473
reimbursements, 7
remote access VPNs, 595
    change management, 636
    Cisco PIX 501 VPN Client, configuring, 669–670
    Cisco PIX 506 VPN Client, configuring, 669–671
    Cisco VPN 3002 HW Client, configuring, 665–666
    Cisco VPN IOS Client, configuring, 666–668
    Cisco VPN Unity Client, configuring, 663–664
    configuration management, 635
    design objectives, 634–635
    operations management, 636
    security issues, 636
        firewalls, 640–641
        IPSec, 637–638
        NAT/PAT, 639–640
        split tunneling, 640
        user authentication infrastructure, 637
    termination equipment, 641–642
        performance criteria, 646–648
        selecting core devices, 643–646
    versus site-to-site, 633–634
remote control software, 109
Remote Page Accelerator, 28
remote users of Frame Relay, troubleshooting nonpassing traffic in up, up state, 555–556

removing echo with digital pads, 129–130

repeaters, 126

RER (residual error rate), 444

resetting Cisco Easy VPN client connections, 717

restrictions

of Cisco Easy VPN client, 713–714

of Cisco PIX VPN client, 722

of Cisco Unity client, 676–679

retrains, 221–223

reverse route injection, configuring on VPN 3000 Concentrators, 655

RF (radio frequency), 44

narrowband, 46

SS RF transmissions, 48

DHSS, 49

FHSS, 48

Rijndael algorithm, 618

ring options, troubleshooting mandatory user participation, 354–355

router commands

AS5200, 207, 209

AS5300, 209–214

AS5400, 215

routing ISDN BRI, 399

performance issues, 377

routing protocols, discovering network topology information, 104–105

RPA (Remote Page Accelerator), 28

RPC (remote procedure call), 402–403

RTT (round-trip time), 745

verifying Frame Relay service, 567–569

S

SAA (Service Assurance Agent), 117–119

SABME (Set Asynchronous Balanced Mode Extended) messages, 190, 322

sampling, Nyquist's sampling theorem, 39

SAPI (service access point identifier) data types, 189

SAs (security associations), 605–607

configuring on VPN 3000 Concentrators, 659–660

satellite systems, 28

BST protocol, 29, 750

DOCSIS 1.1 standard, 54

FITFEEL protocol, 751

IPA, 28

IPSec, 752–753

LEO satellites, 30

manipulating TCP stack, 749–750

performance, 749

VPNs, 745–746

bandwidth, 747

error control coding, 746

TCP efficiency, 747–748

S-CDMA (synchronous code division multiple access), 742

SCTE (serial clock transmit external) timing, 499

SDSL (single-line DSL), 24

security

authentication

DH algorithm, 624–627

HMAC, 627–628

key management, 624–627

OTPs, 228

PAP, 133

RADIUS, 621–623

resolving issues, 396–398

servers, 133

timeouts, 219–221

VPN client authentication, 619

VPN user/identity authentication, 620

IPSec

AH header format, 614–615

connectionless data integrity, 608

ESP header format, 616–618

ICMP processing, 611–612

ICV calculation, 615

ICV fields, 608–610

IP fragmentation, 610

modes, 612

PMTU discovery, 610–611

ISDN, 305
policies, 8
remote access VPNs, 636
    encryption, 638
    firewalls, 640–641
    IPSec authentication, 638
    IPSec mode, selecting, 637
    NAT/PAT, 639–640
    split tunneling, 640
    user authentication infrastructure, 637
selecting
    CIR
        aggregate CIR, 436–437
        asymmetrical CIR, 437
        flexible CIR, 437
        zero CIR, 436
    compression type for Frame Relay, 538
    core devices in remote access VPNs, 643–646
    IPSec mode for remote access VPNs, 637
    VPN model, 19
serial interfaces
    debugging, 552
    SCTE timing, 499
service architecture (Frame Relay), C-plane,
    417–418
Service Assurance Agent, 117–119
service levels, defining, 7–9
service providers
    future of, 89
    last mile, 90–91
    options, 9
    service offering, 90
service timestamps command, 313
service-provider dependant VPNs, 19
service-provider independent VPNs, 19
services
    Frame Relay, 17
        benefits of, 18
        limitations of, 18
        standards, 17–18
    ISDN, 14
        benefits of, 15–16
        limitations of, 16

technology offerings, 10–11
user- versus corporate-managed, 8
VPNs, 18–19
    cable modem services, 22
    cable modems, 20
    limitations of, 19
    satellite services, 28–30
    standards, 21
    wireless broadband services, 25–27
    xDSL services, 22–25
    Windows 2000, RPC, 402–403
session layer (OSI model), 99
SF (Super Frame), 43
SGBP (Stack Group Bidding Protocol), 278
    queries, debugging, 351
Shannon, Claude, 12
Shannon's Capacity Theorem, 38
shared secrets, PFS, 627
short cable lengths, 183
short command format (Cisco IOS), 102
show cdp neighbors command, 103
show controllers bri0 command, 316
show dialer command, 373–374
show interface serial 0 command, 502–505
show isdn active command, 372
show isdn status command, 315, 320, 360–363
show modem operational status command, 224
signaling (ISDN), D channel, 234
signals
    amplitude, 40
    analog, 37
    frequency, 40
site-to-site VPNs, 596
    versus remote access VPNs, 633–634
size estimates
    of distance vector routing protocols, 467
    of link-state routing protocols, 467–468
sliding windows, 443
slip seconds on T1 circuits, 186
slow busy signals, debugging, 227
slow connection speeds
    increasing, 226
    sources of, 223–224

snapshot routing, 290, 292

sniffing W2K traffic, 402–403

SNR (signal-to-noise ratio), affecting factors, 128–129

soft skills versus technical skills, 95

software
    global dialer, 13
    compression, 542–543

SONET (Synchronous Optical Network), 80

sparse mode (PIM), Frame Relay multicast configuration, 482–483

specifying loopback format of T1 circuits, 183

SPID (service profile identifier), 253, 308
    configuring, 260–262

split tunneling, implementing in remote access VPNs, 640

spoke configuration
    Frame Relay point-to-multipoint connection, 460–461
    point-to-point Frame Relay connections, 465–466

spoofing, 290

SS (spread spectrum) RF transmissions
    DSSS, 49
    FHSS, 48

SS7 (Signaling System 7), 78–79

STAC data compression, 477

Stack Group Bidding Protocol. *See* SGBP

standards
    CATV data transmission, 741–744
    Frame Relay, 415
        IAs, 415–416
            service architecture planes, 417–418

starting Cisco VPN Client Log Viewer, 686

Static RP, 483

statistical multiplexing, 414, 437

Status Enquiry message format, Consortium LMIs, 514–515

Status message format, Consortium LMIs, 515

STS (Station-to-Station protocol), 626

STS-1, 80

subchannels, 42

supervisory messages, 245

supporting remote access services, 7
    defining service levels, 9
    in-sourcing versus outsourcing, 7

SVCs (switched virtual circuits), 17, 418

switched virtual circuits. *See* SVCs

switches, 82
    ISDN, 252–253, 259–260

symbols, 50

synchronization, clocking, 55

synchronous data transmission, 71

syntax, IOS-based ping command, 110

synthesized radio technology, 46

T

T1 circuits, 76–77
    bit errors, checking, 183–184
    controller status, verifying, 181–183
    errors, 187
    framing
        ESF signal format, 63
        SF signal format, 62–63
    linecode violations, 186
    loopback features, identifying, 183
    ones density, 131
    pathcode violations, 186
    physical layer alarms, 184, 186
    slip seconds, 186

T3 framing, M23 signal format, 63–64

tandems, 82–83

TAs (terminal adapters), 238

Tc (committed interval), 434

T-carriers, 75
    E1, 77
    T1, 76–77

TCP boomerangs, 751

TDM (time-division multiplexing), 74, 414
    D channels, 393

TDRs (time domain reflectometers), 23

TE1 devices, 238

TE2 devices, 238

technology offerings, 10–11
    Frame Relay, 17
        benefits of, 18
        limitations of, 18
        standards, 17–18
    ISDN, 14
        benefits of, 15–16
        limitations of, 16
    VPNs, 18–19
        cable modem services, 20–22
        limitations of, 19
        satellite services, 28–30
        wireless broadband services, 25–27
        xDSL services, 22–25
TEIs (terminal endpoint identifiers), 190
Telnet sessions, logging to console, 548
terminal servers, 86
termination equipment, remote access VPNs,
    641–642
    performance criteria, 646–648
    selecting core devices, 643, 645–646
termination sequence (PPP), 352–353
testing
    D channel, 327
    remote user's router on Frame Relay multicast
        network, 577
testing network connectivity
    extended ping command, 111
    Netcat utility, 115–117
    ping command, 110–114
    tracert command, 114–115
text dial-in
    configuring, 150–151
    network design, 143
text dial-out
    configuring, 164–168
    network design, 144
throughput, Frame Relay, 444
time domain reflectometers, 23
time-division multiplexing. *See* TDM
timeouts, modem authentication, 219–221
timeslots, line code errors, 130
timestamps, applying, 313–314

timing, SCTE, 499
token bucket filters, 483
topologies
    discovering baseline behavior, 103–105
    Frame Relay, 441
T-plane (ISDN), 236
tracert command, 114–115
tracing Frame Relay multicast networks, 577–580
traffic shaping, 483–484
    ELMI, 487–488
    Frame Relay, 441–443, 534
        BECNs, 536
        FECNs, 535
        flapping routes, investigating, 572
        high RTT numbers, investigating,
            567–569
        slow performance, investigating, 569–572
        verifying settings, 566
    generic, 484–486
    map classes, 486–487
transit delay, Frame Relay, 444
transmission rates, Shannon's Capacity Theorem, 38
transport layer (OSI model), 98
Transport mode (IPSec), implementing in remote
    access VPNs, 637
transport mode (IPSec), 612
troubleshooting methodologies, 101–102
    ISDN BRI recommendations, 359
        accessing remote user's router, 365–369
        preconfiguring routers on both ends,
            364–365
        viewing service layers, 360–363
    layered approach, 96
troubleshooting tools
    classifying, 110
    extended ping command, 111
    Netcat utility, 115–117
    ping command, 110–114
        replies, 112
    SAA, 117–119
    tracert command, 114–115
Tunnel mode (IPSec), 613
    implementing in remote access VPNs, 637

tunneling, DPD, 803–804

two-way Internet connections, 744

two-way multicast service, Frame Relay, 440

type codes (ICMP messages), 112–113

U

UHF (ultra-high frequency)

  multiple frequency operation, 47

  narrowband, 46

  synthesized radio technology, 46

UNI (user node interface)

  bearer services, 438

  LMI, 449

    Annex D, 451

    Cisco-Consortium, 451

    ITU-T Q.933 Annex A, 453

Unity client

  Concentrator Event Log, 699–701

    event classes, 702–704

    event security levels, 704–705

  data not passing, causes of, 784

    bad ISP connections, 786–787

    default MTU size, 786

    dropped connections, 786

    inaccessible internal domain, 787–790

    NAT, 785

  Event Log Viewer, 685

    Client Log Viewer, starting, 686

    ISAKMP, 688

    reviewing captured data, 688–699

  extranet issues, 801

    dead peer detection, 803–804

    ESP 50, 801

    tunnel keepalives, 802

    UDP 500 ISAKMP, 801

  failed authentication, causes of

    bad group name, 774–775

    DNE Miniport, 776–777

    misconfigured firewalls, 777–778

    MTU setting too high, 779–784

    MTU setting too low, 784

    RADIUS, 775–776

  inaccessible internal domain, WINS, 788

  incompatible GINAs, 705–706

  PPPoE problems, causes of

    IOS configuration, 793–795

    software, 791–793

  preliminary troubleshooting steps

    creating profiles, 772

    verifying client installation, 771

    verifying Internet connection, 767–770

  restrictions, 676–679

  troubleshooting checklist, 682–685

unnumbered messages, 245

unprotected band (RF), 46

U-plane

  Frame Relay service architecture, 417

  ISDN, 236

upper-layer protocols

  Frame Relay interoperability, 445

    encapsulation, 447

    fragmentation, 448

    multiprotocol support, 445–447

  NCPs, 341–352

upstream PIM neighbor availability, verifying on Frame Relay networks, 574–576

user authentication, remote access VPNs, 637

user participation, troubleshooting ring options, 354–355

user/identity authentication, 620

user-managed services, 8

UWB (ultra wideband) technology, 47

V

V.21 standard, 12

V.32 standard, 12

V.32b standard, 12

V.90 calls, limitations of, 129

Van Jacobson header compression, 477–480

  path characterization model, 105

variable length framing, Frame Relay, 415
VCs (virtual circuits), 415
VDSL (Very-high rate DSL), 25
verifying
    Cisco PIX VPN connectivity, 722–732
    DHCP server reachability, 227
    Frame Relay configuration
        DLCI settings, 556–562
        remote user router status, 553
        serial interface, 551
        service operation, 553–555
        traffic shaping, 566
    incoming connection type, dial-in
      troubleshooting procedure, 192–194
    ISDN configuration
        D channel functionality, 327
        Layer 1 status of PRI circuits, 188
        Layer 2 status of PRI circuits, 188–190
    IP address configuration on Windows operating
      systems, 769–770
    line provision, 354
    MMP configuration, 284–285
    modem operability, dial-in troubleshooting
      procedure, 191–192
    out of order B channels (NFAS), 227
    PPP negotiation, dial-in troubleshooting
      procedure, 194–200
    VPN client installation, 771
viewing
    captured Log Viewer results, 688–699
    ISDN BRI service layers, 360–363
virtual circuits, compression, 477
virtual connections, MLP, 343–344
virtual interface templates, 272
virtual ports, 474
virtual profiles, 273
VoFR (Voice over Frame Relay), 440
voice
    digitalization, 73
    priority over data, 353–354
voice privacy, ISDN configuration, 308–309
VPN 3000 Concentrator, configuring, 648–649
    filters and rules, 650–651
    Group Lock, 662

IKE
    peer identity validation, 662
    proposals, 656, 658–659
  IPSec SAs, 661
  load balancing, 654–655
  redundancy, 653
  reverse route injection, 655
  SAs, 659–660
VPNs (Virtual Private Networks), 10, 13, 18–19
  ADSL, 732
    PPoE, 733–739
  authentication
    client authentication, 619
    DH algorithm, 624–627
    HMAC, 627–628
    key management, 624–627
    RADIUS, 621–623
    user/identity authentication, 620
  cable modem services, 20
    limitations of, 22
    standards, 21
  CATV infrastructure
    data transmission, 740–744
    heartbeats, 745
    two-way Internet connections, 744
  Cisco 3002 HW client, 706
    Event Log, 708–710, 712
    initial troubleshooting checklist, 707
  Cisco Easy VPN Client, 713
    client status, displaying, 716
    debugging IPSec key events, 717–719
    initial troubleshooting checklist, 714–716
    monitoring, 720–721
    resetting connection, 717
    restrictions, 713–714
  Cisco PIX VPN
    connectivity, verifying, 722–732
    restrictions, 722
  Cisco Unity client
    Concentrator Event Log, 699–705
    Event Log Viewer, 685–699
    incompatible GINAs, 705–706
    restrictions, 676–679
    troubleshooting checklist, 682–685

Cisco VPN 3002, connection establishment, 795–800
data not passing, causes of, 784
    bad ISP connections, 786–787
    default MTU size, 786
    dropped connections, 786
    inaccessible internal domain, 787–790
    NAT, 785
enterprise VPNs, 593–594
    categories of, 595
    data link layer, 599–603
    firewall-based VPNs, 597–598
    network layer, 604–607
    remote access VPNs, 595
    site-to-site VPNs, 596
extranet issues, 801
    dead peer detection, 803–804
    ESP 50, 801
    tunnel keepalives, 802
    UDP 500 ISAKMP, 801
failed authentication, causes of
    bad group name, 774–775
    DNE Miniport, 776–777
    misconfigured firewalls, 777–778
    MTU setting too high, 779, 781–784
    MTU setting too low, 784
    RADIUS, 775–776
inaccessible internal domain, causes of, 788
LAN-specific issues
    inability to log in, 760
    MTU settings, 754–758
    NAT, multiple client handling, 753
    packet size, 758–760
latency, 228
limitations of, 19
PPPoE problems, causes of
    IOS configuration, 793–795
    software, 791–793
preliminary troubleshooting steps
    creating profiles, 772
    verifying client installation, 771
    verifying Internet connection, 767–770
remote access

change management, 636
configuration management, 635
design objectives, 634–635
operations management, 636
security issues, 636–641
termination equipment, 641–648
satellite services, 28
    BST, 29
    IPA, 28
    LEO satellites, 30
satellite systems, 745–746
    bandwidth, 747
    BST protocol, 750
    error control coding, 746
    FITFEEL protocol, 751
    IPSec, 752–753
    manipulating TCP stack, 749–750
    performance, 749
    TCP efficiency, 747–748
site-to-site versus remote access VPNs, 633–634
wireless systems, 25, 745–746
    bandwidth, 747
    error control coding, 746
    limitations of, 27
    LMDS, 26–27
    MMDS, 25–26
    TCP efficiency, 747–748
    unlicensed frequencies, 27
xDSL services, 22
    ADSL, 24
    CDSL, 24
    FDIs, 22–23
    HDSL, 24
    IDSL, 24
    RADSL, 24
    SDSL, 24
    TDRs, 23
    VDSL, 25

W

WAN links
   PRI circuits
      Layer 1 status, verifying, 188
      Layer 2 status, verifying, 188–190
      troubleshooting, 188
   T1 circuits
      alarm states, 184, 186
      BERT testing, 183–184
      line code violations, 186
      loopback features, 183
      pathcode violations, 186
      slip seconds, 186
      T1 errors, 187
      troubleshooting, 181–86
      verifying controller status, 182
well-known ports, 403–405
Whitecamp network protocol, 53
WIC T1 pinouts, 499
wi-fi, 44
windowing, 443
Windows operating systems
   verifyingIP address configuration, 769–770
   Windows 2000
      DDR, 399–408
      ports, 403
      RPC, 402–403
      well-known ports, 403–405
wireless broadband services, 25
   3G, 91–92
   limitations of, 27
   LMDS, 26–27
   MMDS, 25–26
   unlicensed frequencies, 27
wireless cable, 26
wireless VPNs, 745–746
   bandwidth, 747
   error control coding, 746
   TCP efficiency, 747–748
WISP (wireless ISP), 54

WLANs
   802.11a, 51–52
   802.11e, 53
   802.11g, 52
   barker sequence, 50
   IR radio-channel, 45
   line-coding techniques, 44–48
   LTI systems, 47
   modulation, 44–45, 48
   narrowband technologies, 46
   photonic, 45
   SS RF transmissions
      DSSS, 49
      FHSS, 48
   UHF, multiple frequency operation, 46
   UWB technology, 47

X

X.25 protocol, 17
   versus Frame Relay, 414–415
XAUTH, 623
xDSL services, 22
   2B1Q coding, 55, 58–59
   ADSL, 24
   CDSL, 24
   coding schemes, 41–42
   FDIs, 22–23
   HDSL, 24
   IDSL, 24
   provisioning enterprise remote access services,
      33–34
   RADSL, 24
   SDSL, 24
   TDRs, 23
   VDSL, 25

Y-Z

yellow alarms, 185
zero CIR, 436
zero-suppression schemes, 61–62

☐ **YES!** I'm requesting a **free** subscription to *Packet™* magazine.

☐ No. I'm not interested at this time.

☐ Mr.
☐ Ms.

First Name (Please Print) _____ Last Name _____

Title/Position (Required) _____

Company (Required) _____

Address _____

City _____ State/Province _____

Zip/Postal Code _____ Country _____

Telephone (Include country and area codes) _____ Fax _____

E-mail _____

Signature (Required) _____ Date _____

☐ I would like to receive additional information on Cisco's services and products by e-mail.

1. Do you or your company:
- A ☐ Use Cisco products
- B ☐ Resell Cisco products
- C ☐ Both
- D ☐ Neither

2. Your organization's relationship to Cisco Systems:
- A ☐ Customer/End User
- B ☐ Prospective Customer
- C ☐ Cisco Reseller
- D ☐ Cisco Distributor
- E ☐ Integrator
- F ☐ Non-Authorized Reseller
- G ☐ Cisco Training Partner
- I ☐ Cisco OEM
- J ☐ Consultant
- K ☐ Other (specify):
  _____

3. How many people does your entire company employ?
- A ☐ More than 10,000
- B ☐ 5,000 to 9,999
- c ☐ 1,000 to 4,999
- D ☐ 500 to 999
- E ☐ 250 to 499
- f ☐ 100 to 249
- G ☐ Fewer than 100

4. Is your company a Service Provider?
- A ☐ Yes
- B ☐ No

5. Your involvement in network equipment purchases:
- A ☐ Recommend
- B ☐ Approve
- C ☐ Neither

6. Your personal involvement in networking:
- A ☐ Entire enterprise at all sites
- B ☐ Departments or network segments at more than one site
- C ☐ Single department or network segment
- F ☐ Public network
- D ☐ No involvement
- E ☐ Other (specify):
  _____

7. Your Industry:
- A ☐ Aerospace
- B ☐ Agriculture/Mining/Construction
- C ☐ Banking/Finance
- D ☐ Chemical/Pharmaceutical
- E ☐ Consultant
- F ☐ Computer/Systems/Electronics
- G ☐ Education (K–12)
- U ☐ Education (College/Univ.)
- H ☐ Government—Federal
- I ☐ Government—State
- J ☐ Government—Local
- K ☐ Health Care
- L ☐ Telecommunications
- M ☐ Utilities/Transportation
- N ☐ Other (specify):
  _____

CPRESS

PACKET

Packet magazine serves as the premier publication linking customers to Cisco Systems, Inc. Delivering complete coverage of cutting-edge networking trends and innovations, *Packet* is a magazine for technical, hands-on users. It delivers industry-specific information for enterprise, service provider, and small and midsized business market segments. A toolchest for planners and decision makers, *Packet* contains a vast array of practical information, boasting sample configurations, real-life customer examples, and tips on getting the most from your Cisco Systems' investments. Simply put, *Packet* magazine is straight talk straight from the worldwide leader in networking for the Internet, Cisco Systems, Inc.

We hope you'll take advantage of this useful resource. I look forward to hearing from you!

Cecelia Glover
Packet Circulation Manager
packet@external.cisco.com
www.cisco.com/go/packet

PACKET